The Hitler Era

Philosophical, Psychological,
and Historical Reckonings

Also by Mitchell D. Ginsberg

Mind and Belief:
Psychological Ascription and the Concept of Belief
(1972)

The Far Shore:
Vipassanā, The Practice of Insight
(1980; 4th ed., 2006)

The Inner Palace:
Mirrors of Psychospirituality
in Divine and Sacred Wisdom-Traditions
(2002; 8th ed., 2013)

Calm, Clear, and Loving:
Soothing the Distressed Mind,
Healing the Wounded Heart
(2010; 2nd ed., 2012)

Peace and War and Peace:
The Heart in Transformation
(2012; 2nd ed., 2015)

Mindful Raft over Troubled Waters
(2015)

Editor of and contributor to the 2nd, 3rd, and 4th editions of
Effective Psychotherapy: The Contribution of Hellmuth Kaiser
(1965; 4th ed., 2018)

The Hitler Era

Philosophical, Psychological, and Historical Reckonings

Mitchell D. Ginsberg, Ph.D.

Wisdom Moon Publishing
2019

THE HITLER ERA
PHILOSOPHICAL, PSYCHOLOGICAL, AND HISTORICAL RECKONINGS

Copyright © 2019 Mitchell D. Ginsberg

All rights reserved. Tous droits réservés.
No part of this work may be copied, reproduced, recorded, stored, or translated, in any form, or transmitted by any means electronic, mechanical, or other, whether by photocopy, fax, email, internet group postings, or otherwise, without written permission from the copyright holder, *except for brief quotations* in reviews for a magazine, journal, newspaper, broadcast, podcast, etc., or in scholarly or academic papers, *when quoted with a full citation to this work.*

Published by Wisdom Moon Publishing, Inc.
San Diego, CA, USA

Wisdom Moon™, the Wisdom Moon logo™, *Wisdom Moon Publishing*™, and *WMP*™
are trademarks of Wisdom Moon Publishing, Inc.

Wisdom Moon Publishing is a nonprofit literary and educational publisher, designated by the IRS as 501.c.3 tax-exempt. We invite and welcome all interested individual, trust, and foundation contributions, tax-deductible under US tax law, to help support our mission.

www.WisdomMoonPublishing.com

ISBN 978-1-938459-63-4 (hardcover, alk. paper)
ISBN 978-1-938459-65-8 (softcover, alk. paper)
ISBN 978-1-938459-68-9 (eBook)
LCCN 2019000029

The Hitler Era

Epigrams and Dedication Page	
First Questions (Introduction)	i
Furious Rage: The Rage of the Greek Furies (Seeds for Revenge)	i
A Personal Note (Preface)	xxii
Buchenwald, April 1945	xxii
Nuremberg Trials, other Key Documents, and *Mein Kampf*	xxv
The NT, IMT, TWC, NCA, TTFR, ICC, UNWCC, &c. Transcripts	xxv
The Nuremberg Trials	xxv
Printed Text Collections of These Trials (NT)	xxvi
Further Collections of Documentation	xxvii
Other War-Crimes Trials, Including French and German Trials	xxviii
UN War Crimes Commission	xxx
Cold War Complications	xxxi
Other European Post-War Trials	xxxi
Citing *Mein Kampf*	xxxii
Hitler-Era Suicides & A Reich's Gallery of German Rogues	xxxiii
Acknowledgments	xxxvi
Howl, O Adelwolf: A Poetic Prologue to *The Hitler Era*	1
1. A Blitzview of the Hitler Era	2
2. Facts, Myths, Disinformation; "Lies" and Lies	6
Catharsis, Form, and Tenor	10
A Philosophy of History: Time, Nietzschean Powder, Field Theory	11
Names to Insult By and Functions of Hate Speech	17
The Romanies, Called Gypsies (An Exonym Misnomer)	18
Complexity and Understanding the Hitler Era	20
3. A Philosophy of History for the Hitler Era	21
The Historical Context of the Hitler Era	23
Wilson's Fourteen Points: Unfulfilled Proposals	31
Contentious Articles in the Treaty of Versailles	33
Ludendorff and the Stab in the Back	39
4. The European Context through the Franco-Prussian War	43
Early Wars in Europe with Religious Overtones	43
European Geopolitics and the Peace of Westphalia (1648)	44
Germany's Dream of a Place in the Sun (1890s)	45
5. The Years to World War I	48
The Ottoman Empire and the Armenians	49
European Treaties, Openly Declared or Secret	50
A Balkan Spark Sets Off the Great War	51
Pre-War Tensions between Austria-Hungary and Serbia	52
The proposed Berlin-Baghdad Railway	53
6. The Great War, 1914-1918	63
Segregated Administration of American Soldiers in the Great War	68
Battles of the Great War	70
Innovations for Warfare	72
Les Gueules Cassées, Die Zerbrochene Münder	75

BELLEAU WOOD AND THE US MARINES	81
FINAL GERMAN OFFENSES, 1918	84
THE MANY TOLLS OF THE GREAT WAR	85
7. Turkey, After the Great War, and the 1920s	**91**
TALAAT PASHA AND THE TRIAL OF SOGHOMON TEHLIRIAN	95
THE DISSOLUTION OF EMPIRES AND THE FLOURISHING OF NATIONALISMS	100
ZEITGEIST OF THE ROARING AND CONSERVATIVE TWENTIES	103
REDEFINING MEN AND WOMEN IN THE TWENTIES	108
ON THE DIPLOMATIC FRONT AND 1920S NAZI ORGANIZING	115
Early SA (*Sturmabteilung*), Modeled on the War's *Stoßtruppen*	119
GERMANY AND THE VISION OF A FUTURE WORLD IN *MEIN KAMPF*	123
THE PSYCHOLOGY OF GROUP UNITY IN PEACE AND IN VIOLENCE	127
HITLER AS MESSIAH AND SAVIOR (*RETTER*) AND AS KNIGHT (*RITTER*)	131
GERMANY GETTING RESTARTED, THE EARLY INFLUENCE OF HITLER	143
THE RUHR, 1923-1924	148
1920S, BEYOND GERMANY	154
HYPERINFLATION AND VOTING	156
8. Conceptual Foundations (Worldview) of the Third Reich	**160**
NIETZSCHE ON GERMANY, NATIONALISM, AND ANTI-SEMITISM	161
BAEUMLER: NIETZSCHE NAZIFIED	167
LESSING, DOHM, DARWIN, SPENCER, CHAMBERLAIN, AND PAMPHLETEERS	176
THE VATICAN'S BURNING WORRY ABOUT CATHOLICS IN THE GERMAN REICH	185
NAZI RACE STUDIES AND DEFINING JEWRY	190
THE FINE AND NOT-SO-FINE ARTS OF PROPAGANDA	200
9. Pre-war 1930s: The Tumultuous Birth of the Third Reich	**203**
THE INTERNATIONAL GEOPOLITICAL CONTEXT	203
GERMANY PRIOR TO JANUARY 30, 1933	204
IG FARBEN AG ESTABLISHED, DECEMBER 1925	208
DEEP POCKETS: EARLY CONTRIBUTORS TO THE NAZI PARTY	209
THE MOMENTOUS INVITATION OF JANUARY 30, 1933	211
ROBERT KEMPNER AND HEYDRICH'S LAKESIDE VILLA	214
EARLY DECREES RIGHT OUT OF THE STARTING BLOCK	214
THE TRANSFORMATIVE REICHSTAG FIRE, FEBRUARY 27, 1933	218
THE *MACHTERGREIFUNG* FOLLOWING THE REICHSTAG FIRE	224
SA CRUSHED: THE NIGHT OF THE LONG KNIVES, JUNE 30-JULY 3, 1934	231
GROWING TENSIONS AND THE NUREMBERG LAWS OF 1935	238
ENTER VARIAN FRY (AND ERNST HANFSTAENGL)	238
POLISH FEARS, MATHEMATICIANS, AND CRYPTOGRAPHERS	243
LIMITING FREEDOMS IN THE THIRD REICH	244
EINSTEIN AND THE FIRST CONCENTRATION CAMPS, MARCH 1933	245
DEFERENCE AND THE RAPID TRANSFORMATION TO A NEW WORLD	246
GOOD GERMANIC BREEDING AND THE IDEAL OF THE *VOLK*, THE PEOPLE	254
THE 1933 CONCORDAT: THE VATICAN AND THE REICH IN EARLY AGREEMENT	255
SECRET WAR PREPARATIONS, 1925-1936: *DIE SCHWARZE REICHSWEHR*	258
LIPETSK (USSR) FLIGHT TRAINING SCHOOL AND THE *WELTBÜHNE* TRIAL	260
THE RUHR AND THE RHINELAND BLUFF	265
THE *ANSCHLUß*—ANNEXATION—OF AUSTRIA	271
THE SPANISH CIVIL WAR AND US BIG BUSINESS	273
THE GEOPOLITICAL CONTEXT OF THE SPANISH CIVIL WAR	276

THE MADAGASCAR OPTION	289
THE MUNICH CRISIS AND THE OSTER CONSPIRACY	289
NAZI ATTITUDES AND PROPAGANDA: GÖRING VS. STREICHER	301
MEANWHILE, BACK IN THE LABS OF EUROPE	305
KRISTALLNACHT, HITLER'S WAR PROPAGANDA, AND THE ÉVIAN CONFERENCE	306
10. World War II Starts: Poland & the West, 1939-1940	309
FOG FOILS ASSASSINATION ATTEMPT, NOVEMBER 8, 1939	310
THE VENLO INCIDENT	313
EXPANSION OF THE WAR 1940-1941	314
US BIG BUSINESS IN GERMANY	319
A GLIMPSE OF ANTI-SEMITISM IN THIRD REICH FILMS	322
CONCENTRATION AND EXTERMINATION CAMPS IN THE EAST (POLAND)	323
MONTHS OF PREPARING TO INVADE THE USSR: OPERATION BARBAROSSA	327
NO MORE MADAGASCAR	333
POLAND AND THE GREAT POPULATIONS OF THE USSR TO BE KILLED	340
FOG, THE MECHELEN AFFAIR, AND THE GERMAN INVASION OF THE WEST	344
11. Focus on the Invasion of the USSR, 1941	346
MASTER RACE SPACE: LEBENSRAUM, LEBENSBORN, MASS KILLINGS	346
THE MILITARY CONTEXT ALLOWING THE APPLICATION OF THIS RACE THEORY	353
TOUCHING ON DISCUSSIONS AT THE WANNSEE CONFERENCE	357
SCENES FROM THE EASTERN FRONT, WITH ITS MASS MURDERS	357
JEWS AND PEACHUM'S UNFEELING-AT-WILL GERMANS	360
HITLER, THE LEADER STILL COMMITTED TO PEACE (SAYS HE)	368
ON WHY GERMANY WOULD DECLARE WAR ON THE USA	372
VERMICIDE TO THE "RESCUE" OF THE PROBLEM OF ROMANIES AND JEWS	378
ON THE REICH'S FINAL MASS, METHODICAL MASSACRES	384
DEEP POCKETS PROFITING FROM CONCENTRATION CAMPS' SLAVE LABOR	385
MEDICAL EXPERIMENTATION WITH CONCENTRATION CAMP PRISONERS	389
A WEAK AND SPINELESS GERMANY DESERVES TO BE ANNIHILATED	390
JURIDICAL DOCUMENTATION AND PREPARATIONS	392
EARLY ALLIED RECOGNITION OF MASS KILLINGS IN THE USSR	393
INVASIONS: COLLABORATION, RESISTANCE, NEUTRALITY	393
THE RIGHTEOUS: LAY PERSONS, CHURCHMEN, POPES, IMAMS, AND MUFTIS	397
VARIAN FRY AGAIN, THIS TIME IN MARSEILLE, FRANCE	401
12. Reversals to German Military Successes, 1942-1943	405
NUCLEAR FUSION, DER URANVEREIN, SKIING, & THE MANHATTAN PROJECT	407
SURRENDER AT STALINGRAD, TOTAL WAR SPEECH IN BERLIN	408
13. War's End, 1944-1945: Downfall, Devastating Defeat	413
OVERCAST SKIES AND THE BATTLE OF THE BULGE	414
NAZI VALUES AND WORLDVIEW: A SYNOPSIS OF GLOBAL SHIFTING SANDS	422
CONTINUED MASS KILLING VERSUS A FOCUS ON THE DEMANDS OF WARFARE	425
REFOCUSING DURING THE MOROSE TWILIGHT OF DISCONSOLATE IDOLS	426
HITLER'S MUTATING IDEAS DURING THESE DISTRESSING TIMES	427
VITAL FINAL NON-MILITARY PROJECTS: JUDA VERRECKE, ONCE AND FOR ALL	428
LAST SURGES OF MASS KILLINGS & DESTROYING EVIDENCE (AKTION 1005)	432
AUSCHWITZ ZIGEUNERNACHT, AUGUST 2-3, 1944	438
THE LOGIC AND THE PSYCHOLOGY OF THE NERO DECREE	445
THE PSYCHOLOGY AND THE POWER OF HITLER	447
A BRIEF EXCURSUS INTO PSYCHOPATHOLOGY	456

THE SURPRISINGLY SIMILAR PSYCHOLOGY OF GOEBBELS	469
THE *KREISAUER KREIS*, THE WHITE ROSE, AND JUDGE ROLAND FREISLER	471
DIE ROTE KAPELLE AND JUDGE MANFRED ROEDER	474
BERLIN'S *DIE FREIE PRESSE* AND OTHER RESISTANCE IN GERMANY	475
HIMMLER, COUNT FOLKE BERNADOTTE, AND NORBERT MASUR	476
MISCALCULATION: WHERE 1,000 = 12	484
THE JULY 1944 ASSASSINATION ATTEMPT AND JUDGE ROLAND FREISLER	486
WHO KNEW? DID HITLER?	494
14. The Reich's Death Twitches and the Aftermath	**508**
AXIS WAR-TIME ATROCITIES ANSWERED WITH WARNINGS BY THE ALLIES	509
THE WANNSEE CONFERENCE AS AN ADMINISTRATIVE GATHERING	517
ADOLF EICHMANN'S RETROSPECTIVE ATTITUDE	517
ROMANIES AND JEWS IN THE DOMAINS OF THE THIRD REICH	519
CRYPTOLOGY IN THESE WAR THEATERS	523
KEY DECISIONS FOCUSING ON THE EXTERMINATION OF THE JEWS	524
SCENES FROM THE RUSSIAN FRONT	528
JOSEPH GOEBBELS AND THE CALL FOR TOTAL WAR	529
THE IMMEDIATE POST-WAR TIMES	534
POPULAR RETRIBUTION AMIDST RUBBLE, SCARS, AND MOURNING	540
THE VATICAN RATLINE AND OPERATION PAPERCLIP	542
THE NUREMBERG TRIBUNAL AND LEGAL ISSUES OF PRECEDENCE	545
PRE-1933 INTERNATIONAL CRIMINAL LAW	546
CUSTOMARY INTERNATIONAL LAW	547
15. Yesterday, Today, and Tomorrow	**552**
THE POST-SHOCK TURBULENCES OF THE NEXT CENTURY	552
DPS AND GLOBAL REVERBERATIONS INTO THE 1950S	559
THE UNPRECEDENTED, UNBELIEVABLE ORGANIZED MASS KILLING OF JEWS	562
ARISTOTLE, NIETZSCHE, PERLS: GROUP COHESION TRUMPS MORAL ISSUES	562
POST-WAR FILMS ON THE THIRD REICH AND THE HOLOCAUST	565
WHAT DOES THIS MEAN? WHO ARE WE? WHAT ARE WE?	568
STYX, THE GREEK RIVER OF ANGER: MISERY, STRIFE, OBLIVION, DEATH	584
BEYOND THE QUESTION OF EVIL	587
THE PSYCHOLOGY OF BEING DECENT (*ANSTÄNDIG*) AND CRUEL, TOGETHER	592
REICH ARYANS VS. JEWS, HALF-APES, AND CHRISTIANS MONGRELS	595
THE HITLER FASCINATION—SO WHAT?	598
OUR HEALING AFTER THE TRAUMA OF IT ALL	603
ANCIENT GREEK AWARENESS OF WAR TRAUMA	606
CHILDREN SCHOOLED WITH A STRAP (AND OTHER VIOLENCE)	609
ANCIENT GREEK EPIC ANTIDOTE TO RAGE: THETIS, ACHILLES, AND PRIAM	614
FINALLY RISING ABOVE RAGE THROUGH ADAPTABILITY OF MIND	624
MINDFULNESS AND INSIGHT MEDITATION, HEALING THE RAGEFUL MIND	628
ETHICS IN A POST-REICH WORLD: SOME FINAL CONSIDERATIONS	633
ISSUES ON THE HORIZON FOR OUR SPECIES, IN CLOSING	637
About the Author	641
Bibliography	642
Index	657

The Hitler Era

Philosophical, Psychological,
and Historical Reckonings

Ah, horrible war, amazing medley of the glorious and the squalid, the pitiful and the sublime, if modern men of light and leading saw your face closer, ordinary folk would see it hardly ever.

> Winston Churchill (1874-1965), on the field of dead after the Battle at Trichardt's Drift, in the Boer War, 1900; from *London to Ladysmith, via Pretoria* (1900), p. 292, entry dated January 22, 1900.

Let's not talk high-sounding phrases. Let's not use old words, shop-worn words, words like "glory" and "peace," without thinking just exactly what they mean. There's no "glory" in killing. There's no "glory" in maiming men.

> General John J. Pershing (1860-1948), Commander-in-Chief of the AEF, the American Expeditionary Forces in Europe (1917-1919), quoted in *The New York Times*, Sept. 7, 1924, p. XX3.

War plays havoc with the refinements of conscience.

> British Prime Minister (1916-1922) David Lloyd George (1863-1945), *The Truth about The Peace Treaties*, Vol. 2 (1938), p. 765.

Business complications do strange things to our patriotism and to our ethics.

> Eleanor Roosevelt (1884-1962), "Ford in Germany" (article in her syndicated column, "My Day"), September 20, 1945, *New York World-Telegram*, p. 17.

The purpose of stripping men of their past is to reshape them into whatever form their elite rulers choose. The result, however, is not a new man, but a lost and dying man ... a barbarian, a slave.

> Rev. Rousas John Rushdoony (1916-2001), *The Roots of Reconstruction* (1991), p. 347.

Dedication: to
Solomon Vulfovich Dobkin (Krasnoyarsk, 1888 – Philadelphia, 1966)
Maurice Polen (Shpola, 1890 – Miami, 1997)
Olga Rosenfeld Simon (Mostar, 1902 – Mill Valley, 1985)
Hans Simon (Charlottenburg, 1904 – Pittsburgh, 1975)
Boaza/Basia Litmanowicz Bendien (Łódź, 1915 – London, 1992)
Henry Hiż (St. Petersburg, 1917 – Cape May Point, 2006)
Milton Michael Dobkin (Philadelphia, 1922 – Rackheath, 1944)
Philip Slier (Amsterdam, 1923 – Sobibór, 1943)
Pierre Henri Bohin (Paris, 1924 – Chaville, 2010)
... among the tens of millions of individuals whose stories include the life-uprooting impact of the violence, inhumanity, death, and killings that are wildly unleashed in societal unrest, intergroup hatreds, pogroms, massacres, revolutions, and great or localized wars, with some surviving these and some not.

First Questions (Introduction)

Hitler and the National Socialist (Nazi) Party and government saw themselves as the defenders of European civilization against the mortal threat of the armies of nomadic warriors—barbaric hordes—from the Asiatic steppes: Slavs, Russians, Bolsheviks, Jews, Asians.[1] The Third Reich was claimed to be led by members of a *Herrenrasse*, a supposedly pure, superior race of Aryans (Noble Ones).[2] What came to pass was quite different: These self-declared Aryans were themselves violent hordes—Germanic, murderous warriors who acted on an unprecedented level of savagery, viciousness, and remorseless brutality, stunning the world, which could only comprehend the extent of this violence, years if not decades later. Hitler and his hordes have impacted our entire planet.

How could this have happened? To understand the fuller reality, with a palpable, nuanced sense of that past, we might best investigate this history with focus and attention to the various specifics that led to the Third Reich and its destructive actions. I am investigating here records and other traces from the past century and more, to study the Third Reich through the group (societal) processes that brought it to its greatest power, *to recognize the diverse, multi-faceted cultural and historical background of the Hitler era*, the Hitler years, *and to appreciate the horrific consequences of the resultant events of those times with their strange, largely unforeseen, interlocking synergy.* Our current world has significant questions that persist as we make sense of this period and its historical impact, and cultivate a decent life in their aftermath.

FURIOUS RAGE: THE RAGE OF THE GREEK FURIES (SEEDS FOR REVENGE)

The Greek mythological Furies personified furious rage: fierce, sweet dreams of revenge personified. Here, in considering the Hitler era and the perhaps surprisingly short life of the Third Reich, it is the frustrations, the fury, and the wrath of many Germans at how Germany was treated at the Versailles Treaty and afterwards that stand out as powerful, if not pivotal. The agitated and tormented German times of *Sturm und Drang* (storm and drive, or urge)—of great emotionalism and an honoring of intuitive perception in revolt against society and its rational norms—and the related rage experienced by many Germans of that period simmered for years until the time came when the power of the Third Reich was enough to have Germany call forth the angry spirit of Achilles, as in Homer's *Iliad*. So central to the *Iliad* is rage to the story of war between the Greeks and Ilios (Troy), that the very beginning of the opening verse—the *Iliad* being written in poetic meter—starts with the word *Mēnin* (from *mēnis*, rage,

---

[1] In 1945, 15-year-old Adolf Gladding, questioned by a US intelligence officer, said of Jews, "They wanted to grab Germany. They are a bad race from East Asia. They are a bastard race." Saul K. Padover, *Experiment in Germany* (1946), p. 44.

[2] The Aryans were the noble ones of their Indo-European culture. Relatedly, in Indic Buddhism, there are the *catvāri āryasatyāni* (Skt.) or *cattāri ariyasaccāni* (Pali), the four noble truths, or the four truths of the noble ones.

wrath, anger), and calls on a goddess or muse to chant out the rage of Achilles, son of Peleus. The rage here is not a matter of momentary, passing outbursts of anger. What interested the Greeks (among many other things) was the state of mind that could drive men to extreme violence, often in the context of exhibiting great bravery in battle, as in the mind-state of fury in battle.[3] There was a longer-term, background concern that could keep this wrath present for years, and, with it, the hate-filled urge for an intense and unconstrained revenge. Here, fury is represented as a cohort of goddesses, the Furies, who represent much more than fury understood as simply extreme anger. In Classical Greek literature and mythology, fury is also a drive for rage-filled vengeance against acts that went against the basic social fabric—as in patricide or breaking a solemn oath. It is a drive that can take the most violent (or "blood-thirsty") forms, harking back to the literally bloody source of the Furies, born of the blood of the Greek immortal Uranus when castrated by his son Cronos (himself father of Zeus and Hera).[4]

---

[3] Classical Greek, *Erinúes*. In Homer's *Iliad*, fury was an intense, energizing state of mind that could inspire men to great courage and never-shaken fearlessness, provoking in warriors unswerving courage, especially when defending one's homeland, an excited state that was frenzied, wild, unlimited in its potential, a unifier of fellow warriors into an unstoppable juggernaut of assault, bringing a thrill to battle, and bringing the brave to be braver still. And yet, with its bitter gall, it could drive men to blindness (metaphorically speaking), insatiable until fully satisfied, and that might be fatal in its frenzy, bringing on death. (More just below.)

Note: Quotes from the *Iliad* are in the Robert Fagles tr., with its 62-pg. Intro. by Bernard Knox (1990), and its own book-and-verse count. *The 24 books—or chapters—and verses of the Greek text* are indicated in many publications, such as in Caroline Alexander, *The Iliad: A New Translation* (2015). Passages comparable to the Fagles text are cited as "BK.vv"; see also bilingual texts of the *Iliad*, such as the 2-vol. 1924-1925 tr. by Augustus T. Murray, in the *Loeb Classical Library*, No. 170-171, and HOMER ENGLISH ILIAD, PERSEUS.UCHICAGO.EDU. *Also:* AS HERE, websites are cited in this book in SMALL CAPS. On the comments in this note, see Homer, *Iliad*, 16.193-194, 249-260, 304-317, 651-657, 701-702, 799-802; 17.179-181; 18.126-129, 302-306, 21.78-85. (BK.vv: 16.198-206, 258-267, 302-309, 644-655, 702-711, 822-826; 17.182-186; 18.108-119, 310-313, 21.169-175).

[4] Classical Greek (as above), *Erinýs* (in English, Erinys and also Erinyes), then, in Latin, *Furiae*. These were at first an unnumbered cohort of goddesses (immortals) who were personifications of curses on guilty criminals. Early on, they were seen as avengers or revengers for patricide and against those who had broken solemn oaths (Homer, *Iliad*, 3.332; 9.553-558; 19.305-306, 495-501 (BK.vv: 3.320-323; 9.537-543; 19.258-265, 418-423). In the plays of Aeschylus (ca. 525-455 BCE), esp. in his *Eumenides*, the Erinys or Furies were presented as quite intent on blood revenge. (Aeschylus, *Eumenides*, esp. verses 245-370, with the Furies or Erinys seeking blood in revenge for blood.) Then, through time, their vengeance-taking role, re-establishing justice, was generalized and the specific number of the Furies was made explicit (three) in the texts of various Greek and Roman authors and poets, each with areas of special interest. See "Erinyes," THEOI.COM; "Erinys," MYTHAGORA.COM; "Agamemnon," WIKIPEDIA; and *Eumenides* by Aeschylus, rev. of Cynthia Bannon and Gregory Nagy, KRONOS SOCIETY (HARVARD).

Considering this mythological presentation, from a point of view that sees the storyline without believing it as literal truth, *the Furies are, more fundamentally, rageful urges for revenge*. For the Greeks, these were personified, in a concrete (bodily) form. They represented urges to revenge, or states of mind that are rage-filled and violence-prone. In this way, they were understood as features of thinking that can show up in any person at any time. *Thus, they do not die, unlike people, and in this way are said to be deathless.* This is often expressed as their being immortals. As immortals, they are called gods, so that instead of thinking of them as personifications, we might say that they are deifications. And yet, most importantly here, although these immortals (gods in this particular sense) might perhaps at times show some divinity, some enlightening vision of reality, they are not at all typically manifesting the sacred dimension of reality. In this way, these gods are quite different from the Abrahamic God.[5] *As representations of a driving urge for violent, rage-filled revenge, Furies are an ancient metaphor for that human state of mind,*[6] which, in some cases, can bring down a person or an entire army, or an entire society. *We will see this in an extreme case with Hitler and the German people of the Third Reich.*

Considering here the darker side, to use the Jungian concept of the shadow[7]—the complement to what is honored and lauded in a society's spotlight—we may see this darker side being glorified in the Nordic, the Aryan, ideal, the *Herrenrasse* (Master Race), with its right to *Lebensraum* (living space). Here, what is honored is rage and the fierce, sweet dream of revenge. This was subsequently carried out in reality, with those held to be inferior beings, *lebensunwertes Leben* (lives not worth living): a form of dehumanization. Among these was a group of people who become the target of this unbridled sense of revenge that we will consider in this book, people that the more vehement National Socialists experienced viscerally with repulsion and disgust, as the vermin and the disease of European and Germanic civilization.

We can see in looking back over these several decades since the end of World War II, that for long periods of time, the documentation and other writings from various countries, often stepped very lightly on certain events that did not shine an honorable light on that nation. One example that stands out is the rather cooperative spirit of the French police and Vichy administration in arresting the Jews in France—ultimately both French and foreign Jews—and then delivering these Jews to the Gestapo,

---

[5] For an extended discussion applying the distinction between divine aspirations (using the metaphor of light or seeing) and sacred aspirations (using the metaphor of the sacred or the holy), see Mitchell Ginsberg, *The Inner Palace: Mirrors of Psychospirituality in Divine and Sacred Wisdom-Traditions* (2013).

[6] As a metaphor, this refers to the wrath that is a murderous, rage-filled urge for revenge, with pride reborn and fed by brutal violence, machines of the Hitler era.

[7] Christopher Perry, "The Shadow," THE SOCIETY OF ANALYTICAL PSYCHOLOGY (SAP)— JUNGIAN ANALYSIS AND PSYCHOTHERAPY.

with their being sent by train to camps in Eastern Europe, carried out with a dedication that surprised even the Germans. (Similarly, the Dutch police rounded up Dutch Jews for the German occupiers.[8]) In contrast, there were many French resistance fighters, members of the French *maquis*, to acknowledge in bringing the French story into more balance.[9] Some of these groups are known in only very specific circles.[10]

While we can recognize that this and similar bendings to power and ruthless authority are what we might call normal human tendencies, "normal" here does not mean good or accurate, or well-rounded and balanced, or free of distortions and mystifications. Normal in this context is perhaps merely equivalent to usual. The enormity of the disasters the Hitler era helped bring about can still be felt in our world, the better part of a century later. Many of those still alive who lived through it, in Germany itself, or in the lands attacked or invaded by the Reich military, regularly have nightmares to this day. One such man, from Będzin, a town less than 50 kilometers or 30 miles north of Auschwitz (in Polish, Oświęcim), where the Third Reich was later to set up a double camp, serving both as a concentration and as an extermination center. When asked about focusing on those difficult and tormented times, he spoke of his being drawn to understand the context of that camp. This man, Samuel Pivnik, offered his response to that past experience: "Having seen the worst that humanity can become, I was naturally curious to get a wider perspective on the events I had witnessed."[11] There is something quite natural about trying to make sense of what at first strikes us

---

[8] See extended presentation in *Goodbye Holland: The Destruction of Dutch Jewry*, a film of Willy Lindwer (2004), 8:15-8:30, 31:40-38:45 with discussion of the razzia (*rafle*, round-up) of the Jews of the city of Groningen by the Dutch police.

[9] On July 16, 1995, Jacques Chirac, French President (1995-2007), in a speech in Paris, expressed full recognition of the collaboration of the Vichy Government with the Third Reich. This was on the 53rd anniversary of the *Rafle du Vél d'Hiver* (the Raid of the Winter Velodrome), a massive round-up of Jews in Paris on that date in 1942. See "Discours de Jacques Chirac sur la responsabilité de Vichy dans la déportation, 1995," FRANCE 2: JOURNAL TÉLÉVISÉ. On Oct. 29, 2016, the treatment of "nomads" (*tsiganes*, Romanies) was acknowledged by François Mitterrand, the French President (2012-2017) of France, who declared, *Le jour est venu et il fallait que cette vérité soit dite* (The day has come and it was necessary that this truth be stated): Alexandra du Boucheron, "Les nomades internés sous Vichy: l'histoire oubliée," FRANCE INTER (FRENCH RADIO NETWORK).

[10] The MOI (*la Main d'œuvre immigrée*), better known as the Manouchian Group: the poet Missak Manouchian, Arsène Tchakarian, Spartaco Fontano, Marcel Rajman, Tamás Elek, Olga Bancic, and others ("foreign Jews, Armenians, and Communists"). Some 22 were arrested by the French, and executed by the Nazi military at Fort Mont-Valérien, in Suresnes, on Feb. 21, 1944. See esp. the 2009 film *L'Armée du crime* (*Army of Crime*), and Jason Dawsey, "All Those Who Fight for Freedom: Resisting the Germans Before D-Day," Feb. 26, 2019, NATIONALWW2MUSEUM.ORG.

[11] Sarah Judith Hofmann, "Why one of the last remaining Auschwitz survivors wrote a memoir decades later," DEUTSCHE WELLE/DW, Jun. 13, 2017. Samuel Pitnik is author of *Survivor: Auschwitz, the Death March and My Fight for Freedom* (2013).

powerfully, but in a way that we cannot at all make sense of and comprehend. As one contemporary author has written, "Ignorance is man's worst enemy, whereas the greatest desire a man may have is to learn more. Curiosity and the urge to understand are intrinsic feelings akin to the instincts of thirst and hunger."[12] In contrast, some say it is best not to look back at such horrors, to look only to the present and to the future, and to the good sides of life. And yet, there is a pull to those years and those extreme conditions that is stronger than such advice. This interest is rarely out of a masochistic urge to make ourselves feel bad, miserable, depressed, or hopeless. Mostly, it is the human attempt to understand how our world could possibly become something so violent and so thorough in its hatred. As was written in 1951:

> We can no longer afford to take that which was good in the past and simply call it our heritage, to discard the bad and simply think of it as a dead load which by itself time will bury in oblivion. The subterranean stream of Western history has finally come to the surface and usurped the dignity of our tradition. This is the reality in which we live. And this is why all efforts to escape from the grimness of the present into nostalgia for a still intact past, or into the anticipated oblivion of a better future, are vain.[13]

We might begin thinking of history as a complex collection of individual occurrences, each fully independent from all else, isolated within a discrete bubble in time, each fully self-contained, self-defined, and self-determined (in the history of philosophy, defined as Leibnizian monads[14]).

Considering further, however, we may come to sense that each such reality is actually *a constituent of a larger phenomenon whose parts have an intricate and at times subtle interconnectedness*. Events understood this way are semi-permeable,[15] in which their existence may have impact beyond themselves across a wide span of time, ghost-like and yet quite real and even palpable. Events, which we may think of as occurring at some given specific time, may echo and reverberate through time, in part through the memories, recollections, stories told by elders to younger family members, records, and monuments built to commemorate them. All of these have a defining impact on later personal, social, political, and even international or global contexts. Italy under Mussolini harkened back to the grandeur that was the ancient Roman Empire; the German World War I victory at the Battle of Tannenberg in late August 1914 over the Russian Armies was understood in the Second Reich as a sweet, satisfying

---

[12] Dr. Amal Al-Hazzani, "The Israel We Do Not Know," *Social Media News and Discussion Forum* (Pakistan), Mar. 18, 2013.
[13] Hannah Arendt, *The Origins of Totalitarianism* (1951), Preface to the First Ed.
[14] *La Monadologie* (1714), by Gottfried Wilhelm Leibniz (1646-1716); Eng. ed., *The Monadology*, tr. by Austrian Jewish philosopher and Prussian Academy editor of the works of Leibniz, Paul Schrecker (1889-1963), who fled Germany in 1933 and then France at the occupation in 1940.
[15] This concept of semi-permeability is borrowed from cellular biology.

vengeance for the Teutonic Knights at the earlier Battle of Tannenberg, which had been fought, and which the Knights had lost to their Slavic enemy, some five centuries earlier, in mid-July 1410. We can see by such examples, that such associations can span literally millennia.

One such very recent association to an event from about 1000 BCE—the story of the young shepherd, David with his sling and five smooth stones taken from a nearby stream, to attack and kill Goliath, the Philistine warrior—is with a missile defense system used by the Israeli military, which was given the name David's Sling.[16] And so forth.

The ways of thinking of any given time—the social concerns, frustrations about an unjust world, worries, fears, hopes, and desires for revenge and for power, and for self-protection, which were all in play in the early twentieth century—can be a starting point developing into a deep interest in learning and understanding about the Hitler era that is alive and of vital significance to many people to this day.

If we look at the huge number of books and journal articles, and newspaper articles, diaries, memoirs, and blogs, that continue to be published with a focus on the Third Reich and the events of those years, material that is still coming out year after year, decade after decade,[17] it is clear that the interest in the world of the Hitler era is not just a dead remnant of a dry and dusty past. The interest in this period and its specific structures of operation have become the province of young researchers and readers. Some recent books still offer fresh insights and appreciations of the way that world evolved, and how it came to a crashing ending, with Germany being overwhelmed by Allied military both by the Soviet Army from the east, and from the Western Allies from the south and west.

More information from a possibly wide range of sources is to come, but in some cases not for years; and this, even though the better part of a century has already gone by since the end of World War II. How is that?

First, there are documents that have been made unavailable (legally controlled) for years. Some of these are held as "Classified" or "Closed" or "Secret" material by various government agencies. Documents that are held in Great Britain by the royal family, for example (many at Windsor Castle, under lock and key), are prohibited from publication for a full one hundred years. *This is not limited to personally embarrassing information being kept private.* There are large numbers of informative documents from the era of the Third Reich kept unknown to the general public and

---

[16] The biblical passage is at 1 Samuel 40-58. Tamir Eshel, "Following a successful test series, David's Sling to become operational this year," DEFENSE UPDATE, Apr. 1, 2015. In Hebrew, David's sling is *kalah david* (or *qala' david*). On this missile system, see the report from Ratheon Corp., RATHEON: DAVID'S SLING WEAPON SYSTEM: MEDIUM-RANGE AIR DEFENSE.

[17] Among many texts, consider, from the point of view of concentration-camp prisoners, Charlotte Delbo (1913-1985), *Auschwitz and After* (a trilogy); Tadeusz Borowski (1922-1951), *This Way for the Gas, Ladies and Gentlemen;* Olga Lengyel (1908-2001), *Five Chimneys;* Ka-tzetnik 135633 (Yehiel De-Nur, 1909-2001), *House of Dolls.* Other such writings are mentioned in various contexts, below.

even to scholars focused on gathering a more complete and coherent sense of the era. Before such information can be considered, it has to be known about, and access must be established.

The amount of information that is held in closed vaults is perhaps beyond our imagination; we only come to know of them decades after the fact, and then there is often a struggle to have those documents available for research. In short, the general public, and even historians and other researchers, *do not have ready access to many relevant sources of information* we might be interested in learning about in greater depth.

It might seem unlikely that a huge mass of organized, researched, and documented texts would remain basically unknown, and yet, *we might be wary of believing that we already have all of the important information about the Third Reich.* A large number of documents that organized information about war crimes, assembled during and just after the end of the war, were classified secret and closed to the general public.

These were documents of the UNWCC (United Nations War Crimes Commission), established on October 20, 1943, and working into 1948-1949. This collection, gathered by researchers of twenty-six countries, contained more than 2,240 UNWCC documents, on 22,184 pages, concerning many international criminal cases—*no small collection of information on war crimes through Nazi-dominated Europe*. Now, the fact that there are documents even as extensive as this collection containing over 22,000 pages does not necessarily mean that there is anything of value or interest in those pages. Here, however, we have the dedicated work of people from a large number of countries who committed their professional abilities to a careful documentation that could be used as solid evidence in war crimes trials for Nazi perpetrators.[18]

This certainly suggests that these pages are not some wild ramblings of people in deep ignorance about the activities and actual actions of those in power, but, rather, documentation taken down in ways that would allow legal criminal evaluation and use. On the other hand, some information is far from being accurate in ways that are not always obvious.

For example, with the joy at the ending of World War II, details of the surrender agreements with the Japanese Empire were just that: details. If, however, we can see the power of language and respect it fully, we can be more alert to its distortions (from the misleading names given to laws and treaties, to the declarations of politicians, not only the Third Reich, but in a much more general way throughout the world). This calls on us to be acutely attentive to what we and others are actually saying, and to appreciate the way in which what is said, and thought, has a powerful impact on us, and on others.

We can be wary and attentive to such possibilities without becoming hysterical or paranoid: As Leningrad-born Joseph Brodsky (1940-1996), Nobel Laureate in Literature (1987), stated, "A political system, a form of

---

[18] "UN War Crimes Commission's archive is now available in the ICC Legal Tools Database," COUR PÉNALE INTERNATIONAL/INTERNATINAL CRIMINAL COURT, ICC-CPI.INT, Jul. 4, 2013; more below in "UN War Crimes Commission" (in the Front Matter).

social organization, as any system in general, is by definition a form of the past tense that aspires to impose itself upon the present (and often on the future as well) .... I am speaking ... of the education in speech, the slightest imprecision in which may trigger the intrusion of false choice into one's life."[19] We may consider here the example of the unconditional surrender of the Japanese agreed to by all signatories was of all armed forces under Japanese control. It was unconditional *in military ones—but not in governmental ones*. Thus, Prince Hirohito (1901-1989), Emperor (1926-1989), was allowed to keep his honorary title, as part of a desire to establish acceptance of the surrender and cooperation in the post-war reconstruction of Japan by American military forces.[20] The Emperor was also exempt of any charges of war crimes. And his uncle, Prince Yasuhiko Asaka (1887-1981), despite being the General and commander of the Japanese forces at the Battle of Nanking (now Nanjing), often referred to as the Rape of Nanking—was interrogated by Allied military but did not face trial. Rather, it was General Iwane Matsui (1878-1948) who accepted responsibility and blame for not advising Prince Asaka more wisely, and was found guilty in the Nanking Massacre. Mastsui was hung on December 23, 1948. Relatedly, another member of the imperial family also in the military, Prince Nashimoto Morimasa (1874-1951), a Marshal General in the Imperial Japanese Army, was arrested by MacArthur on war crimes charges, imprisoned for four months, and then released in April 1946 by American authorities, with no charges made. Perhaps it was an arrest meant to assure the cooperation of the Japanese Imperial family to the conditions of surrender that were formally signed aboard the USS Missouri on September 2, 1945.[21]

In a much more general perspective here, the period of time during which given documents may be classified as closed (secret or top secret, etc.) is typically 30, 50, or 100 years—after the event or after the death of the last person involved in the document at hand—by governmental agencies (the Foreign Office, the UK Public Records Office/PRO, the US

---

[19] "Joseph Brodsky, Nobel Lecture, Dec. 8, 1987," NOBEL PRIZE, NOBELPRIZE.ORG.

[20] See the role of US Army Colonel Sidney Mashbir (1891-1973), a Japanese-language, -culture, and –business expert, and colleague in 1930s peace efforts with Japanese Emperor Hirohito and Prince Tokugawa (1863-1940). Cf. Stan S. Katz, *The Art of Peace: An Illustrated Biography about Prince Tokugawa* (2019); more on Tokugawa, his untimely death, and the subsequent signing of the Tripartite Pact between Germany, Italy, and Japan, below. During the war, Mashbir, a close associate of General Douglas MacArthur, was a key member of the Japanese-American Military Intelligence Service (decoding and interpreting captured Japanese documents). It was Mashbir, on MacArthur's appointment, who acted as US Military liaison to greet the Japanese envoys aboard the USS Missouri for the signing of the Japanese Military surrender to the USA on Sept. 2, 1945: see *The Emperor and The Spy Book Promo*, YOUTUBE, at 0:15-0:35. Cf. Stan S. Katz, *The Emperor and the Spy* (2017), pp. 439-515, esp. pp. 455-458, 503.

[21] "Japan: Instrument of Surrender, September 2, 1945," pp. 625-627 in US Congress, *A Decade of American Foreign Policy: Basic Documents, 1941-49* (1950).

Department of State, the FBI, the CIA, the US Library of Congress, the French *Archives nationales*, the Russian Archives, etc.), by royal families holding their own private communications and other material (the British and Dutch royal families,[22] etc.), by military organizations (in the UK, Canada, US, France, USSR/Russia), by private entities (such as archives at various universities), etc. The policy of the Vatican Secret Archives is to release information 70 years after the end of any pontificate. For Pius XII (1939-1958), this would be 2028. The Vatican has declared that it will open these documents from the pontificate of Pius XII—some 16 million pages of documents—to scholars (not to the general public) on March 2, 2020.[23] That promises new information for many years to come.

Freedom of Information (FOI) laws are being passed in numerous countries, with an impact still to be seen,[24] as with the documents of British World War II governmental organizations such as the JPS (Joint Planning Staff) or the JIC (Joint Intelligence Committee), now within the UK Cabinet Office.[25]

Other governments may keep documents classified as Top Secret and so forth, or may have them destroyed when their disclosure might prove unacceptably embarrassing for those involved, or embarrassing for the institution of government itself. (Personal or institutional interests at times have a way of trumping historical inquiry).

There are, we see, governmental and other institutions and even individuals who may find ways of blocking access to many documents in their possession; of course, in some cases important documents may be burned or otherwise destroyed (as in many bureaucratic departments in the Third Reich as the end of the war was fast approaching). Here, we might also consider the case of the former Soviet Union, with its own vast collections of documents pertaining to the Hitler era. *What impacted and impeded this information from being widely investigated and propagated was in part the significant shift after the defeat of the Third Reich, in which ideological issues between the Western Allies and the Soviet Union*, a tension that lead to a new Red Scare, the first being early in the life of the Soviet Union—and in the USA, McCarthyism and Communist witch-hunts). More on this, below. These post-war concerns made for a hostile,

---

[22] *Edward VIII: The Traitor King* (1995, CHANNEL 4 UK), at 1:32:00-1:32:20.

[23] James Reynolds, "Pius XII: Vatican to open secret Holocaust-era archives," *BBC News*, Mar. 4, 2019; Christopher Wells, "Pope Francis: Pius XII archives to open next year," *Vatican News*, Mar. 4, 2019, VATICANNEWS.VA; Elisabetta Povoledo, "Pope Francis to Allow Access to Holocaust-Era Documents of Pius XII," *The New York Times*, Mar. 4, 2019.

[24] Mark Strauss, "Eight Historical Archives That Will Spill New Secrets," *Smithsonian Magazine*, Oct. 27, 2017; "Unlocking the secrets of government," BBC NEWS, Jan. 1, 2001; and "France: des archives présidentielles sur le génocide rwandais restent fermées," *Le Point*, Sep. 15, 2017; Sheila Fitzpatrick, "Impact of the Opening of Soviet Archives on Western Scholarship on Soviet Social History," *The Russian Review*, vol. 74, Jul. 2015, pp. 377–400.

[25] "Joint Planning Staff" and "Joint Intelligence Committee," UK NATIONAL ARCHIVES.

suspicious attitude toward anything—including documents and other information seized from the Third Reich's organized and quite thorough bureaucracy and record-keeping—coming from the other side of the Iron Curtain (a name introduced in Churchill's speech, March 5, 1946).

Documentation held in Soviet Union archives has been inherited by the successor of the USSR, the Russian Federation, and its State Archives. Some of its documents have been released for public study by researchers such as Slavic and Russian Scholar Patricia Kennedy Grimsted and others, while others were still in closed files (as of 1997).[26] This research is rather recent, given the lack of cooperation beginning with Western-Soviet hostilities in the post-war 1940s and continuing for decades: but with economic and voting crises and unrest, the DDR, the German Democratic Republic, or East Germany, on December 9, 1989, allowed its citizens to cross over into West Berlin, with the destruction of the Berlin Wall. Germany was reunited on October 3, 1990. The USSR formally ended on December 26, 1991, with the birth of the Russian Federation. All of these changes were part of the start of new availability of East German and USSR secret archives to Western scholarship. (And vice versa.) As well, important sources of information about the Hitler era were intentionally not shared because of personal or geopolitical issues. And so, *despite the common idea that all that there was to be discovered about the Third Reich has long been discovered, some newer publications expose us to information that was simply not available in earlier decades.*

Another limitation in the making use of wartime documents is that some documents were in a condition that made almost all of the text illegible. One example of this is the set of notes written by Marcel Nadjari, a Greek Jew from Thessaloniki. Nadjari had been shipped to Auschwitz in April 1944, when he was 26, and was to put to work there as part of the Jewish *Sonderkommando*, transferring Jewish corpses from the gas chambers to the crematoria. He wrote twelve pages of notes on what he had witnessed there, in (modern) Greek. In November 1944, he placed them in a container and buried them near Crematorium III. They were discovered in some excavations near Auschwitz in 1980. With their having spent decades in the dank soil at Auschwitz, only some 10-15% of their text was at all legible. These notes might have remained only a mere hint of a violent past, but—*with radical advances in technology*—in 2013, the text was made mostly readable—85-90% of it—using the contemporary technology of multispectral image analysis.[27]

---

[26] Patricia Grimsted, *Archives of Russia Five Years After: "Purveyor of Sensations" or "Shadows Cast out to the Past"?* (1997), IISG RESEARCH PAPERS; see Chap. 1 (Why Is Stalin's Archive Still Locked Away?) and Chap. 7 (Archival Destruction and Retention Policies); *Archives of Russia: A Directory and Bibliogaphic Guide to Holdings in Moscow and St. Petersburg*, P. K. Grimsted, ed. (2000); Sheila Fitzpatrick, "Impact of the Opening of Soviet Archives on Western Scholarship on Soviet Social History," *The Russian Review*, vol. 74, Jul. 2015, pp. 377–400.

[27] Dagmar Breitenbach, "Reconstructed Auschwitz prisoner text details

The Hitler Era   xi

This is one example of the way in which advances in science can have an impact on our access to information and can also give form to some earlier questions that were not answerable given limits to our knowledge and applicable technology. Some documents were simply hidden away, often for safety during the war, and only discovered decades later, in the context of tearing down old buildings, of descendants having a chance to look through old papers never discussed earlier, and so forth. Some of the information was not seen or appreciated, or was perhaps misplaced.[28]

Recent theoretical break-throughs can (perhaps surprisingly) help our understanding of various historical mysteries, as in our appreciation of the physical and psychological problems that philosopher, philologist, and psychologist Friedrich Nietzsche experienced, made significantly clearer in the last two decades, based on genetic distinctions and discoveries that shed light on what was otherwise not understood at all or understood in very distorting ways.[29]

Further, here, some sources we now have access to, show their own historical bias: those who were targeted as members of specific groups were *described without indicating these specifics*, as in a nationalist framework, with people described merely as being citizens of one country or another. Thus, a Romani (Gypsy) who had been murdered was spoken of as a Pole or a Rumanian or a Russian, and not a Romani; a Jew was often counted as a citizen of the Soviet Union, Poland, Czechoslovakia, Lithuania, and not as a Jew, and so on. *This hides the specificity of the*

'unimaginable' suffering," DEUTSCHE WELLE/DW, Oct. 9, 2017; Brigit Katz, "Reconstructed Auschwitz Letter Reveals Horrors Endured by Forced Laborer: Marcel Nadjari buried his letter hoping it would one day reach his family," *Smithsonian Smart News*, Oct. 11, 2017; Theo Ioannou, "Greek-Jewish Holocaust Survivor's Letter Buried in Auschwitz Uncovered," *Greek Reporter*, Nov. 6, 2017; Laurence Peter, "Auschwitz inmate's notes from hell finally revealed," *BBC News*, Dec. 1, 2017. Based on work by Russian historian and Doctor of Geographical Sciences in the Russian Academy of Sciences, Pavel Markovich Polian, pub. in his text, *Svitki iz Pepla* (2013), *Scrolls from the Ashes*.

[28] One such set of documents was hidden away in the ceiling of a bathroom on the third floor, in a house at 128 Vrolikstraat in Amsterdam. Discovered in the late 1990s, during the demolition of that building, these were letters sent to his parents from Hardenberg (Molengoot camp), where he was a prisoner, by a young Dutch Jew, Philip ("Flip") Slier (1923-1943). He escaped, went into hiding, but was arrested on March 3, 1943, his twentieth birthday, *ohne Stern* (not wearing a Jewish star), and sent untimately by train on April 9 to Sobibór, where he was killed. See Deborah Slier (Flip's first cousin) and Ian Shine, *Hidden Letters* (2008).

[29] Did Nietzsche have an incapacitating mental breakdown from intense empathy on seeing a horse beaten in Milan—or was that incident what we will call a Nietzschean match? Was it divine retribution for his rejecting Christianity? Genetic studies in the 1990s by French researchers Marie-Germaine Bousser and Elisabeth Tournier-Lasserve have led to the diagnosis of CADASIL, Cerebral Autosomal Dominant Arteriopathy with Subcortical Infarcts and Leukoencephalopathy, associating the syndrome with a mutation of the Notch3 gene (on chromosome 19). More on Nietzsche, this condition, and the metaphorical Nietzschean match, below.

killing, of course. That is, when people are killed in virtue of having been identified by their killers solely by their nationality alone, that is the most appropriate way for them to be remembered, reflecting animosities between nations; but, if not, the more specific basis of selection is presumably relevant to indicate explicitly the import of the killing, avoiding a basic misidentification of those targeted, only by national identity, *totally missing the reasoning behind their being specifically selected for mass killing.* As materials come to light, however, wherever they have been filed away, they give us more and more of a broad overview of the world we are investigating. It has even been said, for example, that in terms of Holocaust Studies, "It is difficult to conceive that Holocaust research could have developed [as it has in recent years] without access to the previously closed archives in the former German Democratic Republic, Eastern bloc countries, and Soviet Union."[30]

On the right to—or at least the value of—full information, in Spanish government archives from the Franco era, covering both the years of the Spanish Civil War and World War II, with Franco's remaining neutral despite aid from Germany and Italy, are volumes published with the proviso, "Each document has been carefully reviewed to assure that it appears intact [*aparece integro*]. Neither has there been any pre-selection made [*tampoco existe una selección previa*]—familiarity with an epoch should be based on a review of all perspectives, including those sources favorable [to the Franco regime] and also unfavorable.... The Spanish people have a right to know them [*tienen derecho a conocerlos*]."[31] *As we see old material published for the first time now and in years to come, our appreciation of the machinations of that Hitlerian world will become continually clearer and more comprehensible.*

We are fortunate in this way to be living now, to see so much more proof of what people thought, did, set up as policies, and carried out as projects of great significance in the Hitler era. Some of this documentation is in the way of diaries and memoirs along with other more official records and other new sources that are surprise findings that no one—or only a very small, select group—knew about beforehand.

We might well distinguish between diaries, which are typically more personal and candid, being written primarily for oneself, and memoirs, usually written with an audience in mind. The latter are often more self-protective if not self-glorifying and self-justifying than the former.

One political commentator[32] has suggested that there is a universal pattern to be noticed here, writing of a man who "tried to cast himself as

---

[30] Gerald D. Feldman, "Confiscation of Jewish Assets, and the Holocaust," pp. 1-8, in *Confiscation of Jewish Property in Europe, 1933-1945: New Sources and Perspectives; Symposium Proceedings*, CENTER FOR ADVANCED HOLOCAUST STUDIES, US HOLOCAUST MEMORIAL MUSEUM (2003), at p. 3.

[31] Fundación Nacional Francisco Franco, *Documentos inéditos para la Historia del Generalísimo Franco*, Vol. II-1 (1992), from Notice page, facing the full title page.

[32] Rick Wilson, *Everything Trump Touches Dies: A Republican Strategist Gets Real About the Worst President Ever* (2018), p. 23.

the hero of the piece, as all do in retellings of their story." (Even if not actually true of everyone, this tendency is common and presumably worth remembering when reading autobiographical accounts.)

Here, we might keep in mind that Hitler's *Mein Kampf* was definitely written for a reading public, with a biased, selective, and distorting description of many events: Consider the schematic and rather idealized version of his early life, and the glorified, self-flattering, and importantly exaggerated rendering of his role in the birth and early years of the National Socialist German Workers' Party (the NSDAP). More, below.

In addition, there is also another kind of realization to take into account, where seemingly disparate events and developments end up impacting one another in unexpected ways. (The world and all of reality seem to have connections we do not always see from the start with clarity.)

In any case, we can recognize that a number of the texts that review the Third Reich are quite substantial in size (and content), being in many cases more than 1,000 pages in length each.

Furthermore, an estimate at the turn of the (twenty-first) century concluded that there had been some 120,000 books written by that time on Hitler and the Third Reich. And even that enormous quantity of texts and of pages devoted to the period leaves unsaid much that may be significant and of great interest to us. Texts that examine very particular features of the times continue to be written and released for an interested reading audience. (Our breadth of interest here is wide, to see and appreciate some of the complexity of those events.)

If, in particular, we go back to early books that spoke about Hitler and the rising National Socialist (Nazi) movement in Germany, and then about the first years of the Third Reich, though, we may be impressed by how much was in fact written, published, and available to the public back then.

To take a sampling of some of the more substantial of these books here, there are, looking from 1923 through to recent publications, the following titles, first those published before 1933 (with year of publication in parentheses—*followed, after a comma, by the number of pages*): Adolf Hitler, *Adolf Hitler: Sein Leben und seine Reden*, Adolf-Viktor von Koerber,[33] ed. (1923, 112); Georg Schott, *Das Volksbuch vom Hitler* (1924, 330); and Friedrich Plümer,[34] *Die Wahrheit über Hitler und seinen Kreis* (1925, 71).

---

[33] Von Koerber was editor at the Nazi newspaper, *Völkischer Beobachter*, from which speeches were taken, with Hitler's approval, for incorporation into this book. Konrad Heiden, in *Der Fuehrer* (1944), p. 138, remarks that as the book went into new editions, the texts of the speeches kept changing. (Heiden was among those saved by Varian Fry; more on that, below.)

[34] Friedrich Plümer was a member of the group around Anton Drexler (the founder in January 1919 of the DAP, the German Workers Party, which in February 1920 was to become the NSDAP, the National Socialist German Workers Party). Drexler felt that Hitler was becoming too powerful within the Party. Drexler would be expelled from the new NSDAP on July 29, 1921 when Drexler was negotiating with other right-wing parties and Hitler in reply demanded to be made chairman of the

A new phase of German life began after January 1933, when Hitler became Chancellor. Published in that period, until the end of the Third Reich in 1945, were Leo Motzkin, *Die Lage der Juden in Deutschland, 1933* (1934, 535); Gerhart Seger, *Oranienburg: Erster authentischer Bericht eines aus dem Konzentrationslager Geflüchteten* (1934, 76) and its English translation, *A Nation Terrorized*, Foreword by Heinrich Mann (1935, 204); Wolfgang Langhoff, *Rubber Truncheon: Being an Account of Thirteen Months spent in a Concentration Camp* (1935, 279)—with a 1946, 294-page German ed., *Die Moorsoldaten: 13 Monate Konzentrationslager; The Yellow Spot: The Outlawing of Half a Million Human Beings; A Collection of Facts and Documents relating to Three Years' Persecution of German Jews, derived chiefly from National Socialist sources*, with an Introduction by Herbert Dunelm, Bishop of Durham (1936, 287); Kurt G. W. Ludecke, *I Knew Hitler: The Story of a National Socialist Who Escaped the Blood Purge* (1937, 814); William L. Shirer, *Berlin Diary: The Journal of a Foreign Correspondent 1934-1941* (1941, 626); Fritz Thyssen, *I Paid Hitler* (1941, 281); Institute of Jewish Affairs, American Jewish Congress, *Hitler's Ten-Year War On the Jews* (1943); *The Black Book of Polish Jewry: An Account of the Martyrdom of Polish Jewry Under the Nazi Occupation*, Jacob Apenszlak, ed. (1943, 343); Konrad Heiden, *Der Fuehrer: Hitler's Rise to Power* (1944, 788); American Representation of the General Jewish Workers' Union (the Bund) in Poland, *Geto in Flamen: Zamlbukh* (1944, 205); and Jan Karski, *Story of a Secret State* (1944, 389).

Then, after the war, were Jewish Black Book Committee (World Jewish Congress, et al.), *The Black Book: The Nazi Crime Against the Jewish People* (1946, 560); Saul K. Padover, *Experiment in Germany: The Story of an American Intelligence Officer* (1946, 400); Georges Wellers, *De Drancy à Auschwitz* (1946, 231); Gustave M. Gilbert, *Nuremberg Diary* (1947, 471); Alan Bullock, *Hitler: A Study in Tyranny* (1952, 848); Gerald Reitlinger, *The Final Solution: The Attempt to Exterminate the Jews of Europe 1939-1945* (1953, 622); Joseph Tenenbaum, *Race and Reich: The Story of an Epoch* (1956, 554); William L. Shirer, *The Rise and Fall of the Third Reich: A History of Nazi Germany* (1959, 1245); *Faschismus—Getto—Massenmord: Dokumentation über Ausrottung und Widerstand der Juden in Polen während des zweiten Weltkrieges* (1960, 609); Joachim C. Fest, *Hitler: Eine Biographie* (1973, 1190); Heinrich Himmler, *Heinrich Himmler: Geheimreden, 1933 bis 1945, und andere Ansprachen* (1974, 319); Serge Klarsfeld, *Vichy-Auschwitz* [Vol. 1]: *Le rôle de Vichy dans la Solution Finale de la Question Juive en France, 1942* (1983, 544) and *Vichy-Auschwitz* [Vol. 2]: *Le rôle de Vichy dans la Solution Finale de la Question Juive en France, 1943-1944* (1985, 409), Claude Lanzmann, *Shoah* (1985, 220), Raul Hilberg, *The Destruction of the European Jews* (rev., definitive 3-vol. ed., 1985, 1273); the five-volume *Encyclopedia of*

NSDAP, with dictatorial powers, on the threat of leaving the party totally. On July 29, 1921, a vote gave Hitler total power over the Party. Hitler was then considered the *Führer* (Leader) of the *Party*. He was not referred to as *Führer* of the *nation* for more than a further decade.

the Holocaust (1990, 1,905); Brigitte Hamann, *Hitler's Vienna: A Portrait of the Tyrant as a Young Man* (1999, 482); Richard J. Evans, *The Third Reich Trilogy—The Coming of the Third Reich* (2003, 622), *The Third Reich in Power, 1933-1939* (2005, 941), and *The Third Reich at War, 1939-1945* (2008, 926)—a total of 2,489 pages; Ian Kershaw, *Hitler: A Biography* (2008, 1030), an abridgment of his texts subtitled *1889-1936: Hubris* and *1936-1945: Nemesis* (1998, 2000; total, 1964); Peter Longerich, *Heinrich Himmler: Biographie* (2008, 1035); Dietrich Orlow, *The Nazi Party 1919-1945: A Complete History* (2010, 581); Christian Ingrao, *Croire et détruire: Les intellectuels dans la machine de guerre SS* (2010, 585); Robert Gerwarth, *Hitler's Hangman: The Life of Heydrich* (2011, 336); Jean-Paul Lefebvre-Filleau and Gilles Perrault, *Ces Français qui ont collaboré avec le IIIe Reich* (2017, 540); Laurent Joly, *L'État contre les Juifs. Vichy, les Nazis et la Persécution antisémite: 1940-1944* (2018, 366); *The Oxford Illustrated History of the Third Reich*, Robert Gellately, ed. (2018, 383).

Now, this somewhat random and rather motley sampling can perhaps give an idea of serious authors who have found it appropriate to offer texts of hundreds of pages of information, in order to give a non-superficial understanding of the aspects of the Hitler era that they were discussing, each from a particular perspective and set of interests.

While no one book holds everything we might be interested in knowing about, we can find a good number of publications, each giving a decent sense of certain features of those horrible years, even if limited or biased in various ways. Interests can vary, with some texts focusing on one single event, such as the first torpedoing of the Second World War, on September 3, 1939, with a German submarine (U-boat) sinking the British ship *SS Athenia*, bound from Liverpool to Montréal, with 117 passengers and crew killed, and with 673 saved by other ships in the vicinity,[35] or a text devoted to the night of November 9-10, 1938, called *Kristallnacht* (the Night of the Broken Glass).[36]

The scope of interest in the times of the Third Reich is vast, and each text has its own value, for those who are especially interested in the book's focus, as well as for those who appreciate details that add to the overall understanding of the period.

Beyond all of those authors who have attempted to sieve through the indefinitely large amount of information contained in authoritative texts and documents from the Hitler era itself, and from compilations of very

---

[35] "SS Athenia," WIKIPEDIA. Cmp. a fictionalized account by journalist and author Thomas C. Sanger (grandson of a surviving American passenger, Rhoda Thomas), *Without Warning* (2017), and a BBC report by its Science Correspondent, Jonathan Amos, "Athenia: Is this the wreck of the first British ship torpedoed in WW2?" *BBC News*, Oct. 5, 2017, locating the sunken ship as being 200 m. (656 ft.) down, on Rockall Bank, off the coast of Ireland, and identifying the Captain of the German U-boat as being Fritz Julius Lemp. The Rockall is 263 mi. northwest of Ireland, 440 mi. south-southeast of Iceland, and south-southwest of the Danish Faroe Islands.

[36] Anthony Read and David Fisher, *Kristallnacht: The Nazi Night of Terror* (1989); Martin Gilbert, *Kristallnacht: Prelude to Destruction* (2006).

serious and dedicated researchers (in search of historical understanding), there are those with specific goals of proving someone or some group or country right, justified, and honorable, and another wrong and perhaps horrible.

Facing this issue in a speech given on Oct. 5, 2010, Michael Gove, the British Education Secretary in the UK Conservative Party government (more recently to hold still other posts in the Conservative party), in speaking of education in the UK and public knowledge of history, said, in a moment of candor, "Our history has moments of pride, and [also of] shame, but unless we fully understand the struggles of the past we will not properly value the liberties of the present."[37]

And in a psychological analysis, the philosopher Nietzsche is famous for having spoken to this phenomenon, talking of the individual—and we might see his insight as true, just as well, for groups and even for entire countries, in this vignette of consciousness:

> "I have done that," says my memory. "I cannot have done that," says my pride, and remains inexorable. Eventually, memory yields.[38]

Similarly, the Yale historian David W. Blight wrote, "nations rarely commemorate their disasters and tragedies, unless compelled by forces that will not let the politics of memory rest."[39] And yet, societal and national disasters will not rest quiet, either, and may ultimately impact the world in perhaps even more compelling ways!

Some will hate Hitler and everything in the Reich and others will laud the man and his work; still others will deny that certain events ever took place, in spite of the astonishing precise and definite, formal records that were kept about those events, including film news clips from the period, and the thousands of witnesses, including many Nazi leaders themselves, who have not denied any of these facts (but who come to different judgments or evaluations of their practical or moral merits).

Not all people, and certainly not all people in government positions, are open to recognizing that every single country might well have parts of its history that can be easily acknowledged to be quite respectable and even honorable, and other parts, reflecting something that would have been better not to have happened at all, something to regret, a source of shame, and perhaps something even to make amends about.

This implies that it is important for us to appreciate the sources of information that we are considering. Still, *we can learn something in any case, not only about what someone wants to protect or glorify, or to*

---

[37] "Michael Gove: All pupils will learn our island story" (Speech given by the UK Sec. of Education, Oct. 5, 2010), CONSERVATIVE-SPEECHES.SAYIT.MYSOCIETY.ORG.

[38] Friedrich Nietzsche, *Beyond Good and Evil* (1886), Sect. 68. (Passages in Nietzsche's works are regularly cited for ease of comparison, by the section numbering of the original texts.) This passage and more are discussed in "Nietzschean Psychiatry Revisited," pp. 59-102, in Mitchell Ginsberg, *Calm, Clear, and Loving: Soothing the Distressed Mind, Healing the Wounded Heart* (2014).

[39] *Race and Reunion: The Civil War in American Memory* (2001), p. 9.

criticize or denigrate, but also what is perhaps being acknowledged in that context.

We can be speaking some truths, even as we try to dissimulate, disguise, deny, or glorify something through our story. As an example, if we read, "Hitler as the Führer of the Third Reich always treated the Jews with great respect," we may not find this statement at all true, yet we can see at the same time what is not being questioned at all in this statement: that Hitler was the Führer of the Third Reich, and that the issue of his relationship with Jews is significant.

To consider this basic feature about statements and what we can understand from them, even while questioning something about them, we can say, technically speaking, that statements have presuppositions—independent claims that must be true if the statement we are reading or hearing is to be true, although they are not explicitly stated.[40] *This is just one consideration, that perhaps points to a general factor in our reading any text.* In this we might develop our sensitivity to looking into any given narrative (set of descriptions of the topic at hand) in order to recognize "hidden transcripts," the information we can cull from any text if we are subtle and nuanced in our reading, without, of course, reading into a text anything that provides no hint of being there at all!

If we have an interest in understanding some phenomena rather than in declaring a moral position about them, our judgmental mind is best put aside (remembering: "Someone has said that it requires less mental effort to condemn than to think."[41])

Now, to understand rather than to adjudge Hitler, his thinking, and his actions, to look for what happened, without judgments of a wide variety of sorts, may be quite a challenge for many of us interested in the Reich.

As one German historian wrote, "We are not at this point criticizing Hitler's thought (difficult though it is to present this homicidal nonsense uncritically [*so schwer es fällt, diesen mörderischen Unsinn unkritisiert wiederzugeben*]—we are [merely] presenting it."[42] Here is the need to "interpret events accurately" without presenting "news sensationally."[43]

Similarly, the Hungarian historian Judit Molnár is quoted as noting that the historian is not a judge, prosecutor, or defense lawyer, that his role is, rather, to get to know and analyze the events of a period of history, and to make use of archival materials that are indispensable for understanding the past.[44]

---

[40] A technical discussion of statements and their presuppositions and entailments can be found in Mitchell Ginsberg, "The Entailment-Presupposition Relationship," *Notre Dame Journal of Formal Logic*, vol. 13, Oct. 1972, pp. 511-515.

[41] Emma Goldman, *Anarchism: What It Really Stands For* (1916), p. 2.

[42] Sebastian Haffner, *Anmerkugen zu Hitler*, 1978 ed., p. 106; 1994 ed., p. 82; Eng., *The Meaning of Hitler* (1979), p. 83.

[43] Frank McDonough, "The Times, Norman Ebbut and the Nazis, 1927-37," *Journal of Contemporary History*, vol. 27, no. 3, 1992, pp. 407–424, at p. 409.

[44] Thomas Komoly [speaker on the Holocaust; nephew of Ottó Komoly], "Most misleading book about the Hungarian Shoa," *The Times of Israel*, Aug. 22, 2017.

The issue for anyone trying to get a clear and undistorted sense of what happened at some time in the past *used to be* that there was so little information readily available. To consider one important example, if we look at the immense records contained in the numerous Nuremberg Trials, the problem for decades was that this information was contained in books very difficult to find, or very expensive to purchase. *This paucity of information is no longer the case.* For example, the transcripts of these trials are now available online.[45] At the same time, the communication that has been possible these past brief decades through the internet has also led to the promulgation of many wild ideas with no basis in anything in particular that can be tracked down. While offering up many more points of view than when sources were limited to the printed products of traditional publication houses, we have another important issue to deal with now: "the digital age, where nothing is vetted, context is absent, and lies proliferate."[46] Vetting here sounds perhaps esoteric but is nothing mysterious: it is where nothing is taken for granted as stated, but investigated thoroughly, to confirm or reject the various claims made.

We ourselves can vet issues or claims that are perhaps questionable. It may take some effort on our part but simply involves going to the sources of information on which given claims are made. Some we may appreciate, perhaps after research and in-depth consideration, are based on nothing more than *vint un shtaybl un raykh* (wind, dust, and smoke): imagination lacking any substance.

Claims that have no confirmable basis may be quite questionable. By contrast, one clear example of a very succinct and yet thorough vetting of claims about Hitler's physical and psychological condition can be found in a work by a German Professor of Medicine Emeritus and a historian who have seen the basis (or the lack thereof) of many claims about the Führer. In their work, they put aside many confabulations and confirmed many substantive claims, based on their analyses of primary sources of information and the official medical records that were made through the 1930s and 1940s.

The context of such vetting investigations involves an appreciation of the way in which a theory is constructed, with a search for anomalies

---

[45] "Nuremberg Trials, 1945-1949, Nuremberg, Germany," *Military Legal Resources, Federal Research Division, Library of Congress*, LOC.GOV. Note 2nd-4th links to the Blue, Red, and Green Series, most relevant here. The Nuremberg trials took place from 1946-1949. First was the trial of the major war criminals (Opening Session, October 18, 1945, final session, October 1, 1946), with defendents Göring, Hess, Keitel, Frank, Streicher, Dönitz, Von Schirach, and others). This was followed by a number of other trials (the Subsequent Nuremberg Proceedings), which ran from October 1946 to April 1949. More on these below, in the section "The Nuremberg Trials and other Key Documents." This German city has its name spelled as Nürnberg (the German spelling), as Nuremberg (the English spelling), and also as Nuernberg (an alternative spelling—from when Eng.-based texts had no ü type in its character set).

[46] Robert D. Kaplan, *The Return of Marco Polo's World* (2018), p. 216.

(facts that we do not want to deny but which do not fit neatly into the theory as it stands at a given time in its development).[47]

A classic, brief presentation of these features of theory construction[48] is by Carl Hempel, who had been one of the Vienna Circle (*der Wiener Kreis*), a group of highly respected philosophers and scientists; the group's work was banned and the group dissolved when the Third Reich annexed Austria. Hempel—leaving the Greater Reich: another dogmatic loss of National Socialism becoming a gift to the rest of the world— became a member of the Philosophy Department at Princeton University.

Another clear illustration of theory construction is an application of this thorough, honest questioning to develop a more comprehensive theory, presented in a detailed, reflect essay by psychotherapist Hellmuth Kaiser, "The Universal Symptom of the Psychoneuroses: A Search for the Conditions for Effective Psychotherapy."[49] Kaiser, trained at the Berlin Psychoanalytic Institute, then moved into exile in 1933. In this essay, he presents several versions of a theory of what is actually going on in psychotherapy sessions of psychoanalysis, until he comes to some inclusive conclusions. (Both of these works are worth reading to shed light on theory construction that demystifies the process.)

In our times, *what was a paucity of information has become the deluge of over-abundant information*, much of which demands an approach that is cautious and non-gullible, non-naïve. It has been said, *Caveat emptor* (Let the buyer beware) and this should perhaps be modified here to *Caveat lector* (Let the reader beware)!

The great if not the overwhelming amount of sources for information on the web is in part based on how easily and quickly we can post to the web anything we want: The threshold of time and energy required to put something before a potentially huge audience is minimal; we can send out a message through various social networks or services, with the time from birth of a thought to completion of the transmission to our audience being counted in seconds in some cases.

This easily allows for many an ill-conceived if not insulting comment to go into a real-world (virtual) community, rather than remaining a thought that twirls around in our mind for a moment and that we then simply put aside. This is presumably obvious to most users of the internet in these times, but it is important and relatively new. We need to develop or strengthen our sensitivities to the basis or lack of basis other than someone's imagination, fears, hopes, and fantasies) in what we are now exposed to! Again, *Caveat lector!*

---

[47] Hans-Joachim Neumann and Henrik Eberle, *War Hitler Krank?: Ein abschlissender Befund* (2009); Eng., *Was Hitler Ill?: A Final Diagnosis* (2013), esp. the chapters "Der kranke Hitler: Ein Projekt der Gescfhichtsschreibung," pp. 18-81; Eng., "The Diseased Hitler: A Historiographical Project," pp. 7-45, and also "Der medizinische Befund," pp. 166-223; Eng., "Hitler's Medical History," pp. 104-141."

[48] Carl Hempel, *Fundamentals of Concept Formation in Empirical Science* (1952).

[49] See the thorough discussion in *Effective Psychotherapy: The Contribution of Hellmuth Kaiser*, Mitchell Ginsberg, ed. (4th ed., 2018), pp. 14-171.

The many dimensions or aspects of the history of those times, the Hitler era, the times of the Third Reich, or of any times, are not confined to major political events, or to battles in a war (as history has sometimes been taught in school studies).

A history with a complex appreciation of human societies in action might well include the way given societies understand the world and the past that lie in their background, a past that often leaves sweet or bitter memories that represent unresolved issues the next generations have to deal with or be controlled by; it might include the impact of a region's natural resources, its terrain (some geographical features allowing for natural protections and others laying open its people to invasion from beyond).[50]

While histories of any period, including those of the Hitler era, are often tales of human interests, mutually satisfying interactions, and conflicts, there are typically other features of the overall situation that have an influence in what ends up happening in the fuller story.

In any case, if we glance at religious and political histories, we can appreciate that natural phenomena often have a significant impact on what we as a species are doing, in ways we usually have not planned for, from earthquakes to volcanic eruptions, the impact of the lunar cycle, tidal waves, draughts, or the destruction of plant foods (when cultivated by humans, called crops), with starvation. Then, there are infestations (such as those of locusts), hurricanes, typhoons, torrential rain storms, freezing cold winters, massive blizzards burying human shelters under snow, and stultifying dry heat in the air, to mention a few of nature's contributions to human life. History may also be impacted in unexpected ways, even travel by political figures or military missions, simply by heavily clouded skies (certainly since the age of the airplane). Even small microbes, the source of various infectious diseases from diarrhea to cholera to typhus fever to the Bubonic plague to influenza (the "flu"), can lay havoc to events small and large, from a community's health to an army's decimation that cuts short its victories.

The flow of reality can, and often does, surprise us, since events are not especially what we can imagine or assume ahead of time. So, in terms of our own particular life experiences and our interpretations of them, while a black swan is certainly a rare and unforeseeable phenomenon, events that this metaphor[51] captures do occur, much to everyone's surprise, and while not every butterfly flapping its wings over the Caribbean results in a significant change in the path of a hurricane moving

---

[50] More on this below, in Chap. 3.

[51] Nassim Nicholas Taleb, Lebanese-American statistician and author of *The Black Swan: The Impact of the Highly Improbable* (2007) made the important point "that statistics is fundamentally incomplete as a field as it cannot predict the risk of rare events, a problem that is acute in proportion to the rarity of these events." From "Nassim Nicholas Taleb," OMICS PUBLISHING GROUP CONFERENCES: RESEARCH, OMICS INTERNATIONAL (2014).

The Hitler Era

northwards toward the US East Coast,[52] *there is much in our history that is totally unpredictable on a practical level.*

Some say that the phenomenon of the Third Reich is something that very few foresaw or could appreciate ahead of its evolution.

That special and violent period was perhaps totally beyond the realm of the imaginable, thinking back on the high culture of Germany, or, rather, of Middle Europe, with its vast population speaking German spread across what is now Germany, Austria, the Czech Republic, and neighboring countries, that respected world of world-honored writers, composers, sociologists, economists, philosophers, mathematicians physicists, artists, and film directors, to give a sampling of human inquiry and creativity.

Germanic *Mitteleuropa* attracted the most serious students and scholars from around the world for many decades—*all of this ended with the creation of the Third Reich and its doctrinaire insistence on an Aryan science, thwarting a centuries-long, vanguard tradition in human culture.* The impact of these is part of the overall shift in contemporary concerns and understandings of what is important to address, the past echoing on.

A well-rounded perspective on that history will take into account people's aspirations, fears, and worries, with complex balancing acts between groups within a nation and between nations, and of disputes within a religious tradition or between such traditions, all in a multi-dimensional, multi-faceted vision of this history. *History is certainly best not interpreted as a mono-causal phenomenon.*

In this book, I will be open to considering these and other aspects of our ongoing, never-stagnant world, and, in particular, how these were relevant in the Hitler era. The era we will be investigating is one that reflected broad currents of societal interests in their historical context, but one that could be impacted by individual actions that were unforeseen and yet powerful, changing even a country's sense of its power, but also its sense of its sad and worrisome vulnerability, its perhaps bittersweet mixture of joy and happiness with tears and deep sadness—a painful, hurting joy, its *malegría*, as has been expressed in a Spanish neologism.[53]

---

[52] Benoît Mandelbrot, French-American mathematician famous for introducing the concept of fractals (and the nature of roughness: "Fractal Geometry," IBM.COM), makes the point that a very tiny change in initial conditions may lead to very significant results (outcomes), and, that even systems that are completely predictable in principle may be completely unpredictable in practice (given the impossibility of determining all of the relevant initial conditions). He cites the example of the movement (upwards vs. sideways) of a butterfly in the Caribbean that could affect the process of a storm moving toward the US coast. See the video *The butterfly effect—Benoit Mandelbrot 1998*, YOUTUBE.

[53] Consider here "Malegría" (1998) by French-Spanish polyglot singer Manu Chao (José-Manuel Thomas Arthur Chao Ortega, born 1961, in Paris). The word merges *mal* (bad, poorly, hurt, pain, etc.) and *alegría* (joy); the Eng. parallel, perhaps, might be a neologism such as hurtjoy or painjoy.

A Personal Note (Preface)

Given the events of the years of my life, I have been drawn (or dragged) into this world of political confrontations and great violence. This world filled with its wars has given much basic form to my sense of the world, and perhaps my case is not at all unusual, given the presence of wars in a seemingly never-ending sequence going back into the mists of time.

In particular, as it happens, in my case—born about 16 weeks after Pearl Harbor and other important events of that moment[54]—my first public memory (in other words, my first memory of the world outside of my personal and family life) goes back to less than a month after my third birthday, and was the experience of seeing photographs in some of the various magazines and newspapers that came to our house, images that have been etched into my memory. In particular, I was touched by seeing pictures of the liberation of various concentration camps in western and central Germany by the British and American military, recorded and printed in these and other magazines and newspapers I was exposed to.

What I saw there, long before I could read any of the written comments in the news articles I was looking at, were photographs that were stunning and ultimately inexpungible and indelible from my mind.

BUCHENWALD, APRIL 1945

Buchenwald Concentration Camp, six miles outside of Weimar, was liberated on April 11, 1945. Gen. Dwight D. Eisenhower invited key military and civilian photographers to record the shocking conditions, with the purpose of making denial of these harsh realities impossible.[55]

---

[54] To take a moment in this personal note to orient my own life here in historical context, among events that took place the weekend of December 7, 1941 were the bombing of Pearl Harbor, the declaration of the *Nacht und Nebel Erlaß*, the Night and Fog Decree, and the opening of the first extermination camp at Chełmno. On that birthday (Mar. 30, 1942) were also the arrival of the first SS-RSHA transport of French Jews from Drancy (a suburb northeast of Paris) and Pithiviers (about 53 mi. south of Paris) at Auschwitz Birkenau; in Polish, Oświęcim Brzezinka (see *From the History of KL-Auschwitz*, Kazimierz Smoleń, ed., p. 192), and, worlds away, the forced evacuation from Bainbridge Island in Puget Sound, across Elliot Bay from Seattle, of Japanese Americans to war-time internment camps, an action declared constitutional by the US Supreme Court in Korematsu v. United States, 323 US 214 (1944), while the war was still going on.

[55] Many pictures were taken there on Apr. 16, 1945 (and the following days). The 1st image here is from a photo by Pvt. Harry Miller of the Civil Affairs Branch, US Army Signal Corps (thus, in the public domain), of men lying on 4-tiered bunk beds inside Buchenwald Barrack No. 56. The photo appeared in print that spring, as in "Atrocity Report Issued by Army," *New York Times*, Apr. 29, 1945, p. 20; at "Medicine: Back from the Grave," *Time*, vol. 45, no. 20, May 14, 1945, p. 60, with caption "Ex-Prisoners of the Nazis (Buchenwald Camp)," etc. The 2nd image, digitally refined for this text, is of a wagon piled high with corpses, *is offered with permission* from the USHMM (the United States Holocaust Memorial Museum), with this explicit acknowledgment: "*Credit: United States Holocaust Memorial Museum, courtesy of Arnold Bauer Barach.*" (The photo is part of the Arnold Bauer Barach

The Hitler Era

Resonating in my visual memory are two images that remain in my consciousness, from seeing photographs made public at that time, in spring 1945:

The first of these memory-marking pictures was of cramped and crowded shelf-like tiers of wooden bunks, with expressionless men stretched out on them, staring out at the camera eerily, with powerfully, strangely hypnotizing, deep, blank eyes. Another I recall showed many corpses piled up in a large heap in a cart or wagon, with bare feet randomly protruding skyward. While these are quite clearly defined in my mind's eye, that clarity is of course no guarantee of historical accuracy, although printed records support my recall: in any case, these remain for me clear and powerful memories. The two images just above capture the essence of the printed photos I remember from those days long ago.

Now, one single moment of experience most obviously does not define a person's entire worldview, but these two reflect my first early awakening to something rather eerie and unsettling. I may ask whether these memories had anything to do with religion (given what is now called the Holocaust), but at the time, for me as someone barely three years old, having no sense or understanding of religion, that experience for me consisted only of the images themselves and their mesmerizing impact on my mind, seared deep within. Later, that inchoate sense of the

---

collection.) For several photographs of that very wagon, from different angles, see pp. 4, 7, 8, in *KZ-Bildbericht aus fünf Konzentrationslagern* (1983), as among the many photos and films that were taken at Buchenwald Camp that week, including those of visits of the German residents of nearby Weimar, forced to see the work of the Third Reich. Some were taken by Walter Chichersky (1924-2008), US Signal Corps—the first photographer to enter Buchenwald Camp, authorized by Gen. Eisenhower—his work appeared in "German Concentration and Labour Camps," *The Times* (London), Apr. 19, 1945, p. 6, and in "Nazi Barbarism," *Philadelphia Inquirer*, Apr. 26, 1945, p. 14, and elsewhere.

macabre from 1945 was again brought into focus for me in 1957, when I was fifteen. That year I came across a book by Lord Russell of Liverpool (Edward Frederick Langley Russell,[56] not to be confused with Bertrand Russell[57]). The book was *The Scourge of the Swastika: A Short History of Nazi War Crimes, With 16 Pages of Illustrations*. There I read early testimonies and could study photos of the crematoria at Buchenwald, the razed town of Lidice, a Gestapo thumb-screw torture apparatus from Belgium, a military prisoner mug shot of wife of the Commandant, Ilse Koch (*die Hexe von Buchenwald*, the Witch of Buchenwald),[58] with shrunken human heads, lampshades made of tattooed human skin, among other harsh, compelling visual records of the violence of that world.

I was also exposed in those years to newsreels of Hitler giving one speech or another, *yelling, screaming, ranting, and raving, to me a madman in an incomprehensible expression of frightening hatred!*

All of this, and other events in my life, led me to focused research for some five years, in part as a Visiting Scholar in the History Department, Judaic Studies Program at UCSD (University of California at San Diego) from 1986-1990. That project was put aside, and I later returned to my research and reflections on that era, with appointments as a Research Scholar in the Psychiatry and in the Family Medicine and Public Health Departments in the UCSD School of Medicine over the past several years.

In general, though, and putting my own particular experiences aside now, for many of us as adults there remain questions about some tormented experiences that people have undergone in their lives, and how to deal wisely—with awareness, insight, and compassion—with that past, with the extreme violence of the period of the Hitler era and of the Third Reich being a case we will focus on here.[59]

---

[56] Langley Russell, 2nd Baron Russell of Liverpool (1895-1981): barrister, one of the chief legal advisers for the British Military Tribunals at various war-crimes proceedings, at Nuremberg, etc.

[57] Bertrand Russell, 3rd Earl Russell (1872-1970): 1950 Nobel Laureate, mathematician, philosopher, and social-political activist; a pacifist in World War I, a critic of Hitlerism, Stalinist totalitarianism, and, later, of the US military involvement in Vietnam.

[58] Ilse Koch, war-end icon of Nazi barbaric, brutal sadism, was sentenced to life by a US Army Court in 1947, but a military review court reduced this to a 4-yr. sentence in 1951, after which a German *Landgericht* (State Court) sentenced her to life imprisonment: She committed suicide in 1967. See Michael S. Bryant, "Punishing the Excess: Sadism, Bureaucratized Atrocity and the U.S. Army Concentration Camp Trials, 1945-1947," pp. 63-85 in *Nazi Crimes and the Law*, Nathan Stoltzfug and Henry Friedlander, eds. (2008), at p. 74.

[59] The role and impact of spirituality and religions in world history will be considered in these discussions, and will also be discussed, with more of a central focus, in Mitchell Ginsberg, *Cultivating Spirituality: Religious Teachings and Contemplative Meditations in the Waters of World Cultures* (in preparation).

The Hitler Era

Nuremberg Trials, other Key Documents, and *Mein Kampf*

During and after the years of the Third Reich,[60] both the Germans and the Allies gathered together an immense number of historical documents from that period, laying bare the actions, inter-departmental communications, official cables, and other documents, often originally classified as secret (*geheim*) or strictly secret (*streng geheim*), concerning the goals, projects, actions, and reports of German diplomatic and military activities.

THE NT, IMT, TWC, NCA, TTFR, ICC, UNWCC, &c. TRANSCRIPTS

The written records of a wide range of war crimes trials concerning actions taken by the Third Reich and collaborators (and by the Japanese) are held in a number of transcript collections. There are abbreviated citations for these, mostly being abbreviations for much longer titles of the various collections. *In this book, we will be using these abbreviations and can refer the reader back to this section for the full titles.*

THE NUREMBERG TRIALS

The trials most relevant to the discussions to follow, cited for their richness of documented information and sworn testimonies by leading National Socialist leaders, are the International Military Tribunal (IMT) Trial of the Major War Criminals, and the US Nuremberg Military Tribunal Subsequent Nuremberg Trials, or Trials of War Criminals (TWC).

These were remarkable in the history of jurisprudence, as expressed in the opening address by Robert Jackson, US Supreme Court Justice and Chief Prosecutor at the first trial. He stated, "The privilege of opening the first trial in history for crimes against the peace of the world imposes a grave responsibility. The wrongs which we seek to condemn and punish have been so calculated, so malignant, and so devastating, that civilization cannot tolerate their being ignored, because it cannot survive their being repeated. That four great nations, flushed with victory and stung with injury stay the hand of vengeance and voluntarily submit their captive enemies to the judgment of the law is one of the most significant tributes that Power has ever paid to Reason."[61]

These trials are part of the NT, the Nuremberg Trials as a group. These Trials of War Criminals, addressed war crimes but also crimes against civilians, with entire peoples being annihilated for their social identity, which sorts of actions have come to be called in a more explicit way, crimes of aggression against non-combatants, mass murders of entire groups, and crimes against humanity. *These many mass murders did occur during war, yes; but were crimes against human beings, not war*

---

[60] On some key features of the legal framework of the Third Reich and related orienting background issues, see articulate discussion in James Q. Whitman, *Hitler's American Model: The United States and the Making of Nazi Race Law* (2017).

[61] "Justice Jackson Delivers Opening Statement at Nuremberg, November 21, 1945," ROBERTJACKSON.ORG, Jan. 6, 2016.

crimes as defined by various international treaties. And, decades later, there was the formation in 1998 (and becoming operational in 2002) of the International Criminal Court (ICC), in The Hague, The Netherlands, which has been the site of trials against more recent cases of government-directed mass murders in various countries, against various populations. We will return to the ICC below, in the text.[62]

Some but not all of these very significant trials took place in the German city of Nürnberg, or Nuremberg, in English.[63] These began with what has been known as the Trial of the Major War Criminals, begun in late 1945 and concluded the next year. In this trial, there were 24 defendants, all major figures in the governance of the Third Reich and its political, economic, and military exploits. This ground-breaking trial was conducted in the International Military Tribunal (IMT), with prosecuting attorneys being legal representatives of the major Allied countries of the war: France, the Union of Soviet Socialist Republics (the USSR), the United Kingdom, and the United States of America. Among other trials were those conducted at the US Nuremberg Military Tribunal, under the US Military Authorities, also referred to as the Subsequent Nuremberg Trials; these took place, obviously, in Nuremberg, itself part of the American zone established at war's end. These latter trials followed the authorization of the Allied Control Council Law passed on December 20, 1945, empowering any of the occupying authorities to try suspected war criminals in their respective occupation zones. This was called Control Council Law No. 10.

PRINTED TEXT COLLECTIONS OF THESE TRIALS (NT)

There are several sets of the printed texts of the Nuremberg Trials (in totality referred to in abbreviation as NT), each set frequently referred to individually as IMT, TWC, NCA, and TTFR. These different collections are also cited in terms referring to the color of the covers of the volumes in each series. These collections of trial transcripts are sometimes confused with one another. That caveat made explicit, the three main series or collections of transcripts most relevant for our purposes here are the Blue, Red, and Green Series, to give their brief names. All of these transcripts in these series are available through US Library of Congress websites.[64]

The Blue Series, a set of 42 volumes, which we will refer to here as NT-IMT-Blue, are transcripts of the *Trial of the Major War Criminals*, fuller title: *Trial of the Major War Criminals before the International Military Tribunal* [thus, IMT], *Nuremberg, 14 November 1945-1 October 1946*. There were 24 major war criminals tried in that context.

---

[62] On the 124 Parties to the ICC, the 32 signatories who have not ratified the treaty, and others not at all signatories, see "State Parties to the ICC," THE AMERICAN BAR ASSOCIATION'S ICC PROJECT.

[63] An alternative early spelling in English of Nuremberg was Nuernberg, reflecting the German spelling, Nürnberg, with an ü-umlaut (the *ü* being rendered as *ue*).

[64] "Nuremberg Trials, 1945-1949, Nuremberg, Germany," *Military Legal Resources, Federal Research Division, Library of Congress*, LOC.GOV. Note 2nd-4th links to the Blue, Red, and Green Series, most relevant for our purposes here.

The Hitler Era

The Red Series, a set of 8 volumes in 12 books, which we will refer to here as NT-NCA-Red, are transcripts of Nazi war crimes entitled *Nazi Conspiracy and Aggression 1946-1948* [thus, NCA], a collection of documentary evidence and guide materials prepared by the American and British prosecuting staffs for presentation before the International Military Tribunal at Nuremberg, to be used to support the charges made against Nazi war criminals in their trial at Nuremberg, Germany, 1945-1946.

The Green Series, a set of 8 volumes in 12 books, which we will refer to here as NT-TWC-Green, are *Trials of War Criminals* [thus, TWC] *before the Nuernberg Military Tribunals Under Control Council Law No. 10* (note the two plurals here). These are transcripts of another set of 12 cases or trials, in 15 volumes. They are also called the Subsequent Nuremberg Trials. They lasted from December 9, 1946 to April 13, 1949. The authorization of TWC under Control Council Law No. 10—the Allied Control Council (ACC) Law No. 10—is also used on occasion to identify them. The ACC gave authority to each occupying power to try Nazi war criminals in their respective areas of control, involving almost 200 defendants.

These trials are the sources of much valuable information about the specifics of the actions taken in the master plan of the Third Reich, in a number of areas of application.

The documents that are contained in these records, from National Socialist (Nazi) documents, including internal communications, and from the affidavits (sworn testimony, given under oath) of high officials, can be a source of insight into the practical and express plans and programs of the Third Reich.

FURTHER COLLECTIONS OF DOCUMENTATION

In addition to the Nuremberg Trials and their official transcripts, there are other collections of documentation that did make it as evidence in these trials, but which contain further information about issues that were not addressed at the trials.

In this way, after the war, a committee representing the British Foreign Office, the US State Department, and the French Government gathered some of these and published them in the decade following the war.

One such set of the texts—*Documents on German Foreign Policy, 1918-1945*—was published over the period 1949-1983. These documents are based on German texts from the German Foreign Ministry (*Auswärtiges Amt* or *AA*). This set was divided into several series: Series A covered documents from the years 1918-1925; Series B, from the years 1925-1933; Series C, from the years 1933-1937; and Series D, from the years 1937-1945. Each series was composed of a number of volumes. All were edited by teams of American, British, and French consultants.

There are also the original German-language texts—*Akten zur deutschen auswärtigen Politik 1918-1945*—that are available online. Most relevant here are Series C (six volumes, from January 30, 1933 to November 14, 1937) and Series D (fourteen volumes, including the last as an Index, from September 1937 to December 11, 1941). American-

German historian Christoph M. Kimmich has presented a comprehensive presentation of a large number of such collections of texts concerning the Nazi Movement and the Third Reich.[65]

OTHER WAR-CRIMES TRIALS, INCLUDING FRENCH AND GERMAN TRIALS

In addition to these, we might mention that there were a number of other significant trials both by the British and the Soviets, and also by the German Federal Republic. In addition, a major war-crimes trial also took place in 1961 in Jerusalem, the Eichmann Trial.

This came about through the investigatory work of the Attorney General (*Generfalstaatsanwalt*) of Hesse, based in Frankfurt am Main, Fritz Bauer (1903-1968). Bauer had been an attorney and jurist, and a Social Democrat fighting the Nazis into 1933, when he was arrested, interned at Heuberg KL (concentration camp), released—little-known Jews, homosexuals, and small trouble-makers were not the major focus in those first months of Nazi power—then moved to Norway in 1935, to Sweden in 1943, and did not return to Germany until 1949, to take his part in the search for former Nazis who had become active members of the new West German government, their former work put into the shadows. Bauer was central in the second Auschwitz Trial, in Frankfurt (December 20, 1963-August 19, 1965), which tried 22 of the guards at Auschwitz for individual murders they had committed (a rather small number, you might say).[66] He tracked down Adolf Eichmann, living in Argentina under the assumed name Ricardo Klement, and passed on the information to the Mossad (the Israeli Intelligence Agency), who captured Eichmann and brought him back to Israel for trial (April-December 1961). Bauer had wanted Eichmann then extradited to Germany for trial there, where he might expose others from his earlier powerful organization within the SS: this was blocked by several interests: first, by German ex-SS officers now rehabilitated and working for the Federal Republic of Germany (*Bundesrepublik Deutschland*), second, by the West German government under Chancellor Konrad Adenauer which was in negotiations with Israel to sell arms (military equipment), and third, by Israel (with similar interests, under Prime Minister David Ben-Gurion) and the US (which wanted a strong West Germany and a strong Israel, against the Soviet Union and its sphere of influence).[67]

In France, there was the trial in Lyon from May 11 to July 4, 1987, of Klaus Barbie, head of the Gestapo there (the "Butcher of Lyon") extradited from his refuge-residence in Bolivia, using the name Klaus Altmann, for war crimes; he was found guilty of crimes against humanity—the murder

---

[65] Christoph M. Kimmich, *German Foreign Policy, 1918-1945: A Guide to Current Research and Resources* (3rd ed., 2013). It is a text of 340 pages.

[66] This German trial is presented in the documentary, *The Auschwitz Trial* (2013).

[67] See FRITZ BAUER INSTITUT: GESCHICHTE UND WIRKUNG DES HOLOCAUST (THE FRITZ BAUER INSTITUTE, FRANKFURT), and the 2015 Lars Kraume film, *Der Staat gegen Fritz Bauer* (*The People vs. Fritz Bauer*) which dramatizes this story.

The Hitler Era

of tens of thousands, the arrest, torture, and murder of *maquis* leader and representative of De Gaulle in occupied France, Jean Moulin, and the responsibility for the shipment to their death of the children of Izieu (April 1944)—and sentenced to life in prison.[68]

Earlier, there had been a large number of major French collaborators and members of the Vichy establishment who were either tried under the French court system, in person, or *in absentia*, who fled toward the end of the war and were in hiding, or who committed suicide before trials could be set up. These trials, with over 300,000 French citizens judged, were part of a citizens' action run by the underground in the first parts of a liberated France (called *l'épuration sauvage*, the wild purification),[69] and complemented later by the new government's legal system (called, in turn, *l'épuration légale*, the legal purification).[70]

There were significant trials in Germany itself, both when divided into two countries, the BRD (*Bundesrepublik Deutschland*, the Federal Republic of Germany, or West Germany), and the DDR (*Deutsche Demokratische Republik*, the German Democratic Republic, or East Germany), and also as a single Germany (once East and West Germany were reunited, on August 31, 1990). One of the most significant of these

---

[68] Campbell Page, "From the archive, 28 May 1987: The trial of Klaus Barbie," *The Guardian* (London). BBC-Scenario Films, *The Trial of Klaus Barbie (1987)*, is a reenactment of the trial itself, based on BBC notes permitted by the French court; *the French TV recording of the trial was to be held in closed files for 50 years after the end of the trial—meaning until July 2037*. Cf. *Jean Moulin & Klaus Barbie: The Justice of History* (2018), 3:40-3:55; Serge Klarsfeld, *The Children of Izieu: A Human Tragedy* (1985); the 1983 report by Alan A. Ryan, Jr., *Klaus Barbie and the US Government. A Report to the Attorney General of the United States, Aug. 1983* (re officers of US Gov't protecting Barbie from extradition from Germany to France).

[69] These judgments were against collaborators but also against young women who had had German soldiers as their lovers. This was fictionalized in the 1959 Alain Renais film from a Marguerite Duras screenplay, *Hiroshima, Mon Amour* (*Hiroshima, My Love*), starring Emmanuelle Riva and Eiji Okada. It portrayed how the French woman was treated for having taken a young German soldier as lover, in Nevers (in central France, north of Vichy), her mental breakdown, and her later voyage to Hiroshima to make an anti-war film, where she took a Japanese architect as lover. The similar treatment of women in Sicily after the liberation was shown in the 2000 Giuseppe Tornatore film, *Malèna*, starring Monica Bellucci; Tornatore was also director of the 1988 film, *Cinema Paradiso*.

[70] Less than 800 executions were actually carried out. See "L'épuration légale," WIKIPEDIA. Cf. Herbert R. Lottman, *The Purge: The Purification of French Collaborators after World War II* (1986); Philippe Bourdrel, *L'épuration sauvage* (1988); Peter Novick, *L'épuration française 1944-1949* (1985); Fred Kupferman, *Le process de Vichy: Pucheu, Pétain, Laval 1944-1945* (1980); Henry Rousso, "L'épuration en France: une histoire inachevée," *Vingtième Siècle: Revue d'histoire*, no. 33, Jan.-Mar. 1992, pp. 78-105; Marie-Thérèse Viaud, "L'épuration en Dordogne," *Annales du Midi: Revue archéologique, historique et philologique de la France méridionale*, vol. 104, no. 199-200, 1992, pp. 417-428.

German trials was that of John (Ivan) Demjanjuk (1920-2012). It began on November 30, 2009, and the verdict was read on May 12, 2011. The charges put forth against him were 27,900 counts of acting as accessory to murder. The number corresponded to the number of people killed at the *Vernichtungslager* (extermination camp) of Sobibór while he worked there as a guard. Demjanjuk complained that he did not deserve such special attention, being just a Ukrainian forced to serve at that camp, with a rather minor and trivial job that he carried out—unlike Eichmann, who was an important member of the overall Nazi mass murders of European Jewry—and that, being an old and sick man, he deserved to live the few remaining years of his life in peace. *That said, the court held the trial and in it established a number of important legal concepts and precedents for future trials, not only of Nazi War Criminals but also of others in other contexts who committed genocide or mass murders or other crimes against humanity.* A major principle that was articulated at this trial was based on the concept of institutional function—in particular, the nature of the core function of the establishment in which a given defendant was involved. In the case of Sobibór, its very function as an extermination camp was to exterminate people. People who worked in that context were deemed to be essentially involved in the defining function or purpose of that institution: in this case, an institution of organized, methodical, and immediate killing of each carload of newly-arrived prisoners. On the precedence established by this court ruling, for use in future crimes against humanity and genocide, the argument that one was just doing one's duty or doing what was ordered or was merely "a cog in the gears" (as Demjanjuk put it) was no longer a possible plea for innocence.[71]

UN War Crimes Commission

Major records that were assembled beginning with the establishment of the United Nations, in 1943, have been stored as the UNWCC documents, in the United Nations War Crimes Commission, established on October 20, 1943; this commission was chaired by British judge, Rt. Hon. The Lord Wright of Durley, Wiltshire (Sir Robert Alderson Wright).

There is a collection from *Law Reports of Trials of War Criminals*, in 15 volumes; fuller title: *Law Reports of Trials of War Criminals, Selected and Prepared by the United Nations War Crimes Commission, 1947-1949*. Volume 1 discusses some of the legal principles underlying the trials.

These UNWCC volumes[72] include not only European information, but also, for example, the trials and convictions of General Tomoyuki Yamashita, the Tiger of Malaya (1885-1946, executed by hanging) and Hideki Tōjō, Prime Minister who ordered the bombing of Pearl Harbor, often known simply as Tōjō (1884-1948, also executed by hanging). The subsequent trials were part of the International Military Tribunal for the

---

[71] Lawrence Douglas, *The Right Wrong Man: John Demjanjuk and the Last Great Nazi War Crimes Trial* (2016), esp. pp. 247-260.

[72] The Commission's 15 vol. set is at "Law Reports of Trials of War Criminals, 1947-1949," LOC.GOV/RR/FRD/MILITARY_LAW/LAW-REPORTS-TRIALS-WAR-CRIMINALS.HTML.

Far East (IMTFE), administered by one chief administrator, American jurist Joseph B. Keenam (former Assistant US Attorney General), under the administration of General McArthur. Seven high-ranking Japanese military officials were sentenced to death and sixteen others were given life sentences. There were also other trials of Japanese criminals; some 5,000 were found guilty of war crimes, and more than 900 of those were subsequently executed.[73] The numerous records from this UN collection are found scattered in different government and private repositories.[74]

COLD WAR COMPLICATIONS

Difficulties developed when various collections were closed down, in large part because of the conflicts after the Allied victory in World War II, between the Soviet Union and Communism, on the one hand, and the US, the UK, and France and democracies, on the other. In the USSR and East Germany (including the *Deutsches Zentralarchiv* in Potsdam), access to documents by Western scholars was cut off, and the West was not especially friendlier to Soviet researchers. This ended after the downfall of the German Democratic Republic (East Germany) and the USSR. In the US, anti-Nazi documents were to a noticeable extent put under wraps since the push to end war crimes trials by the US State Department and US Senator Joseph McCarthy, who saw Communism as a threat to the West, overshadowing the pursuit of Nazi war crimes. The US Government, through the OSS and CIA, made use of Nazi criminals because of their shared hatred of Communism and the Nazis' in-depth documentation about Soviet political and military operations: the CIA welcomed former Wehrmacht Gen. Reinhard Gehlen with his vast information about the USSR, becoming their well-paid expert on Soviet operations.[75]

OTHER EUROPEAN POST-WAR TRIALS

Other than the International, the US, and the British war crimes trials, there was, for example, under the (Polish) Supreme National Tribunal, the Auschwitz Trial took place in Kraków (November 24-December 22, 1947). There was also the Second Auschwitz Trial, called the Frankfurt Auschwitz Trials, a set of trials (December 20, 1963-August 19, 1965). These were conducted under the laws of the Federal Republic of Germany.

There was a series of Majdanek Trials (*over the long span of the years 1944-1981*). The camp at Majdanek, nearby to Lublin, was overrun and liberated by Soviet troops on July 22, 1944; with the Germans not having time to destroy anything, *the Soviets found entirely intact its gas chambers and crematoria*. The first of these trials was administered during the war, before the Soviet-Polish Special Criminal Court in Lublin (July 23, 1944-December 2, 1944). The Second Majdanek Trial was a

---

[73] "International Military Tribunal for the Far East," WIKIPEDIA.

[74] Dan Plesch, *Human Rights after Hitler: The Lost History of Prosecuting Axis War Crimes* (2017), "Appendix B" (pp. 214-217).

[75] Reinhard Gehlen, *The Service: The Memoirs of General Reinhard Gehlen* (1972); cf. the documentary, *Superspy: The Story of Reinhard Gehlen* (1974).

series of trials held from 1946-1948 in the Polish cities of Lublin, Radom, Świednica, Kraków, Wadowice, Toruń, and Warsaw). The Third Majdanek Trial was held before a West German Court in Dusseldorf (November 26, 1975-June 30, 1981).

The Chełmno Trials were held, the first, in Łódź (1945), the next four in Bonn (1962) and then the last, in Köln (Cologne, ending in 1965).

Additional war crimes trials of Nazis include the Frankfurt Auschwitz Trials (1963-1965), the Sobibór Trial, in Hagen, Germany (September 5, 1965-December 20, 1966), the Bełżec Trial in Munich (August 18, 1963-January 21, 1965), the Treblinka Trial, in Munich (1964-1965), and one of the Majdanek Trials (1975-1981).

There was also the Belsen Trial (the Trial of Joseph Kramer and 14 Others), which took place at Lüneburg, and was administered by the British (September 17-November 17, 1945). This trial included charges against actions at the Bergen-Belsen Concentration Camp and also at Auschwitz. There were the Dachau Tribunals, administered by the US Military (November 1945-August 1948) and the Flossenbürg Camp Trial (June 12, 1946-January 19, 1947), the two Mauthausen-Gusen Camp Trials, which were held at Dachau (March 29-May 13, 1946, and August 6-21, 1947), the Buchenwald Trial, also at Dachau (April 11-August 14, 1947), and the British-administered Hamburg Ravensbrück Trials, a series of seven trials for war crimes at Ravensbrück Concentration Camp (December 5, 1946-July 21, 1948). We might think that the Nuremberg Tribunal Trials were the only ones after the war, but these many other examples add greatly to the well-known trials that were carried out at Nuremberg.

All of this suggests that while we may speak of and think of the post-war trials of Nazi criminals as the Nuremberg Trials, these in fact include only a delimited although very important portion of all of the trials that were held in a number of countries in Europe after the way.

CITING MEIN KAMPF

There are several editions of both the original German texts to the two volumes of Adolf Hitler's *Mein Kampf* and of the full English text. In this book, the German edition cited will be *Mein Kampf. Zwei Bände in einem Band, Ungekürtzte Ausgabe* (1936).

There is also a scholarly, critical edition now available: Adolf Hitler, *Mein Kampf: eine kritische Edition*, edited by Christian Hartmann, Thomas Vordermayer, Othmar Plöckinger, Roman Töppel, and Edith Raim (2016).

Translations into English, also with the title *Mein Kampf*, are available in an unabridged edition, annotated by Comte Raoul de Roussy de Sales *et al.* (1941), and as well in an unabridged edition, again with the same title, translated by Rudolph Mannheim (1943).

The 1936 German edition and these two English translations are available for complete downloading from the net. Citations for the English will be primarily from the De Roussy de Sales edition, and secondarily from the Mannheim edition. When the Mannheim text is being cited or quoted, that will be made explicit in the given context.

HITLER-ERA SUICIDES & A REICH'S GALLERY OF GERMAN ROGUES

Suicide is an extreme, irrevocable tactic to avoid an unacceptable present or future, but it was not unique to the Hitler era. It did, however, became common late in World War II for Nazis and Nazi sympathizers to take their own lives, rather than face a society that rejected National Socialist values, and a world in which they could readily imagine receiving the wrath, the revenge (*Vergeltung*), and perhaps even a justice from the Europe that the Third Reich had ruled mercilessly. Earlier in the Hitler era, those who committed suicide included many who lived in great fear, terrorized by the Nazi police state.[76] Enemies of the Reich were harassed, beaten, arrested, tortured, with civil rights denied, property confiscated (stolen by the state), forced into ghettos, starved, shipped to slave labor in Germany or in concentration camps, and sent to be exterminated in the *Vernichtungslager*, death camps: many reasons to want to end one's life!

O suicide, found in Germany and worldwide, ubiquitous![77] For French philosopher Albert Camus, "There is only one truly serious philosophical problem: suicide. To decide whether life is or is not worth living is to reply to the fundamental question of philosophy."[78] And while perhaps every person has thought of suicide at one time or another, for many, it has been the best solution for their tormented experiences, their dark night of the soul, as San Juan de la Cruz (St. John of the Cross) wrote in *La noche oscura del alma* (1578). We will return to consider suicide, which always leaves others behind to deal with the resultant vacant aftermath.

In this context, let us consider here the Third Reich and some key individuals in the National Socialist Party, government, or military (some of whom committed suicide, as just noted):

Baer, Richard (1911-1963): Commandant of Auschwitz I from May 1944-February 1945.
Below, Colonel Nicolaus von (1907-1983): Luftwaffe adjutant to Hitler.
Bormann, Martin (1900-1945): Hitler's personal secretary and confidant, Hitler's informal deputy and Head of the Nazi Party Chancellery, carrying out strong anti-Slav and anti-Jewish decrees; committed suicide on May 2, 1945 (confirmed by 1998 DNA testing of his corpse.
Canaris, Admiral Wilhelm (1887-1945): head of the Abwehr (German Intelligence); executed at Flossenbürg Concentration Camp for treason on April 9, 1945, in the last weeks of the Third Reich.
Dönitz, Admiral Karl (1891-1980): Commander-in-Chief of the German Navy; appointed by Hitler as his successor, thus serving in the role of the Führer, very briefly, from April 30-May 7, 1945.

---

[76] On Nazi terrorism and fanaticism, see Saul K. Padover, *Experiment in Germany: The Story of an American Intelligence Officer* (1946), pp. 4, 9, 20-24, 36, 46, 158.
[77] Here, Johann Wolfgang von Goethe, *Die Leiden des jungen Werther* (1774).
[78] Albert Camus, Nobel Laureate in Literature (1957), *Le Mythe de Sisyphe: Essai sur l'absurde* (1942). This quotation is the opening passage of the essay.

Eichmann, Adolf (1906-1962): Head of the RSHA Sub-Department IV-B4 (the Gestapo Office of Jewish Affairs, charged with organizing and administrating the mass deportations of Jews to ghettos and to concentration camps, as part of the Final Solution).

Ernst, Karl (1904-1934): SA officer and SA leader in Berlin.

Freisler, Roland (1893-1945): jurist, State Secretary of the Reich Ministry of Justice, President of and Judge in the People's Court; died in the bombing by US Army Air Force B17s of the People's Court, in session that day, February 3, 1945; presumably he would have been tried for war-criminal and other charges in the Nuremberg Trials after the war.

Gisevius, Dr. Hans Bernd von (1905-1974): German diplomat and Abwehr (German intelligence) agent.

Goebbels, Dr. Joseph (1897-1945): appointed District Leader for the NSDAP in Berlin by Hitler in 1926; founder in 1927 and editor of *Der Angriff;* Minister of Propaganda beginning in 1933; committed suicide with his wife by potassium cyanide capsules on May 1, 1945.

Göring, Hermann (1893-1946): World War I Ace, early head of the SA (Brownshirts), then head of the Prussian Police, creating the Gestapo (*Geheime Staatspolizei*, Secret State Police), Field Marshal and head of the Luftwaffe, the Third Reich Air Force; committed suicide by a potassium cyanide capsule on October 15, 1946, hours before being scheduled to be hung after having been convicted at Nuremberg for crimes against peace, crimes against humanity, and war crimes.

Halder, General Franz Ritter (1884-1972): Chief of Staff (1938-1942) of the OKH/Supreme High Command of the German Army.

Hanfstaengl, Ernst (1887-1975): Foreign Press Secretary to Hitler and later consultant to fellow Harvard-graduate Franklin Delano Roosevelt.

Heydrich, Reinhard (1904-1942): Head of the RSHA, the Reich Main Security Office and acting Protector of Bohemia and Moravia; seriously wounded on May 27, 1942 in Operation Anthropoid, by Czech and Slovak agents of the Czech Government-in-Exile, dying on June 4.

Himmler, Heinrich (1900-1945): Head of the SS, the Gestapo, the concentration and extermination camps, and the *Einsatzgruppen* (mobile killing squads of the SS).[79] Under British arrest, he committed suicide with a potassium cyanide capsule on May 23, 1945.

Hindenburg, General Paul von (1847-1934): Field Marshal during World War I, later President of Weimar Germany.

Hitler, Adolf (1889-1945): Führer of the Third Reich. Committed suicide in the bunker below the Reich Chancellery on April 30, 1945.

Höss, Rudolf (1901-1957): Commandant of Auschwitz I and II (Birkenau). Disguised as a farmer named Franz Lang, he was arrested by British military on March 11, 1946, and handed over to Polish authorities, who tried, convicted, and executed him by hanging at Auschwitz itself, next to the former crematorium of Auschwitz I, on April 16, 1947.

---

[79] For a thorough, in-depth study of the SS mobile killing squads, see French L. MacLean (West Point Graduate and Col., US Army, Ret.), *The Field Men: The SS Officers Who Led the Einsatzkommandos—the Nazi Mobile Killing Units* (1999).

The Hitler Era

Keitel, Field Marshall Wilhelm (1882-1946): Chief of the Armed Forces High Command; executed for crimes against peace, crimes against humanity, and war crimes, on October 16, 1946.

Loerzer, Colonel General Bruno (1891-1960): World War I Ace, officer in the Luftwaffe.

Ludendorff, General Erich (1865-1937): Hindenburg's Chief of Staff, the de facto operational head of the German Army in World War I, later a participant in the Beer Hall Putsch; an influential supporter of Hitler.

Manstein, Field Marshal Erich von (1887-1973): surrendering commander at the Battle of Kursk.

Ohlendorf, Otto (1907-1951): General and commander of *Einsatzgruppe D*, in Moldava, southern Ukraine, and the Crimea; later convicted of crimes against humanity and executed by hanging, in 1951.

Oster, Lieutenant Colonel—later General—Hans (1887-1945): Deputy Head of the Abwehr counter-espionage office under Admiral Wilhelm Canaris, also executed at Flossenbürg Concentration Camp for treason on April 9, 1945.

Ott, Adolf (1904-1958): Commanding officer of *Sonderkommando 7b*, part of *Einsatzgruppe B*, in Russia and Belarus, from February 1942 to January 1943; tried, convicted, and sentenced to death by hanging, which was commuted to life imprisonment, which, in turn, resulted in his being released from prison in 1958.

Paulus, Field Marshal Friedrich (1890-1957): surrendering commander at the Battle of Stalingrad.

Rommel, Field Marshal Erwin (1891-1944): General in the 1940 invasion of France, the Desert Fox (*der Wüstenfuchs*) of the North African campaign, later directing the German defense of Fortress Europa. Part of the July 20, 1944 assassination attempt on Hitler; Hitler proposed an alternative to a disgracing trial: Rommel's suicide to maintain his military honor and spare his family of disgrace for his treasonous actions. Rommel committed suicide with the cyanide capsule provided by his captors, on October 14, 1944.

Schirach, Baldur von (1907-1974): Gauleiter and head of the Hitler Youth (*Hitlerjugend*) and lyricist of its marching song, *Unsre Fahne flattert uns voran (Vorwärts, vorwärts, schmettern die hellen Fanfaren)*.

Seyss-Inquart, Arthur, SS General, Chancellor of Austria, Deputy Governor-General of the *Gouvernement General*, Reich Commissioner for the Netherlands (for the Occupied Dutch Territories).

Speer, Albert (1905-1981): Hitler's personal architect and later Minister of Armaments and War Production.

Stauffenberg, Lieutenant Colonel Claus Graf von (1907-1944): lost his left eye, right hand, and more, on April 7, 1943, in an Allied attack in the North African theater; organized and led the July 20, 1944 attempted assassination on Hitler and subsequent failed coup; arrested within hours, he was summarily executed by firing squad on July 21, 1944.

Acknowledgments

I would like to thank many of my past and current mentors, friends, colleagues, and students, whose inspiration, expertise, enthusiasm, good will, fresh perspectives, encouragement, and advice through the decades have given form to the organization and understanding of my thinking in general and specifically in this book, which began in earnest in early 1986 and is now reaching completion.

I have been repeatedly pushed in my thinking, and inspired to rethink and to reformulate my ideas, in exchanges that offered me replies to my questions, suggestions for further research and reflection on my part, questions that opened up new avenues of consideration, and numerous helpful comments for me to consider, from Henry Abramovitch, Robert Abzug, Jean-Pierre Aharonian, Anastasia Barinova, Heinz Bechert, Frithjof Bergmann, Frank Bellizzi, Ben Bendien, Angelika Betz, Mei-I Chang, Eugenio Chang-Rodríguez, Israel Charny, Noam Chomsky, Will Cummings, Peter Devine, Vichtr R. Dhiravamsa, Alexander Eremenko, Nora Esperguín, Marvin Farber, Manfred Fidorra, Koji Fujino, Esther Gilbert, Anatole Ginsberg, Françoise Ginsberg, Ted Ginsberg, Yvonne Ginsberg, Etienne Ginsberg-Jambou, Tania Ginsberg-Jambou, Angela Graf-Nold, Eric Gruenwald, Joe Hanania, Ian F. Hancock, Alfons Heck, Kathleen M. Higgins, William Hitchcock, Charlene Inouye, Annette Insdorf, Stanley Insler, Sébastien Jambou, Małgorzata Jankowska, Howard Kahn, Carol Kamenstein, Irv Katz, Stan Katz, Hasan Kayalı, Andy Kean, Elise Kert, Victoria Khiterer, Ulrich Knölker, Jerry Krakowski, Robert Levitt, Osi Livni, Frank McDonough, Klaus Meyer, Paul J. Mills, Julius Moravcsik, Glenn R. Morrow, Zhanna Morozova, Loren Mosher, David J. Najafi, Kumbale N. Nayak, K. R. Norman, Sait Özdalkıran, Terry Parssinen, Roland Pfaff, William H. C. Propp, Doris Quintanilla, Elliot J. Rayfield, Regina Reinhardt, Markus Richter, L. Mark Russakoff, Pierre Sauvage, Fred Schwartz, Deborah Shine, Mohammed Siraj, David Slier, Jon Solomon, Robert C. Solomon, Charles P. Stevenson, Jr., J. O. Urmson, and Marin F. Xavier.

I would also like to thank the United States Holocaust Memorial Museum for permission to use the 1945 photograph, part of the USHMM Arnold Bauer Barach collection, found in the discussion above of Buchenwald, and to thank her family for use of the 1930 photograph of Sylvia Dobkin, aged 17, as an example of an "it" girl, found below in discussion of the aesthetics of female beauty of the post-War period.

As well, and most importantly, I have the library facilities at the University of California, San Diego (UCSD), especially their ILL (Inter-Library Loan) Service, to thank for their repeatedly remarkable work at finding texts published through the decades in a number of countries, as well as obscure, rare, and old documents—some more than a century old—for my examination, reading, and use in preparing this work.

Of course, we can all thank the many thousands of scholars and jurists whose research, work, and publications have been preserved as sources of peerless and irreplaceable value to any grounded understanding of this formidable, historically pivotal era.

The Hitler Era

Howl, O Adelwolf: A Poetic Prologue to *The Hitler Era*

A poetic call to fury and war:

> Rage with the Furies,
>> O Adelwolf, O Noble Wolf,[80]
>> O alpha Wolf, decent, *anständig*, yet cruel, *grausam*,[81]
>> meant to be a leader, a *Führer*,
>
> reach with your firmness,
>> O iron-willed son of a strict, brutal civil servant,
>> O Knight (*Ritter*) of Teutonic Glory,
>> O Savior (*Retter*) of the German people,
>
> for divine heights: your historic destiny
>> (animated by unquenchable rage,[82]
>> flooded[83] by gut-wrenching bile).
>
> Howl, O great Wolf, from your lair
>> across the great expanses of Europe.
>
> Gather together your pure yet vicious hordes,
>> O alpha Wolf, to better those from the Asian Steppes,
>> with rage at the injustice
>> you see done to your land and your people.

We can perhaps imagine a passionate latter-day Homeric muse intoning these inspired, visionary words in a whisper to young man Hitler in search of a life mission. Or perhaps howling them out to Adolf/Adelwolf. Or, at least, we can perhaps envision young man Hitler pondering such a divine, daemonic communication meant for him and him alone.

Such an inspiration of unrelenting viciousness could well give direction and definition to the Hitler era.

---

[80] This self-identification of Hitler through his personal name, Adolf, which he understood as a shortened version of Adelwolf (Noble Wolf), reflected either his sense of, or his wish for, his own power and relentless aggressivity.

[81] *Anständig:* decent, respectable, proper; *grausam:* cruel, ruthless.

[82] We also spoke above of the Homeric understanding of the furious rage of the Greek Furies in *The Iliad*, in the Introduction. (More below.)

[83] The flood or great flood (*ogha* or *mahogha*, in Pali, and *ogha* or *mahaugha*, in Sanskrit) is a metaphor for various great mental disturbances that can drive people to turbulent acts lacking calm, insight, and rectitude. They are to be transcended and overcome through meditative pratices. In Pali teachings, see *Dhammapada* 47, *Oghataraṇa Sutta* (*Discourse on Crossing over the Flood*), and *Ogha Sutta* (*Discourse on the Flood*), *Saṃyutta-nikāya*, SN 1.1 and SN 45.171.

1. A Blitzview of the Hitler Era

In short, after the Great War of 1914-1918 came peace. With peace came an onerous treaty attributing guilt and responsibility to Germany, and demanding payment of a heavy financial burden of war reparations. Many Germans felt they had been betrayed, stabbed in the back. The old German government collapsed, the Kaiser fled to the Netherlands for asylum, and a republic was declared in Weimar. The nation saw combat for political control, with extreme leftists (mostly Communists) battling in street fights against extreme rightists (various Germanic nationalist groups). The 1920s saw nonpayment of the war debt, occupation of the Ruhr by the French in 1923, the exporting of coal and lumber as payment, the need for Germany to purchase its basic needs on the open market, a drying up of German governmental wealth, hyperinflation. In late 1923, Hitler and the National Socialists in Munich attempted to take over the government by force; the *Putsch*, their attempted *coup d'état*, ended in defeat, with several National Socialists (Nazis) killed by the police. Hitler was arrested, tried for treason, where he was allowed to give a speech attacking the Weimar Republic and justifying the Nazi vision. Then, with the rather lenient judgment of the court, Hitler ended up spending less than a year in prison, during which time the first volume of *Mein Kampf* was produced, to be published in July 1925, setting forth the political story of his youth, his vision of society and government, and his intense hatred of the Jews, whom he saw as parasites, vermin, germs, to be eliminated totally. Then came financial aid to Germany in the Dawes Plan of 1924, stabilizing the German economy, with several years of a cultural renaissance in the arts, film, literature, followed by a worldwide economic crash in late 1929 in the USA and in European centers of commerce, devastating Germany. Desperate times called for desperate measures. Hitler and his National Socialist Party, at one point almost disappearing as a political force, came to new power. With the disintegrating of the Weimar Republic unable to protect and to sustain itself, Hitler was invited by newly elected President Hindenburg, to be Chancellor: January 30, 1933. Within weeks, the world saw the burning of the Parliament, the Reichstag. In lightning succession, the National Socialists took over the government in the *Machtergreifung*, the Seizing of Power: the elimination of many civil rights, the imposition of law by decree, the arrest of Communist and Socialist Party members and trade unionists, including Deputies elected to the Parliament, the opening of concentration camps, with the installation of a reign of terror for all political opponents (those who disagreed openly with the new government's values and programs), with increasingly severe restrictions on the civil and legal rights of some Germans (the "unworthy of living" and especially the "non-Aryans," that is, the Jews); the *Gleichschaltung*, the switching or transformation of German society and all of its institutions to conform to Nazi values and ideals—all in the first months of 1933, then continuing in scope over the next years. German youth were organized into the *Hitlerjugend*, with a

The Hitler Era

conformity (in uniform and thought), a sense of camaraderie and of a direct link to Hitler in their commitment, with an understanding for them to be obedient, brave, not to be weaklings but to be fit, trim, tough as leather, and hard as Krupp steel. They and the military were pledged to following Hitler as the Leader (*Führer*) of the German people and the Reich. In 1934, infighting brought about the decimation of the *Sturmabteilung*, the SA (Storm Troopers, or Brown Shirts) and its leader Röhm, largely by the hands of the *Schutzstaffel*, the SS (Protection Squadron), originally Hitler's personal bodyguards and later the administrators of the concentration camps and members of the *Einsatzgruppen* (mobile killing squads, to be active in the Eastern Front), all headed by Himmler. In 1935, Jews were stripped of German citizenship. In 1936, German military entered the Rhineland; the British and French offering no resistance or military intervention. In March 1938, claiming the right for Germany to protect all Germans (in a wide sense), Germany entered and annexed Austria: The Greater Reich. In September, the Munich Agreement granted Germany rights to the Sudetenland, also largely populated by German-speaking people. Soon all of Czechoslovakia was invaded and conquered: the first non-Germanic territory now under Reich occupation. Of the 550,000 Jews in Germany in 1933, many who could leave, did (with only 250,000 left in 1938). Hitler declared a German right to *Lebensraum* (living space), territory to support its population—to be applied in an expansionist politics, primarily at the expense of neighboring Slavic homelands; as Russian historian Georgily Kumanev rendered *Lebensraum*, bluntly, "taking other people's territories and enslaving the inhabitants."[84] With this vision, Germany invaded Poland. Great Britain and France demanded that Germany retreat from Poland; with no reply, given their commitment to defend Poland, they declared war. The German occupying army carried out arrests and killings of Polish intelligentsia and Romanies (Gypsies), and set up restricted living quarters for Polish Jews (ghettos), with the death of many Jews by disease and slow starvation, with no means of livelihood, and cramped, unhealthy living conditions. Germany invaded Norway, to protect its access to Swedish iron ore. Then, in a claimed proactive defense against war-seeking Western Europeans, Germany invaded the Benelux countries and France. With similar claims, Germany later invaded the USSR, with SS killing squads organizing mass murders of Jews, Romanies, and Soviets: Babi Yar, Vinnitsa, etc.

---

[84] Georgily A. Kumanev, "Chapter 13. The German Occupation Regime on Occupied Territory in the USSR (1941-1944)," pp. 128-141, in *A Mosaic of Victims: Non-Jews Persecuted and Murdered by the Nazis*, Michael Berenbaum, ed. (1990), at p. 128. See that book's index with links to each section and chap. of the book.

The Baltic States joined in the killing spree. The West learned of all of these mass murders within months. Meanwhile, Germans who were judged to be incurably ill, mentally incapacitated, and others deemed "lives unworthy of life" were killed in a number of hospital-killing centers using carbon monoxide from truck fumes; this euthanasia program, called the T4 Program (or *Aktion Gnadentod*, Operation Mercy Death)—was officially stopped after vigorous complaints by concerned Germans; conclusion: for ease of operations, German killing programs would thereafter best be done out of the German public eye, including mass shootings in the USSR. The Final Solution of the Jewish Question, already begun with the invasion of the USSR, had administrative issues resolved at the Wannsee Conference, held on January 20, 1942, projecting the death of 11,000,000 European Jews.

At first, poisoning in concentration camps was done in gas vans, using the carbon monoxide of exhaust fumes (guided by technicians from the T4 Program); for mass killings this method proved too costly. Furthermore, there was a need for more effective killing methods that were also less onerous (to the German SS and military, who were suffering from the stress of being involved in the work of carrying out so many killings, shooting one victim after another). Karl Fritzsch, an assistant to Rudolf Höss, Commandant at Auschwitz, in searching for killing efficiency, had Soviet POWs murdered in late August 1941 (less than two months after the invasion of the USSR) by a poison chemical, hydrogen cyanide (prussic acid; commercial name: Zyklon B); it proved to be effective and cost-efficient. Second in command at Auschwitz as the Adjutant to Höss, Robert Mulka,[85] was in charge of obtaining and directing the use of Zyklon B at the camp. From early September 1941 on, it would be used at Auschwitz and several other *Vernichtungslager* (extermination camps)—*Totenlager* (death camps)—with the mass, organized process beginning in the first quarter of 1942. Millions of people were killed at these centers after having been transported, largely in train cattle cars, from across Europe. Many of those killed were Jews.

Meanwhile, the invaded European countries responded to the German aggression with compliance and collaboration, but also with fighting the German occupation with militant resistance, sabotage, the creation of anti-Nazi counter-governments, with helping and hiding Jews and those in the underground movements. There were attempts at communication of the dire situation of those targeted by the Nazis. With this, all property, wealth, and real estate of Jews were taken by the Reich or by other nearby residents in unhidden, expropriation (organized stealing). With the Reich invasions across Europe, there was an unbridled despoiling of the wealth and treasures of Europe's conquered lands. This included the taking possession—gratuitous, unwarranted, and illegal by international law—of museum-quality works of art from through the centuries, of financial wealth, real estate, business enterprises, industrial and manufacturing

---

[85] See *The Auschwitz Trial* (2013), at 7:00-9:45.

enterprises (early on, the take-over of the Škoda Works, automobile, tank, and armaments manufacturer in Prague), the appropriation of livestock—both through the Nazi Occupation Administration's interests in keeping the German people well-fed (*unlike the dire situation in World War I due to the British naval blockade of commerce into Germany*)—and directly by the Wehrmacht for its own men, and the deportations of millions of citizens of occupied or conquered countries for slave labor (often worked to death) for German military and domestic needs. These and similar actions were and are considered illegal by international law. Militarily, by late 1942-early 1943, the tides of war shifted and the Germany military began losing its conquered territories in the East. The focus on killing Jews continued. Early that second year, Goebbels called for *Totaler Krieg* (total war), on February 18, 1943—a date that had a double significance, as we shall see; that total war came, but not with German victory; many Germans would commit suicide. Hitler refused to have Germany surrender. Generals attempted to kill Hitler in July 1944; the attempt failed, the culprits were put to a painful death, filmed for Hitler's appreciation. The war continued with ongoing losses by the Reich, in the East by Soviet forces, and in the West and South by the other Allies (along with, we might mention, losses as well for the Allies).

The fervent and dedicated rush to attempt to finish killing off the Jews of Europe (with final transports from Hungary and Greece in Summer 1944) was matched with an attempt to destroy all evidence of these mass killings, at Auschwitz, Treblinka, Bełżec, Sobibór (all in the General Government, in eastern Poland), Maly Trostenets (near Minsk in Belarus), etc., and at Babi Yar, near Kiev (in Ukraine),[86] used for two years to kill enemies of the Reich and to kill prisoners who were witnesses to the mass killings. In September 1944, Hitler called on the German people (at first, boys 13 and older, and older men up to 60) to join in the defense of the Fatherland, creating the *Volkssturm* or People's Home Front Army, and Himmler added his own proposal, Operation Werewolf—the Werewolf Organization or Guerrilla Movement—to provide passive resistance to the coming Allied armies' onslaught. Both proposals were formalized in October 1944. Then, when Berlin was overrun by the Soviets, Hitler and a number of high-ranking Nazi officials and officers, holding out in the Reich Chancellery bunkers, committed suicide. Tens of thousands of Berliners joined them. The Reich was conquered and was no more: It had lost the total war. A total of some 50-60,000,000 people were estimated to have died during the war, most civilians.

---

[86] The largest death camp in Belarus, Maly Trostenets (Polish, Maly Trascianiec), used mobile gas wagons, as at Chełmno. With its first mass killings of Jews on May 10, 1942, it became an extermination camp. Later, Jews from Theresienstadt and from elsewhere in the Protectorate of Bohemia and Moravia, Austria, and Germany were also "processed" there. The SS burned Maly Trostenets to the ground on June 28, 1944, at the approach of the Soviet Army, but evidence of its operations remained to be found by the Soviets. Soviet footage of the massacres in the East is presented in *Shoah: The Forgotten Souls of History* (2015).

2. Facts, Myths, Disinformation; "Lies" and Lies

The activity of coming to an understanding of the past, which we may more commonly think of as learning history, is a rather interesting process of human investigation and organization. It involves considering some of what has happened in days gone by, in ways that we would like to explain, to make use of information we take to be important, and, overall, to make sense of what has happened in the times that have preceded our present world. Relevant to this issue, French historian Marc Léopold Benjamin Bloch (1886-1944) remarked, "Misunderstanding of the present is the inevitable consequence of ignorance of the past."[87] We can say here that having a sense of history may allow us to appreciate in more profound ways not only the past but also the present and the future. *The related organizing of what we take to be relevant to a given understanding of some part of the past is neither automatic or mechanical.* There are many ways to carry out the process of noticing specifics we take to be significant, and many ways to combine them into a coherent whole.

Even the selection of what to notice and give importance to, or not, is something that allows for a number of options. While there may certainly be evidence or other indications of what has happened in the past, it is not as if there are piles of "facts" waiting to be bumped into or to be scrupulously discovered intact. Furthermore, there are several ways in which we avoid certain topics, with a systematic selection of information, at times a narrow funnel that is widely distributed, leading to a distortion that is less obvious, but identified and discussed.[88] (Examples: the silence by the US government and US free press[89] about decades-long CIA international interventions, or political donations determining US election outcomes[90]; or silence by many empires about violence in their colonies.) Then, we can embellish the truth, first, by exaggeration (tall tales). There are complex stories that are mythic in stature, representing an entire vision of the world and its operations, seen by outsiders as ultimately groundless. (Who still believes in Zeus?) People can lie and deny others' statements, calling them lies. ("Liar, liar, pants on fire!") And now, there is "fake news." There is the intentional misrepresentation of events. The KGB, Soviet Secret Police refined this into *dezinformatsiya*, disinformation: organized false claims designed to obfuscate and mislead. The Nazis dismissed some unwelcomed statements as *Greuelpropaganda* (also written *Gräuelpropaganda*), atrocity propaganda.

---

[87] Marc Bloch, *The Historian's Craft* (1954), p. 43; cf. Marc Bloch, *Apologie pour l'histoire ou Métier d'historien* (1949), p. 47.

[88] Walter Lippmann, *Public Opinion* (1922); Edward S. Herman and Noam Chomsky, *Manufacturing Consent: The Political Economy of The Mass Media* (1988).

[89] In 1952, Russell held that the free press was most apparent in England and Scandanavia (Russell did not mention the US press at all): *A Conversation with Bertrand Russell (1952)*, 20:10-20:30, YOUTUBE.

[90] Thomas Ferguson, *Golden Rule: The Investment Theory of Party Competition and the Logic of Money-driven Political Systems* (1995). More on the CIA, below.

One tendency of our thinking that may mislead us is illustrated by visual representations, as in the 1510 *Crucifixion with Saints*, by Leyden artist Cornelis Engebrechtsz (1460s-1527) and in the 1518 *Madonna and Baby on a throne between Saint Vincenzo and Saint Antonio of Padova*, by Cremona artist Boccaccio Boccaccino (1460-1525):

Engebrechtsz   Boccaccino

The tendency here is to fit the past into our sense of the present world. In these paintings, as in many early Renaissance paintings, the dress of the individuals portrayed will usually be that of the contemporaries in the society of the artist. Sometimes there are individuals clothed as nuns, or nobility, or other contemporaries of the artist (but certainly not of Bible times), figures, that is, from much later than the scene being portrayed.

It is a relatively new recognition that different ages and cultures might have differences of social roles and dress. It was a shift in historical sophistication for us to come to question, as one example, the clothing of another age and culture, and to appreciate the time-limited range of some societal roles, such as being a nun, monk, or local noble.

We, too, might think about earlier times without questioning our assumptions, taking them to be obvious truths. This has led to some serious problems, as when people remembered the kind treatment during the Great War (of 1914-1918), in which German soldiers fighting in the East would give bread to the Russian civilians who were starving. When the Wehrmacht, the military of the Third Reich, entered eastern Europe, there was regularly the assumption that German soldiers were (still) kind and respectful—which did not at all apply to the new German military. Most could not believe reports of German atrocities in World War II, holding to this earlier idea of German civility, with deadly consequences.

Our generalizations from one context cannot automatically be applied across time with any guaranteed validity or correctness. Many of what we take to be historical parallels or instances of history repeating itself may be groundless assumptions on our part. This can keep us from seeing what is new, different, and significant about the situation we are now facing. *Some* of the features of an earlier situation may find parallels in a present situation. *That does not mean that everything (or even anything) significant can be deduced about how the present will evolve based on the past story.* In short, not all factors from the past will be found in the later, current reality. *Rather than history repeating itself, particular features may recur.* Their current impact, however, may be quite different, with distinct, new, significant factors that may bring about quite different consequences. Of course, when we have been powerfully influenced by some past situations with their shock and traumas, it is we that are making the link to that past, not that particular past that is reproducing itself. We may respond as if it were the same, and that may, in turn, make differences in how we understand and interpret the present situation, which may, on its own, then influence how we now respond and, consequently, what now comes to pass—but our imagination cannot define and dictate the actual specifics of a full, new present we now face.

In the search for an understanding of the past, and a putting it into its larger context, the perspective of a geopolitical historian is relevant, since "real history is not the trumpeting of ugly facts untempered by historical and philosophical context—the stuff of much investigative journalism. Real history is built on constant comparison with other epochs and other parts of the world."[91] While we may be hesitant about a wide variety of sources that may prove themselves to have little basis beyond a personal opinion or a rich but biased imagination, we can start by respecting the primary relevance of historical sources and philosophical considerations.

In looking for information about the past, we can look to primary sources, original documents, and other evidence from the period being investigated, and to later presentations that give us an integrated sense of the time we are interested in. In this, we may have access to presumably authentic documents from the time period in question.

In this, we can distinguish between different categories of original documents: governmental papers, often bureaucratically conformist and precise (if not dry); newspaper reports, often reflecting one bias or another; as well as sworn testimony and other documents that are part of various court records, all sources of original information from the period in focus. There are also diaries and memoirs written at or about the times in question. In considering these, we might use a rule of thumb (with its limits) the tendency for diaries, typically written for oneself, to be more candid than memoirs, often after-the-fact recountings of the person's life and experiences written to present the person in a particular light (perhaps more powerful, significant, cruel, or gentle, humble, kind, and so forth, depending on what the author wants to portray).

One relevant example here is Hitler's *Mein Kampf*, which contains some significant misrepresentations of Hitler's youth as an autodidact, portraying his life experiences, education, and claims of wisdom. The amount of self-glorification in this work is a study of its own; the image of the poor student in Vienna scraping out a living painting postcards for sale on the street, as one example of retouching reality, was finally discovered to distort that past by avoiding reference in a family account book that records a loan in the spring of 1908 given to Hitler of 924

---

[91] Robert D. Kaplan, *The Return of Marco Polo's World* (2018), p. 155.

Austrian crowns, *enough to support him for a year of independent living in Vienna*, suggesting more the life of a rentier than of a starving but self-determined young student.[92]

Even in the case of memoirs with their potential for distortion, however, there are still bits of information that we might cull that are informative. In any case, what is written may be limited, misleading, distorted, or a work of persuasion to convince the reader of one story or another, as found useful for the authors involved. (Some call this propaganda, etymologically, the propagating of some set of ideas or beliefs.) We can think of propaganda as intentionally distorted information, but sometimes the term has been used in its more etymological sense, as when Joseph Goebbels—"the evil genius of twentieth-century marketing"[93]—described propaganda in functional terms, on January 9, 1928: "Nobody can say that your propaganda is too crude, too vulgar, or too brutal, or that it is not respectable enough, for all these terms do not indicate the variety that characterizes it. It shouldn't be respectable in the first place, nor should it be smooth or gentle or meek; *it should lead to success.*"[94]

Given biases presented as objective fact, how do we have a careful eye, not being gullible and yet being open to considering the claims put forth? Again, the principle of *Caveat lector*, Let the reader beware.

Some research focuses on one aspect of a given period: the speeches and historical context of one important person (perhaps Hitler or Goebbels or Himmler), or the organization of the work world at the time, the differences in rights and privileges of various subgroups of the society, the patterns of abundance and deprivation at any given time—in narrow and world-wide considerations, across time. In developing a sense of some complex society, we may focus on the concerns, interests, hopes, and fears of a society, overall. We may look at the role of violence, both sporadic and organized, in spontaneous mobs or in organized groups,

---

[92] Ian Kershaw, *Hitler: A Biography* (2008), p. 14, cites this loan from Hitler's mother's sister, his Aunt Johanna—congenitally hunchbacked (a problem for Hitler's sense of his pure blood line) and yet apparently kind to Adolf. Cmp. Krysia Diver, "Journal reveals Hitler's dysfunctional family: Beaten by his father, the future dictator used to bully his sister [Paula Hitler]," *The Guardian* (London), Aug. 4, 2005, citing findings by scholars, American Timothy Ryback and German Florian Beierl, who cited the amount of this loan as 900 Austrian crowns.

[93] Niall Ferguson, *The War of the World: Twentieth-Century Conflict and the Descent of the West* (2006), p. 239. Cf. the War School of Land Army of the Spanish Defense Ministry 2013 film, *History's Verdict: Adolf Hitler (WWII Documentary)*, YOUTUBE, at 9:35-9:45.

[94] Edith Roper and Clara Leiser, *Skeleton of Justice* (1941), p. 49; emphasis added. From a talk, "Knowledge and Propaganda," in *Signale der neuen Zeit (Signals of the new Times);* later printed as "Erkenntnis und Propaganda," in *Signale der neuen Zeit. 25 ausgewählte Reden von Dr. Joseph Goebbels* (1934), pp. 28-52. Eng. at "Knowledge and Propaganda, by Joseph Goebbels," GERMAN PROPAGANDA ARCHIVE (CALVIN COLLEGE). Cf. Hans Herma, "Goebbels' Conception of Propaganda," *Social Research*, vol. 10, no. 2, 1943, pp. 200-218, with reflections on Goebbels' pride in the superiority of Nazi propaganda to that of any other nation.

from gangs to the military. With each of these as a focus, we may go in depth into that sub-domain of an overall society or era. We may also look back to see the origins of later tendencies, perhaps reading later developments into earlier beginnings, as in interpreting Hitler's virulent hostility toward Jews from the mid-1920s—as in his speeches of those years and in *Mein Kampf*—as somehow containing the developed system of gas chambers and crematoria of the 1940s. Or even reading the systematic mass killings by SS or other squads into Hitler's vague talk in that book of eliminating the vermin and bacilli that for him were Jewry.

We can develop a sense of when what is being described is unlikely or is overly emphasizing some point of character or of deeds done—or not done; we can sense what the intended goal of the passage is, even if perhaps recognized as disinformation ("fake news").

CATHARSIS, FORM, AND TENOR

The classical Greek pair of the smiling mask (joy and hopefulness) and the frowning mask (sadness and despair) focus on the impact of plays on the audience, in which the emotional experience inspired by the play allows for a deeper appreciation of the significance of what is being presented in one's own life: catharsis. When understanding the form of language used to communicate some situation that may be quite complex and have several sub-sections (or sub-plots), the text may be metered verse, blank verse, or prose, for example. Representations, whether in words, sketches, drawings, paintings, sculpture, in spoken form or in mime (pantomime), may be idealizing, laudatory, cynical, mocking, ridiculing, exaggerating, caricaturing; may be parodies, exposures of hypocrisy, or any combination of these. Films classified as comedies that are not filled with jokes or visual gags may be misclassified, especially if they are sarcastic, sardonic, tongue-in-cheek, or mocking parodies. Some films described as comedies may totally fail as comedies, if we expect to be laughing away in watching the film. They are not comedies in the ha-ha sense at all, but, rather, they are retelling the story with intentional distortions to point out certain features of the actual reality.

We may have a cavalier dismissal of histories, as if every description of the past is quite distorted, even suggesting, perhaps derisively, that a true story might be "so true that it may never appear in a history book" or that in a hundred years people will still be writing about Hitler and actors still depicting him, because "we want to understand what we will never understand."[95] Or, consider the words of the film character Herbert

---

[95] From the film *Mein Führer: Die wirklich wahrste Wahrheit über Adolf Hitler* (2007), at 2:01-2:06 and 1:27:05-1:27:20 (Eng., *My Führer: The Really Truest Truth about Adolf Hitler*). There are relatively few comedies about the Third Reich (perhaps more precisely parodies, spoofs, lampoons, or satires). Still, we may think here of the film, *The Great Dictator* (Charlie Chaplin, 1940). Its dictator dancing with a helium globe is well known, as are perhaps the upside-down airplane, with objects dropping upwards, and the dictation scene, where dictations and the time for typing are out of synch. Chaplin, who was not Jewish and not American, self-

Kropp, returning decades later with his own grown son, Klaus, to Herbert's boyhood German town of Brombach (Lörrach-Brombach, about 11 miles north-east of Basel, Switzerland), to investigate the fate of his mother, Paulina, who had a love relation during World War II with a Polish forced laborer, Stanisław Zasada ("Stani"). We first see Paulina's son Herbert as a boy, under a swastika-emblazoned canopy, licking on an oversized Nazi lollipop, a swastika-emblazoned sweet with little nutritive value:

Stani & Paulina

young Herbert

The adult Herbert concludes at the end of the film, "Many films have been made about that period but I doubt that it's really possible to tell it the way it is."[96] And yet, this sort of consideration puts forth the complex question (of "the way it is") as if simple: a more nuanced idea is that we can come to some initial understanding and that that can grow or be modified through time as we come to appreciate ever-new features of the historical situation we are studying. (A similarly unhelpful question is one we will begin with in a later section of this book, "Who knew? Did Hitler?")

A PHILOSOPHY OF HISTORY: TIME, NIETZSCHEAN POWDER, FIELD THEORY

Aside from these and other pitfalls to avoid in the search for a sense of what has preceded our own time, we can look back from the present, figuratively speaking, to consider the past.

But what counts as the present, what the past, what the future?

We can consider the present in terms of experience, taking it to be this fleeting moment, an instant of experience, in which there is a sound we are now hearing, a smell that catches our attention, a momentary glimpse, a savory taste, a sensation in our body, a thought or image that presents itself fleetingly in our mind. That makes for a very short sense of what counts as the present.[97]

---

financed the film. Chaplin was threatened by pro-Nazis, and Jews in the US film industry also faced hostility in a country where many were neutral if not pro-Nazi. Following the world premiere in NY of *The Great Dictator*, on Oct. 15, 1940, at a luncheon hosted in LA by Jack Warner, Pres. of Warner Bros. Pictures, the US Ambassador to the UK, Joseph P. Kennedy, told the Jewish moguls there, "Unless you stop this anti-Nazi, anti-Hitler propaganda, unless you stop making films like this, you're going to be responsible for pushing the United States into war." He then predicted that, if so, "the outbreak of anti-Semitism in this country will be unimaginable." Tom Putnam, "The Life of Joseph P. Kennedy," *John F. Kennedy Presidential Library and Museum*, JFKLIBRARY.ORG, Dec. 12, 2012. (More, below.)

[96] *Eine Liebe in Deutschland* (*A Love in Germany*), a 1983 German-language film by Polish director Andrzej Wajda, at 1:45:40-1:45:55.

[97] In Abhidhamma, Buddhist theoretical or metapsychology, a *cittakṣaṇa* (Pali,

We can think of the present as extending over anything from weeks to years or even decades. (We can even talk of a present that covers many centuries, such as the time of medieval Europe.) In general, there is the present, a past that preceded this present, and a future that will come later. And, in many cases there will be an influence of what preceded, in which the present makes more sense when we see it as linked to and related to earlier events. This can be a short-term linking, for example: "He was out in the cold rain and got soaked yesterday and today he has the sniffles." Or, our sense of history may involve a linking with quite a long-term span of time envisioned: "The British invaded Ireland in the late 1100s, and a movement came into dynamic focus, primarily in the first quarter of the twentieth century, fighting for Irish independence."

We may focus on aspects of the past that have links, *at least in our thinking*, to present conditions and events. That may distort the original historical situation. (What is important to us is not especially what was important to people in earlier ages and cultures.) We try, nonetheless, to make sense of what we become aware of about the past. When we consider historical events, one tendency in our thinking is to arrange these in a chronological order, earlier events followed by later events. This can give one arrangement to a history, the recounting of some expanse of time as we take it to have unfolded in time. The fuller meaning to us of some past can also make references to what preceded that time, to make a little more sense of how that came to happen, and also to later times, with what are understood as some of the more important consequences of that period (at least from one point of view).

And, as we look back at earlier times, from the standpoint of our own age and its concerns and interests, we may interpret earlier situations in terms of current-day values and understanding. This is often a distortion, an anachronistic misinterpretation of earlier interests and values. As an example, we may appreciate that *what was once understood as political representation in government is not what that generally implies today*. This can help limit our cross-time distortions.

We may also add new considerations to earlier descriptions of past events: in part, we may come to be curious about those times in ways that earlier generations of historians, and others interested in our past, did not consider. Of course, new information about an old topic may put it all in a new context that can change our sense of what was actually going on and its new-found significance.

This is not especially a matter of earlier historians being wrong in their focus, interests, and the issues they investigated, and our present questions being the correct and most important ones. It is more that we

---

cittakkhaṇa) is a mere moment of consciousness, strictly momentary, variously understood as 1/75th of a second, as a discrete irreducible atom of the series in time, or as one billionth of the duration of a flash of lightning. See Surendranath Dasgupta, *A History of Indian Philosophy* (1932), p. 161; A. K. Warder, *Indian Buddhism* (1970), p. 325; Ven. Nyanatiloka, *Buddhist Dictionary: Manual of Buddhist Terms and Doctrines*, 4th enlarged ed. by Nyanaponika (1980), p. 86.

have the opportunity in addressing new considerations, to have an ever-richer sense of the past. As one somewhat random example, in the political sphere, we might become curious about the concept of nationality as it developed in the eighteenth and nineteenth centuries, or how minorities in any given locale were treated and thought of in various particular lands in those centuries, relative to the evolving ideas of nationality we might be considering. And in that research and discovery, we might come to appreciate something important about what life in that context involved and was concerned with, that had not been considered in earlier times. New areas of interest, with new questions and new puzzlements about what was going on in the past, may lead us to notice what was always there but for long periods of time not considered relevant or important. Of course, what is important (to us) depends on what we are interested in, curious about, and wanting to understand. Sometimes these new areas of investigation may not impact our overall understanding of a period of time from the past, but at times may add a significant new sense of something about that historical period. If what we become aware of is significant enough, it may lead us to re-evaluate what we had earlier taken to be the case, leading to what is sometimes called historical re-interpretation.

We may be inspired, with some imagination, to open up new avenues of research, generating new topics and new questions to address. We may also be aware that the way we describe what we are looking at, the way we pose questions and the way we answer them, can give us insight, but can also make it more difficult to appreciate other features of what we taking to have happened that are not in our focused understanding (that are "under the radar").

Importantly, our perspective can both structure and limit our understanding in various ways.[98] Our very way of describing a period under a given name—such as in our speaking of the Franco-Prussian War, what preceded it, and what followed it—may have us assume that there are three distinct realities or periods of reality (one interpretation of the three distinct concepts of past, present, and future), with time defined in terms of certain military confrontations, disregarding all else. Also, we may appreciate that some terms used in political discussions have either vague meanings at any given time or *change meanings through time*. As further examples: leftist vs. rightist, monoculturalism vs. multiculturalism, nationalism vs. internationalism, open vs. closed societies, globalist vs. protectionist, democrat vs. republican, bipolarity vs. multipolarity vs. unipolarity, and liberal vs. conservative—even while accepting that there is also a politics identified as liberal conservativism. *Even democracy has meant different things in different ages and in different political contexts.*

---

[98] On this dual feature, see (1968) paper pub. in *The Human Context*, London (1974); revised ed., "Action and Communication & Schizophrenogenesis" (Chap. 2, pp. 26-38) in Mitchell Ginsberg, *Calm, Clear, and Loving*, esp. p. 36. On approaches to the historical analysis of the Holocaust, see Omer Bartov, *The Holocaust: Origins, Implementation, Aftermath* (2015).

We may take such terms to be more information-rich, constant in meaning, and unambiguous, than they are, leading to reading into one situation what is relevant in another. These considerations, encouraging reflection on and appreciation of the complexity of history and how we understand it using various key concepts and interconnected principles, will, I feel, add clarity and more subtle and complex understanding to our discussions. Here, in coming to appreciate the complexity of this process of developing a sense of history, without getting lost, we might keep in mind (to start with) at least two significant tendencies in our thinking that run counter to the fullest comprehension of which we are capable.

The first of these tendencies can be illustrated by a short story: A nine-year-old is handed back his exam paper by his teacher, and sees that he has a failing score. He is very upset and worried about how his father will react to this. He goes home at the end of the school day and opens the door to see his father standing firmly in the middle of the living room. The father stares at the son and then turns to his wife, mumbles something to her the boy cannot hear clearly, leaves the room, and returns with a small suitcase. Without saying a further word, he leaves the house, never to be seen again. The boy is sure that his father heard of the failed exam, and was so upset that he left the family forever. The boy continues through his life, for more than the next thirty years, with this deep sense of guilt, not only for failing an exam, but, more importantly, for receiving that poor grade that drove his father from the home, leaving him and his mother in dire straits for the rest of his childhood. It was only in reviewing this sense of guilt in discussion that he realized that there was no possibility of his father's knowing about his test results that day, and that, therefore, his father could not possibly have left because of anger and disappointment at the boy's school work. This allowed a re-evaluation of this important aspect of this man's sense of self, allowing little room for guilt over what was not his doing in the first place.[99]

We often go through life with ideas, beliefs, explanations of why what happened in our lives happened as it did, and, in a grander scheme of things, what the world is like (promising, inspiring, threatening, dreadful, incomprehensible, and so on), all based on the particular beliefs such attitudes are based upon. This is true on an individual level, but we might also see such patterns in groups of people, in cliques, in coteries, and in entire societies. *In this, the beliefs that are predominant in the group have an impact that is independent of the truth, falsity, absurdity, or fundamental incoherence of the accepted belief systems.* As historian and psychohistorian Robert Waite (1919-1989) pointed out, "In what follows here, stress will be placed not so much on what actually happened as on what many Germans remember [with or without distortions] about their history—the memories [beliefs about the past] which helped Hitler come to power. For well he knew how to exploit popular history for his own purposes. Our attention [Waite continues] will also focus on the *results* of

---

[99] These are features from a psychotherapy I conducted in the late 1990s.

ideas and actions: on the legacy of Luther and Nietzsche rather than on what they may actually have thought or intended, on the consequences, rather than the causes, of World War I and the Great Depression [and, we may add, on the Hitler era, as well]."[100] Here, there will be a place for considering both, and to acknowledge this distinction Waite presents.

Our accepting what we learned in specific situations—including the teachings of our family and our society, in ways that are not questioned and that are allowed to structure our thinking, speaking, and acting in the world—*is not guaranteed to be the most accurate, insightful, and helpful view of reality*. It is certainly no mere happenstance or accident that we tend to be in overall agreement with our society's beliefs, depending on where we were raised and educated. (And when we have cross-societal contact with others, we are invited to remain firm in our earlier beliefs, or to consider the possibilities that other cultures have something to add to our overall comprehension of the world and of our lives in that world.)

That is one form of thinking we can be aware of and not be controlled by here. Basically, our firmness of belief in what has been passed on to us can be of value, to give a basic orientation to life, but can also be like wearing a pair of horse-blinders through life.

The second of these tendencies in our thinking can be illustrated in its simplest form by an image:

In this photograph, we see a firing squad of German soldiers, rifles pointed at a French resistance fighter, identified as Georges Blind. The photo was taken in October 1944. Georges Blind, defiantly smiling at the squad, would receive a number of bullets, any of which might be sufficient to kill. It also meant that even if several of the rifles were poorly aimed, the deed, the execution of the resistance fighter, would still succeed.[101]

In terms of the structure of the event, here we have a number of sources ("causes") here with the outcome of a dead person, *more than enough to achieve this end*. When we have more than enough contributing causes to a result, the situation is described as overdetermined. This could

---

[100] Robert G. L. Waite, *The Psychopathic God: Adolf Hitler* (1977), p. 246. Italics in original.
[101] Elizabeth Pastwa, "Photographe du fusillé souriant," *Fondation de la Résistance*, FONDATIONREISTANCE.ORG.

also be understood as an event being simultaneously determined in multiple fashions. In the German of Freud and others, this was described as *überbestimmt* or *überdeterminiert* (overdetermined), or, in other terms, as *mehrfach determiniert* (multiply determined). [102] In this example of the firing squad, with a number of possible causes of the outcome, the killing of the Frenchman being shot by this firing squad, we can see that these are repeating the same single kind of cause. *This gives a flat or limited, one-dimensional, sense of what over-determination of a given outcome is*, which may be more complex.

When we look at an immediate context without taking into account the larger picture, we can easily draw conclusions that could, and should, be seriously questioned. For example, an elephant with a flea sitting on its head near its ear is walking slowly across a rope bridge. With each step, the bridge swings from side to side. When they get to the far side of the bridge, the flea whispers into the ear of the elephant, "Wow! We really shook that bridge, didn't we!" What looks like a full, non-distorted, non-one-sided understanding and explanation of some event may be seriously misunderstanding that event. We will see this tendency in looking at various historical incidents and how they have been understood.

Nietzsche made a distinction between a match (*Streichholz*) or burning fuse (*brennender Lunte*) and explosive powder (*Pulverfass, Pulvertonne*). *Here, the match is inoperative if there is not a powder keg to ignite*. We will see small incidents in a context of countries eager for war used as triggers, inspirations, or excuses to go to war; to take what is used by governments and military for their interest in going to war is to misidentify the defining features of the situation: this is confusing the match for powder keg, in Nietzsche's metaphor.[103] We will return to this issue of the incidents that are cited to "explain" going to war in a number of historical contexts, throughout this text.

There are other examples, *where the relevant conditions lie along a variety of dimensions*. For example, if we consider what led to a water pipe cracking on a cold winter night, we might consider the freezing temperature of water and its physics (the expansion of liquid water to frozen water, ice), the thickness and resistance to expansion of the pipe itself, the stress that the walls of the pipe would experience under those

---

[102] See, first, (1-GER.) Josef Breuer and Sigmund Freud, *Studien zur Hysterie* (1895), p. 255 (*überbestimmt*), pp. 185, 229 (*überdeterminiert*; older spelling, *mehr determinirt*) and (1-ENG.) *Studies on Hysteria*, James Strachey and Anna Freud, tr. (1955), p. 290 (re *überbestimmt*), pp. 212, 263 (re *überdeterminirt*), p. 255 (re *mehr determinirt*); and, second, (2-GER.) Sigmund Freud, *Die Traumdeutung* (1900), pp. 195, 280 (*überdeterminirt*), p. 195 (*mehr determinirt*), and (2-ENG.) *The Interpretation of Dreams*, James Strachey, tr. (1961), p. 301, 485 (re *überdeterminirt*), p. 301 (re *mehr determinirt*).

[103] Friedrich Nietzsche, *The Gay Science*—also tr. with the title *The Joyful Wisdom: Gaia Scienza* (1887), 38, 360; cf. Arnout Hostens, "Über Auslösung und Pulverfass," *Engadiner Post* (St. Moritz, Switzerland), Sep. 18, 2010, p. 13.

The Hitler Era

conditions, the resultant cracking of the pipe and the subsequent dripping of water through the cracked pipe when the temperature rose enough to melt the ice within the pipe back into liquid water.

When there are multiple conditions that are all involved in the changes or processes, we would like to understand, one way of conceptualizing this interwoven complexity is *to replace talk of cause-and-effect with that of the "field"* (as in "field theory"), *the overall complex and often multi-faceted, multi-dimensional, context*. This field is the totality of various sorts of conditions that are together the ground or the context in which the events we would be considering can come about, and be understood, *a field potentially of an innumerable number of factors*.[104] This tendency we often see is to go for the simplest answer may have its own value. And yet when the situation does not lend itself to such a simple attitude, something else is more appropriate. *Simple thinking can generate a limited appreciation of the phenomenon at hand, and make use of inadequate ideas for a rich understanding.*

NAMES TO INSULT BY AND FUNCTIONS OF HATE SPEECH

In noticing how people relate to, and speak about, others, in general, and in the violent and hate-filled context of the Third Reich, we are easily aware that there are *exonyms*, names given to some group by outsiders, and *endonyms*, names given by a group to itself.

Sometimes exonyms are innocent, but sometimes they are quite insulting. In that case, they form a group of expressions that are called ethnophaulisms (words or phrases used as ethnic slurs or insults).

The list to follow will include examples that are presumably already familiar to many people, even if to be avoided in polite society. (I consider what follows here to be a sociological resume *that is explicit about nastiness*.) We can quickly come up with terms such as Jewboy, Hymie, Heeb, Sheeny, Christ-killer—a term that regularly has enjoyed more popularity at the time of Easter Sunday, the anniversary of the crucifixion of Jesus of Nazareth as the *Xristos* (the Christ), the *Moshiaḥ* (the Messiah, the Anointed One)—as well as the rather nasty insult term, Kike, and so on, in English. In other languages, we can also find many insult names for Jews: in French (the regular word being *Juif*), insult terms include *youpin, youpe, youpi, youte, youtre, youdi, Feuj* and *Feuje* (*Juif* in verlan,[105]). In Russian and Ukrainian: *Zhid* (the plain word for Jew being *Yevrei*, with its cognate, *Yid*, the ordinary endonym in Yiddish for a Jew). In German, there is *Jüdlein* (little Jew, Jewboy, kike), and terms identifying Jews as pigs: *Judensau, Judenschwein,* and *Saujude*. Even the

---

[104] In psychology, this was largely developed by German-American Kurt Lewin, as in his "Field Theory and Experiment in Social Psychology: Concepts and Methods," *American Journal of Sociology*, vol. 44, no. 6, May 1939, pp. 868–896.

[105] In French, "verlan" is a way of forming slang (at times a secret code) by inverting syllables, or sound sequences; thus, the word *verlan* itself is a "verlan" of *l'envers*—imagine here: *l'en-vers* (reverse) reordered into *vers-l'en*.

regular German word for Jew, *Jüde*, can serve as a hostile insult term, as in the expression *Jude Verrecke!* (Jew, die a miserable death!).[106]

For blacks (formerly respectfully called colored people) some insult terms are boy, nigra, nigga, nigger, coon, and such. We may remember the insulting terms Jap or Nip, Chink, Jerry, Kraut, or *een mof* (Dutch insult term for a German, with connotations of being grumpy or uncivilized), or, in French, *Boche* (especially from the Franco-Prussian War on), as well as Dago or Wop (for those of Italian descent, the latter taken to be an acronym of Without Papers), Spic (for those of Hispanic descent), with even further examples the reader can perhaps easily add.

THE ROMANIES, CALLED GYPSIES (AN EXONYM MISNOMER)

Some issues arise simply from the names by which given groups are mentioned (as suggested just above). One example of this sort of concern that will have important application in this text is that of the peoples quite commonly, though inaccurately, called Gypsies—the Romanies,[107] to give the most widely self-accepted term—an alternative to speaking of the Roma, an often-used PC name actually disliked by some Romanies,[108] such as the Sinti—to give two endonyms here. (Other tribes or groups of Romanies include the Lalleri, Drisari, Kelderari, Lovari, and Medvashi.[109])

Some thought that the Romanies had come from Egypt and so were called Egyptians and then Gypsies, as a shortened form. This is historically incorrect, as we now know, but it is still widely used. Detailed linguistic analysis[110] suggests that the Romanies, who had lived for centuries in the northwestern Indian sub-continent (in Kafiristan, Dardistan, Kashmir, and in the Sindh basin—a regional reference found reflected in the name

---

[106] *Eine Sau*, lit., a sow, is also an insult term for people, and *ein Schwein*, a pig, is also used as an insult term (as "dirty pig"), as is *Schweinhund*, pig-dog.

[107] The term Gypsy, and even more so, the variant common noun, gypsy, are insult terms. One common term, the Roma, is widely accepted (as mentioned just above), but some, such as the Sinti, find the term Roma a misnomer (given its more specific meaning an adult male). By contrast, the term Romanies for the entire group or various sub-parts is acceptable to all; I will use that here for what others have called Gypsies. The related adjective is Romani—also written Romany—as in Romani children, language, culture, or music. Romani is also the name of the language spoken by many Romanies. I will use the term Gypsy here, primarily when quoting the terminology found in Nazi or other sources.

[108] At least part of the basis of the Sinti disagreement with using Rom (or Roms, Roma, etc.) as a name of the entire people is that the term Rom does not mean simply a Romani: it literally means a married adult male; the parallel term for a married adult woman is Romni. See "Roma," WORLD CULTURES ENCYCLOPEDIA. On Roms (or Rroms) in French terminology, see Loïc Le Clerc, "Tsiganes, Roms, gitans ou gens du voyage: les distinctions à faire," LCI SOCIÉTÉ, Oct. 29, 2016.

[109] Donald Kenrick and Grattan Puxon, *Gypsies under the Swastika* (2009), pp. 36-38. Cf. the film, *The Forgotten Genocide: Gypsies in World War II* (2011).

[110] Rajko Djurić, "From Legend to Fact," pp. 13-16, in Nebojša Bato Tomašević and Rajko Djurić, *Gypsies of the World* (1988), discussing the research of Slovenian linguist Franz Miklosich (Franc Miklošič, 1813-1891).

The Hitler Era

Sinti[111]), migrated through Kabulistan, Iran, and Armenia, where many stayed for generations, then through Phrygia and Laconia into the Byzantine Empire (later the Ottoman Empire), living in part on the Anatolian plains, at that time called Rum or Rom[112] (a reference that was perhaps adapted in the names Roma and Romanies, along with the link to Romania), and entered southeast Europe; their presence is documented in Serbia in 1348.[113]

Furthermore, the name *Gypsy* often, usually, has connotations of strange, isolationist, asocial, criminal, violent, and otherwise undesirable people. These are widely assumed associations with the name Gypsy, contributing to these negative and derogatory undertones. We may derive terms for the Romanies such as *Zigeuner* and *tsiganes* from the medieval Greek, *Atsingani*, a ninth-century sect proposing the unity of God (monarchianism), in contrast with trinitarianism, holding the three-fold nature of God; in Classical Greek, *athígganoi*, untouchable. In German, the Romanies have been called *Zigeuner*; in France, *gitanes, tsiganes, bohémiens*, or *manouches;* in Spanish, *gitanos, cíngaros*, or *flamencos;* in Portuguese, *ciganos, calés, calãos*, or *boémios;* in Italian, *zingari;* in Greek, *Athínganos, Tsiggánoi*, or the more derogatory, *Gúphtoi (Gýphtoi)*; in Serbian *Romi*, or the less polite *Tsigani (Cigani)*; in Russian, *tsyganskii;* and so on. Issues of choice of vocabulary aside, there is also the important impact of speech in play here: in twentieth-century British philosophy of language, the use of speech addresses *the capacity of speech to persuade, convince, scare, enlighten, inspire, and so on.*[114]

What is important in this context is the use of such terms and the attitudes that they express and perhaps are intended to encourage in

---

[111] The name, Sinti, is derived from Sindho: those from the Sindh, the area (including present-day Sindh Province, Pakistan) around the Hindus River—the Sindhu River—our words Hindu and Hinduism come from the same source. See Deryck O. Lodrick and Nafis Ahmad, "Indus River," ENCYCLOPÆDIA BRITANNICA.

[112] This location gave the name to the Persian poet, philosopher, and Sufi mystic Jalaluddin Rumi (1207-1273), whose name means one from Rum (Anatolia). Born in Balkh (present-day Afghanistan)—giving him a second name or epithet, Balkhi—his parents fled to the Byzantine Empire, settling in Rum. He is the author of *Mathnawi, Diwan-e Shams-e Tabrizi*, and *Fihi Ma Fihi* (Eng., *Signs of the Unseen*).

[113] Czar Stefan Uroš IV Dušan (ca. 1308-1355), Emperor of the Serbs, Greeks, Bulgarians, and Albanians, wrote in 1348 of presenting Gypsy slaves to the Church monastery of Prizren, in Kosovo province. See Jelena Čvorović, "Sexual and Reproductive Strategies among Serbian Gypsies," *Population and Environment*, vol. 25, no. 3, 2004, pp. 217–242, at p. 219. Slavery of Romanies in Moldavia and Wallachia (Romania) ended in 1855-1856, with complete legal freedom coming in 1864. See Ian Hancock, "Towards Abolition," in *The Pariah Syndrome: An Account of Gypsy Slavery and Persecution* (1987), pp. 30-36, esp. p. 35. Slavery ended in the USA in 1865 (Amendment XIII), and in Cuba in 1886. See Rebecca J. Scott, "Gradual Abolition and the Dynamics of Slave Emancipation in Cuba, 1868-86," *The Hispanic American Historical Review*, vol. 63, no. 3, Aug. 1983, pp. 449–477.

[114] This feature of speech is called a "perlocutionary speech act": See the groundbreaking text by J. L. Austin, *How to Do Things with Words: The William James Lectures Delivered at Harvard University in 1955*, J. O. Urmson, ed. (1962), p. 101.

those hearing such speech. If even the tone in which one of the many exonyms or endonyms is spoken can convey contempt, disgust, hatred, and so forth, we can see that ultimately the attitude and the relationship that is being expressed can convey a great animosity if not open threat to those so called. In Nazi Germany, the repeated call, "*Jude! Jude!*" ("Jew! Jew!), a chant that could make it clear Jews were not safe in that situation.

Furthermore, and importantly, the use of derogatory names can be, and was, used in order to incite and encourage profound hostility against Jews, and similarly, against Romanies (*die Zigeuner*). *We will see many examples of this use of perlocutionary, provocative language, used to instigate repulsion, anger, rage, violence and organized murder.*

COMPLEXITY AND UNDERSTANDING THE HITLER ERA

In attempting to understand the complex story of the Hitler era and the years of the Third Reich, we may become focused on one facet of a complex phenomenon, with our missing what is relevant and illuminating.

Here, and in our coming to an understanding in general, single features, taken as a complete explanation of a complex reality, essentially distort and block any well-rounded understanding.

Was the phenomenon of the Third Reich, World War II, and the Holocaust are all based on the madness of one man, Hitler, a man with great confidence in his wisdom and brilliant understanding of history, a man with a messianic sense of his role and powers for the German nation?

Did it all evolve out of the harsh conditions demanded of Germany by the Versailles Treaty of 1919? Or from the organized and authoritarian nature of German society before the 1930s? Or from the frustrations of a proud nation feeling betrayed and wanting to take significant revenge? Or as Germany's attempt to gain redemption and to prove its worth, an existential question?

We may notice a pervasive issue seen in many countries, where major differences in wealth and power wreak havoc,[115] and, so, here, did such a turbulent disorder lead a fledgling, fringe group of impotent men in Germany to search for their path to power? Or was Germany just trying to find peace in the midst of ongoing, deep hostilities, but beset by hostile neighbors on all sides? Does any one of these allow us to appreciate Hitler and Third Reich years, the cause of the Second World War, and the state-sponsored, -structured, and -implemented program, using modern technology in its most barbaric, powerful, and efficient form, facilitating the killing of millions of civilians?

We can certainly simplify (and oversimplify) events, misidentifying root causes, confusing cause and effect, misunderstanding what we want to understand. We discussed these various features above, as in our considering field theory and the metaphor of Nietzschean matches.

---

[115] Here, see the in-depth analysis of American political economist and social philosopher Henry George (1839-1897), *Progress and Poverty: An Inquiry into the Cause of Industrial Depressions, and of Increase of Want with Increase of Wealth: The Remedy* (1879).

3. A Philosophy of History for the Hitler Era

When we speak of the Hitler era as history, we are perhaps thinking of the many varied events, actions, speeches, laws, decrees, and dictates of that period. But what makes these and related matters history? Why do we think of these as historical at all? *These are questions that can be raised in* a philosophy of history, *attempting to understand the nature, features, and dynamics of history* (as touched on in the previous chapter). To consider some situation, event, or phenomenon as historical is to place it in a complex framework or matrix of time. Something is historical in so far as it has a past (that which preceded it, and in some ways influenced it to come to pass as then happened), a present (the other features of that given period of time in focus that were in interaction with one another), and a future (what then followed as impacted by that present).

Here, we will be considering events that took place during the post-Great-War years (1919-1933), earlier, during the years of World War I, as well as political and geopolitical events of the 1800s, in addition to, as well, events from earlier centuries (these last to a more limited extent).

Looking back at the Hitler era as a history, its recognized features keep being modified through time, meaning that what people have been interested in learning about has evolved, not in a straight line, but in shifts that have arisen in part from new life situations raising new life concerns.

One principle here is that the events of any period, including that of the Hitler era, do not happen in a void: "Nazism was not simply a nightmarish parenthesis in history that bore no relationship to what came before and after; nor was it a completely unexampled racist horror... There *were* continuities between Nazism and came before and after."[116]

As we will see when considering the Third Reich, World War II, the end of the Reich, or the end of the War, these do not neatly refer to sharp shifts from one reality to a totally different reality. We might say that our lives are continua, processes that go through transformations that may be subtle and so slow that we do not even notice them, except perhaps much later, looking back and appreciating our lives' overall evolution.

All of this we can keep in the background of our thinking as we delve into the period at hand. Here, then, in considering the Hitler era, we will maintain an overall chronological arrangement. Within this approach, we will be able to see, when looking in greater focus, a set of various phenomena in complex interaction. This will allow the interweaving of various threads of those particular processes to be more apparent, perhaps referring when helpful to some earlier and later events in the larger story. This will have the text move through time, from relative pasts, presents, and futures, in ways I think will be clarifying.

How do we date the Hitler era and *die Nazizeit* (the time of the Nazis)? We presumably know that this shortened form, Nazi, is often felt to be a derogatory, insulting way of referring to the National Socialists, members of the *Nationalsozialistische Deutsche Arbeiter Partei* (or NSDAP). Actually,

---

[116] James Q. Whitman, *Hitler's American Model*, p. 15.

however, the German roots of the term Nazi go back years before the creation of the NSDAP and its name in 1920. This National Socialism, abbreviated *Nazi* (parallel to *Sozi*, for the *Sozialdemokratische Partei*, the Social Democratic Party and its members[117]) consisted in a doctrine that Germany was under an existential threat—that its very existence was challenged (the "nationalist" part)—and that to achieve this goal required a concerted, coordinated action throughout the society (the "socialist" part). *This second doctrine, importantly, overrode class distinctions in Germany (and Europe, in general) in those years*, continuing a breakdown in class distinctions and separations that began in the late 1800s and continues through current times, in a number of Western countries. Note that this form of socialism is quite different from the concept of socialism as a society in which the major means of production—including factories—are owned by the government. Castro's Cuba involved such a socialism, triggered by the nationalizing or government take-over of its sugar and oil production on August 6, 1960, for example. With these basic Nazi principles, important additional teachings of the NSDAP under Hitler would add to these two core principles, transforming National Socialism into what we now understand it to be, informed by the structure and the history of the Third Reich.[118]

With this as framework, perhaps for Adolf Hitler himself, the Hitler era started with his birth, April 20, 1889, and ended with his feeling betrayed by the German nation and by all those he had put his trust into, with his suicide on April 30, 1945, in the bunker below the Reich Chancellery garden, in the rubble of a Berlin conquered by Soviet troops.

Others may see the roots of the Hitler era going back at least five hundred years, to the time of the Holy Roman Empire. This Empire begun with the crowning in Rome of Charlemagne by Pope Leo III in 800—and especially in its time of greatest territorial control, since the time of Frederick I (Emperor, 1152-1190)—in Italian, Federico Barbarossa (Red-Beard). With a reference to this long German history, Frederick I would be the individual honored by the Third Reich in the code name for its plan to invade the Soviet Union in June 1941, *Unternehmen Barbarossa* (Operation Barbarossa), also known as *Fall Barbarossa* (the Case or Matter of Barbarossa). This Holy Roman Empire during the period of the Hohenstaufen Dynasty (1155-1268) had the Empire ruling the central portion of Europe, including lands that are within present-day France,

---

[117] Kurt G. W. Ludecke, an early supporter of Hitler, would report that in the 1920s, he "heard Sozis attacked as violently as Nazis and the existing [Weimar] government mentioned with contempt rather than fear." In his *I Knew Hitler: The Story of a National Socialist Who Escaped the Blood Purge* (1937), Chap. 21 ("Heil Hitler? Quatsch!"), p. 392—*quatsch* in German means Nonsense! rubbish!

[118] Moshe Zimmermann, "A Road Not Taken: Friedrich Naumann's Attempt at a Modern German Nationalism," *Journal of Contemporary History*, vol. 17, no. 4, 1982, pp. 689–708; Asaf Kedar, *National Socialism Before Nazism: Friedrich Naumann and Theodor Fritsch, 1890-1914* (2010).

Italy, Germany, Austria, and other countries. The question that this posed in a geopolitical sense for Europe was how to have a powerful, organized country in central Europe (*Mitteleuropa*) that would not overpower and dominate neighboring lands and peoples. Perhaps this question has been important for centuries, to the Third Reich,[119] and even to today's world.

The Holy Roman Empire during the Hohenstaufen Dynasty

THE HISTORICAL CONTEXT OF THE HITLER ERA

For others with a very wide vision of history, the roots of the Hitler era lie in pre-Christian German lands, with their rituals (that from a Christian perspective are considered pagan: think, for example, of the Teutonic honoring of fire and of the use of torches in great processions that were seen the night that Hitler was invited to be Chancellor of Germany by President Hindenburg). This pagan period was followed by the conversion of Germans to Christianity by a show of power, around the year 723. (Here, the sacred trees of Teutonic religion, and a holy Teutonic tree called Thor's Oak, were cut down by a Christian missionary, Boniface (later, St. Boniface), who showed the power of Christianity when he was not punished for cutting down Thor's Oak—a sacrilegious act against their pagan gods. Stemming from this source are some of the more pagan-like

---

[119] The Third Empire or Reich (the Nazi Reich) was preceded by the First Reich (the Holy Roman Empire, and the Wilhelmine Empire (the Second Reich).

ceremonies of the Nazis, as well as the Nazi denigration of Christianity as a religion of weakness, to be replaced by traditional Germanic visions respecting strength, imposing violence, and overwhelming power.

A Nazi design with a related inspiration, referring back to the Teutonic script (runes), made use of the form that represented the sun (with a modern association to victory: *Sieg*)[120]: ᛋ, which when doubled in a stylized form was an abbreviation of the *Schutzstaffel* (the SS, or ᛋᛋ).

Histories are not always forgotten. Rather, in fact, their memory— sometimes (if not often) in a distorted form—may well give meaning and significance to later events. In addition to this modified echo of the past, there are also events that take place in one period that have more significance in a later period. In both these ways, historical events have a capacity to be transported into, to find their impact continuing into, other periods: *this is the semi-permeable nature of historical events*.[121]

We will notice this phenomenon at various points throughout this investigation of the Hitler era. We may sense this semi-permeable nature of time in a concrete, specific way when we consider the importance of certain moments in history, some more emphasized in one country or another: October 14, 1066, June 15, 1215, July 4, 1776, July 14, 1789, June 28, 1914, December 7, 1941, November 22, 1963, and September 11, both in 1973 and in 2001 (as a few significant examples).

For still others, the Hitler era has its roots in the years before the Great War of 1914-1918, and the many life-redefining changes that many in Europe experienced, nations gone and new ones created.

Some maps may make the changing political geography of Europe clearer. We can consider here several maps of this period.

Europe 1914, political map

This first map, just above, shows the situation before World War I, considering both a political map of Europe from pre-1914, and a second map, just below, shows the alliances that had been set up by the start of the war, based on treaties for mutual aid in times of international war, an attempt to avoid war by a balance of power, a centuries-old European

---

[120] As in the Nazi exclamation, *Sieg heil!* (Hail to victory!).
[121] This concept of semi-permeability was introduced above.

approach to these concerns: the Triple Alliance (treaties between Germany, Austria-Hungary, and Italy) and the Triple Entente (treaties between the United Kingdom, the French Third Republic, and Czarist Russian Empire). This is the situation defined by these alliances in place in 1914:

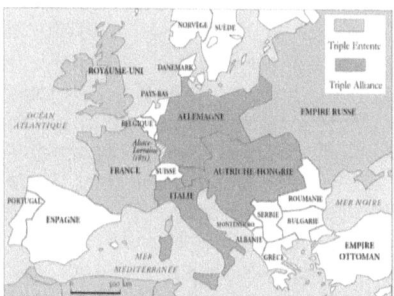

Triple Alliance & Triple Entente 1914

And with that, here is the situation after the war as shown by another map, following the initial restructuring of Europe by the Versailles Treaty:

Europe, post-World War I

As these maps of the period illustrate, at the end of World War I, with the Treaty of Versailles and ancillary treaties of those first years after the Armistice of 1918, new nations were created and others gone.

It looks like Germany had significant parts of its territory taken from it, and what had been Austria-Hungary was now a number of much smaller countries. And, to the east, the former Czarist Russia, which Germany had defeated in war, was now a fledgling Soviet state.

Post-czarist Russia would remain an outcast, for what were couched in political-theoretical terms, but which had an economic basis, worrisome to countries such as the USA and the UK: US Secretary of State Charles Evans Hughes on one occasion explained the US position concerning the Soviet Union. This was commented upon by the Soviet press:

> Moreover, he [Hughes] says himself that the question of the recognition of the Soviet Government is essentially an economic question, in which considerations of humanity play no part at all. That sounds better! Let us speak plainly, without interlarding considerations of an economic character with hypocritical, and therefore merely irritating, humanitarian chatter.[122]

With the USA retreating into an isolationism, refusing to sign the Treaty of Versailles and refusing to join the League of Nations, Germany faced England and France as remaining confrontive states (if not enemies), but there was no longer a Czarist Russia to contend with, and its successor, Soviet Russia, in no position to pose a military threat. Further, Germany now had no large empire to confront in *Mitteleuropa* (Middle Europe)—Austria-Hungary—either. The newly formed Weimar Republic, at first a coalition of left-center parties (the Social Democrats, the Left liberals, and the Catholics), lost its majority a year later, and the Republic, inspired by the form of the German Empire, with its Parliament, was in a precarious position. Field Marshal Paul von Hindenburg, the old war hero, was elected President of Germany in 1925 (after the disastrous hyperinflation of 1923), having through the Weimar Constitution the right to certain emergency powers if the republic was in peril. *Hindenburg used these powers to limit certain rights established under the Constitution, then appointed a number of chancellors who ruled using these emergency powers to limit even further the democratic rights of the Weimar Republic, and this, from the position of a minority government.* It was a slow process. Ultimately, Hindenburg aligned with the National Socialists and Hitler, leading to the further erosion of democratic parliamentary government that was then operating under even more autocratic principles.[123]

One reflection of the hostility toward, or at least lack of enthusiastic support for, the Republic can be seen in the Bavarian government's treatment of Hitler, his co-conspirators, and of the fledgling Nazi Party (the National Socialist German Worker's Party, *Nationalsozialistische Deutsche Arbeiterpartei*, in short, the NSDAP) in the trial for the Hitler Putsch. The court meted out to Hitler (who was not even a German citizen at the time) an extremely light prison sentence for conspiracy to overthrow the government (treason): sentenced to five years in prison, he ultimately spent less than one year in Landsberg Prison (April 1-December 20, 1924). At the time, *The New York Times* would have an article stating (ultimately rather mistakenly) that Hitler left prison "much

---

[122] "Soviet Comments on Our [US Gov't] Russian Policy," *Advocate of Peace through Justice*, vol. 85, no. 7, July 1923, p. 272. Quoted from the March 27, 1923 issue of *Izvestiya* (Moscow). The comments by US Sec. of State Hughes were his response on March 21, 1923, to a delegation of the Women's Committee for Recognition of Russia, an American women's group.

[123] Anthony James Nicholls, *Weimar and the Rise of Hitler*, 4th ed. (2005), pp. 150, 157-160, 165-167, 177-178.

sadder and wiser ... [and] no longer to be feared. It is believed he will retire to private life and return to Austria, the country of his birth."[124]

Also, we can consider the ban ordered by the Bavarian government against the NSDAP (National Socialist German Worker's Party, the Nazi Party), after the failed Putsch: the Bavarian government lifted this on February 25, 1925, some two months after Hitler's release from prison.

The prison in which Hitler was held was in the town of Landsberg am Lech, some 40 miles west of Munich, and his quarters were rather luxurious relative to the prison cell one might imagine. Hitler could have his own library (some 200 books) and was allowed a birthday celebration shortly after being imprisoned (on April 20, 1924, his 35th birthday).[125]

Ernst Hanfstaengl, after a visit to Hitler, spoke of feeling that he had "walked into a delicatessen. There was fruit and there were flowers, wine and other alcoholic beverages, ham, sausage, cake, boxes of chocolates and much more."[126] An image of Hitler and fellow convicted prisoners who had partaken in the Putsch shows them posing in his living quarters:

Hitler with Emil Maurice, Hermann Kriebel, Rudolf Heß, and Friedrich Weber

Germany would have the potential to achieve a geopolitical status of a great continental European power (which it did become in the coming decades). *Furthermore, the onerous reparations payments were to be abandoned in steps, with the US-sponsored Dawes Plan of 1924, the Locarno Treaties of 1925,[127] and then the Young Plan of 1929, undoing and restructuring European international relations.* The two American plans greatly reduced the amount of reparations to be paid by Germany and ultimately, in practice, all but totally eliminated them. The Locarno Treaties, with Foreign Minister Gustav Stresemann negotiating for Germany—who proposed currency reform to help stabilize the German currency—presented himself as a major proponent of a new atmosphere of peaceful resolution of international conflicts. (For his conciliatory work,

---

[124] "Hitler Tamed by Prison: Released on Parole, He is Expected to Return to Austria," *New York Times*, Dec. 21, 1924, p. 16.

[125] Prof. Michael Lynch, interviewed in *Hitler's Circle of Evil 2/10: Regrouping*, YOUTUBE, at 11:20-12:10.

[126] Jan Friedmann, "Adolf Hitler's Time in Jail: Flowers for the Führer in Landsberg Prison," *Spiegel*, Jun. 23, 2010.

[127] These were seven treaties, negotiated in Locarno, Switzerland, Oct. 5-16, 1925, and formally signed in London that Dec. 1.

he shared the award of the Nobel Peace Prize in 1926 with Aristide Briand,[128] French Foreign Minister). In three months, he stopped the hyperinflation that was ravaging Germany: by persuading striking workers in the Ruhr to work (eliminating government payments for strikers), by making a commitment to return to reparations payments, the French ended its occupation of the Ruhr earlier than scheduled, in 1925, and by printing limited amounts of a new currency, the *Rentenmark*, which held its value.

Through the Locarno Treaties, Germany was also invited to join the League of Nations, which it did. *Germany, in effect, was rehabilitated into the community of nations*. The Germans were also safe from the British, who, under Foreign Minister Austen Chamberlain (half-brother of Neville Chamberlain), were not ready to back the French or become engaged in more military strife, feeling the great losses they suffered in the War.

Still, the new Germany of the Weimar Republic had serious problems, with many Germans preferring alternative forms of government, thus making for a weak government even before it acted. Late in the life of the Republic, during the time of the government of Heinrich Brüning—who became Chancellor of Germany on March 20, 1930, and kept that post until May, 1932—Brüning in fact made use of the emergency powers within the Weimar Constitution to have emergency decrees, and operated from a minority government—not a democracy as we might imagine it.

In these and other ways, much of the Republic was already undermined, if not destroyed. Hitler, once he became Chancellor, would continue this erosion, but the governing capacity of the Weimar Republic was quite weakened, if it ever had any significant solidity and strength to govern with basic stability.[129]

Given that context, for some the Hitler era is sometimes dated from the Hitler *Putsch*, the attempted *coup d'état*, of November 8-9, 1923.[130] And have their end dated not on the day of Hitler's suicide, but with the unconditional surrender of the surviving leaders of the Third Reich to the Allied forces, on May 7, 1945—VE (Victory in Europe) Day.

Still others date the Hitler era starting at the end of hostilities at 11:00 am on November 11, 1918 (Armistice Day), the formal moment of the end of military engagements between the Allies and German.

---

[128] "Gustav Stresemann" and "Aristide Briand," THE NOBEL PRIZE. On some of the negotiating and reasoning of the period, see "The French in the Saar," *Advocate of Peace through Justice*, vol. 85, no. 7, July 1923, pp. 270–272; Maj. Bernard Talbot Reynolds, Royal Artillery, Ret., "The Problem with the Saar," *The Military Engineer*, vol. 26, no, 149, Sep.-Oct. 1934, pp. 363-367.

[129] Anthony J. Nicholls, *Weimar and the Rise of Hitler*, pp. 136-163; Sebastian Haffner, *Anmerkungen zu Hitler*, 1978 ed., pp. 66-93; 1994 ed., pp. 52-72; Eng., *The Meaning of Hitler*, pp. 52-67.

[130] This was also called the Hitler-Ludendorff Putsch, the Bürgerbräu-Putsch (the attempted overthrow of the government at the Bürgerbräu Beer Hall), and the March on the *Feldherrn Halle* (the March on the Field Marshals' Hall).

The Hitler Era

Significantly, the armistice took place without General Erich Ludendorff, who had resigned on October 26, 1918, from his post as second in command under General Paul von Hindenburg and fled to Sweden; this also took place without Kaiser Wilhelm II, who had abdicated on November 9, 1918, and fled to the Netherlands the next day.[131] The Triple Alliance was already collapsing before the armistice with Germany: Bulgaria had signed its individual armistice on September 30; Turkey, its treaty, on October 30; and Austria-Hungary, on November 3—changing the pre-War map of Europe, as suggested by the maps just presented.

Or, again, some date the Hitler era as beginning on November 12, 1918, the day following Armistice Day, when the provisional government in Austria renamed itself the Republic of German-Austria: a symbolic attempt at a Greater Reich.[132]

Others date the Hitler story back to the decades preceding the start of World War I, with tensions already recognizable in German society, the arising of a new ethnic nationalism, with new threats to the bureaucratic and authoritarian order that privileged the Junkers (Prussian landed nobility), the alienation of many—leading to extreme leftist and rightist populism from Communism and Socialism in their different factions, to various forms of nationalistic movements of the far right—which would be partially overcome a decade later by a universal conscription that involved an entire young generation in the Great War, World War I, with millions killed in the process.[133]

And still others date the beginning of these years based on a letter by Hitler addressed to Adolf Gemlich and a political group in Berlin with a

---

[131] German newspapers of Nov. 9, 1918, had front-page banner headlines in their evening printing announcing: *Der Kaiser hat abgedankt!* (The Kaiser has abdicated!)—in *Vorwärts*, and *Abdankung des Kaisers* (Abdication of the Kaiser)—in *Berliner Volksblatt* and *Berliner Tageblatt und Handels-Zeitung*.

[132] The Treaty of Saint-Germain-en-Laye (signed Sept. 10, 1919) disallowed any such union. The country name was consequently changed to the Republic of Austria.

[133] See, for example, the multi-faceted analysis of the factors involved in that historical period in Fritz Fischer. His work from 1961, *Griff nach der Weltmacht* (*Grasping for World Power*), questioned the idea that Hitler was a mere *Betriebsunfall* (literally, industrial accident), questioned whether the Nazi grabbing of power (*Machtergreifung*) was either accidental or necessary. *Both attitudes tend to relinquish all questioning about the specifics, how they combined as they did, and how to be alert to such recurrences later in history.* Cf. Fritz Fischer, "Hitler war kein Betriebsunfall," SPIEGEL SPEZIAL, Feb. 1, 1989; Richard Herzinger, "Adolf Hitler war mehr als ein Betriebsunfall [Hitler was more than an industrial accident]," WELT KULTUR, Oct. 13, 2010; "Gedenkveranstaltung für Nazi-Opfer. Lammert: Hitler war kein Betriebsunfall," *Merkur*, Jan. 30, 2013. Cf. Fischer's later work, *Krieg der Illiusionen: die deutsche Politik von 1911 bis 1914* (1969), tr., *War of Illusions: German Policies from 1911 to 1914* (1975); cf. John A. Moses, *The War Aims of Imperial Germany: Professor Fritz Fischer and his Critics* (1975). See further, the in-depth discussion of the many facets of the war, in the DVD series by Vejas G. Liulevicius, *World War I: The 'Great War (Parts I-III)*, THE TEACHING COMPANY (2006), and his text, *The German Myth of the East: 1800 to the Present* (2009).

strong nationalistic and anti-Semitic orientation, containing his first formal declaration of anti-Semitism,[134] on September 16, 1919:

> Anti-Semitism stemming from purely emotive reasons will always find its expression in the form of pogroms. But anti-Semitism based on reason must lead to the systematic legal combating and removal of the rights of the Jew, which he alone of the foreigners living among us possesses (legislation for aliens) [that is, a legal path for excluding Jews from German citizenship and life].[135] Its final aim, however, must be the uncompromising removal of the Jews altogether [*muß unverrückbar die Entfernung der Juden überhaupt sein*].[136]

Here, *Entfernung* in the last phrase of this 1919 document does not at all mean extermination or annihilation, but removal or rendering distant, far away (*fern*). Hitler's attitude here toward Jewry as a noxious intruder into German life, to be removed in its entirety, pre-dates the birth of the Third Reich by some 13-14 years (but without extermination in mind). Its emphasis on a legal framework for racial issues (and hatred) over mob rule (vigilante law in the US, or pogroms) would work to establish central government control over the treatment of those felt to be undesirable, as in the Prussian memorandum of 1933 and the Nuremberg Laws of 1935.

A less-known document from Hitler is a letter he wrote from the Western Front in early February 1915 to Ernst Hepp, his landlord in Munich. This letter included these thoughts by Hitler: "Each one of us has only one wish, that it may soon come to the final reckoning with the gang, to the showdown, cost what it will, and that those of us who have the fortune to see their homeland again will find it purer and cleansed of alien influence [*Fremdländerei*], that through the sacrifices and suffering that so many hundred thousands of us make daily, that through the stream of blood that flows here day for day against an international world of enemies, not only will Germany's eternal enemies be smashed, but that our own internationalism will also be broken. That would be worth more to me than all territorial gains."[137] *Here a vision of a world filled with*

---

[134] Both *anti-Semitism* and *antisemitism* are recognized spellings of this term.

[135] The term here ("legislation for aliens") renders Ger. *Fremdengesetzgebung*.

[136] This nationalistic group was Reichswehr [German Military] News and Enlightenment Dept"; Eng., "Hitler Letter: Understanding the Rhetoric of Hate" (pdf), MUSEUM OF TOLERANCE. Ger., "Hitler-Brief an Adolf Gemlich: Die erste bedeutende Äußerung Hitlers über den Antisemitismus: Antwort an Adolf Gemlich, 16. September 1919," KURT BAUER GESCHICHTE. The path in this early essay—*Fremdengesetzgebung*, formal legislation to accomplish racist policies—will be a focus in *Mein Kampf* and carried out seriously and thoroughly in the Third Reich.

[137] Ian Kershaw, *Hitler: A Biography*, p. 56. Kershaw dates the sending of this letter to Feb. 5, 1915. The copy of the document at the US Library of Congress gives the following information (in a long quote): "Postcard and letter written from the Western Front to Assessor Ernst Hepp in Munich: Adolf Hitler, Ernst Hepp,

The Hitler Era

dangerous, eternal enemies of Germany and of the German people takes form! This international group is presumably a cabal of Jewry postulated to have as its goal Jewish control of government, economy, and a special (degenerate) morality.

If we look, we can find sites online, in film, and in texts that glorify Hitler and the Third Reich and that deny the Holocaust. Consider pages at the Holocaust-denying Institute for Historical Review,[138] the 2013 6.5-plus-hours-long film,[139] *Adolf Hitler: The Greatest Story Never Told!* (the title of which echoes the 1965 film on Jesus of Nazareth, *The Greatest Story Ever Told*), or the text by Benton L. Bradberry, *The Myth of German Villainy* (2012). More on these and similar tracts, below.

Often this sort of perspective is given in a context that denies, minimizes, or does not mention the intense hatred of many nationalistic Germans, including Hitler, toward *all* of the world's Jewry, expressed by Hitler from 1919 on[140] and in detail in *Mein Kampf*.[141]

In *Mein Kampf*, all Jews are presented as completely in agreement among themselves about all important matters of life, as united in all of their opinions, values, interest in controlling the world, as being hostile toward any and all non-Jews, and as having an incurably parasitic nature—such postulated homogeneity of a complex group is a mark of a simplistic, caricaturing, distorting, narrow-minded way of thinking; this came from when Hitler was an unknown on the world stage; his opinions were thus not a reaction to animosity against him that did not yet exist.

WILSON'S FOURTEEN POINTS: UNFULFILLED PROPOSALS

In the political context for the Armistice of 1918, one framework of basic principles had been the proposals by US President Woodrow Wilson, expressed in 14 points that were offered in a speech of his on January 8, 1918, *made without prior consultation with either the British, or the French, or the US Congress*. The Germans found Wilson's proposals appealing as a basis for ending the war; the French, British, and the US

Nationalsozialistische Deutsch Arbeiter-Partei, Hauptarchiv [NSDAP Main Archive], Third Reich Collection, Manuscript. Original postcard has postmark dated Jan. 22, 1915 and envelope has postmark dated Feb. 6, 1916" (end of quote).

[138] Institute for Historical Review (IHR.ORG), with contents such as Harry Elmer Barnes (1889-1968), "Revisionism and the Promotion of Peace."

[139] This extended video was written and produced by Dennis Wise, "an independent film maker with a background in entertainment and media" (from his site, THEGREATESTSTORYNEVERTOLD.TV). Contrast "Dennis Wise: Director, Producer, Writer," IMDB.COM; "Ask Historians: How accurate is Dennis Wise's documentary 'Adolf Hitler: The Greatest Story Never Told'?" REDDIT.COM.

[140] For a filmic presentation of the early years of Hitler, see *Hitler: The Rise of Evil*, a 2003 video production of CBC-TV/CANADIAN BROADCASTING CORPORATION.

[141] The published title of the 1925 first edition, coming from Hitler's publisher, Max Amann, Editor-in-Chief of the Franz Eher Verlag, was changed from Hitler's bulky and clumsy title, *Viereinhalb Jahre des Kampfes gegen Lüge, Dummheit, und Feigheit* (*Four and a Half Years of Struggle against Lies, Stupidity, and Cowardice*) to *Mein Kampf: Eine Abrechnung* (*My Battle: A Settling of Accounts*).

Congress definitely did not. Wilson's principles included the elimination of secret treaties, free trade between nations, freedom of the seas (for ships of all flags), self-determination of minorities in Europe and colonies, reduction in armaments for all countries, the creation of a Polish state in lands which were predominantly Polish in population at the time, the restoration of countries demolished by the war, especially Belgium, as well as Romania, Serbia, and Montenegro, the recognition of a Turkish nation where Turks lived, while calling at the same tune for the liberation and independence of other peoples at the time under the rule of the Turkish Ottoman Empire, the proposal for an international forum for the peaceful discussion and resolution of disputes (a "league of nations"), and so forth. For the Germans, these became the starting point of negotiations to end the war, which became more focused in late October 1918, with exchanges between the US Government and Prince Max of Baden (Prince Maximilian von Baden, 1867-1929)—once he was appointed Chancellor on October 28, 1918 by Kaiser Wilhelm II (before the Kaiser abdicated the throne on November 9).[142] *As it turned out, however, these fourteen points that had served as a starting point in the negotiations to create a treaty were largely ignored or significantly modified in the final accords.*

The negotiations and treaties that then took place made important changes to the political map of Europe, including surprises, especially perhaps, for the Germans.[143] (And, overall, the hopes of many countries in going to war were largely left as unrealized.[144])

What did change involved the creation of a number of nations, some taken from what had been German territory, and others from the Austro-Hungarian Empire, as well as from the Russian Empire, after the successful Bolshevik October Revolution of 1917.

With the evolution of the political situation in the East, the former Russian Czarist Empire became the Russian Socialist Federative Soviet Republic (RSFSR), from 1917-1922, and then, referring to the vast Russian land mass, as the Union of Soviet Socialist Republics (the USSR), the Soviet Union, until its dissolution on December 25, 1991.

Most important perhaps were, first, Britain's refusal to give up its dominion over the seas, and, second, the British and especially the French demands for war reparations, to deal with Britain's great debt from loans from the USA and to help rebuild (the primarily French) Allied industry.

This was a key consideration, especially given that Germany's industrial power was not destroyed at all during the war in the West; it

---

[142] Anthony J. Nicholls, *Weimar and the Rise of Hitler*, p. 55.

[143] See extended discussion in the early text by Émile Joseph Dillon, *The Inside Story of the Peace Conference* (1920), stating, "The Fourteen Points were not discussed at the Conference" (p. 96); for the source document, see *Treaty of Peace with Germany: Hearings Before the Committee on Foreign Relations, US Senate, Sixty-Sixth Congress, First Session* (1919), p. 162.

[144] Barrie Pitt, *1918: The Last Act* (1962); Barbara Tuchman, *The Guns of August* (1964); cf. Fritz Fischer, *Krieg der Illiusionen*, Eng., *War of Illusions*, and John A. Moses, *The War Aims of Imperial Germany* (cited above).

was expected by all sides that Alsace and Lorraine, taken from the French in 1871 at the conclusion of the Franco-Prussian War, would be returned to France. The Allies were strongly against the unification of Germany and Austria, which would have resulted in a post-War greater Germany even stronger than its pre-War power—shades of the Holy Roman Empire! In the background here was respect for the principle of the balance of power that was established and maintained by confrontive alliances, following a model for maintaining overall peace exemplified by the agreements reached in 1648 in the Peace, or Treaty, of Westphalia, these issues still being of serious concern for all countries on the European continent. England and France, for similar reasons concerned with maintaining their sense of security, also wanted there to be a severe limitation on the size of the German Army (unilaterally) and of the German Naval Forces and Air Force. Complicating matters further, on March 19, 1920, the US Senate refused to ratify the Treaty of Versailles, and it would not join the League of Nations, with strong opposition to international involvement with related commitments, headed by Republican Sen. Henry Cabot Lodge (Massachusetts) and progressive Republican Sen. William Borah (Idaho).

Contentious Articles in the Treaty of Versailles

With all of these changes from the Fourteen Points to the ultimate European form of the Treaty of Versailles, there was much disappointment and a sense of what might be called the use of "bait-and-switch," in which one product is offered (as "bait") and where the salesman then talks the potential buyer into an entirely different product ("switch").

The head of the German delegation to Versailles, the German Foreign Minister, Graf (Count) Ulrich von Brockfdorff-Rantzau (1869-1928), was determined that the treaty conditions should be rewritten to conform with Wilson's Fourteen Points, which had been the basis and the readiness of their agreement to end the war. *The British and the French, of course, did not agree in the least.*[145] After all, they had never agreed in the first place to Wilson's unilateral proposal of these principles. (Furthermore, Wilson presented his Fourteen Points to the US Congress on January 8, 1918, but *as a statement* of his vision of a basis for peace negotiations, *and not at all* as something to put before Congress to vote on.)[146] The Versailles Treaty was ultimately signed—without US ratification—by Germany on June 28, 1919, five years to the day after the assassination of the heir presumptive to the Austro-Hungarian throne, Archduke Franz Ferdinand.

It is often held that this treaty set the seeds for World War II. So, it is perhaps relevant here to look at some of the machinations behind the words, and the impact on European countries, especially Germany.

---

[145] Charles L. Mee, Jr., *The End of Order: Versailles 1919* (1980), pp. 11-12, 52-54, 205-226. Georges Clemenceau, the French Prime Minister, said sarcastically of Wilson's Fourteen Points, that this was four more than God needed (referring, presumably, to the Ten Commandments).

[146] "Woodrow Wilson's Fourteen Points' Speech, 8 January 1918." This speech was given before a Joint Session of the US Congress.

Among the most onerous clauses, or articles, of the Versailles Treaty, from the German point of view, were especially, first, Article 231, the so-called War Guilt Clause—which did not actually mention guilt; instead, it spoke, rather, of "the responsibility of Germany and her Allies for causing all the loss and damage to which the Allied and Associated Governments and their nationals have been subjected as a consequence of the war imposed upon them by the aggression of Germany and her allies" (especially Austria-Hungary).

In addition, there were important clauses that declared that the Rhineland would be kept demilitarized, especially Articles 42, 43 (in Part III of the Treaty: *Political Clauses for Europe*) and Article 180 (in Part V: *Military, Naval and Air Clauses*).

These three Articles stated that "Germany is forbidden to maintain or construct any fortifications either on the left bank of the Rhine or on the right bank to the west of a line drawn 50 kilometres to the East of the Rhine" (Art. 42), that "in the area defined above, the maintenance and the assembly of armed forces, either permanently or temporarily, and military maneuvers of any kind, as well as the upkeep of all permanent works for mobilization, are in the same way forbidden" (Art. 43), and that "all fortified works, fortresses and field works situated in German territory to the west of a line drawn fifty kilometres to the east of the Rhine shall be disarmed and dismantled" (Art. 180).

The important issue of debt payments, which was to have such a psychological and practical impact on German society and its thinking about the Treaty involved an original amount to be paid by Germany of 226 billion gold marks ($54 billion), as indicated in the Versailles Treaty. By 1921 this was reduced to 132 billion ($31.5 billion), *with only 50 billion ($12 billion) actually required as payment*, and, in 1924, this was reduced further down to 20 billion gold marks ($4.75 billion)—some 22.1% and 8.8%, respectively, of the original 226 billion.[147]

In this, an important feature in these international debts and their payments, Britain's part of these payments would go toward the immense war debt of $4.7 billion, as of 1919, that it owed for war-time loans it took out from large US banks. We might call this robbing Peter to pay Paul.

The Versailles Treaty documents were signed under threat of renewed hostilities by the Allies (Britain and especially France), who threatened to invade Germany itself—something the German military command knew it could not succeed in defending against—and with a continuing British blockade of food supplies (the "starvation blockade") still in place. The treaty went into effect on January 20, 1920, establishing that the disarming and the dismantling of Article 180 were to be completed by March 20 and July 20, 1920, respectively.

---

[147] Estimates based on the Historian of the US Department of State, "The Dawes Plan, the Young Plan, German Reparations, and Inter-allied War Debts," OFFICE OF THE HISTORIAN, US DEPT. OF STATE. Cf. Alexander Jung, "Nationales Trauma: Millionen, Milliarden, Billionen," *Spiegel Geschichte*, Aug. 27, 2009, pp. 106-115; "Millions, Billions, Trillions: Germany in the Era of Hyperinflation," *Spiegel*, Aug. 14, 2009.

The Hitler Era

A further issue, the creation of a League of Nations, a structure or mechanism by which future wars could be avoided, was made part of the Treaty of Versailles (termed the Covenant of the League of Nations). This was in large part the work of the British lawyer, diplomat, and politician (and three-time Prime Minister of Great Britain), Robert Cecil (1864-1958), who was perhaps an idealist but not naïve: he stated in relation to some sort of international body (as the League of Nations would be), "The great difficulty of all schemes for leagues of nations and the like has been to find an effective sanction against nations determined to break the peace."[148] *That was certainly at the core of the problem (and still is, to this day)*. For his work, Cecil would be awarded the Nobel Peace Prize in 1937,[149] even though, as we know, the League ultimately could not prevent the aggression of a number of states, nor avoid the outbreak of World War II.

Woodrow Wilson was also strongly for this mechanism to avoid war, but the US Congress would refuse to sign the Versailles Treaty or to approve of US participation in the League of Nations spelled out there. Among Wilson's many efforts to convince the American people and the Congress of his position was his address in Omaha, Nebraska, on September 8, 1919, where he stated, "For, I tell you, my fellow citizens, I can predict with absolute certainty that within another generation there will be another world war if the nations of the world do not concert [come into a mutual agreement about] the method by which to prevent it."[150]

With all of this, still others mark the end of the war at the time of the announcement by the German military to the Emperor Kaiser Wilhelm II, on September 29, 1918, informing him that the Germans could not win the war. (The date when those in the know knew!)

They informed him that German military power had been diminished by the great losses of soldiers in those four years, *especially in the last German offensives of 1918 (with the death of one million of the German soldiers in those few months)*, adding that there were severe shortages of important supplies (both for military and for the civilian German population)—in short, that German military power was quite inadequate for the task of continuing the war effort. *Quite importantly, this information was not at all widely shared with the German people, their homeland basically safe, uninvaded, and untouched by enemy fire during the entire war, even if in dire straits.*

---

[148] "Robert Cecil, 1st Viscount Cecil of Chelwood," WIKIPEDIA. His full name was Edgar Algernon Robert Gascoyne-Cecil, First Viscount Cecil of Chelwood.

[149] "The Nobel Peace Prize 1937, Robert Cecil: Nobel Lecture" (Nobel Lecture, June 1, 1938, with audio recording of his acceptance speech), and Robert Cecil—Biographical," both at NOBELPRIZE.ORG; "Robert Cecil," SPARTACUS EDUCATIONAL.

[150] "Woodrow Wilson, XXVIII President of the United States: 1913-1921, Address at the Omaha Auditorium in Omaha, Nebraska, September 8, 1919," THE AMERICAN PRESIDENCY PROJECT. Cf. "League of Nations," THE PRESIDENT WOODROW WILSON HOUSE (NATIONAL TRUST FOR HISTORIC PRESERVATION).

The loss of young men in the war by direct fatal wounds, wound-related infections, plus from the influenza pandemic of 1918-1919—which, importantly and significantly, is held to be responsible for the death of perhaps over 50 million people worldwide. In East and Southern Africa alone, from September 1918 on, some 1.5-2 million people, or 10% of the total population died.[151] Overall, this pandemic, *more than from the war itself*, made the survival of Germany even more precarious.[152] This, as well as the effective blockage of food and other supplies by the British Royal Navy (then still master of the seas), resulted in hunger and starvation for the civilian population ("the home front") in Germany, resulting in strikes and other more violent protestations against the war. The British managed to support its "home front" in ways that encouraged patriotism and related personal sacrifice, along with a commitment to the war effort, *and, importantly, providing them with primary needs*, both adequate food and the satisfaction of key political demands. This was not the case in Germany during those war years.[153]

Hitler would make it a point, as best he could, to be sure the German population did not suffer this same hunger during the next World War.

Pre- and post-war revolts that Germany experienced came from both right and left political extremes, as well as from those simply starving and demanding a change in that situation, and yet there was still a portion of the population (both military and civilian) who believed that the German Army *could win*—or, after the Armistice, *could* (theoretically) *have won*—

---

[151] *The World's War: Forgotten Soldiers of the Empire, Series 1, Episode 2: Foreign Legions* (2014), BBC, at 31:15-32:40.

[152] *Massive epidemics (pandemics)*—cross-species infections to humans from birds, pigs, horses, fruit bats, chimpanzees, etc.—*continue, with virulent, antibiotic-resistant, strains posing ever-more-deadly worldwide infections*. They are One little discussed epidemic was meningococcal infections, often as spinal meningitis, during World war I and again during World War II: see Worth B. Daniels, MD, Chap. IX ("Meningococcal Infections"), in Medical Dept., US Army, *Internal Medicine in World War II, Vol. II: Infectious Diseases* (1963). The "Spanish flu"—first reported by neutral Spain's Madrid paper, *ABC*, on May 28, 1918 (belligerent countries had a censorship blocking all such frightening reports, and hence the name wrongly suggesting a Spanish source to the pandemic: see Antoni Trilla, Guillem Trilla, and Carolyn Daer, "The 1918 'Spanish Flu' in Spain," *CID/Clinical Infectious Diseases*, IDSA/Infectious Diseases Society of America, vol. 47, 2008, pp. 668-673)—spread among the military, with the transport of troops and other military-based sailings taking the disease from Europe to military and civilian populations in South Africa, to Asia, and to America. There are three theories: that it began in British Army bases in Étaples-sur-Mer, France and Aldershot, UK; or, in Kansas; or by laborers shipped from China via Canada to France). See Everett Sharp, "The Etaples flu Pandemic?" ww1centenary.oucs.ox.ac.uk; Frederick Holmes, MD, "The Influenza Pandemic and The War," Essays on First World War Medicine, Univ. of Kansas Medical Center, Dec. 31, 2014; Mark Osborne Humphries, "Paths of Infection: The First World War and the Origins of the 1918 Influenza Pandemic," War in History, vol. 21, no. 1, Jan. 8, 2014, pp, 55-81.

[153] David Reynolds, *The Long Shadow: The Legacies of the Great War in the Twentieth Century* (2014), pp. 423-424.

The Hitler Era

if only they had been allowed to continue in battle, and if only the politicians had not betrayed the loyal and valiant German Army. *This, of course, overlooked the military situation on the ground that perhaps few could appreciate fully, except for high-ranking military, with a distortion in understanding of the general German public, given selected information they were given, minimizing the disastrous situation and military losses.*

While there were some grounds for Germans back home to think the German Army to be in a much more powerful position than it actually was—since the war had been fought almost totally on Belgian and French territory, with Germany never invaded by the Allies—the actual loss of men in the war and the starvation of the overall German population on the home front spoke otherwise. *This false general optimism came in part from a denial, or a public ignorance, of German military intelligence given to the Kaiser that clearly defined the country's dire military position.*

We should note at this point that *Hitler, as a corporal in the German Army,* any more than many, if not most, Germans, *certainly was not privy to such significant information known to the generals.*

Still, given what the general populace of Germany knew, something didn't make obvious sense to the common people! One explanation that many people found somewhat plausible and easy to accept was that German politicians betrayed the German people and army.

Militarily, Paul von Hindenburg and Erich Ludendorff gained much popularity and respect for their early defeat on the Eastern Front of the Czarist Army in fighting from August 26-30, 1914. This was called the Battle of Tannenberg; *the association with Tannenberg added to the idea that here was revenge for a much earlier battle.* Actually, it was fought some 30 km. (18.6 mi.) to the east of Tannenberg, at Allenstein (Olsztyn), now known as Olsztyn, Poland, *but the name Battle of Tannenberg would bring German thinking back to the 1410 battle by that name*—also called the Battle of Grunwald—when German (Teutonic) forces were fully defeated by Slavic armies. (Thus, here: revenge, sweet revenge!)

Furthermore, while the Kaiser was nominally still in power, Hindenburg, functioning as the respected aristocratic, mature, military figurehead, and Ludendorff, his Chief of Staff, were the military leaders in charge of the entire German war effort beginning August 1916.[154] Hindenburg was widely considered to have become the military leader of the Second Reich, the "Field Lord" of the German Armies, or, as he would put it, the "actual dictator of the Central Powers during the latter half" of World War I.[155]

This "Field Lord" (rendering *Feldherr*), declared Ludendorff, is the "man who with head, will, and heart has to lead the total war for the life-preservation of the people (*den totalen Krieg für die Lebenserhaltung des*

---

[154] Lt.-Col. William A. Jones, *Ludendorff: Strategist* (US Army War College, 1992), p. 10.

[155] See the comments of Lithuanian-born Berlin correspondent for the New York Times, who won the Pulitzer Prize in 1940, Otto D. Tolischus, in *They Wanted War* (1940), p. 153.

Volkes zu führen hat) ... No one can relieve him of the responsibility he bears here. (*Niemand kann ihn von der Verantwortung, die er hierbei trägt, entlasten.*)[156]

The sense of total war was explicit in Ludendorff's 1935 book by that name, and certainly not original in the speech in early 1943 by Joseph Goebbels, *Wollt ihr den totalen Krieg?* ("Do You Want Total War?"). It found an important role in the preparation of several nations that participated in the Great War of 1914-1918, presented as the idea that the outcome of the war would involve either total victory or total destruction. This was a prominent idea not only in Germany but also in the Ottoman Empire.

In a similar way, the framing of the conflict as a fight for civilization (or its total absence) was also put forth by the Allies, as in the presentation of the Germans (called "Huns" by Rudyard Kipling[157] and the British, in a misapplication of the original concept of the Huns of Attila), who raped women, including nuns, ate children, and participating in a variety of great barbarities. *Most importantly, and with catastrophic consequences later, this World War I exaggerated reporting, which was recognized later as such, led many to feel that there was also a great distortion and exaggeration in the depiction of Germans in World War II, especially in the reports of mass murders, and then of organized centers for exterminating thousands of prisoners a day.*[158] (This is one more misapplication—and this one a terrible one—of an earlier story.)

Ludendorff came up with the concept of total war: the mobilization and focus of the resources of the entire country on the war effort, making for what came to be called not the civilian nation but the home front, as if one of the theaters of war. For Ludendorff, this total (or totalitarian) war, which we see again in World War II, postulated that "modern war was no longer a conflict between rulers or governments, or even armies and navies, fought frequently for immoral buccaneering purposes." Ludendorff "saw war as an inevitable and a highly moral struggle for survival between nations, which drew within its orbit every man, woman and child and, therefore called on the last moral, physical and material resources of all of them." This vision of nations in mortal conflict with other nations was at its most intense during the nineteenth century, but carried over, even to Hitler's vision of international politics through the years of the Third Reich. For this total war, this moral war, Ludendorff proposed the supreme military role for himself, with a totalitarian responsibility for the conduct of the (next) war, having him supervise the moral, military, and economic mobilization of the nation for that (coming) war.[159]

---

[156] Erich von Ludendorff, *Der totale Krieg* (1935), p. 107. This book was apparently self-published (given the mention of Ludendorffs Verlag, Munich).

[157] From the poem, "For All We Have And Are" (1914), POETRYFOUNDATION.ORG.

[158] On World War I with its visions of apocalyptic warfare, see Stefan Ihrig, *Justifying Genocide: Germany and the Armenians from Bismarck to Hitler* (2016), pp. 93-104 (Chap. 5: Notions of Total War).

[159] See discussion in Otto D. Tolischus, *Thy Wanted War*, pp. 152-156.

LUDENDORFF AND THE STAB IN THE BACK

Ludendorff and Hindenburg maintained that the war was lost not because of their military poor judgments in the closing months of the war.

Historians consider several moments through 1918 when peace could have been arranged on terms much more favorable to Germany than when the Armistice came on November 11, 1918. For example, we may consider here the so-called Ludendorff Offensive, beginning in March 1918, with Ludendorff being of the opinion that a powerful, decisive victory in the west in the next months was the way for Germany to be able to win the war, before the USA—which had declared war on Germany when Germany restarted its policy of unlimited submarine warfare, free to sink Allied and all other ships—could bring in supplies and men to join the Allies. Time was running out, and the German nation began to see the end of a deep cooperation between military and politics under the Kaiser, with the military taking the upper hand.[160] This Ludendorff Offensive took place after the defeat of the Russian armies and the Treaty of Brest-Litovsk, with this German victory freeing up the German troops on the Eastern Front, now available for a quick transfer to the Western Front.

Here, Ludendorff (and Hindenburg) could have sought peace from a position of strength. Or, later, in August of 1918, when the German waves of offensive kept bringing about massive losses of German men (with fewer and fewer reserves to be brought in), there was the possibility of Ludendorff ordering a withdrawal of land gained in 1918, giving the German army relative respite, a chance to regain its physical strength and its morale, and to be better prepared to carry the fight on into 1919. And, at that time, he also still had the option of negotiating a withdrawal to the lines of the German border, with no issue yet of Allied military occupation of the Saar, the heartland of German coal and steel manufacturing.

But Ludendorff took none of these options! By the end of September, he realized that the German military position was untenable; and *on October 1, 1918, he announced to senior officers that he was planning on stopping the fighting.* The situation was frantic, with many German losses, as well as many soldiers simply deserting (these soldiers would later be claimed to be anti-German leftist radicals). *If something at least superficially resembling a parliamentary democracy could be put into place, it could be that government that accepted defeat and a peace accord that would leave the military innocent of those consequences.*[161] All of this was being arranged in ways that would allow Ludendorff and Hindenburg later to place the entire responsibility not on their poor planning and unsuccessful and ill-timed offensives, nor even on superior Allied fighting materiel or greater numbers of soldiers,[162] but, instead, on

---

[160] Lt.-Col. William A. Jones, *Ludendorff: Strategist*, pp. 12-14.

[161] See detailed discussion, for example, by Cambridge Univ. Prof. David Reynolds, *Armistice 1918: The Endgame of World War I*, BBC (2008), esp. 50:45-1:02:00. Cf. David Reynolds, *The Long Shadow* (2014).

[162] On Ludendorff (and Hindenburg) in this propagation of the idea of a political

politicians in Germany who were undermining the German war effort, combined with a far-left infiltration of the military with a thinking that was subversively anti-German.[163] And, as the German forces were decimated in battle after battle, never bringing the Allies to their knees, Hindenburg and Ludendorff concluded—keeping themselves innocent of blundering or miscalculations on the military level—*in ways that Hitler would self-protectively repeat toward the end of world War II*, that the losing situation was due to a lack of a firm, determined will for victory (at any price)—by politicians, not by Ludendorff, Hindenburg, and the German military.

Clearly, for them, their military judgments and operations, their orders not to withdraw, to fight to the last man, were not in any way incorrect or inappropriate, and were not the cause of the end military disaster. We will see a similar story from Hitler in the next war.

The well-used term capturing the idea of this non-responsibility of the military and the responsibility, the guilt, being assigned for the loss to the non-military leaders in Germany—the so-called "stab in the back"—had its origin in testimony given by General Paul von Hindenburg to an investigative committee of the Reichstag (the German Parliament) on November 18, 1919. This idea of military power being undermined by traitorous forces that would stab it in the back was born anew in the closing months of the Great War, but it would carry on into the Weimar Republic. In schools in the 1920s, geography classes would have maps that indicated lost territories in *Mitteleuropa* and in the colonies of the Second Reich, with many Weimar school children seeing a shameful act of betrayal in this stab in the back. Some essays on this topic explicitly address the psychological elements of paranoia and of conspiracy theory in this idea of Germany being stabbed in the back.[164]

In his testimony given before the *Reichstag*, Hindenburg explained Germany's loss of the war, referring to a descriptive phrase of a British General with whom he had recently discussed the end of the war. Hindenburg spoke of the German military Supreme Command (of which he was the head) being betrayed by a revolution back in German society (on the so-called home front). The British General asked whether he meant that he was stabbed in the back. The succinct phrase made an impression on Hindenburg. (This man was Major-General Sir Neill Malcolm, who at the time was the head of the British Military Mission in Berlin.)

But it has been pointed out that the idea preceded that conversation with Major-Gen. Malcolm, and was not in its origins a foreign borrowing,

---

stab in the back, see Anthony J. Nicholls, *Weimar and the Rise of Hitler*, p. 121.

[163] David Reynolds, *Armistice 1918*, esp. 32:30-33:50, 42:50-50:20.

[164] Vinícius Liebel, "Uma facada pelas costas: paranoia e Teoria da Conspiração entre conservadores no refluxo das Greves de 1917 na Alemanha" ("A Stab in the Back: Paranoia and Conspiracy Theory among Conservatives in the Undertow of 1917 Strikes in Germany"), *Revista Brasileira de História*, vol. 37, no. 76, 2017, pp. 45-71.

The Hitler Era

a way of distancing a nation from ideas it claimed were essentially foreign[165]—we will see a similar distancing or dissociation from German ideas with the *Girl* and the *Garçonne*.) Two cartoons of the period illustrate these military-political beliefs. The first cartoon shows Phillip Scheidemann attacking soldiers with a long knife, with Matthias Erzberger in support, behind him; two caricatured Jews sit in the background.[166] The second cartoon shows a caricatured Jew doing the stabbing—this being part of a more general belief, especially among the ultra-nationalist right of Germany and Austria, that the Jews were not loyal to their country and belonged to an international hidden conspiracy to destroy their host nation, its identity, and its morality.[167]

This right-wing belief or doctrine continued, despite the census of Jews, the *Judenzählung*, in the German military, conducted by the German High Command in October of 1916, *which determined that the Jews in the military* corresponded percentage-wise *to the number of German Jews at the time, even though it was meant to prove the paucity of Jews ready to fight for Germany*.[168] The report was therefore not widely disseminated.

---

[165] John W. Wheeler-Bennett, "Ludendorff: The Soldier and the Politician," *Virginia Quarterly Review*, vol. 14, no. 2, Spring 1938, pp. 187-202. On the questioning of the source of the term as British, see Anthony J. Nicholls, *Weimar and the Rise of Hitler*, p. 64 (text and footnote).

[166] The first cartoon, from a May 1924 German newspaper, features Scheidemann and Erzberger, with two caricatured Jews casually witnessing the attack. Scheidemann, a member of the Social Democratic Party, declared the Republic on Nov. 9, 1918, 2 days before Armistice Day; soon thereafter, he was the 2nd *Reichsminsterpräsident* (that is, Chancellor or Prime Minister) of the Weimar Republic, briefly (Feb. 13-Jun. 20, 1919). Erzberger—who spoke out against the war (after initial enthusiasm) before the Reichstag (Jul. 6, 1917), pointing out the severe weakness of the German military effort—was the Vice-Chancellor of Germany (Jun. 21-Oct. 3, 1919) and Reich Minister of Finance (Jun. 1919-Mar. 12, 1920). He was the official who signed the Versailles Peace Treaty *and for all of this was subsequently assassinated, on Aug. 26, 1921*. This and other cartoons are reproduced at "Stab in the Back Images," UCSB HISTORY.

[167] The second cartoon is dated Mar. 26, 1919, Vienna. This and other cartoons are reproduced at "Stab in the Back Images," UCSB HISTORY.

[168] "Deutsche Jüdische Soldaten," BAVARIAN NATIONAL EXHIBITION, HAUS DER BAYERISCHEN GESCHICHTE. The exhibition took place in 2014.

To take an overview here, the number of Jews in the German military was 100,000 men, with 18,000 winning the Iron Cross, more than 35,000 who were formally awarded for bravery, and 12,000 who died fighting for Germany. In addition, there were (an estimated) 275,000-320,000 Jews in the Austro-Hungarian Army, of which 40,000 were killed in battle.[169] These numbers run counter to the German ultra-Nationalist claims that Jews were members of an organized secret conspiracy (cabal) against Germany, with further specific claims of Jews as traitors to Germany and the German people and as shirking their military duties to their Germanic country, in both Germany and Austria-Hungary. And, more inclusively, for all belligerent armies, there was a total of some 1,500,000 Jews, with at least 500,000 in the Russian Army, 250,000 in the US Army once the US declared war on Germany on April 6, 1918, with 40,000 from the British Empire and 35,000 for France.[170]

In a general way, here we can again see in this context something of the breadth of interpretations that a given historical situation can allow. More on this pattern of human reasoning and thinking, with its potential for great distortions, below.

---

[169] "Deutsche jüdische Soldaten," VOLKSBUND.DE; Otto Kron, "Jewish fighters who served in the German and Austro-Hungarian Army during World War I (1914-1918): German/Austro-Hungarian Jewish Soldiers Killed in WWI," GENI.COM; "Jewish Life in the German and Austrian Armed Forces," *The London Jewish Cultural Centre*, JEWSFWW.UK.

[170] Anna Isaacs, "How The First World War Changed Jewish History," *Moment, Journal of Hadassah*, Jun. 16, 2015, MOMENTMAG.COM.

4. The European Context through the Franco-Prussian War

If we look with a grand sense of history, of time, and consider what was often going on among the peoples of Europe, we can see peoples' battles for supremacy and control of large swathes of territory, whether for the thirst for empire, or for religious or nationalistic aspirations. These often were contained to relatively small and limited areas of focus, for locally identified lands or regions, perhaps administered as principalities, dukedoms, kingdoms, and so forth, or as Church-dominated territories. Religion was an important defining concern for centuries.

EARLY WARS IN EUROPE WITH RELIGIOUS OVERTONES

Many wars were fought on a local or regional scale, and for several centuries, often based on which sect of Christianity would be recognized and permitted, which tolerated, and which religious teachings forbidden. And the rise of militant Islam, with the invasion of the Iberian Peninsula in 711 CE, led by the Moors, and in southeast Europe from 1354 CE, led by the Ottomans, was a further significant danger to Christian Europe.

Judaism had its own concerns, living in ultimately unstable conditions, with ebb and high tides—being invited, or tolerated, or expelled, or killed. This was acknowledged by Jews through the millennia, and so, each year at the Seder, the Passover meal service, there is the reminder, "For not just one man has risen up against us, but in every generation, there are those who rise against us to destroy us. But the Holy One, blessed be He, has delivered us out of their hands!"[171] Despite this situation seen as a repeating threat of annihilation, the response, which is expressed later in the service, in the section called the *Hallel*, is not a call for violence or revenge by Jews in their self-defense, but the expression of a faith in God, expressed in the request or plea, "We beseech You, Hashem,[172] save us! We beseech You, Hashem, save us! We beseech You, Hashem, grant us success! We beseech you, Hashem, grant us success!"[173]

This wide-spread hostility toward Jews as a background frame of reference, in Europe in particular, is a rich history, with expulsions of Jews from France, 1254; from Upper Bavaria, 1276; from Napoli (Naples), 1288; from England, 1290; from Bern (Switzerland), 1392; from Spain, 1492; from Portugal, 1496; from Nuremberg, 1499, and so forth. There were also mass killings of Jews, especially by the Crusaders from 1096 on, on their way to kill the Muslim infidels and return the Holy Land to Christian hands, when passing through territories with known Jewish populations. The Crusade declared in 1096 CE by Pope Urban II (Pope,

---

[171] This recitation, as a song (*"V'hi she'amda"*), occurs fairly early in the Passover Haggadah, the text of the Passover or Pesach service, after the Four Questions and the discussion of the Four Sons; in *Ramban Haggadah* (1996), pp. 34-35. Ramban is also known as Rabbi Moshe ben Nachman (1194-1270) or Nachmanides.

[172] *Hashem* is literally "the name" and is a way of referring to God when the tradition suggests avoiding expressing one of God's actual names.

[173] *Ramban Haggadah* (just cited), pp. 108-109. The repetitions here are presumably for emphasis and intensification.

1288-1299) was against the Muslims, but enthusiastic Crusaders killed Jewish populations, as in the Rhineland massacres of 1096: in Worms, May 18; Mainz, May 27; Köln (Cologne), May 30, in the thousands.

EUROPEAN GEOPOLITICS AND THE PEACE OF WESTPHALIA (1648)

Territorial battles were, and still are, not rare. One example is a series of battles between the English and the French over who would rule French territory. These were called the Hundred Years' War (1337-1453). And, if we move forward in time to 1648, also with a general perspective not focused on the Jews of Europe, we can mark an important event, *der westfälischer Friede* (the Peace of Westphalia). This was actually a series of treaties signed during that year in the Westphalian towns of Münster and Osnabrück, ending the Thirty Years' War (1618-1648). *These together are sometimes seen as establishing the first principles for international law.* Some world leaders can still to this day refer back to "the world order based on sovereignty and equality among nations that came into being in the 1600s," as French President Emmanuel Macron mentioned in a speech before the UN General Assembly in New York City in September 2018.[174] A Leibniz scholar was less optimistic: "the Peace of Westphalia did little to allay" that war, "largely an ideological war leaving Europe in a state of tension."[175] The Peace did include the reduction of arms and the recognition of lands that would be home (variously) to Protestantism and to Catholicism. (Judaism and Islam had no recognition.) There were some rudiments of procedures for settling religious differences that could avoid further wars. Still, there would nonetheless be further wars through the next centuries, kept, however, within a framework of a certain constraint. Shifting ahead in time, *given the importance to twentieth-century history that has been granted to the Versailles Treaty and the end of World War I, some details may be helpful to take into consideration here, to give those events context and weight.*

If we look to some of the more recent events that had impacted Europe and how the 1919 Versailles Treaty was defined, we might consider the situation with the Franco-Prussian War (July 19, 1870-May 10, 1871), also called *La guerre franco-allemande de 1870* or *La guerre de 1870*, and *der deutsch-französische Krieg von 1870 bis 1871*.

Appreciating that events can be linked to and experienced as being related to earlier events, Chancellor Otto von Bismarck considered this war a response to the much earlier Prussian defeat to the armies of Napoleon at Jena (French, Iéna) in 1806! The French had renounced their Mexican colonial interests following the Franco-Mexican War of 1861-1867. This war, in turn, began when the government of Mexican President Benito Juárez stopped payments on loans to various European countries

---

[174] Nicole Gaouette, "Macron rebukes Trump's isolationist message," *CNN News*, Sep. 25, 2018.

[175] Paul Schrecker, "Descartes and Leibniz in 1946: On their 350th and 300th Birthdays," *Philosophy*, vol. 21, no. 80 (1946), pp. 205-233, at p. 205.

(including France). The US had been busy with its own Civil War (1861-1865). Soon after, in 1865-1866, it set up restrictions on the rights of the black citizens (the Black Codes[176]). In 1865, it also reaffirmed the Monroe Doctrine; troops were sent to the border and US shipments of arms to Mexico followed. The French Emperor of Mexico, Maximilian I (an Austrian Archduke appointed by Napoleon III) was captured and executed, on June 19, 1867; the French fled Mexico from Veracruz. The French would declare war on Germany,[177] rather nervous about Franco-Prussian relations: Queen Isabela II of Spain had been ousted by a successful rebellion, *La Gloriosa*, in September 1868; she went into exile in France, formally giving up the throne in 1870. One candidate for this vacant position was Prince Leopold of Hohenzollern-Sigmaringen, a relative of the Prussian King, and German Kaiser, Wilhelm I. German Chancellor Otto von Bismarck and the Spanish de facto political leader, Juan Prim, convinced Prussian Prince Leopold to accept. *The French protested against having a German become the king of Spain*, and the offer was withdrawn (July 12, 1870). Then, the French Foreign Minister, Antoine-Agénor-Alfred, Duke de Gramonte, sent a telegram that day to Wilhelm I, asking for a guarantee that the offer to Prince Leopold would never be renewed. King Wilhelm refused, and sent a telegram, the so-called Ems telegram, on July 13, 1870, to Bismarck, reporting this exchange, indicating that there would be no such formal guarantee. The French then declared war on Prussia (which was joined by other German lands) on July 19, 1870. Some French military and political authorities saw that while the German army was quite prepared for war, the French military was seriously unprepared (given the Franco-Mexican losses). The war lasted only several months: France surrendered to the forces of Bismarck on May 28, 1871. (The instabilities of the Spanish government over the next years are another story we leave aside here.) The results of this 1871 surrender were defined in the Treaty of Versailles of 1871, including the loss of Alsace and Lorraine to Germany (later to be returned to France in the Versailles Treaty of 1919), and a war indemnity to be paid to Germany of 5 billion gold francs—*a precedent that would be repeated, with dire consequences for 1920s Germany*. The German Army occupied parts of France until the payment was completed in September 1873. *This issue would return to center stage at the conclusion of the Great War, with a seriousness and insistence that would in turn resonate through the next decades.*

GERMANY'S DREAM OF A PLACE IN THE SUN (1890S)

In those next years, Bismarck continued with his principle of *Realpolitik*, an approach to politics that respected the balance of power and used a variety of political actions and interventions to keep intact Germany's position in the realm of nations, and in an important way, to avoid Germany's involvement in a two-front war. In 1890, however, the

---

[176] Bertram Schrieke, *Alien Americans: A Study of Race Relations* (1936), p. 126.
[177] The British were owed 70 million pesos; the French, owed 3 million, would spend 300 million for the war! See *Patria* (2019), at 28:30-30:10, 1:08:00-1:08:45.

new Kaiser, Wilhelm II, clashing with Bismarck's political approach, forced him to retire. In place of Bismarckian *Realpolitik*, Wilhelm II put forth a *Weltpolitik*, an approach for Germany in world politics that focused on Germany's gaining a greater role with more power through a more aggressive international diplomacy, a colonial empire to equal or even to surpass the colonial empires of the British and the French. This *Weltpolitik* was interested in building a German Navy that could balance the British Navy—something that the British did not look upon with favor. The interest in developing a colonial empire was brought to a focus in a debate in the *Reichstag* (the German parliament) on December 6, 1897: there, German Foreign Secretary Bernhard von Bülow declared, "In a word, we do not wish to overshadow anyone, but we also demand our place in the sun." ("*Mit einem Worte: wir wollen niemand in den Schatten stellen, aber wir verlangen auch unseren Platz an der Sonne.*")[178]

Wilhelm II would go into some details about this concept in a speech to the North German Regatta Association, in 1901: "In spite of the fact that we have no such fleet as we should have, we have conquered for ourselves a place in the sun. [One example, among many in history, of a premature political claim posing as an accomplishment.] It will now be my task to see to it that this place in the sun shall remain our undisputed possession, in order that the sun's rays may fall fruitfully upon our activity and trade in foreign parts, that our industry and agriculture may develop within the state and our sailing sports upon the water, for our future lives upon the water. The more Germans go out upon the waters, whether it be in races or regattas, whether it be in journeys across the ocean, or in the service of the battle flag, so much the better it will be for us."[179]

This was inspiring, perhaps, to the German audience listening to the Kaiser, but not especially to others, concerned with the balance of power and the implications of a German expansionist policy. This issue of a Germany that would satisfy its need for natural resources and its need for a market for its produced goods (as in other industrialized countries, especially those with colonies) reappear in Hitler's central *desideratum* of autarky (a politics-based economic self-sufficiency in its various essential dimensions), on which, more below. One result of this earlier shift by Wilhelm II, with the enthusiastic support of Prince von Bülow, was an increased tension between Germany and its European neighbors, especially Britain but also France and Czarist Russia.

Germany was clearly late in the rush for European colonies to be set up in Africa, primarily a nineteenth-century phenomenon. The British had acquired the colony in South Africa, taking over from the Dutch and the *boers* (farmers, in Dutch and Afrikaans) only in 1806. The Suez Canal had only been opened in 1869. The Belgian Congo was only taken to be a colony, or, rather, the private property of King Leopold II (king, 1865-1909) in 1885. The most intense period for this colonization, called the

---

[178] "Platz an der Sonne," DE.WIKIPEDIA.
[179] "Kaiser Wilhelm II of Germany: Speech to the North German Regatta Association, 1901," FORDHAM UNIVERSITY (MODERN HISTORY SOURCEBOOKS).

The Hitler Era

Scramble for Africa, 1881-1914, had begun with little German activity. In 1870 only some 10% of Africa was under European control, but by 1914, almost 90% of the content was colonialized by European powers, including Kamerun (or German Cameroon), German East Africa, and German South West Africa. This last, a colony beginning in 1884, now called Namibia, saw revolts and the German response under General Lothar von Trotha of a little-known genocide that killed perhaps more than 80% of the native population, with concentration camps insuring death to most of its inmates.[180]

German violence against conquered lands was quite the norm. From Attila the Hun to Genghis Khan with vast murders of the conquered, to US colonization of the continent with the decimation of native American Indian populations and their being confined to reservations, to the wars of extermination against the native Tasmanians in Australia—about which Charles Darwin would remark, "Whenever the European has trod, death seems to pursue the aboriginals" (adding that others also would kill the conquered, as Malay Polynesians against the darker native population), and we could mention here the descent into the Indian sub-continent of Aryans, pushing out the native, also-darker-skinned Dravidians—and the treatment of the Africans of the Belgian Congo: made "rubber slaves," with cages, whipping with a *chicotte*, amputations, or death.[181]

This German appreciation of colonies came with an interest in having a greater stake in the empires and colonies of other Western powers. These ideas about territory as the way to power are very embedded in nineteenth-century geopolitical thinking. Hitler's vision of a greater Germany with lands taken from the Slavic nations for German farmers reflects of this idea that greater land means greater productivity, and focuses on the production of produce and meat products, linked to a certain minimal territory per population—with little sense of urban centers that would change the basics of a nation's productivity and wealth. *This facet of Hitler's vision was more a myopic, an atavistic, antiquated one, even in its own time*. This was a "mixture of naïveté, stupidity, and vanity that all of the conservative participants who collaborated with Hitler" demonstrated [182] —perhaps this was in part modern, avant-garde, retrograde, atavistic, and so forth, but it was ultimately a vision of what humans organized into a State can do to create havoc, fear, hatred, and abundant death, through aggressivity.

---

[180] "Lothar von Trotha: Germany Military Officer," ENCYCLOPÆDIA BRITANNICA; "Namibia's reparations and Germany's first genocide," BBC NEWS, Oct. 12, 2017.

[181] Nemattanew (Chief Roy Crazy Horse), *The North American Genocide* (2002); James Bonwick, *The Last of the Tasmanians; or, The Black War of Van Diemen's Land* (1870); Charles Darwin, *The Voyage of the Beagle* (1845), p. 212; Thomas Pakenham, *The Scramble for Africa: The White Man's Conquest of the Dark Continent from 1876 to 1912* (1991); Adam Hochschild, *King Leopold's Ghost* (1998), with 16 pages of historic photographs inserted between pp. 116-117.

[182] Joachim C. Fest, *Hitler: Eine Biographie* (1973), pp. 666, 1032-1039; Eng., *Hitler*, pp. 485, 756-763.

5. The Years to World War I

In retrospect, after the horrors of the Great War, the years preceding it would be seen as *la belle époque*, the beautiful epoch. This name refers to the period from the end of the Franco-Prussian War to the start of the first hostilities that quickly devolved into World War I. That period was also called *la fin de siècle* (the turn of the century). In Britain, it overlapped the Victorian era (named for Victoria, queen from 1837-1901) and the Edwardian era (named for Edward VII, king from 1901-1910). The time was remembered as peaceful, relatively calm, a time of the development of the arts (painting, literature, sculpture), with high society living out many of its dreams. *It was a period in which the poor did not partake of the best of the epoch (as usual).* It was also a culture in which the beautiful and the reassuring took precedence, with the societies of Europe paying little caring attention to the plight of those in dire straits, to the violence of the streets, to the mistreatment of women (many forced into prostitution and then jailed for their activities), or to the international tensions with their underlying malaise and societal ills and woes that were not being addressed forthrightly.[183] *As with most if not all idealized representations of the past, this too was a romanticized, distorted vision of the period as actually lived across the social spectrum.*

In these years of peace, the military of the European powers were not asleep. One important innovation that was brought about by designers taking advantage of technical innovations was a cannon developed in the French Army by Colonel Albert Deport in 1894. The length of the bore was 11.67 ft. (3.564 m); its bore was 75 mm (a diameter of 2.95 inches). It was produced as the Field Cannon of 75 mm, 1897 Model (*le Canon de campagne de 75 mm Modèle 1897*, referred to as the *Soixante-quinze*, French for Seventy-five[184]). This cannon had the remarkable feature that after being fired, it would return to its original position (through the use of a hydro-pneumatic recoil brake), which eliminated the need to reposition the canon after each firing, and thus made the firing of the next shell a much quicker process. It also used other innovations of the times (such as smokeless powder, a time-delay fuse in the shell allowing a

---

[183] A fictionalized recounting of this era, with a stereoscopic understanding, including both the Victorian era story (set in the Dorset coast and London, in the 1860s) and an integrated commentary from a contemporary point of view (in which Victorian statistics of women with a "bad reputation" were laid out with austere reflections, is contained in John Fowles' novel, *The French Lieutenant's Woman* (1969), made into a film (1981) with screenplay by Nobel Laureate Harold Pinter and directed by Czech-born Karel Reisz, director of *Saturday Night and Sunday Morning* (1960) and *Morgan: A Suitable Case for Treatment* (1966).

[184] Some French web sites request that Belgians and Swiss use this term, *soixante-quinze* (rather than *septante-cinq*, 75 in those dialects). Relatedly, an alcoholic beverage, the French 75, named in honor of this powerful weapon (and more widely known in the USA than in France), was first developed in 1915 by Harry MacElhone in the New York Bar (later, Harry's New York Bar), near Place de l'Opéra, Paris, and later made popular in the Stork Club, New York City.

detonation once in flight, and an integrated structure for the shell and cartridge case). It would be used in the Great War both with poison gas and with shrapnel shells. It also had anti-tank capacities. Here armaments developments during peacetime would have important subsequent military applications.

THE OTTOMAN EMPIRE AND THE ARMENIANS

Meanwhile, of course, what was experienced as peaceful, if not idyllic, in some lands of our world, was not so elsewhere. For example, between 1871 and 1915, there were massacres of at least hundreds of thousands of Armenians in the Turkish Ottoman Empire. (More on the earlier of these massacres, just below.) Shortly after the Great War ended, there was recognition of the great massacres of the Armenians in the Anatolian plains of the Ottoman Empire, and a discussion of creating an Armenian state, along with other self-determined new nations defined along cultural and historical lines. On March 20, 1919, the Supreme Council of the Paris Peace Conference, for example, restated the principle that "it is the purpose of the Conference to separate from the Turkish [Ottoman] Empire certain areas comprising, for example, Palestine, Syria, the Arab countries to the east of Palestine and Syria, Mesopotamia, Armenia [in the eastern Anatolian Plains of the Ottoman Empire], Cilica [south-central Anatolia, north of Syria and south of ancient Cappadocia], and perhaps additional areas of Asia Minor."[185] There is an ongoing debate even to this day about whether these massive, programmed deaths were a genocide of the Armenians or not. The Turkish government says that the killings in 1915 were not a genocide: As recently as December 2018, for example, Turkish President Recep Tayyip Erdoğan, at the G20 Economic Summit in Buenos Aires, declared, "Turkey cannot be blamed of having committed a genocide against the Armenians."[186] The basic position of the Turkish government has been that this was basically a question of the relocation of Ottoman subjects potentially allied with Russia, and who were therefore dangerous to the safety of the Empire. Other groups, including Armenians, say that it was indeed a genocide.[187] Labels aside, no one seems to deny

---

[185] Richard G. Hovannisian, "The Armenian Genocide and US post-war commissions," pp. 257-275 in *America and the Armenian Genocide of 1915* (2003), at p. 261.

[186] "Erdogan Denies the Armenian Genocide During the G20 Summit," *Horizon Weekly* (Canada), Dec. 2, 2018, HORIZONWEEKLY.CA, at 34:00-36:15. Cf. "Erdoğan slams Merkel, EU over Armenian bill," *Hurriyet Daily News* (İstanbul), Jun. 4, 2016; "Erdogan: Turkey will 'never accept' genocide charges," DEUTSCHE WELLE/DW, Jun. 4, 2016. In 2004, DW was chartered for broadcasting by the German Budestag.

[187] John Kitner, "Armenian Genocide of 1915: An Overview," *New York Times*, Nov. 6, 2007; this mentions 145 *New York Times* articles on the topic in 1915. Research cited in that article from the Univ. of Minnesota's Center for Holocaust and Genocide Studies reported that there were 2,133,190 Armenians in the Ottoman Empire in 1914 and some 387,800 in 1922. The numbers are significant whether or not we call this significant loss of Ottoman Armenians a genocide or

that perhaps 1.5 million Armenians died in those years. In addition, there had been earlier massacres of Armenians, occurring in the 1890s.[188]

There were also other Ottoman Christians killed during the Great War: At the start of the war at least 20% of the Empire was Christian, including Armenian Christians, and other Eastern Christian denominations, including the Syriac Church, the Nestorians, the Maronites, and the Chaldean Church. Many of these were also killed, remembered in Syriac histories as Seyfo, Year of the Sword.[189]

It was important and significant that none of this led to any particular response holding the Ottomans responsible for these murders of Armenians and others. *This would be a precedent for Hitler to think—in looking ahead to the Third Reich—that Germany, too, would not have to face any reckoning of its mass killing of the German physically and mentally unfit, of Jews from many European nations, of Gypsies (Romanies), of Slavs, of the Polish intelligentsia, or of Soviet POWs.*

EUROPEAN TREATIES, OPENLY DECLARED OR SECRET

As had been the practice throughout Europe for centuries, there were numerous mutual-protection treaties in which countries committed themselves to coming to the aid of any treaty member that had gone to war against another nation. The idea, of course, was to dissuade potential enemies from starting wars. Before the outbreak of World War I, there were treaties in place by 1914 that basically set up two enemy groups, known as the Great Entente and the Central Powers.

What may be striking is the ease with which these alliances in the decades preceding the outbreak of war in 1914 could be, and were, dissolved, based on changing concerns in the constituent countries over what each took to be the most threatening international threats it faced.

(This same sort of fluidity was later seen beginning with the Molotov-Ribbentrop Treaty, the German-Soviet Non-aggression Pact, formalized the week before the German invasion of Poland on September 1, 1939, starting World War II, followed by its radical, violent reversal in June 1941, in the sudden, massive invasion of the Soviet Union by the Third Reich.)

Some of these pre-1914 treaties were secret accords, *making diplomacy not fully a transparent affair.* The treaties and other documents preceding and at the start of the hostilities included the 1839 Treaty of London (Britain committed to defending neutral Belgium), and the 1873

---

not. Some discussions (as in "Armenian genocide" denials), focus on only whether the term "genocide" is appropriate or not, *distracting from the issue of the massacres themselves.* (Some Armenians escaped to the USA, with large Armenian groups now in Valence and in Paris.) Cf. Vincent Duclert, *La distruzione degli armeni* (2007).

[188] For example, "Fifty Thousand Orphans: Made So by the Turkish Massacres of Armenians," *New York Times*, Dec. 18, 1896, p. 3.

[189] Eli Melki, "In search of Leonard, my martyred ancestor," *BBC News*, Dec. 31, 2018, BBCNews; David Gaunt, "The Assyrian Genocide of 1915," Apr. 14, 2009, SEYFOCENTER.COM; Paolo Maggiolini, "The Forgotten Genocide of the Syriac Christians," Mar. 4, 2015, OASISCENTER.EU.

The Hitler Era

Three Emperor's League, committing the German, Austro-Hungarian, and Russian Empires to mutual defense, in potential opposition to France (valid until Russia withdrew from the agreement in 1878, leaving a German-Austro-Hungarian alliance). In 1879 came the Dual Alliance, put into place after the Franco-Prussian War, 1870-1871, and after Bismarck had united Germany into one Empire, in 1871. This had Germany under Bismarck and the Austro-Hungarian Empire commit to refrain from joining an attack on one of them by other powers, including France; this was in effect a mutual non-aggression pact between the two empires. It also stipulated that if either was attacked, specifically by Russia, there was a commitment to mutual defense. Then came the 1882 Triple Alliance (in which Italy joined in the self-defense pact with Germany and Austria-Hungary). This was counter-balanced (in the geopolitical thinking of alliance-building) by the 1892 Franco-Russian Military Convention, set up after Russia had withdrawn in 1878 from the treaty with Germany and Austria-Hungary. This Accord made a commitment to mutual military support if either was attacked by Germany, or by Austria-Hungary supported by Germany. *It was a secret accord.* Then, there was the 1902 Anglo-Japanese Alliance—renewed and modified in 1905, after the Japanese defeat of Czarist Russia that year)—each recognizing special interests: of the British in China and India, and of the Japanese in Korea, and defining a mutual defense if either would be attacked by another power (having, here too, Russia in mind). In 1904 came the Entente Cordiale (between Britain and France, settling colonial disputes in Africa and setting up a mutual-defense agreement, mostly against Germany, which England saw as trying to confront Britain's naval superiority). This would be expanded to include Russia by the 1907 Anglo-Russian Entente, creating the Triple Entente. At this point in time and changing alliances, there were two grand mutual-defense—mutually mistrustful—agreements: The Triple Entente (between Britain, France, and Czarist Russia), and the Triple Alliance (between Germany, Austria-Hungary, and Italy, called the Central Powers). *With all of these treaties in place, the stage was set for involvements to drag most of Europe into a great war.* This was apparent to many, some with dread and others with great anticipatory excitement.

In this context, in May 1913, Hitler moved from Vienna to Bavaria, leaving Austria-Hungary and its compulsory military service; Hitler was intent on avoiding military service for the Austro-Hungarian Empire. When war came, he requested and was granted permission as a non-German citizen to join a Bavarian Regiment: The political idea of an *Alldeutschland* (Pan-Germanism and an envisioned Greater Germany) strongly attracted Hitler with its idea of fighting for a quite exclusively Germanic vision.

A Balkan Spark Sets off the Great War

Someone died: Ferdinand by name. In the opening passages of the unfinished but widely translated Czech novel *Good Soldier Švejk*,[190] its

---

[190] The author, Jaroslav Hašek (1883-1923), planned this to be a 6-volume work; he died before he could complete his project.

central character, Josef Švejk—or Schweik, in German spelling—a simple man, is told by his charwoman: "They've killed our Ferdinand." Schweik wonders which Ferdinand! Candidly, he asks, "Which Ferdinand, Mrs. Müller? I know two Ferdinands. One is the pharmacist Průša's delivery boy who drank up a whole bottle of hair potion once by mistake. And then I know one Ferdinand Kokoška who collects dog turds. Neither one would be much of a loss." When he is told that it is neither of these two men, but, rather, someone named Franz Ferdinand of Austria, a Ferdinand who was an archduke from far away, whom Schweik did not at all know personally, Schweik's emotional involvement in this man's death, which was not especially emotionally troubling for him even at the beginning of the conversation, drops precipitously.[191]

Now, absurdist literary satire aside, in a peaceful Europe of 1914, this nephew of Austro-Hungarian Emperor Franz Joseph, and so heir to the Austro-Hungarian Empire, on a trip into Serbia, was shot and killed by a nineteen-year-old Bosnian Serb nationalist, Gavrilo Princip. Earlier that day, Nedeljko Čabrinović, his collaborator, threw a bomb that exploded under the Archduke's car, but that attempt was not fatal to the archduke.

This assassination took place in Sarajevo, Bosnia, on June 28, 1914. In the background were the treaties just mentioned, *as well as a secret Turco-German Alliance*, signed soon thereafter, on August 2. This set up an agreement that Germany and Turkey would remain neutral if the conflict remained only between Austria-Hungary and Serbia, but that they would aid one another if Russia entered into the war; Turkey would ultimately enter the war on October 28, 1914. Reactivity was fast and excited. Austria-Hungary made demands on Serbia that it knew would be unacceptable, allowing it to declare war on Serbia. Russia came to aid of its southern Slavic brothers. Germany joined in. France and Britain joined the war, in support of Czarist Russia. The war was quickly moving into high intensity. (We will return to this in greater detail, below.)

Pre-War Tensions between Austria-Hungary and Serbia

Many nationalists were very enthusiastic about the Great War, and the expectations on each side of a quick and thorough victory in a matter of months was widespread. Serbia saw a chance to establish its presence and power in the Balkans, having freed itself from Ottoman Rule during the Balkan Wars of 1912-1913. Austria-Hungary saw its empire challenged and an opportunity to make manifest its power over central Europe. Now, although financial interests cannot fully explain any major political decisions or wars,[192] we often find something of significance in

---

[191] Jaroslav Hašek, *The Good Soldier Svejk During the World War, Book I* (1921), here following the 2018 Zdeněk Sadlon tr., with ref. to the Czech text, *Osudy dobrého vojáka Švejka za světové války*, KCJL2.UPOL.CZ/JAKUBICEK/HASEK1.PDF. Cf. Jan Velinger, "The Good Soldier Svejk: A Literary Character, A Legend," RADIO PRAHA, Apr 2, 2003.

[192] On the economics of the Spanish colonies in Mexico in the 1500s, see the French film, *La controverse de Valladolid* (1992), YOUTUBE, 1:14:15-1:16:45.

The Hitler Era

investigating financial considerations. In the decades preceding the Great War, alongside a superficial peace came great industrial expansion and the search for colonies and spheres of political and economic (financial) influence. We can trace this empire-building back several centuries: early examples are the Spanish Colonies in Latin America, from 1492 on—raising significant moral issues about the treatment of natives[193]; the Portuguese colonies in Africa, Sri Lanka, and Brazil, starting in the early 1500s; the British colonies in North America, soon expanding, especially with the East India Company, founded in 1600 and later to be British India; and the Dutch East Indies Company, founded in 1602 and superseded by the colony of the Dutch East Indies in 1800, with North American colonies first in 1615 (New Amsterdam). In particular here, an important feature of colonization and industrialization in the more recent nineteenth-century was the growth of railroads in Germany, Austria-Hungary, Britain, France, USA, and Turkey. Inter-connectivity in southeast Europe seemed more plausible with Serbian hostility crushed, promising fortunes for German, Austro-Hungarian, and Ottoman interests, in a great project conceived in 1888 of a railway that would run from Berlin into the Middle East.

THE PROPOSED BERLIN-BAGHDAD RAILWAY

Baghdad was decided upon in 1912 as the terminus: thus, the name, the Berlin-Baghdad Railroad. The British were concerned, given their clear awareness that at that time they were importing 65% of their oil from the USA and 20% from Russia.[194] This gave them a serious interest in what is now Iraq (Baghdad, Basra, etc.), with its great oil reserves, then part of the Ottoman Empire. And with this same interest, the oil fields of Persia were also not far from that, if the railroad was set up and operating—

---

[193] The moral question of how to treat native Amerindians, the *Controversia de Valladolid* (Spain), was addressed at the 1550-1551 *Concejo* (Council) of Valladolid, in the debate (*el debate*) before the *Junta consultiva*, the authoritative religious jury—*perhaps the first debate ever on human rights:* Juan Ginés de Sepúlveda held these Indians to be barbarian heathens, sacrificing humans to their plumed-serpent god Quetzalcoatl and, thus, that wars against them were just; Dominican friar (*fray*) Bartolomé de Las Casas held that such wars, with barbaric (dehumanizing) treatment of the Amerindians, their enslavement, torture, and mass killing by the *Conquistadores*, were tyrannical, unjust, and iniquitous, wicked; soon, *Leyes Nuevas* (New Laws, 1552) limited the conquerors' powers earlier granted by the *Leyes de Burgos* (1512). See Bonar Ludwig Hernández, *The Las Casas-Sepúlveda Controversy: 1550-1551* (2001); Paula Andrea Restrepo Hoyos, *Justicia epistémica y epistemología intercultural* (2011); Bartolomé de las Casas, *Brevísima relación de la destrucción de las Indias* (1552); Eugenio Chang-Rodríguez, *Latinoamérica: Su civilización y su cultura* (2008), pp. 5-6, 97, 236; *El sacrificio humano en Mesoamérica*, Guilhem Olivier and Leonardo López Luján, eds. (2010), pp. 19-42.

[194] *Oliver Stone's Untold Story of the United States* (2012), *Season 1, Episode 11 (World War One)*, at 22:40-24:15. Cmp. Australian historian Nigel Davies, "Statistical confusion—whose troops actually did the fighting in World War Two," *Rethinking History*, Feb. 16, 2011, and Ron Klages and John Mulholland, "Number of German divisions by front in World War II," AXIS HISTORY, Jan. 25, 2011.

another threat to British interests. The developing trade connections of Germany and the Ottoman Empire were generally rather disconcerting to the British; Germany had similar, complementary worries about Britain. During the war, Britain would rely mostly on oil (especially for the ships of the Royal Navy), while Germany relied more on coal (especially for its trains). Thus, in a victory banquet one week after the Armistice, on November 18, 1918, George Nathaniel Curzon, Lord Curzon (1859-1925), Viceroy of India (1899-1905), and British Foreign Secretary (1919-1924), would state succinctly, "Truly posterity will say that the Allies floated to victory on a wave of oil."[195] Meanwhile, before the end of the war, if this Berlin-Baghdad railroad could be completed, there were great fortunes to be made in Germany: by Krupp as a manufacturer of steel; Henschel, Borsig, and Maffei as manufacturers of locomotives (*Lokomotivfabriken*, Locomotive Factories), and the Philipp Holzmann Company that carried out railroad construction. *Serbia, however, stood in the way, an unsafe territory the railroad would have to pass through*. A defeat of Serbia, despite its own yearning for independence after the Balkan Wars of 1912-1913 that had pushed back the Ottoman Empire, would make the railroad project much more workable (and lucrative).[196] The line was completed, but only decades later; the first train only arrived at Baghdad in 1940.

Here, as in other contexts, we may see that the motivations for war are typically complex and mixed, with financial considerations being only one dimension of the complex processes that lead a country to war.

Of course, a war needs a justification (or, at least, a pretext). With the murder of the Archduke by Serbian nationalists, the stage was set, even

---

[195] Benjamin Shwadran, *The Middle East, Oil And The Great Powers* (1955), p. 39; Ian O. Lesser, *Resources and Strategy: Vital Materials in International Conflict* (1989), p. 42; Oliver Gliech, "Petroleum," INTERNATIONAL ENCYCLOPEDIA OF THE FIRST WORLD WAR, 1914-1918, Jan. 7, 2015.

[196] Arthur Maloney, *The Berlin-Baghdad Railway as a Cause of World War I* (1959); reprint by CENTER FOR NAVAL ANALYSES, Jan. 1984; *The Great Powers and the End of the Ottoman Empire*, Marian Kent, ed. (1996), p. 112.

though a report, dated July 13, 1914, by Dr. Friedrich von Wiesner, the Chief Austrian investigator of the assassination, stated that while the Serbian government knew ahead of time of the assassination plans (and, in fact, had warned the Austro-Hungarian government in a timely fashion through several diplomatic channels), "there is nothing to prove or even suppose that the Serbian government is accessory to the inducement for the crime, its preparation, or the furnishing of weapons. On the contrary, there are reasons to believe that this is altogether out of the question."[197]

There was further evidence, including testimony by some of the group of assailants, that there was aid given them by some others who had ties with a group called the Black Hand, a shadowy nationalist group within the Serbian military, but not by the Serbian government. *Not letting such acknowledged facts halt their interests for war*, Austria-Hungary, eager to rein in Serbia's aspirations for independence, used this limited and unconvincing evidence as a basis for issuing an ultimatum to Serbia on July 23, 1914, demanding an answer within 48 hours. (The powder keg of the urge for war could still be ignited with the murder of Archduke Ferdinand Incident as its match.)

Several conditions were expected to be rejected by Serbia (most especially Demands No. 5 and 6); the response of July 25 by the Serbian government was quite conciliatory and acquiesced to most demands: in its response to this fifth demand, while questioning its precise import, it stated that the Serbian government was "willing to accept every cooperation which does not run counter to international law and criminal law, as well as to the friendly and neighbourly relations." For the sixth, however—as expected—the Serbian Government (formally, the Imperial and Royal Government of Serbia, or the I. and R. Government) replied, "As far as the cooperation in this investigation of specially delegated officials of the I. and R. Government is concerned, this cannot be accepted, as this is a violation of the constitution and of criminal procedure." The Serbian response at the same time expressed a desire to maintain peaceful relations with the Austro-Hungarian Empire, and to submit any remaining issues, to the International Court at The Hague or to another international body.

Rejecting the Serbian response, Austria-Hungary, with reassurances from Germany of mutual aid, declared war on Serbia days later, on July 28, 1914, exactly one month after the assassination.[198]

In his declaration directed at his subjects (*An meine Völker, To My Peoples*), Kaiser Franz Josef stated, with a leader's initial confidence, "I have examined and pondered everything. With a serene conscience, I

---

[197] Richard C. Hall, "Balkan Wars 1912-1913," INTERNATIONAL ENCYCLOPEDIA OF THE FIRST WORLD WAR/1914-1918; "July 13, 1914, Austrian Investigation into Archduke's Assassination Concludes," HISTORY.COM; "The Assassination of Franz Ferdinand (4): The Smoking Gun," Jun. 23, 2014, FIRSTWORLDWARHIDDENHISTORY.

[198] The ultimatum, "The Austro-Hungarian Ultimatum to Serbia," and response, "The Serbian Response to the Austro-Hungarian Ultimatum" are at BYU LIBRARY.

enter the way that duty shows me."[199] Russia saw a role here in supporting fellow Slavs against those who oppressed them (especially the Austro-Hungarians). Then, Germany saw a chance to define and establish its place in the sun, taking a more prominent and privileged political and economic position in Middle Europe. France saw a chance to defend its national borders and perhaps to regain Alsace and Lorraine, lost in the Franco-Prussian War of 1870-1871. Britain would reassert its dominance over the seas and proclaim its role as protector of small countries being overrun by German power (especially Belgium)—despite questions that this raised about Irish independence.

A background consideration less discussed was the danger that a German-controlled Belgian coast would pose to Britain sea power. This would be relevant to Britain's interest in countering German aggression in Western Europe at the start of the Great War. Then, almost three years into the war, in 1917, the United States, at first maintaining neutrality, would enter the war.[200] In the last two years of the Great War, more immediate political considerations were also in play: The famous Zimmermann telegram of January 1917 (about which more, below) showed German willingness to bargain with Mexico, promising it US territories if the Germans together with Mexico on its side should win the war. This was a promise to give the states of Arizona, New Mexico, and Texas back to Mexico, in part sold by Mexico to the USA in the Gadsden Purchase (or *La venta de la Mesilla*, in Spanish) of 1853, but mostly lost earlier through the Treaty of Guadalupe Hidalgo, signed in early 1848, ending the Mexican-American War of 1846-1848, a treaty which bore the cheery and amical formal name of the Treaty of Peace, Friendship, Limits and Settlement between the United States of America and the Mexican Republic. More urgent as a pressing issue, with more immediate, very practical implications, on January 30, 1917, Germany announced its intention to re-institute the unlimited use of submarine warfare against ships of all nations. The US Government had a strong (commercial) interest to defend its rights to protect US flagships' lucrative commercial transports across the Atlantic. *Here we have a blending of political and economic interests being taken on by the government, not that unusual.* This German announcement and what it foretold became the immediate focus that led the USA to declare war on Germany, on April 6, 1917. The German decision was based on a hope, or an envisioned plan, at least, to bring the war to a prompt end with this escalation in their submarine warfare; but the US finally did bring over arms and men for the last months of the war (with a time lag for the US to organize and give rudimentary training to an army, its reliance on French materials and

---

[199] Declaration of July 28, 2014 at Bad Ischl: "Ich habe alles geprüft und erwogen. Mit ruhigem Gewissen betrete ich den Weg, den die Pflicht Mir weist." See Meret Baumann, "Die Kriegserklärung aus der Sommerfrische," *NZZ (Neue Zürcher Zeitung)*, Jul. 26, 2014.

[200] The US defined its role as that of making the world safe for democracy; Britain would talk more of the war to end all wars.

The Hitler Era

arms when arriving in Europe, with American political and military preferences for limited US military action integrated with British and French troops, and the eventual direct US military involvement in 1918.)

There was much enthusiasm on all sides (each side envisioning in joyful exuberance an easy, prompt victory). Celebrations and military parades, with crisp, inspiring, military marches being played by bands to accompany men going to sign up for the war, or men in uniform ready to go off to the front, can be seen in old newsreels and films.) The glorification of war, with an imagined easy victory, was quite exhilarating. Thus, not long before the war began, General von Loebell[201] stated, "In not long a time [*Lange dauert's nicht mehr*], war will come [*dann kommt's zum Kriege*], and then the world will experience something! [*dann wird die Welt etwas erleben!*] In two weeks we will crush France [*werfen wir Frankreich nieder*], then we will turn around, strike down Russia to submission [*schlagen Rußland zu Bogen*] and then we will march to the Balkans and establish order there [*nach Balkan und stiften dort Ordnung*]."[202] This plan was later known as the Schlieffen Plan, named after Field Marshal Alfred von Schlieffen, who in 1905-1906 had defined this war plan.[203] This inspiring plan envisioned a Germany that would reign over all of Middle Europe, assuring its place in the sun. And yet, here as elsewhere, reality is not always ready to cooperate with any given nation's vision of grandeur and power.

The self-confidence in this vision is remarkable, but not, it turns out, especially unusual in the world of war and the views that support and encourage it. (Who even hints at the possibility of great disasters, rather than victory upon victory, glory upon glory, when about to go to war?)

One of numerous examples of this disappointment in the unpleasant vicissitudes of warfare occurred early in the Great War.

To have a sense of the timing and the sequence of this, the war began on July 28, 1914 with the declaration of war by the Austro-Hungarian Empire on Serbia (after the assassination of Archduke Franz Ferdinand, on June 28). Then Czarist Russia called for a mobilization of troops, on July 30; Germany's ultimatum for Russia to stand down was refused, with Germany then declaring war on Russia, on August 1; at that time France,

---

[201] Major-Gen. Arthur von Loebell was also a *Militärschriftsteller*, an author of military texts, such as *Das deutsche Heer, Mit Berücksichtigung der Heeresverstärkangen 1913; Bücher des Wissen*, Vol. 92 (2nd ed., 1914). His brother was Friedrich Wilhelm von Loebell, the Prussian Minister of the Interior.

[202] Friedrich Wilhelm Förster, *Mein Kampf gegen das militaristische und nationalistische Deutschland* (1920), p. 121. The title predates Hitler's *Mein Kampf*.

[203] This was based on Schlieffen's *Memorandum for a War Against France*, which he had written in December 1905: see "Alfred Graf von Schlieffen, Denkschrift 'Krieg gegen Frankreich' (Schlieffen-Plan), Dezember 1905," 1000DOKUMENTE.DE. Discussions by German historians in the decades after World War I variously interpreted the import of this plan and possible explanations of how Germany lost the war. Cf. Hans Ehlert, Michael Epkenhans and Gerhard P. Gross, *The Schlieffen Plan: International Perspectives on the German Strategy for World War I* (2014).

too, began to mobilize; Germany declared war on France two days later; when German troops went through Belgium on August 4, to get to France; the next day, the UK, having a treaty with Belgium and also seeing in the German control of Belgian ports a threat to British sea power, declared war on Germany. From Germany's side, there were some very early worries following a massive British-French counter-offensive on September 6, 1914, after a promising initial series of great German victories. *These were, of course, not made public at all.* General Helmuth von Moltke,[204] having witnessed this counter-offensive, expressed his first doubts days later, on September 8, 1914, in a letter from Luxembourg. This was only six weeks after the war had begun; Moltke wrote, with fresh hesitation, "The great struggle along the whole of our army's frontline from Paris to upper Alsace [*unser ganzes Heer von Paris bis zum oberen Alsaß*] has still not been decided. It would be horrible if all this blood had been shed without a thorough success."[205] (And of course, this was only the start of much more blood to flow and soak the earth, as was chanted repeatedly in *The Iliad*.[206])

Although the loss of lives is admittedly horrible, the wish that blood should not be shed in vain can be used to inspire continuation of fighting that may greatly exacerbate the situation and increase the losses of life significantly, as we have sadly seen repeatedly through history.

General von Moltke added, with a touch of the paranoia seen in other historical contexts (in which political or military set-backs mean that the whole world is against us): "The whole world has conspired against us [*Die ganze Welt hat sich gegen uns verschworen*]; it looks as if it would be the mission of all the other nations finally to annihilate Germany [*die Aufgabe aller übrigen Nationen wäre, Deutschland endgültig zu vernichten*]." (More on such paranoia, below.) The next day, September 9, 1914, he would write again, also from Luxembourg: "Things are going badly. [*Es geht schlecht.*] ... How different it was [*Wie anders war es*] when we a few weeks ago [*als wir vor wenigen Wochen*] opened the campaign so splendidly [*den Feldzug so glanzvoll eröffneten*] ... and I'm afraid [*und ich fürchte*] that our people in their thirst for victory [*unser Volk in seinem Siegestaumel*] will hardly be able to endure the misfortune [*wird das Unglück kaum ertragen können*]."[207]

And while there were variations in the power and the weakness of each army, relative to the others, neither side was seen to have undisputed

---

[204] Helmuth von Moltke was called Moltke the Younger; his uncle was Moltke the Elder (who was German Field Marshal and Chief of Staff in the German Army in the Franco-Prussian War); his grand-nephew was Helmuth James von Moltke (who would later be in the resistance against Hitler, on whom more below).

[205] Entries for Sep. 18-19, 1914, in Helmuth von Moltke, *Erinnerungen, Briefe, Dokumente 1877 bis 1916* (1922), pp. 384-386.

[206] The *Iliad* is entitled in ancient Greek, Iliás (Ilium/Iliad/Troy), short for *He poiēois Iliás* (*The Poem of Ilium, The Poem of Troy*).

[207] Entries for Sep. 18-19, 1914, in Helmuth von Moltke, *Erinnerungen, Briefe, Dokumente 1877 bis 1916*, just cited.

The Hitler Era

prominence across the Western Front. The various final offensives by the German military, called the Ludendorff Offensives, when German troops had defeated the Russians (Lenin and the Soviets asking for peace after overthrowing the Czar) and were available for transfer to the Western Front, were less than totally successful. In fact, each such offensive found the German Military weaker and weaker. (More on this, below.)

The German public, suffering in its own ways largely from the British naval blockade, was not privy to the negotiations between the German Military and the German political structure of the time. Their own situation did, however, make it clear that all was not going so well in Germany.

Not publicly or widely known, on September 29, 1918, the German Supreme Army Command called for a ceasefire. The German government was to communicate directly with US President Woodrow Wilson to get a sense of his readiness to act on his Fourteen Points (which Wilson had announced in January of 1918). Wilson was, to the surprise of the German military and its diplomat representatives, rather firm in his demands at that time. Only on November 8, 1918, did Germany come to a decision to send delegates to France to sign the Armistice, which of course was done in the next days, to go into effect at 11 am on November 11, 1918.[208]

These inter-governmental exchanges not being available to the public, it was still possible for Ludendorff and others later to claim that if left alone they would have been able to continue and perhaps win the war, had it not been for politicians making vital unilateral decisions.

So, General von Moltke's sense from the first months of the war (quoted just above), that this war was not going to be decided in a matter of weeks, or at most by Christmas 1914, was rather accurate. And yet, the setbacks of the German military in the Great War were not accepted at face value by many in Germany. Furthermore, information was censored, that is, not at all reported or made public.

Those in the know knew! On November 18, 1914, Theobald Bethmann Hollweg (German Imperial Chancellor, 1909-1917) had an important consultation with General Erich von Falkenhayn, earlier Prussian Minister of War, 1913-1915, then Chief of the *Oberste Heeresleitung*, the German Army General Staff, 1914-1917, replacing Helmuth von Moltke the Younger, and was later to be replaced himself by General Paul von Hindenburg, who was assisted by Erich von Ludendorff as *Erster Generalquartiermeister*, Quartermaster General. The next day, November 19, 1914, only some four months into the war, Chancellor Hollweg wrote to Undersecretary of State for Foreign Affairs, Arthur Zimmermann (promoted to Secretary of State in November 1916 and author of the important Zimmermann telegram of January 1917, already mentioned), "Our losses especially in officers are monstrous [*namentlich an Offizieren sind ungeheuer*] and in many cases not replaceable [*vielfach nicht*

---

[208] See both "Extra-Blatt der Leipziger Gerichts-Zeitung: Der Waffenstillstand abgeschlossen (8. November 1918)" and "Supplement to the Leipzig Court Journal: Armistice Accepted (November 8, 1918)," in *Das Wilhelminische Kaiserreich und der Erste Weltkrieg (1890-1918)*, GERMAN HISTORY IN DOCUMENTS AND IMAGE.

ersetzlich]; the strength of the offensives of the troops [*die Stosskraft der Truppe*] is still present, but [is] however, attenuated [*aber doch abgeschwächt*]; a possibility to impose the law of effective management [*das Gesetz des Handelns aufzuzwingen*] on the opponent is no longer perceived, the present numerical superiority of our opponents is at least 200,000 men [*die gegenwärtige numerische Überlegenkeit unserer Gegner wird auf mindestens 200 000 Mann geschätzt*], the leadership of the French and English military is excellent [*die französische und englische Herresleitung sind ausgezeichnet*], their artillery is better and is better used than ours [*und wird besser verwendet als die unsere*]."[209]

In short, the high administration of the German military in the Great War was already demonstrating clear awareness of serious questions about the German ability to win the war, and this, less than four months after the start of the war! We can appreciate here that this awareness by the German generals directly in charge of the war came years before the brutal mutual killings on the war front of the last definitive German offensives in 1918 (with some one million German soldiers additionally killed). This systematic ignorance of major problems in the German war effort among the German populace, as well as in lower-ranking military, contributed in part to the distorted idea that it was not the military but the politicians, especially those of the Social Democratic Party who would sign the Versailles Treaty, who were responsible for the German surrender: *This widespread misunderstanding after the war disregarded the military reasons of the defeat itself and targeted as scapegoat the political group that was left to accept the defeat imposed by the enemy's ultimately superior military power.*

We might appreciate that the German situation was not unique; governments and military can both show an inclination to present the situation in the most honorable light, at least for consumption by its own public. That is, this tendency to ascribe problems to isolated groups is not just German. As one example from more recent history of this tendency to see problems as external (a variant of psychological splitting and projecting), with resultant scapegoating: during the Vietnam Era, President Johnson felt that the organizers of the civilian protests were the Communist governments in Moscow and Beijing, and the comment by Nixon on newspaper reports of the Mỹ Lai Massacre was, "It's those dirty rotten Jews from New York who are behind it!" (Nixon, in his anti-Semitism rather typical of the time, also called Kissinger his "Jew boy.")[210]

---

[209] Document No. 13 (Bethmann-Hollweg letter to Zimmermann), original text in German, in *L'Allemagne et les problèmes de la paix pendant la première guerre mondiale: Documents extraits des archives de l'Office allemand des Affaires étrangères*, André Scherer and Jacques Grunewald, eds., *Vol. 1: Des origines à la Déclaration de la Guerre sous-marine à Outrance; août 1914-31 janvier 1917* (1962), pp. 15-19, at p. 18.

[210] Robert Dallek, *Nixon and Kissinger: Partners in Power* (2007), pp. 169-171, 185-186, 305, 582, 589. Cf. "The Vietnam War—Errors and Omissions—Episode Nine, September 27, 2017," *The Nixon Foundation*, NIXONFOUNDATION.ORG.

The Hitler Era

Looking specifically back to those first few months of the Great War, in 1914, both sides had already suffered a great loss of men, with many killed and even more maimed, disfigured, incapacitated, and dealing with troubling, recurrent traumatic memories of their experiences. That military and governments on both sides remained determined to continue the carnage is a reflection of our common collective capacity to see the nation's interests (in some sense of that offered up in justification of continued warfare) as more important and significant than an interest in the well-being of the people of the nation, it would seem.

This overall pattern, sadly, is a scenario that has been repeated many times, in many wars: the initial exuberance and pride in one's power—it is often joined with an under-estimation of the power of potential enemies and a disregard for problems encountered in warfare, from injuries, death, mutilations, stresses on family, disease, epidemics, and even temporary adverse weather and climatic conditions,[211] and with a related denial of the ways in which warfare could turn unexpectedly into disastrous calamities and losses of great numbers of the nation's soldiers.

This often leads to a creative variety of misplaced, confusing (mystifying) pseudo-explanations that are aimed at maintaining the nation's best possible positive image of itself in the situation and avoiding the underlying harsh processes that were actually taking place. While it would be wise for nations to take this tendency to rather tendentious thinking into account before jumping into war, national political-military decisions are sometimes made with no such wisdom.

The exuberance of war is intense and there is a link between the great intensity of actual battle with significant, palpable changes in adrenalin and other hormones that prepare the body for intense combat.

Berlin-born Albert Otto Hirschman (1915-2012)—a key assistant to Varian Fry helping German refugees escape from Vichy France in 1940-1941 (more on which, below), where he was known as Albert Hermant and especially as Beamish, and later was to be a renowned political economist and Professor at the School of Social Science, Institute for Advanced Study, Princeton—knew about the excitement of threatening situations (war, espionage in enemy territory, and such).

He commented about their time in Marseilles, with marked understatement, "The work was extraordinarily absorbing and often dangerous—and being in danger is always exciting as well as highly memorable."[212]

---

[211] On the significant impact of something as seemingly inconsequential as some transitory fog, we will discuss in detail Georg Eiser (1903-1945) and his attempt to assassinate Hitler on Nov. 8, 1939, on the anniversary of the failed Beer Hall (or Hitler) Putsch of Nov. 8-9, 1923, below.

[212] Dr. Albert O. Hirschman, "Introduction" (pp. v-viii), at p. v, in Varian Fry, *Assignment: Rescue: An Autobiography* (1945; Introduction in 1968 ed.); on the joy, bravery, and fighting fury experienced in warfare (all very energizing), see Homer, *Iliad*, 13.98-99, 334-335, 14.100-110, 15.380-381, 556-557, etc. (BK.vv:

One important pattern is the shift of this warrior excitement into a more sexualized form of excitement, experienced perhaps throughout history, explaining in part not only mutually satisfying sexual intimacy, but also the many stories of war rape, rape being violence carried out forcefully in the sexual dimension of human interaction, manifesting the power of one person over another. (More on this, below.) There, was, for example, this (non-violent) passion as that felt by Paris in *The Iliad*, now with Helen, wife of Menelaus, with her "face that launches a thousand ships"[213]), saying to her: "But come—let's go to bed, let's lose ourselves in love! Never has longing for you overwhelmed me so, no, not even then, I tell you, that first time when I swept you up from the lovely hills of Lacedaemon, sailed you off and away in the racing deep-sea ships and we went and locked in love on rocky island. That was nothing to how I hunger for you now—irresistible longing lays me low!"[214] Or again, there was the driving passion of Zeus for his sister-wife Hera, in the midst of their mutual tactical maneuvering concerning the Trojan War, where he invites Hera with a direct declaration of his intense yearning for her: "Now—come, let's go to bed; let's lose ourselves in love! Never has such a lust of goddess or mortal woman flooded my pounding heart and overwhelmed me so." After mentioning other moments of intense sexual desire, Zeus adds, "That was nothing to how I hunger for you now—irresistible longing lays me low!"[215] Or, still again, also as recounted in the *Iliad*, in a similar state of urgency, Hermes (a son of Zeus) is described as lusting after the mortal Polymela, a gorgeous dancer, going with her to her bed that very night, leading to the birth of their son Eudorus.[216]

Feeling great excitement of one inspiring form or another, it was often relatively easy to enter into war, and not all that difficult to imagine glory on the battlefield (beforehand); it was not so easy to stay alive, to provide for the daily needs of one's family or of one's nation during such a stress on individual and group life, and not so easy to find a path to an acceptable peace treaty, not at all easy to pick up life, for those who survive, after the injuries, the loss of limbs or the loss of their normal use, in additional to the destruction of buildings, roads, and bridges, all of these components so vital to life in our age.

Of course, those killed in the war did not have such post-war problems to face. (We might ponder rhetorically: Who is luckier in such cases, those killed or those who survive?)

Such issues would not die with the dead; they would be inherited by surviving relatives and others who had the strength of will, the good will, and the force to attempt to deal with the destruction on so many levels that war brings about.

13.81-82, 115-119, 330-338; 14.83-100; 15, 365-366, 560-567, etc.)

[213] See the later depiction of Helen of Troy in Christopher Marlow (1564-1593), *The Tragical History of Dr. Faustus*, Scene 13 (publ. ca. 1590-1604).

[214] Homer, *Iliad*, 3.517-524 (BK.vv: 3.437-446).

[215] Homer, *Iliad*, 14.375-393 (BK.vv: 14.341-351.

[216] Homer, *Iliad*, 16.214-219 (BK.vv: 16.380-384).

6. The Great War, 1914-1918

Let us start here with a brief overview, following the introductory comments about World War I in the preceding chapter that considered especially the almost immediate disappointing realizations that each country's vision of a swift and decisive victory was not to come to pass.

The war began with great enthusiasm in the nations and empires of Europe, soon subdued by the unexpected intensity of massive killing and injuries to all participants in the conflict that had erupted. In part, this unexpected intensity was related to the delay between military tactics and the weapons that were used. What does this amount to?

We see an example of this phenomenon, from the nineteenth century, when muskets from the period of the Napoleonic Wars of 1803-1815, and of the US Revolutionary War, as well, determined the distance at which opposing armies would confront each other: perhaps 100 yards (or meters). This was because the accuracy of those muskets was not at all reliable at greater distances. In the US Civil War, some muskets might have been used, but there were new weapons: rifles, so-called because their barrels had rifling, that is, grooves inside the barrel that spiraled, having bullets fired not only with great force (as with muskets) but rotating through the barrel, coming out spinning tightly in a way that allowed much greater accuracy at greater distances. But the military protocols still had armies meeting at the shorter distance that military commanders had learned from earlier times and weaponry. The result was much more accurate shooting, and so, much more killing.

There was also the war-changing invention of machine guns, with earlier versions of a mechanism that would allow multiple bullets (or rounds) being fired without the need to empty and reload with each bullet. One early mechanism was the Gatling gun, invented in 1862, during the American Civil War, by Richard Gatling, with a hand-cranked mechanism rotating ten barrels each with its own capacity to fire bullets. It was used at Wounded Knee (Dakota Territory), on December 29, 1890, by the US Seventh Cavalry (part of the US Army), some 600-men strong, using Gatling guns and Hotchkiss M1875 mountain guns (cannons)[217] against some 300 Lakota Sioux Indians (half men and half women and children): "It had turned into a war of extermination."[218] The Gatling gun was soon widely used in the Spanish-American War of 1898. A more automated gun was used in the Russo-Japanese War of 1904. Earlier automated guns were made obsolete, in turn, by the development of recoil gas-operated guns using smokeless gun powder (as in the French Canon 75). By the start of World War I, the British Vickers machine gun could fire 450 rounds per minutes; by the end of the war this gun had water cooling and a

---

[217] The French-designed Hotchkiss M1875 was a short cannon (length of bore, 3.43 ft. (1.045 m); the diameter of its rifled barrel was 1.65 in. (42 mm).

[218] George R. Brown, "An Account of the Battle," *El Paso Daily Herald*, Jul. 23, 1900, beginning on p. 7, with quotation from closing passages on p. 5. Cf. "Wounded Knee Massacre [aka Battle of Wounded Knee]," WIKIPEDIA.

capacity of 600 rounds per minute. The Germans, for their part, had the Machinengewehr 08; the French, their Canon 75.

The ability of a non-specialist to use these guns and to fight off the enemy, the arc of spray of the bullets killing many soldiers attempting to overcome defended positions, made for a radically different sort of warfare (making attacks on enemy lines quite dangerous). The use of refinements in machine guns would continue into World War II.

The use of the airplane, just a decade after the very first flight in 1904, began as a new form of reconnaissance: seeing enemy positions and movements and reporting them back. Soon, attacks on these (both from the ground and from opposing aircraft) became part of the war scenario. There were even attacks against the ground from machine guns mounted in airplanes and a rudimentary form of aerial bombardment, nothing like what would come to pass in World War II, but using a variety of means of transportation and attack: dirigibles, balloons, zeppelins, bomber airplanes, and seaplanes. These were used in a number of theaters of war: Liège in Belgium was first bombed (by German Zeppelins) on August 6, 1914; Paris was lightly bombed in early September 1914; the British bombed Zeppelin bases in Köln (Cologne) and Dusseldorf, beginning in September 1914. After earlier bombings by Germans elsewhere in England beginning on January 9, 1915, London was bombed first in May 1915—total British casualties from these bombings were less than 5,000 (considerably less than in the next World War); other cities, such as Warsaw, were also to see this early form of aerial bombardment. And yet, certainly, German Lutwaffe planes in the Spanish Civil War (think: Guernica) and in World War II would bring on an intensity of bombing, of both military objectives and of cities of the enemy, that far surpassed that of these early activities of the First War.

Overall, this Great War also saw the organized introduction and use of various poison gases, machine guns, the rudiments of aerial warfare, an intense mechanization of warfare, with the introduction of other new forms of weaponry, including submarines and landships (tanks).

There was also the use of cryptology, the analysis and decoding of messages expressed in a hidden or secret way (from the Greek *kryptós*, hidden, secret). This would prove to be very important both in the interwar period (1919-1939) and also during World War II, when the German highly sophisticated coding system called Enigma would be broken by Polish and then British intelligence, making the British mathematician Alan Turing famous, years later, to the general public.

In World War I, this work was the province of British Naval Intelligence, in a project code-named Room 40. This was aided by coding information captured by the Czarist Russian Navy (on August 26, 1914) and by the British (on October 11, 1914), including German code books, *Signalbuch der Kaiserlichen Marine* (the *Signal Book of the German Imperial Navy*), the *Handelsschiffsverkehrsbuch* (the *Merchant Ship Transportation Book*), and the *Verkehrsbuch* (the *Transportation Book*). Among the important discoveries that could be derived from these texts was information about

The Hitler Era

German naval movements and plans for attacking British Navy ships—leading to the thwarting of the plans for German surprise attacks on the British, the Battle of Dogger Bank (in 1915) and the Battle of Jutland (in 1916)—and, most importantly, diplomatically, was information learned from the Zimmermann telegram of January 1917, mentioned above, which was a secret offer to Mexico of the US territories (not yet states) of Arizona, New Mexico, and Texas, as a promised enticement to join the war on the German side, information passed on the US by the British.

The War of 1914-1918 began with visions of gallantry and heroism and individual courage playing a decisive role in the outcome of any battle. The charge on enemy positions, from an era when well-dressed cavalry could lead the attack, sabers ready to attack, or individual soldiers who were expert marksmen ready to shoot their rifles at the enemy, met with a new form of warfare, primarily, the machine gun. This weapon did not require marksmen, expert shooters, but, simply, soldiers' ability merely to aim their gun in the right direction and to have its bullets spray across the charging enemy. The number of men killed in each charge was enormous, with the command for the next wave of men to go forth ("over the top," to climb up, out, and over the somewhat protective trenches, into the land between the two facing armies, "no man's land").

A new instrument and vehicle of war developed by the British was the landship, mentioned just above, a huge armored land vehicle that was soon given the code name by which we now know of this: tank (perhaps so named because of its resemblance to a steel water-storage tank).

In operational terms, this was an armored, mobile weapon of war, able to cross very irregular terrain, including being able to go over trenches, up and down sharp inclines in the land, and over barbed-wire fences. It was able to hold a small group of soldiers. Its great mobility (although not great speed) was from its design, in which the body of the vehicle was propelled not by wheels, but, rather, by a long, continuous belt of interlocked steel segments called tracks or, more fully, caterpillar tracks. Tanks were supplied both with a cannon and machine guns. They were impenetrable to ordinary firepower (guns, rifles, machine guns), but not to the anti-tank rifles, rockets, grenades, bazookas, missiles, anti-tank weapons that were soon to be developed.

The submarine (or "under-sea boat": *Unterseeboot*, U-boat) was also a new form of machinery, with new employment under rules that were quite natural but shocking: submarines could not warn enemy ships prior to sinking operations, because they themselves were too vulnerable to counter-attacks if their presence was known. One important submarine attack involved the sinking of a British passenger ship—*which was secretly carrying arms*—the *RMS Lusitania*, on May 7, 1915. The German Embassy had placed announcements in New York City newspapers prior to that voyage, making it clear that that ship would be going through waters patrolled by German submarines (and that US citizens traveled there at their own risk). Despite this warning, there was a great uproar after the sinking of the ship, in which more than 120 US citizens lost their lives, which soon led to a temporary halting of German unrestricted submarine warfare, in September 1915. This ban was lifted by Germany in January 1917 (with the encouragement of Hindenburg and Ludendorff, commanding the German military),[219] to cut off British shipping supplies, hoping to end the war quickly before the US could muster a working military to join the Allies, as mentioned above. This change was officially acknowledged on February 1. The US declared war against the German Empire 74 days later, on April 16, 1917.

The War of 1914-1918 was disastrous for all involved. On the Western Front, for over four years German forces faced off against the British and French (with members of their colonies and empires also involved) and then also against American forces (who arrived in numbers in Europe finally in early 1918). The number of casualties was calculated in various ways, leading to different numbers being cited, and yet we can still consider statistics as suggestive estimates (the usual case when considering large populations). Typical numbers—rounding off in each case—suggest that in the War, killed in battle were approximately 1,774,000 soldiers for Germany, 1,700,000 for Russia, 1,358,000 for France, 1,200,000 for Austria-Hungary, more than 908,000 for Great Britain and the Empire, 650,000 for Italy, 336,000 for Romania, 325,000 for Turkey, 117,000 for the USA, 45,000 for Serbia, and, overall, on both sides, some 13,670,000 killed (more on the side of the Central Powers, fewer for the Allies).[220] This was called a world war for good reason: not only did the great countries of Europe enter into an organized, mechanized, and industrialized mutual massacre (with machine guns, tanks, airplanes, submarines, massive cannons, mortars, howitzers, and other arms, with poison gas, and other refinements of sophisticated science applied methodically), but each country as the head of a great empire called on its entire subject population to come to save civilization as each country understood that concept. This involved some 4 million colonial soldiers brought from around the world to support the Great War: 1.5 million East Indians, 2 million sub-Saharan Africans, 100,000 Chinese, and 100,000 Indo-Chinese (from French Indo-China).[221]

There were, we might surmise, multiple interpretations of how these soldiers understood the British slogan describing the war as "the war to end all wars" or the American slogan of "making the world safe for democracy" (from Wilson's request to Congress on April 2, 1917, for a declaration of war against Germany). In any case, some around the world took the Wilsonian phrase quite seriously (as they did his Fourteen Points), only to be disappointed later. A number of colonies around the world,

---

[219] Anna von der Goltz, "Hindenburg, Paul von," INTERNATIONAL ENCYCLOPEDIA OF THE FIRST WORLD WAR: 1914-1918.

[220] "Killing, Wounded, and Missing: World War I 1914-1918," ENCYCLOPÆDIA BRITANNICA; more than 1,000,000 British and Commonwealth soldiers are cited as being killed in the Great War: see *All the King's Men* (1999), at 1:47:05-1:47:20.

[221] *The World's War: Forgotten Soldiers of the Empire, Series 1, Episode 1: The Martial Races*, BBC (2014), at 1:32-2:00.

mostly British and French, would not see their own self-rule democracy as a product of the war. We may consider here British India, French Algeria and French Indochina, and other non-white lands. While after the War there were the new European countries of Poland, Austria, Czechoslovakia, Hungary, the Kingdom of the Serbs, Croats, and Slovenes (later renamed Yugoslavia), peoples longing for their own country and autonomous government would remain with only a hope for the future, including homelands for Armenians, Kurds, Vietnamese, Indians, and Jews, to name a few. And many other lands in Africa and Asia did not see the application of new nationhood come to them at all in the next decades.

One young man from the French colonies in Indo-China, a Mr. Nguyen (Nguyễn Sinh Cung), for example, who had worked earlier as a chef in the Parker House Hotel in Boston, and in the Ritz Hotel in Paris, petitioned President Wilson for an interview during the Peace Conference, pleading the case of his colony. There was no reply; it was decades later, in May of 1941, that this man founded a group with a goal of gaining, finally, independence from French rule, the Viet Minh (its full name means the League for the Independence of Vietnam). This man, later known as Ho Chi-Minh (1890-1969), was quite persistent, although his dream for an independent Vietnam was not quite realized during his lifetime.

The use of non-whites in the Great War had a side-product: The strict colonial prohibition for non-whites against any violence to whites was suddenly voided, and, instead, these non-white soldiers were given orders to kill the (white) European enemy. *This was no small shift!* Also, many of these soldiers from the various colonies were hardly prepared for the conditions in Europe in which they were to fight, including cultural and climatic differences from their native lands. Furthermore, from the European point of view, the presence of non-whites was seen as an additional complication to the war: in Germany, especially, the fact that the French brought in sub-Saharan Africans (from black Africa, as those lands are also termed) was seen as a betrayal by the French of white civilization, with these blacks, referred to indiscriminately as Senegalese (the main black African colony of France, even if the forces included those from others African countries, as the Sudan). Thus, in a German magazine from 1916, a front-cover caricature showed a "Senagalese":

Here we have a caricature of one of these *fusilleurs sénégalais* (Senegalese riflemen), with a rifle, who would also often carry a *coupe-coupe*, a machete-like, short, thick-bodied sabre:

A *coupe-coupe* with its sheath

Above, this Senegalese was shown as a barbaric invader, and even as a cannibal. This front-page cartoon appeared in the edition of July 23, 1916, of a satiric German weekly publication ("daily except work days"), the *Kladderadatsch* (*Crash! Bang! Mess!*). This paper, inaugurated on May 7, 1848, evolved into a pro-Bismarck, and still later into a pro-Nazi and anti-Semitic weekly. In the background context here, we have the principle that while killing the enemy with a short machete was seen as barbaric and an attack on civilization, by contrast, Western weaponry, much more lethal, had no such associations with barbarity. Overall, those who were called upon in one military context or another to take part in the battles of World War I included not only the Germans, Austro-Hungarians, French, and British, but also, as we might already know quite well, the Americans, the Canadians, the Australians, and the New Zealanders. And yet, in addition, other participants in the war included Algerians, Tunisians, Senegalese, Vietnamese, East Indians, Maori (from New Zealand), Intuits and Blood Tribe men (from Canada), West Indians, South Africans, Egyptians, and Chinese.[222] While Germany saw these black soldiers in Europe as a barbarity, the Germans also used African soldiers in their ranks, called Askaris—confined to war in German East Africa.

SEGREGATED ADMINISTRATION OF AMERICAN SOLDIERS IN THE GREAT WAR

Of the many American soldiers who went "over there" (to the war in Europe), there was a significant number of black Americans. Although white American and British officers *refused to lead them in battle* (black American soldiers would have their own units and their own black, low-ranking officers),[223] they were accepted by the French to serve in French uniforms in French units. In this administrative imbroglio, the American military advisors set down strict regulations about how the French were to treat these black American soldiers. (A similar segregation continued in the US military in World War II. This later situation was given a bright, respectable patina in the 1944 Army film directed by Frank Capra, *The*

---

[222] *The World's War: Forgotten Soldiers of the Empire, Series 1, Episode 2: Foreign Legions*, BBC (2014), at 32:40-40:30.
[223] Pellom McDaniels III, "African American Soldiers (USA)," THE INTERNATIONAL ENCYCLOPEDIA OF THE FIRST WORLD WAR/1914-1918.

The Hitler Era

Negro Soldier. There, these problematic features of the life of World War II black service men were thoroughly obfuscated.[224]

Illuminating this situation in the Great War was a report, "Secret Information Concerning Black American Troops" that was *issued by the French Military Mission, dated August 7, 1918*, reporting on how it was advised. The document from the US military delegation made clear their official understanding of some basic truths of 1917-1918 America. These American military advisories to the French made powerful and inclusive generalization speaking of Americans as if all (or even perhaps only all *white*) Americans agreed to the attitudes articulated: "American opinion is unanimous on the 'color question' and does not admit of any discussion.... Although a citizen of the United States, the black man is considered by White Americans as an inferior being, with whom relations of business and service are only possible [but nothing more]. The black is constantly being censured for his want of intelligence and discretion, for his lack of civic and professional conscience and for his tendency towards undue familiarity. The vices of the Negro (*les vices du Nègre*) are a constant menace (*un danger constant*) to the [White] American, who has to repress them sternly (*qui doit les réprimer sévèrement*)." The French are advised to keep contact with black American soldiers to a minimum as required by the military service. The French report continues, "We [the French] must not commend too highly [black American soldiers] in the presence of white Americans.... We must make the point of keeping the native population [the French] from spoiling the negroes [perhaps by treating them with untoward respect or interacting socially with them]. White Americans become greatly incensed by any expression of *public* intimacy between white women and black men (*Les Américains [blancs] sont indignés de toute intimité PUBLIQUE de femme blanche avec des noirs*)."[225] Looking ahead into the 1950s, large segments of US white society who were quite prominent and politically powerful, continued being firmly adamant about maintaining total segregation between whites and blacks. It was only decades after the end of the Great War, and almost a decade after the end of the Second World War, when a pivotal US Supreme Court case[226] initiated a national shift of legal parameters for the treatment of American citizens who were black. Brown v. Board of

---

[224] Frank Capra, Italian-born American director of *It Happened One Night* (1937), *You Can't Take It With You* (1938), *Mr. Smith Goes To Washington* (1939), *It's a Wonderful Life* (1946)—also directed war-time films *Prelude to War* (1942), *The Battle of Russia* (1943), and *The Negro Soldier* (1944).

[225] *The Crisis*, May 1919, publication of the The National Association of Colored People/NAACP (banner title: *The American Negro's Record in the Great World War: A Record of Loyalty, Valor, and Achievement*). Quoted here from article at pp. 16-17, which included the original French and an Eng. tr. (Upper-case French in original text.) Cf. related discussion in *The World's War: Forgotten Soldiers of the Empire, Series 1, Episode 2: Foreign Legions*, BBC (2014), at 44:00-48:20.

[226] This US Supreme Court Case is cited formally as Brown v. Board of Education of Topeka, 347 US 483 (1954).

Education of Topeka, Kansas, was decided on May 17, 1954. Republican President Dwight David Eisenhower in 1957 would send in over 1,000 federal paratroopers in full battle gear with fixed bayonets and rifles to guard the safe entrance of nine black children—there were over 1,500 white protestors held back by the military, with a very small number of them arrested[227]—all to enforce the integration of a public school in Little Rock, Arkansas.

This segregationist attitude in the 1950s was expressed rather vehemently by the self-appointed Executive Secretary of the Alabama White Citizens Council, Asa Carter,[228] putting forth his opinion about blacks and rock and roll, even linking it to Communism: "The obscenity and vulgarity of the rock and roll music is obviously a means by which the white man, his children, can be driven to the level of the Nigger [his choice of vocabulary].... If we choose to call this the Communist ideology [a great American worry, especially during the McCarthy Era], I think we hit it [presumably referring to the proverbial nail] fairly on the head."[229]—This, from another age, and yet, we might acknowledge that even in the present day and age, there are many who long for what they perceive to be the loss of White supremacy in the USA.

Having considered here the Great War, with millions of men killed from many of the countries participating in this organized blood-bath (often counted in the tens or hundreds of thousands killed), and having recognized the status of American black soldiers and their ultimate integration into the French military in that war, we may also consider the several major battles through the war years that are frequently highlighted and discussed in the military literature, and that stand out for their shockingly high number of casualties, especially give how little territory changed hands at the end of each day.

The trauma that went to the core of European countries, from the stunningly high percentage of the young male population killed would strongly and pervasively impact the European attitudes toward war into the late 1930s and beyond.

BATTLES OF THE GREAT WAR

The casualties in the War of 1914-1918, with battles that at sometimes continued over several months, *often ran into the hundreds of thousands of soldiers each, and even to more than one million* in given prolonged and intense battles! *These numbers are individually shocking and, taken*

---

[227] Anthony Lewis, "President Sends Troops to Little Rock, Federalizes Arkansas National Guard; Tells Nation He Acted to Avoid An Anarchy," *The New York Times*, Sep. 24, 1954, p. 1; "On September 25 in 1957: Troops end Little Rock Crisis," BBC News, at CIRCLES (WIJNGAARDS INSTITUTE FOR CATHOLIC RESEARCH); "Eisenhower and the Little Rock Crisis," THE US LIBRARY OF CONGRESS.

[228] An excerpt of Asa Carter's statements is quoted in "White Council vs. Rock and Roll" (*Time*, Apr. 18, 1956); one related article is "Rock n' Roll in the Press," UNIV. OF MISSOURI-ST. LOUIS.

[229] *Rock n' Roll: The Early Days, Documentary* (1984), COLUMBIA PICTURES: ARCHIVE FILM, at 27:30-29:00.

The Hitler Era

all together, truly horrific. In this light, consider the following major battles during the war and the total casualties in each.

Given the lack over several years of any significant changes in the front lines on the Western Front, the hundreds of thousands and millions of men thrown into these battles are a reminder of the tendency to keep at a plan even though it is showing itself to be an unmitigated disaster!

Among these early battles with major defeats were the victories over the Czarist Russian military by German armies led by Lindenberg and Ludendorff, garnering them great respect among all Germans: immediate heroes—*we will certainly see their important roles in the post-war years in Germany.*

These were the Battles of Tannenberg and the Masurian Lakes, August 26-30, and September 7-14, 1914, with 347,000 casualties. Other early battles included the First Battle of the Marne (an Allied victory and a major set-back for the German army, with the failure of the German Schlieffen Plan to conquer the French very quickly, with its idea of a quick Western victory allowing the German military to turn to defeating the Russians on the Eastern Front), September 6-12, 1914, 519,000 casualties; the 1914 First Battles of the Marne (September 5-11), of Aisne (September 13-18), and of Ypres (October 19-November 23), which all marked a stalemate and end of a German hoped-for quick victory on the Western Front. This led to trenches being built September 25-November 22, 1914, all the way to Nieuport on the North Sea Coast ("the Race to the Sea"), September 13-28, 1914; the Battle of Galicia (Lemberg, Lvóv, or Lviv, on the Eastern Front, a Russian victory but with great losses), August 23-September 11, 1914, 655,000 casualties; the Battle of Kolubara (Serbs gaining superiority over the Austro-Hungarian armies), November 16-December 16, 1914, 405,000 casualties.

That's already over a million casualties, and we are only at the end of the first half-year of the war! Moving into 1915, there were the Gallipoli Campaign (British loss against the Ottoman Turks), April 25, 1915-January 9, 1916, 470,000 casualties, and the Gorlice-Tarnów Offensive (German victory on the Eastern Front), May 2-June 1915, 1,087,000 casualties. Then, in 1916, there were the Brusilov Offensive (Russia-Germany, on the Eastern Front, a Russian victory, June 4-September 20, 1916), with 2,317,800 casualties; the First Battle of the Somme, July 1-November 18, 1916, 1,113,000 casualties; and the Battle of Verdun—to be remembered as the longest and the deadliest of all World War I battles (at least in the West), and, in some quarters as an indication of the determination and perseverance of the French military (who lost more men that the Germans)—February 21-December 20, 1916, with estimates of 714,200 casualties (of which, 305,400 deaths),[230] or of 750,000 casualties with 300,000 killed,[231] or of 707,000 casualties,[232] and, in the

---

[230] "World War I: Battle of Verdun Ends," THIS DAY IN HISTORY: DEC. 20.
[231] "Battle of Verdun, World War I [1916]," ENCYCLOPÆDIA BRITANNICA.
[232] "Battle of Verdun, 21 February-18 December 1916," HISTORY OF WAR.

estimate of Gerd Krumeich, German professor of history, who discussed the Battle of Verdun as the most significant battle of the First World War (agreeing with many historians), of 700,000 casualties.[233] And other estimates are even higher, such as one stating "a million and a half young Frenchmen and Germans died within an eight-mile radius."[234]

The year 1917 saw the Second Battle of the Aisne, April 16-May 9, 1917, 355,000 casualties; the Battle of Arras, April 9-May 16, 1017, 278,000 casualties; and the Third Battle of Ypres (Passchendaele), July 31-November 10, 1917, 857,100 casualties.

And with the coming of 1918, there was the disastrous Spring German Offensive (the *Kaiserschlacht* or Ludendorff Offensive), March 21-July 18, 1918, 1,539,715 casualties; the Battle of Lys, April 7-29, 1918, and the Second Battle of the Somme, August 21-September 3, 1918, 804,100 casualties; and, at war's end, the Hundred Days Offensive—beginning with the Battle of Amiens, August 8-11, 1918 and continuing until the Armistice ending the war. *The war from start to its end, Armistice Day, November 11, 1918, resulted in more than 1,855,000 casualties.*[235]

What each side thought would be a pleasant and satisfying summer affair, with its troops in proud victory, medals of heroism pinned proudly to their uniforms, returning home by the fall, or at least by Christmas, for a spiritual, peace-filled family celebration, turned out to be something quite different, as we have just seen. Envisioned quick, decisive victories turned on the Western Front into a bogged-down matter of digging trenches for protection, exchanges of yards or meters: deadly stalemate!

INNOVATIONS FOR WARFARE

The war led to some desperate and creative plans. The medieval use of mining under an enemy position (as in fortressed castles) was made use of by both sides in World War I. One important, major, protracted mining project took almost two years of preparatory digging under a stable German position on the heights near Ypres, in Western Flanders, Belgium. This high position, the Messines (in Flemish, the Mesen) Ridge, gave the Germans a commanding position and excellent visible intelligence on enemy activities. It was located south of the town of

---

[233] "Prof. Gerd Krumeich: Verdun—Attrition Warfare and Site of Remembrance," GOETHE INSTITUTE.

[234] Alfons Heck, *The Burden of Hitler's Legacy* (1988), p. 221.

[235] "10 Significant Battles of the First World War," IMPERIAL WAR MUSEUM, Jan. 3, 2018; Alexander Collin, "15 Bloodiest Battles of World War One by Casualty Figures," MADE FROM HISTORY, JAN. 30, 2015; "World War One—Statistics," FLANDERS FIELD MUSIC; "The First Battle of the Marne," ENCYCLOPÆDIA BRITANNICA; "World War One Great Stories: First Battle of the Aisne," WORLD WAR 1; "Battle of the Aisne," BRITISH BATTLES; "First Battle of the Aisne: Sept. 13, 1914 to Sept. 28, 1914," WORLD HISTORY PROJECT; "The First Battle of the Aisne, 13-28 September 1914," BRITISH POLITICAL HISTORY; "Battle of Amiens," ENCYCLOPÆDIA BRITANNICA. See also *Tunnel Warfare* (2012), NOVA-WGBH, largely on the Battle of Massines, but also on Passchendaele, at 48:50-49:20.

The Hitler Era 73

Ypres—in Flemish, Ypern (called Wipers by British troops)—between the towns south of Ypres, Wijtschaete and Ploegsteert (called Whitesheet and Plugstreet by British troops), in the Ypres Salient.[236] These mines—19 in number, some containing as much as 30,000 pounds (over 13.6 metric tons) of ammonal, and using in all a million tons of these high explosives, creating many huge craters visible today (the largest of which is the Spanbroekmolen Mine Crater, now called the Pool of Peace)—were all exploded in a matter of some 20 seconds, in an orderly sequence according to their position, starting at 3:10 am on June 7, 1917. Thus, each group of Germans would see these massive explosions approaching, but have no time to react or to protect themselves. The vibrations from this attack, said to be largest explosion prior to the use of the atomic bomb, could be felt in London. The Battle of Messines Ridge (*die Schlacht bei Messines*, in German) went on for a week. The surviving German army was overrun by Allied forces. Estimates suggest that up to 10,000 Germans were killed, while completely losing this strategic position on the ridge. Soon to follow was the Battle of Passchendaele (the Third Battle of Ypres), which went from July 31 to November 6, 1917.[237] After several months of fighting in rain-soaked land just northeast of Ypres (with the most rain in thirty years), the clay earth was turned into mud and deep pools of water, often quagmires in which men, horses, and mules were trapped and drowned. *With the loss of about one third of a million men,* the Allies ultimately took the town of Passchendaele.[238]

In addition to rapid-fire machine guns and artillery and cannons of great power, in this war there was the introduction of poison gases. All major parties to the war used poison gases, amounting to being war crimes, violating the 1899 Hague Declaration concerning Asphyxiating Gases and also the 1907 Hague Convention on Land Warfare.

The French made the use of tear gas (gaseous eye irritants), in August 1914; the Germans followed in October 1914, at the battle at Neuve Chapelle. These were all of limited power and impact. No one felt these were against the Hague conventions, being neither asphyxiating nor fatal.

---

[236] In military parlance, a salient or bulge is a battle front that projects out beyond a more linear front of confronting armies, connected to its fellow troops on that front, advancing troops, but in a threatened, vulnerable position, with enemy military almost surrounding it. See the term in the Battle of the Bulge (1944-1945).

[237] "Schlacht bei Messines," DE.WIKIPEDIA; "Schlacht bei Messines: Wir warden die Landschaft verandern," DERSTANDARD.AT; "Battle of Messines," ENCYCLOPÆDIA BRITANNICA; "Battle of Messines Ridge, June 1917," IMPERIAL WAR MUSEUM; "Passchendaele," ENCYCLOPÆDIA BRITANNICA; Neil Shea, "This Explosion Was the Biggest Blast Before Atomic Bombs," *National Geographic*, June 6, 2017; "Spanbroekmolen Mine Crater Memorial," THE GREAT WAR 1914-1918. Cf. *Passchendaele* (2008), a Canadian film rendering of the battle, fought largely by Canadian troops representing the British Empire. This film, as the French film, *A Very Long Engagement*, discussed below, also showed the intense rains of that time and the resultant mud and deep ponds in which mules and men drowned.

[238] Tim Cook, "Passchendaele—grit, muck, blood and victory," *The Globe and Mail* (Toronto), Oct. 26, 2017, THEGLOBEANDMAIL.COM.

The use of chlorine gas was also introduced in the war. This attacked the breathing capacities and caused related chest pains, with nausea, coughing, and vomiting, and could kill. The Germans used this weapon beginning in January 1915, against the Russians, and on the Western Front, near Ypres, Belgium, in large quantities, on April 22, 1915. Winds were unfavorable but then shifted, ultimately pushing the gases onto French troops. The British would use chlorine gas at the Battle of Loos (Loos-en-Gohelle, southwest of Lille), September 25-October 8, 1915, but it was ineffective, given the directions the winds took. (*Weather conditions were not favorable to the British military interests.*) The gas was deadly to men, horses, rats, and insects. In late 1915, the French introduced the use of phosgene (or phosgene mixed with chlorine). Some 80-85% of chemical-weapon deaths in World War I were due to phosgene exposure. Germany also began using gases, shifting to mustard gas (or sulphur mustard), actually fine liquid droplets rather than a vapor. Mustard gas was remarkable for the blistering that occurred on the body, often leading to a painful recovery or death, even though it was responsible for only about 5% of the fatalities from gas exposure (some 4,500 mortalities).[239] The Germans had developed and introduced this mustard gas in the Battle of Passchendaele (the Third Battle of Ypres, Belgium), just mentioned, which began on July 31 and ended on November 6, 1917. It was one of the bloodiest battles of the war, *with lowest estimates of British dead being over 250,000 men—other estimates of deaths are Allies: 275,000, and Germans: 220,000*,[240] *in all, up to 700,000 men were killed or wounded.* Some 5 miles of terrain changed hands.[241] Overall in the war, there were more than one million soldiers exposed to one gas or another, with some 90,000 killed directly from that source.[242] The results of this chemical warfare during the war were devastating, with men being blinded (permanently or temporarily, as was Corporal Adolf Hitler, in his mission as a message-carrier at the

---

[239] Lincoln Riddle, "Chemical Weapons Created and Used During the First World War," WAR HISTORY, Jun. 27, 2017.

[240] Tim Cook, "Passchendaele—grit, muck, blood and victory," just cited.

[241] Kenza Bryan, "Passchendaele 100th anniversary: Why was this one of the most brutal battles of the First World War?" *Independent* (UK), Jul. 31, 2017. See both *Passchendaele* (2010), just cited, and films, *All Quiet on the Western Front* (1930 and 1979), dramatizing the novel by Erich Maria Remarque. This book was burned in Berlin on April 10, 1933. Its initial message, in the epigram preceding Chapter one, declared itself: "This book ... will simply try to tell of a generation of men who, even though they may have escaped shells, were destroyed by the war." The Nazis, *wanting to associate this pacifism with a Jewish militaristic pessimism*, claimed that Remarque was Jewish and that his supposed family name, Kramer, spelled backwards yielded Remarque. Actually, his birth certificate (Jun. 22, 1898, Osnabrück) gave his birth name as Erich Paul Remark. Of a German working-class family, he attended the Osnabrück Catholic Teachers' Seminar. Remarque left Germany in 1932, as did 1929 Nobel Laureate Thomas Mann, in early 1933.

[242] "One Hundred Years Ago: First gas attacks in WW1," *CBS News*, Apr. 18, 2015.

Ypres Salient in Belgium, on October 14, 1918), with others asphyxiated, leading to death or to agonized breathing. Others were wounded by artillery and large cannons used during the war—Hitler would later refer to this as *das Stahlgewitter*, the steel thunderstorm—making an implicit reference to Ernst Jünger, *Stahlgewittern* (1920). As Hitler knew, Jünger (a centenarian: 1895-1998) in his writings defined a man with a new mentality, forged in the violence of this endless onslaught of artillery and cannon shells, which killed or deformed many, on all sides of battle.[243]

LES GUEULES CASSÉES, DIE ZERBROCHENE MÜNDER

Those with grave injuries to the face and head were called *les gueules cassées* (broken snouts, mugs, muzzles; *gueules* being French slang for the mouth or face), termed by the British, broken faces, and, in German, *die zerbrochene Münder* (the shattered mouths). Soldiers on both sides of the war in the West were severely disfigured. These provided medical experience and great advances in reconstructive surgery (as, sadly, many wars provide, each challenging the capabilities of the medical world at the time).[244] Films were made for medical professionals showing damage and disfigurement to the faces of soldiers, some supplied with face masks to hide the disfigurements. Artists portrayed these very real results of warfare, rather shocking, although much less so than seeing actual photographs of mutilated faces, with everything from minor destruction of part of a nose, or of one side of the jaw, to more extreme injuries to large parts of the entire face, or to other body parts.[245]

The unbearable trauma of dealing with these injuries was described in "Grodek"—a final poem of ultimately-suicided Austrian poet Georg Trakl (1887-1914) after his experiences treating the wounded at the battle of Gródek (Aug. 23-Sep. 11, 1914) between Austro-Hungarian and Russian forces—that spoke directly, simply, bluntly, of *sterbende Krieger* (dying warriors), *zerbrochene Münder* (shattered mouths), *blutende Häupter* (bleeding heads), and—appreciating the multigenerational implications of warfare—*die ungeborenen Enkel* (the unborn grandchildren).[246] German

---

[243] The book went through a number of editions (1920-1978), with modifications reflecting the changing politics in Germany; Eng. tr., *Storm of Steel* (1929).

[244] Krupp, the steel manufacturer of weaponry, in a contribution to the healing arts of cosmetic surgery, provided steel jaws for such wounded soldiers!

[245] Sophie Delaporte, *Les gueules cassées: Les blessés de la Grande Guerre* (2004); Andréas Becker, *Gueules: Récit* (2015), has photographs from the period and line drawings to give graphic emphasis to the actual injuries; with an essay by Françoise Hoffman (grand-daughter of the man with a mandolin in the photo on p. 122, taken at the Dresden Hospital during his recovery there after having being wounded in 1916). She wrote of these (p. 125), "*Loin de l'horreur, les visages béants et les yeux perdus de ces hommes ont suscité un sentiment de tendresse, mêlé d'un relent de dégoût face à l'absurdité des guerres.*" ("Far from horror, the gaping faces and lost eyes of these men aroused a feeling of tenderness, mixed with the stench of disgust at the absurdity of wars.")

[246] "Grodek: Poem by Georg Trakl," POEMHUNTER.COM; "Grodek," WIKIPEDIA.

artists who presented these consequences of war were later to have their work declared to be degenerate by Hitler, Goebbels, and others in the Third Reich.[247] In contrast with Nazi kitsch,[248] art and literature that faced the violence of war and questioned traditional mores and recognized roles were understood to be dangerous to the regime and its thinking.[249] Here are images of war injuries and an artist finishing the look of a face mask:

Wounded and *gueules cassées* in art & an artist finishing the look of a mask

By these last months of the war, the German side, especially, had less military materiel and dwindling forces. *By the end of the war, there were 3.5 million German troops facing 6.5 million Allied forces.* German soldiers were surrendering; the higher German military knew it could not continue; the German military commanders realized that it could not maintain fighting, had best not refuse to sign the Versailles Treaty, under threat of an invasion of the homeland of Germany by Allied forces that would bring an invasion of Germany the German military could not stop.

The number of young men who died in that war marked the decimation of their populations in Germany, the UK, and France. (The losses to US military in that war were much less percentage-wise and in terms of absolute numbers, given the relatively short time of US involvement.) Some early estimates of the war dead were published in 1919-1920.[250] It is generally appreciated that the counting of the dead after any great cataclysmic event can only be accurate to a certain extent, rarely giving a precise, correct number—but still giving a reasonable range, whatever the actual, precise total number might have been. That said, some thorough studies done[251] in the late 1920s and 1930s determined:

---

[247] The 2017 German TV series, *Babylon Berlin*, could finally show some faces that had been deformed by the war, as in *Season 1, Episode 6*, at 43:50-44:20.

[248] This plays on a contrast of "uplifting" vs. "demeaning" kitsch, in the distinction by Saul Friedländer, "Preface to a Symposium," *Salmagundi*, No. 85/86, 1990, p. 206; for Milan Kundera, *Acceptance Speech for the Jerusalem Prize for Literature* (1985), kitsch is "the translation of the stupidity of received ideas into the language of beauty and feeling ... The *agélastes* (men who do not laugh, who have no sense of humor) and kitsch are one and the same." Cf his *The Art of the Novel* (1988).

[249] As in the varied work of Dix, Remarque, Hemingway, and Klaus Mann.

[250] Early numbers cited a total for all belligerent forces in the War of about 12-13 million dead, and for Germany alone, losses for the Army, 1,728,246, and for the Navy, 24,112. See Karl Binding & Alfred Hoche, *Die Freigabe der Vernichtung Lebensunwerten Lebens* (1920), pp. 27-28.

[251] See texts by demographers Michel Huber (1875-1947), Dir. of the Institut national de la statistique et des études économiques (1920-1936), *La Population*

The Hitler Era 77

> Among *young men not surviving* the Great War (1914-1918), the noble War to End All Wars, were 32.2% of *all* German men aged 21-26 when the war began, 24.5% of *all* Frenchmen 17-20, and 16.2% of *all* British men 23-27! Leaving aside misery and mourning, hunger, famine, and starvation, orphans, widows, mutilated veterans, and momentous epidemics and horrendous genocidal massacres, estimates of *total* war dead range upwards from 8.5 million military & 6.5 million civilians (non-combatants, but still ending up quite dead)—all solemn tributes to the terrifying gravity of war.[252]

The impact of the war's catastrophic losses resulted not only in a more limited labor force in the 1920s in European countries, especially in Britain France, and Germany—Germany being impacted the most—but also made for many fewer marriages, and with that, a significant drop in the population growth for the next decade or two. This would become a major concern in the Third Reich, with an ambitious variety of decrees, programs, and general societal policies to overcome that tragic decline in population, in a rather ambitious variety of ways. Hitler, once in power, was to address this shortage of young men—for peaceful labor and for employment in the military—with the help of Heinrich Himmler. More on that, below. By comparison to the significant losses of young men by the European combatant nations, given the relatively short time that American forces were in actual combat during the First World War, the loss of young American soldiers of draftable age *came to less than 1.2% mortalities of this young population.*[253] This is perhaps not surprising if we remember that the US did not declare war on Germany until April 6, 1917, and it then had to create a significant army before shipping off large number of soldiers to Europe.

The very first American troops (of the American Expeditionary Forces, the AEF) arrived in Europe in June 1917: General Pershing reached France on June 13; by the end of June, there was one American division landed (about 28,000 men), but it would be "trained intensely for the next four

---

de la France pendant la guerre (1931); Rudolf Meerwarth (1883-1946), Dir. of the Institute for Economics & Statistics at the Univ. of Leipzig, *Die Einwirkung des Krieges auf Bevölkerungsbewegung, Einkommen und Lebenshaltung in Deutschland* (1932); Boris Tsezarevich Urlanis (1906-1981), Sr. Researcher in the Inst. of Economics of the Soviet Academy of Sciences, *Wars and Population* (1971).

[252] Mitchell Ginsberg, *Peace and War and Peace*, from epigram at p. 78.

[253] Based on statistics from US Dept. of Veterans Affairs, "America's Wars (Dead and Wounded Military Statistics)." Cf. Nese F. DeBruyne and Anne Leland, "American War and Military Operations Casualties: Lists and Statistics," *US Library of Congress*, Apr. 26, 2017, based on gov't statistics citing 53,402 Americans killed in combat, with 116,516 military deaths during the war *from all causes*, with some 10 million men of draftable age registering at the time.

months" before being battle-ready; in mid-October the doughboys (US military) were in action, but under French supervision; by the beginning of 1918, there were 175,000 US military in Europe.[254] When the British and the French faced the German offensive, *on March 20, 1918, only one division of the AEF was combat ready, and limited to a back-up role.*[255]

The full force of the AEF came into play as an independent unit (not under British or French commanders) only in the Battle of St. Mihiel (south-southwest of Verdun), on September 12, 1918, and then from September 26 to Armistice Day, November 11, in the Battle of the Argonne Forest, the Meuse-Argonne Offensive (west of Verdun).[256] The great potential of American industry was also of limited value to the Allied war effort, given the great lag time between the entry into war in April 1917 (mentioned just above) and the arrival of tons of war materiel only *after the Armistice* in November 1918. Of this, Prime Minister David Lloyd George later wrote of the US role in World War I, that it is "one of the inexplicable paradoxes of history, that the greatest machine-producing nation on earth [the USA] failed to turn out the mechanisms of war after 18 months of sweating and toiling and hustling."[257] *Such limits on US involvement in these ways are at times left aside with a focus on an image of the US coming into a great stalemate and tipping the scales to bring about an Allied victory over Germany and the Central Powers.* German and Allied forces by summer of 1918 had been facing off in a war to test endurance and the willingness of governments to keep sending young men into battle, for four years, with a very high likelihood that many of them would be destroyed for life, if not killed in battle or ultimately dead because of battle wounds and diseases encountered in trench warfare.

The Germans were able to add to their forces at the Western Front half a million soldiers who had been fighting Russia until the Czar was overthrown, abdicating on March 15, 1917. At that point in time, Vladimir Lenin was transported in a sealed German railway car—the Germans having an interest in a new Russian government that could sue for peace,

---

[254] Maj.-Gen. Hunter Liggett, *AEF: Ten Years Ago in France* (1928), pp. 43-58.

[255] Lt.-Gen. Maxwell C. Bailey, *The Amalgamation Controversy, 1917-1918: America's Fight for Independence* (US Air War College, 1988), p. 59.

[256] The first actions into early 1918 of American forces were only in support of British and French in both defensive and attacking operations against the Germans. US General John J. Pershing (and President Wilson) wanted military independence for American troops, but this did not come until sufficient numbers of trained US soldiers had been prepared and shipped to Europe. This military independence started in May 1918. Finally, on Sept. 12, 1918, Pershing led a force of over 500,000 American soldiers into the Battle of St. Mihiel (south-southeast of Verdun)—*recognized as the first American offensive as an independent army.* See Lt.-Gen. Maxwell C. Bailey, *The Amalgamation Controversy, 1917-1918* (just cited), pp. 63, 71-73. Then, from Sept. 26 to Nov. 11 (the day of the Armistice), Pershing led over one million American and French soldiers in the Battle of Meuse-Argonne (Battle of the Argonne Forest), northwest of Verdun.

[257] David Lloyd George, *War Memoirs*, Vol. 2 (1934), p. 1831; cf. Ronald Schaffer, *America in the Great War: The Rise of the War Welfare State* (1991), p. 61.

The Hitler Era

rather than the Czarist regime that was then collapsing—from Switzerland, through Germany, Sweden, and Finland, arriving on April 16, 1917, at Petrograd train station (whose name had been changed from the German-sounding St. Petersburg in 1914, at the start of the war).

It was the new Bolshevik government that surrendered to the Germans, with the signing the Treaty of Brest-Litovsk (in present-day Belarus) on March 3, 1918. This surrender of Russia, now led by Vladimir Lenin, came with severe terms. Russia lost vast territories—including Riga, Lithuania, Livonia, Estonia, some of Belarus, and some of Ukraine—to Germany, and also to Austria-Hungary. A map shows the losses by Russia after the Treaty:

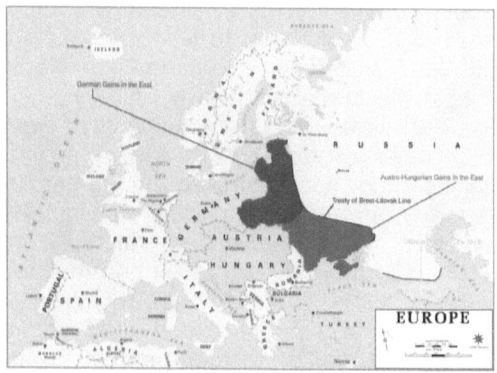

This German victory freed up the German troops on the Eastern Front, now available for quick transfer to the Western Front. At this time, the German was at least on parity with the Allied military. *Here, Ludendorff could have sought peace from a position of strength.* What came to be, for the 1919 Versailles Treaty, had models to inspire it; earlier peace treaties dictated by Germany, most notably, the treaty ending the Franco-Prussian War, with large indemnities in gold demanded of France to be paid to Germany, and the loss of two French provinces, Alsace and Lorraine, and the Treaty of Brest-Litovsk (1918).

The 1919 Versailles Treaty had a degree of harshness that was comparable to the same practice of spoils to the victor of these German-dictated treaties. (This was not typically mentioned by post-World War I German laments or evaluating Versailles 1919 as if this harshness arose in a historical vacuum, or even by other historical recountings.)

Along with the murderous warfare of 1914-1917, the final year of the Great War, 1918, would prove to be quite brutal. The fighting actually became even more intense, with the just-mentioned surrender of Russia.

After the surrender of the fledgling state of Russia, which had just overthrown the Czar, a major German Western offensive in the spring was organized. This offensive began on March 21 under the leadership of General Erich Ludendorff, with an artillery barrage of a million artillery shells being fired on Allied positions, followed by stormtroopers—called *Stoßtruppen* or *Sturmtruppen*—soldiers who carried only their weapons, allowing their movement to be swift and effective.[258] These were men who were ready to go over the top, that is, go over the top of the trenches into no-man's land, controlled by neither army, and recognized as especially dangerous, given the machine gun installations on the other side. Their bravery and readiness to face the ever-present danger of death were later to be taken as a model of the German soldier as a man ready to face the enemy up close, to risk injury and death, undaunted if not thriving on this sort of encounter. Also during World War I, in Italy, a similar group, *gli Arditi* (the Bold Ones, those with ardor for Italy), developed into a group of daring soldiers who saw their role not only to defend the army but also to attack and overcome the enemy.[259]

Keeping up hopes for the German military was the German advance to within 120 km. (75 mi.) of Paris, in what would be the last German offensive of World War I, an offensive that began on March 21, 1918. (The Germans would begin their final withdrawal only by July 18.[260])

At this distance, Paris was within firing distance of Germany's immense howitzers—short-barreled cannons using a high arcing trajectory—the Krupp[261] *dicke Bertha*—known in English as the Big Bertha[262]—whose very name became a synonym for immense artillery power: A Big Bertha, with a barrel length of 10 m. (33 ft) and a diameter of 42 cm (17 in.), could shoot shells 9,300 m. (30,500 ft). With such pummeling of the city (with somewhat limited accuracy), *Paris panicked*. By June 1918, a million or so—one third of the total Parisian population—had fled Paris.

Despite this promising situation, a major and insurmountable problem for the German Army was that *their supplies could not keep up with the advances* of their stormtroopers; thus, armaments and food were not available, and horses were killed for food, slowing down the German advance. This would be a problem to be repeated by the German Army in World War II.[263]

This time also saw the first use of US Marines in battle, alongside British and especially French forces. As part of the German Spring

---

[258] The *Stoßtruppen* of World War I were presented in the 1934 Nazi film, *Stoßtruppen 1917*, YOUTUBE.

[259] Antonio Carioti, "Arditi formidabili in guerra ma ingenui nella lotta politica," *Corriere della Sera*, Jul. 20, 2017.

[260] Maj.-Gen. Hunter Liggett, *AEF* (cited above), p. 78.

[261] Fritz Thyssen, *I Paid Hitler* (1941), pp. 104-105: "The Friedrich Krupp Corporation at Essen has always been Germany's most famous arsenal. As early as the 1860s, when it was still a private firm, it received a subsidy of five million thalers from the Prussian State. All the artillery used by Prussia during the Danish War of 1864, the war with Austria of 1866 and the Franco-Prussian War of 1870-1871, came from the Krupp plants."

[262] The name *dicke Bertha* (known as Big Bertha) means literally fat Bertha.

[263] This also happened briefly for the Allies in Sept. 1944, but this was quickly remedied, given the great manpower and materiel available to the Allies and the significantly weakened German Air Force and Wehrmacht. See Alfons Heck, *A Child of Hitler: Germany in the Days When God Wore a Swastika* (1985), p. 107.

The Hitler Era

Offensive, under General Ludendorff, German military approached Amiens and Paris. They were stopped by combined Allied forces at Château-Thierry at the end of the Aisne defensive operation.

BELLEAU WOOD AND THE US MARINES

The Battle of Belleau Wood (June 6-24, 1918) had great symbolic importance for the US Marines, representing their intense aggressive fighting spirit and ultimate victory over the German forces, which were often seen as threatening Paris. Relatedly, several sources suggest that this brigade of Marines stopped the advance of the German Army and changed the course of the war.[264] One Marine historian of Belleau Wood, Maj. Ralph Bates, Sr., USMC (Ret), wrote of the battle at Belleau Wood, "In its aftermath, the stage was set for an Allied victory in World War I. Indeed, it was the turning point of that war ..."[265] More, questioning this, below. The human cost of these battles was extreme for all involved.

On the first day of battle, there were 1,087 Marine casualties.[266] All told, 904 Marines were gassed,[267] 1,811 Marines and participating US soldiers were killed, with a total of US military injuries of 9,777; while an estimated 8,000 German troops were killed, and 1,000 taken prisoner.[268] The Germans had dug in at Belleau Wood, a relatively small area of 200 acres (0.31 sq. mi., 0.81 sq. km).[269] The US Marines were under the immediate command of the US Army 2nd Division, which, in turn, was under the command of French General Jean Degoutte, commander of the French and American forces. The Marines at this battle were the 4th Marine Brigade, itself made up of the 5th and 6th Marine Regiments and the 6th Marine Machine Gun Battalion, comprising 280 officers and 9,164 enlisted men.[270] As the British and French in earlier years of the war were not yet become familiar with the power of German machine-gun nests that mowed down waves of charging Allied soldiers, so, too, here, the first Marines were similarly åkilled *en masse*. Pershing admitted that he did

---

[264] Staff Sgt. Will Price, "Remembering the Battle of Belleau Wood," *Marine Barracks*, May 28, 2006; Alexander Merrow, Gregory Starace, Agostino von Hassell, "Belleau Wood, From the German perspective," *Marine Corps Gazette*, vol. 92, no. 11, 2008, pp. 43-47; Maj. Ralph Stoney Bates, Sr., USMC (Ret), "Belleau Wood: A brigade's human dynamics," *Marine Corps Gazette*, vol. 99, no. 11, Nov. 2015, pp. 12-19, at p. 12.

[265] Maj. Ralph Stoney Bates, "Belleau Wood" (just cited).

[266] Maj. Ralph Stoney Bates, "Belleau Wood," p. 17.

[267] Mark R. Folse, *The Battle of Belleau Wood, 1-26 June 1918* (Marine Corps History Division, Marine Corps Univ., 2015), pp. 1, 21, 29.

[268] David T. Zabecki, "The US Marines' Mythic Fight at Belleau Wood: Piercing the Fog of War to Separate Legend from Fact," *Military History*, vol. 28., no. 6, 2012, pp. 40-43, 46-49, and Staff Sgt. Will Price, "Remembering the Battle of Belleau Wood" (just cited).

[269] [Author not identified] "Marines in World War I: The Tide Turns At Belleau Wood," *Leatherneck: Magazine of the Marines*, vol. 100, no. 9, Sept. 2017.

[270] David T. Zabecki, "The US Marines' Mythic Fight at Belleau Wood," pp. 40-43, 46-49, and Maj. Ralph Stoney Bates, "Belleau Wood," pp. 14-17.

not appreciate the killing power of German machine guns. (Was there a lack of communication from the Allies, or was their warning not heard?[271]) The shift in the basics of how Marines would fight took place in these several weeks of battle: "On June 6, 1918, the moment they launched their first assault on the dark woodland, the Marines ... entered the industrialized world of massive firepower and wholesale slaughter. Costly mistakes in command, intelligence, and communications reflected their difficult transition."[272]

Finally, by the morning of June 26, 1918, the woods were cleared of Germans except for a few scattered machine guns. In honor of the brigade of Marines at Belleau Wood, on June 30, the French Sixth Army renamed the wood *le Bois de la Brigade de Marine* (the Marine Brigade Wood).[273] The Germans were pushed back, and stopped, at least temporarily, but the total cost for the Marines was high: 9,777 casualties including 1,811 killed. In some cases, there were almost 50% casualties (as for the 2nd Battalion, under Brig.-Gen. James G. Harbord).[274]

We may notice that when there are great losses in warfare, there is a tendency to avoid seeing the large number of deaths in their own right, especially wanting to believe that these men did not "die in vain" but that they gave the "ultimate sacrifice" for the good of their country. Whatever we think of such psychological urges and how they play out in history, here the significant losses of men in the Battle of Belleau Wood defined the courage of Marines for later generations to live up to.

It was also said to have turned the tide of war, stopped the powerful German Army from capturing Paris, changed the balance of power, and brought victory to the Allies over Germany, but this is clearly not an understanding shared by all. The idea that Germany was on its way to taking Paris by military force, in its otherwise irresistible surge of power may make some sense when considering only the immediate period preceding the Battle of Belleau Wood. (More just below.)

In any case, the significance of the Battle of Belleau Wood keeps its importance in US military circles and beyond; on the centenary of the end of World War I, commemorated on November 11, 2018, the US President, Donald J. Trump, cancelled his scheduled visit to the Belleau Wood battle scene and its US cemetery. There were some strong criticisms for this. As

---

[271] Mark Ethan Grotelueschen, *The AEF Way of War: The American Army and Combat in World War I* (2007), p. 31; Frank E. Vandiver, *Pershing and the Anatomy of Leadership* (1963), at pp. 69-87 in the collection, HARMON MEMORIAL LECTURES IN MILITARY HISTORY, 1959-1987 (1988).

[272] Brig. Ben. Edwin H. Simmons, USMC (Ret.), and Col. Joseph H. Alexander, USMC (Ret.), *Through the Wheat: The US Marines in World War I* (2008), p. 100.

[273] Edwin H. Simmons and Joseph H. Alexander, *Through the Wheat*, pp. 119-125, esp. pp. 122-125.

[274] Harbord was Pershing's Chief of Staff. See Dick Camp, *The Devil Dogs at Belleau Wood: US Marines in World War I* (2008), pp. 41, 99, 117-120; George B. Clark, *Devil Dogs: Fighting Marines of World War I* (1999), pp. 62-221.

British MP Nicholas Soames—grandson of Winston Churchill—tweeted of the American losses at that battle and of President Trump's non-visit, "They died with their face to the foe and that pathetic inadequate @realDonaldTrump couldn't even defy the weather to pay his respects to The Fallen #hesnotfittorepresentthisgreatcountry." And another critique added, "Some saw Trump's no-show in Belleau Wood as a sign of disrespect to US soldiers who fought and died in the trenches." In contrast to Trump's cancellation, French President Emmanuel Macron, German Chancellor Angela Merkel, and Canadian Prime Minister Justin Trudeau all visited war memorials that same day, under the rain.[275]

In investigating German military documents from that battle, it is clear that the Germans saw that battle in the context not only of its 1918 Offensive in its various parts, but in the context of the entire war that had been going on for some four years by then. One summary of this by scholars of the war points out that the Battle of Belleau Wood was not that significant for the German overall war effort in 1918. "The difficulties experienced by the German divisions at Belleau Wood betray problems that were systemic throughout the German offensives of 1918. Time and again German divisions advanced, reached their culminating point, stalled, and then could not effectively transition to the defensive. The battle of Belleau Wood was indistinguishable in this regard."[276]

In fact, the Battle of Belleau Wood *took place after the German commanders called off* Operation Blücher (one of the offensives by the German military in 1918 that were all together referred to Operation Ludendorff) *as undoable*.[277] At this time, the German Army needed time to reorganize, set up the logistics of getting food and arms to the military, and time was certainly running out. Furthermore, the entire idea that Germany had as its goal the capturing of Paris (and perhaps with that the surrender of the French) was a misunderstanding of German tactics. From German military papers it is clear that this offensive toward Paris *was actually planned to be diversionary*, to draw Allied troops away from Flanders (which, however, never happened), so that the German Army could push the British (the BEF) out of that territory, to deal then

---

[275] This paragraph is based on the many news sources on this event, esp. Clare Byrne and Francis Curta, "President Under Fire After Canceling WWI Cemetery Visit Due to Weather," *AFP/Agence France Presse*, Nov. 10, 2018, MILITARY.COM, with full quote from British MP Nicholas Soames at Bill Hutchinson, "Trump's rain check on honoring Ametricans killed in WWI prompts backlash," *ABC News*, Nov. 11, 2018, ABCNEWS.GO.COM. Cmp. "Centenary of End of WWI Marked with Paris Ceremony," *Voice of America News*, Nov. 11, 2018, VOANEWS.COM; Ewan Palmer, "Armistice Day: Trump Shuns Trudeau, Gets Thumbs Up from Putin at WWI Memorial Service,"*Newsweek*, Nov. 11, 2018, NEWSWEEK.COM; David Nakamura, Seung Min Kim, James McAuley, "Critics pile on after Trump cancels visit to US military cemetery outside Paris, citing weather," *Washington Post*, Nov. 10, 2018, WASHINGTONPOST.COM.

[276] Alexander Merrow et al., "Belleau Wood" (cited above), p. 46.

[277] Alexander Merrow et al., "Belleau Wood," p. 44.

separately with the French, all before the American Forces (the AEF) could arrive in effective numbers. Despite this, there is still the idea that the ultimate German objective in its recent advance was the capture of Paris, with the conclusion that the Battle of Belleau Wood marked "the closest that they would get to their ultimate objective in this war: Paris."[278]

The overall context here was a number of German military offensives in 1918: Operation Michael (begun March 21), Operation Georgette (begun April 9; a smaller workable variation on what had been named Operation Georg), Ludendorff's Operation Blücher (begun May 27; part of the Third Battle of the Aisne), a short-lived abortive offensive called Operation Gneisenau (begun June 9), Operation Marneschutz-Reims (begun July 15), and, finally Operation Hagen (also called Operation Neu-Georg), which was fully planned but never put into action.[279]

Most relevantly, *Operation Blücher was stopped by the German command on June 5, 1918, the day before the beginning of the Battle of Belleau Wood*. In other words (as mentioned above), the Germans were already shifting from their offensive, which had achieved its tactical goals but not the strategic one of having the British and the French siphon off any of their forces in Flanders to come to the aid of Paris, taken to be under attack. Its position in the Wood was not part of a continuing offensive; it was pushed back, it is generally recognized, and the US Marines showed that they were a formidable force to be reckoned with, but there was already no wind remaining in the sails of the German Army.

Final German Offensives, 1918

Furthermore, in the so-called Ludendorff offensive (of 1918), there were fewer German soldiers in the West than Allied soldiers, even after the transfer of German armies from the Eastern Front, and significantly less war materiel, from machine-guns to artillery, to trucks, and so forth, leading "to the conclusion that the outcomes of battles in 1918 were determined more by material disadvantage than by the actions of men in the field."[280] The four years of trench warfare with horrific losses of men meant a degradation in terms of manpower and the will to fight, for both the German armies and perhaps even more so for the British and French armies; and while the Germans were not impressed by American military tactics, they understood that the lack of experience contributed to their initial questionable approach, despite the American Marines' freshness, vigor, and excellent marksmanship.[281] And so, while a point of honor, not all US military were happy with the special honors given to the US Marines at the Battle of Belleau Wood. US Army troops, for example, claimed that their role, especially at Château-Thierry, had neither been duly reported

---

[278] George B. Clark, *Devil Dogs*, p. 96.
[279] David T. Zabecki, Maj.-Gen., US Army, ret., "The US Marines' Mythic Fight at Belleau Wood," *Military History Magazine*, Mar. 2012, and "Hope is Not a Strategy: Germany's Last Best Shot at Victory," *Military History Quarterly*, Jan. 2015. Both are online at HISTORYNET.COM.
[280] Alexander Merrow et al., "Belleau Wood," p. 45.
[281] Alexander Merrow et al., "Belleau Wood," pp. 46-47.

The Hitler Era 85

nor acknowledged. Later criticism would also include the comment that the US military commanders should have known of the great loss of other Allied combatants in similar, earlier battles of the Western Front, and so should have resisted the French orders to mount an offensive there.

In any case, Ludendorff soon ordered a final major advance, which started on July 15. For German public consumption, this action was termed the *Friedensturm* (The Peace Storm, or the Peace Offensive), with the implications that this offensive was a drive to achieve victory, and with it, peace—that the German military was capable, once again, of surprising the Allied forces, and this time, to strike the death blow to them, having them plead for peace with a victorious Germany. It is perhaps rather doubtful that Ludendorff shared this optimistic confidence, knowing what he did about the massive losses of Germany forces and the difficulty of providing his armies with the materiel they would need to continue fighting, with the diminished numbers of Germans on the Western Front by this time being rather important and significant.[282]

The US Marines and Army in September 1918 were under Pershing—*so were finally fully under American command, as both Pershing and President Wilson had wanted all along*)[283]—and were involved in the important battles of the St. Mihiel Offensive, in mid-September 1918, fighting in coordination with British and French Armies.

The Autumn Offensive, too, was a disaster for the German Army. *In these mere five months of massive military confrontations in 1918, the Germans lost one million men (one-fifth of their remaining Army)!* Their military forces were depleted: war dead of some 1.8 million men, some 4 million wounded.[284]

THE MANY TOLLS OF THE GREAT WAR

Overall in World War I, among the estimates for military casualties (killed and wounded) are these numbers: 9.15 million Russians, 7.14 million Germans, 7.02 million Austro-Hungarians, 6.16 million French, 3.1 million British, 2.20 million Italians, 757,000 British Empire subjects

---

[282] Maj.-Gen. Hunter Liggett, *AEF* (cited above), pp. 90-91.

[283] The reasoning was that an independent US military role would allow for a greater influence that the US could have during the post-war peace conferences. There was also a fear that US servicemen would be used as fodder for the ongoing stagnated trench warfare on the Western Front. The American military, however, was not very well prepared, and the British and French wanted integration (amalgamation) of the various armies. This led to an agreement that was signed in mid-December 1917, stating that "in compliance with the request of Great Britain and France, prompted by the expectation of a strong German offensive, the President [Wilson] agrees to the American forces being, if necessary, amalgamated with the French and British units as small as the company." See Michael S. Neiberg (Prof. of Military History, US Army War College), "Pershing's Decision: How the United States Fought its First Modern Coalition War," ARMY.MIL, Dec. 10, 2010 (quotation in the article's penultimate paragraph); cf. Lt.-Gen. Maxwell C. Bailey, *The Amalgamation Controversy, 1917-1918* (cited above).

[284] Peter Gay, *Weimar Republic: The Outsider as Insider* (1968), p. 147.

(excluding British), 536,000 Romanians, 331,000 Serbians, 323,000 Americans, 267,000 Bulgarians, and 215,000 Canadians.[285]

Furthermore, the influenza pandemic begun in 1918 helped to weaken the German (and other) armies even further. The presence of infectious diseases in the history of warfare is not new; we have seen it through the ages, going back to ancient times. Once again, in this case, it was an ingredient in the weakening of German's military capacity. It was also, perhaps as significantly, widespread in the German civilian population, something hard to deny, but not regularly linked to the vicissitudes of the war.[286] Some of the conditions the soldiers of the Great War encountered were age-old, including inhospitable weather conditions. In the War, these included wet, cold winters, with mud puddles and trenches that were often canals of muddy water, leading not only to feet being exposed to cold, damp, wet conditions but often with a resultant fungal infection of the feet called, in an appropriate way, Trench Foot. There were also vermin, with rats in such a quantity that soldiers would make sport (in a rather macabre way) of hunting rats and hanging them up to display. These rats would carry disease (aside from the Bubonic Plague, which is in a class of its own): the urine of rats, which was present in the wetlands of the trenches and puddles in no-man's land, carried the risk of a bacterial infection, a severe form of leptospirosis called Weil's disease, now treatable with antibiotics, but which then could more readily lead to organ malfunctioning and death. Then, there was an endemic infestation of body lice. These not only fed on the bodies of the soldiers, being very disagreeable in that way, but were also carriers of disease (such as deadly typhus). Lice were also responsible for Trench Fever, which was intensely debilitating and required several months' recovery time. These medical threats were in addition to sexually transmitted diseases that the soldiers may have been infected by and then spread to others.

New sorts of wounds, based on new technological advances in war armaments, military weaponry—not only from the bullets of muskets or rifles (as in earlier times), but now, also from shells from artillery and from cannons—could do massive damage to the bodies of soldiers. These, as in older times, would be wounds that could easily become infected, leading to gangrene and requiring amputation. The fact that these wounds

---

[285] "World War I: Killed, wounded, and missing," ENCYCLOPÆDIA BRITANNICA; "World War I casualties," REPÈRES: PARTENARIAT ÉDUCATIF GRUNDTVIG 2009-2011. To repeat, estimates of such large groups vary depending on sources, system of calculations, and so forth.

[286] Among the civilian population who died from this pandemic—*among literally millions of others!*—were the French poet Guillaume Apollinaire, Austrian artist Gustav Klimt, German philosopher, economist, and sociologist Max Weber, Sophie Freud (Sigmund Freud's daughter and older sister of Anna Freud), and Gwenith Jones (who died in the interwar influenza epidemic of 1928), daughter of English psychoanalyst Ernest Jones. *An ancient truth here is that no family escapes death, as the Buddha pointed out long ago to distraught Kisāgotamī, who at first could not accept the death of her infant boy.* On this story, see *Samyutta Nikāya* 5:3 (at SN.i.129), with Eng. tr. at DHAMMATALKS.ORG/SUTTAS/SN/SN5_3.HTML.

The Hitler Era

were regularly exposed to the dirty water and mud of the trenches led to further infections. *The importance of cleanliness, which was perhaps more carefully respected by the German troops than the Allies, was strongly impressed upon the minds of the German soldiers, including young Corporal Adolf Hitler (and others)*. All of these together made for a reasonable wariness about infections that soldiers who were exposed to those conditions were quite aware of. We might appreciate that what at first can seem a paranoid fear of disease and a compulsive drive for cleanliness and purity found in ex-soldiers after the war is, rather, simply a remembrance of past traumas from the times on the battlefield. *Of importance here is the subsequent attitude of Hitler about purity and the avoidance of vermin, vermin-like beings, and infection.* The linkage of all such concerns with disease and health to an imagined source in world Jewry is a further aspect of Hitler's understanding of such processes.[287]

The ongoing life-threatening everyday life on the Western Front with its trenches and the related stagnant war fronts, hardly moving for much of the several years of the war, led to many soldiers feeling like expendable fodder for a war that they were legally but not morally obliged to fight in. This led to many men trying various ways of getting out of the war, from letting their feet develop Trench Foot (requiring hospitalization) or exposing themselves to cold and threatening conditions, leading to Trench Fever or other illnesses. Still others would inflict wounds on themselves.[288] Another response to these hellish conditions was a growth or intensification in some of a sense of patriotism, a love of one's country, a great vision of sacrifice for the fatherland, and a willingness if not an eagerness to give up one's life for the greatest of causes. This attitude was often matched with an equally intense sense of national identity: "We are but a cog in the great reality of our nation; our role is to support the continuing existence of our nation, even at a cost of our lives."

This firm attitude and serious commitment would be something that Hitler later expected and demanded of his military and, in fact, of all loyal, patriotic German citizens. And that, in turn, led to dire consequences for Germans in 1943-1945. All of these events piled one upon the other

---

[287] On filth and Hitler's fussiness about personal hygiene that approached a cleanliness fetish, see Ian Kershaw, *Hitler: A Biography*, p. 34.

[288] The 2004 French film about World War I, *Un long dimanche de fiançailles* (*A Very Long Engagement*), directed by Jean-Pierre Jeunet and starring Audrey Tautou, showed at length in non-glamorous scenes the dingy, miserable situation French soldiers in the Battle of the Somme endured, with incessant rains and rainwater built up deep in the trenches, with scenes where soldiers intentionally or accidentally inflict minor but incapacitating wounds to themselves in order to be sent back behind the lines for medical treatment.

Depending on the commanding officer, the military alternative could just as well be hospitalization or their arrest and military trial (court martial), as for the five men condemned at the start of this French film, at 2:10-3:00, 3:50-4:15, 5:10-7:00, 9:00-9:20, 11:00-11:50, etc. The so-called Spanish flu (*la grippe espagnole*) is not overlooked in the film, either: It is acknowledged at 22:30-22:40.

certainly made some unusually significant impact on the general psychology of all belligerent nations and of the German people, in particular—not always with the same interpretations or adaptations by those who went through war, all with their particular experiences and contexts, though. Thus, the Great War, World War I—which Professor of History and former US Ambassador to Yugoslavia and the Soviet Union, George F. Kennan, described as "*the* great seminal disaster of this [twentieth] century,"[289] and that has rightly been called a colossal disaster of mutual slaughter.[290]

In retrospect, this Great War of 1914-1918 resulted in total military and civilian deaths for the war estimated at around 18 million; and yet, by comparison, worse was still to come for the unexpecting world, with estimates for World War II military and civilian deaths even greater, put at in the range of 50-60 million,[291] or, in some estimates, more than 55 million dead.[292] In these catastrophes of the Great War, all sides suffered significant deaths of the young men of their society, with many maimed, incapacitated, and disfigured from machine-gun, mortar, cannon fire, and from poison gas,[293] in addition to the psychological traumas that so many men experienced (as did nurses caring for these wounded and mutilated young men), as well as a significant number of deaths in the civilian sector.

It was a time, as one young German Jewish philosopher put it, *when man had become obsolete*, that is, a time when feeling our violence on a human scale, as in our punching or hitting with our fists, was replaced by mowing down tens or hundreds of men with machine guns, or, later,

---

[289] George F. Kennan, *The Decline of Bismarck's European Order: Franco-Russian Relations 1875-1890* (1981), p. 3.

[290] Omer Bartov, *Anatomy of a Genocide: The Life and Death of a Town called Buczacz* (2018); quote from his lecture, Apr. 13, 1997, "Industrial Killing: World War I, The Holocaust, and Representation," MILLERSVILLE UNIV.; Yvonne Chiu, "Conspiring with the Enemy and Cooperating in Warfare: 'Live and Let Live' as a Representative Element in Warfare," *Institute for Advanced Studies, Social Sciences* (2014); Vejas G. Liulevicius, *World War I: The "Great War"* (DVD, 2006) and his text, *The German Myth of the East: 1800 to the Present* (2009).

[291] Comparing the number of people who died as war deaths (soldiers and others directly involved in combat with a military enemy) with those killed in various ideologically-inspired murders, political scientist Rudolph J. Rummel (1932-2014), offering a thorough discussion in *Democide: Nazi Genocide and Mass Murder* (1992), *Table 1.1: Nazi Democide*. His mid-estimate of war deaths was 28,736,000 dead, in addition to genocide, mass murders, euthanasia, and related killings, at 20,946,000 dead. The total here would be 49,682,000 people. *This war killed many more than just the directly engaged military!* Some estimates of total war dead are even higher, as in one total vision of military and civilian dead being put at 64,781,162: see "Bilan de la Seconde Guerre mondiale (en chiffres)," REPERES: PARTINARIAT ÉDUCATIF GRUNDTVIG 2009-2011. In *Lethal Politics: Soviet Genocide and Mass Murder Since 1917* (1990), R. J. Rummel also estimated that in the Stalin era (1929-1953), some 44,451,000 were killed; online at HAWAII.EDU/POWERKILLS.

[292] *13 Minutes* (2015), 1:46-00-1:46-05: more than 55 million killed in WW2.

[293] Discussed above (in sect. "*Les Gueules Cassées, die Zerbrochene Münder*").

The Hitler Era

killing hundreds of thousands with the push of a button that would release an atomic bomb: an unfelt, fantastic intensification of the potential for violence. Human obsolescence here arises from machinery that had significantly surpassed the capacities of mankind, as analyzed by this German Jewish philosopher, husband of Hannah Arendt from 1933-1936, Günther Stein—who later took the name Herr Anders, literally, Mr. Otherwise.[294]

In addition to the physical and psychological impact on those in that technologically overpowering war itself, and on the civilians back home (at that time, redubbed "the home front"), with starvation from lack of food and other deprivations, there were also social changes that were taking place in the context of the war and of the fear of enemy actions that many felt. With this attitude, there was a related, quite intense sense of a nation's need for all its men, at least all able-bodied young men, to join in the military venture.

Those who questioned the sanity or wisdom of war, who spoke out in favor of peace, were looked on quite unfavorably.

In both the USA and the UK, there were laws passed making any speeches that did not support the righteousness of the war effort a crime. The UK on August 8, 1914, in the first month of the war, passed the Defense of the Realm Act (DORA) on August 6, 1914.

Among those who were thus arrested and imprisoned was Bertrand Russell (1872-1970), Nobel Laureate in Literature in 1950. During those war years, Russell, wrote *Principles of Social Reconstruction* (1915), as well as journal articles, declaring (this from one journal's January 1915 issue):

> To begin with the most obvious evil: large numbers of young men, the most courageous and the most physically fit in their respective nations, are killed, bringing great sorrow to their friends, loss to the community, and gain only to themselves. Many others are maimed for life, some go mad, and others become nervous wrecks, mere useless and helpless derelicts. Of those who survive many will be brutalized and morally degraded by the fierce business of killing, which, however much it may be the soldier's duty, must shock and often destroy the more humane instincts. As every truthful record of war shows, *fear and hate let loose the wild beast in a not inconsiderable proportion of combatants, leading to*

---

[294] Anders had studied with Martin Heidegger and written his doctorate in 1923 under the German Jewish phenomenologist, Edmund Husserl. Konrad Paul Liessmann, "Reflexió després d'Auschwitz i Hiroshima: Günther Anders i Hannah Arendt" ("Thought after Auschwitz and Hiroshima: Günther Anders and Hannah Arendt"), *Enrahonar: Quaderns de Filosofia* (Univ. of Barcelona), no. 46, 2011, pp. 123-135; Sal·lus [following Catalan orthography] Herrero, "A propòsit del film sobre Hannah Arendt," *País Valencià, Siglo XXI*, Aug. 25, 2013.

> *strange cruelties*, which must be faced, but not dwelt upon if sanity is to be preserved.[295]

And, in an article of his that appeared in the Spring 1915 issue of *Cambridge Review*, Russell stated further,

> Behind the rulers, in whom pride has destroyed humanity, stand the patient populations, who suffer and die. To them the folly of war and the failure of governments are becoming evident as never before. To their humanity and collective wisdom, we must appeal if civilization is not to perish utterly in suicidal delirium.[296]

Russell would later state that he was against the Great War (but not against World War II), and that if there had been no World War I, there would not have been the Communists, the Nazis, nor World War II (the many deaths among the Czarist armies leading to the overthrow of the Czar; the harsh conditions at Versailles, a step toward the Nazi reign).[297]

Similarly, the United States passed the US Espionage Act, June 15, 1917 and the Sedition Act, May 16, 1918. A target of this patriotic pro-law attitude was labor advocate and Socialist Party candidate for the US Presidency five times, Eugene V. Debs (1855-1926), prosecuted for his anti-war speeches, such as his speech in June 1918:

> They have always taught and trained you to believe it to be your patriotic duty to go to war and to have yourselves slaughtered at their command. But in all the history of the world you, the people, have never had a voice in declaring war, and strange as it certainly appears, no war by any nation in any age has ever been declared by the people.[298]

A number of those speaking out in the US against the war were arrested, and many who were not yet US citizens were deported, including Lithuanian-born Emma Goldman (1969-1940). An anarchist political philosopher, deeply inspired by the Haymarket Massacre or Riot of May 4, 1886,[299] she had to return to Czarist Russia. She criticized Soviet life, and saw Socialists and Anarchists who joined the Soviet Communists[300] as abandoning the anarchists and socialists brutalized by Stalin.

---

[295] Bertrand Russell, "The Ethics of War," *The International Journal of Ethics*, vol. 25, no 2, Jan. 1915, pp. 127-142, at pp. 130-131. Italics added.

[296] Bertrand Russell, "Can England and Germany Be Reconciled after the War?" *The Cambridge Review*, vol. 36, Feb. 10, 1915, pp. 185-186, at p. 186.

[297] *A Conversation with Bertrand Russell* (1952), 10:30-11:10, YOUTUBE.

[298] Eugene V. Debs, "Canton, Ohio" (Speech by Debs, Jun. 16, 1918), ZINN EDUCATION PROJECT.

[299] Ernest W. Puttkammer (Prof. of Law Emeritus, Univ. of Chicago), "[Book Review of] *The [Chicago] Haymarket Riot*, by Ernest Bloomfield Zeisler," *The University of Chicago Law Review*, vol. 24, no. 2, Winter 1957, pp. 390-391.

[300] On anarchism (and esp. anarcho-syndicalism), see Rudolf Rocker, *Anarcho-syndicalism: Theory and Practice: An Introduction to a Subject Which the Spanish War Has Brought into Overwhelming Prominence* (1938).

7. Turkey, After the Great War, and the 1920s

We can see the Great War as an over-riding, if not *the* fundamental and principal context of European post-war attitudes toward war, with a great reluctance by Britain and France to consider war again, and Germany longing for sweet revenge and a re-establishing of its national honor, not deterred by the fact that it had actually lost more young men percentage-wise than even Britain or France. Here, furious rageful revenge trumped mourning. (In the same post-war years, the USA, on its part, returned to its isolationist stance toward European affairs.)

The Great War was not only fought on the Western Front (in Belgium and France), even though that has received perhaps the most recognition, especially in Western European and American consciousness. The Eastern Front brought about the demise both of Czarist Russia and an independent treaty between Germany and Russia, with no inclusion of Russia's Allies. This treaty, the Treaty of Brest-Litovsk, signed on March 3, 1918, freed up German troops for a final offensive on the Western Front, with its own consequences. This led to great confusion, with a wide array of political proposals for how to go on. Even though this Eastern war was over, peace did not find its place. Even before the Armistice of November 11, 1918, there was a Germany Navy mutiny at the Kiel Naval Base, on October 18, 1918. And on November 7, 1918, German Communists declared the Bavarian Soviet Republic. These civil conflicts made their place, leaving Europe unstable. This would continue into the 1920s and even the 1930s, in the shifting politics of a number of countries.

There were other issues to address, as well. For example, with the Ottoman Empire joining on the side of the Central Powers (Germany and Austria-Hungary), there were battles both in what is now Turkey and also in the Middle East, especially from Egypt through Mesopotamia (Iraq and Persia, now called Iran), the first for control of the Suez Canal, an international waterway vital to the free movement of British and other nations' ships. The Ottoman Empire, with help of German battleships, were able to maintain control of the Dardanelles (the passageway between the Black Sea and the Mediterranean)—thus blocking Russian access to the latter. British attempts to invade the Turkish lands, such as the Battle of Gallipoli (at the peninsula at the southern end of the Dardanelle Straits), which lasted from February 17, 1915 until January 9, 1916, were unsuccessful (for the British, that is).

Still, the general alarm within the Ottoman Empire from this invasion by a military enemy, from the south, with the Czarist Army to the north, contributed in part to the Ottoman worry about its citizens who were not Turkish, of which there were between 30-40% at the turn of the twentieth century: a portion of the population that was not Muslim but Catholic, Eastern Orthodox, Protestant, Greek Orthodox, Jewish, among others.[301]

---

[301] *Soghomon Tehlirian: La vengeance des Arméniens*, YOUTUBE, with comments by historian Claire Mouradian of the CNRS (the highly respected French *Centre national de la recherche scientifique*), at 4:38-5:02.

The earlier overthrow of the sultan by the Young Turks in 1909 and the establishment of a constitutional government, was begun on the French principles of liberty, equality, and brotherhood among all citizens, but internal disaccord in 1911-1913 turned the government toward a Turkish-centered nationalist vision, excluding all those who were not Turkish Muslims. The Empire had earlier lost most of the Balkans[302] in the Balkan Wars of 1912-1913 ("prelude to World War I"[303]), with Serbia calling for a pan-Slavic union, a threat to the Austria-Hungary.

Armenians had begun to emigrate in the years before the war; by 1915, those who were Armenian were especially worrisome to the Ottoman Empire, since they had family and cultural links to the Armenians of Czarist Russia—compare current-day Turkish worries about Kurds in Turkey, Syria, and Iraq. This led, first, to arrests of Armenian intellectuals, beginning on April 24, 1915, based on a decree of that date by the Ottoman Interior Minister, Talaat (or Talât) Pasha. To support and formalize these actions, the parliament passed a law days later, on May 27, 1915, the Tehcir Law (the Law on Forced Deportation).

We can repeatedly see this discomfort if not repulsion when one group experiences another group in its presence. The tendency to want to keep other groups away is perhaps rather primordial. *In times of great stress (as in wartime) there can be a limited amount of energy to devote to this effort; it can become a matter of ease and expediency to go from isolation of unwanted strangers (culturally speaking) to eliminating them in their entirety.* There was this evolution of practice in the Ottoman Empire, and we will see it again in National Socialist Germany, especially in relation to the Jews, Romanies, and other intensely hated groups. We see it as well in many other countries, at various periods in their history and changing conditions, even to this day. So, the process is not that rare.

In the following period, 1915-1916, somewhere between one and perhaps two million Armenians (statistics vary) were either killed outright, experienced fatal forced walks, largely from Anatolia, their homeland, to the south, toward the Syrian desert. They were told that there would camps for them there (a transfer to the south, we could say), but there were no such camps.

---

[302] The Ottoman Empire lost almost 75% of its European territories in October 1912 to a military coalition of the Serbs, Bulgarians, Greeks, and Montenegrans. Turkish-German historian Taner Akçam noted that the Young Turks saw Anatolia, with its large Christian-Armenian populations, as the next Ottoman territory to be lost by the Empire, with the Empire becoming more Muslim in the process. Many Turks fled from the Balkans to Asia Minor (Asian Turkey), remembered today by their descendents. See the video *Soghomon Tehlirian* (just cited), at 15:30-16:20.

[303] A phrasing that links the Balkan Wars to World War I was used in the title of my youthful World History essay, "The Balkan Wars of 1912-1913: Prelude to World War I" (1959). The Russian demographer Boris Urlanis (quoted in another context) estimated that in these two Balkan Wars that there were 122,000 killed in action, 20,000 dead of wounds, and 82,000 dead of disease. See Boris Urlanis, *Wars and Population* (1971).

The Hitler Era

The Allies knew of the mass killing of Armenians. US Ambassador to the Ottoman Empire until 1917, Henry Morgenthau, reported back through diplomatic channels about this violence. An American diplomat stationed in Turkey at the same time, Leslie A. David, was eyewitness to a number of killings of Armenians. The Swedish Ambassador to Turkey during the war, Per Gustaf August Cosswa Anckarsvärd, sent reports back to the Swedish Foreign Office in Stockholm on the extermination of the Armenians.[304]

In a more central and potentially more influential position was the German military in Turkey, the two countries being allies in the War. These German officers also saw these massacres, and did nothing to stop these murders of civilians, appreciating the strategic importance of keeping good relations with their allies in the Great War and with an eye to a future German colonial presence in the Middle East (part of Kaiser Wilhelm II's standing interest in creating a German colonial empire to rival those of France, Britain, and Czarist Russia).[305]

This, of course, raises many questions of responsibility of influential bystanders allowing such extensive violence, and of the responsibility of those who carried out the killings themselves. These are both moral and legal questions and apply not only to Germans and Turks.

The British and other Allies responded otherwise. A telegram dated May 29, 1915, from William Jennings Bryan at the Department of State in Washington, DC, to the American Embassy in Constantinople relayed the French position[306] on the killing of Armenians in Turkey by the Kurds and Turks. Bryan wrote of "crimes against humanity and civilization"—using the term "crimes against humanity" long before the Nuremberg Trials that began in late 1945:

> French Foreign Office requests following notice be given Turkish Government. Quote. May 24th. For about a month the Kurd and Turkish populations of Armenia has *(sic)* been massacring Armenians with the connivance and often assistance of Ottoman authorities. Such massacres took place in middle April (new style) at Erzerum, Dertchun, Eguine, Akn [or Eğin], Bitlis, Mush, Sassun, Zeitun, and throughout Cilicia. Inhabitants of about one hundred villages near Van were all murdered. In that city Armenian quarter is besieged by Kurds. At the same time in Constantinople Ottoman Government ill-treats inoffensive Armenian population. In view of those new *crimes of Turkey against humanity and civilization*, the Allied governments announce publicly to the Sublime-

---

[304] "Eyewitnesses: Diplomats and Military," GENOCIDE1915.ORG.
[305] Discussions by historians Raymond Kévorkian and Tessa Hofmann, in the film *Soghomon Tehlirian*, at 37;28-37:52 and 37:53-39:10, resp.
[306] The French request was dated May 24, 1915.

Porte [the central government of the Ottoman Empire] that they will hold personally responsible [for] these crimes all members of the Ottoman government and those of their agents who are implicated in such massacres. Unquote.[307]

In the following months, in late September 1915, the Associated Press published a letter from Lord Bryce (a British jurist, historian, and politician) to Mr. Aneurin William, MP, in which he stated, "Soon after the war between Turkey and the Allies broke out, the Turkish Government formed, and has ever since been carrying out with relentless cruelty, the plan of extirpating Christianity by killing off the Christians of Armenian race. The massacres of this year have, however, gone far beyond even those of 1895-1896. Over the whole of Eastern and Northern Asia Minor and Armenia the whole Christian population is being deliberately exterminated. In Trebizond, a city where the Armenians, numbering more than 10,000, had dwelt in peace with their Moslem neighbours, orders came from Constantinople to seize all the Armenians. The troops hunted them all out, drove them to the shore, placed them in sailing boats, took them out to sea, threw them overboard, and drowned them all, men, women, and children." *This sort of outrage was apparently lost in the context of millions of people, each seeing in their enemy a despicable, brutal, heartless creature not worthy of sympathy or compassion, with millions being killed on many military fronts, people numbed to brutality, maiming, and killing.*

Several years later, writing again of "crimes against humanity," British Solicitor General Sir Ernest Pollock wrote to Arthur James Balfour (earlier British PM, and Foreign Secretary during the War) on February 8, 1919, with an eye to fellow Allied jurists, addressing the significant question of how to prosecute those responsible for "crimes against humanity" that were committed primarily against minority Christians in the Ottoman Empire during the just-ended War, remarked, "I think that a British Empire war tribunal should do it."[308]

These early examples of explicit use of the concept of crimes against humanity—such as from Jennings Bryan and then British Solicitor General Sir Ernest Pollock (just quoted, from May 1915 and February 1919)—clearly predate the use of the term in the 1940s. This history clearly shows the earlier use.

---

[307] "France, Great Britain and Russia Joint Declaration," ARMENIAN NATIONAL INSTITUTE, with link to a fascimile image of the actual telegram, May 29, 1915 (with its ungrammatical "has"). *La Sublime Porte* is a French rendering of Babıali (Bāb-ı Ālī), the Great Gate, entrance to the Ottoman governmental offices. Italics added.

[308] British Solicitor General Sir Ernest Pollock to A. J. Balfour, February 8, 1919, *Bodleian Special Collections, Oxford, Hanworth Papers, 1802–1938, MS. Eng. Hist. c. 943*. Cf. Michelle Tusan, "'Crimes against Humanity': Human Rights, the British Empire, and the Origins of the Response to the Armenian Genocide," *The American Historical Review*, vol. 119, no. 1, Feb. 2014, pp. 47-77.

The Hitler Era

As was said even earlier, addressing some of the roots of such violence, "hatred gives birth to hatred, and here ... hatred not only poisons, but also stupefies; therefore, guard your communities from being stupefied through hatred."[309] This pre-war insight from 1902 Berlin was obviously lost on the belligerent societies. Hatred can endure even in the face of repeated comments about its violent manifestations and the hurt it can cause. As Alfons Heck wrote, "Hatred, I have learned, is bound neither by logic nor reason.... unrelieved hatred is self-destructive."[310] The same is true of rage, a violent manifestation of hatred, of course.

TALAAT PASHA AND THE TRIAL OF SOGHOMON TEHLIRIAN

Before the end of the war, there was the threat (or talk) of judgment and retaliation against those responsible for the killing of the Armenians, and, explicitly, crimes against humanity, as just given in examples. The demands for justice and bringing those responsible for these mass killings, however, did not have much traction.

The three Pashas, as they were called—Talaat Pasha, Prime Minister and Minister of the Interior; Enver Pasha, Minister of War; and, Jemal Pasha, Minister of the Navy (the three being the joint rulers of the Empire during the war)—had all fled from Turkey in early November 1918. Germany refused to institute any extradition processes. Armenians who were not satisfied with this outcome set about in a very carefully secretive plan, Operation Nemesis, to bring these men to justice, to pay for their role in the mass killings of Turkish Armenians. In this operation, Talaat (or Talât) Pasha was killed in Berlin on March 15, 1921, by Soghomon Tehlirian (1897-1960).[311] Jemal Pasha was killed on July 21, 1922, by Stepan Dzaghigian, Artashes Gevorgyan, and Petros Ter Poghosyan, in Tiflis. Enver Pasha, who had fled to Germany with the other two Pashas, soon involved himself with the Soviet government, only to side with Tajiks against the USSR; he was killed by the Soviet military, in August 1922.

Attending the brief trial of Soghomon Tehlirian (June 2-3, 1921) were Max Erwin von Scheubner-Richter, former German Consul in Erzurum (Ottoman Empire) who would later march arms interlocked with Hitler in the march on to the *Bürgerbräukeller* (the Bürgerbräu Cellar or Hall), on

---

[309] Nobel Laureate in Literature (1905) Henryk Sienkiewicz (1846-1916), in a letter dated Sep. 7, 1902, to Karol Rose (1863-1940), publisher of the Berlin Polish-language paper, *Dziennik Berliński*, printed in Berlin Sep. 24, 1902; reprinted in H. Sienkiewicz, *Dzieła: Wydanie zbiorowe, Vol. 53* (1952), pp. 127-134, tr. from text at pp. 129, 131; cf. "The Nobel Prize in Literature, 1905: Henryk Sienkiewicz," NOBELPRIZE.ORG. Quoted in Mitchell Ginsberg, *Peace and War and Peace*, p. 87.

[310] Alfons Heck, *The Burden of Hitler's Legacy*, pp. 219, 233.

[311] Talaat Pasha escaped from Turkey at the end of the war, and lived in Berlin. He was tracked down by Armenians and was killed in Berlin; his assassin, Soghomon Tehlirian, was tried in a German court and judged not guilty. The governments of the world did nothing in particular about the massacres, a lapse in persistent interest that Hitler remarked about, suggesting that the Jews, too, would not be remembered, and no justice or vengeance would be sought.

Rosenheimerstraße in Munich, on November 9, 1923—being shot and killed, pulling Hitler down with him and causing a dislocation of Hitler's right shoulder. Earlier, Hitler attended the two-day June 1921 Tehlirian Trial in Berlin, as did Von Scheubner-Richter, and, separately, a young attorney, Robert Kempner (decades later to be on the American prosecutorial team at the Nuremberg Tribunal after World War II).

Hitler, as became clear later, took the lesson to heart that one could go about the rather methodical work of killing off an entire people during a war context, lose that war (as did the Ottoman Empire), and still not be brought to task for the mass murders that had been carried out. Not one Turkish leader, after all, was executed by any government for his role in bringing about the Armenian massacres.[312]

Furthermore, there was no condemnation, no outpouring of outrage or of moral indignation, either from the overall population and press, or from any of the churches[313] within Eastern Orthodox Christianity,[314] even though Armenian acceptance of Christianity dates back to about 300 CE. *Indifference, here, too, did not extend only to the Jewish plight.*

Through the past century or more, in Turkey, there is still a firm denial that there was a planned genocide of the Armenians.[315] (There may be financial considerations here, in that the current Turkish government might then consider itself responsible for reparations if it admitted that the Ottoman Empire did in fact carry out a systematic killing of Armenians.) And yet, there was evidence presented at a Martial (military) court in the Empire, presided over by Lieutenant-General Mustafa Nazim Pasha, President of the Tribunal, in which it was stated, "Ihsan Bey, Director of the Special Office of the Interior Ministry, confirms that Abulahad Nuri Bey, Kaymakam [the District Governor] of Kili [a border town at the meeting of the Anatolian plateau and the Syrian plains, north of Aleppo, Syria, and west of the Euphrates], who had been sent from Istanbul to take office in Aleppo, had announced that: "The main reason for the deportations is annihilation"; and added that he had been in touch with Talat Bey [that is, Talaat or Talât Pasha][316] regarding this matter, and *that he had received direct orders for the massacres from him* [from Talât Pasha], and that he (Talat) had persuaded him that this was the only way for the salvation of the country."[317]

---

[312] Stefan Ihrig, *Justifying Genocide*, pp. 261-262, 335-336, 351-356.

[313] Stefan Ihrig, *Justifying Genocide*, pp. 353-354.

[314] "Armenian Apostolic Church," ENCYCLOPÆDIA BRITANNICA.

[315] For an overview, see Turkish-German historian Taner Akçam, "The Ottoman Documents and the Genocidal Policies of the Committee for Union and Progress (*İttihat ve Terakki*) toward the Armenians in 1915," *Genocide Studies and Prevention: An International Journal*, vol. 1, no. 2, 2006, pp. 127-148. This short name, *İttihat ve Terakki* (Union and Progress), in full was *İttihat ve Terakki Cemiyeti* (the Committee for Union and Progress).

[316] "Talat Paşa," VİKİPEDİ or ÖZGÜR ANSİKLOPEDİ.

[317] "The Turkish Military Tribunal," AXIS HISTORY FORUM. This presents the verbatim transcripts of the Turkish Military Tribunal Trial (April 27, 1919), in

The Hitler Era

Elsewhere in the war in the remainder of the Ottoman Empire, the British ultimately gained control of the Suez Canal and there was also the defeat of the Ottoman Empire in Arabia, and in Iraq and Iran (and their oil fields). During the war there was also the issuance of what we know as the Balfour Declaration, written by British Foreign Secretary Arthur James Balfour on November 2, 1917. This echoed the letter by Col. Charles Henry Churchill—cousin of Winston Churchill's father—dated June 14, 1841 to Moses Montefiore, with a strong encouraging of the settlement of Jews in Palestine (later, Israel).[318]

While expressing support for the Jewish interest in a return to Eretz Yisrael (the Land of Israel), Balfour's Declaration was intentionally vague. It said, "His Majesty's government view with favour the establishment in Palestine of a national home for the Jewish people, and will use their best endeavours to facilitate the achievement of this object, it being clearly understood that nothing shall be done which may prejudice the civil and religious rights of existing non-Jewish communities in Palestine, or the rights and political status enjoyed by Jews in any other country." It did not talk of a national state (but "a national home") and it expressly underwrote the undiminished "civil and religious rights of existing non-Jewish communities in Palestine"—*Palestine*, we may well note, *in that time and context was understood to include what is now Israel, the Palestinian territories, and the Hashemite Kingdom of Jordan (earlier Trans-Jordan), as well*.[319] While this would be secondary to the situation in the West, especially for Germany, it certainly would have ramifications of major significance: At the end of the Great War, the Ottoman Empire was dissembled, with Turkey limited in its territories, with new countries and mandate areas from Lebanon, Syria, Iraq, Iran, greater Palestine (as just defined), and Egypt, in addition to the new Maghreb countries along the southern banks of the Mediterranean, also former Ottoman lands. At the Paris Peace Conference, Emir Feisal[320] (1885-1933, a key leader in the fight against the Ottoman Turks, and later King of Iraq, 1921-1933) would write of his approval on March 3, 1919, of the British plan for greater Palestine—not all Arab powers at the time were in agreement—to

---

Takvimi Vekâyi (lit. Calendar of Chronicles), Apr. 29, 1919, no. 3540. For an overview of the Gazette's history, see "Takvim-i Vekayi (The Ottoman Official *Gazette),"* IRCICA.ORG. Italics added.

[318] Barbara W. Tuchman, *Bible and Sword: England and Palestine from the Bronze Age to Balfour* (1956), p. 179.

[319] Martin Gilbert, *Atlas of Jewish History* (1976), p. 96: map entitled "Britain and the Jewish National Home: Pledges and Border Changes, 1917-1923."

[320] "Fayṣal I: King of Iraq," ENCYCLOPÆDIA BRITANNICA. Also, Faysal or Feisal. Faisal wrote from Paris, from the *Délégation hedjazienne* (the Hejaz Delegation, referring to the Hejaz, current western Saudi Arabia). Faisal was a close war companion of T. E. Lawrence (Lawrence of Arabia). See silent film from the desert to Paris, *Video of Lawrence in Arabia and Prince Faisal: The Arab Revolt*, YOUTUBE, and, of course, T. E. Lawrence, *Seven Pillars of Wisdom: A Triumph* (private printing, 1926; first publication for public sale, 1935).

Felix Frankfurter[321] (representing the Zionist Organization to the Paris Peace Negotiations). Feisal wrote:

> We feel that the Arabs and the Jews are cousins in race, having suffered similar oppressions at the hands of powers stronger than themselves, and by a happy coincidence, have been able to take the first step towards the attainment of their national ideals together. We Arabs, especially the educated among us, look with the deepest sympathy on the Zionist movement. Our deputation here in Paris is fully acquainted with the proposals submitted yesterday by the Zionist Organization to the Peace Conference, and we regard them as moderate and proper. We will do our best, in so far as we are concerned, to help them through: we will wish the Jews a most hearty welcome home. With the chiefs of your movement, especially with Dr. Weizmann, we have had and continue to have the closest relations. He has been a great helper of our cause, and I hope the Arabs may soon be in the position to make the Jews some return for their kindness. We are working together for a reformed and revived Near East, and our two movements complete one another. The Jewish movement is national and not imperialist. Our movement is national and not imperialist, and there is room in [Greater] Syria for us both. I think that neither can be a success without the other."[322]

Many in Germany saw the agreement to the Armistice (the end of fighting), the surrender of the German forces, in late 1918, and the peace treaty to follow the next year, *all as unwarranted*, as a "stabbing in the back" of valiant Germany soldiers by weak politicians or disloyal Jews. (This term and idea were introduced, above.)

A simple view of German opinion might suggest that there were those who wanted simply to go on with life, making use of the new Constitution and the new Weimar Republic, and others who wanted to avenge the criminal traitors within the country and to build a military that foreign powers could not push around. Among those who were dissatisfied with the new situation and the newly established Weimar Republic, were Communists who wanted to set up a Soviet-style government in Germany; there were also those who desired a reestablishment of the Reich and reinstatement of Emperor Wilhelm II (who had been granted asylum in The Netherlands at the end of the war, where he lived out his life), as well as those who envisioned a military-led society, those who envisioned a society that would give recognition to the German people

---

[321] "Felix Frankfurter: United States Jurist," ENCYCLOPÆDIA BRITANNICA. Frankfurter was born in Vienna; his family moving to New York City in 1893.

[322] *The Israel-Arab Reader: A Documentary History of the Middle East Conflict*, Walter Laqueur and Dan Schueftan, eds. (1969; 8th ed., 2016), pp. 19-20.

The Hitler Era

(*das deutsche Volk*) with power centralized but not with a return of the Emperor and not one run by a military clique. We might see among this last group the political party that came to be known as the National Socialist German Workers Party (*die Nationalsozialistische Deutsche Arbeiterpartei*, the NSDAP)—in short, the Nazi Party. A number of these groups were united in their revulsion at the Weimar Republic, but what each saw as the solution to this problem was quite different from the vision of each of the other groups. *In a confrontive yet ultimately cooperative, synergistic way—certainly not by plan or agreement—the violence from these conflicting groups that Germany would see in the next years, 1919-1933, would all serve to weaken the power and the authority of the Weimar government and its police. It was not long to survive.*

The Treaty of Versailles at the end of World War I was largely seen in Germany as punitive, harsh, and beyond German's capacity to fulfill. In particular, immediately after the Armistice, German troops were required to pull back from Belgian and French territory, and from the lands of western-most pre-war Germany. The four nations (France, Belgium, the UK, and the USA) brought in troops to the Rhineland in December 1918, authorized by treaty for 15 years.

Shortly thereafter, there were the general strike and street violence of the January 1919 *Spartakusaufstand* (the Spartacus Uprising), with some 50,000 men led by Communists Karl Leibknecht (son of a close friend of Karl Marx) and Rosa Luxemburg (Polish-born, one of the few to be against the war from the very beginnings in 1914),[323] lasting from January 4-15, 1919. Then, the Treaty of Versailles came into effect on March 10, 1920. Shortly afterwards, on March 13, 1920, was the Kapp-Lüttwitz Coup, led by Wolfgang Kapp and Walther von Lüttwitz: this time, a right-wing attempt to overthrow the Weimar Republic, with the support of General Ludendorff.[324] It too, was unsuccessful.

At the same time, the Spartacists (Communists, responding to the Kapp Coup, with a general strike involving tens of thousands of workers—miners and others) had a short-lived control of the Ruhr, in the *Ruhraufstand* (Ruhr Uprising), with some 50,000 men in their military.

---

[323] Otis C. Mitchell, *Hitler's Stormtroopers and the Attack on the German Republic, 1919-1933* (2008), pp. 15-16.
[324] "Kapp Putsch: German History," ENCYCLOPÆDIA BRITANNICA.

This was ended in early April, with the Weimar army and then the French occupation army going into action, occupying Western German cities such as Frankfurt and Darmstadt, on April 6, 1920. New Zealand troops left by March 1919; most British left the Rhineland in 1926, totally withdrawing in 1930; American forces completed their withdrawal in January, 1923; staying on were the Belgian and the French. The latter, perhaps some 25,000 strong, were mostly from French colonies—with related German nationalist talk of the *schwarze Schande*, The Black Shame, African troops reputed to have raped many German women.

This post-war period was certainly a time of the violent left and the violent right (politically speaking) taking turns keeping German society in turmoil and armed conflict. (We may think here of Mercurio's curse on the Montague and Capulet families, "A plague o' both your houses!"[325])

THE DISSOLUTION OF EMPIRES AND THE FLOURISHING OF NATIONALISMS

Going into the Great War, Europe consisted of some very large and expansive empires, especially the two large Empires in *Mitteleuropa* (Middle Europe): the German Empire (Reich), ruled by members of the Hohenzollern Dynasty, especially its Roman Catholic Branch,[326] and the Austro-Hungarian Empire, ruled by members of the Habsburg Dynasty.[327]

Given the migrations through the centuries and the significant number of subsequent marriages between people of different cultural, linguistic, and religious backgrounds, there were many people who did not fit neatly and completely into any one cultural group. *Relatedly, Hitler in some candid moments would acknowledge that there was no one in Europe who was purely, totally, of one given nation (or "race")*. Thus: "A people in the current political sense has ceased to be a racial unit, a racially pure community."[328] More on this, below.

In addition, there were also large numbers of peoples from different groups who lived together in larger social units (population centers, regions, lands, nations, or empires), each recognizing and interacting with the others, in ways that were tempered by the overriding centrality of the empire or nation in which they lived. Austria-Hungary was especially noted for having among its subjects those of Germanic, Hungarian, Czech, Slovak, Polish, Serbian, Croatian, Ukrainian, Russian, Jewish, Slovenian, and other origins. While there might be tensions between these groups, their tolerance of one another was encouraged, or at least their mutual violence was contained, by the overriding national or imperial unity to which they all belonged.

We may recall the slogans used during the Great War, including "the war to end all wars" and "the war to make the world safe for democracy"

---

[325] William Shakespeare, *Romeo and Juliet* (1597), Act III, Scene 1.
[326] "Hohenzollern Dynasty, " ENCYCLOPÆDIA BRITANNICA.
[327] John Graham Royde-Smith, "Habsburg Dynasty," ENCYCLOPÆDIA BRITANNICA; "Austria-Hungary," WIKIPEDIA.
[328] Otto Wagener, *Hitler aus nächster Nähe: Aufzeichnungen eines Vertrauten 1929–1932*, H. A. Turner, ed. (1978), p. 288; Otto Wegener, *Hitler—Memoirs of a Confidant*, Henry Ashby Turner, Jr., ed., Ruth Hein, tr. (1985), p. 166.

(the former more a British expression, and the latter more an American one). These are what some might call "high-sounding phrases."

And yet, in terms of practical applications (or non-applications) of these ideals, if we look at what actually came out of the war, first was the loss by Germany with its eastern territory of Prussia being separated from the western portion of Germany by access given to the new state of Poland to the Baltic Sea, a region called the Polish Corridor.

This re-creation of Poland had been one of the explicit desiderata from US President Wilson, as announced as the thirteenth of his famous Fourteen Points. (Other nations would find inspiration in this, seeing it as a precedent for asking for their own independent political existence.) To the east of the Corridor and to the west of German Prussia was an independent Free City of Danzig (whose Polish name is Gdańsk).

Furthermore, the breakdown of the central power of Austria-Hungary allowed the rather immediate creation of a number of new nation states, from Czechoslovakia (bringing Czechs and Slovaks into one nation) to Austria, Hungary, to Poland, to what was soon called Yugoslavia (uniting Serbs, Croats, Bosnians, Slovenes, Macedonians, and others).

These were basically de facto changes on the ground, needing only formalization by the Versailles Conference and the resultant treaty. Many other peoples around the world also expected, or at least hoped for, the creation of new nations, including an envisioned independent Armenia, Kurdistan, Ireland, Vietnam, India, and so on. (That was not to be for many decades, and for some, not even today.)

Even considering the new political structure of Europe, the new nations were not in fact culturally homogeneous, that is, in each country there were now (as before and at all times, perhaps) minority groups living and hoping for equal legal rights and possibilities of fulfilling lives. In the new Czechoslovakia, for example, there were over two million people of German descent, who would be called *Volksdeutsche*, Germanic people (especially when in a basically non-Germanic society). There were also Poles and others who lived in the new Czechoslovakia. In a similar way, each new country would have a number of cultural and religious groups, usually one of which had predominance over the others.

Having cultural oneness (a myth in perhaps every single case) was expected by some to be the solution to earlier multi-cultural societies with their inter-cultural tensions. The idea of such a solution continued into the Hitler era, with the National Socialist vision of a culturally pure (that is, unmixed, homogenized, unified) sameness being a central goal. In a first time, this called for the forced emigration of all German Jews, the Definitive Solution to the Jewish Problem, *die endgültige Lösung*, in the legalistic terms of Eugen Dühring (1881) and Wilhelm Stuckart.[329]

We may have noticed that in every society we can think of or imagine, sameness or identical homogeneity of the entire group is, of course, a

---

[329] Eugen Dühring, *Die Judenfrage als Racen-, Sitten- und Culturfrage* (1881), p. 124; Wilhelm Stuckart, legal expert of race law in the Reich Interior Mininistry, a co-author of the 1935 Nuremberg Laws, and attendant at the Wannsee Conference.

merely theoretical ideal, a myth, a delusion: there are differences between individuals and small groups. Even in such a simple social structure as a nuclear family (parents and children), or in a couple, there will be disagreements about what is right or important or what should be done in given situations. Of course, there are historical examples of when peoples of different communities, even different religious communities, could live together in mutual peace, as a contrast to the idea that all "foreign elements" should be expunged, leaving a "racially" (culturally and perhaps religiously) unified group. One example that stands out in the centuries of such a cohabitation in the Iberian Peninsula, when most of it was known as Al-Andalus. In this society, the Moors from North Africa, having arrived in 711, established themselves and their Muslim religion, and, despite conflicts both within Muslims factions and between Muslim and Christian rulers, overall, for centuries of fundamental stability, the Peninsula survived as a multi-cultural, multi-religious land.

This surprising history was recognized by a young US White Supremist and neo-Nazi as he learned of the wider world that had been outside the focus of his group's isolationist and self-righteousness, leading him into the study of history, into medieval Europe, which he felt would be a high ground of White, Christian domination of the continent. This research would give him time to rethink and reject his earlier hatred.[330]

This opening up to new categories of information is in general a direct pathway to a greater understanding and mutual respect. As the American psychiatrist Oliver Spurgeon English (1901-1993) pointed out in another context, "Misunderstandings which arise through wide separation are cleared up on close contact."[331] This is so much more so when we think of large communities or, in an extended way, entire nations. Even in Great Britain, while all its citizens might consider themselves British, they also have various additional identities such as being Welsh, Scottish, Irish, Yorkie (from Yorkshire), Cornish, or Liverpudlian (from Liverpool).

And even in the rather culturally unified land of Japan, there are those who are considered to be Japanese, in addition to Ryukyuan (Okinawan), Yamato, Ainu, as well as Japan's population having Chinese, Filipino, Brazilian, and American roots.[332] These considerations suggest that dealing with others of different opinions, viewpoints, religions, cultural values, and focused interests at any given time, is possibly a matter of subjugating the less powerful to conform with the interests of the more politically influential, *or, alternatively*, of finding some way in which all can find a basic level of security and satisfaction in their lives in their

---

[330] Eli Saslow, *Rising Out of Hatred: The Awakening of a Former White Nationalist* (2018), pp. 198-203. This retells the story of Derek Black, son of Don Black, who was founder of the white nationalist website Stormfront.

[331] Oliver Spurgeon English (1901-1993), "Sex and Human Love," pp. 96-113 in *About the Kinsey Report: Observations by 11 Experts on "Sexual behavior in the Human Male,"* David Porter Geddes and Enid Currie, eds. (1948), at p. 102.

[332] "Ethnic Groups of Japan," WIKIPEDIA.

society. The first way here has been called a zero-sum game (which assumes that there is only a certain amount to be had and so if one has more, someone else in the same process has less); this is a win-lose model. The second way suggests that I can win and you can win at the same time; this relatively new and novel idea has been described as a win-win model.[333] The issue was important during the Hitler era, and almost always considered from only a self-centered point of view (my group shall have its rights fully respected, whatever the problems for other groups in our achieving that goal). This remains an issue to this day.

ZEITGEIST OF THE ROARING AND CONSERVATIVE TWENTIES

The mentality—the *Zeitgeist* (literally, the spirit of the time)—of postwar 1920s Germany was quite different from and yet strongly influenced by the Great War and its violence. (More on this important aspect of the story of the Hitler era, below.) There was a great sense of loss (along many dimensions), and—in contrast with that—a relief, a vital desire to appreciate life, and to investigate and experiment with new possibilities, now that the war was over. (A similar exuberance could be noticed in many countries at the end of World War II.)

Among the clauses of the Versailles Treaty of 1919 was the demand that Germany pay war reparations. While Germany had obliged France to make payments in the peace treaty ending the Franco-Prussian War of 1870-1871, the current demand was both much greater (at least at first) and also more complex. (More on this, earlier, and below.)

If we look at the USA, it was a debtor nation in 1914, with a debt of $3.7 billion. During the war, it lent vast sums through its major commercial banks, especially that of J. P. Morgan, Jr., to the Allies. And so, consequently, by war's end, Britain owed these banks some $4.7 billion and the Allies in all, owed $10 billion; US banks had also loaned Germany the much smaller sum of some $27 million in all.

If Germany had won the war, presumably these US banks would have had billions in unpayable debt from Britain alone. But the Allies won the war; as a consequence, the war had changed the center of the financial world from London to New York.[334]

Furthermore, interconnected with this, the war reparations demanded of Germany would go in large part to the paying off to US banks of war debt incurred by the Allies, especially Britain, with their loans from these banks. The amount owed by Britain to US banks of $4.7 billion was much less than Germany was asked to pay in reparations—even the subsequent, lower amount of 50 billion marks ($210 billion)! In addition, there were also terms intended to block Germany's ability to make war, limiting the

---

[333] Herbert A. Simon, *Models of Man: Social and Rational, Mathematical Essays on Rational Human Behavior in A Social Setting* (1957); Anatole Rapoport, *Fights, Games, and Debates* (1960) and *Game Theory as a Theory of Conflict Resolution* (1974).

[334] Martin Horn, "War Finance (Great Britain and Ireland)," INTERNATIONAL ENCYCLOPEDIA OF THE FIRST WORLD WAR, 1914-1919 ONLINE.

size of the German Army to 100,000 men, with a ban on conscription (forced militarization of the young adult male population).

A German submarine fleet was banned, as was an air force; the Navy was restricted to vessels of less than 100,000 tons. (*These restrictions would be broken once the Third Reich began*, and, in fact, even before that, in the 1920s, secretly.)

On September 10, 1919, the Allies (except the USA) and the new Republic of German Austria (*Deutsch-Österreich*) signed the Treaty of Saint-Germain-en-Laye, in which it was agreed that the name of the country would immediately be changed to Austria, and its territory limited to a small part of the former Austro-Hungarian Empire. Much of the territory of the former Austro-Hungarian Empire was separated from this new, smaller Austria, which retained Vienna as its capital.

Vienna economically became the capital of a former Empire now without an empire. Its ability to maintain itself through time was in this way seriously challenged. Conscription was abolished and Austria's military made up of volunteers was severely limited. (All of this gave appeal to Austria's becoming part of a larger and more viable economy: As it turned out, after 1933, the most likely candidate for that merger would be Germany, the Third Reich.) In any case, union with Germany was proscribed without the explicit agreement of the League of Nations.

In Germany itself, after the Great War (of 1914-1918), nationalist parties developed with strong resentment about what it considered to be the betrayal of Germany to the Allies (There was also strong nationalist sentiment with some xenophobia thrown in, in other countries as well, across Middle, Eastern, and Western Europe.)

In Germany, one of these parties was the German Workers Party (the *Deutsche Arbeiterpartei* or DAP), which Hitler, once a key member of the group, had renamed *Nationalsozialistische Deutsche Arbeiterpartei* (or NSDAP), the National Socialist German Workers Party, in short, the Nazi Party.

This was in February of 1920. At the important gathering of the small group, on February 24, Hitler is said to have realized his great power as an orator, with both an intense delivery (described by many as hypnotic) and a clear sense of a program of what he and a Party behind him, would like to, and could, accomplish. In this, he incorporated a strong appeal to the profound frustrations and related yearnings of many in Germany.[335] At this gathering on February 24, 1920, the Party declared a 25-point Program which contained some basic position statements as well as a number of demands, some of which may be familiar, including the following, with their original numbering in the Program retained: "(1) We demand the union of all Germans, on the basis of the right of the self-determination of peoples, to form a Great Germany, (3) We demand land and territory (colonies) [*Wir fordern Land und Boden (Kolonien)*] for the

---

[335] Sebastian Haffner, *Anmerkungen zu Hitler*, 1978 ed., pp. 22-23; 1994 ed., pp. 18-19; Eng., *The Meaning of Hitler*, p. 14.

nourishment of our people and for settling our surplus population [*unseres Bevolkerungsüberschusses*], (4) None but members of the nation may be citizens of the State. None but those of German blood, whatever their creed, may be members of the nation. No Jew, therefore, may be a member of the nation, (6) The right of voting on the leadership and laws of the State is to be enjoyed by the citizens of the State alone. We demand, therefore, that all official positions, of whatever kind, whether in the Reich, the provinces, or the small communities, shall be held by citizens of the State alone ..., (17) We demand a land reform [*Bodenreform*] suitable to our national requirements ..., (18) We demand ruthless war upon all those whose activities are injurious to the common interest. Sordid criminals against the nation, usurers, profiteers, etc., must be punished with death, whatever their creed or race, (23) We demand legal warfare against conscious political lies and their dissemination in the press. In order to facilitate the creation of a German national press we demand that: (a) all editors, and their co-workers, of newspapers employing the German language must be members of the nation; (b) special permission from the State shall be necessary before non-German newspapers may appear (these need not necessarily be printed in the German language) ...."[336]

Giving a context to these Twenty-five Points of the National Socialist program, Austrian Jewish psychiatrist and psychoanalyst, Wilhelm Reich (1897-1957),[337] remarked in a 1933 text of his, "The theoretical pivot of German fascism is its race theory. The economic program of the so-called twenty-five points plays no other role in fascist ideology than that of the means to an end... Therefore 'Keeping pure the race and the blood' is the primordial task of a nation [so declares Nazi race Theory] and is worth any sacrifice."[338] Reich continues, "The image of wholesome, healthy, muscular, and fit young couples with several children, the blessings of large Aryan families as a goal for all truly German youth to keep as a foremost ideal, serves in "depreciating woman's sexual function compared

---

[336] Eng. text, Gottfried Feder, *The Program of the NSDAP, The National Socialist Workers' Party and its General Conceptions* (1932); original Ger. text: *Das 25-Punkte-Programm der NSDAP vom 24.2.1920* (1920).

[337] Wilhelm Reich, Univ. of Vienna Medical School, 1922, was an analyst in Freud's out-patient psychanalytic clinic (1922-1930), moved to Berlin in 1930, becoming a training analyst at the Berlin Psychoanalytic Institute, until he fled Germany a day or two after the March 2, 1933 attack on his *Der sexuelle Kampf der Jugend* (1932), in the Nazi newspaper, *Völkischer Beobacher*. Cf. Myron Sharaf, *Fury on Earth: A Biography of Wilhelm Reich* (1994), p. 164. In 1933, Reich published *Character Analysis* (Theodore P. Wolpe, tr., 3rd. rev. ed., 1949), and *The Mass Psychology of Fascism* (Theodore P. Wolfe, tr., 3rd rev. ed., 1945). One analyst in training at the Berlin Psychoanalytic Institute supervised by Reich (and others) was Hellmuth Kaiser (who also fled Germany in 1933), about whom, see *Effective Psychotherapy: The Contribution of Hellmuth Kaiser*, Mitchell Ginsberg, ed. Among many fleeing the Reich in 1933 was also the Leibniz scholar, Paul Schrecker.

[338] Wilhelm Reich, *The Mass Psychology of Fascism*, p. 63.

with her function of procreation."[339] This split is reflected in the dichotomy of mother-whore found in a number of social and religious analyses of female sexuality, a dichotomy we may be familiar with from our own upbringing. (We see this societal-value analysis of society and especially of women not only in Nazi Germany but also in the new motto for occupied ("Vichy") France from 1940-1944, replacing the long-honored French national motto, *Liberté, égalité, fraternité* (Liberty, equality, fraternity) with *Travail, famille, patrie* (Work, family, nation): these slogans had a powerful significance in reorienting the values of the society; they were not empty slogans!

On the psychosexuality of politics, in contrast with Greek orgasms,[340] geopolitical historian Robert D. Kaplan made an understated observation that "sexual frustration can be appeased much more easily by a totalizing ideology than by being able to vote once every four years in an election."[341] These and other themes here were refined in *Mein Kampf* and, later, once the NSDAP took control of Germany, carried into action. This 1920 declaration would limit German citizenship to those of German blood, would exclude Jews from that right, from the right to vote, and from working in the German press. The declaration also claimed the right to a Greater Germany, to land and colonies to satisfy the needs of the German population. The term *Lebensraum* is not used here (unlike its use in *Mein Kampf*); its focus was on colonies to support the country.[342]

The idea of eastern lands for German use was not new with Hitler and the NSDAP: during the Weimar Republic, Chancellor Brüning in 1930 declared that his government saw "the recovery of eastern agriculture as the basis of the national political salvation of the German east."[343] Brüning and other German politicians, and later, Hitler and the Nazis, as well, saw state power in terms of land within its realm, which was presumably more significant in the late Middle Ages and early modern centuries than in the period from the late 1800s on, in which industrial capacity was a more significant measure of a country's strength and economic impact on the world. *This anachronistic (outdated) model of what political and state power amounts to, a serious confusion, would have implications and consequences for political thinking through the period of the Third Reich.*

Some later basic principles of the National Socialists and the Third Reich would not have been a surprise if these 1920 NSDAP points were reviewed and taken at face value. (Of course, many took all of that as hot air, empty bluster, and political posturing without there being any intent

---

[339] Wilhelm Reich, *The Mass Psychology of Fascism*, pp. 88-90.
[340] The concept of the Greek orgasm was introduced above.
[341] Robert D. Kaplan, *The Return of Marco Polo's World*, p. 248.
[342] The term *Lebensraum* is usually rendered in English as living space and in French as *l'espace vital*. In the National Socialist vocabulary its meaning evolved *from an earlier* notion of Germany's option to have colonies in which some nationals could live, helping support the country, *to a newer* sense of Germany's right to take over non-Germanic lands, mostly Slavic lands (Poland and the USSR).
[343] Anthony J. Nicholls, *Weimar and the Rise of Hitler*, p. 190.

The Hitler Era

to carry out in the German society what they were spouting as impressive doctrine. That was ultimately a misjudgment, we can say in retrospect.)

The consequences of the war and of the Treaty of Versailles were still in the background. As part of that, there was a series of trials for war crimes concerning the Great War. At first these were envisioned to be conducted in a non-German context, but the Allies accepted having the trials conducted in Germany. In this way, a set of trials, the Leipzig War Crimes Trials, came before the German Supreme Court (*Reichsgericht*) in Leipzig, and lasted from May 23 to July 16, 1921.

Though brief, and even if only twelve individuals were brought to trial, with acquittals or relatively short-term prison sentences, *these war crimes trials did serve as a precedent to future such trials*—to look ahead briefly here to the next war and future trials—most notably, the Nuremberg Trials, beginning in late 1945, followed by the International Criminal Court (the ICC), with its seat in the Hague.

This is still not a totally settled matter.[344] Even today, not all nations have signed on to and ratified the various treaties that established this ICC. These States are few, but include the USA,[345] China, India, Indonesia, Iraq, Israel, Libya, Qatar, Sudan, and Yemen. Nonetheless, viewed historically, war crimes had already been defined in various international conventions, such as the Geneva Convention of 1864 and the two Hague Conventions of 1899 and 1907, among other formal international agreements.[346]

At the end of World War I, the Allies wanted to put on trial Fritz Haber (1868-1934), Nobel Prize Laureate in Chemistry (1918, for nitrogen fixation), for his role in directing the German poison-gas operations and the use of chlorine gas, to be superseded then by the use of mustard gas, during the war.[347] As well, they had in mind the same for the German Kaiser during the war, Wilhelm II, who had fled Germany for asylum in the Netherlands at war's end, and was welcomed there,[348] since, after all, the Netherlands, although neutral in the Great War, had been blockaded

---

[344] Its authorization, formalized through the signing by signatory States of the Rome Statute (Jul. 17, 1998), has now ratified by 124 states. This Rome Statute became operational as of July 1, 2002. See "ICC 'undeterred' by US sanctions threat," *BBC News*, Sep. 11, 2018.

[345] Following the article in the *New York Times*, Dec. 12, 2000, Robert S. McNamara and Ben Ferencz, "For Clinton's Last Act," the treaty was signed (on Dec. 31, 2000), but never ratified by Congress.

[346] *Substantive and Procedural Aspects of International Criminal Law, Vol. 1: Commentary*, Gabrielle Kirk MacDonald, Olivia Q. Swaak-Goldman, eds. (2000), pp. 276-277; "Laws of War: The Hague Convention of 1899," YALE LAW SCHOOL, AVALON PROJECT; "Chemical Weapons Convention: The Hague Convention of 1907," ORGANIZATION FOR THE PROHIBITION OF CHEMICAL WEAPONS (OPCW).

[347] "Fritz Haber," ENCYCLOPÆDIA BRITANNICA. His son, Ludwig Haber (1921-2004), was to write *The Poisonous Cloud* (1986), a history of the use of gas warfare during the Great War. Fritz Haber, being Jewish, escaped to Switzerland after the Nazi *Machtergreifung* (the Grabbing of Power), where he died in 1934.

[348] "This Day in History: January 23, 1920," HISTORY.COM.

by the British, making it impossible for them to supply the Germans with any food or war materiel. Relatedly, on January 23, 1920, the Netherlands formally rejected the request that the former Kaiser be extradited to stand trial. The international venue was also rejected by various nations, including the USA and Japan. In short, there was not an agreement about which crimes could be tried and punished under international law.

The Leipzig Trial followed (with mixed results), and the proceedings were widely regarded at the time as a failure, but the trials have been seen as a significant step towards the introduction of a comprehensive worldwide system for the prosecution of violations of international law.

REDEFINING MEN AND WOMEN IN THE TWENTIES

While these legalities were being debated and carried out to no one's particular satisfaction, at the same time, there was a crisis of men's understanding of themselves. From the war, there were the experiences and memories of mutilated bodies, limbs lost, facial features destroyed (*les gueules cassées* and *die zerbrochene Münder* described just above), spirits broken—all of these experienced realities raised questions about how wars were decided and directed, about what a man is, about what manliness is, and about what life offers as new freedoms for survivors.[349] A typical shift after any deadly war has ended is for there to be rejoicing at the relief and an eagerness to celebrate having survived! *But the past is relentless; it may be harder to survive than to die, whether killed by others or by suicide.*[350] In the 1920s, men and women who had survived the War were seeking a sense of vitality and life. The war led to women taking over work and to their enfranchisement, or active suffrage, the giving them the right to vote, as was made explicit by the Weimar Constitution in Germany, and in the USA (1920) and the UK (1928).

In the historical background here, the suffragette movement had actually begun in the late 1800s, with limited voting rights granted in Finland, Sweden, Iceland, New Zealand, South Australia, some US western states, and, during the period of World War I, in Norway, Denmark, Austria, Germany, and Poland; during the fall of the Czar, women were granted voting rights in Russia, in 1917, and then in the Netherlands, in 1919.[351]

---

[349] D. H. Lawrence's *Lady Chatterley's Lover* addressed the plight of Lord Chatterley, paralyzed from the waist down from injuries in the Great War, and of his wife, Lady Chatterley. It was banned in the US (until 1959), and the UK (until 1960). Lawrence on obscenity: "you can recognize it by the insult it offers, invariably, to sex, and to the human spirit. Pornography is the attempt to insult sex ... As soon as there is sex excitement with a desire to spite the sexual feeling, to humiliate it and degrade it, the element of pornography enters." ("Pornography and Obscenity," *This Quarter*, vol. 2, no. 1, 1929, pp. 17-27, at pp. 24, 27.)

[350] On the psychological subtleties of survival after the death of loved ones, as in war, see Maurice Rostand, *L'homme que j'ai tué* (1925; play, 1930) and film adaptations, *Broken Lullaby* (US, 1932), and esp. *Frantz* (Fr.-Ger., 2016).

[351] "Women's Sufferage," INFOPLEASE.COM; Thomas Ben Thompson, "Equality

The Hitler Era

For many, this was a time to experiment with life to the fullest possible. Sexual roles were questioned and alternatives considered and acted upon. For men, this would include an openness to intimacy with other men. Clubs were opened in Berlin, for example, that were welcoming of same-sexed couples. One famous club was El Dorado:

 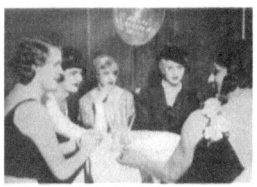 

This would be an avant-garde invitation to those who wanted to open up to experimentation in the sexual and intimacy realms. It would change once the National Socialists came to power in 1933. But during the 1920s, there was no great uproar about this: even the homosexual activities of the SA, the Stormtroopers, were well known and tolerated by those at the top of the NSDAP. That, too, would change with the changing situation and the changing politics of the 1933-1934 period, culminating in the Night of the Long Knives, several days of organized murder of SA and others found to be troublesome in one way or another. More on that below.

For the young women of Germany who made up much of the work force (as a result of the death of so many men, with work still needing to be done) were variations of style defining different types of women, parallel to issues questioning male identity.

As shown here, one type was the *die Girl* (using the English word), as represented by such movie actresses of the period as Louise Brooks, an American starring in several German films of the period. A second was the *die Garçonne* (the feminine form of the French word for boy, *garçon*), who often dressed in men's clothing, as in Marlene Dietrich photographs from the period. There is the unstated implication that these two are foreign imports. The third, by way of contrast, was *die Gretchen*, using a German personal name, a wholesome Germanic woman respectful of traditional German values of a home-centered life.[352] (In literature, the

---

Begets Equality: Women's Suffrage in 1917," WEB.MIT.EDU; "International Woman Suffrage Timeline," THOUGHTCO.COM.

[352] Rüdiger Graf, "Anticipating the Future in the Present: 'New Women' and Other Beings of the Future in Weimar Germany," *Central European History*, vol. 42, no. 4, 2009, pp. 647–673.

introduction of avant-garde or risqué social values through foreign characters allows a distancing from such perhaps questionable practices; the use of members of one's own society taking on the same roles makes the challenge to the reader much more direct and immediate. Both literary conceits are found around the world, used for the different impact each has on its readers. An American type that was free of such a "foreign" sense was the "it" girl. (More, below.) This freedom—or as seen otherwise, this chaotic, amoral, or even immoral, breakdown in traditional cultural values—was powerful, exciting, and also, for some, threatening, as often accompanies rapid significant social changes in mores and practices.

This had a backlash, a strong, emotionally driven counter-trend, which we also often see in cultures. German Penal Code Paragraph 175, first formalized in 1871, forbade male-male sexuality intimacy, and was enlarged during the Third Reich, on September 1, 1935, in its scope to include even "simple looking" and "simple touching." From 1935-1945, some 75,000 men were arrested under this law (with imprisonment, castration, or other consequences). It would remain in force until 1994.[353]

We might note that these changes in society were not born full-grown after the end of World War I. Already during the war, in Germany as in the UK and in France, there was a significant transformation of civilian life (or life on the "home front" as it came to be called, likening the civilian context to a branch of the war effort), in which traditionally men's labor was taken over by women, from work in businesses to factory work to the production of arms and ammunition. This led quite naturally to a change in the clothing of women (bulky long dresses were quite inappropriate and, in fact, quite dangerous for some contexts of work). Furthermore, women began receiving regular pay for their work, even if at a lower rate than for the same position if taken by men. (That continues in many countries to this day, of course.) This pay and this much more prominent societal role of women brought with it a natural sense of societal value and the capacity to take on roles of much responsibility. Women too had seen a new world in which they were not confined to living their lives inside and centered around a home and hearth. They, as the men who had survived either in civilian labor (especially in the manufacture of war materiel) or in the front lines of the war, had seen very dire conditions and were eager for something more satisfying, less draining, miserable, and life-threatening. This general phenomenon took place not only in Germany, but also in other countries that suffered the trauma of large numbers of their young male adults being either mutilated, paralyzed, or killed. In England, as well, the younger generation was eager to live its life in ways that the older generations could not appreciate, respect, or willingly allow! (*The Prince of Wales, later King Edward VIII, suffered from this malaise in the ruling class around him.*) And across the English Channel, Paris of the 1920s was also known to be quite cosmopolitan and

---

[353] "Nazi Germany: Paragraph 175 and other sexual deviance laws," *Fordham Univ. Internet History Sourcebooks Project (IHSP)*, SOURCEBOOKS.FORDHAM.EDU; "Nazi Persecution of Homosexuals 1933-1945," USHMM.ORG.

The Hitler Era

experimental. These were *les années folles* (the wild, crazy years). This desire for full living, including yearnings for a decent, safe, and comfortable life, had its turbulent side: In the US, the situation of the workers was not very secure: There were strikes that began in 1919 of more than 4 million workers, including 365,000 steel workers, 450,000 coal miners, and 120 textile workers. In addition, there were serious clashes between blacks who had moved up from the South during the war to work in factories in the North. The so-called Red Summer (or Blood-Red Summer) of 1919 had beatings, murder, and arson, with whites standing off against blacks, especially in Chicago. The desire for peace and well-being was not going to be easy for everyone![354] Still, this desire to live while life was still possible was very strong, and perhaps is always strong, but after such a survival despite the odds, it is perhaps strongest of all, and most urgent. The flowering of art with a deep searching for new forms—in novels, plays, poetry, paintings, sculpture, film, and music—that could also face the recent disastrous past, looking at those harsh realities without flinching. (These creative works were banned in a general way by the Third Reich as "degenerate" or even as "Jewish" art.)

In Germany, there were interesting variations on this theme of an intense search for meaning, life, full sexuality, and satisfaction, as in the early life of the Storm Troopers (the *Sturmabteilung*, the SA). As mentioned above, these were paramilitary forces with nationalist leanings, called the Storm Detachment or Assault Division (in German, the *Sturmabteilung*, or SA,[355] in English, the Stormtroopers, or the Brown Shirts). *More on its members' sexual mores and proclivities, below.*

The SA was founded in late 1921. In early 1923, Hermann Göring was appointed its leader. Why Göring? Why not Röhm, who was already an army officer? Ernst Röhm, who had joined the Nazi Party by then, in the military in World War I, where he suffered wounds (leaving facial scars), and had received the Iron Cross First Class. And yet, Göring had more of a public profile: he had received the *Pour le Mérite*, the highest German military medal, informally known as the Blue Max; he at war's end was the commander of the fighter wing that earlier was led by the Red Baron (Manfred von Richthofen). Given Göring's higher public respect, Hitler chose him over Röhm to head the SA. (This was not the end of their rivalry.) There was also an informal group called the *Saalschutz* (the Meeting-hall Protection Group) made up of NSDAP volunteers to provide security for party meetings in Munich. These were formalized into groups of eight men at the time, the *Stabswache*, the Headquarters Guard, the personal bodyguards of Hitler, renamed in May 1923, the *Stoßtrupp* (the Collision or Shock Troopers, a term taken from German World War I

---

[354] "The Jazz Age (The American 1920s): Postwar Labor Tensions," DIGITAL HISTORY UK; Eric Arnesen, "'*Red Summer: The Summer of 1919 and the Awakening of Black America*' by Cameron McWhirter," *The Chicago Tribune*, Nov. 18, 2011.

[355] The term *Abteilung* can mean division, department (as in a business), a battalion, and so forth. *Stormabsteilung* is commonly rendered as Storm Troops; the alternative name of Brown Shirts is in reference to the color of their uniforms.

military vocabulary); it was enlarged and called *Stoßtrupp-Hitler*. *These served as the personal bodyguards of Hitler himself, even against the SA, should that happen.* It was disbanded by the Weimar government after the failed Beerhall Putsch, but was reconstituted after Hitler's release from prison, in April 1925, established with independence from the SA, and renamed the *Schutzstaffel*, the Protection Squadron, or SS. There was a fundamental disagreement: Hitler, inclined to pursue a political path to power, and Röhm, still intent, if need be, on a violent overthrow of the government. Some three years later, Hitler gave Röhm the option of towing the line or resigning; Röhm chose the latter, and at first went into private life. In 1928, Röhm became a military advisor in Bolivia, which ended in 1930 as a result of a Bolivian revolt.

At the same time, after the economic crash of 1929, many young men joined the SA, many with dreams of a socialist improvement over the failed capitalist system. The commander of the Berlin SA, Walter Stennes, claiming that Hitler had betrayed the socialist promises of the Nazi Party, began a revolt, which was harshly put down by the SS and the German police. At that point, Hitler took over the SA and invited Röhm, a strict disciplinarian, to return to Germany to put the SA into order.

Meanwhile, after revisions beginning in 1925, the SS, the small squad for personal protection of Hitler, consisting then of 290 men, on January 6, 1929, came under the leadership of Heinrich Himmler, then 28 years old. By the end of the same year, it had a thousand members.[356] The SS under Himmler would grow to gigantic proportions in the next years: By 1939, at the start of the war, it was 250,000 strong and growing.

In Hitler's shifting preferences, Ernst Röhm would be appointed Chief of Staff of the SA on January 5, 1931; by January 1932, the SA numbered about 500,000 men. We will consider some of the implications of these changes, in considering the period of June 30-July 3, 1934, referred to as the Night of the Long Knives, in context, below.

Considering the historical developments for the SS from these times forward, the SS would take a major role with the invasion of the USSR in June 1941, the *SS-Einsatzgruppen* in the Eastern campaign. (More, below.) These *Einsatzgruppen* were also was in charge of general security for the police state of the Third Reich. Beginning with less than 100 men, by war's end, the SS counted over 1,250,000 men, including both Waffen-SS (military) and Allgemeine-SS (administrative and police SS), and, overall, becoming a force to be greatly feared (or greatly admired, depending on one's politics).[357] *All of these men were under the command of Heinrich Himmler, and seconded by Reinhard Heydrich (until the latter was assassinated outside of Prague in the spring of 1942)!*

If we look at the xenophobia and the stereotyping with violence that we think of as the Third Reich, we may recognize that hostility toward various groups within Germany were often clothed in a moral framework

---

[356] Richard J. Evans, *The Coming of the Third Reich* (2004), p. 228.
[357] "List of SS personnel," WIKIPEDIA.

of good versus evil. Thus, the Nazi boycott of Berlin Jewish businesses (April 1, 1933) and the violence of Kristallnacht (November 9-10, 1938) were against what was claimed to be a morally degenerate Jewry.

On Nazi Germany's view of US racial politics, Nazi racist theoreticians recognized the US doctrine of Manifest Destiny[358]—with the presumed divine right to widespread killing of heathen native American Indians— and its ongoing concern with blacks, with Jim Crow laws institutionalizing discrimination against blacks, and with segregation. For Nazi Germany the issue was not one of segregation but of a thorough closing off of Germany to Jews, limiting their work options, denying them citizenship, even banishing immigrant Jews. Yet the USA also codified immigration limits: the Chinese Exclusion Act of 1882, the Geary Act of 1902, the Asiatic Barred Zone Act of 1917, the (anti-Jewish) Emergency Quota Act of 1921, and the Immigration Act of 1924, blocking immigration for various national, racial, and religious groups.[359] And, illustrating racial violence, in the USA, there were Hanging Trees on which blacks were killed in lynchings, sometimes with celebrations and photos:

Lynching of Shipp and Smith, Marion, Indiana, 1930

As shown in this photo, on August 7, 1930, Thomas Shipp (18 years old) and Abram Smith (19 years old), were forcibly taken from the jail where they were being held, and then beaten and hung, with some 7,000 witnesses gathered around. *Some in the crowd can be seen smiling, and one man is pointing to the hung men*, as if to emphasize this to the potential viewer of the photo. Lynching was to be made a federal crime, but only until many decades later, on December 19, 2018.[360]

---

[358] The phrase was first used in 1845 by columnist John L. O'Sullivan, who wrote of "the fulfillment of our manifest destiny to overspread the continent allotted by Providence for the free development of our yearly multiplying millions."

[359] See James Q. Whitman, *Hitler's American Model*, pp. 1-7, 11-14, 137-161.

[360] "US passes first anti-lynching law," *BBC News*, Dec. 20, 2018. As mentioned, slavery of blacks ended in the USA in Dec. 1865; in comparison, the slavery of Romanies in Romania was abolished in 1855-1856, with complete legal freedom in

A somber song that recounted the strange fruit of such trees, meaning dead black men, who had been not only hung but often castrated or had their penis removed, was written in 1937 by Lewis Allan, the penname of Bronx-born Abel Meeropol (1903-1986), which was recorded by Billie Holiday in 1939. The song was and is well known in certain circles.[361]

In the USA there was the peculiar situation in which there was this urge for celebration ("the roaring twenties") at the same time as a national prohibition against all alcoholic drinks, with ratification of the 18th Amendment to the Constitution, on January 29, 1919, was in effect until its repeal on December 5, 1933), even if the trauma of the Great War to the country was much less immediate than in Europe.

In the 1920s, known as a decade of American conservative Republican presidencies and thought of as a time of a return to isolationism, the USA, nonetheless, was instrumental internationally at a number of key points during the decade, including treaties and pacts growing out of the Washington Naval Conference of 1921-1922, especially the Five-Power Naval Limitation Treaty (1922), in which total weight of naval ships for the UK, US, Japan, France, and Italy was established to be in the ratio of 5-5-3-1.67-1.67 (that is, cited in whole-number ratios: 15-15-9-5-5).

Also showing the involvement of the US Government even during this so-called isolationism were the Dawes Plan (1924), with US loans of private money (from major US banks) to Germany, setting up a new reparations payments schedule by Germany to the UK and France; the Kellogg-Briand Treaty (1928), outlawing war as an instrument of national policy—realizing Immanuel Kant's vision in *Perpetual Peace* (1795); the Young Plan, named for the organizer of the international group, Owen D. Young, American industrialist, chief counsel of GE (General Electric), creator of RCA (the Radio Corporation of America), and a member of the Board of Trustees of the Rockefeller Foundation. The Young Plan was finalized in 1929 and went into effect in 1930: a renegotiating of the reparations schedule for Germany, greatly reducing the amount to be paid per year, with much of the debt so structured as to allow its complete non-payment, and the London Naval Arms Limitation Treaty (1930), which added further restrictions on the size of the submarine navies for the UK, US, Japan, France, and Italy. We can look more, below, at what this predominant mentality of the times (*Zeitgeist*) amounted to for the new National Socialists, the leaders of the Third Reich.

This sociopsychological foundation to these events has several strands or features, each of which had its own power and capacity to inform (that is, to give structure or form to) and to define the way of thinking, the language, and the politics of those ultimately leading the Third Reich.

While there were these liberal trends following the end of the war, there were also more critical points of view being expressed. It was in

---

1864. See See Ian Hancock, "Towards Abolition," in *The Pariah Syndrome: An Account of Gypsy Slavery and Persecution* (1987), pp. 30-36, esp. p. 35.

[361] Lyrics and video of "Strange Fruit" sung by Billie Holiday in *Billie Holiday: Strange Fruit*, YOUTUBE; "Strange Fruit Lyrics: Billy Holiday," GENIUS.COM.

May 1920 that the first of the anti-Semitic articles appeared in *The Ford International Weekly, The Dearborn Independent*, owned by Henry Ford, the respected car manufacturer. The headline of the May 22, 1920 issue, for example, read "The International Jew: The World's Problem." Ford's weekly published the *Protocols of the Elders of Zion* as truthful. The writings of Ford's Dearborn weekly[362] and the writings of Houston Stewart Chamberlain (more below) were to have a strong impact on Hitler, and, as well, on other Nazis, such as Baldur von Shirach.[363] Much later, on June 30, 1927, Ford wrote a formal apology, claiming that he was not aware of the content of his paper's articles, that he felt deep mortification at the contents he had just become aware of, and that had he known earlier, he "would have forbidden their circulation without a moment's hesitation," adding that he was fully aware of the virtues of the Jewish people as a whole and of their contributions for civilization and mankind.[364] In any case, the articles were republished in German and made a strong impression on Hitler, Von Schirach, and others—part of a long relationship of mutual respect between Ford and Hitler. Even before the first appearance of *The Ford International Weekly, The Dearborn Independent*, there was a strong undercurrent of anti-Jewish sentiment in both Germany and Austria, where Hitler certainly would have been exposed to many anti-Jewish diatribes and texts, despite his claim to have discovered independently and in a flash of self-generated insight the essentially foreign nature of the Jew, dressed in his Oriental black kaftan and having black curls, as described in *Mein Kampf*—with the suggestion that only then did read pamphlets on Jews, to imply his self-born thinking.[365]

ON THE DIPLOMATIC FRONT AND 1920S NAZI ORGANIZING

On the diplomatic front, on April 16, 1922, Germany and Soviet Russia (known at the time as the Russian Soviet Federative Socialist Republic, the RSFSR—not yet the USSR) signed the Treaty of Rapallo. All territorial and financial claims against the other were terminated, and *there were also secret sections involving military aid between the two*. The German minister Walther Rathenau and the Russian Georgii Vasilyevich Chicherin negotiated the terms of the treaty. Despite the benefits for Germany, including much less encumbered trade with Russia, and secret military support, Rathenau would be killed June 24, 1922 by rightist extremists in Germany shortly after his having laid out the groundwork of the treaty.

In that same year of 1922, there would be an event that was inspiring to Hitler: this was the March on Rome on October 28, 1922, in which

---

[362] "The Dearborn Independent," WIKIPEDIA.

[363] Baldur von Schirach (1907-1974) would become known especially for his role as the Nazi national youth leader, head of the *Hitlerjugend* (Hitler Youth), 1931-1940, and later, as the *Gauleiter* and *Reichsstatthalter* (Reich Governor) of Vienna.

[364] *Statement by Henry Ford* (Pamphlet, 6/30/1927), DIGITAL KENYON COLLEGE.

[365] The black curls are presumably sidelocks (in Hebrew, *payot;* in Yiddish, *payis*), following one interpretation of Leviticus 19:27. Adolf Hitler, *Mein Kampf*, Vol. I, Chap. II (Years of Study and Suffering—*Wiener Lehr- und Leidensjahre*), Sect. "Is This Also a Jew?" at p. 7; Ger., p. 59.

Benito Mussolini, *Il Duce* (The Leader), with almost 30,000 members of the PNF (*il Partito Nazionale Fascista*), had arrived at the capital on foot. King Victor Emmanuele III appointed Mussolini the next day as Prime Minister: a non-violent coup. (The 30,000 was key.)

German nationalists were inspired by the bold moves of Mussolini and his Fascist followers. Focused largely in Bavaria, they too were quite proud of their own traditions and dress. including the wearing of *Lederhosen*, short or knee-length leather pants, a traditional work garment of clothing. Early National Socialist militiamen (the SA, or Brownshirts) would wear this for marches and other events. At first, Hitler, who was at that time still an Austrian, presented himself as a typical Bavarian:

SA Men marching   Hitler among trees and in studio

With less than 7% of Mussolini's 30,000, things certainly did not go the same for Hitler and the relatively miniscule group of fellow Nazis who joined him on their march and attempted *Putsch* (take-over) of the Bavarian government, just over a year later, on November 9, 1923.

This quite unsuccessful *coup d'état* ended with the shooting by Munich policemen of sixteen of the approximately 2,000 Nazis who marched together to take over the Bavarian government. Hitler, who fled into hiding at the home of a supporter, Ernst ("Putzi") Hanfstaengl, was arrested two days later, tried, convicted of treason, and sentenced to time in prison, during which he wrote *Mein Kampf* (*My Struggle*).[366] Meanwhile, Helene Bechstein, wife of Carl Bechstein, the piano manufacturer,[367] who

---

[366] Contemporary German historian Othmar Plöckinger, an editor of the 2016 text, *Hitler, Mein Kampf: A Critical Edition* (pub. by Munich *Institut für Zeitgeschiche*), has strongly suggested that the book did not have a co-author (Rudolf Hess or others discussed in the history of the text) and that Hitler's ideas were found in his earlier speeches or in the then-current literature. See his earlier *Geschichte eines Buches: Adolf Hitlers Mein Kampf, 1922-1945* (2011).

[367] The Bechstein grand piano was (and still is) considered by many the finest in the world. In the 2002 film, *The Pianist*, the central character, Władysław Szpilman, has to sell his piano when the family is forced to move into the newly-created Warsaw ghetto. For his Bechstein piano, he is offered 2,000 Polish złotys (złytoch), less than $575 US dollars at the time; he suggests that the family accept this meager sum (at 13:50-14:35 of the film). The film is based on Władysław Szpilman, *The Pianist: The Extraordinary True Story of One Man's Survival in Warsaw, 1939-1945* (1998), presenting the relation between Szpilman and a German Army officer, Capt. Wilm Hosenfeld (quoted below). The name Szpilman (also spelled Shpilman or Schpielmann) means a musician.

with a motherly caring[368] was an early supporter of Hitler,[369] had sent a chauffeur from Berlin to Munich to hasten him to safety, but Hitler had been arrested before that could help him escape. Hitler had known Hanfstaengl for a year by then: Earlier, soon after meeting Hanfstaengl for the first time in November 1922, Hitler spoke to him of his vision of changing the weekly *Völkischer Beobachter* (which Hitler had purchased in 1920[370]) to a daily, but needed for that to purchase two American rotary presses, which were for sale only with payment in hard currency (US dollars), not the weak and unstable German mark. Hitler did not have the needed US $1,000,[371] Hanfstaengl gave the money on loan with the hope of becoming the editor of the paper. Instead, this role was given to Alfred Rosenberg.[372] In addition to helping make the paper a daily, Hanfstaengl was also behind much of the financing of the publication of *Mein Kampf*, the now-well-known autobiographical political statement by Hitler. (Hanfstaengl would become a close associate of Hitler's, and during the first years of the Third Reich, its Foreign Press Secretary.)

Looking ahead here briefly, *Mein Kampf* ultimately guaranteed Hitler a large part of his income for life: in the Third Reich, the book was given as a government gift to all newly-weds, starting in 1936; free to the married couples—and also given within Germany industry and business as a reward to workers—all such books generated royalties that were paid directly to Hitler as author. Hitler would also receive royalties for the use of his profile on Reich postage stamps, in all denominations and through the years of the Reich.[373] Furthermore, the *Völkischer Beobachter*, which was owned (as above) by Hitler, would become an obligatory subscription item for all Germans, once the National Socialist Party took power.[374] In the early years, Hitler was already developing his political recognition by

---

[368] Margarete Plewnia, *Auf dem Weg zu Hitler: Der »völkische« Publizist Dietrich Eckart* (1970), p. 69.

[369] It was Dietrich Eckart who had introduced Hitler to the Bechsteins. Cf. Ralph Max Engelman, *Dietrich Eckart and the Genesis of Nazism* (1971), pp 94-110. Eckart also had contacts with important industrialists and the military; he also introduced Hitler to General Ludendorff. Cf. Wulf C. Schwarzwäller, *Hitlers Geld: Bilanz einer persönlichen Bereicherung* [*Hitler's Money: Balance Sheet of Personal Enrichment*] (1986), pp. 89-91, Eng. tr., *The Unknown Hitler: His Private Life and Fortune* (1990), pp. 74-75.

[370] This was accomplished with money offered Hitler by Helene Bechstein and other supporters. See Richard Rother, "Ein Auf und Ab wie auf einer Tonleiter," TAZ DEUTSCHLAND (TAZ.DE).

[371] US $1,000 in 1922 would currently be worth about US $14,570; see the conversion rates at INFLATION CALCULATOR.

[372] Wulf C. Schwarzwäller, *Hitlers Geld* [*Hitler's Money*], pp. 94-95, 106-107, Eng., *The Unknown Hitler*, pp. 79, 98-99.

[373] Richard J. Evans, "A Warning From History: A new biography of Hitler reminds us that there is more than one way to destroy a democracy," *The Nation*, Feb. 28, 2017.

[374] Konrad H. Jarausch, *Broken Lives: How Ordinary Germans Experienced the Twentieth Century*, pp. 69-70.

a group of supporters of like-mind. Some ideas were already in place, at least in a simple but recognizable form that would develop in future years, in *Mein Kampf*, and then in the Third Reich itself. Hitler already had a sense of some major issues the Reich would face: In a 1922 interview with Major a.D. (retired)[375] Josef Hell, then a newspaper man, Hitler was asked, imaging a future in which he, Hitler, would have full discretionary powers against the Jews [*wenn Sie erst einmal volle Aktionsfreiheit gegen die Juden haben*], what Hitler would then do with the Jews.

The reply that Hell reported was, "Once I really am in power, my first and foremost task will be the annihilation of the Jews. [*Wenn ich einmal wirklich an der Macht bin, dann wird die Vernichtung der Juden meine erste und wichtigete Aufgabe sein.*]" Hitler went on to describe setting up gallows one after the other [*Galgen neben Galgen*] and hanging Jews in small groups, continuing "until the last Jew in Munich has been blotted out [*bis der letzte Jude in München ausgetilgt ist*]. Other cities will follow suit, precisely in this fashion [*Genau so wird in den anderen Städten verfahren*], until all Germany has been completely cleansed of Jews [*bis Deutschland vom letzten Juden gereinigt ist.*]"[376]

Some question the authenticity of this document, on the grounds that Hell was an anti-Nazi (and so, biased), but these statements are consistent with what Hitler said in other speeches and in his two-volume *Mein Kampf*. For example, announcements showing (limited) hostility against Jews, declared they would not be allowed to attend meetings.

Hitler's talk, Apr. 20, 1923

Hitler's talk, Feb. 22, 1925

---

[375] The German military abbreviation a.D. (*ausser Dienst*) means retired.
[376] Josef Hell, "Aufzeichnung," INSTITUT FÜR ZEITGESCHICHTE (1922), p. 5; the typescript of the interview (prepared Nov. 28, 1955) is at ZEITGESCHICHTE-ARCHIV, p. 5 (Doc. ZS 640). Cf. Gerald Fleming, *Hitler and the Final Solution* (1984), p. 17.

In these two examples of posters announcing Hitler's talks, there was a notice typically added: *Juden haben keinen Zutritt* (No entrance for Jews). These two were for Hitler's talks on Friday, April 20, 1923, *Politik und Rasse. Warum sind wir antisemiten?* (*Politics and Race. Why are we anti-Semitic?*), with the notice below the title of the talk, on the right, and almost two years later, for his talk on Friday, February 22, 1925, *Deutschlands Zukunft und unsere Bewegung* (*Germany's Future and Our Movement*), with the notice similarly placed, on the left (in bold font). Hitler was praised by his many admirers in the Reich as one of the greatest of all German speakers. He was also known, less publicly, for his oratory perseverance. He could give hours-long speeches. Later, when critical comments about him were not fatal to make, he was sometimes described as a *Besserwisser* (literally, a Better-knower, in English, a Know-it-all), perhaps wanting to show those who had a better education that he too had something worth saying.[377]

As Magda Goebbels told Count Galeazzo Ciano, "'It is always Hitler who talks!' Ciano recalled her as saying. 'He can be Führer as much as he likes, but he always repeats himself and bores his guests.'"[378] Hitler's secretary, Christa Schroeder, similarly noted that at the Berghof, "*das Gespräch ... nur noch müde dahinplätscherte,*[379] (with conversations that gradually degenerated into monotonous repetitions, Hitler babbling on boringly).

Early SA (*Sturmabteilung*) Modeled on the War's *Stoßtruppen*

The early Nazi *Sturmabteilung* (SA, Stormtroops) was modeled on these earlier specialized military units: lightly but well-armed, they could move into position for attack suddenly, strike with violence, and then go on to other locations for further confrontations.

To those experiencing the phenomenon, the Nazi Storm Troops were literally remarkable and stunning. They, too, were well organized, their uniforms[380] defined their sameness of purpose, their marching in unison reflected their singleness of cause; their spirited songs reflected the intensity of their commitment. As well, the focus and organization of their

---

[377] For example, this opinion of Albert Speer, expressed after the war. See James O'Donnell, *The Bunker: The History of the Reich Chancellery Group* (1978), p. 315. O'Donnell was German bureau chief for *Newsweek* magazine, from July 1, 1945 on. See also the US TV film based on this book, *The Bunker* (1981).

[378] Ian Kershaw, *Hitler: 1936-45, Nemesis* (2000), pp. 198-199. Cf. Max Domarus, *Speeches and Proclamations, 1932-1945* (2004), p. 2463.

[379] Christa [Emilie Christine] Schroeder, *Er war mein Chef: Aus dem Nachlaß der Sekretärin von Adolf Hitler* (1985), p. 185; Eng., *He Was My Chief: The Memoirs of Adolf Hitler's Secretary* (2009), p. 161.

[380] Large number of these brown uniforms (for the *Braunhemden*, the Brownshirts) were obtained in 1925, from army surplus supplies, originally planned for use in tropical climates; their introduction is attributed to Freilkorps leader Gerhard Roßbach (1893-1967); these uniforms were first issued in 1925. Before then, Stormtroopers were dressed in a motley fashion. See Otis C. Mitchell, *Hitler's Stormtroopers and the Attack on the German Republic, 1919-1933* (2008), p. 77; "Early SS uniforms (1925-1928)" as a sub-section in "Uniforms and insignia of the *Schuzstaffel*," WIKIPEDIA.

attack methods had a power in their instilling fear (or admiration) at their violence: they could arrive in open-back trucks, which held as many SA Men as possible standing side by side, waiting for the trucks to stop at key points. There they could all climb out and charge groups they wanted to attach, most frequently groups of Communist protesters. They could be signaled back to the trucks and be off before any organized resistance by police or others could arrive on the scene. *Their point was in part to show the fundamental inadequacy of the Weimar Republic's police force to protect German citizens.*

In the early years after World War I, there were various right-wing pro-nationalistic, anti-Semitic (and also anti-Polish) groups that worked together. One of these, the *Freikorps*, the Free Corps—also known as the *Freikorps Oberland*, the *Bund Oberland*, and the *Kameradschaft Freikorps*—consisted of ex-soldiers who were independent and who had kept their weapons—and were thus available for providing their services as free, independent units—were invited into the new republic's military, the *Reichswehr* (the National Armed Forces), but many refused. The Free Corps was often supported financially[381] by industry and conservative interests; the Weimar government did not make any concerted effort to eliminate them or integrate them into the government forces, but some *Freikorps*, such as the Ehrhardt Brigade, were paid by the government.

We can get a sense of the political viewpoint of the *Freikorps* through considering early statements by some of its spokesmen: (1) the hero of the Battle of Annaberg and founder and leader of the *Wehr-Wölfe* or the *Freikorps Heydebreck*, Peter von Heydebreck[382] (1889-1934): "But my idea was not to husband and preserve my troops until the new state had established itself. On the contrary it was war against this state of Weimar and Versailles. War daily and by every means. For as I love Germany, so I hated the Republic and November 9th"—the date in 1918 when Kaiser Wilhelm II abdicated and the Weimar Republic was declared. (2) Rudolf Berthold (1891-1920), German flying ace, recipient of *Pour le Mérite* (Germany's highest military medal), and founder and commander of the *Eiserne Schar Berthold*, the Berthold Iron Troop: "I will not forget these days of criminals, lies, and barbarity. The days of the Revolution will forever be a blight on the history of Germany.... As the rabble hates me .... I remain strong. The day will yet come when I will knock the truth into these people and tear the mask from the faces of the whole miserable, pathetic lot." And (3) a member of the Second Marine Brigade, the Ehrhardt Brigade, the *Marinebrigade Ehrhardt*,[383] who later took part in

---

[381] Robert G. L. Waite, *Vanguard of Nazism: The Free Corps Movement in Postwar Germany, 1918-1923* (1952), pp. 78-79.

[382] Heydebreck was author of *Wir Wehr-Wölfe: Erinnerungen eines Freikorps-Führers*, hence this name for these troops. *Wehr-Wölfe* can be rendered Resistance or Opposition Wolves.

[383] This brigade, some 6,000 strong, led by Hermann Ehrhardt (1881-1971), was one of the components of the (right-wing) Kapp-Lüttwitz Putch; the brigade

the Beer Hall Putsch: "Out of the experience of the Revolution came the conviction that our task for the next decade would be: For the Reich! For the Volk! Fight the Government! Death to the Democratic Republic!"[384]

The Freikorps were to form a core element in the early SA. Along with this second paramilitary group, under Ernst Röhm, was the *Bund Reichskriegsflagge* (The Imperial War Flag Society), or the *Verband Reichskriegsflagge* (Imperial War Flag Union). Together with the SA, these were together called the *Kampfbund* (Battle Society or League). These worked together in their violence; they were disbanded after the unsuccessful Putsch of November 1923, but reformed themselves under other names, less obviously militant in nature. And, within the SA were units called *Stoßtruppen-Hitler München* (Munich). These paramilitary fighters were well known as *Schlägertruppe* (gangs of thugs) who engaged in *Zusammenstößen* (street fights).

On a practical level, their "paramilitary rowdiness"[385]—meaning the violence in their street-fighting, mostly with German Communists—resulted in many injuries in those confrontations, which in turn led to a creative insurance coverage for SA injuries, part of their membership benefits for being part of the SA, subsidized by some very rich early donors to the Nazi Party. (The role of these rich providers perhaps made the difference between the SA going under with no funds to pay these fights and the administrators over them, or surviving and even thriving financially, often with hidden strings being involved.)

Freikorps Bund Oberland   Stoßtruppen-Hitler München

One observer described the SA Men in these terms: "the booby-stepping [high-strutting] columns of brown-shirted storm troopers with their red, swastika-emblazoned armbands struck me as being ridiculous as well as repulsive, but there were sinister overtones. A course, mindless follow-the-leader attitude characterized these jackbooted [having knee-high military boots] members of the *Sturm Abteilung* (Storm Squadron), commonly known by its initials as the SA. Their behavior was vulgar, ruthless, and regularly unquestioning in the discipline observed among

---

entered Berlin on March 20, 1920; the Putch was unsuccessful. It was formally banned and disbanded, but continued its position and activities under other names. See "Hermann Ehrhardt" and "Marinebrigade Ehrhardt," WIKIPEDIA.

[384] Robert G. L. Waite, *Vanguard of Nazism*, pp. 50, 56-57. Ellipses in original.
[385] Anthony J. Nicholls, *Weimar and the Rise of Hitler*, p. 158.

their own ranks."[386] In this line of thought, the SA would become known for their military-like organization and chaotic violence, and their use of precise military formations and of marching songs to inspire and to bring a sense of common mission. One very famous song of the SA, actually a variant of a German song from the Baden Revolution of 1848-1849 under the leadership of Friedrich Hecker, *das Heckerlied* (the Hecker Song), was already used with new anti-Semitic lyrics in Munich in the spring of 1919 by the nationalistic military group, the *Freikorps*. In its SA variant, the lyrics read in part: *und wenn's Judenblut vom Messer spritzt, dann geht's nochmal so gut* (and when Jewish blood splashes off of the knife, then things are going quite well once more).[387] What these lyrics perhaps lacked in subtlety, they gained in vehement explicit hatred and imagery.

Here, in a brief overview, the violent, bloody confrontations between Communist demonstrators and Nazi SA Men was well known through the Weimar Republic 1920s. The two groups, wanting to crush the other, actually worked together (not intentionally) in their mutual violence to show the fragility of the Weimar Republic's capacity to keep civil peace.

The Weimar Republic had means, but only limited and ultimately inadequate, to maintain civil order. The Berlin Chief of Police, Friedrich Karl Zörgiebel, a Social Democrat, in December 1928, for example, banned all demonstrations and gatherings in open air, on the grounds that this would eliminate the bloody clashes (*blutige Zusammenstößen*) between Communists and Nazis. Such clashes were between Berlin Weimar police and either the SA or the Communists (or among all three); we can perhaps imagine two-or-three-way violence involving the Weimar Police among Communist, Nazi, and the Berlin Weimar police.[388]

In spite of this ban—and certainly not willing to back down against SA violence—Communists still gathered for traditional annual Communist celebrations on the First of May, Workers' Day, or International Workers' Day, the very next year (1929), in Berlin neighborhoods with significant

---

[386] Henry Simon, *Third Reich Diaries: An Eyewitness Account of the Hitler Years* (1989), p. 25. Californian Simon had moved to Jena in the 1920s, to work with the Zeiss optical company (founded in 1846, Zeiss has made some of the world's most respected microscopes, binoculars, telescopes, and other lenses). Simon remained in Germany as an enemy alien, treated with some relative gentleness, given his importance in writing for foreign markets for Zeiss Works; he nonetheless had a loaded Colt pistol ready for self-defense or suicide (pp. 18-19, 70-75).

[387] "Heckerlied," DE.WIKIPEDIA. For fuller discussion, see Michael Kohlstruck and Simone Scheff, "„Das Heckerlied" und seine antisemitische Variante. Zu Geschichte und Bedeutungswandel eines Liedes," pp. 135-158 in *Ausschluss und Feindschaft. Studien zu Antisemitismus und Rechtsextremismus*, Michael Kohlstruck and Andreas Klärner, eds. (2011); online via a search for Heckerlied Feindschaft.

[388] Wolfgang Zank, "10 981 Schüsse auf die Republik," *Der Zeit*, May 5, 1989. The violent confrontation on May 1, 1929, called *Blutmai* (Bloody May)—also called *Mai-Unruhen* (May Riots), was written up that day in German papers such as the *Berliner Morgenpost* front page article, "Blutige Unruhen in Kreuzberg und Wedding," and is portrayed in *Babylon Berlin, Season 1, Episode 4*, at 13:10-11:40.

working-class populations, such as Kreuzberg and Wedding, which was known as *roter Wedding* ("red" Wedding)[389]:

Weimar Police vs. SA, July 1931   Militants in *roter Wedding*, Berlin

GERMANY AND THE VISION OF A FUTURE WORLD IN *MEIN KAMPF*

By the time of Hitler's speeches of the 1920s, posters for which were shown above, the book *Mein Kampf* was soon to be published.[390] It was not a bestseller; that would come later, in the Third Reich, when the book became the standard gift to newly-weds, signed by the town's mayor, and was even given to workers to reward their good work. Then, and later, the book itself was and is sometimes considered to be the ravings of a driven and twisted mind; or perhaps consisting of the extreme statements of a man wanting to correct the wrongs he saw perpetrated on the German nation during and after World War I, especially by German politicians and then by the government of the Weimar Republic (seeing, or at least imagining, a worldwide cabal of filthy Jews pulling the strings of world politics behind the scenes). Some took *Mein Kampf* quite seriously and saw in it a text that had better not be dismissed as absurd nonsense. For example, the German Jewish philosopher Günther Anders and his wife, German Jewish philosopher Hannah Arendt, conducted a seminar in 1932 "with the aim of convincing the intellectuals among their circle of friends and acquaintances of this book's deadly seriousness."[391]

And one non-German sense of *Mein Kampf* was presented in an article from 1932 by Nicolas Fairweather on Hitler before he became Chancellor, in which he commented on Hitler's thinking, based in large part on his review of *Mein Kampf*, "All his views are energetic, positive, dogmatic, but there is no penetration in his reasoning processes and he is often carried away by the glamour of his own gorgeous phrases.... He has a poor grasp of abstract principles and puts his faith in high feeling and strong emotion. *Not seeing that civilization is a structure slowly built up*

---

[389] Kreuzberg, with a working-class population, in West Berlin, was the site of many street brawls between its left-leaning if not Spartacist (Communists) residents and the SA (Stormtrooopers). Wedding was an area in Charlottenburg, only incorporated into *Groß-Berlin* (greater Berlin) in 1920. Otis C. Mitchell, *Hitler's Stormtroopers and the Attack on the German Repulbic, 1919-1933*, p. 109.

[390] Volume 1 of *Mein Kampf* was published in 1925; Volume 2 in 1926.

[391] Anders' birthname was Günther Stern. Kerstein Putz, "The Letters of Günther Anders: His Corresondence with Hannah Arendt," pp. 131-142, in *The Life and Work of Günther Anders: Émigré, Iconoclast, Philosopher, Man of Letters*, Günther Bischof, Jason Dawsey, and Bernhard Fetz, eds. (2014), at p. 134.

by orderly procedure and respect for law, he is all for immediate action.... Hitler is narrow, seeing only his own national ideal, and would ruthlessly force the human spirit into his mold.... For him there is only one thing in human life to aim at. Race and nation are one, and he has fused them into an idol which he calls Volkstum, the racial community, which becomes an object of fanatical devotion. In short, his political philosophy is a kind of religion, based on pseudo-science and tribal psychology...."[392]

Fairweather continued in the essay's Part II: "With Hitler, what is expedient is right, and any alliance is possible for a limited aim (even with the Devil, says Gregor Strasser) but only for the moment and for the partial goal to be achieved.... Coalitions are dangerous, and any cooperation with others must be temporary, for some special purpose."[393] This is a rather penetrating, early, analysis, from before Hitler became Chancellor.

Others find in *Mein Kampf* words of wisdom. There was enthusiastic praise by those who were inspired by the National Socialist political vision. The book is one way of seeing early negative characterizations of a group (stereotyping in repulsive ways) from Nazi propaganda, in *Mein Kampf* itself, but we also find this in *Der Stürmer*, the weekly newspaper founded in 1923 and edited by Julius Streicher, and in *Der Angriff*, the daily founded in 1927 and edited by Joseph Goebbels, among other sources, and in earlier pre-Nazi formulations, largely from the 1800s.

Mein Kampf was praised by some and harshly criticized by others who resisted the society that was being created by the Nazi worldview. For example, the Munich-centered anti-Nazi group, the White Rose, described *Mein Kampf* in its 1942 Pamphlet 2,[394] as "a book that is written in the worst German (*in dem übelsten Deutsch geschrieben worden ist*) I have ever read (*das ich je gelesen habe*), in spite of the fact that it has been elevated to the position of the Bible in this nation of poets and thinkers."[395] More on the White Rose, below.

In marked contrast to this negative opinion of Hitler's writing style, what Hitler heard was more like the comment Ribbentrop made to him in words of adoration (as recorded in the diary of Eva Braun), "Your German style, my Führer, will last just as long as Shakespeare's English or

---

[392] Nicolas Fairweather, "Hitler and Hitlerism [Part I]: A Man of Destiny. An early 10-point summary of the inspiring dictator's agenda," *The Atlantic*, Mar. 1932. Italics added. (Some cite the author as Nicholas Fairweather, incorrectly.)

[393] Nicolas Fairweather, "Hitler and Hitlerism [Part II]: Germany Under the Nazis. The Führer's early goals included physical education, a return to rural life, health care for all—and foreboding plans for the Jews," *The Atlantic*, Apr. 1932.

[394] These pamphlets originated in Munich, but were distributed to a larger area. The American Henry Simon, who was living in Jena, near Weimar, at that time, remarked, "According to my diary, it was in November of 1942 when our younger daughter Hilda brought home a contraband leaflet printed by the clandestine White Rose opposition group." From Simon, *Third Reich Diaries*, p. 23.

[395] "White Rose: Leaflet 2," CENTER FOR WHITE ROSE STUDIES; Ger. at "Flugblatt II: Flugblätter der Weißen Rose II," BUNDESZENTRALE FÜR POLITISCHE BILDUNG.

The Hitler Era

Racine's French."³⁹⁶ What was in this book? Leaving aside here such critical judgments as just quoted, if we look at some of the major themes in the book, to see topics that were of central importance to Hitler in *Mein Kampf*, we can notice a few concerns that are presented as having an urgent priority, with a call to alarm and emphasis of the need of the people to apply ongoing, enthusiastic diligence to deal with and ultimately to conquer.

This ideal or principle for action addresses the issue of the overriding, global need of a focused commitment to a full engagement in tasks needing society's involvement (from earlier National Socialism). Hitler wrote, "*In all cases which involve the fulfillment of apparently impossible demands or tasks, the entire attention of a people has to be united uniformly on this one question in such a manner as though indeed its existence or its non-existence depended upon its solution* [*als ob von ihrer Lösung tatsächlich Sein oder Nichtsein abhänge*]."³⁹⁷

This principle is joined with the teaching that life is a struggle of the strong against the weak: "If the power to fight for one's own health is no longer present, the right to live in this world of struggle ends" [*Wenn die Kraft zum Kampfe um die eigene Gesundheit nicht mehr vorhanden ist, endet das Recht zum Leben in dieser Welt des Kampfes*].³⁹⁸

Along with this vision, a core concept for Nazi politics presented in *Mein Kampf* was the ideal of the German people as one naturally unified community (*ein Volk*)—a race—with shared ideals, projects, and sense of their history and its future potential. Ultimately this would be woven into a powerfully inspiring slogan defining the Nazi state, "*Ein Volk, ein Reich, ein Führer*" (One people, one empire, one leader).

In this photograph, we see this slogan declared in large banners here, as at important events such as speeches at Berlin's *Sportpalast* and at

---

³⁹⁶ Eva Braun, *The Private Life of Adolf Hitler: The Intimate Notes and Diary of Eva Braun*, Paul Tabori, ed., (1949), pp. 107-108, July, 1940.

³⁹⁷ Adolf Hitler. Editions used cited above; here, in short, *Mein Kampf*, Eng. (1941); Ger. from Adolf Hitler, *Mein Kampf. Zwei Bände in einem Band* (1936). Quotation from Vol. I, Chap. X (Causes of the Collapse—*Ursachen des Zusammenbruchs*), Eng., pp. 302-388, at p. 340; Ger., pp. 245-310, at p. 273.

³⁹⁸ Adolf Hitler, *Mein Kampf*, Vol. I, Chap. X, Eng., pp. 816-845, at p. 257; Ger., pp. 245-310, at p. 282; emphasis original: Ger. spacing between the letters of the text (*Spationierung, Sperrsatz, Sperren*, etc.) for emphasis (as Eng. italics).

the annual Nazi Party Congresses in the years preceding the war, especially those of 1933-1938. In Hitler's words, the government (as in the National Socialist Third Reich), understood as being based on "a folkish-ethnic *[völkisch]* way of life" would have a first obligation to ensure its own perpetuity, "to see to it that the conception of the nature and the purpose of a State receives a uniformly clear form."[399] Furthermore, "the 'folkish' view ... sees in the State only a means to an end, and as its end it considers the preservation of the racial existence of men. Thus it by no means believes in an equality of the races, but with their differences it also recognizes their superior and inferior values [*ihren höherin oder minderen Wert*] ..."[400] This would be explained in *Mein Kampf*, with *radical powers of the state described.*

> National Socialism must, in principle, claim the right [*muß grundsätzlich das Recht in Anspruch nehmen*] to force its principles on the whole German nation [*der gesamten deutschen Nation seine Prizipien aufzuzwingen*], and to educate it in its ideas and thoughts.... [We] must never give up on the reintroduction of a national army [in contrast to the militias of German regional governments] in the future. Then the basic realization is that *the State represents not an end, but a means. It is indeed the presumption [precondition] for the formation of a higher human culture, but not its cause. On the contrary, the latter lies exclusively in the existence of a race* [meaning the German *Völk* or people] *capable of culture.*[401]

For the State to be conceived of as merely a means to a völkisch or racially uniform community, gives to the concept of the Völk, the people, a fundamental, all-contextualizing function and supreme significance. This is no mere after-thought or mere rhetorical flourish! This is serious business! And it touched on something important for many Germans. As an educator would reply, when asked after the war why he as an educated adult had been taken by the National Socialists and had joined the party in 1928, "Hitler appealed to the atavistic instinct in us by not being afraid to shout out loud what we only silently admitted to ourselves—that we Germans were indeed the superior race."[402] *Such delusions of grandeur are more dangerous than they might seem at first blush.*

---

[399] Adolf Hitler, *Mein Kampf*, Vol. II, Chap. II (The State—*Der Staat*), Eng., pp. 584-655, sub-sect. "The State No End in Itself," at p, 592; Ger. pp. 425-487, at p. 431.
[400] Adolf Hitler, *Mein Kampf*, Vol. II, Chap. I (View of Life and Party—*Weltanschauung und Partei*), Eng., pp. 563-583, at pp. 579-580; Ger., pp. 409-424, at pp. 420-421.
[401] Adolf Hitler, *Mein Kampf*, Vol. II, Chap. X (Federalism as a Mask—*Der Federalismus als Maske*), Eng. pp. 816-845, sub-sect. "One People—One State," at p. 845, Ger., pp. 621-648, at p. 648. Emphasis original.
[402] Alfons Heck, *The Burden of Hitler's Legacy*, p. 58.

Hitler's respect for the military and his focus on the establishment of a society of the *Völk* came together in his considering the path to this goal. Writing about the realization of the ideals of a worldview [*Verwirklichung weltanschauungsmäßiger Ideale*] and the implications derived from them, Hitler stated that "only if the ideal urge [or drive] for independence [*der Ideale Drang nach Unabhändigkeit*] receives, *in the forms of military means of power*, the fighting organization [*in den Formen militärischer Machtmittel die kampfesmäßige Organisation*], can the urgent wish of a people be turned into glorious realization."[403]

The Psychology of Group Unity in Peace and in Violence

There is great power in these concepts of the *Völk*, the people, and of the *Völkgeimeinschaft*, the community of the people. The sense of fellowship and intense interconnectedness, in which people experience themselves as part of a group of like-minded and similarly committed people, all of whom ultimately work with and rely on one another, a phenomenon we see in civil life as well as in military contexts, is psychologically an extremely powerful influence and motivation. This sense of a shared mission, whether in a civil or in a military context, can be appreciated as a universal phenomenon, in all group activities and in all military ones, as well.

In the battlefield, there may be a thought now and then about the principles that have been used to define and to justify the violence that is now called for, but there is also the desire to live, simply to survive, which is often joined to a desire to help our comrades survive, or to avenge the injuries or death of these comrades in arms. This was the case not only in the Wehrmacht and in the Waffen SS, or in other branches of the Third Reich military, but in opponent military (the Soviets, the British, the Americans, and others); we can also find this form of camaraderie in other instances of organized, systematic violence, both as formal military confrontations and as rampaging inter-group killing.

In this way, while ideology and a society's moral vision of the world (in some loose sense of what counts as morality) have their role in the more careful presentations of what the violence is all about, *in another way, these are much less important, if not irrelevant, to the reality of organized violence, which has its own patterns of coordinated experience, with psychological, emotional, social, and visceral components:* there can be intense feelings of disgust at seeing comrades dead in one's arms, the rage at this violence—rarely called "collateral damage" when it comes to one's own group and its losses—and feelings of an essentially limited capacity to correct and certainly to undo this damage, with the realization of the (limited) revenge that we might feel strongly driven to impose on those enemies we see as evil for their violence against us and ours.[404]

---

[403] Adolf Hitler, *Mein Kampf*, Vol. II, Chap. I, pp. 563-583, at p. 575; Ger., pp. 409-424, at pp. 417-418. Emphasis (italics) added.

[404] Sönke Neitzel and Harald Welzer, *Soldaten: On Fighting, Killing, and Dying; The Secret World War II Transcripts of German POWs* (2012), pp. 320-343.

While some students of war—military theoreticians, psychologists, historians, and others—may touch on this topic, often many of the most powerful and most impressive presentations of the autonomous, non-ideological nature of violence in war come in the form of art, in novels, and, in more recent times, in film. (More on this role for films, below.)

Some inter-war books have portrayed with precision a wide variety of aspects of war and its consequences for the people that are drawn up into them, whether willingly or otherwise; for an international sampling (some better known than others):[405] *The Fire* (Henri Barbusse, 1916), *The Good Soldier Švejk* (Jaroslav Hašek, 1921-1923), *Seven Pillars of Wisdom: A Triumph* (T. E. Lawrence, 1922), *The Storm of Steel* (Ernst Jünger, 1924), *All Quiet on the Western Front* (Erich Marie Remarque, 1929), *A Farewell to Arms* (Ernest Hemingway, 1929), *Higher Command* (Edlef Köppen, 1930), *Toward the Flame: A Memoir of World War I* (Hervey Allen, 1934), *The Complete Memoirs of George Sherston* (Siegfried Sassoon, 1937), *Johnny Got His Gun* (Dalton Trumbo, 1939), *Ashes and Diamonds* (Jerzy Andrzejewski, 1948), *The Naked and the Dead* (Norman Mailer, 1948), *Two Women* (Alberto Moravia, 1957), *The Painted Bird* (Jerzy Kosiński, 1965), *The Color of Smoke* (Menyhért Lakatos, 1975), *General Escobar's War* (José Luis Olaizola Sarriá, 1983), *Suite Française* (Irène Némirovsky, 2004), *Sarah's Key* (Tatiana de Rosnay, 2006), and so on.

The military can be used not only to reflect the values and social organizations of the society, but it can also be instrumental in giving a nation a sense of its own power, security, and worth, however ultimately limited this sense is in the face of the realities a nation will actually face.

It would seem that Hitler saw the use of military force as a means of bringing about fundamental societal changes (as in the development of a Germany of the *Völk*), the most appealing path, in fact, a path that is quite effective, if not actually essential, to bring about this goal.

We may also find the ideal of the Teutonic Knights having a significant place for Hitler in *Mein Kampf*, in part in the context of the issue of the aggressive acquisition of *Lebensraum*,[406] living space—by then (1924 on, as in *Mein Kampf*) meaning territories for the growing German occupation of vast lands, principally beyond Germany's pre-war borders, especially to the east and in the vast fertile lands of Russia.

On this, Hitler expounded, "The acquisition of new soil [*Grund und Boden*] for the settlement of the excess population [*zur Ansiedelung der überlaufenden Volkszahl*] possesses an infinite number of advantages,

---

[405] Ordered by date of first ed., not by the historical contexts portrayed.

[406] The notion of *Lebensraum* did not originate with Hitler. Friedrich Ratzel (1844-1904) introduced the concept in *Eine biogeographische Studie* (1901), pp. 51, etc., without the later (Nazi) implications of migrationist colonialism. It is also found in the proclamation in Sept. 1928, by a section of the Stahlhelm—an association of veterans founded in late 1918, with monarchist leanings—that Germany needed to win *Lebensraum* in the East. See S. William Halperin, *Germany Tried Democracy: A Political History of the Reich from 1918 to 1933* (1946/1965), p. 366.

particularly if we turn from the present to the future.... If land was desired in Europe, it could be obtained by and large only at the expense of Russia [*im großen und ganzen nur auf Kosten Rußlands*], and this meant that the new Reich must again set itself on the march along the road of the Teutonic Knights of old [*dann mußte sich das neue Reich wieder auf der Straße der einstigen Ordensritter in Marsch setzen*], to obtain by the German sword, sod for the German plow and daily bread for the nation."[407] *There are strong parallels in this with the American doctrine of a divine Manifest Destiny with its own expansionist principles.*

In the German context, the close link between the nation—the people, *das Volk*, identified as a group of one blood—and the soil, was captured by the often-used expression, *Blut und Boden*, Blood and Soil, a nineteenth-century linking of a people or family, a blood-line, with territory, giving rise to the relatedly important legal expression (as in the Nuremberg Laws of 1935), *deutschblütig*, German-blooded, similar to another term defining German racial identity, *deutschstämmig*, stemming from Germans, of German stock, lineage, or ancestry.[408]

This idea of *Lebensraum* found here in *Mein Kampf*, living space for the *Volk*, the German, Aryan people, at the expense of the East, especially of the Soviet Union, *was to remain one of the major principles guiding Hitler and the Third Reich*. The significance of this concept was put forth by Hitler to his military, just months before the outbreak of the war, on February 10, 1939, when he declared, "I have taken it upon myself to solve the German question, that is, to solve the question of space. You must take it as a fact that, as long as I live, this idea will rule my entire thinking."[409] *Imagine the power of such a ruling idea!*

The right to this aggression, we might note, was based on the idea of the superiority of the Germans as the Aryan Race and the supposed inferiority of others, especially Jews, Romanies, and Slavs. And this, in turn, rested upon the Social Darwinist principle of the right of the strongest to dominate all weaker peoples. (In a thorough consistency, when Germany was definitively losing the war against the Soviet Armies, Hitler's logical conclusion was that Germany was in fact a weaker power and so deserved to be destroyed by the Soviets. More on that, below.)

---

[407] Adolf Hitler, *Mein Kampf*, Vol. I, Chap. IV (Munich—*München*), Eng. pp. 126-156, at pp. 138, 140; Ger., pp, 138-171, at pp. 151, 154 (with spacing).

[408] The second part of this, *-stämmig* (stemming from, or originally from), is from *der Stamm* (cognate with Eng. stem): stock, lineage, descent, ancestry, ethnicity, etc. *Deutschstämmig* means being of German lineage, ancestry, roots, parentage, ethnicity. Cf. the Feb. 24, 1934 *Neue Zürcher Zeitung* article "Deutschstämmige Psychotherapie," a critique of Carl Gustav Jung's position by fellow Swiss psychoanalyst Gustav Bally, MD, in tr. as "Gustav Bally and *deutschstämmige Psychotherapie*"—pp. xlviii-lii (presentation, tr. of the Bally article, and discussion, by Mitchell Ginsberg and Angela Graf-Nold, Zurich Jungian analyst)—in *Effective Psychotherapy: The Contribution of Hellmuth Kaiser*, Mitchell Ginsberg, ed. (2018).

[409] Jonathan Steinberg, "The Third Reich Reflected: German Civil Administration in the Occupied Soviet Union, 1941-4," *The English Historical Review*, vol. 110, no. 437, Jun. 1995, pp. 620-651, at p. 621.

The linking of the drive to the East and the centuries-earlier Teutonic Knights made use of the image of the Teutonic Knights, which had its own power and was an inspiration both in propagandistic posters and in the florid imagination of Heinrich Himmler, who saw the SS as a somewhat mystical recreation of these noble Knights.

This interest in the Teutonic Knights, with emphasis on fire rituals, going back to pre-Christian pagan times, was used by Hitler. We have only to think here of the many night-parades with torches and images created by large numbers of SA Men or *Hitlerjugend* marching in formation, or to consider the night rituals of burning of books of "un-German spirit" (that went against National Socialist ideas) to recognize this thread of thinking in the Nazi world.

So, in addition to the National Socialist vehement focus on Jew-hatred, put aside in this present moment, there was also *a tension between the Germanic (Nazi) worldview and that of Christianity as the inheritor of Judaism*.

This tension, already present in the early 1920s, was felt to be quite basic by those at the center of the National Socialist movement and government, although there was ample reference to God and an explicitly pious and respectful attitude toward the teachings of the Christ—often transposed to Hitler as a savior (*Retter*)—a Savior who was nevertheless certainly not presented as the Son of God—and at least presenting Hitler as a holy knight (*Ritter*) in shining armor, for the German people.

There was a fascination about Hitler by those drawn to him. His glance, and his speaking voice, were both said to have a hypnotizing power of captivation and even inspiration for those who could be close enough to him to gaze clearly and intently into his eyes. Hitler, spring 1924[410]:

---

[410] This photograph was taken by Heinrich Hoffmann at a corner of the *Volksgericht* (People's Court) in Munich, at the trial against the participants of the Hitler-Putsch, April 1924 (*das Verfahren gegen die Teilnehmer des Hitler-Putsches April 1924*). The *Bayerische Staatsbibliothek* (Bavarian State Library) or BSB (BSB-MUENCHEN.DE) identifies the photo as hoff 1726, dated spring 1924; coloration of the picture from an unknown source. (Personal communication, Feb. 6, 2018, from Angelika Betz, Diplomate Librarian, *BSB/Bayerische Staatsbibliothek*, Dept. of Manuscripts and Early Printed Books, Map Collection and Image Archive.) See this image at "Adolf Hitler Biography," THEFAMOUSPEOPLE.COM; "Where was Adolf Hitler born," *ProProfs Discuss* (PROPROFS.COM), etc.

The Hitler Era

Hitler was said to have a hypnotic glance, with eyes that were blue— deep blue, steel-blue, ice blue, light greenish-gray blue, or blue-gray. Some sources, found later to be based on forged documents put out by British intelligence to mock Hitler, even claimed that his eyes were brown.[411] Beyond his physical appearance, many Germans perceived him, in part, as precisely such a holy savior or knight, dedicated heart and soul, so many felt, to the well-being of Germany.

HITLER AS MESSIAH AND SAVIOR (*RETTER*) AND AS KNIGHT (*RITTER*)

Hitler was frequently praised as the "coming Messiah" (*preist Hitler als den „kommenden Messias"*),[412] as he was once described by the French noblewoman Marie-Gabrielle-Blanche Comtesse (Countess) d'Allemont de Broutillot (1873-1937)—wife of Graf Ernst Reventlow (1869-1943),[413] a journalist, former German Naval captain, and anti-Semitic Nationalist leader—when she and her husband met Hitler, who was living at the time at the Bechstein home in Charlottenburg, Berlin, in 1921.

In the next decade (1934), Hermann Göring would write, "there is something mystical, unspeakable about this single man [Hitler], ... we love Adolf Hitler, because we believe, deeply and believe steadfastly, that he has been sent to us by God to save Germany [*Deutschland zu retten*]."[414] This is no small compliment, no trifling belief! Now, while some ideas, as just above, were expressed in Christian terminology, there was another dimension of the National Socialist relationship with religion in general, and, in particular, with Christianity.[415]

Here we have a mystical dimension in the thinking of some leading Nazis *involving the alternative ideal of the Teutonic Knights*. (Hitler wrote of them in *Mein Kampf.*) This basic idea was put forth in various forms by

---

[411] The "proof" that Hitler actually had brown eyes, was based on a forged passport created during the war by the UK's SOE (Special Operations Executive) for propagandistic purposes. Hitler is described in that faked document as a painter and as having brown eyes; it has a stamp from Vienna. See "Adolf Hitler's Fake Passport," THE (UK GOV'T) NATIONAL ARCHIVES. It perhaps had more significance during the war than afterwards, but falsified information dies hard.

[412] Wulf C. Schwarzwäller, *Hitlers Geld* [*Hitler's Money*], p. 98; Eng., *The Unknown Hitler*, p. 82.

[413] Also known as Ernst Graf (Count) zu Reventlow, or, Ernst Graf von Reventlow.

[414] Hermann Göring, *Aufbau einer Nation* (1934), p. 52. Ger.: *es ist etwas Mystisches, Unsagbares um diesen einzigen Mann, ... wir lieben Adolf Hitler, weil wir glauben, tief und unerschütterich glauben, daß er uns von Gott gesandt is, Deutschland zu retten.*

[415] Hermann Rauschning reported that in April 1933 Hitler confided to him: "A German Church, a German Christianity, is a distortion. One is either a Christian or a German. You cannot be both." Hermann Rauschning, *Hitler Speaks: A Series of Political Conversations with Adolf Hitler On His Real Aims* (1939), pp. 57-58. Cf. discussion in Samuel Koehe, "Were the National Socialists a Völkisch Party? Paganism, Christianity, and the Nazi Christmas," *Central European History*, vol. 47, no. 4, 2014, pp. 760-790. Christmas: in Ger., *das Weihnachten* (Christmas), in Nazi vocabulary became *das Julfest* (Midwinter Festival).

Joseph Goebbels in the Propaganda Ministry, but also applied seriously by Heinrich Himmler, head of the Schutzstaffel (SS), discussed above.

From the German perspective, Himmler, in particular, would come to adopt a great cultural task, one taking a clear anti-Jewish but also anti-Christian attitude: The romanticizing from the nineteenth century of the great Teutonic Germanic culture was taken in the Nazi context to have had great power before being weakened centuries earlier by Christianity—itself a child of Judaism and its fight against the natural order (as seen by the Social Darwinism of that age, in which the fight for survival was interpreted to be a justification for force over the weak).

This totally overlooks the recognition by scholars such as the German-Russian zoologist Karl Fëdorovich Kessler (1815-1881), who proposed a second principle that complemented that of the Darwinian Law of Mutual Struggle (of competition and strife), in a 1879 paper "On the Law of Mutual Aid" (which he presented in a talk at St. Petersburg University in January 1880). And, concerning the place of Social Darwinism among core ideas for Hitler, psychiatrist Fritz Redlich[416] held that "The centerpiece of his *Weltanschauung* was his social Darwinism and anti-Semitism."[417] (We can compare with this the similar, earlier, comment by another psychiatrist, Wilhelm Reich, quoted above in discussing the 1920 Twenty-five Points of the Nazi Program.) And German historian Peter Longerich wrote of Himmler, that he "wanted to direct the SS to one task above all: it was to act as the vanguard in overcoming Christianity and restoring a 'Germanic' way of living [*einer »germanischen« Lebensweise*]."

As Himmler understood it, this was the actual mission of his *Schutztaffel* [SS]: "it was to this task that it owed its identity and the justification for its existence."[418] Himmler foresaw the SS as leaders of a "cult of the Teutons [*Germanenkult*]".[419] Some 8 years before the end of the Reich, he described this mission in these terms: "We live in an era of the ultimate conflict with Christianity. It is part of the mission of the SS to give the German people in the next half-century [*im nächsten halben Jahrhundert*] the non-Christian ideological foundations on which to lead and shape their lives. This task does not consist solely in overcoming an ideological opponent but must be accompanied at every step by a positive impetus: in this case that means the reconstruction of the Germanic heritage [*die Erschließung des germanischen Erbes*] in the widest and

---

[416] Frederick (Fritz) Redlich (1910-2004) received his MD from the Univ. of Vienna in 1935, followed by training in neuropsychiatry. Emigrating after the *Anschluß* in 1938, he was later Chairman of the Psychiatry Dept. at Yale Univ., from 1950-1967, and then Dean of the Yale Medical School, from 1967-1972. See "Frederick Redlich," WIKIPEDIA, and "Former Medical School Dean Dr. Fritz Redlich dies at age 93," *Yale Bulletin and Calendar*, vol. 32, no. 15, Jan. 16, 2004.

[417] Frederick Redlich, *Hitler: Diagnosis of a Destructive Prophet* (1999), p. 340.

[418] Peter Longerich, *Heinrich Himmler;* Jeremy Noakes & Lesley Sharpe, tr. (2012), p. 265. Ger. text: Peter Longerich, *Himmler: Biographie* (2008), p. 274.

[419] Peter Longerich, *Heinrich Himmler*, p. 269; *Himmler: Biographie*, p. 279.

The Hitler Era

most comprehensive sense."[420] All of this highlights the fact that Hitler and cohorts were not *Christian* anti-Semites! *They were even more radical!*

A popular application of this was in the adaptation of the Teutonic Knights (*die germanen Ritter*) as *das arische Ideal*, the ideal of the Nordic or Aryan man and woman. There was a more profound respect for, and valuing of, the strong and powerful, in the one value system (also found in ancient Roman values), than for the caring and love for the weak and meek, in the other. *For the National Socialists, the first was superior and to be cultivated, while with the former, the weak and destitute were best abandoned, expulsed, or even eliminated (killed)*.

In terms of our being wary of reductive thinking, we might note here a false (incomplete) dichotomy: a society could actually have both of these as respected values: honoring the strong and caring for the weak. As is often the case, *the exhaustive and mutually exclusive dichotomous (or "opposite") categories that we set up for ourselves are in some instances neither exhaustive (there being further alternatives) nor mutually exclusive (there being the possibility of both being present at the same time)*. In the case of the Third Reich, the dichotomous issue of the cultural identity of an individual, the importance of being German (*germanisch*) or being non-German, was of great importance in terms of how people were to be treated by the Third Reich in its political operations. Even such a simple dichotomy of Aryan versus Jewish was in fact never adequately resolved, and caused questions and complications if not confusion among the Nazi administration. (The Wannsee Conference of January 1942, which, in addition to other administrative conundrums, tried to define who was Aryan and who was Jewish, was a case in point.)

While we can approach the issue of personal identity from many interesting and potentially profound starting points (with philosophical, psychological, experiential, social, cultural, moral, and legal issues being variously addressed), and recognizing its importance not only in Nazi Germany but in many societies that were ultimately multi-cultural (and thus having to differentiate between the identities of its various cultural components), the Nazi approach was both simple and casuistic, with Hitler having ultimate say over who would be recognized and treated as an Aryan and who not.

The National Socialist focus on the Teutonic Knights as an alternative to Christianity as "Southern" (from Rome) and inferior, took its admirers back to 723 CE and what was considered from the Germanic point of view a Teutonic disaster, when the Christian Winifred, later called Bishop Boniface of Mainz, as mentioned above, took an axe to the holy oak tree of Thor, chopped it down, and, when he not struck by Thor's thunderbolt in punishment, inspired those around to be converted to Christianity. For the National Socialists, this period of conversion was a turning point from true Germanic values to the values the Nazis saw as imposed by the

---

[420] Longerich dates this as *vermutlich 1937* (presumably from 1937): Peter Longerich, *Heinrich Himmler*, p. 270; *Himmler: Biographie*, p. 280.

inferior, non-Germanic Southerners (that is, coming from Rome), who were inheritors of Jewish "moral" values that protected the weak and constrained the strong (a dichotomy we questioned, just above).

The focus on "Southern" morality is perhaps too limiting and confined in its understanding, given the relevance here not only of Christianity (and Judaism) but also of such teachings as Confucianism, Daoism, Buddhism, Shintoism, the Bahai Faith, Sikhism, and on and on, in a wide range of religious and spiritual traditions around the world and from different ages that each and all honor and encourage its followers, and all people, to be considerate, compassionate, emotionally unrepressed, sympathetic, to have understanding and an appreciation of the other, a sense of the unity of humanity and of basic human worth, a harmony with nature, a sense of hope and of courage, a candidness in many contexts, an honest fearlessness, and a peace-seeking way of dealing with life's issues, and so forth. Behind all of these non-Nazi frames of mind and ways of relating with others, is the question of *what sorts of human beings do we ourselves want to be, and what sort of human beings do we respect, honor, and appreciate for their contribution to our world*. (More on this topic, below.)

In one contrast, the archetypal model representing the Germanic worldview and its values was that of the Order of Brothers of the German House of Saint Mary in Jerusalem, commonly called the Teutonic Order— variously *der deutsche Orden* (the German Order), *Deutschherrenorden* (Order of the German Masters or Lords), or *Deutschritterorden* (Order of the German Knights). This was, perhaps ironically, a Catholic religious order—this was overlooked in the Nazi redefining of the Knights as a purely Teutonic force in contrast to Christianity—which was founded as a military order in 1190 in Acre, in the Kingdom of Jerusalem. In the 1300s, the Teutonic Order took up a call to a crusade, to conquer the eastern Baltic lands and to bring them into the Germanic (*and* the Christian) fold. Their expansion into Prussia and Livonia (Poland, Lithuania, Latvia) preceded their attack and their defeat on July 15, 1410, in the Polish-Lithuanian state near Tannenberg, with half the knights left dead on the battlefield.

(One feature of this history concerns the impact of disease on the outcome of military encounters. In the battles of 1410, there was a major dysentery epidemic among the Slavic troops that helped keep the Teutonic Knights from being even further decimated.) And in a scene that was later repeated after the German defeat in World War I, the Teutonic Knights attributed the defeat to treason on the part of Nikolaus von Ranys (Mikołaj of Ryńsk), the commander of Culm (Chełmno—later, a first extermination center for the Third Reich); he was beheaded.

The Knights saw this surrender as their having been stabbed in the back! (Back-stabbing is thus not a new concept!) Further, war reparations the Teutonic Knights were to pay the victors led to internal dissension and economic hardships among the Teutonic domains. (This might also sound familiar.)

Germans had in the meantime settled in these territories in those centuries, and their descendants were still living there when Hitler and the National Socialist worldview inspired the desire to take back all Germanic lands and to protect the German-speaking populations in Eastern Europe against all of the real and imagined foes out to annihilate the German world.

The victorious and religiously inspired first half of this story—but not the second part (with the destruction of the Germanic invaders), disastrous for the Germans, and preferably left in the shadows—remained in the German consciousness, and Himmler took the Order of the Teutonic Knights as a model for the SS. The story, in any case, remained in the thoughts and understanding of German history, at least among those with strong military interests: the German victory in World War I against the Russians, in the Battle of Tannenberg (August 26-30, 1914), was seen, as discussed above, by some German military as revenge for the Teutonic defeat at Tannenberg of 1410, a full half a millennium earlier!

The German military leaders of this battle, Field Marshall Paul von Hindenburg and Erich Ludendorff had their reputations strengthened through this major victory: It was Von Hindenburg who gave the battle the enduring name of the Battle of Tannenberg, by which name the earlier Teutonic defeat was known (with the alternative name, the Battle of Grunwald), even though the battle took place some 30 km. west of Tannenberg, near the town of Olsztyn (Allenstein), as noted above: names linked to history mean a lot, bringing the past into the present!

The Teutonic knight in medieval armor would be widely used in patriotic images for inspiration in the Third Reich and its dependent states. This use of knights in medieval dress, otherwise an out-of-place atavistic image, was used in posters for Germans, for French anti-Bolshevists, for Nordic populations (showing a SS-Wiking with a Viking ship), and for the Flemish (showing Teutonic-linked SS-Vlaanderen):

When Hitler had himself represented as a knight in shining armor, he presented himself as the guardian and protector of Germany, against all dragons that might present themselves in a belligerent hostility (especially the Jews as a world conspiracy), but, in fact, as one German historian remarked, "the would-be slayer of dragons was murdering the helpless."[421]

---

[421] Sebastian Haffner, *Anmerkungen zu Hitler*, 1978 ed., p. 122; 1994 ed., p. 95; Eng., *The Meaning of Hitler*, p. 95.

One image (on the left, just above) found in publications of the era harkens back to this vanguard Teutonic knight having a shield with an emblem on it that is here a variant on the swastika, with (middle image) one of Hitler as a Knight (*Ritter*), the horse-mounted leader (*Führer*) of these knights. And on the right, we can compare the earlier etching (1494) by Albrecht Dürer (1471-1528) called *der christliche Ritter* (The Christian knight)—from a Nuremberg of another age long ago and from a great conceptual distance, as well.

Such images represented the reconstruction of the pure race, one free not only of Jewish taint but also free of other non-German peoples—the Slavs, most centrally, but also others in Europe, even including Germans who were not up to the standards being envisioned: the weak, the sick, the incurable (both from physical and psychological problems), the Romanies, Southern Europeans (Christians), homosexuals, and so on. *This teaching held sway even though Nazi race scientists and Hitler realized and stated that* there was in fact no pure race to be found *(a consideration often overlooked when convenient)*.

The Nazi doctrine of the inferiority of the Slavs, available for slavery or elimination, was joined with the question of the need of Germany to invade the Soviet Union to obtain *Lebensraum* (space for an expanded German population to live and work the land), as would come to pass. During the war non-Jewish Poles and Russians were sent into Germany to be slave laborers. Any personal contact or respect shown them would regularly result in imprisonment of the Germans involved, and death for the Slavic slave laborer.[422] As we read in *Mein Kampf*,

> If one wanted land and soil [*Grund und Boden*] in Europe, then by and large this could only have been done at Russia's expense, and then the new Reich would again have to start marching along the road of the Teutonic knights [using the word *Ordensritter*, presumably for the more usual term, *Ritterorden*] ... of former times to give, with the help of the German sword, the soil to the plow and the daily bread to the nation."[423]

---

[422] *Eine Liebe in Deutschland* (*A Love in Germany*) presents one such fictionalized loving, tender relationship between a German woman (played by Hanna Schygulla) left to run her small grocery store, her husband away to war in the German military, and a Polish laborer (played by Piotr Lysak).

[423] Adolf Hitler, *Mein Kampf*, Vol. 1, Chap. 4; Eng., pp. 182-183, tr. here slightly modified (re "Teutonic Knights"); Ger., p. 154.

The Hitler Era

In the background here is a vision of a superior Nordic (Germanic) race, with full rights of a *Herrenrasse* (master race), a *Herrenvolk* (master people), to treat inferior races as it would, with steel-like determination.

With this, if we look at the model of the Nordic man and woman, young, tall, blond, healthy, images of power and health, and compare that to the principal leaders of the Third Reich, we may come to the comment once reportedly made by Reinhard Heydrich that most of these men leading the Nazi party hardly fit the image. (Heydrich, in contrast to these leaders, looked like a model for the ideal Germanic man: tall, light-haired, with a fine nose; Himmler, head of the SS and dreamer of the cultivation of a greater Aryan German nation, certainly did not look at all like the fair, tall, clear-sighted, robust German that the Nazis idealized.)

If we put aside (as inconvenient here) the fact that Nazi-oriented authors on race science, as the Nazis called it, had developed an extremely complex system with many races of man (looking only at Central European groups, and acknowledging that there are no longer any "pure" races (races not mixed with others of neighboring or distant races), there was nonetheless the more popular presentation of the *Herrenrasse* or Master Race, to which Germans should aspire, or, rather, should work toward cultivating through the coming generations. It was this simplistic version of idealized Germans that was presented as those worthy of and destined to rule the world, with all other lesser beings either acting as slaves for the German Nation or else killed in the millions, to make way for the taking over of Slavic Russia and its fertile lands that Germans dreamed of and coveted, as Hitler had written in *Mein Kampf*.

All talk of numerous human races will seem quite confused, absurd, and ultimately incomprehensible if we accept the understanding of many, including José Martí (1853-1895), an honored Cuban poet, who wrote "there are no races"—even if this idea was embedded in his claim, going against historical realities, "*No hay odio de razas porque no hay razas*" ("There is no racial animosity, because there are no races.")[424]

There was also the recurrent emphasis on the need for Germany to overcome the shame of the Versailles Treaty. Hitler, reminiscing in *Mein Kampf* about his speech given on February 24, 1920, remarked that the audience "did not want to hear or understand that Versailles was a shame and a disgrace (*eine Schande und Schmach*), and not even that this dictated peace was an unprecedented pillaging of our [the German] people (*eine unerhörte Ausplünderung unseres Volkes*). The destructive work (*Zerstörungsarbeit*) of the Marxists and the poison of enemy propaganda (*feindliche Vergiftungspropaganda*) had deprived the people of any sense."[425]

---

[424] José Martí, "Nuestra América," *La Revista ilustrada de Nueva York* (New York), Jan. 10, 1891, pp. 2-6, at p. 6.

[425] Adolf Hitler, *Mein Kampf*, Vol. II, Chap. VI (The Struggle of the Early Period: The Significance of the Spoken Word—*Der Kampf der ersten Zeit: Die Bedeutung der Rede*), Eng. pp. 463-479, at p. 464; Ger. pp. 518-537, at p. 519.

While Hitler strongly lamented this pillaging, there would be no sense of its wrongness in general, and time would show the ways the wartime Third Reich took the principle of pillaging of conquered peoples to new heights (or depths)! There was, as well—presumably not unfamiliar to the reader—Hitler's great disgust at the Jewish people as a whole, whom he called vermin (*Ungeziefer*) and vipers (*Schlange*),[426] a typical (or eternal, perpetual) parasite (*der ewige Parasit*) similar to a noxious bacillus (*wie ein Schädlicher Bazillus*),[427] which he saw as bringing the plague of syphilis to Germany. Further, Hitler saw in Jews a people that was totally derivative, that had no originality, that never had a homeland (apparently, he did not think here of the ancient kingdom of Israel[428]): "In judging the Jewish people's attitude on the question of human culture, the most essential characteristic we must always bear in mind is that there has never been a Jewish art [*eine jüdische Kunst niemals gab*] … Thus, the Jew lacks those qualities which distinguish the races that are creative and hence culturally blessed…. the Jew never possessed a state with definite territorial limits [*der Jude niemals einen Staat mit bestimmter territorialer Begrenzung besaß*] and therefore never called a culture his own."[429] All of these ideas had already been expressed by Richard Wagner and other anti-Semites. Not that Jews were the only humans that Hitler (and the Nazi worldview) saw as *lebensunwertes Leben*, lives unworthy of living: To be conquered and destroyed were also Romanies, criminals, homosexuals, the mentally retarded, the severely physically handicapped, the Slavs, as well as Jehovah's Witnesses, Quakers, and others. Some of these groups were seen as people to be done away with because of their political opposition to the Nazi regime, some because of their unwelcome actions and interpersonal proclivities, and *some because of their status based solely on birth and "race"—most thoroughly, vehemently, and completely, the Jews and the Romanies*—and with less intense disgust, the Slavs. Those considered to be *lebensunwertes Leben* (lives not worthy of life) would be sterilized or killed. Some 400,000 Germans were forcibly sterilized and up to 250,000 of the sick and disabled murdered.[430]

Anti-Romani (anti-Gypsy) sentiments of nineteenth-century Europe were expressed in published descriptions of the *Zigeuner* (Gypsies), such as texts by Dutch author Richard Liebich in 1863 and by Rudolf Kulemann

---

[426] Adolf Hitler, *Mein Kampf*, Vol. I, Chap. V (The World War—*Der Weltkrieg*), Eng. pp. 157-175, at p. 169; Ger. pp. 172-192, at p. 186.
[427] Adolf Hitler, *Mein Kampf*, Vol. I, Chap. XI (Nation and Race—*Volk und Rasse*), Eng. pp. 389-455, at p. 420; Ger., 311-362, at p. 334.
[428] As in the reigns of Kings David and Solomon. Joshua J. Mark, "[Ancient Kingdom of] Israel: Definition," Ancient History Encyclopedia, Jul. 10, 2010.
[429] Adolf Hitler, *Mein Kampf*, Vol. I, Chap. XI, Eng., pp. 389-455, at p. 303; Ger., pp. 311-362, at pp. 332-333.
[430] Boleslav L. Lichterman, "*Nazi Medicine and the Nuremberg Trials: From Medical War Crimes to Informed Consent*, by Paul Julian Weindling, *British Medical Journal*, vol. 331, Aug. 13, 2005; Aaron Levin, "German Psychiatrists Explore, Acknowledge Nazi-Era Failings," *Psychiatric News*, Jun. 30, 2015.

in 1869.[431] These strong anti-Romani (anti-Gypsy) sentiments matched anti-Jewish sentiments. The Italian criminologist, Cesare Lombroso (1835-1909), in his book *L'uomo delinquente*, wrote (in a critical generalization) of the Romanies (*gli zingari*) that they are always poor because they do not like working except enough to keep from starving to death (*sempre poveri, perche essi non amano di laborare se non quanto baste per non morire di fame*). In cases of "a mixture of the indigenous population with that of the Gypsies" (*una mistione degli indigeni con degli zingari*), "race enters as a factor in the greater criminality in these lands" (*la razza entri come fattore nella maggiore criminalità di questi paesi*). Lombroso added, "The Gypsies could be called, in general, like the Bedouins, a race of associated wrongdoers." (*Gli Zingari, si potrebbero chiamare, in genere, come i Beduini, una razza di malfattori associati.*)[432]

These judgments about the Romanies, overall, are rather harsh, but representative of the then-current European opinion about such matters. Expressing a similar negative attitude, later in that century, the Swabian parliament (Swabia being a land or legal district in southwest Germany) at the turn of the 1890s discussed the problem of *Zigeunergeschmeiß* (Gypsy scum, vermin, riff-raff) and how to deal with them.[433]

And in the broader scheme of things about life and death, an important text from 1920 by jurist Karl Binding and physician Alfred Hoche took the term, *lebensunwertes Leben*, as central to the book's title: *Die Freigabe der Vernichtung lebensunwerten Lebens: Ihr Maß und ihre Form* (*The Deregulation of the Extermination of Lives Unworthy of Living: Their Limits and their Structure*).

The term here would be used in such Nazi-era expressions as: *Vernichtung unwertes Lebens* (the extermination of unworthy lives), *menschenunwertes Leben* (people unworthy of life), and *die Tötung auf Verlangen und die Vernichtung unwerten Lebens* (killing on demand and the extermination of unworthy lives).[434]

---

[431] Richard Liebich, *Die Zigeuner in ihrem Wesen und in ihrer Sprache* (1863). Cf. Helmut Samer, "Racism and Anti-gypsyism," ROMBASE: DIDACTICALLY EDITED INFORMATION ON ROMA, where he mentions that Lieblich wrote of "unworthy lives" (*unwerte Leben*) in 1868, with nothing more specific about the actual source. See also, Rudolf R. Kulemann, "Die Zigeuner," *Unserer Zeit*, vol. 5, no. 1, 1869, pp. 843-871.

[432] Cesare Lombroso, *L'uomo delinquente: Studiato in rapporto alla Antropologia, alla medicine legale et alle discipline carcerarie* (1876), pp. 88, 123-124, 196.

[433] On the Swabian situation and on *lebensunwertes Leben*, see Ian Hancock, *O Porajmos: The Romani Holocaust* (2013), p. 3; cf. Ian Hancock, "Roma in Europe: A Chronology Leading to the Holocaust," ILLINOIS HOLOCAUST MUSEUM; Ian Hancock, "Gypsy History in Germany and Neighboring Lands: A Chronology to the Holocaust and Beyond," *Nationalities Papers: The Journal of Nationalism and Ethnicity*, vol. 19, no. 3 (1991), pp. 395-412.

[434] See Adolf Jost, *Das Recht auf den eigenen Tod* (1895); Jens Grünberg, *Der Wert des Lebens: Euthanasie in der historischen Rückschau, im aktuellen Diskurs sowie in der heutigen Praxis der Sterbhilfe. Eine Aufgabe für die Soziale Arbeit*

There was and is a distinction between aiding those in terminal pain to end their own lives (or carrying out procedures to bring about their death with their authorization) and having specialists decide which people are to live and which are to die. This distinction was sometimes quite clear and explicit, and at other times, as in some Nazi propaganda films—for example, the 1941 film, *Ich Klage an* (*I Accuse*)—twisting the title of an essay by Émile Zola attacking the anti-Semitic court martial of Captain Alfred Dreyfus[435]—which presented the Nazi forced euthanasia plans as reasonable. Then, in October 1939, Hitler initiated the T4 euthanasia program.[436] This involved the early use of truck motor fumes and would later lead to more efficient agents for the quick death of those subjected to those gases, especially Zyklon B. Although public outrage (especially criticisms by Church leaders against the wanton killing of innocents) led the T4 program to be officially stopped by Hitler.[437] It continued in more clandestine forms (ongoing deaths by malnutrition or poison), and led the mass killings to be carried out with any public announcement, and without further ado.

Public criticism simply led to the process being carried out with no public fanfare: patients died from starvation or injection of lethal substances, well below the radar. Overall, some 100,000 Germans were killed in the T4 program.[438] These were German Germans (not Jewish or Romanies) who were also deemed not fit to live!

But, in brief, Jews shared with European Romanies a rather repugnant status in the eyes of some nineteenth-century Germans, among others in Europe and elsewhere who took the despising of Jews and the Romanies as an obvious, reasonable, and respectable attitude to maintain. Still, staying a moment with this focus on the Jews (linked in *Mein Kampf* to Western powers and capitalism, as well as to Soviet Communism, depending on the focus desired), Hitler also wrote:

> Marxism, the ultimate aim of which was and will always be the destruction [*die Vernichtung*] of all non-Jewish national States... But now the time should have arrived

---

(2005); Eberhard Schockenhoff, *Ethik des Lebens: Grundlagen und neue Herausforderungen* (2nd ed., 2013), p. 495; Ernst Haeckel, *Die Lebenswunder: Gemeinverständliche Studien über Biologische Philosophie* (1904); Karin Anna Ertl, *NS-Euthanasie in Wien* (2012), pp. 1-7, 13-20, 29-33, 125, esp. p. 27; Karl Heinz Hafner and Rolf Winau, „Die Freigabe Der Vernichtung Lebensunwerten Lebens": Eine Untersuchung Zu Der Schrift Von Karl Binding Und Alfred Hoche," *Medizinhistorisches Journal*, vol. 9, no. 3/4, 1974, pp. 227–254.

[435] Zola was then found guilty of libel and fled France, finding haven in England.

[436] Also, *Aktion Gnadentod*, Operation Mercy Death. Andreas Schlebach, "Hitler und das lebensunwerte Leben," NORDDEUTSCHE RUNDFUNK (NDR), Aug. 15, 2014.

[437] Cancelled on Aug. 24, 1941, with a documented 70,273 recorded as killed in T4 in 1940-1941: see *Action T4: A Doctor Under Nazism* (2014), 36:00-43:00.

[438] Sebastian Haffner, *Anmerkungen zu Hitler*, 1978 ed., p. 166; 1994 ed., p. 129; Eng., *The Meaning of Hitler* (1979), p. 132.

> for proceeding against the entire fraudulent company of these Jewish poison mongers of the nation [*dieser jüdischen Volksvergifter*]. Now was the time one should have dealt summarily with them without the slightest consideration for the clamor that would probably arise, or, what would have been still better, without the least regard to their initial screaming or whining [*ohne die geringste Rücksicht auf etwa einsetzendes Geschrei oder Gejammer*]....[439] No [rather, the diatribe continues], the Jew possesses no culture-creating energy whatsoever [*der Jude besitzt keine irgendwie kulturbildende Kraft*] ... [The Jew was] always only a *parasite* in the body of other people [*immer nur ein Parasit im Körper anderer Völke*].[440]

Going through the rhetorical flair in such vituperative passages against Jews—as an overall group held to be all cut from the same cloth, a miserable scrap of rag (to offer still one more insulting metaphor)—the prosaic point is not that Jews are literally parasites (or germs, or other dangerous or poison-bearing lower animals), but that they are to be held aside and ultimately eliminated from the body politic, as a matter of what we might call sociopolitical cleanliness.

This of course, makes attributions about Jews as an entirely homogenous group, which in general is a way of distorting the specific variations among subgroups, and distorting differences between particular individuals of the group; instead, here, Jews are considered as a single entity, world Jewry, with some sort of unstated assumption that all Jews are the same (as in the expression of a governor of California long ago that if you've seen one redwood tree you've seen them all).

Leaving aside that this is a confusion or a gross oversimplification, amounting to a distorted caricature of an entire people, we might balance this criticism of Jews as a group with a remark made by a young English essayist in 1888, writing of Jews, "Their faults were many.... Whose faults are few?"[441] *Of course, a group, even if having many faults, does not make them worthy of extermination by mass murder.*

---

[439] The term *die Vernichtung* was used during the war in its literal meaning of annihilation, extermination, destruction; applied to the organized, state-supported mass killing of entire peoples, especially the Jews. Text from Adolf Hitler, *Mein Kampf*, Vol. I, Chap. V, Eng. pp. 157-175, at p. 169; Ger. pp. 172-192, at p. 185.

[440] Adolf Hitler, *Mein Kampf*, Vol. 1, Chap. XI, Eng. pp. 389-455, sub-sect. "The Jewish Ape" and "The Parasite," at pp. 418, 419; Ger., pp. 311-362, at pp. 332, 334. Cf. Eberhard Schockenhoff, *Ethik des Lebens: Grundlagen und neue Herausforderungen* (1993), p. 495.

[441] The essayist was a 13-year-old Winston Churchill (born May 26, 1888). The essay, for a class at the highly respected Harrow School, founded in 1572 under royal charter by Elizabeth I, is dated May 26, 1888. Quoted in Martin Gilbert, *Churchill and the Jews: A Lifelong Friendship* (2007), p. 1.

Hitler also laid the framework for the depriving of certain citizens of full rights, making them subjects of the nation, while leaving as a third category, that of aliens: foreigners whose legal identity is through another country:

> The folkish State divides its inhabitants into three classes: State citizens, State subjects, and aliens [*Staatsbürger, Staatsangehörige und Ausländer*].[442]

This principle would be defined in the Nuremberg Laws that were decreed on September 15, 1935, based on the Prussian Memorandum (of May 1933),[443] and which went into effect on November 14 of that year, with German Jews deprived of their citizenship and reduced to subjects of the Reich, a "health measure" long in need of being implementedThis was not just an image. Hitler had much to say, for example, about syphilis, a "Jewish disease" (*Judenkrankheit*) that was part of the "Jewification of our spiritual life" (*Verjudung unseres Seelenlebens*).[444] He even would devote many words in *Mein Kampf*[445] to this infectious curse he saw as having been brought on by Jews and prostitutes. The focus, with such vehemence, on a disease in a work on politics and government, *may strike us as a remarkably strange diversion*, but the emphatic value given to purity (*Reinheit*, in some sense of this term) in Hitler's thinking is not negligible, casual, or incidental: "The sin against the blood and the degradation of the race [*Die Sünde wider Blut und Rasse*] are the hereditary sin [*Erbsünde*][446] of this world and the end of a mankind surrendering to them."[447] *This particular vision of purity and a pure people would be implemented in the Third Reich*. In addition to its theoretical emphasis, this emphasis on purity and a healthy citizenry would later have great practical ramifications, including the T4 Program—euthanasia of "lives unworthy of living." Hitler remarked about a healthy society:

> This cleansing of our culture must be extended to nearly all fields. Theater, art, literature, cinema, press, posters, and window displays must be cleansed of all manifestations of our rotting world and placed in the service of a moral, political, and cultural idea.... For, if necessary, the incurably sick will be pitilessly separated

---

[442] Adolf Hitler, *Mein Kampf*, Vol. II, Chap. III (Subjects and Citizens of the State—*Staatsangehöriger und Staatsbürger*, Eng., pp. 656-659, sub-sect. Citizens—State Subjects—Aliens), at p. 658; Ger., pp. 488-491, at p. 490.

[443] James Q. Whitman, *Hitler's American Model*, pp. 19-32, with full text of the two key Nuremberg Laws, pp. 29-32; on the Memorandum, pp. 83-90, 135, 196.

[444] Adolf Hitler, *Mein Kampf*, Vol. I, Chap. X, Eng., pp. 302-388, at pp. 247, 253; Ger., pp. 245-310, at pp. 270, 277.

[445] Adolf Hitler, *Mein Kampf*, Vol. I, Chap. X, Eng., pp. 302-388, sub-sect. on syphilis, pp. 246-257; Ger. pp. 245-310, sub-sect., "*Die Syphilis*," pp. 269-180.

[446] An alternate Eng. tr. renders *Erbsünde* as "original sin."

[447] Adolf Hitler, *Mein Kampf*, Vol. I, Chap. X, Eng., pp. 302-388, at p. 339; Ger., pp. 269-180, at p. 272. Emphasis in original.

out [*unbarmherzigen Absonderung unheilbar Erkrankter schreiten müssen*]—a barbaric measure for the unfortunate who is struck by it [*eine barbarische Maßnahme für den unglücklich davon Betroffenen*], but a blessing [*ein Segen*] for his fellow men and posterity. The passing pain of a century [*die vorübergehende Schmerz eines Jahrhunderts*] can and will redeem millenniums from sufferings."[448]

This principle would be defined in the Nuremberg Laws of September 15, 1935, and which went into effect on November 14, with German Jews deprived of their citizenship and reduced to subjects of the Reich. Such passages as these suggest that Hitler was already contemplating the application of what will appear to be barbaric, from one limited point of view (that of those to be mercilessly killed, and of those who have compassion for them), but will be devoutly to be desired, from another (that of those who wish to be free of these hopeless and valueless beings). And Hitler is obviously thinking in wide spans of time here; he will later speak of the thousand-year Reich, giving the Reich literally hundreds of years to realize their vision of a German-led Europe, guided by National Socialist values and political vision.

Here, we have laid out in rather clear German some rather powerful themes that would be carried out in specifics that were partially guided by thoroughly elaborated ideas from *Mein Kampf*, and partially defined by subsequent events on the national and international scene that the Reich encountered and operated within.

GERMANY GETTING RESTARTED, THE EARLY INFLUENCE OF HITLER

If we return to the years that followed the Versailles Treaty and the start of the effort of various groups of Germans to recreate their country in the image of their ideal—whether this was a return to the Kaiser, the creation of Bolshevik communes, or of a militaristic, perhaps a nation-honoring and -glorifying government, one with a strong sense of who belonged and who didn't (whether leftist, centrist, or rightist in politics) or a liberal government with rights to all—and focus primarily on the efforts of Hitler to form a cohesive political group and to head it himself, we see his first significant attempt to take power in the 1923 Putsch.

While one sketch of Hitler's rise to power has him slowly and skillfully insinuate himself into right-wing, anti-Semitic, strong nationalistic (pan-Germanism) politics, stealthily taking over power and getting even the support of gullible industrialists who thought they could control him and bring about through him a successful bulwark against threats from the Bolshevik left, in fact, there were a number of conflicts between Hitler and his early, and later, supporters, beginning already in 1921: for example, early on, there was Hitler's confrontation with Anton Drexler (1884-1942), the founder in January 1919 of the DAP, the German Workers Party. In

---

[448] Adolf Hitler, *Mein Kampf*, Vol. I, Chap. X, Eng., pp. 302-388, at p. 255; Ger., pp. 245-310, at p. 280.

February 1920, this group became the NSDAP, the National Socialist German Workers Party. Drexler felt that Hitler was becoming too powerful within the Party. The conflict was resolved in July 1921 when Drexler was negotiating with other right-wing parties, and Hitler in reply demanded to be made chairman of the NSDAP, with dictatorial powers, on the threat of leaving the party totally. On July 29, 1921, the Party membership voted 543-1 to grant Hitler his demands; Drexler was excluded from the Party.

This would be followed by other conflicts. Another early supporter, Otto Strasser (1897-1974), would split with Hitler over the form of socialism that the NSDAP was developing; Strasser felt that Hitler and the NSDAP were not giving due respect for the perturbing plight of the workers, with Hitler apparently reluctant to stand firm against capitalism; he was expelled from the Nazi Party. Then, he was a founder with his brother Gregor Strasser of a group called *das schwarze Front* (the Black Front) in 1930. The brother Gregor was killed on July 3, 1934, along with many of the SA, in the Night of the Long Knives.

Considering briefly here some later conflicts between Hitler and those of relative power and importance in the National Socialist world—more on these, below—just before the invasion of Czechoslovakia, which the German military were quite aware of ahead of time, there was a plan to capture Hitler and to overthrow the Reich government (another putsch), called the Oster Conspiracy; to be carried out, it required the British to stand up to Germany, which they, of course, did not, thwarting those plans. Then, Fritz Thyssen, the coal and steel magnate, along with others including military career men, would break with Hitler when Hitler went to war against Poland. Thyssen would flee, first to Switzerland, from where he wrote a letter to Hitler December 29, 1939, resigning his position within the Nazi Party and Government. His memoirs, *I Paid Hitler*, rather critical of Hitler (passages quoted above), were published in 1941; he would later escape to Argentina, where he died in 1951.

Of course, there were also the generals who were part of *Unternehmen Walküre* (Operation Valkyrie), the attempted assassination of Hitler at his headquarters, *die Wolfsschanze*, the Wolf's Lair, in eastern Prussia, on July 20, 1944. (Hitler flew to Berlin, on October 14, 1944, abandoning the Wolf's Lair; it was blown up in January, 1945.)

There had been resistance to Hitler throughout the Hitler era,[449] with those in Operation Valkyrie among a long line of those who disagreed vehemently with Hitler.)

---

[449] *Hitler's Bodyguard, Season 1, Episode 11 (Attempt to Kill Hitler at the Wolf's Lair)*, extended discussion at 26:50-37:10, YOUTUBE; "Ludwig Beck" WIKIPEDIA; "Ludwig Beck," SPARTACUS EDUCATIONAL; Anton Drexler," WIKIPEDIA; "German Workers Party," WIKIPEDIA; "Otto Strasser" and "Strasserism," ENCYCLOPÆDIA BRITANNICA; Kathy Warnes, "Fritz Thyssen Helped Finance the Nazi Party, but Later Changed His Mind," WINDOWS TO WORLD HISTORY; "Fritz Thyssen," SPARTACUS EDUCATIONAL; "Operation Valkyrie," WIKIPEDIA; "Unternehmen Walküre," DE.WIKIPEDIA; "Unternehmen Walküre," ÖSTERREICH1918PLUS (POLITIK-LEXIKON.AT).

Such internal conflicts aside, the basic political context certainly allowed a central role for Jew-hatred, as above discussions highlight, but there were other concerns that were perhaps even more pressing in the post-war years of the 1920s.

What might be significant here is to look at a few related events during the post-war years and 1920s up to the elections of 1932 in Germany. While many dismissed Hitler as a harmless side-show comedic anomaly in the history of Germany and Europe, some others saw the coming storm and violence of the National Socialist program quite early.

The Munich newspaper, *Der gerade Weg: Deutsche Zeitung für Wahrfheit und Recht* (*The Straight Path: German Newspaper for Truth and Law*) had a front-page headline on April 2, 1932: "*Hitler der Bankrotteur*" ("Hitler, the Bankrupt"), with the sub-headline, "*Stalin: Mit nationalsozialistisch. Sieg beginnt Europ. Krieg!*" ("Stalin: With a National Socialist Victory, a European War will begin!"), and an image of a Brownshirt (SA Man) giving a Nazi salute, except that the man is not flesh and blood, but a skeleton, representing death. And Kurt Tucholsky—who worked as co-editor of the Berlin publication *Die Weltbühne* with Carl von Ossietzky—being a leftist, an intellectual, and a Jew, was threatened in the 1920s by Nazi activists (the SA).

Ossietzky wrote strong essays criticizing Hitler, including a sarcastic essay, *Hitler und Goethe*, published in May 1932 in *Die Weltbühne* that compared Hitler to Goethe,[450] an essay for which Tucholsky used the penname Kasper Hauser.[451] In it, Tucholsky proposed that Hitler was the greater German. The work ended with a run-on sequence of letters that when separated out into individual words would read: "*Deutschland erwache juda verrecke hitler wird reichspräsident das bestimmen wir!*" ("Germany, awaken! Jews: have a miserable death! Hitler becomes Reich President, that's what we determine!") Tucholsky had emigrated to Sweden under Nazi death threats before Hitler became Chancellor. His works were banned, and burned on May 10, 1933, along with many other books in the famous Berlin book-burning, an intellectual *auto-da-fé*.[452] On

---

And, on these, see also Robert Wistrich, *Who's Who in Nazi Germany* (1982): "Drexler, Anton," "Stauffenberg, Claus Schenk Graf von," "Strasser, Gergor," "Strasser, Otto," "Thyssen, Fritz."

[450] *Die Weltbühne*, No. 20, 1932, May 17, 1932, pp. 751-753.

[451] Kasper Hauser (1812-1833) was well known in Germany. The Austrian poet, Georg Trakl wrote a poem in 1913, *Kaspar Hauser Lied* (*Song of Kaspar Hauser*), which popularized the man, presenting him as a homeless, misunderstood genius, with no roots or personal attachments, living in fear of an uncertain death. Hauser, reportedly growing up in isolation in a dark cell, with a death by stabbing, was perhaps curious, certainly enigmatic, and a source of many rumors and speculations. Some said he was a kind of wolf man; others, a great con artist. This was the Trakl who was famous for his poem "Grodek," giving impressions of the violence at the Battle of Gródek in World War I, where he served as a medic, perhaps the last poem he wrote, committing suicide on November 3, 1914.

[452] Joseph Roth, "L'Auto-da-fé de l'Esprit," *Cahiers juifs* (Paris), vol. 1, Nov. 1933,

Dec. 20, 1935, Tucholsky died, presumably committing suicide, in Hindås, Sweden.[453]

We might imagine here a Germany filled with chaos. And there were, in fact, three prominent attempts to overthrow the government: The first, the Sparticist Uprising in Berlin (January 4-15, 1919), was a left-wing attempt to replace the Socialists of the Weimar Republic by a Communist government. It did not succeed. Then, second, there was the Kapp or Kapp-Lüttwitz coup of March 13, 1920, in which Gen. Ludendorff participated; it too attempted to overthrow the new Weimar Republic, this time to set up an autocratic regime (an envisioned return to the Second Reich). It, too, failed, unable to obtain any effective authority. The two leaders fled the country, leaving the Weimar government intact, while showing the disloyalty and impotence of these right-wing activists.[454] The third was the Munich Hitler Coup (or Putsch), which also failed, even though war hero Hermann Göring, appointed by Hitler in 1921 to give military structure to the SA, was in charge of the 1923 Munich Putsch. Gen. Ludendorff was also a party to this coup.

The Hitler Putsch began in Munich on the evening of November 8, 1923, with hundreds of Nazis taking over of the political meeting in the beer hall. The next morning, November 9, National Socialists marched toward Munich's Bavarian Defense Ministry, but were met by Bavarian police who shot a number of these revolutionaries, seriously wounding Göring in the groin and hip. Göring was carried away by SA Men who noticed a house identified as being a physician's office; two elderly couples named Ballin aided Göring, with Ilse Ballin stopping his bleeding; they did not turn him into the police, even realizing he was a Nazi: these couples were Jewish; Göring later helped them to escape from Germany.[455] He would manage to escape to Austria, where he was treated for the wounds and the pain, becoming addicted to morphine. Ernst Hanfstaengl also escaped to Austria in the next days. Young Himmler, only 23 at the time, would simply return to live quietly with his parents, in Landshut, near Munich; questioned by the Bavarian police, his case was dismissed for lack of compelling evidence. The Bavarian police also shot to death Ludwig Maximilian (Max) Erwin von Scheubner-Richter, former military officer, German Consul at Erzurum (Ottoman Empire) during the Great War and the times of the Armenian mass killings or genocide,[456] and colleague of Alfred Rosenberg. Scheubner-Richter was marching next to Hitler, in a

---

pp. 161-169, Eng. tr., *What I Saw: Reports from Berlin, 1920-1933* (2003), pp. 207-217 (closing essay, "The Auto-da-Fé of the Mind"); Kurt Tucholsky, *Berlin! Berlin! Dispatches from the Weimar Republic* (2013).

[453] "Tucholsky, Famed Anti-nazi Writer, Suicide in Sweden," *JTA (Jewish Telegraphic Agency*, Jan. 12, 1936. Hindås is east of Göteborg (Gothenburg).

[454] Anthony J. Nicholls, *Weimar and the Rise of Hitler*, pp. 70-71.

[455] NT-IMT-Blue, vol. 9, pp. 19-21: testimony of Gen. Karl Bodenschatz, military adjutant to Göring; Anthony Read, *The Devil's Disciples: The Lives and Times of Hitler's Inner Circle* (2003), pp. 101-102.

[456] Stefan Ihrig, *Justifying Genocide*, pp. 15, 130, 132, 264, 336, 352, 359.

The Hitler Era

row of men, locked arm-in-arm. He was shot in the lungs, collapsed suddenly, and died instantly. When he fell, Hitler's right shoulder was dislocated. Hitler, in pain, fled, and went into hiding at the home of Ernst Hanfstaengl. In any case, the Putsch was, nonetheless, *almost* successful.

Considering specifics, the Putsch began on November 8, on the occasion of a meeting in Munich at which a large number of officials were present, along with three major political figures: Gustav von Kahr, the Bavarian Prime Minister, basically with dictatorial powers (who would be killed by the Nazis in the 1934 purge, the Night of the Long Knives), Otto von Lossow, the commander of the Bavarian Army, and Hans von Seisser, the commandant of the Bavarian State Police. Hitler, entering the meeting hall with 600 armed SA troops commandeered by Hermann Göring,[457] interrupted Von Kahr's speech, jumping up on a table and firing a pistol shot into the ceiling, and announcing the take-over of the Bavarian government. Hitler took the three leaders into another room, trying to convince or to threaten them to agree to recognize his coup. They refused. When Ludendorff then arrived, Von Kahr asked him to be allowed to leave, giving his commitment to return. With permission. Von Kahr left and then reassembled Bavarian police, which met the marchers the next day, killing sixteen (who would later be remembered in solemnity as great martyrs each November 11 by the National Socialists, and then by the Third Reich). Four Bavarian police also were killed in that confrontation.

Hitler was arrested, tried for treason, and given a prison sentence.

We may also have the image of a strongly anti-Semitic Germany, with caricatures showing repulsive, hook-nosed Jews stabbing German soldiers of the First World War in the back. And yet, the Weimar Republic did have some Jewish politicians (although not all, and not most, as some versions of the Weimar period might imply).

One important figure was Walther Rathenau (1867-1922), Foreign Minister in 1922 (February 1 to June 24); who was assassinated[458] in the hopes of igniting a revolt against the "Jewish" Weimar Republic. The killing occurred on that latter date by some right-wing activists who pointed out Rathenau's Jewish background and his arranging for trade agreements with Soviet Russia (which was clandestinely already helping the German secret rearmament program). And yet, did the country explode in joyous glee at the death of this Jew in the government? Did his murder provoke the left to revolt, then to have the Army and the right, counter-revolt to set up a rightest government? Not at all! The violence envisioned did not come to pass. Rather, there was a significant demonstration in support of his life and against his having been assassinated, with over a million

---

[457] By the sumer of 1923, there were some 15,000 SA troops under Göring. See Ralph Max Engelman, *Dietrich Eckart and the Genesis of Nazism* (1971), p. 223.

[458] See Martin Sabrow, "Mord und Mythos. Das Komplott gegen Walther Rathenau 1922 [Der Tod Walther Rathenaus 1922]," pp. 321-344, in *Das Attentat in der Geschichte*, Alexander Demandt, ed. (1996), esp. pp. 323-324; 336-337, and Carole Fink, "The Murder of Walter Rathenau," *Judaism: A Quarterly Journal of Jewish Life and Thought*, vol. 44, no. 3, Summer 1995, pp. 259-271.

Germans demonstrating peacefully in the streets. His coffin was given a temporary resting place of honor in the Reichstag building itself.

If we have the idea that the Nazis gained steadily in its following and in its popular appeal to the German society, we might consider the votes they obtained in the years before 1933. The situation had changed in Germany from the time of the unsuccessful Hitler-Ludendorff Putsch of November 1923—also called the Bürgerbräu-Putsch or the March on the *Feldherrnhalle*—to when Hitler had been tried, found guilty of treason, imprisoned, and then released. Hitler, who had begun his sentence at Landsberg Prison on April 1, 1924, was released on December 20 of that year. Meanwhile, Ernst Röhm, who had also been convicted of treason, was given a conditional discharge. *The Germany Hitler found on release was not in the dire, chaotic situation from a year earlier.* The economy of the country had been stabilized, with relief from the war reparations demands and from the significant loan of money generated through the Dawes Plan. The German debt was lowered and the totality to be repaid left indefinite. This plan was formally accepted by the Allies and by Germany on August 16, 1924, and, by 1929, *with the Young Plan, the debt was left basically moot*. Meanwhile, Hitler was banned from giving any speeches in public before 1927, and the SA (the Storm Troopers) were also now illegal. Thus, Joseph Goebbels, along with Gregor Strasser, began giving speeches supporting the anti-Semitic and nationalistic principles of the National Socialists. For the second, another paramilitary organization was created in April 1924, when Hitler authorized Röhm to reorganize the SA. The result was the *Frontbahn* (the Front Track), claimed to be a sports club. Due to disagreements with Hitler, Röhm resigned as head of the SA and the *Frontbahn* in May 1925, going to Bolivia, returning on invitation by Hitler after the elections of September 1930. With Röhm as head of the SA, the SA would grow to 260,000 members by the end of 1931.

The Ruhr, 1923-1924

During those first post-war years, there were repeated defaults by the German nation and government on its war debts, leading to a Belgian-French occupation of the Ruhr beginning on January 11, 1923. Given this default of payments, the French demanded to be paid in raw materials, in lumber and especially in coal. The German miners went on strike; the French replaced them with French workers. No coal was left for the German population; the Weimar government was required to buy coal on the open market. Its reserves quickly dwindling, a hyperinflation of the German currency, the mark, set in. In addition, the Germans of the Ruhr were without coal, and without food, left hungry, cold, disgruntled, and restless.[459] The frustrations of Germans, and in a confrontive way, of the young National Socialist Party, led to its attempt to take over the Bavarian

---

[459] See Isabelle Clarke and Daniel Costelle, *Apocalypse: Hitler. Part I: La menace* (2011), NATIONAL GEOGRAPHIC CHANNELS INTERNATIONAL, TÉLÉVISION BELGE, TÉLÉ-QUÉBEC, TV5 MONDE, etc., at 26:58-30:15.

government later that year. That unsuccessful action, just discussed, led to Hitler's arrest and trial. In addition to having the opportunity of writing the first part of *Mein Kampf*, Hitler would now have another major focus—even more immediate than his hatred of all Jews ("world Jewry"): that of building a voting block to bring him into national power. Hitler gathered loyal supporters to aid in this quest.

Among these was Joseph Goebbels. In his diary—with its shifting between entries of discouraged hopelessness and hurtful disappointments, and entries of self-aggrandizing exuberance and joyous enthusiasm—for April 13, 1926, we read of his meeting with Hitler, as part of a large group in Munich.

In the entry for this date, Goebbels declared his emotionally charged impression of a loveable Hitler: "He shames us with his kindness. (*Er ist beschämend gut zu uns.*) ... We ask. He answers brilliantly. I love him. (*Er antwortet glänzend. Ich liebe ihn.*) ... I bow to his greatness, his political genius (*Ich beuge mich dem Größeren, dem politischen Genie!*)."[460] Then, on June 17, 1926, Goebbels wrote further, "Such a fellow can turn the world inside out. (*So ein Kerl kann eine Welt umkrempeln.*)"[461]—Yes, indeed! Indeed! Hitler (and Germany) certainly managed to accomplish that, we must admit! Later in the 1920s, Goebbels wrote, putting his love of National Socialism into religious terms, in his diary entry for October 16, 1928: "What is Christianity to us today? (*Was ist uns heute das Christentum?*) National Socialism is religion. (*Nationalsozialismus ist Religion.*) ... My Party [the Nazi Party] is my church, and I believe I serve the Lord (*dem Herrn*) best if I do his will, and liberate my oppressed people from the fetters of slavery. That is my gospel (*mein Evangelium*)."[462] Goebbels did have a sense of grandeur!

Heinrich Himmler, too, came to worship Hitler, as described by British historian Richard Evans: "From 1925 onwards, when he joined the newly reconstituted Nazi Party, Himmler developed a boundless hero-worship of the Nazi leader; he kept a portrait of Hitler on his office wall..."[463]

With this adoration, these organized preparations for future power, and more, Hitler developed a speaking manner that was studied and practiced. And, given this new interest, he became focused on cultivating his oratory abilities; he took locution lessons to lessen his off-putting native dialect from rural Austria.

---

[460] The full set of the diaries, in German, is contained in Joseph Goebbels, *Tagebücher, 1924-1945, Five Volumes in One*, Ralf Georg Reuth, ed. (1992). German quoted here from pp. 239, 241; Eng., T*he Early Goebbels Diaries 1925-1926* (1962), pp. 77-78. Cf. *The Goebbels Experiment*, at 8:12-9:35, a joint film by FILMSTIFTUNG-ZDF, SPIEGEL TV (GERMANY), BBC (UK), AND THE HISTORY TELEVISION (CANADA).

[461] See extended discussion on the diaries of Joseph Goebbels by editor for the *Spiegel*, Wolfgang Malanowski, "Meine Waffe heißt Adolf Hitler," *Spiegel*, Sep. 7, 1987, pp. 200-220.

[462] Joseph Goebbels, *Tagebücher 1924-1945*, p. 327. Cf. *The Goebbels Experiment*, at 13:35-14:10.

[463] Richard J. Evans, *The Coming of the Third Reich* (2004), p. 227.

Hanussen   Hitler speech   Photos of Hitler posing for dramatic power

With instruction from psychic and clairvoyant Eric Hanussen, Hitler learned crowd-influencing techniques of gestures and dramatic pauses for improving his performance before crowds and the achievement of dramatic effect; some of Hitler's first speeches as Chancellor, where he stands silently before making a point, show this technique and its impact.[464] As part of this cultivation of a speaking presence, there was also Hitler's attentive study of his speech-making poses photographed by his photographer, Heinrich Hoffman (1885-1957), to develop an oratorical style marrying word with gesture in a powerful synergy of moving rhetoric.

Hitler also began to make use of the very most recent forms of transportation and communication, including the airplane, to allow him to give political talks in distant parts of Germany within short intervals. He would also make use of radio broadcasts, more so after the taking of the government in 1933, with a larger listening audience than in the 1920s, and with monopolistic control by the Nazi Reich over radio and other forms of communication, overseen by Goebbels.[465] Hitler also helped in the development of the Brown Shirts, the SA, a large group of paramilitary personnel, in part by finding financial support for the movement.

Party organization began even before the Putsch of November 1923, Hitler's time in prison, and his writing the first volume of *Mein Kampf*. Already in 1922 there was the founding of a Nazi group for children and adolescents. This was an institution of the youth, later called the *Hitlerjugend*, or *HJ*, the Hitler Youth—for boys 14-18 (and *Deutsches Jungvolk*, or *DJ* or *DJV*, German Youngsters, for boys 10-14), and one for girls, the *Bund deutsche Mädel*, *BdM*, League of German Girls. By 1938, these would have 8.7 million members (girls and boys).[466] They all had regimentation, standardized dress, military-like training, and a total devotion to Hitler.

---

[464] Hanussen (1889-1933), born Hermann (Herschel Chaim) Steinschneider, was assassinated on March 25, 1933. See "Hanussen, Erik Jan (1889-1933)," ENCYCLOPEDIA OF OCCULTISM AND PARAPSYCHOLOGY. (More on Hanussen, below.)

[465] Maria Petrova, "Radio and the rise of Nazis in pre-war Germany," *Center for the Study of Democratic Politics* (WOODROW WILSON SCHOOL OF PUBLIC AND INTERNATIONAL AFFAIRS, PRINCETON UNIV.), Apr. 4, 2013, with link to pdf file.

[466] Hannsjoachim Wolfgang Koch, *The Hitler Youth: Origins and Development, 1922-1945* (2000), pp. 113-114. The film *Hitler's Children* (2004) extensively documents the *Hitlerjugend* and the extreme indoctrination of the German youth to total dedication personally to Hitler. This is a 5-part series by Guido Knopp and the ZDF CONTEMPORARY HISTORY DEPT., not to be confused with a more recent film with this same title, a BBC Productions documentary, *Hitler's Children* (2011).

The power of capturing the hearts and minds of the new generation was something Hitler and associates deeply appreciated and assiduously cultivated. (More on this, below.) Hitler and his associates handled the general confusion, self-doubting, self-searching, and the yearning for acceptance by others of their age, in a remarkable way, giving the young a respected role, and a clear definition of how they should think, act, dress, and deal with social issues.

This is an issue that all societies face, often not quite well, with old and new problems developing including violence, the use of drugs (with all of the various consequences of that—we will see that with Göring and Hitler, themselves, with dire results). *Whether the results of the inviting and incorporating of the German youth (Jews excluded, of course) are ones we admire or dread is another question.*

This education of the young of Germany would continue to take place in formal settings, such as the annual Nazi Party Congresses, as well as in more limited social contexts. Rudolf Höss, later the Commandant at Auschwitz, recounted that in his training as an SS officer, anyone who refused to take part in acts of cruelty forced upon them as educational training (learning how to be cruel without qualms) would be accused of having a bourgeois mentality (that is, one that preferred softness, ease, and gentleness, to harsh and vigorous life pursuits).[467]

The excitement and entertainment at these Congresses were well thought-out and orchestrated. Some of the features that became common fare in the rallies (or Party Congresses) can be traced to their inspired sources. For example, the proposal for making use of one group phenomenon that was later used in Nazi rallies apparently came from Hanfstaengl (mentioned above), a graduate of Harvard College, Class of 1909:

> It was on another occasion, at the house of Heinrich Hoffman, his [Hitler's] photographer friend, that I started playing some of the football marches I had picked up at Harvard. I explained to Hitler all the business about the cheerleaders [Hanfstaengl was one] and college songs and the deliberate whipping up of hysterical enthusiasm. I told him about the thousands of spectators being made to roar, "Harvard, Harvard, Harvard, rah, rah, rah!" in unison and of the hypnotic effect of this sort of thing.[468]

This was to be transformed into the well-known thrice-repeated Nazi salutation, *Sieg heil!* ("Victory, hail!" or "Hail Victory!"). Also designed to inspire great throngs of people was *der Lichtdom*, the Cathedral of Lights: imposing parallel columns of air-raid lights that seemed to disappear in the clouds above the city, devised by Albert Speer.

---

[467] Maria Ossowska, *Social Determinants of Moral Ideas* (1970), p. 160.
[468] Ernst ("Putzi") Hanfstaengl, *Unheard Witness* (1957, NY), pp. 52-53. Similar text in his *Hitler: The Missing Years* (1957, London), p. 51, with the rather minor variation: "... the cheerleaders and marches, counter-marches ...."

And yet, even with all of this committed focus on increasing the sheer numbers of inspired, dedicated followers of the Nazi Party, and the programs (pro-nationalistic, anti-Versailles, and anti-Jewish) that were proposed with great intensity, there was no significant impact by these rallies and their theatricality *on the voting in Germany in the 1920s.*

The Weimar Republic, as is generally acknowledged, came into being with many problems. Its immediate problems were the great loss of young men during the Great War and the starvation of its citizenry, as well as the psychological shame of having lost the war and the need to accept a humiliating treaty.

Anti-Semitism, as shown in the cartoon earlier, was still somewhat of a fringe phenomenon, but one that still could be noticed.

As a politically significant example of this hatred of Jews in German life (and also its pre-Reich limited scope), Walther Rathenau, the Weimar Foreign Minister, who was German Jewish, was assassinated on June 24, 1922 (discussed above, in the context of the Treaty of Rapallo). Nationalist Germans accused Rathenau of being part of a great Jewish-Communist conspiracy, with joy at his murder in those political centers, by those with strong anti-Jewish sentiments—who had chanted, *Knallt ab den Walther Rathenau, die gottverfluchte Judensau!* (Bump off Walther Rathenau, the God-damned Jewish sow!).

The term we find used here would echo to the German consciousness the anti-Semitic teachings, centuries earlier, of Martin Luther (1483-1546), whose church in Wittenberg had one example of this *Judensau* as a statue,[469] with its earlier use of this special term, *Judensau*.[470] The Jew-sow, or Jewish sow, was a sow (an adult female pig) that was typically shown in medieval Christianity.

In one early print, presented below, we can see an adult Jew (typically drawn in Jewish attire, and here, presumably representing a rabbi) focused on the rump of the sow (with variations on the sexual intimacy indicated, from some voyeuristic lusting for the anus, or suggestive of the rabbi's urge to engage in anal intercourse or in some other act seen as repulsive).

And, to add a broader sense of the universal depravity of Jews, the print also shows several Jewish children suckling on the pig's nipples—suggesting early-life depravity, filthiness, bestiality, and more, in Jewish youngsters.[471]

This is a very old metaphoric conceit, as in the insulting image in this 1596 woodcut, below, with an adult Jew shown lifting the tail of the sow to look at what could then be seen, while young Jews suckle.

While over four centuries have gone by since the print shown just below, there are reminders of this old history to this day—letting us appreciate once again the power of the past in our present world.

---

[469] See 1596 Wittenberg sculpture, in Christoph Richter, "Die Welt schaut auf Wittenberg—und sieht eine Judensau," DEUTSCHLANDFUNK, May 24, 2017.

[470] Variations of the term *Judensau* include *Judenschwein* and *Saujude*.

[471] "Judensau in Wittenberg," a sub-sect. in "Judensau," WIKIPEDIA.

For example, in 2017, exactly five hundred years after Martin Luther posted his statement (ban, decree) on the front door of his church (on October 31, 1517), there was the issuance of the *Joint Statement by the Lutheran World Federation and the Pontifical Council for Promoting Christian Unity on the conclusion of the year of the common commemoration of the Reformation, 31st October 2017.*

This inter-Christian document stated in part, "we begged forgiveness for our failures and for the ways in which *Christians have wounded the Body of the Lord and offended each other during the five hundred years* since the beginning of the Reformation until today." And added, "We recognize that while the past cannot be changed, its influence upon us today can be transformed to become a stimulus for growing communion, and a sign of hope for the world to overcome division and fragmentation. Again, it has become clear that what we have in common is far more than that which still divides us."[472]

With this historical contextualization, to consider again the murder of the "Jew-sow" Rathenau: what is remarkable is that it did not spark a general rightist, nationalist uprising leading to the grabbing of power by the National Socialists or other nationalist groups, as some desired.

There was not yet enough support for such an action.

In contrast, among other Germans, there was respect toward this assassinated government official (even though it was well known that he was Jewish) by hundreds of thousands—up to a million in some reports[473]—of mourners who paid their respects at his funeral in Berlin and also in other towns.

---

[472] *Joint Statement*, PRESS.VATICAN.VA. Italics added. These offenses presumably include the massive killings between Catholics and Protestants, with no mention of the violence done by both Protestants and Catholics to the Jews of Europe.

[473] The early biography by Graf (Count) Harry Kessler, *Walther Rathenau: His Life and Work* (1930) cites over one million mourners in Berlin, 150,000 in Munich and Chemnitz, 100,000 in Hamburg and some other cities (at p. 360). "The Murder of Walther Rathenau," ALPHA HISTORY (Australian site) also reports this number.

As German historian Eberhard Kolb expressed it, the "murder [of Rathenau] caused great indignation among the public, including the middle class, by whom he was much respected. 'The enemy is on the right!' Chancellor Wirth [Joseph Wirth, of the Catholic Centre Party] exclaimed in the Reichstag ... thus proclaiming that the whole right wing, in their boundless hatred of the democratic republic and its representatives, were to blame for the unheard-of brutalization of the political conflict."[474]

In that speech, Wirth warned against "this atmosphere of murder, of quarreling, of poisoning in Germany and concluded, declaring, "*Da steht (nach rechts) der Feind, der sein Gift in die Wundes eines Volkes träufeltg.—Da steht der Feind—und darüber ist kein Zweifel: dieser Feind steht rechts!*" "There is (to the right) the enemy who drips his poison into the wounds of a people. There is the enemy, and there is no doubt about this: this enemy is on the right!"[475] A significant point is that *anti-Semitism had apparently not yet widely saturated German society. What could be seen more broadly at the time was a lack of enthusiasm for the new republic and a yearning for a dictatorship primarily envisioned to be monarchical, but a dictatorship, nonetheless. (Germany would get the latter, but not the former.)*

Chancellor Joseph Wirth spoke critically of the comment made by General Ludendorff to an English publication, where he recommended for Germany a dictatorship, a monarchical dictatorship (*für Deutschland die Diktatur zu empfehlen, die monarchistische Diktatur*)—which comment Chancellor Wirth considered unworthy (*unwürdig*) of a German general.

1920s, Beyond Germany

On a grander, international scale of things, Germany in any case could not sustain its payments of war reparations. At first, its lower exchange rate allowed more exports, and in 1922, Germany's unemployment, was cut to 1%. But the superinflation that was to follow in 1923 wrought havoc on the buying power for the German population, and for the German economy overall.[476] The situation became untenable and Germany could not continue to pay the war reparations demands of the Allies: the French and the Belgians came into the Ruhr in 1923 to collect in kind (the region's coal, iron, steel, and lumber) when Germany seemed unable to pay in cash or gold coin. *It was later in 1923, with this occupation ongoing, that Hitler and members of the Nazi Party attempted the coup.*

---

[474] Eberhard Kolb, *The Weimar Republic* (2nd ed., 2005), p. 46.

[475] From speech by Chancellor Joseph Wirth before the Reichstag, June 25, 1922, on the occasion of the assassination of the Reich Foreign Minister, Walther Rathenau. From Verhandlungen des Reichstags. Stenographische Berichte, I. Wahlperiode 1920. Band 356, 236th Session (236. Sitzung), pp. 8054-8058 [*at the website, search for* "236. Sitzung"].

[476] Alexander Jung, "Nationales Trauma: Millionen, Milliarden, Billionen," Spiegel Geschichte, Aug. 27, 2009, pp. 106-115; "Millions, Billions, Trillions: Germany in the Era of Hyperinflation," Spiegel Online, Aug. 14, 2009.

The Hitler Era

A little noticed event also took place in 1923; which was to have a major impact on the course and outcome of World War II. It involved the esoteric fields of the foundations of mathematics, sentential logic, and cryptology. The event was the offering of the first commercial version of a machine invented by a German engineer, Arthur Scherbius, building on the work of Dutch researchers.[477] Scherbius had applied for a patent during the Great War, on February 23, 1918; in 1923 his machine, expensive, bulky, and weighing some 110 pounds, was made available for purchase; this was not very successful: it was rejected by the German Army, and was not economically appealing to businesses. Then, in 1926, a lighter model came out and became economically interesting.

What was this odd machine? It was a coding system, called Enigma: in the business world, banks and other organizations could use it to send encoded messages in private. The potential military use of this machine was not fully appreciated at the time. Still, attracting little attention in Germany or elsewhere, the Enigma kept being revised and made more sophisticated. Finally, the German navy would purchase the most up-to-date version of the machine, in 1926—but would not introduce it into German submarine warfare in the four-rotor M4 version of Enigma until February 1942; the German army would first purchase the machine in 1928. (More on this important encoding and decoding device, below.)

Ultimately, before and during World War II, German military coded communications were intercepted and interpreted by British Intelligence, without the Germans suspecting at any time the lack of security and privacies of their communiqués!

The Germans, from Hitler on down through the generals and admirals were quite convinced that their Enigma machine was so sophisticated a coding that no decoding would ever be possible; Hitler even convinced Mussolini to change from the Italian coding system (which the Allies had not decoded) to the German Enigma machine, which the Allied had been able to decipher—the Germans' quite mistaken assumption, of course.

And, in the early years of World War II, there was another system of coded transmission of information, *using quite different principles.* Its primary inventor, H. K. Markey (née Hedwig Kiesler), was a Viennese-born, assimilated-Jewish inventor, mathematician, and actress, *better known by her stage name as Hedy Lamarr,* called in that era an "it" girl, a magnetically beautiful woman.[478]

---

[477] Dutch naval officers working for the Dutch War Dept. (the *Ministerie van Oorlog*), succeeded in 1915 in work on such a machine; on their work and the link to the German work of Arthur Scherbius, Karl de Leeuw, "The Dutch Invention of the Rotor Machine, 1915-1923," *Cryptologia*, vol. 27, no. 1, Jan. 2003, pp. 73-94.

[478] Hedwig Eva Maria Kiesler (1914-2000), left Austria and was soon employed by Louis B. Mayer (of Metro-Goldwyn-Mayer film studios), who gave her the screen name Hedy Lamarr. See "Hedy Adds New Twist to War: Actress Invents Control Device While Toying With Torpedo Idea, Has Patent to Prove It," *Stars and Stripes (US Military paper), Western European ed. (France),* Nov. 19, 1945, p. 1; Rob

an "it" girl (1930)

Hedy Lamarr

Here we see her most inventive, inspired mind. This coding system used what is termed frequency hopping spread spectrum (FHSS); it is also referred to as frequency hopping and as spread spectrum. It used radio frequencies that were changing ongoingly, with each being used for less than one second, and with some 88 different frequencies used overall—from the number of keys on a piano keyboard, using coding imprinted on perforated paper or metallic rolls, to play the melody on a "player" piano, using the expertise of the second inventor, American avant-garde composer, George Antheil. This complex, pseudo-random, rapid changing of radio frequencies made any jamming of radio signals ultimately ineffective; it also made capturing the signals basically impossible. This American technology ("Secret Communication System") was given US Patent Number 2,2923,387 in August 1942, to H. K. Markey *et al*. This encoding-and-decoding technology is used nowadays, *decades later (suggesting that it was quite an extraordinary invention)*, in the now-familiar GPS (Global Positioning System) technology, as well as secure Wi-Fi technology, Bluetooth, and US military satellites, including the very advanced and most reliable Milstar Statellite System, used for the highest US Presidential and high military secret communications.[479]

Hyperinflation and Voting

More obvious to everyone, and not at all involving any esoteric mathematical or electronic theorizing, there was hyperinflation in Germany, especially in 1923 and 1924, wiping out most Germans' savings, whether meager or significant. (At the end of 1923, the US dollar was at 4.2 trillion marks!)

With the passing of the years (of the 1920s), we hear of Hitler's Brown Shirts (Storm Troopers, the SA) showing their power as a paramilitary

---

Walters, *Spread Spectrum: Hedy Lamarr and the Mobile Phone* (2006); *Bombshell: The Hedy Lamarr Story* (2017), YouTube, at 1:30-3:05, 13:15-14:55, 33:45-45:40, 1:19:20-1:25:10; George Antheil (1900-1959), *Bad Boy of Music* (1945), Chap. 32, "Hedy and I Invent a Radio Torpedo" (p. 327); "George Antheil," Wikipedia.

[479] The invention and its current use in very sophisticated US military applications are acknowledged by Major Darrell Grob, Milsatcom Staff Direction, at 1:20:15-1:21:10 in *Bombshell* (just cited). On Milsatcom in the contemporary international military context, see Mark Holmes, "Government/Military: New Visions Emerge for Global Milsatcom," *Via Satellite*, Nov. 9, 2018, Satellitetoday.com.

The Hitler Era

group ready to enter into street brawls, especially against Communist demonstrators, and, against others the Nazis found to be their enemies, for personal or more militaristic reasons. *And still the Weimar Republic held on.* Then, the US plan, the Young Plan, infused millions of dollars in the German economy in 1924, stabilizing the German economy.

Considering international affairs and tensions, the major military occupation of the Ruhr by the Allies lasted until August 25, 1925. The French would not return in the years following, the occupation seen by all sides as rather unhelpful and rather unsuccessful. The Dawes Plan of 1924 was an attempt to bring these European tensions down and to provide a means for the stability of the region. In 1926, Germany was admitted to the League of Nations. (It would leave the League after Hitler and the Nazi Reich came into being, through a formal letter dated October 19, 1933.)

The war debts imposed on Germany in the Versailles Treaty of 1919 were a reflection of the earlier payment imposed on France by Germany in 1871. The amount of this 1918 indemnity (reparations) was set in the Versailles Treaty at 226 billion gold marks and reduced in the 1921 London Schedule of Payments to (on paper) 132 billion gold marks (vs. the much smaller 1871 French indemnity of 5 billion gold francs).[480]

The amount Germany was required to pay back in this 1921 Schedule was only 50 billion, the rest being a number that could be presented to the French public to show how harsh the reparations were.

Important here was Charles Dawes, who had held the office of Comptroller of the Currency in the US Department of the Treasury, had been US Ambassador to Great Britain, and, later, the 30th Vice President of the USA, 1925-1929. In 1924, Dawes put forth the Dawes Plan, which cut the amount to be paid by Germany to 20 billion gold marks, this amount staggered over the next years, along with loans from various countries totaling $200 million, with J. P. Morgan, Jr., again floating a loan for a large portion of that amount. The plan was approved by all participant nations in August 1924. Dawes received the Nobel Peace Prize for his proposals.[481]

The years 1925-1929 were rather active for Germany, with Berlin becoming again an international center for culture, the arts and literature, and avant-garde civilization, a short-lived experiment that was thoroughly overturned and crushed by the rise to power of the National Socialists.

In any case, something is missing about the way that Hitler finally came to power in this understanding of the rise of National Socialism, when explained only as coming from the shame-inducing Versailles Treaty, the claim of back-stabbing, and the harsh reparations payments of that Treaty.

---

[480] Sally Marks, "The Myths of Reparations," *Central European History*, vol. 11, no. 3, Sep. 1978, pp. 231-255.

[481] "Charles G. Dawes," NOBELPRIZE.ORG.

This is so even if we consider the traditional, Prussian-inspired Germanic sense of authority and obedience to that authority.[482] Rules had a supreme position of respect in this world. As Goebbels' private secretary, Brunhilde Pomsel, wrote of the late 1920s, "Crazy, all the rules in those days that you just unquestioningly obeyed."[483]

The Nazi road to power involved some dips to something close to oblivion. In the elections during the 1920s, for example, the Nazis with Hitler at their head received of only 6.5% of the popular vote (election of May 4, 1924), 3% (December 7, 1924), and 2.6% (May 20, 1928). In short, there were no significant election results from Hitler's focusing on the "back-stabbing" of Germany's politicians, or of Jewry, spoken of as a conspiracy of world capitalist Jewry together with world Bolshevik-communist Jewry, even leaving aside the confused incomprehensibility of trying to understand how those two, held to be paradigmatically Jewish world-hating value systems, could operate together as a unified block.[484]

In 1929, a further emendation in international debt that impacted Germany (among other nations) was made, based on the Young Plan, proposed by US financier Owen D. Young, and put into effect in 1930. This further cut the amount Germany was to pay (on paper) to 112 billion gold marks, but, importantly, this was divided into several sub-categories.

The first part, one third of the new total (or some 37 billion gold marks) was put onto a schedule of a payment of only *2 billion gold marks per year* (with the payments to continue until 1989, which no one in particular expected to be carried out). All payments ended with the birth of the Third Reich, so the indemnity paid out by Germany (from 1919 to 1933) was ultimately *only a small percentage* of the huge number defined in the Treaty of Versailles.

The other two-thirds were set up as a postponable loan (which of course was never paid back), payable to a Bank for International Settlements, established for the occasion in 1930.[485]

---

[482] The 2009 German film, *Das weiße Band* (*The White Ribbon*), about pre-World War I Germany, investigates the implications of this strict upbringing.

[483] Brunhilde Pomsel, *The Work I Did: A Memoir of the Secretary to Goebbels* (2017), p. 12.

[484] One early attempt by Hitler to present Jews as the power behind both extreme capitalism and fervent Bolshevism was in his speech of July 28, 1922, in Adolf Hitler, *Collection of Speeches, 1922-1945*, pp. 19-28, esp. pp. 21-24. Hitler refers back (p. 27) to Bismarck (from a speech by Otto von Bismarck as Prussian Prime Minister, on Sept. 30, 1862) and the idea that some political issues cannot be resolved satisfactory by vote, but only by blood and iron—*Blut und Eisen*. Earlier, the anti-Semite Dietrich Eckart in *Der Bolschewismus von Moses bis Lenin: Zwiegespräch zwischen Hitler und mir* (*Bolshevism from Moses to Lenin: Dialogue between Hitler and Me*), pp. 28-33, merged Jewry and Bolshevism, saw Jews as a threat to all nations, wanting to go beyond world domination to annihilation of the world (*Über die Weltherrschaft hinaus, zur Vernichtung der Welt*).

[485] "World War I reparations," WIKIPEDIA; "Dawes Plan," ENCYCLOPÆDIA BRITANNICA; "Dawes Plan," WIKIPEDIA; "Young Plan," WIKIPEDIA; "Young Plan," ENCYCLOPÆDIA

The Hitler Era

Just before that was the famous economic crash of Wall Street, traditionally dated October 24-29, 1929, with the final collapse that last day, termed Black Tuesday. In those few days, the Dow Jones Industrial Average dropped 25%; investors lost some $30 billion dollars, ten times the US 1929 federal budget and more than the USA had spent for all of World War I.[486] Even before this crash, not everything financially speaking was rosy: Germany was already experiencing a recession, with blame placed on higher wages for workers, higher taxes (from the part of big business), and real wages not rising, with industry skimming off profits (not reinvesting in their businesses). The unemployment insurance program the government had set up was overwhelmed with claims, which its taxes had not been able to keep up with.[487] Overall, the Wall Street crash had world-impacting ramifications, most severely in the US and Germany. One reaction to the crash was the passage in the USA of the Smoot-Hawley Tariff Act of 1930.[488] This set up high tariffs on imported good, leading to a response from other countries setting up their own tariffs; *the result was widely seen as greatly exacerbating the economic situation, with an overall lessening in international trade of perhaps 50% in the next years, a dire intensification of the hardships of countries world-wide.*[489] With this, the repayment of loans by Germany was postponed, out of necessity. Unemployment in the USA was 23.6% in 1932, and 24.9% in 1933.[490] It was more severe in Germany (peaking at 25% in 1932).[491] One study held that unemployment in Germany in early 1933 was 1 in 3 workers; in the USA, 1 in 4; in Britain, 1 in 5; and in France, 1 in 7.[492] Thus, *the Lausanne Conference of 1932 recognized that Germany would not be able to repay these loans*, and lowered them even further, on paper, to 713 million gold marks, *less than 0.006% of the 1921 level of 132 billion gold marks!* Germany's repayment *by that time was a moot issue.* Hitler's coming to power was thus not a direct consequence of onerous reparations demands; still, the terrifying ghost of past realities can long endure!

BRITANNICA; Allan Hall, "Germany ends World War One reparations after 92 years with £59m [£59 million] final payment," *Daily Mail* (London), Sep. 28, 2010.

[486] Kimberly Amadeo, "Black Tuesday: Definition, Cause, Kickoff to Depression," THEBALANCE, Jan. 2, 2018.

[487] Anthony J. Nicholls, *Weimar and the Rise of Hitler*, p. 138.

[488] The two sponsors of this Congressional act, passed on June 17, 1930, were Senator Reed Smoot, Republican, Utah, and Representative Willis Hawley, Republican, Oregon. See "Smoot-Hawley Tariff Act," ENCYCLOPÆDIA BRITANNICA.

[489] Robert Whaples, "Where is There Consensus Among American Economic Historians." *Journal of Economic History*, vol. 55, no. 1, Mar. 1995, pp. 139-154.

[490] Robert A. Margo, "Employment and Unemployment in the 1930s," *Journal of Economic Perspectives*, vol. 7, no. 2, Spring 1993, pp. 41-59.

[491] N. H. Dimsdale, N. Horsewood, A. Van Riel, "Unemployment and Real Wages in Weimar Germany," *Oxford University Discussion Papers in Economic and Social History*, no. 56, Oct. 2004, pp. 1-49, at p. 17. Unemployment was estimated to be 30% in 1932: "Unemployment in Nazi Germany," SPARTACUS EDUCATIONAL.

[492] Eberhard Kolb, *The Weimar Republic* (2nd ed., 2005), p. 111.

8. Conceptual Foundations (Worldview) of the Third Reich

Long ago, more than two and a half millennia ago, it was pointed out by a man known as the Awakened One (the Buddha), that:

> All mental states are preceded by mind;
> mind is their chief, they are made of mind.
> If with a spoiled mind one speaks or acts,
> suffering follows him,
> just as the wheel follows the puller's foot[493] ...
> If with a clear mind, one speaks or acts,
> happiness follows him,
> just as a never-departing shadow.[494]

This looks at the foundation of our speaking and our actions in terms of how we are thinking, what we are thinking, what our thoughts, beliefs, and sentiments are. Here we have the understanding that *we act not in accordance with reality itself but with what we interpret and sense to be the case*. If we join this with our desires, we have a basis for an appreciation of the definitive ways in which what we think, believe to be the case, and what we want, can together direct what we say and do.[495]

That considers our own actions as individuals; we may extend this principle to a societal level, to a society's predominant, guiding thoughts and beliefs. *While not all will necessarily agree with the beliefs directing the society forward, those beliefs will still have their grand power.*

Seen from a broad viewpoint here, each age can be understood as having its own vision of the world, or worldview. The concept comes from the German, *die Weltanschauung*. This sense or spirit of the times, *der Zeitgeist*, consists in how the society thinks, what it is interested in and concerned about, the terms in which it thinks of its situation and possibilities, what its ideals and its horrors are that structure its mindset. This is a way of thinking that involves the complex and interconnected beliefs, ideals, values, morality, *and the key concepts that are used to define this world-as-understood*. (The world may operate applying many different ideas, principles, understanding, fears, and aspirations.)

We can see some periods in the past when a primary issue was how to understand the human race (or races), and others where societies had other preoccupying issues. From a contemporary perspective, we might look back on talk about there being several distinct and mutually exclusive groups of people that were members of different human races as an astonishingly simplistic view of human complexity. More recent work in genetics, with a large number of inherited variables associated with given chromosomes and within genes within each chromosome, have much

---

[493] This refers to the foot of an ox envisioned to be pulling the cart.
[494] *Dhammapada*, verses 1-2. Based on tr. in Mitchell Ginsberg, *The Inner Palace: Mirrors of Psychospirituality in Divine and Sacred Wisdom-Traditions* (2013), pp. 112-113, 423.
[495] This is discussed in detail in Mitchell Ginsberg, *Mind and Belief: Psychological Ascription and the Concept of Belief* (1972).

more exact information than any theory of races ever had. This questioning of the basic simplicity and crudeness of organizing information through the concept of a plurality of human races is not new.

It was already an issue in the 1700s. An early statement by the honored German philosopher Immanuel Kant (1724-1804) that spoke of the superiority of the Caucasian (white) race over the others (the black, yellow, and copper red), which Kant later refined,was confronted by German biologist and essayist Georg Forster (1754-1794).[496] Even Kant, in his later writings (in the 1790s), would begin to talk of international rights: the rights of members and of their entire societies in interaction with other societies, which we would now think of as international rights and international law, but also of cosmopolitan rights: the rights of individuals irrespective of which society or nation they were considered to be members of, which we would now think of as human rights and human rights law.[497] While in retrospect we might now say that *the concept of human races remained rather simplistic throughout its long history* (while continuing in some circles into the present), even in earlier centuries there were subtle variations in how the issue was viewed, and how it was applied in addressing specific issues, as in the insights of the brothers Von Humboldt: Wilhelm on one human race with a common humanity (1836), and Alexander on the unity of the human species (1858).

With this history as background, we can also look in particular at the situation in 1920s-to-1940s Germany. What is there to notice of that time and age, in particular? Let us consider some of the philosophical and scientific underpinnings (to use these terms loosely) to Nazi thinking about history and society. In this consideration, we can look both at teachings that preceded World War I, the Weimar Republic, and the birth of the Third Reich.

NIETZSCHE ON GERMANY, NATIONALISM, AND ANTI-SEMITISM

In tracing some of the ideas that were propagated during the Nazi Era, one early philosopher who is often mentioned is German-born Friedrich Nietzsche (1840-1900).[498] He was a rather brilliant classicist (gaining the equivalent of a Full Professorship at the University of Basle in Switzerland, at the age of 24), familiar with both Roman and Greek literature. After he resigned for poor health at the age of 39, in 1879, he lived in the Swiss Alps and in northern Italy, in the vicinity of Turin. He prided himself on

---

[496] Thomas Strack (Ger.-Amer. scholar in German studies, philosophy, anthropology), "Philosophical Anthropology on the Eve of Biological Determinism: Immanuel Kant and Georg Forster on the Moral Qualities and Biological Characteristics of the Human Race," *Central European History*, vol. 29, no. 3, 1996, pp. 285-308; and Dutch scholar Pauline Kleingeld, "Kant's Second Thoughts on Race," *The Philosophical Quarterly*, vol. 57, no. 229, 2007, pp. 573–592.

[497] Immanuel Kant (1795), *Zum ewigen Frieden: Ein philosophischer Entwurf (Toward Pepetual Peace: A Philosophical Sketch)*.

[498] Passages from Nietzsche's books are regularly cited by title and sect. number, constant through different editions, in various languages (just a reminder).

his Polish background, partly to differentiate and distance himself from his German upbringing (tracing his family name, Nietzsche, back to its Polish origins).[499] During the 1880s, he was prolific in his writing and publishing, in the fields of aesthetics and the theory of music, and in producing significant original books in philosophy and the foundations of psychology.[500] In the last decade of his life he suffered from what was earlier seen to be a mental collapse (*Nietzsches Zusammenbruch*), which was thought to be due to tertiary syphilis. This, however, has been more recently seen as a complex set of symptoms, including severe migraine, psychiatric disease, dementia, visual loss (possibly from a vascular origin), and stroke or stroke-like episodes, which can now be understood as supporting a diagnosis of CADASIL,[501] with further specific features of Gastaut-Geschwind Syndrome, from temporal lobe epilepsy.[502] After this

---

[499] For example, *Ecce Homo* (1908; written, 1888), I.3; Walter Kaufmann, tr. (1967), p. 225: "I, the last anti-political German. And yet my ancestors were Polish noblemen: I have many racial instincts in my body from that source... When I consider how often I am addressed as a Pole when I travel, even by Poles themselves, and how rarely I am taken for a German, it might seem that I have been merely externally sprinkled with what is German."

[500] *Ecce Homo*, V.6; Walter Kaufmann, tr., p. 331: "Who among philosophers was a psychologist at all before me...? There was no psychology at all before me." Cf. "Nietzschean Psychiatry Revisted" (pp. 59-102) and "Commentary on Nietzsche's HAH 379: Survival of the Parents" (pp. 108-116) in Mitchell Ginsberg, *Calm, Clear, and Loving*.

[501] See Dimitri Hemelsoet, Koenraad Hemelsoet, and Daniel Devreese, "The Neurological Disease of Friedrich Nietsche," *Acta neurologica Belgica*, vol. 108, no. 1, 2008, pp. 9-16. CADASIL Syndrome was only defined in the 1990s by French researchers Marie-Germaine Bousser and Elisabeth Tournier-Lasserve, associating the syndrome with a mutation of the Notch3 gene (on chromosome 19). The name CADASIL is short for Cerebral Autosomal Dominant Arteriopathy with Subcortical Infarcts and Leukoencephalopathy. See Jane Qiu, "Marie-Germaine Bousser: Going against the Grain," *The Lancet: Neurology*, vol. 7, no. 10, Oct. 2008, p. 870. The condition may show first signs in one's 30s, with intense migraines with subcortical stroke. The early death of Nietzsche's father in 1849 (apparently from a stroke with loss of sight) when 35, when Nietzsche was 4 years old, suggests a similar condition. The condition is linked to cognitive decline, dementia, loss of sight, and possible psychotic symptoms. Cf. Cyrus S. H. Ho and Adrian Mondry, "CADASIL presenting as schizophreniform organic psychosis," *General Hospital Psychiatry*, vol. 37, no. 3, May-Jun. 2015, pp. 273e11-273e13; Lampros Perogamvros, Stephen Perrig, Julien Bogousslavsky, Panteleimon Giannakopoulos, "Friedrich Nietzsche and his Illness: A Neurophilosophical Approach to Introspection," *Journal of the History of the Neurosciences*, vol. 22, no. 2, 2013, pp. 174-182.

[502] Steven G. Waxman and Norman Geschwind, "The Interictal Behavior Syndrome of Temporal Lobe Epilepsy," *Archives of General Psychiatry*, vol. 32, no. 12, Dec. 1975, pp. 1580-1586; Louwai Muhammed, "A Retrospective Diagnosis of Epilepsy in Three Historical Figures: St. Paul, Joan of Arc and Socrates," *Journal of Medical Biology*, vol. 21, no. 4, Jul. 2013, pp. 208-211; Christian R. Baumann, Vladimir P. I. Novikov, Marianne Regard, Adrian M. Siegel, "Did Fyodor Mikhailovich Dostoevsky suffer from mesial temporal lobe epilepsy?" *Seizure*, vol. 14, no. 5, Jul.

collapse in 1889 at the age of 44, Nietzsche suffered further physical and mental deterioration, and died aged 55 in 1900, after being in the care of his mother and then his sister, Elizabeth Förster-Nietzsche, who took over his estate, including all of his literary works.

The relation between Nietzsche and how he was interpreted by Nazi theoreticians is of significance and so it may be of value to consider what his actual writings offered, for some clarity on this issue. The perennial issue that weighs down Nietzsche discussions of whether he was a proto-Nazi or not, can be answered. We can start with Nietzsche's attitude toward the anti-Semites of his age, those who would visit themselves on the German people at times. Thus, in the late 1950s, *Der Spiegel*, a German publication, suggested, "Hardly any author of the German language has made such spiteful, such devastating, remarks [*so boshaft-zutreffende, so vernichtende Bemerkungen*] about a kind of people Germans are visited by [*heimgesucht werden*] from time to time: about (to be explicit), anti-Semites."[503] We can understand what this meant by considering Nietzsche's writings themselves. To start with, Nietzsche in a letter in late 1887 to his sister about her marriage to Bernard Förster. Nietzsche wrote that to Förster is due [*gebührt*] "the dubious distinction [*der zweifelhafte Ruhm*]" of co-producing the first anti-Semitic mass action in Germany, in April 1881; he went to Paraguay to start a pure Germanic people. This project was a major failure as a sociological experiment and economic venture). Förster subsequently committed suicide in 1889,[504] aged 46, Nietzsche wrote to his sister, "You have committed one of the greatest stupidities—for yourself and for me! Your association with an anti-Semitic chief [her husband] expresses a foreignness to my whole way of life which fills me ever again with ire or melancholy.... It is a matter of honor to me to be absolutely clear and unequivocal in relation to anti-Semitism, namely, *opposed* to it, as I am in my writings. [Nietzsche becomes more specific.] I have recently been persecuted with letters and *Anti-Semitic Correspondence Sheets*.[505] My

---

2005, pp. 324-330; Ivan Iniesta, "La epilepsia en la gestación artística de Dostoievski," *Neurología*, vol. 29, no. 6, 2014, pp. 371-378.

[503] "Philosophen: Nietzsche, Das Lama," *Der Spiegel*, Jan. 29, 1958, pp. 32-41, at p. 32.

[504] "Philosophen: Nietzsche, Das Lama" (just cited), pp. 34, 37.

[505] These were issues of a publication by Theodor Fritsch (1852-1933), a periodical to which Nietzsche's brother-in-law contributed. See Nietzsche's letter to Theodor Fritsch, from Nice, France, Mar. 23, 1887, at "Nietzsche's Letters 1887," THE NIETZSCHE CHANNEL. Nietzsche wrote of his reply to Fritsch: "Recently a Mr. Theodor Fritsch from Leipzig wrote to me. There are no more outrageous and stupid associations [*unverschämtere und stupidere Bande*] in Germany than these anti-Semites. In a written thank-you, I gave him a proper kick [*Ich habe ihm brieflich zu Danke eine ordentlichen Fußtritt versetzt*]. This riffraff [*Dies Gesindel*] dares to put the name (Zarathustra) in his mouth [*in den Mund zu nehmen*]. Disgust! [*Ekel!*] Disgust! Disgust!" See Volker Gerhardt, *Friedrich Nietzsche* (4th ed., 2006), p. 14, with Nietzsche quoted (in German).

disgust with this party (which would like the benefit of my name only too well!), is as pronounced as possible.... I am unable to do anything against it, that the name of Zarathustra is used in every *Anti-Semitic Correspondence Sheet*, has almost made me sick several times."[506] (This refers to the central personage in Nietzsche's four-part work of the 1880s, *Thus Spoke Zarathustra*.)

Nietzsche did not confine his repulsion at anti-Semitism to letters. Similar sentiments are expressed in his published books, as from *The Antichrist* (1895), "An anti-Semite certainly is not any more decent because he lies as a matter of principle."[507]

Or, from *On the Genealogy of Morals* (1887), "I again remind readers who have ears for such things of that Berlin agent of revenge, Eugen Dühring, who employs moral mumbo-jumbo [claptrap, gibberish, nonsense: *Gebrauch vom moralischen Bumbum machen*] [508] more indecently and repulsively than anyone in Germany today. Dühring, the foremost moral bigmouth today [*das erste Grossmaul*]—unexcelled even among his own ilk, the anti-Semites."[509]

There are also Nietzsche's comments about the Jews of Europe, where he wrote in Section 205 of *Daybreak* (1881), "The People of Israel":

> One of the spectacles which the next century will invite us to witness is the decision regarding the fate of European Jews.... In Europe, however, they have gone through a schooling of eighteen centuries such as no other nation has ever undergone, and the experiences of this dreadful time of probation have benefited not only the Jewish community but, even to a greater extent, the individual. As a consequence of this, the resourcefulness of the modern Jews, both in mind and soul, is extraordinary. Amongst all the inhabitants of Europe it is the Jews least of all who try to escape from any deep distress by recourse to drink or to suicide, as other less gifted people are so prone to do. Every Jew can find in the history of his own family and of his ancestors a long record of instances of the greatest coolness and perseverance amid difficulties and dreadful situations.... And above all, it is their bravery under the cloak of wretched submission, their heroic *spernere se sperni* [Latin: to spurn spurning oneself] that surpasses the

---

[506] *The Portable Nietzsche*, Walter Kaufmann, ed., tr. (1959), pp. 456-457 (letter to his sister, Christmas 1887).

[507] *The Antichrist* (1895), 55; in *The Portable Nietzsche*, p. 641.

[508] *Der Fall Wagner* (1888), 6, talks of "Sursum! Bumbum!" as great Wagnerian sounds with no clear meaning. Various Eng. tr. of *The Case of Wagner*, often leave the two terms in the German.

[509] *On the Genealogy of Morals* (1887), III.14; Walter Kaufmann and Reginald J. Hollingdale, tr. (1967), p. 124.

> virtues of all the saints.... On the day when the Jews will be able to exhibit to us as their own work such jewels and golden vessels as no European nation, with its shorter and less profound experience, can or could produce, when Israel shall have changed its eternal vengeance into an eternal benediction for Europe; then that seventh day will once more appear when old Jehovah may rejoice in Himself, in His creation, in His chosen people—and all, all of us, will rejoice with Him!⁵¹⁰

And in *Human, All-Too-Human* (1878), in Section 475 ("European man and the abolition of nations"), Nietzsche again placed European Jewry in its potential role in contributing to a future, trans-national Europe, with an unusual prescience into what might impede that possibility, as will be seen during the years of power of the intensely anti-Semitic Third Reich:

> Trade and industry, the post and the book-trade, the possession in common of all higher culture, rapid changing of home and scene, the nomadic life lived by all who do not own land [this would include both Jews and Romanies]—these circumstances are necessarily bringing with them a weakening and finally an abolition of nations... as a consequence of continual crossing, a mixed race, that of European man, must come into being out of them. This goal is at present being worked against, consciously or unconsciously, by the separation of nations through the production of *national* hostilities... [fostered by those with political or economic vested interests, and] once one has recognized this fact, one should not be afraid to proclaim oneself simply a *good European* and actively to work for the amalgamation of nations....—Incidentally: the entire problem of the *Jews* exists only within national states, inasmuch as it is here that their energy and higher intelligence, their capital in will and spirit accumulated from generation to generation in a long school of suffering, must come to preponderate to a degree calculated to *arouse envy and hatred*, so that in almost every nation—and the more so the more nationalist a posture the nation is again adopting—there is gaining ground the literary indecency of *leading the Jews to the sacrificial slaughter as scapegoats for every possible public or private misfortune*. As soon as it is no longer a question of the conserving of nations but of the production of the strongest possible European mixed race, the Jew will be just as usable and desirable as an

---

[510] Friedrich Nietzsche, *Daybreak: Thoughts on the Prejudices of Morality* (1881), John M. Kennedy, tr. (1911), Sect. 205, pp. 210-211, 215-216.

> ingredient of it as any other national residue. Every nation, every man, possesses unpleasant, indeed dangerous qualities: it is cruel to demand that the Jew should constitute an exception.[511]

Or, from *Beyond Good and Evil* (1886), "I have not met a German yet who was well disposed toward the Jews, and however unconditionally all the cautious and politically-minded repudiated real anti-Semitism, even this caution and policy are not directed against the species of this feeling itself but only against its dangerous immoderation." Nietzsche continues, addressing a particular German thinking from one specific frame of mind:

> Admit no more Jews! And especially close the doors to the east (also to Austria)!" Thus, commands the instinct of a people whose type is still weak and indefinite.... The Jews, however, are beyond any doubt the strongest, toughest, and purist race now living in Europe; they know how to prevail even under the worst conditions...[512]

This interprets the desire to keep Jews out of Germanic Europe not as a reasonable defensive protection of higher culture, but the instinctive reaction manifesting weakness and indefiniteness, a lack of clarity, about one's own identity.

One key distinction between Nietzsche's understanding and that of the applications made by the National Socialists was his concept of the Overman (*Übermensch*). This is one who had overcome or transcended his own personal limitations (by undergoing radical transformation).[513]

This inspired the Nazis in *their* idea of the overman and (more centrally for them) of the superior race, or the *Herrenrasse*, the Master Race, with the Nazi primary contrast, the *Untermenschen*, inferior people.

This calls for two brief comments. First, the Nazi model of the "super" man amounted to one who conformed totally to Nazi demands. This is quite distinct from the Overman (or *Übermensch*) in Nietzsche's writings. Nietzsche would write at length of the *Übermensch* (Overman), and *we can distinguish this concept from* the comic-strip character Superman, *and also from* the Nazis' concept referring to the *Volk* as a unit.[514]

In simple terms, we might note that Superman had one significant difference from Nietzsche's Overman: the special nature of Superman was

---

[511] *Human, All-too-Human: A Book for Free Spirits* (1878), 475; Reginald J. Hollingdale, tr. (1996), pp. 174-175. Italics added.

[512] *Beyond Good and Evil* (1886), 251; Walter Kaufmann, tr. (1966).

[513] We have here the overman (*Übermensch*) with overcoming (*Übergang*), those who go across or transcend (*die Hinübergehende*), the climbing up (*hinaufsteigen*), a transformative downfall (*Untergang*, descent, decline, sinking, destruction, all in one), as of those who go under (*untergehen*) and those who have undergone changes in this self-transformative process (*die Untergehende*), among many related terms illustrating *Nietzsche's love of puns that at the same time carried great significance, one of the distinctive features of his prose.*

[514] *Zarathustra*, I.5.4; *Twilight of the Idols*, I.42; *The Gay Science*, III.143.

not a matter of the shift in consciousness that Nietzsche described in detail, a shift we could describe as non-physical, as psychological, as mental, as emotional—or, use an old term that was the core contrast with the physical, the psyche,[515] the spiritual, to refer to the spirit or soul of a person. Instead, for Superman, the individual specialness was presented as a matter of special physical powers (a body that resisted being shot by bullets, the ability to fly, and so forth). Still, this cartoon character recognized the idea that *it was an individual who was different and special*.

By contrast to both of these, the Nazi idea that was central in National Socialist thinking was, not a special individual, but a group considered to be a race of superior beings (the *Volk*, the pure-German People). Ideal young Nazis were exhorted to be, as Hitler put it, as tough as leather, as swift as greyhounds, and as hard as Krupp steel, and this physical prowess was presented as features of an ideal Germanic group, the *Herrenrasse* or Master Race. This represents two major shifts or changes from Nietzsche's vision: first (for Superman), the special powers became physical, not psychological (or psychospiritual), and second, in Nazi ideology the focus was the superiority of the group, not of the individual.

We may note here that Nietzsche's core contrast with the Overman was with *die Heerde* (the herd) and *Herdenmentalität* (herd mentality), with a second contract, on an individual level, *der letzte Mann* (the last man), one who had given up all vitality and creativity.[516] For Nietzsche, there was the sole individual who has climbed to the mountain tops. For the Nazi vision, there was the superior group, all rather like one another, with the central contrast being of the master race versus inferior humans (*Untermenschen*). With this, the National Socialists avoided questions about individual exceptional excellence that an understanding and consideration of Nietzsche's philosophy would raise—the only individual allowed that vaunted role of exceptionality was Hitler as *der Führer!*

Baeumler: Nietzsche Nazified

The German nationalism that was often accompanied by a xenophobia and especially by a fear, hatred, and repulsion at everything Jewish, called anti-Semitism (we have just seen what Nietzsche himself said about that) had its voices in late 1800s Germany, and also in the years around and especially following World War I. One of the most articulate spokesmen at that time for this anti-Semitism was an early patron and associate of Hitler's, Dietrich Eckart, mentioned above. Eckart saw in Hitler a possible voice for the views that he himself was promulgating, and encouraged Hitler to fill the role of the leader (*der Führer*) of the German nationalist, anti-Semitic political movement. Hitler gave a speech of April 17, 1920,

---

[515] The Greek term *psychē* is rendered as soul, mind, or spirit, or kept as a loan word into modern languages, referring to all non-physical, all psychological, aspects of our existence. In this sense, it is the root of the words psychic, psychology, psychological, psychospiritual, psychotic, and so forth.

[516] *Zarathustra*, Zarathustra's Prologue.5.

before he was very widely known, declaring, "What we need is a dictator who is also a genius, if we ever want to rise up again in the world."[517] Eckart felt he could support and encourage this man. He became a mentor to Hitler, who had little education, a mediocre military career (ending the war as a Corporal), rural manners, and a country Austrian accent. Eckart taught Hitler some more urban manners, tutored him in German, and introduced him to many influential people, from Ludendorff to Helene Bechstein. This first meeting of Hitler with Bechstein was at the Bechstein's villa in Berchtesgaden; Hitler fell in love with the locale and later forced owners of properties he coveted to sell to him. These became Hitler's Berghof, at first a modest retreat, and ultimately a mini-fortress with some 20,000 troops guarding its perimeter and interior.[518]

Eckert would later confide to Ernst Hanfstaengl that on vacation with Hitler at Berchtesgaden, in May 1923, Hitler appeared to him to have a "megalomania halfway between a Messiah complex and Neroism."[519] (More on Hitler and Nero, below.) Hitler's sense of his special, in fact, unique role in German history, was mentioned when, in prison for treason in 1924, Hitler was asked which powers or rights he might pass on to others while he was imprisoned. Hitler "did not say anything which could clarify the issue. Though he was fully informed about the danger [of a split within right-wing German nationalists], he remained stubbornly evasive. After several such fruitless conferences, we [the author, Kurt G. W. Ludecke, includes himself here] were forced to acknowledge that Hitler was prepared to risk everything rather than delegate a portion of his person authority while he remained confined."[520]

With the publication in 1926 of Volume 2 of *Mein Kampf*, Hitler paid tribute to Eckert—but only at the very end of that volume—writing of him as "that man, who, as one of the best, by words and by thoughts and finally by deeds, dedicated his life to the awakening of his, of our nation: Dietrich Eckart."[521] This makes implicit reference to a song written by Eckart in late 1919, "*Deutschland, Erwache*" ("Germany, Awaken"), a later slogan of the National Socialists.[522] Not mentioning Eckart in the text except for this late, closing comment was part of Hitler's overall presentation of his life, in which he portrays himself as a truly self-made, self-educated man, who came to fame and power through his own efforts. There was very little acknowledgment of the help, enthusiastic support, encouragement, and even the financial wherewithal for him to succeed.

---

[517] Thomas Weber, *Becoming Hitler: The Making of a Nazi* (2017), pp. 190-191.

[518] *Hitler's Bodyguard, Season 1, Episode 12 (Nearly Attacked at the Berghof)*, 3:00-3:10, YOUTUBE.

[519] Ian Kershaw, *Hitler: A Biography*, p. 112. Eckart lived only until later that year, dying on Dec. 26, 1923, at age 54.

[520] Kurt G. W. Ludecke, *I Knew Hitler: The Story of a Nazi Who Escaped the Blood Purge*, p 241; in reply, most notably, to Alfred Rosenberg and Gregor Strasser.

[521] Adolf Hitler, *Mein Kampf*, p. 781; Eng., p. 993 (preceding the Conclusion).

[522] William Gillespie, *Dietrich Eckart: An Introduction for the English-Speaking Student* (1975), p. 24 of 42 pp. pdf text: ARCHIVE.ORG.

Relatively short shrift was given to any outside influences on the brilliant insights that Hitler came to, implied to be almost totally self-generated, including the intellectual context (if we can call it that) in which he operated, with widespread nationalist and strongly anti-Semitic, anti-Jewish, teachings Hitler had access to and been exposed to in his years in Vienna and then in Bavaria, implying, instead, that the major features of his vision of society were totally self-created.

Eckart, in any case, saw the answer to all major earthly problems in a *Weltanschauung* (worldview) that held that each nation has a soul, one which also held that in Germany, in particular, the *Volksseele*, the German soul, was in contrast with the Jewish soul. Here we see the application of concepts appropriate to individuals to groups as if one large singular entity. (We speak of the body politic in this same extension or metaphor.)

This Aryan-Jewish split, seeing the noxious influence of the Jew as the basis for the degenerated state of German society, would be the basis of an intense anti-Semitism. Eckart foresaw that Jewry would be condemned to death for its crimes. These views were expressed in a series of articles in the weekly newspaper he had established, *Auf gut Deutsch*.[523] In a later article, "*Das ist der Jude! Laienpredigt über Juden und Christentum*" ("*This is the Jew! A Lay Sermon on Jews and Christianity*"), he declared, "between everything Jewish and everything non-Jewish [*zwischen allem Jüdischen und allem Nichtjüdischen*] is an unbridgeable abyss [*ein unüberbrückbarer Abgrund*].[524] That same year, Eckard in his booklet *Totengräber Rußlands* (*Gravediggers of Russia*), with illustrations by Otto von Kursell, depicted many Jews—as in the distorting caricatures of Julius Streicher's *Der Stürmer*)—all identified as Soviet Jews (Bolsheviks).

Eckert would take from Russian Czarist Secret Police sources the forgery called *The Protocols of the Elders of Zion*, written to suggest that there was a worldwide Jewish conspiracy to control the world. Composed late in the nineteenth century out of earlier works in the 1800s, it was first published in Russian in 1903. Eckart would also introduce Hitler to this work, which gave definition to earlier, less precise visions of Jewry as dangerous to European civilization; Hitler also learned of the teachings of the Thule Society, of which Eckart was a key member. As just mentioned, it was Eckert who introduced the term *Deutschland erwache!* (Germany, awaken!), later used by the Nazis. Eckart took part in the 1923 Putsch, was arrested, but released from prison for poor health, and, a morphine addict and alcoholic, died of a heart attack on December 26, 1923.[525] If we now return to the sources of Hitler's thinking, in general,[526] and, in

---

[523] For example, *Auf gut Deutsch*, vol. 1, 1919, pp. 5-8, 83, 104, 163-164.

[524] *Auf gut Deutsch*, vol. 2, 1920, pp. 337-398, at 358-359.

[525] "Thule Society, Encyclopedia of Occultism and Parapsychology" (2001), ENCYCLOPEDIA.COM; C. N. Trueman, "Dietrich Eckart," HISTORY LEARNING SITE, HISTORYLEARNINGSITE.CO.UK, May 22, 2015.

[526] See discussions in Yvonne Sherratt, *Hitler's Philosophers* (2014) and in Max Weinreich, *Hitler's Professors: The Part of Scholarship in Germany's Crimes Against the Jewish People* (1946); new ed. with Introduction by Martin Gilbert (1999).

particular, to the issue of Nietzsche and the development of his thought as seen through a National Socialist perspective, we may note that there is no reference to Nietzsche in *Mein Kampf*. The source of links of the philosopher with the ideas of National Socialism clearly came from elsewhere, during the 1920s and developed further in the 1930s. Most centrally, on this supposed like-souled connection between Nietzsche and the Führer, Alfred Baeumler saw in Friedrich Nietzsche a proto-Nazi, with his call for the individual to go beyond the herd morality of the masses, to define his own values (the transvaluation or reassessment of all values, *die Umwertung aller Werte*). Baeumler also wrote against Christian values, presenting the foundations of Christian morality as mired in a guilty conscience, meekness, and in an otherworldly concern for salvation in the afterlife of the soul, seeing in them a value system that Nietzsche would intensely criticize and reject. (*In turn, the Nazi rejection of Christian values is something that is often dismissed, with a focus on the National Socialist anti-Semitic obsession.*) Baeumler wrote against Christianity (taking his particular vision of Nietzsche as a support or basis of his claim), "The foundations of Christian morality—religious individualism, a guilty conscience (or a sin-consciousness), meekness (or humility)—all are absolutely foreign to Nietzsche," he wrote.

Relatedly, in Nazi propaganda was a famous photograph taken in 1934, presumably intended to show the profound like-mindedness between the two; we see Hitler staring over toward a bust of Nietzsche, both Hitler and the bust equally mute, admiration neatly hidden, a discreet distance between the two carefully maintained:

Linking Nietzsche to National Socialism in his 1934 essay on Nietzsche and National Socialism, Baeumler wrote referring to Nietzsche specifically as a Nordic man, a special Aryan. Given that terms may have different meanings in different (historical) contexts, it might be important to note that what Baeumler is talking about in writing of the Aryans is radically different from a more contemporary use of the term; worlds apart from its sense for a White Supremacist—Baeumler's category *and that employed during the Third Reich* in general is quite focused, unlike the current sense. The earlier talk of Aryans in National Socialist contexts *most assuredly excluded* English, Scots, Welsh, Irish, French, Italians, Greeks, Spanish, and other "white" peoples such as the Poles, Russians, Czechs, Slovaks, and Serbs. (More below, in discussing Jews, half-apes, others, and Aryans.) The National Social perspective gave no honor to those who see themselves as good Christians. Baeumler in some contexts attacked, not Judaism, but Christianity itself:

> The foundations of Christian morality: religious individualism, consciousness of sin [*Sünden bewußtsein*], humility [*Demut*], distress about the eternal salvation of the soul [*Bekümmerung um das ewige Heil der Seele*] are completely alien to Nietzsche.... Nietzsche speaks contemptuously [*verächtlich*] of Christianity "with its perspective on salvation" [*Seligkeit*]. As a Nordic man [*als nordischer Mensch*], he never understood what he was to be "redeemed" for [*„erlöst"*].... Nietzsche's Nordic, militant evaluation [*nordische, kriegerische Wertsetzung*]⁵²⁷ stands against that of the Mediterranean [as in coming from Catholic Rome] and its priestly values. His critique of religion is a criticism of the priest, and it was the result of the station of the warrior, since Nietzsche proves that the origin of religion lies in the domain of power.⁵²⁸

Finally, Baeumler closes his essay suggesting that there is an intimate link between Nietzsche and the Germany of the National Socialists:

> If today we see the German youth marching under the sign of the swastika [*Hakenkreuz*], we will remember Nietzsche's *Untimely Reflections* ... It is our greatest hope that this youth is open to the [National Socialist] State today. And when we call out to this youth: Heil Hitler!— so we likewise greet Friedrich Nietzsche with this call.⁵²⁹

That is questionable. In Hitler's description of the Nazi flag, the red represented a social movement; the circle represented a nationalistic intensity (the white); and the swastika (in black), for the struggle of the Aryan (Nordic, Germanic) man over other, inferior, races, expressing the Party's anti-Semitic foundation, with relatively recent anti-Semitic overtones, quite foreign to Nietzsche's values and perspective.

Baumler doesn't mention it, but the swastika has pre-Nazi roots. Tracing the use in ancient cultures, in Greek, Semitic, and also in Christian symbolism, as in the miter of Saint Thomas à Becket, fertility represented as sexual intercourse between Mother Earth and God-Father, with the swastika a representation of two intertwined human bodies, originally,

---

[527] The word *Wertsetzung* harkens back to the title *Prinzip einer neuen Wertsetzung* (*Principles of a New Evaluation*), the third part of Nietzsche's unpublished *Der Wille zur Macht: Versuch einer Umwertung aller Werte* (*The Will to Power: The Transvaluation of all Values*).

[528] See here, Alfred Baeumler, "Nietzsche und der Nationalsozialismus," *Nationalsozialistiche Monatshefte*, vol. 5, no. 94 (1934), pp. 289-298, at pp. 293, 296. Reprinted with same title as Chap. 9 in Baeumler's *Studien zur deutschen Geistesgeschichte* (1937), pp. 281-294, at pp. 288, 291. Cf. Max Whyte, "The Uses and Abuses of Nietzsche in the Third Reich: Alfred Baeumler's 'Heroic Realism'," *Journal of Contemporary History*, vol. 43, no. 2, Apr. 2008, pp. 171-194.

[529] Alfred Baeumler, "Nietzsche und der Nationalsozialismus" (journal article, 1934, just cited), p. 298 (and in 1937 reprint, at p. 294).

then, a sexual symbol. The ecstatic gathering of large Nazi groups, in the Nuremberg Rallies, but also in many other contexts, tapped into this urge for sexual, orgasmic excitation and release, but in a sublimated, socialized, large-group, sanitized way.[530] An important contrast here is what Polish MD and sexologist Michalina Wislocka called a Greek orgasm, perhaps referring back to the *Iliad:* "It is about releasing anger."[531]

Baeumler's stress on the posthumous writings of Nietzsche known as *The Will to Power* had him disregard some of Nietzsche's more anti-nationalistic comments, and Nietzsche's more individualistic sense of those few who can go beyond *Herdenmentalität* or herd mentality ("the herd instinct of obedience"[532]). Nietzsche expressed great respect for the strong individual, an individual with an inner understanding and determination, in line with honoring of the élite.[533]

In stark, fundamental contrast with this interpretation by Baeumler, we have Nietzsche himself, in *Morgenröte: Gedanken über die moralischen Vorurteile* (1881), for example, where he writes (with what might strike us as expressing another astonishing prescience about events in Germany in the Hitler era):

> *Haute politique* [*Von der großen Politik*]. However largely the private advantage and vanity—of both individuals and nations—may have influenced the great politics [*in der großen Politik mitwirken*], the most powerful tide which urges them forward is the desire for the sensation of power, bursting forth from inexhaustible wells not only in the souls of princes and rulers, but periodically in an equal measure from among the lowest ranks of the people. *The time will come when the masses will be ready to sacrifice their lives, their good and chattels, their consciences and their virtue, for the purpose of securing that highest of enjoyments and of ruling either in reality or in imagination*[534] *as a victorious, tyrannical, arbitrary nation over other nations.* On these occasions the prodigal,

---

[530] An extended analysis on the symbolism of the swastika referring to earlier studies and continuing into the Nazi era, is in Wilhelm Reich, *The Mass Psycholoogy of Fascism*, pp. 83-87. The concept of sublimation was introduced by Nietzsche and then also found in Freud's writing.

[531] See the Polish film, *The Art of Loving: The Story of Michalina Wislocka* (2017), directed by Maria Sadowska, 1:45-2:05.

[532] Friedrich Nietzsche, *Beyond Good and Evil: Prelude to a Philosophy of the Future* (1886), V.199.

[533] Karl Dietrich Bracher, *The Age of Ideologies: A History of Political Thought in the Twentieth Century* (1984), pp. 1-19.

[534] The power of the imagination freed from constraints of the historical context was recently discussed as "German autistic self-forgetfulness" (*autistische Selbstvergessenheit*), by Joachim C. Fest, *Hitler* (Ger. text), p. 1039; *Hitler* (Eng.), p. 762. Fest understood this as an ongoing, dangerous tendency in German thinking. (*Not that Germans* are the only ones who can shift to what they would wish for as a replacement to what is possible, to be hoped and worked for—with the consequences of such jumps to sheer imagination at times disastrous, *and not that all Germans* without exception have this characteristic.)

The Hitler Era 173

> devoted, hopeful, confident, over-weening, fantastical feelings will spring forth in such abundance as to allow the ambitions or wisely provident prince to rush into a war and to make the good consciences of his people an excuse for his injustice. The great conquerors have always had the pathetic [emotional] language of virtue on their lips: they always had crowds of people around them, who felt as though in a state of exaltation, and who do not listen to any but the most exalted language. Such is the curious madness of moral judgments! [*Wunderliche Tollheit der moralischen Urteile!*] When man feels the sense of power, he feels and calls himself good [*Wenn der Mensch im Gefühle der Macht ist, so fühlt und nennt er sich gut*]: and at the very same time others, who have to endure the weight of his power, feel and call him evil![535]

To be specific here, we can consider what Alfred Baeumler suggested was the proto-Nazi vision of Nietzsche, what Nietzsche (just quoted) said himself, and can compare these two with Hitler speaking in large public forums (as the *Reichsparteitag* of Nazi Congress at Nuremberg). For example, on September 8, 1934, where he spoke to the Hitler Youth at the Congress, emphasizing the Nazi call for their obedience, Hitler declared, speaking to "My German Youth":

> We want to see *one* Reich, and you must even now train yourselves for this in one organization. We want our folk to be loyal, and you must learn this loyalty. We want our folk to be obedient, and you must practice obedience. We want our folk to be peace loving [*friedliebend*], but also brave. Yet ever ready for peace [*friedfertig*]. We do not want our people to be weaklings but that they can be tough in order to withstand the difficulties of life. And you must train yourselves for this in your youth. We want our people to love honor, and you must declare yourselves to the principle of honor already in your youngest years.[536]

Hitler and German spokesmen could speak of being peace-loving, being able to cite (at the time) the ten-year Four-Power Pact (*der Viermachtepakt*) of July 15, 1933, between Germany, Italy, France, and Great Britain—this was never to go into effect, and was effectively annulled when Germany withdrew from

---

[535] Friedrich Nietzsche, *Morgenröte: Gedanken über die moralischen Vorurteile* (1881), III.189; in the 1903 Eng. tr., *The Dawn of Day*, by Johanna Volz, pp. 179-180; italics added. The full title is also rendered *Daybreak: Thoughts on the Prejudices of Morality*, as in the J. M. Kennedy (1911) and R. I. Hollingdale (1982) translations.

[536] Adolf Hitler, "To the Youth of Germany: A Speech by Adolf Hitler, September 8, 1934," Theresa Wettstein, tr., THE BARNES REVUE, p. 57. Cf. video of this at Isabelle Clarke and Daniel Costelle, *Apocalypse: Hitler. Part II: Le Führer*, at 51:15-51:51, and in *A. Hitler in Nuremberg*, YOUTUBE. Ger. text is at "Text nach der gesprochenen Rede auf dem Parteitag in Nürnberg 1934," WISSENREISE.DE.

the League of Nations three months later, on October 19, 1933. Not everyone was convinced of Hitler's peaceful façade. To combat the resultant criticisms that were found in the international press, Hitler's Foreign Press Spokesperson, Ernst Hanfstaengl, in a book meant for a German audience, offered this French cartoon. In questioning Hitler's love of peace, the Parisian newspaper, *L'écho de Paris*, on February 2, 1933 (only days after the *Machtergreifung Hitlers*),[537] published this cartoon, *Le remous* or *Der Strudel* (The Swirl).

Le remous (*L'écho de Paris*, Feb. 2, 1933)

Hanfstaengl added his two-part commentary to this cartoon in the published result of his editing: (1) "Ink sketch (*Tinte*): This caricature, drawn three days after Hitler came to power (*nach der Machtergreifung Hitlers*), wants to make one believe that now European peace would be destroyed in the whirlpool of the swastika (*der europäische Frieden im Strudel des Hakenkreuzes zu Grunde gehen werde*), and (2) Fact (*Tat*): Reality has exposed the cartoonist's lies (*hat den Karikaturisten Lügen gestraft*) and will continue to do so (*wird ihn weiter Lügen strafen*)."[538] To be questioned!

And, maintaining his political stance, on September 14, 1935, addressing the Hitler Youth, Hitler announced the new ideal of the German people [*Volk*]:

---

[537] The rapid and brusque establishment of the Nazi government was called the *Machtergreifung* (the grabbing or seizure of power), and was also known as the *Machtübernahme* (the taking over of power) and the *Machtübergabe* (the handing over of power), involving what was termed the *Gleichschaltung*, the switching into conformity to Nazi values and practices of the entire German society.

For more, see Mitchell Ginsberg and Angela Grof-Nold, introductory comments to "Appendix: Gustav Bally and *deutschstämmige Psychotherapie*," pp. xlviii-lii in *Effective Psychotherapy: The Contribution of Hellmuth Kaiser*, Mitchell Ginsberg, ed.

[538] Ernst Hanfstaengl, *Hitler in der Karikatur der Welt: Tat gegen Tinte* (1933), pp. 90-91. On the Four-power Pact (*Viermächtepakt*), see p. 120.

> In our eyes, the German youth of the future must be slender and supple [*da muss der deutsche Junge der Zukunft schlank und rank sein*], swift as greyhounds [*flink wie Windhunde*], tough as leather [*zäh wie Leder*], and hard as Krupp steel [*hart wie Kruppstahl*]. We must cultivate a new man in order to prevent the ruin of our people [*Volk*] by the degeneration manifested in our age.[539]

Commentators have been divided along a continuum from interpreting Nietzsche as a visionary pre-Nazi, to a thinker who had some few commonalities but also significant differences with the Nazi worldview, to anti-nationalist, in general, and anti-German and anti-anti-Semitic, in particular. Hitler's vision here seems quite far from the Nietzschean honoring of a self-determining thinker, the very opposite of those with herd mentality.

Consider Nietzsche's position—with its strong critique and criticism of herd mentality, of the ease with which many become more obedient, of the readiness of masses of people to give up their own moral judgment, and of their eagerness to partake of the exaltation and a rich sense of an emotionally-charged joy of the self-lauding group. *All of this runs counter to, and is fervently critical of the cultural mindset (the* Weltanschaaung*, the ideology) of the Nazi regime as it was cultivated in the German populace during the Third Reich.* Indeed, this contrast is so intense and fundamental that is not at all easy to maintain that Nietzsche was a proto-Nazi or would have accepted the cultural values of the National Socialist government of Germany's Third Reich. In this context, the process of creating a Nazi state had two distinct parts, in which the right to redefine all values and morality was limited to very few (Hitler, Himmler, Goebbels, and others who made definitive statements about such matters), on the one hand, and, on the other, the pliant, accepting, non-creative followers of the movement, the mass in a unified organization, individuality denigrated and presented as a moral imperfection. *This has very little to do with Nietzsche's comments about petty German thinking and the contrast with a self-defining individual.* In this totalitarian regime, there is a limit to the influence of the intellectuals and other thinking elite (Nietzschean self-defining individuals), and their role is typically quite transient, ending with the firm establishment of the new governing leaders. In this spirit (and unlike Sartre), Albert Camus would place himself *against all forms of totalitarianism, from the Nazi/Fascist right to the Soviet left.*[540] And, similarly, as Hannah Arendt later pointed out,

> In all fairness to those among the elite … it must be stated that what these desperate men of the twentieth century did or did not do had no influence on totalitarianism whatsoever, although it did play some part in earlier,

---

[539] Adolf Hitler, "Speech before the Hitler Youth, September 14, 1935," Neues Europa; cf. Isabelle Clarke and Daniel Costelle, *Apocalypse: Hitler. Part I: La menace*, at 11:35-11:55, with Ger. text at "So geht Deutschland: Flink wie Windhunde: Rede in Nürnberg 1935," *Deutsche Welle*, DW.com.

[540] Michel Onfray, "Monsieur le Président, devenez camusien," *Le Monde*, Dec. 18, 2009.

> successful attempts of the movements to force the outside world to take their doctrines seriously. Wherever totalitarian regimes seized power, this whole group of sympathizers was shaken off even before the regimes proceeded to their greatest crimes. Intellectual, spiritual, and artistic initiative is as dangerous to totalitarianism as the gangster initiative of the mob, and both are more dangerous than mere political opposition.... Total domination does not allow for free initiative in any field of life.... Totalitarianism in power invariably replaces all first-rate talents, regardless of their sympathies, with those crackpots and fools *whose lack of intelligence and creativity* is still the best guarantee of their loyalty.[541]

With that perspective on the contribution (and its limits) of the finer thinkers who were used to support the early Nazi movement, we can look at the context and the reception that such work received. One questioning of the Nazi interpretation of Nietzsche was in the Parisian newspaper *Le Temps* of October 22, 1934, in a letter ("Lettre d'Allemagne: Nietzsche et le troisième Reich") from a Berlin correspondent to the paper, René R. Lauret, who commented early on about the role given Nietzsche by the Nazi Reich, with tongue-in-cheek sarcasm:

> In summary, Nietzsche was anti-socialist, anti-nationalist, and anti-racist. If we leave aside [*si l'on fait abstraction de*] these three tendencies, he could have made an excellent Nazi.[542]

LESSING, DOHM, DARWIN, SPENCER, CHAMBERLAIN, AND PAMPHLETEERS

We may look further to various strands of late nineteenth- and early twentieth-century ultra-nationalism and anti-Semitism. We find strong currents of anti-Semitism, and also hatred of other groups, from country to country, including the hatred and violence against blacks in the USA (think back on the lynchings that took place through much of the nineteenth century into the mid-twentieth century, by groups who thought blacks ("Nigras" in southern US dialect) were becoming too uppity and rebellious, as well as strands of hatred against Catholics (especially Irish and Italian Catholics), against competing sections of Protestantism, of foreigner-born immigrants as they came to America for refuge and a new life. It may be difficult to acknowledge that there is not yet a comfortable acceptance of the cultural preferences in dress and food of all individuals, reflecting the national origins of their ancestors, their religion (or lack of religion), any of which can give rise to a sense of unfamiliarity, with these various groups still to be fully integrated into American practical life and mores. It may be little remembered, if known at all, that for many years there were serious quotas—limits of the number of individuals of various groups that would be allowed into many

---

[541] Hannah Arendt, *The Origins of Totalitarianism* (1951), p. 339. Italics added.
[542] René Lauret, "Lettre d'Allemagne: Nietzsche et le troisième Reich," *Le temps* (Paris), Oct. 22, 1934, p. 6.

US colleges and universities—of Catholics, Jews, blacks (if any were allowed at all), and limited access to society's possibilities to women of all social classes and origins, and so on. Furthermore, until recent decades, there could be contractual limits on sales of property, so that written into such contracts was a commitment never to sell to Jews, Catholics, blacks, and other unwanted people. Social organizations from country clubs to workers' associations had strict or complete, restrictions on membership. In short, a sense of true openness based on individual characteristics and qualities did not have a proper place even in the USA in the past, and many maintain that this is still an ideal rather than a reality. The same can be said for other non-Germanic lands, including Great Britain and France. Speaking candidly as ex-Prime Minister, David Lloyd George stated in 1936, although not addressing the question of the treatment of Jews in Britain over the centuries, "I have always thought, and still think, that the persecution of Jews in Germany has been a great misfortune. But Germany is not the only country that has persecuted Jews. We must not forget the pogroms in Russia and in other European countries." (Lloyd George does not mention the expulsion of Jews from England centuries earlier, or the current restrictions on Jews in many British social circles.)[543]

Lloyd George's point was that the anti-Semitism of Germany in the 1930s did not stand out as an extreme, unique, or unparalleled aberration from a world otherwise radiating tolerance on a grand scale: consider the treatment of Jews, Romanies, the poor, the homeless, the sick, dying, and psychologically disturbed.

Focusing on the German context, it might be pertinent to recall that not all Germans, and not all German authors, thought of Jews as a poison to their world. (As usual, generalizations about the thoughts or opinions or values of an entire people are often distortions of nuanced differences to be found among the populace in focus.)

In 1779, Gotthold Lessing,[544] son of a Lutheran minister-theologian, and himself a theologically educated playwright, published his play, *Nathan der Weise* (*Nathan the Wise*). In this play, Lessing presents a parable, the Parable of the Three Rings.[545] These are presented as three

---

[543] David Lloyd George, "Nazi Regime. Hitler's Hold on People. Desire for Peace," *The Post* (London), Sep. 23, 1936, image of article at "Lloyd George's Impressions of Adolf Hitler," Jan. 23, 2014, THEGREATESTSTORYNEVERTOLD.TV, and quoted at "David Lloyd George's Pro-Nazi Views," FORUM.AXISHISTORY.COM. A similar newspaper report is "David Lloyd George Comments on his visit to Germany and meeting with Hitler," *Daily Express* (London) Sept. 17, 1936, pp. 12, 17, given at "Llloyd George and Hitler," WORLD FUTURE FUND. Cf. Kenneth O. Morgan, "Lloyd George and Germany," *The Historical Journal*, vol. 39, no. 3, 1996, pp. 755-766; articles by Kenneth O. Morgan, "David Lloyd George, 1863-1945," pp. 4-11, and Stella Rudman, "Lloyd George and the Appeasement of Germany, 1922-1945," pp. 38-46, esp. p. 41, in *Journal of Liberal History*, no. 77, Winter, 2012-2013.

[544] Gotthold Ephraim Lessing, 1729-1781.

[545] *Nathan the Wise: A Dramatic Poem in Five Acts*, William Taylor of Norwich, tr.

undifferentiable rings that a father gives to each of his sons (representing the Jews, the Muslims, and the Christians). His point is that each is a gift of the father (the Father) and each has its own validity.

This parable invites an attitude toward tolerance, even while suggesting reasons for any given person to choose one rather than either of the other two, in part, based on education, respect and loyalty to one's parents (and community), and other features. Lessing stresses the importance of the actions emanating from those who follow these traditions, these moral and religious teachings, as what would show their ultimate value.

And two years later, in 1781, Christian Dohm[546] (whom Goethe[547] described as *eine köstliche Gabe*, a delightful gift), in *Über die Bürgliche Verbesserung der Juden (On the Civil Betterment of the Jew)*, declared:

> That the Jews are like all others [*wie alle übrigen, sind*]; that they must be treated like these, too [*wie diese, behandelt werden müssen*]; that only an oppression caused by barbarism and religious prejudice [*daß nur eine durch Barbaren und Religionsvorurteile veranlaßte Drückung*] had degraded and corrupted them [*herabgewürdiget und verderbt habe*]; that only an opposite [approach], in accordance with sound reason and humanity [*der gesunden Vernunft und Menschlichkeit gemäßes verfahren*], could make them better people and citizens ...[548]

In contrast with such non-hostile senses of the relation of one people, the Jews, to others, we can turn to some of the early exponents of a harshly anti-Jewish attitude, in which the exclusion and elimination of Jews from German society was strongly advocated.

Various leading cultural figures in 1800s Germany expressed their anti-Semitic beliefs as if unquestionable and obvious truths. One famous German, much admired by Hitler, was the German musician Richard Wagner (1813-1883). He wrote in his 1850 essay (published using a pseudonym, presumably to hide his identity), *Die Judenthum in Musik* (*Judaism in Music*),[549] that the Jew (a grand generalization) "can naturally only echo and imitate, and is perforce debarred from fluent expression

---

(1893). The parable itself is in Act 3, Scene 7. Cf. Jay Newman, "The Parable of the Three Rings in Nathan Der Weise," *Mosaic: A Journal for the Interdisciplinary Study of Literature*, vol. 12, no. 4, 1979, pp. 1–8.

[546] Christian Wilhelm von Dohm, 1751-1820.

[547] Johann Wolfgang von Goethe, 1749-1832, author of *Faust* (1808, 1832).

[548] Christian Wilhelm Dohm, *Ueber die bürgliche Verbesserung der Juden* (1781; old German orthography), pp. 8-9.

[549] Essay pub. under pseudonym, Karl Freigedank, in *Neue Zeitschrift für Musik*, nos. 19-20, Sep. 1850, pp. 101-107, 109-11. This name, *Freigedank*, literally means free (*frei*) thought (*Gedank*). Presumably Wagner thought of himself as a free-thinker of sorts. *Judenthum* is an old spelling for *Judentum*.

The Hitler Era

and pure creative work [*kann die Jude nur nachsprechen, nachkünsteln, nicht wirklich redend dichten oder Kunstwerke schaffen*]."[550]

One relevant, more scholarly, figure was the Biblical scholar Paul de Lagarde (1827-1891). We can see key features from Lagarde put forth by later writers and political proponents of Nazi values, including Houston Stewart Chamberlain in his *The Foundations of the Nineteenth Century*, Adolf Hitler in his *Mein Kampf*, and Joseph Goebbels in his many speeches and discourses. in Lagarde's *Deutsche Schriften* (1878), he wrote,

> Germany is the totality of all German-feeling, German-thinking, German-acclaiming Germans [*deutsch wollenden Deutschen*]: each and every one of us a traitor to the land [*ein Landesverräther*], if he does not consider himself personally responsible for the existence, happiness, the future of the fatherland [*für die Existenz, das Glück, die Zukunft des Vaterlandes*] in every moment of his life, and every one a hero and liberator when he does [*ein Held und Befreier, wenn er es tut*].[551]

In *Juden und Indogermanen* (*Jews and Indo-Europeans*, 1887), he wrote:

> It takes a heart of the hardness of crocodile skin [*ein Herz von der Härte der Krokodilshaut*], in order not to sympathize with the poor Germans, sucked dry [*mit den armen ausgesogenen Deutschen*] and—which is the same—not to hate the Jews, and not to hate and despise those who—out of humanity!—speak to these Jews or are too cowardly to crush this proliferating vermin [*dies wuchernde Ungeziefer zu zertreten*]. Trichinella and bacilli [*Trichinen und Bacillen*] are not negotiated with; trichinella and bacilli are not cultivated; they are destroyed as quickly and as thoroughly as possible [*sie werden so rasch und so gründlich wie möglich vernichtet*].[552]

We can also see the application of various theories that were being articulated and popularized in the second half of the nineteenth century among other writings that espoused a deep hatred of all things Jewish, Jewry seen as a life-threatening force that would destroy European life and culture if allowed. These ideas filtered into the thinking of those who preceded the National Socialists, who then, in turn, made use of this Jew-hating framework to put forth their own vision of Europe and the Jews.

At about the same period, Adolf Stöcker, the Lutheran court chaplain to Kaiser Wilhelm I, applied his appreciation of the later teachings of his denomination's founder, Martin Luther (1483-1546), expressing an

---

[550] Richard Wagner, *Judaism in Music*, Edwin Evans, Sr., tr. (1910), p. 13; *Das Judentum in der Musik* (1859 ed.), p. 15.

[551] Paul de Lagarde, *Deutsche Schriften* (1878), p. 153.

[552] Paul de Lagarde, *Juden und Indogermanen: Eine Studie nach dem Leben* (1887), p. 339.

intense animosity against the Jews (after earlier having made a failed attempt, up to 1537, to bring Jews to Christianity), writing of them with hostility in his 1543 book *Von den Juden und iren* [modern German, *ihren*] *Lügen* (*On the Jews and Their Lies*). In this same anti-Jewish perspective as Lutheran's founder, Stöcker delivered his first anti-Semitic speech on September 19, 1879, *Unsere Forderungen an das moderne Judentum* (*Our Demands on Modern Jewry*), in which he blamed Germany's recent economic problems—there had been an economic, stock market crash in 1873 (brought on in part by war reparations flooding Germany with money after their victory in the brief Franco-Prussian War of 1870-1871, and the rapid growth of business after that—on the Jews (an old theme).[553] Stöcker suggested:

> Either we succeed: then blessings may come over Germany again [*dann mag der Segen wieder über Deutschland kommen*]. Or, the cancer we suffer from continues to eat away at us [*oder der Krebsschaden an dem wir leiden, frißt weiter*]: then our future is threatened [*dann ist unsere Zukunft bedroht*], the German spirit is judified [*der deutsche Geist verjudet*], and the German economy impoverished [*das deutsche Wirthschaftsleben verarmt*]. Our slogan will be to return to a more Germanic legal and economic life, with reversion to the Christian faith [*Umkehr zu christlichem Glauben*].[554]

Stöcker was also involved in a petition to limit the rights of Jews in Germany and to expel large numbers of Jews who had immigrated into Germany from Russia and Rumania—a petition whose other proponents included Friedrich Nietzsche's brother-in-law, Bernhard Förster, discussed above. Politically a man of limited success, his ideas, nonetheless, had their own appeal, and would be seen reflected in the coming decades.

At about this same time, the German anti-Semitic politician, Heinrich Gotthard von Treitschke (1834-1896) coined the slogan "*Die Juden sind unser Unglück*" ("The Jews are our misfortune"). This expression would be widely used during the Hitler era, seen at important Nazi rallies and speeches such as those given at the Berlin Sportpalast, and as a regular banner statement at the bottom of the front page of *Der Stürmer*, the Nazi weekly newspaper[555]—owned and edited by Julius Streicher, which had its very first copy printed on April 20, 1923, Hitler's thirty-fourth birthday. This hatred of Jewry—which did not saturate Western Europe at this time, where an integration of Jews into society was more the tone of

---

[553] Harold Green, "Adolf Stoecker: Portrait of a Demagogue, *Politics and Policy*, vol. 31, no. 1, Nov. 12, 2008, pp. 106-129.

[554] Adolf Stöcker, "Erste Rede" [Sep. 19, 1879], pp. 3-19, in *Das moderne Judenthum in Deutschland, besonders in Berlin. Zwei Reden in der christlich-socialen Arbeiterpartei gehalten von Adolf Stöcker, Hof- und Domprediger* [*Court and Cathedral Preacher*] *zu Berlin* (1880), at p. 19.

[555] *Der Stürmer* can mean the attacker, the striker, the forward or lineman (in sports), as well as the hothead or hotspur (an impetuous, rash person).

the day—was a reflection of the lives of Jews in Eastern Europe, where they were mostly limited in where they could live (the "Pale"), with Vienna marking the boundary of West and East. As Prince Klemens Metternich— leading diplomat in the Austro-Hungarian Empire, being Foreign Minister, 1809-1848, and Chancellor, 1821-1848 (ended by the revolutionary wave of that year), had said in his years of power that the Balkans begin at the Rennweg, a street in the Landstrasse (the name of the third *Bezirk*, district, of Vienna).

This was to him a precise demarcating of the beginning of the Balkans, representing non-German-speaking Eastern Europe, and seen as the border with the Muslim world of the Ottoman Empire, Vienna having been the far point of the Ottoman invasion into Europe. The intensity of repulsion at the Jews was intense in Vienna, and more so after the exodus from the violence in Czarist Russia in the 1880s. It was into this intensely anti-Semitic environment that Hitler moved as a young man.

Now, while these more elaborated presentations of anti-Semitism were available, we read from Hitler in his *Mein Kampf* that his purchase of inexpensive and readily available pamphlets that were circulating in Vienna during his youth there confirmed his sense of the evils of Jewry. These would include the diatribes against Jews by Viennese authors, Guido von List (1848-1919) and Jörg Lanz von Liebenfels (1874-1954).

Von List put forth such ideas as a call for the destruction of "the hydra-headed international Jewish conspiracy" and the need to establish a racially pure state in which only Aryans had the rights of citizenship, along with a global war against international Jewry that sought to destroy civilization. Von List gave the swastika the German name of *Hakenkreuz* (literally, hook-cross). To this, Liebenfels added the suggestion of a division between the Aryan peoples and the mongrelized inferior beings who were meant to be the slaves of the superior Aryans. We find all of these ideas repeated by Hitler in *Mein Kampf* as his own inspired realizations. The symbol of this higher group was to be the swastika, a form of which was put onto a flag he used, as early as 1907. (In French, *croix gammée*, refers to its composition of gammas, Γ.)

In any case, for Liebenfels, *the swastika (Hakenkreuz) represented a rejection of Christianity*, even though both he and Hitler (as student and choir boy) had spent time at the Abbey at Lambach, Austria, with its unquestioned use in that Christian context of a hooked cross,[556] most prominently in the cenotaph (an empty tomb honoring some important

---

[556] Jagat K. Motwani, *None but India (Bharat): The Cradle of Aryans, Sanskrit, Vedas, and Swastika* (2010), pp. 102-103; Richard Smoley, "The Twisted History of the Swastika," *Quest*, vol. 104, no. 1, 2016, pp. 22-23, THEOSOPHICAL.ORG; Ken Anderson, *Hitler and the Occult* (1995), p. 42; "Flag (Third Reich, Germany): Hakenkreuzflagge," CRWFLAGS.COM; Peter Crawford, *The Occult History of the Third Reich* (2013), THIRDREICHOCCULTHISTORY.BLOGSPOT.COM. See also Robert G. L. Waite, "Hitler's Anti-Semitism: A Study in History and Psychoanalysis," pp. 192–230 in *The Psychoanalytic Interpretation of History*, Benjamin B. Wolman, ed. (1971), esp. pp. 196-198.

figure) of Theodoric Georg Hagn (1816-1872), Benedictine Abbot of the Abbey at Lambach (1958-1872); with the initials TH (for Theodoric Haben), above the *Hakenkreuz*, and AL (for the Abbey at Lambach), below:

We may compare this with two other *Hakenkreuz* (swastika) designs:

Thule Society *Hakenkreuz*   Nazi *Hakenkreuz*

The anti-Semitic *Thule Gesellschaft* (Thule Society), founded in 1918—whose early members included Dietrich Eckart, Rudolf Hess, Hans Frank, and Alfred Rosenberg—also used a form of the *Hakenkreuz*, from as early as 1919, before the Nazi modification of the Swastika.

Given these numerous precedents, the idea that Hitler in a burst of spontaneity drew up the swastika from his self-generated creative imagination one night at a beer hall in Munich may be questioned, if not mocked, and has been. The same can be said for a number of descriptions of Hitler as self-made man that he proposes in *Mein Kampf*.

Furthermore, in the Vienna to which Hitler moved in February 1908 (after his mother's death in December 1907 from breast cancer), there was anti-Semitism and pan-German nationalism already thick in the air[557]: First, the mayor of Vienna, Karl Lueger (1844-1910), cofounder of the Austrian Christian Social Party in 1889, stressed nationalistic and anti-Semitic teachings at the height of his power and influence, including the myth of the blood libel.

Then, there was Georg von Schönerer (1842-1921), son of a wealthy railroad pioneer Matthias von Schönerer (1807-1881). Georg, the son, was a radical pan-Germanic nationalist. An anti-Semitic, anti-Slav, anti-Catholic Prussophile, Georg was a co-founder of the Linz Program of 1882, which required its members to prove their pure German ("Aryan") descent—foreshadowing Third Reich practices.

---

[557] Wilhelm Reich, *The Mass Psychology of Fascism*, p. 31.

The Hitler Era

Georg was called the *Führer* and saluted by his followers with a "Heil!"—*a practice Hitler would adopt much later.* He also felt that there was a war between Germans (in which he counted Austrian Germans as German) and world Jewry; we find a similar, concise statement from November 5, 1906, by Georg Ritter von Schönerer (1842-1921) in his speech before the Reichsrat,[558] with its rather provocative title that touches on male sexual insecurity and fears, *Die deutsche Selbstentmannung* (*German Self-emasculation,* or *Self-castration*): "If we don't expel the Jews, we Germans will be expelled! [*Wenn wir die Juden nicht vertreiben, so werden wir Deutschen vertrieben*]"[559]

Strong anti-Semitic imagery was certainly not lacking in the first decade of the 1900s.

One known text spoke of the influx of Russian Jews from the time of the pogroms of the 1880s that began in 1881, with the death of Czar Alexander II (1818-1881). With that, his son became the new czar, Czar Alexander III (1845-1894), much more traditional and conservative, and set about to annul the various land reforms of his late father, such as the emancipation of the serfs in 1861.

Of course, many peasants rebelled against these retrograde measures, and Jewish Russians were also involved. Many of those who rebelled were arrested on political grounds and sent to serve sentences in Siberia; others escaped to the nearby West, largely to what was Austria-Hungary. Their escaping from Russia was seen as an unwanted intrusion into the life of *Mitteleuropa,* Middle Europe, with a negative attitude toward Russian Jewish refugees.

One text, from 1906—not long before Hitler arrived in Vienna in early 1908—written by Czech author Rudolf Vrba (1860-1939),[560] proposed:

---

[558] The *Reichsrat,* situated in Vienna, was the Austro-Hungarian Imperial Council, a chamber of the Parliament, and represented the Austrian part of the Empire.

[559] This speech was printed as a monograph: Georg Schönerer, *Die deutsche Selbstentmannung: Rede des Abgeordneten Georg Schönerer in der Sitzung des Abgeordnetenhauses vom 5. Nebelungs 1906, nach dem stenographischen Protokolle* (1906); text on pp. 3-11; quotation, p. 10. The quoted German passage is also at "Der Auftakt zur Wahlrechtsreform von 1907, Am 5. November 1906 legte ein Dringlichkeitsantrag den Grundstein," APA/OTS (Austria Press Agency, Original Text Service). On old terms used in this citation: *Nebelung:* an obsolete Germanic-based name for November derived from Nebel (fog); *Wahlrechtsreform:* electoral reform; *Dringlichkeitsantrag:* emergency request.
See also Brigitte Hamann, *Hitler's Vienna: A Portrait of the Tyrant as a Young Man* (2010), pp. 236-244, 343-344, 434; typo at p. 434 citing title of speech, corrected here. Cf. *Georg Ritter von Schönerer, ein Kämpfer für Alldeutschland,* Heinrich Schnee, ed. (3rd ed., 1943). The title identifies Schönerer as a fighter for pan-Germanism (*Alldeutschland*).

[560] This Czech, Rudolf Vrba (1860-1939), *is definitely not to be confused with* Rudolf Verba (1924-2006), a Slovak Jew imprisoned at Auschwitz, together with fellow Slovak Jew Alfréd Weczler, or Wetzler (1918-1988). The two escaped from Auschwitz in April 1944. They presented their information in the Vrba-Wetzler Report, and authored later books. More on these, below.

"The Russian with a strong national sense defends himself desperately against the clutches of the Jewish tentacles."[561] Vrba added the claim that "the Jews don't want 'equality,' but complete control (*die Juden wollen keine „Gleichheit", sondern die volle Herrschaft*)."[562]

Intertwined with the focus on Jewry as the cause of problems in the social fabric, was the surge in nationalism that gained prominence in the nineteenth century. The debate that can be found between the left and the right would make use of historical precedents, each in its own way. For example, the left in the nineteenth century, focused on a rejection of royalty and the Church, both seen as sources of great societal torment, used the example of Joan of Arc (Jeanne d'Arc, 1412-1431), whose life was cut short by a betrayal by the King, followed by her being burned at the stake by the Church; Joan representing a nationalist rejection of religion. At the same time, the right of the nineteenth century, with its own intense nationalism, saw in Joan of Arc a simple girl who represented the people rather than the authorities, and who could inspire the French to the defense of their country, against the British.[563] So, even if Hitler did not study more elaborated texts, he—as he wrote in *Mein Kampf* of his youth in Vienna—did get exposure to core ideas that brought him to his revolutionary realization (whether seen as delusional or not) of the core challenge to German society: the Jewry of the world.

In a broader context, the theory called Social Darwinism found an important role in Nazi thinking, *in that one particular interpretation of Darwinism*. This understanding gave a very particular interpretation of basic Darwinian principles, themselves put forth by Charles Darwin (1809-1882) in his *On the Origin of Species* (1859)— especially the idea that individual variations in given living organisms have the consequence that some such individuals of the species die young (being poorly adapted to the environment in which they are living), and others live to maturity and so procreate (being better adapted to the environment), *the unplanned and effortless consequence of which is called natural selection*.

In Social Darwinism itself, most associated at its origins with Herbert Spencer (1820-1903), as in his *Principles of Biology* (1864), there is the teaching: "This survival of the fittest, which I have here sought to express in mechanical terms, is that which Mr. Darwin has called 'natural selection', or the preservation of favoured races in the struggle for life."[564]

---

[561] Brigitte Hamann, *Hitler's Vienna*, pp. 343-344, p. 443, n. 61, citing Rudolf Vrba and his self-published ("*Selbstverlag*") *Die Revolution in Rußland: Statistische und Sozialpolitische Studien, Vol. 1* (1906), p. 216.

[562] Rudolf Vrba, *Die Revolution in Russland*, Vol. 1 (just cited in full), p. 222.

[563] The German historian Prof. Gerd Krumeich wrote of this and discussed it in interview at the 20th of the History Encounters at Blois, France (*Les vingtièmes rendez-vous à Blois*), Oct. 4-8, 2017. The theme at that year's extensive gathering was "Opinion: information, rumor, propaganda" (*L'opinion—information, rumeur, propagande*). See *Gerd Krumeich: Jeanne d'Arc à travers l'histoire*, YOUTUBE. This is also the Eng. title of his 1993 book on the French maiden, *Joan of Arc*.

[564] Herbert Spencer, *Principles of Biology*, vol. 1 (1864), pp. 444-445.

The Hitler Era

It is relevant and perhaps important that we appreciate that this is not a mere paraphrasing of Darwin, but, actually, *a rather significant reformulation of what Charles Darwin was trying to describe:* for one, the phrase "favoured races" is quite a new addition to Darwin!) In this way, Darwin was much subtler and more nuanced in his thinking than Spencer would suggest here. (We will return to Darwin and Spencer, below.)

Hitler was clearly taken by racial theory and especially of the idea of the superiority of the German people, the *Volk*, presumably in its most idealistic and purified form, the Nordic-Aryan human.

Along these same lines, on January 19, 1937, Himmler was to write to this topic in a formal congratulatory letter about *Der Stürmer:* "If in later years the history of the reawakening of the German people is written, and the next generation can no longer understand that the German people were once friendly to Jews [*einmal judenfreundlich gesinnt war*], then it will be noted that Julius Streicher and his weekly paper *Der Stürmer* accomplished a good deal of this clarification about the enemy of humanity [*ein gut Teil dieser Aufklärung über den Feind der Menschheit geleistet haben*]."[565]

THE VATICAN'S BURNING WORRY ABOUT CATHOLICS IN THE GERMAN REICH

Meanwhile, some of the teachings of the Reich were by this time (1937) of concern to the Catholic Church. In a communication (that is, an encyclical), *Mit brennender Sorge* (*With Burning Worry*), Pope Pius XI spoke to the Church's concerns.

The document is dated "Passion Sunday, March 17, 1937, The Holy See, the Vatican." In part, Pope Pius XI declared to the Catholic Community in Germany, and elsewhere, "No one would think of preventing young Germans establishing a true ethnical community in a noble love of freedom and loyalty to their country. What We [the Pope] object to is the voluntary and systematic antagonism raised between national education and religious duty."[566]

Unlike a vision of all of mankind being the children of God, the proposal that men are of widely varying value as living creatures can be seen in a speech read by Gauleiter Adolf Wagner, on September 7, 1937, at the Nuremberg Congress (Nazi rally), presenting a proclamation by Hitler (as Wagner had done on earlier occasions), which spoke to the overriding importance of the laws defining the purification of the German, presumably Nordic-Aryan, *Volk*—described, quite significantly, as "more significant for the future of our *Volk* than the effects of all the other laws together." In part, that Hitlerian proclamation declared:

---

[565] Letter from *Reichsführer SS* Heinrich Himmler, signed and dated Jan. 19, 1937; letter reprinted in Karl Holz, *Der Kampf geht weiter* (1937), p. 47. The small book was to honor Streicher and the weekly *Der Stürmer* on the 15th anniversary of its first issue, which had been published on April 20, 1923.

[566] *Mit brennender Sorge* (1937), THE VATICAN. This mentions nothing of brutal mistreatment and murder of Socialists, Communists, or labor unionists by the Nazis, nor about the stripping of German citizenship of all German Jews. The range of this religious duty is not stated; presumably the Pope is thinking of Christian practice.

> However, the greatest revolution Germany has undergone was that of the purification of the *Volk* and thus of the races which was launched systematically in this country for the first time ever. The consequences of this German racial policy will be more significant for the future of our *Volk* than the effects of all the other laws together—for they are what is creating the new man. [No small claims!] They will preserve our *Volk* from doing as so many historically tragic past prototypes of other races have done: lose their earthly existence forever because of their ignorance as regards a single question. For what is the sense of all our work and all our efforts if they do not serve the purpose of preserving the German being?[567]

In distinction to the idea that we are all one human race, mentioned above (biblically, all of us as descendants of Adam and Eve), we can see the multiplication of human races to be found in some Nazi texts, with a differentiating between people of the same region because of slight differences in the shape of the forehead, jawline, or variations in hair color.

The species-wide consistencies of the human race (*Homo sapiens sapiens*) are in some of these Nazi analyses denied or given little significance. Even if people are taught that they are different from certain other people (who are at times presented as inferior), it is not that difficult for people at least to recognize in a more self-centered way the pain and torment *of those they see as their own*. Each group, people, or nation has the same sad appreciation of what seems to them to be senseless violence, even if there is not a generalization of this sad truth to all humans. Shylock asks, "Hath not a Jew hands, organs, dimensions [a body in three spatial dimensions], senses, affections, passions [emotions]? Fed with the same food, hurt with the same weapons, subject to the same diseases, healed by the same means, warmed and cooled by the same winter and summer as a Christian is? If you prick us, do we not bleed? If you tickle us, do we not laugh? If you poison us, do we not die?"[568]

This might make us consider that *perhaps all people share a common existential reality, facing the same issues, problems, setbacks, traumas, pains, sicknesses, and death* (in short, that all humans are subject to *la condition humaine*, the human condition—even if denying this of others).

Even Germans suffered at the end of World War II, such as the many women raped (and many gang-raped)[569] in conquered Germany by Soviet

---

[567] "Adolf Hitler: Proclamation read by Bavarian Gauleiter Adolf Wagner, Nuremberg, September 6, 1937," in *Adolf Hitler: Collection of Speeches 1922-1945*, pp. 376-377.

[568] William Shakespeare, *The Merchant of Venice*, Act 3, Scene 1.

[569] The issue of rape as an instrument of violence (rather than of sexual pleasure) is a vast topic, with much literature exploring its important features. For one discussion among many, see Elissa Mailänder, "Making Sense of a Rape Photograph: Sexual Violence as Social Performance on the Eastern Front, 1939–1944," *Journal*

troops, Soviets who remembered the extreme violence to those caught in Eastern Europe by the German troops and especially the *Einsatzgruppen* in Poland and then in the USSR, a creation of Reinhard Heydrich as head of the SD (*Sicherheitsdienst*, the Security Service of the SS), designed to subdue and eliminate Polish resistance through rather direct and brutal methods. Of course, the use of women as sources of sexual satisfaction for men as prizes of war is not new. In Homer's *Iliad*, we read, for example, of those who would be the first to break a peace treaty, that the gods are asked to "spill their brains on the ground as this wine spills [used in a ritual ceremony]—theirs, their children's, too—their enemies rape their wives!"[570] (This violence seen as a source of additional torment to the losing side of the war.) This suggests that we, people, human beings in some situations, and—here, as an open question—perhaps each of us in certain specific situations, would find ourselves treating other human beings as sub-human, as despicable, as better dead than alive. When we think of others as beasts, animals, not fully human, depraved satanic, or as evil incarnate, then we are one step closer to being ready to treat them accordingly: seen as beings that should be attacked if not killed. This is no easy issue. What will lead us to being heartless, to finding the idea of killing others, for what group they belong to, for example?

Even in the case of the Third Reich, the methodical, *somewhat hidden* mass killings that are associated with Heinrich Himmler, Reinhard Heydrich, Himmler's assistant and head of the SD (*Sicherheitsdienst*, the Security Service of the SS), was a main operational structure of the unprecedented genocidal focus of the Reich. Many Germans said they knew of nothing, and the regular German military (the Wehrmacht) was often claimed to be not involved at all in these mass massacres.

And yet, conversations among thousands of German POWs, secretly recorded from 1940-1945 by British intelligence, then transcribed, suggested otherwise. These transcripts were placed into British and American archives as sealed documents, and were finally declassified in 1996; they were only discovered in 2001, by a historian-researcher, Sönke Neitzel.[571] He, together with fellow German social psychologist Harold Weltzer, reported on and analyzed many candid conversations.

---

of the History of Sexuality, vol. 26, no. 3, Sep. 2017, pp. 489-520. The author addresses in part issues about the relationship between gender, sexuality, and war. For a broader perspective, see Gisele Bock, "Women's History and Gender History: Aspects of an International Debate," *Gender and History*, vol. 1, no. 1, Spring 1989, pp. 7-30. (We see in many texts the role rape has as psychological warfare against a perceived enemy. Of course, rape is not limited to war situations; we find it widespread in perhaps every culture and society in the world. I find this a tragic, appalling, deplorable, revolting, lamentable, and shameful story, another facet of the depravity into which our human species is capable of descending!)

[570] Homer, *Iliad*, 3.355-356 (BK.vv: 3.320-323).

[571] Sönke Neitzel (b. 1968) has taught at various universities in Germany and the UK, incl. the London School of Economics. See interview, *Sönke Neitzel: Mindset of WWII German Soldiers: Treasure Trove*, TVO (CANADIAN TV), YOUTUBE.

Their documentation suggested that the mass killing of Jews was not only known by these ordinary, captured German soldiers, but that many of them could joke about the beating, rape, and killing of Jews, Poles, and other Europeans in lands conquered by the German military.[572] This widespread knowledge of what was going on is confirmed by various diaries or letters written to family by German soldiers stationed in Poland, the USSR, and by many reports by Germans, Poles, and others, who saw.

As we see repeated in history, some of a given group cause great loss and death to some of another group, and then, later, others of that second group will (out of rage and an urge for revenge) cause further loss and death to others of that same first group. In this context, if we think clearly about the violence suffered by German women after the Reich was conquered by the Soviet troops in 1945, these raped German women had presumably not done violence to those in the USSR themselves. In addition, there were the *Volksdeutsche* (ethnic Germans whose families had lived, perhaps for generations, in Slavic lands)—of whom some five million were attacked, beaten, killed, or forced to move westward to conquered Germany. These *Volksdeutsche* had been in a relatively more secure, safe, and protected situation when the Third Reich military and administration were in control of their occupied lands; they were then subjected to violence from the other peoples of those lands, even when these *Volksdeutsche* were civilians and perhaps did not in any way help the German occupying forces. This showed that when groups think in broad terms, the actual involvement or roles played by given individuals is not especially an issue of interest or attention.

At the same time, if we return to the Third Reich in its development, the principle of the survival of the fittest, as Spencer, quoted above, phrased it, would, in turn, soon be restated as a moral principle for the Nazis: *the moral right and even obligation of the strongest to survive* (which we see widely in Nazi eugenic theories). This thinking goes from Darwinian adaptive features, to the Spencerian image of power and strength, to becoming a moral principle and justification. In the Nazi reformulation of Social Darwinism, we have a philosophical rendering of the simple idea that might makes right. In this basic form, it was adapted as a justification within the Third Reich for any and all brutalities (against those deemed "weaker" and therefore inferior). This idea was paired with the field of eugenics, popular in the early twentieth century,[573] in which

---

[572] Sönke Neitzel and Harold Weltzer, *Soldaten: On Fighting, Killing, and Dying: The Secret World War II Transcripts of German POWs* (2012). Cf. Ben Hutchinson," *Soldaten*: On Fighting, Killing and Dying by Sönke Neitzel and Harold Welzer: Review," *The Observer*, Sep. 29, 2012; Ian Thomson, "*Soldaten* by Sönke Neitzel and Harald Welzer: Review," *The Guardian*, Jan. 25, 2013.

[573] See Madison Grant, *The Passing of the Great Race: or, The Racial Basis of European History* (1916)—"The man of the old stock ... is to-day being literally driven off the streets of New York City by the swarms of Polish Jews" (p. 81)—and Lothrop Stoddard, *The Rising Ride of Color against White World-Supremacy* (1920).

The Hitler Era

there was the encouragement of those deemed superior, to have offspring, leading to a superior community. A key figure in this was British-born Houston Stewart Chamberlain (1855-1927), married to Eva von Bülow.[574] Chamberlain's major work, claiming the superiority of the Aryan race, was *Die Grundlagen des neunzehnten Jahrhunderts* (1899), in English, *The Foundations of the Nineteenth Century* (1910).[575] He put forth the concept of the *Urarische-Germanische Rasse*, the Proto-Arian-Germanic race. He took Slavs and Celts to be Aryan, unlike the later attitude toward Slavs by Hitler and the Third Reich. In 1915, he renounced his British citizenship, as a rejection of Britain's war position, and became a German citizen in 1916. In this book, he wrote:

> To see in that [the presence of strictly Orthodox Jewish religious observances defining Jewishness] a proof of descent is absurd. It is just the same as if one were to identify the genuinely Slav population of Bosnia or the purest Indo-Aryans of Afghanistan ethnologically with the "Turks," because they are strict Mohammedans, much more pious and fanatical than the genuine Osmans. The term "Jew" is applicable to a definite, remarkably pure race, and only in a secondary and very inexact sense to the members of a religious community.... In this book I understand by "Teutonic peoples" the different North-European races, which appear in history as Celts, Teutons [*Germanen*] and Slavs, and from whom—mostly by indeterminable mingling—the peoples of modern Europe are descended.[576]

Houston Chamberlain misjudged Hitler, writing him some four weeks before the Nazi failed Putsch of November 9, 1923, "You have a great deal to accomplish, but despite your will, I do not consider you a violent man."[577] Still, in balance, Freud is said to have made a similar underestimation, in particular, of the violence in store for the Jews of Europe, mentioning the progress in civilization in which Jews would have been burned at the stake in earlier centuries, but now, in 1933, it was only their books that would go into the flames. In contrast, Heinrich Heine (1797-1856) was perhaps more prescient when he wrote in 1821, "*Das*

---

[574] Eva von Bülow (1867-1942), daughter of Richard Wagner, kept the name of her legal father, Hans von Bülow (1830-1894), orchestra conductor, pianist, and composer; her mother, Cosima von Bülow, was daughter of the Hungarian pianist-composer Franz Liszt. Wagner married Cosima after Von Bülow divorced her.

[575] Houston Stewart Chamberlain, *Die Grundlagen des neunzehnten Jahrhunderts* (1899); Eng., *The Foundations of the Nineteenth Century* (1910).

[576] Houston Chamberlain (1855-1927), *The Foundations of the Nineteenth Century* (Eng. ed., 1911), pp. 207, 257.

[577] "Weltaanschauung, Houston Stewart Chamberlain, Ewige Nacht," *Der Spiegel*, Oct. 2, 1967. Original German: *Sie haben Gewaltiges zu leisten vor sich, aber trotz Ihrer Willenskraft halte ich Sie nicht für einen Gewaltmenschen.*

war ein Vorspiel nur, dort wo man Bücher verbrennt, verbrennt man auch am Ende Menschen."[578] ("That was just a prelude; there where one burns books, one will end in burning human beings.")

At one point in German nationalist race speculations, the Germanic, the Nordic, and the Slavic were on a par, all superior to the Semitic race (referring to Jews)—as in Chamberlain's position. This was to be modified to allow the mixing only of Nordic and Germanic, while, at the same time, placing the Slavs at a lower level of humanity[579]—but still, in the Nazi set of values, Slavs, fit to be slaves, were not quite so despicable as the Jews (and Romanies), who were quite fit to be exterminated.

NAZI RACE STUDIES AND DEFINING JEWRY

In Nazi *Rassenkunde*, Nazi race science[580]—also referred to as race studies, racial science, eugenics, and so forth—one early proponent in this new field, appointed in April 1933 to the Interior Ministry, and who served as a Nazi expert in Racial Theory, was Dr. Achim Gercke (1902-1997), who recommended that a Jew be defined as anyone having at least one-sixteenth Jewish blood (at least one great-great-grandparent who was Jewish). He suggested that the first measures against Jews by the Third Reich were only the beginning of something more extreme, that the *jüdische Ausmerze* (extermination of the Jews, especially by prohibiting all procreation, sexual reproduction, by Jews) was an obvious first step to take in the cultivation of a purer, a higher, Germanic people.

Gercke wrote in the *Völkischer Beobachter*, "We will cultivate by selection a race that will make for the astonishment of the entire world." He was dismissed from his post in early 1935 for allegations of homosexuality (in the year after the Night of the Long Knives that included the murder of Ernst Röhm).[581]

More significantly, perhaps, one German philosopher who was respected and honored by the Nazi government was Hans F. K. Guenther (1981-1968). Guenther traced Nordic blood back to the eleventh century and the reign of Heinrich II (973-1074). This seemingly innocuous or even cute claim would take on special significance in the theorizing of the Nazis. Thus, this early Germanic ruler was a model for another Heinrich, Himmler, who felt that a deep bond existed between him and this early German leader; Himmler actually thought he was both a descendent of this king and also his reincarnation. While many around him did not believe this, he was largely humored, even by Hitler, who could overlook this and keep this loyal Himmler on track to carrying out the mass murder of inferior beings such as the Slavs and the Jews. As Albert Speer, Hitler's main architect and Minister for Armaments and War Production (1942-1945),

---

[578] Heinrich Heine, *Almador* (1821), lines 243-244.
[579] Wulf D. Hund, *Racisms Made in Germany* (2011), p. 19.
[580] Richard Plant, *The Pink Triangle: The Nazi War against Homosexuals* (1986); a German Jewish homosexual (birthname, Plaut), fled Germany on Feb. 28, 1933.
[581] Cornelia Essner, "Le dogme nordique des races," pp. 65-116 in Édouard Conte and Cornelia Essner, *La Quête de la Race: Une anthropologie du nazisme* (1995), at pp. 104-105.

wrote in his memoirs, "Hitler had little sympathy with Himmler in his mythologizing of the SS." And quoting Hitler: "What nonsense! [*Welcher Unsinn!*] Here we have at last reached an age that has left all mysticism behind it, and now he wants to start that all over again [*und nun fängt der wieder von vorne an*]. We might just as well have stayed with the Church. At least it had tradition. To think that I may one day be turned into an SS saint! ... I would turn over in my grave [*Ich würde mich im Grabe umdrehen!*]."[582]

Himmler might have had his share of followers who agreed with his vision of the superior being and his roots in Teutonic warriors of old, but others were not so appreciative: Along with Hitler and Speer, there is also an entry about Himmler in the diary of Goebbels on June 30, 1931: "Himmler hates me [*Himmler haßt mich*] …. This unscrupulous bastard must disappear [*Dieses hinterlistige Vieh muß verschwinden*].[583] Göring agrees with me."[584]

Leaving aside here this mythologizing link to King Heinrich II, Himmler would later be described in some German sources, less glamorously and much more critically and bluntly, as *der wohl grausamste Massenmörder der Weltgeschichte* (perhaps the cruelest mass-murderer in world history).[585]

For Guenther, the Germans were seen as a blond nation contrasted with darker neighboring peoples, such as *die schwarze Gallia* (black Gallia, the French), *die braune Roma* (brown Rome, the Italians), and *die rote Sklavinia* (red Sclavinia: the Slavs).[586]

In addition to physical features that Guenther defined as distinguishing between these different groups, he also pointed out the cultural differences between German and Slavic groups, which were not taken to be definitive features, but were used to emphasize differences between Germans and Slavs:

> One recognizes immediately at the graves and other finds [archeological digs] of eastern German soil that belong to the Slavic nationality. "The Slavs are breaking into a completely foreign culture in East Germany [*Die Slawen brechen mit einer ganz fremden Kultur in Ostdeutschland ein*]. Their ceramics differ so much from the Germanic

---

[582] Albert Speer, *Inside the Third Reich: Memoirs*, R. and K. Winston, tr. (1970), p. 94; Ger., *Erinnerungen* (1969), p. 108.

[583] The literal sense of *hinterlistig* is deceitful/cunning/wily, and of *Vieh*, cattle/beast/dumb animal.

[584] Joseph Goebbels, *Tagebücher 1924-1945*, p. 606. Eng. rendering from *The Goebbels Experiment*, FILMSTIFTUNG-ZDF (GERMANY), BBC, AND THE HISTORY TELEVISION (CANADA), at 21:35-21:55.

[585] Klaus Wiegrefe, "Das Dunkle im Menschen" [The Darkness in Man], *Der Spiegel*, March 11, 2008, pp. 54-66, at p. 54.

[586] Hans F. K. Guenther, *Rassenkunde des deutschen Volkes* (1922; 14th ed., 1930), p. 394.

tradition that one can easily distinguish [the distinct origins of] each sherd [*Scherbe*]."⁵⁸⁷

The combination of various physical features Guenther (and other Nazis) used to define races, focusing on ratio of height to width of skulls (and phrenology), color of eyes, shape of nose, color of skin and of hair, and such, along with cultural features (as the artifacts of ceramic art), is a mixed, somewhat random, and rather limited basis for such classifications, but was used in the general popular culture of the Third Reich. And nothing more sophisticated was needed for popular consumption; no genetic analysis was involved in the applications of these unsubtle ideas.

In practice, however, *ultimately, the issue of who was Jewish, for example, was simplified to that of a familial history:* if one's grandparents were Jewish, then one was Jewish.

One conundrum was how to deal with mixed marriages between Jews and *völkisch* Germans and *Mischlinge* (those of mixed German and Jewish parents). These ended up being treated differently by the administrators of the Third Reich from the treatment of those considered clearly Jewish.

Perhaps not surprisingly, how a grandparent, in turn, would be determined to be Jewish or not, was not a question pushed to any ultimate definiteness. The conflict came when some Jews saw themselves as Christian or non-religious and in that perspective, not at all Jewish, but which the Nazi definitions declared otherwise. Since the difference in treatment could be a quiet acceptance of such *Mischlinge* for most years of the Reich, versus shipment to a *Vernichtungslager*, an extermination center, this was of course an issue with life-changing consequences, no matter how ultimately arbitrary the definition being applied was.

Whatever the specifics that were worked out, there was a strong drive to have a taxonomy (a system of classification) of peoples, as part of a general attempt to gain some comprehension in a world that was quite diverse and complex, upsettingly so for some. This may have been especially so for the Weimar Republic and Berlin, in the 1920s, in contrast with the stable conceptual world of pre-World War I Germany.

That said, the Nazi structure of classification would find its own simplification, as is often (but not always) the case when theories of any subtlety are simplified ("dumbed down") *to the grand public.*

When it came to the later selections of Jews for mass killing, for example, as General Otto Ohlendorf—head of the eastern region SD or Security Service (*Sicherheitsdienst*) and also commanding officer of *Einsatzgruppe D* (Special Attachments Group D, in charge of mass executions in Moldava, southern Ukraine, and the Crimea)— testified in his war crimes trial in Nurnberg after the war, *in practice there was no familial research done in the field to see how many of any given*

---

⁵⁸⁷ Hans Guenther, *Rassenkunde des deutschen Volkes*, p. 399. The source of the quoted passage is Ger. archeologist, Carl Schuchhardt (1889-1943), in his *Alteuropa*, 2nd ed. (1926), although no page in Schuchhardt's text is cited by Guenther. Cf. Hans Günther, *The Racial Elements of European History* (1927).

The Hitler Era

individual's ancestors were (or were considered) to be Jewish. Rather, Ohlendorf explained, concerning the Jews, it was usual that the Kommandos called the Jewish elders of the locale to determine who was Jewish and who not. The possibility to go beyond this decision was not given to the Kommandos. *Therefore, they had to accept the statements of the Jews themselves as a basis of their killing orders.*[588]

In addition to all of these legal-sounding discussions defining Jews and *Mischlinge* (those born of mixed marriages) and the bureaucratic urge for clear, legally-applicable definitions of who should count as a despicable Jew, there was the peculiar (if not astonishing) fact that *Hitler himself could personally declare someone to be Aryan (Germanic, non-Jewish) simply by decree, despite the facts on the ground.*

From among many examples: a decree stating that "the Führer has decided" (*der Führer hat entschieden*) that a Captain (later Lt.-Col.) Walter H. Hollaender, Infantry Regiment 46, is of German blood with respect to racial laws. Then, a Colonel Werner Schmoeckel appealed the case for his half-Jewish wife and quarter-Jewish son Helmut, with Hitler declaring them *deutschblütig* (German-blooded) on September 2, 1939. The son, Helmut Schmoeckel, would later become the captain of U-boat (Submarine) 802. Similarly, Hitler declared Helmut Wilberg to be an Aryan in 1935; Wilberg would go on to be a General in the Luftwaffe.[589]

The case of Luftwaffe General Erhard Milch, prominent in the German aeronautics industry and then in the Luftwaffe, being declared an Aryan is discussed more below. Of course, the orders of the Führer were never to be questioned. *Despite options taken by the Führer himself*, as Germany's one and unquestionable master, *the popular understanding of race (especially of being Aryan versus Jewish) within the Reich stayed rather simple.*

One schoolbook gave a lesson on how to identify a Jew by his nose: *Die Judennase ist an ihrer Spitze gebogen* ("The Jewish nose is bent at its tip"). An illustrated text for children, taught and showed the lying nature of ugly Jews, compared to an idealized Aryan in healthy manual labor.[590]

---

[588] Otto Ohlendorf testimony, p. 289 in NT-TWC-Green, vol. 4.

[589] Bryan Mark Rigg, *Hitler's Jewish Soldiers: The Untold Story of Nazi Racial Laws and Men of Jewish Descent in the German Military* (2002), pp. 39-40, 201-202, 207, 254-255, 293, and photo inserts after pp. 18, 171. This text documents over 1,700 men of Jewish descent who served in the German military, some being quite prominent. For more on these specifics, see talk by Mark Rigg on BOOK TV-CSPAN2, *Untold Story of Hitler's Jewish Soldiers and Racial Laws* (Jul. 22, 2003), esp. 16:30-16:50.

[590] From a 1936 text by Elvira Bauer, a kindergarten teacher (born 1915), *Trau keinem Fuchs auf grüner Heid und keinem Jud bei seinem Eid! Ein Bilderbuch für Groß und Klein* (*Don't Trust a Fox on a Green Heath or a Jew on his Oath: A Picture Book for Old and Young*). This makes reference to passage by Martin Luther in his 1543 work *Von den Jüden und ihren Lügen* (*On the Jews and their Lies*)—here, as quoted in Karl Friedrich Wilhelm Wander (1803-1879), *Deutsches Sprichwörter-Lexikon, Erster Band* (1867), col. 1704, #15: *Glaub keinem Wolf auf grüner Heid'*,

In these same hateful politics, anti-Semitic news articles and cartoons were publicly displayed in prominent places in each town, sponsored by the Nazi publication *Der Stürmer*, in encased boxes called *Stürmerkasten*, *Stürmer* Boxes or Display Cases.[591]

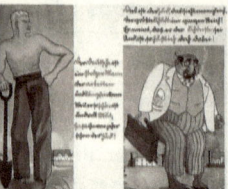

There were, as well, longer tirades in banner form, such as *Helft mit an der Befreiung Deutschlands vom jüdischen Kapital. Kauft nicht in jüdischen Beschäften* (Contribute to the emancipation of Germany from Jewish capital. Don't buy in Jewish shops).[592] Benches in public gardens were often marked *Nur für Arier* (Only for Aryans). Signs in towns, villages, and cities throughout Germany read *Juden sind hier unerwünscht* (Jews are unwelcome here) or *Juden unerwünscht* (Jews unwelcome)—these were *temporarily removed for the 1936 Olympics (August 1-16), and then diligently replaced* soon afterwards.

The New York Times of November 7, 1935, had a front-page article on this situation, "Anti-Jewish Signs Down for the Olympics. Hitler Promises to remove the Placards During the Winter and Summer Games. American Groups Scored. Baillet-Latour Calls the Move Not to Compete Political and 'Based on Lies.'" This was Count Henri Baillet-Latour, Chairman of the International Olympic Committee, quoted as having criticized several national committees that had expressed hesitations about participating in the Games, given the nature of the Nazi Regime.[593]

As part of the systematic teaching of race hatred, a book that was given to graduating German youth during the Third Reich, sketched Germany's pre-Reich and Reich past: "Your fathers displayed unparalleled heroism [*in unerhörtem Heldenmut*] in resisting the attacks of a world of enemies. Your mothers did the work of men behind the plow and at the machines, bearing privation without complaint and overcoming distress. [The romanticizing and obvious idealizing of German men and women can be strongly sensed.] Overcome by superior forces, weakened by hunger,

---

auch kein Juden auf sein Eid, auch keinem München auf sein G'wissen, du wirst sonst von allen drei beschissen (Don't believe any wolf on a green heath, nor any Jew on his oath, nor any monk on his conscience; you will be scammed by all three).

[591] The signs in this photo (Worms, Aug. 1935) read *Mit dem Stürmer gegen Juda* (With the Stürmer against Jewry) and on the box itself, *Die Juden sind unser Unglück* (The Jews are our misfortune). The message was not hidden or subtle.

[592] Robert Gellately, *Backing Hitler*, photos no. 14 and 16, among the photo inserts between pp. 142-143.

[593] "Anti-Jewish Signs Down for the Olympics: Hitler Promises to Remove Placards During the Winter and Summer Games," *New York Times*, Nov. 7, 1935, pp. 1, 6.

The Hitler Era 195

stabbed in the back by traitors at home and abroad [*durch äußeren und inneren Verrat erdolcht*], the old Germany collapsed."[594] The teaching continued, stressing the importance of respecting National Socialist racial principles and laws; the stated position was that the mixing of *some* races (in the Nazi sense of that term) produces fortunate results, as when the Nordic and the Germanic are mixed, but "mixing German people with members of a distant race leads to unhealthy results. Mixing, for example, with blacks, with yellows, and with Jews must be avoided."[595] An Aryan having sexual relations with a non-Aryan—read, in general: "a German having sexual relations with a Jew"—was illegal and was described as *Rassenschande*, racial shame, or *Blutschande*, blood shame.

On one level of greater sophistication, it was acknowledged that the mixture of peoples in Europe had been going on for many centuries, so that the idea of a "pure" race was a fiction that could be useful but could not be accurate; *even Hitler acknowledged at times that there is no pure race at this point in Europe's history*. An early confident of Hitler's, Otto Wagener (1888-1971)—Nazi Stormtrooper Chief of Staff (1929-1930), head of the Economic Policy Section of the party (1931-1932), and head of the Economic Policy Office and Commissar for the Economy (1933)—quoted Hitler as saying:

> A people [*Volk*] in the current political sense has ceased to be a racial unit, a racially pure community [*ist keine rassische Einheit, ist keine reinrassische Gemeinschaft mehr*]. The great migrations of world history, the military expeditions, the times of enemy occupation [*Zeiten feindlicher Besatzung*], and also, of course, the admixture that became ever more frequent as the result of international trade relations [*auch natürliche Mischungen, die durch die weltwirtschaftlichen Handelbeziehungen immer zahlreicher warden, haben sich überall dahin ausgewirkt*], have seen to it that within the borders of any state all sorts of races and racial mixtures live side by side [*innerhalb der Grenzen eines Staates alle möglichen Rassen und Rassenkreuzungen zusammenleben*].[596]

As Hitler further expressed these ideas (here, recorded by his associate and confidant Martin Bormann, head of the Nazi Party Chancellery):

> Our racial pride is not aggressive except in so far as the Jewish race is concerned. *We use the term Jewish race as a matter of convenience, for in reality and from the*

---

[594] From Kurt Schrey, *Du und dein Volk* (1938), p. 8: This was a booklet for young graduating school students during the Third Reich.
[595] Kurt Schrey, *Du und dein Volk*, p. 21.
[596] Otto Wagener, *Hitler aus nächster Nähe: Aufzeichnungen eines Vertrauten 1929-1932*, H. A. Turner, ed. (1978), p. 288; Otto Wegener, *Hitler—Memoirs of a Confidant*, Henry Ashby Turner, Jr., ed., Ruth Hein, tr. (1985), p. 166.

genetic point of view there is no such thing as the Jewish race. (!!) There does, however, exist a community, to which, in fact, the term can be applied and the existence of which is admitted by the Jews themselves.[597]

Looking not so much to Jews by religion or race, but, rather in their mentality (their natural attitudes, sentiments, way of thinking)—their *Gesinnung*[598]—the German psychiatrist, Wilhelm Dolles, wrote in 1921 that he was concerned not at all with religious nor with racial Jews (*weder um Religions- noch um Rassenjuden*) but only with Jews purely in terms of their mentality (*rein um Gesinnungsjuden*).[599] Christian writers such as Hans Blüher (1888-1955), who had been an early Freudian, although he revised his point of view later, rejecting Freudian psychoanalysis as non-German[600]—who would accept the legend of the Jew as failing German soldiers and as betraying Germany—"argued openly for the exclusion of Jews as incapable of integration in to Germany society."[601]

In an odd and perhaps rather unexpected agreement with Blüher—and with Hitler, among others—we find a comment by the British associate of Freud, Ernest Jones (MD, psychoanalyst, and author of the respected 3-volume *The Life and Work of Sigmund Freud*), who in 1945—after the massive killings of Jews (and others) had been made quite public—would manage to make an astonishing suggestion: that anti-Semitism would end only by the total assimilation of Jews into (Christian) society.[602]

---

[597] Adolf Hitler, *Testament of Adolf Hitler: The Hitler-Bormann Documents, February-April 1945* (1961), p. 55. Italics added. Cf. James McGovern, *Martin Bormann: The Life and Disappearance of Hitler's Closest Confidant as Revealed by a former CIA Agent* (1968).

[598] *Gesinnungsbildung*, in the Third Reich meant the inculcation of approved ideas.

[599] Wilhelm Dolles, *Das Jüdische und das Christliche als Geistesrichtung* (1921), p. 9. The pdf is online at GOETHE UNIVERSITÄT. In fn. 1 on p. 9, Dolles makes this point admitting the complication, the difficulty, of making a clear differentiation (clarification, *Scheidung*), given the interplay between the group as the physical race (*die rein körperliche Rasse*) and the group as having a common intellectual perspective (*ein geistige »Rasse«*), with the term *Race* in quotation marks.

[600] Hans Blüher, *Secessio Judaica* (1922). He had written articles published in *Imago*, the literary journal of early Freudian psychoanalysis, in 1912 and 1914; by 1926 he saw psychoanalysis as anti-German. See Sander L. Gilman, "Damaged Men: Thoughts on Kafka's Body," pp. 176-189, in *Constructing Masculinity*, Maurice Berger, Brian Wallis, Simon Watson, eds. (1995), esp. pp. 158, 304, n. 112.

[601] Sander L Gilman, "Damaged Men," pp. 161-162; Yosef Haim Yerushalmi, *Freud's Moses: Judaism Terminable and Interminable* (1993), pp. 23-24.

[602] Ernest Jones, in the wartime 1945 essay "The Psychology of the Jewish Question," reprinted in his *Essays in Applied Psycho-Analysis, vol. 1* (1951/1964), pp. 284-300, states at pp. 296-297, "it follows inevitably that sooner or later assimilation will prove to be the definite solution of our problem," that is, of the Jewish Question of the title. Jones offers this opinion: "With the exception of the Gypsies, the Jews are the only emigrating people who, having no national home, nevertheless refuse to acquire one by assimilating themselves to the people among whom they dwell" (p. 288). Jones makes the point, "Finally, and by far the most

The Hitler Era

And yet perhaps all of these are wrong in thinking that anti-Semitism would end only with all Jews would becoming assimilated into their (non-Jewish) society or otherwise eliminated. There is, after all, anti-Semitism even where there are no Jews: we may consider various Muslim lands as well as the anti-Semitism that at times has appeared in various Oriental countries from Japan to Malaysia to the Philippines, with little history of any significant Jewish presence. If there can be anti-Semitism (hatred of Jews) even where there are no Jews,[603] the ending of this hatred, if it is to occur at all, will presumably happen in some alternative process. On this issue of assimilation, Hans Blüher also followed German nationalist thinking in holding that the Jews, even if visibly assimilated into German culture, were still with a distinct body type and facial features, and that the Jew's westernization was actually quite superficial. It may be helpful at this point to make some distinctions between different intensities of anti-Semitism (the usual way of referring to animosity against Jews). Here, we may also note that another large group of Semites, the Arabs, would be distinguished strongly from anti-Jewish hatred, especially when the Arabs became political allies with Germany, from religious/doctrinaire principles but also from pragmatic considerations.[604]

There are several dimensions to this specifically anti-Jewish hatred: There are personal preferences and dislikes concerning Jews. There are actions meant to avoid contact with Jews. There are stories told, criticizing Jews, characterizing them in critical, nasty, insulting ways. There are the many generalizations about Jews, as if all Jews were alike in all ways. We have the same over-simplifications of our understanding of many groups and nations, in which we might think that all French are elegant gourmets who enjoy the greatest pleasures of daily life, that all Germans are very

---

important, there was what to Christians seemed like the unreasonable contumaciousness [stubborn disobedience] of the Jews in refusing to pursue their own [Christian] Messianic doctrine which had, apart from them, become the essence of the [Christian] religion universally recognized by the white races in every continent. This more than forfeited any advantage the Jews might have gained from their moral primacy" (p. 290). It is not clear, we might comment, what any of those comments amount to in relation to the issue of assimilation, even while he mentions (p. 297) the rather complete earlier assimilation of Jews into German and Hungarian societies (taken as isolated and a "more superficial objection"), which clearly did not make impossible the mass killing of those Jews. Jones makes a random reference (p. 292) to a Jewish immigrant in the UK from Nazi Germany with his personal interests in the foreground, described as focusing on talking of "his chances of evading the military service that has become one of his new civic responsibilities." *This shows the power of "random" examples; here, the implication is gratuitously negative if not also stereotyping.*

[603] Ian Buruma, "The 'Jewish Conspiracy' in Asia," *The Guardian*, Feb. 9, 2009.

[604] Arabs (Semites) and non-Semitic Turks and Iranians were all explicitly exempted from the anti-Semitic (more specifically, anti-Jewish) decrees of the Reich, at the request of the Egyptian, Turkish, and Iranian governments. See Nastassja Shtrauchler, "Interview with historian David Motadel: Hitler's Muslim stop-gaps" (2017), DEUTSCHE WELLE/DW AND THE GERMAN FOREIGN OFFICE, QANTARA.DE.

well organized and like structure and social rules for their own sake, or that all British keep a still upper lip, and so forth.

Then, there are theological issues: that Jews are rebellious and stubborn—contumacious, to quote Ernest Jones, just above—because they do not accept the teaching of Jesus, do not accept the validity of the new testament or the new agreement with God about how we should act.[605] (Muslims can well hold the same position about both Jews and Christians who refuse the teachings of God through Prophet Muhammad as contained in holy teachings recorded in the Qur'an.)

There is also the theological teaching that Jews should be allowed to remain, but only if in miserable conditions; as the French priest Pierre le Vénérable, Peter the Venerable (ca. 1092-1136), Abbot of the Cluny monastery and author of the 1140s *Against the Inveterate Stubbornness of the Jews*, expressed the sentiment: "God wishes them, not to be killed, but to be preserved in a life worse than death, like Cain the Fratricide, for greater torment and greater ignominy."[606] With this comes the teaching that the Jews killed Jesus—which goes back at least to the teachings of Emperor Constantine the Great (ca. 272-337 CE), the first Roman Emperor to accept Christianity,[607] and furthermore, that all Jews of all times are equally guilty of having killed Jesus, even though born centuries or millennia after the execution of Jesus. This teaching has survived into the current centuries, with young Christian boys calling Jews Christ-killers.

Then, more recently, there are the teachings that the Jews are behind capitalist wealth throughout the world (talking incessantly about the Rothschild family—and overlooking the vast majority of Christians in economic power, from John D. Rockefeller to Cornelius Vanderbilt and his son, William Henry Vanderbilt, Andrew Carnegie, Edward H. Harriman, Thomas and Andrew Mellon, J. P. (John Pierpont) Morgan, Henry Ford, and William Randolph Hearst, along with others also insultingly called the Robber Barons, with Jews claimed to control the actions of gullible Christians who passively and dumbly accepted the backroom instructions of this Jewish world conspiracy. There are also teachings that Communism is a Jewish creation (taking Karl Marx as a Jew, even though he was raised Protestant, his father having converted from Judaism when Karl was a boy—and defocusing attention on Friedrich Engels, who was not Jewish at all); focusing on Leon Trotsky, who was Jewish, and whose birth name

---

[605] Consider *A Translation of the New Testament into Hebrew as The Testament of Our Lord and Saviour Jesus Christ, translated out of the Original Greek and with the Former Translations Diligently Compared and revised by His Majesty's Special Command*, with Hebrew title Habrit He-ḥadashah (The New Covenant). Of course, this New Testament was first written in a form of Greek of the century or two after the life of Jesus, called variously Koiné Greek (from *he koinè diálektos*, the common dialect) or Hellenistic Koiné (from *Hellēnistikḗ koiné*, common Hellenistic, a generalized form of Greek for inter-regional communication).

[606] *Against the Inveterate Stubbornness of the Jews* is online at PROJECT MUSE. Quote at Gavin I. Langmuir, *Toward a Definition of Antisemitism* (1990), p. 201.

[607] James Carroll, *Constantine's Sword: The Church and the Jews* (2001).

was Lev Davidovich Bronstein—and overlooking other leaders of the communist world from Vladimir Lenin, born Vladimir Ilyich Ulyanov, to Joseph Stalin to Mao Zedong, all of whom were definitely not Jewish.

This last bit of theorizing, with the idea that Bolshevik Jews were out to conquer and exterminate other nations and peoples, set up an intense sense of *needing to survive by conquering this threat or be annihilated*. Certainly, this was a common theme in the Third Reich.

Relative to this array of attitudes, all being forms of a hatred of Jews, recent scholars have variously proposed a grouping of sub-categories of anti-Semitism in terms of the thinking and goals of the position in question. These varieties of anti-Semitism are known by various (non-synonymous terms) as chimeric (Gavin Langmuir), redemptive (Saul Friedländer), and mystical (Dan Stone) anti-Semitism.[608] In any case, one concern from a National Socialist point of view in all of this is that *the Jews were taken to be a threat to the very existence of Germany*, threatening its ongoing existence, and *posing a serious obstacle* to the German dream of a vast territory for *Lebensraum* (living space), envisioned at least since *Mein Kampf* as involving *the invasion by Germany of the Slavic lands to the east of Germany proper, especially but solely the Soviet Union. This is part of the way two major concerns of the National Socialists—a hatred and fear of world Jewry and the sense of a right to* Lebensraum *in virtue of racial superiority—came together*. The last means of interfering with the lives of Jews took perhaps its most intense form in the Hitler era, following the idea from Hitler's very first anti-Semitic epistle from 1919 (quoted above) that anti-Semitism should not be governed by emotion but by rationality and law. Here, the Third Reich represents a single instance of anti-Semitism being at the core, heart, and essence of a government. If we consider various intensities of anti-Semitism, the hatred of Jews, we may appreciate that they start with relatively innocuous (or non-life-threatening) dislikes of what is identified as Jewish. For example, there may be a general disinclination to want to socialize with anyone known to be Jewish. This would be a rather mild form of this general attitude (*social anti-Semitism*). Then there is an attitude holding that Jews are essentially different (from the rest of the community in question), and incapable of ever becoming full members of that society. This might be termed *societal (or cultural) anti-Semitism*. Then, moving into more hostile attitudes, there is the belief that Jews are the disrupters of society and, importantly, essentially hostile to the group among which they live. This could be termed *xenophobic anti-Semitism*. Moving into an even more intense hostility, there is the attitude that holds that all Jews are responsible for all of a given society's ills and that they should be removed from the society one way or another. This would be *an eliminationist anti-Semitism*. These are general categories, not precisely defined, but can give a sense of the differences between various

---

[608] Gavin Langmuir (just cited); Saul Friedländer, *Nazi Germany and the Jews* (1997); Dan Stone, *Histories of the Holocaust* (2011).

instances of what can be grouped together as anti-Semitism. In the Germany of these years, there were teachings that encouraged *a rather extreme, violent anti-Semitism*. One prolific author, Goebbels' right-hand man, his deputy in charge of anti-Semitic propaganda,[609] was Johann von Leers, who focused on presenting Jews as a bacillus to be removed from the body politic. As early as 1933, he was putting out publications to alert the German people to the dangers of the Jews.[610] One book of that year that makes this point was *Forderung der Stunde: Juden raus!* (*The Demand of the Hour: Jews Out!*). In this, Jews were warned to get out of Germany or to face dire consequences. This little pamphlet of 19 pages of text began stating that there is no race in the world that is more puzzling (*rätselhafter*), richer in its destiny (*schicksalsreicher*), and therefore more interesting, than the Jewish race; the tract concluded inviting Germans who love Germany to join together with Hitler and the Nazi Party, which fights against Jewry, for a free, clean Germany (*für ein freies, sauberes Deutschland*).[611] This man was so intense and so extreme in his hatred of Jews, of Jewry, that the Swiss businessman and supporter of key Nazis and later Arab nationalists, François Genoud (about whom more elsewhere), called him *un obsédé antijuif* (an obsessed anti-Jew).[612]

THE FINE AND NOT-SO-FINE ARTS OF PROPAGANDA

This may be a good place to turn to consider the not-so-fine arts of propaganda. One application will be our considering Streicher's speech of November 10, 1939, immediately after *Kristallnacht*, which we will quote in context, below. We have heard a lot in the context of the Third Reich of propaganda, as coming from the *Reichsministerium für Volksaufklärung und Propaganda* (RMVP), the Reich Ministry for Public Enlightenment and Propaganda. We have the idea of propaganda as the necessarily distorted presentation of half-truths and outright falsehoods in the service of convincing a gullible audience of some distorted sense of reality and of values.

The concept of propaganda can be traced back to the missionary work of the Catholic Church, and, in particular, to what was called the Congregation for Propagation of the Faith, in Latin, *congregatio de propaganda fide*, founded in 1622 by Pope Gregory XV. This congregation was a committee of cardinals, who were responsible for missionary work (worldwide). The word derives from the Latin *propagare* (to propagate). It was presumably in this earlier sense that the Reich saw its propaganda work: the promotion of an organized set of ideas and teachings.

---

[609] Pierre Péan, *L'extrémiste* (1996), pp. 33, 210.

[610] Von Leers would find refuge after the war in Perón's Argentina and then in Nassar's Egypt, applying his anti-Semitic thinking in both countries. On the Jewish expulsion (but not to Palestine), see Dr. Johann von Leers, "Das Ende der jüdischen Wanderung," *Nationalsozialistische Monatshefte,* vol. 38 (May 1933), pp. 229-231; CALVIN COLLEGE.

[611] Johann von Leers, *Forderung der Stunde: Juden raus!* (1933), pp. 3, 22.

[612] Pierre Péan, *L'extrémiste*, p. 247.

The Hitler Era 201

We can see this in a variety of contexts. So, at the turn of the twentieth century, the American Medical Association (AMA) was shifting to the use of pharmaceutical drugs (medicines), based largely on petrochemical products derived from coal tar (crude oil), as lauded by the 1910 *Flexner Report*,[613] sponsored and promoted by Carnegie and Rockefeller (both involved in petroleum products and sales),[614] which called quackery all medical teachings and physicians that did not use these patentable (and therefore commercially profitable) medicines. In this pursuit, the AMA set up a Propaganda Committee to promote these values, and in its journal, it had a recurring column called "Propaganda Reform" that would discuss various new prescription drugs.[615] We may sense an underlying ambiguity here, in which what is seen from its source as simply the putting forth of organized and coherent teachings *is also alternatively understood by others to be an attempt to distort the understanding of any listeners*.

It is in this more critical sense that there was an interest in the 1930s in understanding better just what propaganda was, and how it operated, its techniques and procedures. A classic work in this area was published by the Institute for Propaganda Analysis, *The Fine Art of Propaganda: A Study of Father Coughlin's Speeches*.[616] This institute, which was active from 1937-1942, was established to counter what its members felt was a gradually lessening capacity for the US public to think critically, given the large amount of distorted propagandistic claims being put forth by Nazis, Communists, and other undemocratic parties and countries. The book analyzed a number of techniques used in those speeches, which were taken as concrete examples of how language could be used to insinuate certain values. The techniques illustrated, defined, and discussed included name calling, glittering generalities, transfer by association, testimonials, plain-folk talk, card stacking, and the band wagon. From the perspective of modern philosophy of language, this book looks at language not in terms of the meaning of its parts (from words to sentences, to entire discourses), but focusing on *the use of speech*.

And a more recent text, published in 1955, a decade after the end of the Third Reich, also has philosophical and historical significance. Its analysis considered speech as something that could be (1) the uttering of some statement: *a locutionary act*, such as saying "Shoot her!"; it could be (2) what could be the speaker was doing in speaking: *an illocutionary*

---

[613] *The Flexner Report* (1910), more fully: Abraham Flexner, *Medical Education in the United States and Canada: A Report to the Carnegie Foundation for the Advancement of Teaching* (1910), ARCHIVE.CARNEGIEFOUNDATION.ORG.

[614] "How Rockefeller [and Carnegie] Founded Modern Medicine and Killed Natural Cures," *World Affairs*, Oct. 20, 2015.

[615] See, for example, the column ("The Propaganda for Reform") in the *Journal of the American Medical Association* (AMA), vol. 70, no. 1, Jan. 5, 1918, pp. 48-49, JAMANETWORK.COM.

[616] Its editors were Alfred McClung Lee and Elizabeth Briant Lee. See *The Fine Art of Propaganda* (1939), ARCHIVES.ORG.

act, such as urging someone to shoot her; it could also be (3) a consequence, something brought about in speaking: *a perlocutionary act*, such as persuading someone to shoot her.[617]

If we apply this to some of the speeches of the Third Reich, these various forms of action (words are words but they are more than words when considering their intent, function, and consequences), are used in declaring "The Jews are our misfortune" (a locutionary act), as in encouraging of a hatred of Jews (an illocutionary act), and as in persuading Germans to hate Jews with a murderous intensity (a perlocutionary act). Furthermore, in his dedicated interest in propaganda for the Third Reich, Goebbels not only made available vast numbers of radios provided for use by the vast German public, but introduced the use of public television, even though limited: the use of television, touted by Goebbels as a German first—which, in fact, it was: the first operational television station was the Third Reich's *Fernsehsender Paul Niplow* (TV Transmission Station Paul Nipkow, named after inventor Paul Nipkow), made public on April 18, 1934, and began regular programming on March 22, 1935. Its operations were ended on Oct. 19, 1944. And yet, this technological progress traces back to 1932, when a British physicist, James Chadwick (1891-1974), established the existence of the neutron—for which he received the Nobel Prize in 1935[618]—which would allow in the next years for some remarkable developments in atomic physics, especially through research by Otto Hahn, Lise Meitner, and Fritz Strassmann, with world-changing consequences. (More on these and their impact on world history, below.) And, also—despite the Nazi ideal and claim of keeping all science purely Aryan and Germanic, disposing of any foreign influence (especially Jewish) —German television made use of the invention developed from 1925-1936 by the English inventor John Logie Baird, who called it the Televisor. Baird was awarded a prize by British scientists in 1937.[619] This Nazi doctrinaire principle that ruled out any information seen as coming from non-Aryan (especially Jewish) sources, had serious ramifications. From the perspective of the philosophy of science and of theory construction, this principle was an arbitrary and counter-productive approach to any investigation, a politicized version of holding a personal grudge. This was certainly to the detriment of the Third Reich.

---

[617] These examples are all from the ground-breaking text by J. L. Austin, *How To Do Things With Words*, cited and discussed above.

[618] "The Nobel Prize in Physics 1935: James Chadwick," NOBELPRIZE.ORG.

[619] "Gold Medal of the International Faculty of Sciences [awarded to British television inventor, John Logie Baird]," *Nature*, vol. 139, Feb. 6, 1937, p. 241; cf. "Fernsehsender Paul Niplow," DE.WIKIPEDIA; Vladimir Barović, "Radio and Television in the Nazi Media System," UNIV. OF NOVI SAD, DEPT. OF MEDIA STUDIES, FACULTY OF PHILOSOPHY IN NOVI SAD, 2015, pp. 178-180.

9. Pre-war 1930s: The Tumultuous Birth of the Third Reich

Some of the larger events that brought about shifts in national consciousness in various countries—treaties, military actions, and political movements, etc.—may be considered here. We can start with the financial crash of 1929 and the impact that it had not only on Wall Street, and not only in America (the USA) alone, but in the much wider world.

Germany already had its ups and downs (or, rather, its downs and ups and downs), and its politics were a roller-coaster of changes, with issues shifting erratically through the 1920s.

THE INTERNATIONAL GEOPOLITICAL CONTEXT

If we look at the international dimension of history, we have several events worth noticing. In terms of what is known as international geopolitics,[620] with its vision of large-scale, globally significant events, we can notice that the Great Depression put pressure on countries (and governments) around the globe.

Based on its specific needs and values, Germany took one path. The USA, with its other needs and values, took another, with Franklin Delano Roosevelt being sworn in for his first term as US President, on March 4, 1933. The Soviet Union had still other problems. In its attempt to organize the farm labor of the country, with a focus on the fertile lands of Ukraine, there was instituted a program of collectivization, in which farms were organized into either a collective group (*kolkhoz*) or a socialized group (*sovkhoz*). The first would involve ownership of the land and its products by those working the land; the second would be land owned by the state.

These together would bring about a total dekulakization (elimination of all *kulaks*, peasants felt to be relatively rich: for Lenin, *tuneyadtsy*, freeloaders). This move to living on a *kolkhoz* or *sovkhoz* became obligatory in 1928 and by 1932-1933 there was widespread famine in Ukraine, with many needy peasants moving to cities elsewhere in the Soviet Union. Between forced and voluntary deportations and natural

---

[620] Geopolitics considers the physical features of given lands, their natural defenses such as mountain ranges, their river patterns for transportation, their natural resources. The concept was defined by Swedish political theoretician Johan Rudolf Kjellén (1864-1922) in 1917, inspired by and complementing the earlier use of the term *Lebensraum* (living space), introduced in 1901 by Kjellén's teacher, Friedrich Ratzel (1844-1904). Japan's situation, for example, is very different from that of the USA (with a significant land mass and two oceans giving it distance from potential enemies) or that of the Low Countries, geographically defenseless (with, as Jacques Brel put it, "cathedrals as the only mountains")—lyrics in French, Flemish, and English to "*Le plat pays*" by Jacques Brel, at Christ Breebaart, "Jacques Brel: Le Plat Pays/Mijn vlakke land (My Flat Land)," Jul. 12, 2014, CHRISBREEBAART.COM. See Robert D. Kaplan, *The Revenge of Geography: What the Map Tells Us About Coming Conflicts and the Battle Against Fate* (2013) and *In Europe's Shadow: Two Cold Wars and a Thirty-year Journey through Romania and Beyond* (2016); Tim Marshall, *Prisoners of Geography: Ten Maps That Explain Everything About the World* (2015).

factors, it is estimated that between 1929 and 1933, some 11 million peasants died.[621]

Japan took still another path: in great need of raw materials such as iron, rubber, coal, and oil, to provide a basis for the building of its industry and economy, Japan would make use of a staged attack on September 18, 1931 (the Mukden Incident), on a line of Japan's South Manchuria Railway, near the town of Mukden (now, Shenyang) in Manchuria (northeast China): A full Japanese invasion began the next day.

There was presumably a plan for this invasion (as the 1905-1906 Schlieffen Plan for the German conquest of Europe, mentioned earlier); perhaps, as Chinese diplomats claimed, the 1927 *Tanaka Jōsōbun*, the *Tanaka Report to the Throne*, also called the *Tanaka Memorial* or *Memorandum*, might be interpreted to be the basis of this Japanese military action, although the Report was fundamentally a plan for Japanese economic hegemony, not military conquest.[622]

The Japanese aggression was discussed at length in the League of Nations, ultimately leading to a resolution that Japan should withdraw its forces from Manchuria (or Manchukuo, as the Japanese called it and its puppet government). *Japan did not accept this resolution, casting the sole vote against the resolution; it rejected the position of the League, abruptly walked out, quitting the League completely, never to return.* This Japanese withdrawal occurred on February 24, 1933 (within a month of Hitler's becoming Chancellor of Germany). Japan had maintained its invasion with no peaceful solution. *In this way, the world could see the very serious limits of discussion and peaceful negotiation in the League for dealing with and resolving international disagreements clearly.* Hitler and the National Socialists also understood what this suggested.

Earlier, in December 1930, in an under-estimation about Hitler's political staying power—one of many in the early 1930s—Léon Blum (1872-1950), head of the *Front national*, first Socialist (and three-time) Prime Minister of France—1936-1947,[623] wrote hopefully, "I believe that the Hitlerian comet [*l'astre hitlérien*] has already risen to the maximum of its trajectory [*au plus de sa course*], that it has touched its zenith."[624]

Germany Prior to January 30, 1933

The same year of that Japanese invasion of Manchuria, in 1931, in Germany, the five major German banks crashed; some 20,000 businesses

---

[621] US Congress, Commission on The Ukraine Famine, *Report to [US] Congress: Investigation of the Ukrainian Famine, 1932-1933* (1988).

[622] This was a perhaps spurious document claimed by the Chinese to have been offered on July 25, 1927, by Prime Minister Baron Takaka Giichi to Emperor Hirohito, outlining a plan of economic and military hegemony of Japan over Pacific Asia. See John J. Stephan, "The Tanaka Memorial (1927): Authentic or Spurious?" *Modern Asian Studies*, vol. 7, no. 4, 1973, pp. 733-745.

[623] "Léon Blum: Premier of France," Encyclopædia Britannica, Dec. 19, 2017.

[624] Marc-André Charguéraud, *Les Papes, Hitler et la Shoah: 1932-1945* (2002), p. 20.

in Germany went bankrupt. With all of this misery, there was a major upswing in disgruntled and desperate voters, as shown in the election of September 14, 1930 (with 18.3% of the popular vote to the Nazi Party).

While there had been an attempt by the Weimar government to use its power to give work to the unemployed, the *Freiwilliger Arbeitsdienst* (Voluntary Labor Service, or FAD), established on June 5, 1931, this program under the government of Prime Minister Heinrich Brüning,[625] was of limited success. When Hitler came to power, the unemployed were given little choice; the *Reichsarbeitsdienst* (Reich Labor Service, or RAD) was set up more as a compulsory service, on the model of the Wehrmacht, the German Army[626]; the unemployment rate dropped rapidly, in part in building an infrastructure of highways (the *Autobahn*)—which looked like a civilian project but would allow for the easy movement of trucks and tanks in wartime—and also at the same time reinstituting a German armaments industry in secrecy. (A work program in the USA under Franklin Delano Roosevelt, would include the Tennessee Valley Authority, the TVA, that provided electricity to regions of the Old South of the USA, including part of a rather impoverished Appalachia.)

Before non-Nazi newspapers had their operations shut down in Nazi Germany, there were some published reports suggesting the murderous intent of the German NSDAP Party. The *Münchener Post*, a Social Democratic, strongly anti-Nazi newspaper—which Nazi SA Men had first trashed on November 8, 1923[627]—reported in an article on December 9, 1931 ("The Jews in the Third Reich") that the Nazi party had plans, the *Endlösung*, the final solution, for the Jewish Question, involving confiscation of Jewish property, exclusion of Jews from German economic and political life, prohibitions against Jewish-German (non-Jewish) sexual relations or marriage, using the Jews for slave labor and shipping them off to "swamps" in the East, under SS supervision. These were reported to be secret, that is, not for general open acknowledgment and discussion.[628] *Some other newspapers and the general public of the time did not all appreciate the implications of this report.*[629] And so, seeing such alarming reports as not much more than Socialist propaganda, things continued without any serious anxiety about what the Nazi Party

---

[625] Anthony J. Nicholls, *Weimar and the Rise of Hitler*, pp. 140-189.

[626] "Freiwilliger Arbeitsdienst," WIKIPEDIA; Eng. tr., and "Reich Labour Service," WIKIPEDIA.

[627] Ron Rosenbaum, "Against Normalization: The Lesson of the *Munich Post*," *Los Angeles Review of Books*, Feb. 5, 2017.

[628] Ron Rosenbaum, *Explaining History: The Search for the Origins of His Evil* (1998), pp. 42-43; "Münchener Post," IPFS.IO (INTERPLANETARY FILE SYSTEM).

[629] Some other newspapers came out with related warnings, as, in the *Dresdner Volkszeitung*, Dec. 27, 1932, p. 2: "Die Mutter, deren Nazi-Sohn ermordet wurde, ruft: »Schützt eure Kinder vor den Nazis!«" ("The mother whose son was killed by the Nazis calls out, "Protect your children from the Nazis!"), cited in Wolfgang Hesse, "»Dolchstoß von rechts.« Visuelle Deutungen des Dresdner SA-Fememords von 1932," in *Volkskunde in Sachsen*, vol. 22, 2010, pp. 87-159, at p. 110.

was all about, despite clear statements of political intent being made by the Nazis. Thus, on July 27, 1932, in the campaigning for the next election, Hitler gave a speech in Eberswalde (30 miles northeast of Berlin), in which he stated quite clearly his position on the multi-party system then in Germany and his interest in eliminating it and all opposing parties:

> The enemies accuse us National Socialists, and myself especially, of being intolerant and belligerent people. We don't want, so they say, to work together with other parties…. I have one thing to explain: these politicians are right! We are intolerant. I have set myself one goal: namely, to sweep away the thirty parties out of Germany (*die 30 Parteien aus Deutschland hinauszufegen*)![630]

In this same year of 1932 (before Hitler became Chancellor in early 1933), Winston Churchill, already having doubts about Hitler, made a trip to Germany. Churchill, in Munich, met and was invited by Ernst Hanfstaengl to meet with Hitler personally. Churchill was willing but confronted Hanfstaengl about Hitler's anti-Semitic views; Churchill told Hanfstaengl, "Tell your boss [Hitler] from me that antisemitism may be a good starter, but it is a bad sticker." The meeting was never arranged.[631]

The following final months of the Weimar Republic saw violence, street fights, murders, and an intensifying breakdown of civil society. This violence came from groups of Nazis (largely the SA) and also from Communist partisans. The SA, which was temporarily banned, had been given back its rights by the Chancellor Franz Von Papen, on June 28, 1932, and a fortnight thereafter, on July 17, 1932, there was a major violent confrontation between the SA and Communists in Altona (now part of Hamburg), called Bloody Sunday (*der Altonaer Blutsonntag*). On July 20, Von Papen, using Article 48 of the Weimar Constitution, invoked emergency powers; this was called the Prussian Coup or Putsch (*der Preußenschlag*). The Reichstag was dissolved and another election was held, on July 31, 1932. The Nazi party received more votes than any other party, but did still not hold a majority position: The Nazi Party received 37.3% of the popular vote, and on November 6, 1932, 33.1%. For context, we can mention that there were similar gains for the Communist party during this period of economic chaos.[632]

After the July 1932 elections, with these somewhat promising and yet disappointing results (the latter, from Hitler's point of view), the SA

---

[630] *Hitler's [Eberswalde] Election Speech from [Jul. 27] 1932*, YOUTUBE, 1:28-2:23; text at "1932-07-27. Adolf Hitler, Wahlkampfrede in Eberswalde," INTERNET ARCHIVE.

[631] A story recounted by the historian Sir Martin Gilbert (author of *Winston S. Churchill*, an 8-volume set), in *Churchill and the Jews: A Lifelong Friendship*, pp. 98-99. Cf. "How Far did the UK aristocracy's love of the Nazis really go?" THE JEWISH CHRONICLE ARCHIVES, Jul. 22, 2015. This publication, the long-standing *JC*, a weekly London publication, was founded in 1841.

[632] Cmp. the Communists with 10.6% of the vote (May 20, 1928), 13.1% (Sep. 14, 1930), 14.6% (Jul. 31, 1932), 16.9% (Nov. 11, 1932), 12.3% (Mar. 5, 1933).

actually intensified its violence on the streets, with arson, bombings, and assassination attempts. Given this situation, on August 9, 1932, Chancellor Franz Von Papen put forth *Sondergerichte* (special decrees), which imposed especially severe sentences for those who had committed political violence—from acts of political passion, of causing death by assassination or even by arson, up to the death penalty, and for attacking policemen, where resultant severe wounds called for a minimum sentence of 10 years' imprisonment.[633] These decrees were to apply equally to all such violence, from the right and the left, *at least to appear non-partisan*. In practice, they were used mostly against violence of the left. *Death penalties of Nazis were challenged by Hitler* with his commitment to restore their honor; their sentences were very quickly reduced.[634] The shift of the Prussian government to this accommodating leniency toward the far right would be challenged by the Courts. (More just below.)

At the same time, the increased use of violence by various political factions in these last months of the Weimar Republic suggested that this had become a path to political power, *where such violence was not only exonerated but honored, even before the Third Reich*. German historian Erich Eyck (1878-1964) would write of this, "Never before had a German government bowed so openly to political terror."[635]

Horst Wessel (1907-1930), a 22-year-old Berliner who was one of the SA streetfighters—a "procurer for a bawdyhouse" (pimp for a brothel)[636]— would become transformed into a patriotic hero martyred in his fighting for honorable National Socialist values (the work of Joseph Goebbels): "Horst Wessel's burial was the most perfect creation of the great kitsch myth of the party," as Saul Friedländer later wrote.[637] The song created in his honored memory (*Das Horst-Wessel-Lied, The Horst Wessel Song*), transformed a street ruffian and hooligan into a National Socialist hero and martyr), a marching song of the National Socialists that was used as the party's anthem.[638]

One month after Von Papen's *Sondergerichte* (mentioned just above), in September of 1932, Hermann Rauschning, the Nazi President of the Danzig Senate, visited Hitler at Obersalzberg. Hitler, perhaps impatient with the delay in his gaining power within the Constitutional structure of the Weimar republic, stated, "We must be cruel [*grausam*]. We must

---

[633] Cf. Sigrid Schultz, "Germany Fixes Death Penalty to End Rioting" Special Courts Set Up by Von Papen," *Chicago Daily Tribune*, Aug. 10, 1932, p. 3.

[634] Karrin Hanshew, *Terror and Democracy in West Germany* (2012), pp. 20-23.

[635] Erich Eyck, *A History of the Weimar Republic*, Harlan Hanson and Robert Waite, tr., Vol. II (1963), p. 421.

[636] Elton Groves, "Where the Vatican Rules (Part 2)," *Consolation: A Journal of Fact, Hope and Courage*, vol. 23, no. 582, Jan. 7, 1942, pp. 3-7, at p. 5.

[637] Saul Friedländer, "Preface to a Symposium," *Salmagundi*, No. 85/86, 1990 (cited above), p. 204.

[638] Called both the *Horst-Wessel-Lied* (the *Horst Wessel Song*) and *Die Fahne hoch* (*The Flag on High* or *Raise the Flag*), it became the anthem of the National Socialists from 1930 until the end of the third Reich, played at all major events.

recover the capacity to commit cruelties with a clear conscience [*das gute Gewissen zur Grausamkeit wiedergewinnen*]. Only in this way can we expel our nation's softheartedness [*die Weichmütigkeit*] and sentimental philistinism, this "coziness" [*diese »Gemütlichkeit«*] and easygoing evening-beer mood [*Dämmerschoppenseligkeit*]. We have no more time for fine feelings [*schönen Gefühlen*]. We must compel our nation to greatness if it is to fulfill its historic task."[639]

On October 25, 1932, the Weimar Constitutional Court struck down parts of the Coup, but upheld the transfer of power to Von Papen. Obviously, the structure of society under the Weimar Republic was at an acute crisis point. The next election, in November 1932, also did not produce a majority party. The news from the November 6, 1932 elections was perhaps even more depressing for Hitler and the National Socialist Party: Hitler and the National Socialist Party lost over 2,000,000 votes and 34 Reichstag Deputies.[640] After those elections, Léon Blum would write a front-page article in the Socialist Parisian daily, *Le Populaire*, "La fin de Hitler."[641] (That was of course to be, at best, another bit of premature optimism on Blum's part.) As President Hindenburg continued trying to keep Hitler from the Chancellorship, he replaced Von Papen (not by Hitler, but) by General Kurt von Scheicher (1982-1934), an Army officer. There were pressures from powerful business interests to give Hitler the role of Chancellor. Von Papen joined in, suggesting as well to Hindenburg the idea that Hitler would be able to be controlled by the other members of the government and by business interests with their financial support and the power it was thought this would bring to bear. The political situation in Germany soon changed in favor of the Hitler movement. These political machinations and the elections of early 1933 culminated in Hitler's finally being invited into the government of President Hindenburg, as Chancellor,[642] on January 30, 1933.

IG Farben AG established, December 1925

With the development of industry in Germany, in the 1860s and 1870s, a number of companies were founded that had a common interest in the development of industrial dyes. These were to be into a large conglomerate in December, 1925. (More just below.) The companies here that developed into prominence, with the year of their founding, were Bayer (1863), which also produced a chemical called acetylsalicylic acid, for which Bayer patented the name Aspirin in 1899. A second company

---

[639] Hermann Rauschning, quoted in Joachim C. Fest, *Hitler* (Ger. text), p. 477; *Hitler* (Eng.), p. 343.

[640] On the Jul. 31 and Nov. 6, 1932 elections, for percentage of vote and seats, see "Elections in the Weimar Republic," Deutscher Bundestag (2006); for vote count, see "Weimar Republic Elections," in "Elections in Germany," Wikipedia.

[641] Léon Blum, "La fin de Hitler," *Le Populaire*, Nov. 9, 1932. See Joel Colton, "The Poetry, Prose, and Politics of Leon Blum, 1872-1950," *The American Historical Review*, vol. 79, no. 5, Dec. 1974, pp. 1491–1498; the article is cited at p. 1495.

[642] Isabelle Clarke and Daniel Costelle, *Apocalypse: Hitler. Part II: Le Führer*, YouTube, at 18:30-21:50.

was Hoechst (also, 1863), which integrated two smaller companies, Cassella (1904) and Chemische Fabrik Kalle (1908). BASF (1865) produced gasworks and, using by-products of this for dye production, especially soda and acids from tar. Agfa (1867) produced X-ray plates and photographic film; it was involved in much of the German film industry. The trademark Agfa was taken out in 1897. Fifth here was the *Chemische Fabrik Griesheim-Elektron* (1856), which in 1896 merged to form a larger company that would be known later as *Chemisische Fabrik*, short for *Chemische Fabrik vorm. Weiler Ter Meer*. (The term *vorm.* in full reads *vormals*, formerly known as.) The company produced fertilizers as well as various explosives, used in both civil engineering and in warfare. *In the conglomerate, there are a total of eight components when Hoechst and its two subsidiaries are listed as 3 separate members.* In the legal procedures integrating these, on Christmas Day, December 25, 1925, a new company was created, *Interessengemeinschaft Farbenindustrie AG*, a corporation within the dye industry composed of a community or group of participants having the manufacturing of dye—*Farbe:* color, tint, stain, pigment, paint, dyestuff, etc.—as their common interest; literally, Community-of-Interests Dye-Industry Corporation; in short, IG Farben. An *AG* is a company that has stock; roughly equivalent to a corporation. One corporation, a legal conglomerate, was thus formed, coordinating the five largest chemical and pharmaceutical companies in Germany. At one point, IG Farben was the largest such company in the world.

While the chemical and pharmaceutical industries may seem far from the birth and growth of the NSDAP, the National Socialist German Workers Party, the additional chemical capacities of the various components of this great conglomerate, which also included other subsidiary companies, *would have an important role to play in the support of the fledgling Third Reich and then the exploitation of slave labor and the concentrated production of essential war material.* More on IG Farben, below.

Deep Pockets: Early Contributors to the Nazi Party

IG Farben and other large industries in Germany saw democracy, with the influence allowed of left-wing politics, as a threat to their autonomy. A promising buffer against this—or at least one that was hoped to be so— was the National Socialists representing an opposition to anything that smacked of socialism or communism (Bolshevism). These contributions had begun in the early 1920s. Industrialists such as Fritz Thyssen[643] and Gustav Krupp[644] were such earlier contributors. With the NSDAP being

---

[643] Fritz Thyssen: head of a large steel corporation and of coal production in the Ruhr, contributed 200,000 gold marks to Hitler and the Party in 1923. He was instrumental in convincing Hindenburg to invite Hitler as Chanceller (1933) and in convincing Hitler to carry out the Night of the Long Knives (1934). He left Germany, disagreeing with the invasion of Poland. Cf. Fritz Thyssen, *I Paid Hitler*. See "Fritz Thyssen" and "Thyssen AG," Wikipedia, and "Fritz Thyssen," Spartacus Educational.

[644] Gustav Krupp (who married Bertha Krupp in October 1906, and was given permission by Kaiser Wilhelm II to take her family name as his) would respond

close to broke in 1932 and in need of a more viable financial base, on February 20, 1933, IG Farben would donate (hoping for political and economic benefits) 400,000 reichsmarks to the Nazi Party.[645] Gustav Krupp organized industry contributions, with him as director of the *Hitler-Spende* (the Hitler Donation or Fund), contributing 1 million reichsmarks himself. Altogether, the various industrialists on that date gave a total of 3 million marks to the NSDAP.[646] An overview of some of this extensive industrialist support was given in hearings in the US Senate's Committee on Military Affairs, in July, 1945:

> World War I left German heavy industry with strength unimpaired and the ranks of German industrial organization unbroken. The great industrial leaders, still determined in spite of military defeat to attain world supremacy, cast about for a political figurehead which would enable them to achieve their objectives. There is evidence that even in the early days of the Republic they were seeking a government which could free the country from reparation demands; and embark upon a second attempt at world conquest. By 1919 [Gustav] Krupp was already giving financial aid to one of the reactionary political groups which sowed the seed of the present Nazi ideology. Hugo Stinnes[647] was an early contributor to the Nazi Party (*National Socialistische Deutsche Arbeiter Partei*). By 1924 other prominent industrialists and financiers, among them Fritz Thyssen, Albert Voegler, Adolph Kirdorf, and Kurt von Schroeder,[648] were secretly

---

effectively (discussed next) to the near-bankruptcy of the Nazi Party in 1932. On the centuries-long history of the influential and powerful Krupp family and company, see William Manchester, *The Arms of Krupp* (1968).

[645] "I.G. Farbenindustire AG, German Industry and the Holocaust," HOLOCAUST RESEARCH PROJECT; Urban A. Lester and Richard N. Bagenslos, "[Book Review of] *The Crime and Punishment of I.G. Farben*, by Joseph Borkin, New York, The Free Press, 1978, Pp. 250," *Catholic Univ. Law Review*, vol. 28, no. 3, pp. 711-716.

[646] Ciara Torres-Spelliscy, "How Big Business Bailed Out the Nazis: A tragic tale of what can go wrong when profits are entangled with politics," BRENNEN CENTER FOR JUSTICE, May 20, 2016; "1933-1939: Krupp and the Nazi Consolidation," GLOBALSECURITY.ORG.

[647] Hugo Stinnes was director of companies in the coal industry, with interests in major shipping companies and in electricity production. He was a member of the Reichstag and a newspaper magnate, owning the *Deutsche Allgemeine Zeitung* (Berlin) and the *Münchener Neueste Nachrichtern* and the *München-Augsburger Zeitung* (both, Munich). He was a formidable contributor to the NSDAP.

[648] Fritz Thyssen was just discussed. Albert Voegler: engineer and administrator in the steel and armaments industry (*Vereinigte Stahlwerke*) and major contributor to Hitler from 1930 on. Adolf Kirdorf: leading manager in the textile and coal industries, anti-Empire, anti-Republic, anti-Catholic, extreme ultra-nationalist and supporter of Hitler and the NSDAP. Kurt Freiherr (Baron) von Schroeder: German

giving substantial sums to the Nazis. In 1931 members of the coal-owners' association which Kirdorf headed pledged themselves to pay 50 pfennigs for each ton of coal sold, the money to go to the organization which Hitler was building. A substantial part of the money contributed by the German industrialists was given for the explicit purpose of financing Nazi propaganda. In 1925, Hugo Stinnes' sons and heirs supplied the funds for converting the Nazi weekly paper, the *Völkischer Beobachter*, into a daily publication. [Ernst Hanfstaengl would supply the remaining amount needed for this conversion.][649]

THE MOMENTOUS INVITATION OF JANUARY 30, 1933

Not surprisingly, for the National Socialists, the announcement that Hitler would be the next Chancellor of Germany, which happened on January 30, 1933, was a joyous climax to years of preparatory work. *Changes in the government were to take place in rapid succession those next months.*

That day had its own glory for the National Socialists: Ending that significant day with an emotionally intense pageant, there was an impressive night-time torch-lit parade of Berlin SA-Men, Storm Troopers, in uniform, marching in precise formation for hours in a continuous circling line of flaming torches.

And yet, not all central figures were happy. In particular, General Ludendorff, who had been both a leading general with Hindenburg in World War I and a member of both the Kapp-Lüttwitz Putsch of March 13, 1920, and the Beer Hall Putsch of November 8-9, 1923, wrote to Hindenburg on February 2, "I solemnly prophesy to you that this damnable man will plunge our Reich into the abyss and bring inconceivable misery down upon our nation." [*Ich prophezeie Ihnen feierlich, dass dieser unselige Mann unser Reich in den Abgrund stürzen und unsere Nation in unfassbares Elend bringen wird.*]"[650] We may clearly

---

financier, merchant banker, and nobleman. At Franz von Papen's request (after the losses in the Nov. 1932 elections), Schroeder arranged a meeting at his house with Hitler, Von Papen, Heinrich Himmler, and Rudolf Heß, *pivotal in having Hitler apppointed Chancellor*. See Henry Ashby Turner, "Emil Kirdorf and the Nazi Party," *Central European History*, vol. 1, no. 4, 1968, pp. 324–344; Thomas Ferguson and Hans-Joachim Voth, "Betting on Hitler: The Value of Political Connections in Nazi Germany," *The Quarterly Journal of Economics*, vol. 123, no. 1, 2008, pp. 101–113; "Banker Kurt Baron von Schröder's Report on a Meeting between Hitler and Franz von Papen at Schroeder's House in Cologne on January 4, 1933," GERMAN HISTORY IN DOCUMENTS AND IMAGES, GHDI.

[649] United States Congress, Senate, Committee on Military Affairs, *Elimination of German Resources for War: Hearings Before a Subcommittee of the Committee on Military Affairs, United States Senate, Seventy-ninth Congress, First Session (1945), Session of July 2, 1945, Sect. IV: German Financiers and Industrialists Will Again Lead German Underground*, at p. 648.

[650] Ger. text in "Freiburgs Geschichte in Zitaten: Das 3. Reich oder wie aus

appreciate that Hindenburg remained, nonetheless, with his decision and intention to appoint Hitler Chancellor.[651]

The appeal to spectacle and a sense of group community or a commonality in large crowds were further developed in the pre-Reich rallies of the Nazi Party, but showed themselves in great splendor the night that Hitler was appointed Chancellor (January 30, 1933), and at the extravaganzas of the rallies then held annually from 1933-1938.

The evening display of celebratory triumph for Hitler and the Nazi Party climaxed at the window of Chancellor's new office, with Hitler spotlighted and waving to the adoring crowd:

In some photographs, as above, Hitler stands next to Hermann Göring in the foreground, with Rudolf Hess[652]—who was to be appointed Deputy Fuhrer to Hitler on April 23—behind and partially hidden by Goring's left shoulder. This glamor and the intense group feeling were cultivated rather than being spontaneous; later, there would be many occasions for large gatherings, such as during the subsequent annual Party rallies in Nuremberg (1933-1938): inspiring occasions for strengthening a sense of group unity and conviction in the hundreds of thousands of Nazis who attended. (The last rally, planned for September 2, 1939, was cancelled on short notice, given the invasion of Poland, the day before, and the start of World War II. We can appreciate that Hitler and the military knew of their coming invasion, but could not share that with the general public.)

By way of contrast, the Nuremberg Rallies were not always raving successes. The Third Rally (or Congress) of 1927, the second to be held

---

prahlerischen tausend Jahren nur zwölf wurden," FREIBURGS-GESCHICHTE.DE.

[651] Joachim C. Fest, *Hitler* (Ger. text), p. 564; *Hitler* (Eng.), p. 411.

[652] Hess was the secretary to whom Hitler is said to have dictated *Mein Kampf*, and had been educated in the fear and intense animosity against the Bolsheviks and the Jews in the east by Alfred Rosenberg (a member of the Nazi party from 1919 on and, a fellow member of the anti-Semitic group Thule Society—recently formed in Munich in 1918, by Adam Alfred Rudolf Glauer, using the name Rudolf Sebottendorf (or, Erwin Torre)—along with Hans Frank, Dietrich Eckart, and others. Hess also learned from Karl Ernst Haushofer (1869-1946), a German general in the Great War, and politician, who understood the concepts of geopolitics and *Lebensraum* to include the ideal of autarky (total economic and political self-sufficiency) and the duty of the (German) state to safeguard the right to the soil, to the land in the widest sense, not only the land within the frontiers of the Reich, but also further lands, taken to be the right of Germany's geographic expansion to include *Volksdeutsche* (whatever their citizenship) and culturally Germanic lands. These became important features of the position expressed in *Mein Kampf*.

The Hitler Era

in Nuremberg, apparently had limited impact. This third National Socialist Party Congress (which was given the title "Day of Awakening") was held in Nuremberg over only a short three days, August 19–21, 1927.[653]

It was not considered by some of the German press as very impressive. For example, the *Münchener Post* wrote, at the end of that gathering, "The citizens of Nuremberg are happy to have the party day of the NSDAP behind them.... The working people reacted very coolly to the Wilheminian megalomania[654] of the party members. The parade and review were merely a final demonstration to salvage some of the prestige."[655]

At this rally, Dr. Wilhelm Frick, an *alter Kämpfer* (that is, an Old Guard, one who had participated in the 1923 Munich Beer Hall Putsch), and then leader of the Nazi Party in the Reichstag (1928-1945), who was to be a member of the Hitler Cabinet from 1933-1943 as Reich Minister of the Interior and, after the assassination of Reinhard Heydrich, Frick became Reich Protector of Bohemia and Moravia (1943-1945). He was tried after the war at the Nuremberg Tribunal, along with Göring, Hess, and a number of other then-surviving major Nazis, for planning and initiating aggressive wars and for crimes against humanity. He was hung on October 16, 1946.

Early on, in the Reichstag on May 4, 1924, he had declared his task was not to support, "but to undermine the parliamentary system"; on August 25, 1925, he asked the Reichstag to remove all Jews from public office. A report in 1930 prepared by the Prussian Ministry of the Interior noted that at the 1927 Nazi Party Nuremberg Rally, Frick had said that the Nazi Party would infiltrate into Parliament, then abolish it, and make possible a racial dictatorship; in 1929, Frick announced an envisioned Special Peoples' Court, for trials of the political enemies of the Nazi Party, and that in a 1929 speech in Pyritz (Prussia; now Pyrzyce, Poland), Frick announced that although the Nazi struggle for power would begin at the ballot box, it would be completed in a battle, in which "blood must be shed and iron broken."[656] Frick was also involved in obtaining German citizenship for Hitler in 1932—who had renounced Austrian citizenship in Linz on April 30, 1925 (avoiding impending deportation)[657]—allowing *Hitler to run legally, as a German, for the Weimar Republic Presidency.*[658]

---

[653] A silent film was made of this rally, directed by Julius Lippert. As a video, it is included in a collection, *Nuremburg Rallies, Official Films, 1927-1933*, at ARCHIVE.ORG. The film of the 1927 Rally itself is entitled *III. Reichsparteitag des NSDAP, 19.-21. August, 1927, Nürnberg: „Eine Symphonie des Kampfwillens"*. The title in English would be *A Symphony to the Will to Fight*.

[654] The term refers back to Kaiser Wilhelm II, esp. during the period 1990-1918, known for his public display of grandiose military parades joined with his personal inclination for self-aggrandisement.

[655] Alfons Heck, *The Burden of Hitler's Legacy*, pp. 23-24.

[656] NT-NCA-Red, vol. 2, pp. 653-656. Quotation at p. 655.

[657] Ulrich Menzel, "Professor oder Regierungsrat? Hitlers Einbürgerung in Braunschweig zwischen Provinzposse und Weichenstellung zur „Machtergreifung"" (2013), p. 2. Impending deportation: *drohende Abschiebung*.

[658] NT-NCA-Red, vol. 2, pp. 653-656, at pp. 655-656.

Robert Kempner and Heydrich's Lakeside Villa

Related to Hitler's legal status in Prussia in the 1920s, the German lawyer Robert Kempner (1899-1993), was appointed in 1928 chief legal advisor in the Prussian Ministry of the Interior. In this role, he asked that Hitler be tried for perjury and high treason, that Hitler be deported as an undesirable alien (Hitler at the time still holding Austrian citizenship), and that the Nazi Party be disbanded. Early in the Third Reich, Kempner was arrested, then released to emigrate (to Italy and then to the USA). He returned to Germany to be a prosecutor at the post-war Nuremberg Trials. In March 1947, in his research he came across the important document of the now-well-known notes of the Wannsee Conference of January 20, 1942. This conference took place at the villa Heydrich had arranged to purchase for official SS business and as a resort, in November 1940, for 1.95 million Reichsmark.[659] The document recorded a meeting whose focus was not the creation of a policy of extermination of the Jewish people, but issues having to do with the administration of that policy, including questions that were ultimately never fully answered, defining who was a Jew, who was a half-Jew, and how people with different blood lines including Jewish ancestry should be treated. On a practical level, this would differ from country to country. It reported on the ongoing progress in answering the Jewish Question, with the startling number of 11 million European Jews earmarked for extermination.[660] More, below.

Early Decrees right out of the Starting Block

Of course, Hitler was not deported, the Nazi Party was not disbanded, and by early 1933, President Hindenburg appointed Hitler as Chancellor. Hitler was quick to make his will be known (on February 3, 1933): to rearm the military and the related quest for *Lebensraum*, involving the conquest of living space for the German people, identified in *Mein Kampf* as the fertile lands of the East, especially, of course, the Soviet Union.

This was diametrically opposed by the statement of the head of the NSDAP Press Service in the USA, Kurt Ludecke (who had founded the Swastika League of America in 1932), in an article published on February 12, 1933, where he stated, "Hitler isn't saber-rattling at all…. He is against war for the simple reason that for a long time to come he is going to be so busy with internal problems it would be the utmost stupidity to burden his gigantic task by provoking a war." (We might ask how long "a long time" is?) The article also stated, "To each his own. We believe in that.

---

[659] At Am Großen Wannsee 56-58. See "Wannsee Conference," Wikipedia.

[660] "Robert Kempner," Wikipedia; "Kempner, Robert Max Wasilii," Jewish Virtual Library (AICE); B. Mordechai Ansbacher, "Kempner, Robert Max Wasilii," *Encyclopaedia Judaica*, 2nd ed. (2007), vol. 12, p. 74; Larry Thorson, "Nuremberg Prosecutor Robert Kempner Dies," AP News, Aug. 16, 1993; "Wannsee Conference," Wikipedia; "Reversal of Fortune: Robert Kempner," Holocaust Encyclopedia, USHMM; Robert K. Wittman and David Kinney, *The Devil's Diary: Alfred Rosenberg and the Stolen Secrets of the Third Reich* (2017), esp. pp. 12-18. (Wannsee and Kempner are discussed in various contexts through the book.)

The Hitler Era

Hitler does [too].... We understand under true Socialism the protection of the individual within the state and the protection of the entire nation." Ludecke then adds, "Hitler sees a sharp distinction between Marxian Socialists and those of his own [National Socialist] party. Marxian socialism teaches class hatred and dictatorship of the proletariat."[661] Ludecke does not mention at all the National Socialist disgust, violent rage, and hatred at what they considered to be "unsocial," "foreign," and "inferior" elements in German society (Jews, Romanies, and on and on).

We can at least appreciate that rather different from the picture painted here by Ludecke of social harmony is how Hitler and the Reich would in practice interpret "to each his own" (especially in relation to the "protection" of Jews, Romanies, and other "undesirables") and what would perhaps change in order for Hitler to be ready to provoke a war.

Hitler saw conquering France as the first step in this process. On February 3, 1933, in his very first week as Chancellor, he held two secret meetings, the first was held, formally, at the Armed Forces Ministry (*Reichswehrministerium*), where Hitler presented his overall military program to the select group gathered there, including senior Army and Navy commanders, where Hitler reassured the generals that this development would be carried out by the Nazi organizations (the Party and government), and would not involve the Armed Forces directly. The second gathering was at a dinner party held that evening—also February 3, 1933—at the official residence (*Dienstwohnung*) of the Chief of Army Command, General Kurt von Hammerstein-Equord (or Gen. Hammerstein, 1878-1943). Notes of Hitler's two-and-a-half-hour speech were taken by Lieutenant-General Curt Liebmann.[662]

The National Socialists, once in a position of workable power, began developing decrees that would push their vision, their political agenda, intensely and quite promptly after Hitler's becoming Chancellor. Thus, the day after the secret gatherings on February 4, 1933, was a meeting of the new Cabinet, consisting of Hitler and two other National Socialists,

---

[661] Kurt Ludecke, "Hitler Seen as Savior of Germany," *Pittsburgh Press*, Feb. 12, 1933, p. 31. Cf. his *I Knew Hitler: The Story of a National Socialist Who Escaped the Blood Purge* (1937), and the review of that book with a consideration of the degree to which the claims could be authenticated by correlation with independent sources: Roland V. Layton, Jr., "Kurt Ludecke and *I Knew Hitler:* An Evaluation," *Central European history*, vol. 12, no. 4, Dec. 1979, pp. 372-386.

[662] Peter Hoffmann, *German Resistance to Hitler* (1988), pp. 15-16; Konrad H. Jarausch, *Broken Lives: How Ordinary Germans Experienced the Twentieth Century*, pp. 103, 395-396. Cf. Thilo Vogelsang, "Neue Dokumente zur Geschichte der Reichswehr 1930-1933," *Vierteljahrshefte für Zeitgeschichte*, vol. 2, no. 4, 1954, pp. 398-436 (Dokument Nr. 7, pp. 432-434, and Dokument Nr. 8, pp. 434-435); Andreas Wirsching, "Man kann nur Boden germanisieren. Eine neue Quelle zu Hitlers Rede vor den Spitzen der Reichswehr am 3. February 1933," *Vierteljahrshefte für Zeitgeschichte*, vol. 49, no. 3, 2001, pp. 517-550; "Kurt von Hammstein-Equord," WIKIPEDIA; "Hitler's Comments at a Dinner with the Chiefs of the Army and the Navy (February 3, 1933)," GERMAN HISTORY IN DOCUMENTS AND IMAGES/GHDI; "Curt Liebman," DE.WIKIPEDIA.

Wilhelm Frick (just discussed), Minister of the Interior, and Hermann Göring, Minister without portfolio, with the influence of these three National *Socialists thought to be limited and balanced by the other eight members*, including Franz von Papen, Vice-Chancellor, and seven other additional non-Nazi members, some with no party affiliation. The next 100 days were nonetheless to be transformative of German society and government. As British historian Richard J. Evans has written,

> The story of German politics between January 30 and July 30, 1933, is essentially the story of how the Nazis shut down the country's democratic institutions, destroyed the freedom of its press and media, and created a one-party state in which opposition was punishable by imprisonment, banishment, or even death. It was Hitler's "first hundred days," but the radical changes went on for longer and seemed terrifyingly easy to perpetrate. There was nothing underhanded about these changes: Nazi leaders gave clear warnings about what they planned to do. But too few people saw them as a threat before they came to power.[663]

The power of the these men and their party was exercised repeatedly in those first weeks and months, with Göring, later the commander of the Luftwaffe, the German Air Force, creating on April 26, 1933 the *Geheime Staatspolizei*, the State Secret Police, the Gestapo.[664] A decree was formulated that day by the full Cabinet, and then approved by President Hindenburg; its name declared his authority: the Decree of the Reich President for the Protection of the German People (*die Verordnung des Reichspräsidenten zum Schutze des Deutschen Volkes*). This decree gave police power to ban any publication deemed to threaten public order or to insult leading German politicians; it also authorized arrest and detainment without a warrant for up to three months.[665] This would thus rigorously curtail rights of the press, of assembly, and of free speech, setting the groundwork for the monopolization of news (political information).[666] *The names of laws are often, as here, mystifying misnomers!* The decree, stifling non-Nazi points of view, allowed the blocking of all newspapers with "incorrect news," decided upon by the National Socialist member of the new Cabinet, Reich Interior Minister, Wilhelm Frick (introduced above). Relatedly, this decree would also lay the seeds for the Nazi program of *Gleichschaltung*, the switching into conforming with Nazi principles of all

---

[663] Richard J. Evans, "A Warning from History," *The Nation*, Feb. 28, 2017.

[664] The administration of the Gestapo was handed over to Himmler in April 1934. See "Gestapo: German Political Police," ENCYCLOPÆDIA BRITANNICA. More, below.

[665] Corey Ross, *Media and the Making of Modern Germany: Mass Communications, Society, and Politics from the Empire to the Third Reich* (2008), p. 267.

[666] Militärgeschichtliches Forschungsampt (Research Institute for Military History), *Germany and the Second World War, Volume I: The Build-up of German Aggression, Volume I* (1990), pp. 89-90.

of society. The decree was put into action the next day, on February 5, 1933, when a young Nazi shot and killed the Social Democratic mayor of Stassfurt (a town northwest of Leipzig and east-northeast of Göttingen). The daily of the SPD (Social Democratic Party), *Forwärts* (*Forward*), wrote critically about this, and was banned from publication for a week. Later that month, on February 25, the Communist newspaper, *Neue Zeitung*, was closed by order of the Bavarian Nazi government. [667] And the Socialist newspaper extremely critical of Hitler, the *Münchener Post* (the *Munich Post*—which he called *die Giftküche*, the Poison Kitchen (or Poison Cooking or Cuisine)—referring to their "cooking" of news, filling their reports with venom against him and the National Socialists—was then shut down, on March 9, 1933.[668]

This basic political situation in Germany with its strong repressive measures was very soon to be lampooned in the British press, even if that did not put an end to the repressive measures of this upstart corporal, Adolf Hitler. The satirical paper, *Punch*, on February 18, portrayed Hitler in his SA uniform, sitting on the shoulders of President Hindenburg and Vice-Chancellor Papen, his balance established by his pushing down firmly on the heads of the other two, with SA Men in the background, holding a Nazi banner, looking on:

Punch, "The Temporary Triangle"

---

[667] Richard J. Evans, *The Coming of the Third Reich*, pp. 284, 320, 518; see also, Heinrich Winkler, *Der Weg in die Katastrophe: Arbeiter und Arbeiterbewegung in der Weimarer Republik 1930 bis 1933* (1990), pp. 876-878; Hans Beimler, *Four Weeks in the Hands of Hitler's Hell-hounds: The Nazi Murder Camp of Dachau* (1933), p. 11.

[668] Poison Kitchen: Ger., *Giftküche*; Port., *cozinha venenosa*. See "Münchener Post," WIKIPEDIA; Wolfgang Görl, "Widerstand gegen Nazi-Regime: Publizist gegen Hitler," *Süddeutsche Zeitung*, Mar. 10, 2013, SZ.DE; Silvia Bittencourt, *A Cozinha Venenosa: Um jornal contra Hitler; a história do Münchener Post, o principal inimigo dos nazistas na imprensa* (2013), pp. 12-13; Ron Rosenbaum, *Explaining Hitler: The Search for the Origins of His Evil* (1998), pp. 37-59, esp. p. 53; his interviews with CSPAN TV, 1999, and "Is Trump a Fascist or—Something Even Worse?" THE BIG PICTURE, 2016; and his "Against Normalization: The Lesson of the Munich Post," *Los Angeles Review of Books*, Feb. 5, 2017.

The Transformative Reichstag Fire, February 27, 1933

Within a month of Hitler's becoming Chancellor, there was the significantly transformative *Reichstagsbrand*, the burning of the Reichstag, the night of February 27, 1933, blamed by the Nazis on the Communists, and used to establish even greater political powers for Hitler.

Time magazine (USA) described the fire in these terms: "Starting in four places at once, flames soon swept up to the great square gilded cupola of the Reichstag ... Soon the cupola was a glowing hodge-podge of incandescent girders."[669] One week later, *Time* wrote further, "Before German Democracy could thus be downed [brought down] this week, the Hitler Cabinet had to launch last week a juggernaut of super-suppressive measures and decrees for which they needed an excuse. What excuse could be better than the colossal act of arson which had just sent a $1,500,000 fire roaring through the Reichstag Building ... gutting completely the brown oak Reichstag Chamber and ruining its great dome of gilded copper and glass.... Meanwhile Russian, French, Scandinavian and British newspapers reached press-gagged Berlin with reports that it was not Communists but the Nazis themselves who fired the Berlin Reichstag—for reasons only too obvious."[670] The Nazis claimed that this extensively destructive fire was the work of a single, deranged, young Dutch Communist, Marinus (Rinus) van der Lubbe (1909-1934), who was then tried, to be beheaded in early January 1934; there was serious doubt expressed by some contemporary spectators and later historians about that story, up to the present time.[671] All of this was widely reported on in the press.

One such report, from a Madrid daily newspaper the very next day, speaking of a terrorist plot by communists, also reported that the Berlin police believed the fire had begun—fueled by jars filled with gasoline (*mediante frascos llenos de gasolina*)—in some 20 or 30 distinct places in the building at the very same time (*simultáneamente*).[672] These reported multiple sources of the fire all at one time perhaps suggest that the Reichstag arson was not, could not have been, accomplished by one person alone. And, again, the interest of the Nazis in blaming this on the Communists was "only too obvious," to quote *Time* (as just above).

---

[669] "Flaming Reichstag," *Time*, vol. 21, no. 10, Mar. 6, 1933, p. 22.

[670] "National Revolution," *Time*, vol. 21, no. 11, Mar. 13, 1933, pp. 16-18, at pp. 16, 17. Cf. discussion in Lily Rothman, "Who Started the Reichstag Fire?" *Time*, Feb. 27, 2015.

[671] Whatever its ultimate perhaps limited impact on world history (with questions about possible distortions due to its political bias), in 1933, *Braunbuch: Über der Reichstagsbrand und Hitlerterror* was published, in German and in 24 translations, incl. *The Brown Book of the Hitler Terror and the Burning of the Reichstag*, which suggested a Nazi source to the fire. See questioning by Anson Rabinbach, "Staging Antifascism: *The Brown Book of the Reichstag Fire* and Hitler Terror," *New German Critique*, no. 103, 2008, pp. 97–126.

[672] "Un voraz incendio destruye en pocos minutos parte del edificio del Reichstag alemán," *ABC* (Madrid), Feb. 28, 1933, p. 19.

The Hitler Era

Among the many doubters about this story with van der Lubbe as the person responsible for the fire—including various leftist sources from Germany, from France and the USSR, and from elsewhere—was Ernst Hanfstaengl. In 1957, Hanfstaengl wrote of the Reichstag Fire,

> it would not surprise me in the least, on the strength of the evidence now available, that Göring planned the whole thing himself, necessarily with Hitler's knowledge, as a means of wresting a piece of initiative from his hated rival, Goebbels.[673]

Reichstag fire   Hanfstaengl   Göring   Goebbels

Agreeing with and adding information to Hanfstaengl's position, the Chief of Staff of the German Army (of the *OKH, Oberberkommando des Heeres*, Supreme High Command of the German Army) from 1938 to September 1942, General Franz Ritter Halder (1884-1972), stated in an affidavit presented at the Nuremberg Trial Proceedings, read out by US Chief Prosecutor Justice Robert Jackson to Göring, "On the occasion of a luncheon on the Führer's birthday [April 20] in 1942, the people around the Führer turned the conversation to the Reichstag building and its artistic value. I [General Halder] heard with my own ears how Göring broke into the conversation and shouted: 'The only one who really knows the Reichstag is I, for I set fire to it.' And saying this he slapped his thigh."[674]

Adding information about further involvement by others in the fire, various reports published years later linked the fire to Göring, to his bodyguards, and to other SA, SS, and Gestapo personnel,[675] who were

---

[673] Ernst Hanfstaengl, *Unheard Witness*, p. 213, and *Hitler: The Missing Years*, p. 202. In contrast, Karl Ernst, head of the Berlin SA, is reported to have a signed document that accused Göring and Goebbels of being responsible for the Reichstag Fire, a document *that also incriminated Hanfstaengl*. See Kurt G. W. Ludecke, *I Knew Hitler*, p. 771, and Gilbert Badia, *Feu au Reichstag: L'acte de naissance du régime nazi* (1983), pp. 227-228, 247-248, 296-297. (More in a note, just below.)

[674] In response to this affidavit, Göring denied this, pointing out that many others of course knew of the Reichstag Fire. The quotation suggests the specialness of Göring's "really" knowing about it, with the differentiating information that Göring had set fire to it (and thereby knowing about it in a way that others weren't aware of). NT-IMT-Blue, vol. 9, with affidavit and response by Göring, March 18, 1946, at pp. 435-436. Cf. William Shirer, *The Rise and Fall of the Third Reich*, p. 193.

[675] These include Walter Weber (1895-1945), head of Göring's bodyguards; Bernhard Wilhelm Sander (1895-1934), aide to Röhm and Chief of Staff of the

killed (potential witnesses to the setting the fire of the Reichstag needing to be eliminated) in the murders of the Night of the Long Knives.[676]

A moment-by-moment description of that evening was given by Hans Bernd Gisevius—more on Gisevius just below—who placed the first stirrings (broken windows at the Reichstag), at 9:05 pm, preceding the first glimpses of the fire within the building and the alerting of the fire department at 9:14 pm. The first official of the government to arrive at the scene was Hermann Göring, then Prussian Minister of the Interior. Soon after that, Adolf Hitler and Joseph Goebbels, having been sharing an evening meal at the home of Goebbels, arrived at the Reichstag.[677] The question of who started the fire still remains an important one, with no full agreement about how the fire was started. But, to help us, we now have more precise information than was available in 1933 and in the first decades to follow the event. For a start here, a disclosure in 1983 suggested something more definite, based on a report by a chief German attorney at the Nuremberg Trials that began in 1946, Robert Kempner[678]:

> The Nuremberg prosecutor, Robert M. W. Kempner, said Thursday he has new evidence obtained from a former Nazi Luftwaffe general that Goering himself organized the blaze at the Reichstag, or parliament.... [In a conversation that Kempner had recently had] with former Luftwaffe Gen. Egloff Freiherr von Freyberg-Eisenberg, who now lives near the city of Ulm ... Kempner said [that] Freyberg-Eisenberg [had] told him he discovered the truth about the fire the day after it was set while talking with a Luftwaffe general, Bruno Loerzer, in the Berlin Aero club. Freyberg-Eisenberg said Loerzer told him: "All this about the fire is rubbish. Goering gave me the order to organize the Reichstag fire." Kempner said Freyberg-Eisenberg

---

Berlin SA; and Ottmar Toifl (1898-1934). Toifl was a police spy in the 1920s, in 1931, became an intelligence agent for Göring, and then SS Police Commissar and Criminal Inspector in the Gestapo, as well as being a friend of SS Police Chief, Kurt Daleuge (1897-1946), who later replaced Heydrich and carried out the Lidice massacre in revenge for Heydrich's assassination. See "Walter Weber (SS-Mitgleid)," DE.WIKIPEDIA; "Wilhelm Sander (SA-Mitgleid)," DE.WIKIPEDIA; "Ottmar Toifl," DE.WIKIPEDIA; "Kurt Daleuge," DE.WIKIPEDIA.

[676] Gilbert Badia, *Feu au Reichstag: L'acte de naissance du régime nazi*, pp. 227-228; R. M. Schultz, "Master List of the Blood Purge Victims," *Axis History Forum*, Jul. 10, 2003, FORUM.AXISHISTORY.COM.

[677] Hans Berndt Gisevius, *To the Bitter End* (1947), pp. 6-12; *Bis zum bitteren Ende: Vom Reichstagsbrand bis zum 20. July 1944* (Ger. ed., 1961), pp. 13-18; *Bis zum bitteren Ende* (Swiss ed., 1946), pp. 19-21.

[678] "Nazi leader may have organized 1933 Reichstag fire," UPI, UPI.COM/ARCHIVES, Jan. 6, 1984 (quoting Kempner, the preceding Thurs., Dec. 29, 1983). In 1947, Robert Kempner had discovered the original notes of the Wannsee. See "The Protocol of the Wannsee Conference (January 20, 1942)," DIE DEUTSCHE GESCHICHTE IN DOKUMENTEN UND BILDERN (DGDB), in the introductory "Überblick" ("Overview").

finally confessed to him almost 51 years after the event because by then anyone who could be implicated in the fire was dead, including Loerzer.[679]

(Bruno Loerzer lived from 1891 to 1960; Egloff von Freyberg-Eisenberg, quoted here in Dec. 1983, was born in 1883, died Feb. 11, 1984.)

There is also other, further information on this question: In the Nuremberg Trials of the Major War Criminals, there was testimony by Dr. Hans Bernd Gisevius, who at the start of the war left the Gestapo for the *Abwehr* (the German Intelligence Services) under Admiral Wilhelm Canaris.[680] In the *Abwehr*, Gisevius was assigned to the German Consulate in Switzerland, where he met Allen Dulles[681] in 1943, and where he became a liaison for the German opposition to Hitler. The *Abwehr* was to be dissolved at Himmler's insistence by order of Hitler in February 1944.

On being questioned about the Reichstag fire by US Chief Prosecutor Robert H. Jackson on April 25, 1946, Gesevius stated:

> To speak briefly and to begin with the facts, we ascertained that Hitler in a general way had expressed a wish for a large-scale propaganda campaign. Goebbels undertook to prepare the necessary proposals and it was [also] Goebbels who first thought of setting the Reichstag on fire. Goebbels discussed this with the leader of the Berlin SA Brigade, Karl Ernst, and he suggested in detail how it should be done.[682]

Loerzer & Göring Loetzer Freyberg-Eisenberg Gisevius Ernst Dulles

Relatedly, a document held to have been written and signed by Karl Ernst, which was published in the Parisian *Le Journal* on December 4, 1934— whose authenticity has been denied by some—was to be reprinted in other newspapers afterwards.[683] In this document, Ernst stated that the idea of

---

[679] "Nazi leader may have organized 1933 Reichstag fire," UPI, UPI.COM/ARCHIVES, Jan. 6, 1984 (cited just above). Cf. "Did Goering organize famed 1933 Reichstag fire?" UPI, UPI.COM/ARCHIVES, Jan. 5, 1984, with a preliminary, partial report.

[680] Canaris was later a member of the July Conspiracy, the plot to assassinate Hitler, attempted on July 20, 1944, and was executed on April 9, 1945, for treason.

[681] Allen Dulles was attached to the OSS, US Office of Stategic Services, forerunner of the CIA, of which he became the first civilian director in 1953.

[682] NT-IMT-Blue, vol. 12, p. 252.

[683] Ludwig Lore, "A Nazi Confesses," *New International*, vol. 2, no. 1, Jan. 1935, pp. 19-20. This journal was a publ. of the Trotskyist Communist League of America. Cf. "Reichstag Fire; Nazi Plot Revealed; Confession of a Dead Nazi Leader [Karl

burning down the Reichstag came from Goebbels, in discussion with Göring and Ernst, with the underground passageway from Göring's quarters to the Reichstag to be used by Ernst and other SA members. All of this was to provide Hitler with "convincing grounds for the immediate suppression of the communist movement."

Ernst added that among those who knew of the plan were Göring, Goebbels, Röhm, Edmund Heines (Röhm's SA Deputy), Manfred Freiherr von Killinger (earlier German Naval officer and Freikorps leader, said to have masterminded the assassination in 1922 of Foreign Minister Walther Rathenau, and later a regional SA leader), *Standartenführer* (Regimental Commander) Bernhard Wilhelm Sander, and Hanfstaengl—and Ernst himself—but that Hitler himself was not told about this ahead of time.[684] (*Hanfstaengl would firmly deny knowledge of this when it became public.*)

As well, other more recent evidence, formerly held in closed archives in the Soviet Union (until 1991) and in East Germany (until 1992), also raises more questions about source of the fire. Of course, such archives also give new insight into many other important issues from those years.[685] There have been continuing discussions about this significant event, especially given that it led immediately to the virtual dictatorship in Germany, and the new creation of law by decree, leading in a surprisingly short time to a radical transformation into a Führer state.

Consider these 2014 comments by German scholars Alexander Bahar and Wilfried Kugel, which gave their overview of some recent authors' writings[686] on, and opinions about, the Reichstag fire:

> In his review of Benjamin Carter Hett's book *Burning the Reichstag*, Richard J. Evans is tendentious in his criticism of our research (*LRB*, 8 May).[687] We were the first to evaluate all the historical files on the Reichstag fire, which have been available only since 1991. The "single culprit theory" promoted by Fritz Tobias, Hans Mommsen and others is obsolete. Sven Kellerhoff, a follower of Tobias

---

Ernst]," *The Canberra Times* (Australia), Dec. 6, 1934, p. 1—to retrieve, use this full citation: HTTPS://TROVE.NLA.GOV.AU/ NEWSPAPER/ARTICLE/2380830.

[684] Kurt Ludecke, *I Knew Hitler*, p. 773; Ludwig Lore, "A Nazi Confesses," *New International*, vol. 2, no. 1, Jan. 1935, pp. 19-20; "Wilhelm Sander (SA-Mitglied)," DE.WIKIPEDIA.ORG. On the fire as a plot of a camarilla led by Göring, see Ewan Butler and Gordon Young, *The Life and Death of Hermann Goering* (1989), pp. 107-119.

[685] "Soviet Archives: New Gold Mine for Historians," STANFORD UNIV. NEWS SERVICE, Oct. 8, 1991, and "Germans Remember 20 Years' Access to Stasi [East German Secret Police] Archives," DEUTSCHE WELLE (DW), Jan. 2, 2012.

[686] Consider Alexander Bahar and Wilfried Kugel, *Der Reichstagsbrand: Wie Geschichte gemacht wird* (2001); Sven Felix Kellerhoff, *Reichstag Fire: The Case Against the Nazi Conspiracy* (2016); tr. of *Der Reichstagbrand* (2008); Benjamin Carter Hett, *Burning the Reichstag: An Investigation into the Third Reich's Enduring Mystery* (2014); Tony Paterson, "Historians find 'proof' that Nazis burnt Reichstag," *The Telegraph* (London), Apr. 15, 2001.

[687] *LRB* is short for the *London Review of Books*.

and Mommsen, was not able to "take our work apart," as Evans puts it. The review contains several errors and false suggestions. First, Alexander Bahar was not "a student of the titular head of the Luxembourg Committee." Second, Evans withholds the fact that the "medium" who predicted the Reichstag fire the day before was the world-famous mentalist Hanussen. Hanussen's prediction was not a prophecy: it was based on information that he had acquired from SA inner circles through his friend the SA leader Count von Helldorf (who was not a "police chief" in February 1933, as Evans claims). Hanussen's indiscretion was one of the reasons he was murdered by the SA less than four weeks later.[688] Third, concerning the alleged single culprit Marinus van der Lubbe, Evans leaves out the most important facts. Fingerprints were found inside the Reichstag building, but none of them, including prints on objects he must have touched, was van der Lubbe's. Van der Lubbe's story "that he had acted alone" was inconsistent; he wasn't able to give a plausible explanation of how he had set the fire, and contradicted himself in his various statements. "His confession remains a compelling piece of evidence," Evans claims nevertheless. He also ignores the short time—a maximum of 13 minutes—available to van der Lubbe to set the fire. The experts consulted in 1933 by the Supreme Court in Leipzig weren't the only ones to state that it was impossible for one person to have managed without fire accelerants: [in addition] experts in fire protection and thermodynamics have in recent years reached the same conclusion.[689]

Whatever the particulars of the starting of the Reichstag Fire, there was a fundamental shift of power that it was used to facilitate, with a firm grip now held by the National Socialist Party and the new Nazi Government that would be strengthened even more with further decrees in the next months of 1933.

This Nazi *Machtergreifung* (Seizure of Power) was not just a phrase! It was a quite methodical transformation of the government and of what in legal terms has been called the establishment of hegemony over the

---

[688] Erik Jan Hanussen (1889-1933)—birthname, Hermann (Herschel Chaim) Steinschneider—discussed above, was assassinated on March 25, 1933. See "Eric Jan Hanussen," WIKIPEDIA.

[689] Alexander Bahar and Wilfried Kugal, "Letter," in *London Review of Books*, vol. 36, no. 12, Jun. 19, 2014. At the same *LRB* website are Benjamin Hett, "Letter," in *LRB*, vol. 36, no. 11, Jun. 5, 2014, following the lead article, Richard J. Evans, "The Conspiracists," *LRB*, vol. 36, no. 9, May 8, 2014, pp. 3-9. Orthography modified here to American style.

entire German people.[690] *Time* magazine on March 27, 1933, reported on these very early first steps in this extreme and swift seizure of power: "In Germany last week— ... before the new Reichstag met—nearly all Communist Deputies and many Socialist Deputies were in jail. The Hitler Government announced that no Communist Deputies (even should they break jail) would be admitted to the Reichstag."[691] The very next day after the fire, February 28, 1933, President Von Hindenburg issued two significant decrees that were pivotal in shifting the German government: temporary emergency measures to bring order to the seemingly chaotic violence that would remain in place until the end of the Reich.

The first was the Decree of the Reich President for the Protection of People and the Reich (*die Verordnung des Reichspräsidenten zum Schutz von Volk und Staat*), also called the Reichstag Fire Decree (*die Reichstagsbrandverordnung*). This decree, mentioned above, suspended many constitutional protections and gave the government the power to rule by decree, rather than by the passing of laws. Laws were declared by the executive rather than passed in the legislature. It made explicit the legal possibility of limiting freedom of the press (even severely).[692] This decree, together with the Enabling Act of March 23 (more on this just below), in effect, formalized the creation of a dictatorship in Germany for a theoretically limited but indefinite period of time; the decree remained in effect until the downfall of the Third Reich in 1945.

That same day (February 28, 1933), there was also the issuance of the Decree of the Reich President against Betrayal of the German People and Treasonable Activities (*die Verordnung des Reichspräsidenten gegen Verrat am Deutschen Volke und hoch verräterische Umtriebe*); this defined treason, with the death penalty, as well as outlawing anyone who publicly announced or discussed subjects or reports (*Gegenstände oder Nachrichten*) whose secrecy would be required for the good of the Reich (*für das Wohl des Reich*), whether these subjects or reports were real or false, true or untrue (*ob die Gegenstände oder Nachrichten echt oder falsch, wahr oder unwahr sind*).

THE *MACHTERGREIFUNG* FOLLOWING THE REICHSTAG FIRE

It would not be long before the political situation in Germany changed abruptly and radically, in what was called from very early times, *die Machtergreifung*, the Grabbing or Seizure of Power, of the Nazis. As Brunhilde Pomsel, later to be secretary of Joseph Goebbels, put it, simply, "after Hitler came to power, all the rules and restrictions got going, and a lot of things changed very quickly. Suddenly there was a slew of new

---

[690] The Nazis' hegemony is "the tacit acceptance [by others] of the legitimacy of their acts—and of the dutiful observance to their demands—as the lawful rulers of the German state." From Michael E. Tigar and John Mage, "The Reichstag Fire Trial, 1933-2008: The Production of Law and History," *Monthly Review: An Independent Socialist Magazine*, vol. 60, no. 10, Mar. 1, 2009, pp. 24-49, at p. 25.

[691] "Scared to Death," *Time*, vol. 21, no. 13, Mar. 27, 1933, pp. 17-19, at p. 17.

[692] Richard J. Evans, *The Coming of the Third Reich*, pp. 352-353.

regulations, including emergency regulations."⁶⁹³ In this quite turbulent context, on March 21, 1933, the Day of Potsdam—the celebration in Potsdam, a town some 25 miles southwest of Berlin, of the reopening of the Reichstag—Chancellor Hitler and President Paul von Hindenburg met in official circumstances, symbolically formalizing their relationship. A famous photograph of Hitler, in formal civilian attire, hair neatly combed, head bowed in deference, is shown shaking the hand of Von Hindenburg, dressed in military attire, chest covered with medals from earlier battles.

As it turned out, this Hitlerian deference had strong limits! Two days after the Day of Potsdam on March 23, 1933, came the Enabling Act (*das Ermächtigungsgesetz*), whose more formal name was *Gesetz zur Behebung der Not von Volk und Reich*, known in English as the Law to Remedy the Distress of People and Reich, the Law Removing the Distress of the People and the Reich, or the Decree to Protect the Government of the National Socialist Revolution from Treacherous Attacks. Not indicated by its name, this law gave basically dictatorial powers to Hitler, allowing him to create laws by decree without a supporting vote by the Reichstag. It denied ("suspended"—for what would be the entire duration of the Third Reich) certain civil rights, including freedom of speech, of association, and of the press, citing Article 48 of the Weimar Constitution, as had Chancellor Papen in the *Preußenschlag*, the Prussian Putsch, in 1932, mentioned above. This made it illegal to wear a Nazi uniform in an unauthorized (false) way, and to defame the government in foreign circles,⁶⁹⁴ the latter a serious limitation on free speech. It also put forth the claim that the government had the right to maintain order (with this Enabling Act the means to that end). This Act was to be used harshly against socialist and communist groups, among the many real or imagined "enemies" of the Reich.⁶⁹⁵

With this decree, soon almost all German papers that were not National Socialist in political orientation were eliminated, along with a

---

⁶⁹³ Brunhilde Pomsel, *The Work I Did*, p. 25.
⁶⁹⁴ *Nazi Law, From Nuremberg to Nuremberg*, John J. Michalczyk, ed. (2018), Glossary, p. 1.
⁶⁹⁵Anthony McElligott, "Dangerous communities and conservative authority: The judiciary, Nazis, and rough people, 1932-1933," pp. 33-47, in *Opposing Fascism: Community, Authority and Resistance in Europe*, Tim Kirt and Anthony McElligott, eds. (2004), at pp. 39-40.

strict restriction on foreign reporters. There was one carefully defined exception to this, to show that Germany still actually had an "opposition" press, although it was not actually free at all: Dr. Doerner, the Director of the Reich's Press Division for Justice,[696] which worked in tandem with the Propaganda Ministry, cited two exceptions to this general prohibition: "By special privilege both the *Deutsche Allgemeine Zeitung* and the *Frankfurter Zeitung* are permitted to express views which no other newspaper would be allowed to print" but, he added, that all such articles would be reviewed beforehand by the Ministry of Justice and the Propaganda Ministry, "for approval before publication."[697] There were thus definite limits on what was allowable, even within that focused leniency (just enough to suggest the presence of a free press in Germany itself, with newspapers that did not tow the National Socialist doctrines).

On July 6, 1933, Hitler spoke before a gathering of *Reichsstatthalter* (State Governors), Nazi representatives of Hitler and the Party, a category created by decree on April 7, replacing earlier regional representatives; most of these new officials were Gauleiters within the Nazi Party apparatus). Hitler announced that the Nazi revolution was completed (the *Gleichschaltung*, the bringing of all major aspects of German life into conformity with Nazi values and regulations): "The political parties have now been finally abolished [in practice, and several weeks later, by law] ... The Party has now become the State ... We must now get rid of the last remnants of democracy, especially of the methods of voting and of decisions by the majority..."[698]—*Chilling words, indeed!* And, on July 14 (Bastille Day) of that year, 1933, several laws moving in another direction were declared in the German Reich. There was *das Gesetz gegen die Neubildung von Parteien*, the Law Against the Formation of New Political Parties, making the NSDAP (Nazi Party) the sole political party in Germany; it also stipulated that anyone trying to establish any other party could be punished by three years' imprisonment.[699] That answered the issue Hitler had put forth in a speech in 1932, that there were too many political parties in Germany. Also, on that day, July 14, 1933, there was *das Gesetz über den Widerruf von Einbürgerungen und die Aberkennung der deutschen Staatsangehörigkeit*, the Law for the Repeal of Naturalization and Recognition of German Citizenship (stripping citizenship from Jews who had become naturalized German in the period 1918-1933). In addition, that date saw *das Gesetz zur Verhütung erbkranken Nachwuchses*, the Law for the Prevention of Genetically Diseased

---

[696] German title: *Oberregierungsrat*.

[697] Edith Roper and Clara Leiser, *Skeleton of Justice*, pp. 12, 30. Roper was a reporter allowed to write for both these mentioned newspapers: see also the review of this book of theirs, in Elton Groves, "Where the Vatican Rules (Part 2)," *Consolation*, vol. 23, no. 582, Jan. 7, 1942, pp. 3-7 (cited in full, above), at p. 4.

[698] Milan Hauner, *Hitler: A Chronology of his Life and Time* (2005), p. 94.

[699] *Nazism, 1919-1945, Vol. I: The Rise to Power 1919-1934*, J. Noakes and G. Pridham, eds. (1983), Sect. 114, p. 167; Geoff Layton, *Democracy and Nazism: Germany 1918-45* (2015), pp. 162-164.

The Hitler Era

Offspring, also called the Sterilization Law, requiring sterilization of those with epilepsy, blindness, schizophrenia, and related conditions believed to be hereditarily transmitted: This also applied to "asocial elements," including Gypsies (Romanies). Further, there was *das Gesetz über die Einziehung volks- und staatsfeindlichen Vermögens*, the Law on the Seizure of Assets of Enemies of the State, which was applied primarily to Communists and Jews, especially those who had emigrated (fled).

Later in 1933, on October 13, a related law was established, *das Gesetz zur Gewährleistung des Rechtsfriedens*, the Law to Ensure Legal Peace, or the Law for the Guarantee of Peace Based on Law.[700] This made it illegal to kill any German officials acting in legal capacities, from jurors to political administrators. It went on to make it a crime to disseminate or distribute abroad or inland (within Germany) documents that had treasonous content (that spoke critically of the Reich government). These laws were part of a large restructuring of the German legal system, and with that, German society. These changes were reassuring to those who saw themselves as true Germans, that is, who accepted the teachings and doctrines of the NSDAP Party worldview, with its understanding of the *Volk*, the people. This new Germany promised more economic stability, with jobs that paid decent wages for all, and a greater pride in German power and strength, which would include its military power: After the British and French refused Hitler's demand to be able to increase its military capacities, Germany left the League of Nations (in a curt governmental letter to the League, dated October 19, 1933). All of this was encouraging German national pride. For others, however, from Jews to Romanies, to the socially deviant (in terms of sexual, religious, or political preferences and practices), or were otherwise questionable, things were quite different. Their rights were curtailed, their freedom to various occupations closed off from them, and they were also arrested, imprisoned (in the early German concentration camps), where they were notoriously beaten, tortured, and often killed ("trying to escape"), along with other brutal and even sadistic treatments.[701]

Can we even now come to understand this remarkable idea of a capacity to commit cruelties with a clear conscience, to remain decent people through it all? In Nazi Germany this began in a somewhat sporadic manner, later to be methodically carried out. This violence was known about within the circle of the leaders of the Third Reich: Himmler, as head of the SS, encouraged this attitude, in a speech to SS Major-Generals (high-ranking SS officers), in Posen (Polish, Posnań), on October 4, 1943, and in a similar speech on October 6, 1943. These were meant to remain secret to all others than those in the audience, but later became known to researchers and scholars. Himmler declared: "One basic principle [*ein*

---

[700] "Gesetz zur Gewährleistung des Rechtsfriedens, Vom 13. Oktober 1933," DOCUMENTARCHIV.DE.

[701] Michael S. Bryant, "Punishing the Excess: Sadism, Bureaucratized Atrocity and the U.S. Army Concentration Camp Trials, 1945-1947," pp. 63-85 in *Nazi Crimes and the Law*, Nathan Stoltzfug and Henry Friedlander, eds. (2008).

Grundsatz] must be the absolute rule for the SS men: We must be honest [*ehrlich*], decent [*anständig*], loyal [*treu*] and comradely [or comrade-like, *kameradschaftlich*] to members of our own blood and to nobody else." In that same speech, talking of "the clearing out of the Jews, the extermination of the Jewish race," Himmler remarked, "I also want to talk to you, quite frankly, on a very grave matter. Among ourselves it should be mentioned quite frankly, and yet we will never speak of it publicly."[702] As German journalist and research author, Heinz Höhne (1926-2010), wrote, these killers "reached a level of insensibility surpassed only by those soulless automata, the concentration-camp guards. Here was to be found the elite of that barbaric type of mankind, intoxicated by its own achievements, which Himmler exalted as the SS ideal."[703]

This idea of being decent when at the same time killing literally millions of innocent people is rather strange if not bizarre. Killing millions of people has nothing to do with being decent, and the need to keep this secret does suggest an awareness of its disapproval by general world opinion, so what was Himmler proposing? For this to make sense, there must be a separation of these mass murders and the sense of one's moral status as decent. In psychological terms, this is splitting: a radical separation of parts of our experience and history that are not taken into account in our sense of ourselves. In Sartrean terms, from a phenomenological analysis (of consciousness), this is bad faith (*mauvaises foi*), in which we overlook, disregard, or dismiss some of our experience, thoughts, emotional states, and actions and focus only on other features. It is a form of self-distortion and self-delusion.[704] This Nazi cruelty had its reflection in an intense anti-Semitism, with Jews felt to be threatening the extermination of the German people, and a general intense fear of all others (all non-Germans), all of which can easily lead to an intense, defensively aggressive attitude toward all who were perceived as being foreign, strangers, the unknown other (an intense xenophobia with little limit).[705] Anti-Semitism was taught in a very structured way, by Joseph Goebbels and the Propaganda Ministry, Nazi schooling, press, and the training of the *Hitlerjugend*. Hitler and the National Socialists were quite focused on the young of Germany. Alfons Heck remarked, "More than any other political party, the NSDAP recognized that those who control the children own the future."[706]

Nazi power having been born on January 30, 1933, Hitler made his first radio broadcast as Chancellor two days later, on February 1. In this

---

[702] NT-NCA-Red, vol. 4, pp. 558-572, quoted texts at pp. 559, 563. Cf. NT-IMT-Blue, vol. 29, the Ger. passage at pp. 122-123, quoted Ger. terms, p. 122.

[703] Heinz Höhne, *The Order of the Death's Head: The Story of Hitler's S.S.* (1969), p. 363.

[704] Jean-Paul Sartre, *Being and Nothingness: An Essay in Phenomenological Ontology* (1943), Part I, Chap. 2 ("Bad Faith").

[705] Robert Wistrich, *Demonizing the Other: Antisemitism, Racism and Xenophobia* (1999); "Xenophobia", UNESCO/UNITED NATIONS EDUCATIONAL, SCIENTIFIC AND CULTURAL ORGANIZATION.

[706] Alfons Heck, *The Burden of Hitler's Legacy*, p. 49.

speech, he mentioned that 14 years had gone by since the shameful treatment of Germany at the end of World War I. He does not mention that the reparations payments established in the Versailles Treaty had essentially been annulled by early 1929, given the Dawes Plan of August 1924—developed to counter the hyperinflation in Germany of 1923-1924 after the default of payments by Germany and then the occupation of the Ruhr, with a significant lessening and restructuring of the reparations repayments and loans to Germany of $200 million)—and the Young Plan (written in 1929 and formally adopted by the second Hague Convention in January 1930), both clearly in place before the appointment of Hitler as Chancellor in 1933. Overlooking all of that financial relief from outside Germany, Hitler declared in his February 1, 1933 speech,

> In [the preceding] fourteen years the November parties have ruined the German peasantry. In [those] fourteen years, they have created an army of millions of unemployed. [This was only after the 1929 crash and the great Depression.] The national government will, with iron determination and unshakable perseverance, implement the following plan: Within four years the German peasant must be rescued from impoverishment. Within four years unemployment must be finally overcome. At the same time, this will lay the groundwork for the rest of the economy.... It was not this government which led the German nation into ruin for fourteen years; this government wants to lead the nation to the top once more. It is determined to pay the debt of fourteen years in four years. But it cannot make the work of reconstruction dependent upon the approval of those who are to blame for the collapse.... Now, German *Volk*, give us four years and then pass judgment upon us! True to the order of the Field Marshal [Von Hindenburg], we shall begin. May Almighty God look mercifully upon our work, lead our will on the right path, bless our wisdom and reward us with the confidence of our *Volk*. We are not fighting for ourselves, but for Germany![707]

Hitler's speech touched on one significant part of the National Socialist program, that of eliminating unemployment in a great sense of national unity and an encompassing *Volk*-camaraderie. The full story was more complex: those who benefitted from the resurgence of paid labor, who appreciated the revived sense of national pride, replacing the shame that many felt once the conditions of the Versailles Treaty were announced to the general public and were then imposed on the German people, the people who were comfortable with the regimentation imposed by the Nazi

---

[707] "The first radio broadcast of Adolf Hitler's proclamation. February 1, 1933, 10:00 PM," pp. 105-108 in *Adolf Hitler, Collection of Speeches, 1922-1945*, at pp. 106, 108. Hitler's reference to Almighty God is presumably less than candid.

rather extensive if not intrusive control over social life, could feel a true happiness and appreciation of the benefits of the Third Reich government. Also, however, this was a radically new society in which those who disagreed with Nazi policies and the new body politic were silenced, in which political opponents were arrested, tortured, killed, or otherwise made to disappear, in which Jews were increasingly excluded from participation in the new Germany, humiliated, attacked without police protection as a recourse to justice, and, overall, marginalized from the Germany in which they had lived and grown to adulthood, all signs of a brutal dictatorship. These were the two facets of this new Germany.[708]

If we look at the first six years of the Reich (that is, the first half of the twelve-year "thousand-year Reich"), from 1933-1939, we will see what Hitler was able to claim as his great achievements for Germany. Here was a wild mixture of a great re-stabilization of German society, with full employment in only a few years, in a restructuring of its military and the repossession of some territory lost from the Treaty of Versailles.

At the same time, the leftist opponents to his regime having been crushed (arrested, put into Nazi concentration camps, beaten, tortured, killed, or inspired to emigrate), and "non-Germans" such as Jews and Romanies harassed, persecuted, and deprived of their rights—perhaps something many would see at the time as either a minor nuisance, a regrettable corollary to National Socialist principles (which might be called in more modern terms, "political collateral damage"), or might even be seen as an added value to the Nazi societal restructuring.

Hitler would be able to state on April 28, 1939, *before the war*, in a speech before the Reichstag that included a statement of his many significant accomplishments:

> I have conquered chaos in Germany, re-established order, enormously increased production in all branches of our national economy, by strenuous efforts produced substitutes for numerous materials which we lack, smoothed the way for new inventions, developed traffic [commerce], caused mighty roads to be built and canals to be dug, called into being gigantic new factories and at the same time endeavored to further the education and culture of our people. I have succeeded in finding useful work once more for the whole of the 7,000,000 unemployed who so appeal to the hearts of us all, in keeping the German peasant on his soil in spite of all difficulties and in saving the land itself for him, in once more bringing German trade to a peak and in assisting traffic [commerce] to the utmost.[709]

---

[708] Konrad H. Jarausch, *Broken Lives: How Ordinary Germans Experienced the Twentieth Century*, p. 76.
[709] *Official Translation of the Speech delivered by Adolf Hitler before the German*

The Hitler Era

SA Crushed: The Night of the Long Knives, June 30-July 3, 1934

In a schematic overview, it is often held that the Night of the Long Knives (June 30-July 3, 1934), in which the power of the SA was basically eliminated, was a conflict between the SA under Röhm and the SS under Himmler, and that Himmler was triumphant. The complexities of the story bring in a number of other actors and their interests. Part of this can be understood by our considering the different armed groups in the Nazi world that were responsible for the safety and survival of Hitler.

At the start of the Third Reich, Göring would be appointed head of the Prussian Police, another unit responsible for Hitler's safety, putting Röhm, Göring, and Himmler in tension if not conflict with one another. These tensions and conflicts among the various units, led to in-fighting between Himmler, Göring, Röhm, and others such as the Reichswehr. (This was the name of the German military until its name was changed to the Wehrmacht, on May 21, 1935. *At that time, the number of SA men was five times that of the regular military*).[710] These conflicts involved politics and maneuvering, leaving Himmler one of the most powerful (and ruthless) men in the Third Reich.

We can then see how these interests played out and led to the results that we now know. Units that were responsible for Hitler's safety included (1) the *Stoßtrupp-Hitler*, mentioned earlier; (2) the *SS-Begleitkommando*, the SS Escort Command, established on February 29, 1932, consisting of eight especially chosen, loyal, courageous, and reliable men who would be responsible at close range for the safety of Hitler—later called the *SS-Begleitkommando des Führers* or *Führerbegleitkommando*, the *FBK*, the Führer Escort Command, (3) the *Leibsgtandarte-SS Adolf Hitler*, called for by Hitler on March 17, 1933, and operational in September 1933, at first 120 men under Sepp Dietrich (who took his orders directly from Hitler), enlarged to 1,000 men in the year to follow—these were Hitler's private Chancellery Guards, responsible for Hitler wherever he would be, including at his retreat at Berchtesgaden or in all public appearances; (4) the *Schutzkommando*, Protection Group—this was later to be known as the *Führerschutzkommando*, the Führer Protection Group, and on August 1, 1935, again, renamed the *Reichssicherheitsdienst*, the Reich Security Service, in short, the RSD—this last being set up by Himmler in Bavaria with Bavarian State Police, with authority at first in that area only, commanded by Police Inspector Johann Rattenhuber (who also took his orders directly from Hitler); (5) the Prussian Police, with authority in Prussia, at first under the control of Hermann Göring; (6) the SA; and (7) the SS. *If all of this sounds complex, it was*, and the issue of which particular group had which responsibilities created conflict and an intense competition about who could best act as Hitler's bodyguard. At the same time, Hitler had a declared belief that he was protected by the gods, or

---

Reichstag on April 28, 1939 (1939), p. 69. This was a text of 71 pages, pub. by the German Embassy, Washington.

[710] *Hitler's Bodyguard (2008), Season 1, Episode 4 (Night of the Long Knives)*, 10:25-11:00, YOUTUBE.

destiny, or fate, and that he could not be killed; a reflection of Hitler's two-faceted, polarized, sense of his own invincibility. In this net of competition, Ernst Röhm and the SA remained a powerful force within the party until a serious conflict with the SS and other Nazi key authorities resulted in many of the SA leaders being killed in *die Nacht der langen Messer*, the Night of the Long Knives (June 30-July 2, 1934), also known as the Röhm Putsch, the Blood Purge, and by the code name of *Unternehmen Kolibri*, Operation Hummingbird. The mass murders of that operation were carried out largely, but not solely, by the SS, with the support of Göring and the approval of Hitler.

There were important negotiations and decisions that set the stage for this Blood Purge. Göring had established the Gestapo on April 27, 1933, as a part of the Prussian Police Force. Himmler had the dream of being in charge of all German police operations. That, and more, would change in April 1934. On April 10, Hitler went to the port city of Wilhelmshaven and boarded the battleship *Deutschland*. There he met in secret with Gen. Warner von Blomberg, the Minister of War and Commander-in-Chief of the German Armed Forces, Gen. Werner von Fritsch, Commander-in-Chief of the German Army,[711] and with Adm. Erich Raeder, Commander-in-Chief of the German Navy. At this meeting, Hitler made a commitment to limit Röhm's actions, asking in exchange for a commitment of their military support of Hitler's advancement to President, when Hindenburg would die. (This materialized following Hindenburg's death only several months later, on August 2, 1934. More on that, just below.)

Then, ten days later, on April 20, 1934, Himmler and Göring decided to join together against Röhm and the SA. With that, the two agreed to have the Prussian police and Gestapo, up until then under Göring, transferred to Himmler's portfolio. The two then convinced Hitler to agree to this new arrangement. With that, the SS was now even more powerful than before. Himmler and his assistant Reinhard Heydrich drew up plans for the operation against the SA, with Göring, Himmler, and Heydrich creating death lists of those to be killed for their earlier resistance or opposition to the Nazi Party (*or for the resolution of personal grudges*).

The month of June saw refinements in the issue of what to do with Röhm and the SA. On June 4, 1934, Hitler met with Röhm for some five hours; Röhm agreed to have the SA stand down for the summer, while they vacationed at Röhm's favorite *Kurhaus* (*eine Pension* or Guest House) *Hanselbauer*, at Bad Wiessee with its sulphur baths, about 33 mi. south of Munich. Then, on June 16, on Hitler's first visit to Mussolini, in Venice, he was also advised by the Italian Fascist leader to limit Röhm's actions.

Importantly, on June 21, Hindenburg, arranged for a meeting with Hitler, where he told Hitler that unless Hitler acted immediately against the SA, martial law would be declared and the army would be sent out to

---

[711] Blomberg and Fritsch would later be dismissed by Hitler in early 1938 for their hesitancies about going to war. This was referred to as the Blomberg-Fritsch Affair (or Crisis).

The Hitler Era

crush it. (*We might appreciate with this that Hindenburg was not at all a pacifist nor at all warmly dedicated to the Weimar Republic.*)

The Blood Purge would see a number of close associates of Hitler transformed from bodyguards and political colleagues to assassins on his behalf. These would be personally involved in some of the killings. *Victims included not only SA Men, but also others who had crossed paths with Hitler in one way or another.* Consider here: Gen. Kurt von Schleicher, last Chancellor before Hitler, Gregor Strasser, early member in competition for Hitler in the leadership of the NSDAP (tortured by the Gestapo and then executed), Gustav Ritter von Kahr, earlier Prime Minister of Bavaria, whose speech had been interrupted in the Bürgerbräukeller the evening of the Beer Hall Putsch (November 8, 1923), and who was responsible for the arrest and trial of Hitler and cohorts for that insurrection. Von Kahr's body was found hacked to pieces in a swamp near Dachau, outside of Munich.

Then, specially chosen for execution were Brother Bernhard Stempfle (a Catholic priest who had helped Hitler in the editing for style of *Mein Kampf*, but then who had been involved in extortion demands on Hitler concerning letters writing of his relationship with Geli Raubal, his half-sister's daughter, in which Hitler had mentioned his masochistic and coprophiliac fantasies), Erich Klausener (head of Catholic Action and a critic of Hitler), and Karl Ernst (SA leader in Berlin).

These were assigned to be killed by specifically chosen members of Hitler's entourage: for Stempfle there was Emil Maurice (who had been the head of the SA from 1920-2921, had accompanied Hitler in the Beer Hall Putsch, served a sentence with him in prison in 1924, but who had two marks against him: he was found to have a Jewish ancestor—that is, one great-grandfather, Charles Maurice Schwartzenberger, 1805-1896, making Emil Maurice one-eighth Jewish by ancestry, even if Hitler insisted that Himmler declare him an honorary Aryan. More emotionally significant for Hitler, Maurice had had a love relation with Geli Raubal, much to Hitler's annoyance and rage. Then, Erich Klausener and Karl Ernst were to be killed by Kurt Gildisch (recently demoted for his drinking problem as commander of the select *Begleitkommando*, the Escort Detachment, eight men who were the closest bodyguards that Hitler had, beginning on February 19, 1932, and continuing for most of the Third Reich years).[712]

---

[712] Kurt G. W. Ludecke, *I Knew Hitler*, esp. Chap. 42 (The Blood Purge), pp. 759-780; Konrad Heiden, *Der Fuehrer: Hitler's Rise to Power*, Ralph Manheim, tr. (1944), pp. 385-389 and esp. Chap. 28 (pp. 719-774, "The Blood Purge")—these two mention other men who were killed, who were not members of the SA at all, *highlighting the general tone of revenge and the settling of old grudges.* See also Ronald Hayman, *Hitler & Geli* (1997), pp. 107-115, 142-143; William L. Shirer, *The Rise and Fall of the Third Reich* (1960), pp. 215-226; Alan Bullock, *Hitler, A Study in Tyranny* (completely revised ed., 1962), pp. 133, 305; Ian Kershaw, *Hitler: A Biography*, pp. 98, 128-129, 218-222, 293, 312, 315, 380, 940; and the film, *Hitler's Bodyguard, Season 1, Episode 4 (Night of the Long Knives)*, YOUTUBE.

The new Germany had a new morality: the new German Order was described in a declaration by Hitler's Reich Cabinet, "The measures taken on June 30 and on July 1 and 2, 1934, for the suppression of acts of treason, are legalized as necessary measures for the defense of the State." As Kurt Ludecke wrote in 1937, the "moral order of the Third Reich had sanctioned mass-murder as part of the new German code."[713]

Tensions mounted; then, bringing the issue into focus and urgency, in the first hour of June 30, 1934, Hitler received a phone call from Himmler and told (falsely) that the head of the SA in Berlin, Karl Ernst, had ordered a general mobilization of the SA, suggesting the start of a coup. Adolf Wagner, Bavarian Minister of the Interior (who appeared at various Nazi Party Nuremberg Rallies, at times speaking on Hitler's behalf, as mentioned earlier), also called Hitler to announce (falsely, as well) that the SA Men in Munich were protesting against Hitler.

With these meetings, consultations, and exchanges of information, significant steps were being taken in initiating the Night of the Long Knives. It was generally known that the SA were headed by Ernst Röhm, a recognized *Schwule*, a homosexual. At first, this was not especially an important issue. It was known that Röhm and his companions—in slang, *warme Brüder*,[714] warm brothers—presented an intensely masculine, very aggressive and violent form of what might be called a homoerotic machismo, in stark contrast to a widely understood alternative model of masculinity, the more traditional concept of *kalte Krieger*, cold warriors (hard and ascetic). This unusual image of the SA was quite different from some ideas (caricatures, distorted and insulting stereotypes) of homosexuals as "loose-wristed" (effeminate), anti-social, cowardly child rapists, all loosely associated with one another.[715] (*A note on this terminology: the term "gay" would only become widely used in the 1960s.*)[716] And yet, all of this was ultimately made use of when major figures of the SA were attacked and killed by the SS.

---

[713] Kurt G. W. Ludecke, *I Knew Hitler*, p. 778.

[714] Burkhard Maria Zimmermann, "Was heißt hier 'warmer Bruder'?" ZEIT ONLINE, Jan. 12, 2017.

[715] This is one way to co-opt some understanding: labeling it and simplifying it, eliminating its underlying values, and thus, seriously distorting its core vision. We can understand that in this way the women's movement of the 1960s and 1970s, investigating rigidly sex-defined roles for both men and women, thus defining new possibilities, new freedoms, became distorted and watered down to being merely a narrow issue of women's rights, and this, in turn, reduced to the slogan, "Equal pay for equal work"). *Co-opting is a form of what has been known and explained as mystification*. For an analysis of mystification, see R.D. Laing, "Mystification, Confusion and Conflict," pp. 343-364 in *Intensive Family Therapy: Theoretical and Practical Aspects*, Ivan Boszormenyi-Nagy and James L. Framo, eds. (1965).

[716] The terms *homosexual* and *heterosexual* were only introduced in the 1800s; both were coined by Karl-Maria Benkert, also known as Károly-Mária Kerbeny (born, Vienna, 1824; died Budapest, 1882). The terms became popular in the following decades. See Judit Takács, "The Double Life of Kertbeny," pp. 26-40 in *Past and*

The Hitler Era   235

Hitler and others tolerated Röhm and the SA—composed largely of *Lumpenproletariat* (meaning the class of the unstable, the restless, the changeable, those with nothing to lose, a condition leading to actions of unruly violence),[717] who were widely known and openly acknowledged for their widespread homosexuality—did not make them any less useful in street violence.

Still, when Röhm and many in the SA were later murdered, cartoons were then published that suggested the homosexual interests of Röhm and other SA Men, considered in a critical and mocking light.

In addition to such mockery of the SA (and with that group, of the National Socialists in a more general way)—something the other leaders of the Nazi party and government were interested in dissociating themselves from—the murders were described as a purging "the SA of violent and criminal elements."[718]

The significant weakening of the SA marked the solidifying of the power of the SS in the Nazi State and the elimination of the SA as an operating force. It also represented the suppression of a homosexual masculinity, represented by Ernst Röhm, head of the SA, as an alternative to the typical hard and violent masculinity that was prominent in early Nazi Germany, as mentioned above.[719]

Present Radical Sexual Politics, Gert Hekma, ed. (2004). Cmp. Gert Hekma (Univ. of Amsterdam), *A Cultural History of Sexuality in the Modern Age* (2014). This mutual caring *carried no particular modern connotations defining people essentially by the heterosexual-homosexual contrast.*

[717] Here, the term *Lumpenproletariat* (lit., the proletariat, the working class, the proletariat in rags (*Lumpen*), refers to a class of people living in instability and limited material and political rights. See *Critique of Modern German Philosophy According to its Representatives Feuerbach and Stirner*, pp. 21-452, in Karl Marx and Friedrich Engels, *Marx & Engels, Collected Works Volume 5 (1845-1847)*, esp. pp. 84, 201-202. The "Saint Max" that they mention is the author Max Stirner. Cf. "Lumpenproletariat," ENCYCLOPEDIA.COM. *This contrasts with the modern sense of the Lumpenproletariat:* see Nicholas Thoburn, "Difference in Marx: the Lumpenproletariat and the proletarian unnamable," *Economy and Society*, vol. 31, no. 3, Aug. 2002, pp. 434-460.

[718] *The Yellow Spot: The Outlawing of Half a Million Human Beings* (1936), p. 91.

[719] Eleanor Hancock, "'Only the Real, the True, the Masculine Held Its Value': Ernst Röhm, Masculinity, and Male Homosexuality," *Journal of the History of Sexuality*, vol. 8, no. 4, Apr. 1998, pp. 616-641.

More significantly, Röhm's many SA followers were seen as a challenge to the power of the military, the Reichswehr, the German military. It was also a rival to the growing SS. Hitler was persuaded that Röhm and the SA planned a Putsch, taking over power from the military with the purported goal of ousting Hitler from power. This led to the decimation of the SA, including many high-ranking SA leaders, including Röhm.[720] In the carrying out of the Blood Purge, not only were many SA arrested, shot on the spot, or transferred to the prison in Munich (where they were later assassinated), but others were also killed, in a methodical elimination of political enemies. The SA lost not only whatever prestige and respect they had earlier, but were obliged to relinquish their weapons and their rights as a fighting organization within the Third Reich. As one German anti-Nazi summarized the situation: "The German people breathed a sigh of unutterable relief and hoped that at last peace would be restored. All too soon they discovered that the ill-considered, heavy-handed illegal terror of the SA had been replaced by the calculated and legalized terror of the SS and the Gestapo. These two organizations are virtually identical: The SS is armed with the rights of the Gestapo agent. Every Gestapo agent is a member of the SS. Heinrich Himmler is Reichsfuerer of the SS and at the same time Chief of the Gestapo. The Gestapo keeps every German in fear and terror [including the SA, generals and field marshals, and down to the most insignificant and helpless private citizen] ... Heinrich Himmler has succeeded in forcing the army and all its generals to their knees."[721] *This was no mean feat and meant significant new power for Himmler!*

The murders of the SA (and others) at that time were seen by many as a great act of national strength, warding off an attempt by traitors to overtake the government. Hitler would justify his violence by telling the German people in his July 13, 1934, speech to the Reichstag that Röhm had been planning to have him assassinated.

This apparently largely satisfied the German Reichstag and people.[722] The fact that Röhm was openly, publicly proclaimed as a homosexual added to the sense that here was a trouble-maker to be happily

---

[720] The Night of the Long Knives, *Nacht der langen Messer*, also called the Röhm-Putsch, Operation Hummingbird, *Unternehmen Kolibri*, and the Bloody Weekend of the Nazis (see Henry Simon, *Third Reich Diaries*, p. 46) actually took place from June 30 to July 2, 1934. It was an SS-administered purge of the SA—and of other miscellaneous undesirables—with the assassination of Röhm himself and a number of his higher officers; it took place on the supposed grounds that Röhm was planning a *coup d'état* against Hitler. After these killings, the claimed potential threat of the two million SA Men was eliminated. Many of the SA entered into the Wehrmacht, the regular military. See Isabelle Clarke and Daniel Costelle, *Apocalypse: Hitler, Part II: Le Führer* (2011), FRANCE 2 TV (2011), at 45:25-46:15. Cf. Alan Axelrod, *Encyclopedia of World War II, Vol. 1* (2007), p. 867, and Chris N. Trueman, "The Night of the Long Knives," THE HISTORY LEARNING SITE, Mar. 9, 2015.

[721] Edith Roper and Clara Leiser, *Skeleton of Justice*, p. 177.

[722] Brunhilde Pomsel, later a secretary to Joseph Goebbels, in *The Work I Did*, p. 38. (The book was based on interviews filmed in 2013.)

eliminated; a general wariness about this homosexuality contributed to this feeling. With this attitude, one German would later reminisce about Jule Jaenisch, who was widely liked as the reader of the morning news for the *Rundfunk* (German radio)[723] but who ended up in a concentration camp for his disapproved sexual interests, he "was such a nice, friendly man. Yes, yes, they're friendly, but they're homosexual."[724] A remark, referring to the close-mindedness of many in Germany at that time, was that being "homosexual was something terrible in those days... We really were a repressed bunch."[725]

SA Men were described (or dismissed) as Nazi radicals, as in the report in the US by *The New York Times* (July 1, 1934) under the bold headline as "Hitler Crushes Revolt by Nazi Radicals; Von Schleicher is slain, Roehm a Suicide; Loyal Forces Hold Berlin in an Iron Grip. Police Fill the Streets. Storm Troop Chiefs Die."[726] After this purge, the SS were to become the overriding group of police, including the Gestapo, and the administering of concentration camps and, then, during the war, of the extermination camps as well—their administration was left totally as the special assignment for the *SS-Totenkopfverbände* (the SS Death-head Units).

If we consider President Hindenburg and the German military here, the President's comment on hearing of the mass killings and destruction of the SA as a powerful and therefore threatening, *was not shock at such barbarity, but, rather,* as Hindenburg commented, "When circumstances require it, one must not shrink from the most extreme action. One must be able to spill blood also."[727] And, as for the military, they were pleased that this great threat to their position posed by the SA had been eliminated. As earlier agreed to, when Hindenburg died on August 2, 1934, one month after the Blood Purge, the German Armed Forces gave to Hitler total power, having all military pledge a solemn oath to Adolf Hitler personally. This was carried out as a public ceremony for the first time on August 3, 1934, following the phrasing Hitler himself prepared: "I swear to God this sacred oath, that I will unconditionally obey the leader of the German Reich and people, Adolf Hitler, the Commander-in-Chief of the Wehrmacht, and be prepared as a brave soldier to use my life at any time for this oath."[728] This is quite remarkable as an oath, since Germany was

---

[723] This was the Reich Broadcasting Corporation, *Reichs-Rundfunk-Gesellschaft (RRG)*, administered by the Third Reich's Ministry of Propaganda.

[724] Brunhilde Pomsel, *The Work I Did*, p. 38.

[725] Brunhilde Pomsel, *The Work I Did*, p. 38.

[726] Actually, Röhm refused to shoot himself: He bared his chest to the SS Men who were assigned, if necessary, to shoot him. The *New York Times* article appeared on p. 1 of the Jul. 1, 1934 issue. The headline was thus not accurate.

[727] Albert Speer, *Inside the third Reich*, p. 52.

[728] The original Ger. text reads: Ich schwöre bei Gott diesen heiligen Eid, daß ich dem Führer des Deutschen Reiches und Volkes, Adolf Hitler, dem Oberbefehlshaber der Wehrmacht unbedingten Gehorsam leisten und als tapferer Soldat bereit sein will, jederzeit für diesen Eid mein Leben einzusetzen. Cf. William Shirer, *The Rise and the Fall of the Third Reich*, pp. 226-227, with a slightly variant wording in Eng.

not at war with any other country, nor was any war being publicly contemplated or envisioned! And yet, it was not without precedent: on September 3, 1930, Hitler had demanded that every SA Man swear an oath. Relatedly, the SA *Stabchef*, Chief of Staff, Otto Wagener, then informed all OSAF deputies (deputies of the *Oberste SA-Führer*, the Supreme SA Leader—who, since August 1930, was Hitler himself) that they had "taken an unconditional oath of allegiance [*ein unbedingtes Treuegelöbnis*] to the person of the Party and Supreme SA leader Adolf Hitler." Each member of the SA had to pledge "to carry out all orders undauntedly and conscientiously [*alle Befehle unverdrossen und gewissenhaft zu vollziehen*]."[729]

GROWING TENSIONS AND THE NUREMBERG LAWS OF 1935

Given these comments and requests on the German people, an enthusiastic Nazi might well look forward four years, which would bring us to early February 1937: four years after the establishment of the concentration camp system, the harassment of Jewish businesses and regular insults to German Jews, and the Sterilization Law, two years after the Nuremberg Laws of 1935 that defined Jews as those with three Jewish grandparents, and which deprived all Jews of citizenship in the Reich, the right to legal counsel, to schooling, and other basics of life, and almost a year after the remilitarization of the Rhineland, for example, to mention some considerations if we were to pass judgment on the National Socialist government as of that time.

ENTER VARIAN FRY (AND ERNST HANFSTAENGL)

The Nuremberg Laws decreed on September 15, 1935, were met with some enthusiasm in a Germany that had already seen some of the early violence and pogroms against German Jews—as, for example, in the Berlin riots of July 15, 1935. These were claimed to be a healthy response by the German people to Jews who had hissed their disapproval of a pro-Nazi film Swedish film, *Pettersson & Bendel* (1933),[730] incidents that also provided a pseudo-justification for the Nuremberg Laws of 1935. The resultant riots with violence against German Jews, the evening of July 15, 1935, were reported on by American journalist Varian Fry (more about whom, below), who reported in *The New York Times* (with a similar article in the *New York Post*) under a banner headline, "Berlin Jews Hide from Terror," of crowds along the Kurfürstendamm—a chic avenue in Berlin, "the Champs-Élysées of Berlin," with many shops, cafés, hotels, and other attractions—seeking out Jews (asking for Aryan papers), beating them, with police offering no interference with the violence, the crowd in a call-and-response chant, a leader calling out with the crowd repeating words to the effect of (in Varian Fry's words) "Get the hell out—blood running—noses—the best Jew is a dead Jew." One participant described the event

---

[729] "Der Orden unter dem Totenkopf: 2. Forsetzung," SPIEGEL ONLINE, Oct. 24, 1966.

[730] "Pettersson & Bendel," SV.WIKIPEDIA.

The Hitler Era

to Fry as "a holiday for us." The Germans involved were "old men and young men, boys, Storm Troopers, police, young girls of the domestic servant type, well-bred women, some even in the forties and over—all seemed to be having a good time."[731] Hanfstaengl in the following days told Varian Fry that it was Storm Troopers (the SA) who had hissed (not Jews), in order to create a cause for a response to Jewish insubordination.[732] One author noted the militant power of the SA: "Hitler's second creation of the twenties, his civil war army, the SA, made all other political fighting units of the day—the Nationalist *Stahlhelm*, the Social-Democratic *Reichsbanner*, and even the Communist *Roter Frontkämpferbund*—appear like lame Philistine clubs by comparison."[733]

When there was this outbreak of violence against Jews in Berlin, orders from leaders of the SA stated, "Berlin-Brandenburg Formation ... orders Storm Troops to refrain from all demonstrations and manifestations even when a member is wearing civilian clothes ... the state and the movement ... will cooperate most intensely in order to prevent every disturbance of public order."[734] The issue of whether racial violence would be controlled by the central authorities or by emotional mobs was central.

Some two months later, the 1935 Nuremberg Laws met with some enthusiasm, and widely, with meek or passive acceptance. The first of these, the *Reichsflaggengesetz*, the Reich Flag Law, involved a symbolic move to have the Nazi flag the sole official German flag (prior to that the pre-Nazi flag was also flown and respected), the symbol of a purely Nazi German regime and nation. The second and third took citizenship from Jews and made sexuality between Jew and "Aryan" a crime. In general, German Churches had not spoken out against the early arrests of Communists, Social Democrats, and Labor Unionists in 1933-1934 (including members of the Reichstag, the German Parliament); for the Nuremberg Laws, some described it as Nazi *Rassenwahn* (racial delusion or fanaticism)[735]; there was also a general silence of non-involvement concerning these laws and the rescinding of citizenship to German Jews.

---

[731] Varian Fry, "Editor Describes Rioting in Berlin. Varian Fry of *The Living Age* Tells of Women and Men Beaten and Kicked. Nazis Chanted of Hatred," *New York Times*, Jul. 17, 1935, p. 4; and Varian Fry, "Eyewitness Story of Berlin Horror," *New York Post*, Jul. 16, 1935, pp. 1, 9.

[732] Varian Fry, "Editor Holds Riots Inspired by Nazis: Varian Fry says Hanfstaengl admitted Storm Troopers, Not Jews, Hissed Film. Insists Police Looked On; American Seized for Blocking Party Propaganda by Removing Anti-Semitic Posters," *New York Times*, Jul. 26, 1935, p. 8.

[733] Sebastian Haffner, *Anmerkungen zu Hitler*, 1978 ed., pp. 35-36; 1994 ed., p. 29; Eng., *The Meaning of Hitler*, p. 26. "Lame Philistine clubs": in Ger., *lahme Spießbürgervereine*. A *Spießbürger* or a *Spießer* is someone who is narrow-minded and always does what is conventionally correct.

[734] "Hands Off—[Storm] Troopers Told," *New York Post*, Jul. 16, 1935, p. 9.

[735] The term endures in German consciousness to this day, as in a speech by Chancellor Angela Merkel, "Gegen anti-Semitism: Holocaust-Gedenktag: Mahnung gegen Rassenwahn und Hass," *Zeit Online*, ZEIT.DE, Jan. 27, 2019.

The second of these three laws, as just noted, declared it a crime for there to be any sexual intimacy between Jew and non-Jew. This may remind us of the laws in the US against the marriage or sexual coupling of blacks and whites, laws against what is usually termed miscegenation.[736] Still, one well-known exception to a general silence about these legal innovations is that of Lutheran Pastor Martin Niemöller (1892-1984). At this time, in 1935, from his pulpit, he "turned the fire of his oratory upon the Nuremberg Laws, which he insisted contradicted another established principle of the church, namely, love of neighbor. He cited historical and biblical examples to show that Christians had always survived suppression and terror. It goes without saying that the Nazis were nervously aware of the danger signals in Niemoeller's sermons."[737] Niemöller would spend 1938-1945 in various German concentration camps, and later be well known and quoted for his statement about German cowardice about facing the Nazi rise to power: "When the Nazis came for the Communists (*Als die Nazis die Kommunisten holten*), I kept silent (*habe ich geschwiegen*); I was not a Communist. When they locked up the Social Democrats (*die Sozialdemokraten einsperrten*), I kept silent (*habe ich geschwiegen*); I was not a Social Democrat. When they came for the unionists (*die Gewerkschafter holten*), I did not protest (*habe ich nicht protestiert*); I was not a trade unionist. When they came for the Jews, I kept silent; I was not a Jew. When they came for me there was no one left who could protest (*gab es keinen mehr, der protestieren konnte*)."[738] But Niemöller was unusual; most German Protestant Church leaders understood Hitler well and "readily reconciled their consciences and their Christian identities to the harshness of the Nazi state."[739]

At the 1935 National Socialist Congress (Nazi rally), the crowd there gave an enthusiastic welcome to the speech by Goebbels on September 13. In this speech, "Communism with the Mask Off," Goebbels took the theme proposed by Hitler—Bolshevism as National Socialism's major enemy—and claimed, "Bolshevism is explicitly determined to bring about a revolution among all the nations. In its own essence it has an aggressive and international tendency. But National Socialism confines itself to Germany and is not a product for export, either in its abstract or practical characteristics."[740] (This, in hindsight, would be quite a distorted claim, given the German aggressivity of 1938 and on.) In his diaries about the reception of his speech to the Congress on the morning of September 15, he described its reception: "With dazzling success [*Mit fulminantem Erfolg*].

---

[736] US anti-miscegenation laws were only declared unconstitutional by the US Supreme Court case of Loving v. Virginia (1967).

[737] Edith Roper and Clara Leiser, *Skeleton of Justice*, pp. 117-118.

[738] "Martin Niemöller," WIKIQUOTE.

[739] Robert P. Ericksen, *Christian Complicity: Changing Views on German Churches and the Holocaust*, USHMM LECTURE, Nov. 8, 2007 (2009).

[740] The Sept. 13, 1935, Nuremberg speech by Goebbels, at "Communism with the Mask Off," GERMAN PROPAGANDA ARCHIVE (CALVIN COLLEGE).

The Führer is honestly enthusiastic [*Führer ehrlich begeistert*]. Storms of applause [*Stürme von Beifall*]. My material was deeply moving [*Meine Material wirkt erschütternd*]."⁷⁴¹ At least Goebbels himself was deeply impressed by his speech, although one German later commented more critically that "it was well known that Goebbels was a notorious liar" (*Daß Goebbels ein notorischer Lügner war, ist hinlänglich bekannt*), but that "his records are nevertheless of considerable documentary relevance" (*seine Aufzeichnungen trotzdem dokumentarisch von hohem Belang sind*).⁷⁴² Goebbels continued, building his case: "Swept clear of internal enemies and united under the National Socialist standard, Germany placed herself at the head of the groups marshalled in the fight against the international bolshevization of the world. Herein she is quite aware that she is fulfilling a world mission that reaches out beyond all national frontiers. On the successful issue of this mission depends the fate of our civilized nations. *As National Socialists, we have seen Bolshevism through and through. We recognize it beneath all its masks and camouflages.* It stands before us derobed of its trappings, bare and naked in its whole miserable imposture. We know what its teachings are, but we know also what it is in practice." Here, he become more specific about what is behind (or beneath, as he says) all its masks and camouflages. He mentioned a number of key figures in world Bolshevism that he identifies as being Jews. Generalizing further, he put forward the doctrine, "Almost without exception, the intellectual leaders of Marxist atheism in Germany were Jews, among them being Erich Weinert, Felix Abraham, Dr. Levy-Lenz and others." Then Goebbels brought Jews into the center of his attack on Bolshevism: "While in all the other countries alleged Capitalist and Fascist dictatorships are in power, Russia affords an example of freedom and democratic order.... In reality this land is wilting under the Jewish-Marxist rule of force, which will stop at no means to maintain itself in power." With this, Goebbels intensifies his declaration equating world Bolshevism with Jewry:

> Where are the men behind the scenes of this virulent world movement? Who are the inventors of all this madness? Who transplanted this ensemble into Russia and is today making the attempt to have it prevail in other countries? The answer to these questions discloses the actual secret of our anti-Jewish policy and our uncompromising fight against Jewry; for *the Bolshevik International is in reality nothing less than a Jewish International*. It was the Jew who discovered Marxism. It is the Jew who for decades past has endeavored to stir up world revolutions through the medium of Marxism. It is the Jew who is today at the head of Marxism in all the countries of the world. Only in

---

⁷⁴¹ Joseph Goebbels, *Die Tagebücher: Sämtliche Fragmente, Vol. 2 (1 Januar 1931-31 Dezember 1938* (1987), p. 514.
⁷⁴² "Der Führer ist aufgekratzt," *Der Spiegel*, Jul. 13, 1992.

the brain of a nomad who is without nation, race, and country [all Jews] could this Satanism have been hatched. And only one possessed of a satanic malevolence could launch this revolutionary attack. For Bolshevism is nothing less than brutal materialism speculating on the baser instincts of mankind. And in its fight against West European civilization it makes use of the lowest human passions in the interests of International Jewry[743]

We might note that for Goebbels, as for Hitler and others using the same vocabulary, "international" regularly refers to world Jewry. Goebbels continued, laying at the foot of all Jewry the driving force of all that is destructive to European society, presenting further examples such as the first Communist Party Congress held in Berlin on December 31, 1918, with the Jewish Rosa Luxemburg the elected leader, and the second Congress of the Social Democratic Labor Party of Russia, in 1903, with a split between Menshevik and Bolshevik, emphasizing that in the one as well as in the other of these parties, authoritative positions were held by Jews. Further examples are given to drive home the point. Then, the grand conclusion with its prescription for the defeat of this indefatigable, vicious enemy (which he refers to as International Jewry):

> That is Communism with the mask off. That is its theory, its practice and its propaganda. I have given a bald and staid account of facts which have been gathered mostly from official sources; but this account points to a state of affairs which is so terrible and revolting in all its effects that it must shock the average civilized human being. This gospel of "the emancipation of the proletariat from the yoke of capitalism" ... has been thought out, set afoot and led under the inspiration of the Mammon worship and materialist thought ... incarnated in international Jewry, scattered throughout every country of the globe.... It is nothing else than a mammoth system for the expropriation and despoiling of the Aryan directive classes in all the nations, and the substitution of the Jewish underworld in their place. Those people who put themselves forward here as the apostles of a new teaching and the liberators of mankind are in reality figures that herald anarchy and chaos for the civilized world.... This thing ... must be met with the same ruthless and even brutal means with which it strives to usurp power or hold power in its hands. Here there can be no bargaining; because the danger that threatens Europe is acute.... Those States that make peace with it will soon learn from experience that it is not they who will tame Bolshevism but that Bolshevism will bring them under its heel. It cannot be said that the Komintern

---

[743] The Sept. 13, 1935, Nuremberg speech by Goebbels, just cited. Italics added.

has changed its practices. It is and remains what it always was—the propagandist and revolutionary machinery ... intended to bring about the downfall of the West."[744]

Goebbels perhaps saw his speech as inspiring Hitler to focus in on the danger of world Jewry, when later in that Congress, the Party issued the Nuremberg Laws of 1935. *If so, Goebbels would be exaggerating his own impact on German and world history:* A meeting chaired by Franz Gürtner (Reich Minister of Justice) had taken place on June 5, 1934, with Hitler, Bernhard Loesener (Jewish Expert in the Reich Interior Ministry), Roland Freisler (Secretary in the Reich Ministry of Justice, and later President of the People's Court), and other leading legal authorities in the new Germany, to discuss the structure that laws excising Jews from German life would take, ultimately declared in part as the Nuremberg Laws of 1935. The discussions addressed US Jim Crow laws and other US discriminatory statutes, corroborating the Nazi doctrine of German ("Aryan") racial superiority and the right to consign inferior beings to positions of lesser rights.[745] Goebbels was at least consistent: at the Berlin Sportpalast speech by Hitler on February 10, 1933, for example, Goebbels had introduced Hitler with some threats of his own:

> And if the Jewish newspapers still believe today that they can intimidate [*einschüchtern*] the National Socialist movement with hidden threats [*versteckte Drohungen*], if today they believe they are allowed to bypass our emergency regulations[746] [*Notverordnungen umgehen zu dürfen*], they should beware! Once our patience will be over, and then the Jews will have their impudent lying mouths shut up [literally, stuffed, muted: *und dann wird den Juden das freche Lügenmaul gestopft werden*].[747]

POLISH FEARS, MATHEMATICIANS, AND CRYPTOGRAPHERS

In the meantime, little known by the general public, were the Poles, very concerned with a German threat they felt even in the 1920s, and who were even more concerned through the 1930s about German interests in taking over Polish territory. In that context of pending crisis, in 1932, years before the Nazi invasion of Poland in 1939, some of Poland's most sophisticated mathematicians, logicians, and specialists in cryptography were able to decipher German military messages encoded

---

[744] The Sept. 13, 1935, Nuremberg speech by Goebbels, just cited. The Congress went from Sept. 10 to Sept. 16, with Hitler issuing the Nuremberg Laws (against the Jews) two days after Goebbels' speech, on Sept. 15.

[745] James Q. Whitman, *Hitler's American Model*, esp. pp. 1-7, 22-28.

[746] The reference in this speech by Goebbels on Feb. 10 would be to the Decree of the Reich President for the Protection of the German People, issued on Feb. 4. The Emergency Order, the Reichstag Fire Order, was issued only later, on Feb. 28.

[747] Ger. text of Goebbels' speech on Feb. 10, 1933, at *Goebbels Vorrede zu Hitlers Das Deutsche Volk*, YOUTUBE.

in the latest versions of the coding machine called Enigma, mentioned above. The three credited with this work were Marian Rejewski (1905-1980), Jerzy Witold Różycki (1909-1942), and Henryk Zygalski (1908-1978). That esoteric work aside, there was also a general awareness of German aggressive intentions by the general Polish population: By August 31, 1939, the day before the invasion of Poland by the Third Reich, "everyone in Warsaw had been sure for some time that war with the Germans was inevitable," wrote concert pianist Wladyslaw Szpilman.[748]

LIMITING FREEDOMS IN THE THIRD REICH

To give an appreciation of its historical context, this banning of the press was not totally new under the Third Reich. Freedom of the press was already being limited late in the days of the Weimar Republic; some of this was just discussed. For example, in 1931, well before the birth of the Third Reich in early 1933, newspapers were reporting on the banning of some other newspapers, especially particular issues of extreme left and right newspapers, from the (Social Democratic) *Volkswacht* (People's Watch) and *Rote Fahne* (Red Flag) to the (National Socialist) *Roter Adler* (Red Eagle) and *Angriff* (Attack). In particular, on July 10, 1931, the *Berliner Tageblatt* estimated that up to 100 newspapers throughout Germany were banned per month, for various lengths of time.[749] *This was to be even more intensive and widely inclusive in the Reich, with bans becoming more extreme and then permanent.*[750]

Meanwhile, as part of the fast-moving *Gleichschaltung* or switching all of German law and society into conformity with Nazi principles, on February 22, 1933, Hermann Göring, President of the Reichstag, established an auxiliary police force in Prussia. *This was composed of SA Men, thereby transforming the SA into legally recognized police.*

Two days after Göring's transformation of the SA, on February 24, Brown Shirts (SA Men) went into "legal" action, attacking meetings of the Social Democratic Party at the offices of Albert Grzesinski, formerly the Prussian Minister of the Interior, knowing that protections of the law against their violence had been rescinded by orders of the Reich Interior Ministry. *This was before the burning of the Reichstag, which suggests the equal protections under the law had already been effectively curtailed if not annulled completely* before the Reichstag Fire decree that was announced in the period immediately after the burning![751]

Hitler's *Grundsätzlicher Befehl* (Hitler's Basic Order) of September 15, 1941, after the invasion of the USSR, would complement this. More on this, below.

---

[748] Wladyslaw Szpilman, *The Pianist*, p. 22.
[749] The Communist paper *Rote Fahne*, the SPD's *Vorwärts*, and all Jewish-run newspapers were soon all blocked from further publication, the issue definitively resolved by decree on Feb. 28, 1933. Cf. Bernhard Fulda, *Press and Politics in Berlin* (2009), pp. 220-221, 297; Dr. Wolfgang Bretholz, "Zeitungsverbote," *Berliner Tageblatt und Handels-Zeitung (Abend-Ausgabe)*, Jul. 10, 1931, pp. 1-2.
[750] Richard J. Evans, *The Coming of the Third Reich*, pp. 251, 352-353.
[751] Richard J. Evans, *The Coming of the Third Reich*, pp. 320, 517.

Einstein and the First Concentration Camps, March 1933

With its new, legally instituted exceptional powers, with this greatly extended political and societal control over the nation, the National Socialist government arrested many of "enemies of the state," that is, their political opponents, including Socialists, Communists, politicians, trade unionists, duly elected members of the Reichstag, and other critics of the Nazi Party and program. The vehement rage and organized action of the Nazis now moving into political power, with energizing enthusiasm, however distorted it might be, was already at work in these first weeks of the new Germany. The hatred and mistrust of the Jews was reflected, as an example, in the belief that all of "Einstein's pacifist utterances" were "a mere pose" (as the *New York Times* reported), leading to an inspection by the Brown Shirts (SA) on March 20, 1933 for Einstein's arsenal—with the Prussian police authorized by Hermann Göring to search and seizure of Einstein's home while he was away on tour, without need of a search warrant, having unrestricted rights of search and access, confiscation and arrest[752]—they found nothing closer to an arsenal than a bread knife.[753]

With early arrests of many leading opponents of the Nazis, the month of March 1933 saw the Nazi Party and government then scrambling to find holding centers that were large enough to contain arrested Socialists, Communists, and others in disagreement with the Nazi Party vision for Germany. These centers were soon called *Lager* (storage camps) or, with a fuller name, *Konzentrationslager* (or KL: concentration camps).[754] One understanding of this name at the time was that it was simply to be a gathering together of people who should not be put into prison: these were trouble-makers, and "of course they're not going to put them in prison right away. They were put in a concentration camp to be reeducated. No one gave it a thought."[755] These arrests called for the creation of the first Nazi concentration camps. Some consider the first of these to be KL-Oranienburg, [756] outside of Berlin—not to be confused with the later camp in the same town, KL-Sachsenhausen—with plans for the camp initiated on February 22, 1933, and the opening on March 12. Others cite the more famous KL-Dachau, outside of Munich. It was established on March 10, with the first prisoners arriving March 22. Those

---

[752] Sebastian Haffner, *Defying Hitler: A Memoir* (2002), pp. 118-119.

[753] "Nazis Hunt Arms in Einstein Home. Only a Bread Knife Rewards Brown Shirts' Search for Alleged Huge Cache," *New York Times*, Mar. 21, 1933, p. 10.

[754] Earlier were the precedents of the *campos de reconcentración* of Cubans (1896-1898), set up by Spanish General Valeriano Weyler y Nicolau, and of Boers (1899-1902) in British South African concentration camps (Boer Wars). See Andrés García Suárez, "Reconcentración de Weyler, holocausto cubano," *5 de septiembre* (Cienfuegos), Oct. 23, 2017, 5SEPTIEMBRE.CU.

[755] Brunhilde Pomsel, *The Work I Did*, p. 38.

[756] "Oranienburg Concentration Camp," WW2 DATABASE; Gerhart Seger (Social Democrat member of the Reichstag, soon thereafter an Oranienburg escapee), *Oranienburg: Erster authentischer Bericht eines aus dem Konzentrationslager Geflüchteten* (1934), Eng., *A Nation Terrorized*, Foreword by Heinrich Mann (1935).

held in these camps were political prisoners—mostly Communists, trade unionists (members of workers' trade unions), and Socialists—all of which were viewed with a hostile eye by Hitler and the National Socialists. While these camps were at first run in a harsh if not sadistic manner, the purpose was a re-education through beatings and torture of these so that they would be docile members of the Reich. (The Mohawk Valley Formula for strikebreaking[757] in 1930s USA also aimed at destroying unions.)

It was clear to some by this relatively early moment in the years of the Third Reich that the national revolution, the *Machtergreifung* (the Grabbing of Power) by the National Socialist Party, was pointing to and creating a dictatorship.[758] In addition to Dachau, north of Munich, there were camps opened in Emsland, a region of moors, fens, and bogs, in the northwest of Germany, including Börgermoor and Esterwegen. The famous anti-Nazi song "Die Moorsoldaten" ("The Peat Bog Soldiers"), sung for decades after the camp had shut down, was composed at Börgermoor, expressing the plight of the political prisoners held there.[759] These camps were well publicized to the general German public, unlike the later, more deadly concentration camps and extermination camps, where mass deaths and executions were carried out, kept secret from all but those directly involved in the extermination process. Of early camps, such as Dachau, it is written, "Far from hiding the existence of concentration camps, the Nazi regime used them as its most effective terror weapon to contain so-called People's parasites."[760] These very early arrests of a number of politicians and politically active citizens opposing the Nazis came immediately after the Reichstag fire, preceded the vote already scheduled before the fire, on March 5, in which the Nazis received 43.9% of the popular vote—a plurality but still not a majority. *It was the last vote until the ending of the Third Reich.* On March 21, the Day of Potsdam, the Hindenburg-Hitler relationship was formalized, as just discussed.

DEFERENCE AND THE RAPID TRANSFORMATION TO A NEW WORLD

All well and good, the world thought, seeing in that deferential pose by Hitler, humbled before Hindenburg, the limits to Hitler's craving for power. That said, later that day, Hitler gave Hindenburg two documents,

---

[757] Robert Rodden, "James Rand and the Mohawk Valley Formula," in *The Fighting Machinists: A Century of Struggle* (1984); "Know your propaganda: The Mohawk Valley Formula," *The Forge News*, Nov. 21, 2018. Cf. court case, Remington Rand, Inc., 2 NLRB 626 (Mar. 13, 1937), with the Appeals Court ruling by Judge Learned Hand et al., National Labor Relations Board v. Remington Rand, Inc. 94 F.2d 862 (Feb. 14, 1938). Cf. John Stuart Mill, *Principles of Political Economy* (1884).

[758] Konrad H. Jarausch, *Broken Lives: How Ordinary Germans Experienced the Twentieth Century*, p. 69.

[759] The original German was sung by Ernst Busch. The lyrics were co-written by Wolfgang Langhoff, who later wrote *Rubber Truncheon: Being an Account of Thirteen Months spent in a Concentration Camp* (1935). Lyrics at "Ernst Busch: *Die Moorsoldaten* lyrics + English translation," *Lyrics Translate*, LYRICSTRANSLATE.COM.

[760] Alfons Heck, *The Burden of Hitler's Legacy*, p. 82.

both of which the President signed. The first gave full pardons to all Nazis still in prison. The second authorized the arrest of anyone suspected of maliciously criticizing the new German government and the National Socialist Party. *So much for Hitler's pose of deference!* And yet, in those days, not all Nazis were in accord with the situation. Consider here Karl Heinrich Gustaw Schilke, who had worked in the SS, within the SD[761] as Commissioner of the Security Police.[762] In prison after the war, in a Communist Polish cell with General Stroop and Polish underground fighter Kazimierz Moczarski, Schilke commented, "And the worst part was that my men and I, so-called keepers of law and order, were forced to close our eyes to that lawless SS scum and even to protect them."[763]

In addition to those two documents, a decree was signed by Chancellor Hitler and Franz Von Papen (now Vice-Chancellor under Hitler) that set up special courts for political offenders, to be run as court-martials, *without jury, and with no guarantee of a defense counsel*. The government was reconfirming the Weimar *Sondergerichte* of August 1932.

With all of this, German society and the new Reich government were to undergo radical transformation in the next months at a speed that was quite remarkable: by the time of the Nazi Party Congress in Nuremberg in late summer 1933, Hitler declared the achievement of the submission of all other political parties and the taking of the first major steps intended to marginalize the rather small German Jewish population[764]—some 525,000 or only 0.75% of the overall German population—from government, judicial, and medical professions.

Hitler christened the Congress the *Kongreß des Sieges*, the Congress of Victory (that is, victory over other political parties and over the Jewish presence and criminal control of German society, in National Socialist terms and beliefs). Even by then, so soon after Hitler became Chancellor, the arrest and brutalization of many German Communists and Socialists led many of these to join the Nazis. One early joke about this switching of party affiliation was told in a story: The SA is marching along the street in one of their frequent demonstrations. Some men approach from the opposite direction, loudly cursing the Nazis. The SA leader whispers to them hastily, "For heaven's sake, shut up. A real Nazi is marching in the last row!"[765]

---

[761] SD: *Sicherheitsdienst*, the Security Service, the intelligence service) of the SiPo (*Sicherheitspolizei*, Security Police).

[762] BdS: *Beauftragter der Sicherheitspolizei und des Sicherheitsdienstes*, Commissioner of the Security Police and of the Security Service. See *Kriegsprache*, Thomas L. Houlihan, III, ed., (2009), entry in alphabetical order.

[763] Kazimierz Moczarski, *Conversations with an Executioner*, p. 42. Stroop and Moczarski were cell-mates from March 2 to November 11, 1949, awaiting trial in Communist-dominated Poland, along with Schilke. Moczarski had been in the *Armia Krajowa* (the *AK*, the Polish Home Army), but was accused of being a Nazi. He was ultimately declared innocent, on June 24, 1956, after years of harsh imprisonment.

[764] "Jewish Population of Europe in 1933: Population Data by Country," HOLOCAUST ENCYCLOPEDIA, USHMM.

[765] D. von Schwanenflügel Lawson, *Laughter Wasn't Rationed*, p. 93.

The power and military-like organization of the SA, the SS, and the then-limited Reichswehr, the Armed Forces of Germany, were not only literally paraded in front of Hitler in that Congress, but a film directed by Leni Riefenstahl, *Sieg des Glaubens, The Victory of Faith*, portrayed the adoration of Hitler by the Hitlerjugend and the interminable marching of men in uniform. That 1933 Congress of Victory was clearly a victory over the Weimar Republic and over all of the other political positions held by Germans. The new Germany would be unified and of one mind!

It was possible to see trouble in the making, but many throughout Europe were exhausted physically, emotionally, and spiritually from the devastation to human life from World War I, and hoped for the best. Still, some who had attended this 1933 Congress drew stark conclusions. British historian Philip Ziegler was to write of British Viscount Duff Cooper, an MP (Member of Parliament), "Cooper had recently visited Germany, had attended a Nuremberg rally, and had been appalled and alarmed by what he saw. He warned Churchill that Hitler was preparing for war and continually urged the need for rearmament at a time when this was unfashionable if not politically incorrect."[766] This, in the autumn of 1933,[767] was when Cooper wrote to Churchill that the Germans were focused on "preparing for war with more general enthusiasm than a whole Nation has ever before put into such preparation."[768] And in a letter dated September 11, 1933, Cooper wrote his sister-in-law, Kathleen (Kakoo) Rutland, "The whole of that country [Germany] is preparing for war on a scale and with an enthusiasm that are astounding and terrible. We heard Hitler speak at Nuremberg and were very disappointed. He read his speech, which he doesn't normally do and it aroused no enthusiasm."[769]

Still, whatever Cooper's impressions from the Nazi Rally, something quite significant and revolutionary was happening in Germany. As part of the major project of re-establishing a powerful and proud Germany, to end the disgrace of the Versailles Treaty, this glorification of the military might of the Third Reich continued, as seen in films of the grandiose military and grand public celebrations for Hitler's birthday on April 20, 1939, in the months before the invasion of Poland.[770] The breadth of this

---

[766] Philip Ziegler, "Cooper, (Alfred) Duff, first Viscount Norwich (1980-1954)," *Oxford Dictionary of National Biography, Vol. 13: Constable-Crane*, pp. 240-243, at p. 241, OXFORDDNB.COM.

[767] Given the date of Cooper's letter to Churchill, this Nuremberg Nazi Party Congress (or Rally) would have been the 5th Nazi Party Congress, the Rally of Victory (*Reichsparteitag des Sieges*), Aug. 30-Sep. 3, 1933.

[768] Martin Gilbert, *Winston S. Churchill, Vol. 5* (1976), p. 489. Cf. "Churchill 1933-1934," WINSTONCHURCHILL.ORG, esp. sub-section "Autumn 1933."

[769] John Charmley, *Duff Cooper: The Authorized Biography* (1986), pp. 75, 246.

[770] "20. April 1939," DEUTSCHE WEHRMACHT HISTORY. This film showed appreciative and exuberant crowds, filled with a joyous adoration of Hitler, and differed from the 1933 Riefenstahl film in that it included a subsequent grand display of tanks, other military vehicles, and artillery, in a military parade, Hitler saluting repeatedly to the well-disciplined military. It was all in celebration of Hitler's fiftieth birthday.

restructuring of German society was summarized by terms dear to the National Socialists: the *Machtergreifung* (the Nazi grabbing of power) and the *Gleichschaltung* (the switching of society into Nazi conformity).[771]

Among other decrees that further transformed Germany into the Third Reich that were promulgated in those early months of 1933—which the enthusiastic German attendees and participants at the Congress were quite familiar with—were the Enabling Act of March 23, giving the German legislature's authorization of basically full dictatorial powers to Hitler, allowing the German government to be ruled by Orders (*Befehle*) and other legal documents—decrees (*Erlaße*), laws or statutes (*Gesetze*)—rather than by parliamentarian acts. The next week, on March 31, 1933, Léon Blum would write in the French Socialist Parisian newspaper, *Le Populaire*, with a hopeful sense of rationality and morality that would, despite that hope, be eclipsed by other forces in the next twelve years, "If anything can bring [*peut déterminer*] the racist leaders to take back the raging cruelty of their gangs [*la cruauté déchaînée de leurs bandes*], it is precisely the revolt of the universal conscience [*la révolte de la conscience universelle*] … no power in the world can remain in rebellion indefinitely against the opinion of the world, against universal reason and morality [*contre la raison et la morale universelles*]."[772] Of course, in retrospect, at least, we might sadly appreciate that the key term here, *indefinitely*, does not mean of clearly brief duration, or even of a limited time within our own lifetimes.

Blum's comment aside, the new Nazi government was not slow to act in its own vision. In addition to the arrests of many political opponents, and the other legal transformations of February and March 1933, as discussed above, there was also a one-day boycott of Jewish stores in Berlin, on April 1, 1933, which turned out to be more of a test and a precedent and a warning than a full-fledged attack on Germany's Jews. It was said to be a protest against, and a retaliation for, insulting lies claimed to have been put forth by Jewish-run newspapers in several countries, the so-called *Greuelpropaganda* (atrocity propaganda). To this, *The New York Times* stated, "Not since the early Middle Ages, when the Jew of the ghetto was labeled by being compelled to wear a tall hat and distinctive clothing, has Munich seen such a compulsory setting apart of the whole race."[773] The boycott of April 1, 1933, *with its lack of general support, was stopped after only one day*. In return, there was a significant boycotting of German goods, leading the new German government to come to an accord signed that summer, on August 25, 1933, called the *Haavara* (or *Ha'avara*, Transfer) Agreement, in which German Jews wanting to leave Germany could sell their property in Germany and use

---

[771] These and other closely related terms have been introduced in other contexts.

[772] Philippe Simonnot, "Un désastre nommé Léon Blum," *Nouvelles de France*, Apr. 7, 2016.

[773] "Joins in Boycott but Regards it as 'Much Ado about Nothing,'" *New York Times*, Apr. 2, 1933, p. 28, with dateline Munich, April 1, 1933.

the resultant funds to buy German goods that would be shipped to British Mandate Palestine, keeping German money in Germany while providing Germany with a strong export market!⁷⁷⁴ This early attempt to buoy the German economy in the face of general international disapproval of some of its domestic policies would fade into the background as anti-Semitic measures gained in intensity and in severity in the next pre-war years. At the start of World War II, in September 1939, the program was ended completely (a program presumably more a matter of mutual expediency than an alliance).⁷⁷⁵ On the boycott day of April 1, 1933, for example, Jewish stars and other indications that a store was a Jewish business were painted in whitewash on large display windows; Stormtrooper (SA) Men stood in front, discouraging Germans from entering the store (some entered stores despite that). Signs stated: *Deutsche! Wehrt Euch! Kauft nicht bei Juden!* (Germans! Defend yourselves! Do not buy from Jews!).

This certainly set a tone for state-allowed aggressivity against German Jews. Here, while explicitly anti-Jewish, there was what we might consider to be constrained civility by the SA Men, with no killing of Jews and no shop windows shattered, and no businesses or synagogues put to the torch (unlike November 9-10, 1938, *Kristallnacht*, about which more below). Still, the tension between mob rule and administratively neat violence under central governmental control was still present, and would be for the next years. These events gathered attention, at least through the Western world. Was the boycott a success? It did exhibit the focus against Jews and Jewish businesses, that is clear. But we might wonder why it only happened on one single day. An order to all Party Organizations and members had announced, "The boycott will start all at once at exactly 10:00 am on Saturday, April 1 [1933]. It will continue until the Party leadership orders its cancellation [termination]."⁷⁷⁶

Behind the scenes, there was a lack of unanimity about the whole enterprise. It was called off (abruptly) after that one-day boycott. We

---

⁷⁷⁴ See the perspective of global political economy in Robert Gilpin, *Global Political Economy: Understanding the International Economic Order* (2001).

⁷⁷⁵ "Haavara Agreement," WIKIPEDIA; "Haavara Winds Up Reich-palestine Transfer Operations; Handled $35,000,000 in 6 Years," JTA/JEWISH TELEGRAPHIC AGENCY, vol. 6, no. 33, Sep. 10, 1939, p. 2.

⁷⁷⁶ For Point 8 from the announcement outlining the forthcoming boycott, see "Nazi boycott of Jewish businesses," WIKIPEDIA; "Nazis Boycott Jewish Shops," HISTORYPLACE.COM; "Boycott, Anti-Jewish," YADVASHEM.ORG.

The Hitler Era

might see here the disagreements between various factions of the German government: the SA were a group inclined to express its anti-Semitic opinions with confrontation and violence. But there was also a concern against these actions, at least on a tactical level: Hindenburg, for example, was not at all pleased with this violence. (We may note that Hindenburg tried to make peace with the political forces that he had to deal with, in the years preceding his inviting and appointing Hitler to be Chancellor, similar to the role of a Prime Minister.)

The very apparatus of carrying out anti-Semitic actions was limited, despite the vehemence of Julius Streicher. There was also very little public support by German citizens of that first boycott. Those with a concern for the economic welfare of Germany were also worried that this attack against Jewish businesses was counter-productive.[777] *And there would be ways of eliminating the Jewish presence with less damage to the overall German financial position.* If we look ahead to late 1938, and *Kristallnacht*, the actions throughout Germany given a nod of approval in the speech of Joseph Goebbels, together with the general openness in the SA ranks to violence, resulted in the destruction of many millions of dollars of property within Germany (the final sum was decided to be in the range of 1 billion (thousand million) reichmark, equivalent at the time to US $400 million. Göring and others in charge of German economic stability and growth were quite in disagreement with this quite unruly mob violence. Finally, the solution was offered by Goebbels to have that sum be imposed on the Jewish community of Germany to pay. (More on this, below.) About all of this, *The New York Times* of April 2, 1933, had a front-page headline with its subheadings: "Nazis Hold 1-Day Boycott: Little Violence in Reich; Resumption is Unlikely; Measure is Effective; Jews' Shops, Placarded with Quarantine Sign, Closed Everywhere; Foreign Trade Falls Off; Head of Boycott Thinks That Renewal Can be Avoided as Agitation Diminishes."[778] That headline was overly optimistic!

From the day of the April 1, 1933 boycott, one photograph shows a Jewish lawyer from Munich, Dr. Michael Siegel, who still had confidence in the fairness of the German police, his head shaven and forced to march barefoot in Munich with a sign saying "*Ich werde mich nie mehr bei der Polizei beschweren*" (I will never again complain to the police).

---

[777] Christopher R. Browning, *Fateful Months: Essays on the Emergence of the Final Solution* (revised ed., 1991), p. xi.
[778] "Nazis Hold 1-Day Boycott," *New York Times*, Apr. 2, 1933, pp. 1, 28.

Similarly, another photograph taken that day shows two German Jews being marched down the street by SA Men.

The signs they carry state, *Als Antwort auf die Greuelpropaganda kauft kein Deutscher mehr beim Juden* (As an answer to the atrocity propaganda, no German buys any more from Jews), and *Deutsche wir warnen euch hier zu kaufen! Die Kaufer hier werden photographiert! Kein anständiger Deutscher kauft bei einem Juden!* (Germans, we warn you against buying here! Buyers here will be photographed! No decent German buys from a Jew!). Such actions, and such threats, were prominently carried out on the main streets of Berlin. They made a strong impression, but their impact was more limited than the publicity and notoriety at the time might suggest. Of course, at the time it was interpreted by many as a return to medieval barbarism that had not been seen in such an unsubtle form for centuries.

Shifting from brute force to a more legalistic approach, within a week, the first of the anti-Semitic laws was passed on April 7, 1933, the Professional Civil Service Act, *das Berufsbeamtengesetz, das BBG*, short for *das Gesetz zur Wiederherstellung des Berufsbeamtentums*, the Law for the Restoration of the Professional Civil Service—or, in short, the Professional Civil Service Act, *Berufsbeamtengesetz*. As can be seen repeatedly, *with many laws passed in many countries, the name given disguised the laws' function and significance*. This law basically prohibited those who were Jewish from working in civil service positions, from judges, attorneys, teachers, professors, and such. Hindenburg insisted on certain exemptions (for honored Jewish veterans of the Great War), *which were accorded—but only until his death in 1934*. Then, on April 15, the Law against Overcrowding in Schools and Universities was decreed. Its purpose was focused on limiting the number of Jews allowed into classes at various levels of education.[779] *Despite the number of non-Jews that the*

---

[779] Alfons Heck, *A Child of Hitler*, p. 12.

The Hitler Era   253

Nazis would kill over the next twelve years, at this point in time the focus of their ire was specifically against Jews, not (yet) directed with venom against Slavs, Romanies (Gypsies), or other ethnic groups.

A number of Jews (and many non-Jews who were intensely anti-Nazi) responded to these various restrictions in early 1933 by leaving Germany, mostly to nearby Western European countries (such as France, the Netherlands, and Belgium, but also to Spain, Switzerland, and British-Mandate Palestine, and fewer to the Americas or elsewhere). Many others were not ready to leave their land and lives, some even hoping that the Hitler government would soon end. As has been sung, "Hope springs eternal in a young man's breast, and he dreams of a better life ahead."[780] And on April 22, the Regulation Concerning Admission to the Medical Profession (*Verordnung über die Zulassung von Ärzten zur Tätigkeit bei den Krankenkassen*), prohibited Jewish physicians from practicing in hospitals, and ended reimbursement under the national health plan.

While one facet of these laws (decrees) was the blocking of Jews who had been educated in these professions from practicing, another was an immediate consequence of that blocking: *the opening up of large numbers of positions for non-Jewish Germans across Germany to be hired and promoted. (Those who became members of the Nazi Party were given priority in these matters.)*

None of these laws or actions was done in secret. They were put forth before the public; these laws and the concentration camps, *both being prominently presented in newspapers in Germany*, served as warnings and threats not only to Jews but to all Germans who stepped out of line, even merely by discussing (and perhaps, questioning) anything about what the government was doing—all made criminal acts.

A German publication in 1936, reporting on the changes arising from the application of these 1933 laws, indicated that in the less than nine months, from April 7, 1933 to January 1, 1934, the number of non-Aryan (Jewish) *Rechstsanwälte* (attorneys) in Prussia dropped 39%, the number of non-Aryan—Jewish—*Notare* (Notaries) in Prussia dropped 57% and the number of non-German (Jewish) physicians in Berlin dropped 27%, while the number of German (non-Jewish) doctors there rose 16%.[781]

And so it went; while the main focus of the Nazi government in those first times was to articulate and consolidate the National Socialist vision of society through these various decrees and other legal formulations,

---

[780] From the lyrics of a song in Lindsay Anderson's somewhat surrealistic film, *O Lucky Man!* (1973). In the film, Alan Price performed this song ("Look Over Your Shoulder"). Anderson also directed *This Sporting Life* (1963), among his other respected British-cinema films.

[781] *Antisemitismus der Welt in Wort und Bild*, Dr. Robert Körber, Prof. Dr. Theodor Pugel, eds. (1935; reprint ed., 2015), p. 243. The absolute numbers for these percentages were cited as: non-Aryan attorneys down from 3378 to 2066; non-Aryan notaries down from 2046 to 884; non-German doctors down from 2077 to 1521, and German doctors up from 1404 to 1623.

through the output of the Propaganda Ministry under Joseph Goebbels and of other sources of information for the German people, it did not overlook the role of the Jews in Germany, with a keen interest in excluding them as much as possible (for the time being), and in teaching the root differences in the value of human life in a grand scheme—to be taken as a means of strengthening Germany with a focus on one people, *ein Volk*, a community composed only of people descendant from pure Germanic stock, a people who were purely *deutschblütig*, of German blood, whose ancestry was only German (*deutschstämmig*),[782] one ethnic community.

GOOD GERMANIC BREEDING AND THE IDEAL OF THE *VOLK*, THE PEOPLE

The ideal proposed for this *Volk* was for it to become an even purer, stronger, healthier, and more virile Germanic/Aryan citizenry. This ideal declared the right of the German people to self-fulfillment as a nation, with a community-inspired desire to protect all Germanic populations, no matter where they were located, and the right of Germans to *Lebensraum* (room for living)—the right of Germans throughout Europe to have land on which to live, to cultivate agriculture, and to prosper.

The legalization of this search for Germanic purity was defined at first in the law signed by Hitler on July 14, 1933, the Sterilization Law, formally known as the Law for the Prevention of Hereditarily Diseased Offspring (*Gesetz zur Verhütung erbkranken Nachwuchses*). This law called for the sterilization of all persons who had diseases considered hereditary, including mental illness, learning disabilities, physical deformity, epilepsy, blindness, deafness, and severe alcoholism. With this law the Third Reich stepped up its propaganda against the disabled, identifying them as "lives unworthy of life" (*lebensunwertes Leben*), "useless eaters" (*nützlose Fresser*) and highlighting their fundamental burden upon society.

The idea of sterilization proposed by the Third Reich was not original with that regime. In the first years of the twentieth century, the American Breeders' Association was founded in 1903, with funds provided by Carnegie, Rockefeller, and Harriman.[783] (It was renamed the American Genetic Association in 1914.) A number of states soon passed laws authorizing the forcible sterilization of some criminals, epileptics, and feeble-minded, from the first state to do so, Indiana, in 1907, to New Jersey in 1911 (signed into law by then-governor Woodrow Wilson, later US President—but soon declared unconstitutional by New Jersey state courts, in 1913),[784] to Wisconsin, in 1913. By 1924, a bibliography of eugenics listed over 6,000 titles; the topic was widely discussed and taught in American universities. *Despite some questioning of this doctrine,*

---

[782] See "Gustav Bally and *deutschstämmige Psychotherapie*," pp. xlviii-liii, with tr. and discussion by Mitchell Ginsberg and Angela Graf-Nold, in *Effective Psychotherapy: The Contribution of Hellmuth Kaiser* (cited above).

[783] Talya Nevins, "Eugenics at Princeton," *Nassau Weekly*, Apr. 12, 2015.

[784] Harry H. Laughlin, *Eugenical Sterilization in the United States: A Report of the Pathologic Laboratory of the Municipal Court of Chicago* (1922), p. 80.

sterilizations actually increased in the US in the 1930s, with over 20,000 forced sterilizations, more than triple the number sterilized from 1920-1939.[785] (Significant, but not a T4 forced-killing, "euthanasia" program.)

THE 1933 CONCORDAT: THE VATICAN AND THE REICH IN EARLY AGREEMENT

Meanwhile, on July 20, 1933, the Third Reich and the Catholic Church came to a mutually respectful agreement, assuring each side of its continued rights and freedom of decision-making. For Pope Pius XI (Pope, 1922-1939), his Secretary of State, the Most Reverend Lord Cardinal Eugenio Pacelli (the future Pope Pius XII, 1939-1958) signed, and for the Reich, the Vice-Chancellor, Franz von Papen. Any Catholic clergy in Germany would have to be German citizens; clergy were to be apolitical. This, the Encyclical of Pope Pius XI, of Passion Sunday, March 14, 1937, was entitled *Mit brennender Sorge, With Burning Worry*. Nothing was said about the status or treatment of Jews or others in Germany.[786]

All of these changes were accomplished in less than six months! The next years saw the beginning of intense anti-Semitic indoctrination of the German population, coupled with the teaching of love of the Führer, along with a commitment to help him in his great task of making Germany great again (after, that is, the humiliations, hardships, starvation, and turmoil of the Great War and the instabilities of the period 1919-1929). At the same time there were signs within the Third Reich of the abdication of independent thinking and judgment. The German Jewish philosopher, Edmund Husserl (1859-1938),[787] founder of the approach to philosophy of phenomenology, was removed from his university position. His (non-Jewish) disciple, Martin Heidegger, took over as Rector of the University of Freiburg, on May 27, 1933. Heidegger did resign from this position the next year, but kept his membership in the Nazi Party until 1945—but his enthusiasm expressed in 1933 was definite. Heidegger was perhaps simply sensing the direction of things to come. For example, in his acceptance speech of May 27, he welcomed the new National Socialist regime and its seizure of power (*Machtergreifung*), stating:

> The much-celebrated [or the much-praised] "academic freedom" [*die vielbesungene »akademische Freiheit«*] is being banished [*verstoßen*] from the German university; for this freedom was not genuine, since it was only negative. [These are rather questionable concepts of

---

[785] Thomas C. Leonard, *Illiberal Reformers: Race, Eugenics, and American Economics in the Progressive Era* (2016), pp. 109-117.

[786] From Article 14, 1 (a) in "Concordat between the Holy See and the German Reich, July 20, 1933," NEW ADVENT. The 1937 encyclical is discussed above in the sect. "The Vatican's Burning Worry about Catholics in the German Reich."

[787] See Marvin Farber [early American student of Husserl's], *The Foundation of Phenomenology: Edmund Husserl and the Question for a Rigorous Science of Philosophy* (1943); Jean-Paul Sartre, *Being and Nothingness: An Essay on Phenomenological Ontology* (1943/1956); Mitchell Ginsberg, *Belief: Its Conceptual and Phenomenological Structure* (1967).

freedom and of negativity.] It meant primarily freedom from concern, arbitrariness of intentions and inclinations, lack of constraint in what was done and left undone. [Also, rather questionable claims.] The concept of the German student is now brought back to its truth.[788]

And, also to university students and an academic audience, later that year, on November 3, 1933, Heidegger declared,

> Let not propositions and "ideas" be the rules of your being [*Nicht Lehrsätze und «Ideen» seien die Regeln Eures Sein*]. The Führer alone is the present and future German reality and its law.[789] [*Der Führer selbst und allein i s t die heutige und künftige deutsche Wirklichkeit und ihr Gesetz.*[790]] Learn to know ever more deeply: from now on every single thing demands decision, and every action responsibility. (Signed:) *Heil Hitler!* Martin Heidegger, Rector."[791]

This certainly seems to be a remarkable invitation by a respected philosopher to give up critical, independent thinking in favor of the blind acceptance of the dogmas of the Führer!

Hannah Arendt would describe this departure from the intellect to the mob, in her extended essay, *The Origins of Totalitarianism*,[792] which Karl Jaspers described as a masterpiece of analysis of Nazism.[793] This was Heidegger making a death-defying leap [*einen Salto mortale*][794] from rational, independent thinking into the immediate urges that were felt to

---

[788] Martin Heidegger, *Die Selbstbehauptung der deutschen Universität* (1934; 1983 reprint), p. 15, with *Die Rektoratsrede: Die Selbstbehauptung der deutschen Universität*, p. 3B.

[789] This *Führerprinzip* (the principle of the Führer/Leader) can be traced back to its first use, referring to Hitler, in the work of Dietrich Eckart, discussed above. Cf. Ralph Max Engelman, *Dietrich Eckart and the Genesis of Nazism*, p. 230.

[790] The use in German of wider spacing between letters (*Sperrsatz, Spationierung, Sperren*, etc.) corresponds to italics in Eng.

[791] William S. Lewis, "Martin Heidegger: Political Texts, 1933-1934," *New German Critique*, no. 45, 1988, pp. 96–114, speech "German Students" (Nov. 3, 1933), pp. 101-102, at p. 102. Ger. original text in Guido Schneeberger, *Nachlese zu Heidegger: Dokumente zu seinem Leben und Denken* (1962), Doc. 114: *Deutsche Studenten*, pp. 135-136. Karl Dietrich Bracher, *The Age of Ideologies: A History of Political Thought in the Twentieth Century* (1984), p. 24, n. 1, renders the passage: "Let not theses or ideas be the rules of your being! The Führer himself and alone is today and in the future the German reality and its law."

[792] Hannah Arendt, *The Origins of Totalitarianism* (1973), speaking of the nature of the temporary alliance between the mob and the elite (pp. 326-340).

[793] Sal·lus Herrero, "A propòsit del film sobre Hannah Arendt," *País Valencià, Siglo XXI*, Aug. 25, 2013. Masterpiece (in Catalan): *una obra mestra*.

[794] The term *salto mortale* is Italian. A *salto* is a somersault, but a *salto mortale* means a death-defying somersault (often performed by an acrobat at a height, as on a trapeze): it is a death-defying leap.

The Hitler Era

demand recognition. In this radical shift in the principles of thinking, from doing clear-minded philosophy, was a leap into primitiveness [*in die Primitivität*]," as German philosopher Rüdiger Safranski suggested.[795]

Were such comments remarkable for a sophisticated thinker such as Heidegger, you ask? After all, philosopher Heidegger's suggestion here (quoted just above) was for the replacement of critical thought by an unquestioning respect for the directives of Hitler as Führer.

In balance here, the German philosopher-psychiatrist Karl Jaspers, just mentioned, who had a long relationship with Heidegger, recounted some exchanges between them in early 1933.

On March 18, Heidegger said to Jaspers,[796] "*Man muß sich einschalten*" ("One must join in"—speaking here of the new National Socialist reality.)[797] And in a meeting at the end of June, Jaspers asked Heidegger, "How is a person as uneducated as Hitler supposed to rule Germany?" [*Wie soll ein so ungebildeter Mensch wie Hitler Deutschland regieren?*] Heidegger replied, "Education does not matter [*Bildung ist ganz gleichgültig*]; you should just look at his wonderful hands!" [*sehen Sie nur seine wunderbaren Hände an!*][798] An astonishing reply to a serious question, especially when we consider that this was an exchange between two world-respected philosophers! Certainly, questions about the capability to rule a country cannot be answered by looking at anyone's hands. In any case, the reply certainly ended the discussion of that issue; perhaps it can be read as a sarcastic, absurdist, perhaps mocking reply by Heidegger, his making a joke of a question he did not want to entertain seriously.[799]

Whatever the specifics of that reply, Heidegger's comment apparently abruptly shut down the topic: a non sequitur *that invited no response.* And yet, Heidegger was not the only intellectual, highly educated, and

---

[795] Rüdiger Safranski, *Ein Meister aus Deutschland: Heidegger und seine Zeit* (1994), p. 272; Eng., *Heidegger: Between Good and Evil* (1998), p. 231.

[796] Karl Jaspers, *Notizen zu Heidegger* (1978), p. 13.

[797] The wording here: *sich einschalten* can mean join in; it also means to switch on, and echoes the Nazi term *Gleichschaltung*, lit., the switching into congruence: the bringing of the entire society into conformity with National Socialist values. (Both terms are based on the verb *schalten*, switch, shift, start, enable).

[798] Karl Jaspers, *Philosophische Autobiographie*, pp. 100-101, and also *Notizen zu Heidegger* (1978), pp. 13, 168, 274. Cf. quote and discussion in the work of Chilean-German historian, Víctor Farías, written in Spanish and German, first pub. in Fr. as *Heidegger et le Nazisme* (1987), pp. 129, 319, then as *Heidegger y el nazismo* (1989; enlarged ed., 2009), pp. 198-200, *Heidegger und der Nationalsozialismus* (1989), pp. 175, 418, and with Eng. tr., *Heidegger and Nazism* (1991), pp. 117-119, 319.

[799] Among those who feel that Heidegger was humorless, is Steven Shaviro, author of *Without Criteria: Kant, Whitehead, Deleuze, and Aesthetics* (2009)—in the sub-section "Whitehead vs. Heidegger," *The Pinocchio Theory*—with his comment that Heidegger was "heavy and morbid, without an ounce of humor or irony." From the Steven Shaviro Blog, SHAVIRO.COM.

sophisticated thinker, who would be attracted to the Nazi worldview. As an American who lived in Jena from the 1920s through the war remarked, "it has been my observation that higher education tends to reduce, rather than enlarge, the percentage of individuals with a high immunity against the new barbarisms of our age.... [Consider as a broader consideration that] large segments of the world's academic elite were captivated by the varicolored radical socialist tenets of the 20th century."[800] *Education is no guarantee against one's accepting radical, racist, or unsubstantiated (and perhaps barbaric) teachings; of course;* yet, in a similar way, ignorance is no more of a guarantee of sensitivity to mankind's barbarisms!

That said, with the establishment of all of the many powerful laws or decrees put into place in 1933 and 1934, Hitler effectively transformed his position to that of the single and ultimate leader, *der Führer*, of the German nation. This was made apparent that second summer, when General Paul von Hindenburg died on August 2, 1934.

In a story of world politics that began in late 1931 and continued to its next chapter in early 1933—beginning, therefore, even prior to Hitler's being appointed by Hindenburg as Chancellor on January 30, 1933—Japan invaded Manchuria (oil, lumber, and rubber were three valued resources there) on September 18, 1931. All of Manchuria (a province of China) was under Japanese military control by February 1932. In February 1933, the month of the burning of the Reichstag, an assembly of the League of Nations voted for Japan to withdraw its troops. Japan voted against this motion, abruptly walked out of the international gathering, and promptly ended its membership. This was on February 24, 1933.

SECRET WAR PREPARATIONS, 1925-1936: *DIE SCHWARZE REICHSWEHR*

After the end of the Great War, the destruction of German armaments was not fully carried out, although ships and submarines and some of the larger cannons were ostentatiously reduced to scrap metal. The German Army and Navy would be reconstituted, under the conditions defined by the Versailles Treaty, and renamed the Reichswehr (or Military of the Reich).[801] At the same time, the chief of the Reichswehr (the State Defense, or German Armed Forces) in Bavaria, General Otto von Lossow, told the Chief of Staff of the entire Reichswehr, Generalmajor (Col.-Gen.) Hans von Seeckt, "Millions of rifles, machine guns, and other wartime weapons had never been destroyed or handed over to the Allies. Enormous stores of them were available in all Germany."[802]

---

[800] Henry Simon, *Third Reich Diaries*, p. 91.

[801] These terms have multiple, overlapping meanings. *Ein Reich* can mean a state, realm, empire, kingdom, or reign; *eine Wehr*, an arm, a weapon, military equipment, defense, or resistance. Use of the Reich in English is first of all linked the Third Reich, the Third Empire, with the First Empire, the Holy Roman Empire; the second, the German Empire, lasted from 1871-1918, under Kaiser Wilhelm I—then, briefly in 1888, Frederick III—followed by Wilhelm II; Otto von Bismarck was Imperial Chancellor from 1871-1890, until dismissed by Kaiser Wilhelm II.

[802] Otis C. Mitchell, *Hitler's Stormtroopers and the Attack on the German Republic, 1919-1933*, pp. 72-74.

The Hitler Era

These supplies thus represented a great potential arsenal for unauthorized paramilitary, a large group of which would be known as *die schwarze Reichswehr*, the Black Armed Forces or Defense. In this context, the years 1933 to 1935 and even 1936 saw the further development of the military power of Germany, with a program that began in 1933 as a project of establishing a military air force, *a clandestine extension of training programs begun in 1925*. Hitler would be ready to show some of the development of his military by the Nuremberg Party Rally of 1936, held from September 8-14 of that year. There were a quarter of a million Nazis who took part, with great parades showing off the SS and the military, with 70,000 spectators, who were treated by the glory of the Cathedral of Lights: extremely powerful search lights shining upwards toward the heavens in parallel columns of light, a creation of the personal architect and close associate of Hitler, Albert Speer.

And yet, many still saw Hitler as a force for peace, someone who just wanted what was fair for Germany, with no sense that he was looking with expansionist ideas to take control of much of Europe, by negotiation or by warfare. He could still be presented in the press as a man dedicated to peace, as a *semeur de paix*, a sower of peace, even if tongue-in-cheek:

This is from the March 22, 1936 issue of a satirical paper mentioned above, *Kladderadatsch* (*Crash*), which printed this caricature of Hitler. Despite an image or public positioning as a German leader of reasonable demands, a man of peace, in fact, groups in Germany already during the Weimar Republic had been developing an air force, in large part in Soviet Russia (before the falling out of the two nations took place). This was not a project of the Weimar government itself, but of the just-mentioned military group, *die schwarze Reichswehr*,[803] whose members included a large number of ultra-nationalistic ex-military from the Great War. This project had a non-military, dissimulating name, *die Wissenschaftliche Versuchs- und Prüfanstalt für Luftfahrzeuge* (the Scientific Research and Test Institute for Aircraft), in short, the *Wivupal*. Its more revealing name was *die Kampffliegerschule Lipetzk* (the Lipetsk Fighter-Pilot School). The

---

[803] The *schwarze Reichswehr* was was an illegal group, in contrast with the *Reichswehr*, the Armed Forces during the Weimar Republic, which was a professional, legal army, later to be become the Wehrmacht in the Third Reich.

town of Lipetsk is about 300 km., 185 mi., south-southeast of Moscow. With arrangements made in late 1925, the training of German pilots began in Lipetsk in Spring 1926.[804] Meanwhile, the French and Belgians had ended their occupation of the Ruhr (in German, the *Ruhrbesetzung*), on August 25, 1925, after the British remained neutral and uncommitted on issues related to economic sanctions rather than occupation of the Ruhr, all relative to German war reparations, on January 11, 1923.[805]

LIPETSK (USSR) FLIGHT TRAINING SCHOOL AND THE *WELTBÜHNE* TRIAL

Such activities were recognized by anti-Nazi Germans and publicized, as in an essay, "Windiges aus der deutschen Luftfahrt," that spoke of German air force training in Lipetsk; it was written by aircraft designer and journalist Walter Kreiser (1898-1958)—under the pseudonym Heinz Jäger—which was published in the March 1929 issue of the magazine *Die Weltbühne* (*The World Stage*), by editor, journalist, anti-Nazi, and pacifist, Carl von Ossietzky (1889-1938). Kreiser was tried for this publication (in *der Weltbühne-Prozess*, the *Weltbühne* Trial) and received a prison sentence for treason and espionage of 18 months; Ossietzky was tried for betrayal of military secrets, found guilty, and sentenced to time in Berlin's Spandau Prison.[806] Ossietzky was released in the Christmas Amnesty of 1932, but arrested on February 28, 1933, the morning after the Reichstag Fire, and sent to KL-Esterwegen, one of the first Nazi concentration camps. Later, he would be awarded the Nobel Prize for Peace, in 1936. At first, officially allowed to travel to Oslo to accept the award, Hitler in a speech at the Kroll Opera House, Berlin, on January 20, 1937, announced that Germans would not be permitted to repeat the "shameful events of the past" (implicitly referring to Ossietzky's acceptance of the Nobel Prize, which Hitler interpreted to indicate a Germany humbled if not humiliated by an award by a foreign source).

As Professor of Peace Studies at the Univ. of Bradford, in Yorkshire, Dr. Peter van den Dungen, wrote of this, "The award to Ossietzky led an outraged Hitler famously to forbid any German henceforth to accept any

---

[804] Brian J. Gordan, "Strategic Deception: The Rearmament of the German Air Force, 1919-39," *Studies in Intelligence*, vol. 62, no. 1 (Extracts, March 2018), pp. 1-10, CIA: CENTER FOR THE STUDY OF INTELLIGENCE (CSI). Gordan works at the Defense Intelligence Agency's UFAC (UNDERGROUND FACILITY ANALYSIS CENTER).

[805] Nicholas Roosevelt, "The Ruhr Occupation," *Foreign Affairs*, vol. 4, no. 1, Oct. 1925, pp. 112-122; Sally Marks, "The Myths of Reparations." *Central European History*, vol. 11, no. 3, Sept. 1978, pp. 231–255, esp. pp. 242-244; Mark Harrison, "Myths of the Great War," CAGE/COMPETETIVE ADVANCE IN TH GLOBAL ECONOMY, ESRC/ECOMIMC & SOCIAL RESEARCH COUNCIL, DEPT. OF ECONOMICS, UNIV. OF WARWICK, no. 188, Mar. 27, 2014; "Occupation of the Ruhr," WIKIPEDIA; "Ruhr Occupation," ENCYCLOPÆDIA BRITANNICA; Conan Fischer, "Ruhr Occupation," INTERNATIONAL ENCYCLOPEDIA OF THE FIRST WORLD WAR: 1914-1918 ONLINE; "Ruhr Occupaiton," SPARTACUS EDUCATIONAL.

[806] "Die Weltbühne: „Denn der Geist setzt sich doch durch"—Carl von Ossietzky, Walter Mehring, Kurt Hiller, Ernst Toller," BERENDSOHN-FORSCHUNGSSTELLE FÜR DEUTSCHE EXILLITERATUR—EXILOGRAPH (UNIV. OF HAMBURG), no. 17, Jan. 2009.

The Hitler Era

of the Nobel prizes."[807] Ossietzky was not given the visa permits required to travel to Norway. He died in a Berlin hospital under Gestapo surveillance, on May 4, 1938, of tuberculosis (and of the harsh treatment he suffered while under Nazi imprisonment). The National Socialist German Government forbade any further German citizens from accepting a Nobel Prize.

Meanwhile, these operations in Lipetsk were finally halted on September 15, 1933, because of growing, more mutually abrasive and hostile ideological differences between Nazi Germany and the USSR. A school focused on chemical warfare, and one for training Germans in the operation of tanks (Panzers), were also closed down, in 1931 and 1933.[808]

During those first years of the Third Reich, there was, as well, the organizing of the male population of Germany into military-like groupings, which included both earlier paramilitary street-fighter militias and boy-scout-looking youth activities, organized under National Socialist ideals (part of the switching into societal conformity). The massive gathering at Nuremberg in the late summer (made an annual event in 1933 and continuing through 1938). These events were, first of all, experiences of high drama and enthusiasm-inspiring activities (for those who accepted the Nazi societal vision), which also were recorded and made into very emotionally-charged films showing the prowess, enthusiasm, deeply-felt comradeship among all of the people attending the Congresses, and the strength and military-like organization of the various Nazi organizations, especially the SA (the Storm Troopers)—only through the 1933 Rally: the SA being decimated in late Spring 1934—the SS, and also the military when it was reconstituted and publicly displayed.

There were also powerful laws decreed at those Congresses, especially in the Congress of 1935, when the Nuremberg Laws were presented. As mentioned, these limited the place of Jews in Germany, annulled the German citizenship of all Jews, transformed their legal status to that of subjects of the Reich. The laws also made any sexual intimacy between (non-Jewish) Germans and (German) Jews a punishable offence. This would apply even to intermarried couples and their children. Punishments used were harassment by having couples stand with placards announcing their having committed acts of racial defilement, to arrest, and ultimately, to execution for crimes against the State. These were announced for all the world to know about. Germany had taken off the kid (soft leather) gloves and was serious about putting Jews in their place (as the National

---

[807] "Germany and the Nobel Prizes," *Nature*, vol. 139, Feb. 6, 1937, pp. 228, 241; Peter van den Dungen, "Hitler and the Nobel Peace Prize," *The Guardian* (UK), Feb. 21, 2003; "Carl von Ossietzky: Biographical," THE NOBEL PRIZE ORGANIZATION; Elisabeth Crawford, "German Scientists and Hitler's Vendetta against the Nobel Prizes," *Historical Studies in the Physical and Biological Sciences*, vol. 31, no. 1, 2000, pp. 37–53.

[808] Walter Meyr, "Schulterschluss mit Koskau," *Der Spiegel*, Apr. 26, 2005. Cf. "German schools and training centres in the USSR 1922-1933," AXIS HISTORY, Apr. 7, 2012.

Socialists defined that). *This was common knowledge not only in Germany itself but quite beyond its borders*. Especially in 1935-1936, the actual political situation in Europe was going through obvious, major changes. On January 13, 1935, a plebiscite voted on the status of the highly industrialized Saar. The nation-wide vote in Germany was for the territory to be fully integrated into the Reich. When German troops marched into the region on March 1, 1935, *there were no military confrontations with the Allied Forces.*

As mentioned just above, *die schwarze Reichswehr* (the Black Reich Defense), organized the training of young men as potential soldiers and pilots of military aircraft, during the 1920s Weimar Republic years, at first with the help of the Soviet Union. Hermann Göring was to continue this in a clandestine manner, but what was secret became not-so-secret. By the end of 1934, it was already known among the British, for example, that there was a significant military growth, obviously part of a larger plan.

Thus, on November 29, 1934, MP Winston Churchill spoke before the Parliament about the German Air Force (Luftwaffe), declaring, that "Germany, already at this moment, has a military air force ... and that this illegal air force is rapidly approaching equality with our own."[809] Further, Churchill added, if things stayed on course (as Britain's funding was defined, and Germany's in-place program was understood), "the German military air force will this time next year be in fact at least as strong as our own, and it may be even stronger. Thirdly on the same basis—that is to say, both sides continuing with their existing program as at present arranged—by the end of 1936—that is, one year farther on, and two years from now—the German military air force will be nearly 50% stronger [than Britain's], and in 1937 nearly double [Britain's]."[810]

This startling news was mostly dismissed in British diplomatic circles, given that Churchill was largely discredited for his colonialist stance on India, which he felt should by all means be kept as part of the British Empire—seen by others as an outmoded political position to urge and maintain). PM Stanley Baldwin gave a reply for the British Government, stating, "I say there is no ground at this moment for undue alarm and still less for panic. There is no immediate menace confronting us or anyone in Europe at this moment—no actual emergency."[811]

In Germany, on November 5, 1937, a meeting took place in Berlin, with Hitler and the representatives of the military, including the Navy, Army, and Air Force. There were important notes on this meeting taken by the Army Adjutant to Hitler, Friedrich Hossbach. His memorandum, the

---

[809] Martin Gilbert, *Winston Churchill: A Life* (1991), Chap. 24: "The Moment of Truth," esp. pp. 535-538; Winston Churchill, "The German Air Menace—November 28, 1934," pp. 171-186 in Winston Churchill, *Speeches on Foreign Affairs and National Defense* (1938), at p. 179; Nicholas Rostow, *Anglo-French Relations 1934-36* (1984), pp. 35-38.

[810] Winston Churchill, "The German Air Menace—November 28, 1934" (just cited), pp. 179-180.

[811] Winston Churchill, "The German Air Menace—November 28, 1934," p. 185.

The Hitler Era 263

Hossbach Memorandum, was found among the documents captured after the war from the Reich AA (*Auswärtiges Amt*), the German Foreign Ministry. It stated that present were the Führer and Chancellor (Hitler), the War Minister and Commander in Chief of the Armed Forces (Field Marshal Werner Fritz von Blomberg), the Commanders-in-Chief of the Army (Colonel General Werner von Fritsch), Navy (Admiral Erich Raeder), and Luftwaffe (Colonel General Hermann Göring), the Foreign Minister (Konstantin von Neurath), and the Army Adjutant to Hitler (Colonel Friedrich Hossbach).[812] Hossbach recorded Hitler's remarks about the growth in demand for food of the German people, given the greater employment from the strong development of the armaments industries, which could not be met from within Germany itself, and was precarious because of the British control of the seas. (This had been established by the British blockade of shipments to Germany during World War I.) The solution to Germany's politico-economic dilemmas, in short, lay in creating more *Lebensraum*, living space, for the German people; Hitler stated that "Germany's future was therefore wholly conditional upon the solving of the need for space, and such a solution could be sought, of course, only for a foreseeable period of about one to three generations.... It is not a matter of acquiring population but of gaining space for agricultural use."[813] This focus has been seen as a sign of the nineteenth-century mentality of Hitler's, not consistent with twentieth-century industrialization of much of Europe, a "peculiarly alienated, atavistically reactionary Hitler Germany [*dieses eigentümlich entfremdete, atavistisch rückfällig gewordene Deutschland*]".[814]

Hitler also spoke to the problem of Britain and France: "German policy had to reckon with two hate-inspired antagonists, Britain and France, to whom a German colossus in the center of Europe was a thorn in the flesh, and [with that] both countries were opposed to any further strengthening of Germany's position either in Europe or overseas."[815] As often, Hitler saw the reluctance of other countries to allow Germany free rein in its

---

[812] The Hossbach Memorandum, dated November 10, 1937, gave notes of the meeting of November 5). It is Document 19 in *Documents on German Foreign Policy, 1918-1945; Series D, 1937-1945, Volume I: From Neurath to Ribbentrop, September 1937-September 1938*, pp. 36-37, at THE AVALON PROJECT, YALE UNIV. SCHOOL OF LAW.

[813] Hitler's remarks here from the Hossbach Memorandum, unless otherwise cited.

[814] Richard Weikart, *Hitler's Ethic: The Nazi Pursuit of Evolutionary Progress* (2009), p. 17; Joachim C. Fest, *Hitler* (Ger. text), p. 665; *Hitler* (Eng.), p. 485; Anthony J. Nicholls, *Weimar and the Rise of Hitler*, p. 190; Konrad H. Jarausch, "Removing the Nazi Stain? The Quarrel of the German Historians," *German Studies Review*, vol. 11, no. 2, 1988, pp. 285–301. *In other ways, National Socialism was quite modern*, as in Hitler's use of the airplane in 1920s campaigning, the use of the radio for German propaganda, and then the euthanasia program and train-employed massive deaths by Zyklon B with crematoria to dispose of corpses. See also Richard J. Evans, *The Third Reich in History and Memory* (2015), pp. 12, 75.

[815] Hitler's remarks here also from the Hossbach Memorandum.

desire for expansionism and hegemony as an indication that these countries wanted to annihilate Germany, calling on defensive pro-active attacks by the German military on these enemies before they could strike first. Hitler saw a time constraint, given its present military preparedness, which could become obsolete in time. He, Goebbels, and others were aware of the British Defense White Paper of February 15, 1937, which projected expenditures for military improvement for the five-year period, 1937-1942, to amount to £1,500 million.[816] This was no mean amount!

This re-armamenting or modernization of British military capabilities[817] was a response to the coming to power of Hitler and the National Socialist government, as well as Germany's subsequent withdrawal on October 14, 1933, from both the League of Nations[818] and the Geneva Disarmament Conference.[819] In addition to which there was intelligence of the German beginning to rebuild its army and air force, all prohibited according to the Versailles Treaty. (The Germans knew this; the British knew this; the French knew this; the Poles knew this; it was no secret among intelligence agencies active at the time.) Hitler realized that an arms race was on and that time was not on Germany's side. In short, time was running out. Hitler's remark commenting on this at the Hossbach Conference, in November 1937, was, "Our relative strength would decrease in relation to the rearmament which would by then have been carried out by the rest of the world." Hitler at that meeting also expressed concerns not only about re-armamentation going on by the British and French, but also by the Czechs and Austrians.[820] As Hitler wrote in *Mein Kampf*, "*Deutschland wird entweder Weltmacht oder überhaupt nicht sein*" (Germany will either be a world power or not be at all).[821] Still, there was the development of

---

[816] "The British White Paper on Defense Source," *Bulletin of International News (Chatham House: The Royal Institute of International Affairs)*, Vol. 16, No. 4 (Feb. 25, 1939), pp. 14-17, CHATHAMHOUSE.ORG.

[817] John Paul Harris, *The War Office and Rearmament 1935-39*, KING'S COLLEGE LONDON (OR KCL) (1983).

[818] "The Third Reich: Foreign Policy," *German Culture*, Jul. 15, 2018. This was confirmed in a formal letter dated Oct. 19, 1933, from German Foreign Minister Konstantin Freiherr von Neurath to the Secretary-general of the League of Nations, Joseph Avenol. See image of letter, at "Withdrawal of Germany from the League of Nations: Letter from Konstantin von Neurath," WORLD DIGITAL LIBRARY.

[819] Also called the World Disarmament Conference and the Conference for the Reduction and Limitation of Armaments.

[820] Hitler felt that Germany was already falling behind in this arms race. See Manfred Messerschmidt, "Foreign Policy and Preparation for War," pp. 636-637, in *Germany and the Second World War, Vol. I: The Build-up of Germany Aggression*, Wilhelm Deist, Manfred Messerschmidt, Hans-Erich Volkmann, Wolfram Wette, eds. (1991); cf. William Carr, *Arms, Autarky and Aggression: Study in German Foreign Policy, 1933-1939* (1972), pp. 73-78.

[821] Adolf Hitler, *Mein Kampf*, Vol. II, Chap. XIV (Eastern Orientation or Eastern Policy—*Ostorientierung oder Ostpolitik*), Eng. pp. 933-967, at p. 950; Ger. pp. 726-758, at p. 742. Dietrich Aigner, "Hitler's Ultimate Aim: A Programme of World Dominion?" in *Aspects of the Third Reich*, Hannsjoachim Wolfgang Koch, ed. (1985),

a powerful military in the Third Reich, along with claims for rights to control over lands with *Volksdeutsche* as the majority population. Hossbach, on November 10, 1937, recorded that Hitler estimated that the best time for dealing with this—given his understanding of the European focus on re-armamenting—as no later than 1943-1945. Hitler noted that "the world was expecting our attack and was increasing its counter-measures from year to year. It was while the rest of the world was still preparing its defenses that we were obliged to take the offensive. Nobody knew today what the situation would be in the years 1943-45. One thing only was certain, that we could not wait longer." And so, with this, "the annexation of Czechoslovakia and Austria would mean an acquisition of foodstuffs for 5 to 6 million people, on the assumption that the compulsory emigration of 2 million people from Czechoslovakia and 1 million people from Austria was practicable.[822] (This point assumes the contemplated eventuality of Germany expulsing the populations of those countries to make space for Germans.) The incorporation of these two States with Germany meant, from the politico-military point of view, a substantial advantage, with shorter and better frontiers, the freeing of forces for other purposes, and the possibility of creating new units up to a level of about 12 divisions, that is, 1 new division per million habitants."

The claim of simply wanting to protect German minorities from unjust treatment *was replaced by German interests in taking over the lands of Eastern Europe for an expansion of Germany*, with Germans populating these territories after the natives were expulsed or killed. If Germany made use of this war to settle the Czech and Austrian questions, it was to be assumed that Britain—herself at war with Italy—would decide not to act against Germany. Without British support, a warlike action by France against Germany was not to be expected.

This was late 1937, and Hitler could still imagine that a move against these two neighboring countries would not bring on war with Britain or France. (History would prove Hitler's short-term understanding to be correct.) The next years saw the building up of the German military, the passing of laws against the rights and liberties of German Jews (including many decrees before and after the Nuremburg Laws of 1935 and 1936), the taking over of the Ruhr, and the remilitarization of the Rhineland.

THE RUHR AND THE RHINELAND BLUFF

According to the dictates of the Versailles Treaty (in particular, its Articles 42, 43, and 180, discussed above), which Germany signed reluctantly, and also of the Locarno Treaties (October 1925), which Germany entered into voluntarily, there was to be no militarization of the Rhineland. These treaties held that the Rhineland should remain demilitarized, with guarantees for French and German safety against one another by Italy and Britain, in the case of any aggression. This made the

---

pp. 251-266, at pp. 251-252: to be a *Weltmacht* (world power) is not synonymous with establishing world domination.

[822] "Hossbach Memorandum," AVALON.LAW.YALE.EDU/IMT/HOSSBACH.ASP.

Western border of Germany unprotected (and under potential threat of invasion), *thus guarantor of Germany's not initiating any aggression on its Eastern Front*, which could well have Germany entangled in two wars on two fronts at the same time. And yet, despite these treaty-defined restrictive conditions, on March 7, 1936, several months before the start of the Spanish Civil War, there was the peaceful entry of German military into the Rhineland, which was forbidden by the Versailles Treaty. Despite the breaking of the treaty by Germany, this occupation was not opposed by British, French, or Belgian troops. The Versailles and Locarno Treaties prohibited this occupation, but in Hitler's opinion, the Franco-Soviet Pact (that had declared mutual assistance in case of German aggression) abrogated the Locarno Treaty of 1935. Hitler used his understanding to justify Germany's right to remilitarize the Rhineland.

How was this? Of Hitler's occupation of the Rhineland, his interpreter, Paul Schmidt, wrote that Hitler justified this action by the statement that Franco-Russian Pact constituted such a grave breach of the Locarno Agreement [*einen so schweren Bruch des Lokarno-Abkommens*] that the latter no longer existed [*daß es aufgehört habe zu existieren*], and that therefore Germany was no longer bound by its provisions concerning the demilitarized zone of the Rhineland. To the French communication that Germany has broken the Locarno Treaty [*der Locarno-Vertrag*], Reich official channels replied, referring to the Franco-Soviet Pact, "France broke it first" (*Frankreich hat ihn zuerst gebrochen*). Schmidt placed the occupation on March 7 as occurring "shortly after the ratification of the Franco-Soviet Pact of mutual assistance" (*kurtz nachder Ratifizierung des französisch-sowjetischen Beistandspaktes*).[823] In any case, Hitler ordered the reoccupation of the Rhineland, reserving for himself the right to issue further counter-measures. (These were known to be the order to "a hasty retreat back over the Rhine"[824] in the case of any military opposition by the French, Belgians, or British.) Hitler knew that he had only four brigades of soldiers (at most, 16,000 men), versus much greater armies of potential enemies. Hitler's interpreter, Paul Schmidt wrote, further:

> More than once, even during the war, I heard Hitler say, "The forty-eight hours after the march into the Rhineland [*Einmarsch ins Rhineland*] were the most nerve-racking [*die aufregendste Zeitspanne*] in my life. He always added: "If the French had then marched into the Rhineland, we would have had to withdraw with our tails between our legs [the German has: *mit Schimpf und*

---

[823] Paul Schmidt, *Statist auf diplomatischer Bühne 1923-1945: Erlebnisse des Chefdolmetschers im Auswärtigen Amt mit den Staatsmännern Europas* (1949), p. 320. Eng. partial tr., *Hitler's Interpreter* (1951), p. 40. A literal tr. of the Ger. title would be: *Bystander on the Diplomatic Stage 1923-1945: Experiences of the Chief Interpreter in the Foreign Office with the Statesmen of Europe*. Cf. Alan Bullock, *Hitler: A Study in Tyranny* (1962), p. 345.

[824] William L. Shirer, *The Rise and Fall of the Third Reich*, p. 291.

Schande wieder zurückziehen, more literally: to draw back again with indignity and disgrace], for the military resources at our disposal would have been wholly inadequate for even a moderate resistance [*keineswegs auch nur zu einem mäßigen Widerstand ausgericht*]."[825]

One commentator in Germany remarked about this period, "Amidst all that Olympic goodwill [concerning the upcoming Berlin Summer Olympics of 1936], few observers recognized the importance of Hitler's decision to remilitarize the Rhineland [months earlier] in March of 1936. Strenuously opposed by most top generals, it was a gamble which could have easily brought about his downfall. Had the French decided to send in just a token force to stop the German troops, who were not equipped to fight, it would have been over. But the French did nothing. Hitler triumphed, and his appetite for future adventures was whetted."[826]

This simple matter of not doing anything to confront this German military action—its breaking conditions of the Versailles Treaty—was a great non-action! In the later opinion of an envoy of the Polish-Government-in-Exile during the war, Jan Karski (whose life has been described as "a masterpiece of courage, integrity, and humanism"[827]), in immediate reply to the interviewer's question about whether the Holocaust might have been prevented, stated: "Prevented? Prevented, definitely! If the Western world, particularly France and England, prepared themselves and threatened Hitler, in 1935, 1936, 1937."[828]

So that that relatively minor action, the countering of the entry by German troops into the Rhineland with a stronger force of British and French troops, *if it had taken at the time*, Karski suggests, would have blocked events that later made the Holocaust possible. This is nothing more than a speculation, of course, but, yet, it is from someone who knew the situation at that time quite well.

The geopolitical military significance of Germany's occupying the Rhineland was that it no longer was vulnerable to invasion from the West, and, so, open to breaking the peace on its Eastern front. Germany's becoming remilitarized in the Rhineland was thus a significant step toward the greater eventual threat of German aggression, especially in the east.

There was basically no will by the British, the French, or the Belgians to take military action against this move. For example, in 1936, after former British Prime Minister David Lloyd George (PM during the First World War) visited Hitler in Germany, he was interviewed by the British press. His remarks were then published in a newspaper report, expressing his great admiration for Hitler: "As to his popularity, especially among the

---

[825] Paul Schmidt, *Statist auf diplomatischer Bühne 1923-1945*, p. 320; Eng., *Hitler's Interpreter*, pp. 40-41.
[826] Henry Simon, *Third Reich Diaries*, p. 55.
[827] Elie Wiesel, Foreword to E. Thomas Wood and Stanisław M. Jankowski, *Karski: How One Man Tried to Stop the Holocaust* (1994), at p. viii.
[828] *Karski interviewed on Nashville TV*, 1996, YOUTUBE, at 2:20-2:50.

youth of Germany, there can be no manner of doubt. The old trust him; the young idolize him. It is not the admiration accorded to a popular leader. It is the worship of a national hero who has saved his country from utter despondence and degradation."[829] And yet in another London paper several days earlier, on September 23, 1936, Lloyd George was quoted as saying, in a judgment later proven mistaken, "Germany does not want war. Hitler does not want war. He is a most remarkable personality, one of the greatest I have ever met in the whole of my life, and I have met some very great men." He added, "Affection is a quite inadequate word to describe the attitude of the German people towards Hitler. It amounts almost to worship. I have never seen anything like it."

And, concerning the treatment of Jews, Lloyd George was quoted in this same article, as putting German anti-Semitism into a broader context, and mollifying any criticism of the Third Reich, "I have always thought, and still think, that the persecution of Jews in Germany has been a great misfortune. But Germany is not the only country that has persecuted Jews. We must not forget the pogroms in Russia and in other European countries."[830]

Lloyd George was perhaps thinking of the many pogroms of Jews in Ukraine in the late nineteenth and early twentieth centuries. These included the Kiev pogroms in 1881, triggered by the assassination of Czar Alexander II, in 1905, with some 100 Jews killed, and in 1919, the bloodiest of these three. In these pogroms, Jewish villages (*shtetlekh*) were attacked, pillaged, with murder, serious wounding, and raping of women. There was also a famous pogrom in the *shtetl* (village) of Kishinev, in the spring of 1903, in which 49 Jews were killed, many Jewish women raped, and 1,500 homes damaged, bringing great outrage in some circles. Further, on a Sabbath in March of 1911, a young Russian boy, Andrei Yushchinsky, disappeared and was later found murdered. A Jewish man, Menachem Mendel Beilis, was arrested and tried for a ritual murder. A Kiev detective, Nikolai Krasovsky, concluded that Beilis was innocent. *Consequently, Krasovsky lost his career but continued his investigations, and later named those who had actually killed Yushchinsky.*[831] In the Beilis trial, which did not take place until 1913, there were witnesses who

---

[829] "David Lloyd George, Prime Minister of England during World War I, with comments on a visit to Germany and meeting with Hitler," *Daily Express* (London) Sept. 17, 1936, pp. 12, 17—online at "Llloyd George and Hitler," WORLD FUTURE FUND. His visit was also discussed in "I Just Returned from Germany—I Talked with Hitler," online at NATIONALISTS.ORG (in PDF format). Cf. Kenneth O. Morgan, "Lloyd George and Germany, *The Historical Journal*, vol. 39, no. 3, 1996, pp. 755-766, esp. p. 764.

[830] "Nazi Regime. Lloyd George's Visit. Hitler's Hold on People. Desire for Peace," *The Post* (London), Sept. 23, 1936; passage quoted at "David Lloyd George's pro-Nazi views," FORUM.AXISHISTORY.COM (search text for "pogroms").

[831] See Krasovsky statement at pp. 58-59 in "The Beilis Affair," *The American Jewish Year Book 5675*, Herman Bernstein, ed. (1914), pp. 19–89; "A List of Events of 5762 and Necrology," entry for Oct. 6, 1911, p. 157, *The American Jewish Year Book 5673*, Herbert Friedenwald, ed. (1912).

testified that they had seen Beilis at work that Sabbath—Beilis was known, against pious Jewish practices, to work on the Sabbath, regularly, and hence was not free to have carried out an abduction. Witnesses who presented the belief in Jewish blood rituals on cross-examination showed their ignorance of some basic Jewish principles and teachings; knowledgeable Christian professors explained away the possibility of blood rituals, given basic Jewish law; the jury, composed only of Christians, found the accused innocent! The trial brought worldwide attention, with many criticisms of Czarist Russian endemic anti-Semitism.

And this violence was not especially new in Europe, Lloyd George might have added. After all, looking back, in the 1600s (from 1648-1657), there were major insurrections and battles between the populations of the Polish-Lithuanian Confederation (currently, the Eastern European territories of Belarus, Ukraine, and Moldavia). These lands included Poles, Lithuanians, Ukrainians, Ruthenians, Galicians, and Podolians. In this civil war, both local Roman Catholics and Jews were targeted, among others considered enemies of each group. Earlier in Jewish history was the massacre of Jews by the armies of Bohdan Khmelnytsky (1595-1657), the Ukrainian nationalist. He was also known as Bogdan, with family name also Khmelnitsky or Chmielnicki). However many Jews were actually killed (most estimates are at around 100,000, while a few suggest as few as 20,000), the shock was enough to set off a messianic vision, in hopes of an agent to save the Jews. This led to the declaration by a rabbi, Sabbatai Tsvi (1626-1676), born in Smyrna (İzmir) in the Ottoman Empire, that he was the long-awaited Messiah: hence, the Sabbatean Movement. After various travels, on arrival in Constantinople (İstanbul) in 1666, he was captured by the Ottoman Turks. They offered three options: a test of his messiah status by a volley of arrows shot by Turkish military, to be impaled, or to convert. On September 16, 1666, he converted in front of the Sultan. This ended the hopes some had in him, although some persisted in holding him to be the Messiah, despite this outcome. Even earlier, the Jews were expelled from England by an edict dated July 18, 1290 issued by King Edward I (1239-1307). The Jews had been in England since 1066. They were not invited to return until 1657, under the government of Oliver Cromwell. They were expelled from France in 1182, under Philip II (1165-1223), called *Dieudonné* (God-given), but allowed to return in 1198, presumably for fiscal reasons. Under Louis IX (1214-1270), called Saint Louis, some 20,000 copies of the Talmud were burned in Paris, by his royal order—a saint to some but not to all, we might say. There was a banishment of Jews who had made loans to French Christians, but this was ultimately not carried out in full, Saint Louis leaving for the Crusades, and dying in Tunisia. Of course, the Jews were also expelled from Spain in 1492, given three months to sell their property or to leave behind whatever remained in Spain when they left for other lands.

And, if we focus with Lloyd George on the treatment of Jews in the Western world in the period in which he was discussing, the early middle of the twentieth century, we may note that there were measures taken to limit the position of Jews, which were carried out in the 1930s not only in Third Reich, but also, for example, in Poland, when an anti-Semitic government came into power. This involved *numerus clausus*, which limited the number of Jews who were admitted to various schools of higher education. They came to be known as bench laws. These were made more limiting as the Polish government turned more anti-Semitic during the 1930s, before the invasion by the German military.

In the USA, also in the 1930s, there were quotas limited the number of Jews in clubs, in universities—Harvard, for example, had 25% of its incoming freshman class in 1925, which it lowered by 1933 to 12%—and in property ownership, often with covenants (legally binding clauses for any sale of property) that set restrictions, against Jews, blacks, Catholics, or others the local resident community in question felt to be undesirable in their neighborhoods.

There were also various restrictions on Jews in other lands, including France and Britain. Then, there was the phenomenon of the anti-Semitic Canadian-born Catholic Priest, Father Charles Coughlin, who had a church, the Little Flower Church, in Royal Oak, Michigan, outside of Detroit, who was the leader of the Christian Front, and who also had a radio program spouting vitriolic anti-Semitic messages, garbed in a religious-political-patriotic dress.

So, Lloyd George did have a point, that Hitler and the National Socialists were not the only ones with an anti-Semitic bias, with related actions—even if it had its limits: to be one of several with a fault is not because of that to have no fault at all; that there were other pogroms and programs of violence against Jews, of course, was and is quite true, although we might have an uncomfortable sense that to call the treatment of the Jews of Germany, a great misfortune, even at that *relatively* benign stage in the story, was a nicely delicate understatement. Still, it is understandable that people might not want to criticize another group for their actions, even if despicable and morally reprehensible, especially if any somewhat similar actions were being carried out by one's own people. We are still a species that is very wary of self-questioning, and, even less so, of self-criticism. And yet, David Lloyd George and his politically-nuanced statements aside, during all of this period, the popularity and public support for Hitler and the National Socialist Party and Government did not show any visible signs of weakening.

All was good, perhaps—unless one was sympathetic to the plight of those whose lives were being constrained, limited, and subject to violence, or if one was in fact a member of one of the groups seen as inferior and to be attacked and ultimately eliminated from the German world: this would include not only Jews but those who were physically disabled or mentally ill, homosexuals, those of opposing political viewpoints, the Romani people—including the Sinti, Roma, Romanichal, and related tribes, peoples at least formerly speaking Romani—to be joined by Germans of Slavic ancestry, and on and on. These incidents would fade in the light of what was to come after the German invasion of the Soviet Union!

The Hitler Era

THE ANSCHLUß—ANNEXATION—OF AUSTRIA

The remilitarization of the Rhineland would be followed in early 1938 by the creation of the Greater Reich, resulting from the annexation of Austria. Code-named *Unternehmen Otto* (Operation Otto), it would also be known as d*er Blumenkrieg*, the War of Flowers, given the large number of bouquets of flowers offered the entering German military by the pro-German population.

And yet, this annexation would see intense persecution of Jews and also of others who were not inspired by Nazi values and governance.

In Britain, Winston Churchill wrote about this in "Germany's Discipline for the Old Austria," in the London *The Daily Telegraph and Morning Post* of July 6, 1938, "It is easy to ruin and persecute the Jews, to steal their property; to drive them out of every profession and employment; to fling a Rothschild into a prison or a sponging house [temporary debtor's prison, where the prisoners were "sponged" of whatever money they had on their person at the time of arrest]; to compel Jewish ladies to scrub the pavements; and to maroon clusters of helpless refugees on islands in the Danube, and these sports continue with satisfaction. But 300,000 Jews in Vienna present a problem of large dimensions and [of an] intractable quality to a policy of extirpation [complete surgical excision] .... But it is part of the policy of German Nazism to treat with exemplary rigor all persons of German race and speech who have not identified themselves with Nazi interests and ambitions."[832]

Times changed in the twentieth century, which showed itself to be less disturbed by the killing of innocents (and not only of Jews), perhaps due in part to the slaughter of millions of soldiers and civilians in the Great War. Mass shootings, called the Holocaust (Shoah) by bullets,[833] and continuing with organized mass killings by poison gas, especially Zyklon B and crematoria with their multiple ovens, were at first met with this greater insensitivity, as after the killing of Jews just outside of Kiev, in the ravine of Babi Yar, where in the two days of September 29-30, 1941 (some 38 years after the Kishinev pogrom mentioned earlier), there were 33,771 Jews reported killed—according to precise but perhaps partial, and so overall inaccurate, under-estimations, reports by the *Einsatzgruppen* carrying out the killings—which was more than 669 times the number of Jews killed at Kishinev! *The outrage, when the mass shootings were learned about, was not comparably more intense*. Again, the numbers given in German official reports often quoted, are perhaps underestimates: Other German documents[834] indicated that the shootings took place not

---

[832] Martin Gilbert, *Churchill and the Jews: A Lifelong Friendship*, pp. 63, 145. Full quote of text found in the newspaper article itself.

[833] Patrick Desbois (a French Catholic Priest; founder of Ehad-In Unam), *Porteur de mémoires: Sur les traces de la Shoah par balles* (2007).

[834] *Operations Situation Report No. 106, Einsatzgruppe C [under Col. Paul Blobel]*, Oct. 7, 1941. See Victoria Khiterer, "Babi Yar: The Tragedy of Kiev's Jews," *Brandeis Graduate Journal*, vol. 2, 2004, pp. 1-16, at p. 7.

only on those two days, but continued for five days in all (thus, going from September 29-October 3, 1941, Jews killed in those later days not counted in the earlier counting); this longer time of killings is corroborated by eye-witness reports of Ukrainians. In general, the story of a single tormented family can be more powerful than statistics: "One million human corpses is a concept too bizarre and too fantastical for normal mental comprehension."[835] The total number of Jews killed in mass shootings those five days (not the three of the official statement by the SS) has been estimated from a thorough review of relevant data by the Ukrainian-American historian Victoria Khiterer[836] to amount to more than 100,000 Jews.[837] She estimates the pre-war population of Jews in Kiev to be some 20% (175,000) of the total population; for historian-novelist Anatoli Kuznetsov, things were not much better for non-Jewish residents of Kiev. He wrote, "Before the war Kiev had a population of about 900,000. Towards the end of the German occupation about 180,000 remained, or a great many less than lay dead in Babi Yar alone. One in three of the inhabitants of Kiev was killed and if you add to this figure the number those who died of hunger, who failed to return from Germany and so forth, then it appears that every second person must have perished."[838] In charge of this was Colonel Paul Blobel, later head of *Aktion 1005* (also called *Sonderaktion 1005*). Blobel was tried and hung after the war.[839]

Despite the actual violence, we see a peace-loving façade of Hitler in his speech before the Reichstag on October 6, 1939 (soon after the German invasion of Poland), speaking of a Geneva convention that had outlawed (for "civilized" countries) violence against non-combatants, and spoke of his hope that one day there would be an overall prohibition of "conflict against women and children and against non-combatants in general."[840] *This statement of a civilized attitude on Hitler's part is most remarkable, giving the mass shootings in the USSR and killings in Nazi concentration and extermination camps going on at that same time!*

Here we might consider some events in the 1930s. Earlier—soon after the Nuremberg Party Congress of 1935, with its declarations mentioned above—on October 3, 1935, Italy invaded Ethiopia (Abyssinia) from its neighboring colony, Italian Somaliland, raising alarm in nearby British-controlled Egypt. The League of Nations made its demands; Italy left the League on December 13, 1937. Italy declared victory with the capture of the capital, Addis Ababa, on May 5, 1936, with the final formal battle on February 19, 1937. The war actually dragged on into 1939. In the mid-

---

[835] NT-TWC-Green, vol. 4, p. 427.

[836] Professor of History Victoria Khiterer holds a degree in history from Kiev State Pedagogical Institute, a doctorate from Russian State Humanitarian Univ., Moscow, and a PhD from Brandeis Univ.

[837] Victoria Khiterer, "Babi Yar: The Tragedy of Kiev's Jews" (just cited), p. 7.

[838] A. Anatoli (Anatoli Kuznetsov), *Babi Yar: A Document in the Form of a Novel* (New, Complete, Uncensored Version), David Floyd, tr. (1970), p. 408.

[839] Judge Michael A. Musmanno, *The Eichmann Kommandos* (1961), pp. 145-155.

[840] See *Hitler's Speech 6 Oct 1939, Part 4: A Prophecy*, YOUTUBE, at 7:15-7:50.

1930s in Britain, there was an informal national referendum of the public's faith in the League of Nations, its desire for peace, and its readiness to face down aggressive nations to maintain peace, even while knowing that this confrontation could lead to war. Taken in late 1934, the results were tabulated and released in early 1935. Somewhat surprisingly, 11.6 million British citizens partook in this survey (more than one-third of the adult British population). *In what goes against one understanding of the British attitude against a confrontational attitude*, 60% supported action against aggressor nations, even if it might mean war. *This certainly goes against the idea that the British wanted peace at all costs in those years.*[841] Perhaps Neville Chamberlain's and David Lloyd George's fear-based concerns were not widely shared by the British public.

THE SPANISH CIVIL WAR AND US BIG BUSINESS

Preceding the Nuremberg Congress of 1936, just before the beginning of the 1936 Berlin Summer Olympics (August 1-16, 1936), there was the last of three elections for the Spanish Second Republic, held on February 16, 1936, with leftist parties receiving the majority of seats in the one-chambered Spanish parliament; Manuel Azaña became the new Prime Minister. The rightest parties were quite dissatisfied with these election results; on July 18, 1936, Generalísimo Francisco Franco, calling himself *el Caudillo*,[842] declared his program of freeing Spain from its left-wing government. Franco had the support of the royalty, the *Falange* (the Spanish fascist party), and the Catholic Church—these last two groups were opposed to anything socialist, anarchist,[843] or communist—and, as well, although not formally and not publicly, the German Nazi and the Italian Fascist governments. The Civil War began in Spanish Morocco, on July 17, 1936; the war ended on April 1, 1939. Quite promptly, on July 29, 1936, transports of Spanish soldiers in German Junkers transport planes began, with Italian Savoia-Marchetti SM-81 bombers providing air cover for sea transports of military to support Franco, starting on August 5, 1936. Britain, France, and the United States declared neutrality and

---

[841] J. A. Thompson, "The Peace Ballot and the Public," *Albion: A Quarterly Journal Concerned with British Studies*, vol. 13, no. 4 (Winter 1981), pp. 381-392. Cf. "The 'Peace Ballot' of 1934-35," CHURCHILL COLLEGE, CAMBRIDGE.

[842] The term *caudillo*, a military leader, is said to derive from the Latin (*caput, capitus*, head, and *capitellum*, small head—but this P to a D is a questionable derivation). It was used in the reign (718-734) of the Prince of Asturias, Don Pelayo—in Arabic, Belai al-Rumi, Belai the Roman (non-Muslim), and then in the *Reconquista* (the reconquest of Spain back into Christian rulership, from the Moors). Cf. the Spanish national hero called *El Cid Campeador* (the Champion Cid)—a title for Rodrigo Díaz de Vivar (1043-1099 CE), using an Arabic word (*Cid*, from *sa'id* or *sayyid*, a title of respect). Arabic *qā'id* (plural *quwwād*) means master or leader: from *quwad* to *caud* is not a far shift, and with Spanish *-illo*, a diminuitive suffix, we have *caudillo*. Whatever its etymology, the title for General Franco, *Caudillo*, is parallel to *Führer* (leader)! See "Don Pelayo," ES.WIKIPEDIA.ORG.

[843] Rudolf Rocker, *Anarcho-syndicalism: Theory and Practice: An Introduction to a Subject Which the Spanish War Has Brought into Overwhelming Prominence*.

general non-involvement, while Franco had the support of Mussolini's Italy, Hitler's Germany, and Portugal. *Significantly, some large American companies did not respect the neutrality the US Government had declared.*

Individual citizens from a variety of countries went to fight for the Nationalists (Franco forces), or for the Republicans (Anarchist—more precisely and informatively, Anarcho-syndicalist—Socialist, Catalan, and Communist forces). Thus, some American citizens against Fascism and Nazism went to Spain as part of the International Brigades (many Americans were in the Lincoln Brigade) on the side of the Republicans; citizens of a number of countries, in their own zeal against any Communist governmental power, joined the Nationalist forces under Franco.[844]

As just mentioned, and rather significantly, a number of powerful private US businesses gave extensive support to the Franco side. US commercial interests, wanting to act against Communism and to protect their threatened financial interests, supported Franco and the Nationalists in practical ways. At the very beginning of the war, the Texas Oil Company (also known as Texaco) rerouted tankers that were headed for Spain (and the Republic of those fighting the Nationalists), and had those ships head, instead, to Tenerife (one of the Canary Islands), with the petroleum being processed there (into gasoline) and given to Franco on credit. Ford, Studebaker, and General Motors sold 12,000 trucks to the Nationalists of Franco. Texas Oil Company sold some 2 million tons of oil on credit to the Nationalists during 1936-1939, the years of the Spanish Civil War.[845]

There was a minimal fine for such actions by the US Government but these practices continued through the Spanish Civil War. We would see the same sort of business activities between American corporations and the Third Reich, through to the end of the war—despite the federal prohibition through the Trading with the Enemy Act; Britain had a similar law, for both world wars and beyond. More on that, below.

With an explicit expression of Franco Spain's appreciation to American business, the General Director for Foreign Policy during the Franco regime, a very high-ranking official in the Spanish Ministry of Foreign Affairs, who at the end of the Spanish Civil War was the Undersecretary at the Foreign Ministry (*el subsecretario de Asuntos Exteriores*), José María Doussinague y Teixidor (1894-1967), stated in 1945,[846] "Without American petroleum,

---

[844] The fictional story—and film, *The Prime of Miss Jean Brodie* (1969)—of an Edinburgh school teacher, Miss Jean Brodie (who romanticizes Mussolini and Hitler), with one of her students going to Spain to join her brother, thinking he is fighting for the Nationalists (but, actually, for the Republicans); the girl dies en route in a train crash: a story filled with misunderstandings and distortions of the period.

[845] James W. Cortada, "Economy, Nationalist," in *Historical Dictionary of the Spanish Civil War, 1936-1939*, James W. Cortada, ed. (1982), pp. 178-179.

[846] Ramón Tamames, *La República: La era de Franco* (1988), p. 144. The repeated adjective, *americano*, can mean: pertaining to the Americas, to its early natives, the Amerindians, to the USA (example: *café americano*), etc. See here *Diccionario de la lengua española*, REAL ACADEMIA ESPAÑOLA, 23rd ed. (2014). The context here implies that *americano* is being used in this last, more limited and

without American trucks, without American credits (*Sin el petróleo americano, sin los camiones americanos, sin los créditos americanos*), we never would have won the war (*nunca hubiésemos ganado la guerra*)." *This, of course, represents quite a significant thankful admission.*

Leaving aside the formal neutrality of the US Government and the ways in which some US businesses circumvented that legality, elsewhere, there were other massive loans to Franco; for example, the Vatican joined in, in its animosity to "Godless" Communism.

Helping out Franco's forces was the Luftwaffe, the German Air Force, begun in violation of Versailles Treaty conditions, in 1933, directed by Hermann Göring, and assisted by Erhard Milch (1892-1972).[847] Milch, earlier director of Deutsche Lufthansa (then and now a German national airline), was given the role as State Secretary in the Reich Ministry of Aviation, of the Luftwaffe (RLM), then to manage armament production, and in this, beginning in 1933, secretly to build up the Luftwaffe.[848] (By the beginning of World War II, Milch had attained the rank of General. More on Milch, below.)

Both the Third Reich and Mussolini's Italy contributed warplanes, tanks, and military assistance to Franco. Germany sent the Condor Legion, military personnel from the army and Luftwaffe. With this, the Condor Legion, going against the principle of the military attacking military targets only, bombed a civilian population on April 26, 1937, in the Basque town of Guernica (in Basque, known as Gernikara) in northern Spain. This shocked the world with its attack on a civilian population: 1,654 people were killed, 889 wounded; Franco denied it even took place.

The destruction of the city of Guernica represented the devastating power of bombardment by air over civilian populations. The Luftwaffe in this gained experience and a sense of their own capacities; we would see

---

specific sense here, referring specifically to the USA. The statement by José María Doussinague y Teixidor was quoted by Associated Press newsman Charles S. Foltz, Jr., in 1945. Cf. Juan Manuel Fernández Fernández-Cuesta, *Información y Política exterior en la transición española, 1973-1986* (2015), pp. 207, 211, 235-239.

[847] Milch was generally considered to be half-Jewish, his father being Jewish. But his mother pleaded the case that her children did not have her husband as their father. Instead, she claimed to have borne all six from an incestuous relationship with her uncle, who was also Aryan. *Was bearing a child with a Jewish mate seen as worse than a Christian (Aryan) incestuous birth?* Milch was declared an Aryan and for him to be welcomed into the new Reich. See "Erhard Milch," WIKIPEDIA.

[848] The secret establishment of the Luftwaffe was described as the disguised Luftwaffe (*getarnten Luftwaffe*), already being developed in the 1920s, with the help of the Soviet Union (another one of the apparently incongruous joint ventures of Nazi and a Communist governments, but which served each side temporarily), and certainly by July 1933: see Nicolaus von Below, *At Hitler's Side: The Memoirs of Hitler's Luftwaffe Adjutant* (2001), p. 12; tr. of *Als Hitlers Adjutant 1937-1945* (1980), p. 13. Milch was later in charge of the air campaign in the invasion of Norway, promoted to Field Marshal, and in May 1940, awarded the *Ritterkreuz* (the Knight's Cross, one of the highest military honors in the Third Reich). See Bryan Mark Rigg, *Untold Story of Hitler's Jewish Soldiers and Racial Laws*, BOOK TV-CSPAN2, Jul. 22, 2003, at 17:05-19:55; Fritz Thyssen, *I Paid Hitler*, pp. 136-137.

this played out against Rotterdam, which was heavily bombed in the brief war of invasion by the Wehrmacht on May 14, 1940 (known as the Rotterdam Blitz), which was carried out after a cease-fire had already been negotiated and agreed upon. Pablo Picasso—Pablo Diego Ruiz y Picasso, 1881-1973; taking his mother's name, Picasso, with its Italian spelling—in that same year of 1937 painted a powerful mural-sized image. The mural measured almost 11.5 ft. high by 25.5 ft. wide. It portrayed the suffering and destruction of people and animals of the town.

Meanwhile, in 1937, during the intense internecine fighting of the Spanish Civil War and before World War II, Hanfstaengl, earlier a confident of and Foreign Press Secretary for Hitler, escaped from Germany[849] in fear for his life. In 1942, he became a consultant to fellow Harvard alumnus President Franklin Delano Roosevelt and the US military.

THE GEOPOLITICAL CONTEXT OF THE SPANISH CIVIL WAR

After the fall of Republican Spain (or the victory by Franco's Nationalist forces), some anti-Nazis in Germany drew the conclusion that it would be they alone who could change the politics in Germany, implying the importance of their staying in Germany: "We considered emigration a cowardly flight from responsibility. Who shall change things when the time comes? we argued. Who shall prepare against that time? The democracies are not even thinking about fighting fascism. On the contrary, they are joining forces with Hitler against the bolshevist bogey. Did not the whole world sell out Abyssinia, Austria, and above all, Spain? ... We made one grave mistake. We believed that we alone, and from inside Germany, could change the trend of fascism.... Then came the pogrom of November 1938 [known as *Kristallnacht*] .... The barbaric pogrom forced us to admit that Hitler was now too powerful to be overthrown by the Germans alone."[850] The German use of its military to influence European politics, as in Spain, just discussed, was not the only instance of international

---

[849] Peter Conradi, "The strange, secret tale of Hitler's piano man," *Sydney Morning Herald* [Australia], Jun. 13, 2005.
[850] Edith Roper and Clara Leiser, *Skeleton of Justice*, pp. 13-15.

The Hitler Era 277

violence that the world was facing in those years preceding the invasion of Poland and the outbreak of World War II: Not long after the fall of Spain, in China, after several years of small confrontations between Japanese and Chinese forces, from 1931 on, just over 2 months after the bombing of Guernica, on July 7, 1937, a skirmish between Japanese and Chinese troops escalated into a battle near Beijing, at the Lúgōuqiáo Bridge (Marco Polo Bridge). This focused military confrontation led to a great intensification of military confrontations, with full war breaking out in September. There were major battles at Shanghai (August 13-November 26, 1937), a bloody series of battles later to be called "the Stalingrad on the Yangtse River," with bombings of civilian areas, mirroring that April 1936 German Luftwaffe bombing of Guernica, *but with many more victims.* (More just below.)

While this was going on, the Soviet Union had its own inner issues to address. From early 1936 through 1939 in the USSR, there were a number of purges, basically meaning the expulsion of individuals from the Communist Party, but ultimately in certain cases amounting to the trial, conviction (often based on tortured admissions using beatings, simulated drowning, and threats of violence to family), and execution of unwanted personages.

There were many targeted political murders, perhaps the most famous of which was that of Leon Trotsky who was exiled from the Soviet Union in 1929; he and his wife Natalya were finally given asylum in Mexico, arriving there in January 1937, welcomed by Mexican socialist artist couple Diego Rivera and his wife Frida Kahlo to their home in Coyoacán, a neighborhood in Mexico City. Trotsky was murdered by NKVD operative Ramón Mercader,[851] on August 20, 1940; Trotsky was 60 years old.[852]

These subsequent expulsions and murders have been called the Great Purge, actually several purges, with at least three Moscow Trials (from August 1936 to March 1938), followed by the Purge of Army officers:

> Most of those purged in 1938 were not arrested but merely expelled from the party. Hence, the impact was more limited than once thought.... Estimates have put the figures at somewhere between 3.7 per cent and 7.7 per cent. There are two main reasons for this disparity. One is a previous underestimate of the size of the officer class in the Red Army, the other the rapidity with which many were rehabilitated.... It has now been estimated that 30 per cent of army officers discharged between 1937 and 1939 were reinstated [in relatively short order].[853]

---

[851] Trotsky knew the Spanish-born Stalinist agent Ramón Mercador (aka Jacques Mornard, Jacques Vandendreschd) by a 4th name: Frank Jacson (or Jackson).

[852] "Death of Trotsky: Skull fractured with Pickaxe," *The Guardian* (London), Aug. 22, 1940; Francis Wyndham and David King, *Trotsky: A Documentary* (1972), pp. 144-190. More below.

[853] Stephen J. Lee, *European Dictatorships, 1918-1945* (2008), pp. 72-73.

At the above-mentioned Battle of Shanghai, the Chinese put up a surprising defense to the Japanese, who considered them to be weak and inferior. This led to a desire for a more severe treatment of the Chinese by the Japanese military, which was carried out in December in Nanking. The Chinese government and much of the military abandoned Nanking (then the Chinese capital, now called Nanjing); the Japanese arrived and demanded the surrender of the city. On December 9, 1937, it began a massive assault. By December 13, the Japanese were in control of the city. There followed mass killings (by bayoneting, burning, crushing by tanks, burying, by hand grenades, and by beheadings by *guntō*, Japanese military swords) of Chinese civilians and soldiers, with at least 200,000 Chinese killed, most estimates being 300,000 or more—and with rapes of more than 20,000 Chinese women (many of whom later committed suicide or killed newborn infants conceived in their rapes). This violence went on through January 1938. It is often referred to as the Rape of Nanking (Nanjing).[854] *From the invasion by Japan to the end of the war, at least 14 million Chinese were killed, with 80 million refugees created.*[855]

In Europe, during the last years before the start of World War II, much was happening. *The Thirties (before the invasion of Poland) was a period of Hitler's continuing amalgamation of the National Socialist hold on Germany and on the incremental realization of Hitler's vision of a Greater Germany, one positioned (militarily and otherwise) to protect all concentrations of German-speaking populations, the* Volksdeutsche*, no matter in what country these* Volksdeutsche *were living at the start of the process.* This reflects Hitler's claims that his work on strengthening Germany was purely a defensive approach to ward off the threats of Bolshevism (and of a world conspiracy of Jewish internationalists) against the independence and even the very existence of Germany.

The idea of a unified society, here under German National Socialist rule, can find parallels, as in the Japanese Empire, with an old concept, *hakkō ichiu*, eight corners under one roof, earlier meant to speak of the unification of Japan, but during the war, meant to suggest the world unified under Japanese hegemony. Thus, on October 12, 1943, Okada Tadahiko[856] in a broadcast speech, stated, "From the standpoint of *Hakko Ichiu,* the Emperor of Japan is the Emperor not only of

---

[854] Iris Chang, *The Rape of Nanking: The Forgotten Holocaust of World War II* (1997). See films inspired by events in Nanjing: *Don't Cry, Nanking*—or *Nanjing 1937* (1995); *Nanking* (2007), *City of Life and Death*—or *Nanjing! Nanjing!* (2009); *City of War: The Story of John Rabe* (2009); *The Flowers of War* (2011). A Japanese veteran, Shirō Azuma ("the Conscience of Japan"), published his war memoirs in 1987, and the full diary in 2001, with Eng. tr., *The Diary of Azuma Shirō* (2006).

[855] Rana Mitter, "The World's War-Time Debt to China," *The New York Times*, Oct. 17, 2013.

[856] Tadahiko Okada (1878-1958) was Speaker of the House of Representratives of the Imperial Diet (Japanese gov't legislature). See "Tadahiko Okada," WIKIPEDIA; "Okada Tadahiko," WWW.NDL.GO.JP; "Tenno Heika Grants Audience to Leaders of Government," *The Shonan Times*, Jun. 21, 1943, p. 1, ERESOURCES.NLB.GOV.SG.

Japan but also of all the races of the world."[857] And, earlier, on February 22, 1942, Dr. Saneshige Komaki (1898-1990), of Kyoto Imperial University, in a broadcast, stated, "It is obviously reasonable for us to term America an Eastern Asiatic continent ... We may also consider Europe a part of Asia ... The Pacific Ocean is an Asian sea ... The Indian Ocean must also be a sea for Asia ... There are no seven seas, but only one sea exists and it is connected to Japan where the sun is rising ... All the ocean is to be recognized as the great Japan Sea ... Japan has now become the basic spindle of the world."[858] *(Here again is the compelling power of seeing one's own people as destined to rule over others.)*

As part of an interest in making Germany autarkic (economically totally self-sufficient) and to have the Reich prepared for an eventual war, envisioned as beginning perhaps in 1940, Hitler spoke in an official memorandum issued in September 1936, of the need for Germany to protect itself against a Bolshevik onslaught, the result of which would be the giving up of leadership of humanity to international Jewry. The document also announced a Four-Year Plan, which called for a significant increase in military spending, to develop the German steel industry, to develop the infrastructure of Germany (as in building the Autobahn highways), to develop synthetic materials (needed were oil, fibers, rubber, etc.) and to make secure the access to certain raw materials needed for industrializing Germany and making it war-prepared. The German steel industry was soon developed, the *Reichswerke* Steel Works—known after July 1937 as the *Reichswerke Hermann Göring*—with Göring on October 18, 1936, having been appointed Plenipotentiary (Chief of the Four-Year Plan) by Hitler. Göring saw Austria as a potential source for iron and other raw materials, leading to the *Anschluß* or annexation of Austria:

Greater Germany after Anschluß, 1938   German Confederation, 1815-1871

---

[857] Joel V. Berreman, "The Japanization of Far Eastern Occupied Areas," *Pacific Affairs*, vol. 17, no. 2, 1944, pp. 168–180, at p. 180.

[858] Joel V. Berreman, "The Japanization of Far Eastern Occupied Areas" (just cited), at p. 180. Cf. T. Keiichi, "Geopolitics and Geography in Japan Reexamined," *Hitotsubashi Journal of Social Studies*, vol. 12, no. 1, 1980, pp. 14–2, at p. 19. Cf. W. B. Tibor, "Variations on Geopolitics: A Sleeping Dragon Awakens," Aug. 17, 2017, *Antall József Knowledge Centre*, AJTK.HU. In Japanese and Hungarian, the family name is traditionally given first; thus: Okada Tadahiko, Komaki Saneshige (or Komaki Tsunekichi), Takeuchi Keiichi, and Tibor Wilhelm Benedek.

The envisioned reunification would bring together Germany and Austria into a Greater Germany. On March 9, 1938, Austrian Chancellor Kurt Schuschnigg called for a plebiscite, to be held on March 13, to decide this issue. It was not certain that the outcome of the plebiscite would be in Germany's favor, but this problem was swiftly resolved when *Hitler moved his troops into Austria on Saturday, March 12, 1938, annexing Austria (the Anschluß), before the plebiscite vote could take place.*

This return to the Vienna he had known as youth (wanting to become an artist but being rejected by the Academy) was presumably a powerful experience for him, with many memories, including even earlier times for Hitler to recall as he entered Austria: his youthful days before leaving for Vienna, living with his parents Alois and Klara Hitler.

Hitler wrote publicly only very little of his parents. He wrote of his father's "bitter youth" (*bittere Jugend*), of his father's "pride of the self-made man" (*der Stolz des Selfbstgewordenen*) and of his "domineering nature" (*herrlich Natur*, glorious, lordly, or pompous nature),"[859] and of his son (Adolf, writing of himself in the distancing and objectifying third person) as a rather difficult young man to handle (*ziemlich schwierig zu behandeln*): a boy quarrelsome, stubborn and obstinate (*verbohrt und widerspenstig*, obstinate and unmanageable). Hitler also wrote that he respected his father but loved his mother (*ich hatte den Vater verehrt, die Mutter jedoch geliebt*).[860] Complementing Hitler's own circumspect descriptions of how his father treated him are comments by his sister, Paula,[861] who had a relationship of many decades with her older brother, Adolf. It was he who suggested she change her public family name to Wolf,[862] perhaps for the benefit of her privacy, but also reflecting Hitler's tendency to keep all family history unknown to the general German public. He kept his sister's identity in the shadows, and disowned his relationship with William ("Willie") Patrick Hitler,[863] the son of his half-brother Alois Hitler, Jr.

---

[859] Adolf Hitler, *Mein Kampf*, Vol. I, Chap. I (At Home—*Im Elternhaus*), Eng., pp. 3-25, at pp. 8, 11; Ger., pp. 1-17, at pp. 5, 6.

[860] Adolf Hitler, *Mein Kampf*, Vol. I, Chap. I (At Home—*Im Elternhaus*), at pp. 7, 12, 25; Ger., at pp. 3, 6, 16.

[861] Paula Hitler (1896-1960) was at one time engaged to the psychiatrist Erwin Jekelius (1905-1952). In formerly closed Soviet documents released by Russian authorities in 2005, Dr. Jekelius stated in 1951 that he was responsible for the death of over 4,000 children in his hospital (hence the name "the murderer of Steinhof"). The Steinhof was a psychiatric hospital in Vienna, one of the hospitals in the T4 Euthanasia program. See "Memorial Steinhof," MEMORIALMUSEUMS.ORG; Kate Connolly, "Play turns spotlight on Austrian Nazis experiments on children," *The Telegraph*, Jun. 4, 2018.

[862] "Hitler, Paula (Frau Wolf)," WORLD WAR II GRAVES/WW2GRAVESTONE.COM. Her new family name was also spelled Wolff and Wolfe.

[863] William Patrick Hitler, "Why I Hate My Incle," *Look*, vol. 3, no. 14, Jul. 4, 1939, pp. 16-21, esp. pp. 16-1, 20; cf. Patrick Hitler, "Mon oncle Adolf (Un document inédit)," *Paris Soir*, Aug. 5, 1939, pp. 4-5.

The Hitler Era

The issues stirred up by discussions of Hitler's family were apparently not very agreeable to the Führer. In any case, Paula would later mention the physical harshness against her brother Adolf, by their father Alois Hitler, Sr., in more blunt terms: "Adolf challenged my father to extreme harshness and got his sound thrashing [from their father, Alois] every day."[864] In short, Alois was Germanic, but also brutally nasty, we might say. Despite Hitler's reticence about offering information about his family, it is generally known that Adolf Hitler's father, Alois (1837-1903)—also known as Alois Hitler, Sr., to distinguish him from a son of his from an earlier marriage, Alois Hitler, Jr. (Adolf Hitler's half-brother)—was the illegitimate son of Maria Anna Schicklgruber (1796-1847). His own father was most likely Johann Georg Hiedler (1792-1857), or perhaps Johann Georg's brother, Johann Nepomuk[865] Hiedler (1807-1888), also spelled Hüttler. Alois legally changed his name from Schicklgruber to Hitler, when 40. (This was more than a decade before Adolf Hitler was born, who, thus, was never himself a Schicklgruber by name.) An important further blood relationship was that of his mother, Klara Pölzl (1860-1907), the third wife of Alois: She was a granddaughter of Johann Georg Hiedler's brother, Johann Nepomuk Hüttler, suggesting that Alois was Klara's uncle! Adolf Hitler (1889-1945) was their fourth child; the first three had all died at very young ages before Adolf's birth, and Adolf's younger brother, Edmund (1894-1900), died when Hitler was a pre-teen. Paula, Hitler's younger sister, was his only sibling to live to adulthood (1896-1960), remaining politically loyal to her older brother beyond his death.[866]

Hitler, as mentioned, wrote in *Mein Kampf* that he respected his father but loved his mother. To speak of respect here is a bit one-sided: Alois had a bad temper and for a period he would beat young Adolf, episodes reported both by Hitler's younger sister, Paula Hitler, and by Hitler's (one

---

[864] "He was still my brother: Paula Hitler," AUSCHWITZ.DK/PAULA.HTM. See also Krysia Diver, "Journal reveals Hitler's dysfunctional family: Beaten by his father, the future dictator used to bully his sister," *The Guardian* (London), Aug. 4, 2005. Cf. Oliver Halmburger, Thomas Staehler, Guido Knopp, Timothy W. Ryback, Florian M. Beierl, *Familie Hitler: im Schatten des Diktators* (2007), YOUTUBE, with Eng., *Hitler's Family: In the Shadow of the Dictator* (video title, *1944 Hitler's Family*, YOUTUBE); "Interview with Hitler's sister on 5th June 1946," *Records of the Army Staff (G2), Record Group 319 IRR XE575580*, ORADOUR.INFO; cf. "Paula Hitler," ADOLFHITLER.DK. Further information is in "Interview with Paula Wolf (Hitler's Sister)," in *Berchtesgaden Military Intelligence Records, Ms. Coll. 647, Box 1, Folder 8 (interview with Paula Wolf)*, in the KISLAK CENTER, UNIV. OF PENNA.

[865] Hitler, who was so intent on declaring his own pure Germanic blood, was the great-grandson by his mother of Johann Nepomuk Hüttler. Hitler presumably was quite aware of local common knowledge that a famous Nepomuk—Saint John of Nepomuk (ca. 1340-1393)—was the patron saint of Czechia (also called Bohemia), part, of course, of Czechoslovakia: Does this hint at non-Germanic blood for Hitler?

[866] Ian Kershaw, *Hitler: A Biography*, pp. 1-11; Frank McDonough, *Hitler and the Rise of the Nazi Party* (2012), pp. 19-20; John Toland, *Adolf Hitler*, pp. 3-12, 15-16, 231-232, 246-247, 268.

known) youthful friend, August Kubizek (1888-1956). Adolf would also see his father beat his mother. Neither she nor Adolf could prevent Alois from beating the other. *Such children regularly feel guilt at not being able to protect their mothers, even though they were certainly in no position to be able to block their violent fathers.* Of course, this makes for misery all around in the family. Kubizek quoted Hitler's mother, Klara: "What I hoped and dreamed of as a young girl had not been fulfilled in my marriage, but does such a thing ever happen?"[867] Alois Hitler, Jr., another son of Alois from an earlier marriage, and thus Hitler's half-brother, told his son Patrick Hitler, that Alois had on occasion beaten Alois Jr. into unconsciousness and *at another time had beaten Adolf so severely that Alois Sr. left him for dead*.[868] (Other sources describe this as leaving Adolf in a coma, adding that it was not clear if Adolf would survive.[869]) *Hitler did not write of these beatings*. It was perhaps not a time when such events could be reported without personal shame. It would be many decades before such harshness could be shouted or sung out, with no self-recriminations, as in the lyric, "I was schooled with a strap across my back."[870] That would be a remark made in a rather different age!

The issue of corporal punishment and how beneficial its various forms can be in making a child more obedient and less obstinate has been repeatedly investigated. It is perhaps not surprising that children who are treated with physical abuse may well become rather aggressive adults—Hitler and Stalin are extreme examples of this possibility—and this understanding may rest as an obvious truth, but it has also been studied, as by pediatricians.[871] Important current studies are able to draw some study-based conclusions about the use of physical punishment—spanking, beating, thrashing, whipping, hitting, kicking, burning, scalding, forcing the child to ingest soap, hot spices, or other unpleasant and perhaps noxious substances, or of psychological aggression—humiliating, shaming, ridiculing, denigrating, frightening, or threatening the child. These studies have established that such treatments are at best not very effective.

On a more technical level of investigation, these disciplining actions have now been shown to result in neurological damage to the brain, with life-long consequences. Brain MRIs have shown changes in the child's brain anatomy, including reduced prefrontal cortical gray matter, which has a role in muscular control, sensory perception, emotions, decision-making, and self-control, and changes in the brain's white matter tracts (axons), which effect communication within the brain, speech functions,

---

[867] August Kubizek, *The Young Hitler I Knew: The Memoirs of Hitler's Childhood Friend* (2011), p. 49.
[868] Walter C. Langer, *The Mind of Hitler* (1972), Chap. IV ("Hitler as He Knows Himself"), sub-section, "Father"—p. 104 in Basic Books ed.; p. 110 in Signet ed.
[869] George Victor, *Hitler: The Pathology of Evil* (1998), p. 29.
[870] From "Jumpin' Jack Flash, The Rolling Stones," GENIUS.COM; from 1968.
[871] "Spanking Kids Can Make Them More Aggressive Later," *American Academy of Pediatrics*, Apr. 12, 2010.

The Hitler Era

and when damaged can result in various diseases, from MS to Alzheimer's, lower IQ, and greater cortisol levels, meaning a greater chronic (long-term) sense of stress, as well as a greater likelihood in adulthood of depression, aggression, and addictive behavior.[872] And also, in a perhaps surprising way, there is also *a psychological price for the parents to pay*, with studies showing that many parents become ashamed of their own actions and depressed.[873] (We also saw a strong impact during World War II on those Wehrmacht and *SS-Einstatzgruppen* military involved in repeated shooting of large numbers of civilians in conquered territories, by firing squads, using rifles, with physical and psychological problems).

One response to comments by people who were spanked or beaten as children, that they have survived and are OK now, has been to point out the history of the use of seat belts in automobiles. While many survived those years of driving around without seatbelts, *others did not*, and we might realize now from emergency-room experience through the decades, that using a seatbelt can be the difference, especially in car accidents at high speeds, between surviving and dying. As in using a seat belt while traveling in a car to minimize harm in case of accidents, so too, here, an awareness of the relationship between violent treatment of children and their becoming frightened, aggressive, or hate-filled adults, can minimize the number of those who become such tormented adults.

The impact on a child of having been beaten, as well as seeing his mother beaten, all by the father, is quite complex, but certainly involves much more than being inspired to respect such a father. Aside from all of the issues about who this father is, there are also the experiences of pain and helplessness in seeing the violence carried out, as well, against the mother. The feelings of injustice, of the violence in the world, of a sense of not being worthy of living, all quite experiential, is something we see repeatedly. (This applies, of course, to Hitler, but to millions of others.)

In the 1970s, with the return of so many active and discharged military from experiences in Vietnam during the US military involvement, psychiatrists developed the concept of PTSD (Post-Traumatic Stress Disorder), codified formally in 1980. This was then expanded to include other traumas, especially repeated beatings, deprivation of attention, rapes of young boys and girls, often by family members. Even before

---

[872] Akemi Tomoda, Hanako Suzuki, Keren Rabi, Yi-Shin Sheu, Ann Polcari, Martin H. Teicher, "Reduced prefrontal cortical gray matter volume in young adults exposed to harsh corporal punishment," *Neuroimage*, vol. 47, no. 2, Aug. 2009, pp. T66-T71, NIH PUBLIC ACCESS, NCBI.NLM.NIH.GOV; Marion Smits, Lize C. Jiskoot, Janne M. Papma, "White Matter Tracts of Speech and Language," *Seminars in Ultrasound, CT and MRI*, Jun. 25, 2014, SCIENCEDIRECT.COM.

[873] Robert D. Sege, MD, PhD, and Bejamin S. Siegel, MD, "Effective Discipline to Raise Healthy Chidlren," *Pediatrics* (pub. of the American Academy of Pediatrics), vol. 142, no. 6, Dec. 2018, pp. 1-10; Christina Caron, "Spanking Is Ineffective and Harmful to Children, Pediatricians' Group Says," *The New York Times*, Nov. 5, 2018, NEW YORK TIMES ARCHIVES.

those innovations, such people experienced the deep doubt of one's own value as a human being, the precarious sense of existence, the perturbing issue of what to do with all of the inner agitation, sadness, fear, and rage resulting from such violent, repeated mistreatment—*all of these are the sad mental landscape of someone who has been repeatedly violated in childhood*.[874] We will return to the issue of the psychology of Hitler, below.

One issue for Hitler that haunted him into the early 1940s, leading to his having research done to establish his Germanic pedigree,[875] was the possibility that his father—born Alois Schicklgruber (1837-1903), who changed his name in 1876 to Hitler, long after his own assumed father had died, and long before Adolf's birth in 1889—was the son of a man never definitively identified. This, *in Hitler's worst nightmare*, might have been a young Jewish man from Graz, perhaps one Leopold Frankenberger. *The violence of Alois toward young Adolf in this way could be linked in Hitler's worried thinking of the bad (Jewish) blood his father might have had, and a reason to seek revenge on the entire Jewish people, as carriers of such destructive impulses*. Later research has suggested that there were no Jewish families living in Graz in that period and that his grandmother never worked in Graz. The man who "adopted" Alois, Johann Georg Hiedler (or Hitler), has been taken to be the most likely biological father of Alois. Whatever the reality, which will remain obscure, with no way to establish the identity of Adolf's paternal grandfather, the father of Alois Hitler, Sr., *what is more crucial is how we deal with our situation is what Hitler understood (believed) the situation to be, or to have been, rather than the true historical situation*. As historian/psychohistorian Robert G. L. Waite (1919-1999), wrote, the "crucial question is rather: did Hitler harbor the suspicion that he himself might have Jewish blood? The answer to this question is yes, he did so believe."[876] If, then, Adolf thought that his illegitimate father had himself a Jewish father, the hatred toward Jews (represented in Hitler's thinking by his father) *would not be any the less if, in fact, Hitler had no Jewish ancestry at all*. His doubts reflected the importance of this issue for him. In 1930, for example, Hitler

---

[874] For extended discussion of these processes, see Mitchell Ginsberg, *Calm, Clear, and Loving*, esp. the Foreword by Audrey Rachel Stevenson and Chaps. 9, 16-31. On Complex PTSD (cPTSD), see Julian D Ford and Christine A Courtois, "Complex PTSD, Affect Dysregulation, and Borderline Personality Disorder," *Borderline Personality Disorder and Emotion Dysregulation*, vol. 1, no. 9, 2014.

[875] Results in Karl Friedrich von Frank, *Ahnentafel des Reichkanzlers Adolf Hitler (1933)*, also cited as *Ahnentafeln berühmter Deutscher, No. 3* (1933) and later, in Rudolf Koppensteiner, *Ahnentafeln berühmter Deutscher: Die Ahnentafel des Führers* (1937). These identify Hitler's paternal grandfather—their answer to the big (historical, not psychological) question—as Johann Georg Hiedler, and the maternal grandfather of Klara (Hitler's mother) as Johann Nepomuk Hütler, these two being brothers. These *Ahnentafel* (genealogical tables), cite the family name as Hüttler, Hütler, Hiedler, Huetler, Huettler, and, of course, Hitler.

[876] Robert Waite, "Hitler's Anti-Semitism: A Study in History and Psychoanalysis," in *The Psychoanalytic Interpretation of History*, Wolman, Benjamin B., ed., pp. 192–230, at p. 212.

had his personal attorney at the time, Hans Frank, research the question. Frank reported having found evidence that the mother of Adolf's father Alois, Maria Anna Schicklgruber (the family name Alois had until he changed it many years later to Hitler) was possibly made pregnant by a Jewish man, and that that man supplied money for the care of young Alois. Hitler replied that his grandmother had told him that in fact, this man was not the father of Alois, but, being quite poor, she had accepted payments, letting the man think that he was the father. *All well and good, and a definitive statement, you say?* A significant problem here is that Hitler's grandmother, the mother of Alois, lived from April 15, 1795 to January 7, 1847, dying at 51 years of age. Given that Adolf was born on April 20, 1889, his birth came more than 42 years after Grandmother Maria Anna had died. Hitler's story of her telling him something is therefore rather questionable, but in it, Hitler does allow the mention of a Jew's relationship with his grandmother. (The fact that the Jew is presented as being duped by a needy Austrian unwed mother is perhaps a tolerable way not to deny any such person in his family's history, by showing how that stupid Jew had been tricked.) In any case, the doubt was Hitler's, and his to come to terms with.

It is perhaps not all that unusual that someone would dislike family members disagreeing in heated arguments, members who drank heavily, with wife beating and raping, and merciless floggings of his child, and, by contrast, appreciate the adoration of the masses—especially if one has what is called narcissistic personality tendencies, with their satisfaction in any and all adoration. Reflecting this sense of Hitler's personality, his decades-long (1920-1945) personal adjutant (or *aide-de-camp)*, Julius Schaub, remarked to Hitler's secretary, Christa Schroeder, about Hitler in this triumphant return to his native Austria, of which he was now the Führer, "*Er braucht eben einfach die Jubelrufe wie ein Künstler den Applaus.*" ("He simply needs the shouts of jubilation as the artist needs applause.")[877]

On the geopolitical level, from 1933 to the *Anschluß*, under the Nazi policy of coerced emigration of Jews from Germany, its Jewish population had dropped from about 525,000, or 0.75% of Germany's overall 1933 population of 67 million,[878] to about 390,000 German Jews before the *Anschluß* (perhaps 0.56% of the population). The annexation of Austria by Germany brought about two immediate consequences: there was the enlargement of Germany into the Greater Reich, of course, but there was also the bringing into the new Germany a large number of Austrian Jews, largely concentrated in Vienna.[879] This made for a first significant change

---

[877] Christa Schroeder, *Er war mein Chef*, p. 85; *He Was My Chief*, p. 61.
[878] "Jewish Population of Europe in 1933: Population Data by Country," HOLOCAUST ENCYCLOPEDIA, USHMM.
[879] Most famous might be Sigmund Freud, who daughter Anna was arrested after the Anschluß by the Gestapo; his benefactor Princess Marie Bonaparte—a great granddaughter of Lucien Bonaparte, Napoleon Bonaparte's brother—paid a ransom

in the demographics of Germany: With the Jewish population of Austria added (some 192,000 in 1938), the Jews in Great Germany increased to about 580,000 Jews.[880] This created a major issue for the Reich goal of eliminating Jews from Germany. For this, an office was established to help process the visas for Jews wanting to leave Germany (with the attitude of Good riddance to bad rubbish). At the head of this office was Reinhard Heydrich. Heydrich, earlier, under Himmler, Bavarian Police Chief, became head of both the *Sipo* (German Security Police, *Sicherheitspolizei*) and the *SD* (security Service, *Sicherheitsdienst*, an intelligence-gathering agency). Then, when the invasion of Poland brought on World War II, Heydrich was appointed the head administrator of the new RSHA (*Reichssicherheitshauptamt*, or Reich Security Central Office), which oversaw the *Sipo*, which included both the *Kripo* (*Kriminalpolizei*, Criminal Police) and the *Gestapo* (*Geheime Staatspolizei*, or Secret State Police).

Under Heydrich's watch over and encouragement of the bureaucracy of Jewish emigration from Germany, his office, the *Zentralstelle für jüdische Auswanderung* (the Central Office of Jewish Emigration)—established by decree of Field Marshal Hermann Göring on January 24, 1939[881]—where Adolf Eichmann was his assistant, about 77,000 Jews left the Greater Reich in 1939.[882] This was showing signs of this Office's efficiency but also its limits. (More below on the Jewish population ramifications: especially, the subsequent violence of *Kristallnacht* and its aftermath, and the start of World War II.[883])

While at first Jewish emigration was encouraged and even facilitated by Nazi bureaucracy, on the condition that everything of value, wealth, businesses, personal property, and cash would be left behind as property of the Third Reich, in July 1941, in the first month of the war against the USSR, Göring sent out explicit orders to Heydrich, stating in part, "I entrust you further [*Ich beauftrage Sie weiter*] with the task of presenting to me in the near future an overall draft of the organizational, factual, and material preliminary measures [*die organisatorischen, sachlichen und materiellen Vorausmaßnahmen*] for carrying out the desired final solution of the Jewish question [*zur Durchführung der angestrebten Endlösung der Judenfrage vorzulegen*]."[884] The following autumn, on October 23, 1941,

---

(or bribe) to have her released, and Freud, his wife Martha, and daughter Anna then hastily left Vienna, on June 4, 1938, and arrived in London, on June 7.

[880] "Reich Jewish Population Declined One-third; 135,000 Left [Departed] in 5 Years," JEWISH TELEGRAPHIC AGENCY, JTA ARCHIVE, Jan. 23, 1938; "Jewish Population Drops 44 Per Cent [in 1933-1937] in Hessennassau, Germany," JEWISH TELEGRAPHIC AGENCY, JTA ARCHIVE, Oct. 31, 1937; "Austria," Holocaust Encyclopedia, USHMM.

[881] "Holocaust Chronology of 1939," JEWISH VIRTUAL LIBRARY/AICE.

[882] "German Jewish Refugees, 1933-1939," HOLOCAUST ENCYCLOPEDIA, USHMM.

[883] We will return below to the similarly named *Zigeunernacht* (The Night of the Gypsies), the night of Aug. 2-3, 1944, when all the remaining Romanies at Auschwitz-Birkenau were gassed and cremated.

[884] "Göring an Heydrich über die Endlösung der Judefrage," DE.WIKISOURCE.ORG; with a facsimile of the letter as a JPG file, "Carta Göring," at WIKIMEDIA COMMONS,

The Hitler Era

Chief of the Gestapo, Heinrich Müller (1900-1945),[885] send out Himmler's order that prohibited further emigration of Jews in Germany-controlled Europe.[886] The plan for the final solution of the Jewish problem (the annihilation of the Jews of Europe) called for a concentrating of Jewish populations for more efficient processing, with its mass killings—not their dispersal to distant lands! *The problem was what to do with all of these Jews, growing in number* in German-controlled Europe as Germany invaded and conquered land after land, each with its own population of Jews. On July 6-15, 1938, after the *Anschluß* of Austria in March of 1938, the Évian Conference took place at Évian-les-Bains, France. It had been called for by President Roosevelt on March 22, 1938, ten days after the *Anschluss* (or *Anschluß*), and a number of nations responded, distraught at the treatment of the Jews by Nazi Germany. The focused issue was the question of where German Jews might be able to emigrate. Its envisioned goal was for countries commit to taking some of the Jewish refugees deprived of basic citizen rights in the Third Reich. In responding with a disparaging comment to the announcement of that conference, Hitler proclaimed on March 25, in Königsberg (now Kaliningrad, Russia[887]):

> I can only hope and expect that the other world, which has such deep sympathy for these criminals [*Verbrecher*, meaning the Jews], will at least be generous enough to convert this sympathy into practical aid. We, on our part, are ready to put all these criminals at the disposal of these countries, for all I care [*meinetwegen*], on luxury ships [*auf Luxusschiffen*].[888]

Of all countries at the Conference, it was only the Dominican Republic under Rafael Trujillo, that agreed to admit up to 10,000 Jews (5,000 visas were issued), with Bolivia later allowing Jews in, with much less public awareness.[889] *Hitler took the broad reluctance to help Jews at all to indicate the insincere attitude of these other countries, which criticized*

COMMONS.WIKIMEDIA.ORG.

[885] His appointment in September 1939 was under Reinhard Heydrich, head of the newly formed *RSHA* (Reich Main Security Office), in its Amt 4 (Office 4), the Gestapo (Secret State Police).

[886] Ingrao Christian, "General Chronology of Nazi Violence," Violence de masse et Résistance—Réseau de recherche/sciencespo.fr, Mar. 14, 2008.

[887] Kaliningrad (then Königsberg) on the Baltic Sea is east-northeast of Danzig or Gdańsk (Poland), south-southeast of Klaipėda (Lithuania), and north of Warsaw.

[888] "Hitler Is Pleased to Get Rid of Foes: In Comment on Hull's Plan He Says Some Opponents of Nazis Deserve to Die: US Warned" (buried on p. 25 of *The New York Times*, March 27, 1939); Ger., Max Domarus, *Hitler Reden und Proklamationen 1932 bis 1945. Kommentiert von einem deutschen Zeitgenossen* (1973/1988), in 4 volumes. Speech of March 25, 1938 in vol. 2, pp. 832-837; passage at p. 835. See full text, in Eng., in Propagandaleiter (a penname), *Adolf Hitler: Collection of Speeches, 1922-1945* (2016), Reichsmilitaria.com, pp. 436-440; at p. 438.

[889] "Dominican Republic," *Closed Borders*, Evian1938.de; "Refuge in South America," Encyclopedia.ushmm.org; "Simón Iturri Patiño," Wikipedia.

Nazi Germany but had no more a desire than did Germany for Jews to move to their own countries. The results of the conference suggested that transporting all German Jews to Madagascar would not work. (More just below.) This would have had the advantage of keeping Jews as a hostage, perhaps to attempt to keep non-German Jews from being too hostile toward Germany. Or, in *Amtssprache* (Nazi office talk, bureaucratese, or officialese), July 1940, "*als Faustpfand, um das Wohlverhalten ihrer Rassegenossen in Amerika sicherzustellen*" (as a pawn to ensure the good behavior of their racial comrades in America).[890]

This hope ended definitively when Germany declared war on the USA on December 11, 1941, and the US responded hours later, declaring war on Germany. Then, the very next day in the afternoon, December 12, 1941, Hitler held a meeting with about 50 very high officials of the Third Reich, including Hermann Göring, Heinrich Himmler, Joseph Goebbels, and Hans Frank (Governor of occupied Poland, the *Gouvernement General*).[891] Goebbels wrote in his diary entry about this meeting, "With respect of the Jewish Question, the Führer has decided to make a clean sweep. [*Bezüglich der Judenfrage ist der Führer entschlossen, reinen Tisch zu machen.*] He had prophesied to the Jews that if they again brought about a world war [presupposing that the Jews had brought on World War I], they would live to see their annihilation in it. [*Er hat den Juden prophezeit, daß, wenn sie noch einmal einen Weltkrieg herbeiführen würden, sie dabei ihre Vernichtung erleben würden.*] That wasn't just a catch-word. [*Das ist keine Phrase gewesen.*] The world war is here and the annihilation of the Jews must be the necessary consequence. [*Der Weltkrieg ist da, die Vernichtung des Judentums muß die notwendige Folge sein.*]"[892] For Goebbels here, this extermination of the Jews of Europe was certain, determined, and undebatable!

THE MADAGASCAR OPTION

Later in 1940, the Madagascar option, mentioned just above, was looking less and less a likely solution to the so-called Jewish Question (How to get rid of the Jews definitively?). Unlike the common thought that time heals all wounds, time did not heal all problems, especially not this one of the continuing presence of Jews in Germany's world sphere. In fact,

---

[890] L. J. Hartog, "Als Hitler den Massenmord prophezeite: Zur Rede vom 30. Januar 1939," *Die Zeit*, Jan. 27, 1989, and ZEIT ONLINE, Nov. 21, 2012.

[891] Lorraine Boissoneault, "The First Moments of Hitler's Final Solution," *Smithsonian*, SMITHSONIAN.COM, Dec. 12, 2016.

[892] Christian Gerlach, *Sur la conférence de Wannsee: de la décision d'exterminer les Juifs d'Europe* (1999), pp. 58-59; also, Christian Gerlach, *Krieg, Ernährung, Völkermord: Forschungen Zur Deutschen Vernichtungspolitik Im Zweiten Weltkrieg* (1998), p. 213; and a review focusing on the 1990s research by Christian Gerlach, Volker Ullrich, "Über die Vernichtung der Juden wurde zentral entschieden. Hitlers bösester Befehl" ["The destruction of the Jews was decided centrally. Hitler's worst command"], *Die Zeit*, Jan. 9, 1998. Cf. Ian Kershaw, *Fateful Choices: Ten Decisions that Changed the World, 1940-1941* (2007), pp. 431-483.

time (and events) exacerbated the problem. No country would make any explicit or definite commitment to admitting any Jews at all. Switzerland, for example, declared metaphorically, *"Das Boot ist voll,"* the boat—that is, Switzerland—is full.[893] (This restriction was somewhat loosened in the last part of the war.) Canada would accept only 5,000 Jewish refugees during all the years of the Third Reich.[894] And so on.

The Munich Crisis and the Oster Conspiracy

On the level of geopolitical maneuvering in this context, from Hitler's point of view—after the *Anschluß* of March 1938, which took place, once again, with no military action taken by Britain, France, or Belgium—there were new issues and German interests that were brought into focus. Aside from the nuisance of having more Jews under German governance, and the problem of what to do with them, even more central at the time was the issue of what Hitler spoke of as the mistreatment of *Volksdeutsche* in the Sudetenland, border territories within Czechoslovakia that had a large German-speaking population. Hitler's insistence on the right of the Third Reich to protect these *Volksdeutsche* presented a challenge for the Czechs and, as well, for the British and the French, who saw Czechoslovakia as a free country and ally. On May 23, 1938, Hitler would communicate to Czech government representatives that Germany had no aggressive intentions against Czechoslovakia (a rather short-lived commitment).[895]

That was apparently a public stance with no substance behind it: Generally unknown, just a week later, on May 30, 1938, some five months before the most critical days of late September 1938 and the Munich Agreement, Hitler would declare to a small group of generals, "It is my unalterable decision to smash Czechoslovakia by military action in the near future."[896] Just below we will consider the hidden thinking of the men of the military (and intelligence) who heard this very clear statement by Hitler, especially with those who did not agree with Hitler's aggressive intentions here. German control of the Sudetenland, a physically high-elevation territory that left the remainder of Czechoslovakia relatively open and easy prey, represented a clear threat to Czechoslovakia as a whole. This was presumably not lost on the Czechs, nor on the German military, and was, we might surmise, not unknown to the British and French, either, given their intelligence services.

One significant difference in the question of Czechoslovakia and the earlier claims for the right to German power—the Rhineland, Austria, and even the Sudetenland—was that with the transfer of control over the Sudeten Mountains, a non-Germanic country was left rather defenseless. The claims for the right of Germany to take over all lands where there were significant numbers of Germanic peoples (*Volksdeutsche*) had some

---

[893] This became the title of a 1981 German-Austrian-Swiss film.
[894] Irving Abella and Harold Troper, *None Is Too Many: Canada and the Jews of Europe, 1933-1948* (1983).
[895] William Sherer, *The Rise and Fall of the Third Reich*, p. 365.
[896] NT-IMT-Blue, vol. 3, pp. 42-46; pp. 43, 45 give the dating of this document.

internal logic and validity—not necessarily the preferred situation for peoples who had lived in Slavic lands for many generations—are in contrast with this new threat: German control of a Slavic nation.

This should perhaps have set off alarms, concern that Hitler was now in a different frame of mind, in which his desire for German rule went beyond any pretense of uniting Germans within and without of Germany.

What was the thinking of the leaders, especially in Britain, that could convince them that Hitler was fundamentally peace-loving and desirous only of a fair situation in the European scene? German author in exile, Joseph Roth, wrote back in 1933, "The European mind is capitulating ... out of weakness, out of sloth, out of apathy, out of lack imagination."[897]

Despite that early appreciation of the dangers in Nazism, there was in general a serious lag in time between the new situation and the old understanding. This is a kind of continuing, rote thinking with beliefs that were perhaps once valid and relevant.

On a personal level, this pattern of thinking is understood to be a form of perseveration; perhaps political leaders are prone to suffering from this sort of disjunction from new realities. In any case, however we understand such matters, in the case of the crisis of Czechoslovakia in late 1938, this attitude would have rather dire consequences. The desire to avoid war certainly had a strong role to play in the urge to appeasement (and avoidance of war)—despite Britain's informal national referendum in late 1934, as noted above, that showed most Brits in favor of facing down aggressive nations to maintain peace, even if this might lead to war.

And on to the Oster Conspiracy.[898] Before considering the international sparring that took place in September 1938, culminating in the Munich Agreement at the end of that month, some background events involving some high-ranking anti-Nazi German military—later referred to as the Oster Conspiracy.[899] *The Gestapo and Hitler were not aware of this*

---

[897] Joseph Roth, *What I Saw: Reports from Berlin, 1920-1933* (2003), p. 207.

[898] Terry M. Parssinen, *The Oster Conspiracy of 1938: The Unknown Story of the Military Plot to Kill Hitler and Avert World War II* (2003) and video talk, May 20, 2003, by same title, at THE UNION LEAGUE CLUB OF CHICAGO, CSPANTV.

[899] Toward the end of the war, the Gestapo discovered diaries of Admiral Wilhelm Canarius, head of the German Intelligence Service, the Abwehr, with details about earlier assassination plots against Hitler, leading to immediate focus and violence by the Gestapo. Canarius was executed on April 9, 1945. Others involved were similarly killed, especially, Wehrmacht General Hans Oster (also, April 9, 1945). Two generals also involved in the July 20, 1944 plot to assassinate Hitler, General Ludwig Beck and General Erwin von Witzleben, envisioned as the post-Hitler Commander in Chief of the German military, were killed on July 21 and August 8. Others, less implicated in the 1938 plot, included Ernst von Wiezsäcker (Foreign Office State Secretary), *who survived the war as a guest at the Vatican*, and the German diplomat and intelligence (*Abwehr*) officer, Hans Bernd Gisevius, who in his post-war book stated plainly that *Chamberlain had saved Hitler by his interventions in late September, 1938*. Gisevius wrote, questioning whether it was really "Peace in our time": "as the Parisianers celebrated Daladier [the French

The Hitler Era

conspiracy until the last days of the war. The conspiracy can shed light on the high-tension days before that agreement and what was at stake.

The Oster Conspiracy involved some very high officers in the German military, as well as in the German intelligence service (the *Abwehr*), who were aware from at least early in 1938, of Hitler's plans to invade Czechoslovakia, if changing events would make that at all possible. (*So much for Hitler's repeated claims through the following years that he had never wanted war and that war was thrust upon him*, reluctantly on his part, which he often claimed to be by the war-thirsty machinations of world Jewry, unquestionably taken to be anti-German.)

These generals knew very well the ruthlessness with which Hitler had treated all political enemies, from the first months of 1933, and had seen the political stripping of citizenship of the Jews (which bothered those who had grown up in a spirit of strongly rejecting anti-Semitism, but not all others).

Hitler was making clear to such high-ranking military and intelligence officers that his next target—after remilitarizing the Rhineland, on March 6, 1936, and annexing Austria, on March 12, 1938—was not only the Sudetenland (the Sudeten Mountains encircling Czechoslovakia), but all of Czechoslovakia. This was in their judgment would provoke a war against nations that Germany was not clearly capable of winning: Czechoslovakia had alliances both with France and the Soviet Union, and if those countries and Great Britain were to act against German threats of aggression against Czechoslovakia, this might very well have been a disaster for Germany. They, of course, remembered the bravado and the self-confidence with which the Second Reich had entered into World War I, and the ultimate crushing (if not humiliating) defeat at the hands of a consortium of determined and well-equipped enemy armies.

Furthermore, this group appreciated that for many people in Germany, Hitler had taken the country from its starvation from the British blockade, especially of 1917-1918, with the many dead and mutilated from during the war, the demoralizing Treaty of Versailles, the occupation of the Ruhr by French, Belgian, British, and American troops, along with a period of intense hyperinflation and then a world economic Depression, to a nation of military might and economic stability and growth, a revitalized sense

---

Prime Minister], as in Croyden [location of the airport where Chamberlain landed on his return to Britain from Munich] the same applause sounded out, and as Chamberlain waved in the air a twice-signed little piece of paper: Peace in our time, 'Peace in our time'? Let us, rather, express ourselves a little more realistically: Chamberlain saved Hitler." Tr. from the Ger.: "*wei die Pariser Daladier umjubelten, wie in Croyden der gleiche Beifall ertönte, und wie Chamberlain ein doppelt unterschriebenes Papierschen in der Luft schwenkte... Peace in our time, Frieden in unserer Zeit?* [first in Eng. in the Ger. text and then, questioning it, in German] *Drücken wir uns lieber ein bißchen realistischer aus: Chamberlain rettete Hitler.*" From Hans Bernd Gisevius, *Bis zum bitteren Ende* (German ed., 1961), p. 378. The passage is in the 1946 ed., pub. in Zurich, *Bis zum bitteren Ende*, p. 361; Eng. tr., *To the Bitter End* (1947), p. 326. The book was dedicated to the memory of the Hans Oster ("Who was killed on April 9, 1945 in the death camp at Flossenburg").

of hopefulness for the German people (*Volksgemeinschaft*, Community of the German People), and a place in the sun, *all without going to war*—which from one point of view was quite remarkable and impressive, of course. To attack such a Hitler would not have had popular support at all.

On the other hand, this coterie of German officers that were involved in the Oster Conspiracy also appreciated that many Germans were as hesitant about another war as were the peoples of other countries, all of which had suffered terrible losses of a generation of men, and were not in the least eager to enter into another great war.

With that as the basis of their thinking, it was their conclusion that *only if Hitler would declare war on Czechoslovakia* would the German people find acceptable the overthrow of Hitler. *If, in one possible scenario,* Hitler would declare an ultimatum to Czechoslovakia to give up the protective Sudeten Mountains (thereby exposing itself to a German invasion of the whole country), *and if* England, France, and the Soviet Union (but especially England) would declare their strong opposition to that, including their own threat to go to war against Germany if it followed through on such an ultimatum, *then* the setting was propitious for an overthrow of the Nazi regime in Germany.

So, imagining those conditions, the plan was to wait for Hitler to declare war against Czechoslovakia. In the two days required to put those words of his into military action, this group would attack the Chancellery, which had only 15 SS guards protecting Hitler, to capture Hitler—or perhaps to kill him (to prevent his restoration as Führer)—and to arrest the leaders in the Nazi government, to keep them from initiating Hitler's war plans even with him dead. *This plan required the British to take a clear stand against Hitler's potential threatening of Czechoslovakia*, making a move by Hitler to invade the Sudetenland a unilateral military action that would set off a war. Such anti-Nazis as German diplomat Adam von Trott zu Solz (1909-1944)[900] went to London three times in 1939 to plead with the British—especially with Lord Halifax (UK Foreign Secretary, one of the three most powerful positions of the Cabinet under the Prime Minister, 1938-1940) and with Philip Kerr, British politician and diplomat, earlier private secretary to Prime Minister David Lloyd George (a major contributor to the Versailles Treaty who was afterwards regretful at some of the harsher conditions he had penned, thus later feeling it appropriate to appease Germany)—to end the government's policy of appeasement to Hitler, with no success. These anti-Hitlerian Germans also directly sent a number of communiqués to London, even having Theo Kordt, *Chargé d'affaires* at the German Embassy in London, speak directly to Lord Halifax, the British Foreign Secretary (who was also second in power to the Prime Minister in such issues).[901] Halifax conveyed this information to

---

[900] Adam von Trott zu Solz," WIKIPEDIA, "Adam von Trott zu Solz (1909-1944)," JEWISH VIRTUAL LIBRARY.

[901] Terry Parssinen, *The Oster Conspiracy* (2003) and video talk, *The Oster Conspiracy of 1938*, Mar. 20, 2003, C-SPAN, both cited above; Klemens von

The Hitler Era

Neville Chamberlain, the Prime Minister, who dismissed the group[902] with a quick reference to his being unfavorably reminded of some political agitators from centuries earlier, the dismally failed Jacobites[903]—*again, history and memories of earlier political situations can lead to conclusions and attitudes about a present crisis, not always in insightful or wise ways.*

While Churchill, for one, appreciated the actions of these anti-Hitlerian Germany military and intelligence, it was Chamberlain who was directing the British approach to the challenge and the threat posed by Hitler. As may already be familiar information, Chamberlain went out of his way to insure there would be no war with Germany, abandoning Czechoslovakia, stating that it could resist German demands, but that it would be doing so on its own, without support from the British. The Munich Agreement[904] was signed (in the early hours of September 30, 1938), promising peace (as British PM Neville Chamberlain phrased it, "peace in our time"). In the following days, Eva Braun wrote in her diary that Hitler's comment about those negotiations was "Only now do I know how weak the West is. And now I'll make the war I need to carry out my ideas in the world."[905]

Some two weeks after the agreement was signed, Hitler gave a speech in Saarbrücken, on October 9, 1938 saying "There were weaklings among us, too [*Es hat auch bei uns Schwächliche gegeben*], who possibly did not realize that a stern decision had to be taken [*die vielleicht nicht verstanden hatten, daß ein harter Entschluß getroffen werden mußte*]." Hitler's interpreter, Paul Schmidt, would comment on this, "This Saarbrücken speech was for many Germans [*bedeutete für viele Deutsche*] a rude awakening from the dream that the Munich Agreement had settled everything [*ein hähes Erwachen aus dem Taum, daß durch das Münchener Abkommen alles geregelt sei*], and that peace had been permanently secured [*und der Friede auf die Dauer gesichert sei*]."[906]

Given the earlier expression by Hitler to some of his top generals of his interest to go to war, we may appreciate here what this idea for Hitler to carry out in the world actually amounted to, in major geopolitical dimensions.

The Agreement signed at Munich basically gave Germany the right to annex into a greater Germany the Sudetenland—borderlands of

---

Klemperer, *German Resistance Against Hitler: The Search for Allies Abroad, 1938-1945* (1992), pp. 101-110; Winston Churchill, *The Gathering Storm* (1948).

[902] Letter from Prime Minister Chamberlain to Foreign Secretary Lord Halifax, Aug. 19, 1938. Quoted in Andrew Roberts, *The Holy Fox: Biography of Lord Halifax* (1991), p. 146.

[903] Not to be confused with the French Jacobins, associated with Robespierre (1758-1794) and an initial liberal political stance becoming the Reign of Terror (1793-1794). The Jacobites, in distinction to these Frenchmen, were an earlier group that wanted to reinstall as king the Catholic Stuart King James II of England and Ireland. The group's unsuccessful uprisings occurred in the years 1688-1747.

[904] Munich Agreement or Pact (also, Accords); *Münchner Abkommen*.

[905] Eva Braun, *The Private Life of Adolf Hitler*, pp. 82-83, Oct., 1938, Munich.

[906] Paul Schmidt, *Statist auf diplomatischer Bühne 1923-1945*, p. 419; Eng., *Hitler's Interpreter*, p. 114.

Czechoslovakia held to have a large Germanic, a German-speaking, population. The very next day, October 1, saw the take-over by the German Army (Wehrmacht) of the Sudetenland.

This left the rest of Czechoslovakia very poorly defended militarily, given the resultant new borders and the lay of the land. The lands that were populated by Czechs and Slovaks (making up the name Czechoslovakia) were known in German as Böhmen and Mähren (Bohemia and Moravia). Czechoslovakia (or, by another name, Bohemia and Moravia), a territory largely Slavic in its population, was, basically left at the mercy of the Third Reich's military. (More on this precarious situation, below.) In this Agreement, Hitler was granted access to the Sudetenland; there was no ultimatum, and the German people were once again impressed and very appreciative of a leader (*Führer*) who was capable of fulfilling so many German interests without war.

The take-over of Austria on March 12, 1938, and the occupation of the Sudetenland to Germany, beginning on October 1, 1938, followed by the invasion on March 15, 1939 into Czechoslovakia were accomplished by Germany—with key support by several large US corporations.

For this invasion, Germany needed many military trucks, as well as high-octane fuels for its Luftwaffe fighter planes. The American automobile industry with production of trucks in Germany was able to help out the Germans, and financial arrangements were arranged to allow the use by German industry of patents for lead additives owned by an American company, Standard Oil, needed for the high-performance engines of the Luftwaffe's planes. More on US big business operating in Germany (from the 1920s through the war), below.

The Munich negotiations and Agreement concluded, the opportunity members of the Oster Conspiracy (just discussed) saw in September 1938, with its very well-designed, militarily-savvy plan to rid Germany of its Nazi government was not to return. What followed was a furthering of Hitler's plan for the domination of Europe and the killing off of literally tens of millions of inferior beings, first of all the Jews and the Gypsies (the Romanies), to be exterminated, but also the Slavs, to make room for *Lebensraum* (German living space at the expense of Slavic Europe).

This issue of Germany's attitude toward its neighboring countries was an important one. As early as November 19, 1937, Lord Halifax had been sent to meet with Hitler at Berchtesgaden. There was no agreement reached, but Halifax suggested to Hitler that Britain would acquiesce to further German demands. Halifax reported that Hitler did not appear to be interested in war. (This had perhaps an element of wishful thinking mixed into the judgment by Halifax here.) Relatedly, for Halifax, in early 1939, before the invasion of Poland by Germany, the Soviet Union proposed an international conference to discuss the threat of war coming from Germany, to form a united front against Germany, and to signal to Hitler that there would be clear opposition to any further German aggression. Britain had no particular interest in such a meeting and it was Lord Halifax who told Stalin so, through the Soviet Ambassador in London, on March 19, 1939.⁹⁰⁷ *Stalin, convinced that Hitler only wanted to bluff the USSR* (never wanting to invade it), was regularly skeptical of British and even Soviet intelligence, dismissing them as unreliable or simply fabricated.⁹⁰⁸ The Soviets—it has been learned, from documents earlier classified as secret—two weeks before the outbreak of war, had met with French and British officers, and proposed to them a military, anti-German alliance, with the plan of putting some one million Soviet soldiers on the German frontier (with the permission of the Polish government). Neither the French nor the British took up the offer.⁹⁰⁹ The USSR was quite desperate to contain German aggression, but not ready to do that alone. The very next week, there would be the accords known as the Molotov-Ribbentrop Pact, of August 23, 1939, just one week before Germany invaded Poland.

This agreement was signed two days after Hitler had already spoken to the commanders-in-chief of the Germany military. With his typical self-aggrandizing self-confidence and denigration of his enemies, Hitler discussed with them his sense of the limited capacity of Britain to go to war, suggesting it would take them perhaps two years to build up their military to fighting capacity. He also gave his opinion of the Western powers: "It was clear to me that a conflict with Poland had to come sooner or later. I had already made this decision in spring [1939—obviously months before the excuse of the Gleiwitz Incident the night of August 31, 1939, used to justify the retaliatory attack the very next morning on Poland starting World War II], but I thought I would first turn against the West in a few years, and only afterwards toward the East. [This may remind some of the German pre-World War I plan, the Schlieffen Plan, discussed above.] … But this plan, which was acceptable to me, could not be executed because essential conditions have changed. It was clear to me, that Poland would attack us in the case of a war with the West [perhaps a rather unlikely scenario] …. Essentially it depends on me, my existence, because of my political activities. [Is this a realistic assessment or intense hubris?] Furthermore, the fact that probably no one will ever again have the confidence of the whole German people as I do. There will probably never again be a man in the future with more authority than I have. My existence is therefore a factor of great value…. We have nothing to lose; we can only gain…. Our enemies have men who are below average. No personalities. No masters, no men of action…. The relation to Poland has become unbearable…. This moment is more favorable than in 2 to 3 years…. The enemy did not count on my great strength of resolve. *Our enemies are little worms.* I saw them in Munich."⁹¹⁰

---

⁹⁰⁷ C. Peter Chen, "Halifax," WORLD WAR II DATABASE.
⁹⁰⁸ Stalin: "One can't believe everything the [Soviet] Secret Service says." Heinz Höhne, *Codeword: Direktor: The Story of the Red Orchestra* (1971), pp. 7, 237.
⁹⁰⁹ Nick Holdsworth, "Stalin planned to send a million troops to stop Hitler if Britain and France agreed pact," *The Telegraph* (London), Oct. 18, 2008.
⁹¹⁰ NT-NCA-Red, vol. 3, pp. 581-586; Text No. 420-A: "The Führer's speech to

Returning to the crisis over Czechoslovakia intensifying in September 1938, Chamberlain flew—his first flight ever—on September 15 to see Hitler at Berchtesgaden. Seeking to carry out his policy of appeasement, to maintain the peace of Europe, Chamberlain then flew to Germany twice more that month, first to Bad Godesberg and then to Munich. At that first of three meetings, in Berchtesgaden, on September 15, 1938—this had required Chamberlain a long day's trip: leaving at dawn in London, flying to Munich and then by train, arriving in Berchtesgaden at 4 pm), with a long meeting with Hitler. There resulted an agreement for Britain to agree to giving over to Germany Sudeten Mountain areas (the Sudetenland) with at least 50% Germanic population to Germany, with no consultation with Czechoslovakia. Hitler was offering Chamberlain continuing peace if areas of the Sudeten Mountains with a majority of ethnic Germans would gradually be given over to the Reich. After conferring with his cabinet and the French, Chamberlain returned to confer with Hitler on September 22, at Bad Godesberg. There he agreed to Hitler's proposal of the preceding week. Hitler, however, surprised him by responding with new conditions: the immediate transfer of all of the Sudetenland, by September 28, with a plebiscite only occurring later. Furthermore, Hitler now maintained the option of Germany's going to war unless all of the collateral claims for territory in Czechoslovakia by Poland and Hungary that had significant Polish and Hungarian populations were also complied with. (These claims had been raised in the preceding days by the Polish and Hungarian governments, at Hitler's insistence.) The evening of that meeting at Bad Godesberg, September 22, Chamberlain advised the Czechs to mobilize for eventual war. In a formal document two days later, the Godesberg Memorandum, of September 24, Hitler issued an ultimatum to Czechoslovakia that it must accept these conditions, and, if not done by 2 pm on September 28, 1938, Germany would enter the Sudetenland by force. Chamberlain protested at being presented an ultimatum, to which Hitler responded in a literalist manner that the document in question was entitled a memorandum and not an ultimatum. (They simply have spoken of an ultimatum made within a memorandum.) In any case, this was a shift to a more belligerent stance by Hitler. On September 25, the British cabinet, the French government, and the Czechs rejected Hitler's newest demands. In a speech in Berlin the next day, September 26, Hitler suggested that war might be just days away. On September 28, Czechoslovakia formally rejected the ultimatum; by that date, the French had mobilized their armies and the British Royal Navy was also war-ready.

British intelligence (MI6)—in the person of spy Hugh Christie[911]—had informed the British government in March 1938 that an organized German

---

the Commanders-in-Chief of the Wehrmacht, 22 August 1939," pp. 242-245, in *The Nazi Germany Sourcebook: An Anthology of Texts*, Roderick Stackelberg and Sally A. Winkle, eds. (2002). Italics added.

[911] On August 18, 1939, Hugh Christie would communicate to the British government that Hitler had decided to launch an attack on Poland in September.

anti-Nazi military group was planning the removal (and probably assassination) of Hitler if Britain would join forces with Czechoslovakia against Hitler: the Oster Conspiracy, introduced above. In more detail, members of the Oster Conspiracy also communicated their plans and the need for British resistance to Hitler (to force his hand in declaring war against Czechoslovakia) as part of their understanding of how best to overthrow the Nazi government. At this moment in late September, this group saw that situation realized, with its members in the German military and police forces had foreseen and were timing their attack to being just after Hitler declared war on Czechoslovakia and before the lapse of the two days required to mobilize troops for such an invasion, with a plan to rid Germany of its Nazi government, as described above. Police forces throughout Germany would establish order, and the few SS troops stationed for attack near the Czech border by that time, would be cut off from returning to Berlin by other German military units. This would then involve a change of government (envisioned was a monarchical-legislative structure, modeled on that of Great Britain, with a Kaiser and the Reichstag modeled of the British government with King and Parliament), and their political stance was one of keeping Germany from going to war. This was seen as popular with the German populace since the Germans as well as the British and French and other combatants in World War I still had horrid memories of those times, only two decades earlier.

Hitler, however, did not invade the Sudetenland that day, September 28, as his ultimatum had spoken of, but agreed to hold a meeting with Mussolini, Chamberlain, and Daladier (French Prime Minister), to be held the next day, September 29, in Munich, a meeting that continued into September 30. The Munich Agreement was signed in the early hours of September 30 (but postdated September 29), recognizing German control over the Sudetenland by October 10, with an empty permission to Czechoslovakia to fight against Germany alone (or not at all). Czechoslovakia, which had the strongest military in Middle Europe (except for Germany)—and also had mutual military assistance treaties with both France and the Soviet Union, both of which came to nothing—saw that it would lose its mountainous buffer zone and the fortifications strategically placed there, and, given these new considerations, it capitulated later that day. Chamberlain returned to London, where he famously waved a piece of paper (the Agreement), declaring "Peace in Our Time!" He and others would like to have believed that Hitler was now satisfied and appeased, and would be return to being a civil, peace-loving leader.

The Munich Agreement was signed by Britain (MP Neville Chamberlain), France (Premier Édouard Daladier), Italy (Benito Mussolini), and Germany (Adolf Hitler), on September 29, 1938.[912] The Sudetenland was to be

---

Chamberlain decided to ignore this information, too. See John Simkin, "Hugh Christie," SPARTICUS EDUCATIONAL. Cf. John Simkin, *Hitler* (1988).

[912] David Dilks, "Raleigh Lecture on History: 'We Must Hope for the Best and Prepare for the Worst': The Prime Minister, the Cabinet and Hitler's Germany,

occupied by Germany by October 10. *Czechoslovakia was given notice it could fight on its own or accept the agreement.*

A week after this event, with Chamberlain greeted back in England as a hero and a champion of peace, Churchill would give a speech in the House of Commons in which he would declare, "I venture to think that in future the Czechoslovak State cannot be maintained as an independent entity. I think you will find that in a period of time which may be measured by years, but may be measured only by months, Czechoslovakia will be engulfed in the Nazi regime."[913] We have a detailed sense of the plight of the Czechs at that time in novelized report, *A Stricken Field* (1940), by Martha Gellhorn, author, news journalist, and wife of Ernest Hemingway.

In retrospect, Cambridge University professor of history, Christopher Andrew, would explain, "Appeasement [in the Munich Pact] was based on the belief that *some* of Hitler's demands were, at any rate, reasonable. So, you meet the reasonable demands; Adolf Hitler is going to be satisfied; peace will be break out for the foreseeable future. The thing that was *wrong* with this, of course, is that Adolf Hitler was a profoundly unreasonable person. There was no way that he could be satisfied."[914]

If we look at the changed geopolitical situation in Europe after this agreement, it may be somewhat clear that Britain and France, without one bullet being fired, had ceded to Germany a powerful role in Central Europe, basically placing it within the sphere of influence of the German Reich: in effect, having Germany dominating central Europe. While the Soviet Union might not have been happy or felt secure with these arrangements, the path was basically set for Germany to take a dominant role in the region from France and the Low Countries all the way east to the borders of the USSR. We might say, from this perspective, that war was unnecessary: *the chess game had already been won by the Reich.*

Germany continued its expansionist actions, in 1940, with its invasions of, and surrender by, Denmark (April 9), Luxembourg (May 9), Belgium (May 28), the Netherlands (May 14, with last resistance ended May 17), Norway (June 10), and France (surrender on June 14, 1940). For the French front, a massive German offensive began on May 10, 1940, with 4.5 million Frenchmen already mobilized after the invasion of Poland and the French declaration of war against Germany, leading to some 92,000 French soldiers dying in the first wave of German military attacks, and to some 6.2 million French civilians—including some 2 million Parisians—becoming refugees, along with 1.8 million Belgians and 180,000 Dutch, all fleeing from the Germans, leaving their homes and farms to take to

---

1937–1939," *Proceedings of the British Academy*, vol. 73, 1987, pp. 309-352; "September 1938: FDR Day by Day: US and World Events plus Additional Resources," THE PARE LORENTZ PROJECT, FDR PRESIDENTIAL LIBRARY.

[913] Winston Churchill, "The Munich Agreement," House of Commons, October 5, 1939, INTERNATIONAL CHURCHILL SOCIETY.

[914] *Winston Churchill: The Wilderness Years, 1929-39*, BBC/UKTV (1969), 39:25-39:50.

the roads, mostly on foot.[915] The French military had a seriously flawed sense of what a war with Germany might entail. The French had assumed that the Germans, if they did initiate an offense and invade France, would do so from the east (Alsace-Lorraine) and for this the French had built a set of installments of large artillery, aimed to the east. These were together called the Maginot Line, and were thought to be impenetrable. Of course, the Wehrmacht invaded north of those installments, bypassing them quite thoroughly. In short, "the French High Command had not sufficiently studied or kept up with the new military techniques. They put most of their resources—and confidence—into the Maginot Line, a series of fortifications along the eastern border, little suspecting how vulnerable a fixed fortification was."[916] The invasion of the Low Lands and France, with the capitulation and surrender to the Germans, did not take long. In his own vision of history, shortly after Paris fell on June 14, Hitler would declare in a speech to the *Reichstag*, July 19, 1940, on the victory in the Western campaign, as if ignorant of the harshness, violence, and murders of the German occupation forces in Poland for the better part of a year at that time, "The German Reich, in particular with regard to Poland, has shown restraint [*Selbstüberwindung*, self-restraint or will power] ever since the National Socialist rise to power."[917]

Soon after the fall of France, Maréchal Pétain spoke of his asking for an honorable peace, on June 17; the armistice was signed on June 22. Its significant Article 19 required the French to hand over all German citizens in France upon the request of the German forces.[918] That week, De Gaulle would speak from London offering a rather different attitude, in his *Appel* (call, appeal) of June 18, calling for resistance to the German occupation. With this French surrender and German control over western and northern Europe from the Atlantic coast down to the Pyrenees, the Reich had a basis for a hegemon, simply waiting to be developed.

Politics were changing elsewhere in Europe, as well. Poland decided to annul the citizenship of Polish Jews who had lived in Germany for five years or longer. (Many Jews with Polish citizenship had even been born in Germany.) *This decree took effect on March 31, 1938.*[919]

---

[915] The German invasion of these Western European countries resulted in some 8 million people taking to the roads to escape the Germans. See *En mai, fait ce qu'il te plaît* (*Come What May*), a 2015 French-Belgian-German film, with its depiction of this exodus; statistics at 0:35-0:42. Cf. 2015 film, *Elles étaient en guerre 1939-1945* (*Women at War 1939-1945*), at 7:340-7:40, 15:15-15:25.

[916] Margaret Collins Weitz, "Introduction," pp. vii-xxii, in Lucie Aubrac, *Outwitting the Gestapo* (1993), at p. viii. French title: *Ils partiront dans l'ivresse* (1984). This French title quotes a coded British message. See Aubrac's diary entry for Feb. 8, 1944, at p. 222 (in her book just cited).

[917] *Die Rede des Führers im Reichstag, Berlin, den 19. Juli 1940*, with Eng. tr., "Speech of the Führer, Adolf Hitler, in the Reichstag, 19 July 1940: Declaration of Victory over France and the British Forces in the Western Campaign," WIKISOURCE.

[918] "Convention d'Armistice," *Digithèque MJP*, MJP.UNIV-PERP.FR.

[919] Giles MacDonogh, *1938: Hitler's Gamble* (2009), p. 349.

On October 27, 1938, just weeks before *Kristallnacht* (September 9-10, 1938), the Gestapo began forcing Polish Jews (in the earlier Reich and in its Austrian province) back to Poland. The Polish government, and its border guards, reflecting an anti-Jewish attitude, *would not accept them*. These Jews were literally in no-man's land.[920] Some Jews were able to leave Germany by flight or otherwise, being allowed the clothing they were wearing and 5 deutschmarks. Most Jews did not have this option. One couple among those forced to the Polish border was Sendel and Riva Grynszpan, who had lived in Hanover since emigrating in 1911 from Poland. They had sent their son, Herschel, with no future as a Polish Jew living in Germany, to his aunt and uncle Abraham and Chawa (or Ḥava) Grynszpan; he lived in Paris, illegally, and with no citizenship after the Polish government action of March 31, 1938 (mentioned just above).

His parents, among some 12,000 Polish Jews, were deprived of their possessions and trained to the Polish border town of Zbąszyń (west of the city of Poznań). A postcard dated October 31, 1938, speaking of their plight, was delivered to their son in Paris on November 3. Frustrated and angry at the treatment of the Polish Jews—and of his parents—by the Gestapo and the German government, he went to protest his rage at the German Embassy in Paris. On the morning of November 7, 1938, having purchased a 6.35 mm revolver, he went there, wanting to meet with, and shoot, the Ambassador, Count Johannes von Welczeck. He was shown into the office of a junior diplomat, Ernst vom Rath. With the revolver he had just purchased, he shot Vom Rath four times in the abdomen. Vom Rath was to die shortly thereafter, on November 9. At his death, Ernst vom Rath was 29 years old; the young Herschel Grynszpan was 17.

When the news of this assassination got back to Berlin, the workings of a great pogrom were set into motion, said to be a spontaneous expression of German indignation, but actually a nation-wide action of violence against German Jewry, organized by Joseph Goebbels. This took place that very night, November 9-10, and has been known since then as *Kristallnacht*, The Night of the Broken Glass. In Nazi judgment, the Jews were held responsible; the insurance policies they had for homes and businesses were declared moot, invalid, so that the Jews had to pay for their own losses. In addition, the Third Reich collectively fined the German Jews one billion reichsmarks (or some 400 million 1938 US dollars) for the damages they caused. Some 30,000 German Jews were arrested and sent to concentration camps.

German legal reasoning at the time was quite precise: In a trial in early December 1938, three minors were found robbing a Jewish-owned shop in Berlin's workmen's district. The boys were arrested. Judge Schlehmann, Chief of the Magistrates Court, stated, "The defendants must be punished because they have brought Reich Government measures into ill repute. If the government orders certain measures to be taken against the Jewish enemies of the German people, then individual

---

[920] "The Expulsion of Polish Jews from Germany: Fall 1938," HOLOCAUST.CZ.

folk-comrades (*Volkkameraden*) must not bring these measures into disrepute through plundering or other independent undertakings. *One must remember that only the government can protect the community property stolen from the Jews. Private individuals cannot do this.* But one must not forget either, that the three defendants believed themselves justified in taking away again from the Jews the property which the latter had stolen from the German people. Because of their youth, they were not quite in a position to determine which task belonged to the people and which to the government, The Reich Government ordered the measures taken on November 11, and the [specific] offense of the accused consisted in usurping the power to extend these orders."[921] This was a remarkable admission that the violence on *Kristallnacht* was not a spontaneous reaction but a coordinated action directed from high government sources. The terms *Kristallnacht*, or *Reichskristallnacht*, the Reich's Crystal Night, referring to glass broken that night—involve euphemisms that did not mention the arrests of tens of thousands of Jews, the shipping of many of them to concentration camps, the murders of Jews that also took place in that context—in what were said to be further responses to the assassination of Ernst vom Rath.

For German Jews who had not fully appreciated the intensity of the anti-Jewish values of the Third Reich, this was quite inexplicable. The wife of a Jewish butcher in the town of Wittlich—in the Rhineland-Palatinate not far from the border with Luxembourg (west of Frankfurt, southwest of Koblenz, and northeast of Trier)—Mrs. Marks, her husband thrown into the back of a truck, their shop's front windows smashed, and other local Jews also hit and about to be taken away, asked the SA Men, in despair, "Why are you people doing this to us? What have we ever done to you?"[922]

NAZI ATTITUDES AND PROPAGANDA: GÖRING VS. STREICHER

Concerning *Kristallnacht*, which he heard about the next day, Hermann Göring said to his wife, "Stupid imbeciles! They tell me to organize a four-year plan, to scrape together the smallest bits of iron and old newspapers—and then a band of rowdies goes and destroys an enormous fortune in a single night. And Goebbels just eggs them on."[923] Göring and others in charge of German economic stability and growth were strongly in disagreement with this quite unruly mob violence, much preferring central government administration and control of racial violence. Also on November 10, 1939, Julius Streicher in a speech, declared in part:

> That Jew [the assassin of German diplomat Counsel vom Roth] was the representative and agent of the Jewish people, both through blood and education.... As a bastard, the Jew always follows the dictates of his bad blood.... The Jew ... is not taught "Love your neighbor as yourself" or "If someone strikes you on your right cheek, turn also

---

[921] Edith Roper and Clara Leiser, *Skeleton of Justice*, pp. 146-147. Italics added.
[922] Alfons Heck, *The Burden of Hitler's Legacy*, pp. 61-62.
[923] Emmy Goering, *My Life with Göring* (1972), p. 32.

your left cheek to him." Instead, he is taught: "You may do whatever you wish to a Gentile." ... As I said to you twenty years ago, the time will come when Germans no longer live in barracks, but rather the Jews. Germans will then move into fine houses. And if the Jews now move away, we will be able to give pleasure to some families with many children by allowing them to celebrate Christmas in a decent home, a home in which others previously celebrated a different holiday.... *We could have killed all the Jews in Germany yesterday, but we did not do it* .... Our hope is that the Jewish people will one day receive the penalty they deserve for all the sorrow, misery, and trouble they have brought the peoples. We believe the supreme court is coming that will judge the Devil's people [the Jews]. Then the world will breathe more freely, and there will be peace.[924]

This is a speech whose propagandistic techniques may be studied with some benefit of understanding. This passage is rich in the issues it raises. First, it is clear that Streicher is not interested in explaining what had happened to this young man's parents that led to his despair and anger. This is an example of the art of decontextualizing and abstracting from the specifics being considered, in a way that keeps the significance of the topic at hand from being fully acknowledged. Here, we see the young man characterized as an anonymous representative of the bad blood of all Jews (to use Streicher's terms). This expands the significance by association, a transfer of implied attitude to an entire people. Following the above comments by Streicher, we see him repeat the contrast between Jewish teachings and Christian teachings, which has its own long history. Here is the often-cited supposed contrast between the harshness of Judaism (as a passage from Exodus 21:24, "an eye for an eye, a tooth for a tooth") and the gentler, more loving teaching from the New Testament of turning the other cheek (Matthew 5:39). Again, teachings from long ago and far away are taken as if obeyed to the letter to this day. In Jewish tradition, however, and here we may consider Sforno (an honored medieval Italian rabbi, Ovadio ben Yaakov Sforno, ca. 1470-1550), who commented on this passage in Exodus: "*An eye for an eye*. This would have been the fitting [punishment] according to the strict law of measure for measure, but we have received the tradition [teaching handed down through the generations] that he should pay money, because our conjecture may be at fault [lit., "lacking"—not well-rounded or comprehensive] and we may unwisely exceed the exact measure (in punishing) the guilty (one)."[925]

---

[924] Julius Streicher, "Speech after 'The Night of Broken Glass' [Kristallnacht], 10 November 1938," pp. 86-93 in *Landmark Speeches of National Socialism*, Randall L. Bytwerk, ed., tr. (2008), at pp. 88-92. Italics added.

[925] A modern bilingual edition explained: "Our sages have taught us that an eye

The Hitler Era

In other words, considering a teaching without taking into account its history and subsequent interpretations and applications, may well result (as here) in a radical misunderstanding of the history and the evolving and current status of the teaching in question.

The contrast with the Christian attitude of love and forgiveness is in a way ironic here, given the German reaction to one person being killed, with close to 100 Jews killed immediately, some 30,000 Jewish men arrested and sent to concentration camps, with Jewish businesses, synagogues, schools, hospitals, and homes looted and destroyed, with police and firemen standing by watching but not interfering. Although National Socialist teachings (propaganda) spoke of honoring Christian values, its proclivity toward murder at the least provocation, would reveal the hypocrisy of this association. We have only to think of the response to the assassination of Reinhard Heydrich in Prague, followed by the Lidice Massacre of June 10, 1942, when the entire village of Lidice, north of Prague, was razed, all of its male residents killed, along with some 50 of the women, with the remaining women and children all shipped to a concentration camp, or the massacre of the community of Oradour-sur-Glane, in France, northwest of Limoges, on that same date in 1944, with 642 (almost all) of its population killed most being burned alive, locked inside the village church. A somewhat naïve French pamphlet published later would declare, "*Ce jour-là, l'Armée allemande s'est déshonorée*" (That day the Germans disgraced itself),[926] as if the German military of the Third Reich had otherwise behaved honorably overall. (We discuss other famous Nazi massacres elsewhere.)

Streicher went on to give an old example often claimed of Judaism, that any Jew can treat any non-Jew (Gentile) without any particular moral constraints. Not surprisingly, Streicher does not indicate where this claim is made. He takes a statement he claims is from some Jewish text, not identified; nor does he indicate when such a text might have been written. This is another form of decontextualization, taking something that at most was held (by some, in some contexts) at some time in the past, but implying that it is fully valid in the present. If we do some of his work for him, we might come across a passage held to be from the time of Moses and the Exodus. For example, the principle often cited (that of how to deal with the owner of an ox that gores another ox or a person), is from

---

for an eye means monetary compensation" (Talmud, *Bava Kama* 83b). The Rambam (*Mishneh Torah, Laws of Injuries*, 1:3) states that the person who blinded the eye of another is worthy to have his eye blinded as well (measure for measure), but tradition teaches us not to do so. The reason given in the Talmud cited above is because this kind of punishment would not always be equitable and the Torah teaches us, You shall have one manner of law (Leviticus 24:22). Rambam is an acronym for Rabbeinu (Our Rabbi) Moses ben Maimon, or Moses Maimonides (1135-1204). See *Sforno: Commentary on the Torah/Be'ur al Hatorah l'Rabi Ovad'yah Sforno*, Raphael Pelcovitz, tr. (1997), p. 397, for this explanation and commentary.

[926] *Oradour-sur-Glane (Souviens-toi, Remember): 10 juin 1944* (1945).

Exodus 21:28-37. *Even that was questioned and its principles considered inapplicable, for many centuries.* For example, in the commentary by Rashi (an honored medieval French rabbi, Rabbi Shlomo ben Yitzhaki, 1040-1105) on Exodus, he notes the passage "and its owner shall die" (Exodus 21:29) and explains this as dying "through Heaven" (*bidei shamayim*), that is, it will be God who metes out punishment, not people. At the least, Streicher does not acknowledge the ways in which teachings go through transformations of significance through time.

On the other hand, some link this teaching to the Talmud. The Talmud, we might realize, is not a text which is taken as definitive overall; it is, rather, a collection of a rather large number of opinions, perspectives, interpretations, and proposals about how earlier teachings might be best applied. Its various opinions are not expected to be consistent among themselves. Often its discussions are quite specific, not to be generalized as if applicable to anything slightly resembling what is being discussed.

These limitations or caveats about misinterpreting anything from the Talmud noted, there are statements about keeping one's distance from Gentiles, and being cautious in dealing with them. This is of course *not the same as saying* that Jews can kill Gentiles with impunity before God (or otherwise), *nor as saying* that Jews can treat gentiles any way the Jews' whims dictate. Furthermore, these proposals—which are quite relevant to understand statements in much of the Talmud, understood as the ideas, reflections, and proposals of various individual teachers (rabbis)—are for each person to consider, perhaps debate, and to draw conclusions, especially taking into account other rabbis' comments that are cited in the same sections of the Talmudic text. We are not talking about dogma put forth as indisputable and obligatory in any sense, but as serious comments about the issues at hand, for the serious to debate.

Streicher also talks about violence reported in stories about ancient Persia as if it actually took place and was held by Jews (in general, or all Jews) to be a model automatically followed to this day.[927] That said, even if those events did take place (there is a serious question of how a Jewess could end up being the Queen of the Persian Emperor, for example, which is a key part of the story), there is no continuing suggestion that Jews should repeat the killing that was reported about ancient Persia. It is perhaps interesting that Streicher goes on to talk about the honorable restraint that the German people took in not killing all of the Jews of Germany, in response to the outrage and insult of a young Jew walking into the German Embassy in Paris and killing a German diplomat.

Streicher interestingly goes on to speak of the benefits that the German people are envisioned as receiving as a result of the ouster of the Jews of Germany: Streicher promises, in ways that were not especially carried out, that Jewish homes and property will pass on to the Reich, by laws declared in the Reich by that point in time, which will offer these

---

[927] The events in question were said to have taken place in the fith century BCE; as in many stories, their historical reality has been questioned.

dwellings, and the property left inside by fleeing Jews, to needy German families, especially those with large numbers of children. Himmler and others apparently saw Streicher as overstepping his bounds. Streicher was soon discharged from his status as leader of the Gau (political region) of Franconia. This demotion, in 1940, involved specific charges against him: that he was stealing confiscated Jewish wealth for his own benefit and that of his friends, and that he was repeatedly involved in tax evasion. In February 1940, he was stripped of all of his Party offices. He was, however, allowed to continue publication of the weekly, *Der Stürmer*, with its strong anti-Jewish focus; its last issue was in February 1945.

MEANWHILE, BACK IN THE LABS OF EUROPE

At about that time of late 1939 with the events of *Kristallnacht*, in the laboratories of advanced research scientists, further little-known developments took place; there were discoveries being made that would change the history of the war and of the world: In the years following the discovery and proof of the existence of the neutron, in 1932 (mentioned above), there were some remarkable developments in atomic physics, especially through research by Otto Hahn, Lise Meitner, Fritz Strassmann, with world-changing consequences. Otto Hahn (1879-1968), was later a Nobel Laureate in Chemistry, in 1944.[928] Lise Meitner (1878-1968) was a Viennese-born physicist who had studied with Max Planck in Berlin in 1907. Identified by Nazi criteria as a Jewess, she left for Sweden in July 1938, after the *Anschluß*, when Germany annexed Austria. In 1939, she and her nephew, physicist Otto Frisch (1904-1979)—who had worked in Copenhagen at the institute of physicist Niels Bohr and would later join the US Manhattan Project in 1943[929]—would propose the term fission for the break-up of uranium in the processes the group had studied.[930] Fritz, or Friedrich, Strassmann (1902-1980), would join the team of Hahn and Meitner in 1934, and their discovery of nuclear fission of the uranium atom in late 1938 established the possibility of creating what became known as the atom (or atomic)bomb.[931] There was parallel research begun in Nazi Germany on the project of creating an atomic bomb, starting in April 1939, just months after the Strassmann-Hahn discovery.

The work within the Third Reich was limited, given that those physicists suspected of not being dedicated Nazis and all Jewish physicists were eliminated from the group accepted for this work. Even Werner Heisenberg (of "Heisenberg's Uncertainly Principle") was suspect for the *Deutsche Physik* (German or Aryan Physics), a pro-Nazi group that rejected the theories and work coming from what it termed *jüdische Physik* (Jewish Physics), such as the work of Albert Einstein.[932] In any

---

[928] "The Nobel Prize in Chemistry 1944: Otto Hahn," NOBELPRIZE.ORG.
[929] "Otto Frisch, Physicist, Los Alamos, NM, United Kingdom," ATOMIC HERITAGE FOUNDATION.
[930] "Lise Meitner, Austrian physicist," ENCYCLOPÆDIA BRITANNICA.
[931] "Fritz Strassmann, Chemist, Germany," ATOMIC HERITAGE FOUNDATION.
[932] "The Nobel Prize in Physics 1921: Albert Einstein," NOBELPRIZE.ORG.

case, the project was not seen as significant in changing the course of the war, *and it never obtained clear support from the Nazi regime*. Finally, work was stopped in June 1942 and the project terminated that autumn. And yet, given the secretive nature of such projects, the Allies did not know of the ending of the Nazi project until late 1944, so they were under great pressure to develop a working bomb, which they did through the Manhattan Project. This is a further glimpse of the role that research science plays in the practical world of politics and international relations.

KRISTALLNACHT, HITLER'S WAR PROPAGANDA, AND THE ÉVIAN CONFERENCE

There was an initial conflict among key members of the government about the damage of *Kristallnacht* (with Göring confronting Goebbels), creatively resolved by having the onus of costs of the damages be placed on the German Jews themselves, freeing German insurance companies from being liable for the damages. Then, on November 10, 1939, at the new building for Hitler's official business, the Führerbau, where the Munich Agreement was signed, Hitler and Goebbels spoke before the German press. Hitler spoke of the earlier propagandistic value of talk of peace and of the importance now to use propaganda to prepare the German people for war:

> For decades, circumstances caused me to speak almost exclusively of peace. Only by constantly emphasizing the German *Volk's* desire for peace and peaceful intentions was I able to gain the German *Volk's* freedom step by step and thus to give it the armament necessary as a prerequisite for accomplishing the next step.... In this context, one must not forget one thing which was crucial, namely, propaganda. Not only propaganda in the interior [within Germany] but also in the exterior [internationally]. As I pointed out earlier, the fact that the German *Volk* took a different stance in this case quite different from that of other peoples and of that which the German *Volk* would have taken not so very long ago, is the result of the persistent enlightenment campaign with which we have inundated the German *Volk*. And here the press played a big role.... For years, I spoke only of peace because of this forced situation. Now it has become necessary to slowly prepare the German *Volk* psychologically for the fact that there are things that cannot be achieved by peaceful means.... it was necessary to shed light on certain events abroad in such a matter that the inner voice of the German *Volk* naturally cried out for the application of force.[933]

---

[933] Adolf Hitler, "Speech in Führerbau, Munich, November 10, 1938," NEUES EUROPA. Ger. text in "Rede Hitlers vor der deutschen Presse, 10. November 1938," *Vierteljahrshefte für Zeitgeschichte*, vol. 6, no. 2, 1958, pp. 175-191 (speech itself at pp. 181-191).

The Hitler Era

This may make it clear that Hitler was not dreaming of peace in Europe, as he repeatedly stated, but had other ideas in mind, which he would make public in his own timing. Hitler's vision of propaganda and its ability when organized to persuade a public of its values was also expressed in somewhat similar terms by Hermann Göring in 1946, after his capture, in which he stated,

> Why, of course, the people don't want war.... But, after all, it is the leaders of the country who determine the policy and it always a simple matter to drag people along, whether it is a democracy or a fascist dictatorship or a Parliament or a Communist dictatorship ... the people can always be brought to the bidding of the leaders. That is easy. All you have to do is tell them that they are being attacked and denounce the pacifists for lack of patriotism and exposing the country to danger. It works the same way in any country.[934]

This is quite a powerful global statement about how gullible populations can be. Elsewhere here I give a few examples of later reports from the CIA itself (about wars and other non-declared military operations by US armed forces and the CIA itself). There are further examples of the similar operations of other governments, which I will leave for interested readers.

In the specifics being addressed here, considering the new level of violence seen during *Kristallnacht*, Britain was quite swift to reply. On November 21, 1939, less than two weeks after *Kristallnacht*, the British Parliament allowed for 10,000 Jewish children to come from Germany in the *Kindertransport* program. In this, some Jewish children were given asylum in the UK. The first transport arrived in London on December 2, 1938, just weeks after *Kristallnacht* itself. These continued with persistence into 1940; some 10,000 children were accepted, of which some 7,500 were Jewish. There was vigorous support for this by Jewish and by Quaker organizations in the UK. This joined a policy of domestic-service visas,[935] already earmarked for 20,000 Jewish adult women.[936]

In the USA, there were debates in Congress in an attempt to open up immigration for some of the distressed Jews of Europe—limited to relief for children. On February 9, 1939, the Wagner-Rogers Bill, sponsored by Sen. Robert F. Wagner (Democrat, NJ) and Rep. Edith Rogers (Republican, MA) presented a bill, Senate Joint Resolution 64, on the Admission of German Refugee Children, not "Jewish children"). It would have permitted entry into the USA of 20,000 Jewish children from the Greater German

---

[934] Gustave M. Gilbert, *Nuremberg Diary*, pp. 278-279.
[935] "Kindertransport, 1938-1940," HOLOCAUST ENCYCLOPEDIA, USHMM.
[936] Josie Roberts, "Lisbeth's Apron: Escaping the Nazis," THE JEWISH MUSEUM (LONDON); Sean Kelly, "Review of *Whitehall and the Jews, 1933-1948: British Immigration Policy, Jewish Refugees and the Holocaust* by Louise London," REVIEWS IN HISTORY, REVIEW NO. 221.

Reich, 14 years old or younger, with 10,000 allowed to immigrate in 1939, and 10,000 in 1940. A requirement was that all children who entered would have to have a prior commitment by organizations or individuals to support them fully (a primarily financial commitment). The bill[937] had the support of organized labor, the Federal Council of Churches, the YMCA, a variety of Quaker and Unitarian social workers and Protestant, Catholic, and Jewish clergy, former President Herbert Hoover (Republican), former Governor of Wisconsin Phillip La Follette (Republican, then Progressive), and New York City Mayor Fiorello LaGuardia (Democrat). Opposing the bill were nationalistic groups such as the American Coalition of Patriotic Societies, the American Legion, Ladies of the Grand Army of the Republic, Junior Order of United American Mechanics, Daughters of the American Revolution, and the Patriotic Order Sons of America.

Secretary of State Cordell Hull expressed his opposition to the bill. President Roosevelt would make no comments at all about the bill.[938] The bill was debated but never came to a full-Congress vote. In the Senate Judiciary Committee, its Chairman, Senator Richard Russell (Democrat, Georgia)—US Senator from 1933 to 1971, later a leading segregationist— had the bill significantly modified: the German quota for immigration remained, but German *non-Jewish* children were given priority). Given those significant changes, Sen. Wagner withdrew the bill.

This was one more manifestation of the actual limited power of the so-called global Jewish cabal that was claimed to control all governments and all societies. In fact, Jews, as we might suspect, are one group with its interests, in a context of many more groups and other areas of concern. Jews, by the actual events of history, demonstrate that they are not a super-race that is behind the scenes of all small and great activities on our globe, and are not an omnipotent cabal, no matter how many repeat these claims either in hatred or admiration (both distorted)!

Globally, the Spanish Civil War ended some 14 months after the Rape of Nanking (December 1937-January 1938), on April 1, 1939, months before the German invasion of Poland. Germany now had a much greater Jewish population under its control. *The so-called Jewish question was becoming more serious*, and would intensify considerably when Germany invaded Poland, with its Jewish population of three million; Warsaw had some 300,000 Jews, some 30% of the population of the city, pre-war.

---

[937] Discussed in *The Congressional Record, 76th Congress* (1939), in vol. 84, in Part 2, pp. 1278-1279, Part 11, pp. 641-642, and Part 14, pp. 3980-3982.

[938] FDR was sometimes said to prefer following public opinion than leading it. See James MacGregor Burns, *Roosevelt: The Lion and the Fox* (1956), p. 458.

10. World War II Starts: Poland & the West, 1939-1940

After months of planning and preparations for the invasion of Poland, the last weeks of August saw the final preparations in place. Most importantly, a treaty had just been signed on August 23, 1939 between the German Reich and the Soviet Union, the Treaty of Non-aggression between Germany and the Union of Soviet Socialist Republics, called the Molotov-Ribbentrop[939] Pact. There were public, announced paragraphs, but also secret passages that would divide up German and Soviet spheres of influence (to be invaded without conflict with the other) if a German invasion would take place. In fact, the actual German invasion of Poland (on September 1, 1939) was on the planning board long before the actual start of World War II; the codename for the invasion, *Fall Weiss* (Case White), had first been used on April 11, 1939.[940] Official German sources spoke that summer of Polish killings of *Volksdeutsche*, the German-speaking population. There was often mention of a massacre of Germans, the *Bromberger Blutsonntag*, the Bloody Sunday at Bromberg (Polish name, Bydgoszcz, a Polish city northeast of Posnań, northwest of Warsaw, and southwest of Gdańsk). German authorities claimed that somewhere between 150-300 ethnic Germans were killed in that massacre. In retaliation, 2,000 Polish citizens were chosen and random and executed by the German Army. *Some sources cite this massacre as part of the German urge in protecting ethnic Germans, as part of the justification for the military invasion of Poland. And yet*, given that this massacre took place on September 2-3, 1939—termed by one film source as "one of the most heinous of crimes to be inflicted on a civilian population" (obviously disregarding mass murders by the German military)—with the German army already at war in Poland, it could hardly be the cause or excuse of the initial German invasion.[941] This is not to deny that those German citizens of Poland were ultimately murdered, massacred, followed toward war's end by many Germanic citizens of Poland being killed or expulsed from Poland back to Germany, where they were often treated as second-class Germans.

The plans for the invasion of Poland reflected the seriousness of Nazi dreams of power, even if the lands of the Soviet Union were seen as the real, ultimate prize for *Lebensraum*, living space, for the *Herrenrasse*, the Master Race, and, in other terms, for the establishment and strengthening

---

[939] Ribbentrop, a champagne salesman, married Bettina Henckell of the Henkell Champagne family, and became Foreign Minister of the Third Reich, and, relatedly, was insultingly called Rüpschentropp (*Rüpschen:* a small *Rüpel*, a course fellow or lout). See Eva Braun, *The Private Life of Adolf Hitler*, p. 107, July, 1940.

[940] The planning of the invasion of Poland took form long before the faked attack on the German radio station, justifying the war. See Nicolaus von Below, *At Hitler's Side*, p. 25; tr. of Nicolaus von Below, *Als Hitlers Adjutent 1937-45*, p. 159.

[941] See such retro-causality (causes as later events for earlier consequences) in *Adolf Hitler: The Greatest Story Never Told!* (2013), at 1:05:10-1:14:40; "Bromberg Bloody Sunday," *VNN/Vanguard News Network*, vnnforum.com, 2008.

of the *Volksgemeinschaft*—in the Nazi era, meaning the culturally and "racially" pure community of the *Volk*, the people—the community of the *Deutschstämmige*, those whose lineage was German (not Jewish).

Part of this dream of power defined this path as one of war. As Otto D. Tolischus, mentioned above, wrote of the Reich mentality: "Every human and social activity is justified only if it helps prepare for war. The new human being [in the National Socialist vision] is completely possessed by the thought of war. He must not, cannot think of anything else."[942]

The claim that Germany invaded Poland as a response to an attack by Poles on a German borderland radio station—even put into print in documents by the German Foreign Office (Berlin, 1939) and German Library of Information (New York, 1940), the USA still neutral in the war at that time—was obviously a fabrication to serve as an ultimately empty justification; discussions of the invasion long preceded that supposed attack, faked under the direction of the SS and the German military.[943] This attack was not made on a whim. In the weeks before the invasion, discussions at the highest military levels were held, in which even the eventuality of a two-front war was considered, based on the idea that if the Germans invaded Poland, the French might invade Germany. (This was rather unlikely given the reluctance of the French to get into another great war, and with the British reluctance to become involved, as Hitler was noted to have remarked.) There was even a perhaps needless concern that Belgium could mobilize its army in only four days.[944]

Fog Foils Assassination Attempt, November 8, 1941

Soon after the German invasion of Poland on September 1, 1939, setting off World War II when Britain and France made demands on Germany to withdraw from Polish territory (which the Reich obviously disregarded), there was much jubilation but also hesitation on the part of generals in the military and also of anti-Nazi groups and individuals, seeing the great risks and ultimately a real possibility of German defeat.

The military had organized a plan to overthrow the Nazi Reich, with the possible assassination of Hitler as part of that project; this was the so-called Oster Conspiracy, which came to naught (discussed above). It would only be after the fall of Stalingrad that further plans for the assassination of Hitler were defined. (More on these, below.)

Among the serious assassination attempts against Hitler, a young theology student from Neuchatel in western Switzerland, taking Hitler to be a threat to Catholicism, to Christianity in general, to Switzerland, and to all of humanity, was in Munich to assassinate Hitler during the 1938 annual celebration commemorating the failed Munich Putsch of Nov. 8-9, 1923. He was in the witnessing stand, posing as a Swiss reporter, with a

---

[942] Otto D. Tolischus, *They Wanted War* (1940), p. 53.

[943] German Foreign Office (1939) and German Library of Information (1940), *Documents on the Events Preceding the Outbreak of the War*, pp. 491-504.

[944] Franz Halder, *The Halder War Diary, 1938-1942*, Charles Burdick and Hans-Adolf Jaconsen, eds. (1988), entry, Aug. 14, 1941, pp. 11-27.

The Hitler Era

recently purchased pocket pistol, a 6.35 mm. Schmiesser (with a bore of 0.25 in.); too far to have an accurate shot at Hitler, he did not actually shoot. This was just hours before the violence of *Kristallnacht* broke out. This man, Maurice Bavaud, soon out of money, went ticketless on a train to Paris, was found by a conductor, who turned him over to the police—his gun and other documents brought in the Gestapo, whose torture led him to confess planning to kill Hitler; he was put on trial in the *Volksgerichtshof*, the People's Court, on December 18, 1938, judged guilty, and ultimately executed by guillotine on May 14, 1941; the Swiss government did not come to his aid at the time, only formally apologizing seven decades later, in November 2008.[945]

Precisely one year later, one individual who was not a joiner to political parties (neither that of the National Socialists, nor of the KPD, *Kommunistische Partei Deutschlands*, the German Communist Party, to which he had much more sympathy) saw the already brutal nature of the Nazi regime and sensed the forthcoming disaster to Germany, with severe military losses on the ground, and ultimately to be bombed aggressively (years after German Condor Legion had destroyed the town of Guernica in the Spanish Civil War). This man, a carpenter and laborer with manual skills, was Georg Elser, from Württemberg, a town in Swabia, in southwestern Germany to the west of Bavaria and Munich. Elser saw announcements for the annual event on November 8, to commemorate the anniversary of the start of the 1923 Putsch, at the *Bürgerbräukeller*. He designed and built his own explosive device, and, spending many nights in the hall, when it was closed after hours, he installed a bomb that was set to go off at 9:20 pm, in the middle of Hitler's scheduled speech. The bomb went off exactly on time and did significant damage to the hall and to those present.

As it turned out, however, unexpectedly, Hitler's plan to give his speech and then be flown by Berlin in the late evening had to be changed, because a fog had set in around Munich that made the flight take-off ill-advised (and very dangerous). With advice of his respected personal pilot Hans Bauer, Hitler decided to take an evening train from Munich to Berlin. This required an earlier departure from the hall, so that the talk, originally scheduled for 8:30-10:30, was shifted to run only from 8-9 pm. Because of this change of schedule, Hitler ended his speech[946] at 9:07 pm and left immediately with his entourage that included Joseph Goebbels; Heinrich Himmler; Rudolf Heß (or Hess); Reinhard Heydrich; Alfred Rosenberg, the "philosopher" of Nazism; Julius Streicher, editor of *Der Stürmer*; Robert Ley, head of the German Labor Front; August Frank, a high-ranking functionary in charge of the operation of concentration camps and officer in the *SS-Wirtschafts- und Verwaltungshauptampt*, or *SS-WVHA*, the SS

---

[945] Thomas Stephens, "Switzerland failed would-be Hitler Assassin," SWISS INFORMATION ORGANIZATION (SWISSINFO.CH), Nov. 7, 2008; "1941: Maurice Bavaud, Who Couldn't Get A Shot Off," EXECUTEDTODAY.ORG, May 14, 2008.

[946] Hitler's speech that evening is given at "Adolf Hitler—speech at the Bürgerbräukeller: Munich, November 8, 1938," NEUES EUROPA.

Main Economic and Administrative Office; Hermann Esser, member of the Reichstag and editor of the *Völkischer Beobachter;* and Christian Weber, a very early street-fighter on Hitler's behalf and one of the participants who had gone to Bad Wiessee to kill the leaders of the SA, on the Night of the Long Knives, among others.[947] *All of these would live or die with Hitler that night of November 8, 1939!*

The explosion, consisting of 50 kg. (110 lbs.) of powerful explosives,[948] went off as scheduled, at 9:20, some 13 minutes after Hitler had gone.

There was significant damage to the beer hall, and a number of those still present were killed, but Hitler was quite untouched by the explosion. (Of course, his ire, rage, and desire to track down all of those involved in this act of violence be captured and killed were all quite intense.) This was quite an embarrassment to Himmler and *Reichssicherheitsdienst*—the Reich Security Service, the *RSD*—under his command; it was guessed at first that those responsible must have been an organized team, perhaps with British agents, perhaps with some from Otto Strasser's Black Front, a strongly anti-Hitler group operating out of Switzerland.

The German press linked this assassination attempt to the interference of the British; the next day, two British agents were arrested by Gestapo and SD men at Venlo, in the Netherlands at the German border, events that were called the Venlo Incident (more just below), supposedly as responsible for the Hitler assassination plot.[949]

---

[947] See sub-section "Hitler's Escape" in the article "Georg Elser," WIKIPEDIA.

[948] See major figures seated facing Hitler as he speaks, in video, *Murder Attempt on 8 November 1939 against Hitler*, YOUTUBE, at 0:10-0:15, with his entourage also filmed at 5:35-5:45; on the explosives, see 2:30-3:30. Cf. Nigel Farndale, "The carpenter who almost killed Hitler," *The Telegraph* (London), Jul. 13, 2015; Chris Knight, "The true life story of the man who tried to single-handedly kill Hitler," *National Post* (Toronto), Jul. 6, 2017.

[949] The German film *Elser* (2015), Eng., *13 Minutes*, presents these events in a filmic narrative. See "Georg Elser," WIKIPEDIA. Its director, Oliver Hirschbiegel, also directed *Der Untegang*, *The Downfall* (2004), distortions in which were discussed by David Cesarani and Peter Longerich, "The massaging of history: Review of the film Downfall," *The Guardian*, Apr. 7, 2005. The front page of the Munich ed. of the *Völkischer Beobachter*, dated Nov. 23, 1939, had the headline "*Wiederholte Anschläge auf den Führer. Die britische Mordverschwörung*" ("Repeated Assassination Attempt against the Führer. The British Murder Plot"), linking Georg Elser with these two British Secret Intelligence agents, with photos of the three (entitled "*Der gedungene Mörder und seine Hintermänner*" ("The murderer and his Backers"). The Heidenheim (east of Stuttgart, northwest of Munich) newspaper, *Der Grenzbote (The Border Messenger)*, in its Nov. 22, 1939 issue had the front-page headline, "*Der Münchener Attentäter verhaftet*" ("The Munich Assassin Arrested"), identifying *der Auftraggeber* (mandator or contractor) as the British Intelligence Serivce. These front-page headlines are in *Presse-Berichterstattung am 22./23. November 1939*. See 44:10-44:15 in *13 Minutes*, with several front-page newspapers, including the *Völkischer Beobachter*, with its headline: "*Mit tiefer Genugtuung erfährt das deutsche Volk: Der Attentäter gefaßt. Täter Georg Elser—Auftraggeber Britischer Geheimdienst. Chef des „Intelligence Service" für*

Despite being tortured, mostly at the hands of Arthur Nebe, at the time, head of the Kripo (the Political Police), and Heinrich Müller, head of the Gestapo (the State Secret Police), it became clear that Georg Elser had acted alone: this was made clear when he reconstructed the bomb single-handedly in interrogation. When it became undeniable that it was one person who was responsible for the bomb, and that he had been able to spend many nights in the Bürgerbräukeller preparing his bomb, despite the supposed tight security for Hitler, the incompetence of Himmler, at least in this one incident, was all too apparent. Hitler claimed that he survived not because of the large number of men in his bodyguard, but because of fate (*Schicksal*) or providence (*Vorsehung*), showing his divine mission, as would be his interpretation after the assassination attempt of July 20, 1944. *While Hitler believed in his mission and the fate that would preserve him, he was also protected by hundreds of personal body guards, organized into several groups.* He also had a special train that was highly impregnable to air-borne or ground bombs. His headquarters in Prussia, at Rastenburg (now, Poland), would be reinforced with extra layers of steel and concrete in 1944, and guarded at its peak by some 2,000 guards and 50,000 land mines, when the Allies (the British, Americans, and Soviets) were capable of bombing Hitler's HQ. Hitler left the unimaginable, unforeseeable to fate, perhaps, but he was also quite thorough in his instructions for very extensive protection against potential threats.

THE VENLO INCIDENT

Behind the scenes these first months of the war, there were investigations into whether there could be a peace, especially between Great Britain and Germany. Thus, only weeks after Britain had declared war on Germany, Sigismund Payne-Best, a British secret agent (in the SIS, Secret Intelligence Service, perhaps better known as M-16), was sent to Europe (joined in the Netherlands by Major Richard Henry Stevens—also an SIS officer)—on a mission to enter into peace negotiations with the Germans, ultimately arranged to take place on November 9, 1939. This was for a meeting between Payne-Best and Stevens and German officials, including Walter Schellenberg, a double-agent claiming to be an anti-Nazi, using the name *Hauptmann* (Major) Schämmel, but foremost a member of the *Sicherheitsdienst* or SD, the intelligence service of the SS, at the Dutch town of Venlo, near the German border. (The Netherlands at this point in time was still neutral, and Germans could readily cross the border for visiting and shopping at nearby Dutch towns.) This Venlo Incident, as it was called, was linked to the attempt the evening before on Hitler's life at the Bürgerbräukeller in Munich, just discussed. The interpretation put forth was that it was these

---

Westeuropa in deutscher Hand" ("With deep satisfaction the German people learns: The assassin caught. Offender: Georg Elser—Contractor: British Intelligence. Head of the Intelligence Service for Western Europe in German hands"). Elser was arrested, tortured, and sent to Dachau prison; he was shot to death while a prisoner there on Apr. 9, 1945, just weeks before Dachau was liberated on Apr. 29.

two British agents who orchestrated this assassination attempt, who had ordered (thus making them the backers of the plot (*Hintermänner*) and the contractors, giving the orders (*Auftraggeber*) about the planned assassination.

With all of those issues and anger in the air, the negotiations were broken off, and the British agents ordered to be arrested. On meeting at Venlo, the Gestapo and *Sicherheitsdienst* (SD) men[950] arrested the two British agents, led by Alfred Naujocks, who had just organized the raid on the Gleiwitz radio station on August 30, 1939, to justify the German invasion of Poland. The two would spend years in prison until the defeat of the Reich. Meanwhile, Hitler had had plans to invade the west on November 14, 1939, but these were to be postponed.[951] One German historian has pointed out that before the focused expansion of German power through military means across Europe, it was already widely sensed that Germany had achieved an undisputed hegemony in Europe, which was converted then "into the military conquest and occupation of Europe, a step comparable to the deliberate rape of a woman perfectly willing to surrender [*mit der mutwilligen Vergewaltigung einer vollkommen hingabewilligen Frau vergleichen läßt*]."[952] At the very least we might say that the France that was surprisingly conquered by Germany in 1940 was not the France of 1914, ready to defend its land with its blood, nor the France of 1918, having suffered massive casualties, especially at Verdun, but a different France in 1940 that had seen its defenses against Germany dissolve over the preceding decade, with Britain carrying out a consistent policy of appeasement (perhaps in the hope that Hitler would find his needs for German autonomy and military recognition sufficient). Realizing that, unlike Britain, there were no seas between France and Germany, it was quite unwilling to stand up to Germany on its own.

Expansion of the War 1940-1941

After the conquest of Denmark and Norway (May 9-June 10, 1940), which secured Germany's northern flank from attack, and then of the Low Countries and France (May 10-June 14, with armistice signed June 22, 1940), negotiations to formalize the relationship between what became the Axis Powers took place. When Japanese Prince Tokugawa,[953] who had

---

[950] Sigismund Payne Best, *The Venlo Incident* (1950), pp. 7-8.

[951] Walter Schellenberg, *Aufzeichnungen: Die Memoiren des letzten Geheimdienstchefs unter Hitler* (1985), Eng. *The Memoirs of Hitler's Spymaster* (2006); "The Venlo Sting," The Apricity: A European Cultural Community; Günter Peis, *The Man Who Started the War* (1960) and "Der Venlo-Zwischenfall: Aus der Biographie von Alfred Naujocks", and 'Venlo-Zwischenfall: Synopse" (both at mythoselser.de); cf. Emma Craigie and Jonathan Mayo, *Hitler's Last Day: Minute by Minute* (2015), p. 39.

[952] Sebastian Haffner, *Anmerkungen zu Hitler*, 1978 ed., p. 87; 1994 ed., p. 68; Eng., *The Meaning of Hitler*, p. 67.

[953] Prince Tokugawa (1863-1940)—full name in traditional Japanese order, Tokugawa Iesato—is presented with appreciation for his peace-loving influence on

been a great, powerful, dedicated, and long-time force for peace within the Japanese government, died on June 5, 1940, the Japanese military very soon arranged for the signing on September 27, 1940, of the Tripartite Pact, or the Berlin Pact, between Germany, Italy, and Japan, formalizing the Axis Powers. *The situation was moving toward a more inclusive, intense war.*

A small-time businessman in Newark would make a big impression in some circles, intensifying tensions: In early 1941, Theodore N. Kaufman, owner of a theater-ticket agency in Newark, published a book, *Germany Must Perish*. In this, Kaufman as a self-appointed spokesperson for the Jewish people, declared war on Germany. How an individual with no authority could do this, and how he could do this representing not a country with an army, in fact, representing no country at all, is quite whimsical. And yet, it led to a myth that somehow Jewry had declared war on Germany, even if only somewhat belatedly, in 1941.[954] No matter how absurd that claim and action were, the idea was already in the air, as in a London paper, *Daily Express*, which on March 24, 1933, had published the headline "Judea Declares War on Germany: Jews of All the World Unite in Action." Notice the Teutonic Knight with Christian cross on the shield, at the top of the page, to the right of the newspaper name:

Three versions of the same article, page 1, dated March 24, 1933

Kaufman's concocted fabrications aside, German troops moved closer to the Polish border in the week after the signing of the Molotov-Ribbentrop Pact on August 23, 1939, which paved the way for a German invasion of Poland without a fear of Russian resistance, and before the actual invasion of Poland. In order to give a popular explanation and justification of the invasion of Poland, claimed to be a defensive action of retaliation against the Poles, the SS carried out what was to be known as the Gleiwitz Incident. Information about the organization of this incident was presented on December 20, 1945, at the Nuremberg Trials, in the form of a sworn affidavit, signed and dated November 20, 1945 by Alfred Helmut Naujocks (mentioned just above), the man in charge of the Gleiwitz Incident under direct orders from Heydrich.[955] This mock attack by men dressed in Polish military uniforms involved the capture of a border German radio broadcasting station, on August 31, 1939. A short

---

Japanese until his death, in Stan S. Katz, *The Art of Peace: An Illustrated Biography about Prince Tokugawa* (2019).

[954] Berel Lang, "The Jewish 'Declaration of War' against the Nazis," *The Antioch Review*, vol. 64, no. 2, 2006, pp. 363–373.

[955] NT-IMT-Blue, vol. 4, pp. 242-244.

message was read over the radio in Polish, which acknowledged the violence and the taking over of the station. A number of other similar incidents occurred that same night, together to show unmitigated attacks on peaceful German activity. It was Heydrich who ordered these actions; the men in uniform were prisoners left dead with gunshot wounds, meant to be signs of a battle.

Even though the German military plan, finalized by June 15, 1939,[956] envisioned a sudden and powerful invasion of Poland, the German official position on the start of the war was that it was a firm response to an unwarranted act of hostility against the German Reich. The clear contrast between political positioning and actual events (as here), seems to have guided some of Hitler's statements to the very end of his life, even when they were seen by Hitler's military consultants (Hitler being the Commander-in-Chief) as obviously distorted and an embarrassment.

From another perspective, the idea of Germany having the right if not the natural destiny to take over eastern Europe and especially the rich, fertile lands of the USSR, already clearly presented in *Mein Kampf*, was part of a very long-range vision of Europe.

To consider one dimension of this vision of an expansive Germany (sometimes called Germania), by 1934 if not earlier, the idea of a thousand-year-long Reich was already presented by Hitler to the German People. With this idea that the Reich would last 1,000 years, the Nazis took it that they had time to carry out a long-term project: to repopulate the German stock by encouraging and even organizing the procreation of many pure Aryan children, having pure Aryan young women committed to Nazi values become pregnant with similarly qualified young men. This program, the *Lebensborn*, was initiated by Heinrich Himmler on December 12, 1935.[957] Himmler's idea was to add to good German stock (Nordic-

---

[956] Martin Kitchen, *The World in Flames: A Short History of the Second World War in Europe and Asia, 1939-1945* (1990), p. 12.

[957] NT-TWC-Green, vol. 4: first, at pp. 1028-1029, letter from Himmler dated Jun. 21, 1943, to SS *Standartenführer* (Colonel) Max Sollmann—*Leiter des Lebensborn*, Leader of the Lebensborn Project—stating "The problem to be solved is the care, education and accommodation of Czech children whose fathers or parents had to be executed as members of the resistance movement.... *The children of good racial stock who, unless subjected to proper care and education, are of course likely to become the most dangerous avengers of their parents*, must, I think, be placed into the charge of a 'Lebensborn' nursery on probation for the time being, and if possible, put to a character test, to be distributed among German families as foster or adopted children. Heil Hitler!" (p. 1029; italics added). Then, at pp. 1030-1032, a letter from the Minister of State for the Protectorate of Bohemia and Moravia to SS Colonel Rudolph Brandt (under Himmler), June 13, 1944, mentioned that most of the children being temporarily held in local cites in the Protectorate were from Lidice, which had been razed in retribution for the killing of Heydrich in 1942 (p. 1031). The letter adds (p. 1032, italics added), "It is intended to have *the racially acceptable elements* [children deemed acceptable for Germanization] ... transferred through the Lebensborn to German families or to a children's home whereas the

Aryan blood) by some 300,000 babies. Young Aryan women were selected from Nazi-dedicated members of the *Bund Deutscher Mädel* (League of German Girls); the men were all members of the SS. Various homes were established, within Germany and in other lands under German control, such as Norway.[958]

In a speech in June 1931 to the SS—which had been established in 1925—Himmler stated (in apocalyptic terms), "Shall we, by filtering out the valuable blood through a process of selection, once again succeed in training and breeding a nation on a grand scale, a Nordic nation? Shall we once again succeed in settling this Nordic people in surrounding territory, turning them into peasants again and *from this seedbed* [*aus diesem Saatbeet*] *create a nation* [*ein Volk*] *of 200 million? Then the earth will belong to us!* But if Bolshevism is victorious then this will mean the extermination of the Nordic race, of the last valuable Nordic blood, and this devastation would mean the end of the earth."[959] In this program, we can sense the grandiose nature of this vision of a future Germania (a Europe totally controlled by the Third Reich). It was certainly not a knee-jerk reaction to any events in the East once the war began. *Such a large number of Germans to move into the conquered lands of the East would make feasible the extermination of literally millions of Slavs, with sufficient labor to take over those lands! This was certainly thinking on a large scale!* Soon after the invasion of Poland, Himmler sent an order dated October 28, 1939 to the entire SS and Police Force (*ein SS-Befehl für die gesamte SS und Polizei*), encouraging them to become involved in having children, in order to strengthen the Nordic blood of the nation, and promising SS support for these children, whether they were born in wedlock or not, according to bourgeois laws and customs, or outside of marriage (*bürgerlicher Gesetze und Gewohnheiten hinaus wird es auch außerhalb der Ehe*), and asking for their commitment to the Führer and the Reich by such procreative actions. The order closes addressing the SS Men and these devoted women, to show "your faith in the Führer and in the will to the eternal life of our blood and people" (*daß Ihr im Glauben an den Führer und im Willen zum ewigen Leben unseres Blutes und Volkes*).[960] This was the Order for the Begetting of Children (*Kinderzeugungsbefehl*). This plan, to have SS men and healthy, Nazi-faithful Aryan young women

---

children over 16 years are to be sent to a concentration camp." See Gitta Sereny, "Stolen Children: International Dialogue," *Talk*, Nov., 1999, pp. 104-113, 220-229; "The Nazi Party: The 'Lebensborn' Program (1935-1945)," JEWISH VIRTUAL LIBRARY.

[958] These homes were not at all bordellos: The medical supervision to maximize the likelihood of pregnancy and the routine and efficient manner of intercourse encouraged and focused on that goal, and not on pleasures exotic or bizarre.

[959] Peter Longerich, *Himmler: Eine Biographie*, p. 133, Eng. *Himmler: A Life*, p. 123, italics added. Also quoted in Peter Padfield, *Himmler: Reichsführer-SS* (1990), p. 101, Richard Rhodes, *Masters of Death*, p. 85.

[960] German text: "Heinrich Himmler: SS-Befehl für die gesamte SS und Polizei," Oct. 28, 1939, NS-ARCHIV: DOCUMENTE ZUM NATIONALSOZIALISMUS. Cf. discussion in Otto D. Tolischus, *They Wanted War*, pp. 216-234, esp. p. 218.

procreate to add new pure blood to the German people, was done half in secrecy (many Germans still seeing having children out of wedlock as morally wrong if not sinful), was not enough, especially when German military losses on the Eastern Front were in the thousands each week. This led to a complementary plan, to find and abduct children found to be Aryan, in the conquered Slavic countries, mixed among the Slavic peoples, to have them evaluated and if worthy, of *Germanisierung* (being made into Germans). In this expanded venture, children were abducted from the Soviet Union, Poland, Czechoslovakia, and Yugoslavia. These children were tested for "racial purity" (not linked to family history). Those that passed the tests were sent to *Lebensborn* homes in Germany and lands occupied by German forces, under the control of the SS, given German names, and farmed out to foster parents who were dedicated German Nazis. The plan was to expand the population of Nazi Germany by bringing 30 million people of (apparent) German blood back "home" to create a population of 120 million that would enable the Reich to become the most powerful nation in Europe.[961]

As Hitler had announced at the Nuremberg Rally, on August 7, 1929, printed in *Völkischer Beobachter* on that date, "If Germany every year would have one million children and would eliminate 700,000-800,000 of the weakest, the end result would probably be an increase in (national) strength."[962] Himmler himself would later contribute extramaritally to the next generation of Aryan Germans (perhaps an act of nobility on his part?), having an intimate relationship (1938 on) with his secretary (1936-1941), Hedwig Potthast: The couple had a son, Helge, born in February 1942, and a daughter, Nanette-Dorothea, born in July 1944.[963]

This first period of the war saw the taking over of Poland by the German military. The intelligentsia of Poland were targeted, arrested, held prisoner, or killed, to eliminate Polish leaders of groups that might question and resist German authority. The Soviets, in the part of Poland that had been assigned them in case of invasion by the Reich, also took Polish military and assassinated them once in Russia.

Eva Braun recorded that on the evening of September 1, 1939, Hitler had remarked, "Warsaw is in flames. Scum, Jews, German-haters. In ten days, the whole of Poland will be burning.... In ten years, there won't be

---

[961] *The Last Nazis: Season 12, Episode 3: Children of the Master Race*, BBC DOCUMENTARY; "Lebensborn (Spring of Life)," SPARTACUS EDUCATIONAL; "Nazi 'master race' children meet," BBC NEWS, Nov. 4, 2006.

[962] See *Völkischer Beobachter, Bayernausgabe*, Aug. 7, 1929, p. 1; tr. quoted in Laurence Rees, *The Holocaust: A New History* (2017), p. 98, and in "7 August 1929: Nazi Party Paper Reports on Hitler's Promotion of Eugenics," SKEPTICISM.ORG. Cf. Stefan Ihrig, *Justifying Genocide*, p. 434, n. 77, and Institut für Zeitgeschichte, *Hitler: Reden Schriften Anordnungen, vol. 2, pt. 1*, pp. 374-378. See Adolf Hitler, "Politik der Woche," *Illustrierter Beobachter*, Sep. 7, 1929, pp. 449, 451; Institut für Zeitgeschichte, *Hitler: Reden Schriften Anordnungen, containing vol. 3, part 2 (März 1929-Dezember 1929)*, Klaus A. Lankheit, ed. (1994), at pp. 374-378.

[963] "Hedwig Potthast," IPFS.IO; "Hedwig Potthast," SPARTACUS-EDUCATIONAL.COM.

The Hitler Era

any Polish aristocracy: the formation of an *élite* will be made impossible in Poland."[964] (Another unrealized prophesy.) With these first steps at eliminating those in conquered lands who might prove to be the sources of independent thought and rebellion against the Nazi structure, there was a need of massive camps, with a great expansion of their capacity.

US BIG BUSINESS IN GERMANY

In a synoptic overview, there was a number of US businesses that profited from a range of contracts with German companies, from the 1920s on. These included Standard Oil (founded by John D. Rockefeller; Walter C. Teagle, CEO) that provided to the world's largest chemical cartel, I. G. Farben, lead additives (especially tetraethyl lead) needed for the high-performance motors of military airplanes in the Luftwaffe, and for information about the development of synthetic rubber and fuel; Ford-Werke, a subsidiary of Ford (Henry Ford, President, and James D. Mooney, CEO); and Opel, a subsidiary of General Motors, that manufactured through German subsidiaries some 100,000 military trucks needed for the invasions of Czechoslovakia and Poland).[965] Concerning GM, at a 1974 US Senate hearing, attorney-historian Bradford C. Snell, who had spent two decades researching a history of the world's largest automaker (GM), testified, referring to the long cooperation *that extended into the war years*, "GM is a major force in international affairs. During World War II, for instance, it maximized global profits by supplying both the Axis and Allied powers with armaments. Its auto plants in Germany built thousands of bomber and jet propulsion systems for the Luftwaffe at the same time that its American plants produced aircraft engines for the U.S. Army Air Corps."[966] In another context, Snell also reported, "General Motors was far more important to the Nazi war machine than Switzerland. Switzerland was just a repository of looted funds. GM was an integral part of the German war effort. The Nazis could have invaded Poland and Russia without Switzerland. They could not have done so without GM."[967] Snell also gave other details: "'General Motors was far more important to the

---

[964] Eva Braun, *The Private Life of Adolf Hitler*, p. 90, Sept. 1, 1939, evening.

[965] Dieter Schröder and Joachim Schroeder (father and son German journalists), *Hitler's American Business Partners: US-Company Earned in the War*, at 53:45-55:56. Cf. original Ger.: *Hitlers amerikanische Geschäftsfreunde;* Clive Matthew-Wilson, *Cars & Nazis* (2010), DOGANDLEMONGUIDE-NEW ZEALAND.

[966] *Statement of Bradford C. Snell Before the United States Senate Subcommittee on Antitrust and Monopoly*, Feb. 26, 1974, US SENATE SUBCOMMITTEE &C.

[967] Michael Dobbs, "Ford and GM Scrutinized for Alleged Nazi Collaboration," *Washington Post*, Nov. 30, 1998, p. A01. Cf. Jacques R. Pauwels, *The Myth of the Good War: America in the Second World War* (Revised ed., 2015), p. 40, and Herbert R. Reginbogin, *Faces of Neutrality: A Comparative Analysis of the Neutrality of Switzerland and Other Neutral Countries During WW II* (2009), p. 181; tr. from *Der Vergleich: Die Politik der Schweiz zur Zeit des Zweiten Weltkrieges im internationalen Umfeld* (2006). See, further, "Neutralität im 2. Weltkrieg: Gute Note für die Schweiz," SWI (SWISSINFO.CH), Dec. 8, 2006.

Nazi war machine than Switzerland,' author Bradford Snell told the *[Washington] Post*. He said Nazi armaments chief Albert Speer told him in 1977 that Hitler 'would never have considered invading Poland' without synthetic fuel technology provided by General Motors."[968] *Quite telling!* IBM (Thomas J. Watson, CEO) provided the Third Reich with sophisticated record-keeping to facilitate German census-taking, and, then to track the presence, arrest, and, ultimately, the deportation of Jews from the Netherlands and other countries.[969] There were also the awards of payments from legal actions making claims for reparations filed by the German subsidiaries of these US companies (for damages by the Reich), and by the US (for bombing of their German manufacturing plants).[970]

There was also what is now called money laundering and other transfers of many millions of dollars of wealth for the German industrialist billionaire Fritz Thyssen (1873-1951), a major financier for Hitler, and also of Göring, from the early days of the 1920s.[971] Thyssen would turn against Hitler in 1939, disliking Hitler's policies toward the Jews and other religious groups, and the Reich's great re-armamentation policies (despite the potential for great personal financial gain to him).

---

[968] "Did U.S. Carmakers Help the Nazis?" *CBS News*, Nov. 30, 1998.

[969] After the invasion of the Netherlands by the German Wehrmacht, IBM shipped 132 million punch cards to the IBM subsidiary set up in that country, to help the Reich keep track of the Jews there and of their ultimate transportation to various death camps. See "Secret History: The U.S. Supported and Inspired the Nazis," GLOBAL RESEARCH: CENTRE FOR RESEARCH ON GLOBALIZATION, Mar. 29, 2015.

[970] For example, in Jan. 1945, the German Reich War Damages Agency in Berlin awarded Opel 35 million marks, with 18 million payable immediately: The US had bombed the Brandenburg Blitz Factory, near Berlin, on Aug. 6, 1944, destroying the Opel factory, fully owned by GM (General Motors). See Reinhold Billstein, Karola Fings, Anita Kugler, and Nicholas Levis, *Working for the Enemy: Ford, General Motors and Forced Labor in Germany during the Second World War* (2000), p. 78. Remarkably, the US paid $32 million in compensation to GM. See Dieter Schröder and Joachim Schroeder, *Hitler's American Business Partners: US-Company Earned in the War* (just cited), at 51:00-51:35, Michael Dobbs, "Ford and GM Scrutinized for Alleged Nazi Collaboration," *Washington Post*, Nov. 30, 1998, p. A01, and "Secret History: The U.S. Supported and Inspired the Nazis" (just cited).

[971] Tyssen was to state that he had "personally given altogether one million marks to the National Socialist party. Not more. My contributions have been very much overestimated, because I have always been rated the richest man in Germany." See Fritz Thyssen, *I Paid Hitler*, p. 102. In 1923, Thyssen gave 100,000 gold marks to Ludendorff (not Hitler); later he would support both Hitler and Göring, with Hitler requiring that monies transferred to him be done quite discreetly, in untraceable payments—possible with Thyssen's resources held in a number of countries (including accounts in German, Dutch, Swiss, and American financial institutions). These payments (or gifts) allowed Hitler to find a more suitable apartment, purchase a 100-horsepower *Mercedes Modell 15/70 Kompressor* (Supercharger), to start a magazine, the *Illustrierter Beobachter*, whose photos were all the work of Hitler's personal photographer, Heinrich Hoffmann, and to change his basic level of living. See also Wulf Schwarzwäller, *Hitlers Geld* [*Hitler's Money*], pp. 146-151; Eng., *The Unknown Hitler*, pp. 140-145.

The Hitler Era 321

Thyssen left Germany for Switzerland on September 2, 1939, the day after the German invasion of Poland. France mobilized its troops for war.

The next day, September 3, the British and French sent their formal ultimata—the British in the morning and the French at 12:30 pm—demanding, *on the threat of war*, a response—for the British by 11 am and for the French by 5 pm—by the German government, stating that they "were prepared at once to withdraw their troops from Poland" (as PM Chamberlain put it in his speech, notifying the British of the state of war, at 11:15 am).[972] Germany gave no response. The UK and France (and also Australia and New Zealand) declared war that day. *World War II had begun.* On learning of their declarations of war, Göring remarked solemnly to Goebbels, "If we lose this war, then [may] God have mercy on us." Goebbels remained "downcast and self-absorbed."[973]

Thyssen remained in Switzerland, and the next year, he continued on to France with his wife,[974] with the two planning to go to Argentina. Thyssen's book was published in 1941, even though he and his wife were arrested by Vichy police in August of that year. The two spent the next years in German concentration camps and were freed by Allied soldiers in 1945, then moving to Argentina.[975]

Besides Thyssen's early help, there was also help in transfers of large sums of German money by the Dulles brothers and US Senator Prescott Bush: Prescott Bush, when he met his future wife, Dorothy Walker, was a tire salesman; after their marriage, he was set up in 1924 in the financial world by his father-in-law, George Herbert Walker, a St. Louis investment banker, to work with Averill Harriman, son of railroad magnate E. H. Harriman.[976] In 1926, Prescott Bush became Vice President of W. A. Harriman & Company. Much of the money here came from links to German industry. In particular, in 1928, Fritz Thyssen in Germany formed the United Steelworks, which controlled much of the coal and steel assets there. A business relationship with W. Averell Harriman was formed, the Union Banking Corporation. (Its assets were confiscated by the US

---

[972] "British Declaration of War: 3 September 1939," YOUTUBE; "Édouard Daladier: Discours radiodiffusé du 21 septembre 1939," YOUTUBE.

[973] Christopher Thorne, *The Making of the Twentieth Century: The Approach of War, 1938-1939* (1967), p. 202.

[974] Itamar Levin, *His Majesty's Enemies: Great Britain's War against Holocaust Victims and Survivors* (2001), pp. 162-164.

[975] "Hitler Visits a Thyssen Factory in the Ruhr Region (1935)," GERMAN HISTORY IN DOCUMENTS AND IMAGES (GHDI); Dwight Jon Zimmerman, "The Faustian Bargain: Industrialist Fritz Thyssen and the Nazis," DEFENSEMEDIANETWORK, Aug. 15, 2017.

[976] Antony C. Sutton, *Wall Street and the Rise of Hitler* (2010), Stephen Kinzer, *The Brothers: John Foster Dulles, Allen Dulles, and their Secret World War* (2013), Ben Aris and Duncan Campbell, "How [the 43rd US President, George Walker] Bush's Grandfather Helped Hitler's Rise to Power," *The Guardian* (UK), Sep. 25, 2004, citing sources incl. the Harriman Papers at the US LIBRARY OF CONGRESS, THE US NATIONAL ARCHIVES, and the article "Hitler's Angel Has $3m in US Bank," *New York Herald-Tribune*, Jul. 30, 1942. Cf. *The Bush-Nazi Connection*, YOUTUBE.

Government on October 20, 1942, under the US Trading with the Enemy Act and Executive Order No. 9095.[977])

In this complex business network, working as active attorney at that company, Brown Brothers Harriman, was John Foster Dulles—attorney of Prescott Bush (who was by then a US Senator) and later, US Secretary of State, 1953-1959, and whose brother, Allen Dulles, was later head of the CIA, 1953-1961). Prescott Bush's son, George H. W. Bush, would later be head of the CIA (1976-1977), and then President of the USA (1989-1993). Prescott Bush had other financial connections and positions; for example, he was also Vice President and one of seven directors of Union Banking Corporation, which was seized during World War II by the US Government under the Trading with the Enemy Act.

Eleanor Roosevelt, widow of President FDR, on hearing of US stockholders in Ford making profits from Ford business in the Third Reich, wrote in her syndicated column, "My Day," in the essay dated September 20, 1945 ("Ford in Germany"): "Business complications do strange things to our patriotism and to our ethics!"[978]

The role of the Associated Press (AP) during the Third Reich—before its expulsion when Germany declared war on the USA—has been questioned as well. The AP in reply[979] to a scholarly essay in a German academic journal[980] denied any collusion with the Nazi regime.

A Glimpse of Anti-semitism in Third Reich films

This theme of the repulsiveness of Jews would be taken up in the widely publicized and distributed propaganda film *Der ewige Jude* (1940), in which images of several Jews from occupied Poland—with the Warsaw Ghetto having been decreed by Hans Frank on October 16, 1940, and in operation a month later,[981] with its Jews forced into intensely crowded conditions there earlier by the occupying Reich Army)—were shown in their "Oriental" appearance, with full traditional beards and kaftans, and

---

[977] "Prescott Bush," Sparticus Educational; "United Banking Corporation," Wikipedia; "Trading With the Enemy Act of 1917," Wikipedia.

[978] Eleanor Roosevelt, "My Day: Ford in Germany," *New York World-Telegram*, Sept. 20, 1945, p. 17, col. 1-2 (bottom left of page). In the 2003 documentary by journalists Dieter Schröder and Joachim Schroeder, *Hitler's American Business Partners* (cited above), an image of this Roosevelt article is shown at 42:38-43:01, but cited as being in *The New York Times*, Wed., Sep. 19, 1945. This United Feature Syndicate column (which ceased operations in 2011) appeared in some 62 subscribing newspapers—but not in *The New York Times*.

[979] Paul Colford, "AP statement on historical article," AP—The Definitive Source, Mar. 30, 2016.

[980] Harriot Scharnberg, "Das A und P der Propaganda: Associated Press und die nationalsozialistische Bildpublizistik," *Zeithistorische Forschungen/Studies in Contemporary History*, vol. 13, no. 1, 2016, pp. 11-37, with links (below photo) to both Ger. text and Eng. tr.

[981] Karski was interviewed at USC by Renee Firestone, Mar. 10, 1995: *Holocaust Rescue and Aid Provider Jan Karski Testimony* (1995), USC Shoah Foundation, at 28:50-29:05, YouTube.

The Hitler Era

then, again, clean-shaven in Western clothing.[982] This was a film that was composed by Goebbels with recommendations (or orders) from Hitler about certain scenes that were to be included in the version of the film to be shown to the public. (Here, again, *we see contexts in which Hitler not only knew of what was being done and presented to the public, but in which he took an active role.*) And yet, out-takes from the filming in the Warsaw Ghetto (in May 1942) were found in East German archives after the war, in film cans titled *Ghetto*, showing the reality behind this filmic creation. Its multiple takes and filming of the careful, planned setting up of "candid" scenes by cameramen were composed into *A Film Unfinished* (2010), which shows the art that was behind an apparently candid film shown to audiences throughout lands controlled by the third Reich. We will return to post-war films on the Holocaust, below.

Concentration and Extermination Camps in the East (Poland)

The work on concentration camps in the east began in 1939, to complement all of those already operating within the pre-war Reich. In 1939, the rudiments of a concentration camp were in place in the town of Oświęcim (Auschwitz), which was in Silesia, part of the Reich (in the administrative area or Gau called the Warthegau). An order issued by Himmler, dated April 27, 1940, instructed a large, adequate concentration camp to be built, with Rudolf Höss as its head.[983] The camp's first prisoners were mostly Poles.

The existence of this camp with its early deaths was known by some who were aware. For example, in far-away New York City, on March 14, 1942, a German-language newspaper published an article, "Eine Stätte des Grauens: Bericht aus dem Konzentrationslager Oswiecim (Auschwitz), Polnisch-Galizien."[984]

This newspaper report mentioned, in part, that among the groups there, the Jews rarely come out alive (*kommt nur selten einer mit dem Leben davon*), and that the camp, having room—at that time—for 40,000 men, had an average of 70-80 die daily (*beträgt im Durchschnitt 70 bis*

---

[982] These comparative scenes are at 18:30-20:03 in *Der ewige Jude* (*The Eternal Jew*). On Jewish mimicry with its recognizable features, see Hans Blüher, *Secessio Judaica*, Sect. 1, p. 19: "*Mimikry des Blutes, des Namens und der Gestalt.*" ("Mimicry of the blood, of the name, and of the [visible] form.")

[983] *On the History of KL-Auschwitz* (Polish ed., 1967); Eng. (1982), pp. 1-3.

[984] The English tr. would be: "A Place of Horror: Report on Concentration Camp Oswiecim (Auschwitz), in Polish Galicia." The Polish name is Oświęcim. In Yiddish, it was known as Oshpitsin, but before the destination was clearly known by name, it was called Pichipoy (Pitshipoy), or, in French orthography, Pitchipoï, the name used by the French Jewish children, as at the holding camp of Drancy, just outside of Paris. See the BBC video *Surviving the Holocaust: Freddie Knoller's War* (2015), at 37:50-37:55; Jean-Claude Moscovici, *Voyage à Pitchipoï* (2009), made into a film, *Pitchipoï* (2015). The standardized Eng. of this imaginary destination-village would be *Pitshipoy*. The Polish Yiddish inter-war comedian pair of Szymon (Shimen) Dzigan and Yisroel Szumacher (Shumacher) joked, "*Pitshipoy es iz groys azoy vi a floy.*" (Pitshipoy, it's as big as a flea.)

80 täglich), adding that one day there were 156 people who died.[985] The town of Oświęcim (Auschwitz) was selected by Himmler, who had seen the need for a concentration camp in a convenient area (between the West and the Eastern Front and near major train lines). Initial work on the camp began in 1940, with instructions after an inspection on March 1, 1941, for a significant enlargement to be carried out, with the capacity to hold 30,000 prisoners, with a second camp at nearby Birkenau to hold 100,000 Soviet prisoners of war—*this, months before the actual invasion.* Systematic mass murders at Birkenau began in March 1942.[986]

Himmler and other highest-level administrators of the Racial Policies of the Third Reich, then, were active both before the actual invasion of the Soviet Union. on June 22, 1941—some 129 years after the similar June invasion by Napoleon of Czarist Russia, in June 1812[987]—and in the months that followed. Himmler acted here on Hitler's Reichstag speech that if Jews dragged Germany into a world war, as Hitler threatened (or promised), the Jews would be annihilated. In fact, those in the military high command, such as General Franz Halder, the Chief of Staff of the OKH (the Supreme High Command of the German Army), were familiar with the invasion of the USSR *even before the Reichstag speech!*

Hitler's order for Operation Barbarossa,[988] put into action months later, in June 1941, was formally announced on February 10, 1939. And, even earlier, in late 1940, on December 18, the formal order, Führer Order (*Führerbefehl*) No. 18: "for Russian attack (BARBAROSSA)" had been issued.[989] Then, a two-day conference between Hitler and his generals, which Mussolini also attended, was held at the Berghof on January 8-9, 1941. At this Hitler affirmed his commitment to helping Italian military activity, but also announced to his generals his plan to invade the Soviet Union. The Befghof's manager, Herbert Döhring, saw the maps of the Soviet Union that Hitler had marked in blue, showing his plans for the main routes of invasion. Döhring would call this moment "the beginning of the end of the Third Reich."[990] Such sources as these indicate that those in the military high command, such as General Franz Halder, the Chief of

---

[985] "Eine Stätte des Grauens: Bericht aus dem Konzentrationslager Oswiecim (Auschwitz), Polnisch-Galizien," *Neue Volks-Zeitung*, Mar. 14, 1942, p. 2.

[986] Raul Hilberg, *The Destruction of the European Jews*, 1-vol. ed. (1961), p. 500: "In November 1941, there were as yet no killing centers. Installations for mass killings were not set up in Polish camps until 1942." The first transport from France (Drancy and Pithiviers) arrived at Auschwitz II (Birkenau) on Mar. 30, 1942.

[987] Henry Simon, *Third Reich Diaries*, p. 69.

[988] Barbarossa was the Italian name (lit., Redbeard) given to the German ruler Frederick I, who from 1155-1190 was Emperor of the Holy Roman Empire (said to be neither holy, nor Roman, nor an empire). That was the First Empire (*Erstes Reich*), with the Second Reich (*Zweites Reich*) lasting from 1871-1918, making the Nazi Reich the Third Reich (*Drittes Reich*).

[989] Franz Halder, *The Halder War Diary, 1939-1942*, Appendix, p. 676.

[990] *Hitler's Bodyguard, Season 1, Episode 12 (Nearly Attacked at the Berghof)*, 22:30-25:05, YOUTUBE.

Staff of the OKH (the Supreme High Command of the German Army), were familiar with the Operation even before the Reichstag speech! *No short-term reaction here!* The Führer's adjutant, Nicolaus von Below, present at that conference with its declaration of the forthcoming war with the Soviet Union that Hitler envisioned, remarked, "Hitler stated that he would go to war with the USSR this summer. [This was a declaration, not a proposal or question.] Originally, he intended to start in the second half of May, but because of developments in the Balkans and North Africa he had now had to postpone the attack date—possibly until June. [It took place on June 22, 1941.] Those present listened to all this dumbfounded. Not a word of opposition was raised to any of it. Their faces had a fixed expression. I doubt if any of them saw the need for war against Russia. Only after leaving were the first serious questions asked."[991] Hitler, the *Führer* (Leader) and Supreme Commander-in-Chief of the German Armed Forces, was not asking for support, simply total acceptance, with all appropriate actions expected to be taken when called for. Later that month, on January 27, 1941, in an entry in his War Diary, Halder remarked, "We cannot send to Libya anything more than originally planned, both because time is short and because we cannot cut any further into resources for BARBAROSSA [consistently in upper-case letters in Halder's original text].[992] Further, in an entry made the next day, January 28, Halder mentions that the situation for tires for heavy trucks was serious, with reserves exhausted by the end of February (one month away), and similarly, gasoline was assured for three months, but diesel fuel only for one month. A speculation of the impact of cutting back on domestic diesel fuel quotas and for the occupied countries: "a small reserve of 200,000 tons for the next six months."[993]

Also, in that January 28 entry, Halder writes, concerning a meeting and discussion the preceding January 20, "On this theme [of preparations for Operation Barbarossa] there was a discussion on 20 January [1941] with the Gen Qu [General Staff Administration]" where innumerable questions concerning the military leadership, the armament program, and the economy from the attending officers did not lead to any conclusive results. Halder notes, "This is the purpose of this meeting. You should, in the event that you cannot reach a satisfactory solution for the operational leadership, clarify the issues for a Fuehrer decision." The notes would

---

[991] Nicolaus von Below, *At Hitler's Side: The Memoirs of Hitler's Luftwaffe Adjutant 1937-1945* (2001), p. 85 (notes on the conference of Jan. 8-9, 1941).

[992] Franz Halder, *The Halder War Diary, 1938-1942*, entry, Jan. 27, 1941, p. 313.

[993] Franz Halder, *The Private War Journal of Generaloberst Franz Halder, Chief of the General Staff of the Supreme Command of the German Army (OKH), 14 August 1939 to 24 September 1942: 9 volumes in 1; Vol. V ("The Second Winter. 31 October 1940-20 February 1941")* [PDF, pp. 319-442], Arnold Lissance, ed. (text in microfilm, ca. 1946; pub. ca. 1975), [entry Jan. 28, 1941, pp. 97-98 [PDF, pp. 417-418]. A portion of this passage is given, in an abbreviated form, in Franz Halder, *The Halder War Diary, 1938-1942*, entry, Jan. 28, 1941, p. 314.

continue, focusing on the important logistical problems facing the German military: how to keep the men supplied with arms, food, and other main essentials for continuing the war: "We must destroy the Russian army without pause over the Dnieper-Duna line 9500 kilometers into north Russia and other goals another 500 kilometers."[994] *This major problem was thus clear to Hitler and the top Generals months before their invasion of the USSR.* (The German army was not able to do what it "must" do.)

In short, by January 20, 1941, the Army general staff was quite aware of the forthcoming plans to invade the Soviet Union, with the ultimate authority for specifics being Hitler, the *Führer*, through a Führer Order (*Führerbefehl*), which has *Gesetzeskraft*, the force of law, and is always definitively authoritative. Halder's diary entry that day, January 28, also mentioned a meeting on that date with several army generals concerning the preparations for Barbarossa, and in notes about that conference, he mentions "Mission East (BARBAROSSA) must be assumed to be known" and refers to "around 110 infantry divisions, 20 armored divisions, 13 motorized divisions, 1 cavalry division; total 144 divisional units" with key interests: "Crush Russia in a rapid campaign. Execution [the carrying out of this operation] should evidence the following characteristics: ... *Speed*. No stop! No waiting for the railroad. Depend on motor transport."[995] Compared with these estimates, the German forces that were actually employed on June 22, 1941, at the start of the invasion of the USSR, involved 3 entire Armies, 3 million men, and over 3,000 tanks.[996]

Hitler would later claim that the German invasion of the Soviet Union was actually a defensive action, an action-prone Hitler not willing to be passive in seeing the enemy about to pull the trigger (his metaphor), but would rather fire the first shot (a kind of pro-active defensive, we might say), adding that the enemy (the USSR) "is already broken and will not rise again" (a premature optimism, it turned out), with the German military thus blocking a second invasion of Genghis Khan [metaphorically, the Soviets]. These were laid out for the German public in Hitler's speech at the Berlin Sportpalast on October 3, 1941,[997] after pre-invasion claims of the growing hostility of the Soviets, to prepare the German people for still another war—claims which some Germans believed and others not.

We may also mention that on April 6, 1941, in preparation for the invasion of the USSR, the German Wehrmacht, with military support from its allies at the time, Italy, Bulgaria, and Hungary, invaded Yugoslavia and Greece. Yugoslavia surrendered on April 17; Athens fell on April 27; other Greek soldiers who escaped to outlying parts of Greece had largely

---

[994] Franz Halder, *The Halder War Diary, 1938-1942*, entry, Jan. 28, 1941, p. 315.
[995] Franz Halder, *The Halder War Diary, 1938-1942*, entry, Jan. 28, 1941, pp. 314-315. The word BARBAROSSA is consistently in upper-case letters in text.
[996] *Hitler's Bodyguard, Season 1, Episode 10 (Hitler's Dangerous Train Journeys)*, 20:50-21:05, YOUTUBE.
[997] "Speech at the Sportpalast on the Opening of the *Kriegswinterhilfswerk*," *Neues Europa;* Jacques Pauwels, "Hitler's Failed Blitzkrieg against the Soviet Union: The "Battle of Moscow," Turning Point of World War II," JACQUESPAUWELS.NET.

surrendered by June 12. The time, focus, and related delay of this operation, with Italy not being able to conquer Greece on its own, was later used by Hitler as part of his explanation of why the invasion of the USSR ultimately failed—the fault not lying with Hitler or the Wehrmacht.

MONTHS OF PREPARING TO INVADE THE USSR: OPERATION BARBAROSSA

By the time of the invasion itself, preliminary construction of the bunker system in East Prussia, which began in autumn 1940, would serve as the Eastern Front military HQ for Hitler and the German military. It was operational when Hitler arrived there the first time on July 24, 1941. The center, covering some 250 hectares (about 0.97 sq. mi.) was located near Rastenburg, in East Prussia—now Kętrzyn, in northeast Poland—hidden in the woods at the small village of Gierłoż, some 5 miles east of Kętrzyn (Rastenburg) proper. This location was chosen for its camouflaging woods, in a swamp land. It was given a code name, the Askania Chemical Works, as a pseudo-explanation for the rail lines constructed in the area.[998] Hitler had been planning ahead, realizing that he would need a safe military headquarters in the east for closer observation and control of the fighting on the eastern Front. Hitler called this complex *die Wolfsschanze*, the Wolf's Entrenchment, more usually rendered, The Wolf's Lair.

This name, *Wolfsschanze*, Wolf's Lair, was not chosen at random. Hitler would call himself Wolf, as a nickname. Relatedly, his Eastern Front HQ were known by this fuller name. Hitler, that is, understood his personal name, Adolf, as a shortened form of Adelwolf (Noble Wolf). Of course, in German culture (as in the Grimm Brothers Fairy Tales of Little Red Riding Hood) and in European culture in general, the wolf was seen as a wild, uncontrollable, dangerous, and potentially vicious animal: a formidable foe.

Similarly, with this focus on Wolf as an epithet or name, when Hitler's one full sister, Paula, was fired in 1930 because of her family name, Hitler, suggested that she change her name to Wolff (or Wolf).[999]

---

[998] *Hitler's Bodyguard, Season 1, Episode 11 (Attempt to Kill Hitler at the Wolf's Lair)*, at 3:25-4:10, YOUTUBE.

[999] Later, at the Winter 1936 Olympics at Garmisch-Partenkirchen, in Bavaria, Hitler and his sister Paula again discussed this change of names; she accepted and Hitler, now the Führer, authorized that her name be changed to Paula Wolf. (See "He was still My brother—Paula Hitler," AUSCHWITZ.DK.)

This change of name gave her anonymity during the Third Reich. She added the title Frau (Mrs.) to give an air of respectability that that status provided. This change of names also fundamentally limited awareness of her existence in the public eye, allowing Hitler to dissociate himself from her on a public level.

Hitler, very circumspect about his actual past as a boy and young man, presented in both *Mein Kampf* and in other sources a cultivated image of a self-made, single (unattached) individual who came from poverty to power by his own great, focused will. (This was perhaps not paradoxically like his image of his own father, Alois, whom he said he respected but did not love.) Hitler presented himself as being dedicated heart and soul to the entire German nation and its people (*Volk*). As with

If we look back to earlier that year, to March 1941, Hitler made the important announcement at a conference with a number of high military officers, including Chief of Staff of the OKH (German Army) General Halder, that *Unternehmen Barbarossa* (Operation Barbarossa) would be a *Vernichtungskrieg*, a war of annihilation: annihilation of the Soviet (Communist) East—going beyond the focus on the extermination of the Jews! There, Hitler declared that the war against the Soviet Union "cannot be conducted in a knightly fashion" because it was a war of "ideologies and racial differences."[1000]

We may appreciate that this position derives, of course, from acceptance of the idea of *die Herrenraße* (the Master Race) and the related inferiority of the Slavs, including the Russians—and of their mutual, irreconcilable, unbound animosity, the one or the other destined to be exterminated, all based on the principle and process of dehumanization. Or, as the American historian John Toland (1912-2004) would summarize the point, "The aim of National Socialism was the destruction of Bolshevism. How could he [Hitler] turn his back on his mission in life?"[1001]

As General Holder noted on March 30, 1941, Hitler explained, "It is a fight for extermination (*ein Vernichtungskampf*). If we do not interpret it that way (*es nicht so auffassen*), then we will beat the enemy [now], but in 30 years the Communist enemy will face us again. We do not wage war to preserve the enemy.... Fight against Russia: annihilation of the Bolshevik Commissars and the Communist intelligentsia (*Kampf gegen Rußland: Vernichtung der bolschewistischen Kommissare und der kommunistischen Intelligenz*).[1002]

Hitler was certainly thinking ahead. On April 2, 1941, just days after this diary entry by Franz Holder, Alfred Rosenberg, the "philosopher" of the Third Reich, was invited as a guest of Hitler's. In the two-hour conversation, Rosenberg would write in his diary of "Something I do not wish to record today but shall never forget (*Was ich heute nicht niderschreiben will, aber nie vergessen werde*)." The understood context was the discussion of the extermination of the Jews.[1003] This was to be

---

Eva Braun, about whom the general German public knew nothing, the image for the public of Hitler was of a man all German women could dream about, thinking him to be an eligible bachelor. The fantasy was strongly encouraged with the theme of "Give the Führer a child" as part of the *Lebenborn* Program to increase the German population.

[1000] NT-NCA-Red, vol. 8, Affidavit of Generaloberst Franz Halder, pp. 645-647. Cf. William Shirer, *The Rise and Fall of the Third Reich*, p. 830; Franz Halder, *The Halder War Diary*, esp. entries for March 17 and March 30, 1941 (pp. 335-339 and 345-347, respectively).

[1001] John Toland, *Adolf Hitler*, p. 649.

[1002] "Franz Halder, *Kriegstagebuch, 30.03.1941*, NS-ARCHIV: DOKUMENTE ZUM NATIONALSOZIALISMUS.

[1003] Werner Maser, *Legende, Mythos, Wirklichkeit* (1971), p. 97; tr. *Hitler: Legend, Myth, and Reality* (1973), p. 215. Cf. Robert M. W. Kempner, *Eichmann und*

put into explicit language and into action before the end of the year: Rosenberg—having taken the post of Reich Minister for the Occupied Eastern Territories, created by Hitler in July, shortly after the invasion of the USSR—would be quite ready to discuss this issue, the eradication (*Ausmerzung*, the weeding out) of the Jews of Europe, as in his press conference on November 18, 1941, at which he stated to a select group,[1004] "Some six million Jews still live in the East, and this question can only be solved by a biological extermination of the whole of Jewry in Europe [*eine biologischen Ausmerzung des gesamten Judentums in Europe*].[1005] The Jewish Question will only be solved for Germany when the last Jew has left German territory, and for Europe when not a single Jew stands on the European continent as far as the Urals... And to this end it is necessary to force them beyond the Urals or otherwise bring about their eradication."[1006] *Rosenberg used quite explicit speech here.*

The statement by Hitler of March 30 would be formalized months later as the Commissar's Order (*Kommissarbefehl*) of June 6, 1941, ordering the immediate execution of all Soviet political commissars, reflecting the order's longer, formal name, *Richtlinien für die Behandlung politischer Kommissare* (*Guidelines for the Treatment of Political Commissars*). It was recognized as being in conflict with international law on the treatment of captured enemy combatants (POWs), to which Germany was committed. *It was finally rescinded* by Hitler on May 6, 1942, after he was convinced that news of this practice made Soviet troops more committed to fight until death, *thus, counter-productive to the Nazi war effort.*[1007]

Then, in a surprise event a few days later, on May 10, 1941 (about six weeks before the invasion of the USSR), Hitler's long-time associate Rudolf Hess, an accomplished pilot, flew a Messerschmidt Bff 110 from Bavaria on a five-hour flight to Scotland. His plan was to meet with a British aristocrat he had met at the 1936 Summer Olympics in Berlin, the Duke of Hamilton, at his home at Dungavel Castle. Hess presumably thought this aristocrat would be able to arrange a meeting with Churchill; Churchill was told of the arrival of Hess in Scotland, but was not open to meeting with him. It was long believed that Hess acted on his own, to have Britain at least stay neutral in the forthcoming invasion by the Reich of the Soviet Union—if not to join the Reich (much less likely, of course).

Komplizen (1961), p. 97.

[1004] Beate Kosmala, "[Review of] Rezension von: Frank Bajohr / Sibylle Steinbacher (Hgg.): »... Zeugnis ablegen bis zum letzten«: Tagebücher und persönliche Zeugnisse aus der Zeit des Nationalsozialismus und des Holocaust, Göttingen: Wallstein 2015," in *Sehepunkte*, vol. 18, no. 1, Jan. 15, 2018.

[1005] Ernst Piper, "Die Berufung des Ostens. Alfred Rosenberg und die Vernichtung des europäischen Judentums," STUDGEN.UNI-MAINZ.DE, Nov. 25, 2002; Markus Flohr and Frank Werner, "Niemand sollte überleben [Interview with historian Ulrich Herbert]," ZEIT GESCHICHTE, Feb. 14, 2017; Ernst Piper, "NS-Zeit: Hitlers Vollstrecker," *Der Tagesspiegel*, Jun. 20, 2001.

[1006] Peter Longerich, *Holocaust: The Nazi Persecution and Murder of the Jews* (2010), p. 289.

[1007] "Kommissarbefehl," DE.WIKIPEDIA, and "Commissar Order," WIKIPEDIA.

With this, Goebbels was quick to declare Hess a fool and someone who was mentally disturbed. Stalin so interpreted the flight and while the British did not respond to the offer, the effort by Hess reminded Stalin that the British might not always stay as war allies.

There is some continued debate about the specifics here, especially about the possible expectations of Hess and about whether Hitler knew of this venture beforehand. A 28-page hand-written report from February 1948 that was in closed files in the Soviet Union, was released for scholarly research by the subsequent Russian government, and German historian Mathias Uhl, researcher at the German Historical Institute, Moscow (*Deutsches Historisches Institut, Moskau*). The report that was finally released had been written by Hess' adjutant Karlheinz Pintsch, a Soviet war prisoner from 1945 to 1955. In it, Pintsch reports that Hitler knew of Hess' mission to "use all means at his disposal to achieve, if not a German military alliance with England against Russia, at least the neutralization of England." Pintsch also stated that the day after Hess' departure for Scotland, he handed Hitler a note from Hess, saying that if his mission was unsuccessful, that Hitler should declare him insane, presumably to dissociate himself from what Hess had failed to do. There were similar reports about that moment by Ernst Wilhelm Bohle (1903-1960), head of the *Auslandsorganisation* or *AO* (Foreign Organization) of the NSDAP, and Luftwaffe General Karl-Heinrich Bodenschatz (1890-1979), Adjutant to Hermann Göring. Both were at Obersalzberg when Hitler received the news about Hess and his flight to Scotland.[1008] Also, Mathias Uhl also has written about his findings concerning two intimates of Hitler, Heinz Linge (1913-1980), the Führer's valet and bodyguard, and Otto Günsche (1917-2003), Hitler's personal adjutant. These testimonies suggest that "not only did he [Hitler] know about it in advance, but that he probably even sent Hess to England."[1009] Whatever the details, Hess

---

[1008] At the Nuremberg Trial in 1946, Hess was sentenced to life in prison. Held at Spandau Prison near Berlin, aged 93, he hung himself with an electric cable in 1987. See Jan Friedmann and Klaus Wiegrefe, "Historian Uncovers New Account: Document Suggests Hitler Knew of Hess' British Flight Plans," SPIEGEL ONLINE, May 30, 2011 (quoting Pintsch); Joris Nieuwint, "An Interview with SS Officer Heinz Linge, The Last Person to See Adolf Hitler Alive & the One who Burned his Body," Aug.24, 2016, WAR HISTORY ONLINE; C. N. Trueman, "The Flight of Hess, May 1941," HISTORYLEARNINGSITE.CO.UK; *In the Service of the Führer: Hitler's Shadow (Documentary)*, YOUTUBE. Plus interview (in English), *Interview with Hitler's Valet, Heinz Linge*, YOUTUBE. See also Brian Handwerk, "Will We ever Know Why Nazi Leader Rudolf Hess Flew to Scotland in the Middle of World War II?" SMITHSONIAN.COM, May 16, 2016, with mention of British intelligence MI5 that were declassified in 2004, and other documents made public in the USA in 2014.

[1009] *The Secret Dossier Prepared for Stalin from the Interrogations of Hitler's Personal Aides*, Henrik Eberle and Matthias Uhl, eds., Giles MacDonogh, tr. (2005), pp. xiv, 70. Search "The Unknown Hitler," PRAVDA REPORT, with links to the presentation and discussion by Olga Savka, "The Unknown Hitler reveals curious details about Fuhrer's life," PRAVDA.RU, Sep. 21, 2005.

The Hitler Era

certainly was not able to reach British authorities after his landing in Scotland. In general terms, this and no other peace accord with Hitler was ever seriously considered by the British.

As an operating principle, war against the Bolshevik USSR—and Hitler certainly was ready to launch it, whatever the position of Great Britain, Hess or no Hess—was part of Hitler's vision of the great need for *Lebensraum* at the expense of the Russian Bolsheviks, already made quite explicit in *Mein Kampf*, which had already defined that war as one to be carried out at the right time (from a German military point of view).

Historian Frank McDonough, noted (of the weeks after the invasion), "The first documented written 'order' to kill 'all Jewish males' aged 17 to 45 was given to local *Einsatzgruppen* units by the SS on 11 July 1941. On 17 July 1941, Heydrich gave a set of further instructions which ordered that all Jews found in Russian Prisoner of War camps were to be killed 'straightway'."[1010] The mass killings of Jewish men, women, and children were underway by September 1941, when a quick and total victory over the Soviet Union still seemed quite imminent. Soon, late in 1941, the use of the SS mobile shooting squads, the *Einsatzgruppen*, as the primary method of mass executions was given up, to be replaced by the much less personal, much less stressful (for the SS Men), method of mass gassings by Zyklon B, and destruction of the corpses by crematoria.

Further, historian Christopher R. Browning, in his research on the development of a plan for the extermination of Jews in the second half of 1941, suggested that the first step, shifting to the total annihilation of all Jews, took place after the first astonishing successes of the Wehrmacht in its invasion of the USSR, and led to the second step, *using the mechanized, factory-like efficiency of train shipments to isolated centers with gassing and crematoria facilities to structure the hard work of killing millions of inferior beings*, later in 1941 and put into operation in early 1942.[1011] At about this time, with the radical, complete extermination of

---

[1010] Frank McDonough, *The Holocaust* (2008), p. 51. Cf. Jürgen Förster, "The Relation between Operation Barbarossa as an Ideological War of Extermination and the Final Solution," in *The Final Solution, Origins and Implementation*, David Cesarani, ed. (1994), pp. 85-102, at p. 93; NT-NCA-Red, vol. 2, Chap. XV, Sect. 6: with mention of the *Geheime Staatspolizei* (Gestapo) and *Sicherheitsdienst* (SD), at pp. 284-285, and with text of this July 17, 1942 document (Document 502-PS).

[1011] On Hitler's first authorizations, summer 1941, and authorization of final plans in late 1941, see: Christopher R. Browning, "A Reply to Martin Broszat Regarding the Origins of the Final Solution," *Simon Wiesenthal Center Annual*, vol. 1, 1984, pp. 113-132; Christopher R. Browning, "The decision Concerning the final Solution," in *Fateful Months: Essays on the Emergence of the Final Solution* (1985), pp. 8-38; Heinz Peter Longerich, "Hitler's Role in the Persecution of the Jews by the Nazi Regime," *Holocaust Denial on Trial*, HDOT.ORG; Peter Longerich, *Holocaust: The Nazi Persecution and Murder of the Jews* (2010), pp. 437, 450, 480, 521-522, 541, 589, 592, 605, 628; William D. Rubinstein, "How Murder Became Policy: Review of *The Origins of the Final Solution*, by Christopher R. Browning," *First Things*, June 2004, pp. 52-55; Kevin P. Sweeney, "We Will Never Speak of It: Evidence of Hitler's

the Jews of Europe already begun and waiting for an administrative definition of the operational details (to be defined at the Wannsee Conference in Berlin on January 20, 1942), the SS in the East would be instructed to deal with Gypsies (Romanies) the same way as the Jews: the Reich appointed Hinrich Lohse (1896-1964)[1012] on July 17, 1941, soon after the invasion of the USSR, to the administrative position of *Reichskommissar* for the Ostland (governor of Ostland, which included Estonia, Lithuania, Latvia, and parts of Belarus and Poland). On December 24, 1941, Lohse issued a confidential order to the SS in Lithuania, Latvia, and Belarus, gave his reasoning about the dangers Gypsies (Romanies) posed to the German venture, and then concluded, "I therefore determine that they [the Romanies] should be treated in the same way as the Jews."[1013] In other words, the SS were to eliminate all Romanies, as Jews: with the ultimate intention of realizing a final solution of both the Gypsy and the Jewish Questions (their systematic and total extermination).

This sort of instruction did not go unheard. Across the Eastern Front, there was an attack on Jews, and, as well, on Romanies, all those judged to be part of the Communist political structure, and other undesirables. For example, in the north, in Latvia, shootings began in various regions, such as those centered at the city of Liepāja, on July 5, 1941, continuing for the next months, and reaching one intense killing period in mid-December (December 15-17), when the nearby dunes at Šķēde were the scene of massive killings of Jewish residents of the area.[1014] (Other sites of mass killings are considered, below.)

Relatedly, about formative activities in that first month of war against the Soviet Union, Ian Kershaw wrote about a meeting between Hitler and Croatian Minister Marshal Sladko Kvaternik: "In advising Kvaternik to intervene at home with an iron fist against 'criminals and anti-social elements', Hitler declared that there was only one thing to be done with them: 'annihilate (*vernichten*) them!' It was necessary to 'do away with (*beseitigen*) them' or, if they were not dangerous to lock them in concentration camps from which they must never be left out.' Toward the end of the talks, Hitler turned to the Jews. He called them 'the scourge of mankind'.... [Hitler went on to say] If there were no more Jews in Europe, the unity of the European states would be no longer disturbed. Where the Jews are sent to, whether to Siberia or Madagascar, is immaterial."[1015]

Direct Responsibility for the Premeditation and Implementation of the Nazi Final Solution," *Constructing the Past*, vol. 13, no. 1, 2012, pp. 1-9; Randall L. Bytwerk, "The Argument for Genocide in Nazi Propaganda," *Quarterly Journal of Speech*, vol. 5, no 1, 2005, pp. 37-62.

[1012] His personal name is spelled Hinrich, as above, and not Heinrich.
[1013] Donald Kenrick and Grattan Puxon, *Gypsies under the Swastika*, pp. 87-88.
[1014] "Liepāja Municipality, the Šķēde Dunes," CENTER FOR HOLOCAUST STUDIES AT THE UNIV. OF LATVIA.
[1015] Ian Kershaw, *Hitler, 1936-45: Nemesis*, p. 470. British orthography retained. Cf. photo of Croatian Minister Marshal Sladko (or Slavko) Kvaternik meeting Hitler at the *Wolfsschanze* (at Rastenburg or Kętrzyn), Kvaternik on the right: "Visit of Sladko Kvaternik 21 July 1941" (Photo Code B007645), FRANCE.SCALARCHIVES.IT.

No More Madagascar

It might be relevant to note that at the time, Madagascar was fading as a viable option for the deportation of European Jews, and shipment to Siberia for an unfed and unprotected Jewish population would mean their slow death by freezing. *The simple idea that Europe would be in total internal harmony if only the Jews were gone disregards all of the different interests and concerns of different areas, regions, and groups within the large European community.* We can see that even today, harmony within the EU (the European Union) is not easily approached, even without there being a significant Jewish influence in the issues of today's Europe.

Referring to the spoken (unwritten) orders to kill the Jews of Soviet Russia, given by Reinhard Heydrich to NCOs[1016] at the SiPo[1017] school in the German town of Pretzsch[1018] in May 1941,[1019] Otto Ohlendorff testified:

> The orders for the execution in the past given in Pretzsch went to all Einsatzgruppen commanders or Einsatzkommando leaders who went along during the beginning of the Russian campaign. They were never revoked. Thus, they were valid for the entire Russian campaign as long as there were Einsatzgruppen. Thus, it was ... unnecessary at any time to give another order of initiative and I did not give any individual order to kill people.... My mission was to see to it that this general order for executions would be carried out as humanely [a kind soul!] as conditions would permit.[1020]

Ohlendorff then answered a question about what these orders were:

> These orders had as their purpose to make it as easy as possible for the unfortunate victim and to prevent the brutality of the men from leading to inevitable excesses.[1021] [What would an excess be?]

In considering the issuance of orders, or their felt redundancy, and the expectations of obedience to them, we have often heard the defense of

---

[1016] These NCOs were non-commissioned officers up to the rank of SS-Scharführer, equivalent to US Staff Sergeant or UK Platoon Sergeant Major.

[1017] The discourse was at the Security Police (*Sicherheitspolizei, SiPo*) NCO School.

[1018] Pretzsch is southwest of Berlin, northeast of Leipzig, northwest of Dresden.

[1019] Various sources date this talk that Heydrich gave at Pretzsch in Saxony, to May/June 1941. See Heinz Höhne, *Der Orden unter dem Totenkopf: Die Geschichte der SS* (1984), pp. 328-330 (dating this at the end of May 1941); "Der Orden unter dem Totenkopf. Die Judenvernichtung in Rußland" (pp. 40-61), DER SPIEGEL, Dec. 26, 1966, p. 45; "Einsatzgruppen," WIKIPEDIA; *The SS: Heydrich*, HISTORY CHANNEL (USA), at 24:55-25:35. Christian Ingrao, *La promesse de l'Est. Espérance nazie et génocide 1939-1943* (2016), pp. 428-429, cites June 17, 1941.

[1020] NT-TWC-Green, vol. 4, p. 249.

[1021] NT-TWC-Green, vol. 4, p. 249.

someone accused of wrong-doing claiming that he was "only following orders" and should therefore be completely exonerated and excused from any charges of wrong-doing. Some think that the trials after World War II, such as the Nuremberg Trials, were making illegal and defining crimes actions which at the time of their being carried out were not illegal at all, thus making these unjust charges.

On the other hand, if we look back at this history of this sort of issue, as addressed by countries accepting and signing various international treaties, *long before World War II and the Third Reich*, there has been a legal tradition that proposed otherwise.

One such set of principles was made explicit in a codification of proper conduct during war, in a document signed on April 24, 1863, by US President Abraham Lincoln during the US Civil War (or War Between the States), the Lieber Code[1022] or the Lieber Instructions, known more formally as Instructions for the Government of Armies of the United States in the Field, General Order No. 100. It included passages guaranteeing the protection of civilians. Of course, this was a formal legal precedent *but not part of any international treatises establishing more broadly accepted principles.*

Several decades later, one clear example of legal documents that were international treaties, was the Hague Conventions of 1899, among the first formal statements of principles of international law.

In the Convention with Respect to the Laws of War on Land (Hague II), signed on July 29, 1899, its preamble had a passage known as the Martens Clause.

This Clause was named for its author, Friedrich (or Frédéric or Fyodor) Martens (1845-1909), a diplomat, jurist, scholar of jurisprudence, and specialist on Czarist Russian international treaties. It made explicit the principle that even if in the laws of war agreed to by participating parties (countries) there was no specific mention made of principles or usages (practices) of civilized countries, *these principles were nonetheless to be recognized as operative.* The text itself reads:

> Until a more complete code of the laws of war is issued, the High Contracting Parties think it right to declare that in cases not included in the Regulations adopted by them, populations and belligerents remain under the protection and empire of the principles of international law, as they result from the usages established between civilized nations, from the laws of humanity, and the requirements of the public conscience; They declare that it is in this sense especially that Articles 1 and 2 of the Regulations adopted must be understood [implying *that it is not only* these two Articles that must be so understood].[1023]

[1022] Rick Beard, "The Lieber Codes," *New York Times*, Apr. 24, 2013.
[1023] "Laws and Customs of War on Land (Hague, II)," pp. 247-262 in *Treaties and*

In this historical legal context, the division of Poland in September 1939 between The Third Reich and the Soviet Union, following the secret territorial accords of the Molotov-Ribbentrop Agreement, would have later ramifications. In part, in the Katyń Forest,[1024] the bodies of Polish officers, soldiers, members of the intelligentsia, and others considered dangerous to the Soviet regime (some 22,000 in all) were discovered in spring of 1943. They had been killed several years earlier, in April and May 1940, by Soviet troops. The responsibility and blame fell on Stalin and Beria. This was *short-term good news* for Hitler and the Reich, since they were considered innocent of this massacre, *but—the worrisome aspect*, which was clearly appreciated by leading Nazis (Himmler expressed his concerns about all of this, for example, and Hitler remarked that Germany had better win the war, so as to be able to redefine history, exonerating the Reich from any wrong-doing)—ultimately raised questions of the responsibility of German leaders for the massacres the Reich had carried out, both within Germany and beyond its borders. And, the repulsion at mass murder of innocents, whether codified or not, is clearly against "the usages established between civilized nations, from the laws of humanity, and the requirements of the public conscience" mentioned in the Martens Clause of the 1899 Hague II Convention, quoted just above.

The invasion of Poland by Germany raised a number of political and military issues. On a practical level, German military forces now had to contend with an entire nation of non-Germans (Polish *Untermenschen*), and millions of Polish Jews now raised questions about the treatment of Jews under German command. If the annexation of Austria brought a large number of German-speaking Jews under new Reich control, and the post-Munich-Agreement with the subsequent invasion of Czechoslovakia brought millions more Jews, now, the invasion of Slavic-speaking Poland added a significant burden to the German forces. There was a gathering together or concentrating of Jews from many small villages in Poland to large cities, creating Jewish living quarters or neighborhoods (*jüdische Wohnbezirke*), Jewish ghettos. Among the major Polish ones were those instituted in Warsaw, Łódź, and Kraków.

A program of not giving any food or means of sustenance to the Jews now enclosed in ghettos would lead relatively effortlessly (for the German occupying forces) to the starvation, disease, and death of many Jews, but that was not an efficient plan for dealing with these Jews. Middle and Eastern Europe, especially Poland, with its significant Jewish population (3.5 million Jews), would, serve as slow-death centers and also as the assembling area for later "treatment" of the Jews (mass killing by gas).

Hitler's statement of his interests as a peace-loving man and leader of the German people continued through the invasion of Poland, as he

---

Other International Agreements of the United States of America, 1776-1949, Vol. 1: Multilateral Agreements, 1776-1917, Charles I. Bevans, ed. (1968), from the introductory comments, at p. 248.

[1024] The 2007 Polish film, *Katyń*, dir. by Andrej Wajda, portrays these events.

declared on July 19, 1940 (quoted more fully above), "The German Reich, in particular with regard to Poland, has shown restraint ever since the National Socialist rise to power."[1025] He would maintain this position even after his subsequent invasions of Denmark, Norway, the Netherlands, Belgium, Luxembourg, and France. Given this statement in its historical context, we can perhaps try to imagine what Hitler thought non-restraint in Poland would have been! Presumably it was restraint in contrast with the self-declared absolute German right to remove and exterminate all inferior individuals, groups, nations, and religions it would desire to eliminate from the German world. *Hitler's offer for peace in September 1938 was totally on his terms!* His offer was that Germany would not retreat from Poland, in fact, it would want from Great Britain a recognition of German hegemony (full control) over continental Europe and a commitment to a neutral stance in the case of a German invasion of the USSR. In exchange for this, Hitler would keep in place Germany's formal recognition of the British Empire. If we reflect on the various steps to greater German control over Europe, each step seems to be taken as a given, a *fait accompli*, for future negotiations, not to involve any withdrawal from what Germany had occupied peacefully or conquered in battle. This was a peace that asked other nations to accept all of Germany's expansionist politics and military involvements. *This is perhaps a sense in which Hitler could be seen, and see himself, as truly wanting peace.* Given that it involved encroachment after encroachment of neighboring territories, this is quite a particular, even peculiar, sense of desiring peace and being *friedliebend* (peace-loving) and *friedfertig* (peaceable). If we see all of our neighboring countries as harboring a not-so-secret desire to conquer and to annihilate us, an international stance that guarantees our survival can be quite appealing. And, if we feel we need to attack when we sense that we are about to be attacked, *then we can see as defensive what other countries see as our aggression*.

For context, in the history by the ancient historian Thucydides, an Athenian explained to a Spartan about the Athenian "empire, which we acquired by no violent means, because you [the Spartans] were unwilling to continue the war against the Persians and because the allies attached themselves to us and spontaneously asked us to assume the command. And the nature of the case first compelled us to advance our empire to its present height; fear being our principal motive, though honor and self-interest came in afterwards."[1026] And, in general, even if a given nation sees its development of a powerful military as ultimately an act of defense, this will often be perceived by facing nations as its aggression.

Others voices presented a different understanding of this situation. A civil servant (but non-Nazi) Friedrich Kellner, who lived in the rather small

---

[1025] *Die Rede des Führers im Reichstag, Berlin, den 19. Juli 1940*, with Eng. tr., "Speech of the Führer, Adolf Hitler, in the Reichstag, 19 July 1940: Declaration of Victory over France and the British Forces in the Western Campaign," WIKISOURCE.

[1026] Thucydides, *History of the Peloponnesian War*, Sect. 75. The war took place 431-404 BCE; the *History* covers the war until 410 BCE.

The Hitler Era

town of Laubach, some 46 miles northeast of Frankfurt, wrote in his diary on October 10, 1939 of the use of Jews as scapegoats, "No, not the Jews, but the Nazis are the misfortune for the German people." Kellner went on to write, "Every reasonable person knows that if we had behaved in a decent manner, we could have achieved a satisfactory relationship with England, at least to some extent. Everything with us is weapons and shouts of war and continuous threats—with no suitable middle ground. The purpose is to intimidate the alleged or real opponent to want to be on good terms with us. But eternal saber-rattling leads to one thing, and that is war."[1027]

Given the flow of planning through much of 1939 for further military ventures, and subsequent events, the desire of the Führer for peace is perhaps at least somewhat questionable. Hitler's glorious vision of power with a German ("Aryan") dominance over the world, or at least of all of Europe from the Atlantic to the Ural Mountains, would lead to comments made when the German military began suffering great setbacks and the losses of millions of men: the SS mused, "Enjoy the war while you can, because the peace will be terrible!"[1028] Or, as expressed by *Scharführerin* (Master Sergeant) Monika Mohn to Alfons Heck in a retrospective comment in the first months of 1945: "It was great while it lasted, wasn't it? We almost had the world, didn't we?"[1029]

In any case, in the very first months of the war, the neat partition of Poland between German and Soviet areas of control, soon became a grander issue. In accordance with secret accords within the Molotov-Ribbentrop Treaty, the USSR invaded Poland from the east, on September 17; the division of the country was completed on October 6. Two days later, Germany divided its Polish lands into the western part, which was incorporated into the Greater Reich, calling that the Warthegau, and a large eastern area that would remain conquered territory and was called the *Gouvernement General*. This was established by a decree by Hitler on October 12, 1939, at which time Hans Frank was appointed Gouvernor-General, and Arthur Seyss-Inquart (later to govern the Netherlands at the time of the deportation of many Jews living there) as Deputy Governor General.[1030] This was a gain but a burden for the Third Reich, which now had even more Jews to deal with. At first, the Jews from Poland (and then also from other European lands) were isolated and confined in *jüdische*

[1027] Friedrich Kellner, *My Opposition: The Diary of Friedrich Kellner—A German against the Third Reich*, Robert Scott Kellner, tr. (2018), p. 46.

[1028] Robert Kershaw, "Why the Germans fought to the death," *The Telegraph* (London), Sep. 17, 2004. Cf. similar phrasing, quoted in Alfons Heck, *A Child of Hitler*, p. 110.

[1029] Alfons Heck, *A Child of Hitler*, pp. 180-181; cf. pp. 69, 164, 170, 205. Monika Mohn was secretary of *Sturmbannführer* (Major) Horst Wendt, a professional, high-ranking Hitler Youth leader, who had fought on the Russian front, where he lost his left hand in combat. Wendt, whom Heck described as a merciless disciplinarian, committed suicide the day of the unconditional surrender of Germany to the Allies.

[1030] NT-NCA-Red, vol. 1, p. 1023.

Wohnbezirke, Jewish residential neighborhoods. This could be a holding program, with the question of the ultimate treatment of these unwanted parasites left unanswered for the time being, as mentioned just above. Even so, the shifting of vast Jewish populations into the *Gouvernement General* met the opposition of its new political leader, Rudolf Höss. A meeting was called by Göring, as head of the Ministry of Economics, instructing Himmler to hold off on more transports of Jews, even if the question of what to do with these vermin remained unanswered. And with this, the Blitzkrieg was on! The industrial city of Lwów capitulated on September 22, and the Polish capital, Warsaw, on September 28. Not only was this war a lightning-rapid one (*Blitzkrieg*), but the subjugation of the Polish population, including its considerable Jewish segment, was quite rapid and intense, as well. Jews and Poles (especially the intelligentsia and the clergy, who could not be counted on to be pro-Germany, but, rather, were more likely to support a Polish resistance to the German conqueror) were rounded up; many leaders were taken away, not to be seen again, presumably many of which were killed. The Jews were soon herded into small areas of each city, creating Jewish-only neighborhoods (ghettos). The Germans captured the city of Łódź, on September 8, 1939; it was later to be renamed Litzmannstadt by order of Hitler, on April 11, 1940. Five days after the capture of the city, on September 13, 1939, the Germans appointed Chaim Rumkowski as Eldest of the Jews of Łódź (Litzmannstadt). He would be instrumental in carrying out instructions by Reich representatives, at a time when Jews thought that cooperating with the Germans would guarantee survival. On November 14, a decree was issued that required Jews to wear yellow armbands identifying them clearly as Jews. *This was not understood at the time as the first in a series of increasingly harsh conditions for Polish Jews.* As Jan Karski, an envoy of the Polish Government-in-Exile (birthname Jan Kozielewski, 1914-2000), pointed out, "When we speak about the Jews, keep in mind, that the time is an important factor. 1939: there was no sign whatsoever of what was coming in the next two or three years."[1031]

With the success in Poland, Germany next turned its war aims to Norway and Denmark, attacking after plans were in place, on April 3, 1940. The Norwegian forces finally capitulated to German power on June 10, 1940. By this time, there was also the invasion and conquering of the Western countries of Luxembourg (May 10-May 10), Belgium (May 10-May 28), and the Netherlands (May 10-May 14). France resisted longer (May 10-June 22). This opened up new possibilities for the Jewish Question. Heydrich nurtured the idea of sending all of the Jews of Europe to the French colony island of Madagascar. The inhospitable climate was not a problem, since the survival of Jews was not a concern at all. Of course, the one obstacle to this was transport there, even if Madagascar was now under Reich control, France having surrendered. And that

---

[1031] *Holocaust Rescue and Aid Provider Jan Karski Testimony (Mar. 10, 1995)*, YOUTUBE, at 27:45-28:10.

obstacle of course was the British Navy. Addressing the concern, the obvious solution was to conquer the British and thereby nullify its Navy totally. That was a plan that was to be put into action, even though, of course, the German military, especially the Luftwaffe, which had been so important in all of the confrontations and battles up until then, did not conquer Britain. Hitler, meanwhile, was thinking ahead: The Führer Order (*Führerbefehl*) or Directive No. 16 of July 16, 1940, called for the land invasion of Britain (*Unterfahl Seelöwe*, Operation Sea Lion). This required a preliminary softening of the RAF (British Air Force) defenses, put forth as Führer Order (*Führerbefehl*) or Directive No. 17, of August 1, 1940, known as Operation Eagle Attack (*Unternehmen Adlerangriff*). This began on Eagle Day (*Adlertag*), August 13, 1940. For the English, this operation, known as the Battle of Britain, recognized as the German attempt to wipe out the RAF, the British Royal Air Force—was not a success. German intelligence did not understand the British air defense system, nor the use of radar to identify incoming German aircraft. In addition, the fact that German air power was designed for short-range missions and did not have long-range bombers or fighter planes made the task rather formidable, in fact, ultimately an impossible one. Göring's promise to Hitler to take down the British RAF single-handedly (by the Luftwaffe alone) was to go unfulfilled, which did not help Göring's earlier quite high respect in the eyes of the Führer. And, for Heydrich, it was to become clear—perhaps by October 1940—that Madagascar was ultimately not a solution to the Jewish Question for the Reich. *Something else would have to be devised!* Soon, discussions turned to the invasion of the USSR, code-named Operation Barbarossa. If Germany could defeat the USSR, as it believed it would be able to do in several months at most, then it would have access to vast natural resources, and would have sealed Reich control over continental Europe. Then, either Britain would come to terms to accept some sort of peace accord (Germany and Britain each having its own spheres of interest) or this ever-more-powerful German could then turn to conquer the British Isles. *These are some elements of the strategic thinking in the background here as 1941 evolved.*

While Hitler would repeatedly make it a point to declare that the generals knew nothing of war, but that he, as a soldier who had been in the trenches for four years, and lay suffering from poison gas attacks, knew much better what war was about—on the military front in the east, German Army Chief of Staff Franz Halder, after less than five months of war, considering the logistics of fighting a war, would make a down-to-earth remark on November 4, 1941, "Viewed as a whole, the situation [on the Eastern Front] is determined by railroad capacity and flow of supplies. There is no point in pushing operations outward before we have, step by step, established a solid foundation for them. Failing to do that inevitably would bring fatal reverses down upon us."[1032] Halder also gave a

---

[1032] Franz Halder, *The Halder War Diary, 1939-1942*, entry, Nov. 4, 1941, p. 553.

summary of total German military losses from the start of the Russian invasion to the end of 1941: 830,903 men, which represented 25.96% of the entire German eastern army of 3.2 million men.[1033] By this point in time, Hitler, getting nervous about the limitations of German military success in the East, on November 30, 1941, called in the Commander-in-Chief of the Army, Field Marshal Walther von Brauchitsch (1881-1948). Halder wrote, "The interview appears to have been more than disagreeable, with the Fuehrer doing all the talking, pouring out reproaches and abuse, and shouting orders as fast as they came into his head. Regrettably, the Army yielded to the Fuehrer's insistence and has issued the order not to fall back to the aforementioned line in one move. Field Marshal von Rundstedt's reply was that he could not comply with the order and asked that either the order be changed or that he be relieved of his post." Rundstedt was soon dismissed for this presumed insubordination. [1034] Hitler, breaking military protocol of chain of command, began talking directly with army group commanders,[1035] and on December 19, 1941, took over High Command of the Army, thus appointing himself as its active Commander-in-Chief.[1036] These various interactions also reflect the sense of what was felt to be Germany's core and most vital threat, and the remaining possibility of total victory: its life-or-death struggle with the world of Bolshevism (the world of Jewry-and-Bolshevism): if one half of this identity (Jewry equals Bolshevism) would be conquered, the other would necessarily also be destroyed, being ultimately the same.

Here, if the gloves were not off before, the implementation of mass killings began. The *Einsatzgruppen*, under the direction of Heydrich (and above him, in the background, Himmler), begin inclusive killing of Jewish men, then Jewish men, women, and children, *and by September of 1941, mass murders of tens of thousands of Jews took place and were soon reported in Allied sources*. Certainly, the German communications system, from newspapers, to the radio, to film, all under the absolute control of Goebbels, said nothing explicit about this.

POLAND AND THE GREAT POPULATIONS OF THE USSR TO BE KILLED

Things were not yet quite going into high gear in Poland. That would take a system of convenient, inexpensive, and effective mass killings, which was not developed until the following year, 1942, with the killing in the Soviet Union, the very heart and soul of Bolshevism, taking priority.

Meanwhile, in what may seem like an aside here, the Germans were finding that in Czechoslovakia (renamed the Protectorate of Bohemia and Moravia), which housed the most advanced manufacturing facilities,

---

[1033] Franz Halder, *The Halder War Diary, 1939-1942*, entry, Jan. 8, 1942, p. 599.
[1034] Franz Halder, *The Halder War Diary, 1939-1942*, entry, Nov. 30, 1941, p. 571.
[1035] Franz Halder, *The Halder War Diary, 1939-1942*, entry, Dec. 7, 1941, p. 582.
[1036] Franz Halder, *The Halder War Diary, 1939-1942*, entry, Dec. 19, 1941, p. 592.

including the Škoda factory, very soon after the invasion of the Soviet Union experienced popular unrest, the presence of saboteurs, and the encouragement of resistance and striking from work. Heydrich and others judged that the German civilian administration was insufficient for the job. After addressing this concern with Bormann and then with Hitler directly, Heydrich was appointed Reich Protector of Bohemia and Moravia, on September 29, 1941. *One consequence of this very significant appointment was that he was now to report directly to the Führer, bypassing Himmler.* He took a further independent step forward in calling the Wannsee Conference in January 1942, at which his assistant Eichmann took official notes and a list of 11 million Jews to be eliminated from Europe was outlined and discussed. (Heydrich would retain this position until his death on June 4, 1942, after Operation Anthropoid, an ambush attack on him in Prague, seriously wounding him, on May 27.)

The decree for Jews in occupied Poland to wear identifying armbands was replaced on December 11, 1941, with a decree that Jews would have to place a Star of David on their chest and back. This also applied to the Jews of Warsaw. Polish Jewish concert pianist Wladyslaw Szpilman would write, "So we were to be publicly branded as outcasts. Several centuries of humanitarian progress were to be cancelled out, and we were back in the Middle Ages."[1037]

Between those two decrees about visible identification of Jews, there was an important meeting, on October 13, 1941, set up between Heinrich Himmler and Odilo Globocnik (Globočnik). Globocnik, an SS officer, had been Gauleiter of Vienna; he was Police Chief in the Lublin District at the time of the meeting—the first Jews had been shipped to Lublin on October 18, 1939, with the idea of creating a reservation of Jews: the area was swampy and ideal as a location for speeding the natural death of those sent there for "work"—and, on October 13, 1941, Globocnik proposed the idea of exterminating Jews in mass, using gas chambers to Himmler. He was then authorized to begin building the first of the extermination camps, *Vernichtungslager* Bełżec. Globocnik was later involved in the liquidation of the Warsaw ghetto and in the killing work of other extermination camps: Majdanek, Sobibór, and Treblinka. The next day, October 14, 1941, Himmler had an extended (5-hour) meeting with Reinhard Heydrich on the issue of the eliminating the Jews in the *Gouvernement General*.[1038] After Heydrich was assassinated, Globocnik would have a major role in the general extermination of the Jews (a project that, in commemorative memory of Reinhard Heydrich, was called "Operation Reinhard").[1039] As

---

[1037] Wladyslaw Szpilman, *The Pianist*, p. 54.

[1038] Christopher Browning, *The Origins of the Final Solution: The Evolution of Nazi Jewish Policy, September 1939-March 1942* (2004), pp. 359-369.

[1039] Gord McFee, "The Operation Reinhard Extermination Camps," THE HOLOCAUST HISTORY PROJECT—PHDN.ORG (2008). Note: given that Operation Reinhard is understood to have been named in memory of Reinhard Heydrich, head of the RSHA (Reich Main Security Office) until his assassination in 1942, the correct

an overview, it is estimated that while at Auschwitz somewhere around 1 million people were killed; at other dedicated extermination camps the killings are estimated at: Treblinka (750-870,000), Bełzec (600,000), Sobibór (250,000), Majdanek (also referred to as KL-Lublin, given that it was located within Lublin's city limits), with an early Soviet estimate of some 1.7 million people killed, subsequently revised to something more like 300-350,000,[1040] at Chełmno, about 365,000 killed, including 4,300 Romanies, and at Maly Trostinets, the largest death camp in Belarus, 65,000 at the camp and perhaps a total of 206,000 including murders in nearby forests.[1041] Relatedly, a secret communique intercepted by British intelligence (and later declassified from material at the National Archives, Public Record Office, in Kew, UK), dated January 11, 1943, relayed information concerning Operation Reinhard (*Einsatz Reinhard*, *Aktion Reinhard*, and *Sondersaktion Reinhard*). This presented the plan for the extermination of Polish Jews, stating that as of the end of 1942, there was a total—the coded message identified each camp only by its initial— of 1,274,166 sent to L (Lublin), 24,733; B (Bełzec), 434,508; S (Sobibór), 101,370; T (Treblinka), 713,555.[1042] Several of these had their operations stopped, with the camp and all of its buildings razed, leaving no signs of their earlier existence, as part of Himmler's concern about reprisals, given the world's reaction to the Soviet killing of Polish military and intelligentsia, found in April 1943 at the Katyń Woods (discussed earlier). With dates of closure, daily killing capacity (D), and total killed (T), these include Treblinka (October 19, 1943; D-25,000; T-700,000), Bełzec (late June 1943; D-15,000; T-600,000), Chełmno or Kulmhof (March 1943, except for brief operations June 1944-January 18, 1945; T-152,000), and Sobibór (October 17, 1943; D-20,000; T-250,000). Majdanek (Lublin)

---

spelling is presumably Reinhard (the spelling for the personal name) and not Reinhardt (which is more typically a family name), but even German sources vary in how the name of this operation is spelled.

[1040] Martin Gilbert, *Holocaust Journey: Travelling in Search of the Past* (1997), p. 280; "Treblinka Concentration Camp, Poland," ENCYCLOPÆDIA BRITANNICA; "Treblinnka," HOLOCAUST.CZ; "Belzec Concentration Camp, Poland," ENCYCLOPÆDIA BRITANNICA; "Majdanek," JEWISHVIRTUALLIBRARY.ORG.; "Chelmno Death Camp," *Holocaust Education & Archive Research Team*, HOLOCAUSTRESEARCHPROJECT.ORG; "Killing Operations Begin at Chelmno," USHMM.ORG.

[1041] "Auschwitz Concentration Camp," "Bełzec Extermination Camp," "Treblinka Extermination Camp," "Sobibór Extermination Camp," "Majdanek Extermination Camp," and "Höfle Telegram" (with statistics on Treblinka), all at WIKIPEDIA; "Treblinka Concentration Camp, Poland" and "Belzec Concentration Camp, Poland" at ENCYCLOPÆDIA BRITANNICA; "Majdanek" and "Concentration Camps: Maly Trostenets" at JEWISHVIRTUALLIBRARY.ORG; "Killing Operations Begin at Chelmno" at USHMM.ORG; "Treblinka" at HOLOCAUST.CZ; and "Chelmno Death Camp," *Holocaust Education & Archive Research Team*, HOLOCAUSTRESEARCHPROJECT.ORG.

[1042] Peter Witte and Stephen Tyas, "A New Document on the Deportation and Murder of Jews during 'Einsatz Reinhardt' 1942," *Holocaust and Genocide Studies*, vol. 15, no. 3, Winter 2001, pp. 468-486, at pp. 469-470.

was closed on July 22, 1944; T-200,000. The estimate for total deaths in these and some ancillary death camps has been given as 3,115,000-3,215,000.[1043] Auschwitz and Auschwitz II (Birkenau), its extermination camp, continued with its much greater and more efficient facilities until the arrival of Soviet troops on January 27, 1945. The total killed at Birkenau: more than 1 million.[1044] All of this is, of course, separate from and in addition to the mass murders by the *SS Einsatzgruppen*, operating in the Soviet Union, as well as murders in the Balkans and Baltic states, and in Western occupied Europe.

A relatively early order was issued on February 8, 1940, a small area of Łódź was defined to be the ghetto for the Jews. Within the month, on March 1, Jews were forbidden to go outside of the ghetto confines. At the end of April 1940, the ghetto area was cut off from the rest of the city with barbed wire and armed German guards. In October and November of 1941, German and Austrian Jews joined the Polish Jews of the ghetto; as well, a small area was set aside for Austrian Gypsies (Romanies). On the weekend of December 7, 1941, Jews and Roma were transported to Chełmno from Łódź for killing by gassing in gas wagons, trucks with its exhaust fumes used to kill those put into its hermetically-sealed back space—a lesson learned from the T4 Program in Germany itself, to rid the nation of the burden of seriously incapacitated Germans, seen as "worthless lives." The conditions in these Polish ghettos allowed no means of livelihood, no sources of food or other needed goods. The Jews were crowded into areas designed to bring about their slow death. The opportunity to show off the disgusting living standards of Jews, their indifference to the death of other Jews around them, their ugliness, had come. The showing of Jews at their most repulsive was at hand! The film for this would be entitled *Der ewige Jude*, *The Eternal Jew*. It would be shown in theaters throughout the German sphere of control, being released in 1940. This film ultimately contained some scenes that Hitler personally insisted upon, but remained largely in the style of propaganda that Goebbels personally preferred.

This makes it clear that *Hitler knew of the basic actions of the German Wehrmacht and the SS, and the organized concentration of Jews leading to deaths, as shown in a number of scenes in the film that he had discussed with Goebbels before its final version was established* and the film distributed throughout the German-dominated countries of Europe. More on what Hitler knew, below. On a military level, Germany had its eyes not only on Poland, and the Soviet Union, too, was looking further afield. Thus, some three months after that invasion of Poland by the Reich, the USSR invaded Finland, in the Russo-Finnish Winter War, November 30, 1939 to March 13, 1940. From a Soviet point of view, this was a way of making Leningrad more secure. This raised a parallel question for the

---

[1043] "Extermination Camp," WIKIPEDIA.
[1044] Heinz Höhne, *The Order of the Death's Head*, pp. 376, 380.

Reich of the security of the supply of iron ore that Germany was obtaining from neutral Sweden,[1045] now more vulnerable itself to an invasion by the USSR through its neighbor Finland. To insure the continuation of this supply, Germany, in turn, on April 9, 1940, invaded Norway, which soon capitulated, securing Germany's military position in northern Europe.

FOG, THE MECHELEN AFFAIR, THE GERMAN INVASION OF THE WEST

Only weeks after the Norway invasion, on May 10, 1940, the German Wehrmacht and Luftwaffe, in *der Fall Gelb*, Operation Yellow, invaded the Netherlands and Belgium. (This sequence of events was discussed more briefly above.) The plans for this invasion had been developing for several months. Two German officers, the pilot, Major Eric Hönmanns, and Major Helmuth Reinberger, Adjutant to Colonel Bassenge, were transporting copies of these plans, in a secret flight, on January 10, 1940.[1046] They landed mistakenly under rather foggy conditions at Mechelen-aan-de-Mass, in Belgium, and were arrested; the event was to be known as the Mechelen Affair. The German military learned of this forced landing almost immediately. On January 12, Gen. Franz Halder, noted in his War Diary, "It must be assumed that at least parts of the documents are in the hands of the Belgians."[1047] And on January 20, referring to a conference that day with the Führer, Halder noted, "Enemy has a fair idea of our plans. That plane accident has made everything very clear to the enemy."[1048] Some sources suggest that the Duke of Wales (formerly, King Edward VIII) disclosed this information to the Germans, but it seems clear that German (or Belgian or French) military and intelligence had no need at all for information here that the Duke might pass on to them, drunk or sober, intentional or by slippage of a loosened tongue.[1049]

It is sometimes held that the French were totally surprised by this path of invasion, and had assumed that the Germans, if they attacked, would attack from the east, and in that, would face the formidable Maginot Line, a series of fixed-position pillbox defenses, with cannons facing the east and Germany. For years there was an understanding that Belgium and France might have to face any invasive German military together, as coordinated action. This was set up in its basics in the Franco-Belgian Accord of 1920. Then, on March 6, 1936, Belgium took a position of total

---

[1045] Martin Gilbert, *Churchill: A Life*, p. 635.

[1046] Hugh H. Sebag-Montefiore, "The Mechelen Affair," *The Quarterly Journal of Military History (MHQ)*, vol. 20, no. 3, Mar. 2008, pp. 48-55. This article was based in part on "recently discovered documents in *Reichskriegsgericht* (German War Tribunal) files in the former Czechoslovakia" (as indicated at p. 50).

[1047] Franz Halder, *The Halder War Diary, 1939-1942*, entry, Jan. 12, 1940, p. 86.

[1048] Franz Halder, *The Halder War Diary, 1939-1942*, entry, Jan, 20, 1940, p.90.

[1049] See film, *Edward VIII: The Traitor King* (1996). Cf. such printed material as Kashmira Gander, "Duke of Windsor 'wanted England to be bombed', international archives reveal," *Independent* (London), Jun. 8, 2015; Tom Sommer, "What 'The Crown' Got Wrong: The Duke of Windsor's (Not So) Secret Nazi History," *Observer* (London), Dec. 1, 2017, etc.

neutrality, but the French continued with plans to respond to the possibility of this more northern German invasion. After January 10, 1940, however, when the military secrets and plans being carried on that German aircraft were captured by the Belgians and then passed on to the French, the Ardennes Offensive was known of ahead of time. In the activities of intelligence and counter-intelligence, Hitler was to modify plans for the attack of the west on February 13, 1940, continuing with the movement of some troops, in accordance with the plans known to be known by the Belgians, as a decoy, and to add a more focused thrust further to the south, through the Ardennes (and not attacking the Maginot Line at all).[1050] This was basically accepting a plan already drawn up by General Erich von Manstein. This would take place not when the Belgians and French were expecting it, but on May 10, 1940. *This German offensive ended the* drôle de guerre *(in which French and German armies, formally at war with one another, did not have any battles: the "Phony War") that had lasted eight months.* This German offensive included the devastation by aerial bombing of Rotterdam; the Dutch surrendered on May 14. It also involved the escape of Allied forces at Dunkirk, including some of the British Expeditionary Force (BEF). In this action, lasting from May 26 to June 4, 1940, some 198,000 BEF and some 140,000 French and Belgian troops escaped, a rather remarkable operation with cooperation from many British (and French) civilian sailors using their small boats. Belgium surrendered on May 28. On that day, before the French surrendered, nearly 100 British and French troops, surrounded and without ammunition, surrendered to Waffen SS from the First SS Division *Leibstandarte SS Adolf Hitler* (in short, the *LSSAH*, which before the war had been chancellery bodyguards for Hitler); in their zeal (and against the Geneva Conventions for the treatment of POWs), they drove these soldiers into a barn, near the northern French town of Wormhoudt, and killed some 90 of them by grenades and then machine guns.[1051] By mid-June, France having been overrun in the north, Paris surrendered on June 17, 1940; the formal armistice was signed on June 22, 1940.

Meanwhile, all of these military and political transformations of Europe, for these first years, with the realization of one military victory by the German Reich after another, had not only geopolitical implications, with German hegemony or control established over much of continental Europe,

---

[1050] "French war planning 1920-1940," WIKIPEDIA; "Les allies savaient! The allies knew! (Messerschmitt Bf 108)," WW2LIAISONAIRCRAFTS.E-MONSITE.COM; Hugh Sebag-Montefiore, "The Mechelen Affair," *MHQ: Quarterly Journal of Military History*, vol. 20, no. 3, Mar. 2008, pp. 48-55; "Mechelen Incident," WORLDWAR2-NET.COM; "Mechelin Incident," HISTORYNET.COM; "France stops the blitz 1940: A Stalemate on the Western Front," HISTORUM.COM, Feb. 27, 2016; "Mechelen Incident, January 1940" WW2TIMESLINES.COM; "Military Living in the Netherlands: The Mechelin Incident," US-MIL-IN-NL.BLOGSPOT.COM; Glenmore S. Trenear-Harvey, *Historical Dictionary of Military Failures* (2015), "Gelb," p. 77; "Erich Hoenmanns," WIKIPEDIA.

[1051] "Wormhoudt Massacre Site and Museum," DUNKIRK-TOURISM.COM; Leslie Aitken, *Massacre on the Road to Dunkirk: Wormhoudt 1940* (1977).

but also created a new, more threatening status for the Jews of the lands recently conquered. These included many Jews who had escaped from Germany and were again brought under the hostile control of the Reich.

11. Focus on the Invasion of the USSR, 1941

The invasion of the USSR, even more than the earlier invasion of Poland (and other countries in northern and western Europe), presented a new dimension of Master Race principles and the program of the elimination of inferior beings, from all Jews and Romanies, to Poles and other Slavic groups, especially the Ukrainians, in addition, as earlier, of those Germans who were held to be lives unworthy of living (which had been largely killed off in the T4 killing program described as mass euthanasia). Here was a great challenge, given the literally millions of more people to have to be dealt with in a final solution of mass killings.

MASTER RACE SPACE: *LEBENSRAUM*, *LEBENSBORN*, MASS MURDERS

In this context, the key context of a living space for the master race (the German people), *Lebensraum*, was a self-defined and self-declared right of the German people to take whatever lands it needed to provide for its people as it itself envisioned. This concept was presented in some detail in *Mein Kampf*, quoted above, with the explicit mention of the Soviet Union as the prime land that would serve the purpose of this great German nation, envisioned long before the start of World War II. The fact that this land was not barren and uninhabited, but, rather, the vast territories of Slavic peoples for many centuries, was not seen as an issue or an obstacle: the Slavs would either be turned into slaves for the superior German people or race, or they would be eliminated, killed in the tens of millions: there were, after all, many Slavs to the east of the German lands. This superior German nation was somewhat of a dream or *an ideal to be achieved, rather than an actual, present given*. Hitler and others were quite clear that there were among the German population those who met Nazi Aryan standards (to be encouraged to reproduce) but others who did not meet those standards (requiring some selective elimination, that is, organized killing, as in the T4 Euthanasia program). In addition, then, to these inferior beings, there were also large numbers of people with physical defects, either congenital or developed in life, incurable diseases, mentally weak individuals as well as mentally disturbed individuals. All of these were a serious problem and concern of the Nazi government during the 1930s, before the invasion of Poland. There was a flood of claims coming from the Propaganda Ministry of Joseph Goebbels about the burden that these people put on the entire German society, including graphic films that showed incapacitated individuals, filmed with harsh lighting, described as living beings unworthy of living, as useless mouths to be fed off of the labor of healthy Germans. And, relatedly, the *first organized mass killings* in the Third Reich *were directed against these German lives deemed worthless*. A program that had Nazi doctors evaluate who would live and who would die was instituted, and gas chambers of a primitive sort were installed, with fake

The Hitler Era

shower heads, and using carbon monoxide fumes from a motor running outside the chamber's walls. Bodies were then cremated and the ashes sent back to family, who were required to pay a fee to receive the remains of their dead member. This program, called the T4 Operation—the name comes from the street address (Tiergartenstraße 4, or T4) of the villa that had been taken over from its earlier, Jewish owners, of course with no monetary compensation, and transformed into a government ministry.[1052]

In any case, people were told that the unfortunate deaths of relatives came through disease or particular illnesses. Some churchmen spoke out against this barbaric and unchristian practice—including August Clemens von Galen, Bishop of Münster (in his sermon, August 3 1941), Pastors Dietrich Bonhoeffer, Ludwig Schlaich and Paul Braune, and Cardinal Adolf Bertram of Breslau[1053]; it was then officially terminated by Hitler, without acknowledging any role in T4 himself.[1054]

Himmler applied this technique of truck exhaust fumes as a killing method for concentration camp prisoners, in the *Aktion 14f13* (or *Sonderbehandlung 14f13*, Special Treatment 14f13), beginning in Spring 1941.[1055] The design these mobile killing vans took was the creation of Walther Rauff, assistant to Heydrich and head of *Gruppe II D* (Section for Technical Affairs) in the RSHA. He was responsible for the death of more than 97,000 Jews (people "who have been processed," a report says).[1056]

Soon thereafter would be the issuance of Hitler's *Grundsätzlicher Befehl* (Hitler's Basic Order) of September 15, 1941, mentioned above, that dictated, "Nobody (*Niemand*), no official (*keine Dienststelle*), no employee (*kein Angestellter*), and no worker (*kein Arbeiter*) may know of any secret matter *dürfen von einer geheimzuhaltenden Sache erfahren*) that is not absolutely necessary for that person to know in the course of his or her duty."[1057] This acknowledged secret operations and aimed at keeping information withheld unless absolutely needed for specific tasks.

In those early months of the war on the Eastern Front against the USSR, there was much optimism in Germany, a celebratory mood that seemed to confirm the invincibility of the Reich military and the inferiority of its enemies. In early October, the *Völkischer Beobachter* had a front-page headline in its North-German Edition: *Die große Stunde hat geschlagen. Der Feldzug im Osten entschieden!* (The great hour has come.

[1052] Michael Berenbaum, "T4 Program: Nazi Policy," Encyclopædia Britannica.

[1053] Michael Burleigh, "Between Enthusiasm, Compliance and Protest: The Churches, Eugenics and the Nazi 'Euthanasia' Programme," *Contemporary European History*, vol. 3, no. 3, 1994, pp. 253–263.

[1054] *Action T4: A Doctor Under Nazism* (2014), at 36:00-37:30.

[1055] "14f13," Holocaust Research Project.

[1056] "Walther Rauff: Letters to the Gas Van Expert," *Holocaust Education & Archive Research Team*, HOLOCAUSTRESEARCHPROJECT.ORG. He died in 1984 of a heart attack in Santiago de Chile, where he lived for decades, protected by Pinochet.

[1057] Christa Schroeder, *Er war mein Chef*, pp. 48, 328-329; *He Was My Chief*, p. 26.

The campaign in the East decided!")[1058] That may be seen as a public stance, a political declaration. In contrast to this stance of optimism, there are reports that months earlier, on July 13, 1941, "The Führer is again nagging about the slow development of the attack on [Field Marshal Wilhelm Ritter] von Leeb's right wing,[1059] and demands that the 19th Armored Division[1060] strike northward to encircle the enemy."[1061]

Given the vision of a great German population of model "Aryan" youth, firm, fit, blonde, slim, muscular, and fertile (old age was not at all in focus in this ideal and imagery), and the vast territories from earlier Germany to the Asiatic steppes, and the thousand-year period of time to realize this vision, there was an interest not only in purifying, improving the German people by eliminating those who did not meet certain key criteria, but also a program for the intense increase in the number of pure Aryan-Germans. This was to be accomplished by an organized selection of loyal Nazi youth who were physical representations of the German ideal: blonde, with blue eyes, a firm body composition (especially for the men), a certain height and height-weight relationship. This need for a great increase in the truly German population was a very strongly felt need: after all, Germany, like other European lands, had a great depletion of young men after the mutual organized and mechanized killing in the Great War.

The project, while not announced publicly, had a definite organization. The young women were to be picked by their Nazi teachers and superiors. There was an inspired metaphor for the work of these fertile young women of producing German babies for the Reich, which would need not only laborers, farmers, factory workers, but also soldiers defending Germany and Europe from inferior hordes trying to exterminate German and European culture. They were spoken of as "giving the Führer a baby" and with that metaphor was the perhaps unexpressed suggestion that they would be having an intimate sexual relation (at least on the level of fantasy) with the Führer himself. Hitler was making this easier by keeping all of his sexual life an unknown, including his relationship with Eva: his being in a relationship would dampen the fantasies of the women of Germany of being the one that the Führer would want to be married to.

The fantasy aside, these young women were selected and taken to special centers, administered as hospitals. They were being tracked for their ovulation cycles, so that when the time came of their greatest fecundity, they would be matched with male Germans chosen by similar criteria and offering the seed for a greater, purely Aryan population. These centers were all part of a program called the *Lebensborn*, the Fount, Fountain, or Source of Life. The men chosen for this procreative task of helping to enlarge the German population were mostly SS Men, whether married or not. This was understood to be part of a patriotic duty of those

---

[1058] *Völkischer Beobachter, Norddeutsche Ausgabe*, Oct. 10, 1941, p. 1.

[1059] This was in Army Group C, attacking the Baltic States and Leningrad.

[1060] This was also called the 19th Panzer (tank) Division, involved in the battles of Moscow and, later, Kursk.

[1061] Franz Halder, *The Halder War Diary, 1938-1942*, entry, Jul. 12, 1941, p 467.

The Hitler Era

best equipped to help improve the German stock. Heinrich, who was the head of the SS and also of the *Lebensborn* Program, decided that there were some children of Slavic parents who actually displayed fine Aryan features and could be raised to be true Nazi-inspired Germans. Among those who were chosen in this search were children of a small town in Czech Bohemia, near Prague. The situation was that Reinhard Heydrich, who was the brutal SS administrator of what had been western Czechoslovakia, was ambushed and shot in Prague, dying of serious wounds in the next days. It was decided to retaliate for this one death: a town was selected, with no particular direct link to the assassination, Lidice. It was razed to the ground, all of the men shot, and the women and children taken off to concentration camps. Some of these children were chosen, given new, Germanic names, and adopted by good Nazis to be raised as true Germans. Germany needed a strong next generation, especially with the many deaths of German military on the Eastern Front taking their toll. Now, in addition to eliminating pitiable specimens of German people (the T4 Action), the encouraging of all German women to bring forth as many babies as possible, in the clandestine *Lebensborn* program with its organized reproduction centers, and adopting Slavic "aryanizable" children as future Nazis, there was also the persistent, nagging issue of eliminating Germany's so-called eternal enemies (world Jewry) and the subjugating of Slavic populations of eastern Europe, with an ultimate goal of exterminating Slavs by the tens of millions.

These key concepts with their racial implications (involving the subjugation or elimination of inferior beings) were finally applied in a focused, methodical, thorough way in Soviet-occupied lands by German SS *Einsatzgruppen* of small groups and massive killings, in fields and ravines, begun shortly after the initial invasion of the USSR—before the comments from Hitler, Himmler, Frank, in December 1941, quoted above, and before those at the Wannsee Conference, in January 1942.[1062]

In the southeast, in Ukraine, there was an intense and bloody defense of Kiev by the Soviet forces, against an unrelenting attack by German armies there. The battle for Kiev began at its outer defenses at the end of July. The Germans would finally surround the inner city of Kiev by the start of September. Finally, after a period of siege, with the reluctant

---

[1062] As mentioned above in another context, Robert Kempner, assistant US Chief Counsel in the Nuremberg Trials, discovered the Wannsee Protocol in Berlin in 1947, with the document then used in later Nuremberg Trials. The Wannsee Conference Minutes document was entered into the records of the Nuremberg Trials Ministries Case, NT-TWC-Green, vol. 13, pp. 210-217, as "Document NG-2586-G, Prosecution Exhibit 1452: Extracts from the Minutes of the Wannsee Conference, 20 January 1942, with Fifteen Persons Participating, including Defendant Strackart, at which Plans for the 'Final Solution of the Jewish Question' Were Discussed." Cf. "The Protocol of the Wannsee Conference (January 20, 1942)," DIE DEUTSCHE GESCHICHTE IN DOKUMENTEN UND BILDERN (DGDB), introductory "Überblick" ("Overview"). See also Christian Gerlach, *Sur la conférence de Wannsee*.

withdrawal of remaining Soviet troops, the German Army entered Kiev on September 19, 1941. Anti-German forces, in part Soviet troops, then carried on four days of arson and sabotage, with fires raging and no one to attempt to put them out, which led to an even higher level of violence. In response, the German military posted announcements on September 28 for all Jews of Kiev to assemble on the corner of Melnikovskaya and Dohturovskaya Streets at 8 in the morning the next day, September 29, 1941.[1063] This meeting place was near the Lukyanovka Railroad Station, suggesting (at least to the optimistic) that train transport would take the Jews to some unknown destination for productive. (This was not to be.) The Jews that assembled were led west-northwest down Melnikovskaya Street to the edge of town and the ravine at Babi Yar. In the two days of September 29-30, 1941, German military records reported that 33,771 Jews had been shot to death. The ravine would be used for more killings the next days and for two more years; estimates of total murders are from 100,000 to 200,000 people in all.[1064] This showed what the military of the Third Reich, the Wehrmacht, and especially the *SS Einsatzgruppen* (along with help from willing locals), could do when focused on mass killings. This was just the start, since there were more efficient and easier (on the SS soldiers) methods later developed for these mass killings.

In January 1942, a half-year after the Babi Yar massacre, and the organizational meeting of top Nazi officials in Berlin at the Wannsee Conference, it was taken as an obvious given that there was a violent, a disastrous, time ahead for the Jews (along with Slavs and other sorts of undesirables from the Nazi perspective).

For example, Goebbels, in his diary entry for March 27, 1942, knew of a treatment so harsh that he hesitated to describe it, even when writing for himself: "The Jews are now being deported from the General Government, beginning at Lublin, to the East. Here a rather barbaric and unspecified procedure not described in detail [*nicht näher zu beschreibendes*] is used, and there is not much left of the Jews themselves. On the whole, one can say that 60% of them have to be liquidated [*60 % davon liquidiert werden müssen*] ... The Jews are punished by a judgment that is barbaric, but which they have fully earned [*das zwar barbarisch ist, das sie aber vollauf verdient haben*].[1065]

This echoed the prophecy in Hitler's speech before the Reichstag on January 30, 1939—more on this, below—threatening that if the Jews drew Germany into a world war, the result would be the annihilation of the Jews

---

[1063] There are various spellings of these two streets, some in Russian and some in Ukrainian: Melnikov, Melnikovskaya, Melnikovsky; Dohturovskaya, Dokhturov, Degtyarev, Degtyarivska, Decktiarovska, etc.

[1064] See *Soviet Storm: WW2 in the East, The Battle of Kiev (Episode 2 of 18)*, YOUTUBE, at 41:24-42:45 for the murders of those first 33,771 at Babi Yar, and at 41:24-43:50 for the fuller story. This film series is a 2011 Russian production.

[1065] Joseph Goebbels, *Tagebücher, 1924-1945*, pp. 1776-1777; Claus-Ekkehard Bärsch, *Der junge Goebbels: Erlösung und Vernichtung* (2004), pp. 100-101.

The Hitler Era 351

of Europe "that the Führer gave them for their bringing on a new world war [*für die Herbeiführung eines neuen Weltkriegs*] begins to be realized [now, continued Goebbels in his diary] in the most terrible way. One should not let sentimentality prevail in these matters. [*Man darf in diesen Dingen keine Sentimentalität obwalten lassen.*] The Jews, if we did not resist them, would destroy us. [*Die Juden würden, wenn wir uns ihrer nicht erwehren würden, uns vernichten.*] It is a life and death struggle [*ein Kampf auf Leben und Tod*] between the Aryan race and the Jewish bacillus [*zwischen der arischen Rasse und dem jüdischen Bazillus*].[1066] The reasoning that justified this intense murder plan, that the Jews of the world were united in their controlling history and dragging a reluctant civilized Europe (and especially its pinnacle, the German nation) into a devastating world war, through greed and hatred of true culture (from the Nazi point of view), is a particular kind of reasoning, one which basically attributes our own hateful inclinations on another group, and then responds to this self-created sense of a threat to our existence by taking what we see to be defensive self-protection in the face of such a potentially enormous threat. More on those psychological and sociological processes, below. *This task of purifying German and Europe of the vermin of Jewry with all of its nefarious manifestations, was not going to be an easy one.* But it could be met head-on by determined National Socialists grounded in their reasoned justification for this mass murder.

With this same sense of mass murder as justified self-defense, General Otto Ohlendorf would testify that German soldiers "felt that their work was necessary even if it opposed their own inner tendencies and interest, because the existence of their people was in deadly peril."[1067]

Along with a continuing success on the military front, which was assumed as obvious, this task would demand diligence, imperturbable determination, and perseverance, but many SS were up for this daunting challenge. For example, one of the select participants at the Wannsee Conference, Otto Hofmann, Head of the *Rasse- und Siedlungshauptamt der SS*, or *RuSHA* (the SS Race and Settlement Main Office) from 1940-1943, in late September 1942, would speak to a meeting of SS officers:

> They will no longer recognize any Jewish danger. In twenty years there may not be a single Jew left. In the European part of Russia there are a total of eleven millions [of] Jews.[1068] So there is still plenty of work to do.

[1066] Joseph Goebbels, *Tagebücher, 1924-1945*, pp. 1776-1777; Claus-Ekkehard Bärsch, *Der junge Goebbels: Erlösung und Vernichtung* (2004), pp. 100-101.

[1067] NT-TWC-Green, vol. 4, p. 389.

[1068] At the Wannsee Conference that January, the total number Jews in Europe was cited as 11 million, of which there were listed 5 million in the USSR, among which there were 2,994,684 in Ukraine, and 446,484 in White Russia (Belarus). The statement here by Hofmann mentions 11 million in the USSR, not the 5 million cited at Wannsee. Christian Gerlach, noticing this discrepancy, remarked, "The mistake may have been made by the individual who prepared the minutes of the

> I cannot believe that we have exterminated more than one million of them thus far. It will take some time until we have freed Europe from this pestilence.[1069]

This mass killing that had already begun in earnest was known not only to the SS, its *Einsatzgruppen*, but to family and friends of those who returned from the Russian front who learned personally about the situation, and to those impacted by this task of extermination.

Information was also in the hands of the Soviet government and also the British government, who learned in part through developments decoding the Enigma Machine, which was discussed earlier: Bletchley Park, the center in England that had broken the Enigma Code, transmitted decrypted German military messages to the British government—its intelligence had earlier helped the British know of Rommel's plans in north Africa, the movement of the "packs" of German submarines, allowing their significant destruction, and so forth. They also intercepted reports of the killings of Jews in the first months of the German invasion of the Soviet Union, such as the killing of more than 5,000 Jews near Kamenets-Podolsk on September 11, 1941. Receiving such intelligence, Prime Minister Winston Churchill announced as early as August 14, 1941, that "whole districts are being exterminated" ... We are in the presence of a crime without a name."[1070] And when news of the Babi Yar massacres came to Britain, Churchill had this statement published on November 14, 1941:

> None has suffered more cruelly than the Jew the unspeakable evils wrought on the bodies of spirits of men by Hitler and his vile regime. The Jew bore the brunt of the Nazi's first onslaught upon the citadels of freedom and human dignity. He has borne and continues to bear a burden that might have seemed to be beyond endurance. He has not allowed it to break his spirit; he has never lost the will to resist. Assuredly, on the day of victory, the Jew's sufferings and his part in the struggle will not be forgotten.[1071]

---

speech." Christian Gerlach, "The Wannsee Conference, the fate of German Jews, and Hitler's decision in principle to exterminate all European Jews," *Journal of Modern History*, vol. 70, no. 4, Dec. 1998, pp. 759-812, at p. 800, n. 190; reprinted in *Holocaust: Critical Concepts in Historical Studies*, vol. 3, 2004, pp. 66-120, at p. 116, n. 190. Cf. Christian Gerlach, *Die Wannsee-Konferenz, das Schicksal der deutschen Juden und Hitlers politische Grundsatzentscheidung, alle Juden Europas zu ermorden* (1998); Fr. ed., *Sur la conférence de Wannsee*.

[1069] See Christian Gerlach, "The Wannsee Conference" (just cited); cf. David Redles, *Hitler's Millennial Reich: Apocalyptic Belief and the Search for Salvation* (2005), p. 185 (in Chap. "Final Empire").

[1070] Martin Gilbert, *Churchill and the Jews: A Lifelong Friendship*, p. 186.

[1071] Martin Gilbert, *The Churchill War Papers: The Ever-widening War, 1941* (2001), reprint of article: "Winston S. Churchill To the *Jewish Chronicle* (*The Jewish Chronicle*, 14 November 1941)," p. 1454.

The Hitler Era

To give context for pronouncements sympathetic to the massacres of the Jews, if needed, Churchill would decades later be described by General Sir Edward Louis Speaks, Churchill's fellow soldier, historian, and parliamentarian, who confided to Martin Stuart, on September 12, 1969, that Churchill "was too fond of Jews,"[1072] presumably a conservative evaluation reflective of an anti-Semitic attitude common in the 1930s.

THE MILITARY CONTEXT ALLOWING THE APPLICATION OF THIS RACE THEORY

Of course, the Third Reich, as usual, had more on its mind than only the Jewish question. It was also focused on its military prowess and its continuing conquests. In the first months of the war against the USSR, it quickly took military control over much of European Soviet Union. While its original date of invasion was pushed back, as German forces were focused on supporting its Italian ally to the south, it was early summer (June 21, 1941) when it did attack. It had several months to gain as much territory as it could before the Russian winter set in. Hitler would be quite consistent in his principle that the strong deserve to win and have the right to destroy the weak—no matter who the strong and who the weak! Even at the time of the invasion of the USSR, Hitler said, "If the German people is not strong enough and devoted enough to give its blood for its existence, let it go and be destroyed by another, stronger man. I shall not shed tears for the German people."[1073] We might feel an urge to respect a man who can be so consistent, but at the same time, there is a cold-blooded great indifference to the suffering of those he is talking about, who, in this case, are the very German people he declared to be his mission in life, to protect them and to further their interests. This suggests a difference, or hierarchy, of values that inspired (or drove Hitler). A respect or admiration of the principle of the rights of the strong was apparently more significant to him than his love of his adopted nation, Germany. (We will return to a discussion of Hitler's psychology, below.)

Before the most intense days of the Russian winter (which Napoleon had found to be a major obstacle in his invasion of Czarist Russia, a lesson not to be forgotten), there was the rainy season with the clay-rich earth not absorbing the water, leading to great muddy roads. Termed *rasputitsa* in Russian, this condition meant that German foot soldiers, and the army carts, tanks, artillery, and other parts of the invading army would find themselves stuck. This had also occurred in battles in World War I, the most famous perhaps being the 1917 Battle of Passchendaele (also called the Second Battle of Flanders and the Third Battle of Ypres). The severe winter might not have yet set in, but the rain, the snow, the wet, melted conditions soaking boots and feet during the day would freeze up at night, an annoyance and a serious threat to health, stamina, and the will to fight.

Such details were not part of the original German military thinking and planning, but, as in many other cases, battles could impacted by the

---

[1072] Martin Gilbert, *Churchill and the Jews*, p. xv.
[1073] Timothy Snyder, *Black Earth: The Holocaust as History and Warning* (2015), p. 242.

vicissitudes of weather, and relatedly, from contagious and other diseases that thrived in the close quarters of the military in war. *And, in addition, military and political leaders seem to be widely susceptible to an over-estimation of their own powers, and under-estimation of the enemy's capacity to resist, and a disregard for important factors such as weather.*

In any case, Hitler was expecting a quick victory, as had occurred in Poland, Denmark, Norway, Belgium, the Netherlands, and France. Troops had two issues to contend with, in addition to the Soviet army opposing them. First was the need to have access to supplies (weapons and their shells, fuel for their trucks and tanks, and food). This had been a problem for Germany in World War I, when its storm troops, men traveling only with their immediate arms, with food and supplies not able to keep up with them, leading to abortive offenses by the Germans that left these men stranded and easily captured or killed in warfare. *This was a lesson that presumably would be important to keep in mind in any future war that Germany might undertake or find itself involved in, although unpleasant and a fetter to enthusiasm and unlimited confidence.*

As Germany had secured its northern flank, that is, occupied Denmark and Norway, to stop aggression from that direction, now it would see the relevance of securing its southern flank, making sure (by forced control, alliances, or occupation) that Hungary, Romania, Bulgaria, Yugoslavia, and Greece, lands important also for easier access to the Soviet Union, and also to the grains, minerals, and oil from in that region of southeast Europe and into the Middle East. This would be partly resolved in the first half of 1941, before the invasion of the USSR on June 20, 1941.

On the Russian front itself, there was also the need to establish solid front lines in order to have a sense of success and, on a more practical level, a firm control over important urban centers in the USSR. And while Moscow, Leningrad, and Stalingrad all had symbolic importance, their strategic value was less obvious. As Army Chief of Staff General Franz Halder put it on March 17, 1941, in his *War Diary*, long before the actual invasion of the USSR, "Moscow is of no importance whatsoever."[1074] And, of course, the German Wehrmacht never did capture Moscow or Leningrad.

At first, the German Armies advanced with great success, seen as a repeat of the *Blitzkrieg*—the war (*Krieg*) that was lightning-fast (*Blitz*)— against Poland, and, then again, against the Low Countries and France, in the West. The Wehrmacht, together with the powerful Luftwaffe, seemed invincible. And certainly, the German populace, with Hitler directing as Supreme Commander in Chief of the Armed Forces, filled with confidence, basked in the glory of glorious power.

Hitler would very soon make his attitude known—his vision of the great German potential to fulfill its rights as the *Herrenraße*, the Master Race, to realize *Lebensraum*, living space, in the lands of the East, as he had

---

[1074] Franz Halder, *The Halder War Diary, 1939-1942*, entry, Mar. 17, 1941, p. 337.

written in *Mein Kampf*. In the first months of the invasion of the USSR, on his visit to Ukraine, on August 6, 1941 at Berdychiv (Berdichev),[1075] he stated, as recorded by Martin Bormann:

> The German colonist ought to live on handsome, spacious farms. The German services will be lodged in marvelous buildings, the governors in palaces.... What India was for England, the territories of Russia will be for us. If only I could make the German people understand what this space means for our future! Colonies are a precarious possession, but this ground is safely ours. Europe is not a geographic entity, it's a racial entity.[1076]

June 1941 saw the invasion of Russia, with German military power and conquests starting off again with rapid victories. The next fifteen months or so were decisive: After the seemingly temporary stalling of Wehrmacht (Army) victories by the Russian winter of 1941-1942, the Third Reich military reached their greatest success in the autumn of 1942.

In this, the question of the Jews, Romanies, Poles, and Ukrainians were an auxiliary, non-military focus: German Gauleiters (administrative heads of various lands in Germany) wanted to expel these lower beings to the East; those administering the situation (such as Hans Frank, Governor General of occupied Poland) were having difficulties with the potential huge influx of people to be dealt with. In this context, the Minister of Justice in the Third Reich, Otto Thierack, would write to Martin Bormann, secretary and confidant to the Führer, on October 13, 1942, stating, "With the intention of liberating the German area from Poles, Russians, Jews, and Gypsies ... I envisage transferring all criminal proceedings concerning [these people] to Himmler. I do this because *I realize that the courts can only feebly contribute to the extermination of these people* ... There is no point in keeping these people for years in prison. I ask you to let me know if the Führer approves of this way of thinking!" *Thierack's proposal was soon approved by Hitler by November 5, 1942.*[1077]

At this same time, on October 18, 1942, Hitler issued a secret order, prepared in only 12 copies, stating, "From now on all enemies on so-called commando missions in Europe and Africa, even if, to all appearances, soldiers in uniform or demolition troops, whether armed or unarmed, in battle or in flight, *are to be slaughtered to the last man*. It makes no

---

[1075] "Life and Fate (Berdychiv, Ukraine): Vasily Grossman, *The Last Letter* and *A Mother's Love*," Oct. 29, 2014, EUROPEBETWEENEASTANDWEST.WORDPRESS.COM.

[1076] Martin Bormann, *Bormann-Vermerke*, Eng. tr., *Hitler's Table talk 1941-1944: Secret Conversations*, H. R. Trevor-Roper, ed., New Updated 3rd ed., with new Introduction by Gerhard L. Weinberg (2007), p. 21.

[1077] Donald Kenrick and Grattan Puxon, *Gypsies under the Swastika*, pp. 33-34, italics added. Cf. Nikolaus Wachsmann, "'Annihilation through Labor': The Killing of State Prisoners in the Third Reich," *The Journal of Modern History*, vol. 71, no. 3, 1999, pp. 624–659, esp. pp. 628-632, with, at p. 632, "Both Thierack and Himmler were aware that they were translating Hitler's will into reality."

difference whether they landed from ships or aeroplanes, even if they apparently are prepared to give themselves up. *No pardon is to be granted on principle.*"[1078] This would be a principle of engagement or combat applied to Bolshevik agents and Jews (who were automatically suspected of being Bolshevik enemies of the Reich).

By autumn 1942, there were logistic problems for the Wehrmacht that had been discussed earlier by Hitler at meetings recorded by Franz Halder, discussed above: The Wehrmacht was soon in dire straits on the Eastern Front; it was determined that for the Wehrmacht, 300 tons of supplies were required for daily minimal maintenance, and, to be fully operational, 500 tons.

Some analyses suggested that even this was inadequate, considering the weight of artillery, its shells, food for the men, horses, and other military requirements. On November 25, 1942, Field Marshal Hermann Göring promised Hitler he could provide a minimum of 300 tons of supplies per day. However, on November 26, the Soviet military destroyed 29 Junker-532 and Heinkel-111 German aircraft caught on the ground; on December 25, 60 Junker-52s were similarly destroyed on the ground by Soviet forces. *Things were not boding well for the Luftwaffe's operations.* Hitler summoned Luftwaffe Field Marshall Erhard Milch, a former executive of Lufthansa, introduced above, to come to the aid of the Luftwaffe, but there were simply not enough German airplanes (counting even mail planes that might be adapted to support the German troops focused around Stalingrad). As an average, the Luftwaffe only supplied some 118-120 tons per day, hardly enough for the situation.[1079]

At this same time, on the Southern Front, in North Africa, the Allies invaded North Africa on November 8, 1942,[1080] against the German forces in North Africa, meant to protect the Axis southern flank controlled by its Fascist ally, Italy. This ended with the defeat of General Rommel in North Africa, with the surrender of German troops on May 10, 1943—the British victory having been helped in part by their decoding of secret German military messages using their Enigma machine, discussed earlier.

In this same period, unexpected and shocking to the German Reich, came the German military collapse: The German defense of Stalingrad was impossible; it was soon a disaster for the Wehrmacht. On January 31, 1943, General Von Paulus with the German Sixth Army surrendered to

---

[1078] "Massacre of 5000 Jews Described: Shot in Groups Near Large Pit," *The Advocate* (Burnie, Tasmania), Jan. 3, 1946, p. 1, TROVE.NLA.GOV.AU. This reported on testimony given at the Nuremberg Tribunal on Jan. 2, 1946. Italics added.

[1079] Mike Yoder, "Battle of Stalingrad," MILITARY HISTORY ONLINE, Feb. 4, 2003; Nikola Budanovic, "10 Things You Should Know about Göring" (see Sect. 4. "Decline on All Fronts!"), WAR HISTORY ONLINE, Jul. 17, 2016; "Airbridge (Logistics)," WIKIPEDIA; "Hitler Trusts Göring to Supply Stalingrad by Air: Nov. 25, 1942," WORLD WAR II TODAY; Ben Hanvey, "The Stalingrad Airlift," GERMAN WAR MACHINE: WEHRMACHT IN ACTION, Dec. 3, 2014.

[1080] Alfons Heck, *The Burden of Hitler's Legacy*, p. 87.

The Hitler Era

the Soviets; pockets of Germans surrendered in the next days. The Sixth army was decimated: some 300,000 dead, some 91,000 taken prisoner. Gen. Kurt Dittmar on the German propaganda radio program, *Stimme des OKW* (*Voice of the Supreme High Command of the Armed Forces*, or *Voice of the Wehrmacht*), lauded this disaster as a *taktischer Rückzüg* (tactical retreat).[1081] But the Munich underground anti-Nazi group, the White Rose, distributed a more pessimistic reading in its six leaflets from June 1942 to February 1943. In crisis, Goebbels gave his speech calling for total war, on February 18, 1943. Soon there was the Warsaw Ghetto uprising (April 19-May 16, 1943). Basically, the Soviets gained air superiority over the Luftwaffe, definitively after the failure at Kursk of Operation Citadel.[1082]

Touching on Discussions at the Wannsee Conference

A German diplomat, Otto Bräutigam, wrote on December 18, 1941, "as for the Jewish question, oral discussions have taken place [and] have brought about clarification"[1083] (and definiteness about the Final Solution). Also, on December 18, at 4 in the afternoon, Himmler, after a private meeting with Hitler at the *Wolfsschanze* in East Prussia, wrote of Hitler's idea: "Jewish Question, to be exterminated like the partisans [*Judenfrage, als Partisanen auszurotten*]."[1084] More, below.

Scenes from the Eastern Front, with its Mass Murders

Film was not the only means by which the German public learned of the events in the east, first in Poland, and later in the Soviet Union. *Many of those who returned from Slavic lands brought back first-hand reports, as well as photographs taken from their experiences.*

For example, we may consider Wilhelm Adalbert Hosenfeld (known as Wilm), who was brought up as a Catholic, with strict Prussian values. He joined the Nazi party in 1935, at first filled with enthusiasm for German militarism, in 1940 calling Hitler a true genius. He would have his values questioned and radically changed by his experience in Poland. In 1942 *Hauptmann* (Captain) Wilm Hosenfeld would note, seeing the treatment of the Jews: "You cannot believe it all; I refuse to accept it [*ich wehre mich dagegen*], because I do not want to believe that Hitler wants

---

[1081] Johann Anthaus, "Russland-Feldzug 1942: Die Chance zum Ausbruch aus Stalingrad wurde vertan," *Welt*, Nov. 23, 2017, WELT.DE.

[1082] Military superiority had shifted in 1942 and 1943 to the Soviets. By the end of July 1943, "Operation Citadel was over. The Soviets had gained air superiority and went on full offence." Quoted from Ralph Wetterhan, "Kursk," *Air & Space Magazine*, May 2015, AIRSPACEMAG.COM.

[1083] Christian Gerlach, *Sur la conférence de Wannsee*, pp. 63-64.

[1084] Christian Gerlach, "The Wannsee Conference, the Fate of German Jews, and Hitler's Decision in Principle to Exterminate All European Jews," *The Journal of Modern History*, vol. 70, Dec. 1998, pp. 759-812, at p. 780; Volker Ullrich, "Über die Vernichtung der Juden wurde zentral entschieden. Hitlers bösester Befehl"; Gordon McFee, "The Holocaust Began Because of Circumstances Rather than a Long-standing Plan," pp. 95-100, in *Genocide and Persecution: The Holocaust*, Jeff Hay, ed. (2014), at p. 98; Christian Gerlach, *Sur la conférence de Wannsee*, p. 61.

something like that, that there are German people who give such orders [*daß es deutsche Menschen gibt, die solche Befehle geben*]." In this context, starting on January 18, 1943, an uprising by the Jews in the Warsaw ghetto began. On January 21, German forces retreated (to "regroup"), meaning that the Jewish fighters were inflicting unexpected damage on the German military. And on February 16, Heinrich Himmler issued an order for the emptying of the ghetto and its total razing.

The idea was to have Warsaw *judenrein* (free of Jews) by April 19, to offer that accomplishment as a gift to Hitler on his birthday the next day. This military action, *die Großaktion*, with Gen. Stroop assigned to obliterate the remaining Jews in the ghetto, began at 6 am on April 19, with what Stroop later described as a German "early-morning defeat,"[1085] but with its mission not accomplished that day. On April 22, Stroop began burning down buildings. It was not until May 16 that Stroop could declare that the ghetto no longer existed.[1086] A report on the total destruction of the remains of the Warsaw Ghetto was published in a book, with the 2002 Roman Polanski Film, *The Pianist*, telling of the survival of Polish Jewish concert pianist, Władysław Szpilman, helped to survive by a German officer who found and saved the Jewish pianist. This officer was Wilm Hosenfeld, quoted just above. Precisely a month after the completion of the *Großaktion*, on June 16, Hosenfeld wrote, "The entire ghetto is in ruins from fire. (*Das ganze Getto ist eine Brandruine.*) We want to win the war this way. (*So wollen wir den Krieg bewinnen.*) These brutes! (*Diese Bestien!*) With this appalling mass murder of Jews (*Mit diesem entsetzlichen Judenmassenmord*), we have lost the war. An irredeemable shame (*Eine untilgbare Schande*), we have brought an indelible curse (*eine unauslöschlichen Fluch*) on ourselves. We deserve no mercy (*Wir verdienen keine Gnade*); we are all complicit (*wir sind alle mitschuldig*). I am ashamed to go to the city (*Ich schäme mich, in die Stadt zu gehen*); every Pole has the right to spit on the likes of us (*jeder Pole hat das Recht, vor unsereinem auszuspucken*)."[1087] Presumably he writes of Poles alone

---

[1085] Kazimierz Moczarski, *Conversations with an Executioner* (1961), pp. 118-121.
[1086] "Heinrich Himmler," *World War II Database* (re Feb. 16, 1943), WW2DB.COM; David Kopel, "The Warsaw ghetto uprising: Armed Jews vs. Nazis," *The Washington Post*, Oct. 10, 2015; David B. Kopel, *The Morality of Self-Defense and Military Action: The Judeo-Christian Tradition* (2017), pp. 112-114; "The Warsaw Ghetto: Himmler Orders the Destruction of the Warsaw Ghetto (February 16, 1943)," JEWISHVIRTUALLIBRARY.ORG; ghetto fighter survivors report their experience in the documentary *Diary of the Last Heroes: The Warsaw Ghetto Uprising 1943* (1993).
[1087] Hermann Vinke, *"Ich sehe immer den Menschen vor mir": Das Leben des deutschen Offiziers Wilm Hosenfeld, eine Biographie* (2015), p. 225; Eng., *Defying the Nazis: The Life of German Officer Wilm Hosenfeld* (2018), pp. 112-113; "„Wir sind alle mitschuldig." Aus dem Tagebuch des Wehrmachtsoffiziers Wilm Hosenfeld," *Spiegel*, Feb. 23, 1998, p. 214. Yad Vashem recognized Hosenfeld as a Righteous Among the Nations in 2008: "Wilhelm (Wilm) Hosenfeld," YAD VASHEM (2018). Roman Polanski received the 2003 Academy Award for Best Director for *The Pianist*, the film of Wilm Hosenfeld and Władysław Szpilman. 1933-Paris-born Polanski

having the right to spit on German soldiers, knowing Gen. Stroop had declared on May 16 that the Jewish population of Warsaw was no more! Hosenfeld was later recognized by Yad Vashem in Jerusalem as one of the Righteous Among the Nations.[1088]

The destruction of the Jewish ghetto of Warsaw has also been the subject of poetry. And, after all, perhaps it is the poets who can best recall certain tragedies with their sensitive and elegant, even godly,[1089] use of language. One such poem about the fall of the Warsaw Ghetto is by the 1980 Nobel Laureate in Literature, Czesław Miłosz (1911-2004), entitled "Campo dei Fiori." The poem refers to the field in Rome where Giordano Bruno (1548-1600), an Italian Dominican Friar, was burned at the stake by the Catholic Church for heresy, his mathematics and cosmology supporting the heliocentric understanding of the Pole Nicolaus Copernicus (1473-1543), and rejecting the geocentric model of the world then held by the Church. The poet, Miłosz, then returns to the present: "But that day I thought only of the loneliness of the dying, ... Those dying here, the lonely forgotten by the world, our tongue becomes for them the language of an ancient planet."[1090]

On further German massacres, there is also "Babi Yar," a poem written in 1961 by Russian Yevgeny Yevtushenko (1933-2017), for which he was a 1963 Nobel Laureate Nominee—more on Babi Yar, mentioned above, below—partly in protest of the refusal by the Soviet Union to recognize the site as the killing ravine of tens of thousands of Jews; the USSR held the killing to be of undifferentiated Soviet citizens, with nothing being acknowledged in official contexts about the victims being Jewish.[1091] The poem received a very enthusiastic response from Russian audiences (much to the chagrin of the Soviet authorities); it would also inspire Soviet composer Dmitri Shostakovich to produce his Symphony No. 13 ("Babi Yar"), the next year, in 1962. The poem begins with an unhesitating declaration: "No monument stands over Babi Yar. A steep precipice as the rudest tombstone. I am afraid. Today, I am as old in years as the entire Jewish people itself." And ends with: "In my blood there is no Jewish blood. In their vicious rage, all anti-Semites must hate me now as a Jew. For that reason, I am a true Russian!"[1092]

(Rajmund Roman Liebling), returned to Poland with his Jewish parents in 1936; he escaped from the Kraków ghetto. Cf. *The Krakow Ghetto*, YOUTUBE, 16:40-17:20.

[1088] See preceding footnote, and also "German Officer who Helped 'The Pianist' Recognized as Righteous Among the Nations," YAD VASHEM, Feb. 16, 2009.

[1089] As in the Hebrew prayer: "Blessed are You, Lord our God, King of the universe, through Whose word everything comes into being [*shehakol nih'yah bid'varo*]."

[1090] "Campo dei Fiori: Czeslaw Milosz, translated by David Brooks and Louis Iribarne," POETRYFOUNDATION.ORG.

[1091] The unacknowledged Jewish identity of Soviet victims in popular Soviet media is discussed in *Shoah: The Forgotten Souls of History* (2015).

[1092] "Yevgeny Yevtushenko," WIKIPEDIA. This tr. is based in part on George Reavey, *The Poetry of Yevgeny Yevtushenko, Revised and Enlarged Edition* (1967), pp. 144-149, and on "Babi Yar, by Yevgeni Yevtushenko, Translated by Benjamin Okopnik,

Jews in Eastern Europe, living largely as poor laborers or artisans in towns and villages (*shtetlekh*), would be described by the Nazi occupiers as filthy, vermin-like, living complacently in squalor and filth.[1093]

These Jews in these conditions—taken by Nazi propaganda to represent their natural way of being—were powerfully portrayed in *Der ewige Jude* (1940), mentioned above. While we can appreciate the setting up of scenes to be filmed in a way that would highlight such features of the groups of Jews shown, how could they be made to be so filthy, unkempt, indifferent to the dead on the streets that they walked by? We can keep in mind that these living conditions were not the ones in which the Jews of Poland lived before the Nazi invasion and being forced into specific neighborhoods, with a very intense concentration, with no recourse to leaving or to bringing in needed food, clothing, and such.

For those who have lived in, worked in, studied, or visited institutional living, from jails and prisons, medical and psychiatric hospitals, nursing and old-age homes, and such, the impact of such environments on the mental state and the physical appearance of its residents is quite obvious.

Victor Hugo wrote, "There are no weeds (*mauvaises herbes*) or bad men. There are only bad farmers (*cultivateurs*)."[1094] Or, as Croatian social worker Ladislav Lamza has stated, "It's very easy. If we put people in human conditions, they become more human. If we put them in inhuman, confined conditions, they become less human."[1095] Putting Jews into crowded ghettos and then presenting the visible consequences as indicating the essential nature of those people distorts that process, with the intentional purpose of defining Jews as disgusting and vermin-like.

This propagandistic vision of Jewry was already expressed as core dogma and worldview, we may recall, in Hitler's *Mein Kampf*, with some of these themes depicting Jews as less than human strongly expressed.

JEWS AND PEACHUM'S UNFEELING-AT-WILL GERMANS

The laws in Germany concerning the status, limited rights, and the vulnerability of the Jews of Germany, had evolved over a period of years in the Third Reich; they were soon to be applied in newly conquered lands. Jews were to register, to wear the Jewish star, to have limits on the possessions they were allowed and the money or gold they could hold in their possession. Throughout Western European lands, Jews had a relative respite from spring 1940 until early 1942. The German focus on the Eastern Front and the invasion of the USSR, postponed further action against the Jews in the West. By contrast, this was not at all the case on the Eastern Front.

10/96," REMEMBER.ORG. Cf. Victor Erlich, "Post-Stalin Trends in Russian Literature," *Slavic Review*, vol. 23, no. 3, Sep. 1964, pp. 405-419: in the context of the distinction between reading poetry for its literary value vs. as a political positioning, see esp. discussion of "Babi Yar" at p. 413.

[1093] Yehuda Bauer, *The Death of the Shtetl* (2009); cf. Yehuda Bauer, *A History of the Holocaust*, Revised ed. (2002).

[1094] Victor Hugo, *Les Misérables*, vol. 1, Book V, p. 311 in 1890 Fr. ed.

[1095] Linda Pressly, "Escape from the asylum," BBC WORLD SERVICE, Feb. 1, 2018.

The Hitler Era

Given the German occupation of Slavic lands to its east, the vastly increased number of Jews that now fell under control of the Reich led to new developments. Forcing Jews to emigrate was no longer a viable approach. Even the idea of transporting them *en masse* to the African island of Madagascar was no longer feasible, both because the island was a French colony, and the British Naval forces were also not ready to allow that German plan for deporting and colonizing Jews (to that island or elsewhere). With increased demands on the Reich administration concerning the Jewish Question, the intensification of the violence—some call it a war against the Jews—led to seeking a means of efficient mass murder. Part of the problem was the use of the *SS Einsatzgruppen*, which was having a rather deleterious impact on these soldiers. They were suffering from having to shoot so many civilians, even if the killed were largely part of the hated Jewish community. It was very draining work! In the early part of 1942, gas vans were also used, a practice developed during the organized killing of "lives not worth living" (T4), but this was too costly, and fuel was needed for the war.

Most importantly, from the standpoint of the Reich keeping an efficient working force addressing the Jewish Question (the extermination of the Jewish people in Europe), the results of the face-to-face murder of hundreds, thousands, or tens of thousands of Jews at one time, was taking a toll on the German military. *It was necessary to double their daily rations of vodka, and with that came alcoholism (serious drinking and a habit, an addiction to alcohol, with many soldiers having such experiences needing to be sent back to German hospitals, with serious psychological (and physical) impairment, unable to perform their duties.*

It was disheartening for them to have to kill so many—even if only of disgusting Jews—in such an intense, focused manner, seeing the victims fall over or seeing the bodies jerk in reaction to being shot to death. As Canadian historian Ronald Headland reported,

> At the Eichmann trial one witness testified that some SS men got almost hysterical and were close to nervous breakdowns. A witness to massacres in Uman [a town holy to some Jews, with its links to Rebbe Nachman of

Breslov, 1772-1810, great-grandson of the Baal Shem Tov, the founder of Chasidism] and Winnitsa [Vinnitsa] in September 1941 stated that some of the men did have complete nervous breakdowns because of the shootings. One official testified that certain people "went to pieces" and that there were "individual catastrophes." Arthur Nebe's chauffeur committed suicide. Ohlendorf himself claimed that the Einsatzgruppen leaders "were inwardly opposed to the liquidation."[1096]

In this light, as Jonathan Peachum, the father of Jenny Peachum (the wife of Mackie Messer, in English, Mack the Knife), in his opening speech to the audience in *Dreigroschenoper* (*The Threepenny Opera*), states, "man has the horrid capacity (*die furchtbare Fähigkeit*) of being able to make himself unfeeling (*gefühllos*) at his own discretion (*nach eigenem Belieben*), and that some "can instigate misery (*das Elend anstiften können*), but they cannot face it (*aber sehen können sie das Elend nicht*)."[1097] (This would later apply to Himmler, the first time he saw Jews being shot and killed, when witnessing a demonstration of the SS early killing method at the time, near Minsk, discussed just below.)

Other signs of the psychological impact (on some but not all German soldiers) of being directly involved in the mass shootings of Jews, Bolsheviks, and others perhaps randomly finding themselves dying in these massive shooting actions include not only Ohlendorf (just above) and Otto Köhn (in related note), but also Bach-Zelewski himself, who replied to a question about being in a great state of fear, "Thank God, I'm through with it. Don't you know what's happening in Russia? The entire Jewish people ... is being exterminated there."[1098]

At the Nuremberg Trials, Bach-Zelewski would explain the thinking that was employed in the task of these mass killings. In examination (on

---

[1096] Ronald Headland, *Messages of Murder* (1992), p. 211. Nebe's chauffeur was Otto Köhn of Kripo (Criminal Police, part of the Gestapo), who "had shot himself in horror at the anti-Jewish atrocities." Quoted at Heinz Höhne, *Der Orden unter dem Totenkopf: Die Geschichte der SS* (1967); Eng., *The Order of the Death's Head* (1969), Chap. 16 ("The Final Solution"), p. 363.

[1097] Bertolt Brecht, *Dreigroschenoper*, Act I, Scene 1, and Act. III, Scene 1. Eng., *The Threepenny Opera*, with Foreword by Lotte Lenya (wife of Kurt Weill), Desmond Vesey, tr. (1949); also in the 1931 film of *Die Dreigroschenoper*, a "play with music" by Bertolt Brecht and Kurt Weill, directed by G. W. Pabst—mentioned above—at 1:29:55-1:30:11. The opera premiered on Aug. 31, 1928, in Berlin's *Theater am Schiffbauerdamm*, and was banned in August 1933 under the Third Reich—Brecht fled Germany in Feb. 1933, and Lenya and Weill, the next month—with all printed copies of the score to be handed over for burning; the original negative and all copies the Nazis could find were destroyed, *but some survived!*

[1098] Heinz Höhne, *The Order of the Death's Head*, p. 363; Heinz Höhne, *Der Orden unter dem Totenkopf*, p. 334. Other examples of such statements of unreadiness to continue these massacres are given there. Further examples are given at Martin Gilbert, *The Holocaust: The Jewish Tragedy* (1986), p. 188.

January 7, 1946), the Chief Soviet Prosecutor, Colonel Yuri Pokrovsky asked SS General Erich von dem Bach-Zelewski for a clarification about his activities as head of counter-partisan activities on the Eastern Front:

> If I understood you correctly, you replied to the question by my colleague, the American prosecutor [Col. Telford Taylor], by saying that "the struggle against the Partisan Movement was a pretext for destroying the Slav and Jewish population?"[1099]

Bach-Zelewski responded, "Yes." This testimony of Bach-Zelewski was used to refute a claim set forth by several Nazi officers who attempted to excuse their genocidal murders as military operations.[1100] The change from considering the people being killed as Jews to considering them as partisans, or *francs-tireurs*—to use a term that had its origins in the Franco-Prussian War of 1870-1871, meaning a free (or self-regulated) shooter, an irregular soldier, a sniper, etc.—recategorized Jewish victims into a military framework.

While being made use of in *Amtssprache* (or bureaucratese), this was much more powerful than a mere cosmetic change: it presented the confrontations between Reich and Jewry conceptually as warrior against warrior. Of course, when confronting an enemy warrior, it is appropriate, justified, and called for, to shoot to kill.

What did this amount to, in specific situations? One report, also given in testimony at the Nuremberg Trials, brought on a silence in the courtroom: "An eyewitness report by a German of how a comparatively minor mass execution was carried out in the Ukraine brought a hush of horror over the Nuremberg courtroom when it was read by the chief British prosecutor, Sir Hartley Shawcross."

This report was presented to the court as a sworn affidavit by Hermann Friedrich Graebe, manager and engineer for a German construction firm,"[1101] working as a civilian at a branch of this German firm, nearby to Rowno (or Rovno), in Zdolbunow, testified, describing his witnessing the attack on the Jews of Rowno in rather vivid, even gruesome, stomach-churning terms:

> During the night of 13 July 1942, all inhabitants of the Rovno Ghetto where there were still about 5,000 Jews, were liquidated.... At the corner of a house lay a baby, less than a year old with his skull crushed. Blood and brains were spattered over the house wall and covered the area immediately around the child. The child was dressed only in a little skirt.... I walked around the mound and found myself confronted by a tremendous grave. People were closely wedged together and lying on top of

---

[1099] NT-IMT-Blue, vol. 4, p. 484.
[1100] Ronald Smelser and Edward J. Davies, *The Myth of the Eastern Front: The Nazi-Soviet War in American Popular Culture* (2008), p. 43.
[1101] William Shirer, *The Rise and Fall of the Third Reich*, p. 961.

> each other so that only their heads were visible. Nearly all had blood running over their shoulders from their heads. Some of the people shot were still moving. Some were lifting their arms and turning their heads to show that they were still alive. The pit was nearly 2/3 full. I estimated that it already contained about 1000 people....
> I looked into the pit and saw that the bodies were twitching or the heads [of others were] lying already motionless on top of the bodies that lay before them. Blood was running down their necks. I was surprised that I was not ordered away, but I saw that there were two or three postmen in uniform nearby.... 10 minutes later we heard shots from the vicinity of the pit. The Jews still alive had been ordered to throw the corpses into the pit—then they had themselves to lie down in this [pit] to be shot in the neck.[1102]

While some German soldiers were sickened by carrying out these shootings (as suggested above and in other contexts), many managed to carry on, however they were experiencing their actions and seeing all of the dead lying before them. Now, *while some may have found a kind of sadistic pleasure in such violence, there is little to suggest that this was the primary experience of most of those involved in this mass killing*. This suggests that other psychological factors, such as a profound hatred of Jews, seen as National Socialism's most vicious enemy, as well as group pressure issues, were at play in bringing men to such violence.

If we look a moment at the experience of many who have fought in any of a number of wars, in their recounting of the situation, there comes a moment when death seems imminent, when they realize that they could be dead at any moment, when the focus is one of survival, and perhaps of killing before being killed. In such anxious situations, whatever moves could be taken to be enemies ready to kill, with their death the only way of eliminating that threat with certainty. The sense that what is killed was a threat to one's own life and that of one's co-combatants, one's fellow soldiers, can act as an inspiration and a justification.[1103]

Hitler and others linked the extreme nature of this policy of annihilating entire peoples (especially the Jews, in this context, and also the Romanies, called Gypsies, among other Nazi undesirables) to the ways of the ancient world, where entire peoples who were conquered were then regularly annihilated.

This was not totally reassuring to the military. On February 2, 1940, General Johannes Blaskowitz wrote to his superiors in Berlin:

> The attitude of the troops toward the SS and the police fluctuates between loathing and hatred [*schwankt*

[1102] In order quoted above: NT-NCA-Red, vol. 5, pp. 700, 702, 698, 698-699.
[1103] For a discussion of extreme thinking in various wars, see Sönke Neitzel and Harald Welzer, *Soldaten: On Fighting, Killing, and Dying*, pp. 320-343.

zwischen Abscheu und Haß]. Every soldier feels disgusted and repelled [*fühlt sich angewidert und abgestoßen*] by these crimes that are committed in Poland by members of the Reich and representatives of the state authority. He does not understand how such things, *especially as they are, so to speak under his protection, are possible with impunity.*[1104]

Furthermore, significant numbers of officers were rendered incapable of further service, dealing with their experiences with large amounts of vodka, having nightmares, hallucinations, and exhaustion. These men were suffering from what was called psychic exhaustion, emotional breakdowns, and so forth, such as (earlier) soldier's heart, in the US Civil War; shell shock, in World War I; battle fatigue, in World War II, and more recently, with such diagnostic labels as PTSD or Post-Traumatic Stress Disorder), acute stress disorder (ASD), Developmental PTSD, Complex PTSD (cPTSD), and so forth.[1105]

As some examples, we can consider Arthur Nebe, earlier head of the Kripo, Nazi Criminal Police, who was in charge of Kripo interests in *Einsatzgruppe B*, which covered central USSR (now, Belarus), which reported 41,000 victims killed by November 1941, still in the first months after the invasion of the USSR.

German soldiers would be quite aware of the mass killings. One, interviewed, preferred not answering whether he had personally been involved in the execution of Russian civilians who were resisting the German invasion ("partisans"); another stated without hedging the issue, "They were not resettled [*umgesiedelt*], but were systematically decimated (*systematische dezimiert wurden*)."[1106]

Then, at a demonstration attended by Himmler, on August 15, 1942, of the killing of Jews in Minsk (in Belarus), Himmler had strong visceral

---

[1104] Helmut Krausnick, *Hitlers Einsatzgruppen: Die Truppen des Weltanschauungskrieges 1938–1942* (1981), p. 84. Italics reflect German text.

[1105] "Post-Traumatic Stress Disorder," *National Institute of Mental Health*, NIMH, NIMH.NIH.GOV; John W. Barnhill, MD, "Acute Stress Disorder (ASD)," *Merck Manual*, MERCKMANUALS.COM; Debra Kaminer, Soraya Seedat, Dan J. Stein, "Post-traumatic stress disorder in Children," *World Psychiatry*, vol. 4, no. 2, Jun. 2005, pp. 121-125; "Complex PTSD," *UK National Health Services*, NHS.UK; Janina Fisher, *Healing the Fragmented Selves of Trauma Survivors: Overcoming Internal Self-Alienation* (2017).

[1106] The Resettlement of Jews (*Umsiedlungsaktion*)—to the Lublin Reservation or on Madagascar—was soon a euphemism for the planned extermination of Jewry: Christopher R. Browning, "Nazi Resettlement Policy and the Search for a Solution to the Jewish Question, 1939-1941," *German Studies Review*, vol. 9, no. 3, Oct. 1986, pp. 497-519. Quote from *Mein Krieg: WW2 Films by German Soldiers, a documentary by Harriot Eder and Thomas Kufus* (1990), at 35:15-36:45, YOUTUBE; edited from private films of six former soldiers, one with clear discomfort at what he remembered and another with a conscience that was clear as crystal, totally devoid of any problems about his times in the Wehrmacht (1:28:15-1:29:15).

responses.[1107] A video of this visit of Himmler's to the Minsk camp has him rub his nose as his passes before some prisoners (who remain behind a wire fence), presumably a reflex to the strong, disturbing odors of men in captivity.[1108] (This relates to the Bertolt Brecht text quoted just above.) Himmler still seems to be in decent shape at that moment, so apparently the killing demonstration came later that day.

Later that day, that is, Himmler was shown the method used at the time for the shooting of Jews. SS General Karl Wolff—appointed by Himmler as his personal adjutant in June 1933, and who in August 1942 was SS Liaison Officer to Hitler—gave his eyewitness account of the demonstration that day. Describing Himmler's witnessing Jews forced to jump into a shallow grave to be shot in the head, where Himmler stood up to the edge of the grave, looking in to see clearly. Wolff stated,

> While he was looking in, he had the deserved bad luck that from one of those who had been shot in the head, he got a splash of brains on his coat, and I think it also splashed onto his face. And he went very green and pale. He wasn't actually sick, but he was heaving, and turned around and swayed. And then I had to jump forward and hold him steady and then I led him away from the grave.[1109]

After that demonstration, Himmler contracted Heydrich to discuss ways of mass killing that would be less traumatic (for the German troops).[1110]

General Erich von dem Bach-Zelevski (also known by the shorter name, Erich von dem Bach) was in charge of *Einsatzgruppe B*, operating in Belarus, overseeing the mass killings of Jews in Riga, two examples of which were the Rumbula Massacre, the name given to two separate days of killing a total of about 25,000 Jews, on November 30 and December 8, 1941, in the nearby Rumbula Forest, and in Minsk, with some 2,000 Jews murdered there on July 3, 1941, with similar experiences at Mogilev, Pinsk, Białistok, Grodno, and other cities.

He would be hospitalized in Berlin in February 1942, with the diagnosis of intestinal ailments; more precisely, with severe hemorrhoids (or impacted stools), and, rather separately, as having dreams and hallucinations connected with the shooting of Jews.

[1107] Mario R. Dederichs, *Heydrich: Das Gesicht des Böse* (2005); Eng., *Heydrich: The Face of Evil* (2009). Mario Dederichs (1949-2004) was a German political commentator, author, and biographer.

[1108] In the 26-episode Thames TV series, *The World at War* (1973-1974), *Episode 20: Genocide (1941-1945)*, at 17:33-17:35, and in *Leo's Journey: The Story of the Mengele Twins* (2001), at 16:50-16:55, Himmler walks past prisoners behind a wire fence, and rubs his nose with his fingers, presumably as a reflex. This is presumably KL-Maly Trostenets (Polish, Maly Trascianiec), 6 mi. from Minsk.

[1109] *Episode 20: Genocide (1941-1945)*, in the Thames TV Series, *The World at War*, just cited, at 18:10-18:37.

[1110] Peter Longerich, *Heinrich Himmler: A Life*, p. 547.

Dr. Ernst-Robert Grawitz, Himmler's medical consultant, head of the German Red Cross, physician in the T4 pre-war euthanasia program for the "incurable"—in which some 400,000 men and women were sterilized (about half and half) and then in the T4 program itself, starting in 1939, some 200,000 men, women, the old, the infirm, those considered incurably sick or mentally disturbed were killed[1111]—described Von dem Bach's hospitalization as due to psychic exhaustion and hallucinations connected with the shooting of Jews that he was in charge of, and his grievous other experiences in the East.[1112]

Some of those involved in the administration of the T4 Program moved into positions of power in the extermination camps: physician-psychiatrist Irmfried Eberl, MD (1910-1948),[1113] director of the Brandenburg killing center, near Berlin, became Commandant of the Treblinka extermination camp, and Christian Wirth (1885-1944),[1114] also active in the T4 Program, became the first Commandant at Bełżec Extermination Camp.[1115]

Did Hitler by this point in time give the full weight of his position to the extermination of Jews at the Eastern Front? It would seem so, based on notes and communications especially in December 1941, as well as other documentation, such as the statement attributed to Himmler: When Bach-Zelewski asked Himmler in early 1942 about ending the killing of the Jews in the East (especially as defined by his command post in Ukraine), Himmler replied defining the situation in terms of a *Führerbefehl*, an order from Hitler, which was expected to be followed fully and promptly.

> That is an order of the Führer. The Jews are the carriers of Bolshevism...If you don't let go of that Jewish matter, you'll see what happens to you.[1116]

The *Judenangelegenheit* (Jewish concern/matter/affair/business) was a term that was used during the Third Reich, exchangeable with *Judenfrage* (Jewish question), and, ultimately, both were used as euphemisms, at least after 1939, for referring to the *Entlösung der Judenfrage* (the Final Solution to the Jewish Question); these, in turn, actually referred to what in even more blunt and explicit terms was called

---

[1111] See the 2015 FRANCE TÉLÉVISIONS film, *Elles étaient en guerre 1939-1945* (*Women at War 1939-1945*), at 15:25-15:50.

[1112] Robert Jay Lifton, *The Nazi Doctors: Medical Killing and the Psychology of Genocide* (1986), p. 156.

[1113] "Irmfried Eberl," WIKIPEDIA.

[1114] "Christian Wirth," WIKIPEDIA.

[1115] See photographs No. 31-32, among the inserts between pp. 240-241, in Laurence Rees, *The Holocaust: A New History*.

[1116] Heinz Höhne, *The Order of the Death's Head*, p. 363: "That is a Führer Order. The Jews are the disseminators of Bolshevism... if you don't keep your nose [lit., your fingers] out of the Jewish business, you'll see what'll happen to you!" Ellipsis in original; *Der Orden unter dem Totenkopf*, p. 334: "*Das ist ein Führerbefehl. Die Juden sind die Träger des Bolschewismus... Wenn Sie Ihre Finger nicht aus den Judenangelegenheiten draußen lassen, dann sollen Sie sehen, was Ihnen passiert!*"

the *Vernichtung der jüdischen Rasse in Europa* (the extermination of the Jewish race in Europe), a term Hitler used on January 30, 1939, in a very public context, as part of his famous, filmed, and often-quoted speech to the *Großdeutschen Reichstag* (a full session of the German Parliament):

> If world Jewry drags Europe into a war, the result will not be the bolshevization of Europe, but the extermination of the Jews of Europe.[1117]

HITLER, THE LEADER STILL COMMITTED TO PEACE (SAYS HE)

This statement was hypothetical, seven months before the invasion of Poland. Hitler claimed that he wanted only peace up until August 1939. On April 28, 1939, he declared before the Reichstag:

> Jewish parasites, on the one hand, plundered the nation ruthlessly and, on the other hand, incited the people when it had been reduced to misery. As the misfortune of our nation became the only aim and object of this race, it was possible to breed among the growing army of unemployed suitable elements for the Bolshevik revolution.... The return of the Saar territory has done away with all territorial problems in Europe between France and Germany [until a year later, with the invasion of France in May 1940] .... This is, however, not the way to look at the matter. It was not for fear of France that I preached this attitude.... No, I have confirmed this attitude to France as an expression of appreciation of the necessity to attain peace in Europe, instead of sowing the seed of continual uncertainty and even tension by making unlimited demands and continually asking for revision. [We might wonder how Hitler is denying his ongoing, evolving, ever-increasing demands for more and more German control in central Europe in this claim.] If this tension has nevertheless now arisen, the responsibility does not lie with Germany [Hitler manages to claim this, even after the annexation of Austria, the Munich Accords, and the invasion and conquering of formerly independent Czechoslovakia], but with those international elements which systematically produce such tension in order to serve their capitalist interests. I have given binding declarations to a large number of states. None of these states can complain that even a trace of a demand contrary thereto has even been made to them by Germany. None of the Scandinavian statesmen, for

---

[1117] Adolf Hitler, "Speech delivered before the German Reichstag on January 30th, 1939," ARCHIVE.ORG. Original German, published that year by M. Müller & Sohn, KG, Berlin, under the title, *Rede des Führers und Reichkanzlers Adolf Hitler vor dem Reichstag am 30. Januar 1939* (1939); at pp. 48-49 in scanned version of this 1939 book, IA802603.US.ARCHIVE.ORG. KG is equivalent to LLC.

example [a marginal example, at best], can contend that a request has ever been put to them by the German government or by German public opinion which was incompatible with the sovereignty and integrity of their state. I am pleased that a number of European states availed themselves of these declarations by the German government to express and emphasize their desire, too, for absolute neutrality. This applies to Holland, Belgium, Switzerland, Denmark, etc. I have already mentioned France.... I need not repeat once more that in May of the past year [1938] Germany had not mobilized one single man [totally disregarding the enormous German military built-up that was going on for years by then], although we were all of the opinion that the very fate of Herr Schuschnigg should have shown all others the advisability of working for mutual understanding by means of a more just treatment of national minorities. I for my part was at any rate prepared to attempt this kind of peaceful development with patience and, if need be, in a process lasting some years. However, it was exactly this peaceful solution which was a thorn in the flesh of the agitators in the democracies. [Hitler and the Wehrmacht invaded Austria when a plebiscite was scheduled in the next days, Hitler being worried about the outcome of this plebiscite, not confident that the result would be a decision to join the Reich voluntarily.] They [the Jews] hate us Germans and would prefer to eradicate us completely. [This way of thinking has Germany's focus on exterminating the Jews reversed, as if the Jews or others of the "democracies" wanted to annihilate Germany.[1118]] What do the Czechs mean to them [to the Jews]? They are nothing but a means to an end. And what do they care for the fate of a small and valiant nation. Why should they worry about the lives of hundreds of thousands of brave soldiers who would have been sacrificed for their policy? These Western European peace mongers were not concerned to work for peace but to cause bloodshed, so as in this way to set the nations against one another and thus cause still more blood to flow.[1119]

[1118] Consider discussions relevant to Hitlerian and Third Reich thinking: esp. Robert S. Robins and Jerrold Post, *Political Paranoia: The Psychopolitics of Hatred* (1997); Richard Hofstadter, *The Paranoid Style in American Politics* (1963); N. McConaghy, "Modes of Abstract Thinking and Psychosis," *American Journal of Psychiatry*, vol. 117, no. 2, Aug. 1960, pp. 106-110.

[1119] See note above for Ger. text citation. Eng.: Adolf Hitler, "Official translation of the speech delivered by Adolf Hitler before the German Reichstag on April 28,

The insistence on being a man, a leader, and a nation desiring only peace and avoiding all bloodshed, can be judged in terms of what followed later that year (1939) and for the next six years. *But it also contrasts with Hitler's more candid statements in private contexts.* As an example, on January 21, 1939, a week before Hitler's prediction before the Reichstag on January 30 of the extermination of European Jewry if there should be a world war, itself months before the German invasion of Poland, Hitler told the Czech foreign minister František Chvalkovský, "We are going to destroy the Jews. They are not going to get away with what they did on 9 November 1918. The day of reckoning has come."[1120]

In terms of Hitler's public stance, placing all blame on those interests that would want the nations of Europe to feel tension, animosity, and even warlike hatred, leaves Germany an innocent victim of those who want to eradicate Germans and Germany completely: a mental somersault! With this condescending attitude and its blanket judgments about such groups quite often comes an underestimation of their capacities. This, we can find, is a repeating pattern, as with the German plan before the First World War, the Schlieffen Plan, discussed earlier, with the expectation of conquering France in two weeks before turning to Czarist Russia in the East. For the Third Reich, there was the added component of a belief in its own superiority as the *Herrenrasse*, the Master Race, and the backward, primitive nature of Jews, Romanies, Soviets, half-Asiatic, and half-civilized. From the peculiar, particularly National Socialist dehumanizing understanding of reality, these inferior beings had a core desire, if allowed, to destroy the superior German race. Such a sense of being the target of ill-willed others is sometimes traceable to one's own aggressivity against others, put out on others what is basically one's own hostility (in psychoanalytic terms, called projection).

We might think here of paranoia. This very old term, from the Classical Greek (paránoia, beside or outside one's mind) has a few senses. There are common understandings, and there are clinical (psychiatric) senses of the word.[1121] One clinical sense is that paranoia involves some sort of delusion or psychotic belief. It may be one of persecution, but not necessarily. This differs from the more lay sense of the term in which a delusion of persecution defines paranoia. In talking about the distortions of the mind when they take place in political figures, in a political context, we are most usually referring to the tendency to see what happens as the

---

1939," ARCHIVE.ORG, pp. 5-6,10-11, 19-20. This tr. by the German Embassy, Washington, was *excluded (!)* from *Documents on the Events Preceding the Outbreak of the War, German Foreign Office* (Berlin 1939, New York, 1940). Parts of the speech are in Adolf Hitler, *Collection of Speeches, 1922-1945* (2016), ARCHIVE.ORG, but not key passages quoted above in the text here.

[1120] Helmut Krausnick and Martin Broszat, *Anatomy of the SS State* (1968), p. 44; in 1982 ed., p. 62. (Prague was 20% Jewish in 1938 and 6% Jewish in 1945.)

[1121] See discussion in political scientist Robert S. Robins and psychiatrist Jerrold M. Post, MD, *Political Paranoia: The Psychopolitics of Hatred*, cited just above.

intentional malevolence of someone or of some group. Here, it may be appropriate to talk of a paranoid personality, a general tendency to feel subject to the hostilities of others, in a repeating and often central mode of thinking that can pervade a person's overall relationship to others and to the world in a broader sense.

These features of an organized sense that all others want to annihilate oneself or even one's people, a political dimension of paranoia, are often found together with a self-aggrandizement[1122] and with an exaggerated sense of one's own prowess, intelligence, and abilities, which goes with a complementary sense of the inherent inabilities of one's presumed-hostile neighbors. *While this clearly seems to apply to Hitler, we can find this pattern of thinking in many people, and often in powerful political leaders.* Of course, as was once said, the fact that I'm paranoid does not mean that others are *not* out to get me. Huey P. Newton, founder and president of the Black Panther movement, once described the situation that can give rise to what is seen as paranoia in these words: "I have been tailed for most of my adult life, and the effect was both exhausting and terrifying. People think that you're being paranoid when you describe these situations to them. FBI agents would tail me everywhere—into a grocery or a doughnut shop.... Their blatant lack of indiscretion would be hard to exaggerate."[1123]

Of course, the fact that someone is paranoid does not mean, either, that others are necessarily after him. Hitler saw a world conspiracy of Jews in a global attack on "civilization" and especially on the German nation. Without assuming any psychiatric diagnosis here, we can perhaps agree that the "murderous hatred and wish to exterminate them [the Jews] that Hitler evinced from the very beginning [*denn die Juden mit dem mörderischen Haß und Vernichtungswillen zu vergolgen, den Hitler ihnen von Anfang an entgegengebrachte*]" and the "existence of a world-wide Jewish conspiracy to exterminate all 'Aryans' are not just a misconception but paranoid nonsense [*deutlich nicht einfach Irrtum, sondern paranoider Irrsinn*]."[1124]

As with all belief systems, there is something or other in the life context that supports that conceptual construction of reality. When the selection of supporting considerations is limited and perhaps biased in particular ways, disregarding counter-indications that would modulate or perhaps annul such beliefs, we can hold perhaps many questionable ideas of what the world is like. In Hitler's case, for example, he might have had some disagreeable experiences with some Jews, or heard stories of some

---

[1122] George C. Sisler, "The Concept—Paranoid," *Canadian Psychiatric Association Journal*, vol. 12, no. 2 (Apr. 1967), pp. 183-187.

[1123] "*West Magazine* Interview with Panther Party President: A Conversation with Huey P. Newton," *The Black Panther* (Feb. 18, 1978); reprinted in the collection, *The Black Panther: Intercommunal News Service, 1967-1980*, David Hilliard, ed. (2007), pp. 130-137, at p. 134.

[1124] Sebastian Haffner, *Anmerkungen zu Hitler*, 1978 ed., pp. 121-122; 1994 ed., p. 94; Eng., *The Meaning of Hitler*, p. 94.

Jews who were nasty or otherwise presented as untrustworthy (or perhaps not).

Of course, not everyone who has disagreeable interactions with those of a certain group will jump to a generalization covering all members of that group. This may be a quick and rather lazy way to come to generalizations, but is not that rare. *What is less frequent is a focus that becomes a driving force in one's general thinking and life activities overall.*

We can see the focus that Hitler placed on Jewry—seen as noxious, pathogens, with ill will toward all non-Jews—starting from early diatribes and speeches in the 1920s through his years as Führer, as in his obsession that intensified during the 1943, when the Wehrmacht was clearly losing in its battle to conquer and subjugate the inferior Slavs of the Soviet Union,[1125] and, finally, to his very last formal statements, as in his Political Testament,[1126] which was dictated and signed the day before his suicide. *This was no passing diversion on his part!*

In this context, as September 1939 approached, and the German military was preparing for an invasion of Poland, they carried out a staged incident the day before the actual invasion of Poland on September 1, 1939 (mentioned above).

This was actually a faked assault on a German radio station near the Polish border; Himmler arranged for SS men wearing Polish uniforms and using Polish weapons to kill those in the radio station. An announcement was made in Polish that Poles had attacked the German station. Dead men in Polish military uniforms were left at the site.

Actually, these men were concentration camp prisoners Himmler had transported to the site, dressed in those uniforms, and shot dead. This was the Gleiwitz Incident, used by Goebbels to stir up German anger and to justify a "retaliatory" attack on Polish territory, the next day, September 1, 1939, with 1.8 million soldiers![1127] (Even if a response, this would be a stupendous example of over-reacting to a rather small story.)

The importance of a resolution of the Jewish Question remained paramount in the thinking of both Hitler and his associates, including Heinrich Himmler, Reinhard Heydrich, Adolf Eichmann, and others. Hitler on January 30, 1942, at a speech at the Berlin Sportpalast, repeated his earlier claim that the result of this war (*das Ergebnis dieses Krieges*) would be the extermination of Jewry (*die Vernichtung des Judentums*).[1128]

This issue of what to do with all of the inferior peoples that were coming under the control of the Third Reich, was becoming critical, it being obvious soon after the first actions of the Einsatzgruppen that shooting people individually (with rifles as the instrument of death) had strong disadvantages, in part, the fact that there were so many people to kill with so few *SS Einsatzgruppen* Men to do the work (even though there were many, the number to be killed, in the tens of millions when Slavs

---

[1125] Laurence Rees, *The Holocaust: A New History*, p. 333.
[1126] "My Political Testament," THE ADOLF HITLER MEMORIAL MUSEUM/HITLER.ORG.
[1127] *History's Verdict: Adolf Hitler* (WWII Documentary), YOUTUBE, at 17:50-18:00.
[1128] Online at CHRONOLOGIE DES HOLOCAUST.

The Hitler Era

were counted in), making that approach not only ineffective and tedious, but also quite inoperable, given the immense task at hand.

On Why Germany Would Declare War on the USA

By the time of the events of early December 1941—the bombing of Pearl Harbor on December 7, the US declaration of war against the Empire of Japan on December 8, and the German declaration, as the ally of Japan, of war against the US on December 11—the time was appropriate to see about that earlier statement to the Reichstag promising the extermination of European Jewry if the Jews should drag Germany into another world war.

It is sometimes held to be an inexplicable event that Germany should rush to declare war on the United States after the bombing of Pearl Harbor. An accord had guaranteed mutual assistance to Japan by Germany and Italy, if Japan should be attacked, not if it would wage aggressive war.

What might be appealing to Hitler about declaring war on the USA? First, there was Hitler's low estimation of the USA, its level of mongrel culture (Jews, blacks, and all sorts of mixed peoples), its frivolity, and its incapacity to present a serious military threat, given this superficial American Zeitgeist. When on May 16, 1940,[1129] Roosevelt announced his plans for 50,000 planes a year, Hitler called the number of 50,000 a fantasy. Hitler scoffed, "What is America but beauty queens, millionaires, stupid records, and Hollywood?"[1130] Hitler's distorted, mocking caricature of the US represented quite an underestimation of what US industry and organization were capable of. In a similar even if more cautious attitude, Army chief of Staff, General Franz Halder, in his entry for March 30, 1941, in a review of US military production capabilities (the US not yet having entered the war), wrote, "Maximum output not before end of four years; problem of shipping."[1131] And yet, in terms of actual warfare, while there had been no war declared formally by either Germany against the USA, nor by the USA against Germany, by the time of Pearl Harbor, the US was not a simple by-stander to the war in Europe. It had been shipping war material to the British, often with stop-overs in Greenland and Iceland.

The US Government had also made a unilateral declaration of "waters of self-defense-surrounding outposts of American protection in the Atlantic" (as Roosevelt put it in a Fireside Chat on September 11, 1940). In that chat, Roosevelt spoke of the attack on a US destroyer, the US Greer, described as carrying US mail to Iceland (a totally innocent activity). FDR added, "The United States destroyer, when attacked, was proceeding on a legitimate mission."

[1129] In "Roosevelt's Message to Congress on Appropriations for National Defense, May 16, 1940," The American Presidency Project.

[1130] See Chap. XII (Circus at the Chancellery) in Ernst Hanfstaengl, *Hitler: The Missing Years* (1957), p. 222, and in *Hitler: The Memoir of the Nazi Insider Who Turned Against the Fuhrer* (also 1957). Cf. Arthur Herman, *Freedom's Forge: How American Business Produced Victory in World War II* (2012), p. 13.

[1131] Franz Halder, *The Halder War Diary*, entry for Mar. 30, 1941, p. 345.

*What Roosevelt did not mention—significantly—*was that the US Greer had been notified by RAF pilots that there was a German submarine not far away, and that the Greer then picked up the submarine with its radar, and continued following and tracking the submarine, sending information about the location of the German ship to the British RAF nearby in the skies. The RAF used this information to drop depth charges attempting to sink the sub. The sub, aware of a ship tracking it, sent off two torpedoes, both of which were seen and avoided by the US Greer's maneuvering, itself dropping depth charges against the submarine, likewise ineffective.

After mentioning other incidents of aggression of German submarines against US ships, Roosevelt added, "It is no act of war on our part when we decide to protect the seas that are vital to American defense. The aggression is not ours. Ours is solely defense." He offered up a metaphor that he then made explicit: "But when you see a rattlesnake poised to strike, you do not wait until he has struck before you crush him. These Nazi submarines and raiders are the rattlesnakes of the Atlantic." FDR also announced that he was ordering the Navy to protect itself from any German or Italian ships that moved into this "US Defensive Protection Zone." This order was known as Roosevelt's "Shoot on Sight" Order.[1132]

Shoot on Sight   Attack the Rattlesnake

That Fireside Chat took place on September 11, 1940. On the evening of September 17, less than a week later, there was the torpedoing of a British ship by a German submarine (U-boat), in which 293 passengers, including 83 children, drowned when the ship sunk; 113 were reported saved.[1133] *The sea lanes between North America and Britain for transport*

[1132] Franklin Delano Roosevelt, "Fireside Chat, September 11, 1941," THE AMERICAN PRESIDENCY PROJECT.

[1133] "293, Including 83 Children, Perish When Ship is Torpedoed," *Daily Pantagraph* (Bloomington, Illinois), Sep. 23, 1940, p. 1. The British gov't had contacted family individually before publically announcing this attack on the *SS City of Benares* the following Monday, Sep. 23.

of men, arms, food, and other supplies were definitely not safe at this time. The US was still formally a neutral country at this time, but the US government was more inclined to see the Reich as a hostile nation. The US was being asked vehemently by the UK to join in the war against the Third Reich. Thus, US Ambassador to the UK, Joseph P. Kennedy, a Nazi sympathizer, was asked to resign his post, which he did in November 1940: his idea, expressed in a warning at a luncheon in Los Angeles hosted by Jack Warner, earlier in November, 1940, that the Hollywood moguls, largely Jewish, could drag the US into war, largely overestimated the power of these men and the films they could produce, *and thus, underestimated other factors in operation.* On March 11, 1941—*Jewish film inaction aside*—the US passed into law what is known as the Lend-lease Policy, An Act to Promote the Defense of the United States. This supplied food, oil, and military materiel to Great Britain and France, and later, to the USSR. In exchange, the US was given free use of army and naval bases. Overall, some 11% of US war expenditures went into this program. Some $31 billion went to the UK and its Empire, and (beginning later) $11.3 billion to the USSR. During the war, other countries received less, such as $3.2 billion to Free France (not Vichy France) and $1.6 billion to China.[1134] The program aided the Soviet military, confronted by great concentrations of German military, with the greatest losses of men, significantly more than the losses of all other Allies. Some say that *the war against the Third Reich was won by Soviet blood*, with good reason. *There was already open hostility between the Third Reich and the USA,* and once war between the US and Germany began, German U-boats in *Operation Paukenschlag* (Operation Drumbeat) from mid-January-March 1942, sank almost 40 US merchant ships, from Boston to the Carolinas, mostly along so-called Torpedo Alley, waters off the Carolina coast.

Hitler in deciding to declare war on the USA was not doing much more than making formal the open hostility and mutual attacks between the two countries already ongoing for some months. Hitler, not feeling that US military capabilities presented a serious worry for the Reich, also could appreciate that bringing Japan into the war would draw some of the US (and British and British Commonwealth) Armies and Navies to the Pacific, splitting their power by dealing with two theaters of war. *This would be of benefit both to the German and the Japanese military positions*—if both went to war against the USA together.[1135]

Certain documents substantiate these basic considerations and the actions that followed. These documents make all of this less of a mystery that it might seem to be at first blush: In particular, in transcripts of the trial at Nuremberg (1946) is testimony confirming German commitments

---

[1134] "Lend-Lease," WIKIPEDIA.

[1135] See discussion and elucidation of the negotiating between the Third Reich and the Japanese Empire prior to the bombing of Pearl Harbor in *World War II Myths, Misconceptions, and Surprises* (Nov. 1, 2011), YOUTUBE, with German-born American historian and expert on Nazi Germany, Gerhard Weinberg, at 31:45-35:45, 1:06:45-1:13:00, with co-panelists Mark Stoler and William Hitchcock.

to declare war on the USA, expressed and then reaffirmed to Japan when Japan double-checked to be sure they would be joined militarily by the Reich, just before bombing Pearl Harbor:

> On 4 April 1941, Hitler told [Yōsuke] Matsuoka, the Japanese Foreign Minister, in the presence of the Defendant Ribbentrop, that Germany would "strike without delay" if a Japanese attack on Singapore should lead to war between Japan and the United States. The next day Ribbentrop himself urged Matsuoka to bring Japan into the war.... On 28 November 1941, 10 days before the attack on Pearl Harbor, Ribbentrop encouraged Japan, through her Ambassador in Berlin, to attack Great Britain and the United States, and stated that should Japan become engaged in a war with the United States, Germany would join the war immediately. A few days later, Japanese representatives told Germany and Italy that Japan was preparing to attack the United States, and asked for their [reaffirmed] support. Germany and Italy agreed to do this, although in the Tripartite Pact [signed on September 27, 1940], Italy and Germany had undertaken to assist Japan only if she were attacked. When the assault on Pearl Harbor did take place, the Defendant Ribbentrop is reported to have been "overjoyed," and later, at a ceremony in Berlin, when a German medal was awarded to Oshima, the Japanese Ambassador, Hitler indicated his approval of the tactics which the Japanese had adopted of negotiating with the United States as long as possible, and then striking hard without any declaration of war.... Although it is true that Hitler and his colleagues originally did not consider that a war with the United States would be beneficial to their interest, it is apparent that in the course of 1941 that view was revised, and Japan was given every encouragement to adopt a policy which would almost certainly bring the United States into the war. And when Japan attacked the United States fleet in Pearl Harbor and thus made aggressive war against the United States, the Nazi Government caused Germany to enter that war at once on the side of Japan by declaring war themselves.[1136]

Earlier Japanese war planning was aware of the Tydings-McDuffie Act (also called the Philippine Commonwealth and Independence Act), signed into law by President Roosevelt on March 24, 1934, establishing Philippine Independence on July 4, 1946.[1137] This would be a time after which the

---

[1136] "War against the United States," in NT-IMT-Blue, vol. 22, pp. 457-458 (transcript of Sep. 30, 1946); italics added.
[1137] "Tydings-McDuffie Act, United States (1934)," ENCYCLOPÆDIA BRITANNICA.

Japanese could attack the Philippines—*without at the same time attacking the USA*—in Japan's goal of hegemony over the Western Pacific and security for its envisioned Empire.

But American and German actions changed the situation. The US, here, was already more favorable to the Chinese than to the Japanese, in their conflict.

Within weeks of the surrender of France to the Third Reich (June 22, 1940), the Japanese Empire invaded French Indochina, on July 2, 1940, which was perceived by opposing countries as a significant intensification of Japanese aggressivity; the US, in particular, would stop sales of aviation fuel to Japan that month, and, a year later, on July 26, 1941, all Japanese assets in the US were frozen by order of President Roosevelt.

This meant that dollars were no longer available to Japan to make further purchases from the USA of important prime resources (iron, steel, oil, and so forth). This blocked Japan's access to US commodities—it had been importing more than 80% of its oil, 74% of its scrap iron, and 93% of its copper from the USA (the new American stance also involved closing off the Panama Canal to Japanese shipping)[1138]—and all of this was in the context of Germany's committed encouragement, for its own reasons, for Japan to take action and to go to war against the USA.

Bombing Pearl Harbor was certainly a shock to the American public, but ultimately it was not the most effective warfare: the ships at the harbor were in very shallow water (six feet of water below the ships),[1139] so that bombing and torpedoes could not sink them, but only partially submerge them in the harbor's waters. The only ship that was not able to be used (rehabilitated) later during the war was the USS Arizona, which had been bombed and then exploded, and could not be restored for use; its parts not used for other ships still sit at the harbor. Ideal would have been for the Japanese attack to have been in the open seas, where there was the possibility of sinking the entire US fleet it would have met there.

A question that is repeatedly raised is whether the US Intelligence knew of the attack on Pearl Harbor before it took place. Certainly, there was the ongoing work of cryptologists to decipher Japanese military codes, which were often being revised and even replaced. The version used at that time was named Purple. One of the key cryptologists, on September 20, 1940,[1140] *more than a year before Pearl Harbor*, saw key patterns in the coded communiques among Japanese military using Purple, was Genevieve Grotjan, part of the US Army SIS (Signal Intelligence Service).

[1138] David C. Gompert, Hans Binnendijk, and Bonny Lin, "Japan's Attack on Pearl Harbor," pp. 93-106 in their *Blinders, Blunders, and Wars* (2014); "Events leading to the attack on Pearl Harbor," WIKIPEDIA.

[1139] Matt Saintsing, "Pearl Harbor Survivor Remembers 'Day of Infamy' 76 years later," Dec. 7, 2017, CONNECTINGVETS.COM.

[1140] Ann Whitcher Gentzke, "An American Hero: Genevieve Grotjan applied her dazzling mathematical skills to unraveling enemy codes during World War II," *At Buffalo (Magazine of the State University of New York at Buffalo)*, BUFFALO.EDU.

She was one of many women used as cryptographers, both in US Military Intelligence, and also in the UK's Blatchley Park, famous for having cracked the German Enigma Machine, usually associated with Alan Turing; there had also been important women cryptographers (behind the scenes) who worked for military intelligence in earlier wars.[1141]

While there are various conspiracy theories about all of this (as is often the case when some details are fuzzy about some historical situation), it seems that there was advance warning of a Japanese attack on US military installations, *but the information was rather vague.*

Thus, in an FBI file of 20 pages, the Office of Naval Intelligence warned President Roosevelt (on December 4, 1941, a few days before the attack on December 7),[1142] "In anticipation of open conflict with this country, Japan is vigorously utilizing every available agency to secure military, naval and commercial information, paying particular attention to the West Coast, the Panama Canal and the Territory of Hawaii." This report was of limited value, since not focused on military concerns and including the Territory of Hawaii only as one of three potential target areas.

VERMICIDE TO THE "RESCUE" OF THE PROBLEM OF ROMANIES AND JEWS

To the rescue of this centuries-old problem, in one sense, there had been a use of a vermicide (a chemical regularly employed to kill vermin, as a poison against rats) at Buchenwald Concentration Camp, but applied to humans, killing Romani (Gypsy) children. Now, hatred of the Romanies has a centuries-long history that may remind some of the anti-Jewish sentiment in European history. In 1416, for example, an anti-gypsy law was passed in Germany accusing them of being foreign spies, being carriers of the plague (joining the Jews as disease-carriers), and that they were traitors to Christendom. Romanies, a rather small minority in Europe, have had their share of hatred directed against them!

As mentioned above, on July 14, 1933, a law was passed against the propagation of "lives not worthy of life" (*lebensunwertes Leben*), the Law for the Prevention of Hereditarily Diseased Offspring (as often, a misidentification of the purpose of the law). *It called for the sterilization for certain people, specifically gypsies and most of the Germans of black color*—this latter category referred to the children parented by German women and African soldiers who were part of the French occupation forces (the "Senegalese") in the 1920s. In 1935, the Vatican would complain of sterilization of Catholics: a front-page headline in the *New York Post*, July 16, 1935—under a banner headline, "Pope Protests Nazi Church War"—was: "Faith Breach Laid to Berlin in Strong Note. Sterilization and

---

[1141] Chris Baraniuk, "The female Code-breakers Who Were Left Out of History Books," *BBC Future*, Oct. 10, 2017, BBC.COM/FUTURE.

[1142] Paul Bedard, "Declassified Memo Hinted of 1941 Hawaii Attack," *US News*, Nov. 29, 2011, USNEWS.COM/NEWS. See further analysis in Erik J. Dahl (Naval Postgraduate School), "Reassessing the Intelligence Failure at Pearl Harbor," *2011 Annual Meeting of the Amer. Political Sci. Assoc., Sep. 2011*, ACADEMIA.EDU.

The Hitler Era 379

Oppression of Lay Units Cited. Hostility to Clergy Now Held Official." The article stated, "Pope Pious XI was viewed today [July 16] as determined to defend zealously the rights of Catholics in Germany" and added that whereas earlier the Church had held extremist elements (not the German government itself) responsible, it now held that "today the [German] government not only tolerated such actions, but inspired them.[1143] *The Vatican limited its criticisms to Catholics in Germany, and did not address the use of sterilization and other harsh measures against non-Catholics occurring in Germany.*

The Nuremberg Laws of 1935, prohibiting sexual relations between Aryans and non-Aryans applied not only to Jews but also to Romanies (Gypsies) as non-Aryan. Other restrictions and mistreatment followed. In December 1939, Hitler issued an order restricting movement of Romanies and putting into practice their transportation to occupied Poland, along with German Jews. And in 1938, Himmler, referring to the Romanies in the popular jargon as Gypsies, *Zigeuner*, in German, addressed the issue of *die endgültige Lösung der Zigeunerfrage* (the Final Solution of the Gypsy Question) in documents dated March 24 and December 8. This latter document ("Combatting the Gypsy Nuisance"), offered one vision of the Final Solution of the Gypsy Question, involving the isolation of Gypsies (part Gypsies, and even those only with Gypsy-like behavior!) and their ultimate sterilization.[1144] *By 1945, more than half of the Romanies of Europe had been exterminated.*[1145] In comparison with the doctrine that one Jewish grandparent established one's Jewishness, for gypsies, "one eighth 'gypsy blood' was considered strong enough to outweigh seven-eighths of German blood."[1146]

> The Nazis defined a Gypsy half-breed using the following criterion: two persons classified as Gypsies among the individual's sixteen great-great grandparents. This criterion is narrower [even more draconian and inclusive] than the "one of four grandparents" rule defining Jewish half-breeds [*Mischlinge*]. At the same time the Nazi aim of keeping the German race pure was radically upside down here. Whereas those named by the Ministry of the Interior as half-Jews could often survive, albeit not in absolute security, even until the end of the War, and

---

[1143] "Pope Protests Nazi Church War," *New York Post*, Jul. 16, 1935, p. 1.

[1144] Michael Burleigh and Wolfgang Wippermann, *The Racial State: Germany 1933-1945* (1993), pp. 120-122; cf. "Himmler's Circular of December 8, 1939, 'Combatting the Gypsy Nuisance,'" US HOLOCAUST MEMORIAL MUSEUM.

[1145] Ian F. Hancock, *We Are the Romani People: Ame sam e Rromane džene* (2002), p. 34, in the chap. "O Baro Porrajmos—The Holocaust." The word *porrajmos* can mean devouring, rape, gaping (as in horror); *baro* means great.

[1146] Donald Kenrick, *Historical Dictionary of the Gypsies (Romanies)* (1998), pp. 74-75. Cf. Ian F. Hancock, *We Are the Romani People*, pp. 41, 163; Donald Kenrick and Grattan Muxon, *The Destiny of Europe's Gypsies* (1972).

persons with only one Jewish grandparent were on the whole not affected by the Nazi persecution, in a classification defined in 1943 [it was worse for Romanies] —as [being] even one-eighth Gypsy meant deportation to Auschwitz. It must be emphasized that Nazi ideas could be implemented more drastically in relation to Gypsies because no one in Germany or abroad was likely to object.[1147]

A key document was the 1939 statement by Dr. Johannes Behrendt of the Office of Racial Hygiene, declaring that "All Gypsies should be treated as hereditarily sick; the only solution is elimination. The aim should therefore be the elimination without hesitation of this defective element in the population."[1148] Then, in early 1940, 250 Romani children, who were prisoners at Buchenwald Concentration Camp,[1149] were killed using Zyklon B,[1150] *the first known use of that chemical on humans, to be widely used at other death camps, including Auschwitz*.[1151] Later, an experiment on sick prisoners and Soviet POWs at the concentration camp at Auschwitz, using poisonous pellets that were rather inexpensive, proved to be not only economically feasible, but also quite efficient in the speediness of the process. The Commandant of Auschwitz, Rudolf Höss, wrote about a visit by Himmler to him on March 1, 1941, and informed him that Auschwitz should be built up to hold 30,000 prisoners, and that a second camp at Birkenau (Auschwitz II or Auschwitz-Birkenau) should be built to hold up to 100,000 POWs.[1152] (And this, three months to the forthcoming invasion of the USSR, already envisioned, and known by many in the Reich.)

Then, in the summer of 1941, Himmler revised the project for Auschwitz. Höss wrote, "I was suddenly summoned to the Reichsführer SS [Himmler], directly by his adjutant's office. Contrary to his usual custom, Himmler received me without his adjutant being present."

[1147] Karola Fings, Herbert Heuss, Frank Sparing, *The Gypsies During the Second World War. Volume 1: From Race Science to the Camps*, Donald Kenrick, tr. (1997), p. 32. British orthography retained.

[1148] Johannes Behrendt, "Die Wahrheit über die Zigeuner," *NS-Partei Korrespondenz*, vol. 10 (1939), no. 3.

[1149] Brian Kenety, "The 'Devouring': A look at the Romani Holocaust 27-01-2005," *Radio Praha*, ROMOVE.RADIO.CZ; Julia Hajdu, "The Roma and the Holocaust of World War II: Victims, Then and Now," HISTORY.UCSB.EDU.

[1150] The gas used in the concentration camps was hydrocyanic acid (HCN), which evaporates—becomes a gas—at 25.6° C (78.1° F). In contrast, cyanide capsules— an aqueous solution of potassium cyanide (KCN)—have been used in numerous cases, including the suicide deaths of Rommel, Hitler, Braun, Goebbels, Himmler, Göring; later, British mathematician known for cracking the German military message-encoding Enigma Machine, Alan Turing (1954), as well as (much more recently) Bosnian Croat war-crimes general, Slobodan Praljak (2017).

[1151] Ian Hancock is Professor of Linguistics, English, and Dir. of the Romani Archives and Documentation Center, all at the Univ. of Texas. See Ian Hancock, "O Porrajmos: The Romani Holocaust," PRESENCIAGITANA.ORG (2013).

[1152] "Heinrich Himmler Visits KL Auschwitz," ASG/AUSCHWITZ STUDY GROUP.

The Hitler Era

Himmler then said in effect: "The Führer has ordered that the Jewish question be solved once and for all and that we, the SS, are to implement that order. The existing extermination centres in the east are not in a position to carry out the large actions which are anticipated. I [Himmler] have therefore earmarked Auschwitz for this purpose, both because of its good position as regards communications and because the area can easily be isolated and camouflaged.... I have now decided to entrust this task to you [to Höss]. It is difficult and onerous and calls for complete devotion notwithstanding the difficulties that may arise. You will learn further details from Sturmbannführer Eichmann of the Reich Security Head Office who will call on you in the immediate future. The departments concerned will be notified by me in due course. You will treat this order as absolutely secret, even from your superiors. After your talk with Eichmann you will immediately forward to me the plans of the projected installations. [Himmler continued:] *The Jews are the sworn enemies of the German people and must be eradicated. Every Jew that we can lay our hands on is to be destroyed now during the war, without exception*. If we cannot now obliterate the biological basis of Jewry, the Jews will one day destroy the German people."[1153]

Höss continued: "In the autumn of 1941 a special secret order was issued instructing the Gestapo to weed out Russian *politruks*, commissars and certain political officials from the prisoner-of-war camps and to transfer them to the nearest concentration camp for liquidation.... When I was absent on duty, my representative Hauptsturmführer Fritsch,[1154] on his own initiative, used gas for killing these Russian prisoners of war. [This is regularly dated to September 3, 1941.] He crammed the underground detention cells with Russians and, protected by a gas mask, discharged Cyclone B [now more generally known by the German name, Zyklon B] into the cells, killing the victims instantly. Cyclon B gas was supplied by the firm of Tesch & Stabenow[1155] and was constantly used in Auschwitz for the destruction of vermin, and there was consequently always a supply of these tins of gas on hand. In the beginning, this poisonous gas, which was a preparation of prussic acid, was only handled by employees of Tesch & Stabenow under rigid safety precautions, but later some members of the Medical Service were trained by the firm in its use and thereafter the destruction of vermin and disinfection were carried out by them. During Eichmann's next visit I told him about this use of Zyklon B and we decided to employ it for the mass extermination process."[1156]

[1153] Rudolf Höss, *Commandant of Auschwitz: The Autobiography of Rudolf Hoess* (1959), Appendix 1, pp. 206-226 (signed "Rudolf Hoess, Cracow, November 1946"), at pp. 206-207. The name is spelled Höss, Höß, or Hoess. Italics added.

[1154] Variant Ger. spellings include Fritzsch, Fritsche, Fritzsche, and Fritsch; the rank of *Hauptsturmführer* is equivalent to Captain.

[1155] UN War Crimes Commission, *Law Reports of Trials of War Criminals* (1947), vol. 1, *Case 9: The Zyklon B Case*, pp. 93-103; see links in the Front Matter.

[1156] Rudolf Höss, *Commandant of Auschwitz*, pp. 208-209. Cf. alternate tr. in

As historian Richard Evans stated, "The total numbers of non-Germans killed by these various methods were staggering; if pistol-shots, firing-squads, injections, and hanging accounted for *hundreds of thousands*, then starvation and epidemics brought on through deliberate overcrowding and neglect accounted for *millions*. Up to *four million* soviet prisoners of war were killed by these means, shootings being carried out mainly against those suspected of being political commissars, while the majority were simply starved to death or died through disease and neglect.... [As for the Jews:] In scale and scope, *it [their extermination] puts the history of formal capital punishment even in the Third Reich into the shade.*"[1157]

Of course, people were later to be regularly cramped into a large hall often described as a shower room for disinfecting people, the doors locked tight, and the pellets (HCN: hydrogen cyanide, prussic acid, or hydrocyanic acid, whose German name, *Blausäure*, would be given the commercial name of Zyklon B) were dropped in through an opening.

The pellets quickly evaporated, turning to a gas (at 25.6° C., 78.1° F.) that those who were locked inside would breathe in: "Hydrocyanic acid interrupts the release of oxygen in the blood to the cellular tissue; death comes with symptoms of fear and paralysis, and vomiting."[1158]

Death took place within about fifteen minutes. A fan system expelled the gases, then the doors were opened and the cadavers removed (mostly by Jewish prisoners forced to do this work—*too disturbing for the SS camp guards to carry out*), to be taken to a nearby crematorium, where the bodies were burned, the ashes then dumped into nearby ditches, streams, or small rivers nearby.

Once these *Vernichtungslager* (extermination camps)—including especially Bełżec, Sobibór, Majdanek, and Treblinka, as well as Auschwitz II (Birkenau)—were in place, it was possible to accelerate the murder of Jews from throughout German-controlled Europe.

Some Jews were killed where they were before being transported to these camps in Eastern Europe; others committed suicide instead of suffering what many sensed was in store for them. Still others arrived with hopes of being able to survive the war by offering labor for the German war effort, and therefore (they presumably thought) making them more valuable in living as slave labor.

They did not give due importance to the serious devotion of the Nazi killing apparatus (the work of many dedicated men certain that they were doing a great deed that would later be appreciated by all of the European community. Here are photos of photographs of two individual from those transports:

Nazism 1919-1945, Vol. 3: Foreign Policy, War and Racial Extermination, J. Noakes and G. Pridham, eds., Doc. 889, pp. 1174-1177.

[1157] Richard J. Evans, *Rituals of Retribution: Capital Punishment in Germany, 1600-1987* (1996), p. 731. Italics added.

[1158] Harry Mulisch, *Criminal Case 40/61, the Trial of Adolf Eichmann* (2005), p. 171.

Woman with Jewish star, Prague   Dutch Sinti girl, Westerbork[1159]

Scheduling of train transport of Jews to these camps often took precedence over the movement of Wehrmacht troops, reflecting the importance that the Nazi government saw in the final elimination of all Jews from the continent. The organized transportation of Jews (and Romanies) would lead to the decimation of these two populations: The usual estimates are in the range of 6 million Jews, and more than half of all European Romanies also exterminated in the Nazi death machine.

At this same time, Jews from Germany were also transported out to these Polish centers, as well as to the concentration camp at Terezín (Theresienstadt), north of Prague, in Bohemia (Czechoslovakia), a holding camp for Auschwitz. *The reality of this camp was expressed in a poem by young Hanuš Hachenburg:* "What good is a world when there are no rights? What good is the sun when there is no day? What good is God? Is he only to punish? Or to make life better for mankind? … What good is life when the living suffer? Why is my world surrounded by walls?"[1160] And yet, the camp was presented as an undeniable demonstration of the pleasant ease in which Jews in these camps could live in peace, a heaven on earth for Jews. This camp was especially prepared for a visit by Swiss delegate-physician Maurice Rossel of the ICRC (International Committee of the Red Cross, and two Danish observers, on the invitation of the SS.[1161] *The visit took place on June 23, 1944, and was the only camp ever inspected at all by this international organization.* Where they went and what they saw was under careful organization and surveillance of the SS at the camp. Goebbels and the Propaganda Ministry made a film of this camp, called *Der Führer schenkt den Juden eine Stadt* (*The Führer Gifts a City to the Jews*).[1162] Unlike *Der ewige Jude* (*The Eternal Jew*), constructed out of

---

[1159] Long thought to be a Jewish girl, she was identified in 1994 as Anna Maria Steinbach, known as Settele, a Dutch Sinti Romani, gassed when 9 years old. Cf. Dutch video *Beeldfragment Settela Steinbach in de trein*, YOUTUBE.

[1160] "The Young Poet Hanuš Hachenburg," *hanushachenburg.org*. Cf. his poems and other works (by him and others) in *I Never Saw another Butterfly: Children's Drawings and poems from Terezin Concentration Camp* (1993).

[1161] Claude Lanzmann, *A Visitor from the Living* (1999). This interview was filmed in preparing *Shoah*, but was ultimately an out-take, that is, was not included in that long film; cf. "Claude Lanzmann and Maurice Rossel, Complete Transcript of *Shoah* Interview (1979)," ARCHIVES.ORG.

[1162] Katja Iken, "SS-Propagandafilm 'Theresienstadt': 90 Minuten Lüge," *Spiegel*, Jan. 14, 2015. The site has links to excerpts from the original 90-min. film.

film taken in occupied Warsaw, showing the filth, squalor, moral weakness, and rampant death of this species of rat-like vermin, *Der Führer schenkt den Juden eine Stadt* (*The Führer Gifts a City to the Jews*) presented a distorted, pleasant image of Jews living in relative comfort, Jews actually held captive in a "city" in Bohemia (outside of Prague).

Presumably (unlike *Der ewige Jude*), this film was meant for foreign audiences, to show how gentle and respectful and helpful the Reich was toward the Jews in its ward: given productive but not harsh work, gardens, libraries, showing Jews reading, women chatting, sewing, and knitting, children in the sunshine, men caring for cows and cattle, a sports event with a full, enthusiastic crowd, a philharmonic orchestra, a lecture offered by a man looking like a learned professor, and so on. If a regular German audience had seen this film at that time (1944), they would have been puzzled and perhaps disturbed that Hitler was treating the Jews so nicely, when German cities were being leveled by ongoing bombing raids of the Allies. At Theresienstadt was the former German theater- and film-star and director Kurt Gerron (1897-1944)—who had sung, and made famous, "Mäckie Messer" ("Mack the Knife"), in *The Threepenny Opera*, and was director of *Der blaue Engel*, *The Blue Angel*, starring Marlene Dietrich and Emil Jannings—and was now a Jewish prisoner. Obliged to be the film's director, he and the cast at Theresienstadt were given extra food to show their healthy diet during the making of the film; all were all sent to Auschwitz soon after the ending of the film, where Gerron was killed on October 28, 1944. These ruses were apparently quite successful, perhaps aided by a lack of a focused, determined interest by the International Red Cross to see more fully the concentration-camp world.

ON THE REICH'S FINAL MASS, METHODICAL MASSACRES

This period of mass, methodical massacres, largely from late spring 1942 through late 1944, overlapped the zenith of German power, followed by counter-offensives, by the Soviets in the East—the repulsion of the German Armies at Stalingrad, from late 1942 to early 1943, held to mark the reversal of German military might. At this same time, the mass killing of Jews continued: 46,000 Jews from Northern Greece were gassed at Auschwitz in 1943, and in 1944, some 424,000 Hungarian Jews.

SS-Helferinnen, July 1944

Baer, Mengele, and Höss (L to R)

In July 1944, SS staff were given a vacation at the Solahütte SS-resort at Porąbka, south of Auschwitz. The left photo shows happy *SS-Helferinnen*, women in the SS supporting staff at Auschwitz. On the right, the central figure is Mengele, between Commandants Richard Baer (Auschwitz I) and

Rudolf Höss (Auschwitz II, Birkenau).[1163] These *SS-Helferinnen* reported to Berlin the number of Jews delivered to Auschwitz in each carload shipment and the number killed immediately, and so were quite familiar with the precise details of the massive killing operations taking place there. *While these SS were posing, the extermination of Hungarian Jews was at its most intense:* From May 14 to July 9, 1944 (after the German invasion of Hungary, on March 19), 434,351 Hungarian Jews were deported, to be gassed.[1164] The Reich military was in retreat, *but this was a project dear to Hitler, as in his very last written declarations of the centrality of the elimination of European Jewry to his legacy to Western civilization.*

Not well known, the *Vaʿada* (the Budapest Jewish Rescue Committee, a Zionist group), chaired by Ottó Komoly, with Rezső Kasztner as spokesman, together negotiated with Adolf Eichmann for the release of some Hungarian Jews for war materiel, gold, and other wealth. *These were the most Jews saved from the Nazi killing machine by fellow Jews.* The "Kasztner Train" left Budapest with 1,684 Jews, arriving in Bergen-Belsen on July 9. Of these, 1,670 made it to Switzerland: some children on August 24, and others, including Yoel Teitelbaum, the Satmar Rabbi, on December 7. Kasztner also paid millions of deutschmarks (in valuables) to SS Kurt Andreas Becher, Commissioner of Concentration Camps, for 18,000 Jews to be sent to Strasshof Concentration Camp, near Vienna, many surviving the war. Unlike Oskar Schindler, who also negotiated with Nazi authorities to save Jewish lives, and was recognized as one of the Righteous Among the Nations, Kasztner was widely seen in 1950s Israel to be a collaborator; he was assassinated in Tel Aviv on March 3, 1957.[1165]

There were also massive transports from the Warsaw ghetto to Treblinka.[1166] The first left on July 22, 1942; it arrived the next day at Treblinka. (Adam Czerniaków, Chairman of the ghetto's Jewish Council, then committed suicide with a cyanide pill.[1167]) And in 1943, the few Jews still in the Warsaw ghetto fought against the Germans in an uprising that lasted from April 19 (Passover Eve) to May 16; in June 1944, Himmler ordered the Łódź ghetto to be liquidated, its inhabitants to be killed at Auschwitz. On January 19, 1945, the Soviets liberated Łódź.[1168]

DEEP POCKETS PROFITING FROM CONCENTRATION CAMPS' SLAVE LABOR

The German approach to the wartime shortage of manpower, due to the fact that so many young men were entering into the Wehrmacht and

---

[1163] From Wilhelm Brasse, *Photographer 3444, Auschwitz 1940-1945* (2012).

[1164] Judit Molnár, "Nazi Perpetrators: Behavior of Hungarian Authorities During the Holocaust," *Jewish Virtual Library*, JEWISHVIRTUALLIBRARY.ORG.

[1165] Anna Porter, *Kasztner's Train: The True Story of an Unknown Hero of the Holocaust* (2008); *The Kasztner Report: The Report of the Budapest Jewish Rescue Committee, 1942-1945*, László Karsai and Judit Molnár, eds. (2013); *Killing Kasztner: The Jew Who Dealt With Nazis* (2009), VIMEO.COM.

[1166] "Le camp de Treblinka," UNLIVREDESOUVENIR.FR.

[1167] *The Warsaw Diary of Adam Czerniakow: Prelude to Doom*, Raul Hilberg, Stanislaw Staron, Josef Kermisz, eds. (1982); last entry, Jul. 22, 1043, p. 385.

[1168] "The Final Days of the Lodz Ghetto," *Yad Vashem*, YADVASHEM.ORG.

the Waffen-SS as soldiers, was a choice between having German women go into factory work (as was done in the Great War), or, alternatively, to respect women's National Socialist role as householders and, especially, as mothers of young children. The second option was encouraged, and this meant that labor had to be obtained by other means. The obvious alternative was the peoples dehumanized as inferior (*Untermenschen*) who were now under German jurisdiction and all subject to arrest and imprisonment, their countries having been conquered by Germany. There was an initial idea of killing off these unwanted subhumans by working them to death, while giving them insufficient nourishment to maintain life. (The average life-span of someone young and healthy upon entering the concentration camp has been estimated at 3 months; the weak, sick, or elderly died more quickly, even without the use of gas chambers.) In any case, the labor was there pretty much for the asking. A list of companies using slave labor during the Third Reich includes the Siemens electronics and industrial manufacturing company (formerly, Siemens-Schuckert), Volkswagen (VW),[1169] Bosch, Dr. Oetker foods,[1170] Mercedes, Deutsche Bank, VW, Audi (formerly, Auto Union AG),[1171] Ford (through its German subsidiary, Ford-Werke) and also GM (through its German subsidiary, Opel),[1172] Shell (or Royal Dutch Shell, through its German subsidiary, Rhenania-Ossag, providing fuel and lubricating oil),[1173] IG Farben, Krupp, among others. The London-based Holocaust Education Trust (HET) reports that 51 companies used slave labor at Auschwitz, with 92 companies thus benefitting, at Buchenwald, 52 at Dachau, and 57 at Mauthausen-Gusen.[1174] The IG Farben complex supplied the Reich with coal as well as synthetic oils and fuels, synthetic ersatz rubber for tires, and poison gas for killing of pests, applicable as Zyklon B to the gas chambers of the extermination camps. For the use of slave labor, they paid a minimal amount (3-4 marks) per worker per day to the SS, who

---

[1169] "Siemens Offers $12 Million to WWII Slave Labor Victims," *LA Times*, Sep. 24, 1998; "Siemens Creates a Fund For Nazi Slave Workers," NEW YORK TIMES ARCHIVES, Sep. 24, 1998.

[1170] Christian Ignazi, "Another German company reveals is Nazi past," DEUTSCHE WELLE, Oct. 22, 2013.

[1171] Alan Hall, "Revealed: How the Nazis helped German companies Bosch, Mercedes, Deutsche Bank and VW get VERY rich using 300,000 concentration camp slaves," *Daily Mail*, DAILYMAIL.COM, Oct. 13, 2018.

[1172] Michael Dobbs, "Ford and GM Scrutinized for Alleged Nazi Collaboration," *Washington Post*, Nov. 30, 1998, p. A01; "Defense News: Nazi atrocities at Ford-Werke studied," *UPI News*, Dec. 6, 2001, UPI.COM/NAZI-ATROCITIES-AT.

[1173] Evidence suggests that the German subsidiary was using Jewish slave labor even before the outbreak of World War II: see John Donovan, "Royal Dutch Shell and Nazi slave labor, ROYAL DUTCHSHELLPLC.COM, Oct. 1, 2016. *Note or Disclaimer* by the site: "*This is not at all a Shell website.*"

[1174] Adam LeBor, "Slave Labour at Auschwitz Used by Ford," *Independent* (London), Aug. 20, 1999. For the experiences of Spanish and Catalan prisoners there, based on a true story, see film, *El Fotógrafo de Mauthausen* (2018).

were the administrators of the concentration camp system throughout the empire of the Third Reich. Of course, the slave laborers were paid none of this. At its height of activity during the war, in 1943, for example, *IG Farben used 165,000 prisoners as slave laborers (half of its total labor force), including some 30,000 prisoners at Auschwitz alone.* That year, its products involved *3 billion marks of business.* By the end of the war, IG Farben manufactured all of the Reich's synthetic rubber and methanol (as a fuel) in Germany, 90% of Germany's plastics and related products, 84% of Germany's explosives, 75% of its nitrogen and solvent products, about half of its pharmaceuticals, and about a third of all of its synthetic fuel. We may note that slave labor was not confined to the camps in Silesia in and near to the camp at Auschwitz, although these provided the largest source of free labor. Other camps even in Germany proper had their own labor market, such as at Essen, which provided workers for enterprises of the Krupp organization.[1175]

Krupp, as a major operator in the use of concentration camp and other forms of slave labor during the war, had long been a provider to Germany of weaponry—as Fritz Thyssen would write in 1941: "The Friedrich Krupp Corporation at Essen has always been Germany's most famous arsenal."[1176] Krupp, now a major supplier of arms and artillery, including howitzers and other cannons, tanks, submarines, anti-aircraft artillery, and other military products of steel, made use of slave labor in perhaps 100 factories, which were not only in occupied Poland, but also in Germany, Austria, France, and Czechoslovakia. *Involved as slave laborers for Krupp were a total of some 100,000 persons.*[1177] One of the largest of the Krupp factories was the *Berthawerke*, located in Upper Silesia at Markstädt (Laskowice Oławskie, Laskowitz, etc.), southeast of Wrocław (Breslau). *Berthawerke*—named after Bertha Krupp, as was *dicke Bertha* (Big Bertha), a famous short-barreled cannon (howitzer) of World War I—operated from summer 1942 until March 1944. One camp, Nordhausen-Dora (or Mittelbau-Dora, near Nordhausen, German)—which was built as an underground facility in the Kohnstein mountain, in the Harz Mountain range, some 5,000 m. long (16,400 ft.) and covering some 50,000 sq. m. (539,000 sq. ft. or 59,800 sq. yards)—in operation from mid-1943 to late 1944, called *Mittelwerk*. Its underground facilities, to keep them safe from Allied bombing, were known for using slave labor for the production of V-1 flying bombs or ballistic missiles (7 m. or 23 ft. in length) and V-2 rockets (14 m. or 46 ft. in length). This involved big business: on October 19, 1943, a contract for 12,000 A-4 missiles was granted *Mittelwerk*, with a cost of 40,000 Reichsmarks each.[1178] The V-2 rocket, a model in the A-

---

[1175] NT-NCA-Red, vol. 7, pp. 2-7 (Doc. D-288).

[1176] Fritz Thyssen, *I Paid Hitler*, pp. 104-105 (quoted more fully, above).

[1177] *The Holocaust: An Encyclopedia and Document Collection*, Paul R. Bartrop and Michael Dickerman, eds. (2017), *Vol. 1: A-K*, p. 378.

[1178] Józef Garliński, *Hitler's Last Weapons: The Underground War against the V1 and V2* (1978), pp. 107-110 and illustrations inserted after p. 110, esp. no. 6.

4 series, attained speeds greater than 3,500 mi. per hour, and could carry 2,200-pound warheads 200 miles. It was used during the war from October 1942 on, and using some 1,500 V-2 rockets, to attack Britain, from September 1944 on, killing some 7,500 British civilians.[1179]

One of the engineers working on these rockets was Wernher von Braun, who decades later became director of NASA's Marshall Space Flight Center and the chief architect of the Saturn V launch vehicle, used in the first manned flight to the moon. (This led to political jokes at the time.[1180])

IG Farben was also involved. A US Justice Department lawyer who investigated IG Farben in the late 1970s, stated, "Without I.G.'s immense productive facilities, its far-reaching research, varied technical expertise and overall concentration of economic power, Germany would not have been in a position to start its aggressive war in September 1939."[1181] Among the Nuremberg Tribunal Trials after the war, one was focused on executives of IG Farben. A volume in this legal collection contains the transcripts of that trial.[1182] IG Farben requested that a camp be built, and the SS set up the camp in October 1942. The camp/factory was focused on the production of synthetic rubber, natural rubber not being available for German military purposes (as mentioned by Franz Halder in his notes to meetings with Hitler and the German Military Command). The name *Buna* is short for butadiene-based synthetic rubber. Also produced there (among other sources) was Zyklon B, a chemical produced by a subsidiary of IG Farben, Degesch, *Deutsche Gesellschaft für Schädlingsbekämpfung GmbH* (German Society for Pest Control, Ltd.), with IG Farben holding a major investment position. Its *Buna Werke* (Buna Works) factory was an auxiliary camp to Auschwitz. The camp was located near the town of Monowitz (Monowice), not far from Auschwitz. (Among its prisoners were Elie Wiesel and Primo Levi.[1183]) It also was known as Auschwitz III, to

---

[1179] Harriet Arkell, "Death from above without warning: 70 years after the first one fell, interactive map reveals just where Hitler's V2 rockets killed thousands of British civilians in final months of WW2," *Daily Mail* (London), Sep. 10, 2014, MAILONLINE.

[1180] One joke, perhaps sardonic, had an American politician speaking to a Soviet politician, saying, "Our German rocket scientists beat your German rocket scientists to the moon."

[1181] Joseph Borkin, *The Crime and Punishment of IG Farben: The Startling Account of the Unholy Alliance of Adolf Hitler and Germany's Great Chemical Combine* (1978). The Introduction begins with this quote, p. 1. Cf. Richard Pearson, "Joseph Borkin, Antitrust Lawyer, Dies," *The Washington Post*, Jul. 6, 1979. See also Edmund L. Andrews, "IG Farben: A Lingering Relic of the Nazi Years," NEW YORK TIMES ARCHIVES, May 2, 1999.

[1182] NT-TWC-Green, vol. 8 (The I.G. Farben Case). This trial is also referred to as The United States of America v. Carl Krauch, *et al*. Ten of the original twenty-four defendants were acquited of all charges. No one received a sentence of more than 8 years imprisonment. See "Nazi War Crimes Trials: IG Farben Trial (August 27, 1947-July 30 , 1948)," JEWISH VIRTUAL LIBRARY, AICE.

[1183] Elie Wiesel (1928-2016) came to Auschwitz among the Hungarian Jews

distinguish it from Auschwitz, or Auschwitz I, and Auschwitz II, better known as Auschwitz-Birkenau, the extermination camp set up nearby to the first Auschwitz Concentration Camp. In addition, it is referred to as Buna Monowitz. There were also some 45 subcamps set up in the vicinity. (This was a rather large operation.) The camp had as many as 11,000 prisoners at any time, whose ongoing deaths meant that many more prisoners were actually involved overall. While Monowitz was mostly for IG Farben, the area would also provide slave laborers for some of the camps used by Alfred Krupp (son of Bertha Krupp, by then in charge of the Krupp's industries), who also set up factory facilities, nearby.

MEDICAL EXPERIMENTATION WITH CONCENTRATION CAMP PRISONERS

Consider people who are seen as inferior beings, as sub-human (*Untermenschen*), or dehumanized, held to be non-human, to be seen and understood more as vermin of superior groups, as poisoners of the *Herrenrasse* (Master Race), individuals not worthy of life (the common phrase for this in German was *lebensunwerte Leben*). If there is a need or a desire or even simply a whim to try various sorts of intervention in such worthless beings, for the purpose of learning about human limits (along various dimensions), what might prevent such experimentation?

In the concentrationary world, MDs and other scientists had rather broad allowance to experiment as they would like. The extensive list of experiments includes experiments with prisoners to see how little air pressure a person could survive (as in those in the Luftwaffe who might fly at extremely high altitudes), or to see how cold a human body could be lowered to and still survive (as in those who might be downed at sea and have to survive extremely cold ocean water). Prisoners were injected with bacteria or other disease-causing preparations (to test human resistance, to experiment with possible cures); prisoners underwent surgical procedures (removal of an organ, or of muscle tissue, as the calf muscles on one leg), to compare the ways the body would try to recuperate from such physical traumas or injuries. These were carried out at a number of concentration camps. At Auschwitz, the site of many experiments with identical twins, in which one twin underwent some procedure, to compare that twin's health (or death) course with that of

---

transported there in 1944. He would later be among those transferred to Buchenwald; he is author of *Night*, first written as a 900-page manuscript in Yiddish, for which there was little interest, but was radically shortened to 253 pages, and published in Argentina, in Yiddish, in 1956. Wiesel then translated the text into French, published in 1958 as *La Nuit* (121 pages). It was then published in a variety of languages: *Night* (1958), *La notte* ((1958), *Die Nacht* (1980), along with many other books; he received the Nobel Peace Prize in 1986. Primo Levi (1919-1987), an Italian Jewish chemist and writer, was prisoner at Monowitz-Auschwitz from February 1944 to the camp's liberation on Jan. 18, 1945 by Soviet troops. He was author of *Se questo è un uomo* (1947), with tr. *And If This is a Man* (1959), *Survival in Auschwitz* (1959), *Ist das ein Mensch?* (1958), and *Si c'est un homme* (1987), among more than 25 foreign-language editions. His death from falling down a flight of stairs in his home (Apr. 11, 1987) is considered a suicide.

the untouched twin. These were a favorite focus of interest of a famous physician, Dr. Josef Mengele (1911-1979), later known as the Angel of Death, who was never captured or arrested—although he was reported to have been spotted decades later in his home town of Günzburg (in Bavaria, southeast of Stuttgart and northwest of Munich). He had escaped to South America. There he lived under the name of Wolfgang Gerhard. Many decades later, on February 9, 1979, while visiting Austrian friends, Wolfram and Liselotte Bossert, in the coastal resort town of Bertioga (in Brazil, southeast of São Paulo), Mengele was swimming and had a stroke and drowned. He was buried under his assumed name. There are many sources that go into the variety of medical violence of the Nazis, but this gives a basic overview of this domain of human violence of a rather gratuitous sort.[1184] A trial at the Nuremberg Tribunal focused specifically on doctors' rather barbaric concentration camp experiments.[1185]

A WEAK AND SPINELESS GERMANY DESERVES TO BE ANNIHILATED

At a time when the German advances were halted, but before the Soviet counter-offensive, where Hitler saw the first obstacle to military advances, and the first hint that things were not quite going according to plan, having received reports in a war council meeting on November 24 [1941] that arms production were down and mentioned the "necessity to make peace!" It added, "On 1 April [1942] we shall be 180,000 men short in the east army." At that meeting, General Paulus raised the topic of the German military issues for the coming winter (which would prove rather disastrous for German troops and their equipment, not adequate for the Russian winters where temperatures went down to -30° centigrade, and even to -40°.[1186]

Days later, on November 27, 1941, Hitler met with Foreign Ministers Erik Scavenius (Denmark), Mladen Lorković (Croatia), Rolf Witting (Finland), László Bárdossy (Hungary), and Ivan Popov (Bulgaria), and made a rather remarkable comment expressing his view of Germany and the Germans, in the context of his deeply held principle that victory and power come to the strongest, who deserve what they have obtained, while

---

[1184] An early small text with a number of photographs, including those of some medical experiments, was by Edward Frederick Langley Russell, Lord Russell of Liverpool, *The Scourge of the Swastika: A Short History of Nazi War Crimes, with 16 Pages of Illustrations* (1954). A major study was done by Yale psychiatrist Robert Jay Lifton, *The Nazi Doctors: Medical Killing and the Psychology of Genocide* (1986). Cf. "Dr. Josef Mengele: the Cruelest Nazi Doctor of the Holocaust," Nov. 3, 2014, MEDICALBAG; Kenneth Mellanby, "Medical Experiments on Human Beings in Concentration Camps in Nazi Germany," *British Medical Journal*, Jan. 25, 1947, pp. 148-150; Volker Roelcke, "Nazi medicine and research on human beings, *The Lancet (Theme: Medicine, Crime, and Punishment)*, vol. 364, Dec. 2004, pp. 6-7, THELANCET.COM; "Medical Experiments," AUSCHWITZ.ORG.

[1185] NT-TWC-Green, vol. 1: The Medical Case, aka The Doctors' Trial.

[1186] Franz Halder, *The Halder War Diary, 1938-1942*, entry, Nov. 24, 1941, p. 564.

the weaker, the vanquished, deserve whatever they would then be subjected to. Hitler stated, "On this point, too, I am icily cold. [*Ich bin auch hier eiskalt.*] If one day the German nation is no longer sufficiently strong or sufficiently ready for sacrifice to stake its own blood for its existence [*Wenn das deutsche Volk einmal nicht mehr stark und opferbereit genug ist, sein eigenes Blut für seine Existenz einzusetzen*], then let it perish and be annihilated by some other stronger power [*so soll es vergehen und von einer anderen, stärkeren Macht vernichtet werden*] .... In that case, I shall shed no tears for the German nation [*Ich werde dann dem deutschen Volk keine Träne nachweinen*]."[1187]

There was a strict inner coherence to this attitude, we must admit; it would have ramifications later in the war.

There was the significant precedent of the Napoleonic War (the Napoleonic Russian Campaign, the Patriotic War of 1812, etc.) and the fact that Napoleon's troops were as much conquered by the Russian winter as by the Russian armies—if not more so. It was not for nothing that Nietzsche later in the nineteenth century wrote of Russian fatalism: the ability "to cease entirely from reacting," a "self-preservative measure" to preserve one's limited natural energy, and to avoid being "used up too quickly if one reacted."[1188] (In the Daoism of Lǎo Tzu (Lǎozi), this is called *wúwei*, non-action, non-coercive action.[1189]) At the time of the Napoleonic invasion, the peasants destroyed their crops; the Russians allowed the enemy to be destroyed by the weather: the Russians knew how to dress for that condition and wait; the Germans (and earlier, the French) did not.

The mechanization of the German military was a technological advance over the cavalry and foot soldiers of Napoleon, but the autumn rains made the land mud, capturing heavy equipment, from trucks to artillery to tanks, making them of little use. The supply of fuels was not maintained as needed, and the Russian winter was so cold that lubricating oils for tanks froze, making tanks unusable. In addition, of course, there was the bitter cold that each soldier had to fight against, just to stay alive.

In short, the fact that the Wehrmacht together with the Luftwaffe could not achieve their goals that first half year, to the end of 1941, would prove disastrous. Neither Leningrad not Moscow was captured.

This gave the USSR time to regenerate its factories, moved far away from the front, and to begin manufacturing significant numbers of tanks, fighter and bomber planes, and arms of various dimensions, from rifles to mortars to cannons. While the front lines or the eastern campaign were much advanced from the state of affairs at the start of the invasion in late June 1941, this was to be a rather short-lived victory.

[1187] Sebastian Haffner, *Anmerkungen zu Hitler*, 1978 ed., p. 152, cf. p. 197; 1994 ed., p. 118, cf. p. 153; Eng., *The Meaning of Hitler*, p. 120, cf. p. 160; George F. Will, "Nazism Wasn't Nationalism," *Washington Post*, Aug. 11, 1991.

[1188] Friedrich Nietzsche, *Ecce Homo: Wie man wird, was man ist* (1888), Par. 6 of Sect. "Why I Am So Wise"; Eng., *Ecce Homo: How One Becomes What One Is*.

[1189] Lao Tzu, *Tao Te Ching: The Classic Book of Integrity and the Way*, Victor H. Mair, tr. (1990), Chap. 2 (*Mǎ-wáng-tuī* manuscripts, Chap. 46), p. 60.

JURIDICAL DOCUMENTATION AND PREPARATIONS

We sometimes have the idea that the world's realization of the Nazi atrocities came with the liberation by Western Allies of camps in Western Germany in April of 1945.

Often cited, with videos of the camps as discovered by the American and British Armies that gave testimony to the condition of surviving prisoners. The first of these camps liberated in the west was an abandoned camp at Ohrdruf (southwest of Leipzig, north of Nuremberg), discovered by American Army units on April 4, 1945, followed by their liberating Buchenwald, near Weimar, and also the slave-labor camp at Nordhausen, on April 11. The British forces liberated Bergen-Belsen on April 15, and Neuengamme, near Hamburg, on May 4.

These were not the first concentration camps or extermination camps that were liberated from Nazi control. The Russian Armies, moving into Poland, discovered several extermination camps, the first in early 1944 and the others by that July. Located in Poland, these were, first, Majdanek, and then Chełmno, Bełżec, Sobibór, and Treblinka; they had been partially or totally destroyed and then camouflaged by the Nazis before the arrival of Soviet troops.

One estimate suggests that some 1,7000,000 Jews killed in these camps, which were operational in the extermination primarily of Polish Jewry, along with Sinti-Roma/Gypsies and Jews from other countries.[1190]

Auschwitz was liberated by Soviet troops, on January 27, 1945. Some 1.1 million people had been gassed to death there. In particular, in some 8 weeks in spring and summer 1944, 424,000 Hungarian Jews were trained to Auschwitz to be killed; in all, 565,000 Hungarian Jews were killed by the Germans and its allied governments in Middle Europe.[1191]

As the Soviets approached Auschwitz, many prisoners were force-marched from there west to other camps, some arriving ultimately at Bergen-Belsen, Buchenwald, and other camps in western Germany. Films of various scenes at Auschwitz only became available to Western European allies decades later, although shown earlier in exhibits at Auschwitz itself, for those who could visit that camp in person.

Even before the actual liberation of these camps, however, there was clear information of the mass killings of Jews in Europe.

Reports from the Eastern Front mass murders and of the operations at Auschwitz and other concentration and extermination camps, including photographs taken clandestinely in August 1944, and smuggled out of Auschwitz inside of toothpaste tubes destined for the Polish Underground, were also made available to those who were ready to consider this evidence. These included photographs of Jewish women, naked, being

---

[1190] "The Death Camps," YAD VASHEM; "Extermination Camp" (sub-section Death Toll), WIKIPEDIA; Emily Fuggel, "Liberation of the Concentration Camps," IMPERIAL WAR MUSEUMS (IWM), Jan. 12, 2018.
[1191] "Murder of Hungarian Jewry," YAD VASHEM.

driven into the gas chambers, and photographs of dead bodies being burned in various crude pyres. Some of these were published in 1945.[1192]

Much earlier in the war, there was information diffused by government sources, including the release on November 28, 1940 by the Third Reich Propaganda Ministry of *Der ewige Jude* (*The Eternal Jew*), showing the miserable living conditions of the Jews who were crowded into the Warsaw ghetto, meant to suggest that here was the repulsive lack of cleanliness and civility and decent living of these Jewish vermin.

EARLY ALLIED RECOGNITION OF MASS KILLINGS IN THE USSR

Within months of the beginning of Operation Barbarossa, the Wehrmacht invasion of the Soviet Union initiated on June 20, 1941, the SS Einsatzgruppen were operating intensely by late summer 1941—with mass killings of Jews in the Babi Yar ravine, outside of Kiev[1193] (these killings referred to in a more general way as occurring in and near villages and ravines on the Eastern Front). And, in late 1941 and early 1942, various death camps of different sizes and killing capacities began receiving Jews locally or by train transport, where they were gassed and later cremated. The British and the Soviets both made public declarations of their knowledge of Nazi atrocities on the Eastern Front. More, below.

INVASIONS: COLLABORATION, RESISTANCE, NEUTRALITY

The invading armies of the Third Reich took over a number of countries, from Austria, with many welcoming arms and straight-armed salutes, and then, Czechoslovakia, with no military confrontation but many crying faces, and continuing after that in warfare with Poland, Norway, the Low Countries and France, followed by the great invasion of the USSR.

Some welcomed the take-over of their countries, not just in Austria, but also, for example, by nations that had been earlier invaded and occupied by the Soviets, in the period from the invasion of Poland in September 1939 until the invasion of the USSR by the Reich in June 1941.

This included such peoples as the Lithuanians, the Latvians, and the Estonians as well as the Ukrainians, who were part of the USSR but with a history of great mistreatment, as in the famine of 1932-1933. These earlier occupations could be, and were, used by the political apparatus of

---

[1192] Jean-Claude Pressac, *Auschwitz: Technique and Operation of the Gas Chambers* (1989), with copious, very convincing documentation of the mundanity and shared knowledge among many (not only in the inner circles of the SS) that these arrangements called for, with significant civil involvement in the workings of the SS-administered extermination camps—architect's designs and formal, correspondence to the administrative offices at Auschwitz from private German companies involved in the construction of the gas-chamber buildings, the crematoria, the ovens themselves, their ventilation systems, and general operating efficiency, including exchanges with the civil engineering firm of Huta, Kattowitz (Polish name, Katowice), and J. A. Topf & Söhne, Erfurt, Germany. Cf. Edward Frederick Langley Russell, Lord Russell of Liverpool, *The Scourge of the Swastika: A Short History of Nazi War Crimes*, pp. 422-423, with photos.

[1193] See *Spell Your Name: Surviving the Darkest Days of Human History* (2006) with heartfelt, eyewitness interviews with survivors of the 1941 massacres in Kiev.

the Third Reich to create allies of these peoples (using the old principle that the enemy of my enemy is my ally). This can make sense of the willingness of many of these non-Germans to side with, and act in coordination with, the Reich, complementing wide-spread hatred of Jews.

The urgency of taking a position in the face of great political pressures and demands to collaborate (or to resist, or to try to survive the ordeal with as little involvement and recognition by conflicting parties) was a universal issue. As Martin Emil Marty, the American theologian, Lutheran pastor, and emeritus professor of religion at the University of Chicago, remarked in 2007, "(We) Lutherans are not proud of East German clerics who cooperated even minimally with the hated Stasi, their secret police. *It is likely that in almost all cases of totalitarian inflictions some who are weak, or who find it convenient, play along.* So, they did in Hitler's Germany, on a scale that still is haunting. Recovery, if any, is slow."[1194]

In contrast with such examples in their historical contexts, we can see the case of Denmark, which clearly had not been invaded by the USSR in the period of 1939-1941. One explanation for the ability of the Danes to stay fundamentally united against the Reich, with King Christian X of Denmark said to have responded to the Nazi orders for Jews to wear the Jewish star by declaring that we Danes are all Jews (and with almost all Danes then putting the Jewish star on their outer garments).[1195] That story is inspiring, and yet, fictional: The Danish Jews were not required to wear a star, the King and other non-Jewish Danes did not wear stars (nor did the Jews), *but the Danes did stand by the Jews in support of these fellow Danish citizens.*[1196]

There is, we might add to this understanding, the fact that the Danes were not Slavic, which meant that they were not seen as the *Untermenschen* that *Mein Kampf* and German propaganda promoted. Even the Dutch and the French (who were not to be classified as Germanic in any sense) were understood in Nazi theory as less inferior than the Slavs, and certainly much less inferior than Jews, Gypsies, and other worthless beings. Unlike events in Poland, the USSR, the Baltic States, and other Slavic nations in eastern Europe, there were no mass killings in these countries, even if the Third Reich saw itself as their superior and master. We may consider all of this a reflection of a sense of racial superiority, in which civilization was taken to be best represented by Nordic Germans, then western Europeans, and then, moving into the groups taken to be worthy only of being slaves, worked to death, or killed outright. (Rare exceptions include the burning on June 10, 1944, of the central French village of Oradour-sur-Glane, 13 mi. northwest of Limoges, described as the day that the German Army disgraced itself—showing a disregard of the complete razing of the Czech village of Lidice, on June

---

[1194] Martin E. Marty, "Sightings: January 15, 2007, Troubles in Poland," *Sightings* (2007), UNITED-FULFILLMENT.COM. Word in parentheses in original; italics added.

[1195] Timothy Snyder, *Black Earth*, pp. 207-325.

[1196] "King Christian X of Denmark," HOLOCAUST ENCYCLOPEDIA/USHMM; "The Holocaust: The Rescue of the Danish Jews," AUSCHWITZ.DK.

10, 1942, exactly two years earlier, or the killings of hundreds of thousands, in fact, millions of civilians on the Eastern Front.)

This suggests that what the people of an invaded nation are called upon to do by the occupier nation depends on a number of specifics that make significant differences in the constraints on the population and the violence of the occupier. In some cases, the history can go back many centuries. For example, although the Serbs and the Croats are very close (their languages are mutually intelligible, even though Serbian uses a Cyrillic alphabet and Croatian, the Latin alphabet—related to the fact that Serbs are largely Eastern Orthodox and Croats Catholic—the mutual animosity, largely based originally on their different religious positions, was exploited by occupiers, in which (as elsewhere) one social group was favored and protected by the occupier, and the other subjugated.

(We see the same in the earlier British colonies, with the consequence that when the controlling minority group supported by the British was left on its own, the controlled majority frequently went on killing sprees to revenge earlier mistreatment.)

In the Balkans, the Croats had been subject allies of the Ottoman Empire, and the Serbs, the conquered; with the Third Reich presence during World War II, the Croats became supportive allies to the Reich, ahd the Serbs, the subjugated. The mass murders by the Croatian Ustaše (Ustashi), led by dictator Ante Pavelić, perhaps surpassed that of Nazi machine in brutality: Serbs, Jews, and Gypsies were easy targets for the intensely murderous attitude of this regime.[1197]

The Poles had a special position in German eyes: the entire Polish people were held to be prime examples of *Untermenschen*, lesser human beings. The Nazi military and administration had no particular interest in having any major collaboration with the Poles (unlike, for example, their relation with the French or the Norwegians). The entire eastern portion of Poland was to be used as a dumping ground to hold Jews and other fundamentally worthless peoples; this region was also designated as the location for the extermination camps: These were German-administered by the SS under Himmler.

It is perhaps more precisely correct to speak of the Nazi camps in Poland, rather than the Polish camps, given the insinuation in the latter term that it was the Poles who had organized and were running these camps. (Recent reaction in Poland against calling Majdanek and other camps Polish extermination camps comes from this concern.[1198])

The story was different in the Baltic states, as the locals, who had been conquered earlier by the Russians, saw the Germans as liberators (as unlikely as that idea might seem at first); the same was true in southern USSR, with the Ukrainians having their own hatreds of the harsh treatment the Russians had imposed on them, including Stalin's agrarian reforms that resulted in massive starvation, especially in 1932-33. And,

---

[1197] *The Vatican Ratlines: Smuggling Nazis to Safety*, YOUTUBE; on the Jasenovic Croatian death camp, see "Jasenovic Concentration Camp," WIKIPEDIA.

[1198] "Polish jail terms for Nazi camp slurs," *BBC News*, Aug. 16, 2016.

again, the position of Jews and other small groups was made quite precarious under those conditions.

How various countries participated in the killing of Jews ranged from those who strongly resisted German actions (as Denmark) to those who participated actively in the rounding up, holding in camps, and then shipping Jews off to eastern concentration camps (as France and the Netherlands), to those who were given free rein to act on their intense anti-Semitism or to become part of the concentration camp staff carrying out the work of these camps (such as Lithuanians and Ukrainians), to countries that were active in their direct murder of Jews.

An example of this is Rumania, under the leadership of Ion Antonescu, with the activity of the nationalist, anti-Semitic Iron Guard. In various massacres and by other means (such as death of Jews locked in train cars), a recent Romanian report estimated that between 280,000 and 380,000 Jews, along with over 11,000 Romanies, were thus killed.[1199] One such killing was the Jassy (Iaşi) pogrom, which took place on June 29, 1941, in which at least 13,266 Jews were killed. Raul Hilberg reported of Rumania that "no country, besides Germany, was involved in massacres of Jews on such a scale."[1200] And that "Besides Germany itself, Romania was thus the only country which implemented all the steps of the destructive process [of the systematic killing of the Jews], from definition to killings."[1201] Hungary had its own nationalist organization, the Arrow Cross, which is known for its mass shootings of Jews in Budapest, with the wounded or killed Jews then pushed into the Danube. In 2005, a memorial was created on the east (Pest) bank of the river, with cast-iron shoes to be reminders of the murdered Jews, adults and also children.[1202]

In general, the somewhat straight-forward methodology of the Third Reich to gain cooperation from its various rather subservient allies involved the direct confrontation by Hitler or other high-ranking Nazis with the leaders of each such country, persuading them on the wisdom of full cooperation with the National Socialist regime and its programs.[1203]

[1199] International Commission on the Holocaust in Romania, *Final Report of the International Commission on the Holocaust in Romania, Presented to Romanian President Ion Iliescu*, Nov. 11, 2004 (2004), esp. p. 2, USHMM.ORG; "Romania in World War II," WIKIPEDIA; "The Holocaust in Romania," INTERNATIONAL COMMISSION ON THE HOLOCAUST IN ROMANIA (Nov. 11, 2004), esp. pp. 15-16; "Wiesel Commission: International Commission on the Holocaust in Romania," WIKIPEDIA; "Iaşi Pogrom," WIKIPEDIA; Dennis Deletant, *Hitler's Forgotten Ally: Ion Antonescu and his Regime, Romania 1940-1944* (2006).

[1200] Quoting Raul Hilberg, *Final Report of the International Commission on the Holocaust in Romania* (just cited), p. 1. From Raul Hilberg, *The Destruction of the European Jews*, Vol. 2 (1985), p. 759.

[1201] Raul Hilberg, *The Destruction of the European Jews*, 1-vol. ed. (1961), pp. 485-509, at p. 485. Hilberg uses the alternative spelling, Roumania.

[1202] "Arrow Cross Party," ENCYCLOPÆDIA BRITANNICA; "Shoes on the Danube Bank," WIKIPEDIA; Áron Szele, *The Ideology of Hungarian Fascism* (2015), ETD.CEU.HU.

[1203] See "Killing, and Persuading Others to Help (1942-1943)," Chap. 14, pp. 314-

France had surrendered to the Germans on June 17, 1940, signing surrender papers on June 22 at Compiègne—in the very train car where the Germans had signed the surrender documents in 1918. It was made effective as of June 25, 1940. This was sweet vengeance for Hitler's Third Reich over the disgrace (in German eyes) of that earlier surrender. The *Völkischer Beobachter* had a front-page headline: *Schande von 1918 in Wald von Compiègne gelöscht: Waffenstillstandsbedingungen überreicht* (The Shame of 1918 in the Compiègne Forest Blotted out: Armistice Conditions Submitted). The southern half of conquered France was administered from the town in Vichy, in south-central France, by the French themselves, under Marshal Pétain—until the Germans took over direct military control of all of France, on November 10, 1942, two days after Allied landings in French North Africa (Operation Torch). Meanwhile, Vichy France passed many laws conforming to German values, including strong anti-Jewish laws. Many French denounced Jews (as did the Dutch), from hatred against Jews, for personal revenge, or for payment.[1204] One of the most significant laws was *le Statut juif*, the Jewish Statute, issued on October 3, 1940,[1205] which defined Jews in conformity with Third Reich suggestions. As word-artist Céline[1206] penned his *youpin*-hatred, so acted the Vichy regime against the Jews of France, as in the massive arrest of Jews by the French police, including *la Carlingue*, the French SS,[1207] on July 16, 1942—two days after an undisturbed celebration of the French national holiday, *le Quatorze juillet* (Bastille Day)—held in a large sports stadium, *le Vélodrome d'hiver*, the Winter Velodrome, the *rafle*—the Italian term is *razzia*, a hostile raid—consisted of major arrests of Jews in Paris, with deportations to death camps in Poland.[1208] Meanwhile, the German Luftwaffe was attacking Britain. The *Völkischer Beobachter* of June 23, 1940, page 1, read: "*260 Flugzeuge erbeutet, 765 in 14 Tagen vernichtet. Erfolgreiche Luftangreiffe auf England*" ("260 aircraft captured, 765 destroyed in 14 days. Successful air strikes on England").

THE RIGHTEOUS: LAY PERSONS, CHURCHMEN, POPES, IMAMS, AND MUFTIS

There were many involved in the mass killings of entire peoples during the Third Reich, especially in the years starting with the invasion of the Soviet Union (1941-1945). These required the definite assistance in the numerous activities involved in this organized killing. These included police in various countries to keep records of and to arrest and finally

---

333, in Laurence Rees, *The Holocaust: A New History*.
[1204] Laurent Joly, *Dénoncer les Juifs sous l'Occupation: Paris, 1940-1944* (2017); *Goodbye Holland: The Destruction of Dutch Jewry*, 8:15-8:30, 31:40-38:45.
[1205] "Le Statut des Juif est promulgué," *Le Matin* (Paris), Oct. 19, 1940, pp. 1-2. The byline read: ("Jewry is hencefoth excluded from every public function, besides some few exceptions"), including in the press, theater, cinema, and education.
[1206] Novelist-essayist Louis-Ferdinand Céline (L. F. Destouches, MD); see esp. his vitriolic anti-Semitic diatribes, *Bagatelles pour un massacre* (1937), *L'ecole des cadavres* (1938), and *Les beaux draps* (1941).
[1207] See documentary, *Silent Saviours: Surviving in occupied France* (2016).
[1208] "The Vél d'hiv Roundup," WIKIPEDIA; "Rafle du Vél' d'hiv'," UNIVERSALIS.FR.

deport Jews to the death camps in the East. It included all of those involved in the actual logistics of transportation. It involved all of those who worked in the death camps, keeping the process moving ahead, maximizing the number of Jews to be gassed and cremated. During the war, and also after the war, there were also many involved in protecting, hiding, or welcoming former Nazi criminals. Many spoke out in words and actions that accepted and even lauded Reich violence, as in the activities of various political groups and of some in positions of power within religious communities. We mentioned the Vatican Ratline and the US Intelligence community's Operation Paperclip. There was also the alliance between Hitler and the Mufti of Jerusalem and Grand Mufti of Palestine, Haj Amin el Husseini (1895-1974), sharing an intense hatred of Jews and of the British.[1209] (More, just below.)

There were, however, others who aided, hid, and protected Jews at the risk of their own lives, otherwise possibly in no imminent jeopardy. Well known is Oskar Schindler (1908-1974), who helped over a thousand Jews, providing them with work and work permits that prevented their being taken away to the gas chambers of Auschwitz; Raoul Wallenberg (1912-1947: arrested by Soviet authorities in 1945?)—a Swedish diplomat who gave out fake Swedish passports to Jews in Budapest, saving tens of thousands of Hungarian Jews; Chiune Sugihara (1900-1986), Japanese consul in Kaunas, Lithuania, who produced permits for Jews to travel safely to Shanghai (occupied at the time by the Japanese); Ángel Sanz-Briz (the "Angel of Budapest"), Spanish Chargé d'Affaires to Hungary, whose visas saved some 5,000 Jews[1210]; the Portuguese Chargé d'Affaires in Hungary, Carlos de Liz-Texeira Branquinho; El Salvadorian Consul General, Col. José Arturo Castellanos[1211]; Gilberto Bosques, Mexican consul in Marseilles, who saved tens of thousands of Jews and also Spanish Republic exiles[1212]; Aristides de Souisa Mendes, Portuguese consul in Bordeaux,[1213] who issued 30,000 visas, mostly to Jews (against his government's position)—"perhaps the largest rescue action by a single individual during the Holocaust"[1214]; or Ho Feng-Shan (1901-1997), the Chinese Consul-General in Vienna who issued 1,900 visas to Jews then able to flee Europe for Shanghai. Carl Lutz (1895-1975), Swiss Vice-

---

[1209] Roger Faligot and Rémi Kauffer, *Le croissant et la croix gammée* (1990); David Motadel, *Islam and Nazi Germany's War* (2014); *Nazi Collaborators: The Grand Mufti of Jerusalem, Haj Amin el Husseini*, at 22:30-30:00, YOUTUBE; "Hitler Presents Confiscated Jewish Villa in Berlin to Ex-mufti of Jerusalem," *Jewish Telegraphic Agency*, Jan. 2, 1942, JTA.ORG.

[1210] "Ángel Sanz-Briz: The Angel of Budapest, Who Saved 5000 from the Nazis in WW2," WAR HISTORY ONLINE.

[1211] See these and others presented at "Raoul Wallenberg, Carl Lutz, Giorgio Perlasca, etc.," BUDAPESTVACATIONSERVICE.WEBSTARTS.COM.

[1212] "Gilberto Bosques [Saldívar]: Biography," RAOULWALLENBERG.NET.

[1213] Tigrane Yegavian, "Saviors in History: Aristides de Souisa Mendes [do Amaral e Abranches]," *Aurora Prize for Awakening Humanity*, AURORAPRIZE.COM.

[1214] Yehuda Bauer, *A History of the Holocaust*, Revised ed. (2002), p. 249.

Consul in Budapest, is credited with saving over 62,000 Hungarian Jews with Swiss *Schutzbriefe*, protective letters, allowing them to emigrate.[1215] Or, in China in its times of turmoil, John Rabe (1882-1950),[1216] a German Nazi-Party businessman and member of the Nazi Party, who worked for Siemens in Nanking (Nanjing) and helped save many Chinese there.

Among Lutheran pastors to mention here were Martin Niemöller (above) and Dietrich Bonhoeffer (below); among Catholics were the Polish Franciscan monk, Maximilian Kolbe (1894-1941),1214 who offered himself to be killed in place of another Auschwitz prisoner, and Joseph Frings, Bishop of Köln, who in 1942-1943 denounced Nazi treatment of Jews "from the deepest reaches of his soul."[1217]

Consider also Martin Niemöller, above, and Dietrich Bonhoeffer, below, both Lutheran pastors, and the Polish Franciscan monk, Maximilian Kolbe (1894-1941),[1218] who offered his own life in place of another Auschwitz prisoner about to be killed.

In the Netherlands, on January 10, 1941, all Jews were ordered to register themselves using the Nazi blood definition of a Jew, including Jews who had converted to Catholicism, the first Dutch deportation of Jews to Auschwitz leaving the next day. The Netherlands Commissioner-General for Political Affairs and Propaganda, Fritz Schmidt, told the Rev. Herman J. Dijkmeester that Jews baptized before January 1, 1941, would be exempt. The Archbishop of Utrecht, Johannes de Jong, had the Nazi treatment of Dutch Jews publicly denounced in a document read by priests throughout the Netherlands on July 25, 1942. This led to orders of the SS (a Nietzschean match) for more than 40,000 Dutch Catholic Jews—Jews for the SS, but Catholics for the Church: *a deadly difference in understanding*—were shipped off to Auschwitz.

If we turn to Pope Pius XII, he has been lauded as a rescuer of Jews[1219] and criticized for his silence at key moments.

Some explained this silence as his being quiet on the political level *to minimize the death of Catholics* under Nazi governance *and to allow more effective and efficient secret aid to the Jews of Europe*. (Given the above Nazi focus on deporting only Jews, we might ask what basis his fear for Catholics might have had.) Still, there have been expressions of deep appreciation for what Pope Pius XII did during the Third Reich by many

---

[1215] Imogen Foulkes, "The forgotten Swiss diplomat who rescued thousand from Holocaust," *BBC News*, Jan. 4, 2018; "Carl Lutz," *Swiss Federal Dept. of Foreign Affairs (FDFA)*, EDA.ADMIN.CH.

[1216] "About Chiune Sugihara," *Sugihara Museum*, SUGIHARA-MUSEUM.JP; "Ho Feng-Shan," *Encyclopaedia Judaica*, ENCYCLOPEDIA.COM; Thomas Keneally, *Schindler's List* (1982); John Rabe, *The Good Man of Nanking: The Diaries of John Rabe* (1998).

[1217] Robert D. McFadden, "Joseph Cardinal [1946 on] Frings Dies at 91; Defied Nazis as Prelate of Cologne," *The New York Times*, Dec. 18, 1978, p. 17.

[1218] "Kolbe, Saint of Auschwitz," AUSCHWITZ.DK; Matthew E. Bunson, "Catholic Martyrs of the Holocaust," *Catholic Magazine*, Nov. 1, 2008.

[1219] A priest [Pope Pius XII] who saved hundreds of Jews during WWII by disguising them as seminarians, YOUTUBE.

Jewish scholars, theologians, and other leaders. For example, Einstein wrote in December 1940, "I feel a great affection and admiration because the Church alone has had the courage and persistence to stand for intellectual truth and moral freedom."[1220] Pinchas Lapide, Consul General of Israel in Milan, scholar, and theologian, wrote that Pope Pius XII "was instrumental in saving at least 700,000, but probably as many as 860,000 Jews from certain death at Nazi hands."[1221] Jenö Lévai, Jewish Hungarian historian, detailed protests to Regent Miklós Horthy, the Hungarian head of government, by Pius XII and many Hungarian clergy, who aided in hiding Jews marked for deportation; Lévai concluded, "One may say that in the autumn and winter of 1944 there was scarcely a Catholic institution in Budapest where persecuted people [Jews] had not found shelter."[1222] And Michael Tagliacozzo, Italian Jewish survivor and historian stated, "Pope Pacelli was the only one who intervened to impede the deportation of Jews on 16 October 1943 [date of a German *razzia* of Roman Jews] and he did very much to hide and save thousands of us."[1223]

A 1963 German play by Rolf Hochhuth, *Der Stellvertreter*, *The Deputy*, portrayed the Pope in a negative, critical light, leading to a serious reevaluation of the role of Pius XII during the war, and yet its accuracy has been questioned by historians.[1224] After all, many priests and nuns who hid Jews in churches, monasteries, and nunneries have been recognized by Yad Vashem as among the Righteous of the Nations.

Also, then, among Muslims and Imams,[1225] consider Abdelqader Ben Ghabrit (Si Kaddour Benghabrit, 1868-1954), the Imam of the Grand Mosque of Paris,[1226] the Iranian (Muslim) diplomat Abdol Hossein Sardari, who issued some 2,000 false passports for Jews in Paris helping them escape,[1227] and the Bosniaks (Bosnian Muslims), who protected some of the small Jewish community from the Croatian Ustashi.[1228]

[1220] Einstein, quoted in "Christian Martyrs," *Time*, Dec. 23, 1940, pp. 38-41.

[1221] Pinchas E. Lapide, *Three Popes and the Jews* (1967), p. 214.

[1222] By the end of July, most Hungarian Jews had already been transported by train to Auschwitz. Jenö Lévai, *Hungarian Jewry and the Papacy: Pius XII Was Not Silent* (1968), p. 99; David Dalin, *The Myth of Hitler's Pope: Pope Pius XII and His Secret War Against Nazi Germany* (2005), pp. 11-12, 168.

[1223] Michael Tagliacozzo, quoted from "Jewish Historian Praises Pius XII's Wartime Conduct," *St. Michael's College*. Cf. Dimitri Cavalli, "The Good Samaritan: Jewish Praise for Pope Pius XII," EWTN.COM; "Pope Pius XII and the Holocaust," WIKIPEDIA.

[1224] Leonidas E. Hill, "History and Rolf Hochhuth's The Deputy," *Mosaic: A Journal for the Interdisciplinary Study of Literature*, vol. 1, no. 1, 1967, pp. 118–131.

[1225] Marc David Baer, "Muslim Encounters with Nazism and the Holocaust: The Ahmadi of Berlin and Jewish Convert to Islam: Hugo Marcus," *The American Historical Review*, vol. 120, no. 1, Feb. 1, 2015, pp. 140–171

[1226] Ofer Aderet, "The Grand Mosque of Paris That Saved Jews During the Holocaust," *Haaretz*, Mar. 23, 2012; "Si Kaddour Benghabrit," WIKIPEDIA.

[1227] C. N. Trueman, "Abdol-Hossein Sardari," *The History Learning Site*, May 22, 2015, HISTORYLEARNINGSITE.CO.UK.

[1228] Kate Bartlett, "Why Sarajevo's Tiny Jewish Community Believes It's in the

The Hitler Era

In contrast, the story that Hitler was convinced by his meeting with Haj Amin al-Husseini, the Grand Mufti of Jerusalem on November 28, 1941, to begin a program to exterminate the Jews, cannot be supported. Hitler's focus on the *Vernichtung*, extermination, of Jews, already in operation by that point in time, with mass killings beginning soon after the invasion of the USSR in June of that year. This is not to deny the interest of Al-Husseini in resisting the implications of the Balfour Declaration, which he saw as a betrayal of Arab interests, his support of the anti-Jewish, anti-British, and anti-Soviet position of the Third Reich, and his desire to extend the German Final Solution to the Jews of the Middle East,[1229] nor his knowing of the Third Reich's crematoria to burn Jews after their being gassed to death, nor his wish for an Auschwitz-like crematoria to burn Jews in a crematorium he envisioned being built in the Dotan Valley—but a wish is not an accomplishment[1230]—in Samaria (north of Hebron), then part of British-Mandate Palestine, should the Reich continue its expansion through North Africa into Palestinian territories.[1231]

VARIAN FRY AGAIN, THIS TIME IN MARSEILLE, FRANCE

In that context, with the US still a neutral country, 1940 saw a concern by a small number of American civilians about the plight of Jews who were stateless or foreign nationals. One man who was inspired to act to attempt to find ways of getting Jews out of France was a classics teacher and

---

Safest Place in Europe for Jews," *Haaretz*, Jul. 19, 2017, HAARETZ.COM.

[1229] This idea that it was Al-Husseini who convinced Hitler to adopt a policy of the physical extermination of the Jews of Europe (an instance of the tail wagging the dog) is refuted in Jeffrey Herf, "Haj Amin Al-Husseini, the Nazis and the Holocaust: The Origins, Nature and Aftereffects of Collaboration," *Jewish Political Studies Review*, vol. 26, no. 3/4, 2014, pp. 13–37; *Time of Israel* Staff, "Full official record: What the mufti said to Hitler [from the official German record of the unique meeting of Al-Husseini and Hitler, Nov. 28, 1941]," *Time of Israel*, Oct. 21, 2015; Christopher R. Browning, "A Lesson for Netanyahu From a Real Holocaust Historian," *Foreign Policy*, Oct. 22, 2015; Ofer Aderet, "Yad Vashem's Chief Historian [Dina Porat] on Hitler and the Mufti: Netanyahu Had It All Wrong," *Haaretz*, Oct. 22, 2015, HAARETZ.COM. On Al-Husseini's visit to Sachsenhausen in 1942, see Klaus Gensicke, *The Mufti of Jerusalem and the Nazis: The Berlin Years* (2011), esp. pp. 118-119, 169 (n. 54), cf. pp. 212-248. See further, US Dept. of State, *Haj Amin al-Husayni, the Mufti of Jerusalem, Biographical Sketch No. 60*, April 24, 1951 (Confidential until declassified by the CIA, 2006), retrievable online by a search for "CIA, Husseini, Amin El, Vol. 4"; Jeffrey Herf, *Nazi Propaganda for the Arab World* (2009); David Motadel, *Islam and Nazi Germany's War* (2014); Nastassja Shtrauchler, "Interview with historian David Motadel: Hitler's Muslim stop-gaps" (2017), *Deutsche Welle/DW-German Foreign Office*, QANTARA.DE.

[1230] Arabist Raphael Patai (1910-1996), *The Arab Mind* (1983), Chap. IV (Under the Spell of Language) and Chap. X (Extremes and Emotions, Fantasy and Reality).

[1231] Daniel Siryoti and Erez Linn, "The mufi planned to build crematorium in Dotan Valley," *Israel Hayom*, Oct. 23, 2015; "Mufti Planned 'huge Auschwitz' near Nablus to imprison and exterminate Jews said senior Arab Officer in Mandate Palestine," *Adara Press*, Oct. 25, 2015, ADARAPRESS.COM; Shiryn Ghermezian, "Report: Jerusalem's Grand Mufti Planned Construction of 'Auschwitz-Like' Crematorium in Israel," *The Algemeiner*, Oct. 27, 2015, ALGEMEINER.ORG.

graduate of Harvard, Varian Fry (mentioned above). Aged 32, he set up an office in Marseilles, which was at that time under Vichy administration, and began receiving requests from many wishing to flee German-controlled France. In the US State Department, Secretary of State Cordell Hull's assistant Breckinridge Long (1881-1958) became the Supervisor of the State Department's Immigrant Visa Section; he would use his position to instruct US embassies and consulates in Europe and elsewhere *to do their utmost to delay any applications, even to so act repeatedly, creating bureaucratic hurdles ("red tape") to drag on the handling of requests by foreign Jews for visas or other legal entry into the USA.*

This anti-Semitic bias of the US state department was well known by those who kept abreast of such issues. On September 18, 1940, US Secretary of State Cordell Hull sent a telegram to Hiram Bingham concerning the activities of Varian Fry and Dr. Frank Bohn (of the AFL, the American Federation of Labor, concerned with the plight of trade unionists, a prime political enemy of Hitler's National Socialism), stating: "You should inform Dr. Bohn and Mr. Fry in personal interview if this can be arranged immediately that while Department is sympathetic with the plight of unfortunate refugees, and has authorized consular officers to give immediate and sympathetic consideration to their applications for visas, *this Government cannot repeat not countenance the activities* as reported of Dr. Bohn and Mr. Fry and other persons, however well-meaning their motives may be, in carrying on activities evading the laws of countries with which the United States maintains friendly relations." Reflecting this same attitude were the US Consular officers in Stuttgart, who claimed in 1939 that the quotas allowed about 120,000 visas for Germans (including Jews); less than 20,000 were filled.[1232]

Furthermore, Fry would be told directly by a low-ranking member of the US Consular Corps (the only one willing to talk to him), the Third Secretary to the US Chargé d'Affaires at Vichy, "You must understand that we maintain friendly relations with the French government. Naturally, under the circumstances, we can't support an American citizen who is helping people evade French law. We sympathize with the desire of these poor unfortunates to find a haven overseas, but there is nothing we can do."[1233] Fry had originally been sent by the US-based Emergency Rescue Committee with an agreement from the State Department for 200 visas to be handed out at his discretion. Fry ended up helping some 4,000 desperate people, among which were many artists, poets, essayists, philosophers, authors, musicians, sculptors, and others renown in the arts: Lion Feuchtwanger, Marc Chagall, Hannah Arendt, Marcel Duchamp, Heinrich Mann and Golo Mann (Heinrich's nephew, Thomas Mann's son), André Breton, Jacques Lipchitz, Max Ophuls, Dadaist artist Max Ernst,

---

[1232] Timothy W. Ryback, "Evidence of Evil," *The New Yorker*, Nov. 15, 1993. See esp. discussion about German-Jewish, Manheim-born Ernest Wolfgang Michel.

[1233] Varian Fry, *Assignment: Rescue*, pp. 82, 119; text at "Cordell Hull's Telegram to Hiram Bingham, September 18, 1940," FACINGHISTORY.ORG. Italics added.

Wanda Landowska, Franz Werfel and Alma Mahler Werfel—bringing with her the score of the final Symphony, No. 10, of her first, late husband (1902-1911), Gustav Mahler.[1234] Fry also rescued Alfredo Mendizabel (leading Spanish Catholic philosopher), 1922 Nobel Laureate in physiology and medicine, Otto Meyerhoff, Jacques Hadamard (the "Einstein of France"), Hans Habe, Siegfried Kracauer, Ferdinand Springer, Hans Bellmer, André Masson, Wilfredo Lam, Heinz Jolles, and others renowned in their respective fields, and many others with no fame at all.

Fry was forced to leave France (to which the American Embassy readily agreed), so that his work in Marseilles lasted only a little more than a year, from his arrival on August 14, 1940, until his work was ordered stopped by the French government in August 1941. After necessary paperwork was completed, which took a fortnight or so, Fry was given an updated US passport on September 5, 1941 (some sources say he left France in August 1941). Dr. Frank Bohn, mentioned in the telegram by Cordell Hull quoted above, left France the first week of October 1941.[1235] Once Fry's papers were finally in proper order, he was expelled from France, on Saturday, September 6, 1941.[1236] Fry's work had been accomplished with the personal help (seriously frowned upon by the US Diplomatic Corps) from a Yale graduate inspired by Buddhist teachings of compassion, Hiram (Harry) Bingham IV, US Vice-Consul at Marseilles, who helped provide unapproved documentation (just mentioned). As a result, Bingham's career in the US Foreign Service came to a total halt by

---

[1234] Viennese-born Alma Mahler Werfel (1879-1964), née Alma Schindler, was married to composer Gustav Mahler (1860-1911) from 1902 until his death. She had a love relation (1912-1914) with artist Oskar Kokoschka (1886-1980). Her 2nd marriage (from 1915 until their divorce in 1920) was to architect and founder of the Bauhaus Movement, Walter Gropius (1883-1969). Her last marriage (1929-1945) was with Prague-born novelist, playwright, and poet Franz Werfel (1890-1945). Alma Mahler Werfel's full life with its creative men, incidentally, may remind us here of another exceptional woman, Russian-born psychoanalyst Lou Andreas-Salomé (1861-1937), who had intense relationships (1882 on) with philosopher, philologist, and psychologist Friedrich Nietzsche (1844-1900), and later (1897-1926) with Prague-born poet and novelist Rainer Marie Rilke (1875-1926), and (1911-1937) with Sigmund Freud (1856-1939). See *Sigmund Freud and Lou Andreas-Salomé: Letters*, Ernst Pfeiffer, ed. (1972); Lou Andreas-Salomé, *Nietzsche* (1988); Yves Simon, *Lou Andreas-Salomé* (2004); *Rainer Maria Rilke and Lou Andreas-Salomé: The Correspondence*, Ernst Pfeiffer, ed., Edward Snow and Michael Winkler, tr. (2006).

[1235] Varian Fry, *Assignment Rescue*, pp. 57-68, 92, 139-143, esp. p. 182 (partial list of those rescued); Donald Carroll, "Escape from Vichy," *American Heritage*, vol. 34, no. 4, Jun./Jul. 1983; Ronald Weber, *The Lisbon Route: Entry and Escape in Nazi Europe* (2011), pp. 73-75; Pierre Sauvage, "Varian Fry in Marseille," VARIANFRY.ORG; "Varian Fry," HOLOCAUST ENCYCLOPEDIA/USHMM; Barry Gewen, "For the American Schindler, Writers and Artists First," LITERATURE OF THE HOLOCAUST: WRITING.UPENN.EDU; Ginia Bellafante, "[Varian Fry:] A True Hero, For His Time and for Ours," *New York Times, Late Edition (East Coast)*, Sep. 10, 2017, p. MB1.

[1236] Varian Fry, *Assignment Rescue*, pp. 174-179, esp. p. 179.

war's end; he resigned his final position in 1945.[1237] And Fry, ostracized by his unpopular actions, died at the age of 59, respected only posthumously. In this late development, Fry has been recognized—as at the commemoration of Place Varian Fry at the Marseilles US Consulate, on October 18, 2000, by Felix Rohatyn, US Ambassador to France (toward the end of his appointment, September 11, 1997-December 28, 2000)—as an early exponent (*précurseur*) of extra-governmental actions (*sans frontières*) on behalf of those in harm's or death's way in countries around the world. To date, there have been three streets or squares (*Plätze, places*) named after him: Varian-Fry-Straße/Potsdamer Platz, in Berlin; Place Varian Fry, in Marseilles; and Varian Fry Way, in Ridgewood, NJ.[1238] The memorial organization in Jerusalem, Yad Vashem, has tried to recognize all of those non-Jewish helpers of European Jews. In this work, Varian Fry was the first American citizen to be recognized by Yad Vashem, as a Righteous Among the Nations. Overall, as of early 2017, Yad Vashem had recognized 26,513 such people, from 51 different countries.)

One lesson offered by these rare and brave people, all non-Jews, who risked their lives to help Jews facing an otherwise dreadful death is that we must never assume that the unthinkable will not occur where we live—an invitation not to fall into a comfortable complacency and perhaps also a warning to aid us in being more attentive to worrisome tendencies in the society and world in which we live.[1239]

[1237] Varian Fry, *The Peace that Failed: How Europe Sowed the Seeds of War* (1939); Varian Fry, *Surrender on Demand* (1945); *Varian's War* (film, 2001); *Varian & Putzi*, YOUTUBE; *Varian Fry 01*, YOUTUBE; Nicholas Fox Weber, "Art: A Rescuer of Intellectuals from Vichy France," WIKIPEDIA; *Hiram Bingham IV, Diplomat Rescuer in Nazioccupied France*, YOUTUBE; "State Department Memorandum Outlines Ways to Obstruct Granting of US Visas (June 26, 1940)—Memo from Assistant Secretary of State Breckinridge Long, to State Department Officials," JEWISH VIRTUAL LIBRARY; "Varian Fry: USA," YAD VASHEM.

[1238] "Varian-Fry-Straße," BERLIN.KAUPERTS.DE; "US Embassies and Consulates in France," FR.USEMBASSY.GOV; "NJ Town Names Street After Holocaust Rescuer Varian Fry," RAOULWALLENBERG.NET, Jun. 26, 2005. Cf. *Varian & Putzi*, YOUTUBE, 4:10-5:15.

[1239] See Denis Avey, *The Man who Broke into Auschwitz: A True Story of World War II* (2011). Avey (1919-2015), a British POW at Auschwitz. Wanting to become an eye-witness to the horrors of the Jews in the Auschwitz camp complex, Avey exchanged himself with a Jewish prisoner at Auschwitz, in order to enter Auschwitz III (the Monowitz Concentration Camp, built by IG Farben). Cf. video, *The Man Who Broke into Auschwitz WWII British POW Denis Avey*, at Oxford Univ. Chabad Society, CHABAD.ORG. It was only when he was 90 that Avey was finally ready to write his story. Cf. video, *The Man Who Broke into Auschwitz WWII British POW Denis Avey*, a presentation at Oxford Univ. Chabad Society, CHABAD.ORG. Cf. Susan G. Baird, "The Man Who Broke into Auschwitz," *Library Journal*, vol. 136, no. 19, Nov. 15, 2011, p. 43, LIBRARYJOURNAL.COM, with Avey's teaching summarized by Baird; Charmaine Chan, "The Man Who Broke into Auschwitz," *South China Morning Post* (Hong Kong), Jul. 10, 2011, p. 15. Chan's closing comment touches on the power of the book: "This book commands your attention to the end, which will make you weep."

12. Reversals to German Military Successes, 1942-1943

As the situation became less favorable to the German military, marked especially by some key battles in 1942 and into 1943 (less than two years after the initially successful invasion of German forces), tensions grew within the German headquarters, in part, between Hitler's sense of his superior wisdom on how to run a war, greater than that of his generals and his general staff. His generals could remind themselves, but not him directly, that Hitler had been a private first class (or corporal) in the Great War, and had no further training as a military leader.

The winter of 1941 with the rainy season and then the intense Russian cold had stopped the German advances, but with the coming of spring 1942, German morale was high, once again. When German troops reached the Volga, Hitler ordered the capture of Stalingrad. This had great symbolic value (as would the capture of Moscow or Leningrad, neither of which ever occurred), but beyond Stalingrad were the rich oil fields to the south, in the Caucasus, especially at Maikop, Grozny, and Baku.

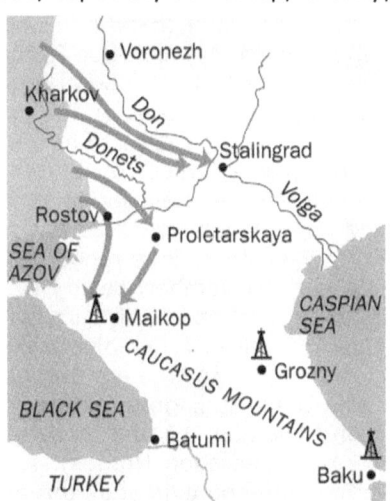

Oil fields at Maikop, Grozny, and Baku

These plans were together called *Fall Blau* (Case Blue), and later *Unternehmen Braunschweig* (Operation Braunschweig). Authorized by Hitler on July 23, 1942, it had two parts. The drive to the south, to capture important oil fields seen as necessary for continued German mobility, was called *Unternehmen Edelweiß* (Operation Edelweiss). The more northern action, called *Unternehmen Fischreiher* (Operation Heron), focused on the capture of Rostov-on-the-Don and Stalingrad. (Stalin died in 1951; the city was renamed Volgograd, in 1961.) In the most southernly Operation Braunschweig, on August 9, 1942,[1240] the German Army was able to capture Maikop, but found it destroyed; it did not reach Grozny. Baku was

---

[1240] Franz Halder, *The Halder War Diary, 1938-1942*, Appendix, p. 680.

never reached by German Army forces and was never even within the range of German bombers (whose range was notoriously limited compared to the Allies' bombers). By November 1942, the German army was on the defensive. (By September 1943, German withdrawals marked the rather definitive end of the Reich's hopes for victory there.)

But already in September 1942, there were significant related tensions between Hitler and the German High Command. On September 24, for example, the notes by Gen. Franz Halder (as he was about to resign his post), addressed "The Idea"—this was basically the idea that Germany would ultimately be victorious, and that, therefore, there was a need on the part of the German army and people for an absolute commitment to fight to the death for the ultimate victory of the Fatherland, the German Reich—as was presented by Joseph Goebbels in his famous Total War speech in February 1943. Halder noted that the Führer was firm in his intention to inculcate "fanatical faith in The Idea. He [Hitler] is determined to enforce his will also into the army." This was when Halder also noted, "My nerves are worn out; also, his [Hitler's] nerves are no longer fresh. We must part" (which happened later that day, as also noted).[1241]

Meanwhile, in the more northerly Operation Heron, the German Army captured Rostov at the very start of this operation, then moved east to the Volga River and approached Stalingrad, which extended over an area some 15 miles long. Germany's over-extended forces with strained supply lines limited its offensive power, while Soviet replacements and new equipment kept being sent in to the area. *By November 18-19, 1942, the German Army reached its greatest advance, controlling some 90% of Stalingrad*. The Luftwaffe was still in its strength and contributed to the bombing of the city. In early November, seeing victory over Stalingrad close at hand, a substantial portion of the Luftwaffe was withdrawn to support Axis operations in Tunisia. Hitler also transferred some of the mechanized divisions of the Army to Western Europe, trying to deal with more than one front at a time. Stalingrad had not, in fact, fallen to the German military, and on November 19, the Soviets launched a counter-offensive, *Operatsiya Urán* (Operation Uranus). A quarter of a million German soldiers, together with approximately three quarters of a million Italian, Rumanian, and Hungarian Axis soldiers faced over 1,400,000 Soviet military. Hitler demanded that the remaining German Armies resist and not surrender, naming the defending forces under Paulus as *Festung Stalingrad* (Fortress Stalingrad). Then, late in these battles, Hitler ordered an increase in the supply by air of military aid to the beleaguered German Army. Hermann Göring as head of the Luftwaffe reassured Hitler, but the Luftwaffe did not have the planes to carry this out. The Russian Air Force, meanwhile, was by now a serious threat and danger for any Luftwaffe flights in the area. Taking all of that into account, *by November 23, 1942, the Axis had been definitively surrounded by the Soviets and had been*

[1241] Franz Halder, *The Halder War Diary, 1938-1942*, entry, Sep. 24, 1942, p. 670.

The Hitler Era

definitively defeated. Hitler repeatedly refused to authorize any retreat. Then, in a final gesture, Hitler promoted Paulus to *Generalfeldmarschall* (General Field Marshal), remembering that no German Field Marshal had ever surrendered to its enemy. Perhaps Hitler expected Paulus somehow to turn the tide of the battle, or, more likely, to commit suicide (to avoid having the military shame of being the first German Field Marshal ever to surrender). On learning of this rather late promotion, Paulus, declared (presumably thinking primarily of Hitler) that he would not do them the favor of killing himself. Paulus then went to meet the Soviet forces and to surrender. When Hitler heard the news of this surrender, he "flew into an indescribable rage, the effects of which fill no less than eight pages of the stenographic record that was taken of his statements." Hitler's offer of one sort of honorable suicide for Paulus was not accepted. To this, Hitler remarked, "How cowardly you must be to flinch before such a deed!"[1242] The surrender took place on January 31, 1943: The Armies under General Paulus that were captured and who surrendered, consisted of between 250,000 and 300,000 Axis soldiers. The news soon reached the German heartland, with the public shocked, realizing that the German military had turned out not to be invincible or unconquerable. (More below.)

Nuclear Fusion, *der Uranverein*, Skiing, & the Manhattan Project

Far from the political confrontations and then the open warfare between armies on the continent, in December 1938, two German physicists, Otto Hahn and Fritz Strassmann, had come across a phenomenon they weren't expected, and which surprised them. Consulting with some colleagues who had left Germany because they were Jewish, or otherwise not ready to live in Nazi Germany, especially their colleague Lise Meitner, who had also been assistant to Max Planck. Hahn and Strassmann published their findings in January 1939. The Reich also set up a secret research project in January 1939, called *der Uranverein*, the Uranium Club. Meitner would analyze the findings of Hahn and Strassmann; with her nephew, physicist Otto Frisch, she would publish the conclusions in February 1939, calling the process nuclear fission. Frisch himself had been forced to leave Germany in 1933; he would determine that a chain reaction using uranium-235 was possible and would release enormous amounts of energy (as in a bomb). He later became a naturalized British citizen and part of the US Manhattan Project.

The power of an atomic explosion was understood as involving one of two paths: one involved manufacturing large amounts of heavy water, or D_2O—the D here is deuterium, an isotope of hydrogen (water itself being, of course, H_2O). Heavy water would slow down neutrons, more effective in invading uranium-235 atoms. The other involved using refined graphite and enriched uranium (uranium-238), which did not require heavy water. *The Germans opted for the first*, and established a secret center in Norway, located in a very remote and inaccessible site, at Vermork, in Telemark, Norway (previously a center for the production of artificial fertilizer. All of

---

[1242] Lt.-Colonel Eddy Bauer, *The History of World War II* (1979), p. 319.

this would be soon known by the intelligence services of various countries. After an unsuccessful British attempt on November 19, 1942 to destroy the facilities at Telemark, Norway—the glider planes used crashing into the Hardangervidda Mountains, the British agents captured, tortured, and killed—a Norwegian effort, Operation Gunnerside, had expert skiers dropped nearby to the German facilities on February 27, 1943. They skied down the ravine, mounted the other side, were able with intelligence to enter the facility, plant bombs, and leave, with the explosion destroying the facility. They then escaped, skiing some 200 miles across land to Sweden, later to rejoin their fellow Norwegian military in the UK. The operations at Telemark began again, after repairs, but intensive Allied bombing of the area inspired the Germans to stop production in Norway and transport its supplies of heavy water to be stored in France. A ferry, the *SF Hydro*, crossing nearby Lake Tinn with this supply of heavy water was sunk by Norwegian saboteurs on the night of February 20, 1944, in effect ending German focused efforts to produce an atomic bomb.

Among the physicists now dispersed around the world, given Germany's limitation of its science to "Nazi science" (with the exclusion of all Jewish and other anti-Nazis of *Mitteleuropa*), were Ernrico Fermi, Niels Bohr, Wolfgang Pauli, Viktor Hess, Gustav Born, and Rudolf Peierls; another was a disciple of Einstein, Leo Szilard, a Budapest-born Jew, who was instrumental in encouraging Einstein to write a letter to the US President, Franklin Delano Roosevelt, dated August 15, 1939, also before the German invasion of Poland. This letter informed the President that the Germans were starting research work with the intention of using new-found physics to produce a bomb with an explosive force quite beyond anything mankind had previously envisioned. Roosevelt responded and set up what was to be known as the Manhattan Project, which produced several atomic bombs, not in time to be used against the Germans, but employed for the first time against the Empire of Japan, on August 6, 1945 (at Hiroshima) and on August 9 (against Nagasaki).[1243]

Surrender at Stalingrad, Total War Speech in Berlin

Meanwhile, only a fortnight after the surrender of Field Marshal Paulus, on February 18, 1943, Joseph Goebbels gave a speech In the Berlin Sportpalast, scene of many glorious moments in earlier years, calling for

---

[1243] "Nuclear Fusion," ATOMIC HERITAGE FOUNDATION, Jun. 4, 2014; "German Atomic Bomb Project," ATOMIC HERITAGE FOUNDATION, Oct. 18, 2016; Timothy J. Jorgensen, "How a Sneak Attack by Norway's Skiing Soldiers Deprived the Nazis of the Atomic Bomb," SMITHSONIAN.COM, Feb. 27, 2018; "Lise Meitner," ATOMIC HERITAGE FOUNDATION; "Lise Meitner (1878-1968)," ATOMICARCHIVE.COM; "Otto Frisch (1904-1979)," ATOMICARCHIVE.COM; "Rudolf Peierls," ATOMICARCHIVE.COM; Sean Coughlan, "The scientists who escaped the Nazis," BBC NEWS, Jul. 17, 2013; "The Atomic Bomb," HISTORY.SANDIEGO.EDU; "Heavy Water," ENCYCLOPÆDIA BRITANNICA; Alan Bellows, "Heavy Water and the Norwegians," DAMNINTERESTING.COM; Joe Duggan, "Adolf Hitler was a ferry ride away from Nazi atomic BOMB material to blow up London," *Express* (London), Sep. 1, 2018.

what he called Total War (with some vagueness about what it amounted to), asking his select audience if they were ready to accept hardships beyond their limited imagination. In his emotionally intense speech, he intended to rouse the German people to an even more intense eagerness to fight on. His secretary, Brunhilde Pomsel, saw him become a *tobender Zwerg*, a raging dwarf.[1244] (More on Goebbels speech and his slip of the tongue, below.) Some kept their questionable belief in an ultimate Nazi victory, despite learning of more losses in the next two years. Not all kept this confidence. For example, in the months after this loss, there would be the White Rose pamphlets discussing the losses at Stalingrad, and the retreat of the German Army from Tunisia (which began on March 2, 1943), along with other military defeats, as well as mentioning the killing of tens of thousands of Polish Jews (from eye-witness reports), found later to be a rather low estimate. Basically, it was a disappointing year for the Reich.

We have seen in other historical situations that a closed group of decision-makers, inspired by a desire for unanimity—whether in the honoring of a leader held to be absolutely infallible, or as a group wanting internal harmony—can lead to systematic distortions of what could otherwise be recognized and dealt with appropriately.[1245] (Once again we can see the power of hope and a drive for conformity of opinion in one's group overriding observation of what is there at the time to take into account.) And here, with the confidence that earlier victory has installed, firm despite changes in the military position on the ground, Hitler was not ready to accept the ancient advice of Sarpedon, son of Zeus and ally to the Trojans, to Hector, Supreme Commander of the Trojans, "Beware the tolls of war, the mesh of the huge dragnet sweeping up the world, before you're trapped, your enemies' prey and plunder—soon they'll raze your sturdy citadel to the roots!"[1246] Most relevant here, of course, is the case of Hitler. Despite limited experience and expertise in the various branches of government, Hitler became in effect the Commander-in-Chief of the Armed Forces (even though his own military experience was limited to the First World War, in which his role was that of a regimental runner,[1247] carrying messages in person from regimental HQ to battalion staffs,

---

[1244] *A German Life* (2016), 6:00-6:10. Pomsel was 103 at the time of the filming. She also called Goebbels a *Kaulquappe*, tadpole: a large head plus a long tail.

[1245] "Group Dynamics and Behavior" (Sect. 6.2), in *Sociology: Understanding and Changing the Social World*. Text modified for web use, UNIV. OF MINNESOTA LIBRARY PUBLISHING/OPEN.LIB.UMN.EDU. Based on book by sociologist Steven Barkan (2014).

[1246] Homer, *Iliad*, 5.559-562 (BK.vv: 5.647-655).

[1247] Georg Bönisch, "Front in Flandern: Hitler-Mythen aus dem Ersten Weltkrieg," *Spiegel*, Mar. 9, 2011; Georg Bönisch, "A Hero in His Own Mind: Hitler Biography Debunks Mythology of Wartime Service," *Spiegel*, Mar. 10, 2011; Dalya Alberge, "Adolf Hitler a war hero? Anything but, said First World War comrades," *The Guardian* (London), Aug. 16, 2010. Cf. Thomas Weber, *Hitlers erster Krieg: Der Gefreite Hitler im Weltkrieg: Mythos und Wahrheit* (2011), Eng., *Hitler's First War: Adolf Hitler, the Men of the List Regiment, and the First World War* (2011), and his *Becoming Hitler: The Making of a Nazi* (2017).

behind the front lines, ultimately promoted to the rank of *Gefreiter*, equivalent to Private First Class in the US military[1248]; he was also wounded in his left thigh from an exploding shell, at the Battle of La Somme, in October 1916, and suffered exposure to mustard gas during the *Flandernschlacht*, the Battle of Passchendaele, also called the Third Battle of Ypres, on October 15, 1918, which rendered him temporarily blind—he was awarded the Iron Cross Second Class, in 1914, and the Iron Cross First Class, in 1918). He also took on the role of the chief economist for the Reich (even though he had no experience in this area); he was chief city planner and architect (even though also lacking training in these specialized areas).[1249] And, as well, he was the supreme decree-maker, the one-man head of the German executive branch, we might say.

At first, all seemed to go well and respect for his astute judgment was quite widespread in Germany. The first year after the invasion of the Soviet Union in June 1941, saw a rapid advance of German troops, similar to the successes of the Blitzkrieg against Poland, Norway, and the Western countries of the Netherlands, Belgium, Luxembourg, and France.

With this recent history of the very rapid conquering of the Low Countries and France by the Wehrmacht together with the Luftwaffe, and the less than splendid way the Soviet Union conducted its war with Finland—and thinking of the Bolshevik USSR as an ultimately core enemy of Nazism and what it stood for—the Hitler and the Nazis saw theReich as the bulwark of European (that is, Germanic) civilization against the inferior beings comprising the Slavic and the Jewish peoples, sometimes referred to as the Asiatic hordes. In brief, Hitler expected to conquer the Soviets and capture Moscow in just a few month in the middle of 1941, after their invasion begun on June 22 of that year.

This was clearly one of Hitler's great miscalculations, fitting into the pattern of over-evaluating one's own power, strength, and superiority, and minimizing the military and moral fiber of the supposedly inferior enemy. This systematically distorted thought would also rear its ugly, distorting head when Hitler considered the UK, the USA, and most significantly and disastrously for the Third Reich, the USSR.)

At this time, a focused and intense program of eliminating undesirable and inferior beings, the Jews, the gypsies, and the Slavs, went into effect by the late summer and fall of 1941. There were reports from a number of governments and resistance movements that were disseminated and

---

[1248] "Comparison of ranks German Army-US Army," TASKFORCEBAUM.DE.

[1249] The billionaire Fritz Thyssen wrote in *I Paid Hitler* (1941), in the chap. "Nazi Economy" (pp. 133-140), at p. 135, of Hitler that "besides the fact that he knows absolutely nothing about matters economic, he cannot even fully understand his economic advisors. He is impulsive and always follows his last impressions... His constant worry [concern] has ever been to keep himself in power. In addition to this, he believes that he alone is a great man, and all others non-entities." Thyssen adds, in the chap. "Nazi Quack Economy" (pp. 141-157), at p. 157, "Taken as a whole, these Nazi achievements are a farrago [a confused mixture] of economic absurdities."

The Hitler Era

were familiar to the various powers. By the end of 1942, for example, a joint statement was made and was presented forcefully in the House of Lords by the Lord Chancellor, Viscount Simon, in the following:

> My Lords, a statement has just been made in the House of Commons on this subject and I am grateful to the noble Lord the Leader of the Opposition for providing the opportunity to make an announcement to your Lordships in the same terms. Trustworthy reports have recently reached His Majesty's Government regarding the barbarous and inhuman treatment to which Jews are being subjected in German-occupied Europe. In particular, we have received a Note on this subject from the Polish Government, which was also communicated to others of the United Nations and has received wide publicity in the Press. His Majesty's Government in the United Kingdom have been in consultation with the United States and Soviet Governments and with the other Allied Governments directly concerned, and a Joint Declaration has been agreed between them, which is being published to-day in London, Moscow and Washington and broadcasted throughout the world. The Declaration is as follows: The attention of the Governments of Belgium, Czechoslovakia, Greece, Luxembourg, the Netherlands, Norway, Poland, the United States of America, the United Kingdom of Great Britain and Northern Ireland, the Union of Soviet Socialist Republics and Yugoslavia and of the French National Committee has been drawn to numerous reports from Europe that the German authorities, not content with denying to persons of Jewish race in all the territories over which their barbarous rule 608 has been extended, the most elementary human rights, are now carrying into effect Hitler's oft-repeated intention to exterminate the Jewish people in Europe. From all the occupied countries Jews are being transported, in conditions of appalling horror and brutality, to Eastern Europe. In Poland, which has been made the principal Nazi slaughter-house, the ghettos established by the German invaders are being systematically emptied of all Jews except a few highly skilled workers required for war industries. None of those taken away are ever heard of again. The able-bodied are slowly worked to death in labour camps. The infirm are left to die of exposure and starvation or are deliberately massacred in mass executions. The number of victims of these bloody cruelties is reckoned in many hundreds of thousands of entirely innocent men, women, and children. The above-mentioned Governments and the French National

Committee condemn in the strongest possible terms this bestial policy of cold-blooded extermination. They declare that such events can only strengthen the resolve of all freedom-loving peoples to overthrow the barbarous Hitlerite tyranny. They re-affirm their solemn resolution to ensure that those responsible for these crimes shall not escape retribution, and to press on with the necessary practical measures to this end."[1250]

And yet, although quite explicit and threatening, such statements would do little to impede the determined efforts of the Third Reich and its allies to continue their well-organized operations of mass killing in the East, especially by this time, late 1942, with the industrial-sized, factory-like, efficient gas chambers and crematoria of the extermination camps.

[1250] "Persecution of the Jews: Allies' Declaration" in *HL Deb [=House of Lords, Debate]*, Dec. 17, 1942, vol. 125, col. 607-612; at col. 607-608.

13. War's End, 1944-1945: Downfall, Devastating Defeat

The last, painful period of the Nazi state before its complete destruction, d*er Untergang* (the downfall) or *die überwältigende Besiegung* (the overwhelming defeat), has also been called *der Zusammenbruch des dritten Reiches* (the collapse of the Third Reich).[1251] The end of the predominant power of the Reich could be clearly seen coming, if not from the defeat of the Wehrmacht at Stalingrad in early 1943, then surely by 1944, when German forces were being overcome both by the massive manpower and military readiness of the Soviet forces, from the east, taking military control over much of Estonia, Latvia, Lithuania, and the *Gouvernement General* (eastern Poland). The Wehrmacht was left free to destroy the Polish Warsaw Uprising (August 1-October 2, 1944), *with the Soviets doing nothing to stop the crushing of the Uprising, finally entering Warsaw only on January 14, "liberating" Warsaw on January 17, 1945.*[1252] This, despite Churchill's strong requests for aid from Stalin.

After significant defeats of the German Wehrmacht by the Soviets at Stalingrad and in the tank battles of Kursk, many of the German military were persuaded that Hitler was leading Germany into disaster; and, in addition, by this time, many of those who had served on the Eastern Front had seen the massacres of thousands of civilians (especially Jews, shot point-blank in ravines or pits, in forests, or in other terrains). One of these was a Captain Axel von dem Bassche-Streithorst, who had seen the SS- and-SD massacre of over 5,000 Jews shot at the Dubno airport, on July 13, 1942,[1253] several weeks after the massacre of some 3,800 Jews at that airport, on May 27, 1942—the day Reinhard Heydrich was shot by British-trained Czech soldiers. (Heydrich died on June 4.)[1254] Bassche-Streithorst, encouraged by Count Klaus Graf Schenk von Stauffenberg (who later would organize the attempt on Hitler's life in the Wolf's Lair on July 20, 1944—Hitler having left the Berghof, for the last time, for the Wolf's Lair, on July 14, 1944), planned to use an occasion of being close to Hitler—he was to demonstrate new-design Wehrmacht wool overcoats (at 6-feet-5-inches tall, with stereotypical "Aryan" features) on November 16, 1943. He would have two hand-grenades with four-second fuses; he could pull the safety pins when next to Hitler, grabbing Hitler, with both of them dying. The day before, the trainload of uniforms was bombed by an Allied air attack on Berlin; the demonstration was cancelled.[1255]

[1251] Helmut Kistler, "Der Zusammenbruch des dritten Reiches," BUNDESZENTRALE FÜR POLITISCHE BILDUNG (BPB), Apr. 27, 2005.

[1252] Maciej Siekierski, "Remembering the Warsaw Uprising," *Hoover Digest*, HOOVER.ORG, Oct. 30, 2004.

[1253] "Massacre of 5000 Jews Described: Shot in Groups Near Large Pit," *The Advocate* (Burnie, Tasmania, Australia), Jan. 3, 1946, p. 1, TROVE.NLA.GOV.AU.

[1254] "Dubno—Guidebook," SHTETLROUTES.EU and TEATRNN.PL; "The Liquidation of Lidice," HISTORYPLACE.COM.

[1255] "Axel von dem Bussche," WIKIPEDIA; "Axel von dem Bussche," IMDB.COM; Adelheid Gowrie, "Obituary: Axel von dem Bussche," *Independent* (London), Feb.

In late 1944, with the Soviets advancing on Germany and Berlin itself, Hitler would leave the Wolf's Lair, in Rastenburg, Prussia, for the last time, on November 20, 1944, flying back to Berlin. Then, Hitler, moving to the Western Front HQ, the Adlerhorst (the Eagle's Eyrie) near Bad Nauheim, ordered an offensive in the West—seen as futile by most German military—hoping to split the British from the American forces, and to make possible an armistice with these Western Allies. That contemplated—so Hitler surmised—he and the German military would be able better to fight back against the Soviet armies. (Hitler's imagination had few bounds.) This began with a Wehrmacht offensive in the Ardennes on December 16, 1944. Not only did the Allies have advance information that was being communicated among German Army posts using the Enigma Code (which the Allied were able to decipher, as discussed above), but the Germans were also largely outnumbered in men and vastly under-equipped in arms, tanks, artillery, and, in addition, the Luftwaffe was by then basically non-existent. It was a hopeless Hitlerian chimera (one of Hitler's several of these, especially in the military situation in 1944-1945).

OVERCAST SKIES AND THE BATTLE OF THE BULGE

This final German offensive in the west, formally commanded by Heinrich Himmler, in his debut appearance as a military general, was called *Unternehmen Nordwind*, Operation Northwind, and in English, the Ardennes Counteroffensive or Battle of the Bulge. The hope (or wish) of the Reich was that this would bring the Western Allies to accept a separate peace with Germany, allowing German forces to mount a counter-attack against the Soviets, who were threatening the very existence of the Reich.

The next day, December 17, 1944, surprised by this attack, some American military were captured by an army unit, the First Panzer Division, *Leibstandarte SS Adolf Hitler*, under General Sepp Dietrich (known from a number of earlier contexts). They, too, were not accorded protections under earlier Geneva Conventions on the treatment of POWs, but machine-gunned to death, an event known as the Malmédy Massacre (to join with the massacres at Babi Yar, Wormhoudt, Lidice, and Oradour-sur-Glane, among many others, as discussed earlier). This last German offensive had some good days, but when the cloud cover cleared, and Allied bombers and fighter planes could come back into action, this battle soon ended, officially on January 25, 1945. When it became clear that the German offensive was a failure, Hitler returned to Berlin on January 15, 1945. He used his specially-armored train, *der Führersonderzug*, the Führer's Special Train, knowing a flight back was not safe, the Allies having full control over the skies. This was on January 16, 1945. During those last days of the Battle of the Bulge in the west, the Soviets began

---

20, 1993, INDEPENDENT.CO.UK; Craig R. Whitney, "[Obituary Notice] Baron Axel von dem Bussche, 73; Joined Officers' Plot to Kill Hitler," *New York Times*, Jan. 20, 1993, p. 11; *Hitler's Bodyguard, Season 1, Episode 11 (Attempt to Kill Hitler at the Wolf's Lair)*, at 15:20-16:50, YOUTUBE.

a major offensive, on January 11, 1945. This would soon lead to their final push to conquer Berlin.[1256] Despite the major destruction Hitler could see on his train return to Berlin, with news of the Soviet offensive adding to the overall military picture, he was still determined that a firm will (his strong will, perhaps with the support of the German people) would triumph. Or at least so he spoke in his last radio address to the German people, on January 20, 1945, almost six years after his Reichstag speech predicting the end of European Jewry, and three years after his Reichstag speech echoing that declaration. Speaking of Asiatic bolshevism, the hurricane from Central Asia, the Jewish international world plot, Jewish Asiatic bolshevism, Hitler took a millennial-large view and declared, "However grave the crisis may be at the moment, it will, despite everything, finally be mastered by our unalterable will, by our readiness for sacrifice and by our abilities. We shall overcome this calamity, too, and this fight, too, will not be won by central Asia but by Europe, and at its head will be the nation that has represented Europe against the East for the last 1,500 years and shall represent it for all times: our Greater German Reich, the German nation."[1257] *We may well ask how much of this was bluff and blunder*, a pure posturing of confidence for the encouragement of the German nation to continue its fight, by now understood by Hitler to be unwinnable: After all, some two years earlier, on Corpus Christi Day, June 24 (1943), Hitler had stated to Baldur von Schirach (at their last meeting ever) that "there was no way out. I might as well shoot myself in the head as think of negotiating peace."[1258]

This was not the first or only time that Hitler would go into a suicidally depressed state of mind: When he escaped from the 1923 Putsch to the house of Ernst Hanfstaengl—Hanfstaengl and Göring escaped into Austria—he was welcomed by Hanfstaengl's wife, Helen, blond and American-born, whom Hitler apparently adored, once falling on his knees and declaring himself her slave.

There is also a (perhaps unreliable) story about that time that Helen Hanfstaengl prevented Hitler from blowing his brains out.[1259] Hanfstaengl, for example, had written explicitly about this, stating that his wife, Helen, had received word from Hitler's lawyer, Lorenz Roder,[1260] that Hitler in

---

[1256] *Hitler's Bodyguard, Season 1, Episode 13 (Poison Gas Plot in the Bunker)*, at 1:25-3:00, YOUTUBE.

[1257] Adolf Hitler, "Radio Address to the German Folk, January 30, 1945," ARCHIVE.ORG.

[1258] Nicolaus von Below, *At Hitler's Side*, p. 173.

[1259] Andrew Nagorski, *Hitlerland: American Eyewitnesses to the Nazi Rise to Power* (2012), and "The Woman Who Prevented Hitler's Suicide: How did Hitler's relationship with a young American woman change history in the 20th century?" The Globalist, Apr. 7, 2012. Cf. "Without hindsight," *The Economist* (London), Mar. 31, 2012; Ian Kershaw, *Hitler: A Biography*, pp. 115, 130-132, 175, 218.

[1260] On Lorenz Roder, defense attorney of Hitler in the Beer Hall Putsch Trial, see David King, *The Trial of Adolf Hitler: The Beer Hall Putsch and the Rise of Nazi Germany* (2017), p. xvii (in "Munich, 1923-1924: Cast of Characters").

prison had decided to starve himself to death; she "sent a message through to say that she had not prevented him [Hitler] from committing suicide in order to let him starve himself to death and that this was the very thing that his worst enemies wished for."[1261]

Was Hanfstaengl writing here for melodramatic flair? In any case, given the situation, Hitler had good reason (if reason, good or otherwise, is needed), given his recent totally unsuccessful attempt to take over the Bavarian government with his Putsch, to be despondent and quite hopeless. We discussed the details of the failed Putsch, above. Moving forward in time, the much later victories of the Allies in 1942 continued into 1943. In the south, the Allies came north via Sicily, with Operation Husky, initiated the night of July 9-10, 1943. These certainly could add to Hitler's sense of the failures and miseries of life.

Only days before, on July 6, 1943, Captain Wilm Hosenfeld wrote his overview of the Reich: "At the time the Nazis came to power, we did nothing to prevent it. We have betrayed our own ideals [*Wir haben die eigenen Ideale verraten*], the ideals of personal freedom, of democratic freedom, and of religious freedom…. We allowed the unions to be smashed, religious denominations to be oppressed. There was no freedom of opinion in the press or broadcasting. In the end, we allowed ourselves to be driven to war [*Zuletzt ließen wir uns in den Krieg treiben*]."[1262]

Meanwhile, from initial positions in the boot of Italy, on a mission to attack a Fascist military camp on August 27, 1943, Allied forces *by mistake strafed a concentration (internment) camp not far from Bari, at Ferramonti di Tarsia*, in Calabria—known as the largest Fascist internment camp in Italy—filled with Jews and other anti-Fascists from various countries. Most, 3,823, were Jews; most, 3,682, were foreign-born.[1263] The Allies moved north from the boot of Italy on September 3, 1943, with the British liberating the camp on September 14, 1943. Of those strafed at Ferramonti by Allied fighter plane machine guns (known to be an American fighter plane), some would die, and others would survive with the help of co-prisoner MDs, lacking, of course, any significant medical supplies. Incidentally, when the American pilot noticed children running around in panic, he drew back and stopped his attack.[1264]

Those same months, Mussolini, suffering pressures from within Italy, resigned on July 25, 1943; he was later arrested, aided in an escape that September by German commandos, then finally recaptured and killed, on May 28, 1945; his lifeless body was hung by the feet in Milan the next day, the corpse beaten and spat upon. Hitler learned almost immediately

---

[1261] Ernst Hanfstaengl, *Hitler: The Missing Years*, p. 117.

[1262] Hermann Vinke, *"Ich sehe immer den Menschen vor mir,"* pp. 231-232; Eng., *Defying the Nazis*, p. 116; "Historisches Sachbuch: Wilm Hosenfeld, 13/3/2016," Mar. 13, 2016, HISTORISCHES-SACHBUCH.WEEBLY.COM.

[1263] "Ferramonti di Tarsia," WIKIPEDIA.

[1264] Carlo Spartaco Capogreco, *Ferramonti: La vita e gli uomini del più grande campo d'internamento fascista, 1940-1945* (1987), pp. 145-146, 167; "Interview: Ferramonti di Tarsia: servizio da 'Sorgente di Vita' del 06.05.13," YOUTUBE.

The Hitler Era

of Mussolini's end, certainly giving Hitler room for thought in his remaining two days before committing suicide, thus avoiding any such similar treatment by Soviets, Allies, or even Germans. And, in Operation Overlord, the Allies invaded the continent of Europe coming across the English Channel, with the D-Day operation of June 6, 1944 along the French coast, at Normandy, then sweeping eastward, with some troops swinging south to liberate Paris (the honor of entering the city in victory being given to Gen. Charles De Gaulle) on August 25, 1944, until entering into Germany, crossing the Rhine River on March 22, 1945.

This invasion was carefully planned and involved (as in many battles) a great deal of what we now call misinformation, that is, reports from the intelligence community that were actually planted to mislead the enemy. In the case of the Normandy invasion, the Allies also did much false preparation of an invasion elsewhere, especially suggesting that the Pas de Calais, not the beaches of Normandy, would be the invasion landing site. The Pas de Calais is located southeast of Dover, a rather direct route into France, slightly over 33 km or 20 mi. (18 nautical miles). By contrast, the Normandy beaches are more than 220 miles to the west of Pas de Calais. British counter-intelligence planted stories of the plans for the invasion at Calais, carried out in part by a double agent code-named Agent Garbo by the British. (His British *nom en clau*, code name, was inspired by Greta Garbo.) To the Germans he was known as Arabel. He real identity was Juan Pujol. His full Hispanic name[1265] was Juan Pujol García (1912-1988). The family name of Puig, and its diminutive here, Pujol, are both Catalan; Pujol was from Barcelona and his Catalan name was Joan[1266] Pujol Garcia.[1267] Pujol, who was both strongly anti-Fascist (anti-Franco and anti-Hitler), and strongly anti-Communist (anti-Stalin), wanted to work against Hitler and the Third Reich. Pujol had escaped Spain to live in Portugal, where he convinced the German intelligence services that he could be of aid to them. With German support, he moved to London, to further his spying (being awarded the Iron Cross) and set up a phantom network of spies (all his invention). In London he could have more direct access to English military and political secrets. Pujol gave much false information in his role as spy for the Third Reich that

---

[1265] In hispanic culture, a person's name consists of his personal name or names, followed by his family name, which is either his father's family name alone or a fuller family name composed of the father's and then the mother's family name (both the child's full family name). Thus the author of *Don Quixote*, Miguel de Cervantes (1547-1616), had the full family name of Cervantes Saavedra, and so is also known as Miguel de Cervantes Saavedra. Here, the shorter family name would be Pujol, and the full family name, Pujol García.

[1266] A more famous Catalan with the personal name of Joan (Catalan for Juan) was the painter and sculptor Joan Miró i Ferrà (1893-1983), known as Joan Miro.

[1267] See Catalan TV interview with him by Josef Maria Espinàs on Sep. 14, 1984: *Joan Pujol Garcia (Garbo), amb Josep Maria Espinàs*, YOUTUBE; Mercè Ubach Dorca and Javier Juárez Camacho, *Garbo, l'espia català que va derrotar a Hitler* (2004); and Spanish film, *Garbo: El Espía;* Eng. version, *Garbo, the Spy* (2009).

finally led the British to contact him. One true gem he reported to Berlin was Operation Torch, the invasion of North Africa by the Allies that began on November 8, 1942. This was sent via mail, through British intelligence, with a postal mark predated from before the invasion, but actually sent after it had begun. His inside information about the Allied invasion of France at Pas de Calais was so convincing that when Hitler heard news of the Normandy invasion—he had gone to bed at about 3 am, and was still asleep at 10 am the next morning—he did not at first believe it.[1268]

This reflected Hitler's usual sleep pattern: His maid at the Berghof said that (typically) Hitler would not get up before 10 am, and not go to bed before 4 am. Dinner would regularly be served at 9:30-10 pm.[1269] That morning (June 6, 1944), Hitler was not awakened until later, with his subordinates respecting his standing demand not to be awakened; on finally hearing the reports, Hitler was even then sure for several key hours that this was a diversionary attack, and that German forces should remain concentrated at Pas de Calais. (By evening, some 156,000 Allied troops had landed on the Normandy Beaches.[1270])

Some took this stubbornness to be just one more example of his living in *Wolkenkuckucksheim* (cloud-cuckoo land, a fool's paradise[1271]). And some powerful Germans of the time appreciated that the actions of Third Reich were even beyond the violence of Attila the Hun,[1272] wrote of Hitler's ideas as in "cloud cuckoo land" (*Wolkenkuckucksheim*). General Rommel in December 1943, after inspecting the German defenses of the Atlantic Wall, described Hitler's idea of an invincible Atlantic wall as farce, as a figment of Hitler's "cloud cuckoo land."[1273] Field Marshal Günther von Kluge (1882-1944) remarked to Hitler in summer 1944, "Yes, my Führer, that is the situation. You must come down from your cloud cuckoo home."[1274]

[1268] Ian Kershaw, *Hitler: A Biography*, p. 804.

[1269] *Former Maid to Hitler Interview*, at 6:45-6:55, 7:55-8:15, YOUTUBE. The maid's name was Elizabeth Kalhammer.

[1270] Ian Kershaw, *Hitler: A Biography*, p. 805.

[1271] This phrase "cloud cuckoo home" refers back to Arthur Schopenhauer's *Wolkenkuckucksheim*, found in *Die Welt als Wille und Vorstellung* (1819), and succinctly, in his letter to Julius Frauenstädt, Aug. 21, 1851: "*Meine Philosophie redet nie von Wolkenkuckucksheim, sondern von dieser Welt.*" ("My philosophy never speaks of cloud-cuckoo land, but of this world.") This, in turn, is traceable to the Greek term *nephelokokkygía* in Aristophanes' *The Birds* (414 BCE).

[1272] Attila the Hun, known for his murderous ways that were ultimately limited to intimidate enemies into accepting military defeat, not aimed at their extermination.

[1273] Stephen Ambrose, *D-Day, June 6, 1944: The Climatic Battle of World War II* (1994), p. 58; Samuel W. Mitcham, *The Desert Fox in Normandy: Rommel's Defense of Fortress Europe* (1997), p. 7.

[1274] Wolfgang Malanowski, "Schluss mit dem Krieg, Ihr Idioten" ["Stop the war, you idiot]," *Der Spiegel*, May 30, 1994, pp. 116-131, at p.131. Kluge's words to Hitler were: "*Ja, mein Führer, so ist die Lage. Sie müssen von Ihrem Wolkenkuckucksheim herabsteigen.*" Kluge had honored himself in the invasions of

The Hitler Era

Again, in 1945, in the last days before the fall of Berlin to Soviet troops, Gen. Gotthard Heinrici (1886-1971), in a meeting with Hitler and other generals in the Berlin Bunker, would comment, "I realized that they were all living in a cloud-cuckoo-land."[1275] Various military advisors had seen the inevitability of the defeat of the Wehrmacht, if not in 1943, then surely by 1944. Hitler would have nothing of that. In his mind, he was not ready to admit defeat when he had dedicated his vital energies for the restitution and ultimate dominance of Germany, giving the German *Volk* its sense of honor and power, while getting rid of inferior beings, subjugating minority cultures, with much slave labor helping to support the German economy, and making free use of crops, livestock, bank wealth, real estate property, and the finest of art collections, garnered from occupied lands.

Hitler, in his own eyes, had not dedicated his life to a German people that would not live up to the demands he had imposed on them—for him, a fair and equitable exchange. But the Eastern Front, where the Third Reich invaded the Soviet Union was soon to be the scene of great military confrontations, with some 200 German Divisions often facing the Soviets. (The Western Allies in the Mediterranean would rarely face more than 10 German Divisions.) As for soldiers killed, some 6 million German soldiers died on the Eastern Front, compared with about 1 million against the Western Allies.[1276] In this time of major set-backs to the German military offensives on the Eastern Front, German generals *who had doubted the wisdom of Hitler's plan to attack the Soviet Union even before it began*—perhaps having a greater vision of the much larger Soviet population and capacity for warfare than the German soldiers and their armaments—came to consider seriously how to end Hitler's power, focusing on how to kill Hitler. There were several plans and attempts at this in 1943 and 1944.

Among the several plots among generals (none of which was successful, we know in retrospect) was one organized by Generals Hubert Lanz, Hans Speidel, and Hyacinth Graf Strachwitz, generals at Kharkov, who planned to arrest and kill Hitler on his visit on February 17, 1943, to Poltava. But Hitler changed his plans to meet at Zaporozhye. Then, Generals Henning von Tresckow and Fabian von Schlabrendorff, meeting with Admiral Wilhelm Canaris of the *Abwehr* (German Military Intelligence) and his assistant Gen. Hans Oster (of the "Oster Conspiracy" from the time just before the Munich Agreement), had bombs to explode during on Hitler's flight on March 17, 1943, to Smolensk. But the bombs planted did not go off, due to the extreme cold in the airplane; the bombs were recuperated and planned to be used again. With an operation designed

---

Poland, France, and the Soviet Union, and had been made OB West (Supreme Commander, West), on July 3, 1944. Suspected of conspiracy and traitorous contact with the Allies, Hitler dismissed him on August 17, 1944; Kluge committed suicide two days later, taking potassium cyanide capsules.

[1275] Cornelius Ryan, *The Last Battle: The Classic History of the Battle for Berlin* (1966), p. 273.

[1276] *Oliver Stone's Untold Story of the United States (2012), Season 1, Episode 1 (World War Two)*, at 51:05-57:55, YOUTUBE.

by Henning von Tresckow and Fabian von Schlabrendorff, days later, on March 21, 1943, Colonel Rudolf Christoph Freiherr von Gersdorff accepted to go on a suicide bomb mission, with the intention of killing Hitler as he attended an exhibition for *Heldengedenktag*, Heroes Memorial Day—the equivalent of Memorial Day, a Nazi term replacing in 1935 the earlier *Volkstrauertag*, People's Day of Mourning—in Berlin, exhibiting captured Soviet war booty. Present would be not only Hitler, but also Göring, Himmler, and Wilhelm Keitel (General Field Marshal and Chief of the OKW, the *Oberkommando der Wehrmacht*, the High Command of the German Armed Forces). This attempt was thwarted by Hitler's change of plans, cutting the meeting short[1277] (recognizing the Allied air superiority by then, the Allies bombing Berlin at will. This began with a wave of attacks on January 30, 1943 (the tenth anniversary of Hitler's becoming Chancellor), with the impressive British de Havilland DH-98 Mosquito, a twin-engined, high-performance plane that as a bomber, reached speeds of 415 mph,[1278] making for an unpredictable, but serious, danger for those on the ground, such as for Hitler and his companions that day. *It was not for lack of plans or efforts that Hitler managed to survive all of these attempts.*[1279] The best-known attempt of that period of the war was on July 20, 1944, and it too did not succeed in killing Hitler. The attempt did come close to succeeding. Those involved were arrested and killed in large numbers, some by murder, others by forced suicide, and others by trial in the People's Court, under Judge Roland Freisler, followed by gruesome death sentences. (More, below.)

Things were not easy for the German military from late 1942 and especially from mid-1943. Hitler's response was to order that no general surrender and no army retreat from any land still held. In tandem with this, Goebbels had a great chore on his hands: it had been relatively easy for Goebbels to generate great enthusiasm on the part of the German people, when he spoke of one military success after another. He certainly had a captive audience (the source of information in the Third Reich was a controlled monopoly, with all communication by newspaper, newsreels, films, and in radio and large public speeches supervised and defined by Goebbels and his Ministry. His task was much more difficult when the German public knew of the losses on the Eastern Front, first the defeat and surrender at Stalingrad (August 23, 1942-February 2, 1943) and then, perhaps militarily more significant, with the Wehrmacht loss at Kursk, in

---

[1277] *Hitler's Bodyguard, Season 1, Episode 9 (Flights into Danger)*, esp. 31:45-38:45, YOUTUBE; "6 Assassination Attempts on Adolf Hitler," HISTORY.COM, Apr. 29, 2015 (esp. #3-6; "List of assassination attempts on Adolf Hitler," WIKIPEDIA.

[1278] "30th January 1943—Mossies [slang for mosquitos] put the kibosh on Herr Göring & Goebbels," PEOPLESMOSQUITO.ORG.UK, Jan. 29, 2014; Robert Dowson, "Berlin bombed by British; Goering 'pep talk' halted," UPI ARCHIVES, Jan. 30, 1943.

[1279] On these various assassination attempts, see William L. Shirer, *The Rise and Fall of the Third Reich*, pp. 1018-1022; Alan Bullock, *Hitler: A Study in Tyranny*, pp. 736-738; Ian Kershaw, *Hitler: A Biography*, pp. 820-824.

The Hitler Era

the world's largest tank battle ever, involving 6,000 tanks, 4,000 aircraft, and 2,000,000 soldiers (July 5-August 23, 1943). These were immense battles. In the long Battle of Stalingrad, the estimate of Axis soldiers, from Germany, Romania, Italy, and Hungary who were killed, wounded, or missing in action (MIA) was 750,000-800,000. On the Soviet side, the numbers were 1,100,000-1,130,000, plus some 40,000 civilians killed. (By comparison, the total number of American armed forces lost in all of World War II was estimated to be just under 417,000.)[1280] There were some 15 million US in the military, some 12% of the population, representing some 25% of Allied military. Other comparisons here are informative: The Soviet countering of the Summer 1944 German Central Group Army led to some 900,000 German casualties. By comparison, the total number of German soldiers facing the Allies in the West totaled only 700,000. And in the Battle of Stalingrad alone there were some over 290,000 Soviet soldiers killed. While the US did supply about two-thirds of all war materiel (guns, artillery, cannons, trucks, and so on), the actual number of soldiers killed was much greater for the Soviet Army.

The pivotal battle of Kursk, which also ended in a Soviet victory, began as the start of what the Germans called *Unternehmen Zitadelle* (Operation Citadel), on July 5, 1943. Days later, Hitler learned of the Allied invasion of Sicily on the night of July 9-10, 1943. He judged that German troops on the Eastern Front would be needed to aid the Italian military in resisting these Allied offenses. Hitler called for the temporary pause in the Operation on July 17; the last battles are reported to have occurred on August 23. In that time, on July 25, 1943, Mussolini was ousted from power in Italy; Wehrmacht paratroopers and SS Men, rescued Mussolini on September 12, 1943; on September 14, he and Hitler met at the Wolf's Lair. The reprieve was short-lived; Mussolini was captured by Italian partisans on April 28, 1945, shot, hung by his feet in Milano, and beaten bloody, even though already dead. *(News of this violence against the corpse of Mussolini was known to Hitler before his decision to commit suicide.)* And, as Sicily was being invaded by the Allies, on July 24-25, 1943, RAF and US bombers attacked the city of Hamburg with more than 5,000 tons of bombs and incendiaries; 50,000 citizens of Hamburg were killed and many more left homeless. (We might mention here the later bombing of Dresden by the Allies, on February 13-15, 1945, perhaps killing many more, with estimates running from 35,000-150,000 civilians killed.) All in all, the Axis military position was being pushed back along several military fronts. Whatever the details, Operation Citadel was not a successful German operation; the Soviets had withstood the offensive, *the last major German offensive in the Soviet Union.* For the Germans, there were immense losses of men, tanks, and Luftwaffe warplanes. *This*

[1280] "Battle of Stalingrad: World War II," ENCYCLOPÆDIA BRITANNICA; "Battle of Stalingrad Facts: Soviet Russia, Part 2," HISTORY/RUSSIA; "Death Tolls for the Man-made Megadeaths of the 20th Century: Pieces of Wars," NECROMETRICS.COM; "World War 2 Statistics," *Second World War Statistics* estimates 395,000 UK, 405,000 American, 5,530,000 German, and 9,750,000 Soviet military deaths.

battle, the battle of Kursk, would destroy German offensive capabilities in the East and no further major offensive operations were undertaken from that time on. Operation Citadel began on July 5, 1943; with a successful Soviet counter-offence to the south, at Kharkov, August 12-23, 1943, ending with a significant German defeat (Fourth Battle of Kharkov; Belgorod-Kharkov Operation). Thus began the Soviet drive to Berlin.[1281]

With these losses in the awareness of the German people, Goebbels' work was cut out for him: he had given a rousing speech on February 18, 1943, after the loss at Stalingrad, but before the subsequent loss at Kursk, showing to Hitler his resolute commitment to stand by his Führer to the very end, with the concept of Total War being presented explicitly to the German people, carefully orchestrated and recorded for transmission by radio and for distribution in newsreels. What this total war was to be was left vague, but it did make clear that this was asking for a commitment of the German people to give their full focus to helping the war effort and being ready to sacrifice absolutely everything for the Führer (presumably even their property, lives, and loved ones). One German was to comment about Goebbels in this speech, "What did that demagogue demand? For us the war was very 'total' already. An elite German army had just been annihilated, sacrificed by Hitler, and we civilians were being bombed with greater force and frequency than ever before."[1282] On the day of Goebbels' Total War speech, February 18, 1943—and, likewise in response to the disastrous loss of the German Army to the Soviets, Sophie Scholl and her brother Hans distributed leaflets at the University of Munich, holding that the war was lost, that continuing it would only result in many more deaths (as came to pass), and calling for a rejection of the entire Nazi project.

Nazi Values and Worldview: A Synopsis of Global Shifting Sands

It is helpful to recognize the understanding that was influencing the extremes of Hitler's thinking in the final weeks of the war: significant shifts in his focus and in his reading of the situation, of the German military and public, and of his basic relationship with the German people, in the light of basic Nazi values, in a situation that had not been envisioned during the zenith of Hitler's power and popularity. And so, if we start with the first years after World War I, there was the conviction that that war had been lost not by a valiant army but by treacherous forces on the home front, liberal politicians, and, ultimately, the Jews (the Jews of Germany and the cohort of international Jewry). There was the belief that the core enemy of National Socialism was the Bolshevik movement—it, too, readily identified as one means world Jewry was using to control the world: an intense hatred of the Jew. There was the central, honored position of the German people, the *Volk*, and the concept (a conceived and theoretically defined ideal) of a *Volksgemeinshaft*, a unified community of equals, consisting only of true Germans, the *Volk*. The

---

[1281] "Battle of Kursk" and "Belgorod-Khar'kov Offensive Operation," both at MILITARY.WIKIA.ORG.

[1282] D. von Schwanenflügel Lawson, *Laughter Wasn't Rationed*, pp. 268-269.

resultant nation would be described in a slogan as *Ein Volk, ein Reich, ein Führer*, One People, One Empire, One Leader. This implied a unified country, with an entire pure, like-minded *Volk* community in full support of the Führer: "*Führer befiehl, wir folgen dir.*" ("Führer/Leader, command; we follow") was an expression repeated with enthusiasm at various rallies and other large events in the Reich. There was an immediate concern with the economic plight of the German people, both in the first years at the end of World War I, and following it, and again, once the Great Depression came on, in late 1929. There was an interest in protecting all ("true") Germans, whether living in Germany or across Eastern Europe.

These ideas did not come out of a vacuum, or full blown out of the head of Hitler (as Athena was said to be born from her father, Zeus). If we look at pre-World War I Germany, there were several key ideas of National Socialism already in the winds. It was not Hitler who created the important idea of a national living space (*Lebensraum*), something in the German consciousness at least since a book was published in 1904, written by the German author Friedrich Ratzel (1844-1904), which addressed the relation of a people and its physical surroundings.

And while hatred of Jews goes back centuries, the concept of anti-Semitism was a nineteenth-century coinage, along with a number of other new terms ending in -ism: nationalism, capitalism, egoism, utilitarianism, socialism, racism, bolshevism, communism, conservatism, agnosticism, determinism, existentialism, solipsism, humanism, idealism, optimism, pantheism, and on and on. The point of this coinage (anti-Semitism) was *to take the idea of hatred (of the Jews) and cast it as a theory or doctrine, not an emotional attitude. It was, thus, a kind of euphemism.*

The idea of a Master Race (*Herrenrasse*), taken to be superior to other races, was not new with National Socialism or with Hitler's writings, either. This too is an idea that came to light during the nineteenth-century. While Darwin, as discussed above, was investigating the way in which different environments made it more likely that certain of a species would live to reproduce, and others less likely, which he called the theory of natural selection, this was taken by fellow British thinker Herbert Spencer and given an ethical interpretation, holding that those who were best adapted to their world were worthier of continued existence. (This is turning a pattern into a value, attempting to derive an "ought" from an "is," as is said in philosophy.) This Spencerian variant teaching was further transformed into a doctrine that claimed that the stronger had the right to exercise their power in the submission of those who were weaker: this was to be interpreted to apply to one nation over others. In simple terms, this was the questionable theory that might makes right. The Third Reich saw itself, at least at first, as this stronger nation with the right to subjugate, enslave, or murder lesser peoples. Hitler made this sort of point in a lecture in the German town of Erlangen, on November 13, 1930, to an audience consisting of primarily university professors and students repeating an idea from *Mein Kampf*. There, Hitler stated, "We know this much: every being strives for expansion and every nation strives for world domination [*jedes Wesen strebt nach Expansion und jedes Volk strebt nach Weltherrschaft*].... A people that is too cowardly or no longer possesses the courage or the strength to meet this goal [*das Volk, das dieses Ziel sich zu stellen zu feige ist, den Mut nicht mehr besitzt oder die Kraft nicht mehr hat, den Weg zu finden*] takes the second path, one of abdication and of personal surrender [*dieses Volk betritt dann den zweiten Weg, und zwar den des Verzichtens, der Selbstaufgabe*], which ends up in annihilation [*der endlich bei der Vernichtung*]."[1283]

These various values that were accepted and promoted by the National Socialists had greater or lesser importance through the time of Third Reich. This was not a random shifting based on whim. It could be seen as a form of responsiveness to changing conditions—a responsiveness that was kept within limits that were tolerable—at least at first. Looking briefly at the history of Reich in this light, we can see that the early actions involved consolidating power and improving the situation of the vast majority of Germans, who in 1933 were still suffering from the consequences of the 1929 economic crash of the New York stock market, felt around the world.

The Jews were a nuisance and an early attempt to gather the German people behind the National Socialist hatred (the boycott of May 1, 1933, administered by the SA, made part of the police force days before by Hermann Göring) *was not a great success* in that many Germans did not go along with SA instructions to keep out of Jewish stores and businesses.

In just two and a half years, though, by the week of the Nuremberg Party Rally of September 1935, Goebbels could give a speech linking the primary enemy of the Reich, Russian Bolshevism and the USSR, with Jews; this was followed two days later by Hitler's issuing the Nuremberg Laws of 1935, stripping all German Jews of their citizenship with its legal rights, and making them subjects of the Reich.

The interest in reestablishing German self-respect, by showing its new strength and military might took center stage. (Not that the condition of the Jews improved at all.) First there was the 1936 remilitarization of the Rhineland, then the *Anschluß*, the annexation, of Austria, on March 12, 1938, with a new problem arising: the significant Jewish population of that land, mostly in Vienna. Soon thereafter, on March 15, Reinhard Heydrich, head of the SD (Sicherheitsdienst, the Security Service, under Heinrich Himmler's SS) issued instructions on the treatment of Jews. He would set up a program to process the application of Austrian Jews to emigrate (leaving their property and wealth behind). This would be followed in later years by a more aggressive approach to the question of

---

[1283] "Document No. 28: 13. November 1930, Rede auf NSDstB-Versammlung in Erlangen," pp. 90-106, at p. 101, in Adolf Hitler, *Reden, Schriften, Anordnungen. Februar 1925 bis Januar 1933. Vol. IV: Von der Reichstagswahl bis zur Reichspräsidentenwahl, Oktober 1930-März 1932. Part 1: Oktober 1930-Juni 1931*, Constantin Goschler, ed. (1994); cf. Jochen Thies, *Hitler's Plans for Global Domination: Nazi Architecture and Ultimate War Aims* (2012), p. 51; Gary C. Fouse, *Erlangen: An American's History of a German Town* (2005), p. 160.

Jews (the Jewish Question).[1284] This was also followed by a series of confrontations with the French and mostly with the British over the Sudetenland, the highlands within Czechoslovakia that gave it a natural protection against possible German aggression; Prime Minister Neville Chamberlain and the British were to negotiate a deal with Hitler that gave him their agreement that he take over these lands, presumably with a high German population, for the safety of those Germans. Then, as the war began, after the invasion of Poland, military expansionist dreams, outlined earlier in *Mein Kampf*, were being realized, with land east of Germany the obvious target for conquering, to realize the goal of more *Lebensraum* for the German population. The new populations of Jews this brought were now a further, increasing problem.

Heydrich developed great plans: France was conquered in June 1940. Its island off the eastern coast of Africa, Madagascar, was eyed as a place where Jews could be deposited, to die in that unhealthy climate. But when the plans to bring Britain to surrender were clearly not going to happen, later in 1940, this Madagascar idea was scrapped (the British Navy being a formidable obstacle to shipping Jews by sea to Madagascar).

With the invasion of the USSR the next summer, millions more Jews were added, making the Jewish Question ever more pressing. Mass murders began, the methodical rounding up and shooting large numbers of Jews. Then, with the development of an organized, factory-like operation of delivery of Jews (and others) by train and killing large numbers in extermination camps, driving them into chambers where they were gassed to death, gave an efficient answer to the question of what to do with all of these vermin (especially the Jews). For that period of time, until perhaps late in 1944, the issue of war aims and the elimination (extermination) of Jews from Europe worked in league with one another.

CONTINUED MASS KILLING VERSUS A FOCUS ON THE DEMANDS OF WARFARE

That said as synopsis, now came a major shift! Conflict arose toward the end of that period: trains used to transport Jews to Death Camps[1285] limited the ability to move the German military efficiently from place to place, as Hitler and military advisors felt was needed for the war effort. Militarily, things were closing in on the Reich, in the west, and, especially, in the east. By the beginning of 1945, the situation had changed for the worse (for the Reich): The Soviets had taken the offensive in the east, taking back the territories earlier occupied by the Wehrmacht, and moved into Poland toward their ultimate target, Berlin. The other Allies had invaded from the south, via Sicily and up the boot of Italy toward Rome.

[1284] "The Establishment of the Gestapo Leitstelle Vienna (regional headquarters)," DOEW.AT (DÖW: DOKUMENTATIONSARCHIV DES ÖSTERREICHISCHEN WIDERSTANDES—DOCUMENTATION ARCHIVE OF AUSTRIAN RESISTANCE).

[1285] Traffic management (train scheduling) was directed by Bureau 33 of the GEDOB (*Generaldirektion der Ostbahn*), Head Office of Eastbound Traffic, under Walter Stier. See *Shoah* (1985), *Second Era, Part 1*, 1:31:25-1:57:20; Stephen Potyondi, "Ziel Treblinka—Final Destination Treblinka" (2006), ARCHIVE.ORG.

On June 6, 1944 ("D-Day"), the Western Allies invaded Fortress Europa (German-controlled Western Europe), landing at beaches in Normandy, to move into Germany itself. There was an important shift in Hitler's focus by this time, and it only became more extreme as the next few months went by. (We know he committed suicide on April 30, 1945.)[1286]

Refocusing during The Morose Twilight of Disconsolate Idols

The ending days of the Third Reich were not very much a twilight of the gods, a *Götterdämmerung*,[1287] with the impetuosity, the high drama, the urge for individual sentimentality, or the weighty pathos of a very German *Sturm und Drang* enactment. It was more a pathetic breaking down of idols, a twilight of the idols, a *Götzendämmerung*,[1288] with, to use a metaphor by Nietzsche, the world acting as a hammer, destroying delusions of self-grandeur, omnipotence, a haughty manner, an attitude of condescending superiority, and a serious underestimation of those dismissed as inferior, dehumanized sub-humans, who proved to be more powerful and resilient than imagined. *What possible shifts or decisions could Hitler make to preserve his sense of his mission, a refocusing that would allow him to carry on in ways that he saw as quite appropriate and ultimately visionary, as always (in his eyes)?*

Propaganda Minister Joseph Goebbels carried out a concerted effort to give the German people hope and even confidence in the ability of their military to come through this war with victory—even after the defeats at Stalingrad and Kursk (both significant as marks of the turning tides of the war). Talk of secret weapons that would destroy England in days and force this Western enemy to surrender, was impressive for those who still had a modicum of desire for hope. At first these were described in rather general, non-specific terms, which allowed for an extensive application of one's imagination. Some ideas that were thrown around were based on early descriptions of these weapons as *Vergeltungswaffen* (vengeance or retaliation weapons), or *V-Waffen*. They were rockets, called V-1 and V2. When the V-1 rockets were first fired on Britain (on June 13, 1944), and

---

[1286] One questionable theory holds that Hitler was drugged (before he could commit suicide), taken away by car through the town of Rottach am Egern (oddly, south of Munich near the Austrian border), transferred by boat to Norway, and to Argentina by German U-Boat, presumably the advanced Type XII submarine. Why would the trip to Norway go from Berlin down to south of Munich? How was a U-boat voyage possible after the end of the war, requiring the (defunct) German Navy to support its sailors, to purchase needed fuel, and to operate its submarines with no Third Reich to support its activities? See Joseph P. Farrell, *Nazi International: The Nazis' Postwar Plan to Control Finance* (2008); Ángel Alcázar de Velasco (a spy and a *falangista*, belonging to the *Falange española*, a fascist group supporting Franco), *Escape From the Bunker*, Harry Cooper, ed. (2010); Harry Cooper, *Hitler in Argentina: The Documented Truth about Hitler's Escape from Berlin* (2014).

[1287] Here we may think of Richard Wagner's 1876 composition by this name.

[1288] We may recall Friedrich Nietzsche's late work (pub. in 1889) by this name (*Götzendämmerung*), with full title (in Eng.) of *Twilight of the Idols, or, How to Philosophize with a Hammer*, punning of the title of Wagner's orchestral opus.

The Hitler Era

V2 rockets deployed in early September 1944 and there was no pleading for peace on the victims' part, the belief (or disappointing delusion) that Germany had a war-turning weapon in its new arsenal lost its footing.[1289]

Even German POWs held in Britain, seeing how little damage was in fact inflicted on Germany's island enemy, were disillusioned: Of the 244 V-1 rockets fired at London on the night of June 12-13, 1944, 45 crashed immediately, and 112 did reach London. By the end of June there had been a thousand V-1 rockets fired at England. (Of course, the British were not at all brought to their knees by these attacks.) As German POW First Lt. Kostelezky put it on July 8, 1944, "When we hear about our reprisal weapon, and the first reports came to us at Cherbourg about London being a sea of flames, we said to ourselves, 'things will be all right after all...' Now I realize that all this reprisal business is only fit for a comic paper [the comic strips]."[1290]

How, though, did these last months, with defeat after defeat of German military force, impact Hitler, his thinking, his judgment, and his new-found attitudes, especially (not toward the Jews, but) toward his Generals and the German people, overall? As the situation in Germany became ever bleaker, a joke was being circulated: Two friends meet on the street. The first asks, "What's new?" "There are two things new," the second responds. "One is good and one is bad." "Oh, let's hear the good news first!" "Hitler is dead." "And the bad news?" "It's not true!"[1291]

HITLER'S MUTATING IDEAS DURING THESE DISTRESSING TIMES

In any case, Hitler was faced with a very fundamental question at this point in time, in light of the events that had been taking place, given his two core visions of the world he would create. First was his vision of a great world-dominant Germany composed of a superior race of humans, in charge over all other peoples, starting with the European nations and peoples. Here, the related ideas of *Lebensraum* (living space) and German (Nordic, Aryan) superiority went hand in glove. Along with this was Hitler's dream of exterminating Jewry, a virus, poison, bacillus, a parasitic, self-centered group. Hitler's anti-Semitism went beyond a desire to avoid contact with Jews, keeping them from his neighborhood or private clubs, or minimizing their presence in government, work, and university settings; it was more than a disgust at Jews: *It was an intense desire to exterminate, to annihilate, to kill the entire Jewish population of Europe; and this, as a most heartfelt drive (if that's the right term here).*

This was a desire that could perhaps be fulfilled if the German military could continue in its crushing all opposition from the Atlantic in the west to the Soviet Union in the east. After, however, the failure of the German offensive (as he expressed in his meeting with a number of allied Foreign Ministers, on November 27, 1941) to achieve its short-term goal of

---

[1289] Alfons Heck, *The Burden of Hitler's Legacy*, pp. 99, 134.
[1290] Sönke Neitzel and Harald Welzer, *Soldaten: On Fighting, Killing, and Dying*, pp. 189, 374.
[1291] D. von Schwanenflügel Lawson, *Laughter Wasn't Rationed*, p. 315.

capturing Moscow in the autumn of 1941, Hitler had apparently rethought some of his basic principles. If we look at Hitler's slowly growing sense that the Germany that he envisioned and wanted to bring the German people to with his guidance, encouragement, and insistence, would not rise to his demands and vision, perhaps deliberating abandoning the vision he had so clearly and strongly set forth for them, we may sense that his disappointment in them was quite intense.

This was in keeping with his firm reluctance to see any problems as his responsibility and doing: if the Jews couldn't be blamed, it was the German people, and certain of the generals or other leaders of the Reich, who had failed (of course not Hitler himself). They had been called to their potential greatness and had not measured up to the task. As such, they were proving their inferiority and, so, were destined to be crushed if not annihilated, as was appropriate (given the basics of Hitler's interpretation of social Darwinism set forth by Spencer and others).

In this way, we can perhaps appreciate that Hitler, in great consistency of thought, came to view ("icily" as he said) that a weak German people deserved annihilation. That's to put it short and sweet. And, given that the German people did not live up to what he dreamt they could be, were incapable of rising to his vision, then they were no longer an inspiring, driving force for Hitler, to support, encourage, and cajole as need be. Let them die, we might say! In short, Hitler would come to the position (or was reinforced in that position) that to the stronger belong the spoils, and to the weaker, submission or even annihilation. If Germany would not rise to the challenge of remaining committed to fight to the death, and there were other forces (most significantly, the Soviet military and its men and armaments), then Germany should accept its failure to be the master race Hitler had taught. This thinking would go through stages in those next years, culminating in a most extreme *Führerbefehl* (Führer decree, absolute orders from the Führer) known as the Nero Order (*Nerobefehl*) on March 19, 1945, within weeks of when Hitler would commit suicide at the end of April 1945.

VITAL FINAL NON-MILITARY PROJECTS: *JUDA VERRECKE*, ONCE AND FOR ALL

Or, as the call against Jews put it, *"Juda verrecke!"* ("Jewry, die a miserable death!" or "Jews, go croak!"). So, with the preceding comments as a framework, we can consider some of the important machinations of Hitler's grand project and the elimination of European Jewry as part of that: The work of resolving the Jewish Question was putting great strain (at first) on the men who were involved in the *SS Einsatzgrupppen* operating primarily in the USSR, on those running the extermination camps located in eastern Poland, and on German military transports, with a conflict of demand for trains, which were in competition for use to transport troops to needed war areas or to transport Jews to the gassing and cremation centers called *Vernichtungslager* (extermination camps).

The demands of the war effort itself, which required the logistics of the transport of men, equipment and ammunition, food, and other supplies needed for the effective operation of the military, called for a certain

The Hitler Era

amount of rolling stock, that is, of railway cars for transporting all of these to the various war fronts.

In vital competition for these cars was the Third Reich's second project of the extermination of European Jewry. In terms of war strategy, we might think that the war effort would hold complete primacy over the problems of transporting Jews from across Europe to death camps (*Vernichtungslager*, extermination camps). What we see, in retrospect, rather, is that the Final Solution (the extermination of European Jewry) *actually took a certain priority over military demands for railway cars*.

What, indeed, was happening? From a military logistics point of view, this made no sense at all, at least at first glance. And yet, if we take seriously the idea that Hitler (and others) had fundamentally (but not publicly) given up on their dream of taking over the Soviet Union and using all of its fertile lands depopulated of its earlier Slavic population, making room for German settlers as Germany expanded its *Lebensraum* (living space)—called for in *Mein Kampf* and through the years—*then we have another appreciation of the times*. That is, if the expansionist dream was not to be realized—this being taken to be the failure of the German people to live up their potential—then what was left? We may appreciate that the murderous repulsion, fear, and disgust at Jewry were still strong sentiments to Hitler and his close associates (such as Himmler and Goebbels), with the power to give *priority to the extermination of Jews, even above the concern to beat back the Soviet armies.*

While the Nazi vision had its own overall integrity and consistency, *the Russian weather and the massive resistance and counter-offenses of the Soviet military* were thwarting Germany's military expansionist vision. And yet, nonetheless, *the operations of the many concentration camps and extermination camps, administered by the SS under Himmler, were going on unhampered.* (There were to be no Allied bombings of any of the camps, deemed secondary to the interest in the war effort itself.)

Despite this, in other targeted areas of the Reich, there was a "devastating scale of Allied attacks [that was so intense that it] did much to undermine ordinary Germans' belief in their government's propaganda." This was so much so that a joke from December 1943 reports Goebbels' distress at losing two suitcases—metaphorically referring to a new, now obvious, inability of the Reich to carry out *Vergeltung* (retaliation, revenge) and to achieve *Endsieg* (final victory).[1292]

The Wehrmacht confrontations with the Soviets, from a tactical military point of view, repeatedly called for a retreat by the Wehrmacht. While Hitler did in fact call for some retreats, and did in fact shift troops from the Soviet front to southern Europe—despite generalizations to the contrary—there were clearly certain battles in which Hitler absolutely forbade any retreat, but, rather, called for the loyal German soldiers to fight to the death.

[1292] Both quotes from Niall Ferguson, *The War of the World: Twentieth-Century Conflict and the Descent of the West*, p. 569.

This was not obviously a matter of sheer ignorance if not stupidity on Hitler's part. If we can give him some credit in this military domain, we would need some other sort of explanation of what led him to put forth many of his orders to the military, as Commander-in-Chief. This may be multifold, that is, it may have a military basis as well as other explanations. The sense on its own that this war was total, a battle to the death, to victory or to extermination, could call for the ultimate sacrifice (as is often said) of the military, to die for the well-being of the country. That would contain its own self-standing rationale. And yet, something else was going on! As one source ponders, "It seems incredible that eleven months before the end of the war it was possible for long trains to travel constantly back and forth between Hungary and Birkenau when one would have thought they were urgently required for the war effort."[1293]

The mystery of this dissolves if we consider the strong drive to eliminate Europe's fundamental enemy, world Jewry, a project with its own, separate influence on decision-making: to hold off the Soviets, giving the blood and lives of millions of young Germans, would keep the extermination operations against the Jews (and others) going on, unimpeded. This is a military consideration, but one that is intimately connected with the desire for continuing mass killings, so long as would be possible. And, if we take the turning point of the war on the Eastern Front (the USSR and neighboring lands) to be either in late 1941, with the halting of the German offensive toward Moscow, or in 1942-1943 with the battles around Stalingrad and Kursk, we find that the killing centers were continuing at full capacity, even into summer of 1944.

We may recall that at that time, Hungary (which had been helped out of the depression of the 1930s by its trade with Germany and Italy, and had sent off troops to fight against the Soviets), in March 1944 began negotiations with the UK and the USA for an armistice. Hitler, on learning of these, on March 12, 1944, ordered *Unternehmen Margarethe, I* (Operation Margarethe, I), the *Deckname* (codename) for the tactical invasion of Hungary by the Wehrmacht, initiated in a week, on March 19.

Soon after this, the Hungarian authorities, under the pressure of the German occupation, gathered together and shipped off Hungarian Jews to Auschwitz, with immediate death for most of the prisoners. This began with Hungarian Jews from an area known as the Subcarpathian Rus' (or Ruthenia).[1294] In the first ten days of May 1944, some 18,000 Jews from

---

[1293] "First Hungarian Jews Arrive in Auschwitz," WORLD WAR II TODAY.
[1294] Yeshayahu A. Jelinek, *The Carpathian Diaspora: The Jews of Subcarpathian Rus' and Mukachevo, 1848-1948* (2007), pp. 227-321, with 54 photos inserted between pp. 218-219; "Hungary," pp. 693-703, in *Encyclopedia of the Holocaust, Vol. 2: E-K*, Israel Gutman, Ed.-in-Chief (1990). This area, in the region of Czechoslovakia, Poland, Romania, and Hungary, was south of Eastern Galicia, east of Slovakia, and north of Northern Transylvania and Romania. Earlier, it had been part of Ukraine, then part of Czechoslovakia, then slowly incorporated into Hungary during Wold War II. Historically, it has also been known as Ruthenia, Carpathian

this area were shipped to Auschwitz.[1295] Then,[1296] during Operation Höß (named for Birkenau's Commandant Rudolf Höß), there was the organized killing of Hungarian Jews, with transports arriving at Auschwitz from May 16-July 26, with the bulk in deportations from Budapest May 15-July 8, 1944 (54 days) of some 437,402 Hungarian Jews, an average of 8,100 Jews each day. By this time, the grounds were prepared to absorb the ashes from the product of the crematoria, whose capacity had been enlarged, along with burning pits to be used to "process" *Stücke* (bodies, cadavers, literally, pieces, logs) into ash. The burning pits had a daily capacity of 10,000 persons and, together with the crematoria of Birkenau, there was a total burning capacity of 15-20,000 persons a day.[1297]

Here we see new arrivals at Auschwitz from Hungary, May 1944, standing in front of their transportation by railway boxcars:

Subcarpathian Jewish brothers

Hungarian Jews

We can certainly appreciate the organized focus on transporting as many European Jews for annihilation as possible, at this point largely using the facilities at Auschwitz-Birkenau, but is there any reason to suppose that Hitler saw this as more important and significant in the large viewpoint of history than the victory (or defeat) or the German military in Europe, especially on the Soviet front?

We may guess, but we may also read the last final, formal statement by Hitler on his life and legacy. Hitler dictated this document himself, and signed it soon before his suicide.

Ruthenia, Carpatho-Russia, Carpatho-Ukraine, etc.

[1295] Birkenau in 1943 had eight gas chambers and four large crematoria with 46 ovens! The crematoria were not always operating at maximum capacity due to damage to the bricks in the chimney system, and other problems. See (NT) *Law Reports of Trials of War Criminals, Vol. 7*, pp. 11-26 (Case No. 38: Trial of Obersturmbannführer Rudolf Franz Ferdinand Hoess, Commandant of the Auschwitz Camp, Supreme National Tribunal of Poland, March 11-29, 1947); "The Holocaust in Subcarthian Rus and southern Slovakia," HOLOCAUST ENCYCLOPEDIA, USHMM; "Auschwitz 1940-1945: the Killing Evolution," *KPBS*, PBS.ORG; "Hungarian Jews in Auschwitz-Birkenau," KONFLIKTUSKUTATO.HU/TÁRSADALMI KONFLIKTUSOK KUTATÓOKÖZPONT; *Swimming in Auschwitz* (2007), at 16:20-16:35.

[1296] These events were published quite soon in the West, as in "Jews in Hungary Fear Annihilation," *New York Times*, May 10, 1944, p. 5. This was not new: we may consider "Poles Ask Allies to Halt Slaughter," *New York Times*, Dec. 11, 1942, p. 8, for a much earlier, also alarming (but basically unheeded) report on mass killings.

[1297] Other estimates of this total capacity are even higher.

He was presumably quite serious in what he dictated and declared. In part, this *Political Testament* stated his belief that Germany never wanted war, but was forced by "the leading circles in English politics wanted the war, partly on account of the business hoped for and partly under influence of propaganda organized by international Jewry." To that he added, "After six years of war, which in spite of all set-backs, will go down one day in history as the most glorious and valiant demonstration of a nation's life purpose, I cannot forsake the city which is capital of this Reich. As the forces are too small to make any further stand against the enemy attack at this place and our resistance is gradually being weakened by men who are as deluded as they are lacking in initiative, I should like, by remaining in this town, to share my fate with those, the millions of others, who have also taken upon themselves to do so. Moreover, I do not wish to fall into the hands of an enemy who requires a new spectacle organized by the Jews for the amusement of their hysterical masses." Here, Hitler does not speak of his interest in destroying the German nation not only morally, psychologically, but also quite physically, as in his Nero Decree of March 19, 1945. More on that, below. Nor did Hitler mention the fact that he had just heard of the treatment of Mussolini, *not by Allies or Jews, but by disillusioned Italians*, who took his body after shooting him to death, hung it upside-down, feet above his head, and beat his corpse to a bloody pulp. (More, below.) Soon thereafter, in his closing summary on his legacy, this *Political Testament*, signed and dated Adolf Hitler in Berlin, at 4 am, April 29, 1945, Hitler made his last appeal to Germany, to continue its unlimited animosity toward Jewry: "Above all I charge the leaders of the nation and those under them to scrupulous observance of the laws of race and to merciless opposition to the universal poisoner of all peoples, international Jewry."[1298] While claiming a glorious defense by the German military and people, stated to be certainly remembered in history as a glorious demonstration (no mention of its being a military failure), *his final stated thought did not concern the remembered glory of the Reich, but the eternal struggle of European (German) civilization against Jewry.*

LAST SURGES OF MASS KILLINGS & DESTROYING EVIDENCE (*AKTION 1005*)

That being the overall context, there were some practical issues that were of concern to the German military and especially the SS and Himmler: After the discovery by German troops, announced on April 13, 1943, in the Katyń Wood or Forest, 12 miles west of Smolensk (itself east of Vilnius and Minsk, and southwest of Moscow), exhuming over 4,000 Polish soldiers as well as journalists and intellectuals killed by the Soviets (in April and May 1940),[1299] it became clear that revelations of mass murder bode ill for the perpetrators.

[1298] NT-NCA-Red, vol. 6, pp. 258-263 (Doc. 3569-PS). Similar texts at "Hitler's Last Will," AUSCHWITZ.DK; Adolf Hitler, *My Private Will and Testament* (WIKISOURCE); Adolf Hitler, "My Political Testament," HITLER.ORG, etc.

[1299] Benjamin Bidder, "Remembering the Katyn Massacre: Putin Gesture Heralds

In the short run, this discovery was good news for Germany, as it was used by the German Propaganda Ministry to good purpose. But the related realization—seeing the possibility that the Reich would not emerge victorious at the end of the World War and that information about the German SS and helpers and their killing of Jews and other undesirables— not counted in the range of the 4,000 of the Katyń Wood, but in the millions!—would bring with it calls for justice, meaning that those responsible for these mass killing could face a day of reckoning! The fear that the evidence of bodies could be used to justify executing the leading Nazis, whether by enraged troops of the enemies, by firing squad, or perhaps by trial (not considered likely in Nazi assumptions), led to an organized attempt to destroy any and all evidence of the Nazi mass killing operations and its extermination camps. This was given the name of *Aktion 1005* (Action 1005), or *Sonderaktion 1005* (Special Action 1005),[1300] whose more telling name was *Enterdungsaktion* (Exhumation Action).

In this Special Action aimed at destroying evidence of mass murders, some extermination camps were closed down; they and other killing sites (such as at Babi Yar) were razed, trying to eliminate all traces of the camp and its operations. (More, below.)

In considering knowledge of the genocide of European Jews, it is helpful not to blur the facts of anti-Semitism and hostility toward the Jews (barring Jews from certain professions within Germany, removing their German citizenship, arrests and confiscation of property and businesses) with the outright massive killing of Jews.

Knowledge of any of the first certainly does not establish knowledge of the second, the organized mass killing of Jews, either in the *Vernichtungslager* (extermination camps), beginning in early 1942, or in the mass shootings of Jews in the Eastern Front (in the war against the USSR), starting with the killing only of Jewish men and then extending to massive killing of Jewish men, women, and children, as in the massacres at Babi Yar, outside of Kiev, beginning on September 29, 1941.

German soldiers from the Wehrmacht and especially from the mobile killing units of the SS, the *Einsatzgruppen*, sent letters from the front back to their families, which sometimes expressed love for the family, so missed, along with a pride in helping to free Europe from the plague of Jews, and even photographs of the shootings. (There had already been this sort of reporting back to families with the shootings of Jews and Poles

---

New Era in Russian-Polish Relations," SPIEGEL ONLINE, Apr. 8, 2010; Guy Walters, "The forest of nightmares: The truth about the Katyn massacres—and why Britain turned a blind eye," *Daily Mail,* Apr. 10, 2010; Benjamin B. Fischer, "The Katyn Controversy: Stalin's Killing Field," CIA LIBRARY, CSI PUBLICATIONS (CENTER FOR THE STUDY OF INTELLIGENCE), Apr. 14, 2007.

[1300] Andrej Angrick, *»Aktion 1005«—Spurenbeseitigung von NS-Massenverbrechen 1942-1945: Eine »geheime Reichssache« im Spannungsfeld von Kriegswende und Propaganda* (2018); cf. Andrej Angrick, *Besatzungspolitik und Massenmord: die Einsatzgruppe D in der südischen Sowjetunion 1941-1943* (2003).

after the invasion of Poland in 1939.) *These basic facts were thus known by some of the German population, but systematically not mentioned by the propaganda apparatus of the Reich.*

Some concentration camps were well known by the German general public, from 1933 on—especially those in Germany proper—when Nazi newspapers reported on the opening of camps and their Socialist, Communist, and trade unionist prisoners. (These politically motivated arrests were widely known throughout Germany.)

Were there many of these camps? There were in fact very many such camps, the *KL*, the *Konzentrationslager*, the concentration camps (also abbreviated *KZ*), which held prisoners who were not bound for immediate killing but were considered criminals and used for forced labor.

Was any of this known? There are indications that information about these camps and about the mass killing of Jews was known at least in high government circles—not to mention residents living nearby to concentration camps throughout Germany—and such information was certainly announced in many non-Axis sources, such as the booklet by the Polish Government in Exile (in London), *The Mass Execution of Jews in German Occupied Poland: Note addressed to the Governments of the United Nations on December 10th, 1942, and other Documents.*[1301]

A map can give somewhat of a hint about the very large number of camps in Greater Germany and the *Gouvernement General* (occupied Poland), within the close vicinity—and easy observation—of German residents throughout Germany.

Here we can also refer to a list provided in 1967 by the German Ministry of Justice,[1302] which cites about 1,200 concentration camps, along with their *Außenkommandos*, outposts, which are also variously referred to as *Außenlager* (external camps) and as *Nebenlager* (subcamps).

A map here shows *some but not all* of the many camps spread across central Europe.

[1301] A PDF version of this booklet is available online at IWP.EDU.
[1302] A list of camps and outposts: "Verzeichnis der Konzentrationslager und ihrer Außenkommandos," BUNDESMINISTERIUM DER JUSTIZ.

The Hitler Era

This can be compared with a more inclusive map of camps across Europe:

Representative concentration camps across Europe[1303]

Given a sense of what German citizens might have noticed or learned—if ready to face the possible death warrant that such investigation and knowledge might lead to by a government eager to limit such information for ordinary citizens—what might Hitler himself might have known? There is some debate about this, with some people suggesting that he was totally ignorant of the mass killings, and that he only was focused on pushing Jews out of his world, that is, only expelling Jews into exile.

There was much information available for those who were open to or curious or engaged politically in the issue of mass killings; there were channels of communication providing access to information the Nazi government did not want to be disseminated. Still, there is another dimension of this process of learning or not learning about what is shocking, revolting, or otherwise disagreeable to contemplate. As two German scholars who studied the topics discussed among prisoners held in the UK who believed their comments to be private, concluded,

> Our source material has led us to conclude that while soldiers were aware of the Holocaust and knew a fair amount about how it was being carried out, that knowledge did not interest them very much. The percentage of conversations dealing with the Holocaust is very small compared to the endless gabbing about

---

[1303] The largest concentration camp in Italy, for example, at Ferramonti, to the west of Bari on Italy's southern Adriatic coast, is not indicated in this map: see Carlo Spartaco Capogreco, *Ferramonti: La vita e gli uomini dei più grande campo d'internamento fascista, 1940-1945*. Cf. United States Holocaust Memorial Museum (USHMM), *Encyclopedia of Camps and Ghettos, 1933-1945, in two volumes (in four parts): Vol. 1, Part A, Part B, and Vol. 2, Part A, Part B*.

weapons and air raid techniques, military honors, ships sunk, and planes shot down. *It was clear to the soldiers that extermination was happening, and the extermination was integrated into their frame of reference.* But it remained quite marginal in terms of what commanded their attention. On the other hand, relatively rare as they are, soldiers' discussions of the Holocaust are usually quite very detailed and considerably more precise than the painstaking reconstructions made by postwar prosecutors."[1304]

There was knowledge, then, even detailed and precise, that might not have held given people's interest or desire to express and discuss. Knowledge of some issue and interest in discussing it are quite distinct.

As for the circle of Hitler, there is ample evidence from a number of people in daily, ongoing contact with Hitler for many of the years of the Reich, that both Goebbels and Himmler were in frequent contact with Hitler, letting him know of their good work, and submitting themselves to his higher authority, in case something needed to be readjusted to fit his sense of the evolution of German society and the Nazi world. The 1940 film *Der ewige Jude*, shown through German-occupied Europe, was a work of great propaganda: Hitler had close-up knowledge of this work, even demanding that certain sequences be included (as discussed above).

If we consider Hitler in the context of his life and especially of the Third Reich, it is no secret that he was a man of great passions and intense, long-lived beliefs, from the idea that the German military in World War I was capable of winning the war had it not been for politicians (and behind them an international Jewish cabal) who betrayed and sold out the army, to the idea of Jewry being a poison, a cancer, a parasite on Europeans and on European culture. His vitriolic hatred of Jews was no secret; it was clearly announced in his talks in the years immediately after the First World War. The repeated and ongoing call for a total elimination of the Jewish population of Europe, intensifying in its nature through the years, was also no secret. It is clear for many decades now that those in his inner circle knew of, planned, and brought about the mass killings after the invasion of the USSR and the establishment of camps whose sole function was the extermination of undesirables (mostly but not only Jews), these being the *Vernichtungslager* (extermination camps). And there is little debate about the role in the society of the Third Reich of Hitler as the Führer, the final and last arbiter of all policies and actions. Here was a man who had his finger in the overall routines and policies of the Reich, as much as might be possible for one man.

Hitler was not isolated: He was helped by many sources of intelligence, from the various establishments under his control, from the Gestapo (Secret Police) to the Kripo (Criminal Police) and then the Sipo (Security

---

[1304] Sönke Neitzel and Harald Welzer, *Soldaten: On Fighting, Killing, and Dying*, pp. 111. Italics added.

The Hitler Era

Police), not to mention having the ear of Heinrich Miller, head of the SS, with information on the KL (concentration camps) and VL (extermination camps), and of the actions of *SS Einsatzgruppen*. It would seem a quite unlikely surprise that Hitler was not kept up to date on the various stages of the evolution of this enormous killing apparatus, especially since he spoke with such hatred of the Jews for well over a decade even before the Third Reich came into existence.

Furthermore, Hitler was not a man who liked being kept in the dark about the machinations and generally hidden activities of the Nazi Government and regime. Clearly in the Third Reich, Hitler was the root inspiration for the extreme killing program of the third Reich.

In this context, Reich Ambassador to Great Britain and then Foreign Secretary, Joachim von Ribbentrop (1893-1946), under arrest after the war and preparing for the Nuremberg War Crimes Trials, had many occasions to speak with Gustave M. Gilbert (1911-1977), an American military psychologist who was a native speaker of German, his parents having been immigrants to the USA from Austria.

In a conversation over the weekend of January 26-27, 1946, Von Ribbentrop remarked, "I cannot understand it. He [Hitler] was a vegetarian... I even had to go hunting secretly because he disapproved of it. Now how can a man like that order mass murder?"[1305] Ribbentrop seems surprisingly naïve here: Ribbentrop certainly knew of the Night of the Long Knives from 1934, and, later of films taken by Goebbels of conspirators of the July 1944 attempted assassination of Hitler being hung on meat hooks with piano wire to die tortured and quite miserable deaths, for Hitler to watch when he wanted. Vegetarian or not, Hitler was not a delicate jellyfish.

Adding some specific information at this point to shed light on this story, Hitler was known to have unusual hours of sleep. This was perhaps due in part to the constant use of drugs, which can alter sleep patterns. In any case, as Hitler's secretary Christa Schroeder remarked, "Hitler spent most of the night studying reports (memoranda: *Denkschriften*) and other documents and slept in more or less until noon."[1306] These hours were filled with focused late-night work. As Eva Braun recorded in her personal diary, Hitler would write mostly after midnight, writing "without corrections and when he finishes a page," she wrote, "he throws it on the ground where it can be collected and put in order later." This does suggest a focused and intense writing process on Hitler's part. He would stay up often until eight in the morning (Braun continued), writing, scrapping, rewriting, and refining a pile of "speeches, orders, drafts of laws" (decrees from the Führer), as well as "queries addressed to Himmler, Goebbels, or to the General Staff," which were then organized and sent out through the teletype machine to the appropriate destinations.[1307]

[1305] "Joachin von Ribbentrop," ENCYCLOPÆDIA BRITANNICA; quotation from Gustave M. Gilbert, *Nuremberg Diary* (1947), pp. 128-130.

[1306] Christa Schroeder, *Er war mein Chef*, p. 195; *He Was My Chief*, p. 171.

[1307] Eva Braun, *The Private Life of Adolf Hitler*, pp. 127-128, Nov., 1941.

Indicating the practice of reports of killings that were relayed to Hitler, Braun also mentions a later event, about which she noticed "a secret report on his table [on Hitler's table] and read it! In the week of the 18th to 25th [1944] there were 2,726 executions inside the Reich, excluding the *Gouvernement General* and the Czech Protectorate. Among them 219 women. The youngest was sixteen, the oldest sixty-three."[1308]

These comments suggest a willingness of Hitler to hear what Himmler, Goebbels, or the military might want to offer up, and a regular, focused practice by Hitler of requesting of such information, and receiving it!

As confirmed in the preceding, as well as in other documentation about and by Hitler, it is not a surprise that Hitler wanted to be in the know about what was going on, especially in those subjects most dear to his heart: the success of Germany in economic, diplomatic, and military affairs, linked to the core program of German expansionism and hegemony over continental Europe, and the status of Jews. Hitler sensed a calling, perhaps even a divine calling to save the German people, and presumably felt that he had a great demand on him personally as father, protector-knight (*Ritter*), and savior (*Retter*) of the German people.

AUSCHWITZ *ZIGEUNERNACHT*, AUGUST 2-3, 1944

All of this was before the night of August 2-3, 1944, remembered as *Zigeunernacht* (the Night of the Gypsies), when the SS in charge of Auschwitz-Birkenau liquidated (gassed to death and cremated) the remaining Romanies in the camp. Of Auschwitz, one Romani wrote:

> Our house in Auschwitz,
> So big and black. So black and big.
> This is where our tears flow,
> Destroying our sight.
> This is where they crushed our pleas
> For no one to hear.
> This is where they turned us to ashes
> For the winds to scatter.[1309]

Prior to that night of mass killing, Romanies were held in various ghettos in Poland and in concentration camps, such as at Łódź, Theresienstadt (north of Prague), and also Dachau, Sachsenhausen, Buchenwald, Mauthausen, Ravensbrück, Bergen-Belsen, Gross-Rosen, Natzweiler-Struthof, Stutthof (at Sztutowo, Poland), and others, including such extermination camps as Majdanek, as well as in their own section of Auschwitz,[1310] the so-called *Zigeunerlager* (Gypsy Camp) *Auschwitz*, or the *Zigeunerfamilienlager* (Gypsy Family Camp) *Auschwitz*. While it is not

---

[1308] Eva Braun, *The Private Life of Adolf Hitler*, p. 158, 1944 (no month); the entry is placed with others of spring and summer of 1944.

[1309] Excerpt from poem "The Terror Years" by Rajko Djurić, p. 88, in *The Roads of the Roma: A PEN anthology of Gypsy Writers*, Ian Hancock, Siobhan Dowd, and Rajko Djurić, eds. (2004).

[1310] Donald Kenrick and Grattan Puxon, *Gypsies under the Swastika*, pp. 124-138, 140-145.

obvious that fewer inmates would have been executed (Romanies and Jews), if there had been damage by Allied bombers, including that of the rail lines bringing more racially-defined prisoners to Auschwitz, that would most probably at least have interrupted and slowed down the killing process. The focus of the Allied military was clearly on the defeat of the Third Reich, without an interest in diverting those efforts to the camps. The claim that this location was beyond the range of Allied bombers (and the precision-targeting British RAF Mosquito fighter-bombers), was shown to be false when US President Carter released earlier secret documents, *US military aerial photography of Auschwitz I and II (Auschwitz-Birkenau)*, thus clearly establishing that bombers could in fact reach that area.

Two considerations are relevant here: first, the photography was done to capture images of various industrial sites nearby (such as the IG Farben and the Buna Werke complexes); not for searching the images for concentration camps and extermination camps. The tactical and the moral question of why there was not more interest in killing centers where thousands of people were put to death daily was not addressed for several decades, until that sort of question was no longer societally too hot and disturbing a topic. Second, the detail that was interpreted with the technology of 1945 was much improved during the following decades, when the photos were once again investigated, with a fresh eye and more sophisticated processing possible. And yet, Dino Brugioni (1915-2005), senior official at the CIA, commented that the photos as viewed with 1944 technology *could have* identified the main buildings (gas chambers, crematoria, etc.), *even with the period's relatively limited technology.*[1311]

Nazi assertions that a world-wide Jewish cabal ruled the West, and the Bolshevik Soviet Union, as well, make no sense if we accept that the Western Allied could not be induced into bombing any of the various killing sites by Jews or those concerned with Jews, and especially if we assume that Jews would act with self-centered and selfish interests in their own preservation no matter what the cost of destruction of lives of others. In fact, *these Nazi ideas were to be disconfirmed by the actual discussions, decisions, and actions of these supposedly "Jew-controlled" countries.*

[1311] Dino A. Brugioni and Robert G. Poirier, "The Holocaust Revisited: A Retrospective Analysis of the Auschwitz-Birkenau Extermination Complex Unclassified," CIA—which discusses the use at the CIA's NPIC (THE NATIONAL PHOTOGRAPHIC INTERPRETATION CENTER) of micro-stereoscopes instead of the 7X tube magnifiers available in 1944. Dino Brugioni, in "Auschwitz and Birkenau: Why the World War II photo interpreters failed to Identify the extermination complex," *Military Intelligence*, vol. 9, no. 1 (Jan.-Mar. 1983), pp. 50–55, stated that mechanisms to enlarge the aerial photographs 7 times were used, but that *it was actually possible with the technology of the time to have enlargements 35 times the originals*. Those examining the over 5 million prints ultimately available for military analysis *were not instructed to try to search out concentration camps or extermination camps (the latter term was not even in usual parlance in the military at the time)*, and these cartographers were not informed or otherwise aware of the human and organizational reports of mass killings at all (see esp. pp. 54-55).

There is an irony, a tragic irony, in here somewhere. The irony is in Hitler's early statement proposing replacing anti-Semitism based on emotive reasons with one based on reason,[1312] when we see that in practice, the central teachings of the Third Reich involved a systematic, prolonged, and consistent insistence and inculcation in the (non-Jewish) German people of a sense of Jews that was an emotionally charged, fear-infused, rageful, condescending disrespect toward Jews—inspired by an image of Jewry being a deadly poison to society, a disloyal, traitorous, untrustworthy foreign intrusion into German life, and, most worrisome (to non-Jewish Germans), a threat to the continued existence of the German people and nation. Creating the image of the Jew as a power capable of destroying the entire German people gave urgent importance to solving the Jewish Question as soon as possible, and as thoroughly and definitively as possible. After defining Jews as intent on destroying the whole German nation, the natural reaction in self-defense was for the German nation to become intent on destroying the whole Jewish people. This is all based on an agitated, fearful, nervous emotionality, even if in the context of a legal (that is, decreed) framework for eliminating Jews in the step-by-step process we have seen from those years. This urgency to destroy was also encouraged by the prediction that if Germany would lose the war, the consequence would be the annihilation of the German people by the Allies, who were described as capable of carrying out the same mass murders of political enemies that had been a hallmark of the Third Reich since the first months of its existence.

And yet there was no tradition of mass killing of a conquered enemy among these Allies, no governmental structure to facilitate the murder of millions of enemies (unlike the organizations created by the SS had established during the 1930s and carried into action once the war began). While there was an urge among a number of Allies to line up the major Nazi leaders and shoot them summarily—an idea that did not prevail—there was, as well, a different value and consideration that was taken into account: the setting up of a legal context, based in part on various conventions on warfare from the late 1800s on.

As a legal process, the accused were given legal counsel. Unlike a kangaroo court (such as the Nazi People's Court), some of the accused were actually found innocent of the charged made against them. In addition, the sentences varied from the death penalty by hanging to several years in prison, a large number of which were reduced in time when reconsidered in the 1950s.

These trials, at Nuremberg and elsewhere in Europe over the next years, were something that we cannot conceive Nazi Germany as carrying out. We have only to look at the practice of killing political enemies, and the tragic farce of the *Volksgerichthof*, the People's Court, with summary

---

[1312] "'Hitler-Brief an Adolf Gemlich': Die erste bedeutende Äußerung Hitlers über den Antisemitismus: Antwort an Adolf Gemlich, 16. September 1919," KURT-BAUER-GESCHICHTE.AT; "Hitler Letter: Understanding the Rhetoric of Hate," MUSEUM OF TOLERANCE.

presentations, badgering by the judge, and swift sentencing, often of death by guillotine, as happened in a trial under Judge Roland Freisler, where key members of the White Rose were arrested on February 18, 1943, put on trial on February 22, and executed by guillotine later that same day. There were several pamphleteers who wrote against the Reich, some quoting news from the BBC: The youngest German executed, found guilty of treason by the People's Court and *guillotined on October 27, 1942*, aged 17, was Helmuth Hübener of Hamburg.[1313]

In the White Rose leaflets was the comment that "our present-day "State" [*unser heutiger "Staat"*—the Nazi, that is, the National Socialist government] is a dictatorship of evil [*die Diktatur des Bösen*]" that you, the German people, permit "to rob you of one sphere of your rights after another, little by little, both overtly and in secret."[1314] The leaflets also declared, "Every word that proceeds from Hitler's mouth is a lie. When he says peace, he means war. And when he names the name of the Almighty in a most blasphemous manner, he means the almighty evil one, the fallen angel, Satan. His mouth is the stinking throat of hell [*Sein Mund ist der stinkende Rachen der Hölle*] and his power is fundamentally depraved [*seine Macht ist im Grunde verworfen*]. To be sure, one must wage the battle against National Socialism using rational means. But whoever still does not believe in the actual existence of demonic powers has not comprehended by far the metaphysical background of this war."[1315] They were not mincing words, and *Hitler and cohorts did not bide well with open criticism*. Then, other White Rose members, including Franz Müller (1924-2015), were arrested some two months later (denounced others under Gestapo torture), two came before Freisler in trial on April 19, 1943: siblings Susanne (1921-2012) and Hans Hirzel, 1924-2006), both good specimens of Germanic youth: blond, blue-eyed, and healthy in stature. Hirzel wore her hair in long braids; Müller was a youthful 18 years old. Freisler remarked to the young woman, with stereotypical, simplistic thinking, "Miss Hirzel, when I see you in front of me, you are the prototype of a Germanic girl! (*Sie sind das Urbild eines germanischen Mädschens!*) You cannot have known of this filth against our Führer! (*Sie können doch von diesem Schmutz gegen unseren Führer nichts gewusst haben!*)" He said to Hans, "You have a good racial appearance (*ein rassisch gutes Aussehen*), how could you be against the Führer? He has saved us all! (*Er hat uns doch alle gerettet!*). We might wonder what one's beliefs have to do with the color of one's hair and eyes and one's physical appearance, although perhaps the answer was obvious within Nazi dogma.[1316]

[1313] "Helmuth Hübener," WIKIPEDIA.
[1314] "White Rose: Leaflet 3," CENTER FOR WHITE ROSE STUDIES. Tr. modified to correspond more closely to the German. See orig. six Ger. pamphlets: "Die sechs Flugblätter der Weißen Rose (Juni 1942 bis Februar 1943," UNIVERSITÄT WIEN, INSTITUT FÜR ZEITGESCHICHTE (KURT BAUER GESCHICHTE).
[1315] "White Rose: Leaflet 4," CENTER FOR WHITE ROSE STUDIES.
[1316] Tim Pröse, "Franz, du lebst! Es ist alles vorbei," *Focus*, No. 23, Jun. 30, 2012; "Franz J. Müller," DE.WIKIPEDIA; "Hans Hirzel," SPARTICUS EDUCATIONAL.

The situation in National Socialist Germany became more and more desperate, despite the best face being put on it by Goebbels and others intensely dedicated to the cause. With this came the prediction of a thirst for bloody vengeance against the entire German nation, an image the Nazis had used to stir the nation to ever greater efforts, more and more out of a fear of their own annihilation in the case of their being defeated. *After the defeat and unconditional surrender of the third Reich to the Allies, this fear was shown to be a chimera of Nazi paranoia.*

On the other hand, the peace was not all peace, joy, celebration, and comfortable living, for either those seen as having been liberated and for the Germans for whom the end of the war brought its own relief, from Allied bombings and military attacks on the ground, but with general uncertainty and worry about what might come next in the chaos.

The celebrations we often associate with the end of the war do not include some features of the conquest of the Nazi Fortress Europe: first, the use of bombardment to weaken the German defenses, along the coast and inland, and second, the terrible displacement of millions of people, from Germans chased from various conquered lands to other Displaced Persons (ultimately, mostly Jews who were now homeless and stateless).

One of the heaviest days of bombing along the French coast, for example, was the day before D-Day, with 5,000 tons of bombs dropped by RAF bombers, attacking German gun batteries along the Normandy coast, and the next two days, June 6-7, 1944, when 2,500 civilians in the Department of Calvados along the Normandy coast were killed by bombings. Overall, some 20,000 French civilians in Normandy were killed during the Allied liberation of the region. *We can say that there were deaths enough to go all around.* On D-Day itself, 1,456 American soldiers were killed and 3,184 wounded, with 1,928 MIA; 26 were captured by the Germans.[1317] Here, let us recall that *the accuracy of bombing during World War II was quite limited*. Many bombs did not land on the defined targets, but in civilian urban and rural areas, with unintended damage now called by the obfuscating term "collateral damage."[1318] (parallel to pharmaceutical "side effects," effects that are no less actual than the advertised "target symptoms" and the advertised purposes of the drugs.)

[1317] William Hitchcock, *The Bitter Road to Freedom: A New History of the Liberation of Europe* (2008), pp. 1-3, 11-13, 27-29, 44-46, 55-57, and "The Price of Liberation," *Quarterly Journal of Military History (MHQ)*, vol. 21, no. 3, 2009, pp. 20-29, at pp. 23, 27.

[1318] The term came to be used by the US military in the mid-1960s (the Vietnam War period) for the wartime unintentional wounding and killing of civilians and unintended destruction of property. Its much earlier use referred to personal property damage due to floods, fires, factory strikes, and related phenomena, as early as the first decade of the twentieth century: *New York Tribune*, Feb. 23, 1905, p. 4; *Daily Public Leader*, May 19, 1905, p. 1; *The Evening Times*, Jul. 11, 1910, p. 1, etc. See Alexa A. Kosarina and A. E. Fedotova, "The Main Reasons and Ways of Term Coinage and their Features," *Filologiya*, Jun. 2015, pp. 206-210, at pp. 207-209; online with the same title at CYBERLENINKA.RU.

The Hitler Era

Other destruction of civilian areas included the use of a new form of bombing, a petroleum jelly that had just recently been developed in US research facilities, in 1942, at Harvard University, led by chemist Louis Fieser (1899-1977).[1319] The jelly was used from May 27, 1944 on, in the bombing of French and German Nazi military targets (just mentioned) and in the fire-bombing in the Pacific Theater, including the bombing of Japan.

Of course, as in the bombing of such cities as Berlin and Dresden, among others, many German civilians were also killed in the violence of war. Dresden—which experienced fire bombing, the night of February 13-14, 1945, in which Anglo-American bombers dropped more than 4,500 tons of high-explosive and incendiary bombs on the city. Dresden, for decades now the icon of massive civilian deaths caused by Allied bombing, with estimates of dead ranging from 35,000 to 100,000, and even, some suggesting 500,000 (now questioned).

The bombing was studied over a four-year period by a group of eleven respected German historians headed by Rolf-Dieter Müller and which included Horst Boorg (1928-2016), both German military historians.

The group was given the formal name of the Dresden Commission of Historians for the Ascertainment of the Number of Victims of the Air Raids on the City of Dresden on 13/14 February 1945. This commission, which was established in 2004, carefully examined many archival sources, as well as burial records and detailed archeological finds. *The conclusion of the commission, reached in 2008, included a lower estimate than earlier reports, suggesting that the death toll was around 18,000 and was no more than 25,000 in total.*[1320] This research was not readily acceptable to either Germans who had lost family that night, nor to the Russians, whose Soviet heritage had painted the Western Allies to be as brutal as the Nazis. In any case, *in a broader scope, one of the lower estimates of total German civilian deaths from Allied bombing was 350,000.*[1321]

If we look to the case of Japan, the fire-bombing of incendiaries on Tokyo the night of March 9-10, 1945, resulted in an estimated 80,000, but perhaps more than 100,000, dead.[1322] (By comparison, one study suggested that in the atomic bombs dropped on Hiroshima and then Nagasaki (August 6 and 9, 1945), the estimated killed were 66,000 and 39,000, respectively.[1323] Then, in the last weeks of the war in Europe, petroleum jelly was also used to blanket bomb a German garrison on the

---

[1319] "Louis Fieser and Mary Fieser," *Science History Institute*, SCIENCEHISTORY.ORG.

[1320] Frederick Taylor, "Death Toll Debate: How Many Died in the Bombing of Dresden?" SPIEGEL ONLINE, Oct. 2, 2008; Kate Connolly, "Panel rethinks death toll from Dresden raids," *The Guardian*, Oct. 2, 2008.

[1321] Richard Ovary, *The Bombers and the Bombed: Allied Air War Over Europe 1940-1945* (2014), p. 255.

[1322] R. G. Grant, "Bombing of Tokyo," ENCYCLOPÆDIA BRITANNICA.

[1323] "The Atomic Bombings of Hiroshima and Nagasaki," ATOMICARCHIVE.COM. These quotes are estimates of the Manhattan Engineer District, the US Army component of the Manhattan Project.

French coast, at La Rochelle, near the town of Royan, on the eastern bank of the Gironde Estuary, in April 1945. This was, in the overall scheme of things, rather unnecessary, since the Germans had already been largely pushed back; this relatively isolated group of Wehrmacht soldiers would have been defeated in the course of things. In these bombings, the city of Royan was largely razed by devastating fire.[1324] Visiting Royan, one will see that many buildings are in the style of the cement-structures built after the war. (This petroleum jelly would find a much more extensive use in the US war in Vietnam, where it became known by the later, more common, name of napalm.) In addition to the destruction by the Allies of towns and villages in France, Belgium, and Italy, there were the deaths of French civilians: in Normandy in 1944, almost 20,000 were killed.[1325] And, while not conforming to the usual image of friendly but respectful Allied soldier-German civilian relations, there were these armies' share of rape,[1326] in addition to the "fraternizing" with willing German women and eager Allied soldiers, all longing for intimacy (or even merely food). The rapes committed by Germans, both in war contexts and in concentration camps, and by Soviet military against German women after the defeat of the Wehrmacht in area after area are widely reported; after the fall of the Reich some 100,000 Berlin women were raped, often gang-raped, with perhaps at least 2 million women throughout the former German Reich raped by Soviet soldiers.[1327]

This was a source of shame for women (as if they were the guilty parties), rather than for the rapists.[1328] As a case in point, one rather educated Berlin woman (speaking several languages, including Russian) wrote of her being gang-raped and then finding the superior Soviet officer in the area, arranging with him to be lovers, on the condition that he forbid any of his military inferiors to touch her, and provide her with food and living quarters. This was published anonymously, first in English, as *A Woman in Berlin* (1954), thanks to Kurt Marek, an author, journalist, and scholar, and then in German, as *Eine Frau in Berlin* (1959), *which led to accusations against the anonymous author of besmirching the honor of German women!* The author died in 2001 and the book was then re-issued in 2003. At that time, her identity was disclosed by a literary agent—without permission nor denial by the editor—to be the journalist, Marta

---

[1324] Howard Zinn, *The Bomb* (2010), "The Bombing of Royan" (pp. 65-87).

[1325] William Hitchcock, "The Price of Liberation" (cited just above), p. 20.

[1326] William Hitchcock, *The Bitter Road to Freedom: A New History of the Liberation of Europe* (2008). See also the Italian film, *Two Women* (1961), set in 1943, portraying the rape of a mother and her young daughter by Allied soldiers in a church, and the psychological consequences for the two. It was directed by Vittorio De Sica and starred Sophia Loren, Jean-Paul Belmondo, and Raf Vallone.

[1327] Antony Beevor, *The Fall of Berlin, 1945* (2002), pp. 434-435.

[1328] We can see throughout many cultures, even to this day, the wide-spread if not universal exoneration of men who rape ("Boys will be boys") and the suggestion that the intercourse might have actually been consensual, and therefore not a rape at all, even suggesting that the women in question actually wanted to be raped.

The Hitler Era

Hillers (1911-2001). In 2008, a film was made that portrayed the key period of her diary that ran from April 20 to June 22, 1945.[1329]

THE LOGIC AND THE PSYCHOLOGY OF THE NERO DECREE

With all of this, we can perhaps sense by spring of 1945 a readiness by Hitler to destroy what was imagined to threaten Germany's very existence (its enemies both real and delusional), a readiness to put the youth of Germany into harm's way for their failure to achieve the National Socialist dream of German autarky, its hegemony over Europe, and its ultimate survival.

If we return to some of the basic principles driving the National Socialist world from its earliest times, we might consider here the guiding principle that is derived from the application of Darwinian ideas by Herbert Spencer, in his Social Darwinism, as it is called (discussed earlier), that this world is meant for the strong and the powerful, to whom the weak and helpless had to submit, in full fairness and justice. A consistent application of this principle, following this logic thoroughly, could well mean for Hitler that if the Soviet Bolsheviks (and Jews) and the Western capitalists (and Jews) should be able to defeat the German military, then this would just show that the Germans were wrong in believing that they were the strong, the justifiably ruling master race (*Herrenrasse*).

We can find this reasoning in Hitler's thinking and in that of the Nazi Party leaders, and, perhaps, among the Nazi Party rank-and-file; as Hitler stated at the time of the invasion of the USSR (quoted above), "If the German people is not strong enough and devoted enough to give its blood for its existence, let it go and be destroyed by another, stronger man. I shall not shed tears for the German people."[1330] The firm (obstinate) attitude of Hitler that this thinking represents was well understood by his generals and also by the general (German) public. He kept this orientation guiding his thinking, decisions, decrees, and actions, to the very end. This is the logic of the Nero Decree, calling for the total destruction of German infrastructure if the Soviet Armies should conquer the once-great German Wehrmacht. Given that, what follows on the psychological dimension of such a position? Hitler saw himself (as he and much of the population of the German Reich did) as a genius and the savior of the *Volk* (the German people). He also "imposed direction, extension, and radicalness upon the course of events [*vielmehr hat er dem Geschehen auch Richtung, Ausdehnung und Radikalität verliehen*]."[1331] Hitler also saw in what he took to be his infallible vision of the future, the final attainment of *Lebensraum* for the *Herrenrasse*.

How was that firm belief undermined by a subsequent recognition that Germany was not up to matching the force and power of the Soviet Armies?

[1329] Cressida Connolly, "She screamed for help but her neighbours barricaded the door," *The Telegraph* (London), Jul. 4, 2005; "Marta Hillers," WIKIPEDIA.

[1330] Timothy Snyder, *Black Earth: The Holocaust as History and Warning* (2015), p. 242.

[1331] Joachim C. Fest, *Hitler* (Ger. text), pp. 1028-1029; *Hitler* (Eng.), p. 754.

Obviously, if we think that one people and its military are invincible, and then we come to see them being roundly defeated in battle, our earlier belief is shown to be quite a mistaken one, more of a hope-based delusion than a brilliant insight into reality. *In that case, if accepting the obvious, Hitler would have his firm beliefs destroyed.* This would change him from a visionary with a mission (and perhaps even a God-given mission, as some Germans felt) into a delusional commander of a delusional people. The greatness of Hitler was thoroughly undermined by the events on the Eastern Front, faced with a much larger population with a deep desire not only to have their own land free from foreign occupation, but with a powerful drive to push that occupation force back and to punish it for its consistently devastating and murderous actions.

We might seriously wonder how Hitler believed firmly that a relatively small nation of somewhere between 66 and 80 million Germans, living on land covering some 244,706 sq. mi., should be able to conquer the peoples of great, expansive Russia—some 193 million in population, the largest country in the world, covering roughly 9,000,000 sq. miles (stretching from its western border at the Baltic to Ukraine and Crimea, to its eastern border, on the Pacific Ocean, some eleven time zones away!), rich in minerals, oil, great agricultural and forest lands, quite self-sufficient.[1332] This was, further, a Russia with a long history of fending off invaders from the north (Sweden) and the west (the Swedes, the Lithuanians, the French, the Germans from the age of the Teutonic Knights through the Second Reich of the Kaiser, and so on), and in 1941, ready once again to defend their homeland with their lives, a people of 190-200-plus-million—more than twice the population of all of Greater Germany. And how could Hitler also firmly believe that the Wehrmacht could complete that conquering of the Soviet Union in a matter of a few months (to add to the imaginary, grandiose vision Hitler cultivated)? This is perhaps a facet of his megalomaniacal exaggeration and his ultimately groundless pride, his unbounded hubris. His intuition and his self-confidence are even more astonishing when we consider his confidence that Germany would conquer the Soviet Union in just a few months, before the Russian winter set in, not thinking that it would necessary for his troops to have winter clothing or equipment capable of resisting Russian winters. As early Nazi Kurt Ludecke (1890-1960) put it in his 1937 book, in terms that would prove to be even more significant and incisive in the following years after the invasion of the USSR, "his [Hitler's] rule was made easy by the fact that Germans were willing to renounce their civil liberty, suffer unbelievable hardships, and submit to a dictator at home rather than bow to a dictator from abroad.... While Mussolini in

---

[1332] "Third Reich," *New World Encyclopedia*, NEWWORLDENCYCLOPEDIA.ORG; *Why We Fight: The Battle of Russia* (dir. by Frank Capra, 1943), esp. 7:15-7:35, 9:45-10:00, 14:30-14:45, ARCHIVES.GOV or YOUTUBE; Bruno Blau, "The Jewish Population in Germany 1939-1945," *Jewish Social Studies*, vol. 12, no. 2, Apr. 1950, pp. 161-172, with the total population for Germany in 1939 cited at p. 162.

The Hitler Era

wise limitation underpinned his new state, building a solid foundation stone upon stone, Hitler [lacking this wisdom of Mussolini] is attempting [Ludecke wrote in 1937] the impossible with inadequate means."[1333]

And yet while this might point to many important distorted evaluations of the capacities and willingness of the German people, of the Russian people, and of many issues subsumed here, this does not make Hitler psychotic or crazy. He might have been prejudiced, driven by rage and a desire for revenge, even if his analyses of the sources of his frustrations led to very distorted conclusions; this is not psychosis. In any case, *the use of such grand categories (as craziness or psychosis) will often shed less light on the thinking of the individuals we are trying to understand than other approaches available to us.*

No matter how inspiring Hitler's vision was to those who accepted its visionary descriptions as future truth, once the ultimately delusional nature of this vision proved itself, and was recognized as such, it could no longer serve as a buttress to defend and support Hitler's sense of his own deep wisdom and power (which were perhaps quite illusionary).

Ultimately, with this overwhelming disappointment and its sense that he had not accomplished his life mission (in his own new pessimistic and defeatist attitude), Hitler ordered that Germany go down into total destruction with him: this was actually codified in a Führer Order, the Decree on Demolitions on Reich Territory, *der Befehl betreffend Zerstörungsmaßnahmen im Reichsgebiet*, referred to as the Nero Decree (referring to Emperor Nero and the great fire in Rome destroying much of the city, in July 64 CE). This decree of March 19, 1945, gave instructions for all buildings, factories, railway lines, electrical sources, roads, bridges, in short, all that was man-made in Germany, to be totally destroyed so that the enemy would come to nothing. Of course, with that, the German people would also face calamity, starvation, and other disasters, but, after all, they deserved it for not meeting Hitler's visionary demands! The extremity of this decree, even by the standards of National Socialism, alarmed some Hitler's closest associates. Albert Speer, in particular, was able to convince Hitler to modify his Decree, stating that "industrial facilities were now only to be 'disabled' and, like supply utilities, were only to be destroyed if they were *directly* threatened by the enemy."[1334]

THE PSYCHOLOGY AND THE POWER OF HITLER

There has been much written about the various particularities of Hitler's personality and his relationships with others, on a personal level and on the grand societal level as Führer of the German people.

While a person's psychology (more on this below) has importance and is one significant influence on that person's way of thinking, acting, and relating to others, certainly we cannot explain any large historical story

---

[1333] Kurt Ludecke, *I Knew Hitler*, p. 789.
[1334] Hans-Joachim Neumann and Henrik Eberle, *War Hitler Krank? Ein Abschliessender Befund* (2009), p. 281; Eng., *Was Hitler Ill? A Final Diagnosis* (2013), p. 180.

by appealing solely to this feature of the situation, however complex it is: many have had miserable, even brutal childhoods—beaten as young Adolf was by his alcoholic, short-tempered and demanding father, Alois Hitler, Sr. The son, Adolf, believing that his society had been intensely mistreated, developed an intense rage that yearned to be expressed and satisfied,[1335] but certainly many similarly treated with violence did not come to such an attitude. The remarkable impact of Hitler on the overall society of Germany following World War I and on European and even on world history, is complex and asks for an appreciation of the many factors that developed as the Hitler era evolved.

It has also been noted, similarly, that Joseph Stalin—born Iosif Vissarionovich Dzhugashvili, and known as Koba[1336]—was brought up in Georgia (on the east coast of the Black Sea, south of the current Russian Federation, and north of Turkey, Armenia, and Azerbaijan) by a cobbler father who insisted that his son become a cobbler, who was also an alcoholic who beat his wife and his son Joseph—shades of Alois and Adolf! Stalin was also beaten by his mother, who, unlike Hitler's mother, left the father and supported herself and her boy as a washerwoman. Stalin, too, had his own physical limitations, with a withered left arm (presumably from septicemia, bacterial blood poisoning), facial marks from smallpox, and (as Goebbels) a club foot.[1337] Here, we might say that despite Stalin's mass trials and executions of those who were political opponents, it took Hitler to put Stalin's violence in the background for many, who focus on the mass murders of the Nazi Era, especially its genocide, and at times leave Stalin's violence, Siberian prison camps (*gulags*), and other murderous patterns in the shadows. And this, even though the murderous regime of Stalin was known by some even in the USA at least from the early 1930s, including the great starvation of the Ukrainians in 1932-1933, the aim of which was the destruction of the social class of farmer-property holders (*kulaks*), with some 3.3 million who died, and in the gulags themselves, perhaps one million dead (in the 1933-1945 period)—perhaps as many as three million in all of Stalin's years in power. There were many targeted political murders, perhaps the most famous of which was that of Leon Trotsky, discussed above. If we add national and social groups (the *kulaks*, farmer-land owners in Ukraine, or conservative

---

[1335] Hitler's one known childhood friend August Kubizek (1888-1956) is an incomparable source of information about Hitler's youth here, as in *Adolf Hitler, mein Jugendfreund* (1953); 1st complete Eng. tr., *The Young Hitler I Knew: The Memoirs of Hitler's Childhood Friend*, with Introduction by Ian Kershaw (2011).

[1336] Koba was a Georgian outlaw, and also a character in a romance by Georgian author Kazbek. See "Stalin, Joseph," *Encyclopedia of Marxism*, MARXISTS.ORG.

[1337] Philip Boobbyer, *The Stalin Era* (2000), p. 101; *The Complete Correspondence Between Franklin D. Roosevelt and Joseph V. Stalin*, Susan Butler, ed. (2005), p. 2. Cf. Jonathan Shaw, "Stalin at Home" (a review of Patricia Blake's work), *Harvard Magazine*, Jul. 1999; cf. "Mary Graham Bunting Institute," *The Chronicle of Higher Education*, Jul. 17, 1998.

The Hitler Era

bourgeois) as groups which when systematically killed as instances of genocide, we have another question to answer of whether Hitler or Stalin (and their regimes) committing a higher number of genocide killings—but this can be done without comparisons.[1338] In any case, we are talking about the dead counted in tens of millions![1339] *As a remark on this sort of question ("Who was worse? A or B?"), the answer risks being a limited and confined one, less significant than it might seem.*

There are a number of considerations that we might address in making such a judgment: "better or worse" is not a single-criterion sort of issue. But, more fundamentally, once we have an answer, or perhaps reach the conclusion that we cannot answer such a question, there is the more basic reality that we are considering (in this case): earth-shaking mass murders. *If one murder is a great crime (or sin), as many civilizations and religions teach, then when we start thinking about the millions that were killed in one specific historical context or another, the question of who between two people was worse is secondary to the sheer horror of both of the situations we are considering.* That said, there can, none the less, be interesting discussions that arise out of such limited starting points, which means that the questions might have value more for what they lead us to consider in trying to answer than their value in their own right. Recent books that take these questions into interesting depths can be found.[1340]

The politics of World War II, however, brought on other concerns beyond the question of whether Hitler was worse than Stalin: military alliances between the USSR, the UK, and the USA, presented Stalin as "Uncle Joe" (a term coined by Churchill during the war, before the post-War conflicts that ultimately led to Churchill's first 1946 reference to the Iron Curtain), *disregarding for pragmatic purposes in this new landscape with its ideological tension between capitalism and communism.*

Some suggest that to understand Hitler is to have sympathy for him and to exonerate or to forgive him for whatever he did. I see no reason to accept this principle. Surely, we can understand what makes a person be mean to another: a frustrating day at work, fatigue, perhaps some background irritations that have not been resolved with the person who is the target of one's meanness (or with someone else), and so forth, without concluding that what this person did was ultimately innocent and uncriticizable. We can see vicious, violent, cruel actions, understand what the person carrying them out was thinking, feeling, judging, *and still see them as what we take them clearly to be: nasty, violent, and even cruel.*

[1338] Political scientist Rudolph J. Rummel (1932-2014) in *Lethal Politics: Soviet Genocide and Mass Murder Since 1917* estimated that in the Stalin era (1929-1953), some 44,451,000 were killed; online at HAWAII.EDU/POWERKILLS.

[1339] Timothy Snyder, "Hitler vs. Stalin: Who Was Worse?" *The New York Review of Books*, Jan. 27, 2011.

[1340] Norman M. Naimark, *Fires of Hatred: Ethnic Cleansing in Twentieth-Century Europe* (2001) and *Stalin's Genocides: Human Rights and Crimes against Humanity* (2010); Timothy D. Snyder's *Bloodlands: Europe Between Hitler and Stalin* (2010) and *On Tyranny: Twenty Lessons from the Twentieth Century* (2017).

If we study some of Hitler's early life, from a variety of sources (considering even *Mein Kampf*—with its many distortions, its idealizing of his youth, his indirect references to his own life experiences expressed as general sociological observations—his later comments to those (relatively) close to him, and so forth, we can perhaps accept that his childhood was no summer picnic. While he said that he respected his father and loved his mother, there is certainly more to the story than that simple resume. It is known from a number of sources, as discussed above, that his father would beat not only young Adolf but also Adolf's mother, Klara. We might see some of the descriptions in *Mein Kampf* as somewhat inspired by the violence of his own youth, as in the description of a working man who was estranged from his wife, and familiar with alcohol (*kommt er dem Alkkohol näher*),[1341] or the description of the crowded basement housing (*Kellerwohnung*) with ongoing cramped fights, leading to the imagined three-year-old who witnessed this (lightly disguised reference to young Adolf?), who would become a youth of fifteen years who would despise all authority (*ein fünfzehnjähriger Verächter jeder Autorität geworden*).[1342] To grow up with such ongoing, chronic, intense rage in the air, to be beaten as a little boy in a confrontation with his equally stubborn and unrelenting father, leading to a youth who despised all authority (in ways that would play out in rather complex if not convoluted ways as Hitler aimed at total authority himself), these can perhaps make some sense of the vicissitudes of Hitler's life and psychology; they may make somewhat intelligible what may otherwise seem irrational, but *they do not by that lead to an exculpation or exoneration or dismissal of the great harm* done as these factors (among many others) played out in European history of the 1920s-1940s.

While Hitler had a significant number of powerful issues that he was dealing with and operating out of, *he was not alone*. We might find such a person ending up as a penniless rambler talking to himself, mumbling in his sleeve, or he might have been a speaker at Hyde Park, in London, where people get up on small boxes (soap boxes) and talk out to whatever crowd they can gather about them—and then go their way, with no greater impact on those who hear them or on the society as a whole.

In the years following the defeat of the Third Reich, there was an initial scholarly focus on Hitler and his personality,[1343] the political context of the people of Germany and the Third Reich in the background. With this came the study in social (political) philosophy of Social Darwinism.[1344]

[1341] Adolf Hitler, *Mein Kampf*, Vol. I, Chap. II, Eng. pp. 37-38; Ger., p. 28.
[1342] Adolf Hitler, *Mein Kampf*, Vol. I, Chap. II, Eng. pp. 42-44; Ger., pp. 32-33.
[1343] See esp. Theodor W. Adorno, *The Authoritarian Personality* (1950; a significant 990 pages long), among other books of the post-war years.
[1344] Richard Hofstadter, *Social Darwinism in American Thought: 1860-1915* (1944) and *Social Darwinism in American Thought* (1955); cf. Greta Jones, *Social Darwinism and English Thought: The Interaction between Biological and Social Theory* (1980); Peter Dickens, *Social Darwinism: Linking Evolutionary Thought to*

The Hitler Era

Then, beyond such theorizing, there was the stunning Reich violence, with mass killings by impressive German power involved thousands of SS Men who were members of the *Einsatzgruppen* in the invasion of the Soviet Union. These—in a rather mundane way involving the practical logistics of mass killing—also required the political-police apparatus of the Reich, including the Gestapo (State Secret Police) and the administration of concentration camps (and especially of the extermination camps). And the organization of these efforts also required the many administrators[1345] in the Reich office focused on dealing with the Jewish Question, especially Amt IV B4: Amt IV was the Gestapo, its B was the office of religions and cults, and B4 focused on the Jewish religion, the sub-department on *Judenreferat*, the Office on Jewish Affairs, established in March 1941, and headed by Adolf Eichmann, under the RSHA, itself directed by Heinrich Himmler. There were, of course, furthermore, all of the bureaucrats who were involved in the routine work of traffic managers (in an old meaning of that work title, those who organized train scheduling to and from the camps), plus railroad employees, which involved hundreds of thousands of Germans—surely not each and every German, but remarkably more than a mere handful—*without whom the dreams of Hitler might have remained festering poisons in his psyche and nothing more.*

To expand our focus beyond that of Hitler himself (to quote historian Werner Maser, 1922-2007), we can start with Hitler's "ability not only to win over the majority of the German people, but to lead them so completely astray, [which] has no precedent in history."[1346] We may consider the audience Hitler was addressing, the impact he had, especially in the years 1919 to early 1933, before he was given the Chancellorship, and, then, as he gathered power and a government to carry out his dreams (nightmares for others). Concerning an overall, life-long view of Hitler and his psychology, psychiatrist Dr. Fritz Redlich (introduced above), among others, addressed key questions about the psychopathology of Hitler; Redlich described his work as a pathography, a biography that focuses on the impact of pathology on the life of the given individual (Hitler).[1347] Redlich concluded that had Hitler survived and been brought before the Nuremberg Tribunal, he would not have pleaded innocence on grounds of insanity (feeling he was quite sane and in fact a genius), would have been declared legally competent to stand trial by the Tribunal, and, that, in short, "Hitler believed he could decide what nations or races should inhabit the earth. But nobody has this right. He was too dangerous

---

Social Theory (2000); Rev. John H. Snow, *I Win, We Lose: The new Social Darwinism and the Death of Love, and Other Writings* (2016). John H. Snow (1924-2008) was Professor of Pastoral Theology, Episcopal Divinity School, Cambridge, MA (1972-1990).

[1345] Raul Hilberg, *The Destruction of the European Jews*. In its rev., definitive 3-vol. ed., 1985, it runs 1,273 pages; 1979 1-vol. ed., 790 pages.

[1346] Werner Maser, *Hitler: Legend, Myth, and Reality*, p. 258.

[1347] Frederick Redlich, *Hitler*, p. xii.

to remain a member of human society."[1348] This understanding of the danger presented by Hitler to the world, echoes other judgments of Hitler and the Third Reich as an appalling evil, as exhibiting utter barbarity, as plunging to the depths of depravity that before its time was simply unimaginable in civilized Europe. This suggests that the issue has not been one focused on debating whether there was violence in the Third Reich but of evaluating it: some (many) holding it to be a radically immoral attitude toward the world that glorified viciousness and heartlessness, and some (others) holding it to be a severe but laudable effort to improve the world by eliminating certain segments of it held to be (in Nazi terms) lives unworthy of living (*lebensunwertes Leben*).

The point of view that glorified the extermination of the Jewish people remained prominent in Hitler's worldview through to his final *Political Testament* (discussed above), which ended, "But before everything else I call upon the leadership of the nation and those who follow it to observe the racial laws most carefully, to fight mercilessly against the poisoners of all the peoples of the world, international Jewry." This may be a grand paranoid delusion, but certainly one with catastrophic consequences.

As what some see as an aside, Hitler and others have been mocked or criticized for their sexual interests. How many lives were impacted in strongly problematic ways by the sexual interests of various world leaders (not to mention others who were not at all in the public spotlight)? We have only to look across today's world and see leader after leader, in country after country, have their careers disrupted if not abruptly ended by their sexual escapades. This may be put down to the moralistic demands of society, especially on its leaders, but also reflects a drive that goes beyond anyone's good sense of what is appropriate to do, or to avoid doing, in given situations.

The sexual drive (referred to in Indic psychology as second-chakra energy) has a power that few are taught to recognize, understand, and come to peace with. In the educational dark about what our human sexuality is all about, we are more easily confused and feeling driven to act one (relatively stupid) way or another. Hitler was no exception to this, even if his peculiar proclivities may strike us as seriously "sick" or, at least, rather bizarre. But if we look somewhat carefully at his relationship with women, we can see a feature of his general way of interacting with others, depending on their social status in relation to his.

Hitler could be subservient if not servile and fawning, or could be quite demanding with little pity for the other; he could demand to be treated with harshness, physical violence, and even filth—a preference for being defecated or urinated on from above by someone else, in what are technically called coprophilia and urophilia; in his case, to have women

---

[1348] Frederick Redlich, *Hitler*, p. 339. Redlich cites Hannah Arendt, *Eichmann in Jerusalem*, p. 279, where a similar statement is made about Eichmann in the words of Arendt, imagining a statement that could have been made by the judges at the trial.

kick him and relieve themselves on top of him. Wilhelm Reich linked such exhibitions of misery as a way of (hopefully) bringing the other person to love the person experiencing such misery.[1349] Or, expressing a straight-forward attitude about urgent sexuality, called lust, a young German, Fred Stein, in conversation with his school friend, Alfons Heck, declared, "Never, but never, let ideology get in the way of lust. They are totally different concepts, no matter what Himmler claims."[1350] A reported case in point in masochistic interactions, among others, was Hitler's relation with German film actress, Renate Müller (1906-1937). She presumably committed suicide after one of their unusual intimate interactions.[1351]

Now, if we draw back from a sexual focus, and look to understand the various extreme demands by Hitler in some of their more extensive applications, we can perhaps see the confluence of three tendencies: (1) his reckless risk-taking, (2) his focusing on, emphasis on, and fascination with death, as in the many elaborate and formalized rituals honoring the dead through the Hitler era, and (3) his involvement in being punished and controlled (in part in some of his sexual interactions with his women intimates)—all of these dovetailing into a drive for self-destruction.

It was not only the German nation that Hitler felt deserved to be crushed by the Soviets if it proved itself weaker than the Slavs (however much this was disturbing to an assumption of Aryans as the *Herrenrasse*, of course). Hitler would speak of his *übergreifender Katastrophenwille* (overarching will for catastrophe)[1352] and of the *Strategie des grandiosen Untergangs* (the strategy of the grandiose downfall), for example, in his

---

[1349] Myron Sharaf, *Fury on Earth: A Biography of Wilhelm Reich*, p. 174.
[1350] Alfons Heck, *The Burden of Hitler's Legacy*, p. 93.
[1351] The Nazi Press declared at the time that Renate Müller had died of epilepsy (avoiding issues of suicide, murder, or drug addiction). She apparently died falling out of a window to the ground far below. Some analyses suggest suicide, others, the action of the Gestapo, and still others, that she lost her drug-inhibited balance while sitting at an open window, causing the fall. The report of Hitler's unusual demands on her, when she came to him expecting simply to have coitus, were reported by the American Alfred Zeisler (1892-1985)—who worked in the German film industry of the 1920s and early 1930s including being the producer of the 1933 film, *Viktor und Viktoria*, starring Renate Müller—remade in 1982 as *Victor/Victoria*, starring Julie Andrews—from a report he later passed on to investigators for the OSS (precursor to the CIA). Zeisler, although American was Jewish, and his Dutch actress wife, Nicolina Dijjers Spanier (1909-1982), known by her German film name as Lien Deyers, who was half-Jewish, would leave Germany in 1935, fearing their Jewish identities would be discovered. See Frederick Redlich, *Hitler*, pp. 81-83; Norwegian journalist and author Mikal Hem, *How to Be a Dictator: An irreverent Guide* (2017), presenting Hitler as one of the kinkiest of all dictators, in the lampooning "Be Sure to Sleep Around" (Chap. 6); cf. "Renate Müller," *Cabaret Berlin*, Sep. 7, 2012; Alison Maloney, "Adolf Hitler had a truly disgusting sexual fetish," *New York Post*, Mar. 7, 2016; "What Hitler's sex life was really like," *The Telegraph*, Jul. 6, 2018.
[1352] Helm Stierlin, *Hitler: Familienperspektiven* (1975); tr., *Hitler: A Family Perspective* (1976), pp. 84-85.

comments to Martin Bormann on February 6, 1945, comparing the Third Reich (and its situation then) to ancient Sparta. Hitler remarked: "A desperate fight keeps its eternal value as an exemplar [a paradigmatic example]. Think of Leonidas and his three hundred Spartans. In any case, it does not fit our style to let ourselves be slaughtered like sheep. One may exterminate us, but one will not be able to lead us to the slaughter."[1353] This fear of being exterminated was quite significant, although often put in the background with a greater focus on the claims to being the leader of a superior race of humans, but can make sense of the radical approach to Jews (and Romanies), wanting to exterminate them, man, woman, and child. *A profound fear of a Jewish plan to kill off Germans and Germany could provide the intense focus seen and heard in some of Hitler's speeches, screamed out in a frenzy, transmitted to a likewise-frenzied audience, his ranting and raving being taken with enthusiasm, as an intense but justified defiance against such horrible dangers.* The fear that Jews across Europe wanted Hitler and the entire German nation to be removed from the earth can strike the outsider as quite delusional! That fear might indeed explain the program of killing each and every Jew in Europe, but Hitler's assumption that all Jews, even babies, were potential sources of future genocidal revenge wanting to exterminate the German people, was "totally a fantasy in his own mind," as historian Christopher Browning put it[1354]; Robert Waite considered this a projection with dire consequences (more just below). We can see similar fears expressed by Himmler, in some of his speeches to SS Men.

These observations and analyses of aspects of Hitler's particular psychological make-up have their own interest, and we may consider which of these, and to what extent, they individually and jointly played a role in the social tendencies of the Third Reich and in the international domain, including World War II. Looking back across these great expanses of time and space, we can appreciate that Hitler was not alone in his Sparta-inspired attitude. The interpretation of a loss in battle (especially definitively) is something few nations are ready to accept without the greatest of reluctance. One recent case in point is the long extension of US fighting against the Vietnamese.

From the Vietnamese perspective, this was the Second Vietnam War, the first being fought to expel France as a colonial power, which lasted from 1946-1954, ending with the fall of the French colonial armies at Điện Biên Phủ on May 7, 1954. The US involvement in Vietnam went from a vested interest that began with support of the French that after the defeat of the French evolved from a US military advisory capacity to open involvement of US military in the early 1960s—intensified by the Tonkin Bay Incident (based on US Navy misinterpretations) and continued through years of indecisive encounters (some quite bloody), until it was

---

[1353] Martin M. Winkler, *Classical Literature on Screen: Affinities of Imagination* (2017), p. 294. Cf. Werner Maser, *Adolf Hitler: Legende, Mythos, Wirklichkeit*, pp. 137-140; Eng. tr., *Hitler: Legend, Myth, and Reality*, esp. pp. 40, 51, 258.

[1354] Christopher Browning, in *After the Holocaust* (2015), at 52:15-53:00.

clear to most that the US military and political will were not up to the task of involvement that would have been called for to defeat the Vietcong led by Ho Chi Minh; the final withdrawal of US troops took place on March 29, 1973.[1355] (The USSR faced a similar quandary in the Soviet-Afghan War of 1979-1989.)

Or, much, much earlier, we can consider the invasions of the Persian army under Darius in the early sixth century BCE against the Scythians (who inhabited the Ukrainian steppe, also called the Pontic steppe or the Caspian steppe, a vast area north of the Black Sea), who refused to battle the Persian armies, withdrawing and attacking in a random fashion, losing nothing significant, and, ultimately, frustrating Darius into retreat. With this we may also think back on Greek ships that were sent to far-away Sicily to support allies there, only to be drawn into their own quagmire. As one geopolitical theoretician commented, with a general principle being expressed in the particular: "With the Athenians, as with Darius, *one is astonished by how the obsession with honor and reputation can lead a great power to a bad fate*. The image of Darius's army marching into nowhere on an inhospitable steppe, in search of an enemy that never quite appears, is so powerful that it goes beyond mere symbolism."[1356] This hubris-based thinking is found repeatedly in decisions made by countries at war.

To give one framework here—we will begin with general comments here and then focus in on Hitler—in an overview of human experience and the impact that that has for us in our lives and dealings with others, we can remark that our human condition has us open to learning from our experience. Part of this is our learning about what is pleasant and what disagreeable, what safe and what dangerous, and, in our first years, our understanding of human relations, that is, how people interact with one another. A large part of this we learn from the particular people we grow up with, whether we are living in a nuclear family, a family with a parent or parents and some children, in an extended family, with people of several generations consisting perhaps us and our parents, our grandparents, uncles and aunts and their children, or whether living our first years in other structures for group activity, from kibbutzim to tribal societies.

And, of course, in our growing up in the group we knew as a child, we also received much in the way of various rituals that became second nature to us, including the manners we were taught about how we were to act, and much in the way of beliefs that our group held, unquestionably. One German writer, reflecting on the Hitler era, said of this familial education, "All children are defenseless receptacles, waiting to be filled with wisdom or venom by their parents and educators."[1357]

[1355] See 1974 film, *Hearts and Minds*, on the US involvement in Vietnam—winner of 1975 Academy Award for the Best Documentary. Cf. Raymond Aron, *République imperiale: Les États-unis dans le Monde, 1945-1972* (1973).

[1356] Robert D. Kaplan, *The Return of Marco Polo's World*, pp. 46-47. Italics added.

[1357] Alfons Heck, *The Burden of Hitler's Legacy*, p. 44.

As children, we are filled with ideas and judgments about what is good, bad, and indifferent, in some instances, a mix of wisdom and arbitrary, quite questionable, and even hate-driven ideas. Some of these limit us in extreme ways, making us rigid in our responses to new situations, self-defeating in our actions, and unhelpfully, unskillfully reactive in ways that reflect earlier education and mis-education.

A Brief Excursus into Psychopathology

Whatever the traumas were that we lived through and came to terms with (or remained tormented by), as adults we are certainly more capable of reviewing our earlier education and seeing the ways in which our past is guiding if not controlling our present. We have the capacity to transform what we were given and how we initially learned to survive—children are quite limited in both their options to confront their situation and in their understanding of what is going on when adults speak or act. (Often as a child, there is a reference back to oneself, as if we were responsible for everything everyone else does, as if everyone else's thoughts and actions were defined and controlled by us!)

While prejudice is rampant among our species, we are also, at least as adults, in the position to revisit our accepted doctrines, and to refine them in ways that are more satisfying for us (and for others).

The Austrian-Jewish physicist, considered by many as the greatest physicist of all times, Albert Einstein (1879-1950), has recently been shown to have had his own set of prejudices against other peoples, especially during the journal he kept on a visit to the Orient from October 1922 to March 1923.[1358] (He would have been in his early 40s at the time.) In the next twenty years, he was certainly given the opportunity to look at the ways in which ethnic and cultural stereotyping can lead to rather dire results, and with the changes in his understanding, he is better known for his criticism of racism, remarking after the war that racism was a disease of the white man. (Even then, he was too narrow in his vision of where racism can develop, we should add.) Of course, we don't have to be an Einstein to open ourselves to a re-evaluation of what we believe, even "the little lies we tell ourselves" and the reactivity we are directed by, which can control us even despite ourselves, even if we want fervently to stop being driven by such distorting and perhaps hate-filled features of our mind, conditioned character, or personality.

Considering some of the abusive treatment meted out on young Adolf by his father, Alois Sr., we may put this into a wider context. That is, while some children who are beaten severely by the adults in charge of them later turn out to be as brutal as adults as those adults, other stay focused on avoiding a repetition of such a horrible way of treating children. In other words, there is much flexibility about how we deal with our past and its conditioning. In this light, we may consider the particular path that Hitler took in his dealing with his violent childhood. We can see many

---

[1358] Alison Flood, "Einstein's travel diaries reveal 'shocking' xenophobia," *The Guardian*, Jun. 12, 2018.

examples of his taking his own unpleasant ("negative") psychological states and emotions and rejecting them, transforming them, projecting them into characteristics of others that he saw as mortal enemies. Here, some authors speak of Hitler as manifesting what is termed a borderline personality.[1359]

This does not mean someone who almost has a personality but not quite, but, rather, someone with a personality that has some hint of psychosis but maintains itself in a rigid but basically viable frame of mind. As one psychohistorian put it, "The most basic characteristic of borderline personalities is a 'splitting of the ego.' Patients exhibit dramatically opposing personality traits: they are cruel and kind, sentimental and hard, creative and destructive: they swing violently between excessive protestations of love and wild outbursts of hate. It often appears, Dr. [Otto] Kernberg[1360] has noted, as if there were in each patient 'two distinct selves ... equally strong, completely separated from each other.' His descriptions correspond closely with Albert Speer's picture of Hitler as a person who has cruel, unjust, cold, capricious, self-pitying, and vulgar [tendencies], but who was also "the exact opposite of almost all of those things ... a [person with a] generous superior, amiable, self-controlled, capable of enthusiasm for beauty and greatness."[1361]

And yet a word of caution is appropriate. Given the complex definition of a borderline personality, as in the DSM (*Diagnostic and Statistical Manual*) used in US psychiatric contexts, the term can be applied if a certain number out of the full list of possible symptoms contributing to the definition of the condition are met. As psychiatrist Fritz Redlich wrote, "It is impossible to handle such a laundry list unless one specifies what items are essential and necessary to arrive at a diagnosis."[1362] This suggests being explicit about specific features of interest, *suggesting that a diagnostic description is in this sense only of secondary value*.

Here, we can notice one such shift as was just described, called splitting (separating oneself from the frame of mind or attitude in question) and projecting them onto others (attributing our own psychological truths to these others), as when Hitler (and others) overlooked their own violent instincts and held that to be a goal held by all the world's Jews—capitalists, Bolsheviks, those in between, and those not fitting into this continuum at all—to wipe out civilized Europe with Germany at its peak.

These attitudes, operating in an alienated and split process, could be managed, although not in a totally comfortable way. In the case of Hitler,

---

[1359] For one group of (phenomenological) descriptions of states of mind related to extremes of temperament, see Sect. III ("Through the Faces of Rage"), pp. 29-70, in Mitchell Ginsberg, *Peace and War and Peace*.

[1360] See Otto Kernberg, *Borderline Conditions and Pathological Narcissism* (1975), and *Aggressivity, Narcissism, and Self-destructiveness in the Psychotherapeutic Relationship: New Developments in the Psychopathology and Psychotherapy of Severe Personality Disorders* (2004)—with numerous translations.

[1361] Robert G. L. Waite, *The Psychopathic God: Adolf Hitler* (1977), p. 357.

[1362] Frederick Redlich, *Hitler*, pp. 334-335.

there was an ongoing tension in his way of being and how he related to those around him, as we have seen repeatedly. As psychohistorian Robert Waite, just quoted, summed this up:

> He [Hitler] projected all the bad onto others, especially the Jews: degeneracy, femininity, softness. Projection produced in Hitler—as it invariably does in borderline patients—a terrifying view of the world as irreconcilably split between good and bad, with the forces of evil constantly conspiring against the good. He felt compelled to fight and destroy the encircling and ubiquitous enemy before it destroyed him. While the split world created in his own image was dangerous and constantly threatening him, it served as an important defense, and hence as a kind of therapy. For it enabled him to externalize [and project] a conflict which, if left bottled up within, could have led to mental disintegration and collapse. The diagnosis of Hitler as borderline personality helps to explain why, though he may have experienced psychotic episodes, he never crossed over the border into full-blown psychosis. He was able to project and externalize his own "neuroses," rationalize them, and proclaim them officially as a "world view" and governmental policy.[1363]

Thus, if we appreciate what any given person has lived through up until the present, in that light we can make sense of what that person is now concerned with. *But we might also keep in mind that how a given individual deals with his past is open to many possibilities*. We can stay on automatic pilot, reacting as we learned to, earlier in our lives, or we can examine this and see ways in which to overcome and transform that sort of reactivity, to come afresh to the present situation.[1364]

When we look at experiences that bring about shifts in individuals' thoughts, values, and attitudes about life in general, and about the social fabric in which they are living, what makes for such shifts is sometimes understandable, but almost never predictable.

The variety of influences that shift our sense and appreciation of our world can be pointed to with specifics: speaking of his shepherd dog Prinz, Alfons Heck wrote, "Prinz's death had done to me what the loss of any human never achieved—because of its very senselessness, it temporarily cracked the armour of my soul. I had long since become immune to the brutality and death which were part of my daily life but animals were not soldiers and they had not sworn an oath of unconditional obedience. Prinz and my horse, Felix, now also charred to the bone [from bombings in the

---

[1363] Robert G. L. Waite, *The Psychopathic God*, p. 358.

[1364] This going beyond our conditioning and the related rotelike automaticity of our thinking and acting (reacting) is perhaps the core project of spiritual teachings that are psychologically focused, recently termed psychospirituality.

war], had been my closest companions."[1365] And so with Hitler, and so with the rest of humanity.

Hitler would develop a number of psychological tendencies that would be largely definitive of how he related to others, how he dealt with changing life situations, and how he acted to preserve some sense of his own worth. There were a number of physical and psychological features that were important in Hitler's comportment. There was his desire to present himself as an all-powerful master, totally sure of himself and identifying himself as the one person capable of leading Germany out of its shame and financial crises (which had happened before he came to power); he also had a rather delicate digestive system with a strong, disagreeable odor from his mouth, constipation, and chronic flatulence. Hitler dealt with these problems with a diet that was vegetarian, high in various legumes, especially beans, not known to minimize flatulence.

When drained by the events of the world that he was attempting to master, he began treatments in the mid-1930s with Dr. Prof. Theodor Morell, a Berlin physician who specialized in treating syphilis (even though it is highly unlikely that Hitler suffered from that condition), who used a wide variety of injections, often multiple times per day. While Dr. Morell was looked on askance by many in Hitler's inner circle, including other physicians, perhaps Morell was not a mad quack. The physician Hans-Joachim Neumann and the historian Henrik Eberle[1366] carried out an extensive and careful study of the various medicines administered by Dr. Morell carried out by Dr. Morell. In part, they concluded that a number of these (even if we might think of them as strange if not bizarre) were basically innocuous, not being especially helpful but not having any significant harmful impact on Hitler. (The use of strychnine was one of the exceptions to this.) Besides his fear that he had contracted syphilis in his young Vienna days (most likely, another of his groundless fears), Hitler first consulted with Dr. Morell about his need to maintain his public image as a strong, independent, indefatigable, and sure-minded leader of his people, ready to devote his entire abundant life energies for the welfare of the German nation. This was quite a task for Dr. Morell, given Hitler's physical problems, some just mentioned. Hitler's fatigue would reach extreme levels, not aided by the intense demands on his life as Führer and then Commander-in-Chief of the Wehrmacht, especially given his insistence that his judgment rule over the advice of his generals. Further, his interest in his masculine prowess, his ability to engage in sexual intercourse, led to further injections, such as processed bull testicles (one of Dr. Morell's more unusual treatments). In addition to laxatives—complemented when needed by a compound with sodium bicarbonate, Yatren, used to combat diarrhea—there were anti-gas pills, begun in 1935 at the suggestion of an earlier physician, Dr. Ernst-Robert

---

[1365] Alfons Heck, *The Burden of Hitler's Legacy*, p. 152.
[1366] Hans-Joachim Neumann is Professor Emeritus of Medicine at Charité-Universitätsmedizin (Berlin); Henrik Eberle is a German historian specializing in research on Adolf Hitler.

Grawitz. A charge that Morell was poisoning Hitler, intentionally or otherwise, with high doses of strychnine, turned out to be unfounded, when lab tests of the suspected medicine showed only trace levels of the substance. To soothe gastrointestinal spasms, another condition that Hitler endured, other drugs were given by IM injections for several years, such as a benzoic acid ester, Progynon-Boleosum. For boosting energy, there were also injections that might include a combination of medicines and several forms of amphetamines and narcotics. One commercial product that was widely used in the Third Reich and was for years available with no prescription throughout Germany, was called Pervitin, a brand name for methamphetamine hydrochloride. This was advertised for hypotonia (low muscle tone) and for syncope (*Kreislaufkollaps*) or transitory lapses of adequate blood to the brain, a central nervous system (CNS) stimulant (*Weckmittel*). It was a powerful stimulant.

Many Germans from that period can remember using Pervitin to energize them; the German military, including the Luftwaffe, would use this stimulant on tense and demanding missions. (We might mention that amphetamines were also commonly used in other countries, sometimes given as injections by physicians, when involved, as a mix of vitamins, claimed to be good for giving healthy energy to the patient.)

One significant moment was when Hitler flew into Treviso, north of Venice, to meet Mussolini, on July 19, 1942. Although there were no specific records of the dosage of Pervitin or other stimulants given Hitler there, Neumann and Eberkle wrote, "It is highly likely that he took some [methamphetamine tablets] because during the meeting Hitler was so euphoric and verbose that Mussolini was barely able to get a word in edgewise." When these stimulants resulted in an inability to sleep, Hitler was given sedatives, a favorite being a tablet containing barbiturates (such as Phanodorm), alternating with a suppository, Tempidorm tablets, containing barbituric acid. *In lay terms*, this was an alternating between "uppers" (stimulants) and "downers" (sedatives), quite draining on the body, as we might know or imagine.[1367] Injections of amphetamines are known to give energy, temporarily overcoming fatigue (but leading to a rather extreme physical weakness, if not collapse), to a highly exaggerated sense of self and of one's abilities and achievements, and to a tendency to be able to talk at great length without the need of any responses that would ease conversation in many situations. In addition, and relatedly, Hitler seemed to show a rather minimal appreciation of others, as when he would talk for hours at dinner gathering, repeating the same stories over and over, much to the boredom of those present, as reported by a number of people who spent considerable time with Hitler through the 1930s and the first half of the 1940s.

[1367] On these many meds, with discussion and comments on their usage and health impact on Hitler, see Hans-Joachim Neumann and Henrik Eberle, *War Hitler Krank?*, Eng., *Was Hitler Ill?*, esp. Chap. 4 ("*Ein Blick in Hitlers Apotheke: Die Medikamente und ihre Auswirkungen*"), pp.125-165, and Eng. Chap. 4 ("Hitler's Medicine Chest: The Drugs and the Effects"), pp. 74-103.

The Hitler Era

The decades since the suicide of Hitler have been filled with a stream of proposed diagnoses. *There are two general caveats or hesitations in going down this path of consideration.* First is the general if not ubiquitous use of psychiatric diagnoses attributing one or another psychopathological condition to given people in ways that look very scientific but are used as moral judgments.[1368] As Austrian professor of neurology and psychiatry, Otto Pötzl (1877-1962), who had associations with the famous Vienna Circle,[1369] noted, "many psychiatric diagnoses are forms of slander" and added, about personality diagnoses, "Nothing is gained by such diagnoses but a false sense of knowledge."[1370] In addition to the issue of the judgmental or insulting associations that various pathological terms have come to carry, there is also the complication that given diagnoses may be understood in one of a number of ways. An example here is classification as a Borderline Personality (addressed just above). There are several interpretations of what this amounts to, from the understanding of various respected psychiatrists to the more formal definition (in the USA) that uses the latest version of the DSM (Diagnostic and Statistical Manual), with what some describe as a shopping basket of criteria. Among others, Dr. Redlich commented on this problem (see above). That said, we can certainly give rather specific descriptions of what made Hitler particular. His belief in his messianic purpose for the German people, his certainty about the poison of world Jewry, his sense of leading the German people to a great territorial realm carved largely out of the Soviet Union in which the Germans would be the masters and others subservient to them, without much thought or concern about how such an idea would be received by those being crushed by the German military—these are a combination of psychological features that could aim for world rule.

Touching on this interest in world domination (within limits), Hitler once was being toyed with by his secretary, Christa Schroeder, who accused him of stealing her flashlight (British English, torch). Hitler showed his particular sense of humor and the seriousness of his intention to carry out international plunder, saying, with a play of words between *Lampledieb*, lamp thief, vs. *Ländledieb*, country thief[1371] (in his dialectical German): "I don't steal flashlights! I steal countries!"[1372]

[1368] See discussion of this issue in "Pathologizing Distress," pp. 145-148 in Mitchell Ginsberg, *Calm, Clear, and Loving*.

[1369] The Vienna Circle, known for its development of Logicial Empiricism, was a gathering of some of the most brilliant philosophers, logicians, and other theoreticians in Middle Europe in those inter-war years, with an interest in understanding the foundations of knowledge and the foundations of mathematics; participants included Gustav Bergmann, Rudolf Carnap, Kurt Gödel, Carl Hempel, Otto Neurath, Alfred Tarski, and Ludwig Wittgenstein. See Friedlich Stadler, *The Vienna Circle: Studies in the Origins, Development, and Influence of Logical Empiricism* (2001), VIENNA CIRCLE INSTITUTE LIBRARY.

[1370] Fritz Redlich, *Hitler*, pp. 334, 336.

[1371] Standard German: Lamp thief: *Lampendieb*, and Land thief: *Landdieb*.

[1372] Christa Schroeder, *Er war mein Chef*, p. 112. Quoted and cited in Fritz Redlich,

On other features of Hitler's psychology, we can consider, as well, his strong need to be correct and faultless, his very short fuse when those around him gave disagreeing opinions about him, the objective situation Germany was facing, or the Reich's harsh treatment of the Jews.[1373] Here, his strong tendency to put blame for any setback or problem not on any role he himself might have played, but on the incompetence, laziness, or treasonous disloyalty of those he put his good faith in, his insensitivity, just mentioned, to those around him who might be bored, uncomfortable, or simply quite fatigued after hours of Hitler's monologue of the night, and his image of a man totally dedicated to his country, taking no wife or mistress (a false front only made public the day before he married his lover Eva Braun, and then committed suicide with her). And so on.

One prominent pattern that was seen in several different contexts during Hitler's adolescence by his friend of the time, August Kubizek,[1374] and that recurred throughout Hitler's life, was the transforming of any disappointment into some theory about the betrayal of Hitler by those in whom he had put his good faith and trust—as in his often-present sense of nefarious, unnamed Jews who were quite malevolently blocking him personally from achieving his dreams. We can see this repeatedly through the years up until his very last days, with his similar conclusion of betrayal by his closest, most trusted fellow Nazis (especially Göring and, perhaps even more so, Himmler) and of all of the generals of his military that Hitler saw as incompetent and envious of his genius.

An overriding feature of Hitler's thinking that can be seen in his various statements and explanations of his past (however contrived and unlikely) explained all set-backs and lacks of success on his part as due totally to outside forces that were blocking his path, often implied or stated to be malicious forces. If we look at the groups that Hitler intensely hated, they include, of course, Jews, but also Catholics, Romanies, bureaucrats, and the bourgeois (the middle-class providers of various services and goods), the Czechs, and later, all Slavs, as well as those with what Hitler saw as disgusting, dirty personal preferences, including any sexuality that disturbed him. These were all shadows to Hitler's personal identity, including his fear of being part Jewish, his unexpressed hatred of his father with his traditional Catholic upbringing and socially-correct respect for civil servants, with links to the Czech people coming at least through his maternal great-grandfather, as discussed above. In contrast, he would find great value and honor in the poor, the laborers, the workers of the land (at least in an abstract, romanticized, idealized version), as well as the lower echelon military (not the generals, whom he felt did not know what war was about, never experiencing artillery, cannon, and poison gas attacks during the First World War—unlike many such as himself).

Hitler: Diagnosis of a Destructive Prophet (1999) p. 334, and in Ian Kershaw, *Hitler 1936-1945: Nemesis*, p. 397.

[1373] More on Hitler's strong rejection of Henriette von Schirach concerning this issue, just below.

[1374] George Victor, *Hitler: The Pathology of Evil*, pp. 36-37, 40-41.

The Hitler Era

Another well-known feature of Hitler's interactional style (if we can call it that) was his short-temper and his intense agitation when contradicted or questioned. We have some prime examples of this, such as in Hitler's calling down Henriette von Schirach (just mentioned) when she flew to Berchtesgaden after being disturbed on seeing Dutch Jews being harshly treated at the train station (on their way to an extermination camp).

Foreign Minister Joachim von Ribbentrop reported another example of a disagreement with Hitler in 1940 (and so, not an artifact from the final months of Hitler's great depression as the war was slowly but inexorably being lost). It was a trivial matter for him, but Ribbentrop threatened to resign. At that, Hitler "got red in the face and screamed and then had some kind of attack. He fell into his chair and said, 'Look what you are doing to me! You are driving me to distraction. Now I've got a roaring in my ears and I am sick. Suppose I should get a stroke. Do you want to ruin Germany? I am the only one who can lead Germany in these dangerous times [this, in 1940, the year before the invasion of the USSR], and you will ruin her [the German nation] by upsetting me this way!' So I [Ribbentrop] promised never to resign or to oppose him again."[1375]

Now, what may strike the reader here is that Hitler attributes to Ribbentrop what is happening to him—we would say nowadays that Hitler takes no responsibility for his own role in this social, interpersonal exchange, including his own agitation and his worry about getting a stroke, all tied to the destiny of Germany. (As an example of denial of responsibility, think of a man who yells out at his battered wife: "You made me hit you!") Some would also see in Hitler's statements here a grandiosity, an extreme form of pompous self-importance.

Hitler gave extreme importance to being correct, even down to some rather minor issues. One illustration of this took place when Hitler was whistling a tune. Eva Braun whistled the melody as she knew it: Hitler insisted that his version was correct. "Well, let's listen to the record. You'll see which of us is right," Eva suggested. The aide-de-camp, Albert Bormann, found the record and put it on the turntable. Eva turned out to be right, but Hitler wouldn't admit that he was beaten: "You're right,' he said, "but the composer was wrong. If he'd been as talented as me, he'd have written my version."[1376] This apparent insecurity and need to be right in all instances and in all situations is rather tiring to maintain, but it did have powerful and deadly ramifications in the workings of the inner circles of the Third Reich.

Important, of course, was Hitler's tendency to refuse teachers as competent in any way, from his father's bureaucratic mentality trying to beat into Adolf the value of becoming a government administrator, to

---

[1375] Gustave M. Gilbert, *Nuremberg Diary* (1947), pp. 128-130.

[1376] Quoted from Gertraud Junge, Pierre Galante, Eugène Silianoff, *Les derniers témoins du bunker: La vérité sur la fin d'Hitler* (1989), pp. 96-97; US ed., Pierre Galante, Eugène Silianoff, with Gertraud/Traudl Junge, *Voices from the Bunker*, p. 71; UK ed., Gertraud Junge, Pierre Galante, Eugène Silianoff, *Last Witnesses in the Bunker* (1989), p. 71.

Adolf's rejection of teachers, sometimes before they could criticize him and sometimes afterwards, his lack of interest in completing even the equivalent of a high-school education, his pride in being an autodidact, a self-taught person, and his position that he knew everything better than anyone else (just mentioned).

A word of advice here from Ben Jonson (1572-1637): "No man is so foolish but may give another good counsel sometimes; and no man is so wise but may easily error, if he will take no others' counsel but his own. But very few men are wise by their own counsel, or learned by their own teaching. For he that was only taught by himself [Greek: *autodídaktos*], had a fool to his master."[1377]

These psychological features were complemented by Hitler's sense that he not only knew better than anyone else, no matter what their training, experience, or expertise, but also that he had been selected to be the savior of the German people, who had been saved by providence from many attempts to assassinate him (creating a sense of ultimate invulnerability). Such a frame of mind can certainly be a driving force to inspire a sense of global rights on behalf of his people (*Volk*), but when he declared that only he could save the German people, only he could direct the German military to ultimate victory, through his will and vision of Germany's place in the world—itself quite kitsch an idea—there was a problem. This becomes clear if we consider both Hitler's firm belief that only he could lead the German people as called upon to do, and also that here was a thousand-year Empire (Reich): Hitler could not have thought that he would have such a long lifespan. That was quite beyond our sense of the limits of human longevity! There was for this reason the serious problem of how to imagine, or how to establish, a political system that could maintain the Reich after Hitler's death. The thought that no one could possibility replace him, even a son which Hitler at some rare moments contemplated having (according to the personal diary of Eva Braun). If even a son could not be taught what only Hitler could see, understand, and have the will to carry out, what conceivable government in a post-Hitler Third Reich, could continue for over nine hundred more years? It is perhaps impossible to hold on to the reins of government with a tight-fisted hand and at the same time discuss or at least announce the structures needed in the long-term Reich government and administration to continue the Reich to its full millennial lifetime!

Whatever the answer to that conundrum (if any), Hitler followed rather attentively what was going on in Germany, even to the extent of reviewing court cases, and inflicting (by Führer decree) a harsher sentence, often committing the accused to death, if he felt that the court had been too lenient, as in two cases in which Hitler, through Himmler, let it be known that he wanted two men shot—Paul Latacz and Edwin Jakobs: they had

---

[1377] Ben Jonson, "Sylva (Timber, or, A Wood)," in Jonson's *Discoveries Made upon Man and Matter* (1892 ed.), PROJECT GUTENBERG (2014); the comments quoted, toward the beginning of "Sylva," were put in the speech of the character Consilia.

The Hitler Era

been convicted of attempted robbery of a Berlin bank on September 30, 1939, and were sentenced to ten years in the penitentiary. This was apparently too light a sentence for Hitler.[1378] It is thus a stretch of the imagination, knowing that Hitler had this sort of involvement in German affairs, that he had no idea of the mass killings of those "lives unworthy of life" (the T4 euthanasia program that was stopped after some Church leaders denounced it) or of the use of railway cars to transport people to the death camps, taking them away from the military need for them.

We can also consider here the speculations of some that Hitler did not actually commit suicide in the Berlin Chancellery bunkers at the end of April 1945, but escaped (perhaps to South America). These speculations suggest that if Hitler did survive, perhaps he laid the foundations for a truly millennial Reich! For some years there might have been the hope in some circles that Hitler would present himself to lead a new Reich; given that Hitler was born in 1889, that is hardly an issue at this point in time. Still, if he had only written down his visionary understanding of a Reich that others could follow, perhaps hope for a resurrected Reich might be maintained. Of course, even if there were such instructions, it is not at all obvious that there would be a groundswell of enthusiasm to try the Nazi Reich once again, given its disastrous consequences for the entire German nation the first time around.

Here, we may bring into consideration what has been discussed as the teachings that were appealing both to Hitler—seeing himself as the knight in Teutonic armoring) and to Himmler—considering himself to be the reincarnation of Heinrich I (876-936),[1379] the Saxon king who united the Teutons. These teachings were Germanic to the core, with a culture and societal value system that was free of "southern" morality—the morality of the Vatican, itself representing that degenerate religion, Judaism (from the Nazi perspective, that is). In this Germanic world, the Judeo-Christian caring for the weak, the defenseless, the poor, and other less powerful individuals, and groups, was rejected as a morality of inferiority. In its place was the honoring of power, force, and the ability to conquer, with the killing that that involved, all to be done in true Teutonic spirit, with no remorse, no regrets, and no guilt. Hitler would declare, "I am freeing

---

[1378] Oxford-educated historian Sir Richard Evans mentions other convicted criminals whose sentences were increased to being executed, at Hitler's orders—one estimation was that there were some 18 such extra-judicial executions ordered by Hitler during the War—and even more whose initial sentences were made more severe by decisions of the Reich Justice Ministry. This is not to mention the number of prisoners shot "while resisting transfer or in trying to excape" (many recognized even by Reich Ministry representatives to be quite unlikely). And, this is all in the context of the extremely high rate of guilty verdicts with the sentence of execution by guillotine from the *Volksgerichtshof*, the People's Court. See Richard J. Evans, *Rituals of Retribution*, pp. 697-701. Cf. Michael Stolleis, "Central European History [Review of Richard J. Evans, *Rituals of Retribution*]," *Central European History*, vol. 31, no. 1/2, 1998, pp. 132–136.

[1379] "Henry I: King of Germany," ENCYCLOPÆDIA BRITANNICA.

men from the wearisome restrictions of the mind, from the dirty and degrading self-mortifications of a chimera[1380] [he said] called conscience and morality, and from the demands of a freedom and personal independence which a very few enjoy"[1381]—demands for an individual's independent thinking to judge what is right and what is wrong.

Instead of the Jewish prophets and Jesus as the Messiah, the Nordic gods were central in this National Socialist theistic metaphor, the most central and powerful being Wotan (also known as Odin), taken already in the nineteenth century as "the personification of that driving force of the Germany people that made them supreme in world history,"[1382] as Wolfgang Menzel (1799-1873) expressed the principle in his book, *Odin* (1855).

Relatedly, Carl Gustav Jung (before the war) would look back in time and see the lack of German colonial development (unlike some other European powers) as linked to German psychology: "and so the Germans got their inferiority complex which made them want to fight the [First] World War, and of course when they lost it [the War] their feeling of inferiority grew even worse, and [they] developed a desire for a Messiah, and so they have their Hitler. If he is not their [Germans'] true Messiah, he is like one of the Old Testament prophets; his mission is to unite his people and lead them to the Promised Land."[1383] (Jung does not explain here what the metaphor of this "Promised Land" might amount to.)

Now, to talk of an inferiority complex is to speak of an abiding *sense of one's being inferior* to others (giving the name to the complex), influential in one's related thoughts and feelings, and in one's overall

---

[1380] A chimera: an imaginary creature; in Greek mythology, a fire-breathing female with a lion's head, a goat's body, and a snake's tail.

[1381] NT-IMT-Blue, vol. 7, p. 153, quoting Hermann Rauschning, *The Voice of Destruction* (1940), p. 225. See partial quotation and discussion in Robert G. L. Waite, "Hitler's Anti-Semitism: A Study in History and Psychoanalysis," pp. 192–230 in Benjamin B. Wolman, *The Psychoanalytic Interpretation of History* (1971), at p. 203; cf. Robert Waite, "Adolf Hitler's Guilt Feelings: A Problem in History and Psychology," *Journal of Interdisciplinary History*, vol. 1, Winter 1971, pp. 229-249, at p. 235. Rausching (1887-1982) was an early Nazi and the Nazi President of the Danzig Senate from June 20, 1933 to Nov, 23, 1934. Resigning his post and his membership in the National Socialist Party, he fled to Poland in 1936, moved to Switzerland in 1937, to France in 1938, to the UK in 1939, and to the USA, in 1941. His writings are questioned if not rejected by many with a favorable bent toward Hitler, his history, and his personality, including Holocaust-deniers such as David Irving, Mark Weber, and the lesser-known Swiss revisionist historian Wolfgang Nänel, with links primarily to the revisionist (often Holocaust-denying) Institute for Historical Review (IHR) and to other institutes as the *Zeitgeschichtliche Forschungsstelle Ingolstadt* (ZFI)—Ingolstadt at the end of this institute name is a town in Bavaria, south of Nuremberg and north of Munich.

[1382] Jay Sherry, *Carl Gustav Jung: Avant-Garde Conservative* (2010), p. 148.

[1383] Hubert Renfro Nickerbocker, "Diagnosing the Dictators—An Interview with Dr. C. G. Jung," *Cosmopolitan*, vol. 106, no 1, Jan. 1939, pp. 116-120, at p. 120.

interpersonal attitude and way of relating to others. Here, this can be applied to an entire people, rather than to relevant individuals, but the metaphoric application of a feature of individual psychology to a group brings on distortions that are background questions here, as well as the direct question: Can a group's sense of its inferiority explain on its own a desire for war? At the least, answers to these questions call for reflection and pondering.

Continuing with Jung's thinking here, in the same pre-war period, in his article "The Psychology of Dictatorship" (1936),[1384] Jung wrote, "There are two types of dictators—the chieftain type and the medicine man type. Hitler is the latter. He is a medium. German policy is not made; it is revealed through Hitler. He is the mouthpiece of the gods, as of old. He says the word which expresses everybody's resentment [especially against the Versailles Treaty]." Jung describes Hitler's solitary reclusion leading to an announcement, with no explanation, that Germany would leave the League of Nations as "rule by revelation."[1385] These descriptions may or may not be highly admirative of Hitler, but the essay is at least (or at most) rather circumspect about putting forth any critical comments about the Führer. For Jung (and for others), events in the important years after 1936-1937, through the end of the Reich in 1945, called for a revisiting of what Hitler signified; Jung was inspired to re-evaluate Hitler: After the fall of the Third Reich, Jung would produce an article called "After the Catastrophe" (1945), which wrote of the twelve years of the Third Reich, entering the subject by declaring, "Unfortunately, for twelve long years it has been demonstrated with the utmost clarity that the official German was no gentlemen." Indeed, and, we can say that to speak of Hitler as "no gentleman" is an almost British extreme understatement. After the war, Jung admitted to the scholar Rabbi Leo Baeck, who had survived Theresienstadt, "*Ich bin ausgerutscht*" (I slipped up, slipped off the path, blundered)—in one interpretation: "probably referring to the Nazis and his [Jung's] expectation that something great might after all emerge."[1386] Jung went further, writing from his own special perspective and understanding of the human psyche, "It is a fact that cannot be denied: the wickedness of others becomes our own wickedness because it kindles something wicked in our own hearts. The murder has been suffered by everyone, and everyone has committed it; lured by the irresistible fascination of evil, we have all made this psychic murder possible; and the closer we were to it and the better we could see, the greater our guilt. In this way we are all inevitably drawn into the

---

[1384] See version in C. G. Jung, "Psychology and Dictatorship: An Interview with C. G. Jung," *Living Age*, Sep. 1936-Feb. 1937, pp. 340-341, at p. 341.

[1385] In chap. "The Psychology of Dictatorship" (based on the text as pub. in *Observer* (London), Oct. 18, 1936), in *C. G. Jung Speaking: Interviews and Encounters* (1977), pp. 91-93, at p. 93.

[1386] From their Introduction to Murray Stein and Henry Abramovitch, *The Analyst and the Rabbi: A Play* (2019), about Jung and Baeck.

uncleanliness of evil, no matter what our conscious attitude may be. No one can escape this, for we are all so much a part of the human community that every crime calls forth a secret satisfaction in some corner of the fickle human heart."[1387] Yes? Really? There is, after all, a difference between some "secret pleasure" in imagining or thinking of some act and actually having committed the act in question. The one who is content in this way—whether secretly or not, at learning after the fact of the murder of someone (or of some group of people)—has not in any way committed murder. Keeping such a distinction may be quite relevant and helpful here. Was Jung searching for deeper psychic truths or, rather, inclined to obfuscate the central issues of what "the catastrophe" involved and what it signified about those individuals and groups most central in its violently intensifying development during the Nazi Years. The issue is shifted in Jung's discussion here from that of the responsibility for some horrendous actions (mass murder being at the center of "the catastrophe") to that of the claimed universal human tendency to be attracted to the violent, in a perhaps voyeuristic joy. Not that a shift of topic is necessarily a way of avoiding the earlier topic; it could add to the appreciation of the complexity of the situation at hand. It is perhaps true that there is an inspired sense of the great sameness of all human beings, and yet the question of what each of us might have done if living in the Third Reich itself or during that period of European history is a valid one, or at least one that would be interest and potential value to pursue. Still, the spreading of responsibility about murders committed by or organized by some and not by others, where all are seen equally responsible, based on some sense of common human interests, feelings, and reactivity, is quite a mental *salto mortale* (a death-defying leap in thought).

On Hitler himself, in this article, Jung writes of Hitler as "this scarecrow" and the effect he had on the masses, speaking of Hitler's "sorry lack of education, conceit that bordered on madness, a very mediocre intelligence combined with the hysteric's cunning and the power fantasies of the adolescent, were written all over this demagogue's face. His gesticulations were all put on, devised by a hysterical mind intent only on making an impression."[1388] Jung did acknowledge that these comments were made *after* the catastrophe (his word) of the Third Reich, *not what was said in 1933 or 1934*.[1389] Jung suggested earlier that Hitler had hysterical tendencies, while recognizing only positive aspects of his psyche, focusing on his special, positive (superhuman or godlike) features; unseen and not in focus, in the shadow of the psyche (that is, everything

---

[1387] C. G. Jung, "After the Catastrophe" (1945), in *C. G. Jung, Civilization in Transition* (1970), pp. 194-217, at pp. 197-198.

[1388] C. G. Jung, "After the Catastrophe" (1945), in *C. G. Jung, Civilization in Transition* (1970), pp. 194-217, at pp. 204-206.

[1389] See the 1934 critique of Jung in "Gustav Bally and *deutschstämmige Psychotherapie*" (presentation, tr. of the Bally article, and discussion, by Mitchell Ginsberg and Angela Graf-Nold, Zurich Jungian analyst), pp. xlviii-lii in *Effective Psychotherapy: The Contribution of Hellmuth Kaiser*.

The Hitler Era

considered embarrassing, uncomfortable to consider candidly and thoroughly, everything felt to be shameful—unacknowledged: in the dark—all of this underlying a corresponding great inner insecurity.

For those in the Nazi political apparatus itself—think here of Joseph Goebbels, Julius Streicher, Alfred Rosenberg, for example—much of the theorizing and political posturing had a focused goal of inculcating a new sense of morality of National Socialist values ("morality'), and took place in the context of a rejection of Judeo-Christian morality in favor of a trans-rational (or non-rational) concept or metaphor of a unity of community, taken to be manifest in the German people (freed of those not worthy of belonging to the *Volk*, the People).

To believe, as Hitler claimed, that he was the messenger of the gods, the supreme voice of German identity, or the agent chosen to lead the German people to ever more magnificent greatness—a great burden or a great challenge—identified him as a unique leader in a thoroughly non-Judeo-Christian society! In this context, the project of exterminating entire peoples was no small matter, even if it was not introduced in its full-fledged form in the proposals put forth by the National Socialists in the 1920s, and not even in the beginning of the Third Reich.

The one attempt to make mass killings public, as in the T4 (euthanasia) program, met with marked criticism by some Church and civil leaders, and was officially ended—when it had largely already accomplished its mission—but went into clandestine activities, leading to the same use of gas (in chambers and mobile trucks) for the killing of Jews and others, from 1941 on. *The National Socialist government learned that some programs were best left unannounced.* These most violent and murderous programs were ideas that had to be introduced gradually and with nuance: The Church, after all, was still a carrier of Christian morality! Such beliefs or metaphors for a moral system, as beliefs, have a strong influence on how we think, speak, come to have certain intentions to action, and so act, as in the case of Hitler.[1390]

THE SURPRISINGLY SIMILAR PSYCHOLOGY OF GOEBBELS

Hitler's thinking in those last, pressured, and threatening times, as the German military were being relentlessly pushed back from lands occupied in the earlier years of World War II, back to its very core, took into account a number of distinct and finally disparate and conflicting concerns that he had in those final months.

The situation had changed from one in which the German *Volk* (People) could be considered a Master Race on its way to world domination, to a nation that could not support its own great expansionist and domineering vision, which begged for a rethinking of some basic principles that had guided Nazi thinking up until that time. For Goebbels, there were similar questions. Here, the Minister of Propaganda had become a cheering section to encourage German perseverance and an unrelenting readiness

---

[1390] For a traditional (Western) analysis of belief, see Mitchell Ginsberg, *Mind and Belief* (1972).

to face whatever horrible events would ensue, in order to avoid defeat and another world war in which Germany would pay dearly for its military limitations. Goebbels would continue calling for a great loyalty of all Germans, young and old. One important venture organized by Goebbels was the production of a film that was a call to courage and determination in the face of what seemed to be overwhelming odds.

The storyline contrasts the surrender to Napoleon after the 1806 Battle of Austerlitz by the last Holy Roman Emperor (1792-1806) and first Emperor of Austria, Emperor Francis (Franz) II (1768-1835)—taken to be a German disgrace. The film honored the heart of the Germans of a small town, ready to be buried in rubble in their fight to the death, rather than surrendering to the French to save their lives. Teachings are inserted that any refusal to obey orders, no matter how questionable, is a major step on the disastrous road to anarchy, and that it is a societal good to love one's country more than oneself. Surrendering to the enemy is equated with destroying one's German identity. In the film—*contrary to history*—the citizens of Kolberg finally break the French will to continue barraging the city; death is claimed to be overcome by victory. *And yet, as an actual historical loss, death was perhaps not overcome at all.* Finally, the will of the German people to be reborn as a phoenix after the fire is foreseen, in the film's closing minutes. The fictional retelling takes place in the German town of Kolberg, during the invasions by the French military under Napoleon, focusing mostly on the year 1813. The film, based in part on the story by the 1910 Nobel Laureate in Literature, Paul von Heyse (who was actually Jewish by his mother—for this, his name was omitted in the film's credits), was begun in 1943. (We might remember that Goebbels gave his stirring speech asking the German people if they were ready for "total war" on February 18 of that year.)

Most of the production of the film took place from October 1943 to August 1944. In terms of the military situation, this would correspond to the times after the early 1943 reversal of German military fortune at Stalingrad, and also after great loss of the German Panzer divisions to the Soviets at Kursk (August 1943), to the month of the Italian declaration of war against Germany (Mussolini having resigned his post), past the 1944 invasion in northwest France by the Western Allies on D-Day (June 6) with the Soviets reaching the Vistula near Warsaw and taken Riga, Latvia. It was clearly a period of a rapidly deteriorating German military position.

The film—directed by Veit Harlan, who had earlier directed *Jud Süß*, the intensely anti-Semitic 1940 film[1391]—was the most expensive film

---

[1391] As with the descendents of some key Nazis, the children and grandchildren of Veit Harlan would have to deal with their genetic heritage. One of his daughters, Susanne Körber (the family name she took was her mother's maiden name), married a survivor of the holocaust and committed suicide in 1989. In the next generation, her daughter Jessica Jacoby, the granddaughter of Harlan, had to reconcile the fact that one of her grandfathers "was complicit" in the death of her other grandfather, who was Jewish. Larry Rohter, "Nazi Film Still Pains Relatives,"

The Hitler Era

ever produced in the Reich, cost over eight million marks—which, because of this high cost, was not made public information. So far, this film seems to be just Goebbels acting as an enthusiastic supporter of the Nazi vision to the very bitter end. And yet, there was something rather unusual about this production: first, artificial snow had to be brought in by train for the film. The filming called for some 100 railway wagons to be diverted from either their use in military transports or their use in transports of Jews to the gas chambers at Auschwitz. *This was presumably a short-term issue, but still represented Goebbels readiness to override military and genocidal activities for his filmmaking.* And, most significantly, there were huge crowd scenes representing the large crowds of happy civilians, before the fighting at Kolberg, and the hundreds of thousands of soldiers who fought in that Napoleonic war. The extras used in the film amounted to several thousand; there were perhaps 5,000 German Wehrmacht soldiers[1392] taken from the field to be filmed as German soldiers fighting the Napoleonic armies.[1393] The use of soldiers that were direly needed on the war front may seem like a diversion from were generally seen as more pressing and fundamental issues can make sense (from the point of view of the Ministry of Propaganda), if we see Goebbels as wanting to provide a legacy of his art, even if the Third Reich would be crushed by its enemy nations. And Goebbels was in charge here.

The film was shown to a limited audience on January 30, 1945, and was never released for general distribution. (January 30—twelve years after Hitler became Chancellor—was also to be the last radio address by Hitler to the nation.) *The end was close at hand.* By the end of January, Soviet troops had liberated Auschwitz and some other extermination camps, and were within 80 mi. of Berlin; Allied Air Forces had free rein over the skies, bombing German sites at will, depending only on weather.

The *Kreisauer Kreis*, the White Rose, and Judge Roland Freisler

During the Third Reich, there was no nation-wide organized resistance (*Widerstand*) in Germany—the White Rose group in Munich, for example,

---

New York Times, Mar. 1, 2010. One film that captures some of the tensions and torments carried on generations later, is *Hitler's Children* (2011), which shows interviews with offspring of Hermann Göring, Heinrich Himmler, Amon Göth (Goeth), Rudolf Höss (Hoess), Ludwig Beck, and Hans Frank. It is not to be confused with (1) another film by the same title (2004), ZDSF and The History Channel, channel4.com, which presents the teaching (or indoctrination) of the *Hitlerjugend*, the Hitler Youth, nor with (2) *Hitler's Children* (1943), ok.ru/video, an American RKO-Radio Pictures film based on *Education for Death: The Making of the Nazi* (1941), by American-born war correspondent Gregor Ziemer, who had also been headmaster of the American Colony School in Berlin from 1928-1939; text and film express his experience of the Reich and of its educational system of those years. Cf. Horace Meyer Kallen, "Review of *Education for Death: The Making of the Nazi*, by Gregor Ziemer," *Social Research*, vol. 9, no. 4, 1942, pp. 562-564.

[1392] The claims of 187,000 extras and 50,000 soldiers are quite exaggerated. See Frank Noack, *Veit Harlan: The Life and Work of a Nazi Filmmaker* (2016), p. 222.

[1393] *Kolberg* (1945), imdb.com/title/tt0036989.

was composed of a handful of young students. There were also isolated individuals and groups who acted to thwart the goals and plans of the Reich, such as workers' slowdowns but not enough to invite strong governmental interventions, avoidance of full involvement as members of the Nazi Party or of becoming active agents in the Nazi government.

Using a Swedish commercial channel of communication to his friend Lionel George Curtis [1394] in the UK, a German conscript into the Wehrmacht, jurist, and the key figure in the *Kreisauer Kreis* (the Kreisau Circle),[1395] Helmuth James von Moltke (1907-1945)—grand-nephew of Helmuth Graf von Moltke the Younger (1848-1916)—wrote on March 23, 1943, "People outside Germany do not realize the following handicaps under which we labour and which distinguish the position of Germany from that of any other of the occupied countries: [here there is a] lack of unity, lack of men, lack of communications... With us, even the martyr is certain to be classed as an ordinary criminal."[1396] The Gestapo arrested Moltke not long after, on January 19, 1944.

Some of the remaining group became associated with Klaus Graf von Stauffenberg and the assassination attempt on Hitler's life of July 20, 1944. (More on the social and political post-Nazi vision of the *Kreisauer Kreis*, and on the July 1944 assassination attempt, below.)

One connection between Moltke and the White Rose pamphlets is that Moltke before his arrest by the Gestapo was also able to send a copy of the sixth pamphlet of the White Rose, again through Scandinavia, to England. *There it was printed in millions of copies and dropped by RAF (the British Royal Air Force) planes over Germany in mid-1943!* That reprint of the sixth White Rose pamphlet bore the title *Ein deutsches Flugblatt. Manifest der Münchner Studenten* (*A German Leaflet. Manifesto of the Munich Students*). What they were not able to do themselves in life, the few members of the White Rose—Hans Scholl, Sophie Scholl, Christoph Probst, and their colleagues (likewise tried and executed, or given rather harsh sentences)—had a vast distribution in the next months!

That was some of the resistance of those against the Nazi regime. But even those closest to the power structure and to Hitler himself became much more questioning of the path the Third Reich was taking, as 1943 moved into 1944 and then to the Reich's final months of 1945, with the ever-advancing Soviet army moving in on Berlin itself.[1397] Consider here

---

[1394] Lionel George Curtis (1972-1955) was a British official, a delegate to the Versailles Peace Conference of 1919, advocate of a federal world government and other structures for more self-rule throughout the British Empire (India, South Africa), who was nominated for the Nobel Peace Prize in 1949.

[1395] This was named after the main meeting place of the group, the estate of Moltke in Kreisau, in Lower Silesia (now Krzyżowa, in southwest Poland), east of Dresden, Germany, and west of Częstochowa, Poland.

[1396] Klemens von Klemperer, *German Resistance Against Hitler*, pp. 4-5, 14.

[1397] "Britisches Abwurfflugblatt, das Auszüge aus dem sechsten Flugblatt der 'Weißen Rose' enthält," DHM.DE/DEUTSCHES HISTORISCHES MUSEUM, HAUS DER

The Hitler Era 473

that very last month. Each news item was communicated that could give a ray of hope to those wanting to overcome the Nazi regime, criticizing the Nazi leaders' fantastic imagination and their rather limited appreciation for the capacities of the dehumanized, held-to-be subhuman, inferior nations had in fighting the Reich.

Then, on April 12, 1945, US President Franklin Delano Roosevelt died. The feeling by some Nazi leaders was that this was a weakening of American power and that a peace could be had with the less impressive new President, Harry S. Truman. (A mistake!)

The final crises for Hitler were intensified on April 22, 1945. On that date, the various generals in the Berlin area reported their isolated efforts at defense, with the conclusion, as Luftwaffe Adjutant to Hitler, Nicolaus von Below wrote, "an organized resistance [to the Soviet advances] was not possible (*keinerlei geordneter Widerstand mehr möglich war*).... It was not clear whether it was a consequence of the Russian superiority or the collapse of our own command structure (if this was still possible). Hitler became very irate (*Hitler erregte sich sehr.*) He ordered everybody from the room with the exception of [Wilhelm] Keitel [Chief of the Armed Forces], [Alfred] Jodl [Chief of the Operations Staff of the Armed Forces], [Hans] Krebs [Chief of Staff of the Army] and [Wilhelm] Burgdorf [Chief Army Adjutant to Hitler] and then unleashed a furious tirade against the Army commanders and their 'long-term treachery' (*und ließ dann eine wütende Kanonade gegen die Führer des Heeres und ihre »langjährige Verraterei« vom Stapel*). I was sitting near the door and heard almost every word. It was a terrible half-hour. (*Es war eine furchtbare halbe Stunde.*) After this outburst (*Nachdem diesem Ausbruch*), however, he had at least made up his mind about his destiny. He ordered Keitel and Jodl to report to [Karl] Dönitz [Admiral, head of the Navy, and later successor of Hitler as Head of State and President of the Reich and Supreme Commander of the Armed Forces] in northern Germany and continue the war from there. He, Hitler, would remain in Berlin and take his own life."[1398] The next day, Göring, as Second in Command of the Reich, sent a telegram to Hitler Headquarters at the Bunker in Berlin, received just before 1 am on April 23.[1399] In it, Göring said that he had heard news of the situation there and added, "I felt obligated to assume, in case by 2200 o'clock [military jargon for 10 pm] no answer is forthcoming, that you have lost your freedom of action [*dass Sie Ihrer Handlungsfreiheit beraubt sind*]. I shall then view the conditions of your decree as fulfilled and take action for the well-being of Nation and Fatherland. You know what I feel for you in these most difficult hours of

---

GESCHICHTE DER BUNDESREPUBLIK DEUTSCHLAND, DAS BUNDESARCHIV; "Ein Deutsches Flugblatt. Manifest der Münchner Studenten. Weiße Rose," LERNEN AUS DER GESCHICHTE; *Sophie Scholl: The Final Days* (cited above), at 1:49:50-1:50:10.

[1398] Nicolaus von Below, *At Hitler's Side*, pp. 236-237; *Als Hitlers Adjutant 1937-1945*, p. 411.

[1399] Telegram image at Melanie Hall (Berlin), "Nazi telegram that sent Hitler into a rage sells for over £35,600 at auction," *The Telegraph*, Jul. 8, 2015.

my life and I cannot express this in words. God protect you and allow you despite everything to come here [to Berchtesgaden] as soon as possible [*Gott schütze Sie und lasse Sie trotz alledem baldmöglichst hierher kommen*]."

The decree mentioned by Göring, written by Hitler himself on June 29, 1941, ordered that if he should ever become kidnapped, incapacitated, or killed, then Göring was to take over his position of power in the Reich. Hitler was irate. He stripped Göring of all power and expelled him from the Party.

Göring's telegram carefully stated that he would take action only if he did not get a reply from Hitler by that evening. *Bormann, however, suggested to Hitler that this was treasonous.* Hitler could have simply sent back a message saying he was still alive and in control of the Reich, but he agreed with Bormann's assessment: by this time Hitler was sensing that there was treason all around him. *Von Below, for his part, felt that Göring's request was respectful and not inappropriate at all*. In reply to Hitler's question about the telegram, he said that he took the telegram literally and that Göring actually believed he could still negotiate with the Western powers.[1400]

Hitler also ordered the arrest of Göring and appointed Joseph Goebbels as his successor. (Göring would escape German arrest and execution, only to be arrested on May 9 by the Western Allies, and later tried for war crimes. He committed suicide by biting on a cyanide capsule on October 15, 1946, the night before he was to be executed by hanging.)

DIE ROTE KAPELLE AND JUDGE MANFRED ROEDER

Active primarily in 1940-1942, an informal network of Germans who were strongly anti-Nazi, who wanted the war to end, and were against the mass killing of Jews happening in the East, were known by the name of *die rote Kapelle* (the Red Orchestra).[1401] These were Germans from a variety of backgrounds, social classes, and careers. Some were in the German military, in Germany intelligence, and in civilian roles giving them access to much information not made available to the general German public. They acted on their viewpoints, helping those in danger from the Nazi apparatus, and in publishing declarations—leaflets (*Flugblätter*) or adhesive slips of paper (*Klebezetteln*)—countering the Nazi propaganda machine. (One such leaflet, from February 1942, declared that a final victory for Nazi Germany was no longer possible, adding that Germany would lose the war. Another, from Spring 1942, stated that in every country (in Europe) "today, daily, hundreds, often thousands of people are shot or hung (*erschossen oder gehenkt*) summarily and arbitrarily

---

[1400] Nicolaus von Below, *At Hitler's Side*, p. 237; *Als Hitlers Adjutant 1937-1945*, p. 412.

[1401] Giles Perrault, *L'orchestre rouge* (1967), tr., *The Red Orchestra* (1969), and esp., Heinz Höhne, *Kennwort: Direktor; die Geschichte der Roten Kapelle* (1970), tr., *Codeword: Direktor: The Story of the Red Orchestra* (1971). Cf. next note.

(*standrechtlich und willkürlich*)."[1402] Another text, also from 1942, was entitled "Nazi-Paradise: Krieg Hunger Lüge Gestapo. Wie lange noch?" ("Nazi Paradise: War—Hunger—Lies—Gestapo. How much longer?"),[1403] writing more specifically of mass murders of Jews and of Soviets by the German forces in the East.[1404] Among those of the Red Orchestra who were targeted by the Gestapo and the Nazi regime were Luftwaffe Lt.-Col. Caesar von Hofacker, cousin of Col. Claus von Stauffenberg (a central figure in the July 20, 1944 assassination attempt on Hitler), Harro and Libertas Schulze-Boysen, Arvid and Mildred Harnack,[1405] Hans Coppi, Cay-Hugo and Erika von Brockdorff, Lt.-Col. Gunther Smend, Ursula Goerze, and Helmut Roloff. *The Red Orchestra was claimed to be responsible for the Wehrmacht defeat at Stalingrad (not very likely)!*

Many of them were tried and convicted by a notorious judge in the Military Court of the Ministry of the Luftwaffe, Manfred Roeder,[1406] known as one of the bloodiest and most virulent of judges against members of the German Anti-fascists. (Roeder was called a *Bluthund*, bloodhound, and also shared the epithet of *Hitlers Blutrichter*, Hitler's Blood Judge, as was Roland Freisler, of the People's Court.) By February 1943, over 100 of these anti-Nazis had been executed. After the War, *for rather different reasons*, both former Nazis who were appreciated by the anti-Communist American intelligence services, such as Manfred Roeder, and also Soviet sources, who wanted to appropriate the German anti-Nazi work within the Communist anti-Capitalist mentality, *made distorted claims about the work of these German anti-Nazis.*[1407]

BERLIN'S *DIE FREIE PRESSE* AND OTHER RESISTANCE IN GERMANY

Other resistance against the Reich in a broad, general way was also part of the history of the Reich. We have discussed the example of the White Rose, a small group of Munich University students who published

---

[1402] "Die 'rote Kapelle': Widerstand im NS," *Bundeszentrale für politische Bildung*, BPB.DE, Dec. 22, 2017. *Kapelle:* orchestra, band; chapel; oratory.

[1403] Rolf Maag, «Das Nazi-Paradies—Krieg, Hunger, Lüge», *20 Minuten*, 20MIN.CH.

[1404] *The Traitors' Children: Sons and Daughters of the Resistance* (2014), at 9:00-9:20; Dirk Baas, "Zweiter Weltkrieg. Widerstand Gegen Hitler. Unterwühlung und Zersetzung weiter Volkskreise," *Die Welt*, Dec. 22, 2017; Uwe Klußmann, "«Rote Kapelle», Die vergessene Widerstandsgruppe," *Spiegel*, SPIEGEL.DE, Mar. 25, 2019.

[1405] Mildred Harnack und die Rote Kapelle in Berlin, Ingo Juchler, ed. (2017).

[1406] From "Was war die rote Kapelle," *Frankfurter Allgemeinen Zeitung*, Apr. 26, 1951, discussed in "Fast vergessen: Die 'Rote Kapelle'," *Deutsche Welle*, DW.COM; cf. Thomas Vogel, "Widerstand gegen den Nationalsozialismus," *Bundeszentrale für politische Bildung*, BPB.DE, Sep. 8, 2015.

[1407] See Heinz Höhne, *Codeword: Direktor: The Story of the Red Orchestra*, esp. Chap. 8 ("Rote Kapelle: Fact and Fiction"), pp. 234-247. Cf. Bernhard Biener, "Ein „furchtbarer Jurist" im Bemeindevorstand," "(A 'terrible lawyer' in the municipality board), *Frankfürter Algemeine*, FAZ.NET, Jan. 20, 2018. The CIA has files recording the (distorted) East German view of these Germans, accepting Soviet-block political propaganda at face value: see "23 June 1967, East German postage stamps honor Rote Kapelle Agents," *Schulze-Boysen, Harrow_0016.pdf*, at CIA.GOV.

their own leaflets, denouncing and questioning the Hitler Regime. In that context we also discussed the work of Helmuth James von Moltke and his sending the final leaflet by way of Sweden to England, where millions of copies were printed and dropped by British RAF airplanes over Germany.

In addition, there was the independent dedicated work of a working-class Berlin couple, Otto Hampel (1897-1943) and his wife, Elise Hampel (1903-1943), who carefully prepared, hand-written cards that were distributed across Berlin giving a non-Nazi version of events, calling the little messages *Die freie Presse* (*The Free Press*). They worked from 1940, when Elise's brother was killed in the invasion of France, until they were denounced and arrested in October 1942. They were convicted in the *Volksgerichtshof* (The People's Court), as were key members of the White Rose, who had been guillotined in Munich on February 22, 1943. The Hampels were sentenced on January 22, 1943, with their execution in Berlin by guillotine on April 8, 1943.[1408]

HIMMLER, COUNT FOLKE BERNADOTTE, AND NORBERT MASUR

Even before Göring's telegram of April 23, another one of Hitler's close collaborators, Heinrich Himmler, was secretly seeking to negotiate with Allies through third parties, to establish his credentials as an honorable friend of the Jews and someone the Allies could negotiate a peace with (envisioning himself as the political leader of a Nazi Germany which would be transformed after the Peace). First, Himmler, through the aid of Walter Schellenberg, head of Himmler's Counter-intelligence Service,[1409] tried to negotiate with a Swiss ex-President, Jean-Marie Musy, whom Himmler had known since the 1930s when Musy was publisher of an anti-Jewish Swiss newspaper, *La jeune suisse*. Evidence suggests that at least 1,200 Jews, most notably from Theresienstadt Concentration Camp, survived the war because Musy convinced Himmler to go against Hitler's orders that all Jews held by the Reich be killed; Hitler was furious.[1410]) Himmler also took up negotiations with Count Folke Bernadotte, of the Swedish Red Cross (and nephew of King Gustav V of Sweden). Himmler met with Bernadotte, on April 21 and then again on the night of April 23-24.[1411] He also met with Norbert Masur, representative of the Swedish Section of the WJC (World Jewish Congress). This took place, with Masur guaranteed safe passage, in the town of Harzfeld, around 70 kilometers north of Berlin. They met on April 21, 1945, in the night—Himmler arriving at 2:30 am—after having attended Hitler's birthday celebrations in the Berlin Chancellery Bunker the evening before: Himmler went from celebrating with Hitler to meeting with an important Jewish representative!

[1408] Hans Fallada (penname for Rudolf Ditzen), *Jeder stirbt für sich allein* (1947), tr. as *Alone in Berlin* (UK, 2009) and as *Every Man Dies Alone* (US, 2009).

[1409] NT-IMT-Blue, vol. 4, pp. 374-386.

[1410] "Jean-Marie Musy (1876-1952), President and Swiss federal councillor," MUSY.NET; "Jean-Marie Musy," FR.WIKIPEDIA.ORG; "Musy, Jean-Marie, *Dictionnaire historique de la Suisse*, HLS-DHS-DSS.CH.

[1411] Peter Longerich, *Heinrich Himmler*, pp. 728-729.

Masur in his report wrote, "in the fall of last year [1944] when Himmler allowed 2700 Jews to flee to Switzerland, upon hearing this Hitler became a raving maniac, and prevented any further planned freeing of Jews."[1412] Other sources suggest that the number of Jews involved were 318 in a first transport and 1,368 in a second, arriving in Switzerland on August 21 and December 7, 1944,[1413] mentioned in Mazur's report.[1414] Again, other more precise sources cite 1,210 Jews having been transported from Theresienstadt ghetto, north of Prague, arriving in Switzerland on February 7, 1945.[1415] This meant that this meeting on April 20, 1945, was not the first attempt by Himmler, however limited, to show a caring side of himself, having good will toward the Jews and their suffering—at least on the level of a gesture, for what that might bring about. Himmler, explaining himself, stated, "After coming into power, we wanted to settle this issue [the presence of Jews in Germany] once and for all, and I was in favor of a humane solution through emigration. I conferred with American organizations, to arrange for a quick emigration, but even countries who claimed to be friendly toward the Jews did not want to admit Jews."[1416] (Remember the Évian Conference of 1939!) Himmler gave his explanation and rendering of the ghetto situation and the cremation of Jews: "Then the war brought us into contact with the Jewish masses of the East, who were mostly part of the proletariat. Because of this many new problems arose. We could not tolerate such an enemy at our backs. The Jewish masses were infected with many diseases, especially typhoid fever. I lost thousands of my SS troops through these diseases. Also, the Jews were helping the partisans."[1417] Masur wanted to get Himmler away from "the unfortunate thought to defend his policies against the Jews in front of a Jew." But Himmler wanted to clear his name, adding, "In order to stop the epidemics we were forced to cremate the bodies of the many people that died of the diseases. That was the reason we had to build the crematoria, and now, because of this, everybody wants to tighten the noose around our neck."[1418] (Is this what those crematoria were built for?) Himmler continued, making a statement of his loyalty to Hitler, remarking, "Hitler will be remembered in history as a great man, because he gave the world the national-socialist solution, the only one which is able to stand up against Bolshevism."[1419] And added,

---

[1412] Norbert Masur, "My meeting with Heinrich Himmler April 20/21, 1945: Report to the Swedish Section of the World Jewish Congress, Stockholm, Sweden," CENTER FOR JEWISH HISTORY (CJH), DIGITAL COLLECTIONS, p. 4; Max Wallace, "When Himmler tried to 'bury the hatchet between us and the Jews'," *The Star*, Aug. 19, 2017, THESTAR.COM.

[1413] "Bergen-Belsen and the Hungarian Jews," SCRAPBOOK PAGES.

[1414] Norbert Masur, "My meeting with Heinrich Himmler" (cited just above), p. 8.

[1415] "Bergen-Belsen and the Hungarian Jews," SCRAPBOOK PAGES.

[1416] Norbert Masur, "My meeting with Heinrich Himmler," p. 5.

[1417] Norbert Masur, "My meeting with Heinrich Himmler," p. 6.

[1418] Norbert Masur, "My meeting with Heinrich Himmler," p. 6.

[1419] Norbert Masur, "My meeting with Heinrich Himmler," p. 10.

"The best part of the German people will be destroyed with us; what happens to the rest of them, is immaterial." Mazur comments, "This certainly agrees with Hitler's assessment of the situation, as we see elsewhere in our discussion here."[1420] Himmler's comments here raised questions for Masur, who speculated: "What reasons would he have had to agree to the small concessions during the last few months of the war and also vis-à-vis ourselves? He did not ask any concessions from us. For sure he did not think that he could buy his own life at this late hour. He was too clever to assume this; he knew very well that his list of sins was too large. Possibly he might have wanted to be judged by history in a better light than the other criminals in Germany."[1421] Through these meetings, in any case, there were finally more than 7,000 women freed from the women's concentration camp at Ravensbrück, for some purpose or hope or other on Himmler's part.[1422] One count reports that about 7,100 women (of which were perhaps 1,000 Jews) were liberated from Ravensbrück between April 22-April 28, 1945.[1423] Relatedly, Ian Kershaw reported that in "January 1945, through a Swiss intermediary acting for rabbis in America and Canada, he [Himmler] agreed to the release of 1,400 Jews a month from Theresienstadt in return for $250,000. No money, in fact, changed hands when 1,200 Jews were released February. But Himmler stipulated that the press in America and Switzerland should report his 'humanitarian' gesture... But when Hitler learnt of the release of the Jews, he was reputedly furious and banned any further releases. By now, Himmler's star was on the wane."[1424] Peter Longerich wrote similarly of Hitler receiving this news, "Hitler flew into a rage. In his *Political Testament*, written the same day—the day before his suicide—he expelled the former Reichsführer-SS and Reich Minister of the Interior Heinrich Himmler from the party and from all offices of state."

In any case, Hitler was most definitely not at all content! He was to learn on April 29 of the meeting between Himmler and Bernadotte. This came from news broadcast by the BBC on April 28 of Himmler's meeting with the Count: reports in the international press, which were not available to the general German public, were scrutinized by the Nazi intelligence, propaganda, and security services. When Hitler learned of this, he exploded, declaring that this was the "most shameful betrayal in human history." (Hitler was prone to hyperbole and an overriding sense of great self-importance.) Himmler, as Göring before him (on April 23)[1425] was stripped of all offices within the Reich. These betrayals were the end

---

[1420] Norbert Masur, "My meeting with Heinrich Himmler," p. 11.
[1421] Norbert Masur, "My meeting with Heinrich Himmler," p. 11.
[1422] Norbert Masur, "My meeting with Heinrich Himmler,", p. 13.
[1423] "Ravensbrück Concentration Camp: History & Overview," JEWISH VIRTUAL LIBRARY (JVL).
[1424] Ian Kershaw, "Himmler's Great Betrayal: Churchill Rejected Peace Overtures in 1944," *Sunday Times* (London), Jan. 7, 2001, 456FIS.ORG.
[1425] Nicolaus von Below, *At Hitler's Side*, pp. 236-237.

The Hitler Era

for Hitler: On April 30, 1945, he committed suicide.[1426] In those last few days of his life, Hitler wrote of Göring and Himmler, "through secret negotiations with the enemy, which they held without my knowledge and against my will, and through their attempt in defiance of the law to seize power in the state" both had "done untold damage to the country and to the entire nation, quite apart from their treachery against me personally."[1427] Overall, it was a tumultuous time for Adolf Hitler. In the final two days of his life, he married Eva Braun (now Eva Hitler), shortly after midnight on April 29, 1945. This was hours after Eva's brother-in-law, Hermann Fegelein, was arrested for desertion, brought back to the bunker, quite drunk, and dealt with harshly. Eva had pleaded with Hitler to spare her brother-in-law (she presumably knew of the pregnancy of her sister Gretl, who was to give birth to a baby on May 5, 1945), but to no avail. Hitler would show no mercy to those he viewed as traitors; he was very focused on all of those he saw as betraying his trust and failing in their military and political commitments. Fegelein was quickly tried in a brief court-martial at the Chancellery and summarily taken outside to be shot.[1428] Eva was reported to be in tears.[1429] Then, only a few hours later, after midnight on April 29, 1945, Hitler and Eva were married. Eva was presumably in shock and mourning over her brother-in-law's execution and the situation it left Gretl in. Hitler no longer would need his loving audience of German women holding the romantic vision of Hitler as an available bachelor, so his political image was no longer at play. The wedding night was preoccupied with the dire situation at the Chancellery bunkers, with Soviet troops closing in on their Nazi enemy. As General Gotthard Heinrici summed up the situation: "Three years ago Hitler had Europe under his command, from the Volga to the Atlantic. Now he's sitting in a hole under the earth."[1430] Hitler went on through his wedding night to dictate to his private secretary Traudl Junge his *Last Will* (signed at 4 am), announcing his decision to marry his companion Eva Braun, and closing with the statement, "I myself and my wife—in order to escape the disgrace of deposition or capitulation—choose death. It is our wish (he writes, speaking for himself and for her) to be burnt immediately on the spot where I have carried out the greatest part of my daily work in the course of a twelve years' service to my people," thus closing his personal will with a political posturing. Also signed and dated April 29, 1945, 4 am,

---

[1426] Ian Kershaw, "Himmler's Great Betrayal" (just quoted). Cf. Ian Kershaw, *Hitler: A Biography*, pp. 943-945.

[1427] Peter Longerich, *Heinrich Himmler*, pp. 729-730.

[1428] Nicolaus von Below, *At Hitler's Side*, p. 240.

[1429] Pierre Galante, Eugène Silianoff [with Gertraud/Traudl Junge], *Voices from the Bunker* (1990), p. 11; also as Gertraud Junge, Pierre Galante, Eugène Silianoff, *Les derniers témoins du bunker: La vérité sur la fin d'Hitler* (1992), with UK ed., Gertraud Junge, Pierre Galante, Eugène Silianoff, *Last Witnesses in the Bunker* (1989).

[1430] Cornelius Ryan, *The Last Battle*, p. 259.

is his *Political Testament*, which closes with his final word of his political vision and his political life: "Above all, I charge the leadership of the nation and their followers with the strict observance of the racial laws and the merciless resistance against the universal poisoners of all peoples, Internatinal Jewry." This was no casual afterthought; Hitler's hatred of Jews, or rather, of world Jewry, was no passing matter. The issue of the Jews for Hitler was certainly one of the driving forces behind his overall political vision, goals, tactics, strategies, plans, and actions.

Historian Michael Berenbaum[1431] wrote in this context, "One should never underestimate Hitler's obsession with Jews."[1432] This may sound extreme when read without context, but may actually be ultimately more like an understatement, once we consider the life career of Hitler and the world he tried to define and bring to realization: In this closing passage of Hitler's *Political Testament*, we can see an expression of the importance in Hitler's view of the world of the issue of a death-battle with what he took to be a worldwide group, Jews ("international Jewry"), an issue that ran through his political life in the late 1910s on, as a major, fundamental leitmotif in his entire career. In one week, two of Hitler's must trusted officials, Göring and Himmler, had, in Hitler's eyes, betrayed him, and had been removed from all ministry roles and all offices within the Party and government. Himmler's "betrayal" was not quite successful: He offered through Count Bernadotte to surrender on behalf of the Third Reich to the Western Allies (as if he had the power within the Third Reich to do so), but stated that he was not ready to surrender to the Soviet forces. This limited proposal was not acceptable to the Western Allies or to the Soviet Union. Bernadotte also made it clear that the Allies would treat Himmler only as a war criminal, certainly not as Germany's head of state.[1433]

Not only had Hitler's generals told him that there were not enough forces left to defend even the Bunker, let alone wage a counter-offensive, but he was now bereft of two of his main three colleagues, only Goebbels remaining. This was in addition to Hitler's greatly incapacitated physical state and low morale. Furthermore, he, perhaps rightly, saw that fleeing to his mountain home and fortress of the Berghof in Berchtesgaden, was an extreme exercise in futility: better to die in his capital, Berlin.

If we think of all these events, of his being abandoned by Göring and Himmler, of the continual victories of his military enemies, the Soviets and the Western Allies, moving ever closer to Berlin and bombing at will,

---

[1431] Michael Berenbaum: scholar, historian, rabbi, Project Director of the USHMM, the US Holocaust Memorial Museum from 1993-1997, having played a key role in the very creation of USHMM. He is author of 18 books, and was the Executive Editor of the 22-volume, 2nd ed. of *New Encyclopedia Judaica* (2006).

[1432] Michael Berenbaum, Foreword to Bryan Mark Rigg, *The Rabbi Saved by Hitler's Soldiers: Rebbe Joseph Isaac Schneersohn and His Astonishing Rescue* (2016), pp. ix-xvii, at p. x.

[1433] "Hitler Deputy Proposes Surrender Terms: Luebeck, Northern Germany, April 24, 1945," THE DAILY CHRONICLES OF WORLD WAR II; "Heinrich Himmler and the SS," HIMMLER.GREYFALCON.US.

The Hitler Era

no resistance from a Luftwaffe now a shell of its earlier power, of his generals who finally could tell him the extremely unwelcome news that Germany had no military capacity to resist the enemy—this all came crashing down. Furthermore, the forces that were bringing down the Third Reich were not Jewish in origin or nature, for European Jewry (whatever else can be said) were largely decimated by the organized National Socialist policies that had been carried out intensely for several years.

Among the fervent and unlikely ideas of these twilight times was Hitler's idea of a *Volkssturm*, a People's Home Front Army, old men and young boys (typically with no uniforms and with only very few days of training—simply cannon fodder of untrained civilians, in destroyed cities!

Old and young in the *Volkssturm*, 1945   Berlin bombed and burning, 1945

This idea of a *Volkssturm* was formulated in late September 1944 and formally announced to the German people by Himmler in mid-October, 1944.[1434] A German propaganda film stated that 70% of the *Hitlerjugend* born in 1928 had volunteered for this military service.[1435]

Himmler, on his part, set up Operation Werewolf (*Unternehmen Werwolf*)—*Organisation SS-Werwolf* (SS-Werewolf Organization) and *SS-Werwolf Freischärlerbewegung* (SS-Werewolf *Francs-tireurs*, Guerilla Movement). At its head was SS-General (Obergruppenführer) Hans-Adolf Prützmann, *Generalinspekteur für den passiven Widerstand*, Inspector General for Passive Résistance (or, *für Spezialabwehr*, for Special Intelligence).[1436] This group was meant to be an elite force of volunteers, commandos behind enemy lines. In all of this chaos, Hitler would make two final efforts, first, to visit German troops facing the Soviet Armies, near the Oder River to the east of Berlin, on March 3, 1945. And on his last birthday, April 20, 1945, he emerged from the bunker to honor and to congratulate very young *Volkssturm* soldiers from that ragtag army of

---

[1434] Winfried Dolderer, "Auf verlorenem Posten für den Endsieg: Vor 70 Jahren erging der Erlass zum Volkssturm," *Deutschlandfunk*, Sept. 25, 2014, DEUTSCHLANDFUNK.DE.

[1435] *A German Life* (2016), 1:22:40-1:24:40.

[1436] Kazimierz Moczarski, *Conversations with an Executioner*, pp. 236-246, esp. pp. 238-241. A late-wartime manual of Operation Werwolf, tr. into Eng., is *SS Werewolf: Combat Instruction Manual*, Lt. Michael C. Fagnon, tr. (1945). It discusses in detail guerrilla warfare (*Kleinkrieg*). Cf. Charles Whiting, *Werewolf: The Story of the Nazi Resistance Movement 1944-1945* (2002); Perry Biddiscombe, *The Last Nazis: SS Werewolf Guerrilla Resistance in Europe 1944-1947* (2004); Lorraine Boissoneault, "The Nazi Werewolves Who Terrorized Allied Soldiers at the End of WWII," *Smithsonian Magazine*, Oct. 30, 2018, SMITHSONIANMAG.COM.

pre-teen and teen boys and old men (and from February 12, 1945, women and girls), called up in the defense of the Reich. In the photo on the left, Hitler salutes his troops. In the two right photos, taken on his birthday, he shows his respect and appreciation for the commitment of these boys of the *Volkssturm*, in contrast with his opinion of a lack of commitment in the regular army, which Hitler sensed had lost a sense of mission and could even contemplate a German defeat! Notice that Hitler had aged considerably in the two years since the German defeat at Stalingrad.

March 3, 1945   April 20, 1945 (Hitler's last birthday)

This meeting with young boys of the *Volkssturm*, meant to show their Führer as protective, was not fully successful in its propagandistic aims; compare the diary entry of Dorothy von Schwanenflügel Lawson:

> Friday, April 20 [1945], was Hitler's fifty-sixth birthday... The radio announced that Hitler had come out of his safe bomb-proof bunker to talk with the fourteen to sixteen-year-old boys who had "volunteered" for the "honor" of being accepted into the SS and to die for their Führer in the defense of Berlin. What a cruel lie! These boys did not volunteer, but had no choice, because boys found hiding were hanged as traitors by the SS as a warning that, "he who was not brave enough to fight had to die." When trees were not available, people were strung up on lampposts. They were hanging everywhere, military and civilian, men and women, ordinary citizens who had been executed by a small group of fanatics. It appeared that the Nazis did not want the people to survive because a lost war, by their rationale, was obviously the fault of all of us. We had not sacrificed enough and therefore, we had forfeited the right to live, as only the government was without guilt. The Volkssturm was called up again, and this time, all boys age thirteen and up, had to report as our army was reduced now to little more than children filling the ranks as soldiers.[1437]

Hitler exhibited an unshakeable conviction that the Third Reich would triumph, despite what was obvious to his generals, to many Germans, and to the Allied military: that the defeat of Germany was obvious. Even

---

[1437] D. von Schwanenflügel Lawson, *Laughter Wasn't Rationed*, p. 341.

in 1943, when German generals and even the German public began to doubt that Germany could resist the war it was then facing, with powerful enemies on the east and the south and the west, Hitler still spoke of his confidence. On June 2, 1944, when it was clear to many that the Third Reich had had its day and was already being defeated militarily (with the D-Day invasion at Normandy on the French Coast only four days away), Hitler had declared to Göring, "Göring, you will see, we shall still win the greatest victory of the century." Emma Göring then comments about this statement, simply, "My husband could only helplessly shake his head."[1438] Others also had strong hesitations, even if they were not ready to speak out directly to Hitler. Thus, on April 23, 1945, three days after Hitler's last birthday, Göring, at Obersalzberg, was to ask Albert Bormann, Martin Bormann's brother, where the minutes of the briefing meetings were kept [*wo die Protokolle der Lagebesprechungen aufbewahrt würden*]. Göring said, "They must be destroyed immediately, or the German people will discover that for the past two years they have been led by a madman! [*Sie müßten sofort vernichtet werden, sonst würde das deutsche Volk erfahren, daß es seit zwei Jahren von einem ›Wahnsinnigen‹ geführt worden sei.*]"[1439] High Nazis were speaking more candidly by that time!

The week of April 23-30, 1945, brought a series of bad news for Hitler: on April 23, he received that telegram from Göring that he interpreted to be Göring's attempt to usurp his power as the Führer. Then, in the afternoon of April 28, Hitler heard a Reuters news report broadcast by the BBC[1440] that Himmler had been attempting to make peace with the Allies behind Hitler's back. And, that very same day in the afternoon, Benito Mussolini and his mistress, Clara Petacci, captured by Italian anti-Fascist groups, were killed by firing squad at the entrance to Villa Belmonte, in Giulino di Mezzegra, by Lake Como. Their corpses, brought to pre-dawn Milan, were strung up at Piazzale Loreto; hanging by their feet, their corpses were pummeled into bloody masses. Many photos displayed this brutal spectacle.[1441]

Hitler learned of this that same day. He stated that he did want to be captured by the Soviets and put on display (as a monkey in a cage) before the Russian people. That did leave something unsaid! It was perhaps unbearable for Hitler to think that he might be treated with such violent contempt as Mussolini had received from his own Italian people.

Decades later, Traudl Junge, Hitler's private secretary, in a filmed interview reported on a conversation she had with Hitler after Hitler learned of Mussolini's fate. She quoted Hitler as saying, "And I would never risk to get captured alive." She added, "because he knew what

---

[1438] Emmy Goering, *My Life with Göring*, p. 67.
[1439] This exchange was dictated later that day, April 23, 1945, by Bormann to one of Hitler's secretaries, Christa Schroeder, and was then printed in her *Er war mein Chef*, p. 210; *He Was My Chief*, p. 186.
[1440] Ian Kershaw, *Hitler: A Biography*, pp. 944-945.
[1441] Photos online; among others: "Morte di Benito Mussolini," IT.WIKIPEDIA.ORG.

happened to Mussolini. He saw the pictures [of Mussolini and Petacci hung by their feet, their corpses beaten to a pulp], and he [Hitler] was very, very frightened to have the same fate if he would be captured."[1442] In the same vein, Hermann Göring in 1946 stated that Hitler had declared about Mussolini's death, "This will never happen to me."[1443] *True to form, Hitler spoke not of his great fear, but of the bravery of a soldier who would commit an honorable suicide instead of being taken prisoner!* Hitler committed suicide on April 30.[1444] Goebbels was appointed as Chancellor. The next day, May 1, 1945, he and his wife committed suicide after their six children were poisoned with cyanide pills. Admiral Karl Dönitz (the next Führer) and General Wilhelm Keitel would surrender to the Allies.[1445]

MISCALCULATION: WHERE 1,000 = 12

The Third Reich was widely referred to as the Thousand-year Reich. This was a phrase found early in the Reich, as in the speech by Hitler in late summer 1933, at the Nuremberg Party Congress (quoted above). With the unexpected, radical shift from the Weimar Republic to a State with emergency powers to make declarations into law with no legislative or other consultations came a sense that the revolution was over, the new order established, and all that was needed was the next ten centuries to carry out the magnificent and rather complete vision of what the German nation should be. Many of the basic ideas in this vision were already expressed in Hitler's *Mein Kampf*, which had been published in the mid-1920s (as discussed above). While there was this vision of the Reich in very early stages of a thousand-year period of world hegemony, what did the Nazi vision miss or distort in this thinking about the future?

The rather closed-circle of opinion that was tolerated in the Third Reich systematically cultivated a rather myopic (and, ultimately, a simplistic) appreciation of the world, which various scholars of the period and of more recent times have described as Aryan solipsism,[1446] German autistic self-forgetfulness,[1447] National Socialist living-space dystopia, and, also,

---

[1442] *Hitler's Bodyguard, Season 1, Episode 13 (Poison Gas Plot in the Bunker)*, 41:30-42:30, YOUTUBE, Junge speaking; film of Mussolini and Petacci hung in Milano.

[1443] Benjamin Soloway, "Did the Brutal Death of Mussolini Contribute to Hitler's Suicide?" *Foreign Policy*, Apr. 28, 2015, FOREIGNPOLICY.COM.

[1444] David Rising, "Hitler bodyguard Rochus Misch dies at 96" (with interview notes), *Associated Press*, Sep. 6, 2013, APNEWS.COM; Rochus Misch, *Hitler's Last Witness: The Memoirs of Hitler's Bodyguard* (2014).

[1445] "Joseph Goebbels," *History*, Mar. 24, 2010, HISTORY.COM; Hans Mommsen, "The Dissolution of the Third Reich: Crisis Management and Collapse, 1943-1945," *German Historical Institute (Washington, DC)*, GHI-DC.ORG.

[1446] Gustav Bally, "Deutschstämmige Psychotherapie," *Neue Zürcher Zeitung*, Feb. 24, 1934, p. 2; Eng.: Mitchell Ginsberg and Angela Grof-Nold, tr., *Effective Psychotherapy: The Contribution of Hellmuth Kaiser*, pp. xlviii-lii.

[1447] Joachim Fest, "Die Unfähigkeit zu überleben," pp. 783-798, in Karl-Dietrich Bracher, *Nationalsozialistische Diktatur 1933–1945: Eine Bilanz* (1983), at p. 796; cf. Joachim C. Fest, *Hitler* (Ger. text), p. 1039; *Hitler* (Eng.), p. 762.

as a nation deluded with settlement fantasies.[1448] We can also consider what these descriptions amounted to in the concrete situation of the twelve years, 1933-1945. Other descriptions are perhaps less specific in their diagnosis of the Reich, but were often contemptuous and acrimonious in their perspective. If we look at the critical characterizations of the Third Reich just mentioned, this solipsism (to apply here this philosophical concept to an entire society) is a variation of a metaphysical principle that only the existence of the individual is reality, and that all supposed others have no independent existence. This philosophical concept when applied to a nation, is the idea that only the nation itself has primary existence or value and that nothing else need be considered or taken into account, as being merely of secondary significance, at best.

A nation that is autistic (to apply a psychological concept to a society) is one that has very little awareness and a very poor sense of the other entities (nations, in this case) with which it interacts; this is a nation with very poor judgment about how its proposals, declarations, or actions will be understood and interpreted by other nations. When such an initial limited understanding of others is combined with a forgetfulness that is presumably a selective process—forgetting what might be uncomfortable or uncomplimentary to the nation—the result, of course, is a distorted, perhaps even Pollyannaish, self-lauding caricature of itself. The related suggestion that Nazi Germany suffered from a living-space dystopia (a great dissatisfaction presuming an inadequate, cramped space) and was deluded with related settlement fantasies, is linked to Germany's focus on what it felt was an unfair, unacceptable state of affairs in Continental European international politics. Underlying this was the frantic sense that more land was needed in order for all Germans to live satisfying lives, and the belief, never to be realized, of being able to conquer broad lands for the removal of the local inhabitants and the making of space for, and the settlement of, a growing German population; this idea itself would inspire Germany's entering into war to gain this living space, this *Lebensraum*. These various driving ideas were shown to be radical misinterpretations of the international situation that the Third Reich was operating within, with its extreme plans for how Europe was to evolve.

The confidence in Germany's ability to have its own individual will recognized by all impacted countries and to have it dictate the course of events, was one part of this dive into *the fantasy of Germany as an irresistible, unconquerable power*. This also required the assumption that the other nations, which Germany would soon confront in battle, were composed at least predominantly of incompetent, stupid, spineless, inferior beings (another National Socialist myth) that could in no way stand up against the superior German *Herrenrasse*, Master Race. That those Germany would have to face and conquer were assumed to be (1) peasants, uneducated, and undisciplined, (2) bourgeois and capitalist

---

[1448] Gerhard Wolf, "The Wannsee Conference in 1942 and the National Socialist living space dystopia," *Journal of Genocide Research*, vol. 17, no 2, 2015, pp. 153-175, at p. 153.

soft-bellied peoples bent on superficial entertainment and aware of nothing practical in the world of warfare, nothing to match the hard-willed German nation that had been forged by National Socialist values and the organized group practices of the *Hitlerjugend*, or (3) enemies ultimately controlled by the world-wide Jewish conspiracy bent on taking over the world that a superior Germany would destroy. There was also the Reich hope that once the world saw this Jewish poison, it would surely join the Nazi fight against this Jewish thirst for world control. In its vision of European hegemony, there was no worry about how those who were killed in mass or reduced to slave labor for the German nation would react: These others should accept the reality that Germany had taken over control and was dictating the roles of all peoples in its domain, all others being undeniably inferior to the Aryans of the Greater Germany. And yet, Hitler had advisors that had warned him of the consequences of Germany's starting a war, back in 1938, long before the invasion of Poland.

THE JULY 1944 ASSASSINATION ATTEMPT AND JUDGE ROLAND FREISLER

The consequences of Germany's use of warfare to gain the vast lands it needed to become self-sufficient and impenetrable were foreseen by some of his military advisors. In 1938, General Ludwig Beck, then Chief of the General Headquarters of the Army (*Chef des Generalstabes des Heeres*), offered a memorandum that stated, in part, that a war that Germany would begin would immediately call up more states than only the attacked one. *Germany would be defeated* in a war against a world coalition and would eventually be at its mercy [*Bei einem Krieg gegen eine Weltkoalition wird Deutschland unterliegen und dieser schließlich auf Gnade und Ungnade ausgeliefert sein*].[1449]

This was certainly not the sort of suggestion that Hitler would have wanted to hear.

Beck would resign when the German decision to invade Czechoslovakia was made, and would later be one of the generals involved in the July Plot, the attempted assassination of Hitler on July 20, 1944. He was ordered to commit suicide; his attempt failed; he was then shot dead by a sergeant that same day.

Furthermore, the head of the German *Abwehr* (Military Intelligence Service), Wilhelm Franz Canaris, before the war had assessed the plan for Germany to initiate a world war by invading Poland *to be a mistake on Hitler's part*.

Canaris later was also a member of the July Conspiracy, that same plot to assassinate Hitler, and was executed on April 9, 1945, for treason, in Flossenbürg Concentration Camp, *on an order from Hitler to execute the last of the surviving members of that failed attempt*.

Similarly, co-conspirator General Erwin Rommel was offered a cyanide capsule, which he took (on October 14). Other participants were less

---

[1449] L. J. Hartog, "Als Hitler den Massenmord prophezeite: Zur Rede vom 30. Januar 1939," *Die Zeit*, Jan. 27, 1989, and ZEIT ONLINE, Nov. 21, 2012.

fortunate, being hung by piano wire until they were dead (more on this particular method of execution, just below).

In the next months, some 400 people were arrested (to give a very low estimate), tried in the *Volksgericht* (People's Court) under the judge who had also conducted the first White Rose Trials earlier,[1450] the so-called "Hanging Judge"—Judge Roland Freisler.[1451] Another high-ranking German who was convicted of being a participant in this same plot to kill Hitler, was Arthur Nebe (1894-1945). Nebe had earlier been a principal—along with Heinrich Müller, Chief of the Gestapo—in the important investigation and prosecution of Georg Elser (in the attempted assassination of Hitler on November 8, 1939, discussed above). Nebe also held the position of Chief of the *Reichskrimialpolizeiamt*, Office of the Reich Criminal Police Department. During the invasion of the Soviet Union, he was commanding officer of *Einsatzgruppe B*, one of the major groups of the *Einsatzgruppen*, responsible for mass executions (primarily by firing squads) of Jews and other anti-Nazis in the Soviet Union (claiming over 45,000 victims in November 1941 alone). It was Nebe who arranged in August 1941 for Himmler to witness a mass killing in person. Nebe later suggested, in 1944, that the Gypsies (Romanies) held in Auschwitz might be good subjects for medical experiments. *Relatedly, but little known, the Japanese had their own medical experimentation, its Unit 731, which infected Chinese with bubonic plague, anthrax, typhus, and other infections.*[1452] Nebe was not given the options of suicide given to Canaris or Rommel: He was convicted of high treason and sentenced to death by an exceptionally tortured hanging, with his execution on March 2, 1945.

He and others would be hung in a rather brutal fashion, the noose around their necks not being rope but piano wire, its top loop attached to meat hooks sitting high off of the ground. The torturous deaths in their ritual entirety filmed for Hitler's later review, which, according to reports, was in conformity with Hitler's unambiguous order: *"Ich will, daß sie (die Verschwörer des 20. Juli) gehängt werden, aufgehängt wie Schlachtvieh."* ("I want them—the conspirators of July 20—to be hanged, hung up like meat-carcasses.")[1453]

[1450] The trial of Sophie Magdalena Scholl and Hans Fritz Scholl, brother and sister, and of Christoph Hermann Probst, their colleague in the White Rose, by Judge Roland Freisler, with judgment, sentencing, and execution by guillotine took place on February 22, 1943. They had been arrested for distributing the sixth pamphlet of their group, the White Rose, a few days earlier, on February 18, 1943, which, as it turned out, was the very same day that Goebbels gave his very famous speech on Total War. More on this, below.

[1451] *Roland Freisler and Sham Nazi Trials*, YOUTUBE.

[1452] Keiichi Tsuneishi, *The Germ Warfare Unit that Disappeared: The Kwangtung Army's 731st Unit* (1982; Jap. ed., 1994). Jap.: *Kantōgun;* pinyin: *Guǎngdōng*.

[1453] *Schlachtvieh*: fat stock, livestock that has been fattened for market and butchering. Dieter Ehlers, *Technik und Moral einer Verschwörung. 20. Juli 1944* [*Technology and Morals of a Conspiracy: July 20, 1944*] (1964), p. 113; Review of Joachim Fest's work: "20. Juli 1944: 'Aufgehängt wie Schlachvieh': Joachim Fest

This may be one indication of a sadistic tendency in Hitler, and of a pleasure found in the pain of others, known in German as *Schadenfreude*. In a recent German film there is a representation of the execution of Nebe at the *Hinrichtungsstätte Plötensee*, the Plötensee Execution Site, in Berlin, showing gruesome details such as the twitching unto death of Nebe.

The film, with dramatic focus on the silent cameraman and his camera on a tripod filming the sequence, draws visual attention to the important role in the story of the filming of the excruciatingly painful hanging.[1454] Hitler's interpretation of this July assassination plot, the *Unternehmen Walküre* (Operation Valkyrie)[1455] concluded, "Now I have proof: the entire General Staff is contaminated. Now I know why all my great plans in Russia had to fail in recent years. It was all treason! But for those traitors, we would have won long ago. Here is my justification before history."[1456]

Furthermore, also executed, at Flossenbürg Concentration Camp, on the same day as Canaris (April 9, 1945) was Dietrich Bonhoeffer, German Lutheran pastor, theologian, and also anti-Nazi dissident (vocal against the T4 euthanasia program and the mass killing of Jews); Bonhoeffer's brother-in-law, Hans von Dohnányi, a lawyer and fellow anti-Fascist, was similarly arrested and executed (at Sachsenhausen, also on April 9).[1457]

We might note that Hitler's great mistrust of not only the Reich military (the Wehrmacht) but also of incompetent Party bureaucrats, the SA in its entirety, the over-reaching aspirations of Himmler, and, finally, the entire German nation, can be understood as a consequence of the basic power structure of the Third Reich, based on rule by decree (the Führer Decrees), in which the will of the Führer, Hitler, would determine law and structure, summarized by the slogan *Ein Volk, Ein Reich, Ein Führer* (One people, empire, and leader), *with Hitler seeing himself, as usual, as flawless.*

In this way, Heidegger in his November 3, 1933 speech to university students expressed the *Führerprinzip*,[1458] the Führer Principle, in a few

---

über den Rachefeldzug des Nazi-Regimes gegen die Männer, die Hitler beseitigen wollten," *Spiegel*, No. 28, Jul. 11, 1994, pp. 42-53; Marion Gräfin Dönhoff, "Um der Ehre willen," ZEIT ONLINE, May 6, 1994; Ian Kershaw, *Hitler 1936-45: Nemesis*, pp. 693, 1006, with Hitler's Ger. words quoted above (in n. 40).

[1454] In the film *13 Minutes* (2015), at 1:38:10-1:40:50.

[1455] This refers to a work by Hitler's favorite composer, Richard Wagner, *Die Walküre* (*The Valkyrie*), the 2nd of four operas that formed Wagner's *Der Ring des Nibelungen* (*The Ring of the Nibelung*). The valkyries in Norse mythology were a group of female figures who decided which soldiers in battle would survive, and which would die. The chosen dead were taken to Walhalla, ruled by Odin (Wotan)— the Nordic god of death, war, and ecstasy (a powerful combination and mixture).

[1456] Ian Kershaw, *Hitler: 1936-1945 Nemesis*, p. 687. Cf. Ian Kershaw, *Hitler: A Biography*, p. 843; Alexandra Richie, *Warsaw 1944: Hitler, Himmler, and the Warsaw Uprising* (2013), p. 92.

[1457] On Bonhöffer, see, further, Sal·lus [following Catalan orthography] Herrero, "A propòsit del film sobre Hannah Arendt," *País Valencià, Siglo XXI*, Aug. 25, 2013.

[1458] This *Führerprinzip* (the principle of the Führer/Leader) can be traced back to the work of Dietrich Eckart, discussed above.

succinct words: "The Führer himself and alone is today and in the future the German reality and its law."[1459] This was a formula for structured chaos: "The Führer dictatorship was essentially based, not upon authority and organization, but on a complete lack of any hierarchy or structure. Nothing was more abhorrent to Hitler than the appearance of new organizational structures, for they would inevitably exert a constricting influence upon what was known as the 'dynamic will of the leadership.' Deliberately and instinctively, Hitler refused to permit any intervening hierarchical level between him and the masses—any such intervention could only have detracted from the unique and supreme position of the Führer."[1460] (Again, a rather kitsch idea.) This demand for maintaining a unique and irreplaceable position for Hitler also meant that those who wanted more power would seek it in ways that would not bring on Hitler's ire and obstruction. There was, furthermore, no structure for dealing with the Reich when Hitler would die (and even he did not think he was an immortal). After the assassination attempt of July 20, 1944, there were many arrests. Hitler's fury knew few restraints.

General Jürgen Stroop, in charge of the destruction of the Warsaw Ghetto, stated to his cell-mate for 255 days in 1949, Kazimierz Moczarski, about the assassination attempt and the work of Judge Roland Freisler,

> How could they consider harming their *Führer?* Adolf Hitler was placed on earth by higher powers, perhaps Wotan himself, to fulfill a sacred mission. [Stroop presumably believed this.] The July conspiracy was an example of the moral decay that proved to be our undoing. It would have been impossible to defeat Germany without German participation, *Herr* Moczarski. If it hadn't been for negligence disguised as tolerance, we could have held off the whole world. Instead, we allowed degenerate forces to pervert our healthy masses. A few weaklings poisoned by enemy agents and infected with subversive ideologies backed by gold [read, presumably: with capitalistic world Jewry] were all it took to undermine us. The minute we suffered our first military defeats, the cancerous elements in our society swung into action, organizing Mafias, and creating 'patriotic discussion groups.' In the end, they destroyed our nation.... We should have started our liquidation program sooner [this hints at Jews as the cancerous elements just mentioned] .... As I learned in the Warsaw Ghetto, a contaminated forest must be

---

[1459] As rendered in Karl Dietrich Bracher, *The Age of Ideologies: A History of Political Thought in the Twentieth Century* (1984), p. 24, n. 1. This was quoted earlier following William S. Lewis, "Martin Heidegger: Political Texts, 1933-1934," *New German Critique*, no. 45, 1988, pp. 96–114, at p. 102.

[1460] Heinz Höhne, *The Order of the Death's Head*, p. 409.

uprooted or burned to the ground. Heinrich Himmler knew this, of course. If only we could have convinced all Germany in 1933 of the need for racial and spiritual purity, if we could only have spread the word [of the need to protect the racial purity of Germany from "foreign" cancers], unhindered, the Reich would have been impervious."[1461]

This commentary represents a level of vehement Jew-hatred blended with an adoration, idealization, and even deification of the *Führer*, rare to find at the end of the war. Stroop also expressed his concern that most of the judges at the US Military Dachau trial[1462] were Jews or Masons, and noted that most had dark hair (presumably suspicious as possibly indicating Jewish blood). In addition, he described the conspirators of the attempt themselves as a "murderous band of generals and Jew-ridden civilians" and stated that Judge Roland Freisler was "a fine judge."[1463] Stroop was sentence to death by hanging by the US Military Dachau court, in 1947, but he was transferred to Polish jurisdiction, where he was imprisoned and tried in 1949. He was convicted of war crimes and sentenced to death, remaining quite without remorse or regret to his end, on March 6, 1952.

Looking at the punishments meted out to those found guilty of the conspiracy to assassinate Hitler, first, there were the key men who carried out the assassination attempt, organized by Colonel Klaus Graf Schenk von Stauffenberg. When Hitler survived the bomb and troops loyal to him secured Berlin, Stauffenberg was arrested, along with three other prime conspirators to the assassination scheme: Col. Werner Karl von Haeften, adjutant to Von Stauffenberg, who had fled the Wolf's Lair with Von Stauffenberg, flying back to Berlin with him; General Friedrich Olbricht, who had also returned to Berlin, separately; and Oberst (Col.) Albrecht Mertz von Quirheim. They were immediately ordered to be arrested by their superior, Gen. Friedrich Fromm, chief of the *Ersatzheer*, the Reserve (or Replacement) Army—who had known of their plans but kept silent (and now, perhaps wanting his passive acceptance not to be known)—had the arrested conspirators condemned to death, quickly taken into the nearby courtyard of the Ministry of War, and shot, shortly after midnight, early in the morning of July 21, 1944. General Ludwig Beck, who was also a background operator in this, was also immediately arrested, allowed to shoot himself, rather than to be shot or hung. He did, but the wound not

---

[1461] Kazimierz Moczarski, *Conversations with an Executioner*, p. 220.

[1462] The findings are recorded in Deputy Judge Advocate's Office, 7708 War Crimes Group, European Command, United States v. Jürgen Stroop *et al.*, Case No. 12-2000 (scanned pdf is only somewhat readable). May be cited as United States Army Investigation and Trial Records of War Criminals, United States of America v. Juergen Stroop *et al.*, March 29, 1945-August 21, 1957, M1095 (Superior Orders Case), 10 rolls; also cited as US Military Court, Dachau, Trial No. 12-3188, United States v. Stroop

[1463] Kazimierz Moczarski, *Conversations with an Executioner*, pp. 220, 224, 249.

fatal; he was then killed by a sergeant acting under Fromm's orders. Fromm's role in the plot would also be discovered, despite his eliminating these three key witnesses; he was shot by firing squad on March 19, 1945.

And because he had at least ordered the execution of the three other conspirators, Fromm was spared the more tortured death by hanging with a thin wire attached to a meat hook that was meted out for other conspirators of Operation Valkyrie.[1464]

Further, other generals were involved: first, General Carl-Heinrich von Stülpnagel, commander of the German troops in Paris, and also Field Marshal Rommel (as just mentioned), famous as the Desert Fox for his victories in tank warfare earlier in North Africa, and then head of the German Wehrmacht in western Europe. Rommel was discovered to have been part of the plot, and was arrested on October 14, 1944, and given the choice of standing trial and disgrace, or committing suicide and keeping his honor, as well as avoiding reprisals to his family. He took poison and died.[1465] Stülpnagel had a part in Operation Walkyrie, and when that action collapsed, he, too, was arrested and shot.

Then: five thousand people are arrested; 200 are executed summarily. In all, in the People's Court, there were more than 30,000 death sentences meted out.[1466] This was the largest mass killing within the Nazi machinery since the Night of the long Knives, and involved many more deaths.[1467] (This does not consider mass murders of Jews and others.)

We may note that *Hitler placed all blame for the German Wehrmacht losses in the USSR on the German Generals, seen overall as a traitorous group, and not on his own poor tactical and strategic planning,* nor on the inhospitable weather, the poor logistical support of food, war materiel, clothing, and equipment needed to allow good functioning of the German military in the deep snow and the -40 C. weather of the Soviet winter, or on the amassing of many millions of Soviet soldiers—fighting in defense of their very lives and the survival of their homeland—to confront the

---

[1464] "Friedrich Fromm," WIKIPEDIA; "General Fromm Executed for Plot against Hitler," *This Day in History: March 19, 1945*, HISTORY.COM; *Hitler's Bodyguard, Season 1, Episode 11 (Attempt to Kill Hitler at the Wolf's Lair)*, 37:15-37:40, YOUTUBE.

[1465] "Carl-Heinrich Rudolf Wilhelm von Stülpnagel," DE.WIKIPEDIA; "Erwin Rommel, German Field Marshal," ENCYCLOPÆDIABRITANNICA.COM.

[1466] Hans Mommsen, "The Dissolution of the Third Reich: Crisis Management and Collapse, 1943-1945," *German Historical Institute (Washington, DC)*, GHI-DC.ORG.

[1467] A text published after the war, *20. Juli 1944*, Hans Royce, ed. (1953), with a preface (*Geleitwort*) by Dr. Robert Lehr, Federal Minister of the Interior (1950-1953)—barred from practicing as a lawyer or professor during the Third Reich—presented resumes with photos (or sketches) of 95 of those convicted and executed in the months following the July 1944 assassination attempt on Hitler, both directly involved in the attempt, and Socialists, anti-Nazi religious leaders, and members of various resistance groups identified as the Kreisauer Circle (*der Kreisauer Kreises*), the Military Circle of the Resistance Movement (*der militärische Kreis der Widerstandsbewegung*), and the Socialist Wing of the Liberation Movement (*der sozialistische Flügel der Befreiungsbewegung*), among other groups.

German armies, nor on the more advanced Soviet military equipment from tanks to artillery to a large and very more effective and formidable air force. From Hitler's perspective, his own responsibility for any setbacks: 0%; the fault of the treasonous Generals: 100%. This not only could have a subsequent (envisioned) function in defining history—if Hitler could control that—but also reflected part of Hitler's personal tendency to place any criticism on the rest of the world, not to attribute any of the problem to himself. (We will return further to this characterological pattern, on the level of one's character and psychology, later.)

Considering the plans for the treatment of those living in the lands to be acquired for German *Lebensraum*, there was the idea that all Jews, even children, would have to be killed, because otherwise Germany would have to face a resurgence of rebellious Jewish intransigence as babies grew into resentful adults with a desire for revenge to be carried out against the German people.

This is actually not very far from the comment made in the USA after *Kristallnacht* and during the Congressional debate about the Wagner-Rogers bill (discussed above) by a cousin of President Franklin Delano Roosevelt, Laura Delano Houghteling (1893-1978, wife of the US Commissioner of Immigration): "20,000 charming children would all too soon grow into 20,000 ugly adults [meaning ugly Jews]."[1468] (Again, the stereotyping of Jews as ugly in some way manages at times to be used as a justification for the social rejection or even murder of Jews.)

This German concern about future generations of Jews, however, was specific and was not applied overall to all of the people of the European land mass. There was, to be sure, a neatness about killing each and every Jew, rather than differentiating between those Jews who were an actual threat to Germany and those who were just living in very rural areas with no group support for such violence, or were people who were apolitical and simply trying to make ends meet and to get through life, offering no threat whatsoever against the German drive for power.

While that may be, and such an understanding is certainly supported by speeches and published material by various high members of the Nazi Party and government, the capacity of the German administration to eliminate literally tens of millions of non-Germans (most of these would be Slavs) was not put in doubt. And yet, there was never a chance for Germany to complete these plans of extermination of peoples and of the enlargement of living space for the German people.

Other nations may have seriously wanted to avoid another war with Germany—after all, the memories among the European countries of the enormous loss of the generation of young men in World War I was quite a deterrent to the urge to go to war once again—a reluctance we certainly saw from Britain to Belgium to France and of course to the USA, which wanted to return to an isolationist international political stance, letting

---

[1468] "Roosevelt, Franklin D.," *David S. Wyman Institute for Holocaust Studies, Encyclopedia of America's Response to the Holocaust*, ENC.WYMANINSTITUTE.ORG.

the Europeans fight their own wars and leaving the US out of the picture and any involvement. But Germany's step-by-step demands for more and more rights for Germanic populations throughout Middle Europe, and its offering peace under the condition that other countries accept each and all of Germany's territorial expansions, and finally its attacking Poland on the excuse that Poland was trying to make war with Germany (the Gleiwitz Incident), finally led to these other countries coming to grips with this new evolution in European politics. While Germany's enemies, these presumed-inferior, presumed-incompetent nations, were relatively late in getting started on their production of weapons and the organizing of men into militarily competent groups, Germany would see their surprising capacity to produce in very short time a host of tanks, planes, rockets, artillery, and manpower.

The military prowess of Germany was perhaps at its height during the period from just before the invasion of Poland, and the Blitzkrieg warfare in Norway, the Lower Countries, and France, to shortly after the invasion of the USSR. The Soviet Union, however, was able to come from June 1941—the time of the German invasion, where the German Wehrmacht and Luftwaffe had relatively easy control over the lands and skies of the war theater—to late 1942 and early 1943, when the Soviets began pushing back and retaking territory earlier conquered. In only two years, the military scene went from the invincible onslaught of the German military into the USSR to Germany's beginning to be on the defensive and retreat. This, of course, was despite Hitler's demands that Germany never retreat and never surrender: better to die in battle, even to commit suicide to avoid the disgrace in those acts of weakness, in Hitler's vision of things, better than to go against his orders and military commands.

That the nations of Europe were ultimately unwilling to let the German juggernaut conquer and have its way indefinitely and boundlessly, and their capacity to organize for war against the Reich, was not an early German consideration, given its presupposition of its own invincibility.

Finally, Hitler and Goebbels and close associates having committed suicide, the man left in charge of the German defense of Berlin, Gen. Helmuth Weidling, surrendered unconditionally in the morning of May 2, 1945, to Soviet General Georgy Zhukov.

(We may recall that it was General Zhukov who had earlier led the defense of Stalingrad, beginning July 17, 1942, and counter-offensive Operation Uranus, launched on November 19, 1942, leading to the capture and surrender of Field Marshal Friedrich von Paulus on January 31, 1943.)

After his formal surrender to Zhukov, Weidling issued the following formal statement, following the Soviet instructions:

> On 30 April 1945, the Führer committed suicide, and thus abandoned those who had sworn loyalty to him. According to the Führer's order, you German soldiers would have had to go on fighting for Berlin despite the fact that our ammunition has run out and despite the

> general situation which makes our further resistance meaningless. I order the immediate cessation of resistance. Every hour you keep on fighting prolongs the suffering of the civilians in Berlin and of our wounded. Together with the commander-in-chief of the Soviet forces I order you to stop fighting immediately.
>
> (signed) Weidling, General of Artillery,
District Commandant in
the defense of Berlin.[1469]

The Third Reich that lasted for some 12 years and 4 months is certainly a long way from a government lasting one thousand years, but there are very few governments that last even 100 years, let along surviving for centuries on end.

It is noteworthy that Hitler would not see a huge difference between a political structure that could last a millennium and the government he had hobbled together, leading to his interpretations of all set-backs as the malevolence, incompetence, or traitorous nature of those around him, and a reflection of the impressively distorted, grandiose assessment of his own impact on a nation and its long-term viability.

To assume that the recent revolution in Germany—from the end of January 1933 to the Nuremberg Party Congress of August 30-September 3, 1933, called the Congress of Victory (meaning presumably the victory over and the eliminating of all other political parties in Germany, given that Germany was not at war with any other country at the time)—would bring about a stability under the ongoing control of the National Socialist Party for one thousand years is an idea that would seem to be grounded on thin air, on a wing and a prayer, as was said in World War II.

Unbounded hubris may quite well be essentially the foundation for subsequent failure of a catastrophic dimension. At least that would seem to be the case for the Third Reich.

Who Knew? Did Hitler?

This concept that the German population was in a state of self-induced ignorance about what was obvious to much of the world, and its tendency to forget what it did not manage to remain totally ignorant about, would be identified as German *autistischen Selbstvergessenheit*, an autistic self-forgetfulness, by the German historian Joachim Fest:

> It is certainly true that the majority of Germans knew nothing of the practice in the extermination camps [*Praxis in den Vernichtungslagern nichts gewußt hat*], and in any case [*jedenfalls*] were far less informed [*weit ungenauer darüber unterrichtet war*] than the world public [*als die*

[1469] Hans Dollinger, *The Decline and Fall of Nazi Germany and Imperial Japan: A Pictorial History of the Final Days of World War II* (1968), pp. 242-243: Weidling had written "former District Commandant" and Zhukov replied, "There is no need to say 'former'. You are still commandant." Cf. Ian Kershaw, *Hitler: A Biography*, p. 959.

The Hitler Era 495

> *Weltöffentlichkeit*], which since the end of 1941 had been alerted in ever-new calls of alarm [*in immer neuen Alarmrufen*] to the mass crime [*das Massenverbrechen*] ... The unresponsiveness [*Die Reaktionslosigkeit*] with which people responded to the unfolding rumors [*unlaufenden Gerüchten*] is inconceivable [*nicht denkbar*] without that tradition which had long since handed over the sphere of the political [*der Bereich des Politischen*] to the exclusive jurisdiction of the state [*ausschließlichen Zuständigkeit des Staates*].[1470]

As mentioned above, this is joined by similar descriptions of Aryan solipsism, Germanic autistic self-forgetfulness, National Socialist living-space dystopia, and a nation deluded with settlement fantasies.

Discussions after the war about what the Germans knew were at times put into unhelpfully simplistic terms, in a context where Germans typically denied being Nazis, where documents and uniforms linking them with the party or the military were burned and destroyed: "We didn't know anything about the T4 euthanasia program! We certainly didn't know about the death camps! We didn't know anything about the Jews!" I was never a Nazi!"[1471] And yet, if this topic is refined to something more specific, a blanket denial makes less sense and is less plausibly accurate a reporting. Of course, the opening of the concentration camps in March 1933 was not secret. In fact, it was widely publicized in the Nazi press, in part as a warning to anyone who might think of disagreeing with National Socialist values and worldview.

Then, the Nuremberg Laws of 1935 that annulled citizenship for all German Jews—they, too, were rather public.

As Joachim Fest suggested just above, there was a societal amnesia in Germany (to generalize), but there was much evidence for those who wanted to know specifics about the organized and planned violence of the National Socialist Party and the Third Reich, with its roots in rage and the fierce, sweet dream of revenge, which developed means to this end.[1472]

We may find more clarity here if we look at what was obvious to anyone living in German during the Third Reich and so what the Germans most assuredly knew, then, next, at what they had hints of, in a less than

---

[1470] Joachim C. Fest, *Hitler* (Ger. text), p. 1039; *Hitler* (Eng.), p. 762. (This gloss is closer to the original German, which is more definite and affirmative than the Eng. text, cited here for cross-referencing.) Cf. Joachim Fest, "Die Unfähigkeit zu überleben," in Karl-Dietrich Bracher, *Nationalsozialistische Diktatur 1933–1945: Eine Bilanz* (1983), pp. 783-798, at p. 796.

[1471] Saul K. Padover, *Experiment in Germany: The Story of an American Intelligence Officer* (1946).

[1472] Sebastian Haffner (British name and penname for Raimond Pretzel, 1907-1998), an attorney who fled to England in 1933, kept papers on the machinations of the National Socialist Party, with text written in 1939). After his death, his son, Oliver Pretzel, found these papers, comprising a memoir; they were published as *Geschichte eines Deutschen* (2000), and in Eng. tr., as *Defying Hitler: A Memoir*.

obvious way but one that might lead to their questioning, and thirdly, at what they did not know at all. First, there were published news announcements by the Nazi press of the creation of a web of concentration camps by the new Nazi Government, from March 1933 on, where torture was rumored to take place regularly. Then, there was the constant berating of Jews as the poisonous enemy of European culture and civilization, most notably in *Völkischer Beobachter*, edited by Julius Streicher, in *Der Angriff*, founded and edited by Joseph Goebbels, and in *Das schwarze Korps*, founded by Heinrich Himmler. There were also high-profile speeches by leading figures of the National Socialist government (including Hitler) against the Jews as the betrayers of the German war effort during World War I, against the Jews as Soviet-agent Bolsheviks, and against the Jews as an essentially foreign element that could never be integrated into the world of the German people, culture, and race, being vermin, poisonous parasites sucking the energy of the civilizations in which they inserted themselves, and so on. (Many of these ideas had already been expressed years earlier in *Mein Kampf*, as above.)

Many signs of state power against the Jews were certainly not hidden: from the rough-handed use of the SA in early April 1933 blocking people from shopping at stores owned by Jews, with the warnings that such transgressors were being photographed, to the laws limiting the rights of Jews in Germany, extended from 1933 laws through the Nuremberg Laws of 1935-1936, and beyond. The hostility toward Jews, after that April 1933 boycott as a weak first attempt at aggression, continued with the forcing of Jews to give up certain items (from sewing machines and typewriters, radios, and fur coats, to financial funds and gold, and so on), to the Jews in Germany to show their identity, first, by having to wear an armband—from late August 1940, to wearing a Jewish star (September 19, 1940)[1473]—to their being strongly encouraged to leave Germany and Reich-controlled lands permanently, while leaving their property behind for the German State, and then to their being deported to the "east" (places and situations left undefined or misidentified).

These actions could not be hidden from friends, acquaintances, and neighbors; if anything, they were in everyone's view, as a sign of the power of determination of the Reich. And, as shown just below, there were further publicly visible signs in many cities and towns across Germany in the so-called *Stürmerkasten*, display cases (*Kasten*) in public areas with copies of the newspaper, *Der Stürmer*, with its anti-Semitic comments, edited by Julius Streicher. The two phrases in the image here mean "With *Der Stürmer* against Judah" (referring to Jewry in general) and "Jews are our misfortune." Note the bulbous-nosed caricature of a cartoon of a Jew in the display case, at the far left. These were found widely in place in the first years of the Reich (with many being taken down for the influx of foreigners to the 1936 Olympic games in Germany).

[1473] Victor Klemperer, *I Shall Bear Witness: The Diaries of Victor Klemperer, 1933-41* (1998), pp. 339, 410; tr. of his *Ich will zeugnis ablegen bis zum letzten* (1995).

The Hitler Era

Stürmerkasten (Worms, Germany; circa 1935-1938)

There was also the closing down of all Jewish businesses, which had to be "aryanized" (sold to non-Jewish interests, usually at very low prices), and signs throughout Germany "Juden unerwünscht" (Jews unwelcome), and parks with signs prohibiting Jews from entering, and so on.

Then, in a gradual escalation of anti-Jewish actions, there was the government-guided expulsion of Jews before and then during War War II, first in a more voluntary way (if that's a word that could be applied for the exodus of Jews in the context of an extremely hostile environment).

With a harsher degree, there were forced evacuations "to the east" in which Jewish property (houses and apartments and such) were taken over by the State, to be given to individuals seen as ideal Nazis[1474] or put before the public for a general auction.[1475] The property transferred in this way was then legally purchased (in one limited sense of "legally"). In this context, the amount confiscated from Jewish sources is estimated as having paid for approximately one third of the Reich's war expenses.

There was also the outright robbery in the east, with the confiscation of factories, land, livestock (cattle, sheep, and such),[1476] and more from

---

[1474] Jack Ewing, "Germany's Central Bank Backs Study of Role in Nazi Crimes," *The New York Times*, Nov. 3, 2017. This discusses the successful Nov. 1941 request by Karl Blessing—CEO of *Kontinentale Öl* (a company exploiting oil in countries conquered by the German Army), after the war, President of the Bundesbank, Germany's Central Bank—to Albert Speer for a property that had been confiscated from its German Jewish owners. There were many such transfers (seizing) of prime Jewish-owned property for German administrative offices (such as the Tiergartenstraße 4 estate) or as gifts to worthy Nazi-supporting individuals.

[1475] Robert Gellately, *Backing Hitler*, photo no. 19 (public auction in Hanau, 1942), among the photo inserts between pp. 142-143.

[1476] Metro-Goldwyn-Mayer/MGM, *The Rise and Fall of the Third Reich* (1968), based on the William L. Shirer book by the same title, with scenes of livestock being driven by German military into train cattle-cars, at 1:42:30-1:43:10.

the conquered lands, from Czechoslovakia to Poland to the USSR, and so forth.[1477] Germans were quite aware of the disappearance from the cities of Germany of Jews and presumed-to-be dissidents, either secretly (applying the secretive December 7, 1941 *Nacht und Nebel Erlaß*, the Night and Fog Decree), or, more usually, in less clandestine ways.

The management, herding, transferring of Jews without their property to transit camps, and their transport to the camps "to the East" and their extermination, created an impressive array of witnesses to the whole process: all of this work required the involvement of many Germans, their allies, and their collaborators across Europe, involving the bureaucratic support of various governmental offices scheduling train routings to the death camps, with all of those who were guards there, or lived near the trains' itinerary able to witness the cattle cars with their human cargo.

Once the war began, there was herding of Jews into confined living quarters and concentration and extermination camps, visible to the non-Jewish populations nearby: Himmler and Hitler discussed this topic of the Jews from the conquered lands (in addition to the earlier problem of the presence of German Jews in the Reich itself), in some specificity. As Russian historian Georgily A. Kumanev has written:

> On May 25, 1941, Himmler informed Hitler in writing of his ideas on this topic. These ideas were affirmed and approved by the Fuehrer in a directive [see just below] known as "Several ideas on Ways to Handle the Local Population in the Eastern Regions."[1478] As this document shows, *Hitler's policies were aimed at the physical destruction and complete annihilation of certain Slavic peoples, in particular the western Ukrainians, Byelorussians [Belarusians], and others.* "We insist that

---

[1477] Steve Mariotti, "The Nazi Tax on Jewish Wealth: An Early Warning Sign of the Holocaust," *The HuffPost*, Mar. 2, 2017; Allan Hall, "Confiscated Jewish wealth 'helped fund the German war effort'," *The Telegraph* (London), Nov. 5, 2017. This reported that nearly 120 billion Reich marks—over £12 billion at the time—was plundered from German Jews by laws and looting. To give an idea of this amount, in 1940, £12 billion was equal to $993.95 billion; equivalent in recent dollar values, to roughly $17.85 trillion. See Eric W. Nye, "Pounds Sterling to Dollars: Historical Conversation of Currency, and conversion to 2018 dollars," DOLLAR TIMES. Cf. *The Plunder of Jewish Property During the Holocaust: Confronting European History*, Avi Beker, ed. (2000); Martin Dean, *Robbing the Jews: The Confiscation of Jewish Property in the Holocaust, 1933-1945* (2008); "Final Sale: The End of Jewish Owned Businesses in Nazi Berlin," AKTIVES MUSEUM FASCHISMUS UND WIDERSTAND IN BERLIN (2010); "Confiscation of Jewish Property in Europe, 1933–1945: New Sources and Perspectives—Symposium Proceedings," CENTER FOR ADVANCED HOLOCAUST STUDIES, USHMM (2003).

[1478] Georgily A. Kumanev, "Chapter 13: The German Occupation Regime on Occupied Territory in the USSR (1941-1944)," pp. 128-141, in *A Mosaic of Victims*, Michael Berenbaum, ed., at p. 130. Cf. *Voenno-istoricheskii zhurnal* [*Military-Historical Journal*], Moscow, 1969, no. 1, pp. 87-88.

every effort be made to prevent the people of the eastern regions uniting; we want to break them up into the smallest groups possible."[1479] (Quotes in text itself.)

There was fertile ground for this project, given that Ukraine had been intensely anti-Semitic for centuries, and still is. During World War II, this was fed by the sense (encouraged by the German occupation forces) that the Jews were reliable and consistent supporters of the Soviet regime; for nationalistic Ukrainians, who had suffered for long periods under Czarist and Russian-led Soviet governments, this made the Jews accomplices of their cultural enemy. Alone in the the Soviet Union, Ukraine in the period of the war saw more Ukrainian Jews killed than survived: of the 2.7 million Jews in Ukraine at the start of the war, 1.6 million were killed by the Germans and Ukrainian allies (collaborators) by the end of the war.[1480]

By comparison, overall, during the war, 2,230,000 Belarusians were killed there. This was one-fourth of the Belarusian total population![1481] The document just quoted by Himmler was presented to the Court during the Nuremberg Trials, and entitled *Reflections on the Treatment of Peoples of Alien Races in the East: A Secret Memorandum Handed to Hitler by Himmler on 25 May 1940.*[1482]

Himmler spoke of the importance of ridding Europe of its Jews, of the use of Slavic peoples in limited numbers to be used as laborers in service of the Reich, and of the importance of discovering Aryan children among the conquered peoples, who could be taken back to Germany and raised as model citizens. These were to be children judged to be of German stock (*deutschstämmige*, of German lineage)—not by tracing family trees, but by a physical exam looking for blond hair, blue eyes, and other features taken to be prototypical Aryan.

At this point in time (May 1940, months after the invasion of Poland but before the attack on the Soviet Union in June of 1941), Himmler's thinking (which Hitler would be in agreement with) was for *die Entfernung der Juden*, the removal of the Jews (as Hitler put it decades earlier, in his statement of September 16, 1919, quoted above) and not extermination.

At the time, then, Himmler spoke of the possibility, still considered at that time, of exiling European Jewry to the island of Madagascar. This idea would fade into the background later, especially after the invasion of the USSR.

Another document discussing the preceding memorandum of Himmler to Hitler, marked Top Secret, and dated May 28, 1940, was also presented to the Court at Nuremberg, entitled *File Note of Himmler, 28 May 1940,*

[1479] See preceding note. Italics added.

[1480] Alexander Kruglov, "Jewish Losses in Ukraine, 1941-1944," *The Shoah in Ukraine: History, Testimony, Memorialization*, Ray Brandon and Wendy Lower, eds. (2008), pp. 272-290, at p. 273.

[1481] Victoria Khiterer, "Memorialization of the Holocaust in Minsk and Kiev," in *Holocaust Resistance in Europe and America: New Aspects and Dilemmas*, Victoria Khiterer and Abigail S. Gruber, eds. (2017), pp. 95-131, at p. 125.

[1482] NT-TWC-Green, vol. 13, pp. 147-150.

concerning the Handling and Distributing of his Memorandum on the Treatment of Alien Races in the East. In this, Himmler stated in part,

> On Saturday, 25 May [1940], I handed my memorandum on the treatment of peoples of alien race in the East to the Fuehrer. The Fuehrer read the six pages and considered them very good and correct. He directed, however, that only very few copies should be issued; that there should be no large edition, and that the report is to be treated with utmost secrecy.[1483]

The Germans and the Soviets were both interesting in controlling how their people and the world in general saw their actions (as is quite usual for governments, especially when they sense that some of their actions will be questioned if not attacked in some possible future).

Thus, Bogdan Musiał, German-Polish historian, professor of law, and chair of Studies on Central and Eastern Europe at the Cardinal Stefan Wyszyński University, Warsaw, has questioned Soviet accounts of the war in the East, including issues of Polish-Russian relations during that period. In a work he edited and contributed to are the remarks (now available in the west in a post-soviet Russia):

> the Nazi-Soviet collaboration, on both official and unofficial levels, was vehemently denied. The Ribbentrop-Molotov Pact of 23 August 1939 was reduced to a communist tactical retreat. The Soviet murder of the Polish officers in the Katyń Forest [some 12 miles west of Smolensk], where the Russians killed Poles, mostly Polish military officers, in April and May 1940 (before the Germans overran the area in August 1941), discovered in April 1943 by German troops, with announcement by Goebbels on April 13, making much of the barbarity of the Soviet atrocities] was denied and delinked from the Nazi mass murder of prominent Poles in the Palmiry Forest [30 miles northwest of Warsaw, where from December 1939 to July 1941 the Germans killed and buried some 1,757 Poles, including many of the Polish intelligentsia], even though both were synchronized crimes whose aim was to exterminate Poland's elite. The memories of the exuberant welcome of the Nazis by Soviet citizens in the summer of 1941 and the massive participation of "the Soviet people" in the Nazi war effort against "the Soviet Fatherland" were buried. The extermination of the Jews was depicted [with less specificity, only] as "martyrdom of Soviet citizens" and stripped of its uniqueness.[1484]

[1483] NT-TWC-Green, vol. 13, pp. 150-151, at p. 150.
[1484] Marek Jan Chodakiewicz, "[Review, in English, of Bogdan Musiał],

The Hitler Era

Of course, another claim of uniqueness is that of the Holocaust (Shoah). In contrast to some German historians who have been understood to claim an equivalence between Nazi perpetrators and Jewish victims,[1485] Eberhard Jäckel asserted "that the murder of the Jews was singular (*daß der nationalsozialistische Mord an den Juden deswegen einzigartig war*), because never before did a state decide with the authority of its responsible leader to announce (*weil noch nie zuvor ein Staat mit der Autorität seines verantwortlichen Führers beschlossen und angekündigt hatte*) the total annihilation of a certain group of people, including the old, women, children and infants (*eine bestimmte Menschengruppe einschließlich der Alten, der Frauen, der Kinder und der Säuglinge möglichst restlos zu töten*), and actually carry out this decision with all possible bureaucratic force (*und diesen Beschluß mit allen nur möglichen staatlichen Machtmitteln in die Tat umsetzte*)."[1486]

Soon after the invasion of the USSR, on August 1, 1941, Heinrich Müller, Chief of the Gestapo under Heydrich, sent an order to the heads of the four *Einsatzgruppen* (the SS mobile killing squads): "The Führer is to be kept informed continually from here about the work of the Einsatzgruppen in the East."[1487]

This sort of consideration goes strongly against the claim by some that Hitler did not or could not have known of the East front atrocities of SS and others. Relatedly, "between 23 June, 1941 and 24 April, 1942, 195 detailed operational event reports were sent [from each and all of the four *Einsatzgruppen*] to Heydrich's staff in Berlin, who circulated them to leading Nazi figures, including Hitler."[1488] *We can say the same here.* These would presumably have had a noteworthy place among the reports that Hitler was known to review late each night into the morning.

Significantly, once the killing operations at Auschwitz got underway, Himmler called Bormann at Berchtesgaden in mid-May 1942 to announce good news for the Führer: 20,000 Jews had been *liquidiert* (liquidated) at Auschwitz. Bormann interrupted and reprimanded Himmler, reminding him that such information should be communicated only by courier, sent

---

Sowjetische Paritsanen in Weißrußland: Innenansichten aus dem Gebiet Baranovici [a name for Belarus, from a town southwest of Minsk, northeast of Brest, and west of Gomel] 1941-1944. Eine Dokumentation," in *The Sarmatian Review*, vol. 26, no. 2, Apr. 2006, pp. 1217-1220, quoted passage at p. 1217. *The Sarmatian Review* is a peer-reviewed scholarly journal on Slavistics (Slavic Studies).

[1485] On Ernst Nolte and other historians, see Konrad H. Jarausch, "Removing the Nazi Stain? The Quarrel of the German Historians," *German Studies Review*, vol. 11, no. 2, 1988, pp. 285–301, at p. 290; Maria Karlsson, *Tall Tales of Genocide: An Argumentative and Comparative Analysis of Western Denial of the Holocaust and of the Armenian Genocide* (2011).

[1486] Eberhard Jäckel, "Die elende Praxis der Untersteller: Das Einmalige der nationalsozialistischen Verbrechen lißt sich nicht leugnen," *Die Zeit*, Sep. 12, 1986, p. 145, ZEITONLINE.

[1487] Gerald Fleming, *Hitler and the Final Solution* (1986), p. xxvi.

[1488] Frank McDonough, *The Holocaust*, p. 52.

to Bormann, who would pass on information to the Führer.[1489] Hitler, quite clearly, *was being advised directly about the ongoing killing of the Jews*. While there is at this time no definitive recorded order *from* Hitler about the work of the *Einsatzgruppen*, the National Socialist attitude toward Jews was not hidden. This does not mean that a program of mass extermination was put forth or even contemplated in the early years of the Third Reich. This obviously intensified after *Kristallnacht* (November 9-10, 1938) and certainly by the beginning of the organized mass killings on the eastern Front in late 1941. The brutality of *Kristallnacht* (which was not only a night of broken glass, as the name suggests, *but also a night of violence against Jews in many towns throughout Germany, not just Berlin*) was to be a clear indication of the potential in the Nazi-cultivated hatred of Jews. A young boy at the time later explained, "Even as a ten-year-old, the events of the *Kristallnacht* ... signified the end of German innocence. From now on, not one of us could ever maintain that we did not know what was in store for the Jews."[1490] (Still, others tried.)

Concerning the subsequent murderous violence against Europe's Jews, one group of historians has proposed, "The decision to kill the European Jews was undoubtedly taken by spring 1941 at the latest."[1491] In any case, we are talking here about a range of a few months: "The first murders of Soviet Gypsies in fact took place in the second half of August."[1492] Soon after, were the indiscriminate killings of Jews at Babi Yar, starting September 29, 1941. This mass killing of Jews involved cities, villages, and *stetlech*. A *shtetl* was typically a township with 10-35,000 Jews (at least a third of its overall population) living a Jewish life.[1493] Relatedly, interviews reveal more of the extensive nature of this killing: Ukrainians have recently spoken, some broken by what they had seen, some with eyes still full of terror, some speaking of being requisitioned to do work (as gathering left clothes or removing gold teeth of murdered Jews). Many were eye witnesses of these mass murders: a Holocaust by bullets.[1494]

Hitler in his famous speech before the Reichstag on January 30, 1939 had forewarned (or threatened) the Jews of Europe with their annihilation

---

[1489] The call was overheard by a telephone operator at Berchtesgaden, Alfons Schulz, who later wrote and spoke of it: Reuven Assor, "[Book Review of] Alfons Schulz, *Drei Jahre in der Nachrichtenzentrale des Führerhauptquartiers* [1997]," *Freiburger Rundbrief*, vol. 5, 1998, p. 309; Simon Wiesenthal, *Hitler's Holocaust* (2000), *Season 1, Episode 4 (Factory of Murder)*, Schulz interview at 36:20-36:35.

[1490] Alfons Heck, *Confessions of a Hitler Youth* (1991), HBO, at 12:10-12:45.

[1491] "The Start of the Mass Murder," HOLOCAUST.CZ.

[1492] Donald Kenrick and Grattan Puxon, *Gypsies under the Swastika*, p. 87.

[1493] Yehuda Bauer, "Nowogródek: The Story of a Shtetl," *Yad Vashem Studies*, vol. 35, no. 2, 2007, pp. 5-40.

[1494] Patrick Desbois, *The Holocaust by Bullets: A Priest's Journey to Uncover the Truth behind the Murder of 1.5 Million Jews* (2009), esp. pp. 74-75; Yahad-In Unum, *Ukraine Trip 27: July 21-August 5, 2011*, and *Summaries of 2018 Investigative Trips*, both at YAHADINUNUM.ORG; interview with Father Patrick Desbois: Lara Logan, "The Hidden Holocaust," *60 Minutes*, Oct. 4, 2015, CBSNEWS.COM.

if they managed to draw Germany into another world war, even if not all Nazi descriptions of their "defensive" war made reference to Jews. (More below.) It could describe aggression as retaliation for Polish violence against Germans (as the Gleiwitz Incident). There was also no attributing to Jews (or to a world-wide conspiracy of Jews, or a cabal of Bolshevik Jews) as the source leading to the annexation of Austria, the taking over of the Sudetenland, the invasion of Czechoslovakia, or the Blitzkrieg against the Polish nation. On its own, though, the idea that it was the Jews who were primarily responsible for the war kept being repeated, and applied with deadly implications. And, in terms of simplifying a complex message down to something simple (here: Jews as the sole source of Germany's problems), Goebbels' comment on Nazi propaganda to Norbert Schultze (composer of the melody[1495] to the earlier melody of "Lili Marleen") was: "Propaganda is like a convoy [of ships] in the war, which must reach its target under heavy military protection. It has to adjust its speed to suit the slowest ship of the unit. That is how it is for us, too. Sophisticated propaganda is [always] out of place."[1496] Hitler, too, spoke of the slowness of the "great masses" to comprehend, and had stated in *Mein Kampf*, "All propaganda has to be popular [*volkstümlich*] and has to adapt its spiritual level [*ihr geistiges Niveau*, its mental level] to the perception [*Aufnahmefähigkeit*, power of absorption] of the least intelligent [*des Beschränktesten*, the most slow-witted] of those towards whom it intends to direct itself."[1497] In short, politically important information (propaganda) should be presented in simple terms and should be repeated in intervals that would overcome the enormous "power of forgetting" of the masses. Both Hitler and Goebbels presented the ideas of invading *Haufen*, hordes, with Hitler referring in *Mein Kampf* and elsewhere to the endless hordes of Russian prisoners from the 1914 Battle of Tannenberg, to the press horde (mostly Jewish), to hordes of rats (fighting bloodily among themselves), to the uneducated hordes of the great masses, to black African hordes, and so on, and Goebbels spoke of his concerns about the red horde, the Bolshevik horde.[1498] Thus,[1499] for *Der ewige Jude*, Hitler demanded that Goebbels insert scenes depicting rampaging hordes of rats among animals, to repeat graphically the metaphor for Jews among humans. (Goebbels reluctantly agreed.)

[1495] Lyrics written in 1915 by Hans Leip, with melody added by Schultze in 1938. It became popular to German troops in southeast Europe and north Africa after its broadcast from Beograd (Belgrade) by German military radio.

[1496] BBC film, *Goebbels, Master of Propaganda*, at 29:45-30:15.

[1497] Adolf Hitler, *Mein Kampf*, Book I, Chap. VI (War Propaganda—*Kriegspropaganda*), pp. 232 234; Ger., pp. 197-198.

[1498] See throughout *Mein Kampf*, Ger., pp. 215, 224, 290, 301, 358, 413, 594, 711, etc., and Eng., pp. 256, 265, 280, 285, 304, 313, 328, 331, 341, 346, 416, 917, etc., in the Reynal & Hitchcock ed. (1941) and pp. 61, 196, 302, 523-524, 629, etc. in the Rudolph Mannheim ed. (1943), referring to *Haufen*, *Horden*, hordes, and masses, resp., for images of hordes to be overcome by Aryan superiority.

[1499] *Goebbels, Master of Propaganda*, 1992 (BBC), YOUTUBE, at 30:45-33:25.

Having seen the runners for the forthcoming film, Hitler was thus intimately aware of the conditions under which the Jews in the Warsaw ghetto lived, and the starvation to death of those filmed. Goebbels, noted in his diary on July 5, 1941, a difference in approach: "The Führer wants more polemical material in the script. I would rather have the pictures speak for themselves... I consider this to be more effective because then one does not notice the intent *(weil man die Absicht nicht merkt)*."[1500]

It is sometimes proposed that if there has been no written evidence of a precise, explicit decree by Hitler to exterminate the Jews, he therefore knew nothing of the process. This is taking one possible piece of evidence and holding it to determine definitively a more complex question. That is an arbitrary narrowing of what counts as evidence. We can see many other indications that Hitler was quite aware of it all, from written notes by a number of Hitler's very close associates in the Third Reich and from other official documents. We can also see Hitler's general interest and desire to be aware of, and in control of, a wide range of activities in the Third Reich, which are in part personality features of Hitler's mentality. We can also note Hitler's claim for total control and awareness of what was going on in the Nazi Party, as in his statement, "Nothing happens in the [Nazi] movement without my knowledge, without my approval. Even more: nothing happens without my wish."[1501] *If we accept this statement, which seems to be consistent with what many around him expressed in official communications, verbal exchanges, and personal notes (including diaries), Hitler would surely know of something so central to his rule, so close to his heart, and so involved as the isolation, concentrating, and shipping off of Jews—with the thousands upon thousands of Germans who would be involved in this process.*

Serious students of the period, including almost all academic historians of the era, take this to be a proven, unquestionable fact. There is a wide recognition by now of some key later steps: Hitler at the Reichstag in January 1939 predicted the extermination of Jewry should it drag Europe into another world war. Hitler knew of the deaths occurring in the Warsaw ghetto, and demanded that the film *The Eternal Jew*, should include images of swarming rats as a metaphor for Jews, just discussed. Rudolf Höss, Commandant of Auschwitz, in testimony after the war, reported on his conversion in summer 1941 in which Himmler spoke of a Führer Order: "Every Jew that we can lay our hands on is to be destroyed now during the war, without exception." In July 1941, there was the written message from Göring to Heydrich about setting up an organized plan to deal with the Final Solution (quoted in detail, above). There was the realization that

---

[1500] Joseph Goebbels, *Tagebücher 1924-1945*, p. 1621; on *Der Ewige Jude*, cf. pp. 1412-1413; *The Goebbels Diaries 1939-1941*, Fred Taylor, ed. (1983), p. 449. Cf. *Goebbels, Master of Propaganda*, at 33:10-33:35.

[1501] From a series of 1932 articles in the *Münchener Post* (*Munich Post*) on death squad killings within Hitler's movement: see Ron Rosenbaum, *Explaining Hitler: The Search for the Search for the Origins of His Evil*, pp. 40-41.

winning the war and conquering the USSR was not going to be easy, was not even guaranteed: on December 5, 1941, General Zhukov initiated a counter-offensive that stopped the Wehrmacht, without its ever being able to capture Moscow.[1502] There was then a flurry of serious meetings concerning the extermination of Jewry in the days following Pearl Harbor and Germany's declaration of war against the USA two days later. On December 12, Hitler gave a talk to major Gauleiters; that same day, Goebbels noted in his diary Hitler's firm position on the extermination of the Jews ("to make a clean sweep of the issue"). Nazi philosopher Alfred Rosenberg, Head of the Reich Ministry for the Occupied Eastern Territories (*Reichsministerium für die besetzten Ostgebiete*) at the time, described a conversation with the Führer on December 14, 1941: "On the Jewish Question [*Über die Judenfrage*], I [Rosenberg] said ... I am of the opinion not to speak of the extermination of Jewry [*die Ausrottung des Judentums nicht zu sprechen*]. The Führer approved of this attitude [*Der Führer bejahte diese Haltung*] and said that they [the Jews] had saddled us with the war [*sie hatten uns den Krieg aufgebürdet*] and they had brought the destruction, [and so] it was no wonder if the consequences hit them first [*wenn die Folgen sie zuerst trafen*]."[1503] This refers explicitly to "the consequences" to the Jews, which Hitler had openly predicted (as "the annihilation of the Jews of Europe" if they should drag Germany into a world war) in his January 30, 1939 speech to the Reichstag. (More below.)

On December 16, Hans Frank, Governor General of occupied Poland reported to his inferiors that the Jews in their territory could not be deported, and would therefore have to be liquidated (another term for being exterminated, killed en masse). On December 18, Himmler in his diary noted Hitler's words: "*Judenfrage / als Partisanen auszurotten*" ("Jewish Question / eradicate them as partisans"—kill all of them).[1504]

Such statements indicate that those high up in the German war machine and occupation administration were aware that Hitler was being informed about, and presumably, as *der Führer*, leading the programs being carried out. We can see here the application of Nazi theories of supremacy as the Master Race, with that concept's corollary of the inferiority of other peoples, especially the Slavs, and the Jews, not worthy of being called human. Yet *Hitler and the Reich did not limit their sights only to the Jews*. As historian Richard C. Lukas has written:

[1502] *Russian-German War: World War 2, The Killing Ground* (1995), CT NEWS/CT TELEVISION NETWORK (CANADA), 20:00-21:50,YOUTUBE.

[1503] NT-IMT-Blue, vol. 27, Doc. 1517-PS ("Vermerk über Unterredung beim Führer am 14.12.1941"), pp. 270-273. Tr. here from the text in German at p. 270. The document (marked "Geheime Reichssache, Top Secret") was signed and dated Dec. 16, 1941 by Rosenberg. The discussion served to refine a forthcoming speech by Rosenberg at the Berlin Sportpalast.

[1504] For these, see discussion above, and Christian Gerlach, *Sur la conference de Wannsee* (1999), pp. 53-57; Christopher R. Browning, *Fatefiul Months: Essays on the Emergence of the Final Solution* (revised ed., 1991) , pp. 23, 33, 86; Gordon McFee, "When did Hitler decide on the Final Solution," *The Holocaust History Project*, archived at *Pratique de l'Histoire et Dévoiements Négationnistes*, PHDN.ORG.

When the Germans shifted their fanatical racial priorities to the Jews, this did not mean that they abandoned their objective of exterminating the Poles. While the Germans intended to eliminate the Jews before the end of the war, most Poles would work as helots until they too shared the fate of the Jews. German officials made this quite clear. Hans Frank, Hitler's viceroy in the General Government— the part of Poland not annexed by Germany but treated during the war as a gigantic labor camp—declared that Hitler had "made it quite plain that this adjacent country of the German Reich had a special mission to fulfill: to finish off the Poles at all cost."[1505]

The treatment of Jews varied depending on the nationality of the Jews in question. In addition, partial Jews (*Mischlinge*) had a special status through the entire war. German Jews, held in Theresienstadt, a camp north of Prague, were not transported en masse until 1944, after the manicured visit of the International Red Cross and the making of the film *Der Führer Schenkt Den Juden eine Stadt* (*The Führer Gifts the Jews a City*), both for non-German consumption. But killing in the Soviet Union began soon after the invasion in late June 1941, first of men only, then also of women and children, with mass killing occurring already in September 1941. Bełżec, for example, established as a labor camp in April 1940, transformed into an extermination camp, began operating on March 17, 1942 (and continued until that December). Treblinka, northeast of Warsaw, and used in part to exterminate the Jews in the Warsaw ghetto, operated from July 23, 1942 to October 19, 1943. Jews from outside of Poland were also shipped to Treblinka, from October 1942 on. Then, Sobibór, another extermination camp, would receive large numbers of Jews from the Netherlands and from France. It operated from May 16, 1942 to October 14, 1943. Auschwitz, on the other hand, was both a concentration camp, at first mostly for Polish prisoners, beginning in May 1940, with the first killings dated to September 1941, with the experimental gassing of Russian POWs in 1941 (testing Zyklon B), and the building of a second large complex, used as an extermination camp (known as Auschwitz II, Auschwitz-Birkenau, or Birkenau). Birkenau was put into operation beginning in March 1942 and continuing through late 1944. With the threatening approach of the Soviet troops, Himmler, in November 1944, ordered gassing operations (organized extermination) to cease. That the Reich would lose the war was quite apparent to many by then, and leaders in the extermination operations were nervous about their fate should the Allies win. The Luftwaffe was no longer even close to being the master of the skies; by the end of 1944, "the life expectancy of

---

[1505] Richard Lucas, "The Polish Experience during the Holocaust," in *A Mosaic of Victims: Non-Jews Persecuted and Murdered by the Nazis*, Michael Berenbaum, ed. (1990), p. 89.

a green Luftwaffe pilot was all of 33 days" with the Luftwaffe being outnumbered by Allied fighter planes, 40:1.[1506]

In late November 1944, there was a meeting arranged between Albert Speer, Hitler's architect, and since October 6, 1943, Reich Minister of Armaments and War, and some leading members of the *Hitlerjugend*. At this meeting, Speer announced, much to the young men's surprise, "*Meine Herren*, we are about to be defeated." These words would, in general, in other contexts, merit a quick execution for encouraging *Wehrkraftzersetzung*, the undermining of the German determination to fight through to final victory), but not there for Speer. He suggested that the situation was grave but that the Reich could be defended if there would be a strengthening of the German Western Front defense (the *Westwall*, the Siegfried Line). Hitler himself then made an unannounced, surprise appearance before the *Hitlerjugend* there, announcing, "We shall launch an all-out offensive which will not only deny our enemies the holy soil of Germany, but will throw them back into the sea. Then we will take care of the savage Bolsheviks in short shrift."[1507] Here is Hitler's final-stage confidence, or at least staged bravado.

Given the proximity of the approaching Soviet military to the camps in eastern Poland, many prisoners were forced westwards into the Reich and to concentration camps there, many dying or being killed on the way. The SS at Birkenau blew up the gas chambers and crematoria II and II, on January 20, 1945, with crematorium IV being destroyed on January 26. The Germans abandoned the camp; the Soviets took possession the next day, January 27, 1945, finding some remaining prisoners there, including some near-death prisoners and some children (mostly twins who were subjects of the medical experiments of Dr. Joseph Mengele). *Meanwhile, the treatment of the Jews, their exclusion from German life, their forceful removal from their homes and their disappearance, only to be seen in transports and in camps, well known to those of the region and to the tens of thousands of SS and others who worked in those camps, including the German soldiers on the Eastern Front who saw mass executions of Jews and other Soviets.*[1508] There were also the White Rose pamphlets on the mass killings of Polish Jews, the many witnesses who spoke of *the stench of the chimneys at Birkenau, so intense that residents in towns miles away complained of the smell*,[1509] and the widespread, ubiquitous public knowledge of the treatment and disappearance of European Jews.

[1506] Alfons Heck, *The Burden of Hitler's Legacy*, pp. 101, 107.

[1507] Discussed in Alfons Heck, *The Burden of Hitler's Legacy*, pp. 124-127.

[1508] The film *Shoah* (1985) records many Poles who saw Jews killed at Chełmno or in trains at Treblinka; Corfu Christians who knew of the roundups of Jews; and the shipment of Jews by cattle cars are discussed by Henryk Gawkowski, Treblinka train conductor, and by Treblinka SS officer Franz Suchomel.

[1509] Denis Avey, *The Man Who Broke into Auschwitz*, at 1:04:10-1:04:25, CHABAD.ORG; cf. Edith Birkin, "Atmosphere of Death," *British Library*, BL.UK (among many reports).

14. The Reich's Death Twitches and the Aftermath

Did the Third Reich die with the suicide of Hitler, on April 30, 1945, or with Goebbels, the next day, May 1? The end of the Reich is usually dated as of the day the surviving German government surrendered to the Allies. That is known as VE-Day (Victory in Europe Day) and is May 7, 1945. We can say that the Reich was already history at the time of the suicide of Himmler (May 23, 1945)[1510] and that of Göring (October 15, 1946).[1511]

What was to become of the world after this deadly exercise in violence that applied the principle that the strong deserve to dictate what will happen to themselves and others? The many photographs and filmed recordings of the celebrations in victorious capitals of the world suggest total relief and great joy. And yet that is certainly not the whole picture.

One German, seeing the occupation of her destroyed land, and noting that Berlin had been devastated by some fifty thousand tons of bombs that had been dropped, wrote, "Thank God, Hitler's short-lived millennium had ceased to exist, but was that the end of one nightmare, or just the beginning of another one? It was a day of great paradoxes for us. Finally freed of Nazi tyranny, we were newly imprisoned by the 'liberators' via a rigorous occupation regime. Peace brought no relief."[1512]

It has been estimated that there were *50-60 million people who died from those years of turmoil, conflict, and intensely barbaric warfare*. In addition to those losses, there was, we might add, the loss of a familiar structure for the lives of countless millions more. In addition, entire cities and villages were razed to the ground by bombing and more immediate army combat across Europe: homes, buildings, and factories destroyed, people dislocated, their former lives eradicated, a whole new life to face, even for those who were not wounded, maimed, disfigured, or otherwise seriously disabled. Millions could not return to the homes and lives from before the birth of the Third Reich in early 1933. For context here, in the war years continuing beyond, there were many declarations indicating an acute and troublesome awareness of Nazi atrocities.

[1510] Himmler, his mustache removed, a patch over his left eye, and in civilian clothing, was arrested on May 22, 1945, at the town of Bremervörte (northeast of Bremen and west-southwest of Hamburg), with demobilization papers from the military giving his name as Heinrich Hitzinger, unusual in not being stamped by the German Armed Forces (Wehrmacht) but by the SD (the Security Service, part of the SS). The attentive arresting officer was the polyglot Sgt. Arthur Britton of the British Intelligence Service; his (Dutch) civilian name was Arthur Verdun Britton Schrijnemaakers, changed for use in the British military. Himmler, interrogated the next day at the British interrogation centre in Lüneburg, declared his real name and, during examination, bit down on a cyanide capsule, dying within minutes.

[1511] Göring committed suicide (by biting down on a cyanide capsule) just hours before he was to be executed by hanging after his conviction at the Trial of the Major War Criminals held before the International Military Tribunal at Nuremberg. This first of 13 trials held at Nuremberg began on Nov. 20, 1945, with the Court's verdicts being declared on Oct. 1, 1946.

[1512] D. von Schwanenflügel Lawson, *Laughter Wasn't Rationed*, p. 362.

The Hitler Era

AXIS WAR-TIME ATROCITIES ANSWERED WITH WARNINGS BY THE ALLIES

The British and the Soviets both made early public declarations of their knowledge of Nazi atrocities on the Eastern Front (in the invasion of the USSR, carrying out Operation Barbarossa). Churchill and Molotov both described their sense of what was happening in the actions of the German Wehrmacht (Armed Forces) and the *Einsatzgruppen*. There were signs of things to come, from as early as August 1941, less than a month after the Third Reich attacked the USSR. For example, there were very early reports from the German military that were intercepted by British intelligence. This led Prime Minister Winston Churchill to make a public declaration on August 24, 1941, in a broadcast about his meeting with President Roosevelt, in which he said in part:

> The whole of Europe has been wrecked and trampled down by the mechanical weapons and barbaric fury of the Nazis. The most deadly instruments of war science have been joined to the extreme refinements of treachery and the most brutal exhibitions of ruthlessness and thus have formed a combine [a coordinated group] of aggression, the like of which has never been known, before which the rights, the traditions, the characteristics and the structure of many ancient, honoured States and peoples have been laid prostrate and are now ground down under the heel and terror of a monster.... This frightful business is now unfolding day by day before our eyes. Here is a devil who, in a mere spasm of his pride and lust for domination, can condemn two or three millions, perhaps it may be many more, of human beings to speedy and violent death. Let Russia be blotted out. Let Russia be destroyed. Order the armies to advance. Such were his decrees.... As his armies advance, whole districts are being exterminated. Scores of thousands, literally scores of thousands of executions in cold blood are being perpetrated by the German police troops upon the Russian patriots who defend their native soil. *Since the Mongol invasions of Europe in the sixteenth century there has never been methodical, merciless butchery on such a scale or approaching such a scale. And this is but the beginning. Famine and pestilence have yet to follow in the bloody ruts of Hitler's tanks. We are in the presence of a crime without a name.*[1513]

From the Soviet perspective, there was also to be a declaration of German war crimes. Articles in Soviet newspapers in November 1941[1514]

[1513] "Prime Minister Winston Churchill's Broadcast to the World About the Meeting with President Roosevelt, August 24, 1941," BRITISH LIBRARY OF INFORMATION. Italics added.

[1514] "Zverstva nemtsev v Kieve," *Pravda*, Nov. 19, 1941, p. 4; Maior P. Stepanenko, "Chto proiskhodit v Kieve," *Pravda*, Nov. 29, 1941, p. 3.

reported on the mass murder of Jews at Babi Yar, and on January 7, 1942, Vyacheslav Molotov, the Commissar of Foreign Affairs for the USSR, issued a note to all ambassadors and ministers of countries with which the USSR had diplomatic relations. This was intercepted quite soon by high-ranking German Intelligence, of course. Molotov's note said in part:

> The liberation by the Red Army, in the course of its continuing successful counter-offensive, of a number of towns and rural localities which had been temporarily in the hands of the German invaders has revealed and continues to reveal increasingly every day an unheard-of picture of pillage, general devastation, abominable violence, outrage and massacre, perpetrated by the German fascist occupants upon the noncombatant population during the German offensive, occupation and retreat.... Abundant documentary material at the disposal of the Soviet Government testifies to the fact that plunder and ruination of the population, accompanied by bestial outrage and massacre, are widespread in all districts which have fallen under the Nazi heel.... The Soviet Government and its organs keep detailed records of all the villainous crimes of Hitler's army, for which an indignant Soviet people justly demands retribution and will attain it.... A horrible massacre and pogrom were perpetrated by the German invaders in the Ukrainian capital, Kiev. Within a few days the German bandits killed and tortured to death 52,000 men, women, old folk, and children, dealing mercilessly with all Ukrainians, Russians, and Jews who in any way displayed their fidelity to the Soviet Government. Soviet citizens who escaped from Kiev gave an agonizing account of one of these mass executions: A large number of Jews, including women and children of all ages, was gathered in the Jewish cemetery of Kiev. [*This is a public acknowledgement of the Babi Yar massacres* of Jews *that began on September 29, 1941, made less than four months after the killings.*] Before they were shot, all were stripped naked and beaten. The first persons selected for shooting were forced to lie face down at the bottom of a ditch and were shot with automatic rifles. Then the Germans threw a little earth over them. The next group of people awaiting execution was forced to lie on top of them, and shot [a method known as sardine packing, on which more just below], and so on.... Many mass murders were also committed by the German occupants in other Ukrainian towns. These bloody executions were especially directed against unarmed and defenseless Jewish working people. According to incomplete figures, no less than 6,000

persons were shot in Lvov, over 8,000 in Odessa, over 8,500 killed or hanged in Kamenets-Podolsk, over 10,500 persons shot down with machine guns in Dniepropetrovsk, and over 3,000 local residents shot in Mariupol, including many old men, women, and children, all of whom were robbed and stripped naked before execution. According to preliminary figures, about 7,000 persons were killed by the German fascist bandits in Kerch.[1515]

While it is often held that Russian statements about Nazi atrocities keep generic its mention of victims, meaning that the victims would be identified only as Soviet citizens and never as Jews, *this statement from January 7, 1942, is a clear counter-example to that general claim.*

As for the sardine packing (*Sardinenpackung*), just referred to by Molotov, this was a method developed by General Friedrich Jeckelm (1895-1946),[1516] head of the *SS Einsatzgruppen* in Latvia, personally responsible for the assembling and murder of over 100,000 Jews, Slavs, Romanies, and other undesirables. The packing was already being applied during the Rumbula massacre, carried out on November 30 and December 8, 1941 in the Rumbula forest near Riga, Latvia.

Months after these statements by Churchill and Molotov, on August 21, 1942, US President Roosevelt spoke explicitly of "barbaric crimes of the invaders, in Europe and in Asia."[1517] This was followed on December 17, 1942, by mention in the British House of Lords of the concentration camps.[1518] On this same date, the Foreign Secretaries of the United Kingdom, the USA, and the USSR, issued a joint declaration explicitly noting the mass murder of European Jews, with the stated intention of prosecuting those responsible for crimes against civilian populations.[1519]

In late 1943, the attitude of the United Nations (the formal name of the Allies in World War II) was put forth in what is known as the Moscow

---

[1515] "Molotov's Note on German Atrocities in Occupied Soviet Territory," *Embassy of the Union of Soviet Socialist Republics Information Bulletin*, Jan. 7, 1942. This also appeared that same day in the Russian press: "Nota narodnogo komissara inostrannykh del tov. V.M. Molotova," *Izvestiia*, Jan. 7, 1942, p. 2.

[1516] Jeckelm was arrested on Apr. 28, 1945, by Soviet troops, tried (Jan. 26-Feb. 3, 1946), convicted, and hanged in Victory Square, Riga, Latvia.

[1517] *Public Papers of the Presidents of the United States: Franklin D. Roosevelt, 1942 Vol. 11* (1942), "Statement Warning Against Axis Crimes in Occupied Countries. August 21, 1942," pp. 329-330, at p. 330; W. H. Lawrence, "President Warns Atrocities of Axis Will Be Avenged," Aug. 2, 1942, NEW YORK TIMES ARCHIVES.

[1518] As is clear from the transcript of the debate (House of Lords, "Persecution of the Jews: Allies' Declaration"). The transcript is in *HL Deb* [House of Lords, Debate], Dec. 17, 1942, vol. 125, col. 607-612; at col. 607-608.

[1519] Andrew Buncombe, "Allied forces knew about Holocaust two years before discovery of concentration camps, secret documents reveal," *Independent*, Apr. 18, 2017. See esp. Univ. of London professor Dan Plesch, *Human Rights after Hitler: The Lost History of Prosecuting Axis War Crimes* (2017), pp. 74-76; Timothy Snyder, *Black Earth*, p. 216.

Declaration. This was finalized on November 1, 1943, and included an understanding that the leaders of the Third Reich, and all those who were responsible for the planning and carrying out of mass murders, would be held legally accountable. It stated specifically that the three Allied powers (the UK, the US, and the USSR) were aware of the atrocities carried out by the Nazi regime, and that they "will pursue them to the uttermost ends of the earth and will deliver them to their accusers in order that justice may be done." Perpetrators of atrocities, massacres, and cold-blooded mass executions—Germans as well as other nationals joining in these actions—would be brought to trial either in the by-then-freed states that had been occupied by the German Reich, or tried by the military authorities of the major forces of the United Nations.[1520] Both the British and the US Government gained eye-witness information about the Warsaw ghetto and about the Bełżec death camp from Jan Karski, mentioned above, who had been approached by Polish Jewish resistance leader, Leon Feiner, about being helped to enter these sites safely. Karski was told, "Unless the Allies take some unprecedented steps—regardless of the outcome of the war, the Jews will be totally exterminated." Karski then visited both safely in the summer of 1942. He was then sent by the Polish underground to the UK, meeting with Foreign Secretary Anthony Eden, and to the USA, meeting personally with President Roosevelt on July 28, 1943. Karsky could only say briefly that without outside help the Jews of Poland would perish. In reply, Roosevelt asked no questions about the situation of the Jews. Karski also spoke with US Supreme Court Justice Felix Frankfurter, who replied that he could not believe him—not that he thought Karski was lying, but that he simply could not believe him.[1521]

The years 1942 and 1943 saw a number of public statements by the United Nations (the Allies), as here. On October 7, 1942, a statement from President Roosevelt was made public: "On August twenty-first I said that this Government was constantly receiving information concerning the barbaric crimes being committed by the enemy against civilian populations in occupied countries, particularly on the continent of Europe. I said it was the purpose of this Government, as I knew it to be the purpose of the other United Nations, to see that when victory is won, the perpetrators of these crimes shall answer for them before courts of law.[1522] On December 17, 1942, the US Department of State made public

---

[1520] "The Moscow Conference, October 19-30, 1943," pp. 9-14 in US Congress, *A Decade of American Foreign Policy: Basic Documents, 1941-49* (1950). Quoted passage, p. 14. The text contains many important documents on US Foreign Policy in the 1940s. This text is at "The Moscow Conference," AVALON.LAW.YALE.EDU, and as "Statement of Atrocities, Moscow Conference, October 1943," LEGAL-TOOLS.ORG.

[1521] *Interviews with Lanzmann: Jan Karski: Warsaw Ghetto* (not included in the film, Shoah), YOUTUBE, at 6:30-6:45; Jan Karski about his meeting with President Franklin D. Roosevelt, 1943, YOUTUBE, at 3:05-4:25, 7:30-8:33; Jan Karski about his meeting with Supreme Court Justice Felix Frankfurter, 1943, at 5:10-8:57.

[1522] Franklin D. Roosevelt, "Statement on the Plan to Try Nazi War Criminals,

The Hitler Era 513

this statement: "The attention of the Belgian, Czechoslovak, Greek, Luxembourg, Netherlands, Norwegian, Polish, Soviet, United Kingdom, United States, and Yugoslav Governments and also of the French National Committee has been drawn to numerous reports from Europe that the German authorities, not content with denying to persons of Jewish race in all the territories over which their barbarous rule has been extended the most elementary human rights, *are now carrying into effect Hitler's oft-repeated intention to exterminate the Jewish people in Europe*. From all the occupied countries Jews are being transported in conditions of appalling horror and brutality to eastern Europe. In Poland, which has been made the principal Nazi slaughterhouse, the ghettos established by the German invader are being systematically emptied of all Jews except a few highly skilled workers required for war industries. None of those taken away are ever heard of again."[1523] The next year, a joint statement made public by the US State Department on November 1, 1943, signed by President Roosevelt, PM Churchill, and Premier Stalin stated in part: "The United Kingdom, the United States and the Soviet Union have received from many quarters evidence of atrocities, massacres and coldblooded mass executions which are being perpetrated by Hitlerite forces in many of the countries they have overrun and from which they are now being steadily expelled. The brutalities of Hitlerite domination are no new thing and all peoples or territories in their grip have suffered from the worst form of Government by terror. What is new is that many of these territories are now being redeemed by the advancing armies of the liberating powers and that in their desperation, the recoiling Hitlerite Huns are redoubling their ruthless cruelties. This is now evidenced with particular clearness by monstrous crimes of the Hitlerites on the territory of the Soviet Union which is being liberated from Hitlerites, and on French and Italian territory. Accordingly, the aforesaid three Allied Powers, speaking in the interests of the thirty-three United Nations, hereby solemnly declare and give full warning of their declaration as follows: At the time of granting of any armistice to any government which may be set up in Germany, those German officers and men and members of the Nazi Party who have been responsible for or have taken a consenting part in the above atrocities, massacres and executions will be sent back to the countries in which their abominable deeds were done in order that they may be judged and punished according to the laws of these liberated countries and of the free governments which will be erected therein…. The above declaration is without prejudice to the case of major criminals, whose offenses have no particular geographical localization and who will be punished by joint decision of the Governments of the Allies."[1524] And,

---

October 7, 1942," THE AMERICAN PRESIDENCY PROJECT; also in *Report of [Justice of the US Supreme Court] Robert H. Jackson, United States Representative to the International II Conference on Military Trials, with information on the agreement and charter of the International Military Tribunal* (1945), p. 9; italics added.
[1523] Robert H. Jackson, *Report of Robert H. Jackson* (just cited), pp. 9-10.
[1524] Robert H. Jackson, *Report of Robert H. Jackson* (just cited), pp. 11-12.

even earlier, there was published information about the camp at Auschwitz in the New York City newspaper (as discussed above), *Neue Volks-Zeitung*. In its March 14, 1942 issue was an article that stated that Jews there rarely come out alive (*kommt nur selten einer mit dem Leben davon*), and that the camp, with a capacity at that time for holding 40,000 men, had an average of 70-80 die daily (*beträgt im Durchschnitt 70 bis 80 täglich*).[1525]

News came to the west to a much wider audience after the escape from Auschwitz on April 7, 1944 by two Slovak Jews, Walter Rosenberg (1924-2006)—penname, Rudolf Verba—and Alfréd Wetzler (or Weczler, 1918-1988). They provided eye-witness information of the mass murder of Jews, with news of the forthcoming arrival of perhaps a million Hungarian Jews (according to comments they heard from drunken guards at Auschwitz). Their 40-page report to Rabbi Leo Baeck and others is called the Vrba-Wetzler Report or the Auschwitz Protocols.[1526]

We can also go back to September 1935 with the declaration of the Nuremberg Laws and their definitions of Aryans and removal of citizenship and its rights to Jews, and, three months earlier, to July 16, 1935, when young journalist Varian Fry (Harvard, '31) met with Ernst Hanfstaengl (Harvard '09), Foreign Press Secretary to Hitler, where he was told that it was Nazis (the SA) who had hissed in the movie house against a 1933 pro-Nazi Swedish film, *Pettersson & Bendel* (discussed above), but that the German propaganda machine attributed this to German Jews, a confabulation that was then used as the explanation for subsequent anti-Jewish rioting in Berlin.[1527] Fry also quoted Hanfstaengl as saying "that there were two anti-Semitic groups in the Nazi Party, one the radical section that desired to solve the Jewish Question with bloodshed and the other a moderate group that wishes to segregate the Jews by law into a specified area."[1528] This interview between these two Harvard grads was in English. Fry would later report that Hanfstaengl told him—in words more powerful and explicit than those in the *New York Times* 1935

[1525] "Eine Stätte des Grauens: Bericht aus dem Konzentrationslager Oswiecim (Auschwitz), Polnisch-Galizien," *Neue Volks-Zeitung*, Mar. 14, 1942, p. 2.

[1526] "Report by Alfred Wetzler and Rudolf Vrba, two Escapees from Auschwitz," GERMAN HISTORY IN DOCUMENTS AND IMAGES, GHDI. They also authored several books, incl. *Escape from Auschwitz: I Cannot Forgive* (Vrba), *Escape from Hell: The True Story of the Auschwitz Protocol* (Wetzler, also pub. using the penname Jozef Lánik). For more, see Walter Laqueur, *The Terrible Secret: Suppression of the Truth about Hitler's Final Solution* (1980); Martin Gilbert, "Rudolf Vrba and Alfred Wetzler's Escape from Auschwitz, April 1944," Apr. 1, 2016, MARTINGILBERT.COM.

[1527] Varian Fry, "Editor Holds Riots Inspired by Nazis," *New York Times*, Jul. 26, 1935, p. 8.

[1528] This further quotation is also from Varian Fry, "Editor Holds Riots Inspired by Nazis" (just cited); Abraham J. Peck, "Reflections: Meetings with Hiitler's spokesman were confrontations of good and evil," *Press Herald* (Portland, ME), Sep. 30, 2017; Varian Fry, "The Massacre of the Jews," *The New Republic*, Dec. 21, 1942, pp. 816-819.

The Hitler Era

article—that "the more radical Nazi leaders, Hitler and Goebbels among them, were determined to exterminate the Jews."[1529] Fry wrote that he was almost certain that the exact word that Hanfstaengl used was extermination.[1530] In a 1942 review of the conversation, Fry stated, "Yet, when Hanfstaengl told me, in his cultured Harvard accent, that the 'radicals' among the Nazi Party leaders intended to 'solve' the 'Jewish problem' by the physical extermination of the Jews, I only half believed him."[1531] In his 1945 autobiography, Fry was even more explicit, writing of his meeting with Hanfstaengl without mentioning him by name, "During that same visit [to Germany in 1935], I talked to a high German official who told me that what was in store for all the Jews of Europe. One group in the Nazi party wanted to send them to Palestine or Madagascar. Another group was in favor of exterminating them—murdering every Jew in Europe. Hitler sided with this second group, and since no one argued with Hitler, there was no question that, if he won the war, all the Jews in Europe would be put to death."[1532] These later, more explicit, statements by Fry suggest that perhaps the description in the 1935 *New York Times* article quoted just above with its somewhat vague talk of bloodshed[1533] was to protect Hanfstaengl, or perhaps was a hesitation on Fry's part to use the much stronger term that he would later attribute to Hanfstaengl ("extermination"), or perhaps an editorial decision by the *New York Times* to avoid shocking its readership. Even earlier than these events of 1935, we can return to the start of the Third Reich concentration camp system, in March 1933, with books written by those who survived or escaped, about the brutality, sadism, and murders carried out there regularly.[1534] Related to these issues is the post-war Nuremberg Tribunal with its various trials against major war criminals. We will discuss those trials in its historical context of pre-1933 international criminal law, below.

What was the historical context of these various numerous reports and the subsequent formal governmental declarations by the Allies?

Hitler's "prophesy" in his speech to the Reichstag on January 30, 1939, had stated that if the Jews dragged Germany into another world war, the result would not be the Bolshevizing of the earth, but the annihilation of the Jews of Europe [*die Vernichtung der jüdischen Rasse in Europa*].[1535]

[1529] Barry Gewen, "For the American Schindler, Writers and Artists First," *New York Times*, Nov. 25, 2001.

[1530] Sheila Isenberg, *A Hero of Our Own: The Story of Varian Fry* (2005), p. 64.

[1531] Varian Fry, "The Massacre of the Jews" (cited above), p. 816.

[1532] Varian Fry, *Assignment: Rescue*, p. 2.

[1533] The core text of the article in *The New York Times* is shown in the 2003 Richard Kaplan film, *Varian & Putzi: A 20th Century Tale*, at 2:15-2:35; with related information at 0:45-1:10.

[1534] Jews and also Christians were both subject to Nazi brutality and sadism: see *The Ninth Day* (2004), dir. by Volker Schlöndorff, also dir. of *The Tin Drum* (1979).

[1535] NT-TWC-Green, vol. 13, p. 131, with Eng. excerpt. The text was pub. in *Völkischer Beobachter, Berlin ed.*, Jan. 31, 1939, reporting on the speech given the day before. Tr. from *Nazism 1919-1945: A Documentary Reader*, vol. 3,

The war had become a world war—by the declaration of war by Britain, France, Australia, and New Zealand after the invasion of Poland, and certainly by the time of the invasion of the USSR. *Hitler's words were not written orders, but a filmed, well-publicized speech before the Reichstag!*

One question arises concerning a note by Himmler in late November 1941: As 1941 came to its end, there was a transport of German Jews to the East. Concerning that transport, on November 30, 1941, Heinrich Himmler, at the Führer Headquarters in the East, the Wolf's Lair, telephoned an order to Reinhard Heydrich. Himmler's handwritten telephone log recorded this order: *Judentransport aus Berlin. keine Liquidierung.* ("Jewish transport [in the singular]; no liquidation.") There is some debate about what this meant specifically, especially in the larger context of the message. This instruction for there not to be any liquidation had a special, specific status, explicitly talking of a transport of Jews out of Berlin, and so, not meant as a statement covering all treatments of all Jews, under Heydrich's authority or otherwise. We know that by that time, for months, the Eastern Jews—Jews of Poland, called the West Polish Jews, and especially of the Soviet Union, called the Barbarossa Jews, after the code name of the invasion of the USSR—were being systematically killed.

The order reflects the difference at that time between the Reich's attitudes and policies about the treatment of German Jews, in contrast with non-German Jews: those from Slavic lands, and especially those of the Bolshevik concentration in the USSR. Furthermore, there are a number of statements from Hitler himself that made it clear that, to consider one feature of Hitler's thinking, Hitler was not overly romantic even in his attitude about the loss of large numbers of young German soldiers in the east: In late 1941, after months of military gains at a high price of men killed, Hitler remarked, "But that's what the young people are there for!"[1536] Relatedly, we can sense Hitler's attitude on the issue of the extermination of Jews from his comments to the Czech Foreign Minister, František Chvalkovský, in January 1939, "We shall exterminate the Jews. The Jews will not get away with their responsibility for November 9, 1918—this day will be avenged."[1537]

The often-cited remark by Hitler before the Reichstag, on January 30, 1939 (the sixth anniversary of Hitler's becoming Chancellor), and printed the next day in the Berlin edition of the *Völkischer Beobachter*, as indicated just above, used the term *die Vernichtung*, explicitly speaking

---

Foreign Policy, War and Racial Extermination, John Noakes and Geoffrey Pridham, eds., Doc. 770, p. 1049. Cf. the German text at "Adolf Hitler's Address to the Reichstag (30 January 1939)," WIKISOURCE.

[1536] Gordon A. Craig, *The Germans* (1982), p. 73.

[1537] Andreas Hillgruber, "War in the East and the Extermination of the Jews," pp. 85-114, in *The Nazi Holocaust: Historical Articles on the Destruction of European Jews; Part 3: The "Final Solution": the Implementation of Mass Murder, Volume 1,* Michael Robert Marrus, ed. (1989). Note 36 on p. 91 cites *Akten zur deutschen auswärtigen Politik, 1918-1945, Serie D (1937-1941), Vol. IV* (1951), p. 170.

The Hitler Era

of extermination or annihilation. The speech would be quoted by Hitler and others repeatedly, including on January 30, 1941 and January 30, February 24, September 30, and November 8, 1942.[1538] So, the idea of exterminating the Jews of Europe was not a hidden agenda at all!

Among formal statements envisioning the complete elimination of Jewry from Europe—along with the Romanies, who for centuries were denied a place in Europe and were also seen as a foreign, inferior people[1539]—was the statement by Reinhard Heydrich of July 31, 1941, to carry out the final solution in all of (German-controlled) Europe, in which Heydrich communicated that the Einsatzgruppen (in the USSR at that time for just over one month) were to kill all Jews, Gypsies (Romanies), and mental patients, in line with the T4 euthanasia program.

Waffen-SS Generalmajor (Major Gen.) Otto Ohlendorf (1907-1951) described the significance of the direct orders from Hitler, the Führerbefehls (the Führer Orders), which were to be followed unquestionably. Ohlendorf had been appointed in 1941 as commander of Einsatzgruppe D (in the Crimea). At the start of the Nuremberg Trial, US v. Otto Ohlendorf et al. (the Einsatzgruppen Trial), on September 15, 1947, he testified, "There is nothing worse for people spiritually than to have to shoot defenseless populations." (Nor was it healthy for those "defenseless populations"!) He then stated that "during my time in Russia there is no condition which is not connected with the Fuehrer Order.... Himmler came to me and ordered that these Jews were to be treated according to the Fuehrer Order, without any further discussion, and without any further consideration of circumstances...." Questioned about the basis on which he killed Gypsies, Ohlendorf replied, "It is the same as for the Jews... There was no difference between gypsies and Jews. At the time the same order existed for the Jews."[1540]

THE WANNSEE CONFERENCE AS AN ADMINISTRATIVE GATHERING

In this context, to carry out his orders to organize the Final Solution of the Jewish Question (the extermination of European Jewry, and, as we see, also of the Romanies population of Europe), Heydrich organized the Wannsee Conference of January 20, 1942. This was a meeting on the ministerial level, to coordinate all of the government agencies that would need to cooperate in order to carry out this transfer of Jews and their ultimate elimination, as decided earlier.

ADOLF EICHMANN'S RETROSPECTIVE ATTITUDE

Eichmann, who was in charge of the Jewish Question under Heydrich, would later state that in a meeting to which he was called by Heydrich, in

---

[1538] Gordon A. Craig, The Germans, p. 73.
[1539] "Gypsies and the Holocaust," New York Times, National edition, Aug. 14, 2000, p. A00022, NEW YORK TIMES ARCHIVES.
[1540] NT-TWC-Green, vol. 4, pp. 179, 284-286.

late summer 1941, that Heydrich had said to him "the Führer has ordered the physical destruction of the Jews."[1541] This was no longer speaking in bureaucratese or using insinuation! Concerning Eichmann's own attitude toward the Jews and the Final Solution, in testimony before the Nuremberg Tribunal, Dieter Wisliceny, a subordinate of Eichmann's, spoke of this. When asked by US Lt. Col. Smith W. Brookhart, Jr., Assistant Trial Counsel, "Did he [Eichmann] say anything at that time [late February 1945] as to the number of Jews that had been killed?" Wisliceny answered, "Yes, he expressed this in a particularly cynical manner. He said that he would leap laughing into the grave because the feeling that he had 5 million people [that is, Jews, given the question] on his conscience would be for him a source of extraordinary satisfaction."[1542]

An editorial in *Life* remarked, "The Eichmann story reveals how evil can be rationalized because it has been codified."[1543] Eichmann himself stated (humbly?), "In actual fact, I was just a little cog in the machinery that carried out the directives and directives of the Third Reich. I am neither a murderer nor a mass-murderer. I am a man of average character, with good qualities and many faults." [1544]

Eichmann gave his own version of what Wisliceny had testified about (quoted above): "I will gladly jump into my grave in the knowledge that five million enemies of the Reich have already died like animals. ('Enemies of the Reich,' I said, not 'Jews.')"[1545] Despite this joy at thinking of his contribution to the murder of millions of Jews—Hatreds can run quite deep, it would seem!—Eichmann had a sensitivity, like Himmler on being shown an execution, getting particles of brain splashed on his uniform, and becoming faint, with his own limits to what he could personally watch (as reported by SS General Karl Wolff, personal adjutant to Himmler[1546]). In speaking to Avner Less about his experience at Chełmno, the first operational of the extermination camps (on December 7, 1941, 700 Jews arrived from Koło; all gassed the next day), in questioning to prepare for his trial in Jerusalem in 1960, when asked

---

[1541] *Eichmann Interrogated: Transcriptions from the Archives of the Israeli Police*, Jochan von Lang and Claus Sibyll, eds. (1983), p. 114; "Adolf Eichmann Testimony (interrogated by Avner Less)," HOLOCAUST RESEARCH PROJECT; "Eichmann Says He Accepts Death Penalty; Admits 6,000,000 Jews Were Killed," *JTA/Jewish Telegraphic Agency, Daily News Bulletin*, vol 28, no. 78, Apr. 20, 1961; "Reinhard Heydrich, German Nazi Official," ENCYCLOPÆDIA BRITANNICA; "Reinhard Heydrich: Key Dates," HOLOCAUST ENCYCLOPEDIA, USHMM; "Heydrich, Reinhard," SHOAH RESOURCE CENTER, YAD VASHEM; "Adolf Eichmann," WIKIQUOTE.

[1542] NT-IMT-Blue, vol. 4, p. 371.

[1543] "Eichmann and the Duty of Man" (editorial), *Life*, Dec. 5, 1960, p. 46.

[1544] "Eichmann Tells His Own Damning Story," *Life*, Nov. 28, 1960, pp. 19-24, 101-102, 104, 106, 109-110, 112, at p. 21.

[1545] "Eichmann's Own Story: Part II," *Life*, Dec. 5, 1960, pp. 146-148, 150, 152, 155-156, 158, 161, at p. 150.

[1546] *Episode 20: Genocide (1941-1945)*, in the Thames TV Series, *The World at War*, cited above, at 18:10-18:37.

The Hitler Era

how many people the killing vans could hold, commented, "I can't say exactly. I couldn't bring myself to look closely, even once. I didn't look inside the entire time. I couldn't, no, I couldn't take any more. The screaming and, and, I was too upset and so on. I also said that to [SS-Obergruppenfuehrer] Mueller when I submitted my report."[1547] Eichmann is referring here to Heinrich Müller, Chief of the Gestapo (within the RSHA, the Reich Security Office)[1548] and Eichmann's immediate superior.[1549]

ROMANIES AND JEWS IN THE DOMAINS OF THE THIRD REICH

There was the targeting of Romanies as well as Jews, from Riga (Latvia) to France: The Reich Commissar for the Ostland (Eastern Territories), writing to the Higher SS and the Police Leader in Riga, ordered in July 1942 that "the treatment of Jews and Gypsies were to be placed on an equal footing (*gleichgestellt*),[1550] which is to say, that both groups were to be totally and indiscriminately annihilated.

Similarly, in Vichy France, the Commissar for Jewish Affairs, Xavier Vallat, considered treatment of the Romanies to be part of his jurisdiction, and called for measures to maintain racial purity (*Massnahmen zur Reinhaltung der rassischen Substanz*).[1551] The treatment of Romanies as marginal and suspicious (in France as in many other countries, including, of course, Germany) goes back at least several centuries, as does the hostility against Jews by non-Jewish communities.

France, with its own ideals of a homogeneous nation, was hostile on its own (without any push or encouragement of the occupying Third Reich) to what it perceived as alien or foreign populations, from the Jews to the Romanies, who "were rounded up and interned, often under harsh conditions," and to the Spanish who had fled from Franco's Spain, who "aroused considerable popular hostility."[1552]

[1547] *The Good Old Days: The Holocaust as Seen by Its Perpetrators and Bystanders*, Ernst Klee, Willi Dressen, Volker Riess, eds. (1991), "Interrogation of Adolf Eichmann," pp. 221-222; "Global Holocaust Primary Source and Documents: "What is the 'Jewish Problem'? How Do They Propose to Solve That Problem?" WHITEPLAINSPUBLICSCHOOLS.ORG, at pdf p. 54 of 82 pp.

[1548] "Gestapo-Müller: Kein Nazi," *Spiegel*, Oct. 16, 1963, SPIEGEL.DE.

[1549] "Eichmann Tells His Own Damning Story," (cited above), at p. 22.

[1550] Romani Rose, *Bürgerrechte für Sinti und Roma: Das Buch zum Rassismus in Deutschland* (1987), p. 30; Sybil Milton, "The Context of the Holocaust," *German Studies Review*, vol. 13, no. 2, 1990, pp. 269-283, at pp. 276, 280, 283. Cf. YIVO INSTITUTE (NYC), BERLIN COLLECTION, Occ E 3-61: "Reich Ministry for the Occupied Eastern Territories to Reich Kommissar Ostland, 11 June 1942."

[1551] Michael R. Marrus and Robert O. Paxton, *Vichy France and the Jews* (1981), pp. 363-370, quotations at p. 366; Sybil Milton, "The Context of the Holocaust," just cited, pp. 276, 283; Sybil Milton, "Gypsies and the Holocaust," *The History Teacher*, vol. 24, no. 4, 1991, pp. 375-387.

[1552] On the situation of Romanies—in French, *gitanes, tsiganes, manouches* (this, perhaps from the Sanskrit *mānuṣya*, person, man), *bohémiens*, etc.—see also Donald Kenrick and Grattan Puxon, *Gypsies under the Swastika*; Joachim Stephan Hohmann, "Le génocide des Tsiganes" (pp. 263-277), in *La politique nazie*

And about the time of the meeting between Heydrich and Eichmann, German Justice Minister Dr. Otto Georg Thierack would meet with Joseph Goebbels on September 14, 1942. Of this exchange, Thierack noted, "With regard to the destruction of asocial life, Dr. Goebbels is of the opinion that the following groups should be exterminated: Jews and gypsies [*Zigeuner*] unconditionally .... The idea of exterminating them by labor is the best." Or, in a close paraphrase, that "Jews and gypsies must be unconditionally exterminated" and forced labor is understood here as a means to extermination, not an alternative.[1553] Following this idea, Thierack also noted, in summary of his meeting with Reich Leader SS Himmler and three other high Nazi officials four days later, on September 18, 1942, the policy to deliver "asocial elements [*asozialer Elemente*] while servicing penal sentences to the Reich Leader SS to be worked to death [*zur Vernichtung durch Arbeit*].[1554]

How many Romanies were killed by the Nazis and their collaborators? One low estimate suggests that about 200,000 were deliberately killed or were basically worked to death with a starvation diet. There were, as well, Romanies forced into military service: By official policy, Romanies were excluded from military service, but this was not universally followed, as mentioned in Martin Bormann's letter to Himmler, referring to Himmler's position that in certain cases, Gypsies (Romanies) "will serve in special units of the army"[1555]—in work brigades, plus others who were killed in bombings; the total figure of European Romanies dead approaches 500,000, including more than half of all Romanies in Germany in 1933.[1556]

---

d'extermination: *État des travaux et perspectives de recherche, journées d'étude tenues les 11, 12, et 13 décembre, 1987 à Paris*, François Bédarida, ed. (1989); Emmanuel Filhol, "La France contre ses Tsiganes," *La Vie des idées*, Jul. 7, 2010, IDÉES.FR, which looks back to the early fifteenth century and the arrival of Romanies (*Tsiganes*) in France, to the Vichy years, and also to the situation for Romanies in France after World War II. The situation of the Romanies continues being an issue in recent decades, as discusssed in Patrice de Beer, "Haro [a sound of indignation] britannique sur les immigrants tsiganes," *Le Monde*, Oct. 28, 1997, p. 32, with the front-page banner headline, "Vichy vu par Valéry d'Estaing." More precisely, the presence of Romanies in France can be dated to 1419 (in Hamburg to 1417 and in Rome, to 1422): see *Key Writings on Subcultures, 1535-1727: Classics from the Underworld, Volume 1. The Elizabethan Underground: A Collection of Tudor and early Stuart Tracts and Ballads*, Arthur Valentine Judges, ed. (1930), pp. xxiv-xxv.

[1553] Both quoted from NT-NCA-Red, vol. 3, Nuremberg Doc. 682-PS ("In discussion of Thierack with Dr. Goebbels on Sept. 14, 1942 in Berlin"), p. 496. Cf. Ian Hancock, *The Romanies in the Holocaust—Le rromane dukhadile and'o Baro Porrajmos*, p. 8. See also the discussion in Nikolaus Wachsmann, "'Annihilation through Labor': The Killing of State Prisoners in the Third Reich," *The Journal of Modern History*, vol. 71, no. 3, 1999, pp. 624–659.

[1554] NT-NCA-Red, vol. 3, Nuremberg Doc. 654-PS (no title), pp. 467-470, at p. 468.

[1555] Donald Kenrick and Grattan Puxon, *Gypsies under the Swastika*, p. 35 (see also pp. 29-30).

[1556] Emma Brockes, "We Had the Same Pain," *The Guardian*, Nov. 29, 2004; see

The Hitler Era 521

And, adding specificity, Thierack wrote to Reich Minister of Justice [*Reichsleiter* Martin] Bormann on October 13, 1942, expressing his official, legal opinion, writing in part, "With a view to freeing the German people of Poles, Russians, Jews, and gypsies, and with a view to making the eastern territories incorporated into the Reich available for settlements of German nationals, I intend to turn over criminal proceedings against Poles, Russians, Jews, and gypsies to the Reich Leader SS. In so doing I work on the principle that the administration of justice [by the police] can only make a small contribution to the extermination of members of these peoples (*Angehörige dieses Volkstums auszurotten*) [better administered by the SS] .... I am ... of the opinion that considerably better results can be accomplished by surrendering such persons to the police, who can then take the necessary measures [concerning the administration of justice, but not of extermination] ... On the other hand, the police may prosecute Jews and gypsies irrespective of these conditions."[1557] This use of the terms *Vernichtung* (extermination) and *auszusrotten* (to eradicate, to exterminate), with noun form, *Ausrottung* (eradication, extermination) are used here instead of a euphemism. *Bormann obviously understood Thierack's quite explicit comment.*

In accordance with this, a secret directive, Berlin, November 1942, issued to the heads of the SS and to the police services stated, in part: "Re: Jurisdiction over Poles and Eastern nationals. [Point] I. The Reich Leader SS [Himmler] has come to an arrangement with the Reich Minister of Justice Thierack whereby the Justice waives the execution of the usual penal procedure against Poles and eastern nationals. These persons of alien race are in the future to be handed over to the police. Jews and gypsies are to be treated in the same way. [This refers to the policy of annihilating all Jews and Romanies without exception.] *This agreement has been approved by the Fuehrer.* [Point] II. This agreement is based on the following considerations: Poles and eastern nationals are alien and racially inferior people living in the German Reich territory."[1558]

Relatedly, the next year, on April 25, 1943, the German Ministry of the Interior added specificity to earlier regulations of the German citizenship law in which there had been no mention of the Romanies (Gypsies), *now including them explicitly as non-citizens:* "Jews and Gypsies cannot become German citizens."[1559] Heydrich, on July 31, 1941, is also quoted as having said, "The *Einsatzkommandos* received the order to kill all Jews, Gypsies and mental patients."[1560] The Commander of the Wehrmacht in

---

also Donald Kenrick and Grattan Puxon, *Gypsies under the Swastika*, pp. 47, 153.

[1557] NT-IMT-Blue, vol. 3, Nuremberg Doc. NG-558 ("Letter from Reich Minister of Justice Thierack to Bormann, 13 October 1942, concerning the Administration of Justice against Poles, Russians, Jews, and Gypsies"), pp. 674-675.

[1558] NT-IMT-Blue, vol. 23, p. 1073, quoting Doc. L-316; italics added; cf. Gunter Lewy, *The Nazi persecution of the Gypsies* (2000), pp. 168-170.

[1559] Gunter Lewy, *The Nazi Persecution of the Gypsies*, p. 195.

[1560] Ian Hancock, *O Porrajmos: The Romani Holocaust* (2013), p. 8.

Belarus stated on November 24, 1941, "The Jews must disappear from the countryside and likewise the Gypsies must be eradicated."[1561] This would be *Generalmajor* (Major Gen.) Gustav von Bechtolsheim, responsible for many war crimes in his area of command, who wrote in an earlier communiqué, dated Oct. 19, 1941, that Jews were the mortal enemy of the Germans [*Todfeinde der Deutschen*] and "are no longer people in the European sense of culture but youths educated to be criminals [*auf zu Verbrechern erzogene*], and trained from youth to be beasts. Beasts, however, must be destroyed [*Bestien aber müssen vernichtet werden*]."[1562] The ultimate source for this, a *Führerbefehl* (Führer Order), was recognized as defining the work of the SS: as Adolf Ott—commander of *Sonderkommando 7b* (part of *Einstatzgruppe B*, in Russia and Belarus) from February 1942 to January 1943, who directed the mass killing of Jews in those areas—later, in trial, stated, "every Jew who was apprehended had to be shot. Never mind whether he was a perpetrator or not ... I told my Sub-Commando leaders that Jews after they are seized and do not belong to a partisan movement or sabotage organization must be shot on the basis of the Fuehrer-Order."[1563]

This was an oft-repeated mantra: in his speech on January 30, 1939, Hitler predicted "that this war will not turn out as the Jews imagine it [*daß dieser Krieg nicht so ausgehen wird, wie die Juden sich es vorstellen*], that the European Aryan peoples will be exterminated [*daß die europäischen arischen Völker ausgerottet werden*], but that the result of this war is the annihilation of Judaism [*sondern daß das Ergebnis dieses Krieges die Vernichtung des Judentums ist*]. For the first time ... the old Jewish law will be applied: eye for eye, tooth for tooth! [*sondern zum erstenmal wird diesesmal das echt altjüdische Gesetz angewendet: Aug' um Aug', Zahn um Zahn!*]"[1564] Later, on January 30, 1942, in his speech at the Sportpalast in Berlin, Hitler quoted this earlier speech, but he misdated it to September 1, 1939. Then, on February 24, 1942 (the anniversary of the founding of the Nazi Party in 1920), a speech by Hitler, read, as on various other occasions, by Gauleiter Adolf Wagner (Hitler not

---

[1561] Ian Hancock, *O Porrajmos*, pp. 8-9. See also Ian Hancock, *The Romanies in the Holocaust*, p. 8; Ian Hancock, "The Gypsies/Roma," and "Gypsies, Jews and the Holocaust," *Shmate: A Journal of Progressive Jewish Thought*, no. 17, 1987, pp. 6-7, 8-15, resp.

[1562] Gustav Von Bechtolsheim was the military name of Gustav Freiherr von Mauchenheim. See *Die Verfolgung und Ermordung der europäischen Juden durch nationalsozialistische Deutschland 1933-1945: Sowjetunion mit annektierten Gebieten II, Vol. 8*, Bert Hoppe, ed. (2015), pp. 28-29. Cf. Timm C. Richter, "Byelarussian [Belarusian] Partisans and German Reprisals," pp. 207-232 in Stalin and Europe: Imitation and Domination, 1928-1953, Timothy Snyder and Ray Brandon, eds. (2014), at p. 220.

[1563] Judge Michael A. Musmanno, *The Eichmann Kommandos*, pp. 147-148; "Adolf Ott (SS-Mitglied)," DE.WIKIPEDIA.ORG.

[1564] "Adolf Hitler Rede am 30. Januar 1942 im Sportpalast in Berlin," WORLDFUTUREFUND.ORG.

being able to attend the celebration in person), included, again, a statement about Hitler's prophetic abilities: "My prophecy will be fulfilled that this war will not destroy the Aryan, but, instead, it will exterminate the Jew."[1565] Again, at Hitler's speech in Munich on the anniversary of the 1923 Putsch, on November 8, 1942, referred to as the Stalingrad Speech, he again referred back to the Reichstag session of 1939, predicting the extermination of the Jews in Europe' [*daß die europäischen arischen Völker ausgerottet werden, sondern daß das Ergebnis dieses Krieges die Vernichtung des Judentums ist*]."[1566] Similarly, Adolf Eichmann in his memoirs wrote, "At the turn of the year 1941/1942 [*Etwa um die Jahreswende 1941/42*], ... Heydrich informed me orally [*teilte mir Heydrich, mündlich mit*] that the Führer had ordered the physical annihilation of the Jewish enemy [*daß der Führer die physische Vernichtung des jüdischen Gegners befohlen habe*].[1567]

CRYPTOLOGY IN THESE WAR THEATERS

The use of cryptology was to be very significant in the following months, when advance information on Japanese warship activities was used to US advantage in the important Battle of Midway (June 4-7, 1942), the first US victory over Japanese Naval Forces in the war.

When the US entered into World War II, both the German and the Japanese military were formidable war machines with seasoned military, and talk by the Allies was not yet based on confidence but perhaps by determination; of course, for their part, the German and the Japanese military and governments were convinced at the time of the certainly of their final victory. The German military had occupation and military dominance over Europe from Norway to the north, down to the Balkans and Greece in the South, and west to the Atlantic. They were focused on expanding their dominion into the Caucasus with its oil fields, and, beyond that, into Iraq and Iran, also with rather impressive reserves of oil.

The Japanese, who had been fighting the Chinese and Koreans for years by that time, would soon occupy many lands in South and Southeast Asia, including Hong Kong, Singapore, the Philippines, French Indochina (Vietnam, Laos, and Cambodia), Burma, the Dutch East Indies (Indonesia), part of New Guinea, and a large swathe of Pacific Islands to the west of Hawaii. They would have plans for the invasion of Australia, once the shipping lanes between the USA and Australia would be cut, using the obscure island of Guadalcanal—one of the Solomon Islands—

[1565] "Adolf Hitler's Speech on the 22nd Anniversary of the National Socialist Party (23 February 1942)," WIKISOURCE; Ian Kershaw, *Hitler, The Germans, and the Final Solution* (2008), p. 144.

[1566] "Adolf Hitler: Speech on the 19th Anniversary of the Beer Hall Putsch" (November 8, 1942)," JEWISHVIRTUALLIBRARY.ORG; "Radio Address: November 8, 1942," COMICISM.TRIPOD.COM; "Adolf Hitler's Stalingrad Speech: Adolf Hitler's Speech on the 19th Anniversary of the Beer Hall Putsch (1942)," WIKISOURCE.

[1567] Adolf Eichmann, *Ein historischer Zeugenbericht* (1980), pp. 177-178. Eng. in italics in text here reflects emphasis in the German.

with a Japanese military airfield to be built there as the home base for that activity. That was settled by the bloody battles on that island that lasted from August 7, 1942 to February 9, 1943, with an American victory.

The German plan for hegemony over Europe and larger parts of the world (including Canada and the USA),[1568] and the Japanese plan for great hegemony over the Western Pacific were taken at the time to be all-too-realizable, and something that it would take great manpower, weaponry, cooperation, and many deaths to overcome. *With that giving a basic orientation to the situation as the US entered the war*, in December 1941, Germany had been at war with the Soviet Union for several months, since its invasion. Here, we have Japan entering into war with the USA and Germany and Italy joining in, making World War II even broader and inclusive. *This shift into such an inclusive World War was the occasion for some important decisions about the Jewish Question for the Third Reich:* and this suggests that the policy of full extermination was not fully in place, at least not in a definitive form, as the invasion of the USSR was being planned in the months before that invasion. After the invasion of the USSR, the mass killing by *SS Einsatzgruppen* in newly conquered lands, including the massacres in late September 1941 on the outskirts of Kiev, at Babi Yar, and elsewhere, there was established a new policy of how to treat the Jews of conquered lands. (Many killings by the *Einsatzgruppen* do not establish an overall policy being in place for the total extermination of European Jewry, we might point out. Still, the Wannsee Conference in late January 1942, several months after the Babi Yar massacres, formulated an overall program with focused attention on the administrative issues needing clarity and precision for efficiently carrying out the task of annihilating some 11 million European Jews, as made clear in the notes taken by General Eichmann that were preserved.)

Key Decisions focusing on the Extermination of the Jews

The very next day after declaring war on the USA, Hitler called a meeting at the Reich Chancellery, and Goebbels in his diaries, wrote in his entry for December 12, 1941: "With regard to the Jewish question, the Führer is determined to make a clean sweep of it (*ist der Führer entschlossen, reinen Tisch zu machen*). He prophesied to the Jews that if they ever again brought about a world war, they would experience their annihilation. That was not a phrase. (*Das ist keine Phrase gewesen.*) The World War is here, the annihilation of Judaism (*die Vernichtung des Judentums*) must be the necessary consequence (*muß die notwendige Folge sein*)."[1569] This is using a logical vocabulary that implies necessity in what is fundamentally a fervent desire for a focused and yet quite

---

[1568] Leyland Cecco (Toronto), "Nazi blueprint for North American Holocaust acquired by Canada archive," *The Guardian* (London), Jan. 25, 2019; Kelly Egan, "Holocaust remembrance cast against Hitler plan to purge Canadian Jews," *Ottawa Citizen*, Jan. 28, 2019.

[1569] Alan Cowell, "Hitler's Genocide Order: Five Days after Pearl Harbor?" *New York Times*, Jan. 21, 1998, p. A4.

extensive massacre: *to use Hitler's distinction from his statement of September 16, 1919, to Adolf Gemlich (quoted above), the passion is the force here, not the logic.* Or, as Christa Schroeder, one of Hitler's private secretaries put it, logic did not have a dominant role, writing of Hitler, "As his intuition could not be faulted by logic [*Und da Hitlers Intuitionen an sich nicht mit Logik zu bekämpfen waren*] because it has a visionary origin [*sie aus einer seherischen Vorsetellung heraus entstanden*] and lacked any basis of logic [*einer logischen Basis entbehrten*], he considered them [early associates of Hitler, Franz Pfeffer von Salomon and Gregor Strasser] to be fault-finders and pedants [*Nörgler und Besserwisser*] and eventually he cast them aside."[1570]

Logic, aside, then, and back to the passions of the day: The next week, on December 18, 1941, after a conversation with Hitler at the *Wolfsschanze*, Himmler wrote down notes[1571] of a telephone call with Heydrich, mentioning a key point by Hitler concerning the Jewish Question: "Jewish question: eradicate as partisans (*als Partisanen auszurotten*)."[1572]

This meant that German communiques that mentioned the killing of partisans often referred explicitly and plainly to the organized killing of Jews. The issue of which direct expressions were allowed would undergo changes as the military and political situation on the ground changed; on November 20, 1941, SS Obersturmbannführer Arthur Liebehenschel (1901-1948), acting inspector of concentration camps, sent his underling, commandant of Groß-Rosen Concentration Camp, Obersturmbannführer Arthur Rödl (1898-1945) these guidelines and limits:

> In the lists of recommendations [for medals], under "reasons" enter: "completion of vital war assignments." The word "execution" should under no circumstances be mentioned."[1573]

Despite Liebehenschel's work, Eichmann was to remove him from his position on May 8, 1944, for what he felt was incompetence, given the non-optimal state of the crematoria at Birkenau.[1574]

In general, there was to be no public talk of extermination (*Ausrottung, Vernichtung*, etc.)—although had spoken of the *Vernichtung* of European Jewry in his speech of January 30, 1949—but even Goebbels, in his excited speech of February 1943 (the "Total War" discourse), let slip the

---

[1570] Christa Schroeder, *Er war mein Chef*, p. 29; *He Was My Chief*, p. 5.

[1571] The note was discovered in Western scholarship after it could examine documents that had been held by the Soviets. See Alan Cowell, "Hitler's Genocide Order: Five Days after Pearl Harbor?" *New York Times*, Jan. 21, 1998, p. A4.

[1572] Volker Ullrich, "Über die Vernichtung der Juden wurde zentral entschieden: Hitlers bösester Befehl" ["The destruction of the Jews was crucially decided upon: Hitler's most evil command"], *Der Zeit*, Jan. 9, 1998; Alan Cowell, "Hitler's Genocide Order: Five Days after Pearl Harbor?" (just cited).

[1573] Gerald Fleming, *Hitler and the Final Solution* (1984), p. 100; cf. earlier, original Ger. ed., *Hitler und die Endlösung* (1982).

[1574] "Hungarian Jews in Auschwitz-Birkenau," KONFLIKTUSKUTATO.HU/TÁRSADALMI KONFLIKTUSOK KUTATÓOKÖZPONT.

first part of the word *Ausrottung* ("*Ausrott-*") and corrected himself in mid-word by ending that with "*-schaltung*," thus trying to replace *Ausrottung* (eradicating) by *Ausschaltung* (switching out of or excluding from Nazi German life). Some but not all edits of this recording and video deleted the slip, but diligent research can find the unexpurgated actual, full speech.

While some reports back from the Eastern Front (the USSR) were direct in speaking of the number of Jews killed, others used various terms that lightly softened the harshness of the reality. Eichmann, and others, would make convenient use of clichés, and especially of euphemisms (or misnomers): thus, finding a value in *Redensarten* (stock phrases), *Schlagworte* (slogans), and, in general, *Amtssprache* (office language, officialese, or bureaucratese).[1575] This would lead, for example, to talk of special treatment rather than mass murders.

On December 18, 1941, as well, Hans Frank, Governor General of Occupied Poland (the *Gouvernement General*), in his *Diensttagebuch* (work diary), wrote of his speech that day to his cabinet, in which he stated, *also in conjunction with mention of Hitler's statement of January 30, 1939*, "As far as the Jews are concerned, I want to tell you quite frankly that they must be done away with one way or another (*muß so oder so Schluß gemacht werden*).... We must annihilate the Jews (*Wir müssen die Juden vernichten*) wherever we meet them and wherever possible, to maintain the overall framework of the empire here (*um das Gesamtgefüge des Reiches hier aufrecht zu erhalten*)."[1576]

While these do not amount to a formal document signed by Hitler, Himmler and Frank would presumably not be taking on themselves the fabricating and carrying out of such a program. And, of course, *there are many statements by Hitler declaring his vision of the complete eradication, extermination of all of Europe's Jews, some of which we have quoted here*.

What we see here, overall, is the transformation of the practical situation on the ground, calling for new thinking that would keep in central focus the ultimate goal of ridding German-controlled Europe of its Jewish vermin. We can see what followed at the highest levels of the German occupation of eastern Europe: the refinement of an initial, general, intense hatred and fear of Jewry into an organized program of mass extermination. Gone were the times when the Reich was thinking of isolating German Jews, and then of driving them to leave Germany.[1577] Gone were the speculations about transporting the Jews of Europe to the east African island of Madagascar. Gone were thoughts of non-Nazi nations taking in Jewish emigrants out of compassion for them. A new

---

[1575] Hannah Arendt, *Eichmann in Jerusalem: A Report on the Banality of Evil* (1963), quoted from *Eichmann in Jerusalem* (2006 ed.), p. 48.

[1576] "Diensttagebuch Hans Frank 26.12.1041: Regierungssitzung," NS-ARCHIV: DOKUMENTE ZUM NATIONALSOZIALISMUS.

[1577] There being about 500,000 Jews in Germany in 1933, about half had managed to emigrate (leaving their material wealth behind for the Reich) by the start of World War II. See *Apocalypse: Hitler*, at 37:10-38:00, YOUTUBE.

demand came with the number of Jews to be dealt with greatly increasing with the conquering of Poland, then western Europe, and, finally and significantly, the great Soviet Union. The killing by *Einsatzgruppen* of large numbers of Jews throughout the east horded into compact groups and driven to a ravine or gully would prove too difficult (on the soldiers, having to live with their spending their military days shooting defenseless and unarmed civilians), ultimately leading German military-scientific research to develop more efficient and less personal ways of killing thousands of Jews at a time, in a clean and pure way (the gas chambers).

One month after the above discussions, diary entries, and other written notes, there would be the famous Wannsee Conference[1578], on January 20, 1942 (mentioned above), chaired by Reinhard Heydrich, head of the RSHA (Reich Main Security Office), and attended by high-ranking Nazi officials, recording the plans for the extermination of some 11,000,000 Jews, with notes taken by Lt.-Colonel Adolf Eichmann. We might point out that in the break-down of the number of Jews to be eliminated in Europe, this list, significantly, listed the number 330,000 Jews in England, reflecting the expectations of these high-ranking Nazis that Great Britain would be among those countries conquered by, and under the domination of, the Third Reich. Jews in the USSR were numbered at 5,000,000. The listing of 4,000 Jews in Ireland and 18,000 in Switzerland as among those to be exterminated suggests a very inclusive sense of future German power.[1579]

Furthermore, as others have pointed out, the Wannsee Conference, held in late January 1942, came months after the first mass killings of Jews (and Poles, Russians, Romanies, and other undesirables), beginning after the invasion of the Soviet Union in late June 1941.

As Dutch historian Leendert J. Hartog remarked on some key features of this story, "the destruction of millions of Jews [*die Vernichtung von Millionen von Juden*] was organizationally and technically 'no trifle' [*»keine Kleinigkeit«*], and four of the five extermination camps—Bełżec, Lublin, Sobibór, and Treblinka—were established in Frank's territory alone."

Hartog continues driving some points home: "It can therefore be said that Frank himself heard HIlter's extermination order [*daß Frank den Vernichtungsbefehl von Hitler selbst gehört hat*] and in passing [*en passant*] heard that Heydrich had been hired as a 'European Jew Commissar' [*daß Heydrich als »europaischer Judenkommissar« angestellt worden war*], whose competence [and authority] Frank had to accept in the territory of the *Gouvernement General*. When did Hitler pass this

---

[1578]Christian Gerlach, "The Wannsee Conference, the Fate of German Jews, and Hitler's Decision in Principle to Exterminate all European Jews," *Journal of Modern History*, vol. 70, no. 4, Dec. 1998, pp. 759-812.

[1579] See transcript of the Wannsee Protocol, p. 4 of 9 pp., GERMAN HISTORY IN DOCUMENTS AND IMAGES (GHDI); Ger. text of page 4, "Das Protokoll der Wannseekonferenz (20. Januar 1942)," GHDI.

order on to Frank? [*Wann gab Hitler diesen Befehl an Frank weiter?*] It will have been on December 12 [*Es wird am 12. Dezember gewesen sein*], when Frank was received by his Führer in Berlin [*als Frank von seinem Führer in Berlin empfangen wurde*]."[1580] Hartog quotes a later statement by Hitler, from February 1945, on this same topic of Jewry and Germany at great odds: "If we lose this war [*Verlieren wir diesen Krieg*], then the Jews will be the victors [*dann werden die Juden die Sieger sein*]."[1581]

The same concern was expressed by Goebbels on March 27, 1942, "The Jews, if we did not fight back [*Die Juden würden, wenn wir uns ihrer nicht erwehren*], would destroy us. It is a life-and-death struggle [*Es ist ein Kampf auf Leben und Tod*] between the Aryan race and the Jewish bacillus [*zwischen der arischen Rasse und dem jüdischen Bazillus*]."[1582]

We might also quote here a significant statement, also by Goebbels, in his famous Total War speech at the Berlin Sportpalast on February 18, 1943.

This speech by Goebbels came after the development of mass killing operations in concentration and extermination camps, innovations in technique that were developed largely during the collapse of the German military might—marked by the Battles of Stalingrad, Kharkov, and Kursk—a downfall (*Untergang*) that came to pass only some 12 years after the Nazi *Machtergreifung* (the taking of power), something leading Nazis never expected, given their talk of a "Thousand-year Empire." (*While the term may be mocked, it was taken quite seriously and literally.*)

SCENES FROM THE RUSSIAN FRONT

It was on the Russian front that the German military suffered 80% of their losses; it was here, after the Battle of Stalingrad, that the German advance toward Iran and its rich oil fields was stopped. With a German defeat in the offing, Hitler took the pre-emptive step of promoting General Friedrich Paulus to the rank of Field Marshal. In the background of this was the historical fact that no German Field Marshal had ever surrendered in battle.

The option Hitler presumably envisioned was for Paulus to fight on to victory or to commit suicide. (Hitler would not accept the idea that the German Wehrmacht should be seen as defeated in any battle; he had refused the request by Paulus on October 4, 1942 to surrender.) Some two hours after his promotion, Paulus did neither one nor the other: he surrendered to the Soviet Military, along with his 91,000 German troops, including 24 generals, on January 31, 1943; February 2, 1943 marks the formal end to the battle.

[1580] Leendert J. Hartog, *Hoe ontstond de jodenmoord?: Hitler, Amerika, en de Endlösung [How did the murder of Jews originate: Hitler, America, and the Final Solution]* (1994); Ger. tr. from the Dutch: *Der Befehl zum Judenmord: Hitler, America und die Juden* (1997), p. 74.

[1581] Leendert J. Hartog, *Der Befehl zum Judenmord*, p. 79.

[1582] Joseph Goebbels, *Tagebücher aus den Jahren 1942-1943* (1948), pp. 142-143.

The Hitler Era

Hitler's secretary, Christa Schroeder, succinctly and bluntly called this *die Katastrophe von Stalingrad* (the disaster at Stalingrad on 2 February 1943). She added that after Stalingrad, Hitler could no longer relax to music.[1583] Historian Louis Snyder wrote about the Russians—that is, the Soviet Army—at this decisive battle at Stalingrad (which has since been renamed Volgograd), that they "lost more men at Stalingrad than the United States lost in combat in all theatres of the entire war. Stalingrad was one of the great turning points not only of the war but of world history."[1584] It was a long battle—or series of battles—beginning July 17, 1942, with General von Paulus surrendering on January 31, 1943, as just noted.[1585] In these military confrontations in and around Stalingrad, the total of civilian and military deaths came to almost 2 million persons (one estimate gives 1.9 million killed overall).

It was only 16 days after the German capitulation at Stalingrad, on February 18,[1586] that Goebbels tried to inspire the German population to carry on despite these serious setbacks, in his speech filmed at the Berlin Sportpalast to a select audience[1587] of loyal and die-hard Nazi Germans.

JOSEPH GOEBBELS AND THE CALL FOR TOTAL WAR

At this occasion, where below a huge banner stating "*Totaler Krieg—Kürzester Krieg*" (Total War—Shortest War), Goebbels, *after the murder of millions by the Einsatzgruppen in the Soviet Union and the operation of the extermination camps in Poland for almost a year, was apparently prepared to speak of finally taking off the kid gloves!* In his careful words, he stated that "the time had come to remove the kid gloves [*die Glacéhandschuhe auszuziehen*] and prepare to use our fists [*die Faust zu bandagieren*]."[1588] Such a cavalier and ruthless bravado with its bold

---

[1583] Christa Schroeder, *Er war mein Chef*, p. 130; Eng., *He Was My Chief*, p. 105.

[1584] Louis L. Snyder, *The War: A Concise History, 1939-1945* (1964), p. 382. Snyder (1907-1993) received his doctorate from the Univ. of Frankfurt-am-Main.

[1585] Georgii Drozdov and Evgenii Ryabko, *Russia at War 1941-45* (1987), Carey Schofield, ed., p. 130.

[1586] The speech by Goebbels on Total War was given on February 18, 1943. On that very same day, Sophie Scholl and her brother Hans distributed a large number of the final, sixth pamphlet by their group, the White Rose, at the University of Munich and were arrested that same day. There were tried only days later, along with their White Rose colleague Christoph Probst, by Judge Roland Freisler, on February 22, and that day all three were executed by guillotining. In the film, *Sophie Scholl: The Final Days* (2005), as Sophie is taken from one police agent to another, the radio broadcast of Joseph Goebbels is heard in the background (at 29:00-30:30). What might seem to be a sheer coincidence is actually, we might see, two actions taken in response to the same event: the disastrous defeat of the Wehrmacht at Stalingrad, with, obviously, rather different attitudes expressed.

[1587] Alfons Heck, *A Child of Hitler*, p. 88, noting a "carefully chosen audience" who roared out their agreement with Goebbels' proposition, "not surprisingly."

[1588] Randall Bytwerk, "Goebbels' 1943 Speech on Total War" (1998), CALVIN COLLEGE GERMAN PROPAGANDA ARCHIVE. Cf. discussion in "Sportpalast speech," WIKIPEDIA.

defiance is the material for great speeches, we might admit, and yet, there is a bleaker, more direct reality than this vision of glory: as Eva Braun wrote in her diary, quoting an unnamed "sad-faced woman on the tram," who put it differently, stating about final victory (the hoped-for outcome of total war), "What's the use of final victory to me? I have lost my father, mother, sisters, husband, and children. My house is in ruins. And in the end, I might be sent to the east somewhere, so that I'll even lose my country!"[1589] Nothing glorious or inspiring in any of that!

In this historical context of significant German war defeats, unlike any of the earlier confrontations and military victories, from 1936 through 1941, Goebbels asked the people if they were ready for a total war—*Wollt ihr den totalen Krieg?* (Do you want total war?)—"through thick and thin, even if this should mean the heaviest contributions on your part ... Do you want it, [even] if it need be more total and radical than we are capable of imagining today?" The audio portion of this speech records the crowd roaring out their strong agreement with this, even though it amounted to a *carte blanche*, a blind check to take on burdens undefined, beyond what could be imagined at all at the time. All of the audience also responded with gesturing as with a firm Nazi salute, a sea of stiffly outstretched arms. Albert Speer was to write later that Goebbels articulately analyzed what seemed to be "a purely emotional outburst" that touched on primordial hate and defiance as a carefully constructed presentation. Goebbels commented, "It was the politically best-trained audience you can find in Germany."[1590] In this speech on total war, Goebbels quoted Hitler's viewpoint on the war. Goebbels declared, "A merciless war is raging in the East [*Im Osten tobt ein Krieg ohne Gnade*]. For his part, the Führer correctly characterized this when he declared that in the end there would not be winners and losers, but [only] the surviving and the annihilated [*Der Führer hat ihn richtig charakterisiert, als er erklärte, es werden aus ihm nicht Sieger und Besiegte, sondern nur noch Überlebende und Vernichtetet hervogehen*]."[1591]

Here, among the intentions of the Third Reich, as put forth by Goebbels in this speech, was an interesting claim with a slip of the tongue, or at least a modification of one word in mid-speech to another, less direct and more euphemistic. This shift can be heard in some audios of the speech itself, but not in others, and not in the slightly revised renderings for print. The full, unedited rendering, however, is found in some recordings and published texts that convey this spoken passage in its full, original form:

> We see Jewry as a direct threat to every nation. We do not care what other peoples do about the danger. What we do to defend ourselves is our own business, however,

---

[1589] Eva Braun, *The Private Life of Adolf Hitler*, p. 167, 1944 (no specific date).
[1590] Albert Speer, *Inside the Third Reich* (1970), p. 257.
[1591] Joseph Goebbels, "*Rede im Berliner Sportpalast (Wollt Ihr den totalen Krieg)*, 18. February 1943," 100(0) SCHLÜSSEL DOKUMENTE ZUR DEUTSCHEN GESCHICHTE IM 10. JAHRHUNDERT. Cf. NT-IMT-Blue, vol. 27, p. 270 (re discussion between Rosenberg and the Führer, Dec. 14, 1941), NT-IMT-Blue, vol. 11, pp. 606-608.

The Hitler Era 531

and we will not tolerate objections from others. Jewry is a contagious infection. Enemy nations may raise hypocritical protests [*scheinheilig Protest einlegt*, insert sanctimonious protests] against our measures against Jewry with crocodile tears [*heuchlerische Krokodilstränen vergießt*], but that will not stop us from doing that which is necessary. Germany, in any event, has no intention [*hat nicht die Absicht*] of bowing before this Jewish threat [*dieser jüdischen Bedrohung zu beugen*], but rather intends to act at the right moment, using if necessary the most total and radical measures to [extermin-, to] deal with Jewry ["*Ausro-, -schaltung des Judentums*"]. [1592]

Here is the slip of the tongue, the misspoken word that Goebbels took back as best he could. He seems to be moved momentarily by his enthusiasm to speak directly and explicitly, but he presumably felt this phrase in appropriate for a general German public. Goebbels perhaps stumbled in his speech, his tongue getting the better of his careful speech, but did catch himself quickly (and yet without being able to undo what he had started). As just indicated, Goebbels began the word "*Ausrott-*" (the

---

[1592] The relatively short passage with the slip of the tongue being discussed here occurs at about one-third into the speech, after Goebbels mentions the third thesis (*die dritte These*) and before his talking about the struggle for Stalingrad (*das Ringen um Stalingrad*)—even though that battle had already been lost by the German military to the Soviet armies. See Joseph Goebbels: "People, Rise Up and Storm, Break Loose" [or "Total War"] 18 February 1943," pp. 112-139 in *Landmark Speeches of National Socialism*, Randall L. Bytwerk, ed., tr. (2008), at p. 121. The part in Eng. in brackets at the end of this excerpt of the speech was edited out of the German printed text (see remarks by the ed./tr. at p. 113). A Ger. text that retains this change (or slip of the tongue) is Iring Fetscher, *Joseph Goebbels im Berliner Sportpalast 1943: 'Wollt ihr den totalen Krieg?'* (1998), p. 73: "*unter vollkommener und radikalster Ausrott-, -schaltung des Judentums*"; in "Aufruf zum totalen Krieg. Vor 70 Jahren hielt NS-Propagandaminister Goebbels die brüchtigte Sportpalastrede," DEUTSCHLANDFUNK, Apr. 4, 2018; and in "Stichtag: 8. Februar 1943: Joseph Goebbels hält die 'Sportpalast-Rede'," WDR/WDR.DE, Feb. 18, 2006. *A site that preserves the audio of the key passage* is "Sportpalastrede von Joseph Goebbels (am 18.02.1943)," WDR/WDR.DE (15:01); in the discussion, esp. at 9:05-10:20, this slip of the tongue ("*Ausro-, schaltung*") occurs at 9:17-9:20. The shortened, amended audio to "Ausschaltung" is heard at 10:09-10:12. Cmp. the anniversary interview of filmmaker Lutz Hachmeister by Matthias Hanselmann about this Feb. 18, 1943 speech, at Matthias Hanselmann, "Die berühmteste deutsche Rede, die jemals gehalten wurde," DEUTSCHLANDFUNK KULTUR/WDR.DE, Feb. 18, 2013. Online audios (most being exactly 1:48:50 in length) of the "full speech" often delete this key passage: notice split audio at 21:55 in such recordings. The 1944 printed, edited text of the speech, Joseph Goebbels, "Nun, Volk steh auf, und Sturm brich los! Rede im Berliner Sportpalast. 18. Februar 1943," is at Joseph Goebbels, *Der steile Aufstieg. Reden und Aufsätze aus den Jahren 1942/43* (1944), pp. 167-204; at pp. 178-179. The crowd breaks out here in cheering. The printed, modified text reads: "*mit den radikalsten Gegenmaßnahmen entgegenzutreten*" (to oppose with the most radical reprisals). More in the above text.

first part of the word *Ausrottung*, eradication), stopped, and continued with "-schaltung" (the second part of the word *Ausschaltung*. In Nazi jargon, the primary word here, for which *Ausschaltung* is the contrast, is *Gleichschaltung*, switching into conformity of all dimensions of life in Germany to be in congruence with German ideology; hence, *Ausschaltung* is the switching off or disconnection from this conformity: less severe for the Jews in question than their being eradicated or exterminated.

This February 18 speech took place more than two full weeks after the German Wehrmacht at Stalingrad was known to have fallen to Soviet troops. Misrepresenting in a more optimistic light the military position of the Third Reich on the Eastern Front, Goebbels then states that Germany has no intention (*hat nicht die Absicht*) to bow to the Jewish threat (*dieser jüdischen Bedrohung zu beugen*), but intends, rather, to counter this threat punctually, if necessary, with the most complete and most radical extinc- [Goebbels changes here in mid-word, as just discussed, to] switching off or disconnecting of Judaism.

Later generations have focused on the significance of this speech and especially of this specific phrase, even if at the time of the speech itself that one sentence did not stand out. Still, even without this speech or this slip, Germans knew of the Nazi hatred for Jews, whether they were spoken of as the supposed masterminds behind capitalist or Bolshevik opposition to the Reich, and knew of the Nazi image of the Jews as vermin or a cancer (in each case, best eliminated). Despite Goebbels' call for a readiness to face the harshest of wars, in the following months, there was some important set-backs for the Wehrmacht, especially the Battle of Kursk-Orel, of which Harrison E. Salisbury, head of the Moscow Bureau of the *New York Times*, wrote (in 1987) as the "titanic struggle of tanks and armour, the like of which has never been seen, was fought (and is hardly known in the West) at Kursk-Orel, *breaking Hitler's armoured back*. Never again would the Wehrmacht mount a massive offensive."[1593]

This battle was fought in the region between Kursk and Orel; Kursk in Russia is about 285 air miles south-southwest of Moscow, with Orel 85 air miles north of Kursk.

The Battle began as part of what would be the last great German offensive on the Eastern Front, the *Unternehmen Zitadelle* (Operation Citadel), and ended with the last withdrawal of significant troops by the Germans, on July 17, 1943. Despite this loss, and its implication for those high in the German and Soviet military that Germany had lost the war, the Germans (read: Hitler) did not sue for peace and the war went on for two more years, with many more dying and with many more cities destroyed, with the following by the German military leadership of resolute and sometimes frustrated and explosively angry orders[1594] from

---

[1593] Harrison E Salisbury, Preface (pp. 7-11) in Georgii Drozdov and Evgenii Ryabko, *Russia at War 1941-45*, p. 7. Italics added.
[1594] This is well portrayed in scenes of the closing period of the war in Berlin in the German film, *Der Untergang* (2004), Eng. title, *Downfall*.

an irate Hitler, who called himself not only *der Führer*, the Leader) but also gave himself the title and the position of the *Oberste Befehlshaber der Wehrmacht* (the Supreme Leader of the German Armed Forces, the Wehrmacht).[1595]

Those who had lost faith, respect, and confidence in Hitler, especially after the defeat at the Battle of Stalingrad, came up with a term that was a mocking title for Hitler, *Gröfaz*, short for *der Größter Feldherr aller Zeiten*, the Greatest Commander-in-Chief of all Times.

It was at Stalingrad that the Germans basically lost the war, bringing about the end of their Reich. But, the cost to the Soviet Union was more than twenty million who died during the entire war fighting the Germans; this was some 40% of the death toll in the entire war![1596]

While it was clear to both Russian and German generals that the end was approaching, Hitler was to remain adamant about fighting to the end; the accurate but pessimistic reports of Reinhard Gehlen, head of the FHO (*Fremde Heer Ost*, Foreign Armies East) Wehrmacht Intelligence led Hitler—refusing the information—to fire him, on April 9, 1945.[1597] (This is perhaps killing the messenger.)

When the concept of total war was put before the German people in the earlier context by Goebbels, the extreme stakes were made explicit but kept quite vague. Whether Goebbels or they appreciated what would come in the next two years is not obvious, since inspiring rhetoric does not especially dwell on the specifics of the possible extreme devastation to life, homes, cities, roads, or manufacturing facilities, what we now call a nation's infrastructure.

Himmler's similar thinking in early 1941 about the war was described by SS General Erich von dem Bach-Zelewski, who testified on January 7, 1946 at the Nuremberg trial of major war criminals. Bach-Zelewski reported what he had heard from Himmler at the beginning of 1941 (months before the invasion of the USSR)—at the Castle at Wewelsburg, which Himmler had transformed into the spiritual home of the SS as the embodiment if not the actual reincarnation of the medieval Teutonic Knights. In that context, Himmler presented the idea that the purpose of the Russian campaign would be to decimate the Russian population by 30 million people—a grand program of what is now called ethnic cleansing, *one that dwarfs the 6 million Jews that are much more often referred to*— and that "the struggle against the partisan movement was a pretext for destroying the Slav and Jewish population."[1598] A variant of this approach and the language describing the murderous actions taken was used in the Wehrmacht attack on the Warsaw Jewish ghetto in spring 1943, with its

---

[1595] See the document on Hitler's military letterhead, dated Berlin, Nov. 11, 1939, in the photo section after p. 171, in Bryan Mark Rigg, *Hitler's Jewish Soldiers*.

[1596] Vladimir Karpov, Introduction (pp. 13-17) in Georgii Drozdov and Evgenii Ryabko, *Russia at War 1941-45*, p. 17, and also résumé on front dust jacket.

[1597] Jeffrey T. Richelson, *A Century of Spies: Intelligence in the Twentieth Century* (1995), p. 233; Nikita Kusnezov, *Reeds in the Wind* (2011), p. 316.

[1598] NT-IMT-Blue, vol. 4, testimony, 7 January 1946, p. 484.

goal of killing the last of its residents, mostly young adults who saw no reason not to fight back. The ghetto was totally razed and the remaining Jews removed. The uprising went from April 19-May 16, 27 days. (By comparison, Warsaw had been attacked the day the war began, September 1, 1939, and had surrendered September 27, the same length of time.)

The General in charge of the operation of destroying the last Jews in the Warsaw ghetto, Gen. Jürgen Stroop (1895-1951), then prepared a photo album, *Es gibt keinen jüdischen Wohnbezirk in Warschau mehr!* (*The Jewish Quarter of Warsaw Is No More!*), commonly called *The Stroop Report*, in which the Jews were not described as partisans—which would be rather unlikely in their confined and desolate conditions in the ghetto—but as bandits (*Banditen*).[1599]

This report was sent back to the authorities in Berlin, as a photo album reporting on the successful destruction of the Warsaw ghetto and the last of the young Jews who fought to death.

The violence that had one major focus in the elimination of the Jews of Europe extended, perhaps with less of a sense of urgency, to the removal as best possible, as a second-level focus, of other detestable groups (Romanies, Slavs, homosexuals, the deformed, retarded, and incurably sick). It has been suggested that such a hatred had to be cultivated, or learned, but in the Nazi Germany that began in 1933, many young soldiers and SS Men knew no other values. Teaching hatred and violence was not an especially difficult task for the leaders of the Reich with these young, open-minded, belief-free souls as ready students.[1600] Was it a doctrine or worldview, or was it a teaching of hatred? (It might be both, actually.)

After the many horrifying events of the war years, with the Reich crushed and conquered, with Hitler and others dead or captured, survivors in many lands faced the question of how to bring a people back to civilization, or at least to societies in which basic human rights and personal dignity could be reestablished, in which a social web of mutual respect, if not support, could be recreated.

THE IMMEDIATE POST-WAR TIMES

The war in Europe officially ended with VE-Day ("Victory in Europe") on May 8, 1945. *This treaty was signed by the military, marking a total military defeat, not a repeat of the 1919 surrender by German caretaker politicians!* The war in the Pacific, VJ-Day ("Victory over Japan") was on August 14, 1945.[1601] Later, in 1967, a farmer in Luxembourg summed it

---

[1599] *The Jewish Quarter of Warsaw Is No More! The Stroop Report* (1979), facs. ed. and tr. Reporting the viewpoint of the Bund (a Socialist, integrative, non-Zionist, Workers' Union), in Yiddish: American Representation of the General Jewish Workers' Union—known as the Bund—in Poland, *Geto in Flamen: Zamlbukh* (1944).

[1600] Richard Rhodes, *Masters of Death: The SS-Einsatzgruppen and the Invention of the Holocaust* (2002), p 22.

[1601] The Soviet Union continued fighting against the Wehrmacht in Silesia until

all up, in a succinct synopsis: "God, what a waste of everybody's time."[1602] (Yes, a waste of time—at the cost of at least fifty million people's lives!)

A good number of the major individuals of the Third Reich committed suicide in those final days of the war, including Adolf Hitler and Joseph Goebbels at the Chancellery Bunker in Berlin, overrun by Soviet forces.

Hitler had survived to the end, killing himself—and so not attaining the awe-inspiring status of a martyr. He stayed until the end of the total destruction of large German cities, which had become piles of rubble and bricks. This loss could not be denied nor dismissed as back-stabbing! In addition, other notable Nazis also committed suicide, including Martin Bormann (Hitler's Private Secretary), Heinrich Himmler, Hermann Göring (in 1946), General Hans Krebs, last Chief of Staff of the *Oberkommando des Heeres* or *OKH* (Supreme High Command of the German Army), Theodor Dannecker (an associate of Eichmann's), Odilo Globočnik (SS officer, Gauleiter of Vienna, later Police Chief in the Lublin District, involved in the liquidation of the Warsaw ghetto and the idea of exterminating Jews *en masse* using gas chambers, an idea he proposed to Himmler on October 13, 1941), and high-ranking members of the Wehrmacht (Armed Forces): 53 generals of the *Heer* (Army), 14 generals of the Luftwaffe (Air Force), and 11 admirals of the *Kriegsmarine* (Navy).

Many officials committed suicide along with their wives, the most well-known, perhaps, of these being Joseph and Magda Goebbels, with Magda killing her six children, aged between 4 and 12 at their deaths, placing cyanide capsules into the mouths of their drugged children and crushing them open. As she put it, in thinking about her children,[1603] "I would rather have my children die than live in disgrace, jeered at. Our children have no place in Germany as it will be after the war." (She was imagining the imminent defeat of the Third Reich, but perhaps also feeling resentful about her husband's earlier desire to leave her and the family, to be appointed Ambassador to Japan, taking along his lover, the Czech actress, Lída Baarová—killing the children would also be hurting him, their father; Hitler had demanded that the affair be stopped and that Goebbels return to his wife, as was befitting of a leading figure of the Reich.[1604])

Goebbels' secretary, Brunhilde Pomsel, wrote: "Hanna Reitsch had offered to fly them out. Supposedly she[1605] could have landed her little

---

May 9, 1945, the end of its war in Europe, the Great Patriotic War. The Japanese surrendered on August 14, 1945, US time (for Japan, August 15). The signing of documents by General Douglas MacArthur and Japanese Foreign Minister Mamoru Shigemitsu and Army Chief of Staff Yoshijirō Umezu, marked the surrender of the Japanese Empire and its military, aboard the *US Missouri*, on September 2, 1945.

[1602] Alfons Heck, *The Burden of Hitler's Legacy*, p. 222.

[1603] Traudl Junge, *Until the Final Hour*, p. 175.

[1604] "Obituary: Lida Baarova: Beautiful Czech actress who turned down Hollywood to become Goebbels's mistress," *Guardian* (London), Nov. 9, 2000, p. 28

[1605] Hanna Reitsch (1912-1979), an experienced test pilot for the Luftwaffe, wrote in *The Sky My Kingdom* (1955), pp. 202-214, that in Hitler's last days, she flew to Berlin on April 26, with Col.-Gen. Robert Ritter von Greim, overpasssing the

plane to fly out the children. It's the attitude of the mother that I really don't understand.... It's unimaginable."[1606]

Imaginable to Brunhilde Pomsel or not, the children's mother, Magda Goebbels, then bit into a cyanide capsule, after which Joseph, her husband, shot her in the head, and then used the double method suggested by one of Hitler's personal physicians, Dr. Werner Haase, to bite down on a cyanide capsule and to shoot himself in the head at that moment (a method Hitler also apparently used).[1607] This desperation arose in part from the shock of realizing that the end of the Reich was at hand. As the Luftwaffe pilot Hanna Reitsch put it:

> All of us knew beyond a shadow of a doubt that the end was coming hourly nearer.... Although the occupants of the Bunker were confined in the smallest space and would share the same fate, perhaps in a matter of hours, von Greim and I, because we had just arrived from the outside world, felt ourselves separate from the others, as if we were onlookers. This sense of distance increased as the tension mounted. To us, it was clear that Hitler and his immediate circle were living in a world of their own, far removed from the reality outside, where a desperate battle raged for what remained of Berlin and Germany. Hopes of rescue, nourished by rumour and occasional items of favourable news, led them to adopt a fantastically distorted picture of the truth.[1608]

That is, they held that distorted picture of the truth, but only *until* the ever-tighter ring of Soviet soldiers, the artillery, and other sounds of warfare, made it harshly evident that Hitler's final hope that General Walther Wenk would come and rescue those in the Chancellery was not going to happen—Wenk was finally able to communicate on the evening

---

Tiergarten (Zoo), and landing the *Fieseler Fi-156C Storch*—named *Storch* (Eng. Stork), for its leggy landing gear and minimal runway needs—on the Carlottenburger Allee, near the Brandenburg Gate.

She offered to take Hitler to Berchtesgaden. Hitler was despondent at Göring's telegram, stripped Göring of all his offices, expelled him from the Party, and made von Greim head of the Luftwaffe, or, as Reitsch put it (p. 208), "Commander-in-Chief of an Air Force that no longer existed!" On April 28, news came of Himmler's peace negotiations on his own (and of Mussolini's murder and the brutalization of his corpse in Milan). Hitler refused to leave with Reitsch and von Greim. On May 24, von Greim—who in 1920 had given Hitler his very first airplane ride—would commit suicide with a cyanide capsule given him by Hitler. See Michael D. Hull, "German Female Glider & Fighter Pilot Hanna Reitsch," *WWII History, vol. 4*, no. 3, May 2005, pp. 16-21, 77, WARFARE HISTORY NETWORK, Aug. 14, 2014; "Meeting Hanna Reitsch," *Air & Space Magazine* (SMITHSONIAN INSTITUTION), Nov. 23, 2015.

[1606] Brunhilde Pomsel, *The Work I Did*, pp. 105-106, 196.
[1607] James O'Donnell, *The Bunker*, p. 323.
[1608] Hanna Reitsh, *The Sky My Kingdom*, p. 210.

The Hitler Era

of April 28 to Keitel that his army had been pushed back by Soviet troops along the entire front near Potsdam (some 25 miles southwest of Berlin)—and that there was no defense against the Reich's formidable enemy.

The small group who chose suicide along with Hitler and Eva Braun were among thousands of Germans who preferred death to living after the fall of the Reich. There were others, as well, non-Germans, for whom the violence and organized killing of the Third Reich, was also overwhelming. Ukrainian Anatoly Kuznetsov would write, feeling his own good luck, "It was purely a matter of luck that I arrived in this world not a Jew, not a gypsy, not old enough to be sent to work to Germany, that bombs and bullets missed me, that patrols didn't catch me, that I escaped from under a tram by a miracle and fell off a tree without killing myself. My God, what luck! … Unhappy people: what have you done to deserve such a fate? … You can't escape anywhere; there's nowhere to hide. So where is all the justice you talk about, where are you all, clever people of this world? … There is no such counter-balancing thing. There is no compassion on this earth."[1609] Beyond this vision of hopelessness and complete heartlessness among our species was a force of life that had Kuznetsov live until 1979. Of course, there were millions of Germans who did not prefer death to life, either, and who mostly lived merely to deal with the consequences of the years of the Reich and the reconstruction of Germany which took place in the following decades.

The end of the war for Germans was a time of peace in a country that had many of its cities reduced to rubble, with no basic infrastructure: with food shortages, no water, electricity, or livable quarters for the population, no organized labor to be found, and so on. The same was true of other countries that had suffered from the massive destruction from armies fighting on their land and in their cities.

It is a commonplace thought that when the Western Allies entered Germany, there were practically no people who identified themselves as Nazis, for practical, self-serving reasons. Private opinions were a different story: One survivor of the war, Alfons Heck, quoted above, wrote, "In a survey carried out by the American occupation forces six months after the end of the war, more than 50 percent of those questioned thought the idea of National Socialism was good, but had been badly administered. While 40 percent conceded it had been a bad idea, only 20 percent accepted Germany's responsibility for the war."[1610]

Heck added that the age of persecution of ordinary Germans had ended by 1948, that "the prosecution of Nazis, which had never been popular in the *Bundesrepublik* (why foul our own nest), ranked in importance somewhere below traffic offenses in public opinion polls."[1611]

In addition, the number of persons who had been displaced by the war, as in forced laborers shipped to Germany and other Axis-controlled lands

---

[1609] A. Anatoli, *Babi Yar: A Document in the Form of a Novel* (1971), pp. 295-296. This was published under the penname of Anatoly Kuznetsov (1929-1979).

[1610] Alfons Heck, *The Burden of Hitler's Legacy*, p. 1.

[1611] Alfons Heck, *The Burden of Hitler's Legacy*, p. 209.

to replace men who had gone off to war for the greater power and success of the Reich would not find easy ways to return to their homelands.

In this significant sense, there was often no home to come to home to. Here there will be many people dislocated (if surviving) by the war; they would be called DPs (displaced persons). In the first years after the end of the war, many would return to their homes. Jews had special, particular problems. In Europe, people had taken over the cottages, homes, apartments, or other living quarters of the Jews when the Jews were removed by German or German-administered "relocation" actions (*Umsiedlungsaktionen*). This led to a reluctance of former neighbors to welcome these surviving Jews back, at times leading to violence in defense of their recently acquired residences. There were even some pogroms in which returning Jews were killed, such as the pogroms in Przedbórz (May 27, 1945), in Rzeszów (June 11, 1945), in Kraków (August 11, 1945), and in Kielce (on July 4, 1946), along with other violence against returning Polish Jews in Bytom, Białystock, Częstochowa, Sosnowiec, Szczecin, Tarnów, and in other Polish locations.[1612]

Committing suicide avoided further problems and nasty experiences for some of the most powerful members of the Third Reich, including, of course Hitler, Goebbels, and Himmler, who never faced trial or the mixed emotions of the German people, from sadness to wrath and rage.

We may consider worst-case scenarios, from the National Socialist understanding (or misunderstanding), with its self-assumed obvious truths (which from the outside could be seen as sheer distorted dogma). With that, we can think of two key elements that were part of a dogmatic Nazi delusion. Fundamental here was the idea of a relentless, revengeful attitude of world Jewry, with the prediction of its annihilating the German nation if it had the chance. In this Nazi viewpoint, there was a corollary: that if Germany lost the war and world Jewry had the chance, it would inflict a bloody repayment—with the annihilation of the German nation— in retribution for the enslavement and the annihilation of entire European groups, especially the Jewish and the Slavic peoples, but also of the rebellious nationals of a number of other countries that the Reich had rather harshly subjugated, tortured, and often killed in mass. *None of these imagined outcomes was to come to pass. How could this be?*

The starting point here is the National Socialist distorted assumption that the Jews of the world were in fact the masterminds behind all anti-Nazi governments, from the USA, the UK (believed within Nazi circles to be controlled by a presumed coterie of Jewish capitalists), and also from the USSR (likewise assumed to be controlled by Bolshevists, other Slavs, and especially Russian Jewry). Given this delusion of grandeur of the

---

[1612] Earlier had been the Jedwabne killings: "75. Anniversary of the Jedwabne pogrom, 10 July 1941," *Polin*, July 10, 2016, POLIN.PL. See Joanna Tokarska-Bakir (Polish historian), "Cries of the Mob in the Pogroms in Rzeszów (June 1945), Cracow (August 1945), and Kielce (July 1946) as a Source for the State of Mind of the Participants," *East European Politics and Societies*, vol. 25, no. 3, Aug. 2011, pp. 553-574; "Anti-Jewish violence in Poland, 1944-1946," WIKIPEDIA.

hated Jewish enemy—which could make a nation ready to defend itself tooth and nail, then: *If the Jews were also* as vengeful and violent against the Germans as the Germans were against them, *then surely* the German nation would have been exterminated, to the best of the powers of such imagined vengeful Jews! But the mass killings in the hundreds of thousands and millions that were carried about within the context of the Third Reich has not seen a parallel since those years of dedicated, mass genocide. As Wehrmacht Generalleutnant (Lieutenant-General) Friedrich von Broich (1896-1974) put it, on Jan. 21,1944,[1613]

> All we've achieved is that our reputation as soldiers and Germans has been completely besmirched. People say: "You carry out all the orders when people are to be shot, whether it is right or wrong." No one objects to the shooting of spies, but when whole villages, the entire population, including the children, are wiped out, or the people are sent away, as in Poland or Russia, then, my God, one can say it is pure murder, it is exactly what the Huns of old did.[1614] But then of course we are the most civilized people in the world, aren't we?"[1615]

He was certainly not alone in his rejection of the wanton killing of entire populations (of various sizes); many in the German military found the killings repulsive to partake in, leading either to a refusal to so act (not that widespread a response), to imbibing significant amounts of numbing alcohol, to hospitalization for mental anguish or for some physical somaticizing of the stress, to suicide, or to other dire actions.

We have here humanity in a very upsetting, unnatural context, when the killing of others is done nonchalantly and even with a sense of self-righteousness. The natural response that we see again and again, despite the admonitions of superiors (such as Himmler at his famous discourses in Posnań in October 1943), is this repulsion at seeing shot, *en masse*, men, women, the old and the young, including children and babies. This does not minimize the horrors of being herded together and shot, but it is its own living hell, a return to savagery and barbarity of the cruelest and most vicious of all war-hungry peoples we can remember throughout all of history (as Lt.-Gen. von Broich, just quoted, recalls of the Huns,

---

[1613] Lt.-Gen. Broich surrendered to the British Army on May 12, 1943, in Tunisia. He was interned as a POW at Trent Park until the end of the war. This and many other statements were recorded by British intelligence, unbeknownst to the German prisoners, who thought they were speaking privately among themselves.

[1614] These were led by Attila the Hun (born ca. 406, ruler of the Huns, 434-453), with barbarian attacks on the Roman Empire, invading northern Italy in 452, remembered as having declared, in English rendering, "There were I have gone, the grass will never grow again!" In French, "*Là où passe mon cheval, l'herbe ne repousse pas!*" ("There, where my horse goes, grass does not grow again!")

[1615] Sönke Neitzel and Harald Welzer, *Soldaten: On Fighting, Killing, and Dying*, p. 147; citing as source the National Archives, Kew Gardens, London, War Office.

referring to the followers of Attila the Hun. *This is no small indictment by this Wehrmacht general!* Also here, in hopelessness for the future of the Reich, Fritz Steffen (1893-1979), a German member of the *Volkssturm*, the People's Militia, consisting mostly of ill-equipped young boys and older men, wrote on Hitler's birthday, April 20, 1945, that "we have to go to the Party for the Führer's Birthday in the mess [military-like dining hall]. A *Kreisleiter* [a county leader, a civilian Nazi Party official, not having any military standing] talks about the final victory! The free bottle of red wine and small portion of ham and sausage with bread weren't enough to persuade us of it."[1616] (Just about everyone in Germany realized by that time that the end was very close by—except those who would refuse to recognize that the third Reich might go down in flames to dust and rubble.)

POPULAR RETRIBUTION AMIDST RUBBLE, SCARS, AND MOURNING

Almost immediately after there was liberation in the various countries that had been under the control of the Third Reich, there was widespread retribution carried out by various individuals, groups, and even newly victorious Allied armies. This happened on its own, along with formal procedures meant to bring those guilty of war crimes to justice in preparation. (More on those, below.) These popular acts were at times against collaborators in the running of the German political machine, who had posts in the governments that were under Nazi control, or who acted in a more accessory fashion that made the Nazi governance more efficient. Some of these were put on trial in the various now-liberated countries, but some of those targeted for retribution had not participated in any actions against the populations now intent on meting out justice or revenge, once again using a context of great politically-motivated violence as a time for a settling of scores (as in the Night of the Long Knives, discussed above). There were certainly cases of individuals taking justice into their own hands, having summary hearings with what was felt to be just retribution. Some suggested allowing those who had suffered the most at the hands of this inhumane treatment of other human beings—such as the survivors of the concentration camps—to be the ones to be allowed to wreak revenge, allowed, that is, to beat their former torturers and killers to death, then and there (in concentration camps or throughout Europe). Not all such survivors had an interest to return like for like, did not have the energy for such actions, or just wanted to go on with life. In towns and cities through formerly Nazi-occupied Europe, people were beaten, some were hung, others killed by other means.

One way of coming to terms with the suffering that had been endured in those years of Nazi occupation was to attack anyone thought to have had any relation with the Nazi occupiers (mostly with the German military). The repulsion that many felt against local young women who had been friends with, or lovers of, these foreign occupying troops, had a visceral dimension, as if these friendships or love relationships were the most despicable of all treasonous acts against the population. Of course,

---

[1616] "Volkssturmmann Fritz Steffen," p. 6 in Walter Kempowski, *Swansong 1945*.

such women were rather defenseless against the treatment they would receive from others.

Often the punishment for such local women would involve their being variously humiliated: some were sheared, having their locks shaven off, exposing a bare scalp, others were stripped naked and forced to walk among the local crowd in their shame, often while being beaten and spit upon.[1617] While the act of being friendly toward the enemy or becoming lovers was breaking solidarity with the rest of the population, it rarely involved acts of violence against them. The immediate expression of frustrated rage, in any case, was readily and easily expressed against such women, who are regularly defenseless. (More just below.)

One further important example of the popular violence at the time of liberation from Nazi control was the situation for ethnic Germans throughout Europe, but mostly in Eastern Europe. Their mistreatment in Czechoslovakia was significant, perhaps even more so than in Poland. Here, as elsewhere, it seems that the innocent are often punished for the wrong deeds of the guilty who were responsible for earlier violence, sometimes attacked randomly, and sometimes when being individuals seen as being of the hated group. This generalized violence is not new and not unique to post-Reich Europe. In earlier and in more recent times, we can recognize extensive violence, as in mass massacres (or "ethnic cleansing" or "genocides").[1618]

Those subjugated to Nazi violence in the conquered territories of Europe had been beaten, put into concentration camps, or shot without further ado, with some who saw in those murders the brutality, barbarity, and total lack of moral restraint.

Ethnic German in eastern Europe were massacred, in turn, by the Soviet army.[1619] And after the war, *Volksdeutsche*, too, would have occasion to moan, and cry, and wonder, as did Emil Pupip, a *Volksdeutscher* from Brno, who was 16 in 1945, and later remembered ethnic-German children, 6-11 years old, beaten by Czech patriots. Pupip commented between sobs, "It was awful. What had the children—how could someone be so sadistic? It was terrible. Children! They can't defend

---

[1617] Fabrice Virgili, *La France virile: des femmes tondues à la Libération* (2000); Eng. tr., *Shorn Women: Gender and Punishment in Liberation France* (2002). The film *Hiroshima, Mon Amour* (1959) portrays in part the earlier life of one of its two principal characters, and her treatment in France after the Liberation. A similar theme is presented in the later Italian film, *Malèna* (2000).

[1618] Edmund O. Stillman and William Pfaff, *The Politics of Hysteria: The Sources of Twentieth-Century Conflict* (1964); William Pfaff, *The Wrath of Nations: Civilization and the Furies of Nationalism* (1993); David Treuer, *The Heartbeat of Wounded Knee: Native America from 1890 to the Present* (2019); Timothy Snyder, "Redrawing Nations: Ethnic Cleansing in East-Central Europe, 1944-1948 (review)," *Forum: Perspectives on Redrawing Nations*, a special issue of *Journal of Cold War Studies*, vol. 5, no. 3, Summer 2003, pp. 102-105.

[1619] See the German film of overpowered Wehrmacht on the Oder and the German refugees fleeing the Soviets, *Lost in Klessin* (2018).

themselves! What have they ever—they couldn't have done anything! Such little children!"[1620] *As part of the violence done to others*, there would be reports from the period immediately after the end of World War II in Europe—as in the report a young Czech witness, Meda Mladek (born 1919)—that Czechs took some ethnic Germans, *Volksdeutsche*, and "they carved swastikas into their flesh and rubbed salt in the wounds."[1621]

This was part of the treatment of some civilian ethnic Germans in Eastern Europe, said to be in retaliation for the German military practices earlier, inspired and encouraged by Hitler and the Nazi government. This paralleled earlier German military carving Jewish stars and similar designs into the scalp or forehead of Jews in Warsaw. There was a wave not only of expulsions of ethnic Germans from the Slavic countries the Reich had conquered, but also brutal killings. A BBC film reports that three and a half million ethnic Germans were stripped of their citizenship and expelled from their homes with no compensation (in Czechoslovakia alone),[1622] and that overall more than 12 million ethnic Germans were expelled from Eastern Europe, with more than a quarter of a million ethnic Germans dying in forced marches.[1623] *The targets of this violence were in some cases guilty only by association and group identification, even if others had supported the German occupation.*

French woman   ethnic German   Warsaw Jews

Here are photos of the treatment of a French woman, of an ethnic German in Prague, both in 1945, and of Jews in the Warsaw ghetto,[1624] in 1939.

The Vatican Ratline and Operation Paperclip

At the same time, there were major war criminals who had never been captured or put on trial. Many of these went into hiding, either in Europe, or by using a communication system called the Ratline, run by the Vatican,[1625] with the aid of the US Army Counter-Intelligence Corps

---

[1620] From BBC film, *1945: The Savage Peace* (2015), from the interview with Emil Pupik, at 25:40-26:59.
[1621] *1945: The Savage Peace*, at 9:00-9:45.
[1622] *1945: The Savage Peace* (just cited), at 43:57-44:37.
[1623] 1945: The Savage Peace, at 45:14-46:00.
[1624] "SS-Männer schnitten den Juden Sterne in die Haut" ("SS-Men Cut the Jewish Star into Skin"), photo in *Faschismus—Getto—Massenmord. Dokumentation über Ausrottung und Widerstand der Juden in Polen während des zweiten Weltkrieges*, Jüdisches Historisches Institut, Warschau (1960; pub. in East Berlin, DDR), p. 42.
[1625] *The Vatican Ratlines: Smuggling Nazis to Safety*, YouTube, 16:30 on. A well-

(CIC)—now INSCOM, the US Army Intelligence and Security Command—which ran Operation Paperclip, bringing German rocket scientists to the USA.[1626] Those fleeing were given false papers and were able to travel incognito to various countries in South America. Among those helped to escape from Europe were Soviet informers and military; there were also hundreds of Croatian nationalists—including Croatian leader Ante Pavelić, founder of the Ustaše, an ultra-nationalist fascist party banned in May 1945); Klaus Barbie, SS head in Lyon, France, with the help of Croatian Roman Catholic priest Krunoslav Draganović; and Nazi collaborators accused of massacring 30,000 Jews, whom Tito would have arrested and tried for massacring several hundred thousand Serbs.[1627] And so, in the de-Nazification program going on in the post-war years in Germany, with legal hearings of thousands of Germans to determine their involvement in the National Socialist bureaucracy and administration, and many identified as committed Nazis, many others were exonerated, meaning they could partake in the new society and its system of administration and government. On local applications in 1947 of this de-Nazification, former Hitlerjugend and Luftwaffe pilot, Alfons Heck, wrote, "That was the end of the de-Nazification era—a true farce since so many of the Nazi mass murderers had long since vanished and would never face any judge."[1628] As for those who committed this post-war violence out of a sense of vengeance, the carrying out of moral retribution, perhaps some were self-satisfied and feeling moral and honorable, but others, might well have experienced a state of mind in which "anger and repentance neutralized each other," as Romani Hungarian author Menyhért Lakatos wrote in his 1975 novel.[1629] *But what came to pass was not at all what the Nazi propaganda ministry focused on in intending to encourage the German population to give no thought to a surrender that would (so the story went) lead only to the complete annihilation of the German people and nation.* In contrast to this apocalyptic vision, in 1947, not very long after the end of hostilities in Europe, a plan was set into motion called the European Recovery Program, known as the Marshall Plan, after the US Secretary of State George C. Marshall, who devised the idea. Between

---

known pro-Nazi Austrian priest in that network was Alois (Luigi) Hudal (1885-1962).

[1626] On the Vatican, the US and British secret services, Argentina, and its Nazi fugitives, see *The Vatican Ratline—Primetime Live! with Sam Donaldson*, YOUTUBE.

[1627] Thomas O'Toole, "'Operation Ratline' Was Barbie's Ticket Out," *Washington Post*, Aug. 21, 1983; Carl Savich, "The Rat Lines, the Holocaust in France, 1940-1944, and the Klaus Barbie Case, Part II [with vivid details of the treatment of Jean Moulin and others in the *maquis*]," *Serbianna*, Jul. 8, 2016; Col. James V. Milano, USA (Ret.) and Patrick Brogan, *Soldiers, Spies, and the Rat Line: America's Undeclared War Against the Soviets* (2000); Dalya Alberge, "Red Cross and Vatican Helped thousands of Nazis to Escape," *The Guardian*, May 25, 2011; British-French barrister Philippe Sands, "BBC Radio 4 Presents Intrigue: The Ratline: A new 10-part podcast," Sep. 18, 2018, BBC.CO.UK.

[1628] Alfons Heck, *The Burden of Hitler's Legacy*, p. 184, re his home town, Wittlich.

[1629] Eng. tr., *The Color of Smoke: An Epic Novel of the Roma* (2015).

1948 and 1952, West Germany, including West Berlin, received some $1.4 billion.[1630] This was in addition to monies that were earmarked for other European countries devasted by the war. The occupying forces also supplied great manpower to re-establish order and civil security, in a time when they were rare realities. But what was to be done with those who had directed or committed heinous crimes that were of a scope and an order grander than anything our species had experienced? What might be the balance created between the urge for revenge and the desire for justice? Some leaders of the world wanted to finish off with the issue in the most efficient and quickest way possible: to line these men up who were seen as vicious criminals against a wall and finish them off by a firing squad. Others suggested a system of trials that were led by internationally respected jurors and lawyers, with a defense counsel in support of those accused of various crimes. This was ridiculed or dismissed in some circles as a way of camouflaging what they saw as simply vengeance of the victor. *Surprising from that perspective, as it turns out, some of those tried were declared innocent, others were found guilty; furthermore, the sentence was not always death: this would vary from accused to accused* from a given number of years in prison to death (often by hanging).

That taken into consideration here, in any case, there was an attempt to follow earlier international treaties and ratified documents, and an attempt to refine further what was to be understood, in the particular cases of the specific trials that were being held, and also for future reference, *to establish legal precedents*. This would lead decades later to the establishment of the International Court of Justice, where those who were charged with having committed ethnic cleansing, crimes against humanity, or genocide could be brought to trial. These trials have continued until very recent years, and perhaps there will be more, until those being accused of these crimes have all died, given the flow of time.

In this light, some say that it is better to let old people die in peace (and certainly all those who were active in the period up to 1945 have seen their prime, even if they have managed to stay alive at this time). What, after all, is the purpose of such trials? Is it to harass tired old men (and women), a kind of nasty sadism, perhaps? This is a question, when we consider that these same people when they were younger had no such sympathy for the men, women, and children, the healthy and the sick, the young and the old that they harshly treated (including murder, in many cases). Not that cruel behavior should be taken as a model to follow!

If we look at what happens during such trials, we may notice another feature of the whole process. Yes, there is the confrontation of the legal system challenging these people and accusing them of criminal acts from long ago. And in trials that respect Western legal procedures, the accused can give voice to their understanding of that past long-ago, or not.[1631]

[1630] Michael Brettin & Peter Kroh, *Berlin 1945: World War II. Photographs of the Aftermath: Pictures from Berliner Verlag and Soviet Army Archives* (2014), p. 195.
[1631] For example, in the trial under German law of Ivan (John) Demjanjuk, a

While that is certainly at the center of any trial, something else resulted from such legal proceedings. What remained were the transcripts of the trials, the questions asked, the documents presented for inclusion in the trials' records, the answers supplied (when they were). This means that there was a recorded, often printed, trace of what was discussed during these trials, what was alleged to have happened, the viewpoints, opinions, explanations, and justifications of the people involved. All of these provide information that can later be read, reviewed, considered carefully, judged, and explained, for an indefinite time into the future, for those who would be interested in investigating some of the specific actions and events that were deemed of significance during those trials.

Individuals had to face charges that were unpleasant, and yet those trials created records for future generations to have access to. *The courts and their transcripts may have a great value for those not even born at the time of those trials.* As an old Sufi expression puts it, "Talk to the wall so the door can hear."[1632] Here, the exchanges between the court and the accused will allow others from around the world and through the years and decades, if not centuries, to come face to face with the events of those earlier times. For example, through the Demjanjuk Trial, *new principles and precedents for international law, especially focusing on the issues of war crimes, crimes against humanity and genocide, have come to be recognized*, with more refined criteria for war crimes, including violations of the principles of distinction (where combatants distinguish between enemy combatants and civilians) and proportionality (keeping civilian losses at a minimum relative to direct military targets).[1633]

The Nuremberg Tribunal and Legal Issues of Precedence

Perhaps most recognized among these various post-war trials are those that took place in Nuremberg, the earlier honored city of early

---

Ukrainian who worked at the Sobibór and Majdanek death camps, Demjanjuk remained mute throughout the trial. He was convicted on May 12, 2011, as an accessory to the murder of 27,000 Jews at Sobibór. He appealed the conviction, but died (March 12, 2012, aged 91, before that appeal could be heard and adjudicated. Significantly, *a new principle of international law* was established in this trial: *active participation in an institution (in this case, the Extermination Camp whose very essence is the efficient killing of people) was held to be grounds for guilt in the criminal functions of that institution*. This principle has now been established for future application (not only for Nazi crimes of the 1930s and 1940s). For further discussion, see Lawrence Douglas, *The Right Wrong Man: John Demjanjuk and the Last Great Nazi War Crimes Trial* (2016).

[1632] Idries Shah, *Tales of the Dervishes: Teaching-stories of the Sufi Masters over the Past Thousand Years* (1967), p. 116.

[1633] "Yemen conflict: UN experts detail possible war crimes by all parties," *BBC News*, Aug. 28, 2018. On International Humanitarian Law (IHL), consider such documents as the 1977 Additional Protocols to the Geneva Conventions Protocol I and II, with discussion in Marco Alberto Velásquez-Ruiz, "The Principles of Distinction and Proportionality under the Framework of International Criminal Responsibility—Content and Issues, International Law," *Revista Colombiana de Derecho Internacional*, No. 14 (2009), pp. 15-42, Scielo.org.co.

modern German culture, and then the location of most of the National Socialist Party Rallies that preceded World War II. Here, the Nuremberg Tribunal with its various trials against major war criminals is helpfully considered in its historical context of pre-1933 international criminal law.

In the introductory comments to this book, we mentioned a rather large, impressive set of documents gathered by the UNWCC (United Nations War Crimes Commission) from representatives of 26 countries, with more than 2,240 UNWCC documents, on a total of 22,184 pages, concerning more than 36,000 international criminal cases, and then noted that these had been kept as closed files until 2013, for more than sixty-five years. Let us consider now how and for which reasons these were suppressed from public awareness for so long. The holding of these documents in closed files (among others) was in part because of the influence of a political position taken in Western Allied countries, especially the USA, *holding that these issues and files if released would be damaging to the rehabilitation of Germany (West Germany) in the recently developed hostility between Western Allies and the Soviet Union*, and especially by the US Central Intelligence Agency (the CIA), with its much greater focus on anti-Communism and its strong interest in keeping some of its more secret operations from being subject to scrutiny and indictment by any international judicial power.[1634] It was argued that some charges in the Nuremberg Trials were for actions that were not crimes at the time; others recognized there was an earlier international understanding of war crimes, identifying the mistreatment of POWs, but, Jews, Romanies, and others who were mistreated and killed were not POWs, so their being killed was not against established international law.

Pre-1933 International Criminal Law

We might forget in all of this debate that we are talking about large sets of actions that individually are, and have been, seen as crimes for millennia. *Killing did not become a new crime with the Third Reich*, nor did assault (attacking or threatening to attach) and battery (actually physically harming). Aggravated assault (as in the treatment of anti-Nazis by the SA, the SS, and other Nazi organizations) was already a well-recognized crime throughout the world. While there may be a relatively new vocabulary that was brought into common use during and especially

---

[1634] Paired with *negligible US economic aid or focus on human-rights abuses (a practice that—significantly—continues to this day)* are CIA and related US military operations aimed at influencing the national affairs of Iran (1953), Guatemala (1954), Laos (1955-1974), Indonesia (1958), Cuba (1964), Chile (1973), Jamaica and Guyana (1976), Grenada (1983), Panama (1989-1990), among other interventionist actions: See Anthony Lake and Roger Morris, "The Human Reality of Realpolitik," *Foreign Policy*, no. 4, 1971, pp. 157–162; Casey Gane-McCalla, *Inside the CIA's Secret War in Jamaica* (2016); *Massacre at the Stadium* (2019), a film on the 1973 killings and torture at the Estadio Nacional de Chile in Santiago. Cf. all of the following found at CIA site, CIA.GOV: "Central Intelligence Agency, Timeline," and, authored by William M. Leary, "CIA Air Operations in Laos, 1955-1974," "CIA role in Chile exposed," and "Destabilization in the Carribean."

after the violent machinations of the Third Reich, *these basic component actions were already widely recognized for centuries as crimes*, even if the new concepts of Genocide and Crimes Against Humanity put those various actions into a new vocabulary with new defining features: these are based firmly on what were, and are, recognized as crimes. These considerations largely undermine the claim that new crimes were being invented; rather, there were *old, well known crimes that are now being considered in their much greater extension and international impact*. This goes against the maxim of François-Marie Arouet, known as Voltaire (1694-1778), "Here is a case of law to consider: It is prohibited to kill; every killer is punished, unless he has killed in great military campaigns, and to the sound of trumpets. This is the rule."[1635] Here, in contrast, mass killings are recognized as being greater crimes than single murders.

In a more general way, the world has certainly seen the rights and obligations of all members of society, respected in various ways in cultures already in the ancient world, as in the *Vedas* and *Dharmaśāstra* (*Dharmashastra*) of ancient India, the *Babylonian Code of Hammurabi*, the *Analects of Confucius*, the discourses of the Buddha (such as in the collection of verse teachings, the *Dhammapada*), and in the Hebrew and Christian Bibles and the Qur'an, as well as the discussions of the rights, protections, privileges, and obligations of the members of a society that were part of the Inca, Aztec, and Iroquois nations (with its Constitution) as codes of conduct and justice,[1636] complemented by legal instruments in various countries, such as the *Magna Carta* (1215), the English *Bill of Rights* (1689), the French *Declaration on the Rights of Man and Citizen* (1789), the US Constitution and its first ten amendments, the Bill of Rights (1791), precursors to current interest in universal human rights.

CUSTOMARY INTERNATIONAL LAW

In addition to such formalized discussions of this issue, there is the legal recognition of law as established through acceptance by the society in its customs, reflecting values to be adhered to and recognized, as part of common law practice, and referred to as Customary International Law. The recognition of Customary International Law adds an important dimension to the discussion of how a continuation of early international criminal principles was embodied in the Nuremberg Tribunal and its various trials. These considerations strongly suggest that we do not have here a radical departure from what in legal circles were recognized as valid principles for the operation of international criminal law: the issue of human rights and what is recognized as proper interactions among people and peoples was not born *ex nihilo*, out of a void, in 1945. A sense

---

[1635] Voltaire, *Dictionnaire philosophique* (1764), from the entry: *DROIT. Droit des gens, droit natural, Section première*.

[1636] Louise Burkhart, "Nahua Moral Philosophy," AZTECS AT MEXICOLORE; Ralph Miller, "The Inca Way of Life: To Live In A Better Way," HEARTOFTHEINITIATE.COM; Gerald Murphy, "About the Iroquois Constitution," SOURCEBOOKS.FORDHAM.EDU.

of minimal propriety in our behavior, in our ways of interacting, locally and internationally, is *something that lies deep in our societal universe that goes back into the mists of time*. In any case, these issues are not a creation of World War II, although perhaps some will credit Hitler with bringing these issues into much greater prominence in our thinking about our world and how we might best carry on in our relations with one another (individually, socially, nationally, internationally, globally).[1637] Furthermore, in the years since 1945, a number of crimes have been formulated and are now recognized throughout the world, through formal declarations, treaties, and other instruments of the law. A related topic of discussion starts from holding that the taking of the property of conquered countries is an age-honored practice, going back to the ancient world: the right of the victor to booty, in all forms, as desired by those now in control. And, yet, there are traditions in international law on these issues, as well. For example, there is a tradition that discusses the rights and limits of expropriation (the taking of property by a government).[1638] *There were definite limits on what was considered allowable, and what transgressed those limits.* To focus on the international political situation after the fall of the Third Reich (and the Japanese Empire), especially as it manifested itself in the USA: Joseph McCarthy (1908-1957), Republican Senator from Wisconsin (1947-1957)—who gave birth to the term McCarthyism, with its smear campaigns that radically altered the lives of a number of prominent individuals, including black lists such as the Hollywood black list, which led to a number of respected writers being refused work in the USA; some were sent to prison for Contempt of Congress, some had to go abroad to find work, and others used fronts to present their work in a camouflaged way, McCarthyism, with its incendiary and demagogic attacks on those he suspected of being Communist agents—claimed there was a significant number of "card-carrying" members of the Communist Party in the State Department, in the US Army, in organizations such as the ACLU (American Civil Liberties Union), among teachers, university professors, members of the entertainment industry seen as localized in Hollywood, and on and on.[1639]

[1637] See Mark Mazower, "The Strange Triumph of Human Rights, 1933-1950," *The Historical Journal*, vol. 17, no. 2, 2004, pp. 379-398; cf. the overview in Dan Plesch and Shanti Sattler, "Changing the Paradigm of International Criminal Law: Considering the Work of the United Nations War Crimes Commission of 1943-1948," *International Community Law Review*, vol. 15, no. 2, 2013, pp. 203-223.

[1638] See B. A. Wortley, Geoffrey Cheshire, R. K. Kuratowski, Alfred Drucker, Erwin H. Loewenfeld, W. Adamkiewicz, & Alexander Weinreb, "Expropriation in International Law," *Transactions of the Grotius Society (aka the Society of Comparative Legislation, London)*, vol. 33 (1947), pp. 25-48.

[1639] "McCarthyism & Blacklisting," LIB.BERKELEY.EDU; *The Hollywood Ten* (1950), BING.COM; *The Front* (1976). Cf. President Truman on not transforming "our fine FBI into a Gestapo secret police … not going to turn the United States into a right-wing totalitarian country in order to deal with a left-wing totalitarian threat" (in his "Address at a Dinner of the Fed. Bar Assoc., Apr. 24, 1950," TRUMANLIBRARY.ORG).

In this heated context, McCarthy sent a telegram to President Truman (February 11, 1950), repeating his statement from a speech days earlier that "the State Department harbors a nest of Communist and Communist sympathizers who are helping to shape our foreign policy" and that he had a list of 57 Communists in the State Department, telling Truman that he should demand that Acheson give a full accounting of the Communist infiltration in the State Department.[1640] In reply, Truman drafted a letter, which he did not finalize or mail out, calling McCarthy's telegram "an insolent approach."[1641] Truman did send a letter dated March 31, 1950, to Secretary of State Dean Acheson and members of the State Department, who had resisted Roosevelt's attempts to bring attention to the plight of European victims of Nazi atrocities, especially European Jews, a State Department many of whose members were seen as being more interested in focusing on "the Communist threat" (to use a phrase of the period) rather than in prosecuting Nazi war criminals. Truman wrote, "Privately I refer to McCarthy as a pathological liar."

We can also perhaps appreciate the strong interest by those who had domestic issues including the suppression of American blacks (with often totally arbitrary and promiscuous beatings, drownings, and hangings) in removing German war crimes from a national or worldwide focus on those crimes, with trials ongoing—after all, if extralegal murders by Nazis in Germany were to be taken to be indictable crimes, then perhaps the same should apply to those in the USA taking violence and murder as their extra-legal rights. Here, there may be a strong mutual interaction between international and national processes. While there were strong vested interests in downplaying the focus on and legal prosecution of Nazi war criminals (in large part based on a new concern with confronting the Soviet Union, once the war against the Third Reich was won), there were also those in the US government who saw a great value in following through with these legal proceedings. ("Justice, justice, shall you pursue" as was said at Deuteronomy 16:20, also spoken of as righteousness, as at Matthew 5;6, Romans 14:17, 2 Corinthians 9:9, James 1:20, and elsewhere.[1642]) Among those in the US government who spoke out on the barbarity of the Nazi regime in Europe and on the importance of making use of the vast documentation mostly by Europeans about these war crimes and crimes against humanity was Herbert Claiborne Pell, Jr. (1884-1961). Pell was a member of the US House of Representatives (1919-1921; Democrat, New York) and then US Ambassador to Portugal (1937-1941) and to Hungary (1941-1942), after which he was also a member of the United Nations War Crimes Commission (UNWCC), many of whose

---

[1640] "Telegram, Joseph McCarthy to Harry S. Truman, February 11, 1950, with Truman's Draft Reply," TRUMANLIBRARY.ORG, pp. 2-7.

[1641] "Telegram, Joseph McCarthy to Harry S. Truman" (just cited), p. 1.

[1642] John J. Parsons, "The Call for Righteousness: Further Thoughts on Parshat Shoftim," HEBREW4CHRISTIANS.COM; Joseph A. Grassi, *Informing the Future: Social Justice in the New Testament* (2003).

documents are significant to our focus. Pell wrote to Congress, commenting on the US State Department and its anti-Semitic stance during the Nazi Years.[1643] As part of these politically motivated actions, much evidence that was relevant to the trials at Nuremberg and elsewhere was not made available to the prosecution teams. Among the documents *put into closed files, sequestered for many decades*, many were released (made public) after years of procedures and demands by scholars Dan Plesch and Shanti Sattler.[1644] These two prevailed upon diplomats, including US Ambassador to the UN, Samantha Power,[1645] who pushed for the release of these documents, leading to the public availability of these documents some seventy years after the UNWCC collected information for future war crimes trials.[1646] One item that was picked up by news services in reviewing the 2017 publication by Dan Plesch[1647] noted that there was a document revealed there that had been submitted to the UN War Crimes Commission by Czechoslovakia (as a Government-in-exile), dated December 15, 1944, with mention of Nazi crimes including murder, massacres, and systematic terrorism, that the Czech Commission had presented a first list of war criminals that same month, and that by March 1945, the Commission had put forth at least seven separate indictments against Hitler for war crimes (while Hitler was still alive).[1648] *What happened to various Nazis was quite inconsistent.* Some were arrested (if found) and put on trial for war crimes. Others were protected by those who sympathized with the social values that the Nazis and their collaborators were carrying out. Some of these were

---

[1643] See extended discussion in "Dan Plesch: The Lost History of Prosecuting Axis War Crimes," *Carnegie Council for Ethics in International Affairs*, Mar. 15, 2018, esp. 2:45-7:20, 30:40-32:30, and Dan Plesch, *Human Rights After Hitler: The Lost History of Prosecuting Axis War Crimes* (2017), pp. 127-128, 143, 148, 160-171, 181, 194-196. Dan Plesch is War Crimes Project Dir., and Dir. of the Centre for Internat'l Studies and Diplomacy, SOAS/School of Oriental and African Studies.

[1644] Shanti Sattler: War Crimes Project Assistant Director, Univ. of London.

[1645] Samantha Power: Irish-born, graduate of Yale Univ. and Harvard Law School; US Ambassador to the United Nations, 2013-2017.

[1646] On documents kept under wraps, unavailable to scholars, researchers, and the general public, see "UN War Crimes Commission's archive is now available in the ICC Legal Tools Database," *International Criminal Court*, Jul. 4, 2013; Dan Plesch and Shanti Sattler, "Changing the Paradigm of International Criminal Law: Considering the Work of the United Nations War Crimes Commission of 1943-1948," *International Community Law Review*, vol. 15, no. 2, 2013, pp. 203-223; William Schabas, Carsten Stahn, Joseph Powderly, Dan Plesch, and Shanti Sattler, "The United Nations War Crimes Commission and the Origins on International Criminal Justice," *Criminal Law Forum*, Jun. 2014, pp. 1-7; Owen Bowcott, "Opening of UN files on Holocaust will 'rewrite chapters of history'," *The Guardian*, Apr. 17, 2017; Melissa Coade, "Archive sheds historic light on UN war crimes files," *Lawyers Weekly*, Apr. 27, 2017.

[1647] Dan Plesch, *Human Rights After Hitler: The Lost History of Prosecuting Axis War Crimes* (2017).

[1648] Samuel Osborne, "UN indicted Adolf Hitler for war crimes before his death, secret documents reveal," *The Independent* (London), Apr. 19, 2017.

private individuals, but there were also organizations that helped former Nazis (presumable criminals) to stay in hiding or to escape Europe, often to South America. There was the famous Ratline, established by the Vatican, as mentioned just above. In addition, the US and the USSR were interested in having the help of various individuals in what soon turned into a hostile relationship between East and West (with the naming of that difference as the Iron Curtain, Churchill's phrase perhaps intending to imply that it was the Soviet Union that was clearly responsible for this ending of the relationship as allies against the Reich). The reasons for these hostilities influenced the post-war situation, with the various nations *each having its own national interests in the foreground of any decision-making*. Agents were developed who could help the intelligence (or spy) service of these different countries in their national security interests. Both the US and the USSR made use of such expertise, each in its own way. Furthermore, there was the issue of advanced military expertise. There was an interest in finding who was most knowledgeable about such things as the V-2 Rockets and rocketry in general. One of the key members of this program, Wernher von Braun (1912-1977), had been involved in research for the Heinkel group in liquid-fueled rockets. Von Braun became head of the NASA program and director of the moon landing (begun by President Kennedy), and realized on July 20, 1969, during the Nixon presidency. In the larger scheme of things, *there was a tension that began in the late 1940s that lasted for much of the rest of the twentieth-century*. This polarity with its own built-in fears and hostilities also led to the development of "neutral countries" (which maintained their independence from either of the two major spheres of influence). Tito in Yugoslavia and Nasser in Egypt were rare examples of statesmen balancing relationships between the West and the Communist East. In the current situation, with governments claiming autonomy, irrespective of how its own citizens are treated, with the demand that other countries have no say whatever in any internal concerns that might arise, we are perhaps not much beyond the situation in the world during the 1930s. People are certainly mistreated, even ostracized, beaten, or killed, even in today's world. Can we develop a moral sense that honors and respects all people? Elie Wiesel said in 1986,

> Neutrality helps the oppressor, never the victim. Silence encourages the tormentor, never the tormented. Sometimes we must interfere. When human lives are endangered, when human dignity is in jeopardy, national borders and sensitivities become irrelevant. Wherever men or women are persecuted because of their race, religion, or political views, that place must—at that moment—become the center of the universe.[1649]

[1649] Elie Wiesel, "Acceptance Speech on the award of the Nobel Prize," NOBEL PRIZE.

15. Yesterday, Today, and Tomorrow

The violence of the regime of the Third Reich had ramifications that impacted hundreds of millions of people. Even if we focus on just those who had a personal, familial relationship with those involved—both the key members of the Reich and its violent establishment and also those relatively few who survived from the camps—we can see that people responded to what they experienced, or, in later generations, to what the learned had happened to their ancestors. There are documentaries that interview a number of the children and other relatives of Nazi leaders of the organized killings.[1650] The torments of these surviving relatives, even though dealt with in a variety of ways, was a legacy they each inherited, leading them to come to know that they were family of some rather unusually violent men. Some would want to change their names, or would want to sterilize themselves, or to use their lives to compensate for the heartless violence of their ancestors, as the daughter of Albert Speer, Hilde Schramm[1651]—while others would strive to preserve the honorable memory in question, unbesmirched by anything negative.[1652]

These who did not inherit the guilt of their elders (while others might hold the same attitude and continue that murderous hatred) show another way in which descendants can suffer from the past, although innocent of the enormous guilt (if not sins) of their predecessors: One author wrote, "The innocents most burdened by the past are the children of survivors and the children of former Nazi officials or war veterans."[1653] Descendants can sense the importance of this issue for the family through the generations, rather than a literal "inheritance" of guilt. In this there is perhaps a balance to be reached: seeing the past with the guilt of earlier generations, without shutting down discussion (in German, *Schlussstrich*), which Chancellor Merkel spoke out against in 2014.[1654]

THE POST-SHOCK TURBULENCES OF THE NEXT CENTURY

We may find many indications that while the Hitler era, the Nazi years, in an obvious way came to an end in 1945, yet in another way, we may also recognize that our awareness and sensitivities have been strongly informed (given form) by the period of the Third Reich. One such

---

[1650] *Hitler's Children* (2012) interviews families of Hans Frank (Hitler's attorney and Governor General of occupied Poland), Hermann Göring, Amon Goeth (commandant of the Kraków-Płaszów Concentration Camp), Heinrich Himmler, and Rudolf Höss (commandant of Auschwitz I and II (the extermination camp, Birkenau). There is another German film (2001) by the same title with a different focus, the education of the young Germans in the *Hitlerjungend*. On the impact on 3rd-generation Germans, see *Descendants of Nazis: An Infernal Legacy* (2011).
[1651] "Hilde Schramm," WIKIPEDIA; Abby d'Arcy, "Speer's daughter and the Syrian refugees," *BBC World Service*, Sep. 11, 2015, BBC.COM.
[1652] Ties Ramekers, "Hoe verging het de kinderen van bekende nazi-leiders?" ("How did the children of famous Nazi leaders fare?"), HISTORIEK.NET.
[1653] Alfons Heck, *The Burden of Hitler's Legacy*, p. 243.
[1654] "Merkel erteilt „Schlussstrich"-Denken eine Absage," Jul. 1, 2014, *welt.de*.

manifestation of this is in the way in which refugees and those seeking asylum are treated in recent years, as compared with the way Jews were treated in the 1930s. (Here we have the example of the Évian Conference of summer 1939, in which no country—except a limited invitation to Jews by the Dominican Republic (discussed above)—made any specific commitment to allow in any Jews at all in those times of great persecution—even before the mass killings began: and later, after *Kristallnacht*, the main country to step forward was the UK, certainly not the USA.) In a second, related film narrative, *What Our Fathers Did: A Nazi Legacy* (2015), we see interviews and discussions with Niklas Frank and Horst von Wächter.

These are sons of Nazi war criminals: Hans Frank was head of the *Gouvernement General* within which Auschwitz-Birkenau and a number of extermination camps in eastern Poland operated. Otto von Wächter was governor of Kraków, whom the post-war Polish government claimed was responsible for the death of more than one hundred thousand Poles; he was given refuge by the Vatican and died before he could be brought to trial. The rather different attitudes of these two sons toward their fathers is rather striking. Niklas Frank stated that his father committed horrible war crimes; Horst von Wächter focused intently on his son's love for his father, and would not address the question of whether his father was (also) guilty of great crimes against hundreds of thousands of civilians in eastern Europe. For this, in part, Wächter cites the Jewish commandment,[1655] that thou shalt love thy father and thy mother (in what is perhaps a terribly ironic use of Jewish teachings in such a context).

To consider those who survived the camps, and their descendants, they, too, had a range of attitudes that they developed. In the 2012 film, *Numbered*,[1656] which presented a number of survivors of the tattooing of numbers on the left forearm (something done in Auschwitz for those who were determined to be capable of work, at least temporarily, rather than being sent straight to the gas chambers and then to the crematoria with their immense chimneys belching the smoke of burned flesh), and their descendants, we see some who want to remove the number, being mocked by those who claimed that only the most cruel and insensitive survived, given the camp conditions, to others who felt the number to be a badge of honor, of being a survivor. Some were firm that the shame belonged not to them for being tattooed, but to those who had done the tattooing. Others felt the relevance, appropriateness, and importance of

---

[1655] In the Hebrew bible, in the Torah, this is the fifth commandment, found at Exodus 20:12. This is a conditional commandment, with a reason for following it explicitly given, which has basically nothing to do with what von Wächter was talking about; in any case, his love and desire to honor his father clearly trumps for him any issue distancing himself from his father's murderous role. Two later teachings are relevant here: one is that a parent should so act as to inspire respect; the second is that one can honor one's parents as one's progenitors, one's source of life, without honoring their harmful and even evil actions.

[1656] This 2012 film *Numbered* was directed by Uriel Sinau and Dana Doron.

finding joy: life being a one-time gift. Some joked lightly of the fact that by tattooing the left forearm, the right arm was left free to do a Hitler salute. Here we are considering a very select and limited groups of people impacted by the genocidal activities of the Third Reich or people otherwise impacted by living under terrorist regimes and violence within the civilian sectors of society.

In such a synoptic overview, there are also the millions of soldiers and other people directly involved in the military actions in various war theatres across the globe during World War II, and also the families and friends of all of those who partook of those actions, including many who would live with those who had been wounded or who suffered severe psychological traumas, and those who survived those killed in battle.

One remaining remembrance is contained in the cemeteries and memorial structures found in many countries. A 1956 publication, *Cambridge American Cemetery and Memorial*, from the American Battle Monuments Commission,[1657] shows World War I and II cemeteries and memorials in northern Europe:

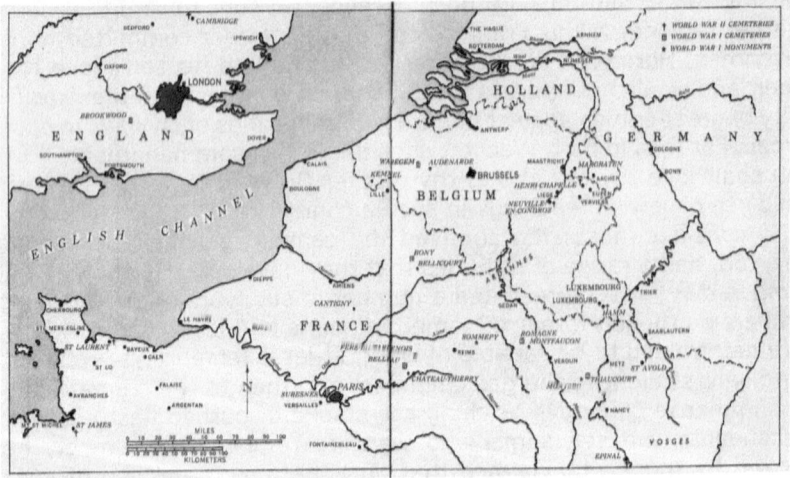

Cemeteries and Memorials in Northern Europe (1956)

It may be obvious that memorials concerning the war and the Third Reich are dedicated to the victims of Nazi policies, both in Germany, and, certainly, in other lands where millions were killed.

But there is also the question of what do with locations that are associated with the Reich and its power, not where massive killings took place, but which nonetheless can carry historical significance. For example, one issue was what to do with the house where Hitler was born, or with Hitler's Bavarian retreat of the Berghof at Berchtesgaden. The issue is whether to demolish and destroy everything that could be identified with that immense residence (with its underground bunker included) or to

---

[1657] This commission was established by the US Congress, March 1923.

mark the area. If so, in a country now that does not want to glorify Nazism and Hitlerism in any way whatsoever, how can it be made clear that the memorial is to remember atrocities and savagery and not to glorify them?[1658]

If we look in some specificity to present-day Germany, we can see (as elsewhere in other countries) neo-Nazism, a resurgence of Nazi ideology, especially of its xenophobia. This at times is anti-Semitic or anti-Romani in focus, but other neo-Nazi groups may be galvanized around a hatred of foreigners from particular neighboring countries, or by a generalized hatred of strangers, frequently accompanied by violence and killing. In these past decades, there have been skinheads and other Neo-Nazis in Germany (especially in former East Germany) and in Russia, Belarus, Ukraine, and other lands of the former USSR, as well as Neo-Nazis around the world, in the USA, Britain, France, Italy, Spain, Greece, Austria, Hungary, the Czech Republic, Slovakia, Slovenia, Bulgaria, Herzegovina, Serbia, Croatia, Bosnia, Lithuania, Estonia, Latvia, in Argentina, Brazil, Chile, Venezuela, Colombia, Ecuador; in Australia, in Mongolia, Nepal, Japan, and elsewhere. The possibility of cultivating hatred and rage against one group or another has not ended, and will perhaps never be confined to the past. In this way, there are the recurring questions of *what to do with our urges and hostile inclinations, and of how to come to deal better with our own frustrations than through expressions of rage and consequent violence.*

On many levels, we do not teach this calmer and more efficient way to deal with our inner turbulence in any systematic or effective way. When a parent in frustration sees that a child is *doing* something that the parent does not want done, or is *not doing* something the parent instructs the child to do, and responds with yelling, insulting, threatening a physical attack, or carrying out some form of violence, as in slapping or beating, or in verbally insulting or denigrating the child, then the child is not given much of a chance to learn to deal wisely with tension and disagreement.

While a young child is not in the best position to deal elegantly with this aggression (given a child's limited understanding of why people do what they do), the means to deal skillfully with such tensions has been developed in the past decades, often under the term NVC (Nonviolent Communication). This is quite a thorough approach; here, we might say that *at its core is the principle that behind insult and violence is a person's (or a group's) unmet, often non-acknowledged needs*. The path to mutual understanding here involves going beyond the insult or threats to what is going on in terms of needs unmet or threats experienced (although not explicit in the insult or aggressive speech or actions). To describe this sort of process, as here, is quite bland compared to seeing the impact that this approach can have when brought into practice. A main proponent of this approach, Marshall Rosenberg, who worked in the tradition of

---

[1658] See discussion of this issue in Timothy W. Ryback and Florian M. Beierl, "A damnation of memory," *The International Herald Tribune*, Feb. 13, 2001.

Mohandas (or Mahātma) Gandhi and Martin Luther King, Jr., was a mediator with a background in Clinical Psychology. Rosenberg worked for almost half a century with groups having intense mutual hatreds, from Ireland, to Israel and the Palestinian lands, to the Balkans, to Africa, and to South Asia, in a large number of areas of conflict where he has offered his approach to conflict and to conflict resolution (NVC), whose immediate interest is in determining the needs of the people in conflict, what they have experienced, what they feel lacking in the situation and its interactions. This process can lead to a sense of connectedness between the people involved, when they feel that they are understood, and when they understand the others, allowing an interest in allowing *everyone's needs* to be met, where *everyone* does whatever he does, willingly.[1659]

We can look still further into the consequences of the Nazi era. Beyond those in the middle of that vortex, there are the millions who lived through the Hitler era, both those subjugated by the Reich and those who lived within the Reich as Germans. For decades in Germany, for example, there was a hushed silence about what had been done by the young adults during the Third Reich who were now parents of the next generation. Those who attempted to investigate such matters were not welcomed with warmth and enthusiasm. A film portrayal of this in a small German town after the war, with more than one secret to want to keep hidden, was *Das schreckliche Mädchen* (*The Nasty Girl*).[1660]

In other countries, there was a lack of ease at discussing anything that resembled collaboration with the Nazi enemy. The instance of the French avoiding that history in various ways, such as not having classes in school go to World War II ("Oops! Sorry! We somehow let the semester fly by with our detailed analysis of earlier periods of French and European history!") and with politicians not touching the subject for decades.

The collaboration that took place by some in Eastern European countries was considered an insult to the fact that so many in so many countries were tortured, starved, killed, and otherwise intensely mistreated, even if managing to survive.

It is as if a country wants to present itself as absolutely pure with not even one instance of one person who committed criticizable actions. There

---

[1659] Among his presentations of NVC are *Nonviolent Communication: A Language of Life* (2003), and videos *Nonviolent Communication with Marshall Rosenberg: A Brief Introduction*, YOUTUBE, and *Marshall Rosenberg: The Purpose of Nonviolent Communication*, YOUTUBE. Other videos of teachers with kindred orientations include Ken Butigan, *Mainstreaming Nonviolence*, YOUTUBE; Amy Scott, *Build don't break relationships with communication*, YOUTUBE, etc. More on NVC below.

[1660] This 1990 film directed by Michael Verhoeven was based on a true story of a young German student named Anna Elisabeth Rosmus (born 1960), who was raised and educated in Passau, Bavaria. Her 1993 dissertation at the Univ. of Passau, *Gedenkstätten für die Opfer des Nationalsozialismus in der Region Passau* (*Memorials for the victims of National Socialism in the region of Passau*) was followed by published books: *Against the Stream: Growing Up Where Hitler Used to Live* (2002), *Out of Passau: Leaving a City Hitler Called Home* (2004), and *Wintergreen: Suppressed Murders* (2004).

The Hitler Era

is at times little interest in nuanced analyses that allow the people of each country to understand what happened and what didn't. (Our imagined ogres are often more horrible that the realities we might be inclined to avoid, even if perhaps remaining heavily depressing).

The families of millions of people traumatized by the war in any of a variety of ways are known to be dealing with the significance of those events and those experiences.

It may be that every single human being has had one trauma or another, but there are some events that are overwhelmingly intense and leave their mark, their psychological residue, alive and active, not only for those directly involved (in what some call primary trauma), but also those who experience those people, who hear about those shocking if not mind-boggling events, in what some call inherited or vicarious trauma, even if these terms are perhaps somewhat misleading.

Contact with present-day Germany and its citizens can quickly make it quite clear that the impact of the Nazi Years is still a significant feature of the current German population. In the first decades after the fall of the Third Reich, some young Germans left Germany and refused to return, even for a visit. Others were bewildered by what had happened, especially if they had not lived through that period themselves. Others would be defensive. More recently, some declare that they have done penance for a long enough time and needed to reassert their own worth, with some turning to neo-Nazi rituals in a modern dress (the so-called "skinheads" that have many from former East Germany, the German Democratic Republic or DDR as members; there are even skinheads in the former Soviet Union). In addition to that general phenomenon, which some fear to be a resurgence of theories of superiority and related violence against so-considered inferiors, there is serious investigation of the Nazi Era by German and other scholars and other researchers, having new material being made public by descendants of those who kept diaries or other records of the Nazi era, or that have been made available from formerly closed archives. For example, a ten-volume work on the German Military of the Second World War (Volume 1 itself is some 800 pages long), addressed itself to the "central part that Germany played in bringing about and waging the Second World War, with its far-reaching consequences for so many nations, and the heavy burdens endured by the German people itself during the war and subsequently." It noted, "It is a special responsibility of German historians to investigate these fateful events."[1661] German investigation and analysis of this period is at the forefront of ongoing research, even if other countries also contribute significant work here. (We may notice that Germany is not predominantly into denial, whitewashing, or self-justification, but is more interested in understanding this remarkable and horrendous past: I find this to be one promising model of a search for truth.)

[1661] Militärgeschichtliches Forschungsampt (Research Institute for Military History), *Germany and the Second World War, Volume I*, Preface to the German Edition, p. ix.

When we hear of new violence, it is now with a backdrop of the earlier traumas, death, incapacitation, starvation, serious illness, and other forms of threatening experiences. From the trench warfare on the Western Front in World War I, we have the memory of massive killing with effective machine guns and artillery and cannons and rockets, and, from World War II, the factory-efficient killing and related establishment of disregard for human dignity and rights. The world has been traumatized by two astonishly violent wars (some call them together the twentieth-century's Thirty Years' War).[1662]

The plight of those who were trapped in the territories under the control of the Third Reich during the 1930s and early 1940s was an unsettling and unsettled matter. The world in later decades would advocate at least token action for the protection of refugees, considering the plight of Jews, and others, in the years 1933-1945. The 145 nations that signed the 1951 Refugee Convention,[1663] under the auspices of the United Nations Refugee Agency (UNHCR), established certain basic rights of refugees and obligations of the signatory nations, including the obligation not to send refugees back to countries where their lives would be in danger, setting some limits on how countries around the world treat refugees who have fled their native lands under great duress.

When we consider some of the globally significant events of the past years, we might appreciate that these relatively contemporary events are strongly influenced if not structured by what happened the greater part of a century ago. The treatment of Jews and others by the Reich and collaborative nations has perhaps brought to our general attention the plight of many around the world, even today. When we look at situations that are driving people away from their homelands (such as persecution of a given group, or a civil war that does not allow a peaceful and secure life), and we see these people seeking refuge from the violence of hostility they were experiencing, we may see that the world does not treat these in quite the same way as the Jews were treated in the 1930s. We can see a change from the Évian Conference of 1938, where almost no nation was ready to make any specific commitment to helping Jewish refugees at all, compared to how we now see nations opening their doors (some in a limited way—but anything is more than zero) to those in dire distress.

When we see what is now called ethnic cleansing (as in the former Yugoslavia in 1992-1995),[1664] we can see countries attempting to stop the blood-baths and even bringing some military leaders to trial (at the International Tribunal at The Hague). And this, even when the victims were Muslims. This does suggest a significant shift in world consciousness

---

[1662] Widespread war deaths left almost every family in Europe bereft: see Claudia Siebrecht, "Imagining the Absent Dead: Rituals of Bereavement and the Place of the War Dead in German Women's Art during the First World War," *German History*, GERMAN HISTORICAL SOCIETY, vol. 29, no. 2, Jun. 1, 2011, pp. 202-223.

[1663] "The 1951 Refugee Convention and 1967 Protocol," UNRA/UN REFUGEE AGENCY.

[1664] "The Bosnian War and Srebrenica Genocide," ENDGENOCIDE.ORG.

The Hitler Era

or awareness of violence against groups and the importance of attempting to intervene to minimize further loss of life, limb, and property. A question we might ask is whether the actions of a given nation would inspire us to say respectfully, "No country in the history of the world ever contributed more to the welfare of humankind in such a short period than did this nation."[1665] I suspect that few would cite the Third Reich here, even those who venerate Hitler and the Reich; Hitler himself might well have been insulted if anyone had proposed such a description to him.

And yet, at the same time, we see a new growth of the fundamental attitude of being firmly self-protective, self-defensive, derived in part from a sense of a limit to the goods of the world, as if someone else's presence in my land is preventing me from achieving what I would like to achieve. And while there is at least a thread of truth in this cautious and perhaps xenophobic attitude, *this is not the only consideration we have to face as human beings, as moral creatures with a sense of right and wrong*. Those who helped the victims who were attacked, badgered, arrested, and killed during the Hitler era were often doing what they did in spite of any consideration for their own well-being, in spite of the dangers posed to themselves and their families.[1666]

Often such people would make a simple remark by way of explanation that they were just being decent human beings, or just doing what they knew was right. We can often see in life that doing what is right is not always doing what is comfortable to do—that it may create animosity on the part of others, and perhaps bring on violence against us and those we love.

Those of us who have the luxury of living a relatively safe and secure existence may ask whether we would be ready to risk danger or threats in order to be of help to others in need.

DPs and Global Reverberations into the 1950s

As happened after the ending of World War I, there were also waves of celebration of relief in much of the world after the defeats of the Axis Powers that ended World War II, as well as the different set of issues that those nations who were defeated in the war had to face. In many if not most countries, there was a reluctance to look into the violence and the mass murders that took place during the war. The displacement of literally millions of people in concentration camps and slave labor meant there were remaining issues for such persons, called DPs (displaced persons).

The next years after the war saw the repatriation of many of these various nationals. Many fled countries where they were not welcome; ironically, going to Germany (especially to the areas administered by the Western Allies). As DPs, Jews in particular were often left stateless and

---

[1665] Eliana Rudee, "Alan Dershowitz on Israel at 70," JNS/Jewish News Syndicate, Mar. 20, 2018, quoting Harvard Law Professor Alan Dershowitz.

[1666] *No. 4 Street of Our Lady* (2009) retells the caring good-will and the protective and skilful bravery of Franciszka Halamajowa and her daughter, Helena Liniewska-Halamajowa, recognized as Righteous Among the Nations in 1984.

with no property remaining, so that DP camps by the late 1940s and early 1950s were predominantly populated by Jews.

Among the many post-war DP Camps for Jews were camps at Feldhafing (one of the first DP camps), Landsberg, Föhrenwald (or Foehrenwald, one of the largest, in Wolfratshausen, Upper Bavaria, closed in 1957), Tempelhof (in Berlin), and Bergen-Belsen (the concentration camp during the Third Reich that was later turned into a DP camp).[1667]

Furthermore, they were not always welcome back when they did return to where they had lived before the war. Aside from such problems, some survivors focused on following through on issues that the violence in the war raised, including the demands of the Allied Powers that those responsible be brought to face charges against them and to be dealt with appropriately (with some differences of opinion about what that might be). But others were more inclined to want to forget it all and get on with life. After so many years of dealing continually with the political and moral issues raised by the disturbing actions the world was (or was becoming) aware of, some wanted just to look elsewhere, and to look at what was reassuring, non-disturbing, and simple.

We can even see this in the politics and the popular entertainment of the 1940s and especially the 1950s. Politics became rigidified, with strong moralistic positions being taken by various factions. An anti-Communist attitude found in the USA, was spearheaded by Senator Joseph McCarthy in the Senate, and by HUAC (the House Un-American Action Committee) in the House, with freshman Congressman Richard M. Nixon coming to national attention in his vigorous role in those activities.[1668]

Questions arose about who was a collaborator with the Nazis, who might be useful in America's geopolitical conflict with the Soviet Union, who was a leftist, who might have been considered a loyal American during the war (when Stalin was referred to in a familial way as Uncle Joe) but would now have his loyalty to America put into serious question. Those who were seen as bystanders during the war were questioned for their lack of caring for those being oppressed by the Nazis, but there was a limit to the criticisms that could be expressed.

After all, remembering the passivity and non-involvement of the non-Nazi countries of the war, most clearly represented by the non-action and overall lack of commitment to being of aid in the Évian Conference, could easily vitiate otherwise vehement and passionate political positions. Western powers, for example, had perhaps more power to act than did the population of Poland under the regime of the Third Reich. In July 1978, film-maker Claude Lanzmann made a statement on this issue:

> The official Polish point of view on this issue—and I agree personally very much upon it—is that if there is any guilt

---

[1667] On the DP camps, see also Judith Nadich, *Eisenhower and the Jews* (1953).
[1668] "House Un-American Activities Committee," *The Eleanor Roosevelt Papers Project*, GEORGE WASHINGTON UNIVERSITY, WWW2.GWU.EDU.

of non-assistance to persons in danger [we may think here of European Jews, among others massacred by the Nazis], this guilt is to be found much more in the attitude of the Western World than in the Polish one.[1669]

The overall desire for something other than an omnipresent focus on violence, brutal regimes, and mass killings from during World War II, can even be seen in the 1950s world of popular music, with a predominance of sweet, simple, and reassuring themes expressed.

For example, in the US and also in the UK, songs tended to be cute, respectful, sentimental, pleasant, mundane, often with a touch of innocent relationships, with much talk of straight-forward romantic longings—dreams to be realized only after marriage—between men and women (boys and girls).

As examples of some lyrics from songs from the 1950s, UK: "You're a pink toothbrush, I'm a blue toothbrush, have we met somewhere before? You're a pink toothbrush and I think, toothbrush, that we met by the bathroom door. Glad to meet, toothbrush, such a sweet toothbrush."[1670] US: "They try to tell us we're too young, too young to really be in love. They say that love's a word a word we've only heard, but can't begin to know the meaning of."[1671] UK: "My son, my son, my son, my son, you're everything to me. My son, my son, you're all I hoped you'd be. My son, my son, my only pride and joy, God bless and keep you safe."[1672] And US: "Life could be a dream, life could be a dream, Do, do, do, do, sh-boom, Life could be a dream sh-boom, if I could take you up in paradise up above sh-boom, if you would tell me I'm the only one that you love, life could be a dream, sweetheart."[1673]

These were often pleasant, and some, heart-felt, inspiring, and respectful of traditional familial values. Some were trite; some were musically inventive, with unusual harmonies (as in the singing of the Everly Brothers).[1674]

This, in turn, would set the grounds for shifts in the 1960s, from the political realm (in the US, Eisenhower followed by John F. Kennedy), in the musical world (pop music stars like Doris Day, Perry Como, and others followed by Bob Dylan, Simon and Garfunkel, Joan Baez, Carole King, the Beatles, the Rolling Stones, Donovan, the Kinks, Cream, the Doors, and so on. We can sense in all of these waves of interests and values being

---

[1669] E. Thomas Wood and Stanisław M. Jankowski, *How One Man Tried to Stop the Holocaust*, p. 253. More on Lanzmann, below, in discussion of the film *Shoah* (1985).

[1670] Max Bygraves (1922-2012), British variety performer and pop singer, "You're a pink toothbruth lyrics" (1959), GENIUS.COM; "Max Bygraves," WIKIPEDIA.

[1671] "Too Young: Nat King Cole" (1951), GENIUS.COM.

[1672] "My son, my son; Vera Lynn" (1954), GENIUS.COM. Dame Vera Lynn was born Vera Margaret Welch.

[1673] "Sh-boom (Life Could Be A Dream)" (1958), GENIUS.COM.

[1674] Paul Simon, "The Everly Brothers," *Rolling Stone 100 Greatest Artists*, Dec. 2, 2010, ROLLINGSTONE.COM.

expressed and modified in an ongoing fluctuation, through what seem like haphazard shifts: the vicissitudes of style, societal values and mores, political and geopolitical concerns—a byzantine labyrinth of culture.

THE UNPRECEDENTED, UNBELIEVABLE ORGANIZED MASS KILLING OF JEWS

As Jan Karski, mentioned above, later commented, emphasizing the unprecedented nature of the genocide of the Jews of Europe, "A question could be asked ... Is there any comparison between what happened to the European Jews during the Second World War? Could it be compared with *any* happening in the past history? Whatever I know about history—totally unique! It was a problem in itself, unprecedented! ... Healthy humanity, rational humanity, which did not see with their own eyes, were not actually there—they had no precedent to compare it."[1675] Overall, there were 9.5 million Jews in Europe in 1930, and 3.5 million in 1950 (a difference of some six million Jews who died during those years). Before the war, 60% of the world's Jews lived in Europe; afterwards, only one third—in those years, some 30%-90% of their Jews were killed in some countries—with the majority living after the war in the Americas.[1676]

It may be hard for contemporaries to think that the entire world would not believe reports of the organized, mechanized and massive killing of the Jews of Europe simply because they were Jews. In today's world, there is the powerful memory of the Hitler era and the defined goal of exterminating the Jewish population in Europe. At the time, however, reports of these killings—a Holocaust by bullets with mass shooting of Jews in villages, forests, and ravines, and an industrialized massive gassings of Jews—sounded fantastic, a gross exaggeration attempting to gain sympathy for what could not possibly have taken place. The people of 1940s Europe were not obstinate, blind, or cold-hearted, but nothing in earlier history gave them a context in which such an aberration of civilization could be placed, understood, recognized, and dealt with as it certainly deserved to be dealt with. This incredulity was even stronger for those who had not lived under Nazi governmental control, who perhaps did not even see the war itself with their own eyes, but could only try to grasp what seemed to be only a horrible nightmare.

ARISTOTLE, NIETZSCHE, PERLS: GROUP COHESION TRUMPS MORAL ISSUES

With the killing of literally millions of people as a reflection of the hatred, disgust, and condescending brutality that the world experienced during the war-time Third Reich, we have a question of how it could be that an entire nation, in fact, several nations in consort, in coordinated action, could be so focused on killing and so diligent in their efforts, could be so content and even proud of what they were doing, as some would say of their actions, predicting that Europe would later be appreciative in retrospect of this great deed of purifying Christian Europe.

[1675] *Wednesday March 18th, Film by Claude Lanzmann: Jan Karski Report* (1979), YOUTUBE, at 58:45-1:00:00.

[1676] "The Holocaust: Facts and figures," *Haaretz*, Jul. 24, 2013; "Remaining Jewish Population of Europe in 1945," USHMM, THE HOLOCAUST ENCYCLOPEDIA.

The Hitler Era

As Brecht's Peachum acknowledged, the hearts of many can be made quite numb (*Unsinn*), at their will and whim. And Peachum (Brecht) stated this, on stage, even before the beginning of the Third Reich.

There are several aspects of this sort of process, and the eclipsing of any moral standards does not especially stand alone. While a strong foundation in one's beliefs helps, but not if in the education we are taught, and become convinced of, is that we as one people or group are superior to others and have rights over others (including, in the extreme case, rights over their lives, as we wish). Still, from feeling superior to organizing a systematic annihilation of those we deem inferior, dehumanized, is a big step. What can have us not only believe that we are superior and have rights over those who are quite inferior to us, but also has us ready and willing, if not eager, to focus our live energies on a massive killing process?

There is a very profound, that is, deep-rooted, sense in our species, at least in general, of our societal nature. Now, Aristotle spoke of the human as a political/societal animal: the Greek term *polītikós* refers to the *pólis*, the small, independent community that defined its own social legal framework, and for which the greatest punishment was banishment: making the person who had gone against basic values of the group leave and be on his own, an outcast, someone who might well be rejected by all human groups and be a target of their violence. This exclusion was a very frightening state to be forced into by one's society. This treatment came from a deep, even if intuitive, sense of the need of the person for a group to be a part of, and accepted by, if not held in honor there.

This is the social cohesion we touched upon earlier in the discussion here. This is hardly a new realization, but, as is often the case, if we take it into consideration, it has much less of an influence on us, if any. The important difference here between what we can be said to know or to believe, and what we think about in a given context, can give rise to thinking and acting that is consistent with some of our beliefs but which might go strongly against others that we are not considering in the given context. *This phenomenon has our thinking and our actions skewed or biased in one way or another, not balanced by taking all of what we know into account.* Some call this splitting. We may have situations in which sets of our beliefs are in conflict with one another and we focus on one, or do not consider others. In this light, *much of psychotherapy can be seen and understood as an attempt to allow us to make use of our full resources and all of the information we have potentially at our service.* There is information we know but that is not taken into account, unless we shift our focus to a broader awareness.

In one school of therapy, we can interpret the goal as being the integrating of all of our information, all of our tendencies, interests, and desires into harmony, into forming one form (or, using the German term, *Gestalt*), as in the psychotherapeutic approach of Fritz Perls (1893-1970)—a psychiatrist and analyst, who had studied at the Berlin Psychoanalytic Institute before it was taken over the National Socialist government in 1933—which he called Gestalt Psychotherapy.[1677] Or, in Virginia Satir's "parts" party, an aid in becoming congruent,[1678] there is focusing on the different parts of our overall psychological existence and seeing their interactions. A similar approach is found in the work of Italian psychoanalyst and family therapist Maurizio Andolfi, who is an expert in bringing focus to the differences within a family and then bringing these differences into communication with one another, in order to have a more nuanced, clear, explicit understanding of each family member's viewpoint and interests, bringing about greater awareness and mutual respect.[1679]

Millennia after the ancient Greek city-states and their concept of people as essentially political, Nietzsche suggested that mores, guidelines for thinking and action, have as a fundamental role the establishing of reliable expectations about how the members of the group (or society) will act. This set of shared expectations can encourage cooperation, mutual aid, reciprocal appreciation and acceptance among its members, and other benefits. In so far as this hampers or even totally eliminates our own self-determined sense of values, Nietzsche sees this process as introducing a fundamental incompatibility between the group-based morality and individual autonomy.[1680] When we apply this to the situation in Europe under the Third Reich with the pervasive attitude of hatred toward ("inferior") others and the taking of action against them, there is an element here that has its power and force without considering any moral issues about what is being encouraged.

Or, alternatively, there is a way of thinking about what is happening and what we are being encouraged to do that has us believe and feel that we are doing right, if not doing God's duty. A basic point beyond all of this is that if we act on the need for support and approval of what we are doing, then we may well be giving importance to group opinions over our own beliefs, intuitions, moral sense, or awareness of what our words and actions might mean about what kind of a person we are, or are becoming, that if we were to contemplate with a clear mind, we would see it to be actually abhorrent to us. But to do that, we have to be ready to question what our group is asking for us, at the risk of being rejected, and, in the case of violent societies and regimes, at the risk of being killed. This is at the same time a societal issue and also an individual, introspective one, with important stakes at play. From this, we can appreciate the courage that paying attention to our own full thinking and morality and sense of self-respect can lead to, in ways that can be literally life-threatening. It is

---

[1677] Frederick Perls, *Gestalt Therapy Verbatim* (1969), and *In and Out the Garbage Pail* (1969).

[1678] Virginia Satir, *The New Peoplemaking* (1988), p. 94; "Parts Party," SATIRWORKSHOPS.COM; Jesse Carlock, "The Solo Parts Party," *Satir International Journal*, vol. 3, no. 1, 2015, pp. 36-57.

[1679] Maurizio Andolfi, *Family Therapy: An Interactional Approach* (1979), *Behind the Family Mask: Therapeutic Change in Rigid Family Systems* (1983), and Maurizio Andolfi and Anna Mascellani, *Teen Voices: Tales from Family Therapy* (2013).

[1680] Friedrich Nietzsche, *On the Genealogy of Morals*, II.1-3.

for good reason that people who have turned out to be brave and guided by courage in such contexts deserve to be deeply respected. These are the individuals we can see as saintly or heroic, discussed more, below.

Post-War Films on the Third Reich and the Holocaust

The years immediately after the end of World War II had many of the European populations, survivors, bystanders, and perpetrators want to put the past behind, to keep from thinking about the horrors they and the world at large had lived through during the venomous and power-driven era of Hitler, to avoid dealing with their responsibility for many deaths, or their other roles in the period of Nazi domination of Europe. We may look at the history of Hitler era and the way what seemed so appealing to many Germans in National Socialism turned to a world of power, fear, threats, murders, and great mutual distrust—as in many a police state, where anyone could report what was said or even merely suspected to go against the thinking, speaking, and acting that were permitted by the government; even fabricating stories for personal vendettas).

We may compare the films of the Third Reich with those in other countries. During the Depression, films could be used to invite people into lovely fantasies of the rich, or with extravaganzas, along with pleasant romance comedies. (Consider the Hollywood films of Busby Berkeley here.) Once the war had begun, German films would include pseudo-documentaries against lives not worth living, such as *Ich klage an! (I Accuse!)*, discussed earlier, arguing for the rationality of the right of physicians to end the lives of people with incurable degenerative diseases (as in the film's specific story), as justification for physician-authorized euthanasia. There were strongly anti-Semitic films, as well, such as *Jud Süß* (1940), about a German Jew, Süß Oppenheimer, presented as corrupt, untrustworthy, and as raping the blond Aryan heroine of the story, with a climax of trial and execution, and *Der ewige Jude, The Eternal Jew* (1940), widely distributed through all of Reich-controlled Europe, also discussed above.

The Western world not under Nazi occupation put out a number of films, such as *London Can Take It* (1940), *Winning Your Wings* (1942), *Casablanca* (1942), *Yankee Doodle Dandy* (1942), *For Whom the Bell Tolls* (1943), *Education for Death: The Making of the Nazi* (1943), *Thirty Seconds over Tokyo* (1944), and *They Were Expendable* (1945). A diet of only war films was never appealing, though, and we see also murder mysteries, romance, and other topics being covered in film, in both the Allied and the Nazi German film industries.

The world was largely not ready to face the full violence that the Third Reich brought on Europe. It is certainly true that there were the Allied governments that had earlier made pledges to bring to trial, or otherwise hold to full responsibility, those guilty of great, almost unheard-of, and unspeakable crimes, with trials carried out both by international tribunals as well as by various governments in their spheres of operation. And yet, the attitude of many was not one of forgiving and forgetting, but of simply forgetting and getting on with life, or of starting life all over again, when peoples' earlier worlds had been shattered forever.

With some interest in bringing those guilty for great crimes to justice, and to create a formal, written record of their deeds, through official governmental documents, sworn testimonies and affidavits, and other tangible sources, and others in looking elsewhere, the film industries in the first years after the war, presented films that looked back at the Nazi Era, or at the consequences of war, such as the American Academy-award winning *The Best Years of Our Lives* (showing recent US veterans with amputations and other physical consequences of war returning to civil life). European cinema would have films that addressed the Nazi occupation period with various specific issues to present, from occupation to the life in the underground, to post-war concentration camp survivors and contributors to the Nazi war machine and its mass murders, to the Aryanization of Jewish property under Nazi regimes.

Consider here such films as the 1946 German film, *Die Mörder sind unter uns* (*The Murderers Are Among Us*), or the Italian film, *Germany Year Zero* (1958), and the 1965 Czech film, *The Shop on Main Street*. Films depicting the war and its specifics have continued through the decades, some carefully researched historically and some fictionalized. Some such contributions to this include *Nuit et Brouillard, Night and Fog*[1681] (1956), *D-Day, the Sixth of June* (1957), *The Longest Day* (1962), *Das Boot, The Boat* (1991), *Saving Private Ryan* (1998), *Die Untergang, Downfall* (2004), *Inglourious Basterds* (2009), and *Dunkirk* (2017).[1682]

The actual events of the Holocaust, the death camps, the forced labor of those related to those killing operations or to IG Farben and Krupp factories that used slave labor, were at first taboo subjects. A film, *Das Tagebuch der Anne Frank* (1958), was produced in the German Democratic Republic (DDR, East Germany), and the following year, 1959, in the USA, a major break-through came with the film *The Diary of Anne Frank*. This opened up in US film the subject of the treatment of Jews

---

[1681] This French documentary film about Auschwitz and Majdanek death camps, *Nuit et Brouillard*, takes its name from the Frech for *Führererlaß*, Hitler's Decree, known as *der Nacht und Nebel Erlaß*, the Night and Fog Decree, of December 7, 1941, mentioned above. The French singer Jean Ferrat had a song by the same French title, *Nuit et Brouillard*, released in Dec. 1963, that sang a lament about those who went off and were never seen again, "a meditation on the Holocaust and its consequences" ("Jean Ferrat: Biography," OPEN.SPOTIFY.COM). Ferrat was born on Dec. 26, 1930 in Vaucresson, just to the west of Paris; his birth name was Jean Tenenbaum. His father, a Russian Jewish immigrant to France, was captured by the police and sent to Auschwitz in 1942, where he was murdered. Ferrat himself was hidden and protected by Communist resistance fighters in the French *maquis* (underground), where he survived the war.

[1682] See Mira Liehm and Antonin J. Liehm, *The Most Important Art: Eastern Europe Film after 1945* (1977); *The German Cinema Book*, Tim Bergfelder, Erica Carter, and Deniz Göktürk, eds. (2002); and Leen Engelen and Roel Vande Winkel, *Perspectives on European Film and History* (2007).

The Hitler Era 567

under German occupation brought before a popular audience. And while this film addressed the plight of a small group of Dutch Jews in hiding, its central themes investigated the fear of this group and the saving grace of an uncrushable hope and faith in the goodness of mankind, its central characters were not shown at their lives' end: After their arrest, they were shipped to Bergen-Belsen Concentration camp, or the brutal beatings, starvation, and diseases there, where all but Anne's father died.[1683]

Other films followed: The year 1960 saw the film *Exodus*, the story of which took place in 1948, with Jewish survivors shown determined to get to the Holy Land, away from the catastrophic past they had survived. In 1961, there was *Judgment at Nuremberg*, which placed the trial in the context of post-War hostilities between the Western Allies and the Soviet Union. The 1964 film The *Pawnbroker* focused on the life of a man who was a camp survivor, but the film's story took place in post-War Harlem.

In the next decades, the greater public would be more open to learning about the Holocaust. In part, survivors, earlier avoiding at all costs, were more open to talking about their past, now that the next generation became interested in that past, and people saw their lives coming closer to their end. In 1978, a 4-part series, *The Holocaust*, presented some events, fictionalized, of the Holocaust, which revolutionized German self-perception.[1684] A later film depicting Auschwitz was not about Jews but about a Polish servant and her experiences helping in the Höss household, called *Sophie's Choice* (1982). These two films starred Meryl Streep.

Then, on April 30, 1985, a film was released in Paris that was unique in its approach to the war years and the Holocaust. It had no historical film footage at all. It was banned in Poland, so that some Poles, such as news reporters, traveled to Paris to see the film.[1685] The film, *Shoah* (the

---

[1683] The family went into hiding on July 6, 1942. The secret annex was raided on August 4, 1944. The group were sent via Westerbork Camp to Auschwitz. In early November, 1944, Anne and her older sister Margot were transferred to Bergen-Belsen. They both died of typhus before the liberation of the camp on April 15, 1945. Anne was 15. It is now thought that the two died in early February of that year. "The short ife of Anne Frank," *Anne Frank House, Amsterdam*, ANNEFRANK.ORG.

[1684] Watched by 20 million Germans, about a third of the population. *But much earlier, in 1965*, I learned from discussions with German students at the Univ. of Lausanne, that some young Germans were quite aware of the Holocaust and some even refused to live in Germany. See "Holocaust (miniSeries)," WIKIVISUALLY.COM.

[1685] From my discussion that spring with a Polish newspaper reporter, in line with her to buy tickets for the film, in Paris; she couldn't see the film in Warsaw. See a discussion by Agnès Poirier, "Claude Lanzmann: the man who told the story of the Shoah; The Holocaust documentarist, who died in Paris last week aged 92, is remembered by his friend Agnès Poirier," *The Guardian* (London), Jul. 8, 2018: "*Shoah*, both an important historical document and an original work of art, was based on [many] hours of testimonies both from survivors of the concentration camps and former Nazis whom he filmed secretly, as well as Polish villagers living near the camps of Treblinka, Chełmno, Auschwitz and Birkenau. Polish antisemitism was so starkly demonstrated by *Shoah* that Warsaw demanded the film be banned after its premiere in Paris." The Paris premiere was in April, 1975.

Hebrew word for the Holocaust), by the director, Claude Lanzmann,[1686] which ran 566, consisted totally of new interviews conducted over an 11-year period, by its stunning specificity of information, its interviews both with camp survivors and perpetrators, and its many on-site filmings (as of the train directed by the conductor into Treblinka), gave a sense of the reality of the mass killing system of Jews during the reign of the Third Reich. It is sometimes considered the best documentary on the Holocaust, and perhaps even the best documentary ever.[1687]

Following this ground-breaking filmic presentation of Holocaust events and experiences, other films and TV movies followed, presenting various perceptions of the Holocaust, the concentration camp system, and the Jewish resistance, most prominently: *Playing for Time* (1980), *The Wall* (1982), *Das Boot ist voll, The Boat is Full* (1981), *The Final Solution: The Wannsee Conference* (1984), *Escape from Sobibor* (1987), *Murderers Among Us: The Simon Wiesenthal Story* (1989), *Europa, Europa* (1990), *Schindler's List* (1993), *La vita è bella, Life is Beautiful* (1997), *The Truce* (1997), *Sunshine* (1999), *Uprising* (2001), *The Pianist* (2002), *Amen* (2002), *Rosenstraße* (2003), *Defiance* (2008), *The Boy in the Striped Pajamas* (2008), *Esther's Diary*, also entitled *Forgiveness* (2009), *The Courageous Heart of Irena Sendler* (2009), *The Roundup* (2010), *Sarah's Key* (2010), *Son of Saul* (2015), *Denial* (2016), *The Zookeeper's Wife* (2017), *The Man With the Iron Heart* (2017), and *Sobibor* (2018).[1688]

WHAT DOES THIS MEAN? WHO ARE WE? WHAT ARE WE?

We may look at the history of the Hitler era as simply a story, horrid though it might be, from the past, a story that we can ponder in our leisure, but that has no particular immediate relevance to us in our own lives, and in our own world, at this time in history. It, like other events, has its own uniqueness, perhaps the special one of being "a failure of all civilization."[1689] *But we might see in more recent events that civilization is failing repeatedly amidst all of its successes.* And if, as author Nicolas Fairweather wrote in 1932, "civilization is a structure slowly built up by

---

[1686] Lanzmann was born in 1925 in Bois Colombes, just northwest of Paris, of eastern-European Jewish immigrant parents. The family fled for the south of France with the occupation by German forces in 1940, where Lanzmann became part of the French resistance, at Clermont-Ferrand, southwest of Vichy in central France. He was an intimate of philosophers Jean-Paul Sartre and Simone de Beauvoir, essayist, and, after the war, Editor-in-Chief of the literary review, *Les Temps Modernes*, founded in 1945 by Sartre and de Beauvoir. See "Claude Lanzmann, intellectual vagabond who captured horror of Holocaust, dies at 92," *France 24*, May 17, 2018, FRANCE24.COM.

[1687] Joe Sommerlad, "Claude Lanzmann dead: French director's 9-hour Holocaust documentary 'Shoah' still stands as greatest of all time," *Independent* (London), Jul. 5, 2018, INDEPENDENT.CO.UK; "Shoah (1985)," IMDB (INTERNET MOVIE DATABASE), IMDB.COM (which describes the film as "an epic documentary").

[1688] See Annette Insdorf, *Indelible Shadows: Film and the Holocaust* (1983).

[1689] Alfons Heck, *The Burden of Hitler's Legacy*, p. 237.

orderly procedure and respect for law,"[1690] then its delicate fragility may be sensed and recognized to be quite significant. *This makes civilization a delicate rose in need of careful attention, protection, and cultivation.* It has been pointed out, "A physician, in order to be admitted to practice, must demonstrate his theoretical and practical knowledge. A politician, however, who unlike the physician, proposes [plans, intends] to decide the fate not of hundreds of people, but of millions, does not have to show such proof of any knowledge, insight, or compassion. This is presumably one of the basic reasons for the tragedy that for thousands of years, has devastated human society with periodic outbreaks."[1691] Keeping this weak point of civilizations in mind, we may not be surprised that wide-spread tragedy does indeed continue to plague our species and the world.

The violence around the globe of the Second World War—the mass bombings of many cities, with killings and executions in retaliation for violence against the Nazis or their war machine, the organized, systematic use of modern technology from train service, to modern poisonous chemicals, to mass killing chambers and crematoria, in a class quite its own, a government-encouraged, government-defined, and government-implemented program with a thorough dedication—may mark it out as special. But the First World War also had its own killing machine, with men charging against machine-gun nests only to be mowed down, the use of poison gas, with men blinded or otherwise seriously incapacitated, with major deformations of the body, including of the head, from mortar and cannon fire removing at times significant parts of soldiers' faces, and the endless fighting over a very limited area of terrain in Western Europe, which was its own form of hell.

And we can even go back millennia to reports of the decade-long violence between the Greeks and the Ilians (Trojans), with its own form of rather gruesome death, as in the precisely described passage, in which the warrior Meriones attacks Menelaus, brother of Agamemnon, both also called Atrides (son of Atreus), as Menelaus is fleeing:

> But Meriones caught him in full retreat, he let fly with a bronze-tipped arrow, hitting his right buttock up under the pelvic bone so the lance [the bronze tip of the arrow] pierced the bladder. He sank on the spot, hunched in his dear companion's arms, gasping out his life as he writhed along the ground like an earthworm stretched out in death, blood pooling, soaking the earth dark red....[1692]

It may be difficult to judge which might be the most gruesome among these various sorts of death in war: the bloody, painful death by the bronzed-tipped arrow just described, the machine-gunning or gassing in asphyxiated agony or the being hacked to death with the coupe-coupe of

---

[1690] Nicolas Fairweather, "Hitler and Hitlerism [Part I]: A Man of Destiny," *The Atlantic*, Mar. 1932.
[1691] Wilhelm Reich, *The Mass Psychology of Fascism* (3rd ed., 1970), p. 312.
[1692] Homer, *Iliad*, 13.749-755 (BK.vv:13.646-655).

the Senegalese fusiliers, both in World War One, or the mass shootings (the Holocaust by bullets) or the organized gas chambers of the Nazi extermination program. There is no best here, no solace in seeing how given deaths might have been even more excruciating or torturous as the last experiences of many human beings; mass murders do not especially allow for significant comparisons in ways that could make some seem tolerable or acceptable. The whole idea of these mass killings is barbaric, savage, abhorrent. With this, shall we be reduced to saying, in the words from the highly respected Syrian-French poet, Adonis, that civilization is a vehicle of the wounded, that a function of blood is to bathe grieving faces in the hemorrhage of the ages?[1693] While we may be bleeding ourselves to death, there are also other forces at play *as we continue through time in our limited wisdom and our vast ignorance*. (A know-it-all, after all, is certainly not someone who actually knows everything!)

For a moment, we can look at all of the particulars, as succinctly stated in the early section giving a Blitzview of the Hitler era, and in other earlier passages describing that historical context. And yet, the specificity of this thinking, which can make the German phenomenon of the first half of the twentieth century unique, may be a confused way of reassuring ourselves. There are some specifics about the period of 1933-1945 with the rise and development of the Third Reich that have left some terribly powerful remnants, memories, and even societal adaptations to that history.

More to the point, some of the explanations that try to capture the thinking and issues of Europe in the 1920s and 1930s, in an attempt to make sense of the rise of Hitlerism, Nazism, have a strong façade but sometimes less significance than we might expect. Thus, as was pointed out long ago, to talk of "Hitler psychosis" or "mass psychosis" does not explain very much at all.[1694] And, aside from the question of whether Hitler was psychotic or not, *one man's craziness or delusions do not lead to an entire society devoting a large part of its energies to mass killing.*

There were disparaging remarks made later about Hitler, even by those in his closest circles: Alfred Rosenberg (author of the 1930 text, *The Myth of the Twentieth Century*), wrote after capture by the Allies in 1945, "What Hitler did, what Hitler ordered, how he burdened the most honorable men [such as Rosenberg himself], how he dragged into the dust the ideals of a movement created by himself, all this is of such ghastly magnitude that no everyday adjective is adequate to describe it." Rosenberg then wrote of Hitler's end of life as a "paroxysm of self-intoxication," with Hitler's remarks "the explosions of a man who no longer seriously bothers to seek counsel from anyone but still believes he is listening to his inner voice; they are soliloquies, in part still logical, in

---

[1693] Adonis, *A Time Between Ashes & Roses: Poems* (2004). Adonis, born into an Alawite Syrian family in 1930 with the birthname of Ali Ahmad Said Esber, has since lived in Lebanon and France. From poems [8] and [9] in this collection.

[1694] Wilhelm Reich, *The Mass Psychology of Fascism* (1933, 1945 ed.), pp. 11-15.

part merely extravagant."¹⁶⁹⁵ Such end-of-the-story comments are far from rare. Whatever the components of a particular individual's (Hitler's) mind-set, beliefs, frustrations, emotional agitation, virulent hatred, and dedication to freeing his world from what he saw as threat to his and his society's very existence, others were of the same mind: We might think here especially of Joseph Goebbels, Heinrich Himmler, Julius Streicher, Alfred Rosenberg, and, then again, Reinhard Heydrich, Adolf Eichmann, and a host of other key figures we might see as sadistic and cold-hearted toward those they excluded from the ranks of humanity, perhaps most prominent among which was Josef Mengele, MD, or Julius Hallervorden, MD, head of the prestigious Neuropathology Department at the Kaiser Wilhelm Institute for Brain Research.

Still, we might consider here that a relatively small number of men in a society of many tens of millions, however, no matter how influential, does not, and cannot, on its own, determine the ideals, organization, plans, and operations of that entire nation. We are advised not to dismiss these actions and apparent rantings of lunatics as nonsense or pure incoherent lunacy.

Wilhelm Reich wrote, "We must get into the habit of paying strict attention to precisely what the fascist has to say and not to dismiss it as nonsense or hogwash. Now [with this approach] we have a better understanding of the emotional content of this theory, which sounds like a persecution mania when it is considered together with the theory of the poisoning of the nation. The swastika also has content capable of stirring the deepest reaches of one's emotions, but in a way completely different from what Hitler could ever have dreamed."¹⁶⁹⁶

Here we can perhaps see how Hitler was represented in Nazi circles and in the third Reich as the ideal male, the protective father of his nation (and called by some, as we have seen, the great Teutonic knight (*der Ritter*) and the Savior (*der Retter*) of the German people.

He was also presented, with an appeal to women taken to sexual daydreaming, as an unmarried, solitary bachelor, calling forth the fantasy of him as an ideal partner for available German women, wrapped in the wide-spread propagandistic proposal of "dem Führer ein Kind schenken" (giving the Führer the gift of a child), as an invitation for young women to become pregnant by good specimens of Aryan manhood, but as a solemn if not sacred offering to Hitler, the State taking possession of the new-borns these young women gave birth to.

This takes sexual fantasy to new levels, here, in the service of the National Socialist State!¹⁶⁹⁷

[1695] *Memoirs of Alfred Rosenberg*, Commentary by Serge Lang and Ernst von Schenck (1949), pp. 201, 248; cf. Robert Wittman and David Kinney, *The Devil's Diary: Alfred Rosenberg and the Stolen Secrets of the Third Reich* (2016), p. 428.
[1696] Wilhelm Reich, *The Mass Psycholoogy of Fascism* (1933; 3rd rev. ed., 1945), pp. 85-86. Passage quoted from the online version at IA800402.US.ARCHIVE.ORG.
[1697] We discussed the *Lebensborn* Project earlier. See here, Volker Koop, *Dem*

To review briefly the historical context, setting the stage for more philosophical, psychological and moral questions, Germany after the Great War had many former German soldiers who did not disarm, as a counter-balance to Communist-inspired uprisings. In particular, the street-fighters that some might call hooligans of the Brown Shirts (the Storm Troopers, or SA) were seen, or presented, as heroes striving for rule and order. It was a time of extremes and people tended to see the choice having to be one or the other: the Communists or the Nationalists (including the Nazis). The more moderate factions in German society were being silenced, especially after the collapse of the economic system of the Western world in 1929.[1698] Given the apparent yet ultimately limiting choices between such extreme political positions, the poorest tended to vote for the Communists, but the lower middle classes, the bourgeoisie, the rural populations, the religious Germans who longed for a strong and clear morality, and those in privileged positions who thought they could control Hitler, all shifted to supporting the National Socialist Party. It is of course of interest to consider the ways in which the various segments of German society—and, more generally, of European society—found appeal in the values that the Nazis were putting forth. There can be an inconsistency that is operating here, as when one doctrine is put forth before one audience, and others, before others. This is not at all unusual in politics, as when a speech in one region caters to the interests and concerns of that group, and another speech elsewhere addresses rather different issues. This is also found in the difference between speeches meant for a local audience and those meant to be heard by the international community—this continues to this day! With Hitler and the Nazis, there was, for example, one attitude expressed to the great lower-middle class, who were suffering under painfully low wages with resentment at the large industrialists, and another attitude that was presented to the large donors of the Party, including powerful industrialists, the military, the nobility, and other groups with an interest in maintaining their various privileged positions.[1699] (We see such maneuvering in many other countries, as well.)

We had in the case of the Hitler era a phenomenon that has its own unique status in the world. While dictatorial regimes have governed in a number of lands through the centuries, this one demanded not only

---

Führer ein Kind schenken: Die SS-Organisation Lebensborn eV (2007). The *"eV"* here is a German legal abbreviation for *"eingetragener Verein"* (registered association, which has with it certain legal advantages not granted to what is simply a *Verein*, an association).

[1698] Richard J. Evans, "A Warning from History," *The Nation*, Feb. 28, 2017. This reviews the book by German journalist-historian Volker Ullrich, *Hitler: Ascent* (2017).

[1699] There are a number of such analyses of the complex political posturing of Hitler and his playing off of one group against another, keeping the loyalty of all, each with its own limited sense of what Hitler was about, wanted, and would and would not do. One such early analysis, from 1945, is that of Wilhelm Reich, *The Mass Psychology of Fascism*, just cited.

The Hitler Era

passive acquiescence, but a deliberate if not enthusiastic participation, which entered into the lives of the young, of manual laborers, of the military, of factory workers, of the activities of attorneys, judges, physicians, and those in academia, from teachers in elementary schools to professors in the universities. It presented a state-encouraged sense of unity (in conformity) while defining the outsider as one who should be quite thoroughly eliminated from society, from those of unwelcome political views to those who were physically limited or mentally disturbed, to those who were not clearly heterosexual in their comportment, as well as those seen as not stemming from a purely German lineage, as not German-rooted (*deutschstämmig*), including Jews, Romanies, and Slavs. It came to accept the solution of re-purification—the elimination and extermination of all such dehumanized inferiors, offering up the time and focus required for such grand schemes to be realized. *In moral terms, it rejected many core values of Western civilization*, with its respect for compassion, understanding, caring for those in need, and peace, human dignity, the existence of a conscience, valuing empathy and sympathy with a concern for fellow members of one's society and of all mankind.

In their stead, other values that were presented as Nordic (the *summum bonum* of Germanic culture, in one sense of that term, at least): the closeness to nature and to ritual fire, the respect for strength, diligence, hardness to overcome strife, indifference to violence, if not a love for it as a sign of power, the value of self-sacrifice if for the good of the group, an intense fear and hatred of everything perceived as different and not in accord with these values. *This was done at times using Christian terms and values, but with an end-point of a rather different attitude* than that expressed in Christian ideals of patience, tolerance, non-violence, and caring for the weakest among us. This is the context!

So, what does this mean in this current time—as I write or whenever you are reading this? We may conceive of this as a conflict between two different systems of value, two different moralities. We could also see this as a conflict between a way of organizing a society that takes values that raise the human above a savage, which we often think of as values that express a civilization: a world of civil, mutually respectful, caring, good-willed people, not just for a certain small group with which we identify, but for others in a more inclusive sense. We can see this as an issue of whether or not to take the survival of one's particular tribe as paramount and to be fought for tooth and nail, intensely and without restraint.

There is a deep-rooted sense of what is proper, just, fair, kind, and so forth, that many if not most of humanity feel quite deeply. Not that this establishes the correctness (if that is the way to describe this) of such values, but it does ask for recognition.

Consider a recent analysis of Nazi German values, which stand in sharp contrast with the vast tradition of morality seen around the world and through the millennia. This analysis focuses on when German soldiers would criticize the way in which Jews were being treated (killed en masse). It considers even Himmler's comments about the weighty task of annihilation and the difficult challenge of remaining morally upright, remaining fundamentally decent people, while killing large numbers of others. This analysis points out what for the Reich was "the *overarching* definition of what was just and unjust"; in this German military discourse, this definition "had already been turned on its head."[1700]

While the number of 6 million Jews killed in the German genocide of the Jews, the Holocaust[1701] is no small sum—the number 6 million is widely accepted, at least as approximate: sources that try to be more precise range from 5.3 million[1702] to 6.2 million[1703]—it was in the context of a war that resulted in a total of some 50-60 million dead. Still, even five million Jews, guilty only of being Jews, is a large number of human beings to be murdered in a program that was designed, promoted, and administered by a government! (This was discussed in detail, above.)

While we can see in the astonishingly violent events of those years something about the destructive potential of people and of groups working together toward violent goals, in a way that was unimaginable before the turn of the twentieth century, we may now be aware of what is possible, and *to act for* such mutual destruction *or to act against* such dire outcomes.

This may sound easy to do, and yet, in looking at the way in which people and groups and nations manage to convince themselves that they are right and just and reasonable in their actions—or, in religious terms, that God is on their side—we may realize that there is some serious self-questioning that is called for, *on everyone's part*.

This is not an impossible task, but it does call for a self-inspection (to repeat, on individual, group, party, and national dimensions) that is probing and requiring us to come to terms with our own limiting beliefs, judgments, critical viewpoint of others we do not know, and so on, along a number of dimensions we have touched on in these discussions, as well as others that might arise in given future, presently-unimaginable circumstances.

Another way to approach the history we are all born into—at whatever time and year, but during or after the Third Reich—is to consider the issue of how we are going to live, knowing that at least one organized society (one government) before it was ended made it a primordial policy to design and carry out the mechanized, methodical, efficient murder of millions of people. This consideration is for all people: for Germans who

---

[1700] Sönke Neitzel and Harald Welzer, *Soldaten: On Fighting, Killing, and Dying*, pp. 120-125.

[1701] The genocidal murder of millions of Jews during the Third Reich, the Holocaust, in Hebrew is called *ha-Shoah*, the calamity, or *ḥurban*, destruction of the Temple in Jerusalem, and in Yiddish, *khurbn*, disaster.

[1702] Alfons Heck, *The Burden of Hitler's Legacy*, p. 266: Post-war German governments have accepted Jews killed by the Third Reich to be least 5.7 million.

[1703] "Holocaust Facts: Where Does the Figure of 6 Million Victims Come From?" *Haaretz*, Jun. 17, 2018.

knew the Third Reich and who came after its end, for Jews, who knew at some early time, or later in life, about the killing of millions of Jews because they were Jews, for peoples around the world who know of these events or who have lived through other regimes and lifetimes of violence, murder, indeed, organized murder, systematic murder, of which there are, sadly, many examples since after the end of World War II.[1704]

Some may think that this comes down to a question of whether we are religious or not. And that has some appeal to it. And yet, let us look here at how differently different religious groups, *even within one religious tradition*, interact with one another, and with those who are not perfect examples of their particular understanding of religion—in behavior, rituals, dress, forms of authority and hierarchy, degrees of strictness and sobriety, or flexibility and gaiety, and so forth. And let us also look at how different groups within different religions think of and deal *with those of other religions or deal with those who are not readily identified with any religion*—whether with friendship and openness and perhaps curiosity, or with condescension or irritation or rage or hatred or violence. In all of this, there is no clear, consistent correlation between religious affiliation and people being kind, considerate, caring, welcoming of others on their different personal, psychological, societal, religious, or spiritual, paths.

How are we at this point in time to understand and deal with the possibility of a society in which organized, government-administered murder is made rather grotesquely into a civic virtue? This may strike us as a bizarre question, but it is one that we have seen presented to us within the last century in great clarity and frightful force.

Here we are facing, in part, the issue of genocide. Now, for many, the paradigm case of genocide is that of the Jews during the reign of the Third Reich in Europe: The term was coined in 1944 by Polish Jewish jurist Raphael Lemkin (1900-1959), but his focus was actually on the mass killing of the Armenians in the Ottoman Empire in 1915. This defined and identified government-designed, -sponsored, and -administered killing of an entire people, or its intending to kill an entire people (often defined as a national, ethnic, racial, or religious group), because of who they were, not what they had done or not done. There were already what many consider to be genocides in the nineteenth and twentieth centuries: of the Tasmanians by the British; of Amerindians in California; of Ukrainians, Jews, and Kazakhs by the Soviets; of Jews, Serbs, and Romanies by Nazi-

---

[1704] These run through the decades in the last century and some, include (as a small sampling out of many other organized killing sprees across the globe): the murder of the Armenians, of Jews, of Romanies, of Slavs, then of ethnic Germans in lands liberated from Third Reich occupation after the war, and of others, more recently, discussed above in the text. *Whether these are termed ethnic cleansing, genocide, or simply organized, systematic mass killings, the dead are dead*, and this use of our human capacities to kill fellow human beings remains astonishing, repulsive, abhorrent, *almost inconceivable and yet quite conceivable*. (Much ink has been spilled quibbling over the most appropriate term to use here, *obscuring the fundamental issue of mass killing, which is, itself, not frequently denied*.)

affiliated Croatian Ustaše, of Bangladeshis by Pakistanis; of East Timurs in Indonesia. While the genocide of Jews by the Third Reich is given the specific name of the Holocaust, there are other mass killings that are considered genocides, including the genocide of the Armenians by the Ottoman Turkish Empire, in waves during the period 1894-1922, of perhaps 1.5 million Armenians in all, but most intensely in 1915-1916. We may also consider the dirty war (*la guerra sucia*) in Argentina in 1976-1983, with 30,000 "disappeared" (*los desaparecidos*), the auto-genocide in Cambodia in 1975-1979 (Cambodians killing Cambodians, with more than 1.7 million fellow Cambodians dead); the killing of the Tutsis by the Hutu, focused in Rwanda in 1994, with between 500,000 and 1 million Tutsis killed; the genocide of Bosnian Muslims (Bosniaks) in the former Yugoslavia in 1995, with some 100,000 estimated dead; the genocide of the Yazidi in modern-day Iraq by the so-called Islamic State (Daesh, ISIL, ISIS, and IS, varying through time) with the sexual enslavement of Yazidi young women and the mass murder of Yazidis, in the years 2014-2017, with more than 10,000 killed or kidnapped. And the astonishing mass killing of entire groups (ethnic, cultural, religious, or otherwise defined) has not ended. What does this mean to us? What is there to do other than wringing our hands in despair? *(Or, rather, what is there to do after that?)*

Soon after the war, in 1945, Jung returned to reflect on the actions of the Third Reich and its leaders, referring to all of that as a catastrophe.

Having expressed a more admirative attitude toward Hitler earlier on (discussed above), Jung returned to the question after the fall of the Reich, pondering whether his own country, Switzerland, could have carried out something as evil as the killing of millions. He asked: "Who are we to imagine that 'it couldn't happen here'? ... Do we seriously believe that *we* [Swiss] would have been immune [from committing the crimes of the Third Reich, given the right conditions and an imagined much larger Swiss population]? ... It has filled us with horror to realize all that man is capable of, and of which, therefore, we too are capable."[1705]

Concerning Jung's theoretical questioning about Switzerland here, while the size of a population has something to do with what it as a coordinated unit (nation) can do, there is of course much more involved in the organized government-designed and –administered killing of millions. Many conditions came together to co-appear in European society (and German society, in particular) to lead to the genocide and other mass killings perpetrated by the Third Reich and collaborators.

Others have seen the issue of the Holocaust as a watershed in violence, a turning point that marks its own Before and After. Some have said that after Auschwitz (representing the Holocaust), there can be no poetry. Perhaps the source of this is a statement in the 1951 essay "Cultural Criticism and Society" by German philosopher, Theodor Adorno (1903-

---

[1705] C. G. Jung, "After the Catastrophe" (1945), at pp. 194-217 in C. G. Jung, *Civilization in Transition* (1970), at p. 200.

1969): "after Auschwitz, to write poetry is barbaric (*nach Auschwitz ein Gedicht zu schreiben, ist barbarisch*).[1706] And, similarly, French-American essayist George Steiner (born 1929) remarked in 1966, "We know now that a man can read Goethe or Rilke in the evening, that he can play Bach and Schubert, and go to his day's work at Auschwitz in the morning.[1707] To say that he has read them without understanding or that his ear is gross, is cant [hypocritical, sanctimonious talk]. In what way does this knowledge bear on literature and society, on the hope, grown almost axiomatic from the time of Plato to that of Matthew Arnold, that culture is a humanizing force, that the energies of spirit are transferable to those of conduct?"[1708] (*The events in Europe and elsewhere during that period certainly suggest a limit to the power of culture and education.*)

And again, more recently, in a 1995 speech, Romanian-American Elie Wiesel (1928-2016), survivor of Auschwitz and Buchenwald, and 1986 Nobel Peace Laureate, stated, "After Auschwitz, the human condition is not the same, nothing will be the same."[1709] We can see that education and a cultural sensitivity (or intelligence, or familial tenderness) are no guarantees of a civilized approach to the limitation of violence in society. That is, education and a foundation in culture (*Kultur*), are consistent with, compatible with, a daily life of focused violence. That is clear from the

---

[1706] "Theodor W. Adorno: Kulturkritik und Gesellschaft—Gedichte nach Auschwitz (1951)," LITERATUREPOCHEN.AT. This is Ger. text of *Cultural Criticism and Society*.

[1707] We may think here of Rudolf Höss (1900-1947), Commandant of the Auschwitz Concentration Camp, who enjoyed a family life close by the crematoria of Auschwitz. And of the son of Richard Heydrich, composer and founder of the Halle Conservatory of Music, Reinhard Heydrich (1904-1942), founder and head of the SD (Security Service), an organizer of the Night of the Long Knives, chairman of the Wannsee Conference of Jan. 20, 1942, that defined fundamental administrative aspects of the Final Solution (the planned elimination of 11 million Jews of Europe), and Reich Protector of Bohemia and Moravia after Czechoslovakia was conquered and restructured by the Reich; Heydrich himself carried a passion for the violin through his adult life, which he played with some proficiency. *In a familial contrast*, after Reinhard's death, *his younger brother Heinz* (1905-1944) learned of the extent of the Final Solution from Reinhard's personal papers, passed on to him, and, disgusted, printed false documents to help Jews escape the Nazi regime; suspecting (wrongly) that he had been discovered by the Gestapo, he committed suicide: see "Heinz Heydrich," WARHISTORYONLINE.COM. We may also think here of *Hermann Göring's younger brother, Albert Göring* (1895-1966), who signed travel documents simply as "Göring" (which bureaucrats took to be Hermann's signature) helping Jews and dissidents escape: see "Albert Göring," AUSCHWITZ.DK. Or again, we may consider physicians at relative ease in conducting rather gruesome experiments on human beings, as the well-known Auschwitz physician Dr. Joseph Mengele (1911-1979), who was especially interested in experiments on twins.

[1708] George Steiner, *Language and Silence: Essays on Language Literature, and the Inhuman* (1970), Preface (in 1966 ed.), p. ix.

[1709] "The Life and Work of Elie Wiesel" (Speech delivered in 1995, at the ceremony to mark the 50th anniversary of the liberation of Auschwitz): PBS.ORG.

Third Reich experience. *And yet lack of education is also not a hindrance to violence.* Hitler, for example, never completed the equivalent of high school, and held himself to have a better understanding of society than all of those around him who had earned law, economics, and other higher degrees. He has relatedly been described by some as *ein Halbgebildeter, ein Besserwisser* (a half-educated individual, a know-it-all).[1710] Perhaps, however, the inspiration and beauty of (some post-Auschwitz) poetry are counter-examples to the idea that any and all poetry after Auschwitz is barbaric. And to the idea that nothing is the same after Auschwitz, we can perhaps agree that awareness of the violence that spread across Europe with millions of civilians deliberately killed with forethought and full intentionally *will, in fact, make a difference in how we view society, the world, society, and ourselves*—with new possibilities for us if we stay with these considerations long enough to gain some self-awareness about how we ourselves are actually impacted and influenced by this history.

It may be, from one perspective, that "every period in history has been more or less tragic," as a character in the film *Masked and Anonymous* remarked.[1711] Or, as Bertolt Brecht has the character Jonathan Jeremiah Peachum declare in his opening monologue (quoted above) in *Der Dreigroschenoper* (*The Threepenny Opera*), "*Denn, der Mensch hat die furchtbare Fähigkeit, sich gleichsam nach eigenem Belieben gefülllos zu machen*" (for man has the horrid capacity to make himself unfeeling at his own discretion).[1712]

Now, while this observation by Brecht's character Peachum does seem to be the case in certain circumstances, this is not always so, not always the way people deal with the torments, adversities, and violence they might experience in the course of their lives.

We might consider this whole question with another focus. One significant and original study, by contemporary psychologist and genocide scholar, Israel Charny,[1713] ponders the question of whether this readiness, or ability, to commit mass murder is a potential in all of us, and if so, what will influence us to act with this barbaric cruelty, *or to avoid such actions, or to stand up against such actions when we see them occurring.* Can we act, in words spoken on March 4, 1865, "with malice toward none, with charity toward all"?[1714]

The values of which these words are a sample are not mild, pleasant, or cute issues; in investigating these, we might know ourselves better

---

[1710] Karl-Heinz Janßen, "Adolf Hitler in Volksausgabe," ZEIT ONLINE, Mar. 14, 1980.

[1711] *Masked and Anonymous* (2003), at 17:00-17:15.

[1712] Bertolt Brecht, *Dreigroschenoper*, Act I, Scene 1; variant Eng. in *The Threepenny Opera*, Eric Bentley, tr. (1949), Act 1, Scene 1.

[1713] Israel Charny is an American-Israeli psychologist, founder of the Israel Family Therapy Assoc., President of the International Family Therapy Assoc., and co-founder of the International Assoc. of Genocide Scholars.

[1714] Abraham Lincoln, "Second Inaugural Address of Abraham Lincoln, Saturday, March 4, 1865," THE AVALON PROJECT, YALE LAW SCHOOL.

and appreciate with more nuance, subtlety, and depth, the stresses that we as individuals, as groups, as nations, as a species, may experience.[1715]

We may consider here some of the values that were discussed and formulated by the anti-Nazi group, the *Kreisauer Kreis* (the Kreisau Circle), under the leadership of the jurist Helmuth James von Moltke, discussed above. Moltke, who had studied at Oxford University as well as at the University of Breslau, wrote in 1942 to a British colleague, Lionel George Curtis, a reader and historian at Oxford University, "Today, not a numerous, but an active part of the German people are beginning to realize, not that they have been led astray, not that bad times await them, not that the war may end in defeat, but that what is happening is *sin* and that they are personally responsible for each terrible deed that has been committed—naturally, not in the earthly sense, but as Christians."[1716]

Some of basic principles articulated during meetings of the Kreisau Circle over the weekend of June 12-14, 1943, half a year before Moltke's arrest, included *a peace not based on force but on a recognition of man's inward (psychological or spiritual) and outward (interpersonal, social, and societal) existence*. In this envisioned restructured society, there would be recognition of the special link of each to his nation, his language, and his spiritual, religious, and historical traditions, *but totally avoiding the amassing of power through those links and the avoiding of degradation, persecution, and oppression of foreign peoples*.

These principles recognized that this vision was quite incompatible with each government having absolute sovereignty; instead, a set of autonomous and yet interdependent units from the family up through small communities to nations and the larger group of many or all nations. This is a vision of *a cooperative community in which smaller units of identity could be recognized and respected, without this being transformed into the violent, confrontive, and combative interactions that had been so prominent in the first part of the twentieth century*.

Furthermore, in this vision of post-World War II Europe, Germany was seen as a mediator between the revolutionary East (the collective socialism of Soviet Russia) and the remains of the restorative West,[1717] seen as maintaining outworn forms of individualistic liberalism. Germany could thus act to bring peace in a way that could avoid another intense animosity and confrontational relationship between the nations of the West after the fall of the Third Reich. Of course, what came to pass,

---

[1715] Israel W. Charny, *The Genocide Contagion: How We Commit and Confront Holocaust and Genocide* (2016). He is author of many works, including *Fascism and Democracy in the Human Mind: A Bridge between Mind and Society* (2008), *Psychotherapy for a Democratic Mind: Treating Intimacy, Tragedy, Violence, and Evil* (2018), and Editor-in-Chief of *Encyclopedia of Genocide, 2 vol.* (2000).

[1716] Hans Rothfels, *The German Opposition to Hitler* (1961), p. 112.

[1717] Jianhong Liu, "The roots of restorative justice: Universal Process or from the West to the East?" *Acta Criminologiae et Medicinae Legalis Japonica*, vol. 81, no. 2, Jan. 2015, pp. 1-14, RESEARCHGATE.

instead, was the establishing of barriers based on the fears of the West against Soviet Russia and the fears of Soviet Russia of hostile nations wanting once again to invade and conquer the Russian homeland.[1718]

We are still at a point in which the nationalistic value of total autonomy, in which no other nation has any say whatever over what happens or does not in one's country, and in which the moral, political, and other values that influence the inclinations of a given country are untouchable by these values as held by other countries. *The world still does not have the mechanisms, the internationally recognized principles and structures, by which each country does not complete power of how it acts toward other nations and how treats its citizens*, for example. The basic values that the Kreisau Circle proposed (just above) are still important considerations that await their day in the world arena. How these principles might have worked out if Hitler had been taken from power after the Stalingrad defeat in early 1943, for example, or even if the assassination attempt of July, 1944, had succeeded, there might have been the option for a surrender of Germany under a new government that declared its new acceptance of European harmonious co-existence. *Given the history of those last two years of the war, this is all mere speculation.*

We may not yet imagine clearly how to answer these sorts of questions, and may have no clear answers yet, but they have their own significance for us as individuals and as societies. Now, to answer any questions about who we are, as moral beings and about how we act in our innermost thinking and in society, requires us to be able to look at ourselves. And yet, these questions are not that simple. While we are much of the time quite civil and mutually respectful, events can suggest that this touch of civility, of civilization *is at times only a thin, fragile patina*. A goal: never to undergo oppression and never to oppress, as Albert Camus expressed the idea.[1719]

It has been noted—especially in carefully structured psychological experiments (as in experiments at Yale by Stanley Milgram and then at Stanford by Philip Zimbardo[1720]—that how we human beings act depends to a large extent on how our society understands its own workings, what it takes to be laudable, what tolerable, and what unacceptable. What we find ourselves ready to do, or refusing to do, can be largely influenced by what we are told the situation to be. A high school teacher in Palo Alto, California—the location of Stanford—Ron Jones, carried out a similar experiment (then losing his position and never teaching in a public school

---

[1718] Klemens von Klemperer, *German Resistance Against Hitler*, pp. 327-340.

[1719] Albert Camus, "Réflexions sur la guillotine," pp. 123-180, in Arthur Koestler and Albert Camus, *Réflexions sur la peine capitale* (1957), at 176.

[1720] The classic experiments are by Yale psychology professor Stanley Milgram (1933-1984) and by Philip Zimbardo, Yale Ph.D. and Prof. Emeritus at Stanford, in the 1971 Stanford Prison Experiments. See Stanley Milgram, *Obedience to Authority* (1974); Philip Zimbardo, *The Lucifer Effect: Understanding How Good People Turn Evil* (2007).

after that), which in 2009 was made into a German film—*Die Welle* (*The Wave*)—that took place in current-day Germany, adding a sense of history to the story.

Relatedly, a French psychologist, Franck Pavloff in 1998 wrote a short story, fictionalizing such psychological processes, using the metaphor of the changes in a society in which everything had to be brown (an implicit reference to the SA, the "Brownshirts").[1721] *The ease of being drawn into a world of distorted values may make our self-confidence and assurance of our deep moral values at least slightly more questionable.*

Confidence certainly has its value, within limits. Famously, the French philosopher Descartes (1596-1650) would claim to have begun in doubt and ended, logically speaking, with certainty: *Je pense donc je suis*,[1722] or *Cogito ergo sum*, I think, therefore I am. The patina of certainly is certainly there in his essay by Descartes, and in most ordinary situations this patina is not scratched at all to expose what else there is. And so, in opposition to the Cartesian reasoning here, we can consider the Russian dissident poet, Sergei Dovlatov,[1723] who was expelled from the Soviet Union of Journalists in 1976, and whose very existence was symbolically denied by the Soviets, who is quoted as saying, "I existed, I was thinking, I disappeared like smoke."[1724]

The possibility of this transitory sense of our very existence points out that it may seem automatic, natural, and effortless, for us to maintain our sense of who we are: This is when that sense is not threatened by any of a number of features of our life, including those of being in a political environment that is dedicated to deny part of what we know ourselves to be. And, perhaps, we can maintain our deepest values, our core morality, even in the face of such great pressures, threats, imprisonment, organized disappearances, and so forth, but that is not a certainty, either.

Can we maintain that basic sense of morality that was preached long ago? In the Sermon on the Mount, is the parable:

> How can you say to your brother, 'Let me take the speck out of your eye,' when all the time there is a plank in your own eye? You hypocrite, first take the plank out of your own eye, and then you will see clearly to remove the speck from your brother's eye.[1725]

[1721] The book appeared in French in 1998 as *Matin Brun* and in a bilingual English-French edition, in 2003, as *Brown Morning*.

[1722] René Descartes, *Discours de la Méthode pour bien conduire sa raison, et chercher la vérité dans les sciences* (1637), in Part 4, *Preuves de l'existence de Dieu et de l'âme humaine ou fondements de la métaphysique*.

[1723] Sergei Dovlatov (1941-1990), son of an Armenian mother and Jewish father, was expelled from the Soviet Union of Journalists in 1976; he emigrated with his mother in 1979 to the USA, and finally achieved recognition in Russian-language Western publications. He died of a heart attack when 48 years old.

[1724] As quoted in the Russian film, *Dovlatov* (2018), at 15:55-16:10.

[1725] Matthew 7:4-5, NIV (New Internatinal Version) Translation.

For those who have felt themselves to be outsiders or the objects of group hatred, making life more difficult, we might imagine a day where every group receives "acceptance as real and feeling members of the human community."[1726]

Contemporary political commentator, Noam Chomsky,[1727] in reply to a student's earnest question, asked us to move to a level of civilization and culture that would honor this parable, taking into account some quite contemporary issues about the ways in which various nations (governments) act in the international arena: "We have to reach a level of civilization in which we are able to think about *ourselves* and what we do. It's really easy to blame others, but there's another question: What about ourselves? Can we reach a level of culture in which we can ask ourselves really simple questions, like the kind you're asking …? It's really hard."[1728] Further, about this yearning for civilization, Ian Hancock has added: "You should, as a human being, be concerned about that, about the treatment of others, because if not for historical, social circumstances that could be you … You could be the one with no home, if history happened to be a little bit different."[1729]

Complementing these concerns, Romanian-American attorney Ben Ferencz, when only 27 years old the Chief Prosecutor for the US Army at the Nuremberg Einsatzgruppen Trial (the biggest mass murder trial in history), in his opening speech, made "a plea of humanity to law," with a large vision of history, and stated much more recently, "I'm also always mindful of the fact that we are, believe it or not, making very significant progress toward creating a more humane and peaceful world."[1730]

Different visions of ideal societies are in play here. Bertrand Russell held that world peace required approximate economic equality, to end the great envy of the very poor.[1731] And yet, others noted that in the US, "a heightened sense of job insecurity … [led to] subdued wage gains."[1732]

With this, there are in some quarters an appreciation and honoring of civilization as we usually understand the term, a rising out of savagery and barbarism, with core values that can orient life such as love (think here of the teachings of Jesus, among many others), kindness, gentleness, and compassionate caring for the "least" in society, or, to quote: "The

---

[1726] Ian Hancock, Introduction, *The Roads of the Roma: A PEN anthology of Gypsy Writers*, Ian Hancock, Siobhan Dowd, and Rajko Djurić, eds., pp. 9-21, at p. 20.

[1727] Noam Chomsky, Prof. Emeritus of Linguistics at MIT, developer of the theory of transformational grammar, philosopher, and political commentator.

[1728] *Noam Chomsky at St. Olaf College, May 4th, 2018*, YouTube, at 1:09:50-1:10:20, Lecture followed by Q&A with students, 1:01:00-1:28:40.

[1729] *About Human Rights—Ian Hancock* (2018), 0:15-0:56, YouTube.

[1730] "Opening Statement of the Prosecution," NT-TWC-Green, vol. 4, p. 30; *Prosecuting Evil: The Extraordinary World of Ben Ferencz* (2018), 3:40-3:50; Ben Ferencz, *Enforcing International Law—A Way to World Peace* (1983).

[1731] *A Conversation with Bertrand Russell* (1952), 22:15-22:50, YouTube.

[1732] "Testimony of Chairman Alan Greenspan," Jul. 22, 1997, FEDERALRESERVE.GOV; "The great American jobs machine," *The Economist*, Jan. 13, 2000.

King will reply, 'Truly I tell you, whatever you did for one of the least of these brothers and sisters of mine, you did for me.'"[1733] Consider here saints and heroes. One philosophical analysis suggests that saints and heroes are unusual in the way they deal with moral duties (as understood by them and the culture) in certain contexts, in which most people will avoid doing their duty for one reason or another.

This philosophical analysis, by Oxford Classics and Philosophy Fellow J. O. Urmson (1915-2012) considering moral codes, proposed, "The basic moral code must not be in part too far beyond the capacity of the ordinary men on ordinary occasions, or a general breakdown of compliance with the moral code would be an inevitable consequence ... A moral code, if it is to be a code, must be formulable, and if it is to be a code to be observed it must be formulable in rules of manageable complexity." The code must be relatively easily understood. For Urmson, a saint, or an action that is saintly, is when a duty is carried out where personal inclination, desire, or self-interest would lead the person not to bother so acting, and that a hero, or an action that is heroic, is when a duty is carried out where fear or a drive for self-preservation would lead the person not to so act, or, further, for these to be done effortlessly, with no inner turmoil or conflict, even if what is done is far beyond what could be considered one's duty.[1734]

Thinking of the danger to people in acting against the Third Reich's policies, we may appreciate the heroic measures taken by those who helped those hunted by the Reich (whether political or military enemies, or Jews, Romanies, and others the Nazi Government had intentions to destroy and to annihilate). Some of these have been honored by a memorial group centered in Jerusalem, Yad Vashem, recognizing these heroes, calling them *Ḥasidei umot ha ʽolam*, the Righteous Among the World (referring to honorable non-Jews).

And if we start by a simple mental exercise in the imagination, we may get *a deeper sense here of what possible actions in a moral context actually amount to*. There is a power in this imagination that has been recognized in its moral dimension. The American philosopher John Dewey (1859-1952) wrote of the power of imagined scenarios in giving us a grounding and palpable sense of our own deepest moral sentiments.[1735] This is placing ourselves in a position to correct our biases with an "intelligent updating of moral beliefs," using "experiments in living."[1736] And, if we apply this mental exercise to an imagined (or remembered)

[1733] Matthew 25:40. In the NIV (New International Version) tr.

[1734] J. O. (John Opie) Urmson, "Saints and Heroes" (pp. 198-216) in *Essays in Moral Philosophy*, Abraham I. Melden, ed. (1958), esp. pp. 200-203, with quoted passage at p. 212.

[1735] John Dewey, *The Middle Works* (*MW*), vol. 14, pp. 132-133, suggested that "deliberation is a dramatic rehearsal (in imagination) of various competing lines of action.... An act carried out in the imagination is not final or fatal."

[1736] As elaborated in Elizabeth Anderson, "Moral Bias and Corrective Practices: A Pragmatist Perspective," Presidential Address in *Proceedings and Addresses of the American Philosophical Association (APA)*, vol. 89, 2015, pp. 21-47.

situation, we can perhaps appreciate the anguish and the torment felt by the members of a family in which its basic context of life was destroyed overnight, where the basic security the family had felt was gone in a very short period of time, in which they were forced to leave their familiar surroundings and go out into the world with no goods or supplies, and we can add that some members of the family were either taken away by hostile forces, or had disappeared in the rush of chaos, or had been killed.

We can perhaps in this way have some sense of their anxiety, whether this family was a French family forced to leave everything, to escape an invasion by the Wehrmacht, a family in the Netherlands, Belgium, Norway, Denmark, Austria, Czechoslovakia, Poland, the Soviet Union, in Romania, Hungary, or elsewhere in Eastern Europe, or even a family in Germany whose city was bombed to rubble or burned to ashes. *And this is imagining only one family at one moment.* Next, imagine how the family would try to deal with their torment not only in those first days, but in the months, years, and even decades that followed. The impact of this line of thought can be staggering, but can give a glimpse into that torment.

Anyone who has had a family member die a violent death (even in a freak automobile accident, let alone in the violence of war) has first-hand experience of how long the memories of loss and a sense of anguish that will not go away for good (even if being out of focus for part of the time). And, while death has a finality about it for the deceased, the survivors usually remember their loved ones for the rest of their lives.

And, if we can manage to stay with this intense, imagined torment—rather than dismissing it as a frustrating, silly, and futile exercise best avoided for our own calm and peace of mind—we can perhaps reflect on these deaths to understand better the impact of war on those who have survived and are now living with lingering memories, including those who have had their bodies wounded or mutilated. If we take the deepest sadness, grief, and turbulence of each of the members of each such family, and multiple that by a hundred, things start to look much worse; by a thousand, even more so, and if we can get any sense of what this would be like if it involved a million or even ten million people, we can start to appreciate the real impact of war: its psychological and societal costs.

STYX, THE GREEK RIVER OF ANGER: MISERY, STRIFE, OBLIVION, DEATH

The Russian officer Andrei in the film *A Woman in Berlin* (2008) stated, "Every newborn child yells for war ... and nothing, no person or nation, could stop that cycle. Except death"[1737]—the death that filled the ancient Greek gods with loathing.[1738] And, on the heart in this anguished state, *in extremis*, an Armenian proverb states: "How to go on living with a heart that is decomposing?"[1739]—a lament on the difficulty of living after the

---

[1737] *A Woman in Berlin* (2008), 1:37:00-1:37:17. Compare the 1945 Soviet military-political documentary, *The Fall of Berlin* (1945).

[1738] Homer, *Iliad*, 20.73-80 (BK.vv: 20.54-66).

[1739] I was introduced to this Armenian expression by my French friend, Jean-Pierre Aharonian, in the late 1970s.

heart has been ripped apart. And yet, wounded in body and often in mind, we do carry on, in each our own modified and altered ways, attempting to live with some glimmer of hope and—perhaps surprisingly—perhaps an even deeper appreciation of the value of life.

This Greek image of the immortals (gods with human-like foibles) having a loathing of death, mentioned above, speaks of *stugéousi* (citation form, *stugéō*).[1740] This verb means to hate, abhor, dread, fear. It is etymologically related to such words as *stúgos*, hatred, abhorrence; *stugētós*, hated, abominated; *stugerós*, hated, loathsome; *stúgios*, Stygian, dark and gloomy, as of the nether world; and is related to *Styx*, literally, The Hateful, the name of the River Styx.[1741] This river encircles the Underworld seven times. This represents a boundary or border to darkness, to death, a descent (*katábasis*), and a place for retrieving (as in the mythic voyage of the heroic quest).[1742] Hence, the River Styx here also symbolizes this quest, with the hero understood as a boundary-crosser and a seeker on a quest.[1743] The River Styx is literally the River of Hate, suggesting a link between hatred and death (*thánatos*). When we consider the five rivers of the Underworld in Greek mythology, we have a further sense of an extended and complex metaphor: the names of these other rivers add detail to the nature of the Underworld: a place of wailing (*Cocytus* or *Kōkutós*), of misery (*Acheron* or *Akhérōn*), of flaming fire (*Phlegéthōn* or *Pyriphlegéthōn*), and of oblivion of the past and an extreme forgetfulness (*Lḗthē*). Further, given that a second name for this river was *Amelḗs potamós*, the river of heedless, negligent carelessness—the daughter of strife or contention, *Eris*—this last river or aspect of the Underworld, suggests a state of mind marked by a profound lack of mindfulness, born of strife.

In a psychological interpretation of this set of rivers in the underworld, we can interpret this Greek mythology as suggesting the way in which hatred brings about a death of clear consciousness, overshadowed by a dark gloominess (*stúgios*), which closes people off to human contact,

---

[1740] Homer, *Iliad*, 20.65 (BK.vv: 20.63-65). This verb is also found in variant forms in the Koine Greek of the New Testament, as in *Apostugountes tò ponērón* (Romans 12:9); the King James Version reads: "Abhor that which is evil." This word, *apostugountes*, is an intensive of *stugeō*.

[1741] I would like to thank Jon Solomon, Classics Professor at the Univ. of Illinois, Urbana, for his help in this passage of the *Iliad* and pointing out the etymological link of the verb to *Styx* (the River Styx), opening up the interpretation to follow.

[1742] Mareile Haase, "Catabasis [Katábasis]", Brill Online, Religious Studies, Religion Past and Present (2011); Marco Antonio Santamaría Álvarez, "The Parody of the *Katábasis*-Motif in Aristophanes' *Frogs*," *Études classiques* (Namur, Belgium), vol. 83, no. 1-4, Jan. 2015, pp. 117-136.

[1743] On the hero as quest-seeker, see Gestalt Psychologist and educator Claudio Naranjo MD, *The Divine Child and the Hero: Inner Meaning in Children's Literature* (1999). In particular, on Abraham, consider the Hebrew (ha'ivri), literally, Abraham, the Boundary-crosser ('ivri), as in R' Gershon Winkler, *The Way of the Boundary Crosser: An Introduction to Jewish Flexidoxy* (1998).

empathy, sympathy, mutual good will, respect, and love, and (as in the above imagery); leaves them with wailing, gloominess, misery, burning torment, and a contention-born heedlessness.[1744] And if anything can be of help in these tormented realities, it is the caring, gentleness, sympathy, understanding, and encouragement that people can receive from others. In the above Christian terms, it is truly treating the least as if the greatest.

This model of certain psychological truths suggests a contrast in how we might deal with life and its various concerns: All of the attitudes just discussed are in sharp contrast with the honor that could be given to bitterness, greed, a self-righteous sense of superiority over other human beings (with the corollary of condescension and hatred against whichever group is picked out as the inferior other), to cynicism, a justification of power as a source of any and all rights and privileges, typically driven by a sense of need, hostility by others, and the related dangers and call for self-protection (to be found both individually and in entire societies, often in justification of war).

On a psychological plane, a caring heart, an openness to the suffering of others, can be difficult (but not impossible) if we ourselves are sensing an intense lack of security, a great fear, or a hopelessness, a traumatic state of mind that *can structure individuals for decades*, and, indeed, *can structure entire societies overall, as they address future tension-filled situations*. This is a powerful consideration for all societies.

Thus, in recalling his experience during the War of 1918-1918, at Verdun, Field Marshal Philippe Pétain would describe the young twenty-year-old Frenchmen he encountered and acknowledged, returning from battle, their elusive gaze seemed to be transfixed in a vision of terror (*leur regard insaisissable semblait figé dans une vision d'épouvante*).[1745]

If, in this context, we see the shifts in overall human consciousness as going toward a realization of human love, or, alternatively, as a going toward a sense of the rights of some over others, dehumanizing those we hate; toward mutual support and good will, or, alternatively, toward hatred and violence against those we feel to be a threat to us, sensed to be endangering our own well-being, *then there is a choice here* of what sort of mind-set we will encourage in ourselves and in others, a choice

---

[1744] Christopher John Mackie, "Scamander and the Rivers of Hades in Homer," *The American Journal of Philology*, vol. 120, no. 4, 1999, pp. 485–501.

[1745] The Battle of Verdun lasted from Feb. 21-Dec. 18, 1916, the longest and costliest battle of World War I, *with more than 700,000 casualties in all*. The French had 377,231 casualties, with 162,440 dead; the Germans had 337,000 casualties with 143,000 dead. In the related offensive by the British BEF that set off the Battle of the Somme, to divert some Germany military from Verdun, the British on the first day alone (July 1, 1916) had 57,470 casualties, with 19,240 deaths. By comparison, US military losses of the AEF in combat totaled 53,402 *in battle for the entire war*, in addition to 63,114 deaths due to the influenza pandemic of 1918 (a grand total of 116,516). See "Les Grands Hommes de Verdun: le Général Pétain," LESFRANCAISAVERDUN-1916.FR; David Wilcock, "Battle of the Somme in numbers: Key facts as the battle marks its centenary," *Independent*, Jun. 29, 2016; Carol R. Byerly, "War Losses (USA)," 1914-1918 ONLINE, Oct. 8, 2014.

between being guided (or driven) by fear and hatred, or being guided by a respect for all human beings.

This raises questions of how we are to deal with conflicts and tensions between people, but this is something we confront ongoing in life, first, within ourselves, when our various desires, beliefs, hopes, and fears are not in mutual harmony, and then in any couple we form part of, when what we are interested in or attracted to at any point in time is not what our partner is focused on, and then in families, which can be quite complex and complicated. Finally, we have entire groups or societies that have contact and interaction with others, and this same form of question presents itself: how do we modulate and take into account others' desires and interests, in ways that allow us to stay true to, and to be at peace with, our own most central values about how we want to be, act, and live.

BEYOND THE QUESTION OF EVIL

In our putting forth basic questions in this domain, for those who think in terms of God (or a god), one question that we all face here is how if there is a God, can the mass killing of the Holocaust, or of other genocides, have happened? How could a caring God have allowed this? This may call up a centuries-old specific question, the Question of Evil. The answer to this specific question is said to be that God gave humans free will: the option to choose good or to choose evil. *And yet the answer to such a question, whatever it might be, does not at all answer a broader and more inclusive question*, namely: How can disasters that cannot be attributed to some nasty or deeply malicious person or persons be explained? Why do any die from earthquakes or volcanic eruptions? Why do babies sometimes die before they can become children, let alone adults with a full life? Why are children born with what we call birth defects, some minor, some life-disturbing and life-altering? There are many questions like these, we might be able to acknowledge.

One answer here (as an example) is that there is no God. This very idea leads quite immediately for many to the question of what any basis of morality would be if there is no God. We might consider that either we live our lives in a moral way, for its own value, or we do not. Our sense of morality in this way would not depend on fear of punishment for wrongdoing, or, in religious terms, for sinning. There is here a further question that we can ponder on our own: Do we act in an honorable, civilized, moral way because we are afraid of a bolt of lightning coming down on us (just a metaphor here) or because we want to do good, to act morally and honorably?

A related question concerns the foundation of morality in general. Some say we are all inherently good and caring, open to and needing love and good will, and that only harsh and violent treatment can move us from that to a sense of hatred and a need for intense self-protection. If we have an inherent potential, at least, of good will (in its most modest form being perhaps what we think of as civility), and this sense of moral existence is inborn, how do we nurture it? It has been said, "Neither shall they say, 'See here! or See there!' For, behold the kingdom of God is within you."[1746] And if what some call the divine spark is within (that is, within in our very own individual consciousness), can we see this same potential in others, even others who are not part of what we experience as our own particular group? This basic concept proposes that all humans have this potential in their consciousness to uncover, or to develop (in another model of the mind), a calm and clear awareness that is not controlled by what we have lived through and have been hurt (or scarred) by, that we can become fundamentally free of reactive thinking and consequent acting—no longer driven by this conditioned past (something we might understand with a moment's thought but which is typically a years-long process of refining our consciousness),[1747] in which we can stay in touch with what is enlightening and inspiring and life-encouraging.

Some call this enlightened consciousness, awakened mind, or Christ-consciousness, and so on, with different names and variations on this idea in a wide number of religious and spiritual traditions, with at times subtle but important differences in methodology, all toward rather similar goals.[1748]

A deeply human sense of morality, of a noble, admirable, kind, good-willed person, not driven by hatred or inner frustration put out onto others as the cause of their own frustration—cutting across most categories of humanity. As Jan Karski (whose official visit to Roosevelt was discussed above) put it once, "There is no such thing as bad nations and good nations; there are bad people and good people; not nations."[1749] Or, we could say, people at times are good, in some basic sense, and perhaps at times, bad, in some parallel basic sense. This presumably applies to all of us. This is not especially frightening, but it does suggest the need for our paying attention to all of our various inclinations, some likely to bring about more torment in the world, which some traditions call being unskillful, and others, that lessen anguish and torment in the world, or at least do not intensify the difficulties of living life, in parallel called being skillful in our thoughts, words, and actions.

Among the values that are widely shared we might see those that are stressed by those who value civilized life—such as was said of a woman by her husband at the time of his mourning her shortly after her death, that she had "a personal conviction that the world needed more kindness." Here, we may see civilized life as opposed to barbaric, murderous, hate- and fear-inspired forms of group life: civilized as shown by kindness, sympathy, understanding, helpfulness to the less fortunate, appreciation of the most sublime contributions to our species and culture that we can

---

[1746] Luke 17:21, in the AKJV (American King James Version).

[1747] This was discussed in a chapter on the gradual and the sudden paths to awakening or enlightenment, in Mitchell Ginsberg, *The Inner Palace*.

[1748] For an extensive presentation and detailed discussion of these and related transformations in consciousness, see Mitchell Ginsberg, *The Inner Palace*.

[1749] *Holocaust Rescue and Aid Provider Jan Karski Testimony* (Mar. 10, 1995), at 15:35-16:15, YOUTUBE. Cf. E. Thomas Wood and Stanisław M. Jankowski, *How One Man Tried to Stop the Holocaust* (1994/2014).

think of or imagine. We might also see other values that we may not think of or at first as essential to civilized life (but which can add something of value to it, even so), such as being resourceful, having passion for one's life and one's activities, appreciation for the contributions of others, creativity, determination, the readiness if it is called for sacrifice (in general, acting in ways of benefit not so much for ourselves but especially for others), a sense of solidarity, a full utilization of each person's inner potential, a readiness to be helpful to those who are making a contribution to the well-being of others, a willingness to be open to others that we do not initially see as part of our particular group. The reader will presumably be able to add a number of further characteristics of value here.

That said, if we look in a more general (non-specific) way, we can see other societies in which a strong government became dictatorial, with little influence of the greater population, in which one group or another was brought into focus as the major source of the country's problems (scapegoats), and with actions, if not laws, that made the lives of such groups miserable, intolerable, and even life-threatening.

If we have not experienced such similar societal situations ourselves, can we imagine what it would be like to live day after day in such a hostile, noxious, even murderous environment? Can we get a sense of what it must be like for those around the world, even in today's realities, who are suffering without relief, with fear of death a constant companion?

And if we can put ourselves into such situations, either through memory or imagination, are we sure of how we would act in those situations? Can we in all honesty answer the question of whether we would stand up for human rights, or silently try to get by as best we can, join in while the joining is good, for the mundane, social benefits that are promised to us? Would we cooperate with such societal demands, or even become enthusiastic about the rights, benefits, and power that we are being given by engaging ourselves fully in that society and its values? Would we show a blind eye to the distortions that often come with governmental bias and a State's desire to establish itself as honorable, trustworthy, and truthful? We may be reminded, "There are times when the truth—frequently in the interests of a State [*auch von Staats wegen*]—grows dim [*verdunkelt*], when it becomes a target for destruction. But some day it comes back into the light [*aber kommt sie doch wieder ans Licht*]. The same may be said for our private and business lives."[1750] Something we would do well not to forget, of course.

Would we be able to bear torture to remain true to our sense of justice, fairness, and compassion, despite the society's values that are declared and put into operation? Can we consider such a situation with sufficient detail, with enough felt detail, in a way that would allow us to come up with a definitive answer to the question of how we would be in that situation? This is not obvious. What we can recognize here, in any case,

---

[1750] Christa Schroeder, *Er war mein Chef*, p. 8; *He Was My Chief*, p. xvi. From her comments about a newspaper article cutting, saved in her papers. Schroeder was a private secretary of Adolf Hitler for many years.

is that there are societies that put great demands on its population, in ways that are demanding, harsh, and even unrelentingly cruel.

Perhaps the issue is better addressed not as a question of how each of us as an individual would deal with such violent societies, but what can we do to prevent such societies from developing, or, if we realize that such a society is in the process of being established, where it had not been before, that we as a group act against this nascent hell on earth.

In looking back at the Third Reich, it had two well-established churches, the Catholic Church and the Protestant Church, the latter primarily Lutheran in teachings and rites. Neither of these raised any questions with the Nuremberg Laws of 1935, stripping German Jews of citizenship, with all related rights also taken from them, and reducing them to subjects of the Reich. So, the presence of solid religious communities is not enough. Furthermore, if we consider education, not only were some the top Nazis quite educated, some with the equivalent of JD (Doctor of Jurisprudence) or of the PhD (Doctorate in Philosophy, with specializations in many fields), but, in addition, there was the overall respected German educational system with its *Gymnasia* (academic pre-university schools, parallel to French *lycées*). None of this could protect the German people from what happened in the *Machtergreifung* (Taking of Power) by the National Socialists beginning in 1933. As Alfons Heck, a member of the *Hitlerjugend* quoted earlier, wrote to this issue: "The only hope is to maintain unrestricted, unlimited freedom of speech, especially for those who don't share our beliefs."[1751] This is not to deny the ultimate individual evaluations of our situation, our decisions of what to do about that, and our actions following from that perspective. It is simply to say that society-wide processes are perhaps addressed in similar terms: with large groups sensing that something has gone awry in the culture.

As in other contexts, a teaching from long ago can touch on issues that are personal and moral, together. We may compare a value system (which calls itself a moral vision) in which the weak and non-conforming are to eliminated from society, perhaps by prison or execution, with one in which there is the encouragement of compassion and tenderness toward those who are the weakest and most vulnerable.

US Circuit Judge Learned Hand (who is often quoted respectfully in legal contexts for his articulate observations) once declared to a large audience,[1752] in a reference to Mathew 25:40, 45,[1753] that "the spirit of liberty is the spirit of Him who, near two thousand years ago, taught

---

[1751] Alfons Heck, *The Burden of Hitler's Legacy*, p. 266.

[1752] Judge Learned Hand, "The Spirit of Liberty" speech given at the "I Am an American" Ceremony, in Central Park, New York City, on May 21, 1944. It is reported that there were 1.5 million people on hand, with 150,000 immigrants who became naturalized citizens that day.

[1753] Matthew 25:40: The King will reply, "Truly, I tell you, whatever you did for one of the least of these brothers and sisters of mine, you did for me." And Matthew 25:45: He will reply, "Truly I tell you, whatever you did not do for one of the least of these, you did not do for me."

mankind that lesson it has never learned, but has never quite forgotten; that there may be a kingdom where the least shall be heard and considered side by side with the greatest."

What will appeal to us may rest in our own sense of morality, but may be strongly influenced by the culture in which we find ourselves, *for better or for worse!* In a spontaneous way, groups of people during the Hitler era would sense who was of like mind, and ready to discuss, plan, and act in ways to bring about the end of that Nazi-directed world. These were often called the resistance—in France, *maquisards* (French Resistance fighters), the movement, *le maquis* (the French Resistance), which worked with the British.[1754] A variation of this in Spain (and in South America) is referred to as *la red antimilitarista* (the network of anti-militarists).

In terms of how populations can be led to have certain attitudes about international relations and about the issue of war, there are some repeating patterns that are used by those with an interest in stirring up hatreds. During World War I, the mathematician and philosopher Bertrand Russell wrote of the machinations of political motivation,

> When I say that the war has been brought about by Governments, I do not mean that it has been brought about without the participation of popular passions. What I mean is that those passions ... have been incited by Governments and the newspapers which support them, partly by means of professed opinions, but still more by carefully selecting the information which was given to the public. I do not deny that, by these means, the instinct of group-hostility has been aroused; but I maintain that in each nation a comparatively small number of men are responsible for arousing it.[1755]

A related statement of how to incite a desire for war was made by Hermann Göring after his capture in 1945, in preparing for his defense at the Nuremberg Tribunal trial. He spoke frequently with the American military psychologist Gustave Gilbert, a native speaker of German, his parents being immigrants to the USA from Austria. In his cell, on the evening of April 18, 1946, Göring said to him,

> Why, of course, the people don't want war! Why would some poor slob on a farm want to risk his life in a war

---

[1754] "Noor Inayat Khan: remembering Britain's Muslim war heroine," *The Guardian* (London), Oct 23, 2012. She was the first woman SOE wireless operator, the sole link to this British sabotage intelligence after the Gestapo arrests of most of the Paris *maquis*. Raised in Suresnes—her father, Hazrat Inayat Khan founded the Sufi Order in the West—the Gestapo arrested her in Oct. 1943 as a *Nacht und Nebel* prisoner, *spurlos*, with no trace; executed at Dachau on Sep. 13, 1944.

[1755] Bertrand Russell, "The Reconciliation Question," *The Cambridge Review*, vol. 36, Mar. 10, 1915, pp. 250-251; reprinted at pp. 100-104 in Bertrand Russell, *Prophecy and Dissent, 1914-1916* (1988), at p. 102.

when the best that he can get out of it is to come back to his farm in one piece. Naturally, the common people don't want war; neither in Russia nor in England, nor in America, nor for that matter in Germany. That is understood. But, after all, it is the leaders of the country who determine the policy and it always a simple matter to drag people along, whether it is a democracy or a fascist dictatorship or a Parliament or a Communist dictatorship ... voice or no voice, the people can always be brought to the bidding of the leaders. That is easy. All you have to do is tell them that they are being attacked and denounce the pacifists for lack of patriotism and exposing the country to danger. It works the same way in any country.[1756]

Perhaps this is not a universally effective methodology, but if we look at the contexts in which numerous nations have come to a war-frenzy and a demand for war, these features are quite regularly present.

These considerations place us at the borderline between national politics and international politics, which moves our focus into the realm of international relations. It is one thing to be alert to the tendencies of those who would like great power to do their best to obtain that power, and to keep our own nation away from such tendencies. It is another to see such developments in other countries, as did the nations neighboring Germany in the 1920s and 1930s. *In a way, our world is in its infancy in trying to establish and maintain just, fair, and equitable societies*—we might ask if there is even one such country in the world, beyond what each country in its proudest and most self-righteous moments says of itself. This is an issue for all of us worldwide. Perhaps we will develop, or, put optimistically, continue to develop, a general consensus of opinion about eliminating the power of prejudice and denigration of other peoples, along with their mistreatment. This is perhaps a desideratum to be attained.

Prejudice is a pervasive element in our thinking, if for no other reason than our inclination to guess at what we do not know, which can readily be transformed from a guess to an opinion, and from that, to an obvious and even undeniable truth. It is a form of mental lassitude and laziness. It is not new and if seen (more easily in others than in ourselves, as was said at Mathew 7:3), prejudice can have a repulsive aspect to it.

THE PSYCHOLOGY OF BEING DECENT (*ANSTÄNDIG*) AND CRUEL, TOGETHER

Himmler suggested in a speech at Posnań to the SS in 1943 that they must be "honest [*ehrlich*], decent [*anständig*], loyal [*treu*] and comradely [or comrade-like, *kameradschaftlich*] to members of our own blood and to nobody else."[1757] When people torture other people or have people killed in front of compatriots (as in the camps), often with music, is this simply sadism at play? Is this simply a denial of the cruelty about to

---

[1756] Gustave M. Gilbert, *Nuremberg Diary*, pp. 278-279; punctuation modified.
[1757] NT-NCA-Red, vol. 4, pp. 558-572, esp. pp. 559; this sect. at pp. 563-564. Cf. NT-IMT-Blue, vol. 29, the Ger. passage at pp. 122-123, quoted Ger. terms, p. 122.

happen? Will such people see themselves as dishonorable? Now, while a moral sense may have a role in this for some, many are not ashamed but, rather, proud of what they are doing and have done. To call them sadistic does not capture these other features of the situation and their understanding of their actions. *This is a perplexing question, but we can come to have a sense of what is going on here.* As Hitler proposed, Germans must be *grausam*, cruel, ruthless[1758]—not with a gratuitous cruelty, but with one rooted in the strength of character that can be applied when one must fight tooth-and-nail for one's most profound (if not sacred) values and understanding of life. One master of this ruthless sadism was the *Teufel/Bestie* (Devil/Beast/Tiger) of Auschwitz, Wilhelm Boger, SS officer in the Gestapo there, inventor of a torture device, the Boger Swing (*Bogerschaukel*).[1759] Such violence had an important role in showing prisoners who is in power, who has the right to do as they wish (shoot someone at whim or beat someone to lifelessness), and that all of this violence is in the honorable name of individual and national pride. We can refer to images from the Third Reich of men being hung by their arms tied behind their back and being beaten, or being burned alive, or pushed off of cliffs, or attacked by guard dogs trained to bite into the crotch, of people being shot in mass, or shipped like animals to death camps. The examples are many and are readily available for those interested in seeing more. In such a mind-set, the violence is often understood in its function and purpose, all honorable and worthy when seen in that light. The sort of internal consistency here requires a limiting of one's thinking, so that other aspects of the thinking and action are not given any attention. This may be seen as part of human capacity to stay focused on one topic, or as part of what can understood as the process of repression or of splitting. This inner coherence loses its force when the human impact of such actions is evaluated for its sheer violence, its criminal nature.

The establishment of the International Court of Justice is one powerful action in the direction of holding governments and also their leaders responsible for the cruelties and killing that they direct. It is just one step, obviously. And it is of limited power and applicability at this time, at least.

One new type of organization in these past decades has been the establishment of research institutes that keep track of violence in different parts of the world. Some of these groups focus, in particular, on what can be the first warning signs of an organized killing program, either for ethnic cleansing, for group massacres, or for genocide, in the more extreme version of this inter-group murderous violence.[1760] What we do not have at this point in time, in human structures for dealing with enormous problems of violence, is an established and readily applied system of intervention, including a system of early warnings about incipient genocides that can be effectively activated. At the same time, UN Peace-

---

[1758] Hermann Rauschning on Hitler, quoted in Joachim C. Fest, *Hitler* (Ger. text), p. 477; *Hitler* (Eng.), p. 343.
[1759] See articles "Wilhelm Boger," at DE.WIKIPEDIA.ORG and at WIKIPEDIA.ORG.
[1760] Such as the organization, Genocide Watch, GENOCIDEWATCH.COM.

keeping missions are a weak and limited application of this international interest in the protection of peoples persecuted and killed. This interest is counter-balanced, after all, by each state, which wants to preserve its self-direction, its autonomy, even if its path is one of horrible violence. We can see in the past, and, perhaps more palpably, in the present, the rape, murder, and attack on civilian populations. Recent mass murders include those by the so-called Islamic State in Syria and Iraq, or the rape, sexual slavery, and murder of civilians in the Central African Republic or CAR (south of Chad, north of the DRC, the Democratic Republic of the Congo) or in the DRC itself (east of the Republic of the Congo, west of Rwanda and Burundi), or of Rohingya Muslims in Myanmar (Burma).

The current state of international understanding and policies is such that there is simply no mechanism, no established system for what some refer to as low-level prosecutions, referring to the foot soldiers and others who carry out these violations of basic human rights, such as colonels, majors, and others in charge of the actual rape and killing of civilians in various countries in the world. This point has been clearly made by Dan Plesch, Professor at SOAS.[1761]

These considerations raise perhaps more questions, both about our own individual inclinations that would influence if not determine how we would respond to some sort of violent crisis in our immediate world, but also about the group, national, and international structures that would allow a means of saving people's lives and caring for the distressed, the forced migrants, those seeking safety and promise of a full life but being in a political and military situation not permitting any of that. Differently expressed, we have here questions both about our own sense of who we are and how we would deal with such stressful situations, and also about the ways in which we might have a greater impact on our world, if we can work together with others of similar values.

Fundamental here is the issue of what these values are. The question of human morality is a great one, and while some feel that it is necessary to have a religion to supply a foundation for one's morality, and others feel that religions encourage dogmatism and rigidity in the name of morality, there is the general human recognition of what is kind, or just or fair, and what is cruel, nasty, or vicious. This may be clear whatever one's relation is to religion (or to a variety of religions around the world).

Of course, not everyone wants a just and fair world, not everyone wants people to be given a basic amount of respect, to be treated with a minimal amount of civility, even. Perhaps there is some justice, but certainly, a deep longing for justice, for kindness, and for support from others when needed, even if only for ourselves, in the most selfish variations on these desires. Perhaps there is also a human drive for fairness and kindness, a balance between justice and loving compassion. One option for us is the small and gradual retuning, refining, of how we

---

[1761] *Dan Plesch: The Lost History of Prosecuting Axis War Crimes, Carnegie Council for Ethics in International Affairs*, Mar. 15, 2018, YOUTUBE, at 10:00-12:00. SOAS is the School of Asian and African Studies at the University of London.

The Hitler Era 595

treat one another, and how we think about society as human beings trying to get through life, individually and collectively.

And this may be so even if Homer was correct in writing, "There is nothing alive more agonized than man of all that breathe and crawl upon the earth."[1762] Even in the face of such a reading of our human condition, as was said traditionally, our task stands firm, to repair the cosmic cracks to let the divine light shine through. As Canadian poet and songwriter Leonard Cohen (1934-2016) expressed this mystical vision, "There is a crack in everything. That's how the light gets in."[1763] And the wish of Chilean poet and songwriter Víctor Jara (1932-1973) was the dream of the simple right to live in peace (*el derecho de vivir en paz*).[1764]

REICH ARYANS VS. JEWS, HALF-APES, AND CHRISTIAN MONGRELS

There are informative passages from Hitler's opus of speeches and writings, which has him discuss his Germanic ideal of a community of pure Germans (Aryans), all of whose members are of pure German blood, whose ancestry stems back only to those who are fully and completely German. This vision sees a pure and elevated, superior group (or race), identified in Nazi thinking with the *Herrenrasse* (the Master Race) with others, assumed to be clearly inferior to the pure German, some held to be inferior groups, some to be subhuman, and some to be more animal than human in any form, dehumanized.

This, is of course in stark contrast with not only a Jewish idea, but a Western, and, in fact, a world-wide respect for all of humanity, with the corollary that all people are human and therefore equal. Hitler would express his views on this topic in clear terms throughout the years. In some of his literature put up in posters, with announcements on the contents of his speeches, he wrote,

> A state of intimate fraternalization is to arrive between Englishmen and Hottentots [early twentieth-century Germany's paradigm example of a primitive African tribe], between Chinese and Zulu Kafirs, French and Japanese, Russians and Germans, etc. They are all human beings and therefore all equal! Although the colors are different, the quantity of brains and the physique do not correspond, the way of thinking and the achievements are not the same [so writes Hitler].... A consequence of this equality is therefore the "international solidarity." But while the peoples dream of this, the same Jew smashes the only

---

[1762] Homer, *Iliad*, 17.515-516 (BK.vv: 17.440-447).
[1763] Leonard Cohen, "Anthem," in Leonard Cohen, *Stranger Music: Selected Poems and Songs* (1994), p. 373. Cf. the Lurianic concept of *zimzum:* "Zimzum: God and the creation of the world," JEWISH MUSEUM BERLIN (with DEPT. OF JEWISH STUDIES AND RELIGIOUS STUDIES AT THE UNIV. OF POTSDAM). This refers to the teachings of Rabbi Isaac ben Solomon Luria Ashkenazi (1534-1572) of Safed (Tsfat), referred to by his students through the centuries as *ha-Eloki Rabbeinu Yitzchak*, Our Holy Rabbi Isaac, or shortened to an anacronym, *ha-Ari*, the Lion.
[1764] Víctor Jara, "El derecho de vivir en paz," GENIUS.COM (with lyrics).

natural and most intelligible solidarity which ought to exist, that of every nation in itself. Immeasurable misery has come over Germany today. In Upper Silesia, in continued slaughter, thousands of fellow citizens sink into the grave. The black disgrace [French African colonial troops in the 1920s occupation] works havoc on the Rhine. Women, girls, and children pay for the bestial negroes' lust with their death. [A commonly used image of the black as having unusually strong sexual drives and capacity, enough to put envy if not hatred into self-questioning white men, either in Germany or elsewhere.] An uninterrupted stream of poison and disease flows into the blood of our people. Moroccan syphilis drives thousands of victims towards a cruel death.[1765]

Goebbels would write of National Socialism as Germany's religion, freed from Christian teachings.[1766] And Alfred Baeumler wrote that Christian morality was f and the stupid German *bourgeoisie*,oreign to Hitler, using a Nazified Nietzsche as model.[1767] Hitler would speak of freeing Germans from Jewish and Christian morality, "from the dirty and degrading self-mortifications of a chimera called conscience and morality.[1768] (We discussed these above.)

Mein Kampf offers Hitler's a consistent attitude about the suffering German nation and the stupid German *bourgeoisie*, about the Jew, the half-ape, and the doctrine of the equality of all mankind that Hitler takes

---

[1765] From an Appendix of early Hitler speeches, included in Adolf Hitler, *Mein Kampf*, Eng. tr., in "Poster Appendix" (pp. 516-559), at p. 540, entitled "National Socialist German Workers' Party. Slogan after slogan rain down on our people: International Solidarity!" (Hitler will speak against this proposition.)

[1766] Joseph Goebbels, *Tagebücher 1924-1945*, p. 327. Cf. *The Goebbels Experiment*, at 13:35-14:10.

[1767] Alfred Baeumler, "Nietzsche und der Nationalsozialismus," in *Studien zur deutschen* Geistesgeschichte (1937), pp. 281-294 (Chap. 9), at pp. 288, 291.

[1768] NT-IMT-Blue, vol. 7, p. 153, quoting Hermann Rauschning, *The Voice of Destruction* (1940), p, 225. See partial quotation and discussion in Robert G. L. Waite, "Hitler's Anti-Semitism: A Study in History and Psychoanalysis," pp. 192-230, in Benjamin B. Wolman, *The Psychoanalytic Interpretation of History* (1971), at p. 203; cf. Robert Waite, "Adolf Hitler's Guilt Feelings: A Problem in History and Psychology," *Journal of Interdisciplinary History*, vol. 1 Winter 1971, pp. 229-249, at p. 235. Rauschning (1887-1982) was an early Nazi and the Nazi President of the Danzig Senate from June 20, 1933 to Nov. 23, 1934. Resigning his post and his membership in the National Socialist Party, he fled to Poland in 1936, moved to Switzerland in 1937 to France in 1938, to the UK in 1939, and to the USA in 1941. His writings are questioned if not rejected by many with a favorable bent toward Hitler, his history, his personality, and such, including Holocaust-deniers such as David Irving, Mark Weber, and the less-known Swiss revisionist historian Wolfgang Nänel, with links primarily to the revisionist (often Holocaust-denying) Institute for Historical Review (IHR) and to other institutes such as the *Zeitgeschichtliche Forschungsstelle Ingolstadt* (ZFI). Ingolstadt is a city in Bavaria.

The Hitler Era

to be a distorted doctrine, all in an inter-related if not totally coherent fashion:

> The folkish state ... has *to put the race into the center of life in general. It has to care for its preservation in purity. It has to make the child the most precious possession of the society. It has to take care that only the healthy beget children.*[1769] A further example [Hitler waxes moralistic here] shows how boundlessly today's mankind sins in this direction. From time to time it is demonstrated to the German petty *bourgeoisie* in illustrated periodicals how ... a negro has become a lawyer, teacher, even clergyman, or even a leading opera tenor[1770] [*daß da oder dort zum erstenmal ein Neger Advokat, Lehrer, gar Pastor, ja Heldentenor oder dergleichen ist*].... While the stupid *bourgeoisie*, marveling, takes recognizance of this miraculous training, filled with respect for this fabulous result of our present educative skill, the Jew knows very slyly how to construe from this a new proof of the correctness of his theory of the *equality of man* which he means to instill into the nations. It does not dawn upon this depraved *bourgeois* world that here one has actually to deal with a sin against all reason; that *it is a criminal absurdity* [*daß es ein verbrecherischer Wahnwitz ist*], to train *a born half-ape* [*ein geborenen Halbaffen so lange zu dressieren*] until one believes a lawyer has been made of him.[1771]

There is also the question suggested by this passage of Hitler's attitude toward those who would now fashion themselves after the original Nazis: the neo-Nazis, skinheads, White Supremacists, the American Nazi Party (founded by George Lincoln Rockwell), and other such groups. Whatever their inner strife and debates about correct doctrine and leadership, they all feel they are the inheritors and the continuing force for the ideas of National Socialism as known during the Third Reich. Many of its members are either of Slavic descent (as in skinheads in the Russian Confederation, neo-Nazis in Ukraine, etc.) or many in the USA with an Anglo-Saxon ancestry, often with family from a rich variety of cultures: English, Irish, French, German, Italian, Czech, Polish, even Cherokee, Seminole, and other native American, Amerindian peoples.

[1769] Here we see the seeds of what will later be the third Reich's T4 euthanasia program. Italics in original. Adolf Hitler, *Mein Kampf*, Vol. 2, Chap. II, at p. 608. Ger., *Mein Kampf*, Vol. 2, Chap. II, at pp. 478-479.

[1770] A *Heldentenor* (here, "operatic tenor"), lit., a heroic tenor, is an operatic singer with great ease of a non-stressed voice through the full ranges of a tenor. Such a singer is quite rare and often highly appreciated in operatic circles. See David L. Jones, "Understanding the Helden Tenor," VOICETEACHER.COM.

[1771] Adolf Hitler, *Mein Kampf*, Vol. 2, Chap. II, p. 639-640. Ger., *Mein Kampf*, Vol. 2, Chap. II, pp. 478-479.

While neo-Nazis would mostly agree with a rejection of the brotherhood of man, many of them might find the Nazi denigration of Christianity to be quite uncomfortable to consider; in any case, such religious beliefs would have them dismissed by those in the Third Reich as inferior and to be made into slaves or murdered in mass.

This interwoven thread can be seen in many of Hitler's many vituperative, venomous, hate-filled, repulsion-rich, disease-phobic, anti-Semitic declarations in *Mein Kampf* and throughout Hitler's speeches through all the Hitler era from 1919 to his final Political Statement dictated and signed the day before his suicide. The power of this concern, which was injected into all Nazi thought and programs is no passing, no superficial matter. In keeping this complex, hateful vision in mind, the unity of Third Reich (despite its inner conflicts between key players and their particular interests) can be traced and recognized.

THE HITLER FASCINATION—SO WHAT?

Hitler certainly has attracted the attention of millions upon millions of people, before and after his death. There are thousands of books written, some backed by great, extensive, and serious research into Hitler's life and world, which give a rather well-defined and precise sense of what Hitler and the world he impacted so powerfully, and destructively, meant.

One glimpse at what role Hitler saw himself taking in the grand history of Europe can be seen by his comment as recorded by Martin Bormann, dated February 26, 1945, only months before Hitler's suicide death; Hitler remarked, speaking of Europe, "It could not be conquered by charm and persuasiveness. I had to rape it in order to have it. [*Man mußte ihn vergewaltigen, um ihn zu haben*]."[1772] In the larger context, there are many works that researched Hitler's medical conditions, his medical treatment, his psychology and his psychosexuality, and his relations with women. Some of these can prove to be quite specific and engaging, and run from his early relationships with a romantic touch to them, typically with women significantly his junior, and often focus on his relation with his half-sister's daughter, Geli, his relation with the famous German actress Renate Müller, sometimes mentioning the English socialite, Unity Valkyrie Mitford, sister-in-law of Oswald Mosley, leader of the British Union of Fascists (never to be a dominant force in British politics), a young woman who seemed to like to *épater la bourgeoisie*, to scandalize the bourgeoisie, as the French say.

And, again, we can consider here Hitler's longer-time companion, Eva Braun, who was kept in the shadows from the public (and even of visitors to Hitler's residence, the Berghof, near Berchtesgaden in the Bavarian Alps) until the day before their joint suicide in the Chancellery bunker in Berlin, as Soviet troops approached Berlin (the glory of the Third Reich),

---

[1772] Joachim C. Fest, *Hitler* (Ger. text), p. 1032; *Hitler*, (Eng.), p. 757; Fr. text from Adolf Hitler, *Le testament politique d'Adolf Hitler: Notes recueillies par Martin Bormann* (1959), being Bomann's notes from Feb. 4-Apr. 29, 1945, quoted from an entry dated Feb. 26, 1945, in French: *il fallait la violer pour la prendre*.

The Hitler Era

and then captured the remains of the bunker, Hitler and Eva Braun to be found dead. There are reports of Hitler having one gonad, of his penis being ill-formed anatomically (one explanation of why he rarely undressed fully in front of others, even his valet—his typical pose, with his hands an improvised codpiece, joined over his groin, adding to this interpretation), of his having distinctively enjoyable interactions with women, including being kicked and receiving their expelled feces or urine from above, and on and on. (The anatomical abnormalities reported were apparently fabrications, as indicated by careful analysis of medical reports from Dr. Morell when he examined Hitler.[1773])

Now, *all of this is perhaps rather interesting and unusual, and yet, while possibly a magnet for attention and curiosity, we might ask what role these changes played in the basic structure of his world and of the Third Reich?*

These may serve to dismiss him, as calling him crazy, insane, or psychotic might serve to do, but this is *a distraction from understanding just what was going on in that world and how personalities meshed with* cultural yearnings in a time of great conflict, confusion, and an unresolved sense of national identity, as was typical of the time from the mid-1800s to late 1900s. Such claims are perhaps not only dismissive of any understanding of what was going on for Hitler, but may also turn out to be quite groundless.

A summary of Hitler's health at the end of his life and his suicide on April 30, 1945, is given in the following points: "1. Hitler suffered from gastrointestinal cramps, an irritable bowel syndrome that seems to depend on his mental constitution, 2. The tremor in his left arm and leg was not what Morell described as a 'variety of shaking palsy' but a symptom of Parkinson's disease that first manifested itself in 1941, 3. Without doubt he also suffered from high blood pressure and a deteriorating coronary sclerosis, 4. There is no scientific medical proof that Hitler suffered from any mental disease."[1774]

Reviews of Morell's medical records concluded that Hitler suffered from a blockage to the bile flow, as in an inflammation of the bile ducts: In Morell's suspected diagnosis (*Verdachtsdiagnose*), a closed or obstructed jaundice (*ein Verschloss- oder Obstruktionsikterus*), which may develop through a mechanical obstruction of the bile flow, an organ malfunctioning would explain some of Hitler's long-term gastro-intestinal problems from some of Hitler's medical symptoms: chronic flatulence, constipation, diarrhea, and irritable bowel syndrome.[1775]

There is much debate about details. The blood at Hitler's left temple was at first taken to be where he shot himself; this would have had him

---

[1773] Hans-Joachim Neumann and Henrik Eberle, *War Hitler Krank?*, pp. 52-60; Eng, *Was Hitler Ill?*, pp. 27-32.

[1774] Hans-Joachim Neumann and Henrik Eberle, *War Hitler Krank?*, p. 290; Eng, *Was Hitler Ill?*, p. 186.

[1775] Hans-Joachim Neumann and Henrik Eberle, *War Hitler Krank?*, p. 183; Eng., *Was Hitler Ill?*, p. 113.

use his left hand to hold the pistol. This seems unlikely. It would be more reliable for Hitler to use his right hand to aim the pistol, the hand that did not have the tremor. Relatedly, an examination by a Soviet forensic pathologist, Pyotr S. Semenovski, who examined the left parietal bone found *typical signs of an exit wound*. This would support the idea that Hitler had shot himself from under the chin upwards toward his skull using his right hand, aiming up toward the middle of his head. Hitler also might have followed the advice of Dr. Werner Haase, one of remaining Hitler's personal physicians (after Hitler fired Dr. Theodor Morrell April 21, 1945), that Hitler use a dual method for his suicide (advice followed by Joseph Goebbels the next day, May 1), biting down on a cyanide capsule, which did not necessarily kill immediately, and at the very same time, shooting himself with the gun, which might be poorly aimed perhaps because of the tremors from which Hitler was suffering. This method would presumably have made death more certain.

In the last days of his life, on April 22, 1945, Hitler himself had declared, "the war is lost ... I shall commit suicide." And, even after this, the façade continued: the next day, for example, on April 23, 1945, Joseph Goebbels in a proclamation to the people told them that he called upon them to defend Berlin with everything within their power, to protect their wives, daughters, children, and parents, stating, "The battle for Berlin must become the signal for the whole nation to rise up in battle" (a rather absurdist and futile thought at that stage of the war, we might comment). And, a few days later, on April 27, as the Soviets were moving in on Berlin, the Berlin paper, *Der Panzerbär: Kampfblatt für die Verteidiger Gross-Berlins* (*The Tank Bear: The Battle News-sheet for the Defenders of Greater Berlin*)[1776] could still propose the ultimately empty front-page headline, "*Bollwerk gegen den Bolschewismus. Berlin Massengrabb für Sowjetpanzer. Berlin kämpft für das Reich und Europa*" ("Bulwark against Bolshevism. Berlin: mass grave for Soviet tanks. Berlin is fighting for the Reich and Europe"). Who in all of Berlin or Germany believed any of this propaganda by that time?

Three days later, Hitler and his newly-wed bride would commit suicide, with Goebbels and family following, one day later, on May 1, 1945.[1777] Hitler abhorred the idea of being captured by the Soviets and displayed in a cage in Moscow as a prize capture: On April 29th, Hitler had announced to his longtime body guard, Hans Rattenhuber, "Everything is ruined, there is no way out, and to flee means falling into the hands of the Russians."[1778] Furthermore, after hearing of Mussolini's capture, execution, with his corpse then being taken to Milan to be hung by his

---

[1776] The bear has been the symbol of Berlin for several hundred years.

[1777] Hans Dollinger, *The Decline and Fall of Nazi Germany and Imperial Japan*, pp. 230-231.

[1778] V. K. Vinogradov, J. F. Pogonyi, N. V. Teptsov, *Hitler's Death: Russia's Last Great Secret from the Files of the KGB* (2005), p. 193; cf. "Johann Rattenhuber," WIKIZERO.

feet and beaten repeatedly (April 27-29, 1945), Hitler also remarked to his secretary Traudl Junge, "I will not fall into the enemy's hands either dead or alive. When I'm dead, my body is to be burned so that no one can ever find it. He then added, "The best way is to shoot yourself in the mouth. Your skull is shattered and you don't notice anything. Death is instantaneous."[1779]

Confirming this plan, a later examination by forensic expert Professor Viktor Zvyagin, head of the Russian Forensic Medical Expertise Institute, noted that the yellow color of the skull was typical of a vegetarian (as was Hitler); it also suggested that Hitler died, an ampule of cyanide in his mouth and his pistol shot upwards from the underside of his chin.[1780] Close examinations and comparisons between the X-rays of the jaw and teeth of the corpse with closely matched sketches drawn by Hitler's dentist, Dr. Blaschke, determined that *the jaw and head of the cadaver were indeed those of Adolf Hitler*. A significant documentary made by Judge Michael Musmanno interviewing those in the Bunker with Hitler at the end, gives direct reports of the death of Hitler, containing much of the key information given above, from those directly involved.[1781]

The particular anatomy of the teeth was not possible to reproduce in a look-alike for Hitler, even if the substitution could made—would Eva Braun have been fooled and gone to her death with someone who was not quite Hitler? Would others not have noticed Hitler slipping out and another man standing in his place? Would everyone involved be able to keep the same story containing this confabulation, composed of speculations about such a substitution? Against this unlikely scenario, later reports by Reidar F. Sognnaes and Ferdinand Ström,[1782] and by forensic biologist Mark Benecke,[1783] each confirmed the identity of the corpse as that of Adolf Hitler himself.

Details aside, the suicide of Hitler was definitively established, while his focused hatred of world Jewry as the source of all of Europe's distress remained central in his thinking through his very last documents the day before his suicide for the world to read and presumably (from Hitler's perspective) to be a source of inspiration for this continued racial fight for centuries to come. However we now understand Hitler's death and

---

[1779] Traudl (Gertraud) Junge, *Until the Final Hour: Hitler's Last Secretary* (2003), p. 177.

[1780] Hans-Joachim Neumann and Henrik Eberle, *War Hitler Krank?*, p. 286; Eng., *Was Hitler Ill?*, p. 183. Among many other discussions, see Ada Petrova and Peter Watson, *The Death of Hitler: The Full Story with New Evidence from Secret Russian Archives* (1995), esp. pp. 38, 69, 73-74, 118, 121, with excerpts at "Tales from the 'Myth File'," *Newsweek*, May 7, 1995.

[1781] Michael Musmanno and Herbert N. Holsten, the late 1940s film documentary, *Witnesses of Doom: The Lost Interviews from 1948* (2014).

[1782] Reidar F. Sognnaes and Ferdinand Ström, "The odontological identification of Adolf Hitler: Definitive documentation by X-rays, interrogations and autopsy findings," *Acta Odontologica Scandinavica*, vol. 31, 1968, pp. 43-69.

[1783] Mark Benecke, "Hitler's Skull & Teeth," *Annals of Improbable Research*, Mar.-Apr. 2003, pp. 9-10 (with mention of work of his colleague, Michel Perrier).

however we might come to revise our sense of that particular moment, the question here still to be addressed is that of what we are to think and to understand of the Reich in its aggressive violence against other European nations and against its minority populations once its conquering of most of Europe had taken place: especially the millions of Jews, Poles, Romanies of various nations, Czechs, French, Dutch, Belgians, Russians, Serbians, Hungarians, Lithuanians, Latvians, Estonians, plus those of threatening sexuality (mostly homosexual men who were seen as not contributing to the next generation of boys, ultimately the next generation of soldiers for the Reich), those who resisted war (Jehovah's Witnesses, Quakers, and others), and various other nationals. Now, we are still dealing with many issues defined by the Hitler era: there those who are still alive (fewer and fewer) who lived through that period; families remain aware of the impact of that society on their present world. As one description summarizes this era, the Hitlerian regime, and his life, "In retrospect his life seems like a steady unfolding of tremendous energy [*und im Rückblick erscheint dieses Leben wie eine einzige Entfaltung ungeheurer Energie*]. Its effects were vast [*Ihre Wirkungen waren gewaltig*], the terror it spread enormous [unprecedented, unparalleled: *der Schrecken, den sie verbreitete, beispiellos*]; but when it was over there was little left for memory to hold [*aber jenseits davon ist wenig Erinnerung*]."[1784] At this time, in retrospect, while the Nazi regime is now over, having ended rather abruptly, there are repeated parallels drawing our thinking back to those years: "So-and-so a leader is another Hitler" and "That country is a Nazi regime, or a fascist regime" and so on. There is much that is widely established about the general flow of events, as well as concerning many details from the Nazi years, established by multiple testimonies and documents in those years, even if German propaganda and publications continued with optimistic statements through most of April 1945.

These claims reverberate through time: In pro-Nazi and Holocaust-denying sources, Hitler may be presented as a peace-loving, politically astute, economic genius, who recognized the hidden control by Jews in many nefarious ways that threatened European culture, who was a kind, sweet, child-adoring, intelligent, compromise-seeking political leader who simply wanted the best for the Germany he so dearly loved. In such sources, we find little of Hitler's being subjected to a demanding, violent, alcoholic father, or of his being required to repeat a year in middle school for poor work, his sexual interests in coprophilia, urophilia, and related self-humiliation practices, the suicides (or hidden murders) of a number of women he was interested in, his need to prove himself incessantly (his *Besserwisserei*, his know-it-all attitude), his inability to accept any criticism or suggestions in the military sphere, his autocratic, dictatorial sense of entitlement, his demands for a total to-the-death attitude on the part of all German military and civilians alike, or his fears in the motivation

---

[1784] Joachim Fest, *Hitler* (Ger. text), p. 1042; *Hitler* (Eng.), p. 764.

leading to his suicide death of retaliation by Soviets and Germans alike. These have been overlooked or claimed to be distortions and fabrications with no significant or convincing historical basis. Perhaps a most high-profile source on this issue was the British law case of David Irving suing Penguin Books and the author Deborah Lipstadt (Jan. 11-Apr. 11, 2000) for what he claimed was a defamation of character.[1785]

While Hitler and the violence of the Third Reich that made use of an organized, mechanized, and industrialized system of mass murders—less in number than the killings by Stalin or Mao, but with an organization that is without comparison—is still astonishing, and something that all of mankind is called upon to come to some resolution and clarity, there is everything else that is happening in the world that also invites us to consider with as much non-distorted understanding as we can muster.

It may be possible to put this violence into a larger context, in which other concerns put this mass murdering into perspective.

As German philosopher Hannah Arendt (quoted above) pointed out, "The fascination was not simply Stalin's and Hitler's mastery of the art of lying [*Stalins und Hitlers Meisterschaft in der Kunst des Lügens*], but the fact that they were able to organize the masses so that their lies actually materialized [*dass sie es vermochten, die Massen so zu organisieren, dass ihre Lügen sich in Wirklichkeit umsetzten*]."[1786]

And from a theological perspective, the American theologian Martin E. Marty offered these reflections: "Five hundred years from now, it won't be Hitler we remember. Hitler may have set the century's agenda; he was a sort of vortex of negative energy that sucked everything else in. But I think God takes fallible human beings like Roosevelt or Churchill and carves them for his purposes. In five centuries, we'll look back and say *the story of the century was not Hitler or Stalin; it was the survival of the human spirit in the face of genocide.*"[1787]

OUR HEALING AFTER THE TRAUMA OF IT ALL

We have still not come to peace with, to complete resolution about, that period of world history, and may never do so. What can change is our overall sense of what that time means for us now, and how we can act, recognizing what that period showed was possible for mankind (in some of its darkest, least civilized moments and frames of mind).

So, can we remember, do healing, and come to societal ease, without forced forgetting of what humankind has lived through?

One expression we often hear is the advice to forgive and forget. For some perhaps not surprising reason, those who call for this are often those who have brought on torment on others, who have transgressed

---

[1785] "Irving v Penguin Books and Deborah Lipstadt," OXFORDREFERENCE.COM; "Irving v Penguin Books Ltd," WIKIPEDIA.

[1786] Harald Weltzer, "Was Hitler sagt, das glaube ich" (2: NS-Jargon)," *Zeit Geschichte*, 2017, no. 3, Aug. 22, 2017; same, at ZEIT ONLINE, Oct. 17, 2017.

[1787] Quoted in Nancy N. Gibbs, "The Necessary Evil? Why all of Adolf Hitler's destructiveness is no enough to make him the Person of the Century," *Time*, vol. 154, no. 27, Dec. 31, 1999, pp. 132-133, at p. 132. Italics added.

some sort of basic social mutual civility and respect: So, it was significant that on September 1, 2019, commemorating the eightieth anniversary of the Reich invasion of Poland, German President Frank-Walter Steinmeier spoke of the initial Luftwaffe *Terrorangriff* (terror attack) and asked forgiveness for the *deutsche Vernichtungskrieg* (the German war of annihilation), and Polish President Andrzej Duda referred to German *Kriegsverbrechen* (war crimes) and of German *grausame Barbarei* (cruel barbarity).[1788] For those who have experienced anguish, fear, loss of security and home, with injury or death to dear ones, though, it is not so easy either to forgive or to forget. There are, fortunately, other paths to resolution available in these contexts.[1789] Still, repeatedly, people have a readiness if not an eagerness to enter into one more war, freshly seen as just, appropriate, and not to be delayed. It is as if no one remembers what the terrible and costly consequences of entering into war brings with it. The comment made at Fredericksburg by General of the US Confederacy, Robert E. Lee, is, alas, often disregarded: "It is well that war is so terrible, or we should grow too fond of it."[1790] (It seems that many become too fond of it, despite that consideration.)

Perhaps we spend much focus on how wars start, but little on how they end—despite the fact that their ending is pivotal in whether there will be peace; after the Great War, French General and Marshal Ferdinand Foch (1851-1929), Commander-in-Chief of the Allied Forces in the West, stated, with prescience, "*ce n'est pas une paix, c'est un armistice de vingt ans*" (it's not a peace; it's an armistice of twenty years).[1791]

Such a concern is not new: In writing about the Peloponnesian Wars and the Peace of Nicaea (or Nicias), signed in March 421 BCE, Thucydides, similar to the comments of Maréchal Foch of the Great War quoted just above, would suggest that the Peace did not deserve to be taken for a peace, given that both sides would for the next years infringe on that Peace, with continued hostilities and perturbations of the peace—in short, it was a treacherous armistice, an unstable peace.[1792] We can recognize the usual eagerness to enter into war, and then a different eagerness to put a war behind us and to go on to living life as best we can. This can easily involve a neglect of issues that if settled at the time would eliminate later complications. But we seem to prefer to take the way of least effort.

[1788] "Steinmeier bittet Polen am 80. Jahrestag des Kriegsbeginns um Vergebung," *Arte Concert*, Sept. 1, 2019, ARTE.TV/DE/AFP/NEUIGKEITEN.

[1789] An alternative to an approach that neatly sweeps important and unresolved, unsettled issues under the rug, is the chapter, "Forgive and Remember," pp. 247-257, in Mitchell Ginsberg, *Calm, Clear, and Loving*. Note: *This process, accepting the hurt and then working at transforming our attitudes is not a project for a day!*

[1790] Roy Blount, Jr., "Making Sense of Robert E. Lee," *Smithsonian Magazine*, Jul. 2003.

[1791] "Un armistice de vingt ans," *France Loisirs*, Jan. 8, 2016; "Ferdinand Foch," HISTOIREDUMONDE.NET, Aug. 17, 2007; "Ferdinand Foch," FR.WIKIPÉDIA.ORG.

[1792] Thucydidies, *History of the Peloppenisian Wars*, 5.26. See thorough discussion in Karl Walling, "Thucydides on Policy, Strategy, and War Termination," *Naval War College Review*, vol. 66, no. 4, Autumn 2013, pp. 47-85, esp. p 48.

The Hitler Era

In a British economic metaphor, in this sort of procrastination we may be penny wise and pound foolish: we are saving the time and work of addressing something important now, and in the long run, the issue will (not always but) many times not go away but become more complex, more convoluted, and more difficult to resolve.

On an individual level, we ourselves may have issues whose solution does not appear immediately to us, and we find it easy to put the whole concern aside. When it comes to overwhelming situations, which we call traumas, this attitude of avoidance and postponement can have rather dire consequences. Of course, sometimes issues do go away and basically resolve themselves on their own, or become unimportant or irrelevant to our later lives. But, as we often come to recognize reluctantly, some problems just stay in the background and fester, waiting for a next crisis before we will address them. *It is said that time heals all wounds and yet that is only true in some cases and not in others.*

The phenomenon of psychic trauma is certainly not new. It was in the wake of the Vietnam War this was at first informally called Post-Vietnam Syndrome, until US psychiatrists came up with the new category of PTSD (Post-Traumatic Stress Disorder), formalized in the 1980 updated, third edition of the DSM (*Diagnostic and Statistical Manual*). Perhaps this new term clarified what the condition amounted to, in ways that improved on more imagistic and less informative earlier names such as soldier's heart or irritable heart (US Civil War), shell shock (World War I, a 1915 terminological contribution of English physician Lt. Col. Charles Myers) and Hysterical Disorders of Warfare (coined in 1918 by Canadian-British neurologist, Lewis Yealland, who used ECT or electroconvulsive therapy, more known popularly as Shock Therapy, to get what he thought were great cures), and Battle Fatigue or Combat Fatigue (World War II).

There has been some presentation to the general public of what in warfare experiences might be linked to these psychological difficulties. Some popular renderings of the treatment of severe psychological problems are rather more theatrical and entertaining than having much to do with what goes on its actual treatment. (We may think of the widely enjoyed book and especially the film derived from it, both entitled *One Flew Over the Coocoo's Nest* (film, 1975). An earlier film, *Let There Be Light*—from the actual treatment of World War II soldiers at the end of the war, directed by John Huston, director of *The Maltese Falcon* (1941), *The Treasure of the Sierra Madre* (1948), and *The African Queen* (1951)— was produced in 1946, copyrighted in 1948, but only finally released to the general public in 1980! It can give a sense of the initial ("presenting") conditions of many men dealing with psychological anguish, even if the less violent treatments focused on and their easy successes may strike us as rather optimistic and quite atypical.

What is most significant is that the severity of psychological problems (constant fear, ongoing hypervigilance, lack of security, absence of ease of spirit and relaxed enjoyment, among other features) is quite real, and can be more debilitating of the human being, the human spirit, than even bodily injuries (not to make light of them in this context, either).

With these considerations, we might mention another film that was made just after the end of World War II, by another well-known director, William Wyler, born in Mülhausen (Mulhouse), German and later French Alsace-Lorraine—director of *Wuthering Heights*, with Lawrence Olivier (1939), *Mrs. Miniver* (1942), *Roman Holiday* (1953), *Ben-Hur* (1959), and *Funny Girl* (1968)—was also director of the 1946 film, *The Best Years of Our Lives*, winner of eight Academy Awards. In this (mentioned above), veterans with various handicaps from injuries in the war are shown appreciating life, although they are shown now dealing not only with physical handicaps but with the worries of how others will relate to them differently, in a more guarded and distancing way, than if they had had no injuries. This overall storyline too had a post-war optimism about it, but still showed what some people were actually dealing with, and did not give in to a public squeamishness and lack of eagerness to look at some of the more devastating consequences of war, of those who were actively involved in combat and its context of ongoing life-threatening danger.

These debilitating changes from warfare, understood as a militarily created condition, were already described in ancient texts. How the torment is presented and how it is dealt with in these texts varies, but the world seemed to continue on its own way, not fully appreciating the lessons illustrated in those stories and reports. This suggests that although approaches to dealing with various sorts of trauma have by now been described for millennia, until recently there has not been a concerted effort to present paths to healing, and even less, not any attempt to teach these to a wide audience, much in need of healing through many centuries. (More on recent developments, below.)

ANCIENT GREEK AWARENESS OF WAR TRAUMA

In Classical Greek literature, there was Herodotus, often considered to be the first historian, and his reports about the Battle of Marathon (490 BCE), describing the loss of sight without any actual physical injury of an Athenian warrior, Epizelus, son of Cuphagoras.[1793] Then, in Xenophon's *Anabasis* (composed ca. 370 BCE) is a description of the Spartan general, Clearchus, representing a grim, solitary warrior, filled with anger and bitterness, an urge to return to war, and an inability to re-establish personal relationships and friendship.[1794] Other historians have suggested that even Alexander the Great (a student of Aristotle) suffered from symptoms we identify with PTSD.[1795] And, more recent discoveries of

---

[1793] Heroditus, *The Histories*, 6.118, reflecting war events from about 400 BCE. Cf. Lawrence A. Tritle, *From Melos to My Lai: War and Survival* (2000), pp. 60-61.

[1794] Alan M. Greaves, "Post-Traumatic Stress Disorder (PTSD) in Ancient Greece: A Methodological Review," pp. 89-100, esp. pp. 89, 96-97, in *Warfare and Society in the Ancient Eastern Mediterranean* (colloquium at the Univ. of Liverpool, June 2008), Stephen O'Brien and Daniel Boatright, eds. (2013).

[1795] Heather Sebo (Univ. of Melbourne), "Review of *Experiencing War: Trauma*

texts from ancient Mesopotamia, during the Assyrian Dynasty (1300-609 BCE), suggest recognition of PTSD-like responses to the intense hand-to-hand combat of those wars.[1796] Those reports offered up observed phenomena, worthy in their own light of being recorded and described.

And the *Iliad* of Homer (Greeks called Troy, Ilios), which is considered the first epic poem, the first work of Western literature, memorialized the war that ended in 1184 BCE between the Greeks and the Trojans.

That such ancient texts can still touch us and raise issues that are alive and significant in our own lives, in our current world, suggests the power of expressions of human issues to transcend time and culture. This does not mean that this is a simple or easy project. Quite long ago,[1797] French scholar and classicist Anne Le Fèvre Dacier, known as Mde (Madame) Dacier (1651-1720), wrote, "Nothing is more difficult than bringing men into a true taste for epic poetry and to have them know its essence (in old French, *de faire bien entrer les hommes dans le véritable goût du Poëme Epique, & de leur faire connoître son essence*)."[1798]

My own interest here with Greek epic poetry, and especially Homer's *Iliad*, is more limited: I merely want to make use of Homer's *Iliad* to draw attention to some features of human interaction when rage is playing an important role.

The *Iliad* is dated at about 750 BCE. It is a long epic poem of some 12,000 lines of metered verse, which we find used in Greek, Latin, and also in Classical Sanskrit literature. In the *Iliad*, each line is in dactylic hexameter (more common in English, as in Shakespeare, is iambic pentameter[1799]): in this there is a measure (or meter) of six dactyls.[1800]

In this epic, there were detailed descriptions of a war-based great driving rage, one we could see as a poetic composite summarizing a

---

and Society from Ancient Greece to Iraq, Michael B. Cosmopoulos, ed. (2007)," in *Bryn Mawr Classical Review*, Feb. 25, 2009, BMCR.BRYNMAWR.EDU. Cf. Louise Gaston, "Challenging Beliefs" (2018), TRAUMATYS.COM, questioning recent PTSD treatments.

[1796] Walid Khalid Abdul-Hamid and Jamie Hacker Hughes, "Nothing New under the Sun: Post-Traumatic Stress Disorders in the Ancient World," *Early Science and Medicine*, vol. 19, no. 6, 2014, pp. 549-557, NCBI/PUBMED.ORG.

[1797] First ed. of *L'Iliade d'Homere. Traduction de Dacier*, in 3 vol. (1719). Other eds., 1731, 1766, 1771, 1779, etc.

[1798] *Les Œuvres d'Homere. Traduites du Grec par Mde. Dacier, avec l'Introduction. En Sept Volumes* (1771), *Vol. 1: L'Introduction*, p. 1 of Préface de L'Iliade.

[1799] Iambic pentameter is a poetic form with five measures or meters (or feet) per line, consists of iambs, sequences of one short and then one long syllable. (*In English, stress serves as a parallel to length*.) for example, "But, soft! What light through yonder window breaks? It is the east, and Juliet is the sun." (*Romeo and Juliet*, Act 2, Scene 2. Or: "Midway on our life's journey, I found myself in dark woods, the right road lost. To tell..." (Eng. in iambic pentameter, *The Inferno of Dante*, Robert Pinsky, tr.). On this meter in Eng., see Kristin Hansen, "From Dante to Pinsky: A theoretical perspective on the history of the modern English iambic pentameter," *Rivista di Linguistica*, vol. 9, no. 1, 1997, pp. 53-97.

[1800] A dactyl is a sequence of one long syllable followed by two short ones, with an alternative meter also found, the spondee, a sequence of two long syllables.

variety of warriors' experiences. The Greek warrior Achilles is presented portraying his complex response to events centered on the Trojan War, including his coming to have a great, driving rage. So central to the *Iliad* is rage to the story of war between the Greek and Ilios (Troy) that the very beginning of the opening verse—the *Iliad* being written in poetic meter—starts with the word *mēnin* (from *mēnis*, rage, wrath, anger), and calls on a goddess or muse to chant out the wrath of Achilles, son of Peleus (as mentioned above in introductory passages).[1801]

This invitation sets the context for recounting the story of the war, beginning after years of the war had already transpired. What is noteworthy is the way this issue of wrath or violent rage is dealt with in the *Iliad*, especially in its closing Book 24. (More on this, below.)

In much more recent times, there has been further investigation of what had been described and defined as PTSD, when it was realized that in civilian life, there are also major traumas, some of these similar in the acuteness of the violent contexts, and *some continuing on for years and years*.

Many childhood traumas are just this sort of tragic occurrence, not just once, termed an acute trauma (as in a car accident), but repeatedly, termed a chronic trauma, and often carried out by those who society sees as the children's caretakers, the providers for these children. Often this will involve violence by the father, other family member, or close friend.

The situation for young Adolf Hitler, who for years would see his father, often drunk, beating and raping his own wife (Hitler's mother) and thrashing Adolf, reportedly at least once until the boy collapsed into a coma for several days, with his ultimate survival not obvious at the time.

We might consider this violent contact in the larger context of primate behavior and needs. It has been known for some time, at least for several decades now, that the cuddling of an infant with its mother, a gentle, firm, warm, secure touch, is a sight that can bring a sense of warmth to the viewer, and is even more moving and important for the mother, and, most centrally, for the baby. Primate studies compared neonates that were given plentiful nutrition but had no touch with adult or other primates, with others who had a chance to be in touch with a warm, cuddly adult, even with only little food. The first group would frequently die, while those of the second would thrive.[1802]

[1801] In the Robert Fagles tr. of the *Iliad*, the opening reads: "Rage—Goddesss, sing the rage of Peleus' son Achilles." Peleus—son of Aeacus, grandson of Zeus himself—with his goddess wife, Thetis, were parents of Achilles. Achilles was thus a mortal born from (descendents of) immortals, both through his father and his mother. See Homer, *Iliad*, 21.212-214 (BK.vv: 21.184-190).

[1802] Harry F. Harlow, "The Nature of Love," *The American Psychologist*, vol. 13, no. 12, Dec. 1958, pp. 673-685; Harry F. Harlow, "Love in Infant Monkeys," *Scientific American*, vol. 200, no. 6, Jun. 1959, pp. 68-74; Harry F. Harlow and Margaret Kuenne Harlow, "Social Deprivation in Monkeys," *Scientific American*, vol. 207, Nov. 1962, pp. 136-146; M. F. Ashley Montague, "The Sensory

CHILDREN SCHOOLED WITH A STRAP (AND OTHER VIOLENCE)

What we see when this nourishing, literally life-preserving, touch is replaced by violent and brutal touch in the form of beatings (with the hand, the fist, with a switch, a strap,[1803] or other forms of inflicting pain), is a doubly-intense betrayal of the care adults could give to the young, first, in that the tenderness of a gentle touching is missing, and second, in that what touch there is a matter of rage, frustration, and violence on the part of the adult, all of which is received by the youngster.

The justifications for such behavior go back to ideas of needing to toughen up the young (claimed to be for the youngster's good), since the world is a harsh and cruel place. Or to the idea that discipline is a good in and of itself.

As a seventeenth-century expression put it, "Spare the rod and spoil the child."[1804] This, even if meant satirically, was taken to be literal advice by many parents and teachers over the next centuries. It made as much (or little) sense as the comment, "This will hurt me more than it will hurt you," said when a parent was about to inflict physical punishment on a child. (Has any child ever responded spontaneously thanking the parent for doing the child a favor by being so harshly "caring"?)

Now, some children who are treated with such intense forms of violence (often with rape as a constant feature) in later years will act as their despicable parent had earlier on, only this time the now-grown child is the one meting out this violence; *but not all do so.* Some, rejecting the violence vehemently, become kind and caring adults who treat their family with respect and basic politeness, gentleness, and civility, at least.

This can be a haphazard phenomenon, or *it can be an object of interest that leads people to ask some basic questions about how they themselves want to be in the world and especially how they want to relate to those they have the most interactions with.*

Study of thousands of adults who as children faced various sorts of what have been termed Adverse Childhood Experiences (in short, ACEs) have a much higher rate of various diseases, including asthma, heart conditions, depression, and suicidal impulses. (Some of the physical, neurological, and psychological problems that have been identified as consequences of such harsh treatment were discussed above.) As Robert Block, MD, who was the President of the American Academic of Pediatrics, said, "Adverse childhood experiences are the single greatest unaddressed public health threat facing our nation today."[1805]

Influences of the Skin," *Texas Reports on Biology and Medicine*, vol.11, no. 2, Summer 1953, pp. 291-301—based on a seminar talk Montague gave Apr. 1, 1952 at Univ. of Texas, Galveston, with the intriguing title "The Mind of the Skin"; Ashley Montague, *Touching: The Human Significance of the Skin* (1971, 2nd. ed., 1974).

[1803] From the 1968 song "Jumpin' Jack Flash, The Rolling Stones," GENIUS.COM.

[1804] Samuel Butler (1613-1680), *Hudibras* (1663-1678), *a work of satirical polemics*, in Part II (1664), Canto I, line 844; modifying Proverbs 13:24.

[1805] Sherry Peters, "Who Needs to Pay Attention to the ACE [Adverse Childhood

This generalization extends over college-educated individuals as well as those living in poverty and those with little formal education. And, we might suspect, this pattern that highlights the danger to individuals and to entire societies stresses the importance of educating the public about these harmful ways of treating children. The old adage "Spare the rod and spoil the child" is a recipe for disaster on the personal and societal level.

The damage to children, which will have its own deleterious second-wave consequences, is no small matter. The more that children are abused, the more difficult their lives will be, with some consequences that may not be obvious but will impact their well-being through life. We can address this in an individual way (helping one child and family at a time), but there is something more systematic, addressed more on a systemic level of interest, that might be of great value here. When we see a parent, often the father, who deals with his own frustrations and anger by frightening outbursts and perhaps with intense and even harmful physical aggression against his family members (we saw this with the fathers of both Hitler and Stalin), we can see an entire family that is distraught, chronically anxious, and hyper-vigilant in search of the next explosion.

As one family with parents and three children was described, "all three children had entered the family business, and all three had difficulties working with their father who was very controlling, as well as being highly reactive emotionally when they did things which he didn't agree with."[1806] This story is not one of a kind, but brings our attention to an important pattern to be investigated and understood, to be transformed into something less harmful, more respectful and loving, more skillful! Such ideas are only relatively recently being reformulated for today's age and times, hopefully in ways that will be effective in bringing about such changes on a wide scale.

The idea of letting a family raise its children as it sees fit has major, significant, and important limits, and people could benefit greatly from being educated about alternatives when there is physical abuse to the child, ongoing repeated rape of children and adolescents still under the care of adults, psychological neglect, nutritional neglect, and so on (as discussed along a number of dimensions in ACE studies just mentioned). Of course, in extreme cases, children are taken from abusive parents or other adults who are the care-takers of these children, and this, in many

---

Experiences] Study?" *Georgetown Univ. National Technical Assistance Center for Children's Mental Health*, Mar. 5, 2015. This is not only of importance to mental health, as the discussion above suggests.

[1806] Aldo Gurgone, *Psychotherapy Tales: The Making of a Family Therapist* (2018), p. 95 (in the chap. "Unbearable Anxiety"). Another family tale he presents (at pp. 90-93, in the chap. "The Peaches Were Delicious") involved a very punitive and demanding father who at one point in therapy recounted an incident involving his own father, when he himself was an adolescent, in which he was taught a lesson (as the expression goes) by his father that was very harsh and frightening for the son, and in that retelling, realizing the fear and dread that he felt, on reflection realized that this was not a fully loving demonstration of the father's caring for him.

countries at this time. While instances of child abuse continue to this day, it is certainly not at all new to the world.

We may look at the way we treat children, and others in positions of low respect or down on their luck, from the point of view focused on the values we want to live by in our world. We may refer to the values already spoken of: the respect for compassion, understanding, caring for those in need, and mutual concern for fellow members of one's society, if not of mankind in general.

Some fundamental values that are encouraged and honored in many world traditions are being considerate, compassionate, emotionally unrepressed, sympathetic, having understanding and appreciation of the other, a sense of personal autonomy and independence, of self-worth, of creativity realized through meaningful activities, of the unity of humanity and of basic human worth, a harmony with nature, a sense of hope and of courage, a candidness in many contexts, an honest fearlessness, and a peace-seeking way of dealing with life's issues, and so forth.

And in Christian terms, recognizing the human brotherhood and sameness of all, St. Paul said, "There is neither Jew nor Gentile, neither slave nor free, nor is there male and female, for you are all one in Christ Jesus."[1807] A complement to this vision of human brotherhood is the Buddhist verbal expression[1808] of universal good will, "May all beings be happy."[1809]

Behind all of these frames of mind and ways of relating with others, *is the question of what sorts of human beings do we want to be, and what sort of human beings do we respect, honor, and appreciate for their contribution to our world.*

We may approach this net of issues from a variety of perspectives. One natural (usual) approach is to consider these values in a judgmental way: that they represent what is good (if not pure and holy), with their lack representing what is bad (if not evil).

We may put this judgment into moral terms, defining for ourselves what is right and honorable, and what is wrong and shameful. This is certainly a grounding, orienting beginning in our thinking about these matters. As we know perhaps all too well, this model or ideal of how people should be, can lead in two principal directions: one, in which we judge people overall as being either good or evil, perhaps with a self-confidence if not a self-righteousness in our sense of ourselves. This perhaps involves a particular understanding of what ideals are: if we take them to be absolute measurements of goodness as people, we may feel we are never good enough. This is a source of much self-attacking and self-denigration, if not a feeling of being totally worthless as a person. This is using an ideal as an absolute that we cannot possible succeed in satisfying. This becomes a burden rather than a desirable goal to move

---

[1807] Galatians 3:28 (NIV: New International Version); cf. Romans 10:12.

[1808] A *mantra*, lit., an instrument (*tra-*) for thinking or remembering (*man-*).

[1809] This is an aspect of *metta-bhāvanā* (the cultivation of loving kindness, or selfless friendship). In the Pali of Theravāda Buddhism, *Sabbe sattā sukhi hontu*.

towards in our life. A related consequence of this can be our blinding ourselves to our own foibles (as Jesus is reported to have said about the ease of seeing a splinter in our neighbor's eye).

In psychological terms this is our tendency to avoid looking at what is less than admirable in our own thinking and comportment. As Nietzsche put it, "'I have done that,' says my memory. 'I cannot have done that,' says my pride, and remains inexorable. Eventually—memory yields."[1810]

Or, as Carl Gustav Jung would say, what we are not comfortable with acknowledging in our thinking or acting, we keep out of clear perception. (This is rather close to Freud's concept of repression.) Jung called these facets of our mental life that we are not at ease in acknowledging, the shadow. This is part of the process by which we maintain our comfort with who we think we are, in a way that often flares up in ways we cannot at all control.

A second course of action that can be taken here can be of great value to us (individually and in our social life): to become clear about what we are dissatisfied with, in order to allow us focused action to change that.

This amounts to an archeology of the soul, as some would say, and is part of many spiritual traditions found throughout the world.[1811] This inner research can be more effective if we free ourselves to bear witness to the world we see, in all of its important specifics; or, we can soften its edges, avoid the discomfort that some realities will have us face. This openness to seeing what is interesting but perhaps unpleasant to consider is something we can become comfortable undertaking, although it may be disturbing at first.

But by being focused on making our current moment more pleasant, no matter what, we may well miss the key, present, powerful opportunity to see into what is driving us in ways that are short-sighted, that bring on greater problems in their wake.

After all, some issues do resolve themselves without our attention (in this, showing themselves to be transient and not deep-rooted), but some tend to return with the same or perhaps even greater agitation, anxiety, and crisis than before (showing themselves to be intransigent and calling for resolution, waiting for an ultimate confrontation that one day can no longer be avoided).

In the case of Adolf Hitler, we can perhaps feel sympathy for the poor boy that received the frustrated demands of his father with an intense violence when the father's way was not followed to the T. At the same time, if we focus on how the boy responded to this violence against him and his mother, we see that Hitler turned this hurt into a deep violence. This was a violence that would become focused against those that Hitler concluded were inferior and dangerous. These judgments were to have a

---

[1810] Friedrich Nietzsche, *Beyond Good and Evil*, Walter Kaufmann, tr., 4.68. See extended discussion in "Nietzschean Psychiatry Revisited," pp. 59-102, in Mitchell Ginsberg, *Calm, Clear, and Loving*.

[1811] A discussion of these practices in traditions around the world is found in Mitchell Ginsberg, *The Inner Palace* (in its pdf format, 900 pages).

The Hitler Era

great influence on other people who became powerful in the Third Reich, with their own frustrations and hatreds.

This contributed to the later readiness in the Third Reich to organize mass killings calling for total murder as a central component in a total war, not seen before. After all, even looking back in history to the Mongol sackings of the mid-1200s, or the invasions of the Huns centuries earlier, in the mid-400s, under Attila, *they were not designed to exterminate entire peoples*, but, rather, to bring them into total submission to the awesome, horrible power of their respective armies.

Power and control of vast lands might have inspired violence, but hatred of other peoples did not have the same sort of importance earlier, did not give the same sense of urgency found in the Nazi war of extermination of entire groups of people killed during the mass killing by German military (including of course the SS) in World War II. This was claimed to be done as a defensive operation against peoples believed to be set on exterminating the German people, an extreme case of seeing other people with the hatred that we feel toward them, a process well known at this point in time as projection, putting forth of one's own sentiments onto others: mental gymnastics, a contortion of the mind!

Our societies do not yet seem to take fully into account the impact of such violence, sometimes calling a contrasting caring attitude a softness, an attitude or frame of mind that is weak and unable to show its strength and power. Better, it is often proposed, is to be determined and resolute, hard-hearted, firm, definitive in one's sense of what needs to be done.

While some of us at times are trying and perhaps managing to avoid facing our limitations—none of us is omnipotent, far from it, and none of us is immortal, as we all will see within the next decades of our life—and trying, as well, to avoid facing the considerable ignorance of our human condition. After all, *with all of us facing our mortality and ultimate death, we are all operating on limited information*, with conclusions regularly not capable of taking into account some of the most important consequences of what we are envisioning, given the way reality is more complex and involves many unforeseeable factors that we cannot even imagine.

That said, what are we as people in society going to do to lessen the torment people experience following the infliction of pain, fear, confusion, hatred, perhaps uncontrollable rage at a world that we take to be deeply flawed and unjust? We might stay focused here, at least as a start, on the issue of trauma, especially in the context of the violence of wars. When a village or a larger group of people has been attacked, raped, killed, or left perhaps to recover from their wounds, memories remain for long periods of time, in some cases, literally for centuries! In what was Yugoslavia, the lands of Serbia, Croatia, and Bosnia, for example, there are memories of the societal splits when the Ottomans invaded the Balkans, with some siding with the Ottomans and others resisting. Or, if we look in the same area of the world, there is still a great dispute or disagreement about the many Armenians who died in the period from the late 1800s and reaching a peak in 1915-1916. There is still no sense of completion or resolution, on either the side of current-day Turkey or of the Armenian community that has been dispersed to a number of countries. There are, of course, many examples of violence in the past that live on in hurt, pain, resentment, and *a strong yearning and urge for some sort of bringing the issue to some sort of resolution.*

How can this be done? *Can* this be done? What is the alternative? One alternative, of course, is to let things sit, let people deal with their own rage about the past, and for the rest of the world to get on with its own concerns and interests. We can say that in a couple, only when both are finding satisfaction (perhaps in different ways from one another) is the overall situation basically agreeable. And *in our societies, if some of the people are happy with things as they are and others are in dire straits and anxious and fundamentally insecure, the overall society is not a happy one*. It may be easier to disregard and to make it a point not to consider the problems of others (so long as we are comfortable), but this is easier only in a rather limited way, often calling on us to become numb (Peachum's *gefüllos*) to the concerns of others, and with this, the ways we experience others and interact with them, tinged with heartlessness, a total lack of caring about others, a cold harshness, or even malice and agitated harmful actions against them.

What would be healing here? What would be coming to societal ease? In a simple way, all we need to do is to look at what we can sense is the core issue of disgruntlement or more intense agitation. In one vocabulary, there is no resolution of past pain. Which, of course, leads to the question of how do we bring about a sense of completion, a sense of peace (finally) about what was never settled. *One key into all of this is the consideration that when there are complaints or criticisms or laments, there is something very important that is not being realized, a need that is being frustrated.* If we can turn from the complaint or criticism, we may begin to appreciate what is bothering the person we are interacting with. Until those needs are brought into focus, acknowledged (recognized), and responded to, the person will certainly not feel heard, understood, or respected. *If an old pain is not recognized, if ignored by those around that person or that group, and let be, it will not especially go away.*

So, how can we acknowledge what is important and allow that sense to have an impact on those in pain, on us, and on how things can go on from here? It may seem an impossible task, but this has been worked on for decades now (in fact, for millennia). We are not totally in the dark.

ANCIENT GREEK EPIC ANTIDOTE TO RAGE: THETIS, ACHILLES, AND PRIAM

Rage uncaged, rage given free rein, rage gone rampant, rage: it has been shown through history in its more virulent forms, especially when taken over by large groups, or countries, or even groups of allied nations working together, that it can do remarkably vast damage, including millions of dead, more millions wounded, mutilated, tormented or incapacitated for life, even more families that will carry forth the scars of the damage from such rage carried out in organized fashion. War, after all, has been seen (by some) since early in the twentieth century as a crime against humanity, as in the 1921 declaration in Bilthoven, Netherlands, by the group *Paco* (the Esperanto word for Peace).[1812]

Rage can be held within limits, reined in, and kept from dictating what the world then has to do deal with. This is not necessarily suppressing by violence or other means of force, but, rather (preferably and more elegantly and efficiently), making use of our awareness and our understanding of the processes and operations of frustration, irritation, agitation, resentment, fantasies of striking back, intentions, and finally actions on an individual and group level that carry out violent reactivity in lesser or greater levels of intensity and violence.

This way of considering the issue may seem quite modern, with much said especially in the past few decades about this general societal issue, and yet statesmen, poets, novelists, and artists have variously known of and expressed themselves in the various media available to them in their times and cultures for millennia.

We may take a clue here from the oldest epic in Western literature, the *Iliad* of Homer, discussed just above,[1813] which recounts the Greek-Trojan war. This work, the *Iliad*, begins with the rage, the wrath of Achilles, a mighty warrior for the Greeks—who are referred to in the *Iliad* as the *Achaioi*, *Argeioi*, and *Danioi* (selected to keep the meter of the recited story).[1814] Achilles is directed by his rage and resentment, feeling a loss of well-earned war booty, the beautiful Briseis—Achilles had first killed her husband, Prince Mynes[1815]—then she was taken by Agamemnon,[1816] with Achilles feeling insulted, with a rage that he was not ready to give up.[1817] His rage would keep him from fighting in the war until after the death of his closest friend, Patroclus.

The tensions between certain central characters in the *Iliad* are intimate; the relations, complex.

The human complexities that result from such different people locked in intense and demanding situations, as presented by Homer, can give such a palpable sense that we can imagine actual people (the characters in the *Iliad*) in such a web of desires, demands, fears, rage, and hopefulness—this making for grippingly powerful imaginary scenarios that we can learn much from if we apply them to ourselves or to the present world and its machinations.

The relation of Achilles to Patroclus, for one, is complex, and reflects the different people these two characters are: bitter, resentful, wrathful, pitiless, versus considerate, compassionate, emotionally unrepressed.

[1812] The group was later renamed the War Resisters' International, the WRI. Quoted at p. 80 in Mitchell Ginsberg, *Peace and War and Peace* (2015).

[1813] Homer, *Iliad* (bilingual), at *Homer English Iliad.1*, PERSEUS.UCHICAGO.EDU.

[1814] Key features are presented in *Iliad*, 1.1-100 (BK.vv:1.1-120).

[1815] Mynes was son of King Evenus of Lyrnessus: *Iliad*, 19.348-349 (BK.vv: 19.291-300).

[1816] Homer, *Iliad*, 1.203-221 (BK.vv: 1.172-187).

[1817] Homer, *Iliad*, 1.350-3, 16.50-65 (BK.vv: 1.342-412; 16.11-22).

Patroclus is considerate: stopping from going to battle to heal a wounded compatriot, Eurypylus, a spear in his thigh, bleeding profusely[1818]—even if mocked when he came to Achilles with flowing tears, as a girl who comes needing the care of her mother, until the mother picks her up and holds her in her loving arms[1819]—and yet, perhaps ironically, earlier in the *Iliad*, Achilles had been portrayed crying to his mother.[1820] And to this mocking criticism, Patroclus replies directly and non-agressively, expressing the wish that he will never hold on to wrath as does Achilles, who is pitiless, who feels no pity.[1821]

Having started from the wrath of Achilles, we find a complementary vision of life, which we can consider at this point: beginning with great intensity, the *Iliad* now has two powerful scenes (among many): one, when Achilles later in the *Iliad* has learned of the death of his close friend Patroclus and is then visited by his mother, the goddess Thetis, who realizes she cannot prolong her son's life nor help to avoid the death that will meet him soon after he avenges his friend's death by killing the murderer of Patroclus, Hector.

She comes to him, knowing her impotence in the face of this fate, "to hear what grief has come to break his heart while he holds back from battle," and, as Homer describes it here, "her words were all compassion, winging pity." *This is a powerful example of the power of compassionate listening to the woes and torments of another, even if there is a realization that nothing can be done to change the situation this tortured soul is experiencing.*[1822]

And, following up on that, the second scene mentioned above: After Achilles has killed Hector, the last chapter of the *Iliad* ends with a very emotionally powerful meeting. Unlike some epic stories whose high point is a focusing on glorifying the conquering hero-warrior, the *Iliad* continues, presenting psychological issues that remain centrally important![1823]

At that meeting, presented in the final Book of the *Iliad*, Priam, the king of Ilios, of Troy, having lost sons in the war with the Greeks, is tormented by the death of his beloved son Hector, killed by Achilles.[1824] That murder, in turn, was in revenge for Hector's earlier having killed Patroclus (just mentioned), the closest of friends of Achilles.

The meeting, then, is between a king facing the man who had killed his beloved son and between a warrior facing the father of the man who had killed his own dearest friend. The story has Zeus, the highest of the

---

[1818] Homer, *Iliad*, 11.961-1005 (BK.vv: 11.804-840).
[1819] Homer, *Iliad*, 16.1-21 (BK.vv: 16.1-19).
[1820] Homer, *Iliad*, 1.422-429 (BK.vv: 1.413-420).
[1821] Homer, *Iliad*, 16.30-37 (BK.vv: 16.20-35).
[1822] Homer, *Iliad*, 18.67-86, 19.3-42 (BKvv: 18.52-64; 19.3-69).
[1823] See discussion in Caroline Alexander, *The War That Killed Achilles: The True Story of Homer's Iliad and the Trojan War* (2009), esp. pp.192-195.
[1824] Priam expresses his forthcoming deep loss, in Homer, *Iliad*, 22.68-92 (BK.vv: 22.69-78).

gods, help to resolve this conflict by ordering messages to be given to Achilles, by the goddess Thetis, mother of Achilles, and to Priam, by Iris, the goddess messenger of Zeus, to arrange for a ransom to be offered by Priam to Achilles in return for Achilles giving over the body of Priam's son, Hector, to Priam and the Trojans for an honorable cremation.[1825] *The two speak to one another with sensitivity and directness of their distress, loss, and deep mourning. They cry together:* Priam, the father, for his son, Hector, killed by Achilles, and Achilles, the warrior, for his foster brother, Patroclus, killed by Hector, and for his own father, Peleus, the father who will also never again see his son, Achilles, alive. Priam expresses unresolved needs, pleading earnestly for support or acquiescence in recognizing those needs, and, with each intensely experiencing, appreciating, and respecting the loss of the other—in modern terms, with each appreciating the humanity of the other—they come to a shared sense of mutual respect, and from this, are inspired to aid in carrying out what was needed to be completed.

In particular, Priam is given permission to take the body of his killed son Hector for ritual cremation on a pyre and a solemn burial to take place later,[1826] which is then allowed to happen.

And so ends the *Iliad:* "And so the Trojans buried Hector, breaker of horses."[1827] Here, compassion and empathy overcome rage. While we can find some descriptions from ancient literature that suggest PTSD-like consequences to war experiences, this long passage closing the *Iliad* is special in its illustration of one way in which deep loss and hurt and unresolved frustration, resentment, anger, and rage, with their stirring up of urges to violence, to lies,[1828] and to still other problems, can be addressed and transformed. Or, in another metaphor, the character for fire (Mandarin, *huǒ*) when written upside down is taken in some teachings to represent the need to master fire, by patience, self-control, and temperance, these being antidotes to the violent raging-fire state of mind that sometimes controls us.[1829]

And while we can say that this lesson has largely been lost on human cultures since then, there is a recent development that comes to a new formulation and understanding of how such transformations and a sense of resolution can be achieved.

In contemporary times, there has been work done, for example, with the Catholics and Protestants in Northern Ireland, with the Serbs, Croats, and Bosnians in the Baltic, with Israelis and Palestinians in the Holy Land,

---

[1825] Homer, *Iliad*, 24.78-271, esp. 24.93-95, 142-146, 168-176, 188-192, 207-223, 258-261 (BK.vv: 24.64-227, esp. 24.63-64, 133-148, 184-187, 217-246).

[1826] This is presented with powerful eloquence in the closing Book 24 of the *Iliad*, at 24.1-55, 280-410, 550-710, 775-805, esp. 24.550-560, 625-640, 786-804 (BK.vv: 24.1-50, 272-348, 468-607, esp. 24.468-478, 534-550, 659-684).

[1827] Homer, *Iliad*, 24.944 (BK.vv: 24.804).

[1828] Homer, *Iliad*, 20.282-295 (BK.vv: 20.244-258).

[1829] "Fire Character," *Shaolin Kung Fu Institute*, SHAOLINKUNGFU.BIZ.

and in a large number of other countries where there were ethnic and cultural groups in murderous conflict with one another.

We should mention here the work of Marshall Rosenberg and the Center for Non-Violent Communication (NVC), of the USA,[1830] and Scilla Elworthy (three times Nobel Laureate nominee) and the Oxford Research Group of the UK.[1831] This work is rather comprehensive, *taking into account the sense of injustice that can be the basis of great anger and rage, but not being driven into violence*—as in the metaphor of the Greek river of the Underworld, *Pyriphlegéthōn* (flaming fire), and the Chinese teaching of mastering fire, by patience, self-control, and temperance, both discussed above—*applying this anger, rather, in more skillful ways.*[1832] A methodical appreciation of communication, of what works and what is counter-productive, a sense of what is best called for in given contexts and times of tension and anger can bring some human understanding to apply here: We can imagine two people, or two groups who are in tension with one another, perhaps with histories of violence and the death of members of both groups. With the arranging of the two to come together, in the same place and the same time, in a context of basic safety—a question of logistics—which may involve having the group travel to a less hostile region somewhere else in the world. *Part of what is most powerfully helpful is the establishing of a sense of the humanity of the other group.* In such a context, there is the opening up of the telling of stories, including simple stories about the violence each group has experienced. This violence need not be by actual members of the other group who are now coming together for these discussions. But those in each group can sense that they are part of one of two groups that have wreaked violence on the other group. In this way, there could theoretically be the gathering of Turks and Armenians, say, in which none in either group was involved in the violence of 1915. It can also involve groups in which members of each were involved themselves in violence against some of the other group. One tendency or inclination that people who partake in such groups may experience is an urge to debate, to deny, to put forth counter-examples that would defocus the story being told and to keep from appreciating it in its own right; this can be limited by skillful moderation, allowing the story to be completed that someone is telling about an important situation or experience that they underwent or that they remembered from their group. *The art of listening, simply listening,*

[1830] The topic with citations appears above. See Marshall Rosenberg, *Speak Peace in a World of Conflict: What You Say Next Will Change Your World* (2005); *The Surprising Purpose of Anger: Beyond Anger Management: Finding the Gift* (2005).

[1831] Scilla Elworthy, *The Business Plan for Peace: Building a World without War* (2018); "Scilla Elworthy (3 Dec 2015)," *Department of Political Science, School of Public Policy (UK)*, VIMEO.COM; *Dr Scilla Elworthy—Stirring the Waters—Making the Impossible Possible*, YOUTUBE; Dylan Mathew, *War Prevention Works: 50 Stories of People Resovlving Conflict*, with Intro. by Scilla Elworthy (2001); Desmund Tutu, *Truth and Reconciliation Commission of South Africa Report* (1998-2003).

[1832] Scilla Elworthy, *Fighting with Non-violence* (2012), YOUTUBE, at 7:15-12:10.

The Hitler Era

not making judgments, refraining from replying with moralistic, perhaps even condescending comments, is actually simpler than putting ourselves into a debate, questioning whose traumas were more severe, who was most ill-treated, and so forth. When the exchange remains focused on the remembered and reported anguish of one group, it can stand on its own, with its own validity. *The recognition, acknowledgment, and sympathy for what other human beings have gone through can have a powerfully soothing if not healing function.* When complete in this way, the conversation can then shift to stories of some from the other group. In this entire process there is an awareness, a consciousness of the past of those of each group and the human frailty that is our condition. In this very real and very intimate expression of what has remained and not acknowledged in our ordinary life contexts and limited communication, this can now be uncovered, no longer hidden, denied, obfuscated, or distorted in ways that prevent the experienced pains from being put forth.

The healing and the coming to a much greater sense of peace that can result from this has changed groups' senses of those they saw as enemies, especially when feeling that these people have heard and shown a realization of the pain those others have experienced.

Most important, and to kept in awareness as this sort of interaction or process evolves, is *the maintaining of a structure in which all those present are willing to listen to the agony and torment of the others, without going into self-defensive comments or counter-attacks.* Each story is given its own weight and the time to have it be expressed fully, to the satisfaction of those speaking, and to the willingness of those listening to appreciate the human suffering that is being expressed. *There is certainly enough pain to go around; that people in one group have suffered in no way has to deny the fact that people in the other group also suffered.* A further part of this process is the expression of a recognition of the deep sadness that is being expressed in each story. This can allow a very profound appreciation for our universal human situation, subject to fears, violence, and even disruption of entire lives.

While memories of earlier losses will remain even after such important transformations, those memories tend to have less power over our thinking, making for less reactivity in self-defensiveness and criticisms of the wrongs of the others, making for more of a sense of human sharing and true intimacy, with those involved feeling respected for what they or their group have lived through. The meeting face-to-face of those who were on opposite sides of violence, with individuals speaking out their experience and injuries suffered by those being addressed has both an individual aspect (the person speaking) and a group aspect (those who listen and take in what is being described). This helps in the process of coming to a resolution or less agitated frame of mind, for these more or less subtle experiences jointly shared by the those in the group.

In addition to this sort of process, there can also be statements by those respected in their own community expressing an appreciative understanding of the plights of another group. Thus, in a visit in 2013 to

Third-Reich concentration camps in Germany and Poland, Imams and Muslim intellectuals from Bosnia, India, Indonesia, Jordan, the Palestinian Territories, Saudi Arabia, Turkey, and the United States knelt in solemn prayer for Holocaust dead at Auschwitz on May 22 and offered a statement, signed by ten leading Islamic figures, including Imam Mohamed Magid, President of the Islamic Society of North America, and Umer Ahmed Ilyasi, India's Chief Imam, which read:

> "We bear witness to the absolute horror and tragedy of the Holocaust where millions upon millions of human souls perished, more than half of whom were people of the Jewish faith. We acknowledge, as witnesses, that it is unacceptable to deny this historical reality and declare such denials or any justification of this tragedy as against the Islamic code of ethics," they said, adding that they "stand shoulder to shoulder with our Jewish brothers and sisters in condemning anti-Semitism in any form. [They then join anti-Semitism to Islamophobia.] *With the disturbing rise of anti-Semitism, Islamophobia, and other forms of hatred, rhetoric, and bigotry, now more than ever, people of faith must stand together for truth, peace, and justice.* Together, we pledge to make real the commitment of 'never again' and to stand united against injustice wherever it may be found in the world today."[1833]

In our world with its good share of inter-group violence, there can be these and other steps that move the world toward a sense of shared humanity if not community, a lessening in the driven anxieties and impulses for revenge or further violence from the past traumas that were presented, a bringing people together to heal themselves and to heal one another, and, so, to more of a societal ease.

There have been Jewish calls in support of Muslims, as well. For example, the Executive Director of T'ruah, The Rabbinic Call for Human Rights, has stated that on the local level, "we're hearing about on-the-ground-cooperation that's happening between Jews and Muslims, whether it's a Jewish congregation supporting Muslims after an attack on a mosque or Muslims supporting Jewish victims of hate crimes."[1834] Or, again, in

---

[1833] Italics added. "Muslim religious leaders condemn Holocaust deniers," *The Express Tribune* (Pakistan), Jun. 4. 2013; cf. "Statement of Muslim American Imams and Community Leaders on Holocaust Denial," *Forward* (New York City), Aug. 18, 2010; Eliad Benari, "Muslim Leaders Condemn Holocaust Denial," *Arutz Sheva*, Jun. 4, 2013; Stuart Winer, "Muslim religious leaders denounce Holocaust denial," *The Times of Israel*, Jun. 4, 2013; Susan Barnett, "For Immediate Release: Statement of Muslim American Imams & Community Leaders on Holocaust Denial," *Politico*, Aug. 7-11, 2010. Susan Barnett is a journalist and TV anchor.

[1834] "Muslims find Jews standing behind them in opposition to Pomeo's confirmation," RELIGION NEWS SERVICE (RNS), Apr. 12, 2018.

West Philadelphia, after an Islamophobic attack on a local mosque, the Mosjid Al-Jamia Mosque, weekly groups of Jews stood outside the mosque to express support of the peaceful Muslim community there. The Jewish supporters were joined by local Quakers (Pennsylvania is the Quaker State, given the religious practices of William Penn). The director of the mosque, Shuja Moore, commented that West Philly (Philadelphia) and the city overall were very supportive of Islam, putting the anti-Muslim hostilities in context.[1835]

And after a March 15, 2019 attack on two mosques in Christchurch, New Zealand, by a self-proclaimed White Supremacist, hater of Islam, and admirer of Oswald Mosley, leader of the British Union of Fascists, with 50 or more killed and many wounded, the local community and people from around the world denounced this as a hate crime and terrorism.[1836]

These are only a small sampling of the support which groups are beginning to show for others who are being mistreated with hostility and violence. We may also consider the important and significant political and national dimensions here, in which such cooperation (or solidarity) among large groups has led to the collapse of a significant number of dictatorships these past 40 or more years, from Europe to Africa, to South America, the Middle East, and Asia.[1837]

If we return here to Charles Darwin, we may remark that his sense of what would allow an individual, and a group, to survive was not only the "fittest" in the sense of the most powerful, and certainly not more powerful in a physical, brute-strength concept of being powerful. Darwin pointed out that man is the only species that is "enabled through his mental faculties 'to keep an unchanged body in harmony with the changing universe.'"[1838] Man has great power of adapting his habits to new conditions of life: Darwin discussed the human instinct or tendency to a social connectedness. (Aristotle long before had said that man is a *politikòn*, a social or societal animal.[1839])

[1835] Grace Shallow, "Jews support Muslims after anti-Islam rally in Philadelphia, amid Middle East conflict," DELAWARE ONLINE (USA TODAY NETWORK), May 17, 2018.

[1836] "World leaders condemn massacres at Christchurch mosques," *The New Daily* (Australia), Mar. 16, 2019; "Christchurch shootings: Jacinda Ardern calls for global anti-racism fight," BBC.COM, Mar. 20, 2019.

[1837] Gene Sharp, *From Dictatorship to Democracy: A Conceptual Framework for Liberation* (2012), presenting Nonviolent Action (NVA) against political violence.

[1838] Charles Darwin, *The Descent of Man and Selection in Relation to Sex*, Revised ed. (1874), p. 124 in Chap. V, pp. 124-141 ("On the Development of the Intellectual and Moral Faculties during Primeval and Civilized Times"); the quoted phrases are from British anthropologist and biologist Alfred Russel Wallace (1823-1913), "Alfred R. Wallace on the Origin of Human Races &c.," *Anthropological Review (Journal of the Anthropological Society of London)*, vol. 2, 1864.

[1839] Aristotle, *Politics*, 1253a7-11; Roger Crisp, "Compassion and Beyond," *Ethical Theory and Moral Practice* (Annual Conference of the British Society for Ethical Theory, Bristol, July 2007), vol. 11, no. 3, Jun. 2008, pp. 233–246. We can distinguish compassion from pity, seen as a distorted excess of compassion.

Darwin proposed that "that any animal whatever, endowed with well-marked social instincts, the parental and filial affections being here included, would inevitably acquire a moral sense or conscience, as soon as its intellectual powers had become as well, or nearly as well developed, as in man. Darwin noted that the social instincts lead an animal to take pleasure in the society of its fellows, to feel a certain amount of sympathy with them, and to perform various services for them, adding that "for those communities, which included the greatest number of the most sympathetic members, would flourish best and rear the greatest number of offspring."[1840] Darwin wrote of groups whose members felt a mutual sense of love, leading to warning each other of danger, and to giving mutual aid in attack or defense. Darwin was speaking of such states of mind or attitudes as sympathy, fidelity, and courage. Whatever the considerations he presented to support his understanding, what is at the core was his respect for certain moral virtues (using old terms), *which would not be honored or respected in the National Socialist worldview*, but which would honor sympathy, mutual support, suggesting that a measure of civilization would be the degree to which all in the society (or world, in very modern terms) would be granted this sort of mutual respect and caring.[1841] In a further, quite modern-seeming text—especially when compared with the reduction of Darwin by Spencer and then even more so by the National Socialists—Darwin addressed the value, importance, and evolutionary significance of several special emotions, especially love, tender feelings, and devotion.[1842] Darwin spoke in deep respect for the role that sympathy can play in the life of our group, that is, in our interpersonal life: "We readily perceive sympathy in others by their

---

[1840] Charles Darwin, *The Descent of Man*, pp. 95, 103, in Chap. IV, pp. 94-123.

[1841] See the discussion in Charles Darwin, *The Descent of Man*, Chap. V.

[1842] Charles Darwin, *The Expression of the Emotions in Man and Animals* (1897), Chapter VIII, pp. pp. 196-219, "Joy, High Spirits, Love, Tender Feelings, Devotion." The theme has been brought into more refined focus recently by those who are investigating neuropsychology and the emotions. See UC Berkeley Prof. of Social Psychology, Dacher Keltner, *Born To Be Good: The Science of A Scientific Life* (2009) and his article "Darwin's Touch: Survival of the Kindest," *Psychology Today*, Feb. 11, 2009, PSYCHOLOGYTODAY.COM.

As the neurological basis of sympathy, empathy, and compassion, neuroscientists have identified the mirror neurons, the periacqueductal gray matter in the midbrain, the Vagus nerve, and the cerebral cortex: Mirror neurons, which have us be aware of the experience of another we are looking at, discovered in the 1980s by a team at the Univ. of Parma headed by Kiev-born Giacomo Rizzolatti. The periacqueductal gray matter operates to control pain, alters the heart beat, and also is involved in neuro-emotional circuits and in experiences of empathy. The Vagus nerve communicates to heart and other muscle tissues, regulates stress and relaxation, and guides digestive processes. The cerebral cortex, the frontal lobes, allow for higher conceptual understanding and judgment.

expression; our sufferings are thus mitigated and our pleasures increased; and our and mutual good feeling is thus strengthened."[1843]

Clearly missing from the Nazi worldview and its respected values are these attitudes of love, caring, tenderness, and devotion to all!

If we return to specific societal conflicts, some deep-rooted conflicts have periods of a relatively peaceful relationship, as in the period after the Irish Catholic-Protestant conflicts (this being at least the way the tensions were conceptualized and taken to be basic) of 1968-1998,[1844] interspersed with periods of flare-ups of violence, as in more recent years.[1845] We might also consider in this context, Sunni-Shia violence in various predominantly Muslim countries, the tensions between various groups (castes) in India, and so on.

How do the countries of Europe, and the rest of us, deal with the mixture of cultures found in every land? One answer to this, looking back at the past century in Europe, is by Bulgarian-born French psychoanalyst, philosopher, linguist, social commentator, and novelist, Julia Kristeva:

> Today, European identity is comprised of many national identities. Europe needs to be federal—made up of different nations that are open to one another and respect one another. I believe that there is a need to highlight the uniqueness of each nation and make it feel self-confident. Self-respect is an antidepressant, and it as important as it gets in building identity, but on condition that it doesn't turn into arrogance but rather openness to the other. That national self-respect will allow nations to create a rich, heterogeneous European identity in which each has its own uniqueness, language, and culture.[1846]

It is not an easy path and it does not work in a straight-line fashion, there being much resistance in all times to such an openness and non-hostile attitude toward the "other" (however defined in contrast to what we take ourselves to be).

But various paths that can be helpful can be marked out for use, at least partially. We may appreciate that some of these paths are defined by what should, or could, be done in given situations to increase a sense of mutual concern and respect.

We can say that perhaps *a minimal goal would be to have civility in our social universe*. And yet this can be clear as a principle and yet not clear in specific contexts how to bring about such a desired goal.

[1843] Charles Darwin, *The Expression of the Emotions in Man and Animals*, p. 364, in Chap. XIV, pp. 347-366 ("Concluding Remarks and Summary").

[1844] "Two Tribes: A divided Northern Ireland," *The Irish Times*, Apr. 1, 2017; "The Troubles 1968-1998," BBC HISTORY; "Northern Ireland: A brief background to the conflict," *Passage Engelsk*, PASSAGE-NEW.CAPPELENDAMM.NO.

[1845] Andrew Coffman Smith, "Catholic-Protestant feud flares anew in Northern Ireland," *USA Today*, Jul. 11, 2014.

[1846] "Julia Kristeva: The humanities can help thwart the destructive depression that feeds fanaticism," KRISTEVA.FR.

For example, we can say to a child, "Be good," or "Be nice to your sister," or "Respect your elders" (or whatever), and this may well leave the person (child or adult) being told what to with no idea whatsoever of *how to fulfill that bit of instruction.*

As at Valentine's Day, when a woman may tell a man that he can give her whatever he would like to, and yet, have a different reaction to different sorts of gifts, with the man often in the dark, in total ignorance, of what would please her; here, too, we may understand the instructions or request or demand, and yet not have the least idea of how to comply.

FINALLY RISING ABOVE RAGE THROUGH ADAPTABILITY OF MIND

In this way, we may look at a core phenomenon that all human beings experience, that of frustration, meaning that there is a difference between what we would like and what is the actual situation. Frustration (or agitation, disturbance, or what in Buddhist psychology is called *dukkha*, or *duḥkha* (disturbance, agitation, unpleasantness, life turbulence, torment, anguish, or "rough riding") is in this way a universal feature of human experience—not that it is constant or omnipresent in our lives.

The issue facing us is not how to avoid frustration completely (even if we can do it briefly at times, at least partially), but how we deal with frustration, or pain, that is there for us to deal with, or to try to avoid or disregard. How do we keep from being dragged about, guided, and even controlled by rage? How do we experience frustration without violent reactivity defining how we experience and act in the world? How do we shift our consciousness so that rage is not our master, our harsh dictator? How do we transcend this realm of conditioned, nasty, petty rage? How do we rise above rage, being free to act in a way that is more satisfying for us and for others, that is more harmonious to the overall situation we are in, that is alive, vibrant, satisfying, and lived in profound ease?

If we look to the starting point (or a very early point in the process, at least) of violence in society, much of which we have seen in considering the Hitler era, we are facing the issue of how we can come to deal with our frustrations and modulate or otherwise take control over our easy tendency to explode in some form of violence.

This is a general issue, since every living person at least from time to time, if not frequently, or predominantly, may become aware that the anger, turbulence, and rage that can become alive and exciting but also potentially dangerous (for others and also for us) *is itself a key pivotal point.* With this, we have a second question that complements the question of how to deal with trauma deeply and skillfully.

In the *Iliad*, to return to that old text, we began the story in midstream with the announcement of the violent rage of Achilles. His rage would keep him from fighting in the war until after the death of his closest friend, Patroclus. After the death of Patroclus in battle at the hands of Hector, Achilles finally decides to focus on revenging this murder.

And yet, how was this done? How did Achilles achieve this shift? This rather significant transformation required a refocusing of his thinking. He declared, going beyond his anger at Agamemnon for taking Briseis from him, "Enough. Let bygones be bygones. Done is done. Despite my anguish I will beat it down, the fury mounting inside me, down by force. Now, by god, I call a halt to all my anger—it's wrong to keep on raging, heart inflamed forever."[1847] With this he called on the Greeks and himself to mount an attack on the warriors of Troy, with Hector the target of Achilles' desire for revenge. In this context, Agamemnon swore an oath before Zeus that he had never laid a hand on Briseis, never forced her to serve his lust, and so forth.[1848] This would suggest that his taking Briseis was his show of power earlier on, rather than involving a carnal desire for her.

Such details aside, this dramatic presentation of a profound shift in consciousness has a powerful function in the story of the attack on Troy. Now, in general, what is not so easy, of course, is the shift away from being wildly enraged, uncontrollably furious. In modern terms, we should just let it go, and of course that, too, is not so easy—but still, doable![1849]

In the *Iliad*, in part, Achilles decided to let go his earlier rage and to focus on issues at hand. *Quick, impulsive judgment had ceded to reflective awareness*. This impetuousness in strong emotions may be a sign of youth: as the young Antilochus, son of Nestor, spoke of the whims of youth, which "break all the rules. Our wits quicker than wind, our judgment just as flighty."[1850]

This may evolve into a more nuanced and sophisticated understanding of life and people, unless one is, like a spoon in soup: "Even though an immature person associates throughout his life with one who is wise, he does not thereby perceive the truth, as a ladle does not perceive the flavor of soup."[1851] *Wisdom does not come simply by staying alive a long time*, so we might look to other influences in our potential to become more discerning, subtle, understanding, and, in short, wise, rather than hoping it will come if we just wait long enough.

It might be helpful here to look at the process of *being less enthralled by our sweet rage and the power we feel when experiencing its intensity*, and to investigate not whether this can happen (it can), but under which conditions this shift happens more easily than under others. In another way of asking questions, What is it that shifts us out of our focused anger to a broader sense of our situation?

It has been said that we can push an alcoholic to stop drinking alcohol through one method or another (hypnosis, court orders, bodily threats, societal opprobrium or insults, electro-shock therapy when that person starts drinking, prescribing a substance such as disulfiram[1852] that would cause great discomfort or vomiting if anyone drinks anything alcoholic,

---

[1847] Homer, *Iliad*, 19.64-78, esp. 74-78 (BK.vv: 19.50-55-70, esp. 65-70).
[1848] Homer, *Iliad*, 19.208-211, 304-314 (BK.vv: 19.175-176; 258-265).
[1849] See Mitchell Ginsberg, *Mindful Raft over Troubled Waters* (2015), esp. "On the Far Shore: Let go the future" (p. xix), "Memory in the Present" (p. 89), "Power of the Now, Prison of the Now" (pp. 98-99).
[1850] Homer, *Iliad*, 23.652-655 (BK.vv: 23.585-590).
[1851] *Dhammapada*, verse 64.
[1852] The substance disulfiram is commonly marketed as Antabuse.

and so forth), but this may be like kicking out the crutches of someone needing the crutches at the time to maintain enough stability to be able to walk. Better is to help develop other means of being able to walk with stability; then there will be no need for crutches. This leads to asking the important question of what purposes the drinking is serving: perhaps numbing of physical or emotional pain, relief from the intense work, interpersonal pressure, or demands that overwhelm someone.

Taking this idea as a model, we can see that in some cases, an urge for violence, rage, and violence impulses, can be eliminated or relieved by *a sense or realization of something more important*, from the point of view of the person in question. *This was the case of Achilles, just noted.* In other instances, there is a feeling of danger or of personal inadequacy or lack of societal respect. And so on. And, in each such case, looking at what is felt to be lacking, or is overpoweringly present, can give a sense of what would be called for *to improve the situation*.[1853]

There are obvious advantages to the development of patience and a relaxed state of mind in the midst of a frustrating situation, which can in some instances be compared with a short-fused violence that can erupt quickly and perhaps violently, to the detriment of all those involved. We have a wide variety of potential responses: We can focus on an appreciation of everything that is going well in our world along with this frustration. We can focus on how the world is violent and ill-willed, and perhaps destroying any joy and happiness we might have. We can go into activities that numb our awareness, such as drinking large amounts of alcohol or taking drugs that decrease our attentiveness to our situation. We can go into a sleeping binge. We can even go into sexual excitement, the sexualization of turmoil, shifting to a sexual focus to avoid some real issue (the opposite of sublimation: the taking of sexual energy and redirecting that energy into non-sexual activities and interests).

If we take seriously this idea that *frustration can be dealt with in a skillful way*, or, in contrast, in a way that increases the torment of those around us and of ourselves, this becomes *an ongoing exercise in self-awareness and self-appreciation*. These practices can be simple in their parts and application. In Western philosophy, Immanuel Kant gave insight into the structures of the mind, of our processes of thinking, our worldview (the basic concepts or categories that we use to comprehend reality), concluding that these are our contribution to understanding, not given in reality itself; and C. I. Lewis pointed out that these basic categories of thought can be modified through time and experience.[1854]

In addition, in an even wider perspective, religious and spiritual (or psychospiritual) teachings have taught the learning of new consciousness

---

[1853] More on this, just below.

[1854] Immanuel Kant (1724-1804), *Kritik der reinen Vernunft* (1781, 2nd ed., 1787); Eng., *Critique of Pure Reason*, Norman Kemp Smith, tr. (1929), and Clarence Irving Lewis (1883-1964), *Mind and the World-order: Outline of a Theory of Knowledge* (1929) and *An Analysis of Knowledge and Valuation* (1946).

since ancient times.[1855] One such simple practice, defined in the 1800s by the philosopher and psychologist Friedrich Nietzsche, is termed Russian fatalism, the ability to refrain from reacting to whatever we are being faced with in our world. In contrast here, the opposite of that would be a hair-trigger readiness to go into some reaction that occurs to us, whether based on excited joy and high expectations, or in an attack and violence at the least provocation or disagreement of opinion from another.[1856] (Hitler's reactive rage is well known, and we have seen a number of other world leaders who are rather practiced at, and ready to go into, this violent reactivity to what is not quite perfectly as they desired.)

This concept that encapsulates the human possibility of *refraining from reacting with an immediate, automatic, conditioned violence*—in a grand scheme, being something that drags many in with it, such as going to war—is a promising alternative to ending up repeating something like World War II, with estimates, as cited above, for World War II military and civilian deaths being put at 50-60 million dead.[1857] *In this context, there is a great potential for a more human, humane, and civilized way of dealing with the many forms of tension, hostility, and conflict in our world, through looking to some of the world's great religious practices and spiritual (or psychospiritual) practices that address this issue, in ways designed to make our world more civilized and more loving.* This is not to deny that any among us might have a perhaps fleeting or even persistent thought of bringing harm to others, or to ourselves, which, in more traditional terms would be to acknowledge the evil or harm-focused urges and actions we might take. And yet, *we do not have to follow those urges*. In a way, the more we are aware of these impulses, the better we are able to evaluate them and to let them be without acting on them, and the less we are living our lives in a reactive, somewhat myopic, if not blind, way. We can be attentive to our potential to make our world more harmonious, respectful, and civilized, or, to make it a barbaric domain of rage and violence. *This is a choice we can address consciously.* In looking at the world's religious and spiritual traditions, we can see explicit

---

[1855] See extended discussions in Mitchell Ginsberg, *The Inner Palace: Reflections of Psychospirituality in Divine and Sacred Wisdom-Traditions*.

[1856] This is discussed in "Nietzschean Psychiatry Revisited," Chap. 3 in Mitchell Ginsberg, *Calm, Clear, and Loving*.

[1857] One analysis of war dead (both military and civilian) put the mid-estimate of war deaths at 28,736,000 dead, *in addition to* genocide, mass murders, euthanasia, and related killings, at 20,946,000 dead. The total here would be 49,682,000 people, at Rudolph J. Rummel, *Democide: Nazi Genocide and Mass Murder* (1992), Table 1.1. Cf. 64,781,162 cited as total military and civilian dead in "Bilan de la Seconde Guerre mondiale (en chiffres)," REPERES: PARTINARIAT ÉDUCATIF GRUNDTVIG 2009-2011, with more than half of total war dead in China and the USSR. A total of over 60 million killed is given at "Tote des Zweiten Weltkrieges," DE.WIKIPEDIA, and at "World War II Casualties," WIKIPEDIA. In these last sources, estimates for French, UK, and US total (military) dead put the numbers up to 600,000, 450,000, and 419,500. Total dead overall is given in recent sources as up to 65 million.

guidelines for the cultivation of compassion—known in Latin as *misericordia*, in Hebrew as *raḥamim*, in Arabic as *raḥ'mah*,[1858] in Indic Buddhist terms, as *karuṇā*.[1859] These can be counter-balances to another one of our states of mind, known in German as *Schadenfreude*, the joy at seeing another person's misery.

MINDFULNESS AND INSIGHT MEDITATION, HEALING THE RAGEFUL MIND

An issue underlying all of these considerations is whether, and how, we might stop being reactive, stop being controlled by the impulses created by what we have variously experienced in life, from parental guidance, education, inspiring and fearful events, and even acute (short-term) and chronic (repeating through time) traumas, that have us hyper-vigilant, anxious, fearful, and readily shifted into rage and an urge to attack, often in a sense of the vital need to preserve ourselves and to survive some new threat to our existence or to maintain self-pride.

As noted above, attention to how we are interpreting and reacting to our given situation can *improve the situation*. That is on the level of thinking and deliberating. There are also considerations of the various states of minds—from being relaxed to jittery, from good-willed to rage-filled—that are also important in *our understanding of the factors that define our ways of thinking, speaking, and acting*,[1860] in ways that are at times elegant, harmonious, contributing to the well-being of ourselves and also of others, which can be described in a general way as our being skillful in that moment. Attention that notices everything, with no filters, even the harsh features of our world, is powerful: "Attention is the rarest and purest form of generosity," said French Jewish philosopher Simone Weil (1909-1943).[1861] The opposites here are our being clumsy, abrupt, aggressive, disturbing, agitating, destructive, and so forth. These latter considerations address the general category of what is understood to be unskillful mind. (More on that, directly below.) And, as we have seen, the issue of rage, in particular, a tendency that is not new and has been recognized as being a source of many further problems, for ourselves and for others, some minor but others, significant even on a global level. This phenomenon and psychological pattern have been addressed for literally millennia, in an attempt to understand their nature and to learn how to

---

[1858] These two terms, *raḥamim* and *raḥ'mah*, are derived from *reḥem* and *raḥmi*, both meaning womb, etymologically linking compassion with the female.

[1859] An extended discussion of the specific practices of a wide range of religious and spiritual practices around the world is in Mitchell Ginsberg, *The Inner Palace: Mirrors of Psychospirituality in Divine and Sacred Wisdom-Traditions*.

[1860] Seeing the interrelatedness between the conditions present and required for a given state of mind is powerful in coming to clarity and non-driven consciousness. Sariputta, later an honored disciple of the Buddha, learned from a new student of the Buddha, Assaji, "Whatever phenomena arise from cause, their cause and their cessation, such is the teaching of the Tathāgata [the Buddha], the great contemplative." In the *Mahavagga*, 1.23.1-10, in the Pali Canon's *Vinaya Piṭaka*.

[1861] Simone Weil and Joë Bousquet, *Correspondance* (1950/1982), p. 18.

The Hitler Era

keep their noxious power from controlling what we think and do. In recent decades, there has been the re-introduction of the concept of being mindful, or mindfulness.[1862] This is one of several core practices within what is known as Insight Meditation,[1863] which is a particularly Buddhist practice[1864] later adopted by various other systems of practice and theory.

The term Insight Meditation renders Pali *vipassanā-bhāvanā* (Sanskrit, *vipaśyanā-bhāvanā*), which more literally can be understood as meaning cultivating insight, or the cultivation of insight. The insight spoken of here is insight into the workings of the mind in the context of our consciousness as created through sense experience with the world in which we live.

There is a goal proposed within this perspective of coming to understand (not simply experiencing moment by moment). This is an understanding that appreciates the ways in which the various parts or components of our experience have consequences. Thus, if grounding, calming, features are strengthened, we can have more of the sort of consequences we find appealing. Complementing this, in appreciating what the foundations are of certain problematic states of mind, thoughts, imagined plans, intentions, and actions—in removing those underlying conditions, their consequences will not come to pass.[1865] Here we have the opportunity of appreciating an ancient teaching on the overcoming of

---

[1862] Pali, *sati*, Sanskrit, *smṛti*, mindfulness, remembering, remembrance; in Buddhism, esp. a state of mind that can be attentiveness to the experience of the present moment. Its grounded form, usually rendered as right mindfulness, is called *sammā-sati* (Pali), *samyak-smṛti* (Sanskrit). *Sammā-* or *samyak-*, the first part—whose root is *sam + añc*, turn together, etc.—means right, but also correct, precise, complete, thorough, etc. The whole term, then, means a well-rounded mindfulness that can see from various perspectives in a comprehensive way.

Consider here such texts as Jiddu Krishnamurti, *The First and the Last Freedom* (1954), *The Awakening of Intelligence* (1973); *Beyond Violence* (1973); *Secrets of the Lotus*, Donald K. Swearer, ed. (1971), chap. on Theravāda Meditation by Chao Khun Sobhana Dhamasudhi, aka V. R. Dhiravamsa; Joseph Goldstein and Jack Kornfield, *Seeking the Heart of Wisdom: The Path of Insight Meditation* (1977); Mitchell Ginsberg, *The Far Shore: Vipassanā, The Practice of Insight* (1980); Eckhart Tolle, *The Power of Now: A Guide to Spiritual Enlightenment* (1997).

[1863] Shunryū Suzuki, *Zen Mind, Beginner's Mind: Informal talks on Zen Meditation* (1970); Thích Nhất Hạnh, *Miracle of Mindfulness: A Manual on Meditation* (1975); Dalai Lama XIV, *Opening the Eye of New Awareness* (1985); V. R. Dhiravamsa, *Healing through Pure Mindfulness* (2014); Claudio Naranjo, *Healing Civilization* (2009); Mitchell Ginsberg, *Mindful Raft Over Troubled Waters* (2015).

[1864] A traditional, classic source of this practice is in the Pali Canon—the traditional collection of the core teachings of Theravāda Buddhism—in the *Satipaṭṭānasutta, The Discourse on the Foundations (or Establishing) of Mindfulness*. This appears with this title in *Majjhima-nikāya, Sutta* 10, and as *Mahā-satipaṭṭānasutta, Dīgha-nikāya, Sutta* 22. For a bilingual ed. with traditional commentaries, see Soma Thera, *The Way of Mindfulness: The Satipaṭṭāna Sutta and Commentary* (1975).

[1865] Mitchell Ginsberg, *Calm, Clear, and Loving*, Chap. 10, "The Liberating Power of Mindfulness," and Chap. 11, "Inter-Personal Mindfulness Practice (IPMP)."

a variety of negative mind-states, negative in that are found to lead consistently to more torment for ourselves and others, to what is termed *dukkha* (Sanskrit, *duḥkha*). Relatedly, thoughts and actions that lead to more *dukkha* (torment, discomfort, anguish, and such) are considered to be unskillful, as mentioned above. One goal we can set is to minimize our unskillful moments and to maximize our skillful ones.[1866]

With that as a general context that addresses our ability to modify our consciousness, our states of mind, our particular experiences, thoughts, intentions, and actions, we can look specifically at anger or rage (rage being an intense form of anger, regularly leading to violent outbursts or even carefully planned actions designed to hurt others).

Seeing such features of our experience is quite difficult unless we at first have a mind calm enough to notice its nuances. This leads to the practice of developing calm.[1867] How do we come to calm?

Traditionally, any practice that has us bring our minds to calm, by focusing on some given particular experience as our object of concentration,[1868] will serve this purpose well. This object of focus can be the light of a burning candle, a geometric design, a repeated sound (*mantra*), or a sensation that is ongoing, as our breath.[1869] As we focus in on one such part of our experience, we can develop calm and inner quiet. Once we have come to such a relatively stable mind-state, we can be less reactive and self-defensive than we might experience in our usual state of mind. When we can look at what thoughts, images, memories, and associations come to us in our mind, without jumping to one or another evaluation or judgment (horrible, wonderful, exciting, boring, inspired, reprehensible, saintly, and so forth), we can see into what the memories and other reflections of our earlier experiences actually are.

This ability to see what our thoughts and memories are, without going into a judgmental stance, is sometimes quite difficult, even in its ultimate simplicity. Now, in terms of our reactivity to what we interpret to be hostile, dumb, stupid, threatening, insulting, immoral, or even evil—some of the more usual starting points for anger or rage—if we can pause and remain with a focused awareness on the actual words or actions we are concerned with, we may experience that we do not have to respond immediately. This opens up the space, with practice, to be able not to

---

[1866] Pali, *kusala*; Skt., *kuśala*: skillful, healthy, proper, suitable, competent, clever, morally good, etc. Its contrast is Pali *akusala*; Skt., *akuśala*: unskillful, unwholesome, inauspicious, not clever, etc.

[1867] Calm or tranquility: in Pali, *samatha*; in Sanskrit, *śamatha*.

[1868] Concentration: in Pali and Sanskrit, *samādhi*.

[1869] A geometric design or an image for focus or inspiration in various practices: in Pali and Sanskrit, *yantra*. See Donald K. Swearer, *Becoming the Buddha: The Ritual of Image Consecration in Thailand* (2004), p. 70. A sound used in a repeated concentration or to bring the mind to a particular focus: in Pali and Sanskrit, *mantra*, lit., a means or instrument (*-tra*) for the mental (*man-*). See Donald K. Swearer, *Becoming the Buddha*, just cited, p. 69.

respond at all, at least in a violent way. This first step, freeing ourselves from knee-jerk reactivity with a potential explosion of frustrated violence, can then be strengthened by our cultivating an understanding and insight into this pattern that we keep repeating that brings hurt or injury to others, and leaves us to deal with our own possible shame at what we keep doing, as well as any angry, hostile responses to our actions we may receive as target of others' hurts and anger, in turn.

This much broader insight is based on *our ability to compare various particular moments and contexts with reactions*, to see more inclusive patterns of our thinking and reacting. This involves the use of memory and our comparative (diachronic) mind to see repeating regularities.[1870]

Further along here, we may come to see what underlying issues there are in our past that keep being touched upon or triggered, having us deal in the present situation with what was unresolved earlier on. This sort of analysis, the breaking-down into the components that make up a basis for anger, resentment, and rage, *is only part of what is called for here*. Still, there is much to say that makes the idea of being awakened (or, to use a more Western term, "enlightened") appealing, with its clear perception and lack of distortions about what is actually the case in our experience and world. Seeing that the direct expression of anger is not a constructive response to real-life problems, how do we transform misdirected pain and its tormented wrath into skillful action? Here, we may think of awakening as a total shift in consciousness, occurring instantaneously ("the sudden path"),[1871] which in ways it is, although our turbulence does not end with that process.

As Meditation Master and founder of Korean Sŏn[1872] Buddhism, Chinul (1158-1210), pointed out, "one should illuminate and examine [one's mind] long after the enlightenment: if deluded thoughts suddenly arise, one should not follow them but reduce them until one reaches non-action [and non-reactivity]. *Only then will one have reached the final realm*. It is precisely this that is called the act of 'cow-tending' by all men of good learning in the world." And in an extended metaphor, Chinul spoke of "prior enlightenment and later cultivation ... the mind already without delusion and ignorance is like the sudden cessation of the wind ... the natural gradual release of attachment to conditions after enlightenment is like the gradual calming down of the waves."[1873] Beyond this metaphor, then, there is the basic idea that there is no immediate resolution through this psychospiritual awakening to some important problems facing us.

[1870] See esp. Mitchell Ginsberg, *Mindful Raft over Troubled Waters*, "Power of the now, prison of the now," pp. 98-99.

[1871] See extended discussion in Chap. 12 ("The Gradual and the Sudden") in Mitchell Ginsberg, *The Inner Palace*.

[1872] *Sŏn* in Korean is equivalent to *Chan*, in Chinese, and *Zen*, in Japanese.

[1873] Both quotes at Hee-sung Keel, *Chinul: The Founder of the Korean Sŏn Tradition* (1984), pp. 115-116. Italics added. Discussed in Mitchell Ginsberg, *The Inner Palace*, pp. 193-194, 483-484.

As the French philosopher and psychiatrist Pierre Janet (1859-1947) expressed a similar point, discussing thinking that created ongoing problems, "I do not think cure is that easy and that it suffices to bring about the expression of the fixed idea [the verbal, explicit rendering of some thought] to eliminate it [unlike Freud]; treatment is unfortunately much more delicate."[1874]

And so, a first caveat here: Long-time and deeply-embedded patterns of reactivity that are unskillful in various ways do not end simply because we are now clearly aware of them and of their detrimental nature; our becoming aware of them may even be experienced at first as a nuisance. ("In ignorance, bliss.")

And, thus, a second note of caution: We are an impatient species, with pervasive hopes for a quick fix to any and all problems. As Nietzsche remarked, certain people "believe that they have helped most when they have helped most quickly."[1875]

If we can refrain from being driven by our impatience, we may be more successful in taking a slow, steady approach, watching an unwanted pattern of thought and action, wanting them to be gone but realizing that they merely become less intense in time. When we see a problem recurring, we may feel it will be there forever. And yet, the first significant signs of change may be a subtler pattern that does not go to the same extremes, or does not last so long as it did earlier.[1876]

A contemporary poet sketched this gradual task in our overcoming the human possibility of becoming a vicious wolf (as in Hitler's ideal):

> A tenacious wolf, said a wise man once, is hidden deep within each of us. Hence, a struggle is ongoing, day and night, between the wolf and the human being. Force alone will not subdue this wolf. It is through the mind that we confront it. Whoever defeats his wolf, gradually becomes a true human. But one who is always defeated by his wolf may be dressed in the robes of man: he's a wolf! One who compromises with his wolf, becomes wolf-like inside.[1877]

Part of the process of shifting the way we respond to given situations involves a re-evaluation of their significance to us. When there are underlying frustrations, if we appreciate what they are and how we might better deal with them, perhaps facing them directly rather than distracting ourselves with anger at some outside forces, we do not change the

---

[1874] Pierre Janet, *État mental des hystériques* (1892), p. 352 in 2nd, 1911 ed. See discussions in *Calm, Clear, and Loving*, Chap. 3, "Nietzschean Psychiatry Revisited," p. 73, and Chap. 6, "Pierre Janet: Misleading Concepts and Integration."

[1875] Friedrich Nietzsche, *The Gay Science*, Walter Kaufmann, tr. Sect. 338. Cf. *Calm, Clear, and Loving*, Chap 3, "Nietzschean Psychiatry Revisited," at p. 77.

[1876] *Calm, Clear, and Loving*, Chap. 26, "Options when Overwhelmed."

[1877] Fereydoun Moshiri (1926-2000), "Gorg" ("The Wolf"). This text based on several glosses: "Fereydoon Moshiri—Gorg," AMARA.ORG; "Fereydoon Moshiri and the wolf within," PARSOLOGY.ORG; "The Wolf, by Fereydoon Moshiri," CAAM.RICE.EDU.

disturbing past, but do give it a different significance and degree of importance in our lives.[1878]

ETHICS IN A POST-REICH WORLD: SOME FINAL CONSIDERATIONS

In looking at recent events in today's world, we may be reminded of earlier times and earlier situations. For example, there is a wave these years of a strong resurgent nationalism, found in many countries with differing particulars but an overall yearning for a well-defined national identity and a re-establishing of the rights of those native to a region, *or at least considered native and original*, whatever the limited actual historical basis for that might be.

One thought that has occurred after the Hitler era and the attempts of the Third Reich and its allies during World War II to exterminate inferior beings (an effort focused most intently and vehemently on the Jews and Romanies) is that what happened there could happen in other contexts. As Churchill scholar and biographer Sir Martin Gilbert wrote in 2011, "It could happen anywhere where the veneer of civilization is allowed to wear off, or is torn off by ill will and destructive urges."[1879] This is so even if we might sense that some steps have been taken to move our species worldwide to an overall more civilized stance. If we review and reflect on the paths that cultures have taken in recent centuries, we may notice that the twentieth century saw the dissembling and the demise of many empires, with the establishment of independent nations, and we may find some comfort in the nineteenth century as a century in which slavery perhaps peaked and then lost its last significant stronghold (as discussed above). Yet, in seeing at the same time the intensification of brutality with the increased efficacy of sophisticated weaponry and other means of mass killing, we may appreciate, nonetheless, that the path toward civilization is not a straight path with steady improvements unmarred by outbursts of savagery. The search for a worldwide civility is certainly not simple, and not at all easy or guaranteed. And, yes, the patina can be easily destroyed, as we have seen in the Hitler era and in so many other more recent shifts toward violence in governments and less formalized groups.

At the same time, it is easy to call one leader a new Hitler, a new Mussolini, or a new Stalin, but we may want to look in the various particulars that were present in the years of Hitler and these others, however, before making a total equation here. Germany after the First World War, for example, was a strong industrial country located in the center of Europe. It also had a government, the Weimar Republic, that was basically established when the leading military were nowhere to be found (Hindenburg, Ludendorff, and the Kaiser dodged the limelight). In particular, many were against the Weimar Republic, wanting either a

---

[1878] *Calm, Clear, and Loving*, Chap. 18, "Forgive and Remember," Chap. 12, "The Pivot of the Dao," and Chap. 13, "The Second Transformation: Our Third Nature & Recalibration."

[1879] Foreword (Feb. 8, 2011) by Sir Martin Gilbert, in Denis Avey, *The Man who Broke into Auschwitz*.

return to a nation ruled by a Kaiser, or a Bolshevik-like government, or a strong and determined nationalistic leader. The relatively few Germans in "the middle" were squeezed by incompatible demands from the political far right and far left. Many groups wished for the end of the Weimar Republic, but wanted a wide variety of different resultant forms of government to replace it. Further, there was a built-in mechanism to close down the free press, even during the Republic's years, as discussed above.

To attempt to see one or two features in a present-day country as resembling pre-Nazi Germany as proving that here we go again, with a new Hitler on the horizon, takes what may be a rather limited similarity to be an absolute equivalence or an exact repetition of an earlier situation. While we may have reason to worry in the present, it may be helpful to see the ways in which this current problem, whatever we take it to be, might also be significantly different from the Germany of the 1920s that paved the way for the Third Reich of the 1930s and 1940s.

In all of this, we have looked at the historical roots that impacted the millions of several generations since the fall of the Third Reich, making clearer which issues people at various times felt to be important and what they saw as improvements or remedies to at least some of their concerns. We have taken here a broad perspective, considering the thousands and even millions of people who were either killed, maimed, incapacitated, or left with life-long torments from those years.

We have also considered individuals as they dealt with what the Hitler era presented to them. (Individual stories can have their own particular poignancy and palpable power.) Those conditions led some to commit suicide, many at the time of great crisis, but others only years or even decades later. What leads people to find life unbearable, knowing their own past, may operate in a number of ways, from guilt to unbearable torment, to appreciation at having survived the crises they experienced.

And, noticing the numerous new illiberal democracies of current times may give pause in thinking about the paths taken in the past.[1880] Here, while poetry is ultimately still possible after Auschwitz (despite claims to the opposite), there is the question of how we are going to live our lives, given this past of the violence of the Third Reich.

Ethics, the investigation into systems of morality, asks us to consider here which guidelines we will take into account and respect at this time in the history of the world, to become people we ourselves respect. We may take a broad view of the relationship between a grounded morality with our own reflective sense of what is right and wrong and of what sorts of persons we want to be, and also at the demands of any group or society for strong cooperation and harmony, with these two being at times in conflict with one another, and so the value of having some balance between the two can be quite helpful. The process of accepting and taking into account both our own moral sense and the demands of the society in

---

[1880] James Traub, "Irony is the Secret to Saving Democracy," *Foreign Policy*, Jan. 28, 2019, FOREIGNPOLICY.COM.

which we find ourselves in can be a subtle and difficult task. Here, we can see the society's mores and values as a demand for stability, while our own deepest values may call for modification in either small or staggering, life-changing, ways. Speaking here in a theoretical way of the relationship between a system that asks for imitation, continuity, and stability, and at the same time, requires non-imitation, innovation, and adaptation to new contexts, Danish professor Svend Østergaard expressed this principle in these more general, inclusive terms:

> Imitation secures stability ... [that continues] from generation to generation, ... [but if] too strong there would be no innovation and society would perish, a development that is counteracted by non-imitative behavior which is the source for new ideas and new behavioral strategies ...[1881]

Coming to resolution when there are these conflicting considerations to take into account is not always an easy affair, and in the case of extreme pressures in some societies, such as we saw during the Third Reich, this may involve literally life-and-death decisions. Even in the aftermath of such situations, the drain on our hearts and souls can be overwhelming. *Many of those who survived the war would find living on to be too great a burden, harder than being killed or committing suicide!*

Within the overall story of the Reich, there was a smaller world that those who were there know in a way that no one else does: the extremely violent world that has been called the concentration-camp universe (*l'univers concentrationnaire*).[1882] This world, terrible and macabre, with a level of harshness if not sadism meted out with no constraints, is difficult and uncomfortable to imagine,[1883] and even then, the imagination can almost never capture the full horror of what was lived through moment by moment, ending often in death within the camp system. By one name or another, the memories that many were disturbed by, ultimately led to many a suicide in their gigantic weight, even if some were able to contribute to society and to its understanding of the war.

One such example is Jewish, Viennese-born, Bruno Bettelheim, who was arrested when Germany annexed Austria in 1938. From May 1938 to April 1939, he was imprisoned in Dachau and Buchenwald, before being released; he fled to America, where he was accepted as a political refugee.

After leaving Europe, Bettelheim wrote a number of articles and books on psychology that were widely read, such as a war-relevant article and his analyses of children's fairy tales.[1884] He also proposed his perspective

---

[1881] Svend Østergaard, "The Dynamics of Interaction and Consciousness," *Cognitive Semiotics*, vol. 1, Fall Issue (2007), pp. 111-122, at p. 116.
[1882] As in David Rousset, *L'univers concentrationnaire* (1946).
[1883] The Russian film, *Sobibor* (2018), dramatizes the sober and the drunken sadism of the SS at that death camp, in the long sequence at 1:09:30-1:21:40.
[1884] Bruno Bettelheim, "Individual and Mass Behavior in Extreme Situations,"

on and interpretation of Freud, making use of his native-speaker familiarity with Austrian German. Bettelheim suggested that Freud had a more spiritual (*seelisch*) viewpoint of the human being, and had a focus on man's psyche, or soul (*die Seele*). This went against the interpretation of Freud as embodied in the particular translation used in the *Standard Edition of the Complete Psychological Works of Freud*. Freud's writings in these official translations into English presented Freud as a physician specialist with interests focused in investigating the scientific, medicalized, psychological domain of the mind in its psychopathological manifestations (the *Seele* or Psyche interpreted as the locus of the psychological).[1885]

The significant difference that Bettelheim was suggesting in that discussion of Freud called for a radical re-reading of Freud's works.

Finally, Bettelheim would contribute a Foreword to a book by a Hungarian Jewish physician at Auschwitz, Dr. Miklós Nyiszli, who worked as an assistant to Dr. Mengele, and survived to write his story. And yet, after contributing a number of original and insightful works, long after World War II and the Third Reich, Bettelheim committed suicide, in 1990.

In the words of Bettelheim, we are even today faced with a life context that invites us, even demands of us, that we look seriously at the way civilization can and has been so quickly and perhaps surprisingly undermined. *This is taking stock of what our species is, and who we are within that context.* Bettelheim wrote in his Foreword:

> Years before Hitler sent millions to the gas chambers, Freud insisted that human life is one long struggle against what he called the death instinct, and that we must learn to keep these destructive strivings within bounds lest they send us to our destruction. The twentieth century did away with ancient barriers that once prevented our destructive tendencies from running rampant, both in ourselves and in society. State, family, church, society, all were put into question, and found wanting. So, their power to restrain or channel our destructive tendencies was weakened [thus shown to be less stable and durable than we might have thought]. The re-evaluation of all values which Nietzsche (Hitler's prophet, though Hitler, like others, misunderstood him abysmally) predicted would be required of Western man, were he to survive in the modern machine age, has not yet been achieved ...[1886]

Journal of Abnormal and Social Psychology, vol. 38, no. 4, Oct. 1943, pp. 417–452; Bruno Bettelheim, *The Uses of Enchantment: The Meaning and Importance of Fairy Tales* (1976).

[1885] Bruno Bettelheim, *Freud and Man's Soul* (1983).

[1886] Bruno Bettelheim, Foreword to Dr. Miklós Nyiszli, *Auschwitz: A Doctor's Eyewitness Account* (1960). Cf. Petruska Clarkson, "War: Bystanding and Hate—Why Category Errors are Dangerous," *Psychotherapy and Politics International*, vol. 1, no. 2, 2003, pp. 117-132.

In this context, speaking of Anne Frank and her family who had gone into hiding in an annex in Amsterdam, where they stayed until captured and sent to Auschwitz and then Bergen-Belsen, Bettelheim continued, recognizing the urge for life to go on, hopefully with as little disruption as possible:

> All the Franks wanted was to go on with life as much as possible in the usual fashion. Little Anne, too, wanted only to go on with life as usual, and nobody can blame her[1887] ... I have met many Jews, as well as gentile anti-Nazis, who survived in Germany and in the occupied countries. But they were all people who realized that *when a world goes to pieces, when inhumanity reigns supreme, man cannot go on with business as usual.* One then has to radically re-evaluate all of what one has done, believed in, stood for. In short, one has to take a stand on the new reality, a firm stand, and not one of retirement [withdrawal] into even greater privatization.[1888]

Bettelheim here invites the reader into a more direct confrontation with a world in which inhumanity rules, "a world gone to pieces," as he expresses it. More on these questions, just below.

Issues on the Horizon for Our Species, in Closing

We can see that we are facing not only the recurrence of mass murders and genocides, investigated here in focusing on the Hitler Era, and not only the concerns of mankind for millennia of shelter, food, survival of natural disasters, avoidance of wild animals, safety from petty familial violence and from plundering marauders, organized formal and guerilla wars, or practical issues of the meager wages of so many in the world.

Could some of that be set aright if there were more self-determination, cooperative engagement in production, with perhaps more artisanal workmanship having its place, with mutual agreement by all involved on the structure of decision-making?[1889]

This may seem a pipe-dream but has already been realized in various countries in their history.[1890] Here, we can imagine the elimination of systemically skewed power and coercion as a way of life.

[1887] She and her family were arrested on Aug. 4, 1944, and transported via Westerbork to Auschwitz, then to Bergen-Belsen, where Anne died of typhus in Feb. 1945. See "Who Was Anne Frank?" *Anne Frank House*, ANNEFRANK.ORG.

[1888] Bruno Bettelheim, Foreword to Dr. Miklós Nyiszli, *Auschwitz*. Italics added.

[1889] For several frameworks in which these issues are addressed, see Pëtr Kropotkin, *Mutual Aid: A Factor in Evolution* (1902); Emma Goldman (founder of the journal *Mother Earth*), *Anarchism: What It Really Stands For* (1916); Rudolf Rocker, *Anarcho-syndicalism: Theory and Practice: An Introduction to a Subject Which the Spanish War Has Brought into Overwhelming Prominence* (1938); Noam Chomsky, *Chomsky on Anarchism*, with Intro. by Nathan Schneider (2013).

[1890] In Tito's Yugoslavia and in other countries, workers set production goals, prices of goods produced, payment for work, and all such administrative issues.

In addition to all such issues, we may see on the horizon entirely new life-threatening issues for us to deal with. First, we were introduced several decades ago to the idea that the earth is not unlimited as a source of sustenance, but an environment with important limits: we are on spaceship earth, as inventor, historian, and visionary R. Buckminster Fuller wrote.[1891] Furthermore, separately, our world population is growing at an exponential rate. These ever-larger numbers of people—the world population in 1950 was 2.56 billion; in 1970 was 3.71 billion; in 2010, 6.85 billion—need living space and a way of providing for themselves and the families they in turn create, as Stanford Professor of Biology Paul Ehrlich discussed.[1892] In addition to that, we have faced the annihilation of our species in ways unprecedented in history. First, after August 6, 1945 (with the world witnessing the devastating power of the first atomic bomb, exploded over Hiroshima), we have been able to contemplate *the possibility of the complete extinction of all human life*, which was given the name of omnicide by philosopher John Somerville (1905-1994),[1893] who focused on the destructive capacity of atomic bombs.

More recently, there is also the possibility of biological warfare ending up creating a worldwide pandemic of a scale never seen. In addition, there are the changes to our planet, usually referred to as Climate Change phenomena. Current information that has been gathered over at least the past half-century may not guarantee our extinction as a species, but all of this careful, extensive research, however, does strongly suggest the likelihood of major disruptions. These include intense weather conditions from hurricanes and typhoons to precipitation changes and drought or flooding in different areas from the expected rise in worldwide sea level, given the noticeable melting of the polar caps, especially around Antarctica. These would involve massive flooding and the consequent migration of the millions who might survive such occurrences.

In short, even if the most worrisome statements by the broad consensus of world scientists are overly pessimistic, it seems quite clear that the planet and we humans as some of the earth's inhabitants will face some unparalleled disasters (if we or future generations are around to experience them).[1894] These are certainly worrisome if not frightening

---

[1891] R. Buckminster Fuller, *Operating Manual for Spaceship Earth* (1968).

[1892] Paul Ehrlich, *The Population Bomb* (1971); Paul Ehrlich and Anne Ehrlich, *The Population Explosion* (1990); *Betrayal of Science and Reason: How Anti-environmental Rhetoric Threatens our Future* (1996); *One With Nineveh: Politics, Consumption, and the Human Future* (2004); *The Dominant Animal: Human Evolution and the Environment* (2008); Paul Ehrlich and Robert Ornstein, *Humanity on a Tightrope: Thoughts on Empathy, Family, and Big Changes for a Viable Future* (2010), and other works.

[1893] John Somerville, "Einstein's Legacy and Nuclear Omnicide," *Peace Research*, vol. 18, no. 1 (Jan. 1986), pp. 20-25, 53-58. Cf. John Somerville, *Philosophy of Peace* (2nd ed., 1954), with Introductory Comments by Albert Einstein.

[1894] See esp. documents of the UNFCCC (UN Framework Convention on Climate Change): *Kyoto Protocol* (1998), *Doha Amendment* (2012), and *Paris Agreement*

possibilities. Given that, as might not come as a total surprise, there are those who personally would rather not consider any of this seriously, and those who would for various economic considerations not want to admit that any of these scenarios are at all plausible. Given the preponderance of those who have studied these issues for decades now, it would perhaps be at least cavalier and rather nonchalant, insouciant, and complacent to dismiss all of the recognized science out of hand. So, considering all of these possible scenarios of our future, can we come together as a species to allow our preservation? This is no rhetorical question!

To these considerations based on extensive, worldwide research for decades, we may add the concern that have touched many people in waves for the past two thousand and more years: that of eschatology, the study of the last things, that is, of the ultimate end of life as we know it, the ending of days, the final battle between the forces of good and evil, and the second coming of the Christ and the Rapture, the gathering in the pious, religious, and God-fearing, separating them from the Devil-driven, evil, and godless others.[1895] This phenomenon was most prominent as the years 1000 CE and 2000 CE approached (marking the millennium, held to be significant as a predictor of the end of days).

Now, with all of this in mind, what can we learn from considering the workings of the Third Reich (and other regimes that have police-state features), noticing the respect given to Hitler as the Führer, the Leader, as the *Ritter*, the Knight, and as the *Retter*, the savior of Germany, his authority largely unquestioned? We may address this issue on a direct, experiential level, with clear thinking, and on a more comprehensive, global, moral level. This German story is an important example of the fact that from one given person (or group), there may be some ideas, some plans, some actions, that are wonderful and inspiring, and others, not at all. *If we can judge ideas each in its own right and value (or lack thereof), we can help ourselves avoid many problems in our understanding.*

As we can say that a people, a nation, is not good or bad (overall), we can continue to see clearly that even one person does not have only brilliant, creative, inspired, and valuable, beneficial ideas, but that in an extreme case, but also ideas that might be nasty, cruel, horrid, and even murderous. We can, that is, judge each idea on its own, without having our understanding influenced, perhaps distorted, by other considerations distinct from the idea actually being judged. As in general, our perception and thought would perhaps be much wiser if they went beyond "good" people and "bad" people, and considered, rather, particular proposals and actions and such, and *judge each of them on its own*. That calls for our cultivating an understanding that can evaluate each idea on its own.

(2015), all at UNFCCC.INT; cf. Kate Marvel, "Climate Change: We're Not Literally Doomed, But …," *Scientific American*, Jul. 30, 2018.

[1895] Revelation (or Apocalypse) 20:1-10; Starr Meade, "[Book Review] These Last Days: A Christian View of History," *Ligonier Ministries*, May 30, 2012, LIGONIER.ORG; John Currid, "Will People Die During Christ's Millennial Reign? Perplexing Passages," *TGC (The Gospel Coalition)*, Jan. 16, 2017, THEGOSPELCOALITION.ORG.

On more interpersonal, group, and societal dimensions of our human condition, we may consider what sort of world we hope for and aspire to. Here, in addressing the challenge of Bettelheim, one possibility is that we feel that such events and issues do not impact us on a gut or emotional level; they may leave us blasé; we may not want to bothered with others' problems. For these or other reasons, we may be inclined to continue on a life path that we feel is satisfying for us, already in synch with our basic values. (We may feel that all is well and wish to leave well enough alone.)

Or, perhaps we come through this reckoning to a sense of a life to be guided by an ethical intuition that takes a stand on such violence, perhaps finding inspiration by our sense of the highest potential of the human being and society, and perhaps by something in the fundamental guidelines that the world's great civilizations have delineated.

The issues presented in this book, along with many other texts that discuss and present detailed information about the murderous years of the Third Reich, and about the extensive violence in many decades now since the Hitler era,[1896] harshly assault us—they might even stun, shock, or nauseate us (or, depending on our values, moral attitude, and beliefs about power and destruction of enemies of the state, might actually have us admire the genocidal policies and actions of the Third Reich)—and, in facing such harsh realities, demonstrating the fragility of civility and of free societies (not directed by police-state tactics and violence)—perhaps in that we can come to a more grounded, coherent sense of who we are, and of what is fundamentally and profoundly important to us, our grounding life values in this reality of ours, *la condition humaine*,[1897] our human condition, "a calamitous race, both cursed and blessed," in the provocative, questioning words of the Swedish ex-theologian, Hitler-Era journalist, Togny Segerstedt.[1898]

[1896] On limits to "Never Again": Anthony Lake and Roger Morris, "The Human Reality of Realpolitik," *Foreign Policy*, no. 4, 1971, pp. 157–162; Samantha Power, "Bystanders to Genocide," *The Atlantic*, Sept. 2001; Abraham H. Foxman, *Never Again? The Threat of the New Anti-Semitism* (2003); Scott Lamb, "Genocide Since 1945: Never Again?" SPIEGEL ONLINE, Jan. 26, 2005; Former UN Secretary-General Kofi A. Annan, "The Myth of 'Never Again'," *New York Times*, Jun. 7, 2010; Larry May, "Bystanders, the Rule of Law, and Criminal Trials," *Nomos, American Society for Political and Legal Philosophy*, vol. 50, 2011, pp. 241–264; UN Secretary-General Ban Ki-moon, "World Not Fulfilling 'Never Again' Vow, Secretary-General Tells General Assembly Meeting on Responsibility to Protect," Sep. 5, 2012, UN.ORG; Charles Ehrlich, "Learning from the Past: Promoting Pluralism and Countering Extremism," *Salzburg Global Seminar* (2010); Gerald Caplan, "Never Again? With Rohingya crisis, we're once again bystanders to horrific atrocities," *The Globe and Mail* (Toronto), Mar. 23, 2018; Josh Rogin, "The vow of 'never again' is dying in Assad's prisons," *The Washington Post*, Feb. 7, 2019.

[1897] The phrase is taken from the 1933 French novel by André Malraux (1901-1976), *La Condition humaine*. In that same year, Belgian artiste René Magritte (1898-1967) created a painting with this same name.

[1898] See 2012 film, *Dom över död man* (*The Last Sentence*), at 1:08:10-1:08:22. One answer to this issue posed by Segerstedt was given by a Kraków survivor: Ben Lesser, *Living a Life That Matters: From Nazi Nightmare to American Dream* (2012).

About the Author

Mitchell D. Ginsberg, PhD, studied world literatures, languages, the physical sciences, and the foundations of mathematics, with an ultimate focus in philosophy and psychology, and also received extensive clinical training in psychotherapy. His interest in the Third Reich and the violent, murderous treatment of individuals across Europe and across a number of cultural, religious, and other lines, goes back many decades.

He has been a licensed psychotherapist in California since 1981. His clinical training, from 1968 on, includes work at CMHC, the Connecticut Mental Health Center (Yale University); at CVH, the Connecticut Valley (State Psychiatric) Hospital; in an APA-approved Clinical Psychology Internship through the Yale Psychology Department, at the Psychiatry Department of the West Haven VA Hospital; at the NIMH-designed Soteria Project Alternative Treatment for Schizophrenia, in San Mateo; as well as later advanced studies in Rome, Italy, at the Istituto di Terapia Familiare. He has also been an authorized teacher in the Thai Buddhist Vipassanā (Insight) Meditation tradition since 1975, leading workshops and residential retreats in the UK, France, Norway, and USA.

He studied at the Universities of Pennsylvania and of Michigan, as well as at the Universidad Nacional Autónoma de México (UNAM) and at the Université de Lausanne, Switzerland. He subsequently has held post-doctoral and research scholar positions in Psycholinguistics (MIT), in Complicated Grief Disorder—before PTSD was recognized—at the Langley-Porter Institute of Neuropsychiatry (UCSF Medical School), in Buddhist Studies (University of Texas), in Indic Studies (Yale University), and at UCSD over the past several decades, in History, Judaic Studies, and Middle East Studies, as well as in Psychiatry and in Family Medicine and Public Health (two Departments in the UCSD Medical School).

He has taught at the University of Michigan, Yale University, the American Institute of Buddhist Studies, Antioch University, the University of Massachusetts, the University of Humanistic Studies (UHS), the International University of Professional Studies (IUPS), and elsewhere, in the fields of Western Philosophy, Philosophy of Mind, Ethics, etc., and in Buddhist Philosophy and Phenomenology, in Systemic Family Therapy, and in Clinical, Transpersonal, and Buddhist Psychology. He has served as an Expert Witness before the US Immigration Court, providing testimony in court and Psychological Evaluations for individuals seeking asylum in the US from over 15 countries (from the Caribbean to sub-Sahara Africa, to the Middle East, Eurasia, and the Far East), and provided psychotherapy for these same groups of people. The author has a number of scholarly articles published from 1966 on, in academic journals in four countries. His published texts are listed above, before the full title page.

This text is a product of the author's long-time interest in the workings of the Hitler era, the Third Reich, and the culture of Germanic superiority and privilege, along with the hatred, violence, and killings that they cultivated, leading to genocide, the Holocaust, and millions of dead.

Bibliography

Abella, Irving, and Troper, Harold. *None Is Too Many: Canada and the Jews of Europe, 1933-1948* (1983).
Adonis (Ali Ahmad Said Esber). *A Time Between Ashes & Roses: Poems* (2004).
Aeschylus. *Eumenides* (458 BCE).
Alexander, Caroline. *The War That Killed Achilles: The True Story of Homer's Iliad and the Trojan War* (2009).
Anatoli, A. (Anatoly Kuznetsov). *Babi Yar: A Document in the Form of a Novel* (1971).
Andolfi, Maurizio. *Behind the Family Mask: Therapeutic Change in Rigid Family Systems* (1983).
Andolfi, Maurizio. *Family Therapy: An Interactional Approach* (1979).
Andolfi, Maurizio, and Mascellani, Anna. *Teen Voices: Tales from Family Therapy* (2013).
Andreas-Salomé, Lou. *Nietzsche* (1988).
Angrick, Andrej. *»Aktion 1005«—Spurenbeseitigung von NS-Massenverbrechen 1942-1945: Eine »geheime Reichssache« im Spannungsfeld von Kriegswende und Propaganda* (2018).
Angrick, Andrej. *Besatzungspolitik und Massenmord: die Einsatzgruppe D in der südischen Sowjetunion 1941-1943* (2003).
Antisemitismus der Welt in Wort und Bild, Robert Körber and Theodor Pugel, eds. (1935).
Arendt, Hannah. *Eichmann in Jerusalem: A Report on the Banality of Evil* (1963).
Arendt, Hannah. *The Origins of Totalitarianism* (1951).
Aristophanes. *The Birds* (414 BCE).
Aristotle. *Politics* (350 BCE).
Aspects of the Third Reich, Hannsjoachim Wolfgang Koch, ed. (1985).
Aubrac, Lucie. *Outwitting the Gestapo* (1993).
Avey, Denis. *The Man who Broke into Auschwitz: A True Story of World War II* (2011).
Azuma, Shirō. *The Diary of Azuma Shiro* (2006).
Badia, Gilbert. *Feu au Reichstag: L'acte de naissance du régime nazi* (1983).
Baeumler, Alfred. *Studien zur deutschen Geistesgeschichte* (1937).
Bärsch, Claus-Ekkehard. *Der junge Goebbels: Erlösung und Vernichtung* (2004).
Bartov, Omer. *Anatomy of a Genocide: The Life and Death of a Town called Buczacz* (2018).
Bartov, Omer. *The Holocaust: Origins, Implementation, Aftermath* (2015).
Bauer, Yehuda. *The Death of the Shtetl* (2009).
Bauer, Yehuda. *A History of the Holocaust*, Revised edition (2002).
Becker, Andréas. *Gueules: Récit* (2015).
Below, Nicolaus von. *Als Hitlers Adjutant 1937-1945* (1980); *At Hitler's Side: The Memoirs of Hitler's Luftwaffe Adjutant* (2001).
Best, Sigismund Payne: see Payne Best, Sigismund.
Bettelheim, Bruno. *The Uses of Enchantment: The Meaning and Importance of Fairy Tales* (1976).
Bettelheim, Bruno. *Freud and Man's Soul* (1983).
Billstein, Reinhold; Fings, Karola; Kugler, Anita; and Levis, Nicholas. *Working for the Enemy: Ford, General Motors and Forced Labor in Germany during the Second World War* (2000).
Binding, Karl, and Hoche, Alfred. *Die Freigabe der Vernichtung Lebensunwerten Lebens* (1920).
Bittencourt, Silvia. *A Cozinha Venenosa: Um jornal contra Hitler; a história do*

Münchener Post, o principal inimigo dos nazistas na imprensa (2013).
Bloch, Marc Léopold Benjamin. *Apologie pour l'histoire ou Métier d'historien* (1949); *The Historian's Craft* (1954).
Bonwick, James. *The Last of the Tasmanians; or, The Black War of Van Diemen's Land* (1870).
Borkin, Joseph. *The Crime and Punishment of IG Farben: The Startling Account of the Unholy Alliance of Adolf Hitler and Germany's Great Chemical Combine* (1978).
Bormann, Martin. *Bormann-Vermerke; Hitler's Table talk 1941-1944: Secret Conversations*, H. R. Trevor-Roper, ed. (2007).
Bracher, Karl Dietrich. *The Age of Ideologies: A History of Political Thought in the Twentieth Century* (1984).
Brasse, Wilhelm. *Wilhelm Brasse Photographer 3444, Auschwitz 1940-1945* (2012).
Braun, Eva. *The Private Life of Adolf Hitler: The Intimate Notes and Diary of Eva Braun* (1949).
Brecht, Bertolt. *Dreigroschenoper* (1928); *The Threepenny Opera*.
Brettin, Michael, and Kroh, Peter. *Berlin 1945: World War II. Photographs of the Aftermath: Pictures from Berliner Verlag and The Soviet Army Archives* (2014).
Breuer, Josef, and Freud, Sigmund. *Studien zur Hysterie* (1895); *Studies on Hysteria*, James Strachey and Anna Freud, tr. (1955).
Browning, Christopher R. *Fateful Months: Essays on the Emergence of the Final Solution* (1991).
Browning, Christopher R. *The Origins of the Final Solution: The Evolution of Nazi Jewish Policy, September 1939-March 1942* (2004).
Bullock, Alan. *Hitler, A Study in Tyranny* (1962).
Burleigh, Michael, and Wippermann, Wolfgang. *The Racial State: Germany 1933-1945* (1993).
Burns, James MacGregor. *Roosevelt: The Lion and the Fox* (1956).
Camus, Albert. *Le mythe de Sisyphe: Essai sur l'absurde* (1942).
Camus, Albert: see also as second author with Arthur Koestler.
Carr, William. *Arms, Autarky and Aggression: Study in German Foreign Policy, 1933-1939* (1972).
Carroll, James. *Constantine's Sword: The Church and the Jews* (2001).
Céline, Louis-Ferdinand. *Bagatelles pour un massacre* (1937).
Céline, Louis-Ferdinand. *Les beaux draps* (1941).
Céline, Louis-Ferdinand. *L'ecole des cadavres* (1938).
Chamberlain, Houston. *The Foundations of the Nineteenth Century* (1911).
Chang, Iris. *The Rape of Nanking: The Forgotten Holocaust of World War II* (1997).
Chang-Rodríguez, Eugenio. *Latinoamérica: Su civilización y su cultura* (2008).
Charguéraud, Marc-André. *Les Papes, Hitler et la Shoah: 1932-1945* (2002).
Charmley, John. *Duff Cooper: The Authorized Biography* (1986).
Charny, Israel W. *Fascism and Democracy in the Human Mind: A Bridge between Mind and Society* (2008).
Charny, Israel W. *The Genocide Contagion: How We Commit and Confront Holocaust and Genocide* (2016).
Charny, Israel W. *Psychotherapy for a Democratic Mind: Treating Intimacy, Tragedy, Violence, and Evil* (2018).
Chomsky, Noam. *Chomsky on Anarchism*, with Introduction by Nathan Schneider (2013).
Chomsky, Noam: see also as second author with Edward S. Herman.
Churchill, Winston. *London to Ladysmith, via Pretoria* (1900).
Churchill, Winston. *Speeches on Foreign Affairs and National Defense* (1938).
Craig, Gordon A. *The Germans* (1982).

Craigie, Emma, and Mayo, Jonathan. *Hitler's Last Day: Minute by Minute* (2015).
Dalai Lama XIV. *Opening the Eye of New Awareness* (1985).
Dalin, David G. *The Myth of Hitler's Pope: Pope Pius XII and His Secret War Against Nazi Germany* (2005).
Dalin, David G. *The Pius War: Responses to the Critics of Pius XII* (2004).
Darwin, Charles. *The Descent of Man and Selection in Relation to Sex*, Revised ed. (1874).
Darwin, Charles. *The Expression of the Emotions in Man and Animals* (1897).
Darwin, Charles. *The Voyage of the Beagle* (1845).
Dean, Martin. *Robbing the Jews: The Confiscation of Jewish Property in the Holocaust, 1933-1945* (2008).
Dederichs, Mario R. *Heydrich: Das Gesicht des Bösen* (2005); *Heydrich: The Face of Evil* (2009).
Delaporte, Sophie. *Les gueules cassées: Les blessés de la Grande Guerre* (2004).
Deletant, Dennis. *Hitler's Forgotten Ally: Ion Antonescu and his Regime, Romania 1940-1944* (2006).
Desbois, Patrick. *Porteur de mémoires: Sur les traces de la Shoah par balles* (2009); *The Holocaust by Bullets: A Priest's Journey to Uncover the Truth behind the Murder of 1.5 Million Jews* (2009).
Descartes, René. *Discours de la Méthode pour bien conduire sa raison, et chercher la vérité dans les sciences* (1637).
Dewey, John. *The Middle Works* (1983).
Dillon, Émile Joseph. *The Inside Story of the Peace Conference* (1920).
Dohm, Christian Wilhelm. *Ueber die bürgliche Verbesserung der Juden* (1781).
Dolles, Wilhelm. *Das Jüdische und das Christliche als Geistesrichtung* (1921).
Dollinger, Hans. *The Decline and Fall of Nazi Germany and Imperial Japan* (1997).
Domarus, Max. *Hitler Reden und Proklamationen 1932 bis 1945. Kommentiert von einem deutschen Zeitgenossen*, in 4 vol. (1973).
Domarus, Max. *Speeches and Proclamations [of Adolf Hitler], 1932–1945* (2004).
Dorca, Mercè Ubach: see Ubach Dorca, Mercè.
Douglas, Lawrence. *The Right Wrong Man: John Demjanjuk and the Last Great Nazi War Crimes Trial* (2016).
Drozdov, Georgii, and Ryabko, Evgenii. *Russia at War 1941-45* (1987).
Duclert, Vincent. *Affaire Dreyfus* (2006).
Duclert, Vincent. *La distruzione degli armeni* (2007).
Dühring, Eugen. *Die Judenfrage als Racen-, Sitten- und Culturfrage* (1881).
Ehlert, Hans; Epkenhans, Michael; and Gerhard P. Gross. *The Schlieffen Plan: International Perspectives on the German Strategy for World War I* (2014).
Ehrlich, Paul. *The Population Bomb* (1971).
Ehrlich, Paul, and Ehrlich, Anne. *The Population Explosion* (1990).
Ehrlich, Paul, and Ehrlich, Anne. *Betrayal of Science and Reason: How Anti-environmental Rhetoric Threatens our Future* (1996).
Ehrlich, Paul, and Ehrlich, Anne. *The Dominant Animal: Human Evolution and the Environment* (2008).
Ehrlich, Paul, and Ehrlich, Anne. *One with Nineveh: Politics, Consumption, and the Human Future* (2004).
Ehrlich, Paul, and Ornstein, Robert. *Humanity on a Tightrope: Thoughts on Empathy, Family, and Big Changes for a Viable Future* (2010).
Eichmann, Adolf. *Ein historischer Zeugenbericht* (1980).
Eichmann Interrogated: Transcriptions from the Archives of the Israeli Police, Jochan von Lang and Claus Sibyll, eds. (1983).
Elworthy, Scilla. *Pioneering the Possible: Awakened Leadership for a World That Works—Sacred Activism, with Desmond Tutu* (2014).

Engelen, Leen, and Winkel, Roel Vande. *Perspectives on European Film and History* (2007).
Engelman, Ralph Max. *Dietrich Eckart and the Genesis of Nazism* (1971).
Ertl, Karin Anna. *NS-Euthanasie in Wien* (2012).
Essner, Cornelia. *La Quête de la Race: Une anthropologie du nazisme* (1995).
Evans, Richard J. *The Coming of the Third Reich* (2004).
Evans, Richard J. *Rituals of Retribution: Capital Punishment in Germany, 1600-1987* (1996).
Evans, Richard J. *The Third Reich in History and Memory* (2015).
Eyck, Erich. *A History of the Weimar Republic*, Harlan Hanson and Robert Waite, tr., Vol. II (1963).
Faligot Roger, and Kauffer, Rémi. *Le croissant et la croix gammée* (1990).
Farber, Marvin. *The Foundation of Phenomenology: Edmund Husserl and the Question for a Rigorous Science of Philosophy* (1943).
Faschismus—Getto—Massenmord: Dokumentation über Ausrottung und Widerstand der Juden in Polen während des zweiten Weltkrieges, Jüdisches Historisches Institut Warschau, ed. (1960).
Ferencz, Ben. *Enforcing International Law—A Way to World Peace: A Documentary History and Analysis*, 2 vol. (1983).
Ferguson, Niall. *The War of the World: Twentieth-Century Conflict and the Descent of the West* (2006).
Ferguson, Thomas. *Golden Rule: The Investment Theory of Party Competition and the Logic of Money-driven Political Systems* (1995).
Fernández Fernández-Cuesta, Juan Manuel. *Información y Política exterior en la transición española, 1973-1986* (2015).
Fest, Joachim C. *Hitler: Eine Biographie* (1973); *Hitler*, Richard and Clara Winston, tr. (1974).
The Final Solution, Origins and Implementation, David Cesarani, ed. (1994).
The Fine Art of Propaganda, Alfred McClung Lee and Elizabeth Briant Lee, eds. (1939).
Fings, Karola; Heuss, Herbert; and Sparing, Frank. *The Gypsies During the Second World War. Volume 1: From Race Science to the Camps*, Donald Kenrick, tr. (1997).
Fischer, Fritz. *Krieg der Illusionen: die deutsche Politik von 1911 bis 1914* (1969); *War of Illusions: German Policies from 1911 to 1914* (1975).
Fisher, Janina. *Healing the Fragmented Selves of Trauma Survivors: Overcoming Internal Self-Alienation* (2017).
Fleming, Gerald. *Hitler und die Endlösung* (1982); *Hitler and the Final Solution* (1984).
Foxman, Abraham H. *Never Again? The Threat of the New Anti-Semitism* (2003).
Freud, Sigmund. *Die Traumdeutung* (1900); *The Interpretation of Dreams*, James Strachey, tr. (1961).
Freud, Sigmund, and Andreas-Salomé, Lou. *Sigmund Freud and Lou Andreas-Salomé: Letters*, Ernst Pfeiffer, ed. (1972).
Friedländer, Saul. *Nazi Germany and the Jews* (1997).
Fry, Varian. *Assignment: Rescue: An Autobiography* (1945).
Fry, Varian. *The Peace that Failed: How Europe Sowed the Seeds of War* (1939).
Fry, Varian. *Surrender on Demand* (1945).
Fuller, R. Buckminster. *Operating Manual for Spaceship Earth* (1968).
Garliński, Józef. *Hitler's Last Weapons: The Underground War against the V1 and V2* (1978).
Gehlen, Reinhard. *The Service: The Memoirs of General Reinhard Gehlen* (1972).
Gellately, Robert. *Backing Hitler: Consent and Coercion in Nazi Germany* (2001).

General Jewish Workers' Union (the Bund) in Poland. *Geto in Flamen: Zamlbukh* (1944).
Genocide and Persecution: The Holocaust, Jeff Hay, ed. (2014).
Gensicke, Klaus. *The Mufti of Jerusalem and the Nazis: The Berlin Years* (2011).
George, David Lloyd: see Lloyd George, David.
George, Henry. *Progress and Poverty: An Inquiry into the Cause of Industrial Depressions, and of Increase of Want with Increase of Wealth: The Remedy* (1879).
Gerlach, Christian. *Die Wannsee-Konferenz, das Schicksal der deutschen Juden und Hitlers politische Grundsatzentscheidung, alle Juden Euroopas zu ermorden* (1998).
Gerlach, Christian. *Krieg, Ernährung, Völkermord: Forschungen Zur Deutschen Vernichtungspolitik Im Zweiten Weltkrieg* (1998).
Gerlach, Christian. *Sur la conférence de Wannsee: de la détermination d'exterminer les Juifs d'Europe* (1999).
German Foreign Office, Berlin, and German Library of Information, New York City. *Documents on the Events Preceding the Outbreak of the War* (1939/1940).
Gilbert, Gustave M. *Nuremberg Diary* (1947).
Gilbert, Martin. *Atlas of Jewish History* (1976).
Gilbert, Martin. *Churchill: A Life* (1991).
Gilbert, Martin. *Churchill and the Jews: A Lifelong Friendship* (2007).
Gilbert, Martin. *The Churchill War Papers: The Ever-widening War, 1941* (2001).
Gilbert, Martin. *The Holocaust: The Jewish Tragedy* (1986).
Gilbert, Martin. *Holocaust Journey: Travelling in Search of the Past* (1997).
Gilbert, Martin. *Kristallnacht: Prelude to Destruction* (2006).
Gilbert, Martin. *Winston S. Churchill*, in 8 vol. (first two vol. by Churchill's son).
Gilpin, Robert. *Global Political Economy: Understanding the International Economic Order* (2001).
Ginsberg, Mitchell. *Belief: Its Conceptual and Phenomenological Structure* (1967).
Ginsberg, Mitchell. *Calm, Clear, and Loving: Soothing the Distressed Mind, Healing the Wounded Heart* (2014).
Ginsberg, Mitchell. *The Inner Palace: Mirrors of Psychospirituality in Divine and Sacred Wisdom-Traditions* (2013).
Ginsberg, Mitchell. *Mind and Belief: Psychological Ascription and the Concept of Belief* (1972).
Ginsberg, Mitchell. *Mindful Raft over Troubled Waters* (2015).
Ginsberg, Mitchell. *Peace and War and Peace* (2015).
Gisevius, Hans Berndt. *Bis zum bitteren Ende: Vom Reichstagsbrand bis zum 20. July 1944* (1946); *To the Bitter End* (1947).
Goebbels, Joseph. T*he Early Goebbels Diaries 1925-1926* (1962).
Goebbels, Joseph. *Der steile Aufstieg. Reden und Aufsätze aus den Jahren 1942/43* (1944).
Goebbels, Joseph. *Tagebücher, 1924-1945: Five Volumes in One*, Ralf Georg Reuth, ed. (1992).
Goebbels, Joseph. *Die Tagebücher: Sämtliche Fragmente, Vol. 2 (1 Januar 1931- 31 Dezember 1938* (1987).
Goering, Emmy. *My Life with Göring* (1972).
Goethe, Johann Wolfgang von. *Die Lieden des jungen Werther* (1774); *The Sorrows of Young Werther* (1779/2005).
Goldman, Emma. *Anarchism: What It Really Stands For* (1916).
Goldstein, Joseph, and Kornfield, Jack. *Seeking the Heart of Wisdom: The Path of Insight Meditation* (1977).
The Good Old Days: The Holocaust as Seen by Its Perpetrators and Bystanders,

The Hitler Era

Ernst Klee, Willi Dressen, and Volker Riess, eds. (1991).
Göring, Hermann. *Aufbau einer Nation* (1934).
Grant, Madison. *The Passing of the Great Race: or, The Racial Basis of European History* (1916).
Gurgone, Aldo. *Psychotherapy Tales: The Making of a Family Therapist* (2018).
Haffner, Sebastian. *Anmerkugen zu Hitler* (1978).
Halder, Franz. *The Halder War Diary, 1938-1942*, Charles Burdick and Hans-Adolf Jaconsen, eds. (1988).
Halperin, S. William. *Germany Tried Democracy: A Political History of the Reich from 1918 to 1933* (1946).
Hamann, Brigitte. *Hitler's Vienna: A Portrait of the Tyrant as a Young Man* (2010).
Hamans, Paul. *Getuigen voor Christus: Rooms-katholieke bloedgetuigen uit Nederland in de twintigste eeuw* (2008); [text adapted, with rather different title, as] *Edith Stein and Companions: On the Way to Auschwitz* (2010).
Hancock, Ian F. *O Porajmos: The Romani Holocaust* (2013).
Hancock, Ian F. *We Are the Romani People: Ame sam e Rromane džene* (2002).
Hanfstaengl, Ernst. *Hitler in der Karikatur der Welt: Tat gegen Tinte* (1933).
Hanfstaengl, Ernst. *Hitler: The Memoir of the Nazi Insider Who Turned Against the Fuhrer* (1957).
Hanfstaengl, Ernst. *Hitler: The Missing Years* (1957).
Hanfstaengl, Ernst. *Unheard Witness* (1957).
Hạnh, Thích Nhất. *Miracle of Mindfulness: A Manual on Meditation* (1975).
Harris, John Paul. *The War Office and Rearmament 1935-39* (1983).
Hartog, Leendert. *Hoe ontstond de jodenmoord?: Hitler, Amerika, en de Endlösung* (1994); *Der Befehl zum Judenmord: Hitler, America und die Juden* (1997).
Hašek, Jaroslav. *Good Soldier Švejk* (1921).
Hauner, Milan. *Hitler: A Chronology of his Life and Time* (2005).
Hayman, Ronald. *Hitler & Geli* (1997).
Headland, Ronald. *Messages of Murder* (1992).
Heck, Alfons. *The Burden of Hitler's Legacy* (1988).
Heck, Alfons. *A Child of Hitler: Germany in the Days When God Wore a Swastika* (1985).
Heidegger, Martin. *Die Selbstbehauptung der deutschen Universität* (1934).
Heiden, Konrad. *Der Fuehrer: Hitler's Rise to Power*, Ralph Manheim, tr. (1944).
Herman, Arthur. *Freedom's Forge: How American Business Produced Victory in World War II* (2012).
Herman, Edward S., and Chomsky, Noam. *Manufacturing Consent: The Political Economy of The Mass Media* (1988).
Herodotus. *The Histories* (440 BCE).
Hilberg, Raul. *The Destruction of the European Jews* (1985).
Hitler, Adolf. *Mein Kampf* (1925, 1926).
Hitler, Adolf. *Mein Kampf: eine kritische Edition*, Christian Hartmann, Thomas Vordermayer, Othmar Plöckinger, Roman Töppel, Edith Raim, eds. (2016).
Hitler, Adolf. *Official Translation of the Speech delivered by Adolf Hitler before the German Reichstag on April 28, 1939* (1939).
Hitler, Adolf. *Rede des Führers und Reichskanzlers Adolf Hitler vor dem Reichstag am 30. Januar 1939* (1939).
Hitler, Adolf. *Testament of Adolf Hitler: The Hitler-Bormann Documents, February-April 1945* (1961).
Hitler, Adolf. *Le testament politique d'Adolf Hitler: Notes recueillies par Martin Bormann* (1959).
Hochhuth, Rolf. *Der Stellvertreter: Schauspiel* (1963); *The Deputy* (1964).
Hochschild, Adam. *King Leopold's Ghost* (1998).

Hoffmann, Peter. *German Resistance to Hitler* (1988).
Hofstadter, Richard. *The Paranoid Style in American Politics* (1963).
Höhne, Heinz. *Der Orden unter dem Totenkopf: Die Geschichte der SS* (1984); *The Order of the Death's Head: The Story of Hitler's S.S.* (1969).
Höhne, Heinz. *Kennwort: Direktor; die Geschichte der Roten Kapelle* (1970); *Codeword: Direktor: The Story of the Red Orchestra* (1971).
The Holocaust: An Encyclopedia and Document Collection, Paul R. Bartrop and Michael Dickerman, eds.
Holz, Karl. *Der Kampf geht weiter* (1937).
Homer. *The Iliad*, Robert Fagles, tr., Introduction by Bernard Knox (1990).
Homer. *The Iliad: A New Translation*, Caroline Alexander, tr. (2015).
Höss, Rudolf. *Commandant of Auschwitz: The Autobiography of Rudolf Hoess* (1959).
Hugo, Victor. *Les Misérables* (1862).
I Never Saw another Butterfly: Children's Drawings and Poems from Terezin Concentration Camp, Hana Volavková, ed. (1993).
Ihrig, Stefan. *Justifying Genocide: Germany and the Armenians from Bismarck to Hitler* (2016).
Ingrao, Christian. *La promesse de l'Est. Espérance nazie et génocide 1939-1943* (2016).
Insdorf, Annette. *Indelible Shadows: Film and the Holocaust* (1983).
International Commission on the Holocaust in Romania. *Final Report of the International Commission on the Holocaust in Romania, Presented to Romanian President Ion Iliescu*, Nov. 11, 2004 (2004).
Janet, Pierre. *État mental des hystériques* (1911).
Jaspers, Karl. *Notizen zu Heidegger* (1978).
Jaspers, Karl. *Philosophische Autobiographie* (1977).
The Jewish Quarter of Warsaw Is No More! The Stroop Report (1979).
Joly, Laurent. *Dénoncer les Juifs sous l'Occupation: Paris, 1940-1944* (2017).
Joly, Laurent. *L'État contre les Juifs. Vichy, les Nazis et la Persécution antisémite: 1940-1944* (2018).
Jones, Ernest. *Essays in Applied Psycho-Analysis, vol. 1* (1964).
Kaiser, Hellmuth. *Effective Psychotherapy: The Contribution of Hellmuth Kaiser*, Mitchell Ginsberg, ed. (2018).
Kant, Immanuel. *Kritik der reinen Vernunft* (1781, 2nd ed., 1787); *Critique of Pure Reason*, Norman Kemp Smith, tr. (1929).
Kant, Immanuel. *Zum ewigen Frieden: Ein philosophischer Entwurf* (1795); *Perpetual Peace: A Philosophical Sketch* (1796, 1884, 1891, 1897, 1903, 1914, 1932, 1948, 1957, 1972, 2012, etc.).
Kaplan, Robert D. *In Europe's Shadow: Two Cold Wars and a Thirty-year Journey through Romania and Beyond* (2016).
Kaplan, Robert D. *The Revenge of Geography: What the Map Tells Us About Coming Conflicts and the Battle Against Fate* (2013).
Karsky, Jan. *Story of a Secret State* (1944).
The Kasztner Report: The Report of the Budapest Jewish Rescue Committee, 1942-1945, László Karsai and Judit Molnár, eds. (2013).
Kempner, Robert M. W. *Eichmann und Komplizen* (1961).
Katz, Stan S. *The Art of Peace: An illustrated Biography about Prince Tokugawa* (2019).
Keel, Hee-sung. *Chinul: The Founder of the Korean Sŏn Tradition* (1984).
Kellner, Friedrich. *My Opposition: The Diary of Friedrich Kellner—A German against the Third Reich*, Robert Scott Kellner, tr. (2018).
Keltner, Dacher. *Born To Be Good: The Science of A Scientific Life* (2009).

Keneally, Thomas. *Schindler's List* (1982).
Kennan, George F. *The Decline of Bismarck's European Order: Franco-Russian Relations 1875-1890* (1981).
Kenrick, Donald. *Historical Dictionary of the Gypsies (Romanies)* (1998).
Kenrick, Donald, and Puxon, Grattan. *The Destiny of Europe's Gypsies* (1972).
Kenrick, Donald, and Puxon, Grattan. *Gypsies under the Swastika* (2009).
Kershaw, Ian. *Fateful Choices: Ten Decisions that Changed the World, 1940-1941* (2007).
Kershaw, Ian. *Hitler: 1936-45, Nemesis* (2000).
Kershaw, Ian. *Hitler: A Biography* (2008).
Kessler, Graf Harry. *Walther Rathenau: His Life and Work* (1930).
Kimmich, Christoph M. *German Foreign Policy, 1918-1945: A Guide to Current Research and Resources* (2013).
Kinzer, Stephen. *The Brothers: John Foster Dulles, Allen Dulles, and their Secret World War* (2013).
Kitchen, Martin. *The World in Flames: A Short History of the Second World War in Europe and Asia, 1939-1945* (1990).
Klarsfeld, Serge, *Les enfants d'Izieu: Une tragédie juive* (1984); *The Children of Izieu: A Human Tragedy* (1985).
Klemperer, Klemens von. *German Resistance Against Hitler* (1992).
Koch, Hannsjoachim Wolfgang. *The Hitler Youth: Origins and Development, 1922-1945* (2000).
Kochavi, Arieh J. *Prelude to Nuremberg-Allied War Crimes Policy and the Question of Punishment* (1998).
Koestler, Arthur, and Camus, Albert. *Réflexions sur la peine capitale* (1957).
Kolb, Eberhard. *The Weimar Republic* (2005).
Koop, Volker. *Dem Führer ein Kind schenken: Die SS-Organisation Lebensborn eV* (2007).
Kopel, David B. *The Morality of Self-Defense and Military Action: The Judeo-Christian Tradition* (2017).
Krausnick, Helmut. *Hitlers Einsatzgruppen: Die Truppen des Weltanschauungskrieges 1938–1942* (1981).
Krausnick, Helmut, and Broszat, Martin. *Anatomy of the SS State* (1968).
Krishnamurti, Jiddu. *The Awakening of Intelligence* (1973).
Krishnamurti, Jiddu. *Beyond Violence* (1973).
Krishnamurti, Jiddu. *The First and the Last Freedom* (1954).
Kropotkin, Pëtr. *Mutual Aid: A Factor in Evolution* (1902).
Kubizek, August. *The Young Hitler I Knew: The Memoirs of Hitler's Childhood Friend* (2011).
Kundera, Milan. *Acceptance Speech for the Jerusalem Prize for Literature* (1985).
Kundera, Milan. *The Art of the Novel* (1988).
Kusnezov, Nikita. *Reeds in the Wind* (2011).
Lagarde, Paul de. *Deutsche Schriften* (1878).
Lagarde, Paul de. *Juden und Indogermanen: Eine Studie nach dem Leben* (1887).
Lakatos, Romani Menyhért. *The Color of Smoke: An Epic Novel of the Roma* (2015).
Landmark Speeches of National Socialism, Randall L. Bytwerk, ed., tr. (2008).
Langer, Walter C. *The Mind of Hitler* (1972).
Langhoff, Wolfgang. *Rubber Truncheon: Being an Account of Thirteen Months spent in a Concentration Camp* (1935).
Lanzmann, Claude. *Shoah* (1985).
Lao Tzu [Lǎozi]. *Tao Te Ching [Dàodéjīng]: The Classic Book of Integrity and the Way*, Victor H. Mair, tr., Introduction by Huston Smith (1990).
Lapide, Pinchas E. *Three Popes and the Jews* (1967).

Las Casas, Fray Bartolomé de. *Brevísima relación de la destrucción de las Indias* (1552); title in old Spanish: *Breuissima relacion de la destruycíon de la Indias*.
Laughlin, Harry H. *Eugenical Sterilization in the United States: A Report of the Pathologic Laboratory of the Municipal Court of Chicago* (1922).
Lawrence, D. H. *Lady Chatterley's Lover* (1928).
Lawrence, T. E. (Lawrence of Arabia). *Seven Pillars of Wisdom: A Triumph* (1935).
Layton, Geoff. *Democracy and Nazism: Germany 1918-45* (2015).
Lee, Alfred McClung, and Lee, Elizabeth Briant. *The Fine Art of Propaganda* (1939).
Lee, Stephen J. *European Dictatorships, 1918-1945* (2008).
Leibniz, Gottfried Wilhelm. *La Monadologie* (1714); *Monadology and Other Philosophical Essays*, Paul Schrecker and Anne Martin Schrecker, tr. (1965).
Leonard, Thomas C. *Illiberal Reformers: Race, Eugenics, and American Economics in the Progressive Era* (2016).
Lesser, Ben. *Living a Life That Matters: From Nazi Nightmare to American Dream* (2012).
Lessing, Gotthold Ephraim. *Nathan the Wise: A Dramatic Poem in Five Acts*, William Taylor of Norwich, tr. (1893).
Lévai, Jenö. *Hungarian Jewry and the Papacy: Pius XII Was Not Silent* (1968).
Levi, Primo. *Se questo è un uomo* (1947); *And If This is a Man* (1959); *Survival in Auschwitz* (1959).
Levin, Itamar. *His Majesty's Enemies: Great Britain's War against Holocaust Victims and Survivors* (2001).
Lewis, Clarence Irving. *An Analysis of Knowledge and Valuation* (1946).
Lewis, Clarence Irving. *Mind and the World-order: Outline of a Theory of Knowledge* (1929).
Lewy, Gunter. *The Nazi Persecution of the Gypsies* (2000).
Liebich, Richard. *Die Zigeuner in ihrem Wesen und in ihrer Sprache* (1863).
Lifton, Robert Jay. *The Nazi Doctors: Medical Killing and the Psychology of Genocide* (1986).
Liehm, Mira, and Liehm, Antonin J. *The Most Important Art: Eastern Europe Film after 1945* (1977).
Lippmann, Walter. *Public Opinion* (1922).
Liulevicius, Vejas G. *The German Myth of the East: 1800 to the Present* (2009).
Lloyd George, David. *War Memoirs*, Vol. 2 (1934).
Lombroso, Cesare. *L'uomo delinquente: Studiato in rapporto alla Antropologia, alla medicine legale et alle discipline carcerarie* (1876).
Longerich, Peter. *Himmler: Biographie* (2008); *Heinrich Himmler*, Jeremy Noakes and Lesley Sharpe, tr. (2012).
Longerich, Peter. *Holocaust: The Nazi Persecution and Murder of the Jews* (2010).
Ludecke, Kurt G. W. *I Knew Hitler: The Story of a National Socialist Who Escaped the Blood Purge* (1937).
Ludendorff, Erich von. *Der totale Krieg* (1935).
MacDonogh, Giles. *1938: Hitler's Gamble* (2009).
MacLean, (Col., US Army, Ret.) French L. *The Field Men: The SS Officers Who Led the Einsatzkommandos—the Nazi Mobile Killing Units* (1999).
Maloney, Arthur. *The Berlin-Baghdad Railway as a Cause of World War I* (1959).
Malraux, André. *La Condition humaine* (1933).
Manchester, William. *The Arms of Krupp* (1968).
Mann, Klaus. *Der fromme Tanz: Das Abenteuerbuch einer Jugend* (1926); *The Pious Dance: The Adventure Story of a Young Man* (1987).
Marshall, Tim. *Prisoners of Geography: Ten Maps That Explain Everything About the World* (2015).
Marrus, Michael R., and Paxton, Robert O. *Vichy France and the Jews* (1981).

Maser, Werner. *Legende, Mythos, Wirklichkeit* (1971); *Hitler: Legend, Myth, and Reality* (1973).
Mathew, Dylan. *War Prevention Works: 50 Stories of People Resolving Conflict, with Introduction by Scilla Elworthy* (2001).
McDonough, Frank. *Hitler and the Rise of the Nazi Party* (2012).
McDonough, Frank. *The Holocaust* (2008).
McGovern, James. *Martin Bormann: The Life and Disappearance of Hitler's Closest Confidant as Revealed by a former CIA Agent* (1968).
Mee, Charles L., Jr. *The End of Order: Versailles 1919* (1980).
Milano, James V., and Brogan, Patrick. *Soldiers, Spies, and the Rat Line: America's Undeclared War Against the Soviets* (2000).
Mill, John Stuart. *Principles of Political Economy* (1884).
Misch, Rochus. *Hitler's Last Witness: The Memoirs of Hitler's Bodyguard* (2014).
Mitchell, Otis C. *Hitler's Stormtroopers and the Attack on the German Republic, 1919-1933* (2008).
Moczarski, Kazimierz. *Conversations with an Executioner* (1981).
Moltke, Helmuth von. *Erinnerungen, Briefe, Dokumente 1877 bis 1916* (1922).
Montague, Ashley. *Touching: The Human Significance of the Skin* (1974).
A Mosaic of Victims: Non-Jews Persecuted and Murdered by the Nazis, Michael Berenbaum, ed. (1990).
Moscovici, Jean-Claude. *Voyage à Pitchipoï* (2009).
Motadel, David. *Islam and Nazi Germany's War* (2014).
Motwani, Jagat K. *None but India (Bharat): The Cradle of Aryans, Sanskrit, Vedas, and Swastika* (2010).
Mulisch, Harry. *De Zaak 40/61: Een Reportage* (1961); *Criminal Case 40/61, the Trial of Adolf Eichmann* (2005).
Musmanno, (Judge) Michael A. *The Eichmann Kommandos* (1961).
Naranjo, Claudio. *The Divine Child and the Hero: Inner Meaning in Children's Literature* (1999).
Naranjo, Claudio. *Healing Civilization* (2009).
Nazi Crimes and the Law, Nathan Stoltzfug and Henry Friedlander, eds. (2008).
The Nazi Germany Sourcebook: An Anthology of Texts, Roderick Stackelberg and Sally A. Winkle, eds. (2002).
Nazi Law, From Nuremberg to Nuremberg, John J. Michalczyk, ed. (2018).
Nazism 1919-1945, Vol. 3: Foreign Policy, War and Racial Extermination, Jeremy Noakes and Geoffrey Pridham, eds. (1988).
Neitzel, Sönke, and Welzer, Harald. *Soldaten: On Fighting, Killing, and Dying; The Secret World War II Transcripts of German POWs* (2012).
Nemattanew (Chief Roy Crazy Horse). *The North American Genocide* (2002).
Neumann, Hans-Joachim, and Eberle, Henrik. *War Hitler Krank?: Ein abschlissender Befund* (2009); *Was Hitler Ill?: A Final Diagnosis* (2013).
Nicholls, Anthony James. *Weimar and the Rise of Hitler* (2005).
Nietzsche, Friedrich. *Also Sprach Zarathustra; ein Buch für Alle und Keinen* (1883); *Thus Spake Zarathustra: A Book for All and for None*.
Nietzsche, Friedrich. *Der Antichrist* (1895); *The Antichrist*.
Nietzsche, Friedrich. *Ecce Homo: Wie man wird, was man ist* (1888); *Ecce Homo: How One Becomes What One Is*.
Nietzsche, Friedrich. *Der Fall Wagner* (1888); *The Case of Wagner*.
Nietzsche, Friedrich. *Die fröhliche Wissenschaft* (1887); *The Gay Science*, or *The Joyful Wisdom*.
Nietzsche, Friedrich. *Götzendämmerung, oder, Wie man mit dem Hammer philosophirt* (1889); *Twilight of the Idols, or, How Man Philosophizes with a Hammer*.

Nietzsche, Friedrich. *Jenseits von Gut und Böse: Vorspiel einer Philosophie der Zukunft* (1886); *Beyond Good and Evil.*
Nietzsche, Friedrich. *Menschliches, Allzumenschliches: Ein Buch für freie Geister* (1878). *Human, All-too-Human: A Book for Free Spirits.*
Nietzsche, Friedrich. *Morgenröte: Gedanken über die moralischen Vorurteile* (1881); *Daybreak: Thoughts on the Prejudices of Morality.*
Nietzsche, Friedrich. *Zur Genealogie der Moral: eine Streitschrift* (1887); *On the Genealogy of Morals.*
Nuremberg International Tribunal. *Nazi Conspiracy and Aggression 1946-1948* [The Red Series: NT-NCA-Red].
Nuremberg International Tribunal. *Trial of the Major War Criminals before the International Military Tribunal, Nuremberg, 14 November 1945-1 October 1946* [The Blue Series: NT-IMT-Blue].
Nuremberg International Tribunal. *Trials of War Criminals before the Nuernberg Military Tribunals Under Control Council Law No. 10* [The Green Series: NT-TWC-Green].
Nyanatiloka, Venerable. *Buddhist Dictionary: Manual of Buddhist Terms and Doctrines* (1980).
Nyiszli, Miklós. *Auschwitz: A Doctor's Eyewitness Account* (1960).
O'Donnell, James. *The Bunker: The History of the Reich Chancellery Group* (1978).
Opposing Fascism: Community, Authority and Resistance in Europe, Tim Kirt and Anthony McElligott, eds. (2004).
Oradour-sur-Glane (Souviens-toi, Remember): 10 juin 1944 (1945).
Ossowska, Maria. *Social Determinants of Moral Ideas* (1970).
Padfield, Peter. *Himmler: Reichsführer-SS* (1990).
Padover, Saul K. *Experiment in Germany: The Story of an American Intelligence Officer* (1946).
Pakenham, Thomas. *The Scramble for Africa: The White Man's Conquest of the Dark Continent from 1876 to 1912* (1991).
Pali (Theravāda Buddhist) Canon. *Dhammapada.*
Pali (Theravāda Buddhist) Canon. *Mahā-satipaṭṭāna Sutta.*
Pali (Theravāda Buddhist) Canon. *Ogha Sutta.*
Pali (Theravāda Buddhist) Canon. *Oghataraṇa Sutta.*
Pali (Theravāda Buddhist) Canon. *Satipaṭṭāna Sutta.*
Parssinen, Terry M. *The Oster Conspiracy of 1938: The Unknown Story of the Military Plot to Kill Hitler and Avert World War II* (2003).
Past and Present Radical Sexual Politics, Gert Hekma, ed. (2004).
Patai, Raphael. *The Arab Mind* (1983).
Pauwels, Jacques R. *The Myth of the Good War: America in the Second World War* (2015).
Pavloff, Franck. *Matin Brun* (1998); *Brown Morning* (2003).
Payne Best, Sigismund. *The Venlo Incident* (1950).
Peis, Günter. *The Man Who Started the War* (1960).
Perls, Frederick (Fritz). *Gestalt Therapy Verbatim* (1969).
Perls, Frederick (Fritz). *In and Out the Garbage Pail* (1969).
Perrault, Giles. *L'orchestre rouge* (1967); *The Red Orchestra* (1969).
Pfaff, William. *The Wrath of Nations: Civilization and the Furies of Nationalism* (1993).
Pitnik, Samuel. *Survivor: Auschwitz, the Death March and My Fight for Freedom* (2013).
Plant, Richard. *The Pink Triangle: The Nazi War against Homosexuals* (1986).
Plesch, Dan. *Human Rights after Hitler: The Lost History of Prosecuting Axis War Crimes* (2017).

Plewnia, Margarete. *Auf dem Weg zu Hitler: Der »völkische« Publizist Dietrich Eckart* (1970).
La politique nazie d'extermination: État des travaux et perspectives de recherche, journées d'étude tenues les 11, 12, et 13 décembre, 1987 à Paris, François Bédarida, ed. (1989).
Pomsel, Brunhilde. *The Work I Did: A Memoir of the Secretary to Goebbels* (2018).
Pressac, Jean-Claude. *Auschwitz: Technique and Operation of the Gas Chambers* (1989).
The Psychoanalytic Interpretation of History, Benjamin B. Wolman, ed. (1971).
Rabe, John. *The Good Man of Nanking: The Diaries of John Rabe* (1998).
Ramban (Moshe ben Nachman). *Ramban Haggadah* (1996).
Rauschning, Hermann. *Hitler Speaks: A Series of Political Conversations with Adolf Hitler On His Real Aims* (1939).
Read, Anthony, and Fisher, David. *Kristallnacht: The Nazi Night of Terror* (1989).
Redles, David. *Hitler's Millennial Reich: Apocalyptic Belief and the Search for Salvation* (2005).
Redlich, Frederick Fritz. *Hitler: Diagnosis of a Destructive Prophet* (1999).
Rees, Laurence. *The Holocaust: A New History* (2017).
Reginbogin, Herbert R. *Faces of Neutrality: A Comparative Analysis of the Neutrality of Switzerland and Other Neutral Countries During WW II* (2009).
Reich, Wilhelm. *Character Analysis* (1933).
Reich, Wilhelm. *The Mass Psychology of Fascism* (1933).
Reitlinger, Gerald. *The Final Solution: The Attempt to Exterminate the Jews of Europe 1939-1945* (1953).
Reitsch, Hanna. *The Sky My Kingdom* (1955).
Restrepo Hoyos, Paula Andrea. *Justicia epistémica y epistemología intercultural* (2011).
Reynolds, David. *The Long Shadow: The Legacies of the Great War in the Twentieth Century* (2014).
Rhodes, Richard. *Masters of Death: The SS-Einsatzgruppen and the Invention of the Holocaust* (2002).
Richelson, Jeffrey T. *A Century of Spies: Intelligence in the Twentieth Century* (1995).
Rigg, Bryan Mark. *Hitler's Jewish Soldiers: The Untold Story of Nazi Racial Laws and Men of Jewish Descent in the German Military* (2002).
Rilke, Rainer Maria, and Andreas-Salomé, Lou. *Rainer Maria Rilke and Lou Andreas-Salomé: The Correspondence*, Ernst Pfeiffer, ed., Edward Snow and Michael Winkler, tr. (2006).
The Roads of the Roma: A PEN anthology of Gypsy Writers, Ian Hancock, Siobhan Dowd, and Rajko Djurić, eds. (2004).
Roberts, Andrew. *The Holy Fox: Biography of Lord Halifax* (1991).
Robins, Robert S., and Post, Jerrold. *Political Paranoia: The Psychopolitics of Hatred* (1997).
Rocker, Rudolf. *Anarcho-syndicalism: Theory and Practice: An Introduction to a Subject Which the Spanish War Has Brought into Overwhelming Prominence* (1938).
Rodden, Robert. *The Fighting Machinists: A Century of Struggle* (1984).
Roper, Edith, and Leiser, Clara. *Skeleton of Justice* (1941).
Rose, Romani. *Bürgerrechte für Sinti und Roma: Das Buch zum Rassismus in Deutschland* (1987).
Rosenbaum, Ron. *Explaining Hitler: The Search for the Origins of His Evil* (1998).
Rosenberg, Alfred. *Memoirs of Alfred Rosenberg* (1949).
Rosenberg, Marshall. *Nonviolent Communication: A Language of Life* (2003).

Rosenberg, Marshall. *Speak Peace in a World of Conflict: What You Say Next Will Change Your World* (2005).
Rosenberg, Marshall. *The Surprising Purpose of Anger: Beyond Anger Management: Finding the Gift* (2005).
Rosmus, Anna Elisabeth. *Against the Stream: Growing Up Where Hitler Used to Live* (2002).
Rosmus, Anna Elisabeth. *Out of Passau: Leaving a City Hitler Called Home* (2004).
Rosmus, Anna Elisabeth. *Wintergreen: Suppressed Murders* (2004).
Rostand, Maurice. *L'homme que j'ai tué* (1925).
Rostow, Nicholas. *Anglo-French Relations 1934-36* (1984).
Roth, Joseph. *What I Saw: Reports from Berlin, 1920-1933* (2003).
Rothfels, Hans. *The German Opposition to Hitler* (1961).
Rousset, David. *L'univers concentrationnaire* (1946).
Rummel, Rudolph J. *Democide: Nazi Genocide and Mass Murder* (1992).
Russell, Bertrand. *Prophecy and Dissent, 1914-1916* (1988).
Russell (Edward Frederick Langley Russell), Lord of Liverpool. *The Scourge of the Swastika: A Short History of Nazi War Crimes. 16 Pages of Illustrations* (1957).
El sacrificio humano en Mesoamérica, Guilhem Olivier and Leonardo López Luján, eds. (2010).
Safranski, Rüdiger. *Ein Meister aus Deutschland: Heidegger und seine Zeit* (1994). *Heidegger: Between Good and Evil* (1998).
San Juan de la Cruz. *Noche oscura del alma* (1578).
Sartre, Jean-Paul. *L'Être et le néant : Essai d'ontologie phénoménologie* (1943); *Being and Nothingness: An Essay on Phenomenological Ontology* (1956, 2003).
Schellenberg, Walter. *Aufzeichnungen: Die Memoiren des letzten Geheimdienstchefs unter Hitler* (1985); *The Memoirs of Hitler's Spymaster* (2006).
Schmidt, Paul. *Statist auf diplomatischer Bühne 1923-1945: Erlebnisse des Chefdolmetschers im Auswärtigen Amt mit den Staatsmännern Europas* (1949); *Hitler's Interpreter* (1951).
Schneeberger, Guido. *Nachlese zu Heidegger: Dokumente zu seinem Leben und Denken* (1962).
Schroeder, Christa. *Er war mein Chef: Aus dem Nachlaß der Sekretärin von Adolf Hitler* (1985); *He Was My Chief: The Memoirs of Adolf Hitler's Secretary* (2009).
Schönerer, Georg. *Die deutsche Selbstentmannung: Rede des Abgeordneten Georg Schönerer in der Sitzung des Abgeordnetenhauses vom 5. Nebelungs 1906, nach dem stenographischen Protokolle* (1906).
Schopenhauer, Arthur. *Die Welt als Wille und Vorstellung* (1819).
Schrieke, Bertram. *Alien Americans: A Study of Race Relations* (1936).
Schwanenflügel Lawson, Dorothea von. *Laughter Wasn't Rationed: Remembering the War Years in Germany* (1999).
Schwarzwäller, Wulf C. *Hitlers Geld: Bilanz einer persönlichen Bereicherung* (1986); *The Unknown Hitler: His Private Life and Fortune* (1990).
The Secret Dossier Prepared for Stalin from the Interrogations of Hitler's Personal Aides, Henrik Eberle and Matthias Uhl, eds., Giles MacDonogh, tr. (2005).
Secrets of the Lotus, Donald K. Swearer, ed. (1971).
Seger, Gerhart. *Oranienburg: Erster authentischer Bericht eines aus dem Konzentrationslager Geflüchteten* (1934); *A Nation Terrorized*, with Foreword by Heinrich Mann (1935).
Sforno, Ovadiah. *Sforno: Commentary on the Torah*, Raphael Pelcovitz, tr. (1997).
Shah, Idries. *Tales of the Dervishes: Teaching-stories of the Sufi Masters over the Past Thousand Years* (1967).
Sharp, Gene. *From Dictatorship to Democracy: A Conceptual Framework for*

Liberation (2012).
Sherratt, Yvonne. *Hitler's Philosophers* (2014).
Shirer, William. *The Rise and Fall of the Third Reich* (1960).
Shwadran, Benjamin. *The Middle East, Oil and The Great Powers* (1955).
Sienkiewicz, Henryk. *Dzieła: Wydanie zbiorowe, Vol. 53* (1952).
Simon, Henry. *Third Reich Diaries: An Eyewitness Account of the Hitler Years* (1989).
Smelser, Ronald, and Davies Edward J. *The Myth of the Eastern Front: The Nazi-Soviet War in American Popular Culture* (2008).
Snyder, Louis L. *The War: A Concise History, 1939-1945* (1964).
Snyder, Timothy. *Black Earth: The Holocaust as History and Warning* (2015).
Soma Thera (Soma, the Thera, the Elder Theravāda Monk). *The Way of Mindfulness: The Satipaṭṭāna Sutta and Commentary* (1975).
Somerville, John. *Philosophy of Peace*, with Introductory Comments by Albert Einstein (1954).
Speer, Albert. *Erinnerungen* (1969); *Inside the Third Reich: Memoirs* (1970).
Stein, Murray, and Abramovitch, Henry. *The Analyst and the Rabbi: A Play* (2019).
Spencer, Herbert. *Principles of Biology* (1864).
Stalin and Europe: Imitation and Domination, 1928-1953, Timothy Snyder and Ray Brandon, eds. (2014).
Steiner, George. *Language and Silence: Essays on Language Literature, and the Inhuman* (1970).
Stillman, Edmund O., and Pfaff, William. *The Politics of Hysteria: The Sources of Twentieth-Century Conflict* (1964).
Stöcker, Adolf. *Das moderne Judenthum in Deutschland, besonders in Berlin. Zwei Reden in der christlich-socialen Arbeiterpartei gehalten von Adolf Stöcker, Hof- und Domprediger [Court and Cathedral Preacher] zu Berlin* (1880).
Stoddard, Lothrop. *The Rising Ride of Color against White World-Supremacy* (1920).
Sutton, Antony C. *Wall Street and the Rise of Hitler* (2010).
Suzuki, Shunryū. *Zen Mind, Beginner's Mind: Informal talks on Zen Meditation* (1970).
Swearer, Donald K. *Becoming the Buddha: The Ritual of Image Consecration in Thailand* (2004).
Tamames, Ramón. *La República: La era de Franco* (1988).
Tenenbaum, Joseph. *Race and Reich: The Story of an Epoch* (1956).
Thorne, Christopher. *The Making of the Twentieth Century: The Approach of War, 1938-1939* (1967).
Thucydides. *History of the Peloponnesian War* (431 BCE).
Toland, John. *Adolf Hitler* (1976).
Tolischus, Otto D. *They Wanted War* (1940).
Tolle, Eckhart. *The Power of Now: A Guide to Spiritual Enlightenment* (1997).
Tomašević, Nebojša Bato, and Djurić, Rajko. *Gypsies of the World* (1988).
Treaties and Other International Agreements of the United States of America, 1776-1949, Vol. 1: Multilateral Agreements, 1776-1917, Charles I. Bevans, ed. (1968).
Treuer, David. *The Heartbeat of Wounded Knee: Native America from 1890 to the Present* (2019).
Tritle, Lawrence A. *From Melos to My Lai: War and Survival* (2000).
Tsuneishi, Keiichi. *The Germ Warfare Unit that Disappeared: The [Japanese] Kwangtung Army's 731st Unit* (1982; Jap. ed., 1994).
Tuchman, Barbara. *Bible and Sword: England and Palestine from the Bronze Age to Balfour* (1956).

Tuchman, Barbara. *The Guns of August* (1964).
Thyssen, Fritz. *I Paid Hitler* (1941).
Ubach Dorca, Mercè, and Juárez Camacho, Javier, *Garbo, l'espia català que va derrotar a Hitler* (2004); *Juan Pujol, el espía que derrotó a Hitler* (2004).
UN War Crimes Commission. *Law Reports of Trials of War Criminals* (1947).
Urlanis, Boris. *Wars and Population* (1971).
Victor, George. *Hitler: The Pathology of Evil* (1998).
Vinogradov, V. K.; Pogonyi, J. F.; and Teptsov, N. V. *Hitler's Death: Russia's Last Great Secret from the Files of the KGB* (2005).
Virgili, Fabrice. *La France virile: des femmes tondues à la Libération* (2000); *Shorn Women: Gender and Punishment in Liberation France* (2002).
Voltaire. *Dictionnaire philosophique* (1764).
Vrba, Rudolf. *Die Revolution in Russland* (1906).
Vrba, Rudolf. *Escape from Auschwitz* (1964).
Wagener, Otto. *Hitler aus nächster Nähe: Aufzeichnungen eines Vertrauten 1929–1932* (1978); *Hitler—Memoirs of a Confidant*, Henry Ashby Turner, Jr., ed.
Waite, Robert G. L. *The Psychopathic God: Adolf Hitler* (1977).
Waite, Robert G. L. *Vanguard of Nazism: The Free Corps Movement in Postwar Germany, 1918-1923* (1952).
Warder, A. K. *Indian Buddhism* (1970).
The Warsaw Diary of Adam Czerniakow: Prelude to Doom, Raul Hilberg, Stanislaw Staron, and Josef Kermisz, eds. (1982).
Weber, Ronald. *The Lisbon Route: Entry and Escape in Nazi Europe* (2011).
Weber, Thomas. *Becoming Hitler: The Making of a Nazi* (2017).
Weikart, Richard. *Hitler's Ethic: The Nazi Pursuit of Evolutionary Progress* (2009).
Weinreich, Max. *Hitler's Professors: The Part of Scholarship in Germany's Crimes Against the Jewish People* (1946); ed. with Introduction by Martin Gilbert (1999).
Wetzler, Alfréd. *Escape from Hell: The True Story of the Auschwitz Protocol* (2007).
Whitman, James Q. *Hitler's American Model: The United States and the Making of Nazi Race Law* (2017).
Wiesel, Elie. *Night* (1958).
Winkler, Gershon. *The Way of the Boundary Crosser: An Introduction to Jewish Flexidoxy* (1998).
Wittman, Robert K., and Kinney, David. *The Devil's Diary: Alfred Rosenberg and the Stolen Secrets of the Third Reich* (2017).
Wistrich, Robert. *Demonizing the Other: Antisemitism, Racism and Xenophobia* (1999).
Wistrich, Robert. *Who's Who in Nazi Germany* (1982).
Wood, E. Thomas, and Jankowski, Stanisław M. *Karski: How One Man Tried to Stop the Holocaust* (1994).
Wyndham, Francis, and King, David. *Trotsky: A Documentary* (1972).
Xenophon. *Anabasis* (ca. 370 BCE).
The Yellow Spot: The Outlawing of Half a Million Human Beings; A Collection of Facts and Documents relating to Three Years' Persecution of German Jews, derived chiefly from National Socialist sources, with an Introduction by Herbert Dunelm, Bishop of Durham (1936).
Yevtushenko, Yevgeny. *The Poetry of Yevgeny Yevtushenko, Revised and Enlarged Edition; With 61 poems in the original Russian and translated into English*, George Reavey, ed. and tr. (1967).
Ziemer, Gregor. *Education for Death: The Making of the Nazi* (1941).
Zimbardo, Philip. *The Lucifer Effect: Understanding How Good People Turn Evil* (2007).

Index

6 million (estimate), 383, 498, 533, 562, 574
1,000-Year (or 12-Year) Reich, 143, 230, 316, 348, 464, 484-486, 528, 602; cf. Third Reich
AA *(Auswärtiges Amt)*, xxvii, 263
Abbey at Lambach, 181-182
ABC (Madrid newspaper), 36, 218
abhidhamma (abhidharma), 11-12; cf. Buddhism and the Buddha
Abramovitch, Henry, 467
Abwehr (Third Reich Military Intelligence), xxxii-xxxiii, 221, 290-291, 419, 486
Abyssinia: see Ethiopia
ACE (Adverse Childhood Experiences), 609-610
Acheson, Dean, 548
Achilles, i, 607-608, 616-617
ACLU (American Civil Liberties Union), 548
Act to Promote the Defense of the United States, 375
Action 1005 or Special Action 1005: see *Aktion 1005* or *Sonderaktion 1005*
Addis Ababa, 272
Adelwolf, 1, 328; cf. Hitler; wolf
Adenauer, Konrad, xxviii
Adonis (Ali Ahmad Said Esber), 569
Adorno, Theodor, xxi, 576
AEF (American Expeditionary Forces), 77-78, 84
Aeschylus, ii
Agamemnon, 569, 615, 624
agélastes (men who do not laugh, who have no sense of humor), 76
Agfa, 209
Aisne, Battle of, 71-72, 81, 84
Aktion 14f13 (Action 14f13), 347; cf. T4 program ended
Aktion 1005 or *Sonderaktion 1005* (Action/ Action 1005), 432-433; cf. Blobel, Paul; *Enterdungsaktion* (Exhumation Action)
Aktion Gnadentod (Action Mercy Death), 4, 141
Aktion Sonderbehandlung 14f13 (Action Special Treatment 14f13), 347; cf. T4 program ended
Aktion T4 (Action T4): see T4 program
Alabama White Citizens Council, 70

Alexander the Great, 606
Alexander II, 183, 268
Alexander III, 183
Alexander, Caroline, ii, 616; cf. Homer and the *Iliad*
alien races, 498-499, 520; cf. hordes
Alldeutschland (pan-Germanism), 51
Altona and Bloody (Altona) Sunday *(Altonaer Blutsonntag)*, 206
American Academy of Pediatrics, 282
American Battle Monuments Commission, 554
American military: see US military
American Nazi Party, 597
Amerindians: see native American Indians (Amerindians)
Amtssprache (bureaucratese), 288, 363, 525
anarchism and anarcho-syndicalism, xvii, 70, 90, 274, 637
Ancient Greece, 58, 234, 504, 564, 584, 606-608, 614-617; cf. Athens and the Athenians; Aristophanes; Aristotle; Greece and the Greeks; Homer; *Iliad;* Marathon, Battle of; Menelaus; Patroclus; Phlegéthōn or Pyriphlegéthōn; Priam; Scythians; Sparta; Styx; Thucydides; Xenophon; Zeus
Anders (Stein), Günther, 89, 123
Andolfi, Maurizio, 563
Angrick, Andrej, 433
Angriff, Der, xxxiii, 124, 244, 495
Annexation (*Anschluß*) of Austria, 271, 279-280, 285, 287, 289, 305, 424
Anschluß: see Annexation
anständig (decent, respectable, proper), 1,228, 252, 592
Antarctica, 639
Antheil, George, 156; cf. FHSS; GPS; Lamarr, Hedy; Milsatcom; wifi and Bluetooth
Antilochus, 625
Loving v. Virginia (1967), 240
anti-miscegenation laws, 240
Anti-Semitism: see Jews, Judaism, anti-Semitism, and anti-Semites, Holocaust; Holocaust by bullets
Antonescu, Ion, 396
Apocalypse (Revelation), 640; cf. New Testament, Christianity, and Jesus

Appel, 299; cf. De Gaulle, Charles
Arabel: see Garbo, Agent
Ardern, Jacinda, 621
Arendt, Hannah, v, 89, 123, 175-176, 256, 402, 603
Argentina, xxviii, 144, 555, 576, 601
Ari, ha- (the Lion): ha-Eloki Rabbeinu Yitzchak, 595; cf. Lurianic Kabbalah
Arian, der: see Aryan
Aristophanes, 418
Aristotle, 562, 606, 621
Armenians, 19, 49-50, 67, 92-96, 101, 146, 447, 575-576, 584, 613, 618
Armia Krajowa (*AK*, Polish Home Army), 247
Armistice of 1918, 25, 28-29, 31, 36, 39, 54, 59, 72, 78, 91, 98-99, 397, 604
Armistice of 1940, 299, 314, 345; cf. Article 19 of the Armistice of 1940
armistice (hopes for, 1944-45), 414, 430, 512
Aron, Raymond, 454
Arrow Cross, 396; cf. Hungary
Article 19 of the Armistice of 1940, 299
Aryan solipsism, 483-484, 494
Aryan (*der Arian, Ārya;* root meaning: honorable, noble One) and the Aryans, i, iii, xxi, 1-2, 7, 47, 105, 113, 129-130, 133, 137, 169-170-171, 181-182, 185, 189, 193-195, 202, 233, 238, 242, 253-254, 275, 305, 316-318, 328, 337, 348, 350, 371, 378-379, 413, 428, 453, 485, 496, 498, 502, 513, 521-522, 527, 533, 565-566, 571, 595
Asiatic Barred Zone Act of 1917, 113
aspirin (Bayer), 208
Assaji, 628
Askania Chemical Works, 327
Athena, 423
Athens, 326, 336, 454, 606
Atlantic Wall, 418
Atrides, 569
atrocity propaganda: see *Greuelpropaganda*
Attila the Hun, 38, 47, 418, 539, 612
Audi, 386
Auschwitz (Oświęcim), iv, x, xiv, xxiv, xxviii, xxxi-xxxiii, 4-5, 151, 323-324, 341-342, 379-387, 389-390, 392-393, 398-399, 401, 430-432, 438-439, 471, 486, 501, 506, 513, 552-553, 567, 576-578, 619, 633-634, 636-637; cf. Birkenau
Auschwitz Protocols, 513
Auslandsorganisation (AO), 330
Ausmerzung, 190, 329
Ausrottung, xiv, 504, 520, 525, 530-531; cf. Goebbels, Joseph
Ausschaltung, 530-531
Austerlitz, 470
Austin, J. L., 19, 202
Austria, xviii, xx, 3, 22, 27, 29, 33, 41, 67, 104, 108, 115-116, 146, 149, 166, 168, 181-182, 213-214, 264-265, 271, 276, 279-280, 285-287, 289, 291, 294, 300, 305, 335, 343, 368-369, 387, 390, 393, 415, 424, 437, 502, 555, 570, 583, 591, 634-635
Austria-Hungary and the Austro-Hungarian Empire, 25-26, 29, 32-34, 42, 45, 51-57, 66, 68, 71, 75, 79, 85, 91-92, 100-101, 104, 181, 183, 470
Austro-Hungarian Archduke Ferdinand assassination as an incident leading to the Great War, 55
autarky, 46, 279, 444
autistic self-forgetfulness, 483-484, 494
Autobahn, 205, 279
autodidact, 8, 463
Avey, Denis, 404
Azaña, Manuel, 273
Azuma, Shirō ("the Conscience of Japan"), 278
Baal Shem Tov (Besht), 361
Baarová, Lída, 535
Babi Yar Massacre, 3, 5, 271-272, 350, 352, 359-360, 393, 414, 433, 501, 509, 523, 536; cf. Blobel, Paul; Kiev
Bach-Zelewski, Eric von (or Erich von den Bach), 362-363, 366-367
bad faith (*mauvaise foi*), 228; cf. Sartre, Jean-Paul
Bad Wiessee, 232, 312
Baeck, (Rabbi) Leo, 467
Baer, Richard, xxxiii, 384-385
Baeumler, Alfred, 167, 170-172, 596
Baghdad, 53-54
Baku, 405-406
Baldwin, Stanley, 262
Balfour, Arthur James, 94, 97, 401
Balkan region, 51-52, 54-55, 57, 92, 181, 324, 343, 395, 522, 556, 613

Balkan Wars of 1912-1913, 52, 54-55, 92
Bally, Gustav, 129, 174, 254, 468; cf. Jung, Carl Gustav
Bancic, Olga, iv
barbarism, barbaric actions, and barbarians, i, xxiv, 20, 53, 68, 143, 228, 258, 276, 347, 350, 390, 507-508, 510, 512, 539, 570, 576, 578, 588, 604, 627
barbarization, 53; cf. dehumanization; inferior beings, *Untermenschen*
Barbie, Klaus (Klaus Altmann), xxviii-xxix, 543; cf. Izieu, the children of; Khan, Noor Inayat; *maquis* and the French *maquisards*; Moulin, Jean
Bárdossy, László, 390
Bartov, Omer, 13, 88
BASF, 209
Battle of the Bulge, 414; cf. Operation Northwind
Bauer, Fritz, xxviii
Bauer, Yehuda, 360, 398, 502
Bavaud, Maurice, 311
Bayer, 208-209
Beamish: see Hirschman, Albert Otto
beaten children, 9, 282-283, 447, 450, 456, 541
Beauvoir, Simone de, 567
Becher, Kurt Andreas, 385
Bechstein, Carl and Helene, and the Bechstein piano, 116-117, 131, 168
Bechtolsheim (Mauchenheim), Gustav von, 521
Beck, Ludwig, 144, 290, 470, 485, 490
BEF (British Expeditionary Forces), 83
Behrendt, Johannes, 380
Beijing, 60
Beilis, Menachem and the Beilis Trial, 268-269
Belarus, xxiv, 5, 79, 269, 332, 342, 351, 365-366, 498-499, 522, 555
Belgian Congo, 47; cf. rubber slaves
Belgium and the Belgians, xxiv, 32, 37, 47-48, 50, 56-57, 64, 72-74, 91, 99-100, 148,154, 253, 260, 266-267, 289, 291, 298, 310, 336, 338, 344-345, 354, 368, 410-411, 443, 492, 512, 584, 602, 638
Belgorod-Kharkov Operation, 422; cf. Kharkov, Battle of
Belgrade: see Beograd
Belleau Wood: see US Marines

Below, Nicolaus von, xxxiii, 275, 309, 324-325, 415, 473-474, 477
Bełżec, xxxii, 5, 341-342, 367, 392, 505, 511, 526
Benkert Karl-Maria (Károly-Mária Kerbeny), 234-235
Beograd (Belgrade), 502; cf. Yugoslavia
Berchtesgaden, 168, 231, 281, 294, 296, 462, 473, 479, 501-502, 535, 554, 598
Berdichev (Berdychiv), 355
Berenbaum, Michael, 3, 347, 478, 497, 505
Bergen-Belsen, xxxii, 385, 392, 438, 475, 560, 567, 636
Bergen-Belsen DP Camp, 561, 637
Berghof, 119, 168, 324, 413, 418, 479, 554, 598
Beria, Lavrentiy, 335
Berlin Psychoanalytic Institute, xix, 105, 563
Bernadotte, (Count) Folke, 476, 478-479
Bertram, (Cardinal of Breslau) Adolf, 347
Besserwisser (know-it-all, pedant, half-educated person), 119, 524, 578, 602
Best, Sigismund Payne: see Payne Best, Sigismund
Bettelheim, Bruno, 636-638, 641
Białistok, 366
Birkenau, xxxiii, 324, 343-344, 380, 382, 385, 389, 430-431, 438-439, 505-506, 525, 552; cf. Auschwitz
Binding, Karl, 76, 139-140
Bingham, Hiram, 402-404
BK.vv (for references to the Greek-based text of the *Iliad*, citing Book and verses): see Homer and the *Iliad*
black American troops, 68-70
blacks, Americans and Africans, 18-19, 70, 67-70, 111, 113, 161, 171, 176-177, 185, 195, 270, 373, 378, 549; cf. Alabama White Citizens Council
Black Codes, 45; cf. US Civil War
Black Front *(schwarze Front)*, 144
black Gallia, 191
Black German Military *(schwarze Reichswehr)*, 259, 262
Black Hand, 55
black list, 548; cf. Hollywood black list; McCarthy, Joseph
Black Panthers, 371

Black Sea, 91, 446-447, 454
black shame (*schwarze Schande*), 100, 506
black swans, xx
Black Tuesday, 159
Black War, 48; cf. Van Diemen's Land
Blaskowitz, Johannes, 364
Blessing, Karl, 496
Bletchley Park, 352; cf. Enigma Code; Turing, Alan
Blight, David, xvi
Blind, Georges, 15
Blitzkrieg, 338, 354, 410, 492, 502, 570
Blobel, Paul, 271-272; cf. *Aktion 1005 (Sonderaktion 1005);* Babi Yar Massacre
Bloch, Marc, 6
bloodhound (*Bluthund*), 475
Blood Purge (Röhm Putsch), xiv, 22, 168, 215, 220, 232-233, 236-237; cf. Night of the Long Knives
Bloody Sunday: see Altona
Blomberg, Warner von, 232, 263
Blüher, Hans, 196-197, 323
Blum, Léon, 204, 208, 249
Blumenkrieg, 271
Bogdanivka massacres, 501
Boger, Wilhelm, 593
Bogerschaukel (Boger Swing), 593
Bohm, Frank, 402-403
Bohr, Niels, 305, 408
Bolivia and Simón Iturri Patiño, 287
Bonhoeffer, (Pastor) Dietrich, 347, 399, 487
Boniface, (Saint) Winifred, 23, 133
Bonwick, James, 48
borderline personality (in lay sense and technical senses), 456-457, 461
Borkin, Joseph, 210, 388
Bormann, Albert, 463, 481
Bormann, Martin, xxxiii, 195-196, 340, 355, 454, 473-474, 481, 501-502, 519-520, 534, 598; cf. Schulz, Alfons
Bosniaks (Bosnian Muslims), 400, 576
Bosques Saldívar, Gilberto, 398
Brauchitsch, Walther von, 340
Braun, Eva, 124-125, 293, 309, 318-319, 327, 348, 381, 437-438, 461, 463-464, 477-478, 529, 536, 571, 601
Braun, Wernher von, 388, 551
Braune, (Pastor) Paul, 347

Brecht, Bertolt, xxi, 362, 366, 562, 578
Breton, André, 403
British Union of Fascists, 598, 621
Briseis, 615, 624-625
Brno, 541
Brockdorff, Cay-Hugo von, 475
Brockdorff, Erika von, 475
Broich, Friedrich von, 538-539
Bronstein, Lev Davidovich: see Trotsky, Leon/Lev
Brown v. Board of Education of Topeka, 69
Browning, Christopher, 251, 331, 341, 365, 401, 454, 504
Brownshirts (*Braunhemden*), xxxiii, 116, 119, 581; cf. SA
Brüning, Heinrich, 28, 106, 205
Bruno, Giordano, 359
brutality, i, iii, xxiv, 1, 9, 60, 79, 89-90, 94, 154, 187-188, 227, 230, 242, 247, 281, 311, 333, 348, 395, 411, 443, 447, 456, 458, 482, 486, 501, 508, 512, 514, 541-542, 561-562, 609, 633; cf. sadism
Bryan, William Jennings, 93-94
Bryant, Michael S., 227; cf. sadism
Bubonic plague, xx, 86
Buchenwald, xxii-xxiv, xxxii, xxxiv, 378, 380, 386, 389, 392, 438, 577, 635
Budapest (Buda-Pesht), 385, 396, 398, 400, 408, 431
Budapest Jewish Rescue Committee, 385; cf. Kasztner, Rezsö
Buddhism and the Buddha, 11-12, 86, 134, 160, 403, 624, 627-628, 630-631, 642; cf. *Dhammapada;* Pali (Theravāda Buddhist) Canon
Bulgaria and the Bulgarians, 19, 29, 86, 92, 326, 354, 390, 555, 623
Bullock, Alan, xiv, 233, 266, 420
Buna Werke, 388, 438; cf. IG Farben
Bund (Socialist, non-Zionist, General Jewish Workers' Union), xiv, 533
Bürgerbräu Putsch: see Hitler Putsch
Burgdorf, Wilhelm, 473
Burleigh, Michael, 347, 379
Burma, 523
Bush, George Herbert Walker (41st US President), 322
Bush, George Walker (43rd US President), 321
Bush, Prescott Sheldon (US Senator),

321-322
Butler, Samuel, 609
bystanders and uninvolved witnesses, 93, 266, 518, 560, 565, 636, 640
CADACIL, xi; cf. Nietzsche, Friedrich
Calabria, 416
Cambodia, 523, 576
Camus, Albert, xxxiii, 175, 580
Canaris, Wilhelm Franz, xxxiii-xxiv, 221, 290, 419, 486-487
Carlingue (the French SS), 397
Carter, Asa, 70; cf. Alabama White Citizens Council
Carter, Jimmy (39th US President), 439
Castellanos, José Arturo, 398
castration by the Third Reich, 110; cf. sterilized for sexual preferences
category mistakes or errors, 636
Cathedral of Lights, 151, 259
Caucasus, 405, 522
caudillo, 273; cf. *Cid Campeador* (Díaz de Vivar, Rodrigo); Franco, Francisco
causality, xxi; cf. retrocausality
Céline, Louis-Ferdinand, 397
Cervantes Saavedra, Miguel de, 417
Cesarani, David, 312, 331
Chagall, Marc, 402
Chamberlain, Austin, 28
Chamberlain, Houston Stewart, 115, 179, 189-190
Chamberlain, Neville, 28, 273, 290-291, 293, 296-298, 321, 425
Chang-Rodríguez, Eugenio, 53
Chao, Manu, xxi
Chaplin, Charlie, and *The Great Dictator*, 10-11
Charlottenburg, 122, 131
Charny, Israel, xxxiv, 578-579
Chełmno (Kulmhof), xxii, xxxii, 5, 134, 342-343, 392
Chemische Fabrik Griesheim-Elektron, 209
Chemische Fabrik vorm. Weiler Ter Meer, 209
Cherbourg, 427
chicotte (whip), 47
children, beaten: see beaten children
China and the Chinese, 36, 51, 60, 107, 204, 258, 277-278, 375, 627; cf. Nanking
Chinese Exclusion Act of 1882, 113
Chinul, 631
Chmielnicki, Bogdan, 269

cholera, xx
Chomsky, Noam, 6, 581-582, 637
Christian X, 394
Christianity: see Boniface, (Saint) Winifred; Crusades; New Testament, Christianity, and Jesus; Pius XII; Teutonic Knights; Thor's Oak; Urban II; Vatican; White Supremist Christians vs. Reich Aryans; Wotan (Odin)
Churchill, Charles Henry, 97
Churchill, Winston, x, 83, 206, 248, 262, 271, 293, 298, 329, 352-353, 449, 508, 510, 512, 551, 603, 633
Chvalkovský, František, 370, 515
CIA (Central Intelligence Agency), ix, xxxi, 6, 307, 322, 439, 475, 546; cf. OSS
Ciano, (Count) Galeazzo, 119
CIC (US Army Counter-Intelligence Corps), 542
Cid Campeador (Díaz de Vivar, Rodrigo), 273; cf. *caudillo*
civility, 7, 250, 393, 580, 587, 594, 604, 609, 623, 633, 640; cf. free press and societies; police states
Clarkson, Petruska, 636
cloud cuckoo home (or land), 418-419
civilizations (and their discontents and vulnerable patina), i, iii, xxv, 18, 38, 66-68, 90, 93, 115, 124, 157, 169, 181, 189, 241-242, 272, 334-335, 351, 370-371, 385, 394, 410, 433, 448, 451, 457, 495, 534, 539, 562, 568-570, 577, 573, 580, 582, 587-588, 603, 622, 627, 633, 636, 638
climate and its changes, 339, 426, 639
Clinton, Bill (42nd US President), 107
Cluny monastery, 198
Cohen, Leonard, 595
colonies and colonial empires, 6, 32, 40, 44, 46-47, 53, 66-67, 100, 104, 106, 262, 272, 338, 355, 361, 395, 454, 466; cf. hegemony
colonies (non-German) and violence, 6, 47, 51, 67, 454
Complex PTSD (cPTSD), 284; cf. Complicated Grief Disorder; Gaston, Louise; PTSD
Complicated Grief Disorder (CGD), 641; cf. Complex PTSD (cPTSD); Gaston, Louise; PTSD
Concejo de Valladolid: see Council of

Valladolid, Spain
concentration camps, iv, xiv, xxii, xxviii, xxxii-xxxiv, 2-4, 47, 227-228, 230, 237-238, 240, 245-246, 253, 260, 272, 300-301, 303, 311, 321, 323-324, 332, 343, 347, 349, 372, 378, 380-381, 383-387, 389-390, 392, 396, 416, 429, 434-435, 437-439, 444, 451, 476, 478, 486, 488, 495-496, 498, 506-507, 511, 515, 525, 528, 540-541, 559-560, 566-568, 620, 635
conceptual frameworks, structures of thinking of Hitler and others, and worldview (Hitlerian, Nazi, and other), ii-iii, v-vi, xvii, xx, 6, 12, 13-17, 21, 31, 34, 37, 40, 42, 47, 51, 53, 61, 106, 114-115, 123, 129-131, 133, 136, 138, 142-143, 160-161, 166-167, 169, 172, 175, 179, 184-185, 188, 192, 196-197, 199-200, 255-257, 268, 276, 284, 289-290, 292, 294, 317, 327-328, 339, 346, 353, 355, 362, 364, 369-372, 375, 410, 422, 427, 441, 445-449, 455, 458, 462, 465-467, 469, 483, 498, 515-517, 525-526, 532-533, 535, 547, 551, 563-564, 570, 580-581, 583, 588, 592-593, 595, 601-602, 611-612, 619, 622-624, 627-628, 630-631, 634, 637; cf. worldview (*Weltaanschauung*)
Concordat between the Holy See and the German Reich (1933), 255
Condor Legion (Luftwaffe), 275, 311
Conquistadores (Spanish colonizing military), 53; cf. Las Casas, Bartolomé de
Controversia de Valladolid, 53; cf. Council of Valladolid, Spain
Cooper, Duff, 248
Copernicus, Nicolaus, 359
Coppi, Hans, 475
coprophilia, 233, 452, 602
Coughlin, (Father) Charles, 201
Council of Valladolid, Spain, 53; cf. human rights; *Junta* (authoritative religious jury) *de Valladolid;* Quetzalcoatl (plumed-serpent god)
Crimea, xxxiv, 192, 446, 517
crimes against humanity, xxv, xxix-xxx, xxxiii-xxiv, 93-95, 213, 544-546, 549, 614; cf. genocide; human rights

Croatia and the Croatians, 100, 332, 360, 390, 395, 400, 543, 555, 575, 613; cf. Serbia and the Serbians; Ustaše (Ustashe)
Cromwell, Oliver, 269
cruel: see *grausam*
Crusades, 44-45, 134, 269
cryptology, 64, 155, 377, 522
Cuba and Cubans, 19, 23, 137, 245; cf. slavery and slave labor; Spanish-American War; Weyler y Nicolau, Valeriano
Curtis, Lionel George, 471-472, 579
Curzon, George Nathaniel, 54
Customary International Law, 547
cyanide capsules (potassium cyanide), 380, 385, 419, 474, 482, 486, 507, 534-535, 600-601; cf. Zyklon B
Czechoslovakia and Czech Republic, xi, 3-4, 67, 101, 144, 265, 281, 289, 291-294, 296-298, 316, 318-319, 335, 340, 344, 349, 368, 383, 387, 393, 411, 425, 431, 485, 496, 502, 540, 542, 550, 570, 577, 584
Czerniaków, Adam, 385
Częstochowa, 472, 537
Dachau, xxxii, 217, 233, 245-246, 313, 386, 438, 489
Daladier, Édouard, 288, 290-291, 297, 321
Daleuge, Kurt, 220
Dannecker, Theodor, 534
Danube River, 271, 396
Danzig: see Gdańsk
Darius, 454
Darwin, Charles and Darwinism, 47, 176, 184-185, 423, 444, 621-622; cf. Kessler, Karl Fëdorovich; Social Darwinism; Spencer, Herbert
Dawes Plan, 2, 27, 34, 114, 148, 157-158, 229
Dawsey, Jason, iv
D-Day, 417-418, 426, 441-442, 470, 481, 566
DDR (*Deutsche Demokratische Republik*), x, xxix, 541, 557
Dearborn Independent, 114-115; cf. Ford, Henry
death camps: see extermination camps
debate de Valladolid, 53; cf. Council of Valladolid, Spain
Debs, Eugene V., 90
decent: see *anständig*

The Hitler Era 663

Decree of the Reich President against Betrayal of the German People and Treasonable Activities, 224
Decree of the Reich President for the Protection of People and the Reich (Reichstag Fire Decree), 216, 243; cf. Reichstag Fire
De Gaulle, Charles, xxix, 299, 417
dehumanization, iii, 53, 328, 370, 386, 389, 426, 472, 516, 563, 573, 586, 595; cf. barbarization; inferior beings; *Untermenschen*
De Jong, (Archbishop of Utrecht) Johannes, 399
Demjanjuk, John, xxix-xxx, 544-545
Denmark and the Danes, 108, 298, 314, 336, 338, 354, 390, 394, 396, 584
Definitive Solution to the Jewish Problem (*die endgültige Lösung*), 101; cf. Final Solution of the Jewish Problem (*die Endlösung*); Stuckart, Wilhelm
depression (economic), 15, 203, 229, 291, 423, 430, 462, 564; cf. economic crashes; economics; Great Depression
The Deputy (Der Stellvertreter), 400; cf. Pius XII
Desbois, (Father) Patrick, 271, 502
Descartes, René, 44, 581
Desert Fox (*Wüstenfuchs*), xxxiv, 418, 491; cf. Rommel, Erwin
deutschblütig, 129, 193, 254
deutschstämmig, 129, 174, 254, 310, 468, 483, 498, 573
Dewey, John, 583
Dhammapada, 1, 160, 546, 625; cf. Buddhism, conceptual frameworks, the structure of thinking, worldview
Díaz de Vivar, Rodrigo: see Cid Campeador; caudillo
dictators and dictatorships, 37, 144, 147, 154, 168, 213, 215, 222, 224-225, 230, 241, 246, 249, 307, 395, 446, 466, 483, 488, 572, 589, 591, 602, 621
Dien Bien Phu (Điện Biên Phủ), 454
Dietrich, Marlene, 109, 384
Dietrich, Sepp, 231, 414
dignity, v, 267, 352, 534, 551, 558, 573
Dijkmeester, (Rev.) Herman J., 399

dirty war (*la guerra sucia*), 576
disappeared (*los desaparecidos*), 576; cf. *spurlos* (traceless)
disasters: see disease; natural phenomena
disease: see natural phenomena; specific diseases (by name)
disinformation, 6, 10
display cases by the publication *Der Stürmer:* see *Stürmerkasten* (display cases of *Der Stürmer*)
Dittmar, Kurt, 357; cf. *Stimme des OKW* (Voice of the Supreme High Command of the Armed Forces)
Dix, Wilhelm, 76
Djurić, Rajko, 18, 438, 582
Dniepropetrovsk massacres, 510
Dohm, Christian, 176, 178
Döhring, Herbert, 324
Dohnányi, Hans von, 488
Dolles, Wilhelm, 196
Dominican Republic, 287, 553
Dönitz, Karl, xviii, xxxiii, 473, 482
Dotan Valley, 401; cf. Samaria
Doussinague y Teixidor, José María, 274-275
Dover, 417
Dovlatov, Sergei, 581
DPs (displaced persons) and DP camps, 537, 559-560; cf. DP camps by name
Draganović, (Father) Krunoslav (Croatian Roman Catholic priest), 543; cf. Barbie, Klaus
Drancy, xiv, xxii, 323-324
Dravidians, 47
Dreigroschenoper: see *Threepenny Opera*
Dresden, 75, 333, 421, 442-443, 472
Drexler, Anton, xiii, 143-144
Dreyfus, Alfred, 140; cf. Zola, Émile
Duchamp, Marcel, 402
Duda, Andrzej, 604
Dühring, Eugen, 101, 164
Dunelm, Herbert: see Durham, Bishop of (Herbert Dunelm)
dukkha (duḥkha), 624, 628-629
Dutch: see Netherlands and the Dutch
Dulles, Allen, 221, 321-322
Dulles, John Foster, 321-322
Dunkirk, 345, 566
Durham, Bishop of (Herbert Dunelm), xiv; cf. *The Yellow Spot*
Dutch: see Netherlands and the Dutch

Dzhugashvili, Iosif Vissarionovich: see Stalin, Joseph
Eberl, Henrick, xviii, 447, 459-460, 599; cf. Neumann, Hans-Joachim
Eberl, Irmfried, 367
Eberswalde, 206
Eckart, Dietrich, 117, 147, 158, 167-169, 182, 212, 256, 488
economic crashes, 159, 180, 229, 291, 424, 570; cf. Great Depression; economics &c.
economics and economic stressors, x, xxi, xxvi, 2, 25-26, 31, 38, 46, 49, 53, 56, 61, 77, 86, 104-106, 112, 134, 148, 154-155, 158-159, 163, 165, 180, 195, 198, 204-206, 210, 227, 229, 250-251, 260, 263, 279, 291, 311, 325, 338, 380, 388, 410, 419, 423-424, 438, 570, 572, 602; cf. autarky; depression (economic); economic crashes; political economy or economics; US big business
Edward VIII: see Windsor, castle/Duke
Ehrlich, Charles, 640
Ehrlich, Paul, 639
Eichmann, Adolf (Ricardo Klement), and the Eichmann Trial, xxviii, xxx, xxiv, 286, 329, 341, 361, 372, 381, 385, 450-451, 517-519, 522-523, 525, 534, 571
Ein Volk, ein Reich, ein Führer, 125, 423, 488
Einsatzgruppen (SS mobile death squads), xxxiv, 3, 112, 187, 192, 271, 331, 333, 365, 428, 522, 533; cf. Heydrich, Reinhard; Himmler, Heinrich
Einstein, Albert, 245, 305, 400, 403, 408, 456, 637
Eisenhower, Dwight David (34th US President), xxii, 70, 560-561
Elders of Zion: see *Protocols of the Elders of Zion*
El Dorado, 109
Eiser, Georg, 311-313, 486
El Salvador, 398
Elek, Tamás, iv
Elworthy, Scilla, 617-618
Emergency Quota Act of 1921, 113
emigration, coerced emigration, and emigrants, 90, 92, 113, 132, 145, 196, 214, 227, 230, 265, 276, 285-286-288, 300, 360-361, 382, 398, 424, 475, 526, 581; cf. immigration and immigrants; race laws
Ems telegram, 45
Enabling Act (Law to Remedy the Distress of People and Reich, Law Removing the Distress of the People and the Reich, Decree to Protect the Government of the National Socialist Revolution from Treacherous Attacks), 224-225, 249
English Channel, 110, 417
Enigma code and machine, 64, 155, 352, 356, 377, 380, 414; cf. Bletchley Park; Turing, Alan
Enterdungsaktion (Exhumation Action), 433; cf. *Aktion 1005 (Sonderaktion 1005)*
Erdoğan, Recep Tayyip, 49; cf. Turkey
Erfurt: see Topf, J. A., & Söhne
Erlangen, 423-424
Ernst, Karl, xxxiv, 219, 221, 233-234
Ernst, Max, 403
Erzberger, Matthias, 41
eschatology, 640; cf. Rapture
Esterwegen, 246, 260
The Eternal Jew (*Der ewige Jude*), 322-323, 343, 360, 383, 393, 436, 502-503, 565
ethics and ethical issues, 53, 90, 322, 423, 549, 594, 620-621, 632, 634, 637, 641; cf. moral groundedness
Ethiopia (Abyssinia), 272, 276
ethnic cleansing, 533, 541, 544, 558, 593; cf. genocide; massacres; pogroms
eugenics, 188, 190, 254-255, 318
Eurypylus, 615
euthanasia: see T4 euthanasia program
Évian Conference (Évian-les-Bains), 287, 306, 475, 553, 558, 560
Evil, the Devil, and the Question of Evil, xvi, 9, 27, 31, 89, 113, 128, 146, 166, 172-173, 181, 187, 205, 214, 217, 257, 282, 302, 352, 365, 402, 451, 457, 462, 467, 474, 483-484, 503, 508, 514, 517, 524-525, 553, 570, 576, 579-580, 585, 587, 603, 611-612, 627, 630
ewige Jude, Der: see *The Eternal Jew*
extermination (death) camps and centers (*Vernichtungslager*), iv, xxii, xxix-xxx, xxxiii, 4-5, 134, 192, 237, 246, 272, 323, 341-342, 347, 367,

The Hitler Era 665

380, 382, 384-385, 389, 392-393, 395, 401, 412, 421, 425, 429-430, 433, 436-439, 450, 462, 471, 493, 497, 505, 518, 526-528, 552-553; cf. concentration camps
facts, xiv, xvi-xviii, 6, 8, 55, 193, 221, 223, 242, 256, 433, 480, 574, 586
Fagles, Robert, ii, 608; cf. Homer and the *Iliad*
Faisal (Faisal I, King of Greater Syria, and then of Iraq) bin Hussein bin Ali al-Hashemi, 97; cf. Feisal, Emir
fake news, 6, 10
Farben, IG, 208-210, 319, 386-389, 566
Farber, Marvin, 255; cf. Husserl, Edmund
Federal Reserve Board, 582
Fegelein, Hermann, 477
Feisal, Emir, 97-98; cf. Faisel I
Feldhafing DP Camp, 559
Ferencz, Ben, 107, 582
Ferguson, Thomas, 6
Fermi, Enrico, 408
Ferramonti, 416, 435
Fest, Joachim, xiv, 47, 172, 208, 212, 263, 445, 483, 487, 493-494, 593, 598, 602
Feuchtwanger, Lion, 402
FHSS (Frequency Hopping Spread Spectrum], 156; cf. Antheil, George; Lamarr, Hedy; Milsatcom; wifi and Bluetooth
Field Cannon of 75 mm (*le Canon de campagne de 75 mm*), 48
Fieser, Louis, 442
Final Solution of the Gypsy Problem, 379
Final Solution of the Jewish Problem (*die Endlösung*), 4, 286-287, 349, 372, 516; cf. Definitive Solution to the Jewish Problem (*die endgültige Lösung*)
Financial debt and war reparations: see economics
Finland, 79, 108, 343, 390, 410
fire as rage: see *huŏ* (fire and rage, inverted); cf. rage (*mēnis*) and outrage
Fireside Chats, 373-374
Fisher, Janina, 365
Flossenbürg, xxxii, 486-487
Foch, Ferdinand, 604

Fontano, Spartaco, iv
Ford, Henry, 115, 198, 319; cf. *Dearborn Independent*
Ford Motor Company, 274, 319-320, 322, 386
Förster, Bernard, 163, 180
Fortress Europa, xxxiv, 418, 426, 441
France and the French, iii, viii, xiv, xxvi, xxviii-xxix, xxxi, 3, 19, 22, 26, 33-34, 42-47, 51-53, 56-57, 59, 61, 66-67, 76-77, 79, 91, 93, 99, 103, 106, 110, 114, 157, 159, 173, 177, 204, 215, 219, 253, 263, 265-267, 269-270, 273, 287, 289, 291-292, 297-299, 303, 310, 314, 321, 336, 338, 344-345, 354, 368, 370, 374-376, 387, 393, 396-397, 401-404, 408, 410, 417-418, 425, 443, 454, 470, 482, 492, 505, 515, 518, 555, 591, 641; cf. *maquis* and the *maquisards*
Franco, Francisco, xii, 273-274, 426
Franco-Mexican War, 44-45
Franco-Prussian War, 13, 18, 33, 43-44, 48, 51, 56, 58, 79-80, 103, 180, 363
Franco-Soviet Pact, 266
Frank, Anne, 566-567, 636-637
Frank, Hans, 182, 212, 284, 288, 322, 337, 355, 470, 504, 525, 552-553
Frank, Niklas, 553
Frankfurter, Felix, 97-98, 512
Franz Joseph II (Emperor), 52
Franz Ferdinand (Archduke of Austria-Hungary), 33, 52, 55, 57
free press and societies, 6, 108, 110, 117, 176, 185, 200, 216, 224-227, 241, 244, 255-256, 289, 306, 352, 375, 400, 412, 416, 446, 513, 590, 634, 640; cf. civility; police states
Freie Presse, 482
Freikorps, 120-122, 222
Freisler, (Judge) Roland, xxxiv, 243, 420, 441, 471, 475, 485-486, 488-489, 528; cf. Roeder, Judge Manfred; *Volksgericht* (People's Court)
Freud, Anna, 16, 86, 635
Freud, Sigmund, 16, 86, 196, 285, 403, 612, 632, 636
Freyberg-Eisenberg, Egloff, 220-221
Frick, Wilhelm, 213, 216; cf. Stuckart, Wilhelm
Friedländer, Saul, 76, 199, 207
Frings, (Bishop of Köln) Joseph, 399

Frisch, Otto, 305, 407-408
Fritsch, Werner von, 232, 263, 381
Fritzsch, Karl, 4
Fromm, Friedrich, 489-490
Frontbahn, 148; cf. SA
Fry, Varian, xiii, 61, 238-239, 401-404, 513-514; cf. Bingham, Hiram
Führer (Leader): see *Führerbefehls* (Führer Orders); Hitler, Adolf
Führer Gifts a City to the Jews, The (Der Führer schenkt den Juden eine Stadt), 383, 505
Führer schenkt den Juden eine Stadt, Der: see *Führer Gifts a City to the Jews, The*
Führerbefehls (Führer Orders), 238, 244, 249, 317-318, 326, 329, 339, 347, 357, 367, 428, 447, 517, 522-523, 527, 533; cf. *Gesetzeskraft* (the force of law); *Nerobefehl* (Nero Order)
Fuller, R. Buckminster, 639
fury and the Furies, i-iii, 1, 488, 508, 541, 624
Galen, (Bishop of Münser) August Clemens von, 347
Gandhi, Mohandas (Mahātma), 555
Garbo, Agent (Arabel; Juan Pujol), 417
Garbo, Greta, 417
Gaston, Louise, 606
Gatling gun, 63
Gawkowski, Henryk, 506
Gdańsk (Danzig), 101, 207, 287, 309, 465
Geary Act of 1902, 113
gefühllos (numb, insensitive, callous), 360, 362, 614; cf. Peachum
Gehlen, Reinhard, xxxi, 533
Gemlich, Adolf, 30, 440, 524
General Motors (GM), 274, 319-320, 386
Geneva Disarmament Conference, 264
Genghis Khan: see Khan, Genghis
genocide, xxiv, xxx, 47, 49, 77, 96, 146, 187, 363, 379, 433, 448, 471, 540-541, 544, 546, 554, 561-562, 574-576, 578, 587, 593, 603, 619, 633-637, 640-641; cf. crimes against humanity; ethnic cleansing; Holocaust; Lemkin, Raphael; massacres; pogroms
geopolitics, xi, 8, 21, 23, 27, 44, 47, 51, 106, 203, 212, 267, 276, 279, 285, 289, 293, 298, 345, 454, 560-561
George, David Lloyd: see Lloyd George, David
George, Henry, 20
Gerlach, Christian, 288, 349, 351-352, 357, 504, 526
German Cameroon, 47
German East Africa, 47
Germanisierung, 215, 318
Germans and Germany, i, iii-vi, x, xii-xviii, xx-xxii, xxv-xxix, xxxi-xxxiii, 1-5, 7, 11, 14, 16-42, 45-47, 50-61, 64-68, 71-93, 95-101, 103-164, 166-169, 171-175, 177-197, 199-200, 202-282, 284-333, 335-341, 343-402, 405-447, 450-453, 455-545, 549-580, 583, 586, 590-603, 606, 613, 619, 627, 633-641
Gerron, Kurt, 384
Gesetzeskraft (the force of law), 326; cf. *Führerbefehls* (Führer Orders)
Gesevius, Hans, 221
Gestalt Psychotherapy, 564; cf. Naranjo, Claudio; Perls, Fritz
Gestapo, iii, xxiv, xxxiii, 216, 219-221, 232-233, 236-237, 261, 285-287, 290, 299-300, 311-314, 331, 362, 381, 425, 436, 441, 451, 472, 486, 500, 518, 548, 577
Gierłoż, 327
Gilbert, Gustave, xiv, 591; cf. Göring, Hermann
Gilbert, Martin, Sir, xv, 97, 141, 169, 206, 248, 262, 271, 342-343, 352-353, 362, 513, 533, 633
Gilpin, Robert, 250
Ginés de Sepúlveda, Juan, 53
Gisevius, Bernd, xxxiv, 220-221, 290-291
Giulino di Mezzegra, 482
Gleichschaltung, 2, 174, 216, 226, 244, 249, 257, 531
Gleiwitz Incident, 295, 314-315, 372, 492, 501; cf. Naujocks, Alfred
global political economy, 250; cf. political economy or economics
Globocnik, Odilo, 341, 534
Goebbels, Joseph, xxxiv, 5, 9, 17, 20, 38, 75, 119, 124, 132, 148-149, 158, 175, 179, 191, 200, 202, 207, 219-222, 224, 228, 236, 240-241-244, 251, 254, 288, 300-301, 306, 311,

321, 323, 330, 340, 343, 346, 350-351, 357, 372, 380, 383, 406, 408-409, 420, 422, 424, 426, 429, 436-438, 441, 448, 468-471, 474, 479, 482, 486, 492, 495, 499-500, 502-503, 507, 514, 519, 523, 525, 527-532, 534-535, 538, 571, 596, 600; cf. Baarová, Lída; Goebbels, Magda; *Kaulquappe* (tadpole); *tobender Zwerg* (raging dwarf); total war
Goebbels, Joseph, and the nightmarish core conviction that the Jews' intention was the extermination of the German people, 350, 528
Goebbels, Joseph, diary entry (Mar. 27, 1942) on the barbaric extermination of the Jews (following Hitler's prophesy on Jan. 30, 1939), 350-351
Goebbels, Magda, 119, 486, 535
Goerze, Ursula, 475
Goeth, Amon: see Göth, Amon
Goethe, Johann Wolfgang von, xxi, xxxiii, 145, 178, 577
Goldman, Emma, xvii, 90, 638
Göring, Albert, 577
Göring/Goering, Emmy, 301, 481
Göring/Goering, Hermann, xviii, xxxiv, 20, 111, 131, 146-147, 151, 191, 212-213, 216, 219-223, 231-232, 244-245, 251, 262-263, 275, 279, 286, 288, 301, 306-307, 320-321, 330, 338-339, 356, 380, 406, 415, 420, 424, 462, 470, 473-474, 477-479, 481, 503, 507, 534-535, 552, 577, 591
Göth/Goeth, Amon, 470, 552
Gouvernement General (General Government), xxxv, 5, 288, 337-338, 341, 350, 413, 434, 438, 504, 525, 527, 553
GPS, 157; cf. Antheil, George; FHSS; Lamarr, Hedy; Milsatcom; wifi and Bluetooth
Graebe, Hermann Friedrich, 363
Grant, Madison, 188
grausam (cruel, ruthless), 1, 191, 207-208, 593, 604
Grawitz, Ernst-Robert, 366, 459
Great Britain's informal national referendum of 1934, 273, 290
Great Depression, 15, 203, 229, 423; cf. depression (economic); economic crashes, economics and economic stressors
Greek furies: see fury and the Furies
Greenspan, Alan, 582
Great War: see World War I
Greece and Greeks, 5, 326-327, 354, 384, 411, 522; cf. Ancient Greece; Nadjari, Marcel
Greim, Robert Ritter von, 535-536
Greuelpropaganda (atrocity propaganda), 6, 249, 252
Greek orgasm, 172, 190; cf. Homer and the *Iliad;* rage (*mēnis*) and outrage; Wislocka, Michalina
Grodek and Battle of Gródek, 75, 145
Gröfaz, 532; cf. Hitler, Adolf
Groningen, iv
Gross-Rosen, 438
Grotjan, Genevieve, 377
group dynamics (cooperation, harmony), 409; cf. Aristotle; herd mentality; moral groundedness; Nietzsche, Friedrich
Grozny, 405
Grynszpan, Herschel, 300-301
Guadalcanal, 523-524
guerra sucia (the dirty war), 576
gueules cassées (broken faces), 75-76, 88, 208
Guernica, 64, 275-277, 311
gulags, 448; cf. Siberia
Gurgone, Aldo, 610
Gürtner, Franz, 243
Gustav V, 474
Gypsies: see Romanies
Haase, Werner, 535, 600
Haavara Agreement, 248-250
Hadamard, Jacques, 403
Haeften, Werner Karl von, 489
Hahn, Otto, 202, 305, 407
Hakenkreuz, 171, 174, 181-182; cf. swastika
Halamajowa, Franciszka, 559; cf. Liniewska-Halamajowa, Helena; righteous and the Righteous among Nations; Yad Vashem
Halbgebildeter (a half-educated person), 578; cf. Hitler, Adolf
Halder, Franz, xxxiv, 219, 310, 324-326, 328, 339-340, 344, 347, 354, 356, 373, 388, 390, 405-406
half-apes, 170, 595-597
Halifax, (Lord) Edward Wood, 292-295
Hallervorden, Julius, 571; cf. Kaiser

Wilhelm Institute; Mengele, Josef
Hamens, (Father) Paul, 399
Hampel, Elise, 482-483
Hampel, Otto, 482-483
Hancock, Ian, xxxiv, 19, 113, 139, 379-380, 438, 519, 521, 581-582
Hand, (Judge) Learned, 246, 590
Hanfstaengl, Ernst/Putzi, xxxiv, 27, 116-117, 146-147, 151, 168, 174, 206, 211, 219, 222, 238-239, 276, 373, 415-416, 513-514
Hanfstaengl, Helen, 415-416
Hanging Trees, 113
Hanussen, Eric, 150, 223
Harnack, Arvid, 475
Harnack, Mildred, 475
Harlan, Veit, 470
Harriman, Averill, 321-322
Hartog, Leendert Johan, 288, 485, 526-527
Hashem (ha-Shem), 43
hatred, ii, v, xvi, xxxi, 2, 17, 20, 30-31, 47, 89, 92, 95, 102, 120, 122, 130, 145, 149, 152, 154, 165, 167, 176, 179-180, 191, 194, 197, 199-200, 202, 215, 219, 228, 239, 245, 263, 280, 283-284, 318, 350-351, 359, 361, 364, 369-371, 378, 394-395, 397-398, 422-424, 436-437, 440, 449, 455-456, 462, 478, 489, 500-501, 518, 526, 529, 531, 534, 541, 552, 555-556, 562, 564, 571, 573, 575, 581, 585-588, 591, 596, 598, 601, 612-613, 620-621, 636, 641
Hachenburg, Hanuš, 383
Hauser, Kaspar, 145
Hawaii, 378, 523; cf. Pearl Harbor
Heck, Alfons, xxxiv, 72, 80, 95, 127, 213, 228, 239, 246, 252, 301, 337, 356-357, 427, 452, 455, 458, 501, 505-506, 528, 534, 537, 543, 552, 568, 574, 590
Hecker, Friedrich, and the *Heckerlied*, 122
Hector, 409, 616-617, 624
hegemony, 204, 223-224, 264, 278, 299, 314, 336, 345, 376, 378, 444, 483, 485, 523; cf. colonial empires
Heidegger, Martin, xxi, 89, 255-257, 488; cf. Jaspers, Karl
Heinrici, Gotthard, 419, 478
Heinrich I, 465
Heinrich II, 190-191

Heisenberg, Werner, xxi, 305
Helen of Troy, 61
Hem, Mikal, 453
Hemingway, Ernest, 76
Hempel, Carl, xviii-xix, xxi, 460
Hera, ii, 62
herd mentality, 167, 170, 172, 175; cf. group dynamics
Hermann, Edward S., 6
Hernández, Bonar Ludwig, 53
Herodotus, 606
Herrenrasse (Master Race), i, iii, 134, 137, 166-167, 309, 328, 354, 370, 389, 423, 445, 453, 485, 595; cf. White Supremist Christians vs. Reich Aryans
Hess, Rudolf, xviii, xxi, 116, 182, 212-213, 311, 329-331
Hexe von Buchenwald (Witch of Buchenwald; Ilse Koch), xxiv
Heydrich, Heinz, 577
Heydrich, Reinhard, xv, xxxiv, 112, 137, 187, 213-214, 220, 232, 286, 303, 311, 315-316, 331, 333, 338-341, 348, 365-366, 372, 413, 424-425, 500, 503, 515-517, 519, 521-522, 524, 526-527, 571, 577; cf. Lidice; Operation Reinhard
Hiedler, Johann Nepomuk, 281, 284; cf. Hitler, Alois, Sr.; Nepomuk, (Saint) John
Hillers, Marta, 444
Himmler, Heinrich, xiv-xv, xxxiv, 3, 5, 9, 20, 77, 112, 130, 132, 135, 137, 146, 149, 175, 185, 187, 190-191, 211, 216, 221, 227-228, 231-234, 236, 286, 288, 304, 311-313, 316-318, 323-324, 335, 338, 340-342, 349, 355, 357-358, 362, 365-367, 372, 379-381, 385, 395, 414, 420, 424, 429, 433, 436-438, 450, 452, 454, 462, 464-465, 476-479, 480-481, 483, 487-488, 490, 496, 498-500-502, 504-506, 508, 516-521, 525-526, 533, 535, 538-539, 552, 571, 573, 592, 597; cf. Posnań (Posen); Schulz, Alfons
Himmler grown faint on witnessing execution, 518; cf. Karl Wolff
Hindenburg, Paul von, xxxiv, 2, 23, 26, 29, 37, 39-40, 59, 66, 135, 208-209, 211-212, 214, 216-217, 224-225, 229, 232, 237, 246, 251-252, 258,

633
Hirohito (Emperor), viii, 204
Hirschman, Albert Otto (also known as Beamish), 61; cf. Fry, Varian; political economy or economics
Hirzel, Hans, 441
Hirzel, Susanne, 441
Hitler, Adolf, i, iii-iv, vi, ix, xi-xx, xxiv, xxxii-xxxv, 1-3, 5, 8-11, 14-15, 20-24, 26-32, 36-38, 40-41, 46-47, 50-51, 57-58, 60-61, 74-75, 77, 87, 95-96, 100-101, 103-104, 106, 111-112, 115-119, 123-138, 140-151, 154-159, 167-175, 177-186, 189-191, 193-196, 199-200, 204-222, 224-240, 242-244, 246-249, 251, 253-254, 256-268, 270-272, 274-276, 278-282, 284-285, 287-299, 306-307, 309-314, 316, 318-320, 323-332, 335-340, 343, 345-358, 360, 367-373, 375-376, 378-380, 384-385, 388, 390-391, 394, 396-398, 401-402, 405-407, 410-430, 432, 435-438, 440, 444-469, 471-493, 497-498, 500-509, 512-516, 521-525, 527-529, 532, 534-536, 538-539, 542-543, 546-547, 550, 552-556, 559, 562, 565-566, 568, 570-572, 576-577, 580, 589, 593, 595-603, 608, 610, 612, 624, 626, 632-634, 636-637; cf. Gröfaz
Hitler, Adolf, and the nightmarish core conviction that the Jews' united intention was the extermination of the German people, 454
Hitler, Adolf, not a martyr, 535
Hitler, Adolf, psychosis, 446, 455-457, 570, 599
Hitler, Adolf, ranting and raving like a madman, xxiv, 453
Hitler, Alois, Jr., 280-281, 284
Hitler, Alois, Sr., 281, 284, 448, 610; cf. Hiedler, Johann Nepomuk
Hitler, Klara, 280-282, 284, 450
Hitler, Paula (Frau Paula Wolf), 9, 280-281, 327
Hitler Oath (Wehrmacht solemn oath taken by all Third Reich military personnel pledging life and limb to obeying and protecting Hitler personally as Führer), 237-238, 458
Hitler (or Bürgerbräu) Putsch, xxiv, xxxiii, 2, 26-28, 61, 112, 116, 121, 130, 143, 146-148, 150, 169, 189, 211, 213, 228, 233, 310-311, 415-416, 500, 522
Hitlerian worldview: see conceptual frameworks, structures &c.
Hitlerjugend, 2, 115, 130, 150, 228, 248, 470, 481, 485, 505-506, 543, 590; cf. Schirach, Baldur
Hitlers Blutrichter: see Hitler's Blood Judge
Hitler's Blood Judge (*Hitlers Blutrichter*), 475
Hitler-Spende, 210
Hitler's Stalingrad Speech: see Stalingrad Speech (Hitler)
Ho, Feng-Shan, 398
Hoche, Alfred, 78, 139-140
Hochhuth, Rolf, and *Der Stellvertreter*, 400; cf. Pius XII
Hochschild, Adam, 47
Hoechst, 209
Hofacker, Caesar von, 475
Hoffman, Heinrich, 130, 320
Hofmann, Otto, 351
Holiday, Billie, 114
Hollywood black list, 548; cf. black list; HUAC; McCarthy, Joseph
Holocaust: see Jews, Jewry, Judaism &c.; Jews stereotyped &c.
Holocaust (Shoah) by bullets, 271, 502, 510-511, 562, 567-568, 570
Holy Roman Empire (Ist Reich), 22-23, 33, 258; cf. Wilhelmine Reich (IInd Reich); Nazi Reich (IIIrd Reich)
Holsten, Herbert N., 601
Homer and the *Iliad*, ii, 1, 58, 61-62, 172, 187, 409, 569, 584-585, 595, 607-608, 615-617, 624-625; cf. BK.vv; Greek orgasm; rage (*mēnis*) and outrage; Wislocka, Michalina
homosexuality, heterosexuality, and variations, xxviii, 109, 136, 138, 190, 234-237, 270, 346, 534, 602; cf. Benkert Karl-Maria; Night of the Long Knives; Paragraph 175; Röhm, Ernst; sexuality, sex roles, and stereotypes
Hong Kong, 523
Hönmanns, Eric, 344
Hoover, Herbert (31st US President), 308
hordes (*Haufen, Horden*, masses), Asian, Aryan-Germanic, and other, i, xxiv, 1, 348, 410, 502; cf. alien races

Horthy, Miklós, 400
Hosenfeld, Wilm, 116, 357-358, 416
Höß/Hoess, Rudolf, xxxiv, 381, 431, 470
Hossbach, Friedrich, and the Hossbach Memorandum, 262-265
Houghteling, Laura Delano, 491
Hoyos, Paula Andrea Restrepo: see Restrepo Hoyos, Paula Andrea
HUAC (House Un-American Action Committee), 560
Hübener, Helmuth, 441; cf. White Rose
Huber, Michel, 76-77
Hudal, Alois/Luigi, 543; cf. Vatican Ratline
Hugo, Victor, 360
Hull, Cordell, 308, 402-403
human brotherhood, 611; cf. New Testament and Jesus; St. Paul
human condition *(condition humaine)*, 186, 455, 595, 613, 619-620, 640
human rights, 53, 161, 411, 512, 534, 547, 589, 594, 620; cf. Council of Valladolid, Spain; crimes against humanity; Ferencz, Ben; ICC (International Criminal Court); Jackson, Robert; Kant, Immanuel; NT (Nuremberg Tribunal trials and transcripts)
Humboldt, Alexander von, 161
Humboldt, Wilhelm von, 161
Hundred Years' War, 44
Hungary, 5, 67, 101, 234, 296, 326, 354, 384, 390, 396, 398, 421, 430-431, 549, 555, 583; cf. Austria-Hungary; Danube River
Huns (an ambiguous term), 38, 512, 539, 612; cf. Attila the Hun
huǒ (fire and rage, inverted), 617-618
Hutus, 576
Husseini, (Mufti) Haj Amin el (the Grand Mufti of Jerusalem), 398, 401
Husserl, Edmund, xxi, 89, 255
hyperinflation: see economics
I Accuse (*Ich klage an*, *J'accuse*), 140, 565
Iberian Peninsula, 43, 102
ICC (International Criminal Court), vii, xxv-xxvi, 107, 550
ICRC (International Committee of the Red Cross), 383
Iliad: see Homer and the *Iliad*
Ilians: see Trojans

illocutionary speech acts, 201-202
immigration and immigrants, 113, 176, 180, 307-308, 402, 437, 491, 591, 641; cf. emigration, coerced emigration, and emigrants; race laws
Immigration Act of 1924, 113
IMT (International Military Tribunal), xxv-xxvi; cf. NT-IMT-Blue; NT-NCA-Red; NT-TWC-Green
incidents (small events "explaining" actions): see Autro-Hungarian Archduke Ferdinand assassination as an incident leading to the Great War; Gleiwitz Incident; Lúgōuqiáo (Marco Polo Bridge) Incident; Mukden Incident; Nietzschean matches and powder kegs; Tonkin Bay Incident
inferior beings, iii, 69, 126, 129, 133-134, 136-137, 166-167, 181, 186, 188, 190, 215, 243, 270, 294, 328, 331, 336, 346-349, 370-372, 386, 389, 394, 410, 419, 426, 428, 465-466, 472, 485, 492, 504, 516, 521, 533, 557, 563, 573, 586, 595, 597, 612, 633; cf. barbarization; dehumanization; *Untermenschen*
influenza: see natural phenomena, disasters, disease
INSCOM (US Army Intelligence and Security Command), 542
Insdorf, Annette, xxxiv, 568
Insight Meditation, 627-629, 641
Institute for Historical Review, 31, 466
insults, xix, 17-18, 21-22, 108, 141-142, 197-198, 216, 234, 238, 249, 304, 461, 555-556, 559, 615, 625, 630
International Court of Justice, 544, 593
International Criminal Law, 107, 514, 545-548, 550
International Humanitarian Law (IHL), 545
International Tribunal, 558, 565
Ireland and the Irish, xv, 56, 12, 101-103, 170, 176, 293, 411, 526, 550, 556, 597, 617, 622-623
Iris, 616
Iron Cross, 42, 111, 410, 417
Iron Curtain, ix, 449, 551; cf. Churchill, Winston
Iron Guard, 396; cf. Romania
Irving, David, 466, 596, 603
Islamic State, so-called (IS, ISIS, ISIL),

576, 594
Israeli Supreme Court, 385
Italy and the Italians, v, viii, xii, xviii, xxix, 11, 18-19, 22, 25, 51, 66, 69, 80, 85, 108, 114, 139, 155, 161, 170, 173, 176, 191, 214, 232, 256, 265, 272-273, 275-276, 297, 302, 315, 324, 326-327, 353, 356, 359, 373-374, 376, 389, 397, 399, 406, 416, 421, 425, 430, 432, 435, 443, 470, 481-482, 512, 523, 539-540, 555, 564, 566, 597, 641
Izieu, the children of, xxix; cf. Barbie, Klaus
Jacson (or Jackson), Frank: see Mercader, Ramón
Jackson, Robert, xxv, 220, 222, 513-514
Jacobins (French), 293
Jacobites (British), 293
Jacoby, Jessica, 470
Jaenisch, Jule, 237
Janet, Pierre, 631
Japan and Japanese Empire, vii-viii, xxii, xxv, xxix-xxxi, 51, 63, 102, 108, 114, 197, 203-204, 258, 277-279, 314-315, 372-373, 375-378, 398, 408, 442-443, 493, 522-523, 534-535, 548, 555, 595, 600, 631
Japanese Americans, xxii
Japanese military experimentation Unit No. 731, in China
Jara, Victor, 595
Jasenovich death camp, 395
Jaspers, Karl, xxi, 256-257; cf. Heidegger, Martin
Jeckelm, Friedrich, 510
Jedwabne pogrom, 538
Jehovah's Witnesses, 138, 346, 602
Jesus: see New Testament, Christianity, and Jesus
Jewish populations before and after World War II, their displacement, 562
Jews, Judaism, anti-Semitism, pro-Nazis and anti-Semites, Holocaust, i, iii-iv, x-xii, xiv, xvi-xvii, xxviii, xxx, xxxiii, 2-6, 10-11, 17-18, 20, 30-31, 41-44, 50, 67, 74, 76, 87-89, 91-92, 95-98, 100, 105-107, 111, 113-115, 118-119, 122-124, 129-130, 132-136, 138-143, 145-147, 149, 151-153, 155, 158, 164-167, 169-170, 176-181, 183-190, 192-200, 202, 205-206, 212-215, 226-228, 230, 233, 238-245, 247, 249-255, 261, 265, 268-272, 275, 278-279, 284-289, 291-292, 294, 299-308, 310, 315, 317-318, 320, 322-324, 328-329, 331-333, 335-343, 345-347, 349-353, 355-373, 375, 378-386, 388-389, 392-402, 404, 407-413, 415-416, 422-425, 427-444, 446, 450-451, 453, 456-457, 461-462, 466, 469-471, 474-476, 478-479, 485-489, 491, 494-506, 509-527, 530-538, 541-544, 546, 549, 553, 558-562, 565, 568, 573-574-575, 577, 581, 583, 585, 590, 595-597, 601-602, 620-621, 633, 635-636; cf. Jewish populations before and after World War II and their displacement; Holocaust by bullets
Jews and the Nazi nightmarish core conviction that the Jews' intention was the extermination of the German people, 350, 454, 528
Jews as a bastard race from East Asia, i
Jews defined racially vs. Jews defined by religious beliefs, 399
Jews not a power behind all governments and all societies, not an omnipotent cabal, 11, 31, 41-42, 123, 135, 169, 198, 308, 375
Jews stereotyped, caricatured, with insulting metaphors (bacillus, cancer, parasites, poison, rats, syphilis-carrier, vermin, virus, etc.), iii, 2, 10, 17-18, 60, 86-87, 138-139, 141-142, 151-153, 162, 179-180, 200, 246, 250, 338, 351-352, 360, 368, 378, 381, 383, 389, 393, 425, 427, 430-431, 436, 488-489, 495, 526-527, 532; cf. half-apes; *Protocols of the Elders of Zion*
Jim Crow laws, 113, 243; cf. Nuremberg Laws of 1935
Joan of Arc, 162, 184
Jodl, Alfred, 473
Johnson, Lyndon Baines (36th US President), 60
Joiner, Fred, 246
Joly, Laurent, xv, 397
Jones, Ernest, 86, 196, 198
Jones, Ron, 580
Jonson, Ben, 463
Juárez, Benito, 44

Jud Süß, 470, 565
Judensau, 17, 152
Jung, Carl Gustav, 129, 466-468, 576, 612; cf. Gustav Bally; Jungian shadow and the shadows
Junge, Gertraud/Traudl, Hitler's private secretary, 463, 477, 482, 600
Jünger, Ernst, 75, 128
Jungian shadow and the shadows, iii, 135, 280, 448, 462, 468, 598, 612
Junkers (Prussian landed nobility), 29
Junta consultiva (authoritative religious jury) *de Valladolid*, 53; cf. Council of Valladolid, Spain
Kahlo, Frida, 277
Kahr, Gustav von, 147, 233
Kaiser (Emperor), 2, 297; cf. Wilhelm I, Wilhelm II
Kaiser, Hellmuth, xix, 105, 129, 174, 254, 468, 483
Kamenets-Podolsk, 352, 510
Kamerun: see German Cameroon
Kant, Immanuel, xxi, 114, 161, 257, 626; cf. *Perpetual Peace: A Philosophical Sketch*
Kapp-Lüttwitz Putsch (Coup), 99, 120, 146, 211
Katyń Wood or Forest, 335, 342, 432-433, 499
Karski, Jan, xiv, 267, 322, 338, 511, 562, 588
karuṇā, 627
Kasztner, Rezső/Rudolf/Yisra'el, 385
Kasztner Train, 385
Katowice (Kattowitz), 393
Kaulquappe (tadpole), 409; cf. Goebbels, Joseph
Kaunas, 398
Keitel, Wilhelm, xviii, xxxv, 420, 473, 536
Kellogg-Briand Treaty, 114
Kempner, Robert, 96, 214, 220, 329, 349, 399
Kennedy, John Fitzgerald (35th US President), 551, 561
Kennedy, (Ambassador) Joseph P., 11, 375
Kerch massacres, 510
Kernberg, Otto, 456
Kershaw, Ian, xiv, 9, 30, 87, 119, 168, 233, 281, 288, 332, 415, 418, 420, 447, 461, 476-477, 481, 487, 493, 522

Kessler, Karl Fëdorovich, 132; cf. mutual aid; Kropotkin, Pëtr
KGB (Soviet Secret Police), 6, 600
Khan, Genghis, 47, 326
Khan, Hazrat Inayat, 591; cf. Khan, Noor Inayat; Sufi Order in the West
Khan, Noor Inayat, 591; cf. Khan, Hazrat Inayat; *maquis* and the French *maquisards;* SOE
Kharkov, Battle of, 420, 422, 528; cf. Belgorod-Kharkov Operation
Khiterer, Victoria, xxxiv, 271-272, 498
Kiev, 5, 268, 271-272, 349-350, 393, 433, 498, 509, 523; cf. Babi Yar
Killinger, Manfred von, 222
Kindertransport Program, 307
King, Martin Luther, Jr., 555
Kipling, Rudyard, 38
Kishinev Pogrom, 268, 271
Kissinger, Henry, 60
kitsch: see Nazi kitsch vs. "degenerate" art, mores, and literature
Kjellén, Johan Rudolf, 203
Kladderadatsch, 67-68, 259
Klaipėda, 287
Kluge, Günther von, 418-419
knight: see *Ritter*
know-it-all: see *Besserwisser*
Koba, 448; cf. Stalin, Joseph
Koch, Ilse (*Hexe von Buchenwald*, the Witch of Buchenwald), xxiv
Koestler, Arthur, 580
Köhn, Otto, 362
Kolbe, Maximilian, 399
Kolberg, 470-471
Koło, 518
Komaki, Saneshige, 279
Komoly, Ottó, xvii, 386
Komoly, Thomas, xvii
Königsberg, 287
Korematsu v. United States, xxii
Körber, Susanne, 470
Kraków, xxxi, 335, 358, 538, 553
Kraków-Płaszów, 552
Krebs, Hans, 473, 534
Kreisauer Kreis (the Kreisau Circle), 472, 490, 579-580
Kristallnacht (Night of the Broken Glass), xv, 113, 200, 250-251, 277, 286, 300-302, 305-307, 311, 491, 501, 55
Kristallnacht and Jewish arrests, 300
Kristallnacht and state-authorized

violence vs. mob violence, 301-302
Kristeva, Julia, 623
Kropotkin, Pëtr, 638
Krupp family (Gustav, Friedrich, Bertha, Alfred) and the Krupp Iron Works, 3, 54, 75, 80, 167, 175, 209-210, 386-387, 389, 566
Kubizek, August, 282, 447, 462
Kumanev, Georgily, 3, 497
Kundera, Milan, 76
Kung Fu and the inverted fire character in Mandarin script: see *huŏ* (fire and rage, inverted)
Kursk (and Kursk-Orel), xxxiv, 358, 414, 422-423, 431, 471, 528, 533
Kursk (and Kursk-Orel), dates of the Battle of, 422
Kvaternik, Sladko, 332-333
Lagarde, Paul de, 179
Lakatos, Menyhért, 128, 543
Lake Como, 482
Lamarr, Hedy, 155-156; cf. Antheil, George; FHSS; GPS; Milsatcom; wi-fi technology and Bluetooth
Landsberg Prison, 26-27, 148
Landsberg DP camp, 559
Landowska, Wanda, 403
Lanzmann, Claude, xiv, 383, 511, 560-562, 567-568; cf. *Shoah*
Lǎo Tzu/Lǎozi, 391; non-action; Russian fatalism; *wúwei*
Lapide, Pinchas, 400
Las Casas, Bartolomé de, 53
Latvia, 134, 332, 393, 413, 470, 510, 518, 555, 602
Law Against the Formation of New Political Parties, 226
Law Against Overcrowding in Schools and Universities, 242
Law for the Prevention of Genetically, or Hereditarily, Diseased Offspring (Sterilization Law), 226-227, 254, 378
Law for the Repeal of Naturalization and Recognition of German Citizenship, 226
Law on the Seizure of Assets of Enemies of the State, 227
Law to Ensure Legal Peace (Law for the Guarantee of Peace Based on Law), 227
Law to Remedy the Distress of People and Reich (Law Removing the Distress of the People and the Reich; Decree to Protect the Government of the National Socialist Revolution from Treacherous Attacks), 225
law-defined racial control vs. mob control, 30, 239, 513-514; cf. Fry, Varian; Hanfstaengl, Ernst/Putzi; mobs, gangs, vigilante violence, lynchings, pogroms; Nuremberg Laws of 1935; Prussian Memorandum of May 1933
Lawrence, D. H., 108
Lawrence, T. E. (Lawrence of Arabia), 97, 128
League of Nations, 26, 28, 32-33, 35, 104, 157, 173, 204, 227, 258, 264, 272-273, 467
Lebensborn (Life Source) program, 316-318, 346, 348-349, 571
Lebensraum (living space), iii, 3, 106, 128-129, 136, 199, 203, 212, 214, 254, 263, 294, 309, 331, 346, 354, 423, 425, 427-429, 445, 484, 491
lebensunwertes Leben (lives unworthy of life), iii, 76, 138-140, 254, 378, 389, 451; cf. T4 euthanasia program
Lee, Robert E., 604
Leibknecht, Karl, 99
Leibniz, Gottfried Wilhelm, v, xxi, 44
Lemkin, Raphael, 575; cf. genocide
Lend-lease Policy, 374-375
Lenin, Vladimir (Vladimir Ilyich Ulyanov), 59, 78-79, 199, 203
Leningrad, 343, 347, 354, 391, 405
Lenya, Lotte, 362; cf. Weil, Kurt
Leonidas, 453
Leopold II, 46-47
Less, Avner, 517-518
Lessing, Gotthold, 176-178
Lévai, Jenö, 400
Levi, Primo, 388-389
Lewis, Clarence Irving, 626
Ley, Robert, 311
Leyes de Burgos, 53
Leyes Nuevas, 53
Lidice massacre, xxiv, 220, 303, 316, 349, 394, 413-414
Liebmann, Curt, 215
Liebehenschel, Arthur, 524-525
Lieber Codes, 334
Liebling, Rajmund Roman, 359; cf. Polanski, Roman
Liepāja, 232

"lies" and lies, 6-10
Lifton, Robert Jay, 367, 390
Lincoln, Abraham (16th US President), 334, 578
Lincoln Brigade, 274
Liniewska-Halamajowa, Helena, 559; cf. Halamajowa, Franciszka; righteous and the Righteous among Nations; Yad Vashem
Lipchitz, Jacques, 403
Lipetsk, 259-261
Lippmann, Walter, 6
Lipstadt, Deborah, 603
Lithuania, xi, 79, 134, 269, 287, 332, 393, 396, 398, 413, 446, 555, 602
lives not worth living: see *lebensunwertes Leben;* T4
living space: see *Lebensraum*
Liz-Texeira Branquinho, Carlos de, 398
Lloyd George, David, 78, 177, 267-270, 273, 292
Locarno Treaties, 27-28, 265-266
locutionary speech acts, 201
Loebell, Friedrich von, 57
Loerzer, Bruno, xxxv, 220
Loesener/Lösener, Bernhard, 243
Lombroso, Cesare, 139
Longerich, Peter, xv, 132, 312, 317, 329, 331, 366, 474, 476-477
Loos, Battle of, 74
Lorković, Mladen, 390
Loving v. Virginia (1967), 240; cf. anti-miscegenation laws
Lubbe, Marinus/Rinus van der, 218-219, 223
Lublin, xxxi, 341-342, 350, 365, 527, 535
Ludecke, Kurt, xiv, 22, 168, 214-215, 219, 222, 233-234, 446
Ludendorff, Erich, xxxv, 28-29, 37-41, 59, 66, 71-72, 79, 81, 83-85, 99, 117, 135, 146-148, 154, 168, 211, 320, 479, 633
Lueger, Karl, 182
Luftwaffe, xxxii-xxxiii, 193, 216, 220, 228, 262-263, 275, 277, 294, 319, 330, 339, 344, 354, 356-357, 389, 391, 397, 406, 410, 414, 421-422, 459, 473, 479, 492, 505-506, 535, 543; cf. Below, Nicolaus von; Göring, Hermann; Reitsch, Hanna
Lúgōuqiáo (Marco Polo Bridge) Incident, 277

Lumpenproletariat, 235
Lurianic Kabbalah, 595; cf. Cohen, Leonard; Ari, ha- (the Lion): ha-Eloki Rabbeinu Yitzchak
Luther, Martin, 152-153, 179, 193
Lutherans, 153, 177, 179-180, 240, 394, 399, 487, 590
Lutz, Carl, 398
Luxembourg, 58, 223, 298, 301, 336, 338, 410-411, 512, 534
Luxemburg, Rosa, 99, 242
Lwów (Lviv), 71, 338, 501
MacArthur, Douglas, viii, 534
Machtergreifung (Grabbing of Power), 2, 29, 107, 174, 223-224, 246, 249, 255, 527, 590
MacLean, French L., xxiv
Macron, Emmanuel, 44, 83
Madagascar, 288, 332-333, 338-339, 161, 365, 425, 498, 514, 526
Magid, Imam Mohamed, 619
Mahler, Gustav, 403
Maikop, 405
Majdanek KL and Trials, xxxi-xxxii, 341-342, 382, 392, 395, 438, 544, 566
Malay Polynesians, 47
Malmédy Massacre, 414
Maly Trostenets (Polish, Maly Trascianiec), 5, 342, 366
Manchuria, 204, 258; cf. Khan, Genghis
Manhattan Project, 305-306, 407-408, 443
Manifest Destiny and the massacres of native Americans, 113, 129
Mann, Golo, 402
Mann, Heinrich, xiv, 402
Mann, Klaus, 76
Mann, Thomas, 402
Manouchian, Missak, iv
Manouchian Group, iv
Manstein, Erich von, xxxv, 345
mantra, 611
maquis and the French *maquisards*, iii, 566, 591; cf. Barbie, Klaus; France and the French; Izieu, the children of; Khan, Noor Inayat; Manouchian Group; Moulin, Jean
Marathon, Battle of, 606
Marco Polo Bridge (*Lúgōuqiáo*) Incident, 277
Mariupol, 510
Marne and Battles of the Marne, 71-72

The Hitler Era 675

Marseilles, 61, 401-404
Marshall, George C., 543
Marshall Plan (post-WW2 European Recovery Program), 543
Martens, Friedrich, and the Martens Clause, 334-335
Martí, José, 137
Marty, Martin Emil, 394, 603
martyrs, xiv, 50, 147, 207, 399, 472, 499
Marx, Karl, and Marxism, 99, 198, 235
Marxism, 137, 140, 215, 241
Maser, Werner, 328, 451, 454
Mashbir, Sidney, viii
Masons, 76, 489
Mass Execution of Jews in German Occupied Poland, 434
massacres, viii, 44, 49-50, 63, 66, 77, 90, 93-96, 187, 220, 270, 303, 309, 335, 345, 350, 352-353, 356, 359, 361-362, 366, 384-385, 411, 413-414, 433, 509-514, 523-524, 538, 541, 546, 550, 561, 593, 621; cf. ethnic cleansing; genocide; mobs, gangs, vigilante violence, lynchings, pogroms; pogroms
Master Race: see *Herrenrasse*
Masur, Norbert, 474-476
Matsui, Iwane, viii; cf. Nanking, Battle and Rape of
Matsuoka, Yōsuke, 375
Mauchenheim, Gustav (Freiherr) von: see Bechtolsheim, Gustav
Maurice, Emil, 27, 233
Mauthausen-Gusen, xxxii, 386, 438
mauvaise foi (bad faith), 228; cf. Sartre, Jean-Paul
Maximilian I, 45
McCarthy, Joseph, and McCarthyism, ix, xxxi, 70, 548-549, 560; cf. black list, Hollywood black list; HUAC
McDonough, Frank, xvii, xxxiv, 281, 331, 500
McGovern, James, 196
McNamara, Robert S., 107
Mechelen Affair, 344-345
medical experiments, 390, 486, 506; cf. Japanese military experimentation Unit 731, in China
meditation: see *metta-bhāvanā; samatha; samādhi; vipassanā-bhāvanā*
Meerwarth, Rudolf, 76

Mein Kampf, xiii, xxxii, 2, 8, 10, 30-31, 57, 106, 115-118, 123-129, 131, 136-138, 140-143, 149-150, 168, 170, 179, 181-182, 184, 199, 212, 214, 233, 264, 280-281, 316, 327, 331, 346, 355, 360, 394, 423, 425, 429, 449, 483, 495, 500, 502, 596-598
Meitner, Lise, 202, 305, 407-408
Mendizabel, Alfredo, 403
Menelaus, 61, 569
Mengele, Josef (Wolfgang Gerhard), 384-385, 390, 506, 571, 577, 635; cf. Hallervorden, Julius
Mercader, Ramón (Jacques Mornard, Jacques Vandendreschd, Frank Jacson/Jackson), 277
Mercedes, 320, 386
Meriones, 569
Merkel, Angela, 49, 83, 239, 552; cf. *Rassenwahn* (racial delusion or fanaticism); *Schlussstrich* (final stroke; closing point; closure of discussion),
Messines Ridge, 72-73
metta-bhāvanā, 611
Mexico, 45, 56, 65, 277, 547, 641; cf. Franco-Mexican War; Juárez, Benito
Meyerhoff, Otto, 403
Milan, 399, 416, 421, 482, 600
Milch, Erhard, 193, 275, 356
Milgram, Stanley, 580
military deaths, World War II, 422
Mill, John Stuart, 246; cf. Mohawk Valley Formula; political economy or economics; strikebreaking
Milosz, Czeslaw, 359
Milsatcom, 156; cf. Antheil, George; FHSS; GPS; Lamarr, Hedy; wifi &c.
Minsk, 5, 362, 365-366, 433, 498, 500
mirror neurons, 622
miscegenation: see anti-miscegenation laws
Misch, Rochus, 482
Mischlinge, 192-193, 379, 505
misericordia, 627
Mitford, Unity Valkyrie, 598
Mitteleuropa (Middle Europe), xxi, 23, 26, 40, 100, 183, 408
Mitterrand, François, iv
Mladek, Meda, 541
mobs, gangs, vigilante violence, lynchings, pogroms, 9-10, 30, 113,

176-177, 183, 238, 268-271, 299-300, 396, 509, 538; cf. Jim Crow laws; *Kristallnacht* (Night of the Broken Glass); pogroms; SA
Moczarski, Kazimierz, 247, 358, 479, 488-489
Mogilev, 366
Mohawk Valley Formula, 246; cf. political economy or economics; Mill, John Stuart; strikebreaking
MOI (*la Main d'œuvre immigrée):* see Manouchian Group
Moldava, xxxiv, 192, 269
Molnár, Judit, xvii, 385
Molotov, Vyacheslav, 508-510
Molotov-Ribbentrop Pact: see Treaty of Non-aggression between Germany and the Union of Soviet Socialist Republics
Moltke, Helmuth von, 58-59, 472
Moltke, Helmuth James von, 58, 472, 482, 579
Moors, 43, 102, 273; cf. Ottomans
Moorsoldaten (Peet bog soldiers), xiv, 24
moral groundedness, 464, 628, 634, 638; cf. ethics and ethical issues; group dynamics
Morell, Theodor, 458-459, 599
Mornard, Jacques: see Mercader, Ramón
Moscow, x, 60, 260, 272, 277, 330, 347, 354, 391, 405, 410-411, 427, 430, 432-433, 504, 532, 600
Moscow Conference & Declaration, 511
Moshiri, Fereydoun (Mushīrī, Farīdūn), 632
Mosley, Oswald, 598, 621; cf. British Union of Fascists
Mosquito fighter-bombers (De Havilland DH-98), 420, 439
Moulin, Jean, xxix, 543; cf. Barbie, Klaus; De Gaulle, Charles; *maquis*
MRIs, 282-283
mud and war, 73, 86-87, 353, 391; cf. Passchendaele, Battle of; *raspútitsa*
Mukden Incident, 204
Mulisch, Harry, 382
Mulka, Robert, 4
Müller, Franz, 441
Müller, Heinrich, 286, 313, 486, 500, 518
Müller, Renate, 452-453, 598

Munich, xxxii, 2, 27, 30, 96, 111, 116-118, 121-122, 124, 129-130, 145-147, 149, 153, 182, 205-206, 210, 212-213, 217, 232-234, 236, 245-246, 249, 251, 310-313, 390, 416, 422, 426, 466, 471-472, 482-483, 503, 522, 528
Munich Agreement/Pact (Accords), 3, 289-298, 306, 335, 368, 419
murdered by the Third Reich for being sick or disabled, 138
Musiał, Bogdan, 499
Musmanno, (Judge) Michael, 272, 522, 601
Mussolini, Benito, v, 116, 155, 232, 273, 274-275, 297, 324, 416-417, 421, 432, 446, 460, 470, 482, 535, 600, 633
Musy, Jean-Marie, 474
mutual aid, 132; cf. Darwin, Charles; Kessler, Karl Fëdorovich
Mỹ Lai Massacre, 60
Mynes, 615
myths, i-ii, 6-10, 29, 31, 81, 84, 88, 101, 147, 157, 182, 191, 260, 314-315, 319, 328-329, 363, 375, 399, 409, 451, 454, 465, 485, 487, 570, 585, 601, 638
Nachman of Breslov, 361
Nachmanides: see Ramban
Nacht und Nebel (Night and Fog) Decree, xxii, 497, 566, 591; cf. *spurlos* (traceless)
Namibia (formerly German South West Africa), 47
Nanking/Nanjing, Battle and rape of, viii, 277-278, 308, 398-399
Napoleon and the Napoleonic Wars, 44-45, 63, 285, 324, 353, 391, 469-471
Naranjo, Claudio, 585, 629
Nasser, Gamal Abdel, 551
National Socialist German Workers Party (NSDAP): see Nazi &c.; NSDAP; Third Reich
native American Indians (indigenous Americans, Amerindians), 37, 113, 575
natural phenomena such as blizzards, disasters, diseases, epidemics, pestilence, volcanic eruptions, xx, 36, 61, 77, 86, 134, 381, 447, 475, 587
Natzweiler-Struthof, 438
Naujocks, Alfred, 314-315; cf. Gleiwitz

Incident
naval blockade, 4-5, 34, 59, 107, 263, 291
Nazi kitsch vs. "degenerate" art, mores, and literature, 31, 76, 111, 113, 169, 207, 464, 489; cf. Friedländer, Saul; Kundera, Milan
Nazi nightmarish core conviction that the intention of the Jews of Europe was the extermination of the German people, 340, 350, 454, 528
Nazi Reich (IIIrd Reich): see Holy Roman Empire (Ist Reich); NSDAP; Third Reich; Wilhelmine Empire (IInd Reich)
Nazi worldview: see conceptual frameworks, structures &c.
NCA (Nazi Conspiracy and Aggression), xxv-xxvi, 213, 228, 295, 328, 331, 337, 387, 432, 519, 592
Nebe, Arthur, 313, 362, 365, 486-487
nephelokokkygía, 418; cf. Aristophanes
Nepomuk, (Saint) John, 281; cf. Hiedler, Johann Nepomuk
Nerobefehl (Nero Order), 168, 428, 432, 445, 447
Nestor, 625
Netherlands and the Dutch, iv, xxv, xxxv, 2, 29, 53, 98, 107-108, 253, 298, 312-313, 320, 336-338, 344-345, 354, 396-397, 410-411, 479, 505, 512, 583, 614, 636
Neue Volks-Zeitung, 324, 513
Neuengamme, 392
Neumann, Hans-Joachim, xviii, 447, 459-460, 599, 601; cf. Eberl, Henrick
Neurath, Konstantin, 263-264, 460
neutrality, xii, 36, 50, 52, 56, 107, 260, 273-275, 310, 313, 319, 329-330, 336, 343-344, 368, 374, 393, 401, 551
New Testament, Christianity, and Jesus, 17, 31, 198, 302, 466, 549, 581-582, 584, 587, 590, 611, 640
Newton, Huey, 371
Newton, Isaac, Sir, v
Nicolau, Valeriano, Weyler y: see Weyler y Nicolau, Valeriano
Nicholls, Anthony, 26, 28, 32, 40-41, 106, 121, 146, 159, 205, 263
Niemöller, Pastor Martin, 240, 399
Nietzsche, Friedrich, xi, xvi, xxi, 15, 161-167, 170-173, 175-176, 180, 391, 403, 426, 562, 564, 596, 611-612, 626, 631-632, 636
Nietzschean matches and powder kegs, xi, 11, 16, 20, 55, 399; cf. incidents
Night and Fog: see *Nacht und Nebel* decree
Night of the Broken Glass: see *Kristallnacht*
Night of the Long Knives, 109, 112, 144, 147, 190, 209, 220, 231-234, 236, 239, 312, 437, 490, 540, 577
Nixon, Richard (37th US President), 60, 551, 560
Nobel Laureates and Nominees, vii, xxxiii, 28, 35, 89, 95, 107, 157, 202, 260-261, 305, 359, 403, 471-472, 577, 618
Noble Ones: see Aryans
non-action, 391; cf. Lǎo Tzu/Lǎozi; Russian fatalism; *wúwei*
non-violent action (NVA), 621; cf. Sharp, Gene
non-violent communication: see NVC
Nordhausen-Dora (Mittelbau-Dora), 387, 392
Normandy, 417-418, 426, 441, 443, 481; cf. D-Day
Norway, xxviii, 3, 108, 261, 275, 298, 314, 317, 336, 338, 344, 354, 393, 407-408, 410-411, 426, 492, 523, 583, 641
NSDAP (National Socialist German Workers' Party), xiii, xxxii, 2, 21-22, 26-27, 99, 104-106, 109, 111, 117, 126, 143-144, 148, 205, 208-210, 213-215, 223, 226-228, 233, 246-247, 270, 320, 330, 465, 493-494, 522, 545, 572, 596; cf. Third Reich
NT (Nuremberg Tribunal trials and transcripts): see NT-IMT-Blue; NT-NCA-Red; NT-TWC-Green; Nuremberg Tribunal and Trials
NT-IMT-Blue, xxvi, 146, 219, 221, 228, 289, 315, 363-364, 376, 465, 474, 504, 517, 520-521, 530, 533, 592, 596
NT-NCA-Red, xxvii, 213, 228, 295, 328, 331, 337, 387, 432, 519, 592
NT-TWC-Green, xxvii, 193, 316, 333, 349, 351, 388, 390, 498-499, 515-516
nuclear fusion, 407-408
numerus clausus, 270

Nuremberg (the city), xviii, xxvi
Nuremberg (Nürnberg) Nazi Party Rallies (or Congresses), 43, 136, 172-173, 175, 185-186, 212-213, 234, 242, 247-248, 259, 261, 272-273, 318, 424, 483, 493
Nuremberg Laws of 1935, 30, 129, 142-143, 238-240, 243, 261, 378, 424, 494-495, 513, 590; cf. Jim Crow laws; law-defined racial control vs. mob control; Prussian Memorandum of May 1933; Stuckart, Wilhelm
Nuremberg Tribunal and Trials, xiv, xvii-xviii, xxiv-xxvii, xxxii, 93, 96, 107, 192, 213-214, 219-221, 307, 315, 330, 334, 349, 356, 362-363, 375, 388, 390, 437, 440, 451, 463, 499, 507, 514, 516-517, 519-520, 533, 545-547, 550, 567, 591-592, 614; cf. Ferencz, Ben; Jackson, Robert; NT-IMT-Blue; NT-NCA-Red; NT-TWC-Green
NVC (Non-Violent Communication) and non-violence, 555-556, 617, 621; cf. Elworthy, Scilla; Rosenberg, Marshall; Sharp, Gene; Tutu, Desmond
oaths, ii, xxvii, 516, 625; cf. Hitler Oath
Obersalzberg, 207, 330, 481
Oder River, 480
Odin: see Wotan
Ohlendorf, Otto, xxxv, 192-193, 333, 351, 362, 516
Ohlendorf, Otto, and mass murders claimed to be justifiable since needed to keep Germany's enemies from exterminating it, 351
Ohrdruf, 392
Olbricht, Friedrich, 489
Olympics, Berlin 1936 Summer, 194, 267, 273, 327, 329
omnicide, 637; cf. Somerville, John
Onfray, Michel, 175
Opel (General Motors), 319-320, 386
Operation (*Unternehmen*): see specific operations
Operation Anthropoid, xxxiv, 341
Operation Barbarossa, 22, 325-328, 331, 339, 380, 393, 508, 515
Operation Blücher, 83-84
Operation Braunschweig, 405
Operation Citadel, 421-422, 532
Operation Drumbeat (*Paukenschlag*), 375

Operation Eagle Attack, 339
Operation Edelweiss, 405
Operation Georg, 84
Operation Georgette, 84
Operation Gneisenau, 84
Operation Gunnerside, 408
Operation Hagen, 84
Operation Heron, 405-406
Operation Höß/Hoess, 431
Operation Hummingbird (*Kolibri*), 232, 236
Operation Husky, 416
Operation Ludendorff, 83
Operation Margarethe, 430
Operation Marneschutz-Reims, 84
Operation Michael, 84
Operation Nemesis, 95
Operation Neu-Georg, 84
Operation Northwind, 414; cf. Battle of the Bulge,
Operation Otto, 271
Operation Overlord, 417; cf. D-Day
Operation Paperclip, 398, 542
Operation Ratline, 543
Operation Reinhard, 341-342
Operation Sea Lion, 339
Operation Torch, 397, 418
Operation Valkyrie (*Walküre*), 144, 487, 490
Operation Werewolf (*Werwolf*), 5, 479
Operation Yellow, 344
Ophuls, Max, xxix, 403
Oradour-sur-Glane Massacre, 303, 394, 414
Oranienburg, xiv, 245
Order for the Begetting of Children (*Kinderzeugungsbefehl*), 317
OSS, xxxi; cf. CIA
Ossowska, Maria, 151
Oster, Hans, xxxv, 290-291, 419
Oster Conspiracy, 144, 289-292, 294, 297, 310, 419
Østergaard, Svend, 635
O'Sullivan, John L., 113
Oświęcim: see Auschwitz; *Pitshipoy*
Ott, Adolf, xxxv, 522
Ottomans and the Ottoman Empire, 19, 32, 38, 43, 49-50, 52-54, 71, 91-97, 133, 146, 181, 269, 395, 575-576, 613; cf. Moors; Turkey
over-determination, 16; cf. retro-causality
Pacelli, (Cardinal) Eugenio: see Pius XII

The Hitler Era

Padover, Saul K., i, xiv, xxxiii, 495; cf. Dittmar, Kurt
Palestine, British-Mandate, 49, 97, 200, 250, 253, 401, 514; cf. Balfour Declaration; Churchill, Charles Henry; Husseini, (Mufti) Haj Amin
Pali (Theravāda Buddhist) Canon, 1, 160, 546, 625, 629; cf. Buddhism
Palmiry Forest massacres, 499
pandemics, 36
Paragraph 175, 110; cf. homosexuality, heterosexuality, and variations
paranoia (lay senses), 40, 58, 370, 441, 571
paranoia (technical senses), 369-370
Paris (in the *Iliad*), 61
Paris and the French, iii-iv, xxi-xxii, 48, 50, 58, 64, 67, 80-84, 110, 140, 174, 176, 208, 221, 249, 269, 280, 291, 298-300, 304, 311, 323, 345, 358, 397, 400, 417, 490, 519, 566-567
Paris Peace Conference, 49, 97-98
Pas de Calais, 417-418
Passchendaele, Battle of, 72-74, 253, 410; cf. mud and war
Pacelli, Eugenio: see Pius XII
Patroclus, 615-616, 624
Paulus, Friedrich, xxxv, 356, 390, 406-408, 492, 527-528
Pavelić, Ante, 395, 543
Pavloff, Franck, 580
Payne Best, Sigismund, 313; cf. Venlo Incident
Peachum, Jonathan Jeremiah (Brecht character), 360, 362, 563, 578, 614
Pearl Harbor, xxii, xxx, 372, 375-378, 504, 524
Peleus, i, 608, 617
Pell, Herbert Claiborne, Jr., 549
perlocutionary speech acts, 202
Perls, Fritz, 562-564; cf. Gestalt Psychotherapy
Perpetual Peace: A Philosophical Sketch (*Zum ewigen Frieden: Ein philosophischer Entwurf*) by Immanuel Kant, 114
Pershing, John, 77-78, 81-82, 85
personal creativity and self-worth, 178, 403, 456, 611, 639
Petacci, Clara, 482; cf. Mussolini, Benito
Pétain, Philippe, xxix, 299, 397, 586
Peter the Venerable, 198

phenomenology, 228, 255, 641; cf. Farber, Marvin; Husserl, Edmund; Sartre, Jean-Paul
Phlegéthōn or Pyriphlegéthōn (Flaming Fire, Greek river of the Underworld), 585, 618; cf. Styx
piano-wire executions by hanging, 437, 486; cf. Freisler, (Judge) Roland
Piazzale Loreto, 482
Picasso, Pablo, 276
Pinsk, 366
Pithiviers, xxii, 324
Pitshipoy/Pitchipoï, 323
Pius XI, 185, 255
Pius XII, ix, 255, 399-400
place in the sun, 45-46, 56-57, 292
plague: see Bubonic plague; natural phenomena, disasters, disease
Planck, Max, 305, 407
Plant (Plaut), Richard, 190
Plato, 577
plebiscites, 262, 280, 296, 369
Plesch, Dan, xxxi, 511, 548-550, 594
Plewnia, Margarete, 117
pogroms, 30, 177, 183, 238, 268-269, 270-271, 276, 299-300, 396, 509, 538; cf. ethnic cleansing; massacres
poison gas, 49, 54, 66, 73, 88, 107, 271, 339, 381, 386, 415, 462, 569; cf. cyanide capsules (potassium cyanide); Zyklon B
Poison Kitchen, 217; cf. propaganda
Poland and the Polish, iv, xiv, xxi-xxxii, 3, 11, 32, 50, 64, 99-101, 120, 134, 162, 172, 187-188, 227, 243-244, 247, 267, 277, 286, 269-270, 295-296, 299-300, 309-310, 315-316, 318-319, 321, 335-337, 340-341, 343, 346, 360, 364, 368, 372, 393, 395, 425, 434, 438, 485-486, 492, 497-498, 501, 504-505, 511, 525, 529, 539, 541-542, 553, 560, 604
Polanski, Roman, 358-359; cf. Liebling, Rajmund Roman
police states, 112, 565, 640; cf. civility; free press and societies
political economy or economics, 61, 246, 250; cf. economics and economic stressors; global political economy; Mill, John Stuart; Mohawk Valley Formula; strikebreaking
Political Testament (Hitler), 372, 432, 451, 476, 478; cf. *Private Will* (Hitler)

Pomsel, Brunhilde, 17, 158, 224-225, 236-237, 245, 409, 535-536
Porąbka, 384
Portugal, 43, 53, 274, 398, 417, 549
Posnań (Posen), 227-228, 309, 539, 592
potassium cyanide capsules: see cyanide capsules (potassium cyanide)
Potsdam, Day of, 225, 246
Potthast, Hedwig, 318; cf. Himmler, Heinrich
Pour le mérite, 111, 120
Power, Samantha, 550, 638
Prague, 4, 112, 303, 341, 348-349, 382-383, 403, 438, 475, 505, 541; cf. Lidice massacre; Theresienstadt
Prague Jewry population in 1938 vs. 1945, 370
Praljak, Slobodan, 380
Pretzsch, 333
Preußische Denkschrift: see Prussian Memorandum of May 1933
Priam, 614, 616-617
pride, iii, xvi, 9, 20, 61, 72, 90, 116, 161, 195, 227, 229, 248, 280, 394, 433, 446, 464, 509, 561-562, 592-593, 612, 628
Private Will (Hitler), 432; cf. *Political Testament* (Hitler)
Probst, Christoph, 472, 486, 528; cf. White Rose
Professional Civil Service Act (Law for the Restoration of the Professional Civil Service), 252
projecting (psychological): see splitting and projecting; scapegoating
propaganda, ix, xxxiii, 9, 39, 124, 130-132, 137, 140, 161, 170, 184, 200-202, 205, 211, 221, 226, 228, 237, 239-240, 242-243, 246, 254, 263, 302-303, 306-307, 312, 322, 332, 343, 346, 360, 378, 383, 393-394, 401, 426, 429, 432-434, 436, 469, 471, 477, 502-503, 513, 529-530, 543, 600, 602; cf. Goebbels, Joseph; *Greuelpropaganda;* Poison Kitchen
Protocols of the Elders of Zion, 115, 169; cf. Jews stereotyped &c.
Prussian Coup or Putsch, 206-207, 225
Prussian Memorandum (*Preußische Denkschrift*) of May 1933, 30, 142; cf. law-defined racial control vs. mob control; Nuremberg Laws of 1935; race theory
Prützmann, Hans-Adolf, 479
psychopathology, 15, 370-372, 451, 453, 456-469, 635
psychospirituality and religious psychological teachings, 167, 458, 626
PTSD, 283-284, 365, 605-608, 617, 641; cf. Complex PTSD (cPTSD); Complicated Grief Disorder; Gaston, Louise
Pupik, Emil, 541
purity (*Reinheit*), pure ones, and the limits of the concept, i, 1, 9, 30, 100-101, 105, 134, 136-137, 142, 163, 167, 178, 181-182, 189-190, 195-196, 202, 254, 281, 310, 316, 318, 348, 379, 423, 556, 573, 595, 611; cf. race theory
Pyriphlegéthōn or Phlegéthōn (Flaming Fire, Greek river of the Underworld), 585, 618; cf. Styx
Quakers, 138, 307-308, 602, 620
Quetzalcoatl (plumed-serpent god), 53; cf. Council of Valladolid, Spain
Quirheim, Albrecht Mertz von, 489
Rabe, John, 278, 398
race laws: see Asiatic Barred Zone Act of 1917; Chinese Exclusion Act of 1882; Emergency Quota Act of 1921; Geary Act of 1902; Immigration Act of 1924; Jim Crow laws; law-defined racial control vs. mob control; Nuremberg Laws of 1935; Prussian Memorandum of May 1933
race theory, i, iii, xiv, xvii, 94, 98, 100, 105, 113, 119, 124-127, 129, 136-139, 142, 160-161, 165-167, 171, 184-186, 189-190, 192-197, 200, 241, 249, 255, 271, 278, 309, 317-318, 328, 346, 350-351, 353-354, 367-368, 370, 379, 389, 411, 423, 427, 432, 445, 451, 469, 485, 493, 495, 498-499, 504, 512, 520, 522, 527, 551, 595-596, 621; cf. alien races; *Herrenrasse;* Jews, Jewry &c.; purity and pure ones (and the limits of the concept); race laws; Romanies &c.; *Untermenschen*
racial delusion or fanaticism: see *Rassenwahn;* Merkel, Angela
Raeder, Erich, 232, 363
rafle (*razzia*, round-up), iv, 397, 400

rage (*mēnis*) and outrage, i-iii, 1, 20, 91, 94-96, 127, 140, 172, 188, 215, 233, 245, 260, 268, 271, 284, 300, 304, 312, 359, 407, 440, 446-447, 450, 456, 473, 476, 494, 509, 538, 541, 555, 575, 607-609, 613-615, 617, 624-631; cf. fury and the Furies; Greek orgasm; Homer and the *Iliad;* torment; wrath
raḥamim, 627
raḥ'mah, 627
Rajman, Marcel, iv
Ramban (Nachmanides), 43
rape, 38, 61, 100, 186-188, 268, 278, 283, 314, 379, 443-444, 593-594, 598, 609-610, 613; cf. Nanking, Battle and Rape of
Rapture, 640; cf. eschatology
Rashi (Rabbi Shlomo ben Yitzhaki), 304
raspútitsa, 353
Rassenwahn (racial delusion or fanaticism), 239; cf. Merkel, Angela
Rastenburg (Kętrzyn), 313, 327, 333, 414
Rath, Ernst vom, 300-301
Rathenau, Walther, 115, 147, 152-154, 222
Ratzel, Friedrich, 128, 203, 423
Raubal, Geli, 233
Rauff, Walther, 347; cf. Heydrich, Reinhard
Rauschning, Hermann, 131, 207-208, 465, 593, 596
Ravensbrück, xxxii, 438, 476
razzia: see *rafle* (*razzia*, round-up)
Realpolitik, 45-46, 546, 638; cf. *Weltpolitik*
Red Orchestra (*rote Kapelle*), 474-475
Red Summer of 1919, 111
Referendum of 1934: see Great Britain's informal national referendum of 1934
Regulation Concerning Admission to the Medical Profession, 253
Reich (Empire): see Holy Roman Empire (Ist Reich); Wilhelmine Empire (IInd Reich); Nazi Reich (IIIrd Reich
Reich Flag Law, first of the Nuremberg Laws of 1935 (*Reichsflaggengesetz*), 239
Reichstag and Reichstag speeches, 2, 40-41, 46, 148, 154, 206, 208, 210, 213, 230, 236, 239, 244-245, 258, 272, 297, 299, 312, 324, 326, 336, 350, 367-369, 372, 415, 424, 501, 503-504, 515-516, 521-522
Reichstag Fire, 218-225, 243, 246, 260
Reichswehr, 30, 120, 215, 231, 236, 247, 258; cf. Black German Military
Reinberger, Helmuth, 344
Reitsch, Hanna, 473, 535-536
Rejewski, Marian, 243
Remarque, Erich Marie, 74, 128
retro-causality, 309; cf. over-determination
resistance and resistance movements, iii, xvii, 3-5, 16, 58, 120, 144, 187, 215, 225, 232, 258, 266-267, 293, 297-299, 315-316, 338, 340, 393, 410, 425, 429, 432, 454, 471-473, 478-479, 482, 487, 490, 493, 498, 511, 566, 568, 579, 591, 623
Restrepo Hoyos, Paula Andrea, 53
retaliation: see *Vergeltung*
retribution: see *Vergeltung*
Retter (savior), 1, 130-131, 438, 571, 640; cf. Hitler, Adolf
Revelation (Apocalypse), 640; cf. New Testament, Christianity, and Jesus
revenge and vengeance: see *Vergeltung*
Reynolds, David, 36, 39-40
Rhine River, 34, 266, 417, 596
Rhineland, 3, 34, 44, 99-100, 238, 265-267, 271, 289, 291, 301, 424
Ribbentrop, Joachim von, 124, 263, 309, 321, 375-376, 437, 462-463; cf. Molotov-Ribbentrop Agreement; Rüpschentropp
Riefenstahl, Leni, 248
Riga, 79, 366, 470, 510, 518
righteous and the Righteous among Nations, 358-359, 385, 397, 400, 404, 559, 583; cf. Yad Vashem
Ritter (knight), 1, 129-131, 133-134, 136, 438, 571, 640; cf. Hitler, Adolf
Rivera, Diego, 277
Rizzolatti, Giacomo, 622
Rocker, Rudolf, 90, 273, 637; cf. anarchism and anarcho-syndicalism
Rockwell, George Lincoln, 597
Roder, Lorenz, 415
Roeder, (Judge) Manfred, 474; cf. Freisler, (Judge) Roland
Rödl, Arthur, 514

Röhm, Ernst, 3, 111-112, 121, 148, 190, 219, 222, 231-232, 234-237; homosexuality, heterosexuality, and variations; Night of the Long Knives; sexuality, sex roles, and stereotypes
Röhm Putsch: see Blood Purge
Roloff, Helmut, 475
Romania, 19, 32, 66, 86, 113, 203, 354, 396, 421, 431, 577
Romanichal, 270; cf. Romanies
Romanies (Gypsies), iv, 3, 18-20, 50, 92, 113, 129, 136, 138-140, 165, 177, 190, 215, 227, 230, 253, 286, 294, 332, 342-343, 346, 355, 364, 370, 378-379, 383, 396, 438-439, 462, 486, 510, 516-521, 526, 534, 546, 573, 575, 583, 602, 633
Romanies stereotyped, caricatured, with insulting metaphors (lazy, a mixed race, unstable vagabonds, unreliable, a band of wrong-doers, etc.) 139-140, 190, 227, 332, 379, 516, 519
Rommel, Erwin, xxv, 352, 356, 380, 418, 486, 490
Roosevelt, Eleanor, 322, 560
Roosevelt, Franklin Delano "FDR" (32nd US President), xxxiii, 203, 205, 276, 287, 308, 373-374, 376, 378, 408, 448, 473, 491, 508-513, 549, 588, 603
Rosenberg, Alfred, 117, 146, 168, 182, 212, 214, 311, 328-329, 468, 504, 530, 570-571
Rosenberg, Marshall, 555-556, 617-618; cf. NVC (Non-Violent Communication)
Rosenberg, Walter: see Vrba, Rudolf (1924-2006)
Rosmus, Anna Elisabeth, 556
Rossel, Maurice, 383
Rostand, Maurice, 108
Rostov-on-the-Don, 405-406
Rottach am Egern, 426
Rotterdam, 276, 345
round-up: see *rafle* (*razzia*, round-up)
Rovno: see Rowno
Rowno (Rovno), 363
Royan, 443
Różycki, Jerzy, 243
RSD (*Reichssicherheitsdienst*, Reich Security Service), 231, 312
RSHA (*Reichssicherheitshauptamt*, Reich Security Central Office), xxii, xxxiii, 286-287, 341, 450, 518, 526
rubber slaves, 47; cf. Belgian Congo
Ruhr, 2, 28, 99, 148, 154, 157, 209, 229, 260, 265, 291, 321
Ruhr Uprising (*Ruhraufstand*), 99
Rumbula Forest Massacre, 366, 510
Rumania: see Romania
Rumi, Jalaluddin, 19
Rumkowski, Chaim, 338
Rummel, Rudolph, 88, 448, 627
Rüpschentropp, 309; cf. Ribbentrop, Joachim von
Russell, Bertrand, xxiv, 89-90, 582, 591
Russell, Edward, Lord, xxiv, 6, 390, 393
Russia, i, v, viii-x, xxxiv, 7, 17, 19, 25, 522; cf. Czarist Russia, USSR
Russian fatalism, 391, 626; cf. Lǎo Tzu/Lǎozi; non-action; *wúwei*
Russo-Japanese War, 63
Ruthenia: see Subcarpathian Rus'
ruthless: see *grausam*
Rwanda, ix, 576, 594
SA (*Sturmabteilung*, Stormtroopers, Brownshirts), iii, xxxiii, 3, 109, 111-112, 116, 121-123, 133, 144-146, 148, 150, 156, 206-207, 223, 231-239, 244, 247, 250, 261, 301, 312, 424, 487, 513, 546, 580; cf. Röhm, Ernst
Saavedra, Miguel de Cervantes: see Cervantes Saavedra, Miguel de
Sabbatean Movement and Sabbatai Tsvi, 269
Sachsenhausen, 245, 401, 438, 488; cf. Oranienburg
sadism, xxiv, 227, 246, 364, 487, 514, 541, 544, 571, 592, 635; cf. brutality
Sadowska, Maria, 172
St. John of the Cross: see San Juan de la Cruz
St. Paul, 611; cf. human brotherhood; New Testament and Jesus
Salisbury, Harrison E., 532
salto mortale, 256, 468
samādhi, 630; cf. *samatha, vipassanā-bhāvanā*
Samaria, 401; cf. Dotan Valley
samatha, 630; cf. *samādhi, vipassanā-bhāvanā*
San Juan de la Cruz (St. John of the Cross), xxxiii

Sander, Bernhard Wilhelm, 219-220, 222
Sanz-Briz, Ángel, 398
Sariputta, 628
Sartre, Jean-Paul, 175, 228, 568
Satmar Rabbi, 385
Sattler, Shanti, 547, 550
savior: see *Retter*
scapegoats and scapegoating, 60, 154, 336, 589
Scavenius, Erik, 390
Scheicher, Kurt, 208
Scheidemann, Phillip, 41
Scheubner-Richter, Max, 95, 146
Schicklgruber, Alois, 281, 284
Schicklgruber, Maria Anna, 281, 285
Schilke, Karl, 247
Schindler, Oskar, 385, 398, 568
Schirach, Baldur, xviii, xxxv, 115, 415; cf. *Hitlerjugend*
Schirach, Henriette, 461-462
Schlaich, (Pastor) Ludwig, 347
Schlieffen, Alfred, and the Schlieffen Plan, 57, 71, 204, 295, 370
Schlöndorff, Volker, 514
Schlussstrich (earlier: *Schlußstrich* or *Schluß-Strich*, final stroke; closing point; closure of discussion), 552; cf. Merkel, Angela
Schmidt, Fritz, 399
Schmidt, Paul, 266-267, 293
Scholl, Hans and Sophie, 422, 472, 486, 528; cf. White Rose
Schönerer, Georg, 182-183
Schopenhauer, Arthur, 418
Schrecker, Paul, v, 44, 105; cf. Descartes, René; Leibniz, Gottfried Wilhelm
Schroeder, Christa (Hitler's secretary), 119, 285, 347, 437, 461, 481, 524, 528, 589
Schroeder, Kurt von, 210-211
Schulz, Alfons, 502
Schuschnigg, Kurt, 280, 369
schwarze Front: see Black Front
Schwarze Reichswehr: see Black German Military
Schulze-Boysen, Harro, 475
Schulze-Boysen, Libertas, 475
Schweik, Good Soldier Josef, 52
Scythians, 454
Second Coming of the Christ, 640
Segerstedt, Togny, 640

semi-permeability, v, 24
Sepúlveda, Juan Ginés de, 53
Serbia and the Serbians, 19, 32, 52-55, 57, 66, 92, 100, 395, 555, 602, 613; cf. Croatia and the Croatians; Yugoslavia and the Yugoslavs
sexuality, sex roles, and stereotypes, xxviii, 19, 61-62, 86, 100, 102, 105-106, 108-109, 111, 122, 136, 138, 152, 171-172, 183, 186-187, 190, 195, 205, 227, 234-235, 237, 261, 270, 346, 348, 378, 452-453, 459, 462, 534, 571, 573, 576, 594, 596, 598, 602, 621, 626; cf. El Dorado; Hitler, Adolf; homosexuality, heterosexuality &c.; Röhm, Ernst
Seyfo, 50
Seyss-Inquart, Arthur, xxxv, 337, 399
Sforno, Ovadio, 302-303
shadow: see Jungian shadow
Shanghai, 277-278, 398
Shaolin Kung Fu and the inverted fire character in Mandarin: see *huǒ* (fire and rage, inverted)
Sharp, Gene, 621; cf. non-violent action (NVA)
Shell Oil Company, 386
Shipp, Thomas, 113
Shoah (film), xiv, 383, 425
Shoah (Holocaust): see Holocaust by bullets; Jews, Jewry, Judaism, anti-Semitism, Holocaust
Shoot on Sight Order, 374
Shostakovich, Dmitri, 359
Siberia, 183, 332-333, 448
Sicily, xxiv, 416, 421, 425, 454
Siegel, Michael, 251
Siemens, 386, 399
Sienkiewicz, Henryk, 95
Singapore, 278, 375, 523
Sinti: see Romanies
SIS (US Army Signal Intelligence Service), 377
Škēde, 332
skinheads, 555, 557, 597
Škoda Works, 4
slavery and slave labor, 5, 136, 205, 209, 246, 382, 385-387, 389, 392, 419, 485, 559, 566
Slavs, i, 50, 55, 129, 136, 138, 189-191, 253, 294, 317, 328, 346, 349-350, 371, 394, 410, 453, 462, 485, 491, 504, 510, 534, 538, 573, 575

Smend, Gunther, 475
Smith, Abram, 113
Smolensk, 419, 433, 499
Smoot-Hawley Tariff Act, 159
Snell, Bradford C., 319-320
Snyder, Louis, 528
Snyder, Timothy, 353, 394, 445, 448, 511, 521, 541
Sobibór, xi, xxix-xxx, xxxii, 5, 341-342, 382, 392, 505, 527, 544, 568, 635
Social Darwinism, 132, 184, 188, 428, 444, 450; cf. Darwin, Charles; Spencer, Herbert
SOE (Special Operations Executive, a secret branch of British intelligence focusing on sabotage in Nazi-controlled Europe), 131, 591
Soixante-quinze: see Field Cannon of 75 mm
Solomon, Jon, xxxv, 585
Solomon Islands, 523
Somerville, John, 639; cf. omnicide
Somme and Battle of the Somme, 71-72, 87, 410, 586
Sonderkommando, x-xi, xxxiv
Souisa Mendes, Aristides de, 398
Soviet-Afghan War, 454
Soviet Union (USSR), ix, xi, xii, xxviii, xxxi, 22, 25, 32, 50, 88, 129, 136, 199, 203, 214, 222, 262, 270, 275, 277, 291-292, 294, 297-298, 309, 318, 324-326, 328, 330-332, 335, 340, 343, 346, 352-354, 357, 359, 393, 397, 410, 413, 418-419, 421, 427-429, 439, 446, 450, 454, 461, 486, 492, 498, 505, 512, 515, 523, 526, 529, 532, 534, 546, 549, 551, 557, 560, 567, 581, 583; cf. Czarist Russia, Russia
Spain and the Spanish, 36, 43, 45, 245, 253, 269, 273-277, 417, 519, 555, 591
Spanish-American War, 63; cf. Weyler y Nicolau, Valeriano
Spanish Civil War, xii, 64, 266, 273-274, 276, 308, 311
Spanish flu (misnomer), 36, 87; cf. natural phenomena, disasters, disease
Sparta, 236, 454, 606
Spartacus, 99, 123, 236
speech as action: see illocutionary speech acts; locutionary speech acts;
perlocutionary speech acts
Speer, Albert, xxxv, 119, 151, 190-191, 237, 259, 320, 447, 457, 496, 506, 529, 552; cf. Cathedral of Lights
Spencer, Herbert, 184, 423, 444
splitting and projecting, 40-41, 60, 228, 456-457, 563, 593, 613; cf. scapegoating
Sportpalast, 126, 180, 243, 326, 372, 408, 504, 521-522, 527-531
spurlos (traceless), 591; cf. disappeared (*los desaparecidos*); *Nacht und Nebel* (Night and Fog) Decree
SS (*Schutztaffel*, Protection Squadron, Blackshirts): see *Carlingue* (French SS); Himmler, Heinrich
Einsatzgruppen
SS-Begleitkommando, 231
SS-Helferinnen, 384
SS-Totenkopfverbände (SS Death-head Units), 237
stab in the back, 2, 39-41, 134, 147, 195
Stalin, Joseph ("Koba"), 88, 90, 145, 199, 282, 295, 330, 335, 395, 405, 413, 433, 447-449, 512, 521, 560, 603, 610, 633
Stalin on Hitler wanting to bluff, 295
Stalingrad and Battle of Stalingrad, xxxiv, 277, 310, 354, 356, 384, 405-406, 408-409, 413, 420-421-422, 426, 430, 470, 480, 492, 522, 527-528, 530-532, 580; cf. Dittmar, Kurt
Stalingrad, dates of the Battle of, 421
Stalingrad Speech (Hitler), 522
Stalingrad of the Yangtse River, 277
Standard Oil, 294, 319
Statut juif, 397
Stauffenberg, (Count) Claus Schenk von, xxxv, 145, 413, 472, 475, 489
Stein, Murray, 467
Steiner, George, 577
Steinmeier, Frank-Walter, 604
Stellvertreter, der (The Deputy), 400; cf. Pius XII
Stempfle, Brother Bernhard, 233
Stennes, Walter, 112
sterilized by the Third Reich for sexual preferences, 138
Stevens, Richard Henry, 313; cf. Venlo Incident
Stierlin, Helm, 453

The Hitler Era

Stimme des OKW (Voice of the Supreme High Command of the Armed Forces; or, Voice of the Wehrmacht), 357; cf. Dittmar, Kurt
Stocker, Adolf, 179-180
Stoddard, Lothrop, 188
Stoßtruppen-Hitler, 121
Strasser, Gregor, 124, 144-145, 148, 233, 524
Strasser, Otto, 144-145, 312
Strasshof Concentration Camp, 385
Strassmann, Fritz, 202, 305, 407
Streicher, Julius, xviii, 124, 169, 180, 185, 200, 251, 301-305, 311, 468, 495, 500, 571; cf. *Der Stürmer*
Stresemann, Gustav, 27-28
strikebreaking, 236; cf. Mohawk Valley Formula
Stroop, Jürgen, 247, 358-359, 488-489, 533; cf. Warsaw ghetto
Stuckart, Wilhelm, 101; cf. Dühring, Eugen; Frick, Wilhelm; Nuremberg Laws of 1935
Studebaker, 274
Stülpnagel, Carl-Heinrich, 490
Stürmer, Der, 76, 124, 169, 180, 185, 194, 305, 311, 495
Stürmer boxes or display cases: see *Stürmerkasten*
Stürmerkasten (display cases of *Der Stürmer*), 194, 495-496
Stutthof: see Natzweiler-Struthof
Styx, 584-585
Subcarpathian Rus' (Ruthenia), 269, 430-431
subdued worker wages based on worker insecurity, 582
subhuman: see dehumanization; inferior beings; *Untermenschen*
submarines and submarine warfare, xv, 39, 56, 64-66, 104, 114, 155, 193, 240, 258, 352, 373-374, 387, 426
Suchomel, Franz, 506
Sudetenland and Sudeten Mountains, 3, 289, 291-294, 296-297, 425, 502
Suez Canal, 46, 91, 97
Sufi Order in the West, 591
Sugihara, Chiune, 398
suicide, xxix, xxxiii-xxv, 5, 22, 28, 75, 108, 146, 163-164, 237, 278, 362, 372, 382, 385, 407, 416-417, 420-421, 426, 428, 431, 453, 461-462, 465, 474, 478-479, 484, 486-487, 491, 493, 508, 528, 535, 537-539, 598-603, 634-636; cf. survival
Suresnes (Paris suburb), iv, 591
survival, iv, xi, xv, xxv, 28, 36, 38, 62, 73, 77, 89, 102, 108, 110-111, 116, 121, 127, 132, 162, 184, 188, 199, 213, 231, 282-283, 290, 313, 321, 323, 336, 338, 358, 362, 364-365, 377, 379, 382, 385, 389, 392-394, 397, 400, 416, 420, 445, 451, 456, 465, 467, 470, 476, 482, 486, 488, 490-491, 494, 499, 508, 515, 530, 534, 537-538, 540, 552-554, 556, 560, 565-568, 573, 577, 584, 603, 606, 608, 621-622, 628, 634-638, 640; cf. suicide
swastika (*Hakenkreuz*), including, pre-Hitlerian contexts, xxiv, 11, 121, 136, 171, 174, 181-182, 214, 542, 571; cf. Abbey at Lambach; Thule Society and its *Hakenkreuz*
Swastika League of America, 214
Sweden and the Swedes, xxviii, 29, 79, 108, 145-146, 305, 343, 408, 446, 474-475, 482, 640
Switzerland and the Swiss, 11, 27, 43, 48, 79, 107, 129, 144, 161, 200, 220-221, 253, 289, 310-312, 319-321, 368, 383, 385, 398, 466, 474-476, 526, 567, 576, 596, 641
syndicalism: see anarcho-syndicalism
Szilard, Leo, 408
Szpilman, Władysław, 116, 244, 341, 358
T4 (Tiergartenstraße 4) euthanasia program (also called *Aktion T4*), 4, 140-142, 255, 280, 343, 346-347, 349, 361, 366-367, 465, 469, 487, 495, 517, 597; cf. *Aktion Gnadentod* (Action Mercy Death)
T4 program ended, 141, 347; cf. *Aktion 14f13; Aktion Sonderbehandlung 14f13*
tactical retreat, 500; cf. *taktischer Rückzüg*
Tadahiko, Okada, 278
Tagliacozzo, Michael, 400
taktischer Rückzüg (tactical retreat), 357; cf. Dittmar, Kurt
Talaat Pasha, 92, 95-96
Talmud, 269, 302-304
Tanaka Memorandum, 204
Tannenberg, Battles of, v, 37, 71, 134-

135, 502
Tchakarian, Arsène, iv
Tehlirian, Soghomon, 91-93, 95
Teitelbaum, Yoel: see the Satmar Rabbi
Telemark, 407-408
Tasmania and Tasmanians, 47, 575
Terezín: see Theresienstadt
Teutonic Knights, v, 128-131, 133-134-136, 446, 533
Texaco (Texas Oil Company), 274
Theravāda Buddhism: see Buddhism; Pali (Theravāda Buddhist) Canon
Theresienstadt, 5, 383-384, 438, 467, 474-475-476, 505
Thetis, 608, 614, 616
Thierack, Otto Georg, 355, 519-520
thinking: see conceptual frameworks, the structure of thinking, worldview
Third Reich, i, iii-iv, vi-vii, ix-x, xiii-xvi, xviii-xxi, xxiii-xxviii, xxxiii, 4, 7, 10, 17, 20-23, 28, 30-31, 38, 47, 50, 75, 77, 104, 106, 111-112, 114, 117-118, 122-124, 126-127, 129, 133-135, 137-138, 142, 147, 149, 152, 158, 160-161, 165, 170-171, 175, 181-182, 187-192, 194-196, 199-203, 205, 207, 209, 214, 216-217, 219, 222, 224-225, 227-228, 230-231, 233-234, 236-238, 241, 244, 246, 248-249, 254-255, 258-259, 261, 263-260, 270, 274-275, 286-289, 294, 300-301, 303, 305, 309, 317, 320, 322-324, 326-328, 334-335, 337, 346, 350, 353, 355, 362-363, 367, 369-370, 372, 375-376, 382, 387, 393-397, 399, 401, 412-413, 417-420, 423-424, 426, 436-437, 440-441, 446, 450-451, 453-454, 459, 463-464, 467-472, 478-479, 481-484, 490, 493-494, 496, 501, 503, 507-508, 511, 514, 517-519, 523, 526, 529-531, 534-536, 538, 540, 546, 548-549, 552, 554, 556-560, 562-565, 568, 570-571, 574-577, 579, 583, 590, 593, 597-599, 603, 612, 619, 633-641; cf. 1,000-Year (12-Year) Reich; NSDAP
Thirty Years' War, 44, 558
Thor's oak, 23
Thousand-Year &c.: see 1,000-Year &c.
Threepenny Opera (Dreigroschenoper), xxi, 362, 384, 578
Thucydides, 336, 604

Thule Society and its Hakenkreuz, 169, 182; cf. swastika
Thyssen, Fritz, xiv, 80, 144-145, 209-210, 275, 320-321, 387, 410
Tiergartenstraße 4: see T4 euthanasia
Tito, Josip Broz, 543, 551, 637
tobender Zwerg (raging dwarf), 409; cf. Goebbels, Joseph; Pomsel, Brunhilde
Toifl, Ottmar, 220
Tokugawa, Prince, viii, 314
Tonkin Bay Incident, 454
Topf, J. A., & Söhne, 393
torment, i, iv, xxiv, 184, 186-187, 198, 283, 455, 487, 551-552, 578, 583-584, 588, 603, 606, 613-614, 616, 619, 624, 626, 629, 631, 634; cf. rage; wrath
Torpedo Alley, 375
total war, 5, 37-38, 77, 88, 357, 406, 408-409, 422, 470, 486, 525, 527-529-530, 532, 612, 627
traceless: see spurlos (traceless)
trade unionists and unions, 2, 239-240, 245-246, 402, 434; cf. anarcho-syndicalism; Mohawk Valley Formula; subdued worker wages based on worker insecurity
Trading with the Enemy Act, 274, 322
Trakl, Georg, 75, 145
Treaty of Non-aggression between Germany and the Union of Soviet Socialist Republics (the Molotov-Ribbentrop Pact), 50, 295, 309, 315, 335, 337, 499
Treblinka, xxxii, 5, 341-342, 367, 382, 385, 392, 425, 505-506, 527, 567-568
Treitschke, Heinrich, 180
Trench Fever and Trench Foot, 86-87
Triple Alliance, 25, 29, 47, 51
Triple Entente, 25, 51
Trotha, Lothar von, 47
Trotsky, Leon (Lev), 198, 221, 277, 448
Trotz zu Solz, Adam von, 292
Trudeau, Justin, 83
Trujillo, Rafael, 287
Truman, Harry (33rd US President), 473, 548-549, 560
Trump, Donald (45th US President), xii, 44, 82-83, 217
Tsuneishi, Keiichi, 486
Turing, Alan, 64, 377, 380

The Hitler Era

Turkey, 29, 49, 52-53, 66, 91-97, 447, 613, 619; cf. Erdoğan, Recep Tayyip
Tutu, Desmond, 618
Tutsis, 576
TVA (Tennessee Valley Authority), 205
Twelve-Year &c.: see 1,000-Year &c.
Tydings-McDuffie Act, 377
Typhoid fever, 475
Typhus, xx, 86, 567
Übermensch (Overman), 166
Ukraine, xxxiv, 5, 79, 192, 203-204, 268-269, 349, 351, 355, 363, 367, 396, 431, 445, 448, 498, 555, 597
Umsiedlungsaktionen, 537
UN Refugee Agency (UNHCR), 558
UN War Crimes Commission (UNWCC), 549
unions and trade unionists: see anarcho-syndicalism; Mohawk Valley Formula; trade unionists and unions
Unit 731: see Japanese military experimentation Unit 731, in China
Untermenschen (inferior beings) stereotyped, caricatured, with insulting metaphors, 166-167, 335, 386, 389, 394-395; cf. barbarization; dehumanization
Uranverein Club, 407
Urban II, 44
Urlanis, Boris, 77, 92
Urmson, J. O., 19, 582-583
urophilia, 452, 602
US big business, 159; cf. economics
US big business and Germany, 210, 294, 319-320
US big business and Spain, 273-275
US Civil War, 45; cf. Black Codes
US Marines and Belleau Wood, 80-82, 84-85
USSR: see Soviet Union; cf. Czarist Russia, Russia
Ustaše (Ustashe), 395, 400, 543, 575; cf. Croatia and the Croatians
V-1 rockets, 387, 426-427
V-2 rockets, 387-388, 551
Va ʿada (*Va ʿadat ha-Ezrah ve-ha-Hatzalah be-Budapesht*), 385
Vallat, Xavier, 518
Van Diemen's Land, 48; cf. Black War
Vandendreschd, Jacques: see Mercader, Ramón
Vatican, viii-ix, 185, 207, 226, 255, 275, 290, 378, 400, 465

Vatican Ratline, 395, 398, 542-543, 550, 553; cf. Hudal, Alois/Luigi
Vatican Secret Archives, viii
VE-Day, 21, 507, 534
Vél d'hiv (*Vélodrome d'hiver*), iii-iv, 167, 197, 397, 456
vengeance and revenge: see *Vergeltung*
Venlo Incident, 312-314
Verdun, Battles of, 71-72, 78, 314, 586
Vergeltung (revenge and vengeance, retribution, retaliation), i-iii, vi, xxv, xxxiii, 20, 37, 43, 91, 95, 127, 135, 164-165, 188, 203, 220, 233, 249, 284, 295, 309, 315-316, 349, 372, 382, 395, 397, 412, 426, 429, 442, 447, 454, 465, 492, 495, 502, 510, 538, 540, 542-544, 569, 603, 616, 620, 624-625
verlan, 17
vermicide, 378; cf. poison gas; Zyklon B
Vermork, 407
Vernichtungslager: see extermination camps and centers
Versailles Conference and Treaty, i, 20, 25-26, 33-35, 41, 44-45, 60, 76, 79, 99, 101, 103, 107, 120, 137, 143, 152, 157-158, 229-230, 248, 258, 264-267, 275, 291-292, 466, 471
vetting, xviii
Vichy France, iii-iv, xiv, xxix, 61, 106, 321, 375, 397, 402-404, 518-519, 568; cf. Pétain, Philippe
Vienna, xiv, 8-9, 41, 51, 97, 104-105, 115, 131-132, 169, 180-184, 234, 271, 280, 285, 341, 398, 424-425, 459, 535
Vienna Circle (*Wiener Kreis*), xviii, 460
Vietnam, xxiv, 67-68, 101, 283, 442-443, 454, 523, 605
viewpoint (point of view, worldview): see conceptual frameworks &c.
Villa Belmonte, 482
Vinnitsa (Winnitsa), 3, 361
violence, i-iii, v, x, xxi-xxii, xxiv, 6, 9, 17, 19-20, 24, 36, 43, 47-48, 62, 67, 75-76, 88-89, 93, 95, 99-100, 103, 112-113, 119-120, 122, 127-128, 145, 147, 151, 176, 186-189, 200, 206-207, 215, 224, 227, 234-236, 238-239, 244, 250-251, 269-270, 272, 276-278, 282-284, 299-301,

304, 307, 311-312, 316, 336, 349-350, 361, 364, 390, 395, 398, 418, 421, 443, 448-450, 452, 456, 468-469, 483, 492, 495, 502, 508-510, 534, 537-543, 547, 549, 552, 554-555, 557-561, 563-565, 569, 573-579, 584, 586-587, 590, 593-594, 602-603, 608-609, 612-615, 617-619-621, 623-624, 626-627, 630-631, 633-635, 637, 640-641; cf. rape
vipassanā-bhāvanā, 628-629, 641; cf. Insight Meditation; *metta-bhāvanā; samatha; samādhi*
VJ-Day, 534
Voice of the Wehrmacht: see *Stimme des OKW* (Voice of the Supreme High Command of the Armed Forces); cf. Dittmar, Kurt
Volgograd, 405, 528
Volk (people, race) and *Volksdeutsche*, 37-38, 55, 58, 76-77, 98, 101, 105, 121, 125-129, 131, 137-138, 141, 154, 166-167, 174-175, 185-186, 188, 191-192, 195, 212, 216, 224-225, 227-229, 237, 243, 254, 265, 278, 289, 292, 300, 306, 309-310, 317, 327, 391, 419, 422-424, 445, 464, 468-469, 481, 488, 521-522, 531, 541
Völkischer Beobachter, xiii, 76, 105, 117, 190, 211, 312, 318, 347, 397, 495, 500, 515
Volksgericht (People's Court), 130, 244, 311, 440, 464, 482-483, 486; cf. Freisler, Roland
Volksseele, 169
Volkssturm (People's Home Front Army), 5, 479-481, 520, 539
Volkstum, 124
Volkswagen, 386
Voltaire (François-Marie Arouet), 547
voting, x, 105, 108, 149, 152, 156, 226, 570
Vrba, Rudolf (1860-1939), 183-184
Vrba, Rudolf (1924-2006), 183, 513
Vrba-Wetzler Report, 183, 513
Wächter, Horst von, 553
Wächter, Otto von, 553
Wagener, Otto, 100, 193, 195, 238
Wagner, Adolf, 185-186, 234, 522-523
Wagner, Richard, xxi, 138, 164, 178, 188-189, 426, 487
Wagner-Rogers Bill, 307-308, 491

Waite, Robert, 14-15, 120-121, 181, 207, 284, 453-454, 457-458, 465, 596
Wall Street, 159, 203, 321
Wallenberg, Raoul, 398
Wannsee Conference and villa, 4, 101, 133, 214, 220, 288, 332, 341, 349-352, 357, 483, 504, 517, 523, 526, 568, 577
war trauma: see Complex PTSD (cPTSD); PTSD
Warner, Jack, and Warner Brothers Pictures, 11
Warsaw, xxxi, 64, 244, 287, 308-309, 318, 335, 338, 413, 470, 487, 499, 505, 533, 587, 619
Warsaw ghetto, 116, 244, 308, 318, 322-323. 341, 357-359, 383, 385, 393, 488-489, 503, 505, 511, 533, 535, 542
Warsaw Uprising (1944), 413
Warthegau, 323, 337
weather: see natural phenomena &c.
Weber, Walter, 219-220
wedding, Hitler's, 477-478
Wedding (neighborhood in Charlottenburg), 122-123
Wehrmacht (Third Reich Armed Forces), 5, 7, 127, 187, 205, 231, 237, 248, 259, 290, 294, 299, 326-327, 331, 343-344, 350, 354-357, 369, 371, 383, 385, 507, 534
Wehrmacht oath: see Hitler Oath
Weidling, Helmut, 492-493
Weil, Simone, 628
Weill, Kurt, 362
Weimar and the Weimar Republic, xxii-xxiii, xxxiii, 2, 22, 26, 28, 32, 40-41, 85, 98-99, 106, 108-109, 112, 120-124, 146-148, 152, 154, 157, 159, 161, 192, 205-208, 213, 217, 225, 232, 244, 247-248, 259, 262-263, 392, 483, 633
Welczeck, Count Johannes von, 300
Weltbühne, 145, 260
Weltpolitik, 46; cf. *Realpolitik*
Wenk, Walther, 536
Werewolf (*Werwolf*): see Operation Werewolf (*Werwolf*)
Werfel, Alma Mahler, 403
Werfel, Franz, 403
Wessel, Horst, 207
Westerbork, xi, 382, 567, 637

The Hitler Era

Westphalia, Peace of (1648), 33, 44
Wewelsburg Castle, 533
Weyler y Nicolau, Valeriano, 245; cf. Cuba and the Cubans; slavery and slave labor; Spanish-American War
White Rose, xxxiii, 124, 357, 409, 441, 471-472, 482-484, 486, 506, 528
White Supremist Christians vs. Reich Aryans, 102, 595-598; cf. race theory
Whitman, James Q., xxv, 21, 113, 142, 243
Wiesel, Elie, 267, 388-389, 396, 551, 577
wi-fi technology and Bluetooth, 156; cf. Antheil, George; FHSS; GPS; Lamarr, Hedy; Milsatcom
Winkler, Gershon, 585
Wilhelm I, Kaiser, 45, 179, 258
Wilhelm II, Kaiser, 29, 32, 35, 37, 39, 46, 59, 93, 107-108, 120, 143, 209, 213, 258, 446, 479, 633
Wilhelmine Empire (IInd Reich), v, 23, 37, 40, 146, 291, 326, 446; cf. Holy Roman Empire (Ist Reich); Nazi Reich (IIIrd Reich)
Wilson, Woodrow (28th US President), 31, 33, 35, 59, 66-67, 78, 85, 101, 254
win-win and win-lose models, 103
Windsor, castle and Duke of (Edward VIII), vi, ix, 110, 344
Winnitsa: see Vinnitsa
Wirth, Christian, 367
Wirth, Joseph, 154
Wisliceny, Dieter, 517
Wislocka, Michalina, 172; cf. Greek orgasm; Homer and the *Iliad;* rage (*mēnis*) and outrage; sexuality, &c.
Witch of Buchenwald (*die Hexe von Buchenwald*): see Ilse Koch
Witting, Rolf, 390
Wivupal, 259
wolf, as metaphor, inspiring image, and name, with wolfpack (*Wolfsrudel, Wolffamilie*), 1, 280-281, 327-328, 632; cf. Adelwolf; Hitler, Adolf
Wolf, Frau Paula: see Hitler, Paula
Wolff, Karl, 366, 518; cf. Himmler grown faint on witnessing execution
Wolf's Lair (*Wolfsschanze*), 1, 144-145, 327, 524; cf. Adelwolf; Hitler, Adolf; wolf, as metaphor &c.
Wolkenkuckucksheim (cloud cuckoo land), 418; cf. Aristophanes; *nephelokokkygía*
worker insecurity: see subdued worker wages based on worker insecurity
World Jewish Congress, xiv, 474-475
worldview (*Weltaanschauung*), xxiii, 124, 127, 130, 134-135, 138, 160, 169, 175, 227, 258, 360, 422, 451, 494, 533, 570, 622. 626
Wormhoudt Massacre, 345, 414
Wotan (Odin), 466, 487-488
Wounded Knee and the Massacre of the Lakota Sioux Indians, 63, 541
wrath, i-ii, 538, 608, 615-616, 631; cf. rage; torment
WRI (War Resisters' International), 614
Wrocław (Breslau), 387, 579
wúwei, 391; cf. Lǎo Tzu/Lǎozi; non-action; Russian fatalism
xenophobia, 104, 112-113, 167, 199, 228, 456, 555, 559
Xenophon, 606
Yad Vashem, 358-359, 385, 392, 400-401, 404, 501, 517, 559, 583; cf. righteous &c.
Yazidis, 501, 576
The Yellow Spot, xiv, 235
Yevtushenko, Yevgeny, 359
Young Plan, 27, 34, 114, 148, 157-158, 229
youpin, 17, 397
Ypres, Battles of, 71-74, 353, 410
Yugoslavia and the Yugoslavs, 67, 86, 88, 101, 318, 326, 354, 411, 512, 551, 558, 576, 613, 637; cf. Serbia and the Serbians; Tito, Josip Broz
Zeitgeist (spirit or mentality of the time), 103, 114, 160, 373
Zeus, ii, 6, 62, 409, 423, 608, 616, 625; cf. Hera
Zhukov, Georgy, 492-493, 504
Ziemer, Gregor, 470
Zigeuner: see Romanie
Zigeunernacht, 286, 438
Zimbardo, Philip, 580
Zimmerman, Arthur, and the Zimmerman telegram, 56, 59-60, 65
Zygalski, Henryk, 243
Zyklon B, 4, 140, 246, 263, 271, 331, 380-382, 386, 388, 505; cf. cyanide capsules (potassium cyanide); poison gas (*Giftgas*)